Fr...aerick Delaware
28th July 2009

NORWAY

A Triumph in Bigotry

by Frederick Delaware

To Rick, Wendy, Jon and Crystal without whose help this book would not have been possible.

NORWAY
A Triumph in Bigotry
Copyright © Frederick Delaware 2008

Too hot to handle?   See what happens when our Freddy, a London lawyer, becomes Public enemy No. 1 in Norway.

Solicitor Frederick Delaware risks his career to expose establishment duplicity in Norway where rampant xenophobia and bigotry subvert the rule of law.

Norway – A Triumph in Bigotry explodes the myth that Norway is a bastion of fair play and even handedness. Rather that it is an isolated, excluded country, which, when the need arises, uses sex and psychiatry on an industrial scale to pervert the course of justice.

ISBN: 978-0-9559841-0-5

Chapter 1

It would all begin shortly ....

I had finished playing tennis with Gilles, my French friend, in Villejuif, a south Paris suburb and hurriedly got dressed as I had a train to catch at Gard du Nord to Boulogne for the ferry back to England. The break in France was just the rejuvenation I needed; it was Spring 1982.

On the train, I felt quite exhausted and settled back in a window seat to the left of the aisle and dozed peacefully. It was a nice trip back to the coast and I reflected on the six incredible months I had spent in Egypt prior to taking up the Law Society Final Examination course for solicitors in September 1981. I left Egypt two weeks before Anwar Sadat, the President, was assassinated and had even passed the parade ground at Heliopolis in Cairo on the way to the airport where Sadat was to meet his bloody end on October 6th 1981. Oh Egypt and its great and friendly people; people who had raised me out of the depths of melancholy that I had descended to in England. What a difference the Egyptians had made to my spirits. I was back on track and full of beans. I was still a student in England, where I was born, to be precise in the London Hospital at Whitechapel.

A pretty, but pale looking blonde passed by me, in my carriage to and from her visit to the toilet. I noticed she sat a couple of rows behind me, beside a very spotty girl; they were obviously friends who had been on holiday together. I wondered where they came from; they did not look English and they were certainly not French. The train eventually pulled into Boulogne Station. I got off with my bag and started chatting to the two girls in the queue to the boat. The pale one was from Norway and her friend was from Sweden. They told me they had had a break in Paris from working in England as au pairs. I wished them well and then we made our separate ways onto the ferry where I had a good meal and a King Edward cigar. Soon we would be back in England and there was Tottenham Hotspur to look forward to in the F.A Cup Final against Queens Park Rangers in May.

The ferry docked at Folkestone and all the passengers congregated on the exit deck. The two au pairs were in front of me and I managed to catch up with them on the gangway. A jolly girl, this Norwegian, very sprightly and talkative and so it was nice that we would be able to sit together and chat on the train journey back to Waterloo. It turned out to be a very warm cosy conversation with the girls and by the time we were back in London we were pals, so I accompanied them on the underground to Kings Cross and on to St. Pancras station where we swapped addresses and telephone numbers and promised to meet again very soon. I quite liked Heidi, who was from Bergen on the west coast of Norway. She had a joie de vivre and an openness that few English girls have. I was genuinely interested in Norway as for a couple of years I had had a wonderful penfriend, a girl, from Hønefoss, a town just north of Oslo.

The following Saturday, I went by train up to St. Albans in Hertfordshire where Heidi lived. I phoned to say I had arrived at the station and 20 minutes later she turned up and greeted me with a lovely hug. Heidi was a delicious girl and was wearing blue jeans and a multi-coloured pullover. We walked into a pub and had a coke each, then wondered what to do. Heidi phoned her host mother and we were given permission to go to the house. St. Albans seemed a very pretty place - lots of trees and winding roads and it was really a pleasant walk to the large house in Sandpit Lane. Shirley Warwick welcomed us in; she was a midwife and her husband, Colin, was a businessman currently away in New Zealand. They had two small children.

Over the next few weeks, Heidi and I met frequently. I always went to see her in St. Albans since it wasn't so far for me to go from Law College in central London. I took her a couple of times to White Hart Lane to watch Tottenham Hotspur with Glenn Hoddle in the side and we stood in the famous old Shelf section of the ground. One of the matches was against Sunderland. John Pratt scored a brilliant headed goal at the Paxton Road end at the near post, straight from a corner. Years later, I met Pratt at East Thurrock United Football Ground in deepest Essex after a benefit match and I told him how sorry I was that he had been sacked as Assistant Manager at Tottenham, along with Peter Shreeves, the Manager, when Spurs had just finished third in the League. Pratt said, resignedly, that the Board at Tottenham always thought the grass was greener on the other side. Poor old Pratt was now running his own cleaning business and offered to clean anything going. Martin Peters, our World Cup hero from 1966 was also there. My best friend, Russell, once lived across the road from Peters and Russell told me he used to kick a ball around with him in Peters' garden. I mentioned this to Peters and told him

Russell was now the drummer with Chris Barber's Jazz and Blues Band, Europe's most successful jazz ensemble. "Are they still going?" Peters asked. Not a surprising question as Chris Barber had started in 1954 and Russell was at the time their latest and youngest member and a star. Dear Martin Peters - he had the humility to confide in me that his going to Sheffield United as the manager was a "big mistake." He "went for the money," he said, and it just did not work. I remembered that one of their goalkeepers, 19 years old, had collapsed and died in training after leaping up to take a ball and United were then relegated to the old Third Division at the end of that season. It finished Peters off and he never went back into management.

Heidi had unfortunately lost her mother three years or so before she came to England as an au pair. She had two older sisters and her parents had been divorced when Heidi had not quite reached her teens. Her father remarried and then had two sons. She told me her mother had a miserable final few years, "always drinking, taking pills and wanting to kill herself." One day, if my memory serves me correctly, Heidi told me her mother had a fall, hit her head on the ground and later died from her head injury after going into a coma. I expressed my deepest sorrow and left it at that. Heidi never referred to her mother again whilst she was in England and indeed her death did not seem to bother her. Perhaps she had got over her grief and had accepted the tragedy with stoicism. I felt sad for Heidi for I myself certainly could not do without my mother. As for her father, who worked for the United Nations, Heidi said she did not get on with him and that in fact he had just had a heart attack and her stepmother told her specifically not to return to Norway to pay him a visit as it would do him more harm than good. So off she went to Paris instead. It was not the greatest of holidays as the weather was bad and accommodation was expensive, she moaned. They had stayed with a Frenchman they had met, in his small flat with only one bed, which the three of them had to share. A threesome, but nothing untoward had taken place, Heidi assured me. However, when she went to the toilet in the middle of the night, she had to go through another room first and received a great shock, she told me, when she disturbed two other men who were staying in the adjoining room and in the act of committing sodomy with each other.

What a comfort it was to be with Heidi. It was a good feeling to hold her hand and hear what she had to say; to share our feelings, to kiss and cuddle. Unfortunately she smoked; you know how it starts - teenage girls trying to look cool and sophisticated and then they become addicted. One day in early May we were in the sitting room exchanging frank views in the late afternoon, when she told me quietly that she had done "something" in her past, which she deeply regretted. I suspected that it was something sexual. At first she was reluctant to come clean but eventually she told me that she had had an abortion when she was 16. Her Norwegian boyfriend, Petter, said he would leave her if she did not go to the hospital for a termination. The contraceptive pill she was taking had not worked in preventing her pregnancy, she said. I was very disappointed to hear this news as I truly despise abortion as a form of contraception. To me only the lowest form of people indulge in abortion of this sort. I would not see Heidi in the same light again.

So Heidi's sad story prompted me to console her for her self-imposed loss and I said it would be a good idea if we went out for a walk to get some air. We went out with our arms around each other and went for a prawn cocktail in a restaurant in town. On the way back to her place, Heidi mentioned that there was something else she had done that was "wrong," although she wasn't going to tell me what it was. Honestly, now that she had wetted my curiosity further, I thought it would be best if I knew what this other 'misdemeanour' was so that we could get things out of the way. So I asked several times what this other thing was and her resistance was eventually broken and she told me in a very pained voice that she had had a second abortion. Her personality then changed completely and she cursed me and broke into a real sob and ran back into the house in utter despair and misery. The second abortion was also at the request of this same boyfriend, who again had warned her that if she did not go to the hospital for a termination he would leave her. What utter cruelty! Heidi's relationship with this boy ended anyway after these traumas, but their relationship had received the highest sanction. Her boyfriend's parents allowed them both to go to their own master bedroom and allowed them to have sex in complete comfort and privacy.

The second time Heidi went to the hospital, she told me that the nurses treated her with extreme discourtesy so annoyed were they that she was in for a second abortion so soon. Heidi said that her stepmother had called her a "whore" and she dropped out of school in Voss, a town close to Bergen, without explanation, as soon as she had had the abortion. The teachers and all her school friends could not understand why all of a sudden she had left and it was then that she came to England to forget everything. No sooner had she got to St. Albans then she picked up another boyfriend in town but they had split up before I came onto the scene. My prompting had brought all the bad memories back to Heidi and she was in a sorry mess. We did not have much more to say and were both in shock for different reasons. I decided to go home and Heidi was good enough to pick herself up and walk me halfway back to the railway station, a walk which then broke into a run as I told her I was close to missing my train, the last one of the night. When we were about to part company (for me to run the rest of the way to the station and for her to go back home), she said she would much prefer it if we did not meet again. Clearly, she was upset and wanted to forget about me now, the person who had brought back memories of her ghastly past. Regarding her as something akin to a delinquent, I wasn't going to protest and I said goodbye and ran as fast as hell back to the station, but it was in vain as I had missed the train. Gingerly, I phoned Heidi's home and Mrs. Warwick answered and gave me permission to return and sleep the night on the sofa. Twenty minutes later I entered the driveway and Heidi was at the upstairs window, which she had opened to welcome me back. I then went up to see her in her room and we tried to talk things over. She was lying face down on her bed in her dressing gown. I lay beside her and put my arms around her as she proceeded to tell me that as everything in her life seemed so futile and proper relationships so impossible to find, she could see no reason why she should not just resort to the pleasures of sex with anyone at all to whom she felt attracted. I really did not think she meant it and was only saying this out of temporary despair and so I told her that eventually she would get over her depression and trauma and would recover to find a nice husband. I went back downstairs to have fitful night's sleep on the sofa.

Heidi was a beautiful girl, with long blonde hair, blue eyes, large firm breasts and strong limbs. She had a fantastic personality. So many men wanted to have sex with her, she told me; she could just "feel it" when she spoke to them. Men were always after her, she said. Indeed, I experienced this one sunny day when I was in the back garden waiting for her to finish her bath and had my stereo headphones on listening to the beautiful tones of David Byron, ex-lead singer of Uriah Heep. I did not hear the front doorbell ring but Heidi had confessed to me after he had gone that a photographer she knew called to say hello, after she had asked him to pop round. He had in fact photographed her for the local newspaper, holding out an ice cream, which Heidi had previously shown me. However, as I was Heidi's favourite at the time she made her excuses to him and told me that he sighed sadly and left. She came down from her bath dressed in crimson leggings with matching dress top and elegant shoes. We joked about how sexually attractive she looked but how it was important that we both be "good." My ardour and potential fondness for her was dampened, however, as I felt she was now 'used goods' and almost a sexual leper. Besides, I had met an incredible girl in Egypt the previous summer and my heart was set on her. But what an illusion, that girl from Cairo later turned out to be. I wrote to her four times without reply and when I eventually phoned her up to see what was up, her protective brother answered the phone and told me his sister had received no letters whatsoever from me. What in fact had happened, was that I had written to the wrong address each time. In September 1981, when I was in Cairo, she had written her address in my address book as 449 Al Ahram Street, Giza, Cairo and yet in my book the '9' looked like a '4,' so I wrote all the time to 444 Al Ahram Street. When I next went back to Egypt, an Egyptian pal of mine came with me to look for 444 Al Ahram Street and we discovered it did not exist. None of the letters even got to the right address. When I went to see her in her home, her brother answered the door and led me in to sit down with him and his father. The girl was in but "not available," so it took me half an hour of explanation and insistence to the father and brother that I just wanted to say hello for "one minute" to the girl. So the father told his daughter to come out, which she sheepishly did, accompanied by her mother. She said only a few words - an attitude that I found disgusting compared with the lively, kind and generous spirit she showed me when I found her in the grounds of the American University in Cairo the year before. So much for the famous Egyptian hospitality. That 12 month total absence of communication had killed her feelings for me and I later found out she had met an Egyptian pilot whom she went on to marry. Nevertheless, to be treated with such contempt by denying me a proper chat after I had come all the way from England, was shameful, and taught me that just because someone 'is a Muslim' does not necessarily give them those endearing qualities of compassion and respect that Islam teaches. It is a lesson that has served me well ever since. Relations between men and women in the educated classes in Egypt would make for a fascinating social study. The men invariably wanted to leave Egypt for a better life. But the women, in my experience, could only function properly on their home turf of Egypt amongst their nearest and dearest. They needed that support network. The girls on the whole did not have the adventurous get up and go attitude that the men had. The women also had too many selfish traits. Self help was not their forte. That came later in life. All too soon they became overweight through lack of exercise.

Heidi and I often kissed and cuddled whilst we were in England. She was always on the phone to me. I was 24 and she was 19. We certainly had a lot of affection for each other and one day at dusk, after we had spent the afternoon in each other's arms, kissing on the large floor cushions, placed appropriately on the carpet, she begged me to stay the night with her. I knew what that might lead to. Half wanting to be with her but half hoping to be rescued from myself, I phoned my mother to say I would probably be staying the night - I would not be coming home. My mother, acquainted with Heidi's past, told me to come home if I possibly could and as my father was standing beside her, she gave the phone to him and his request for me to go home was all the persuasion I needed. Home I went. Close! Heidi was on the pill "just in case" she had told me but I was glad I had avoided the temptation. I doubt I would have gone all the way with her but you never know. Besides, I wanted to set a good example after her past disasters and not be just another prick in for a good time. If I really loved her, then it was up to me to be patient. Certainly, both of us desperately needed love and security. She did not trust men very easily and told me that whilst she was on holiday in Greece in 1981, Greek boys had taken her for a ride in their jeep and they stopped the car in a remote coastal area, got out to go for a walk together and produced a knife to Heidi's throat. They demanded to have sex with her but Heidi responded by saying she was on her period. These boys asked her to prove it and she took down her pants and proved that indeed she was on her period. After that they left her alone and took her back to town. Heidi's fear of men had been compounded some time before, as she told me, a cousin of hers had been raped and killed in Norway. The case had received a lot of press publicity but the perpetrator had never been found.

The Saturday of the Tottenham Hotspur against Queens Park Rangers F.A Cup Final was the last time I saw Heidi in England as I watched the 1-1 draw with her in St. Albans and although I slept on the sofa in the sitting room overnight, I didn't care to impose myself on the family at breakfast so I left as soon as I woke up. It was a Sunday and it was my birthday - a depressing day marked by its emptiness. I left a note for Heidi saying goodbye and good luck. A couple of weeks later Heidi had left back for Bergen on the Newcastle Ferry, herself quite miserable. Her resumed friendship with an earlier boyfriend in St. Albans had not made her any happier.

I must comment on the issue of abortion. As far as I am concerned, abortion should only be permitted when doctors think the mother's life or health is at serious risk or where the foetus is suffering from a congenital defect, preventing the enjoyment of a normal life. The stress imposed on parents in looking after a severely mentally or physically handicapped person is usually debilitating, but the problem with this approach is that a diagnosis of abnormality might be wrong, resulting in a perfectly healthy baby being aborted. Abortion, however, often takes place where the parties aren't married; where there is no commitment and the rules of love and companionship (that should embrace the institution of marriage) are not in the thoughts or minds of the parties. If a girl is stupid enough to have sex with a man who has not committed himself to her and gets herself pregnant, then she should be brave enough to have the baby and take whatever consequences come after that. A soul that is coming here by God's leave should not be killed for social reasons, for example the groundless fear of poverty or the oft quoted reason, "I'm too young to have a baby." Research shows in fact that women who have socially aborted their foetus often suffer post abortion trauma, i.e. severe regret and psychological disturbance for years afterwards. The reasons they gave at the time for having the abortion later appear so ill conceived. Oh, for what might have been! The sweet little smile, the loving grip of that tiny hand around the adult's finger, that God given innocence and trust of the helpless infant, all forgone. All an illusion - as the foetus never became a child - it was crushed and sucked out of the mother's womb and thrown dead into the dustbin.

Brian Sewell, the noted art critic, put it so well in an Evening Standard newspaper article entitled 'Women are the crueller sex' on Tuesday 18th November 1997 when he said:

'The other concept of a woman, as warm, kindly and compassionate, as the mother of us all, as the comforter for whom grown men cry on deathbed and in deep distress, still stands fairly firm, but for some of us is blemished by their attitude to abortion, cosmetics and fur coats, for in all three women demonstrate a measure of heartless selfishness quite alien to the image of woman as universal mother. To many men it is incomprehensible that in the 30 years since abortion was made legal, some five million foetuses, living human beings, whose hearts are functioning and limbs are formed, far from the mere blobs of jelly of which pro-abortionists so often speak, have been ripped from wombs with the compliance and authority of the law and medicine. Are women quite so often sexually had against their will?

That an abortion may save a woman's sanity when she has been assaulted by a stranger, drunk, drugged and perhaps diseased, we may feel compelled to concede, but that abortion should be employed as a primary method of birth control - and that is the implication of this huge and growing number - is surely not acceptable.

Convenience was the reason for 91 per cent of abortions in 1996 - unwanted babies dressed up in the statistics as supposed threats to the physical and mental health of the mothers. These were babies that need not, and should not, have been conceived, but prevented with a moment's forethought and the necessary simple apparatus to keep sperm and egg apart. It is time that we questioned the fancy that women are more compassionate and merciful than men. Are they indeed in any sense the gentler sex?'

***

I wonder how many a man has been deceived by his teenage/twenty-something girlfriend who went behind his back and had their unborn child aborted – only for him to assume everything in the garden was rosy? Quite a few indeed, ignorant of the reality of the girlfriend's 'love.' Gentle in the manner but violent in the deed!

Chapter 2

The greatest night of my young life was one November evening in London's Chancery Lane in 1983 and it came quite unexpectedly. The Law Society Final Examination results were due to be published in the main broadsheet newspapers but unfortunately when I got to The Guardian newsapaper's offices in Grays Inn Road in the evening, I was told that the printers were on strike and I would have to wait at least until the next day to see if they had decided to go back to work. With the tension off for the moment, I recovered my appetite and went for a meal, after which I decided to go straight home. As I crossed the bottom of Chancery Lane I saw that even at this late hour, 9 p.m., the Law Society was open. I walked right into the reading room where all the examination results were posted up. I looked for my name under the successful candidates' list and found it! I had passed all seven papers. Thank you God! I was free. I went out of the hall and danced all the way up the street to the telephone boxes outside the old post office to tell my parents the wonderful news. It was a supreme moment, as the previous year I had failed six out of the seven papers - all the law subjects - and passed only the accounts paper. Students were only allowed three attempts at the time to pass the Law Society Final Examination and after that there was a permanent bar to entry into the legal profession, so there was a lot of pressure on me. Later on the rules would change to allow unlimited attempts.

Come Christmas I went back to Egypt for a holiday to share my joy with all the people who had been so kind to me during my stay in Egypt in 1981.

It was at the famous Gezira Sports Club in Cairo that I came across a petite pretty girl with smooth porcelain-like features, sitting at a table in the Lido, beside the swimming pool. She invited me to sit down and we began to find out about each other and our families. I discovered her father was one of Egypt's best-known architects and a multi-millionaire; a guest on Egyptian TV chat shows. He had made his money from President Sadat's open door policy of allowing investment in Egypt from any quarter. This was a man who came to have three limousines and a luxury flat, yet when he got married he was so poor, he had to live with his mother-in-law. The celebrated confidante of Presidents Nasser and Sadat, Mohammed Hussein Heikal, in his book covering Sadat's life and death, 'Autumn of Fury,' said that when Sadat came to power there were five hundred millionaires in Egypt (1971) but that when Sadat was assassinated in 1981 there were seventeen thousand millionaires. Sayed El Komy, the pretty girl's father, was one of them and he had transacted business with another relative of mine, Mohsin, who was Egyptian Ambassador to the Vatican at the time (1984). So, remarkably, our families knew each other. Her name was Hala. You see, my own father is Egyptian, a Muslim, and he married my mother, a German and born a Protestant. So how come my name is Frederick Delaware? Read on.

A couple of days later I went up to see Hala at her parents' high rise apartment on the Nile, on the off-chance she would be in, just to say hello. Her mother greeted me and welcomed me in and it was then that I saw Dalia, Hala's sister. After only a few sentences from her, I found myself longing to spend the rest of the day with her. I felt completely at one with her and felt that she liked me too. Before long, Hala came in from outside and was most happy to see me waiting in the oak panelled sitting room. I quickly discovered she was very fond of me. She had already told her mother of our meeting in the Gezira Club and we were left alone in the sitting room to talk. Some way into the conversation she said, "You don't love me do you?" and I replied, "No." What does a man do when two sisters like the one fellow? I had instantly liked Dalia and wanted to develop things with her. She was only 17. She desperately wanted to study in England she told me. Hala on the other hand was 19 and I knew for sure that she wanted to get to know me properly. Decisions, decisions. So, I made a decision and carried on to say to Hala, "But I'll come back to Egypt when I have secured a job in England; lets then see if we can get to know each other properly." Dalia had already decided for herself that Hala and I would "probably marry," when I put some feelers out about how nice it would be to see her, Dalia, in England as a student. I saw Hala a couple of more times in the Gezira Club when it soon became clear that the whole family detested the father, who seemed to be a very cruel man. The family had all suffered terribly when as a unit they had been involved in a serious car accident in Egypt a few years before. Hala's uncle was almost crippled and Dalia had sustained extensive injuries to her stomach. They had not got a penny in compensation.

Anyway, I had made a good impression on Hala's sister, mother and grandmother, who all liked me. It made me feel appreciated, particularly as Hala already had an admirer, Amir, who wanted to marry her. But I knew that I had not followed my heart that day in their flat and by more or less committing myself to Hala, I had finished off rather abruptly my longing to get to know Dalia. I really ached for Dalia, and I'd messed up.

I went back home to England convinced it was a formality that I would get a job with Fox & Gibbons, the London solicitors who had a branch office in Cairo. After all, I had passed the Law Society Final Examination and came from a well known Egyptian family on my father's side which comprised of doctors and diplomats and one uncle had been Sadat's Minister for Land Reclamation and later Minister to the Sudan. He had met Colonel Gaddaffi of Libya six times. Most of all, though, my heart was in Egypt. I was sure that once I was at the interview to which Fox & Gibbons had invited me, I would get the job. So the day after returning from Cairo I made an appointment for the following week with Mr. Dunn's secretary at Fox & Gibbons. It was a second chance because a year earlier they had rejected me, but it did not matter then as I had failed the Law Society Final Examination and would not have been able to join the firm in any event. Three days before my interview I came down with chickenpox and was in a dreadful state, covered from head to toe in Calamine cream. What a sight I was! So, on the eve of the 'great interview,' I telephoned Fox & Gibbons and told them regrettably I would have to cancel my appointment because I had caught chickenpox. One of the secretary's replied that they had been trying to contact me during the day to tell me they had to cancel the interview because Mr. Dunn, the interviewing partner had to go abroad. I asked when the interview could be re-arranged for. The secretary had no firm idea but said "in about six week's time." What discourtesy I thought - that is no way to treat prospective employees. When I began to express my disappointment at this extraordinarily long wait, all I got was, "Well you're not the only articled clerk who has applied to this firm." True, but not good form to say it to my face. Still, I would have a direct line into the business community of Egypt and for certain no other prospective articled clerk would have that priceless asset.

The next day I wrote and told the firm what I thought of their attitude. If they treated me like shit at that stage, then what was to come later, I wondered. They seemed to have retained a colonial attitude towards Egyptian workers. It certainly felt like that to me. I burnt that particular bridge to the Cairo workplace, so I settled down to make applications to other London law firms telling them I could start straight away. One interesting interview came up with Masons, the Fleet Street construction law firm. They were at that time based opposite the High Courts of Justice in the Strand. Two of the partners, Mr. Watney and Mr. Roberts were present to interview me and they were lovely chaps. We talked of Egypt and I mentioned that I had an uncle, Ahmed, who was a prominent lawyer in Abu Dhabi in partnership with a certain gentleman, Zaki Hashem. To my surprise and their consternation, this same Zaki Hashem had been in the office of Masons that very morning talking with Mr. Watney. Wow! That can't be anything other than a Godsend. Mr. Watney said he would get in touch with Zaki Hashem tomorrow and get back to me within a week. The rest of the interview went well and I was shown around the whole building. I was happy and I went home supremely confident that I had secured a job.

Two weeks passed and I had heard nothing from Masons. So I wrote to Mr. Watney asking whether I could have some news. I got a simple letter back saying they had decided not to take my application any further and they wished me well. I could not figure out the reason for this at all. It wasn't until three months later that I was lucky enough to find out the apparent reason for my rejection. My uncle, Osman, who had been Sadat's Minister for Land Reclamation was visiting London and told me that Zaki Hashem and my other uncle, Ahmed, had terminated their legal partnership in Abu Dhabi in very acrimonious circumstances. Another desperate piece of bad luck, especially as Masons were later to open up a Cairo office.

It was a frustrating time. I was writing to Hala in Egypt and was never getting any correspondence back at all. Not because I had been rejected but because it wasn't 'good form' for the daughter of a famous Egyptian to put her feelings in writing to someone she was not engaged to, in case the letters were 'used' against her later. So I spent hundreds of pounds phoning her, never receiving a call back. It wasn't really a very productive exercise anyway, as I knew I really liked Hala's sister. I had already spoilt everything for myself with these Egyptian sisters by not having the patience to keep my mouth shut until I had had the time to get to know my true feelings. The trials of long-distance love!

Then one evening, I wondered how Heidi was getting on. Something told me to leave it alone but I was curious so I phoned her up. Her stepmother answered and told me that Heidi was living on her own, that Heidi was not married and that perhaps I had better speak to her father so he could tell me more. He gave me Heidi's telephone number and I eagerly phoned her up. When I spoke to her after a gap of over two years, in amusement, I made her guess who I was. With Heidi, I was not the only chap she had known in England, but when I told her it was me she was very pleased and we spoke for a long time. We had a lot of news to catch up on. Some time into the conversation, she said something traumatic had happened to her that she would rather keep to herself. Once again, having excited my curiosity, I knew this time I would have to bide my time and coax the story out of her bit by bit during the ensuing conversation.

The facts that came out were these. She had met a boy whilst working in a supermarket near her home and had fallen in love with him. He had even asked to marry her but she had refused. What she did not refuse was - yes, you have guessed it - that staple diet of Scandinavian mythology - sex! Five times a day they were at it, she later confessed. Soon our Heidi became pregnant. Lucky girl! Lucky boy! The prospective father had something he must have been looking forward to. As is so often the case when visiting the sweet shop, there are lots of sweets to choose from and Heidi's boyfriend had a very sweet tooth indeed. His name was Gudmund Johannessen. He had also been screwing Heidi's best friend, behind Heidi's back, at the same time. Well, Heidi got to find out about this and the shock made her miscarry. Depression and despair set in quite quickly followed by self-neglect; no washing for a fortnight, locking herself in her flat and seeing no one followed by an overdose of sleeping pills and lying down on her bed preparing for 'permanent sleep.' It was one of her sisters who found her in time and took her down to the hospital to have her stomach pumped. Now Heidi was recovering in her flat and my phone call came as a welcome distraction for her. Once again I found myself thinking, "You do pick 'em." The whole scene disgusted me and I could not understand how a boy could sleep with his pregnant girlfriend's best friend and live with himself. Still, I enjoyed talking with Heidi, as it was very lonely in England as it always had been. Foreign girls, apart from being on average prettier than the British, have certain 'charm' qualities that British girls just do not possess and never will.

I spoke to Heidi several more times and she also regularly phoned me from her father's office in Bergen. I enjoyed it all. We corresponded and I got some lovely photographs of Heidi posing with the family's black Labrador dog by the waters of a fjord. In those photos, Heidi without doubt was the prettiest girl on earth; so extremely beautiful, and yet so abused in the one area that mattered. I told Heidi I had met an Egyptian girl who I was quite fond of but Heidi must have guessed from my voice that I did not love her and said so. In one of her letters, Heidi said it would be nice if I could marry a blonde Norwegian as well as a dark-haired Egyptian girl. I told Heidi that I would still proceed to sort out my feelings for the Egyptian girl but if in the event it did not work out, then perhaps Heidi and I could try again. Besides, when I met Hala, Heidi was pregnant, a fact that I emphasised to Heidi, trying to avoid her accusing finger. I could tell Heidi needed love and companionship and so lonely was I, that I asked her to come and visit me, saying I would pay for her to stay in a hotel. But she hated the idea of staying on her own in a hotel. I was only trying to respect her body and avoid temptation. In the event, we left it that I would try and visit her sometime in the near future and we continued to speak on the phone in the meantime.

By the month of June, I had acquired a job at a small lawyer's office in Wimpole Street in the London's West End. This particular firm were kind enough to offer me a six-month trial period, which I gratefully accepted. Soon, however, Hala, her sister, mother and her grandmother were upon me, over from Egypt and I knew it would be a tiring fortnight working in London and fitting the family in. However, it was a chance for us to become better acquainted, although I was apprehensive about the prospect of any happy outcome. I wished I had not committed myself to Hala, but as one friend had told me earlier, "It is hard to say thanks, but no thanks."

The family took an apartment at Lees Place opposite the United States Embassy at a weekly rental that only millionaires could afford to pay. Even so, the accommodation was cramped and the grandmother and mother had to use the settee, which converted into a double bed, to sleep on. The first day we met, I went up to see these ladies and we caught up on each other's news. The younger sister was in a frantic state because she was anxiously awaiting the results of her GCSE's taken in Egypt. They had come to England out of respect for me in order to convey their feelings over the matter of myself and Hala and the next day we were to discuss it all properly. When the next day came, Mrs. El Komy told me privately that she and Hala did not think it viable that her daughter and I would have a future together - that very probably we were not entirely suitable. Well, I replied that I was not too distressed at this assessment of the situation because I happened to be very fond of her other daughter, Dalia, who in fact seemed a lot more suitable even though she was only 17.

9

There was no denying it, I preferred Dalia, although I was reluctant to make a move on her now. It would be far too undiplomatic and just be so embarrassing as well. I felt I had blown it, but I was prepared to wait and see. You never know. A fortnight still lay ahead of us for their stay in England and we decided to meet up every day and I was going to make the most of their presence in London. Dalia quickly got her exam results and had not done as well as she had expected. After relaying the bad news to her father in Cairo over the phone, she remained rather distressed and unfortunately entered into quite an immature phase, which put me off her totally. That left Hala, who I quite naturally sidled up to whenever we went out for walks in the parks of London and through the streets of the West End. We soon decided, without exactly saying so, to see if we could develop our friendship and indeed I asked my brother over to meet Dalia and all of us had dinner together in a classy restaurant. Dalia and my brother did not hit it off at all.

The family all came to see me at my Essex home a few days later at the weekend and although they liked the beautiful countryside, they were discouraged by the size of my small three bedroomed house; in a way I could understand that. I was by this time seriously exhausted. I was always getting home at midnight from leaving them in London and waking up at 7 in the morning and on my feet again all day at work. I craved sleep, but still there wasn't long to go until the family returned to Egypt. I had always taken a deep interest in Anwar Sadat and gave a book I had read on him called 'Frogs and Scorpions' to Hala. She disagreed strongly with some of the views expressed by the author and I tried then to explain the reasoning behind the author's views, which in turn Hala could not accept from me. So I got Dalia to try and explain to Hala what I meant. Dalia's kind intercession annoyed Hala greatly.

I had introduced my mother to the family and both girls were very pleased to have met her and gave Mum a long hug before she left for home from Lees Place. What I did not want to tell Mrs. El Komy though was that my parents were in the midst of divorce proceedings. I thought I would save this bad news until I had cemented my friendship with Hala, which I was now in fact genuinely set upon. I had truly begun to develop stronger feelings for Hala and we did get much closer having detailed chats about how we would approach her parents over our plans. So close had we become that one evening whilst on our own in the kitchen, Hala took my hand and placed it inside her nightdress to let me feel a nicely shaped pair of breasts. Hala was proud to tell me that the London shop assistant who was helping her to chose a bra had told her she had great breasts and had told Dalia that her bigger breasts were dropping, something Dalia did not like hearing at all.

One evening towards the end of their stay, I sat down in the kitchen of their apartment with Mrs. El Komy and Dalia and discussed what could be done about Hala and me getting engaged and married. The problem of course was that I knew I would not now get a job in Egypt and unless we got married I would not be able to be with Hala at all. Mrs. El Komy said that Hala had to wait for a couple more years until she finished her English studies at Cairo University. I said it would be impossible for me to wait that long and in any case Hala's English was perfect in every way and continuing to study English Literature was a waste of time. Mrs. El Komy then proceeded to tell me that in the interim, whilst Hala was studying, I was free to have sexual relations with other women until Hala was ready. I responded by asking how could a Muslim woman say such a thing, when clearly, sex before marriage was forbidden in the Quran. Even more astonishing was her next comment that sexual relations "in these circumstances" were allowed by the Quran. I could not believe I was hearing this and told her she was talking nonsense and Dalia agreed completely with me and told her mother so. I wanted marriage as soon as possible, because I knew that during the interim all sorts of things would come between us, not least of all being in different countries, which would kill the relationship. So Mrs. El Komy and I were at loggerheads.

Another mistake of mine, which proved decisive in my downfall, was not to tell Mrs. El Komy that my parents were getting divorced. My mother told her herself when they met earlier. This really distressed Mrs. El Komy as she had been completely frank about the state of her marriage with me and obviously expected similar reciprocity on the state of my own parents' marriage. What held me back was the fact that her daughter, in coming to a strange country would have the misfortune of marrying into a broken family, which is a depressing situation to be introduced to and worth keeping quiet for as long as possible. Hala actually supported my reasoning on this point and stood up for me in front of her mother. Besides, the decree nisi had not come through, and indeed as it later turned out, my mother abandoned her divorce proceedings against my father - a decision that was to cost her dearly in the years to come and indeed was not just to affect her health but mine too. My heart went out to my mother. Her father, one by the grand sounding name of Eduard Alexander Von Pahlsberg was killed in Stalingrad fighting for the German Sixth Army under Field Marshall Friedrich Von Paulus, in 1942. Her mother died at age 35 from a fall off her horse. There was not one happy moment in her entire marriage to my father. They were eventually divorced in 1990.

Relations then were deteriorating rapidly between Hala's mother and me and they were not getting any better with Hala. Things came to a head when, in her distress, Mrs. El Komy told Hala that I also liked her sister; something she had kept to herself for 10 days but now had decided to reveal to Hala. Hala and I argued the next day about something or other and then it all came out. She told me her mother had told her I liked her sister also and that, coupled with our own deteriorating friendship, ended with her telling me in the evening that everything was off; no marriage would ever take place between us. I was relieved, as by then I knew I did not love the girl enough. I had had all the time I wanted to discover my true feelings. Conversely, after my initial dislike for her, I had gradually got to know Dalia at a distance and by the end of her trip we had got to like each other very much. There was a marked improvement in her self-control. On the last day of their stay, we all went to the Central London Mosque and for a walk in Regent's Park. I managed to get away with Dalia for a stroll when she put my arm around her and she held my hand. I proceeded to have one of the nicest and most peaceful conversations I have ever had with a girl. I liked what I was hearing and I knew then that I surely should have chosen her instead of Hala. I was in love with Dalia. Indeed, Hala told me that if I had chosen Dalia in the first place, then everything would have been okay - marriage would have been possible. Now it was all over with the family and of course I was in emotional turmoil. There I was with my dream girl arm in arm walking in Regent's Park, but she would never be mine. We sat by the ornamental pond talking openly about our secrets and I cherished the moment. I was never to see Dalia again after her return to Egypt and for years afterwards at night alone in bed I sometimes pretended she was there with me. It gave me peace, as I knew we were kindred spirits.

On the last evening before they went home, Mrs. El Komy, her mother and the two girls accompanied me to a meal in a Lebanese restaurant in Kensington High Street. It was a peace offering by Mrs. El Komy who did not want things to end on a sour note. I was in good spirits. When the meal was over we said our goodbyes and went our separate ways. The next morning, a Sunday, at 10 a.m., I phoned the family from home to wish them a safe flight but decided during my conversation with Hala that I wanted to see her in person just to console her a little and reduce the bitterness. So I raced round to Heathrow Airport in my car and found the check-in terminal for Yugoslav Airlines, but I had missed them. They had already gone through passport control. Shit! I gave a hand-written message to another passenger to pass on to one of the airhostesses to pass on to the El Komys. I then went up to the terminal restaurant, wrote a long letter to Hala and posted it to Egypt. I had done my best and drove home, exhausted, around the M25 motorway.

The next day I phoned Heidi in Norway and explained that I literally had not had a spare moment to phone her. It was true - I had spent the whole of the previous fortnight from the time I got up until the time I went to bed at midnight, going to work or being with the El Komys. However, this was no solace to Heidi who was upset and not a little angry that I had not phoned her in two weeks. I told her that my association with this Egyptian family was over and that I could therefore pay her a visit, adding truthfully that we could try and see if we could resurrect a friendship that might lead to something deeper. But instead of gratitude, she told me she did not like being made "the second choice," the implication being that I should have made her my number one from the start. I just could not win with anybody. With Hala El Komy she already knew a chap who she was thinking of marrying (and eventually did marry). I was in competition with him - Amir, which at one stage I was told by Hala I was winning. Now I was told by Heidi, who had already lost unborn children to men that plainly used her for self-gratification, that I was basically unfair and inconsiderate for getting to know an Egyptian girl (at the time when she, Heidi, was pregnant).

Anyway, Heidi's desperation and frustration subsided a little over the next few weeks and she agreed that I could visit her at Christmas. I could not go before as I was anxious to secure articles of clerkship at the firm I was working with in Wimpole Street. I was still on my trial period.

The trial period eventually became very trying indeed. The practice had two partners and the senior one, Phillip, was good at his job but had a marked 'Jack the lad' approach to his staff and some of his clients. Foul language came much easier to him than the Queen's English, so did lewd talk. For instance, one day all the trainees, including myself, were sitting in his room having a cosy chat, when he said he was surprised that none of us had caught herpes yet, as he had, pointing to the sore on his mouth. Another time, a Lebanese client was in his office with me and a secretary who was taking too long to find a file, when eventually Phillip said to her, "Stop playing with your breasts and bring that file here now." For sure, her breasts were very big indeed but even a 'Jack the lad' should not make such vulgar comments so openly. Luckily, the girl was a family friend of 'Mr. Tact and Diplomacy' and she left it at that. The girl and the client, however, were extremely embarrassed.

Then one day another trainee arrived at the firm. He was the brother of a lawyer that Phillip had previously worked with. The new chap, Adam, had obtained his law degree from the same college as me but was a few years younger and was awaiting the results of his Law Society Final Examination. I could not see that there was room for two articled clerks though. Some time in late October I was sent to get a file, which unfortunately, although I tried hard to locate, I just could not find. I went back into Phillip's room to tell him this, whereupon he went upstairs agitatedly to look for the file himself. He found it immediately and came back down the stairs to tell me he thought I was "fucking hopeless" and added, "I really mean it." He certainly did mean it and I knew then that I was as good as finished at the firm.

A month or so later, just as Adam had found out he had failed his Law Society Final Examination, he was offered articles of clerkship and I was told I had to leave at Christmas (even though I had long since passed the Law Society Final Examination). I stayed on until Christmas, making applications to other firms. I attended the firm's Christmas dinner. It turned out that after Adam had - for the second time - failed his Law Society Final Examination, he in turn foundered on the displeasure of Phillip, the senior partner, and was told to leave himself. Two of my fellow trainees were then made partners, whereupon they told Phillip never again to treat anyone in the way he had treated me and Adam. One of these new partners was Steven Barker who in 2001 defended the then Leeds United footballer, Lee Bowyer, against those well-publicised assault charges and who later successfully defended the Chelsea footballer and future England captain John Terry against assault charges. Steven Barker even took on Ronnie Biggs (the Great train robber) as a client, pro-bono. I had already made my feelings known to Phillip having written him a letter literally wishing him torment in hell and in the meantime if ever he was to see me in London walking on the same side of the street, would he please cross over to the other side so I would not have to face him. Not getting articles of clerkship was affecting my health and I blamed that wanker, Phillip, directly. As it turned out, Phillip himself left the firm a couple of years or so later to go out on his own.

I had the good fortune, however, to meet a very good-looking Lebanese girl on the London Underground before Christmas. She was studying interior design at a college in Willesden and we exchanged telephone numbers on the train. She was staying in a convent in Hampstead and that is where I went to visit her. The nuns were just wonderful and let Leila and I sit in the guest room and chat for as long as we wanted. I must say I liked her, but I don't think she was that keen on me, but I wanted to work on it. I wasn't sure whether going to Norway to see Heidi was a good idea, but I had promised I would go and I had already booked the flight, so yes, I was going to go to Norway.

I knew Heidi was still having difficulty getting herself together. She wasn't working or studying but just trying to get over her last trauma. She hated sleeping in the dark so slept with a table lamp on to give her a feeling of security. When I had spoken to her in the late summer she had told me she was very lonely indeed, so I told her to get a flatmate and she said she had already been trying to get one.

Chapter 3

During the phone call I made to Heidi just before going to visit her, I had been put off by her plea that I should promise not to "argue" during my stay with her. I knew from the past that it wasn't me that started the arguments but that it was her little peculiarities that started her off in directions I hardly knew existed. In England I had only tried to indicate that her way of life wasn't conducive to clean living and it had upset her. So if constructive advice is 'an argument' then I might just as well have no tongue to speak with. Giving any well-meaning advice to 'an independent girl' was obviously classed as intrusive and argumentative and most unwelcome by its recipient.

The night before my flight to Bergen I did not get much sleep - too much was going on in my mind, which was full of nervous tension. I was so tired at Gatwick Airport that I didn't even have the enthusiasm to say hello to my boyhood hero, Martin Chivers, the ex-Tottenham Hotspur and England centre forward who was in the departure lounge with his family.

I arrived in Bergen on a cold misty afternoon on the 23rd December, where Heidi met me at the airport with Knut, a friend of hers who came with his van to take us back to her place. She looked totally gorgeous and once again I wondered at how anyone could use and discard her. She was an absolute dream. I gave her a Christmas present of an expensive bottle of perfume and also three huge Christmas cards which she asked me to bring over from England to give to her friends. The scenery on the way back to her place was breathtaking. I thought Paradise itself couldn't look any better - little lakes, big lakes and mountains with snow on the peaks. So, I was with a beautiful girl in a beautiful country. "A happy ten days this should be," I thought.

Heidi's home consisted of a basement room containing every essential; a big bed built in an alcove on a raised platform, a sofa, wardrobe, cupboards, kitchen and separate toilet and shower room. It was very warm and snug and out of the kitchen window one could see a huge mountain covered in mist. Heidi was a very good artist and had sketched several pencil drawings of herself in the nude in various positions and stuck them up on the wall by her black sofa. I was quite taken aback at these pictures, as it seemed to me that her 'art' was only giving out the wrong signals, but she couldn't make the connection when I asked her why she was putting these pictures up. The pictures stayed up the whole time.

It got dark at around 3 p.m. and Knut stayed with us for a couple of hours chatting. Heidi and I then at last had some time to ourselves and it was then I realised I would be staying with her alone, as her flatmate was visiting relatives.

No sooner had I begun to relax when six of Heidi's friends came round - all men - and as exhausted as I was I chatted for three hours or so with them and then went up to sit on the bed as I was dead beat. I waited another hour until midnight and then asked Heidi if we could all call it a day, as I wanted to go to sleep. Half and hour later she reluctantly obliged and all the boys trooped out into the darkness.

I slept on the couch and Heidi slept on her bed with the table lamp on all night. The next day was Christmas Eve and after breakfast I had a shower, got dressed and waited to see what we were going to do. Heidi surprised me by saying that she wasn't at all happy with my request that her friends go home "early" the previous night as she had not seen them for some time and would have liked to have talked with them through the night. "Till what time?" I asked. "Until about 4 or 5 in the morning," she replied. "But I was exhausted last night - it was my first night and I wanted to go to sleep before midnight," I said. "Oh fuck - what a waste of time your visit is, you had better try to go back home immediately! You have paid for a trip here and it is like all your money has been put in the dustbin," she angrily remonstrated.

This outburst came as such a shock to me that I thought, "Well if that's your attitude you can shove it and I will go home." Besides, her eruption was in keeping with her fucked up character and fucked up life. So, quickly, she rang up the booking agent at Fresland Airport to ask if my return flight could be changed to the evening flight of that same day. The reply came that my ticket was non-changeable, so unless I paid the earth for a one way ticket back home, I would have to see out my full 10 days stay. So that is what I did - I stayed. Heidi resigned herself to this fact but pleaded that I "behave" myself. Me! Behave myself! Fucking cheek!

13

Later that day, Iren came round. She was Heidi's flatmate, a tired looking petite girl who spoke poor but adequate English. Heidi told me that Iren, who was 17 years old, had just finished a stint as a prostitute - "She goes with much older men," said Heidi a touch disgustedly. "And now chosen as your flatmate," I thought, very disgustedly. Fine company for one recovering from a suicide attempt! Great spiritual succour and support Iren, the hooker, would be for her! I learned that fortunately I would not have to put up with Iren's company at night for a few more days yet.

We then went out to begin our walk to the local shopping centre. Tomorrow was going to be Christmas day; a day Heidi was invited to spend with her stepmother and father and her two sisters and two half-brothers. I had not been invited, as it was to be a "family day" but was instead invited to go and eat with them all on Boxing Day. Fair enough. Heidi said it was important I hear what she had to say about her stepmother as I should not be fooled by her stepmother's gossip as she was prone to telling lies and exaggerating. Heidi warned me that if her stepmother was going to subject me to words of censure over Heidi's own behaviour then I should be made aware of her stepmother's own past. She "had been a fashion model in her youth in America and has slept with lots of men and is nothing but a hypocrite." When Boxing Day came upon us and the family had treated me to a traditional Norwegian dinner, I sat down on my own with Heidi's stepmother and we had a friendly conversation. I made oblique mention of my disquiet over Heidi's general situation. Mrs. Overaa was careful not to commit herself too deeply on the subject of Heidi as I could see she was nervous about any repercussions that would come her way if I happened to pass her comments on to Heidi. However, she did have the courage to tell me not to believe everything Heidi told me. Quid pro quo. Heidi's parents had a lovely home on top of a rocky outcrop. It was perfect in every way, neat and tidy, and they clearly took pleasure in its appearance and upkeep. Heidi had two half-brothers, one aged 4 and the other aged 12, both of whom Heidi liked very much. Mrs. Overaa's father lived in a self-contained apartment on the ground floor in the house and concerning whom I was made privy to another of Heidi's secrets. It was that the old man was keen to have sex with Heidi and was always asking for it. He never got his way on actual intercourse, I believe, but one night when I questioned Heidi further on what had taken place between them, she abruptly said, "Don't ask" and turned over to go to sleep. Clearly she did not want to talk about what had taken place. The afternoon that I spent with Heidi's family was rather tense and I could feel their discomfort at having a new face to dinner. Maybe they felt that I knew too much. Heidi later told me that her parents didn't like me.

Boxing Day night was memorable if only for what didn't take place between Heidi and me. In a way I was drawing closer to Heidi but as each day passed it was becoming still clearer that this was not the girl for me, but I was in the fly-trap and further weakened by the knowledge that nowhere in England could a girl be found as bubbly and attractive as Heidi. England just doesn't make 'em. We both needed the warmth of a good kiss and cuddle and we had now taken to sleeping together in her bed. Well, the kissing and cuddling very quickly overcame us that night and Heidi was soon an uncontrollable love bomb getting lost in her passion. It was incredible stuff. Off came her blue dressing gown to reveal her large firm breasts but with very small nipples. Her body was perfect - strong large bones, plenty of meat. But it had a blemish - a very unsightly and large birthmark on her lower back that was rather off-putting and which I told her to have removed, not least because of the risk of cancer. She was now on top of me and clearly I had let myself in for the inevitable - even though before my visit I insisted that she do her best not to let me "touch" her. When I was seconds away from commencing my big entry, Heidi all of a sudden must have remembered my plea and she stopped, saying, "No, this is wrong." This statement made me feel a little guilty but it didn't stop us later continuing exploring each other's bodies in a slightly less - only slightly mind you - pleasurable manner. But the big act itself had not been done. I was in an unfortunate position, sick and tired of meeting trash, but sick and tired of self-restraint and self-discipline. I wanted marriage with a nice girl but was reduced to this because Heidi was all that was available on the planet and dealing with her rationally was impossible.

The next night Heidi and I spent away from each other as she had been invited to go on her own to a mountain lodge for a party and stay over. Apparently there wasn't any sleeping accommodation for me, so I couldn't come. My fears over whether Heidi would be doing any more than partying apparently proved unfounded when she told me the day after that she had genuinely behaved herself and had had to be woken up in the small hours from talking in her sleep about me. She told me she was mentioning my name in her sleep, asking me to help her. "Oh well, it's nice to be dreamed about," I thought. I sometimes dreamed about Heidi myself and one of the first dreams that stuck in my mind was one that featured Heidi and me trying to escape from a house fire. We had lost each other in the confusion and panic. All of a sudden we found each other and hugged and kissed in grateful thanks to God that we were together again. We then found our way to safety. I had written and told Heidi about this dream and related my tremendous feeling of love and tenderness for her. She wrote back with her tender comments. In years to come I had other dreams about Heidi, but those can keep for now.

My conversations with Heidi increasingly reached a quite intimate level and I took this as an indication that Heidi had regretted her rash action in asking me to go back home on my first full day with her. In one such discourse, as we waited at a bus terminal to return home, Heidi revealed that a shopkeeper in Bergen had raped her. He was a young chap, a boutique owner but he wasn't Norwegian and Heidi and him had been at a party together. Heidi told me that she complained to the police about the rape but they questioned her version of events suggesting that she may have encouraged the man by showing him her breasts. She got nowhere in having the police press charges. I also learnt that her last boyfriend, Gudmund Johannessen, had contracted venereal disease and had been treated for it.

Before the old year was out, Heidi took me round to a gathering of her friends, all boys, whom we met outside a bar. She introduced me to them and we chatted happily about this and that. Before going round the corner to one of these friends' flat, Heidi came up to me and quietly pointed to one chap saying that he was the boy who had got her pregnant and made her miscarry - "It was twins," she said matter-of-factly. Twins! "Oh no," I thought. The boy, Gudmund Johannessen, I expected would be nowhere in sight after what he had done - but it was just a case of c'est la vie. Twins! I had thought there was just one foetus miscarried, but the truth was there were two.

New Years Eve was a wonderful occasion in Bergen; but it was bitterly cold and very very icy. Come the night time, Heidi, Iren and I made our way to a party in a house that overlooked a valley. It belonged to the parents of a boy, Bjorn-Morten, who Heidi had quite fancied. Indeed Heidi had informed me on the third or fourth day of my stay that she was in discussions with him over whether they could be boyfriend and girlfriend. He had come up to see her one time in his car and they spent half an hour in the car trying to see if there was a way forward for them. Tonight at the party, talk was still of the two of them getting together and one or two people expressed surprise that I myself had been invited over to Bergen to see her, as they thought she was very fond of this other guy. Anyway, the old boyfriend, Gudmund Johannessen was also at the party and two or three times Heidi came over and implored me in low whispers to tell Johannessen to leave her alone as he kept asking her to go out with him again and resume their relationship. Fate, however, was to come to Johannessen's rescue. Fireworks were part of the celebrations after midnight. It was the most beautiful fireworks party I have ever seen and the whole valley was a sea of glorious light. A loud scream suddenly pierced the celebrations. It was from Johannessen who had injured himself by careless detonation of a firework and was in considerable pain in his upper leg. Heidi, in sympathy, tended to him giving him the chance, I guess, to play on her vulnerable emotions.

As things turned out, Johannessen needed a place to sleep for the night and he asked me if he could come round to stay in Heidi's flat. Heidi was going to sleep at her parents. Not wanting to be difficult, I agreed and he and Iren slept in the big bed and I on the couch. We woke up on New Year's day and soon afterwards Johannessen got himself comfortable with Iren, snuggling up beside her in the bed with his arm around her. She didn't mind at all and said they had even gone out with each other for a short period. After she had left, Johannessen and I had a long talk. He regretted what he had done to Heidi in the past and was keen to make it up to her and get back together with her. I told him his chances were slim indeed and that only last night Heidi had told me she never wanted to go out with him again. He seemed struck by the sincerity of my views and invited me back to his parents' place where I met his family, who welcomed me warmly. I liked his father a lot enjoying his company whilst we ate cheese on toast and drank tea. Their home overlooked a long fjord: a scenic delight. We watched a Charles Bronson video whilst waiting for Heidi and Iren to turn up, but Heidi then phoned through to say she was too tired to come, so eventually I left on my own back to Heidi's flat by bus.

Heidi did her best to entertain me but she knew I wasn't happy with what I was seeing and hearing. Her personal habits left an awful lot to be desired. She used to cook her pork chops frozen, directly from the freezer. Telling her that it was essential to let the meat thaw first so it cooked through when fried had no effect on her. One night, nature got its own back on her with hilarious results. I was woken in the midst of my slumbers by the longest fart I had ever heard. It went on and on and on and the poor girl didn't even wake up! Next morning she complained of a stomach ache.

15

On another occasion, I went back on my own early to sleep on Heidi's bed instead of the couch, this time. Before going to sleep I noticed in the half-light of the table lamp the nicely embroidered bed sheets. The next morning, I woke up and started to play with the embroidery with my fingers, picking at the stitching. On deeper inspection, I discovered the embroidery was not embroidery at all but thick congealed blood deposited during Heidi's recent period. Yuck - the sheets should have been changed immediately by her. When I later mentioned this, she said she had reminded me to change the sheets before I returned to the flat, but I didn't recall being told this at all. Anyway, I was prepared to give her the benefit of the doubt but in truth she should have changed the sheets herself without a moment's delay.

Like so many girls in Norway, Heidi was a smoker – 'Prince' cigarettes were the most popular brand in their attractive red and white carton. She was addicted and had the annoying habit of smoking in bed last thing at night and even in the middle of the night when she couldn't sleep. When Iren slept over with us, the pair of them would sometimes chat away into the night happily smoking their cancer sticks. Both of them were occasional users of cannabis supplied by the ever ready Johannessen, who was proud to smoke the stuff in front of me.

Iren had, remarkably, acquired a boyfriend. He was a couple of years older than she was and extremely handsome. We went around as a foursome and I got to know the chap quite well. I wanted to tell him that Iren had been a prostitute, but knew that if I did Heidi would never speak to me again. It was bad enough when I complained to Heidi about Iren whilst we were all waiting for a bus to pick us up. Iren and her boyfriend were quite unashamedly kissing each other in full view of others at the bus stop; something which always embarrasses me and I feel is really offensive. When I criticised them to Heidi, she lost her temper with me saying I was fussing over nothing and it was up to them what they did.

Even a simple enough event like going to watch a film at the cinema was not without its disruptions. The film we had chosen to see was '1984,' starring Richard Burton and John Hurt. When it came to Winston Smith (John Hurt) being questioned about his greatest fear - that of being tortured by rats - Heidi couldn't bear to watch any more and asked if we could leave. I said that I wanted to stay - so she then got up annoyed and said she would wait in the café whilst I watched the rest of the film on my own. After 10 minutes she came back to take up her seat beside me carrying a nice cup of coffee for me. She seemed to have bucked up and I was grateful for her more relaxed behaviour.

On the last day of my stay, Heidi, Iren and I had some time to kill before Knut turned up in his van to take me back to the airport. The conversation got round to the subject of their sex lives and they both confessed to having slept with a lot of guys for fun. Heidi said she had had sex with a couple of different chaps on the beach whilst on holiday in Rhodes, taken soon after she had returned from being an au pair in England. Two of her other friends who went with her also had sex with the local studs because "they were attracted to them" - these Mediterranean types being a source of fantasy fulfilment. I asked both girls to write down on a piece of paper the names of the boys they had slept with. Iren immediately took up the challenge and returned with a list of exactly 12 boys but said there were one or two more but she needed time to remember their names. Heidi didn't bother with her list but said reflectively that she had been with "about 20." She was only 21 years old.

Heidi's two sisters had fared little better than her. Elisabeth, I had never met, but Heidi told me that she had ditched her husband some time back who then developed quite severe mental problems as a result. One day he came round to see Heidi to try and unburden his heavy soul and ended up "shaking" in grief and despair at his rejection by Elisabeth, desperately wanting his wife back. He never got her back. Heidi's other sister, Rennaug, I did meet twice, once in the garden nursery where she worked and another time when she gave us a lift in her litter-strewn car. She was a slim girl, completely different from the well built Heidi and looked quite tired. In her case, her husband had left her and their three children and not surprisingly Rennaug found it very difficult to cope on her own. She was on prescription pills from her doctor and Heidi said that but for her children Rennaug would have committed suicide.

Knut arrived with a full load of the friends I had made who were all coming to see me off at the airport. They had all been good to me and I had taken it as a sign of their friendship in coming to bid me farewell. This gesture was emphasised when it was announced at the airport that my flight had been delayed by an hour and a half, so instead of going back home they stayed. I shook hands with all of them in turn and could tell they were sad to say goodbye. With about 10 minutes to go before departure time, I took Heidi to one side for a farewell embrace. I will always remember for as long as I live the quality of her kisses at that moment. Her mouth was just made for kissing and when her lips touched mine I felt so happy. God's gift of physical love was truly incredible. The kisses were long in duration and we were finding it difficult to stop. Had I been too hasty in my judgement of her? Was it the case that after all her traumas she needed extra special care and rehabilitation with a caring person over an extended period of time? Even after our final kiss and after I had closed the door separating the public lounge from the departure lounge, I wanted to go back to hold her tight but I said to myself, "No, don't do it. Don't be a Desperate Dan." Besides, there was always the phone - later.

Chapter 4

I was eager to get back to London to try yet again to secure a place for articles of clerkship in a law firm. Most fortunately, I had been recommended by a lawyer immediately across the road from my old office at Wimpole Street to a solicitor in adjacent Queen Anne Street. I went in to see the two partners who within a couple of days decided to take me on for a trial period. I loved the place; I liked all the staff; the place was happy and wealthy but alas dear Jim, the partner with whom I sat, was in no mood to train me. He had made a lot of money in the conveyancing market in the late 70's and early 80's and owned a gorgeous home in Hampstead. It had even been featured in the magazine 'House and Gardens.' He had a tasty wife, three young daughters and a boat; why bother to teach a novice the art of conveyancing? He had just taken on a property solicitor in any case; a recently qualified lady, Frances, who didn't need any supervision. Jim had already done his stint in teaching others at a night school as a part-time law lecturer, where in fact he had met his wife who was one of his students. No sir, things were going fine for Jim and he just left me to read old files, sit in on his meetings with clients and attend simple Court hearings and other legal business when needed. He enjoyed tennis and knew John Lloyd, the former British No. 1. I even answered the phone one time to Mr. Lloyd when he phoned up whilst I was manning the newly acquired reception desk; a reception desk which I chose and ordered.

One of Jim's more alluring clients was Fowzia, a Moroccan student in her 20's who needed some conveyancing done. Did she have style! Fine clothes, well-manicured hands and a good bit of jewellery - all whilst a student. Mind you, she did have extremely large breasts to go with her good looks which might have attracted wealthy admirers. On our first meeting, she was very formal and most concerned to resolve one or two problems she faced regarding a clothing business transaction she had been involved in. Jim left me to deal with her on my own once he had dealt with some formalities on her conveyancing transaction. On the third occasion I saw her she was in a café in Marylebone High Street and I went up to her to say hello while she was sitting with another college friend. They were studying costume design in the nearby American College and Fowzia was already involved in import/export for her clothes. Eventually Fowzia told me she felt there was "something" I wanted to say to her. She could feel it in her bones she said. I knew exactly what she thought she wanted me to say but romance wasn't on my mind. True, I thought she must have been wonderful in bed but my heart lay elsewhere, back in picturesque Norway. I had missed Heidi and remained lonely here in London but still distrustful of my Norwegian friend after all I had seen and heard. London, nay England, was such a lonely, loveless place. The 'island' mentality pervaded all social relationships towards, not just foreigners, but also amongst the British themselves and getting to know strangers in a non-work, non-circle-of-friends environment was next to impossible. Everything was so confrontational. By instinct I turned to the only girl I had feelings for, the delinquent Heidi. I have only seldom come across an English girl with the inspiration of the typical European or South American girl. The English (in general) are socially handicapped in comparison, a view echoed by the numerous European men and Scandinavian au pairs I have talked to on the subject over the years. The au pairs tell me that English girls get jealous in fear of the better looking (or at least friendlier) Scandinavians taking their boyfriends away and that, besides this, the English girls just do not want to mix socially with the invading Scandinavians.

It transpired that the Lebanese girl, Leila, that I had met the previous autumn, was very fond of a Lebanese boy whom she had known for quite some time but as he lived in Lebanon and she studied in London, distance had kept their meetings limited. I had acquired this knowledge on another trip to the convent when the nuns had warmly welcomed me once again. I had been very hopeful up to that moment, but Leila came out with it and said that we had nothing in common. I took this as a sign that she just wasn't really attracted to me. I wasn't an authentic Middle Easterner and my knowledge of the Arabic language was only basic. It was a shame, but I accepted her wishes. The guy she liked also came from a very wealthy family so I was truly a beaten man. She was a good and polite girl. She confided in me about a health problem relating to her thyroid gland for which she had to take medication for the rest of her life and spoke of certain family secrets, so I had no cause to dislike her and I wished her well. I never saw her again but a few years later I went back to the convent and enquired of the Mother Superior, who still remembered me, about the fortunes of Leila. It turned out that she had got married and now had a young baby daughter. But her husband was not the man she told me she was fond of years earlier. No, the Mother Superior told me another Arab man came on the scene who despite initial rejection refused to take no for an answer from Leila. He persisted in trying to win her affections, having ample opportunity to do so as Leila's first love was mostly away doing business in Lebanon and West Africa. Eventually she succumbed and they married. Her first pregnancy ended in miscarriage and the couple were terribly upset, the dear nun told me. When the next pregnancy succeeded the couple were over the moon. They were now living in London.

I still had not finished either with the Egyptian sisters who came to see me the previous summer and was annoyed that I had not received any written communications whatsoever to my pleas on the telephone for them to understand my position. All I wanted was some consolation in writing. I still spent a fortune on the phone on damage limitation but really I was clutching at straws. I was cut off and forgotten in a flash. So, feeling very hard done by, I wrote to their father telling him a few home truths but not the one truth that would have really crushed him, that his wife had never loved him. This mighty Pharaoh had to be told that his peculiar Egyptian ways were wrong and I did this to good effect. The letter made him ill, he surprisingly admitted to me some time later when I phoned him up in his office. Yes, I couldn't believe I had the balls to make that call to him but I did and at the same time I said I was sorry. Sorry for him! Was it really me saying this? Yes, it certainly was. I even got my cousin to phone the man up later to ask how his other daughter, Dalia, was fixed. He said she was too young for marriage - his very polite way of saying she wasn't available for me, as within a year she did get engaged. Well - I had to try.

So naturally my emptiness translated itself into another hopeless cause, the one living in Bergen. Events thrust me in her direction rather unexpectedly. Things were dragging along at work with little to really get involved in. The boss, Jim, out of the blue told me things "aren't working out" and thought it might be better if I found employment elsewhere. I liked life with him but had to admit, without any effort by him to train me properly, I would just get nowhere. He gave me a week to stay on and on my last day gave me a generous tip and wished me all the best. It was the Easter weekend and everybody else in the building went home early. I was the last to leave and had arranged to meet the busty Fowzia in the office from whence we would go to have a cup of coffee in Marylebone High Street. I tidied up, switched off all the lights in the office and waited for Fowzia. She called dead on time - 5 o'clock. I immediately left the building locking the front door and putting the keys back through the letterbox.

Off Fowzia and I went to a café round the corner and discussed everyday mundane things. Fowzia eventually turned the talk directly to her own personal problem of not having a British passport. She wanted one to ensure she could stay in Britain for good but didn't know whether she could convert her present temporary residence permit into permanent residency, in due course. She wanted to deal with the matter once and for all now. Her proposal was this - she would give me £10,000 in exchange for marrying her. We would "have sex and a good time" and she would then get her British passport as my wife. After a decent but minimal interval we would then get divorced, she told me. She was honest enough to say it was simply a business transaction between the two of us and no one else need know. What did I have to say to that, she enquired? I couldn't go along with it, I said. If I were going to marry a girl it would be because I loved her. Did I want to marry Fowzia? No. It was morally wrong to go along with her plan and that if we were to marry it would be on a proper basis. Only the way I put it to her was that the transaction was too risky for me as I was at the beginning of my legal career and I was concerned that the thing would ruin me. I deliberately gave her the impression in the café that "marriage on a proper basis" was something I just might consider, as I did not yet want to go back home. Fowzia then said we would take a taxi back to her place and during the journey I should consider whether to take up her proposal. We got in the taxi and without a second's delay, Fowzia had her hands on my groin and was French kissing me with all but a little resistance from me. I knew it had to stop as it was embarrassing doing this in full view of the taxi driver's rear view mirror. He must have thought we were real shits. I backed off and eventually we arrived at Fowzia's place in West London when the taxi driver showed his disgust by abruptly driving off, almost colliding with me as he sped away after snatching the fare from my hand.

Fowzia and I then crossed the road and at once she stopped and told me that she lived just a little further on. If I was to go any further she required at least my provisional agreement to her little scheme. Seeing a full-scale seduction in her place if I lied and said okay, I knew it would be hypocritical to go with her. Her huge breasts and no doubt horny bedroom action were tempting for any man but for me that day my head ruled my groin fortunately, and we parted company in the street.

I kept this episode with Fowzia to myself until almost exactly a year later when I visited my old principal, Jim, in his office in Queen Anne Street. By then I had obtained articles of clerkship. He and I exchanged each other's news and I asked after Ron his personal assistant and driver. Ron, an out of work actor had got married Jim told me - to Fowzia. "To Fowzia!" I exclaimed. Jim went on. It was Ron's first marriage and he was so in love but as soon as Fowzia had got her passport she had left Ron and then they got divorced. Ron was heartbroken and because he got married for love she didn't pay him a penny for the passport. Jim was astounded when I told him my own story about Fowzia. In keeping the matter to myself as Fowzia had made me promise, I had let her carry off her scheme to fruitful completion with poor Ron. My silence had proved golden indeed for our Moroccan friend Fowzia.

But back to the time when I left Fowzia to go up to her flat on her own in West London. After that I went back home myself. I was so alone and decided I couldn't take Easter by myself. Next day I went straight up to London and bought myself a return air ticket to Bergen from the Norwegian Railways Office. I phoned Heidi to say I was coming the very next day – 11th April – for five days. "Oh shit!" she protested, as at such short notice she said she could not meet me at the airport as she was going skiing but would leave the door key under a stone on the bathroom window-ledge.

Chapter 5

On arrival at Bergen Airport I caught the Flybussen to the town centre and a local bus to Heidi's place. I found the key where Heidi said she had left it and let myself in. A pot of warm blackcurrant tea was left there for me and I helped myself whilst waiting for Heidi to get back from skiing. After an hour and a half she turned up with her male companion who had been on the slopes with her. I had never met him before and he certainly was a jolly nice fellow. "Never had sex with him though," said Heidi when he had left.

"So what's your news then," I asked her, "and how is Iren?"

"Oh you would never guess…" and Heidi proceeded to tell me a story that was in keeping with all that had gone before. Iren also knew that Heidi had apparently been raped by the Bergen boutique owner. A man in fact that Iren knew herself and was very critical of for doing such a "dreadful, despicable thing" as she was keen to tell Heidi when discussing the man's alleged actions. Only trouble was, Heidi told me, that at the same time as telling her this, Iren was also screwing the boutique owner herself. When Heidi found out about this duplicity, she beat Iren up. Iren was history and we would not be seeing her again.

I was only going to stay in Bergen for four days this time. The weather was really nice so Heidi and I went out and about. Her ski partner took us for a fantastic drive around Bergen and its surrounds. Unreal beauty. Down valleys, up mountains, across a suspension bridge. I loved it and I loved being with Heidi who chatted cheerily all the way pointing out the landmarks.

To my surprise, Gudmund Johannessen turned up early on the first evening. He had had his hair permed. He settled down and cheerfully proceeded to roll himself a joint, which he smoked in the room. It seems he had wormed his way back into Heidi's life as I had suspected. Jesus! How desperate must she be! What on earth was going on? When he left, I reprimanded her for continuing to associate with this jerk. She listened and then promptly went to the toilet to retch. Hearing home truths literally made her want to be sick! But she was not sick of Johannessen; just sick from me telling her off. Still, they were not living together.

The second day took us to the Bergen Aquarium which was cut into a rocky outcrop. The high point came when we saw a tank containing lots of fish - drawing the remark from Heidi, "Group sex… the fish are having group sex." Heidi then proceeded to give me a short rendition of Franky Goes to Hollywood's biggest hit 'Relax' - good old-fashioned 'Fuck-the-Girl' lyrics. She knew the words by heart. Clearly Heidi was still a horny bitch whose main interest was sex. As for myself, I was getting really steamed up and simply asked Heidi if we could "do it tonight." She said "No." It wouldn't be right for me because I didn't believe in sex before marriage, she reminded me. "True," I thought to myself, but I also knew that in England I would face a bloody long wait. So I persisted in my request on the way to the cinema where we were going to watch 'The Killing Fields.' I asked Heidi what the matter was as to why we couldn't have sex. She was single, I was single. I liked her. So what was up? Something was up but I couldn't figure out what it was. I was at a loss. We spoke of other things but half way through the film she said, "You can have me as much as you want tonight." I had the condoms and I was really looking forward to it. I had never had intercourse before. The film was really an emotional one and it made a big impact upon me. If only I could have infused Heidi with a sense of spiritual worth, it would have made her a worthwhile human being.

Outside the cinema, after the film had finished, Heidi was in a bad mood. We caught the bus back to her place and on the way she lost her temper over nothing and when we got off the bus she said she had changed her mind about us going 'all the way' that night. A good time girl like her? Does a leopard change its spots? I was mystified. But I accepted it and when I got back to her place, I put the condoms deep into her kitchen refuse bin whilst she was in the toilet. What the hell, she was such a shit that in the final analysis she was not the sort of girl anyone could live with for long; but I had known that for some time anyway hadn't I?

The last hours of the evening we spent chatting away whilst she lay on her bed and I lay on the couch on the other side of the room. I was still however wondering what had happened to turn her off sex and started to probe her again as to what was preventing her. I went over to her bed and got in and we talked easily to each other. I told her that I couldn't understand what she was doing with her life and that the mess she was in seemed so unnecessary. I was weary of the strain of it all and I wept on her shoulder as she genuinely tried to comfort me. Her body also made me horny but realising it was not going to happen, I left the bed to go back to the couch, but I was still horny and again I asked if we could do it.

"No," she said.

"What's the reason?" I asked.

I just got evasive replies so I asked her several times more whilst all the time we were on opposite sides of the room with me on the couch and her on the bed. Eventually, she conceded and called me over saying, "Oh come on then, lets do it....You will see it's really nothing." Over I came and she let me slip into her whilst she lay on her back. She refused to go on top, but in any case I thoroughly enjoyed it but withdrew at the last moment. When it was over, she lay back and sighed, "Oh God. Gudmund and I are finished."

"What do you mean, finished?" I said.

"We resumed having a relationship," she informed me.

"What?" I said incredulously. "And have you had sex?"

"Yes - twice," she said.

I could not believe my ears. "After all he has done to you?" So at last I knew the reason for her reluctance to have sex with me. She didn't want to cheat on the king of cheats, Gudmund Johannessen! But years later I was to discover that Heidi was hiding even more from me, as will be seen later.

She went into the bathroom to wash herself and came back with her blue dressing gown done up and we cuddled up and talked on into the night. After half an hour she looked at my dick to see if it was erect, saying, "Oh, usually guys want it a second time, don't you?" I said no, not wanting to be greedy as she covered my privates with my dressing gown, although to be honest a second time would have suited me fine. I noticed that she had had surgically removed from her back those very unsightly birthmarks. Heidi told me she'd had a local anaesthetic at hospital. They had certainly done a good job.

It was a happy moment and her defences had been lowered. She admitted to me that Gudmund Johannessen had gone to "prison" (military detention to be precise) for six months some time ago. It was for wrecking an armoured vehicle he was driving whilst doing his military service with the Norwegian Army. Heidi couldn't say what sort of vehicle it was called in English but drew it on a piece of paper: it looked like a tank and I told her that's what I thought it was. I think she told me that Johannessen was drunk at the time. She also told me that when he came out of "prison" and had finished his army service, she found that she still liked him.

The next evening, Heidi, myself, Gudmund Johannessen (regrettably) and one of his friends went to have a pizza in Bergen town centre. Heidi and Gudmund sneaked a kiss whilst I was paying the bill. How forgiving they were of each other! We then visited the flat of Johannessen's friend but stayed only for a short while. After that, Heidi and I went home on our own to leave Johannessen and his friend to go and smoke some grass. When we got off the bus, Heidi suddenly remembered that she had forgotten her handbag at the other chap's flat and so had to go back to retrieve it. I was naturally suspicious, thinking it was just an excuse to have a bit of sex with Johannessen, but I didn't say anything and let her go. I made my way back to her place and with nothing to do I just waited in the big bed for Heidi to return, whenever that might be. There was a clothes chest to the right of the bed and I had always wondered what was stored in it. Curiosity got the better of me and I went to have a look. Only clothes and letters were in there, even those letters I had sent her and also I noticed another chap's letters from St. Albans. He was the one she had gone out with for a little while during my friendship with her in England and she had stuck one of his Christmas cards on the wall containing lots and lots of kisses. (Heidi had invited him - his name was Carmine - to visit her after Christmas. After I left for home he turned up and they spent a few days together, she told me, and her parents liked him. I wondered how Johannessen felt at the competition). I then came across a green dildo in Heidi's drawer. The plastic

24

penis was quite big and I wondered why Heidi needed that on top of the real thing. When I asked her the next day she was naturally annoyed I had looked through her drawers and said the dildo was a present from one of her friends. A kind of "joke present" she said.

Anyway, Heidi came back with her handbag a couple of hours later but we slept only towards sunrise and the next day was quite a relaxed one for both of us. It was my last day with Heidi and I asked her to pay me a visit in England. She said she was probably going to go anyway to visit second-hand clothes shops, with the idea of opening a second-hand clothes shop in Bergen herself. I asked her to explain what she had in common with Johannessen and she said, "I sometimes wonder what we ever had in common - we only had good sex in common really. As for his morals he hasn't any. He is worthless compared to you."

Chapter 6

One day in summer a letter from Heidi dropped in through the letterbox. "I am going to have a child," she wrote. It could only be to Johannessen. I couldn't take it in. Again she was pregnant to that scoundrel.

I was furious at the stupidity of the girl; evidently she could never learn the lessons of the past. She just couldn't give a damn. So I wrote to her immediately, a very strong letter telling her that she was basically a sick woman and her being with Johannessen was "shit for shit." I couldn't see how she would have any life now with this man and I told her she would only be in for more trouble. It was a 'Go to hell' letter and she demonstrated her own fury at my words by writing back a defiant letter telling me what an "unlucky day" it was when she met me on the train in France and that I should be happy for her as she was going to have a child. Further, that she was soon coming to England and would certainly not be paying me a visit. Our friendship was over, she said. Well, that wasn't good enough for me. Hypocrisy in a woman I could never accept, so having a fairly good idea where I might find her when she visited England, I decided to confront her in person.

I soon phoned that other chap she had known in St. Albans, Carmine, to ask if he knew of Heidi's whereabouts and he said that in fact Heidi was going out with him and another friend that very evening. Heidi had brought along her best friend, Ann-Kristin, and they would be staying with him at his parents' place but he expressly told me not to pay them a visit as I had been "nasty" to Heidi and she was in no mood to see me. He didn't seem to want to understand my sorrow; he was probably just glad he had got the company of the two girls for himself. Anyway, I wasn't going to be put off and I decided to turn up at his place and rather than confront the girl on his doorstep and risk embarrassment, I was going to follow them in my car and confront them at their destination, wherever that may be.

I arrived in St. Albans after dark and waited down the road from the house where Heidi was staying. I got out and walked up to the house and luckily heard Heidi upstairs in the bathroom where she was brushing her teeth. She sounded very happy. So I went back to my car and waited for them to come out. Four of them left the house, two girls and two men. God knows how they didn't see me reverse and follow them. It soon became clear to me that they weren't going out locally when they took the main road away from St. Albans and into the country. They were travelling far too fast. To keep up with them I had to travel at a dangerous speed and I was not happy at having to do this, but I just couldn't lose them. It turned out they were going to Luton and they parked in a road near the railway station close to a disco. I parked a short way from them, got out of my car and walked towards the group. Heidi, in neat evening dress with her full cleavage on show, ignored me as I tried to speak to her and walked off leaving the two boys alone with me. The driver of the car, who I didn't know, was upset that my high speed pursuit of them could have resulted in an accident. I let them be, bitter that I didn't have the opportunity to confront Heidi. A second chance would be hard to come by and as usual she had got away with it.

A couple of days later, Heidi phoned me from Norway to explain herself. Her evening in Luton had been "a disaster" she said. "Good," I thought. The car chase had made her anxious and too upset to stay in the disco so they all went back home immediately in a state of distress. That same night she said, Carmine, the boyfriend she used to have when she was an au pair in England came into the room in which she and Ann-Kristin were sleeping and proceeded to have sex with Ann-Kristin. Heidi said this was "disgusting behaviour" by Carmine when he already had a girlfriend called Debbie. I believed Heidi on this score and some time later I met Carmine in Chancery Lane, where he was now attending Law School. He cheerfully told me what "a tasty bit of stuff" Ann-Kristin was but he also condemned Heidi for getting pregnant to an "arsehole" like Johannessen. At last he had understood. It turned out, a long time later, that Heidi had lied about his having sex with Ann-Kristin. "If I said this, then it wasn't true," she told me in 1990. Carmine did not have sex with Ann-Kristin. A couple of years after their Luton experience, Heidi's friendship with Ann-Kristin was over. A second-hand clothes shop they had planned together got off the ground but Heidi soon dropped out of the set-up and since then the two former best friends have not spoken.

Going to see Uriah Heep at Hammersmith Odeon a few weeks later in May deepened my distress. Uriah Heep were now fronted by Pete Goalby, their fourth lead vocalist. Two thirds of the way through the concert he dedicated a song to David Byron, Heep's unforgettable first singer. When Goalby said,

"Here's one for David Byron," I thought to myself - "Oh, that's nice, to mention Byron's name"-obviously to honour a unique artist. David Byron was sacked from the band in 1976 aged 28 because his drinking had turned him into "a complete pain in the arse" as his manager, Gerry Bron, had put it. In any case Byron had a reputation for being a difficult man and that didn't help his cause. Uriah Heep were never the same again without Byron. As a supergroup they were finished. I managed to get into the post gig party at the Clarendon Pub in Hammersmith and I met up with drummer Lee Kerslake's girlfriend. I had met her six months before in Brentwood High Street outside Barclays Bank, which Lee and her were just about to enter. Kerslake used to live near Brentwood (in Essex), my home town, and was going to the bank to pay for a property he had recently bought in Lanzarote and I asked after David Byron. The first thing Kerslake said that day was, "He's finished." He explained that Byron was overweight and had narrowly avoided going to prison for drink driving; he had got divorced from his German wife and was "in a right state." For anyone who saw Byron at his peak, it was obvious that he was one of the best front men in the business. His voice was incredible. He had great charisma, good looks and a thick head of hair - perfect for a rock star. He was up there with Robert Plant, Freddy Mercury and, in later years, Joey Tempest of Europe, famous for their worldwide hit 'The Final Countdown.' These singers, for me, had absolutely everything it took. They all mesmerised their audience. (Coincidentally, I got to know Joey Tempest as he lived near my office close to Tower Bridge on the River Thames before he left for Ireland in 1998. He always stopped to have a chat whenever our paths crossed). I had longed to meet David Byron. Ominously, in 1981 in Egypt I had this recurring dream that he would die before I could meet him in person. I woke up distressed on several occasions. It happens that way in dreams sometimes. I had taken with me to Egypt a tape of 'High and Mighty,' Byron's last album with Uriah Heep and I was always playing it. He was like a standard-bearer for me and his fall from grace left me empty. I longed for him to rejoin Uriah Heep and it was with great surprise and sadness years later that I learnt that in 1980 he'd refused an invitation to rejoin when John Sloman left. (Only in 1999 did Heep's bass player, Trevor Bolder (ex-David Bowie), tell me that he and Mick Box went to Byron's home in 1980 to ask him back, only for Byron to put to them that they should join Byron's own band! And that Byron was too stoned to talk sensibly with. Mick Box later told me that Byron had his own agendas away from Heep and a greedy management, and that Byron never came to realise the mistake he'd made in not re-joining Uriah Heep. What a pity Byron never saw sense. Particularly as he thought Uriah Heep were wrong to sack him in the first place.) So back in Brentwood High Street, I asked Lee Kerslake if he knew of Byron's whereabouts, but he didn't. They hadn't kept in touch. Byron was obviously on the rocks and in trouble.

So meeting up with Kerslake's girlfriend after the May 1985 concert, I asked her about Byron. "Oh, David died in February," she said. I couldn't believe it. My dream of 1981 had turned into reality. Just before Lee had his photograph taken with the Nolan sisters, he told me to speak to Mick Box who might know more. Box was Heep's lead guitarist and was not in a good mood that night but managed to tell me they had no idea for a long time that Byron had even got divorced but that he had died as a result of his drinking. Stunned, I left to eat some food at the buffet with my friend, Graham, who came along with me that night. The rock group Motorhead were guests at the party and singer Lemmy was there beside me in his leathers. Motorhead were to take off in a big way a year or so later.

I then resolved to investigate who David Byron's next of kin was so I could find out exactly what had happened to him. I managed to get his will out of the Probate Registry next to Kings College in the Strand in London. It was a short will with just a couple of clauses whereby he gave his estate (a little under £73,000) to his sister, Sally, who lived in Loughton, Essex. I found her name in the phone book and gave her a ring. She thought I was a journalist from The Sun fishing for information on her late brother. I explained who I was and she was frank enough to tell me that for several years she did not keep in touch with her brother but finally they had met up some time just before he died. I told her that I had to know if David believed in God, as it would be consoling to know that we could hopefully meet him in the next life. Sally said that David definitely believed in God. "Good," I said. I bid farewell to Sally. A German rock journalist, Hannah Jordan, who had in fact got me in to Uriah Heep's after-gig party and who I went on to become great friends with, asked me if she could print this information about Byron's belief in God in the magazine she wrote for. I said "No" as I wanted to keep Sally's confidence. Maybe I was misguided in my ethics. It would not be a breach of confidence to tell the world that Byron was God-fearing. It would have reminded rock fans that life did come to an end even for rock stars and that God was their only salvation. The Christmas after, I went to see Sally and gave her a box of chocolates. She didn't want to talk much saying it was the anniversary of the time her brother had last stayed with her before his death. Even when I went to see her yet again a year and a

28

half later, she was in no better mood, wanting to lay his memory to rest, saying, "He has given his public enough and he should be left alone." Byron had died of epilepsy and fatty liver as the office of the Coroner who carried out the autopsy phoned up my secretary to confirm. What follows are the exact words from an article written in March 1985 by Malcolm Dome of Kerrang rock magazine which I have included, with his kind permission, to pay tribute to a man whose singing meant so much to so many.

FIERCE PRIDE

WHATEVER HAPPENED to former **Uriah Heep/Rough Diamond** easy squeezer **David Byron**? I say that because, to be honest, the vocal viper was one of rock's Seventies giants. Yet where is the diamond dreamer in '85? Ah well, time stands still only in the poisoned pouches of innocents and those too dazed to seek the way of the shark-infested sunlight.

FORMER URIAH HEEP vocalist **David Byron** was found dead at his home in Berkshire on February 28. Apparently he was discovered by his former brother-in-law; at present the cause of his death remains something of a mystery, although the possibility of an epileptic fit has been mooted. Already one inquest has been held and at the time of going to press, another one was planned. However, Byron was given just six months to live last Christmas due to the serious deterioration of his liver and was notorious for indulging in heavy alcoholic abuse.

The story of David Byron is one of the most tragic in recent rock history. Born in Epping, he rose to prominence with Uriah Heep in the early Seventies, having previously served out an apprenticeship with Heep precursors the **Stalkers** as well as singing on sessions with such luminaries as **Elton John**. Byron presided vocally over all of UH's early triumphs, including albums such as '**Salisbury**,' '**Look at Yourself**,' '**Demons & Wizards**' and '**Return to Fantasy**.' However, in 1976 (after recording ten LP's with the band), Byron was sacked after a bout of internal feuding. He was replaced by **John Lawton**.

It's probably fair to say that neither Byron nor Heep were ever the same again. The band lurched along with scarcely any sign of their former glory (until guitarist **Mick Box** revamped the outfit in 1982 and recorded '**Abominog**'). Whilst the vocalist disappeared from the scene after a brief liaison with ill-starred 'supergroup' **Rough Diamond**. He briefly resurfaced in the early Eighties with his own band (featuring, among others, **Robin George**), on an album titled '**On the Rocks**' for Creole Records and a short tour. But his career was virtually killed off early in 1981 when he collapsed onstage at London's Marquee Club just a few numbers into the set.

Byron was a victim of his own vast talent. As his former manager **Maggie Farren** commented recently: "David came to prominence when record companies lavished large amounts of money on rock stars and he became used to seeing his name up in lights."

He was caught up in a never-ending whirl of drinking and craziness that became an inextricable part of his character. Even when the merry-go-round ground to a halt in '76, he continued to live in the style of high society, eventually winding up spending money he didn't possess. In the end, he was trapped in a net of his own manufacture, like many before him. Byron had to sell his mansion in Reading and move to altogether more humble dwellings, where he lived out the last part of his 37 years alone and virtually friendless.

There will be those who will look upon Byron's passing as nothing more than a salutary lesson in self-abuse, and to many he'd exhibited a death wish for some little while. Indeed, he probably realised long ago that fame had rested upon him with its feather touch all too briefly before being blown away on the winds of fate, never to return. But, in common with thousands of Uriah Heep fans, I'd like to remember him simply as the man who breathed immortality into one of rock's most emotive of songs, '**July Morning**.' As Maggie Farren so rightly stated: "He had a truly great voice. But in the past few years no-one could spare the time to give him the care and attention required to bring him back to full health and prominence."

MALCOLM DOME

***

Uriah Heep was a band that I came to know personally. It started properly in 1988 when I was coming home late one night from work and was entering Oxford Street Underground Station. Straight ahead of me was Mick Box and I immediately said "Hello Mick." He wouldn't have remembered me from our meeting three years earlier at the Clarendon Pub but he might as well have for all his immediate friendliness. "Hello mate, how are yah? Happy days!" He was a dear fellow who had obviously had a lot to drink. He went to phone his girlfriend and when she answered he immediately told her, "Here, speak to a mate of mine." So I did and explained with gentle diplomacy who I was and in answer to her concern over Mick's ability to get home in one piece, I said I would take him home personally if need be. I put the phone down and was invited for a drink by Mick but knowing this was an offer that had to be refused, I declined. At that moment, a former college friend of mine, Roksana, bumped into the pair of us. We said hello and a delighted Mick said hello too and even gave the girl a kiss goodbye. Nice one! That's my boy! All of a sudden, Mick sobered up enough to have a decent conversation with me, which started at the top of the escalator. They had just toured Russia (1987) with their new lead singer, 32 year old Bernie Shaw, a Canadian, and the country was "dire" according to Mick. I related to Mick my sadness over the death of David Byron and mentioned my efforts to find him before he had died and all that happened afterwards with his sister. Mick was genuinely touched and said, "If you were shocked mate, I was devastated" (at Byron's death). We climbed on to the Central Line train heading out for Essex and continued to talk about Uriah Heep in general. Mick gave me his address and phone number and made me write down mine in his filofax. Before I got off at Stratford, he made me promise not to disclose his address to anyone. I wrote to him the next day and immediately he wrote back enclosing some autographed photos of Uriah Heep and their album 'Live in Moscow.' Ever since then, whenever I have been to a Heep concert, Mick has treated me as if I was his guest of honour and this level of kindness I will never forget. I was just a genuine fan but he made me feel like an important record company executive he needed to impress. He advised me on the merits of demo tapes of bands my best friend, Russell, was drumming for when he was off from Chris Barber tours. Over the years I have chatted at length with all the members of Uriah Heep. Those chaps all confided in me to varying degrees and I felt privileged to be made privy to the voices of their hearts. To say these guys have suffered is an understatement. That Uriah Heep have survived for almost 40 years in the business speaks volumes for the never-say-die attitude of Mick Box, the band leader.

Apart from the delightful melodies of many Uriah Heep songs, I had also been struck by their strong 1970's lyrics, which often reflected an intense appreciation of the power of God. I wrote in to the Uriah Heep Appreciation Society magazine in the early 1990's with my views on the spirituality of the band's lyrics and related my search for David Byron. The response was enormous and in the next two issues my name was mentioned six more times in connection with letters other fans had written, all agreeing that Heep's lyrics made them think of God. In this respect Uriah Heep were unique among the heavy rock groups. Their lyrics did not just go on about women; they also sang of things on a higher plane. Their songs were full of wisdom and reflected the shallowness of human nature and told us there was more to this life than material things. In 1973, for example, the song called Stealin' contained these words:

Stood on a ridge and shunned religion thinking the world was mine.
Made my break and a big mistake stealin' when I should have been buyin.'

In 1975 the song 'A Year or a Day' went as follows:

Seen from a height of a thousand miles the earth looks the same as it did
How is it we can fly faster than day but we can't find the things that we need

Young man said the old man
Let the youth in your heart be at rest
We may all be dead in a year or a day
When the devil is put to the test

The day of creation was our finest hour
It's something that we ought to defend
But it's been so abused since the first day of light
that no glory can come in the end

Young man cried the old man
There is victory in staying alive
And if you care so little for the world we're in
Why and what do you want to survive

Can't we try and let the past go by with its lessons firmly
settled in our minds
To our children one by one and before the darkness comes
let us leave a world full of light of a different kind

In truth they should meet and with love their hearts should beat
And with patience solve the problems of our time
It wouldn't be so hard to do, it's only up to me and you
Let us not bequeath a life that is a crime.

I had the good fortune one day to meet the chap who wrote most of those great lyrics, Ken Hensley, who left Uriah Heep in 1980 having been the focal point of the band's direction since its inception in 1969. He was their keyboard player but also contributed to the vocals and played the guitar too. Russell, my best mate, had invited me up to the British Music Fair at Olympia in the autumn of 1996. He was demonstrating on his drum kit and it was a chance for me to maybe meet some other well-known musicians. The funny thing was that I played Ken Hensley's solo album 'Free Spirit' in the car on the way to the railway station with Russell and his wife beside me. Remarkably, within two hours I was engrossed in conversation with the man himself. Ken was now representing Washburn, the American sound equipment company at the Olympia Exhibition. Ken had become a born again Christian and it was interesting to hear his views, including his abhorrence of homosexuality and the role played by the so-called Gay Christian movement. Ken stressed that these people ignored the Lord's clearly explained teachings in the Bible as mentioned in Leviticus.

Ken Hensley was a major player in rock music in the 1970's. He was frank with me about the past. His behaviour and that of all the other members of Uriah Heep in their glory days was far from praiseworthy he told me; anything but. That the fans just adored them for the sound of their music and nothing more. That there was no one for him to turn to in the band who could give him spiritual succour in times of need. His own behaviour, he confided, towards the other band members fell far short of the standard of a Christian but he was now trying to heal the wounds of the past with all those he had fallen out with.

I asked him what he would like to have done, in hindsight, regarding David Byron. Instead of himself and the management giving Byron the sack, maybe a year's break to let things settle? "Yes - and maybe attend counselling sessions with David," said Ken, "to help him to get off his addiction to booze." I was most impressed with Ken and on the second day of my visit to the Music Fair I gave him a copy of Muhammad Asad's English translation of the Quran – 'The Message of the Quran.' In it there is even a footnote telling the story of the soldier Uriah (the Hittite) and the prophet and Biblical King David (famous for slaying Goliath). Much later, Charles Dickens picked the name Uriah Heep for an obnoxious character in his book, 'David Copperfield,' which was being staged in a London Theatre in 1970, and Uriah Heep, the rock group, chose their name after seeing it on the billboards. I had also given Mick Box the Quran a few years earlier and told Ken that it elicited no response from Mick at all. Ken told me that at least it had sowed a seed in his mind. In winter 2002 when Mick Box was reminiscing, he remarked how dearly he missed David Byron and Gary Thain (Uriah Heep's former bass guitarist who died in 1975) to whom Uriah Heep's 1998 song 'Between Two Worlds' had been dedicated. Said Mick in the Uriah Heep magazine:

> "And I just thought it would be great if you could meet somebody that's passed away and meet them in a world between the spiritual world and the real world and you could just spend five or ten minutes or a couple of hours or something and say 'How're you doing? What's it like up there? Who are you jamming with?' And all that stuff and just have those sort of ordinary exchanges. It would be lovely to meet just once. I dedicated the song to

31

David and Gary but, you know, when you listen to the song it could be any one of your friends or somebody you've lost."

The seed had surely germinated.

Islam had had its sporting superstars: the boxer Muhammad Ali, the greatest athlete of the 20th century and his fellow world champions, Mike Tyson, Hasim Rahman, Chris Eubank and 'Prince' Nazeem Hamed. The world had admired their skills but found it a lot more difficult to look beyond that and examine the beliefs that formed the foundation (in varying degrees) to these men's lives.

Islam also had its own pop star. It was one fine autumn day in 1979 in the foyer of the Regent's Park Mosque in London that I observed a slim, dark-skinned cockney speaking in a group, talking about Islam. I didn't know who he was, but as a Londoner myself I felt drawn to speak to him. He told me he'd recently converted to Islam so I asked him how his parents took it. "Very well – they've accepted it," he said. "Where are they from?" I asked. "One's Swedish and the other's Greek," he replied. "Oh, really!" I said, adding, "My mum's German and my dad's Egyptian." He told me that every Saturday afternoon he had a discussion group at 3 p.m. in the mosque and that I was welcome to come along. We shook hands. His name was Yusef, he said. Two days later on the television, I saw the same man talking about his faith. He was the singer Cat Stevens who had changed his name to Yusef Islam.

I used to sit with Yusef week after week in his discussion group. One time he even stuck up for me when another chap in the circle criticised me for having long hair. "But I can't understand your objection," Yusef told the man. "The Prophet Muhammad himself had long hair." Yusef personally taught me to recite a passage in the Quran. I liked him. He was always available for a chat and always had a kind word when I met him. It was with great sadness that I observed his heartbreak years later at the Bosnia debacle.

Cat Stevens, by the time of his conversion to Islam (funnily enough it was his brother who introduced him to it by giving him a copy of the Quran) had had enough of the music scene and all that went with it: the drugs, drink and women. He even went as far as telling music stations not to play his music as he associated pop music with decadence.

He certainly needed a break to find his feet and recover from the stresses of being a rock star. But the way I felt, as did many others, was that somehow he had to be persuaded to resume his career in order to promote a popular image of Islam to the world. If anyone could do it he could. He was a world superstar and music influences millions of people like no other medium. But I think those around him persuaded him to take a very puritanical attitude. I should've told him myself to get back into music - it always brought me closer to God. But I never got around to doing it. But by the end of the 90's he realised the opportunity he'd missed in giving up singing and said as much publicly. He saw the unbounded happiness that music and song gave the people of Sarajevo in their grief and decided that this sort of entertainment wasn't such a big sin after all. His old record company released a compilation album entitled 'Remember Cat Stevens.' But those lost 20 years could never be made up for, musically. A golden opportunity had been tossed away. Into the new millennium Cat Stevens resumed performing some of his old hits as well as new material. He got a lot of radio play and enjoyed quite a revival. And on the 29th April 2007 BBC2 aired a concert he did at the Porchester Hall in London.

The British establishment's greatest Islamic supporter is, of course, Prince Charles. The Times of 14th December 1996 stated on its front page:

> 'Calling for a renewed "sense of the sacred," the Prince, a practising Anglican, said there had been a "loss of meaning in Western society" and cited traditional Islamic culture as an example of how spirituality can be integrated with modernity.'

But back to 1985. Articles of clerkship on the outskirts of the East End of London had been no fun at all. It had been 18 months from the time I had passed my Law Society Final Examination to the time I signed up for articles (1985) and I was mentally exhausted. Tragically, my poor dear mother had made one of the biggest mistakes of her life. She had dismissed the divorce proceedings against my father out of pity for him and went back to live with him. Within 6 months she was off again to stay with me.

It took three further sets of solicitors (including one whose deceitful conduct I'll never forgive – she knows who she is) and five more years of grinding, hellish struggle to get a divorce and settlement. The second time round my father defended the divorce and those five years of pain, during which I steadfastly supported my mother, did me in. She had dismissed the proceedings before Decree Nisi, whereas if she had applied for Decree Nisi and got the Order first, if any subsequent attempt at reconciliation had failed, it was just a question of applying for a Decree Absolute to make the divorce final. The first time round, my father had inadvertently ticked the box in the divorce petition saying he would not defend it. He hadn't realised he was letting the divorce go through. The second time round when my mother commenced divorce proceedings from scratch, he defended the divorce all the way up to the preliminary hearings at the High Court in London when the judge forced him to see sense and settle. The best years of my life were going down the drain. I wasn't sleeping well at all.

Chapter 7

Heidi was happy to be pregnant to a chap who must have been the biggest cheat in Christendom. However, years later she confessed to me that she was "obsessed" with him. This statement haunted me. It showed me that certain men could get away with anything if the girl was stupid enough. The normal ambition of getting a good education, a good job and a nice girl to marry did not apply in Johannessen's case. 'Fucking' was all that mattered: the beginning, the middle and the end, regardless of the consequences. The Norwegian Welfare State was there to support all single mothers and the unemployed generously. Norway is Europe's richest country, having the benefit of North Sea oil and a small population of 4½ million. It was a relatively easy life for youth in general. The screwing begins early for the girls and boys. By the time they are married, a lot of them have been through so many partners that it totally devalues the institution of marriage. Another au pair I met in the Norwegian Seamen's Church in London was only 19 and she told me she had had "about 40" sexual partners but now every time a man asked her for sex she "closed up" in her words, because she had been put off the act. I wondered if her very handsome Pakistani boyfriend she brought with her, who I spoke to, knew of her past.

I sometimes visited the Swedish Church in London where on a Sunday afternoon the au pairs congregated to drink coffee and read the Swedish newspapers. It was there in early March 1992 that I first set eyes on Josephina, a really beautiful girl who I fancied straight away. She spoke politely, seemed decent and she knew another Swedish friend of mine so I hoped that I would meet up with her again. A fortnight later, I was having forty winks in a pub in Putney on Oxford and Cambridge University boat race day. I was quite tired because it was Ramadan and I was fasting. I was also thinking about Josephina, as she happened to be an au pair in Putney. Incredibly, when I opened my eyes, there she was walking towards me in the pub. A wild co-incidence! I didn't even have to get up and she saw me and came down to sit beside me. We got talking and as it was Ramadan I could not drink anything and we got round to the subject of what Ramadan was all about. We then proceeded to talk about other Islamic beliefs including its condemnation of homosexuality.

"But what about men doing it to women up the arse?" she said. "I do it with my boyfriend. It hurt to begin with but now I love it," she continued. Her boyfriend was a student at Southampton University but lived in Nottingham where she went to see him. She practised anal sex without a condom and for all she knew, she told me, she might have HIV as she had never been tested. This, a girl whose father was a University Professor in Sweden and yet she was incredibly stupid when it came to sex. She told me one night she was lying on her bed naked with her boyfriend when another chap she knew broke into the house where she was working as an au pair by smashing a window. She had seen this 'intruder' from her bedroom window and decided to handle him without the assistance of her boyfriend who had wanted to intervene. She sent the 'intruder' packing, but what explanation did she give to the homeowner? "I told the mother that it was a burglar. What else could I say?" Yes, I do pick 'em don't I? All of a sudden she said it was time for her to go.

"Where to?" I asked.

"Oh, there's a boy in another pub up the road I want to see. I've got an appointment with him."

"Your boyfriend?" I enquired.

"Oh no, it's the chap that broke into the house."

"What!" I exclaimed. "And you want to see him???"

"Oh yes, I quite like him."

And off she went. A week later she phoned me to tell me this:

"Do you know what that boy I met after I saw you said to me?"

"No, what did he say?" I asked.

"You'd make a good fuck," she said.

"What?" I asked again, incredulous.

"He said I'd make a good fuck. I was disgusted and left him with his mates," she said indignantly.

We said our goodbyes and I never spoke to her again but two years later a friend of hers told me she had split up with her boyfriend, the student from Nottingham University, and was working in her home town in Sweden. But I digress.

On 1st April 1986, Heidi gave birth to a son, Daniel Sebastian. She was overjoyed. She had had to stay in a lot whilst pregnant and spend many "boring" evenings with Johannessen. She continued to smoke, however, right through the pregnancy. Johannessen was there at the birth and Heidi stressed to me how "unbelievably well" he had treated her. It appeared all was forgiven of his previous misdemeanours.

For six years I had known another Norwegian girl, Tove, but only as a penfriend. At last in the summer of 1986 we were to meet. I was off to Hønefoss where she lived. It was close to Oslo. However, I wanted to see first how Heidi and her son were getting on. By July of that year, she wasn't living with Johannessen but they still had some sort of relationship. A few days before going to Norway, I telephoned Heidi to say I would be coming soon and said I would phone her again with the exact day and time of arrival. Instead of phoning through this information I in fact wrote to her with it but my letter didn't arrive on her doorstep until the morning of my departure – 15th August – and Heidi wasn't there to receive it. She in fact phoned my mother on that day from somewhere else to see exactly what time I would be arriving in Bergen. When I got to Bergen, I went straight round to her place but she wasn't in, so I went over to her parents' place. They weren't in either but her stepmother's father was. He was really helpful. He didn't speak English but he understood I had come to see Heidi and he got his telephone directory out and, with no alternative, we tried to find Gudmund Johannessen's phone number. I forced myself to speak to Johannessen's father who said Heidi had just left to go back home. I was truly grateful to the elderly grandfather for his help and I thanked him with all my heart and left, glad that social interaction had taken place that ended in a happy outcome.

Heidi was in when I got there and she seemed glad to see me and I gave her a big hug. As usual, she looked simply gorgeous. How sad it was for me that her good looks were her only asset, an asset that was worth nothing without the other attributes that go to making a proper human being. She welcomed me in with open arms. She asked me how things were. Whether I had found a girlfriend yet. Her own 'boyfriend,' Johannessen, was living back with his parents now and she had also left her baby with them to look after. She sometimes slept round at the boyfriend's parents' place. I noticed the huge pile of ironing she had in the kitchen and remarked that it must be tough to do it all on her own. Well, that was the wrong thing to say, as she took it as criticism of her being, in effect, a single mother. "I didn't ask you to visit me," she sniped. Well, what a thing to say to someone who had popped over from another country just to say hello. I thought to myself what a taciturn callous little bitch she was. How quickly her mood changed. A few false apologies from me got her back into a better mood and she spoke on about her pregnancy and family matters. Her boyfriend's mother was due to pick her up soon she said as she was going to stay overnight with her "son's family." She said I could stay the night in her place on my own and gave me the only key to the flat. She asked of me that when the grandmother of her son came round, I was not to mention anything about Gudmund Johannessen. Heidi knew I despised Johannessen and that his mother would not be pleased to hear what he had done to Heidi in the past. "You are a big boy now," she told me, implying that I should be mature enough to hold my tongue. When the mother came round, she shook hands with me and seemed nice enough. I could not help notice how much older she looked than her years, with wrinkled skin and the loss of any semblance of youth. This was something I noticed with so many older Norwegian women. Perhaps it was the cold weather; perhaps it was the drinking or just their genetic makeup which made them age prematurely.

Next day Heidi returned in the late morning and we went out for a walk and something to eat at the shops. She phoned her dad from a callbox and he told her I had been round her place the previous day and also visited the grandfather. Heidi told her father it was all okay as I was with her now. I decided in the circumstances that it would be best if I stayed in a hotel in Bergen and Heidi said she would help me find a cheap one. So round we went to her flat to collect my luggage. And who was waiting in there? None other than Gudmund Johannessen who had let himself in and who sat on the couch in total silence smoking a cigarette. All he said was a cold "Hello" and not a word more. Heidi and I left again with my bag and she told me Johannessen knew exactly what I thought of him. On the way to the bus stop Heidi told me of an Irish guest who recently stayed with her parents. He was a radio journalist and was gobsmacked at how "gorgeous" Heidi was and told her father so, who was quite embarrassed. Heidi talked to the journalist quite a lot and was interviewed about tourism in Bergen and Norwegian matters in general. "I was on the radio all over Norway," she said. Obviously she had managed to blind the Irishman with her good looks and sweet talk, something that in years to come she was to practice with continued success on those who knew no better.

After a little while in Bergen town centre we found a hotel and I dropped my bag off and went to pay for the room. I had explained to the receptionist the anomaly in my passport name and the name on my credit card. I had changed my Egyptian name in November 1982 to Frederick Delaware by statutory declaration in order, basically, to get into Egypt without being drafted into the army. At the time anyone with an Egyptian father, even if the son was born outside Egypt, was conscripted into the army. I had no idea what I would be letting myself in for and in any case I had a legal career to get off the ground in England, so in order to get into Egypt to see my relatives, I had to change the name on my passport. I should have also changed the name on my credit card but I hadn't bothered, so Heidi explained all this to the receptionist in Norwegian as the latter's command of English was not at all sufficient for her to understand me. When Egypt changed their conscription rules exempting the likes of me from the draft I reverted to my original name by swearing another statutory declaration. (For the purposes of this book I have continued to call myself Frederick Delaware). After booking into the hotel we had a cup of tea in the restaurant whilst Heidi confided some more about general family problems. I accompanied her back to the Bergen suburb where she lived. The next night I planned to take the overnight train to Hønefoss to see my penfriend, Tove, and Heidi said she would pass by the hotel at noon to see me. We had a cuddle and a kiss about half a mile from her flat and then I bade her farewell. I turned back to see her waving goodbye to me happily.

The night in the hotel in Bergen was awful. I paid the equivalent of £4 for a glass of lemonade - the bar staff ripped me off - and my room was directly above the stage where a band played until two in the morning. I got next to no sleep. Come midday Heidi hadn't turned up so I phoned her and there was no reply. I went all the way back to her place to see what was up. What would it be this time? My timing was impeccable. As I went up to the flat, Johannessen and a young girl, probably a relative, were taking Heidi's baby, Daniel, in his pram down the stairs. I caught a quick glance of the boy fast asleep. Johannessen didn't want to talk at all and just said Heidi wasn't in and would be back in an hour. So I went off for a walk for half an hour and when I returned a local newspaper lay on her doorstep. I went round the back of the apartment block to peek into the living room and definitely no one was in. I went back and sat on the stairway. Eventually, needing a change of scene I went for a walk just for ten minutes. When I got back the newspaper on her doorstep had gone. Oh good - she must have got in so I rang the doorbell. No answer. That's funny - oh well perhaps someone else had just purloined her newspaper. I carried on waiting but time was running on so I resolved to take the only option left open to me. I went to find Johannessen at the supermarket where he worked to ask him what had happened to Heidi. I knew it would be humiliating to seek Johannessen's help but what alternative did I have? Time was running out. In my own inimitable way, I managed to convince him that I did not hate him that much after he criticised me for "writing all that shit to Heidi." He told me that if I waited an hour he would phone Heidi. He returned to tell me that Heidi said we could go to her for dinner in the evening and I was to return to his supermarket at 5 p.m. After finishing his work he came out of the supermarket, whistled to me to get my attention and beckoned me to follow him. He deposited the day's takings in the local bank's wall safe and off we went back to Heidi's place. I hadn't expected his co-operation at all, but boy, did I have to grovel to get it. He had phoned Heidi to tell her we were coming. Johannessen told me that she was cooking us "a delicious meal of sheep."

On arrival, Heidi was at the door to greet us. The baby was there and we got on as if we were the best of friends. Our differences were put aside. The meal of lamb was absolutely awful - completely tasteless. Heidi was certainly no cook, which wasn't surprising really as she had spent most of her time doing 'other things.' At the end of the meal I relaxed over a John Travolta film. Heidi loved her baby and spoke to it in a very charming and attractive way, a style that bit deep into the loneliness of my soul. Heidi sat beside me whilst Johannessen had gone to the toilet and said that he was soon going back to his parents for the night but I was welcome to stay on for a while. And that's exactly what happened. She sat down on the couch beside me when Johannessen had gone and I then asked her how on earth could Johannessen approve of me staying with her alone. She just replied, "It's none of his business. He doesn't tell me how to run my life." One surprise. The next surprise was that she could see absolutely nothing wrong in what she had done - getting pregnant yet again was all okay as far as she was concerned. This time I just kept my mouth shut and listened. I wasn't going to argue. The third surprise - a shock in fact - was that when I assumed a third party had picked up her newspaper on the doorstep earlier in the day, it was in fact Heidi who had picked it up when she arrived at her flat. In the few minutes I was out stretching my legs she had returned and gone inside. What bad luck for me. She knew I'd rung her doorbell, she said, as she saw me through the spyhole but had decided she didn't want to speak to me. What a mental case, I thought to myself. Now we were alone again talking cosily with my arm around her. This was insanity! One could depend on nothing here with this woman. It was a free for all in the jungle, or was it the asylum?

I had to catch the last bus back to the hotel and for a long time I held Heidi in my arms at the communal entrance to the apartment block. She was in a forgiving mood and very relaxed as it used to be in St. Albans in 1982. As I left, I punched the air in relief. I had turned a potentially sad situation into a happy one. I thanked God for small mercies. I told Heidi that in the circumstances, when I returned to Bergen by train from Hønefoss to take the plane back to England, I would not pay her a visit.

The subsequent trip over the mountains to Hønefoss to see my penpal, Tove, was an anti-climax. I was too tired to enjoy her company and she realised this. Poor girl. Poor me. I never visited her again and shortly afterwards we stopped writing. There was nothing else to say anymore. We had been introduced via the Uriah Heep Fan Club magazine pen-pals section, in 1979.

Back home in England I telephoned Heidi to see how she was. We got talking again. The conversation had turned to Johannessen and why they weren't living together. Heidi said he was miserable and said he felt he had nothing to look forward to in his life. I asked after his habit of hashish smoking and Heidi said he was still at it.

"He has even been injecting heroin," she said.

"What? When?" I asked.

"Oh, before Daniel was born. He bought it in China when he went for a fortnight's holiday there on his own."

Alarm bells rang in my head. Heidi went on to tell me that she knew he was injecting heroin whilst he was sleeping with her and yet she had carried on regardless.

"Deep down I knew I might catch AIDS," she confessed.

Johannessen was, she suspected, also sleeping with other girls at the same time but she just never "dared" to ask him. After her son's birth, she and Johannessen had two AIDS tests each to make sure they were safe. Heidi was more worried for her son than herself, she said. The test results were negative. After we said goodbye, I stopped to think about it all. I had had unprotected sex with her at the time all this was going on. Could you imagine! This first time sex could have been a disaster and I ignored all my own principles and advice. It was my fault, of course; my responsibility and I was furious with myself for letting myself down. I was even angrier with Heidi for not telling me before sexual intercourse of the fact that Johannessen had been taking heroin. In her own mind, she had exposed me to the risk of HIV infection and that was something I could never forgive. Next day I got out my writing pad and wrote to Heidi telling her off in no uncertain terms as to what a dirty bitch she was. I was incensed and told her in my own words that she should have been kicked into orbit for her criminal negligence. A little while later, I also wrote to her father telling him exactly how I felt about his sick minded daughter and all that was going on behind his back. Enough was enough.

Chapter 8

In September 1987 I qualified as a solicitor and immediately joined a sole practitioner in Portland Place in London's West End, just down the road from the Chinese Embassy. One hot summer's day in 1988 I was in my office when Heidi called me, hysterical with grief and sobbing uncontrollably. She explained that Gudmund Johannessen was staying with some friends of his and she had phoned them up to speak to him to ask him to come back home because she needed him, not least to care for their son. These friends of Johannessen were girlfriend and boyfriend and they came back to Heidi on the phone with the message, "Gudmund says that you can both [i.e. Heidi and her son] fuck off " and then the phone was put down on Heidi. When she tried to phone again, the response was equally negative. Well, Heidi was beside herself with rage and despair.

"I've got a little child here who needs his father and now we have both been told to fuck off. Gudmund is a psycho. I want revenge - I want revenge. His brothers think he's an arsehole. You were right all along. I am so so sorry." Her wailing was very genuine and very disturbing and so I asked what she thought I could do. "Come to Norway immediately with your karate friend and beat Gudmund up or take him to the woods and tie him up or something," she pleaded. "But isn't there any one you know in Bergen who can help you?" I queried. "No," she replied, "I don't know anyone else."

I said I would see what I could do and that I would get in touch with my karate friend, who was Russell, the drummer. I told her she would have to reimburse us at least half our joint airfares. That was okay she said. I promised I would phone her the next day to tell her of "my friend's" response and whether he would be available. I had not told her Russell's name.

Russell, my best friend, was at the time the drummer with Alan Price, who was formerly the keyboard player with The Animals. Russell was a black belt third dan in karate. That evening I joined Russell at his karate club, which I also trained at. I had phoned him after receiving Heidi's call and told him there was a need for his services in Norway and asked him to bring his Alan Price tour schedule with him so he could check when he would be free to travel to Norway. Russell was in the middle of a U.K tour and when he handed me the date sheets I could see that only three consecutive days in the next fortnight were available but, like a true friend, he said he would come over to Norway for those three days. I briefed Russell fully on the situation and told him we would give a good lesson to Johannessen but would also have some very strong words with the girl as she was equally to blame for her mess and the shit she had given me. It would be a delicious humiliation for the two delinquents and there would be nothing they could do about it. No one raised their fists to Russell without a six-month stay in hospital afterwards.

Very late in the evening, after I had got home from the karate club, I phoned Heidi to tell her the exact day we would come and that I would proceed to book a flight in the next few days. She was relieved and asked me if I thought she was doing the right thing. She seemed to have a few doubts but I reassured her everything would be okay. She was also getting together half the money for our airfares she said. At one o'clock in the morning, after having done all I could to console her in her enormous distress, I went to sleep.

I was woken by the telephone ringing. I looked at my alarm clock and it was six in the morning. I was quite angry as I was exhausted and needed my sleep, but I knew it had to be Heidi and it was. She had had a complete change of heart. She wanted to call off our expedition.

"You are enjoying my pain," she told me.

"No I'm not," I lied.

"Of course you are ….. after what has happened between us. Don't come over," she said.

"Fair enough," I said, as she firmly explained her change of heart.

She was quite adamant about the whole project being called off. I said goodbye and went back to my slumbers. How perceptive of Heidi to realise I was indeed enjoying her pain. God works in mysterious ways and was giving Heidi a well-deserved come-uppance. Nevertheless, I was disappointed that she

39

and Johannessen were not going to receive a visit from us. I told Russell the whole thing was off. It was just as well. He was sticking his neck out for me in the middle of a concert tour and who knows how things would have gone for us in Norway.

Russell turned out to be a truly steadfast friend and being with him enabled me to meet, over the years, some of the great musicians of our time. I met Russell through his mother who was attending my office during my articles of clerkship in connection with her divorce. It turned out he went to the same school as me but he was five years younger so I'd left by the time he joined the school. This was the school where the celebrated musician Mike Oldfield had been a pupil and where Roxy Music and Supertramp played on the same night together (at the booking cost of £38 for both acts) in 1970 at the school dance! Before they were famous. Also U.F.O. did the school dance a year later, a certain Phil Mogg on vocals – the band were crap. I got to know Alan Price and it was fun to see him criticising and cajoling. He confided in us telling us his hopes and fears, but Pricey refused adamantly when Russell told him at the Towngate Theatre in Basildon to reform The Animals. "Not on your life," Pricey said. "I'd rather be on the fucking dole." In between infrequent Alan Price gigs, Russell drummed for John Farnham on his big hit 'You're the Voice' at the Montreaux Rock Festival in Switzerland (1988) and also on his follow up single 'Age of Reason' on Top of the Pops. Later, Russell joined up with the American duo, Boy Meets Girl for Top of the Pops and the Wogan show. He had also done the first two singles with the short-lived supergroup Five Star. After Alan Price (who also lost the services of both his female backing singers, Deena Payne to the TV soap Emmerdale where she played Viv Windsor, and then, through pregnancy, his wife Alison Thomas, the other singer) the chance came for more regular work for Russell with the evergreen Chris Barber Jazz and Blues Band. They had started in 1954 with Chris Barber and his wife Otterlie Patterson and Pat Halcox. They were the equivalent of The Beatles then and to this day they still draw the crowds in theatres throughout Europe. I joined the band on tours of England, Holland and Germany and these chaps treated me like a brother. There was true camaraderie. Russell was a real star and audiences talked about him wherever we went. Autographs, photographs, girls. The Fortieth Anniversary Tour of Chris Barber put me in touch with Lonnie Donegan, Monty Sunshine and a host of other stars who had played with Chris Barber in the past. All of them signed a Tour Programme, at my request, for the birthdays of Mick Box and Trevor Bolder of Uriah Heep who were both born on the same day, the same day as my mother's birthday – the 9th June. Whilst on the subject of birthdays, Russell's birthday was the 17th May which was also Norway's National Day.

Chris Barber was always good to me and often let me stay in a room for nothing and eat for nothing whilst they were on tour. One day in Germany in 1993, Chris and I were travelling alone together in his Mercedes back to the hotel and he reminded me of the general nature of so many musicians - extremely talented and able on their instruments but lousy and inept when it came to looking after their money. Chris Barber had been careful with his money. He had made a lot of it and kept a lot of it too, in spite of two divorces. His willingness to confide in me touched my heart but I knew from Russell that Chris was an agnostic in religious matters and back in the hotel bar I invited Chris for a drink and told him frankly that I thought it was a shame that for all the happiness and pleasure he had given people over the years, and the kindness he had shown me, it was of little use if he did not believe in an after-life and the existence of God. Chris understood where I was coming from but insisted that only when he died would he find out for sure what was up there. I pressed on and said kindly that the test was to be passed down here on Earth. Facing the unseen based on the teachings of all the prophets was the way forward. When one died and found the truth staring one in the face, it was no longer a test. I promised Chris that the moment we got back to England I would get him the Quran and a video called 'The Message' starring Anthony Quinn telling the story about the origins of Islam and the Prophet Mohammed. This video would touch anyone. Indeed, my own Secretary, Janet, gave it to a friend of hers, an Englishman from Essex, who after watching it told Janet it was the greatest film he had ever seen: the ideal of Islam; a universal message to mankind incorporating the unadulterated word of all God's prophets was portrayed in this film and I was glad to give it out as a gift.

Accordingly, at the next gig in England, I forget where, I gave Chris Barber and Pat Halcox each a copy of the Quran and 'The Message' and it tickled me to see Chris thumbing through the great book before going on stage. I had done my duty to men who had been good to me. The rest was up to them. For Pat Halcox, my efforts had worked. In a concert at Tilbury Fort in Essex in the autumn of 1998, he told me he'd watched 'The Message,' looked at the Quran and confirmed he was "into that sort of thing." And again, spontaneously in December 1999 on meeting him again at a Chris Barber, Kenny

Ball, Aker Bilk triple bill at the Brentwood Centre, the first thing he repeated to me was his fondness for "the book" and "the video." Sweet, dear man, who a few years earlier had survived complicated brain surgery. Unfortunately, Russell himself did not get on with the band musically and was always complaining bitterly to me about Chris's attitude towards his playing. I told him to stick the job out until something better came along. Being with Chris Barber was giving him a wonderful platform and he was getting noticed. Meinl Cymbals of Germany promoted him in 1993 as 'the Best British Drummer of the 90's' purely from the attention he was getting on Chris Barber tours in Germany. There were also the spin-offs of drum clinics, newspaper and magazine articles. Russell also had the opportunity to play in front of 15,000 people with Alan Price in the Brabanthall in Den Bosch in Holland in April 1993 along with the Spencer Davis Group and Hot Chocolate. Russell had got a bigger crowd than for the Deep Purple and Uriah Heep Concert I went to see there a year later; 8,000 had turned up for that which was quite an amazing gig. Heep were brilliant. Later Russell came to the notice of the mercurial artiste Van Morrison whose gigs together included one at the Royal Albert Hall in London.

All of a sudden, it was all over for Russell with Chris Barber. He was going out of his mind staying with the band and he left, a decision that he did not regret but one that hurt him financially. Russell was sick of jazz and reverted to his first love of rock music and was prepared from now on to take his chance in that medium. In the autumn of 1998 he joined a Liverpool band called Deadline that had previously supported Whitesnake. A little dream came true for me in March 1999 when Deadline supported Uriah Heep on a short, three-concert tour culminating at the London Forum on 13th March. My favourite band performing with my best mate's band! Magic! Even better was to come in 2007 when in February of that year Russell joined Uriah Heep on the retirement of Lee Kerslake.

Chapter 9

I didn't have any strong feelings either way for Heidi after her latest come-uppance. I felt a sense of relief, a reward for my patience and suffering that she had been taught yet another lesson by a Norwegian, one of her own. A few weeks later in September 1988 I phoned her up again to see how she was doing, telling her that I was off on a long break of several months to Egypt. What was her news? She told me she had made a suicide attempt after we had last spoken and the method was a repeat of her previous performance; she had swallowed a lot of pills but luckily and in time she had thought better and brought them up. I refrained from expressing my disgust this time but reflected on the consequences of that poor little boy of hers having no mother. What a cruel thing to do to an infant. The mere thought! However, this time, she told me it was all over with Johannessen and that she "hated all men." Tomorrow, she was off to Drammen to stay with her sister, Elisabeth, and to try and find a place of her own. For how long she would be there she didn't know but I could write to her old address and the letters would be forwarded on to her. Heidi sounded cheerful and happy and spoke to me without any trace of resentment. One never knew from one moment to the next how she would react. It was always so difficult to know what to expect. She wished me well in Egypt - "Have a safe trip," were her last words to me before we broke off. I said, "God bless you," meaning it, and rang off.

1988 had been a hard year for me working in the West End. I had just left the firm I was working for as it had been forced to close down its office in Portland Place, at a time which, ironically, saw the height of the property boom. My boss had worked in the same offices in partnership with a couple of other solicitors but unfortunately one of them died suddenly - he was very young. This caused the partnership to dissolve and only my boss remained thereafter. However, he had never managed to obtain the landlord's permission to stay in these offices in the name of the new firm - named after him - where he was the sole practitioner. However, he did manage to delay things for a year and a half and even sublet space in his office to a property developer, Ken Coffee, a strong-minded, amiable Jewish chap who had as his assistant Darren Gayer, who later went on to become the interior designer for and a good friend of Noel Gallagher of Oasis rock group fame.

My boss had found me by contacting the Law Society's job recruitment section. I liked everyone at his firm and the atmosphere was relaxed and very informal. Unfortunately, our clients included some very dodgy customers and I was glad I myself wasn't handling them personally. On one occasion, my boss and I went to a disused Mayfair nightclub, which a consortium of businessmen (including a well-connected Jordanian man - a Muslim - who also invested in pubs!) were trying to re-open. The whole deal eventually collapsed amid accusation and counter-accusation and some of the revelations that were uncovered were most revealing, most unsavoury. What a mess the poor boss had got himself into with this lot. After such high hopes on this "major deal" things only got steadily worse for him.

Bill, the Accounts Officer in the firm, became a great confidante of mine. He was always honest about everything that went on, always giving me good advice. He was a single man in his late forties when I joined the firm but he looked very unwell. His face was covered in red blotches and he was on medication for his claustrophobia and the resultant panic attacks. He shared a flat with a divorced man. I enjoyed his company and came to like him very much. He often told me to say a prayer for him before I went to the Regent's Park Mosque, which was fairly close by.

Then one day, tragedy struck the firm. Kelly, one of our secretaries lost her brother in a road accident outside Blackwall Tunnel in London's East End. Her brother's pregnant girlfriend suffered serious head injuries but she went on to give birth to a healthy baby.

In the summer I was returning home on the train one particular evening. I was sitting on the same couch as a girl who was sitting immediately by the window to my right. I sat at the other end of the seat with a gap between us. Another chap to our left sat across the gangway from us but had his back against the window with his feet up. As the train was approaching Brentwood station she got up - the train was slowing down and the girl went past me to open the door whilst the train was still moving. This was an all too frequent practice with most rail users. She opened the door with one hand while having to cope with a bouquet of flowers in the other and a handbag on her shoulder. This left her with only her feet to push the door outward and fully open. As she did this, she lost her balance. I stretched out my hand to try and save her from falling out as did the other chap but it all happened too quickly for us and she was gone. The door had slammed shut as the train came to a halt. My fellow passenger looked out of the window and turned back towards me with his hand over his face in horror. I looked out of the window; no sign of the girl. She had gone under the train! Then almost immediately she climbed up from the track on to the platform - minus her left arm. It was a sickening scene. The poor girl was screaming hysterically as one would - begging for someone to give her back her arm. The cries of horror were truly heartrending. Oh Lord God have mercy upon this poor soul! A woman station attendant held the girl down to control her panic and at the same time tried to comfort her. Soon the emergency services arrived and after the train was moved out of the way, a fireman recovered the severed arm and put it in a plastic bag. The girl had already gone off in the ambulance to the hospital.

The police came round the next day to interview me as a witness to the accident. It emerged that the girl was a legal secretary in that very big London firm of solicitors, Clifford Chance. She was on her way that evening to her fiancé with some flowers for him. Her severed arm could not be sewn back on as it had been crushed under the wheel of the train. However, the girl was back at work within a fortnight. Her lost arm was not the one she wrote with.

September came and it was time for the Portland Place office in the West End to close. The firm was moving to the wrong side of Liverpool Street to very basic basement premises to begin afresh. It was No. 8 Fairchild Place, Shoreditch, exactly opposite the lock-up garage where Justin Fashanu, the openly gay and first £1million black footballer, was to hang himself in 1998 after spending his last hours in a gay sauna up the road. I stayed on for a few weeks but had made up my mind to leave. I would be off to Egypt for quite some time I decided. A clean break. Bill gave me a watch as a leaving present. He and his flatmate had, some time before, decided they would go on holiday to Egypt and so I booked the same flight with them. At Heathrow Airport I bumped into a client of ours - Sammi, an Egyptian chap who was going to Germany on business.

Within 18 months, Sammi, Bill and his divorced flatmate were all dead. Sammi died 'on the job.' He had a heart attack whilst committing adultery. Bill's flatmate then died. Bill told me that his flatmate had got a bout of shingles and Bill had to treat him and look after him. Then the next thing I heard from Bill was that his flatmate had died. Bill asked me to break the news to his flatmate's former wife who lived not far from me. Bill didn't get on with her, so I obliged. The woman wasn't too upset when I went round to see her but I was surprised to hear that her son wasn't on speaking terms with his late father. Something had happened to cause a rift between father and son but the mother did not elaborate.

Bill was now in the shit as he had to take over his flatmate's share of the mortgage on repayments on their home. The flatmate hadn't taken out life insurance as he hadn't got round to having a medical.

Come January 1990, Bill himself had gone into hospital with pneumonia. It was the Rodney Porter Ward of St. Thomas's Hospital in London. I knew Bill had always looked ill and was on Tamazepan to quell his nerves and panic attacks. I then found out that the Rodney Porter ward was the AIDS ward, although the hospital refused to confirm whether or not Bill was suffering from AIDS. I spoke to him in the early period of his stay; he was tired but hopeful, but he got worse, naturally, as in reality Bill was dying and very quickly so. My boss and a couple of others went round to see Bill but I never managed to do so. I spoke to Bill again the day after returning from yet another trip to Norway, which hadn't gone at all well, and I was relating my misfortune to him in his hospital bed over the phone. I had told him all about Heidi a long time before and he was very sad for my sufferings with her. Well, more bad news about this trip was just too much for Bill and he cut me short, saying, "I feel very tired now - I had better go - I'll speak to you again. Bye."

Next morning Bill was dead. Did my bad news hasten his death? Only Bill and God know for sure and maybe the nurses and doctors at the hospital who witnessed his demise.

Poor Bill and his flatmate were homosexuals. Both had died of AIDS. Kelly the senior secretary at our firm told me that they knew Bill was "a poof" but did not want to tell me as they feared I wouldn't join the firm.

Bill's family had come over from South Wales to the Putney Crematorium for the funeral and were a lovely lot. They behaved with such dignity and I take my hat off to them all. His sister told me how much Bill liked me, which I particularly appreciated. Bill was in the same year at school as Neil Kinnock (the former Labour Party leader) in South Wales and indeed Bill had shown me a school photo from 1961 with the pair of them in it.

I saw my former boss for the last time at Bill's funeral. The boss was a brave fellow always giving a positive side to us in spite of his own severe personal problems. Not much later, his former friend, a partner he had been in association with at a related legal office, was sent to prison for 9 months for fraud. My boss then retired from practice and went into teaching. It was another sad end to a law firm I had been associated with. Bad luck had been a good friend of mine though for quite some time.

The East London firm that I had started my articles of clerkship with rather abruptly terminated my employment only four months before I was to qualify as a solicitor. Why so? Firstly, I had asked the accounts clerk to draw up a cheque in favour of my insurance company regarding the premium for my car insurance. My boss, Peter, had agreed to pay half but unfortunately I had in my memorandum to the accounts clerk completely forgotten to ask him to divide the figure I gave him in half, so the clerk brought the cheque in for the boss to sign which he was about to do when he looked at the amount and saw that it was for twice as much as it should have been. Before I had a chance to explain, Peter stormed out to the accounts room with the cheque in his hand saying, "I'm not having that" and accused me of trying to pull a fast one. Well, I can safely say bollocks to that. For Peter to imagine that I would try to fiddle about £30 out of his firm, I think he must have taken leave of his senses. I protested vigorously but in a few days I found out what Peter really thought of me. I was told to hand the office keys in to him on the flimsy pretext that there was no real need for me to have them as there was always someone in the office before me to open up. I didn't want to rock the boat any further and just gave the keys in and bit my lip.

The second nail in my coffin occurred shortly after the day a girl in her twenties walked out of our office with her mother. I only saw her profile and her long golden hair and barely caught a glimpse of her face. It was enough to attract my interest. I asked the secretaries who this mother and daughter were and it turned out that one of the secretaries knew them. I didn't want to make a fuss and prepared to do things discreetly. I found out the girl's address from our firm's records and went round to see her. When I knocked at the girl's door she answered and of course I could now see properly what she looked like. She had a weather-beaten face, having spent too much time under the sun bed. Her face was already lined. I wanted to go but was decent enough to explain exactly who I was and where I had first seen her. I offered my apologies for arriving unannounced at her doorstep but said that's what sudden impulse is all about and "After all," I said, "that kind of thing makes the world go round." Beginning to feel nevertheless suspicious of the natural inborn tendencies of English girls not to accept 'unusual approaches' (unless it's from the likes of well-known footballers or popstars) I asked whom she was going to tell about my visit. "Only my mother, who I tell everything," she said. It was a Friday night.

I didn't even make it in to work on the Monday morning. I got a phone call early that morning from Peter telling me that the girl's mother had complained to him about my actions on Friday evening. Fucking shit of a woman and daughter! "You had better not come in until I have made some more enquiries," my boss said. "Fucking shit of a boss," I thought, not to support me without at least first giving me a chance to explain. He was adamant. He called later to say I was cleared of any impropriety but he didn't like the fact he had received a complaint and thought it best if I left the firm and sought to continue my training elsewhere. "Well fuck you too," I thought.

I wasn't to learn until a little later from a couple of 'dicky birds' that Peter himself was firstly, under severe strain and "worried sick" about being struck off the Solicitors Roll if he got convicted of assault in the Magistrates Court, which hearing was shortly to take place, on a charge of assaulting his next door neighbour which gentleman had in fact insulted his wife, and secondly, Peter had got involved with a married secretary at work when he was training to be a solicitor himself. He had been caught in the act of having sexual intercourse in the office on a Saturday, when initially just he and the secretary were around. Caught inflagranti. The senior partner transferred him to another branch office to keep him and the secretary apart. Fortunately for him he was found not guilty of the assault after I left the firm. But what stinking hypocrisy towards me even if he was facing a personal crisis. This, the man who had also, a while before, executed a bloodless coup at the firm. Whilst the senior partner's son, who was articled to Peter, went out to attend on a completion of a house purchase transaction, Peter altered the firm's bank account into his own name and changed the locks to the premises. The firm was renamed after him. He'd found a loophole in the partnership agreement to break away from the firm. Pretty neat work in one fell swoop!

How the hell was I going to explain leaving a firm with only four months left to qualify? Luckily, I didn't have to as the boss of my next firm told me it was "too good to be true" that he had found a chap who did probate and conveyancing, which was exactly what he wanted. It was another East London firm and I had no intention of staying there once I had qualified. I was pleased, nevertheless, to stay for 6 months with a happy bunch of people. One colleague was Mark Goldstein, who later came to national prominence as the solicitor for Reggie Kray, the notorious East London gangster on whose patch I was born. Come the conveyancing crash of the late 80's, this firm all but collapsed. Its two branch offices closed down with most of the staff leaving and the only other partner in the firm was banned by the Law Society from working as a solicitor except under supervision. His case files were in a mess and neglected. He couldn't cope at all not least because the loss of his young wife to cancer a few years earlier had devastated him. He was alone with small children to bring up and I felt truly sorry for him. Some people just get dreadful luck. In 1991 he'd suffered the humiliation of all his shortcomings being set out in the Law Society's Gazette, having come up before the Solicitors' Disciplinary Tribunal. He escaped with a fine. And it wasn't his last one either.

When I look back now, quite a few of the solicitors I'd come across personally had appeared before the Solicitors' Disciplinary Tribunal and were thus shamed in the Law Society's Gazette. They were as follows:

- I'm glad to say in 1987 Phillip Proctor (decision 3985) the solicitor who took me on in Wimpole Street, was ordered to pay a penalty of £2,000 for accounting errors in his firm's bookkeeping, and delays in dealing with correspondence. In June 1997, he had another penalty imposed on him for £2,000 and in September 1998 one for £3,500. He had a further disciplinary hearing on 25th January 2000.

- On 20th April 1999, Michael Palmer, solicitor with Palmer Cowan in Mayfair, made The Times newspaper under the headline 'Solicitor stole £150,000 from fund for orphans.' The sub-title was 'Mayfair man who lent cash to Dodi Fayed is jailed for three years,' written by Michael Horsnoll. Palmer had, on 20th August 1997, also made The Times on the same matter under the headline, 'Tory donor and lawyer charged with fraud offences.' I was particularly annoyed with Michael Palmer regarding my application to his firm for articles of clerkship on 4th July 1985. He replied on 19th July asking me up for an interview, which I quickly attended with him. Then I waited until 29th August to be asked up for a second interview with him and his partner, Anthony Cowan. I went up for the interview in early September and saw them both. There was a short list of four for the job. On 16th September, I was informed the position had been offered to another applicant. Just as well in hindsight, but 10 weeks waiting to learn if I'd got a job was too much. On the 14th March 2002 Michael Palmer and Anthony Cowan were struck off the Solicitors Role along with a third member of the firm. The Law Society's Gazette explained how Palmer had been convicted of 15 offences of dishonesty. Would you believe, even the barrister turned solicitor who recommended me for the interview to Palmer Cowan got struck off in 1998. He too was featured in a special Law Society Gazette disciplinary article.

- Also, the solicitor Andrew Warren who recommended me to Jim, my short-lived boss in Queen Anne Street in 1985, was arrested in 1998, together with his Partner (a Magistrate!) and both had their homes raided by officers from the National Crime Squad. They made the Law Society Gazette under the heading 'City lawyers face fraud inquiry' and their arrests followed "a joint U.K and U.S investigation into a share fraud and money laundering scam." In 2002 the British government agreed to a request by the U.S government to extradite Andrew Warren following his indictment for money laundering there in 1999. His former partner was already living in the U.S whilst on bail but was convicted in the autumn of 2002 on money laundering charges. So it was a serious matter for Andrew Warren who had instructed my former colleague Steven Barker to defend the extradition. Steven Barker sought a judicial review of the government's decision to extradite him. But eventually the Americans got their man when he was extradited in early 2003. The Law Society Gazette reported that Warren had "pleaded guilty" to attempted "enterprise corruption" in connection with an international stock fraud conspiracy operating in New York and the U.K. The Gazette continued: 'John Moscow, a deputy bureau chief for the New York District Attorney said, "Lawyers should not falsify documents, set up false companies, lie to the authorities and otherwise assist criminals. They are supposed to be loyal to the law and not to assist crime."' In August 2003 Andrew Warren received a 5 year prison sentence.

- Another one who interviewed me in the Spring of 1984 for articles and never even wrote back to me after my interview – I had to phone them after waiting weeks and weeks – was Amyn Nazerali, the senior partner in his Mayfair, three-partner (family members only) law firm. He was struck off on 9th October 1990 for among other things "calculated dishonesty."

- My former boss from Portland Place twice made the Law Society Gazette Disciplinary Section in 1989 and 1991. He was suspended from practice for an indefinite period until he could sort out his terribly unfortunate personal problems. I won't name him as he treated me like a true friend would. His former partner though, who I knew, although he wasn't associated with the firm when I joined in 1987, was struck off in 1994 after serving 9 months in prison for an offence of dishonesty.

- The pick of the bunch I leave to last; that of Peter Jonathan Denby, who interviewed me in the second week of February in 1984 at his new office in London EC3. Not easy to forget as the receptionist took a liking to me straight away and often phoned me up. Denby made The Sun newspaper in 1987; just a quick paragraph which read:

Runaway is arrested

Runaway solicitor Peter Denby, who vanished after a gun hold-up of two London policemen, was arrested yesterday.

The former parliamentary aid to Enoch Powell was seized in a dawn raid on a house in Richmond, North Yorkshire, after he was featured on the BBC's Crimewatch TV programme.

Denby, 38, nephew of former Law Society President, Sir Richard Denby, has been hunted since last June.

***

The fact was that he was the getaway driver for two I.R.A armed robbers. How he got himself into that position, I never knew, but he made the Law Society Gazette, which reported the fact that he was convicted of a criminal offence and got six months imprisonment. He was struck off in 1989. I was so disappointed in not getting articles with him as he had strong Middle Eastern shipping connections. Another blessing in disguise as it turned out.

Chapter 10

Egypt in October 1988 saw the world karate championships in Cairo and I went to see my own instructor, Simon Kidd, fight for the English team managed by the irrepressible 'Ticky' Donovan. They beat Holland in the final but Vic Charles, the former television 'Superstars' winner, lost his individual world title in the top weight category to a chap called Pinder of France. Vic I really liked; he was full of life and I enjoyed speaking to him at the post tournament party. He was so easy to get on with.

I was not achieving much in Egypt. I was living in a dilapidated apartment with no hot water, a toilet that didn't flush and rising damp everywhere. A pack of stray dogs - all too frequent in Cairo - bayed outside my bedroom window most nights for a good hour or so. It was absolutely awful. I missed Heidi as well. I wrote a few letters to her and asked her to write to an uncle's address in Egypt but didn't receive a single reply. What a difference it would have made to my happiness to hear from her as I had imagined she would be making a fresh beginning in her life. I wrote four or five very generous letters to her consoling and encouraging her. I had also sent a tape of the hit album by Brian Wilson fittingly called 'Love and Mercy' to her before I had left England for Egypt. It was magical music guaranteed to cheer the soul. I genuinely felt for her and longed to hear from her.

I left on a trip for Israel and went to Eilat, Jerusalem and Tel Aviv. I met an English girl from Surrey at the Israeli border. We carried on to Eilat and had dinner together. She later wrote me a most incredible letter (after which I telephoned her in Tel Aviv) which I framed as a memento. It went as follows:

> How are you? I hope this communique finds you well wherever you are.
>
> I hoped very much that you could have contacted me, as I wanted to express my sincere gratitude to you for such a lovely evening. It was as if God chose that direction for me from Mount Sinai in order to meet you, and I was happy to have done so, my only sadness was that I did not hear from you again; if only to know you were safe and happy; that was the important factor. You probably did not realise how strong an impact you had on me, after living in a religiously observant community for six months then going to Sinai for a few days vacation, the finale of my trip was meeting you. You treated me as a lady, something I have not appreciated in a long time. You obviously have the qualities in a man I didn't believe to exist anymore.
>
> It was on that basis I believed that God Almighty had answered my prayers on Rabai Tani 1409 Tuesday 15th November 1988 6 Chistev 5749, between Egypt and Israel. I just want you to know you restored my faith in mankind, to know that men, especially an Englishman, still have the qualities that are so rare to find today.
>
> God bless you …. I pray we will meet again ……
>
> Warmest Regards, Linda

Within two days of being in Eilat a Finnish girl - Tina - befriended me. I found her, her sister and friend bathing topless on the beach whilst armed Israeli soldiers patrolled close by. I doubt I will ever see again a group of three girls who each had simply enormous breasts. Six air balloons. Well, Tina was a quiet, reserved girl. The three girls came to visit me in Egypt a little later after I had obtained for them a visa from the Egyptian Consulate in Eilat. Tina came to my room in the Eilat hostel we stayed in one evening and we did sleep naked together until the small hours but sex did not happen, but it was a close call. I had deliberately refrained from buying condoms during the day to avoid the temptation. It was ironic that after she got back home to Finland she wrote to me and said that on her last day in Egypt they came across three Finnish guys "and of course you know what they wanted," she wrote, "but they didn't get it."

I also met four Swedish girls at the Ein Gedi Kibbutz by the Dead Sea in Israel and they too visited me in Egypt and for ten years afterward I kept in touch with one of them, Victoria. These Swedish and Finnish girls I had no problem with at all. They listened kindly to my views on Islam and dressed decently when we were in Egypt. I treated them all with kindness, generosity and respect and I was proud to have acquitted myself well as a human being in my dealings with them. They all visited my relatives in Egypt and ate dinner with us.

But I missed Heidi and it upset me. I went home to England and left almost immediately for Tunis at Christmas. But I could not stand the loneliness and left early for London after a two hour stop-off in Geneva. In the space of a month, I had sent postcards to Heidi from Cairo, London, Geneva and Tunis, all without response. I had even given a letter to a Norwegian girl who was competing for Norway in the karate championships in Cairo having trained in Drammen. She promised to post it as soon as she got back home. All to no avail. I got no reply from Heidi.

It was time to phone Heidi's sister, Elisabeth, in Drammen. Elisabeth was Heidi's eldest sister but I had never met her. When I spoke to her I explained I had written lots of letters to Heidi but hadn't heard back at all and wondered what had become of her since last autumn.

"Well, she is having professional help. I haven't spoken to her for a little while so when I see her again I will ask if she wants to get in touch and you can ring me back in a few days time. She is not on the phone," said Elisabeth.

It took three more phone enquires from me over the period of a fortnight before Elisabeth spoke to Heidi and after all that the news was that Heidi didn't want to get in touch with me. I was surprised at this and also very annoyed. It seemed my kind letters had obviously meant nothing and I guessed her statement the previous autumn that she "hated all men" now included me, at least to the extent of not caring in the least for even simple courtesy. Talk about beating one's head against a brick wall.

I was furious at these disgusting manners from Heidi. Even accounting for her past, I did not expect to be ignored especially as she was supposed to be putting the past behind her. So I wrote to Heidi and told her exactly what I thought of her cruelty. Just after I posted that letter, as luck would have it Heidi phoned me out of the blue from the Central Hotel in Drammen where she was now working as a night receptionist. She called me for one hour and I then called her for one hour to share the cost. She said she had spent four weeks (or was it eight weeks, I can't recall exactly now) in the BSS Psychiatric Clinic in Lier, not too far from Drammen. She said they had given her the Bible to read but it hadn't done anything for her. We had a nice talk and Heidi was most generous in her speech but alas I knew the rapprochement wouldn't last long because, for sure, the letter I had written her would kill off any reconciliation. So I told Heidi at the end of our two hour conversation that I had written her a letter that she wouldn't like and asked her just to throw it into the dustbin without reading it. She said she would tear it up straight away but I knew the temptation to read the letter would be too much to resist for her. If she was honest with herself, she would realise the error of her ways and accept the harsh truth of my written word. But it didn't work out for me and contact came to an abrupt halt. Heidi then left the employment of the hotel.

In August (1989) I decided to go and visit the Swedish girls I had met the previous year in Egypt. I took the ferry from Harwich to Esbjerg and went across Denmark to Malmö. I stayed for one night with the sister (and her boyfriend) of Victoria. The next day we were to go and see Victoria at her parents' place some way away in Orrefors. She was spending her summer holiday working in a crystal shop. In my hosts' flat I telephoned the Central Hotel to see if Heidi's sister Elisabeth was there. She was working at the hotel also but not on the day I phoned. She was having a few days off, the receptionist, Terri-Ann told me. Elisabeth had also moved house and I had no idea of her new phone number or address. As I recall, the hotel no longer had Heidi's address on their records as she had left their employ. They did have Elisabeth's phone number but wouldn't give it out to me. Terri-Ann agreed to telephone Elisabeth to see if she could get Heidi's address for me. I telephoned Terri-Ann again but it was to hear the bad news which I feared. Elisabeth did not want to speak to me or give any information as to Heidi's whereabouts.

Bad news only puts my back up so I abandoned my stay in Malmö immediately and the same evening took the overnight ferry up to Oslo. I got no sleep at all and felt wretched sailing up Oslo Fjord in the beautiful morning sunshine. I made straight for Drammen via Oslo railway station and went to the Central Hotel to see if I could persuade whoever was on duty to give me Elisabeth's address. Terri-Ann unfortunately was on duty and just confirmed she could not give me Elisabeth's address. No one who knew Heidi was working that day either so the gamble of trying to find someone who could easily tell me where she lived had not paid off.

What was I to do now? I decided to take another gamble and phone Heidi's parents in Bergen to pump them for information. Her half-brother, Christian, was the only one at home and he said he would try and find out where she lived and asked me to phone back later. When I called again, he said he had no record of her address anywhere but said I should try the Central Hotel. I informed him that I had already been there and that Heidi wasn't there. He did, however, offer me Elisabeth's telephone number so that I could ask her where Heidi was living. I took the number without telling him that Elisabeth didn't want to talk to me. Christian thought Heidi lived in Hokksund, a small town not too far from Drammen. I then took the bus from Drammen bus station to the end of the bus route, passing through Hokksund without recognising it. I got out in the middle of nowhere. The local town hall would now be closed preventing me from getting any information from them regarding Heidi's address. I hopped back on the same bus, which was making a return journey to Drammen. I was by now totally exhausted but I was going to make one more phone call. To Elisabeth. I phoned her up much to her surprise as she wondered how I got her number and asked her if Heidi was with her as I was in Drammen now. She said Heidi wasn't with her and still refused to tell me her home address, so I swore at her and put the phone down. Sick of everything, I went straight on to Fornebu Airport in Oslo only to book the most expensive business class seat on an SAS flight back to London as that was all that was available. I just wanted to get out of Norway. The weather was gorgeous. Pretty Norwegian girls were off on their summer holidays to the Mediterranean and they were probably a joy to be with, any single one of them. The only girl I knew was a sick mental case living somewhere outside Drammen.

It was a real low point on that plane trip home and I promised myself that I would return to face Heidi and demand an explanation for all the madness she had foisted on me in the past.

For a long time after that, I had these dreams whereby I was in the snow-filled streets in Norway searching for Heidi in her home town or some other, anonymous, place and occasionally I would catch a glimpse of her a stone's throw ahead of me, sometimes pushing her son in his buggy. Then I would run to catch up with her … … but I never managed to reach her. I just missed her – in every dream. She'd either turned the corner, got lost in the crowd, or simply vanished into thin air.

51

Chapter 11

The first thing I did on my return to England was speak to Stuart, a member of my local karate club. It turned out that he was happy to accompany me to Norway to have words with Heidi. He was a good fighter and ready for the adventure but he did not want to go to Norway until after Christmas. It was a bit too long to wait for my liking but I had no choice.

I then went about contacting Drammen's only private detective with instructions to find Heidi for me. I sent him photographs of her so that he could easily identify her. I then waited. I also got to know very well another Norwegian au pair, Dise, who I had met in a pub in North West London. One evening, I asked her to do me a favour, which she eagerly agreed to do. I explained as much as necessary to her and then from a public phone box in Northwood, she phoned Elisabeth, Heidi's sister, on the pretext of being a friend of Heidi's who she had not spoken to since Heidi left Bergen. Elisabeth dutifully gave out Heidi's address (Heidi was not on the phone). Great! It was just the result I needed. The next day I phoned the private detective at his home to tell him exactly what had happened and obviously marvelling at my technique, he said "Jesus Christ!" in amazement. He told me he had also found out where she lived and confirmed as correct the address I had. I kept my part of the bargain and paid him in full for his services. In return I got a full report and two photos of Heidi's house, which was on a main road. I then discovered from the road map the detective had sent me that I had in fact passed right by Heidi's house on my bus journey the previous August. Indeed, there was a bus stop immediately outside her house.

Stuart and I planned our trip for the first week of February 1990. We went to Gatwick Airport and we bumped into yet another Norwegian au pair I had met in the Norwegian church, Elisabeth Grimstad, who was off back home for good. She had had enough of being a nanny and we were coincidentally taking the same flight. We wished her well and went to check in. To our amazement, Elisabeth was seated right next to Stuart and me on the plane - yet she hadn't checked in with us. On the flight she asked us what we were going to do in Norway and we just said we were going to see a friend of mine who had been a naughty girl and we had to confront her. On landing in snow-covered Oslo the customs officials picked out Stuart and myself and pulled us aside for further questioning. The female officer present even took up a pair of rubber gloves and asked me to follow her into a private room. No way was I going to submit to a strip search. I had very long hair then and looked like a rock musician so I guess they thought I would be a good choice for a random drug search. As my explanation satisfied them, they let me go without a fuss. We met up with Elisabeth again outside and she told me that some customs officials had in fact asked her about Stuart and myself. She told them the truth that she knew me from the Norwegian Church in Rotherhithe, London where I had complimented Elisabeth on her piano playing.

We said goodbye to Elisabeth and went out to look for our Hertz rental car in the freezing weather but we were told we had to pick it up in Oslo town centre. Off we went on the bus. The road conditions were dreadful, thick ice in many places. For the Norwegians who are used to the conditions it was plain sailing but I was going to go as slowly as possible in the car when we picked it up. I needed the company of a fearless fellow like Stuart to ensure I didn't get any stick from Heidi's lot. I was in no mood to take any more nonsense from her or her family or any friends who might care to make things difficult. She needed to be told quite firmly some home truths and questioned properly about everything especially her little stunt about deliberately exposing herself to the possibility of HIV infection. Maybe if she had got a good telling off years ago, I would have saved myself all the anguish that came afterwards.

I had made arrangements whilst in England for bed and breakfast accommodation in Drammen and when we had deposited our luggage and rested we went out to Heidi's place. In time we found it and as I drove past we noticed a light was on. We parked a little way up the road and Stuart and I walked back to the house to investigate. We could see no sign of life from the outside and assumed she had gone out for a late night out or possibly to stay overnight with her sister. We went back to our beds at our landlady's but not before I slid all over the place on the icy roads on the way back. It was pure luck that I didn't have an accident. Our tyres had metal studs in them but it wasn't sufficient for a novice like me.

The next day I was all keyed up and after Stuart consumed a huge breakfast we set out back to Heidi's. The light was still on in the house and still there was no sign of activity in the place. Now there was no alternative but to call on the neighbours and ask as to Heidi's whereabouts. We were greeted by a little girl and boy at the door of one of her neighbours and I asked them to fetch their mother, which they dutifully did. The mother was happy to invite us in and it was evident that Heidi had told her little or nothing about me, or so the mother led me to believe. Heidi was in fact on the other side of the country in Bergen with her parents. Just the news we didn't want to hear, but her neighbour, Heidi-Anita, told us that Heidi had become a Christian. Heidi-Anita was a Christian too and together with her husband had helped Heidi on the way to 'seeing the light.' It had been a difficult time for Heidi of late and Heidi-Anita told us that this Christmas just gone, Gudmund Johannessen had turned up on Heidi's doorstep and beaten Heidi to the ground. Heidi had reported the incident to the police. This news cheered me up enormously. Now the silly fuckers were destroying each other again! They didn't need my help in bringing them to book and the assault on Heidi I strongly suspected had something to do with the letter I had written to Johannessen's parents acquainting them with all the spicy details of their son's relationship with Heidi. Oh for the power of the pen! Johannessen had probably punished Heidi for betraying their nasty little secrets to me.

Heidi-Anita continued. Heidi's eldest sister Elisabeth, an atheist, was furious with Heidi for becoming a Christian and they ended up not speaking to each other. Heidi-Anita was very good to Stuart and myself and made us some tea and prepared some cheese and biscuits for us. She then phoned Heidi up in Bergen explaining that I was with her. Heidi-Anita passed the phone to me. In a cold voice Heidi asked me what I was doing in Norway at her neighbour's place. After making it clear she didn't want to discuss anything she put the phone down on me. I couldn't even make an appointment to see her. After that embarrassment, it was time for a bit more explaining to Heidi-Anita and I told her all about Heidi's past. On the subject of fidelity, Heidi-Anita said, "If my husband slept with another woman, I would leave him." Slightly ironic words these turned out to be too!

When we decided it was time to go, Heidi-Anita hugged both Stuart and myself and insisted that we took some of her Christian literature, which was printed in English, with us. I gave her my business card and asked her to get in touch with me by letter if there were any further developments of note with Heidi. We then made our way over to see Heidi's sister Elisabeth. After a confusing search for her place, we came across her apartment block and I went up and rang the doorbell. No answer. So I knocked on the door of the flat opposite and asked the woman who answered if she knew of Elisabeth. She confirmed she did live opposite but couldn't help any more. Her English was practically non-existent. I went back out into the thick snow to tell Stuart I was out of luck and after we stood wondering what to do someone called from an upstairs window in the apartment block. It was Elisabeth whose neighbour had somehow alerted her to our presence. Perhaps Elisabeth had been unable to answer the door when I rang. Elisabeth, in her now customary rudeness, told us to go away and that she didn't want to speak to us. I had to grovel once again and ask her to have the decency to come down and speak to us if she didn't want us to come up to her. Down she came with her cat and I tried to engage her in some sensible conversation but it was to no effect. She cut me off. It was cold and the cat was distressed and did not want to stay out. The cat was refusing to go off for a stroll, so Elisabeth just picked her up and said, "Look, even the cat doesn't like you" and walked back in. We then left quickly just in case trouble arrived, in the form of the local police.

But what would we do now? Our return flight wasn't for another two days and it was too cold to do anything other than stay indoors. So I decided that we might just as well go over to Bergen to find Heidi. She would either be at her parents' place or her other sister's place whose phone number I had. I got out the road map and plotted our course. We would go north to Hønefoss and then west over the mountains through Gol and into the ski resort of Geilo, then on through to Bergen. I estimated we would be in Bergen for about noon the next day. After all, we had come for a purpose and I was going to see it through.

The journey after Gol saw a dramatic change in our fortunes. So far, the driving was manageable. Stuart was brave enough to take the wheel when the gradient got really steep. The roads were very icy and dangerous and it was also snowing hard. Stuart's very slow speed was still not enough to prevent us sliding off the road when going up one steep mountain gradient and we took out a couple of bollards on the verge in quite dramatic fashion. One of the bollards managed to take off the entire back bumper on our Ford Sierra. It was only hanging on by a couple of rivets on the driver's side of the vehicle when we slid to an abrupt halt in the snow-filled verge. We would have been in real trouble right then but for the greatest good fortune of a pick up truck passing us down the road in the opposite direction. The driver saw our distressed vehicle, stopped and reversed to see what our problem was. He got out and decided that a tow by his truck was the only way to pull us out, so back in he got, turned around and reversed up to the front of our car. Out came his towing rope and soon enough we were out, whereupon I ripped off the dangling plastic bumper. This young mechanic surprisingly didn't speak any English but his sturdy efforts in that freezing snowy weather I will always appreciate. He was our saviour.

Off we went again, Stuart resuming his place at the wheel. As we continued our journey it didn't feel or sound right. We stopped again and I got out to see that our nearside back tyre was flat. The collision with the bollards had punctured it. We drove on until we stopped in the relative safety of a lay-by and tried to change the wheel, but even the strength of Stuart could not budge the wheel nuts. Now we were marooned and before long we were going to freeze. There was nothing else for it so I hailed down a driver and explained our predicament. Fortunately, this chap was a mighty big fellow and his strength managed to dislodge the wheel nuts, using the spanner from the boot of our car. We thanked him profusely and the stranger then left us to change the wheel. The old wheel came off and Stuart and I put the spare one on. It was unbearably cold and it was an enormous relief to get back into the car after our earlier false restart. We drove on into the beautiful winter resort of Geilo at about 8 in the evening and booked ourselves into the Alpine Hotel for the night.

Stuart and I went into the bar and discussed the day's events over our drinks. I just had to phone Heidi though and I got some change from the gentleman at the reception desk. I went into the phone booth and closed the partition door behind me. Phoning her sister Rennaug's number, Heidi answered immediately.

"It's me," I said.

"I thought so - I was expecting your call," said Heidi.

I didn't tell her where I was phoning from but said I was on my way to see her. Without provocation, she immediately raised the level of her voice and launched a hysterical tirade of abuse against me, the content of which was hard to take in. Really shocking stuff. The underlying reason for her dramatic attack on me was because of the letter I had sent to Gudmund Johannessen's parents, which she said had caused her enormous problems. In a booming voice, she told me I was "a miserable pathetic human being." In order that I myself could get a word in, I had to raise the level of my voice to cause the hyena on the other end of the phone to listen and to hear me.

"I'm a useless human being am I? What about you and Johannessen, sleeping with him when you know he is taking heroin? And at least I don't kill my own children!" (A reference to her two abortions). This statement struck a raw nerve and she then went into ballistic mode - "Don't you ever say that to me again, you bastard!"

Everyone in the hotel must have heard my loud protestations and not unexpectedly the hotel manager came over to tell me to quieten down. A little later Heidi put in the final shots and put the phone down on me. This was one shrew that just had to be tamed. I was furious. I went back to an embarrassed Stuart in the bar. We decided then to go out for a walk and went to watch some girls play football in the snow covered floodlit sports ground about half a mile from the hotel. These girls were excellent players and many of them were quite pretty and charming too. They were easy to speak to and once again this contact only emphasised to me the gulf between English and Norwegian women in general.

Before I went to bed, I wrote a letter to Gudmund Johannessen's girlfriend, Nina, telling her all about her 'wonderful' new boyfriend. I had every intention of seeking out Johannessen in Bergen to give him a piece of my mind but in case there was no opportunity for this I was going to tell his girlfriend in writing just what sort of a shithead she had shacked up with. So if I posted the letter in the morning it would reach her after we had left Bergen for home and would not alert them to my presence in the country before I confronted them.

Next day, we set off on the final leg of our journey beginning with a stretch of driving across an unmetalled road in moderate snowfall. Cars were even overtaking us on the snow packed track, which showed us something of the marvellous snow driving skills acquired by members of the Norwegian public. Our journey took us down into steep ravines passing wonderful frozen waterfalls and up and around hairpin bends as we slowly made our way into Bergen. We went to Åsane, a suburb of Bergen where Heidi's family lived. I directed Stuart into the car park of the local supermarket and he turned off the engine and told me he had a splitting headache and had to have some aspirins. We both got out and made our way towards the store. We were no more than 20 yards from the entrance of the supermarket when before my very eyes stood Heidi's father and stepmother. Heidi's father was pushing the trolley and the pair of them saw me coming towards them but I hoped they didn't recognise me. We had met six years earlier and I trusted the passage of time had erased their memories of what I looked like. My hair was now much longer and furthermore they were not expecting to see me. So I whispered to Stuart to keep on walking past the supermarket without having the time to explain why. I had made an instant decision not to say hello to the parents in case they forewarned Heidi of our presence. I had rejected the idea of enlisting their help in getting me together with Heidi and sorting things out as being an unrealistic expectation. A decision in hindsight I came to regret. So we left the area and headed out for Gudmund Johannessen's place in another part of town. When we got to our destination, we discovered that he lived on the first floor of a small apartment block up a narrow set of wooden stairs. He had scribbled his name in blue biro on a sticker by the front entrance on the ground floor. He was living in his girlfriend's flat. Waiting outside in the car for Johannessen to appear would be pointless. We were just too tired for an indefinite wait. The alternative of knocking on the door Stuart dismissed immediately as being too dangerous. Johannessen would have seen us through his spyhole and prepared himself maybe with a knife to confront us. So we left intending to return if we had the time, after dealing with Heidi.

Time was now of the essence. The stepmother of Heidi, Ellin, had looked me in the eye and I could not be sure that she had not recognised me. If she was going to alert Heidi then we had to be quick. It started to rain very heavily. Big freezing droplets. We drove up to Heidi's sister's apartment block and I got out on my own to catch the lie of the land. I went up the stairs in from the cold and found her flat. On impulse I rang the doorbell and waited. There was a spyhole but I turned my head away. No one came to the door. "Damn it," I thought. Just my luck that no one was in. So I went back down the stairs and before going back out into the driving rain stood in the stairwell wondering what to do. The icy weather and driving rain told me not to wait around any longer. I found a phone box and rang Heidi's sister, Rennaug. She answered. Clever girl. She was in after all and obviously knew it was me from looking through the spyhole. Rennaug told me Heidi had gone back to Drammen that morning. I was surprised to hear this but it could have been true although I did have my doubts. I thought she might be at her parents at least. I asked Rennaug if I could come up and see her. I knew I was taking a chance because I didn't trust any of the sisters now. Heidi took my call the previous night in her sister's flat and her emotional rantings would have unnerved anyone present and left them all in a state of high anxiety. Bearing in mind the abuse these sisters had received from their own men and indeed the whole general history of the family, I could not rule out that these trigger happy sisters would call out the police to assuage their fears. I suppose if a man had been present in the flat we could have all talked reasonably and in comfort. So I requested of Rennaug that I come up and talk to her straight away but I did ask if she could promise me she would not call the police. Her reply was that she could not promise this. But I said that I was prepared anyway to come up and this I did. I first went back to the car and told Stuart what had transpired. He advised me not to go up to the flat as he felt it would only be a trap but I told him that we had not come all this way for nothing and I was going to take my chances.

So up I went. Rennaug answered the door and as I entered her warm apartment I greeted her with a hand on her shoulder in appreciation for her letting me in. She led me into her lounge where an extremely deep-breasted girlfriend of hers was sitting. Oh my, they were big! I gratefully accepted their offer of a cup of coffee. I remarked how cold it was outside and how good it was to be able to relax in the warmth. Rennaug brought me the cup of coffee. I made it clear that they had nothing to worry about and they seemed to accept this and chatted quite jovially. A knock at the door then came and Rennaug politely excused herself to say she had to give her neighbour some money to enable him to do some shopping for her, which she could not do herself now that I was with her. Up she got to give, whoever it was, the money and she came back in and continued with the general conversation. I explained all about the situation concerning Heidi from my point of view and said I wanted an explanation for the various injustices she had visited upon me. Some time later, whilst we were discussing the situation, another knock came on the door.

"Ah, my neighbour has returned with the shopping," said Rennaug and she got up to answer the door. Not true! Two policemen in blue uniforms entered the sitting room with pistols in their holsters and batons and handcuffs in their belts. I had been set up. Immediately, the tone of my two hosts changed. The busty one sternly told me to "leave Heidi in peace" and to "let her live her own life" and Rennaug too joined in the reprimands. The police took me out of the flat and I tried to explain to them at the bottom of the staircase why I was in the flat and the purpose of my visit. They were understanding enough but said I had to go down to the police station as they'd received reports of threats I had made. "Threats?" I queried in disbelief. Brilliant tactics I thought. Lies had been told to the police in order to get me into trouble. I explained to the police that I had a friend waiting in the car outside and that I had to tell him to follow the police car which would be taking me to the police station. The policeman let me go to Stuart on my own. Stuart was dozing in the car and I banged on the window to get his attention. I told him what had happened and he just said, "Bastards." He then told me he had seen a young chap running past him down the path and go into a phone box and make his call. This chap then waited around for ten minutes and the police turned up to meet the boy. Stuart's suspicions had been raised by this activity but he thought there would be no time to run up to the flat and get me out by the time the police came. So he stayed put. I told him I didn't think there was too much to worry about. There is no doubt that I could have just got in the car with Stuart and driven off without the police seeing us, but I told Stuart I wanted the chance to tell the police about Heidi and expose her for the black widow she was. So I told Stuart to follow me in the police car to Bergen police station.

When we arrived, Stuart parked the car in the police yard and the policemen told us that they would see it was returned to Hertz Car Rentals in Bergen. I had taken out insurance so we would have nothing to pay save for the excess for losing the back bumper in our accident coming over the mountains. We entered the police station and Stuart and I waited in Reception. "The girl is coming soon," we were told.

"Which girl?" I asked.

"Heidi" a policeman said.

"Heidi? I was told she had gone back to Drammen," I replied.

"No, that's not so, she is in Bergen."

"Where in Bergen?"

"Oh, that we can't tell you," the policeman said.

I later learned that she was in her sister's flat all the time, hiding in one of the bedrooms with her three year old son. There I was, calmly chatting away and all she had to do was come out into the sitting room and sit down and face the music. But no! Her paranoid mind must have been imagining all kinds of scenarios that obviously rendered her incapable of reasonable behaviour. Into the station she came with the young neighbour who had called the police and also another man who was probably in his forties or early fifties. Heidi saw me. She looked well and was calm. The older man was talking animatedly to the police on the other side of the glass partition that separated us from them. A kindly policeman came up to me and asked me what I had to say for myself and casually asked what it was he could do to resolve the problem. I told him to sit me down with Heidi so that in his presence I could go through the whole thing and vindicate myself completely. He went off to put this proposal to her and came back saying she did not agree to this. "Crafty bitch!" I thought.

"But it is the only way to let you see what she is all about," I told the policeman.

"Yes, I understand but she doesn't have to do this. It's her right," he replied.

The slippery eel knew what she was doing. Facing me would have exposed her for the fraud that she was and obviously she wasn't going to let this happen. I waited a few minutes more before a more senior plain-clothes police officer came in to see me.

"You will have to stay the night at the police station and we will take a statement from you tomorrow. We are investigating certain allegations that have been made against you. I'm sorry."

"Why can't you take a statement from me now?" I asked.

"There is no one here available. I can assure you there is nothing you can do now," he said.

With that I looked at Stuart in amazement, told him to make his own way back to England, and said goodbye and good luck to him. I was taken down by lift into the basement of the police station, relieved of my boots and valuables and locked up in a cell with a solid metal door and a small window.

Half an hour later, the cell door was opened, not to explain how sorry everyone was for the misunderstanding, but to give me a note from Stuart who was being sent back home straight away having been declared persona non grata. The note explained that the police were sending him back by train to Oslo that night and he needed some money and could I give him some. So I gave the police officer 200 kroner which he was to pass on to Stuart. I knew for sure then there would be no release for me that evening and prepared myself for a long night.

It was another hour before anyone came to see me, only to tell me again that absolutely nothing could be done that evening as it was now the weekend when few policemen were at the station and that a statement would be taken from me next morning. They gave me a drink and I was then transferred to another cell with metal bars in another part of the basement where I was to sleep.

Chapter 12

Next morning, I was given a cup of tea and a sandwich and was then allowed to have a shower. I then got in touch with a Norwegian lawyer after the police had supplied the names of two to me. Not knowing one from the other, I chose one, a woman, rang her up at home and explained my predicament, taking the lawyer through a brief history of Heidi's past but emphasising the fact that she had spent several weeks in a psychiatric unit and anything she said was liable to be very suspect. The lawyer told me she would talk to the officer in charge of my case and tell him exactly what I had said. An hour later she rang back and said that it would be all okay and that the police would release me as soon as they had taken a statement from me.

At about 2 p.m. I was taken upstairs into an interview room and was joined by a police officer, a typist and an interpreter. The interpreter was a really nice woman and assisted me in making my statement about the history of my friendship with Heidi which was complete and truthful. After that I signed my statement. Heidi had earlier made a statement in Norwegian but I wasn't allowed to have it read out to me. The interviewing officer proceeded to pose some questions to me through the interpreter whilst picking out relevant points in Heidi's evidence.

"Have you been giving trouble to other girls in England?"

In years gone by I'd told Heidi about one or two English girls who had been a real pain in the arse. Heidi was now trying to set me up as a troublemaker.

"No, I haven't," I answered. "Never."

"Why did you travel to Norway in 1986 with a different name on your passport?" I was asked.

"Dirty little bitch, Heidi!" I thought. She had known damn well that it was to avoid going into the Egyptian army but I assumed she had not explained this to the police, otherwise they would not be asking me. Heidi had probably told the police that she simply knew my passport name was different, hoping to make the police suspect I had some sinister ulterior motive for the change of name. So I explained the reason. "In order to avoid being conscripted into the Egyptian army, a fact which I explained in full to Heidi ...." and I proceeded myself to tell the interpreter the full story.

Another police officer then walked in with faxed copies of six of the letters I had written to Heidi and her sister Elisabeth. They were given to the interpreter to read through to see if they contained any threats. I could see they went back to about 1986 and up to 1989. I was aware Heidi had mentioned some years ago over the phone that she would be keeping one of my letters "just in case," but I really could not remember what I had said in it. I had a feeling it was one really condemnatory letter I had written in response to learning that she had been sleeping with Johannessen whilst he was taking heroin, or maybe one that I wrote in reply to her telling me she had got pregnant to Gudmund Johannessen. I waited, with my fingers crossed, to see if that one was included with the pages my interpreter was reading through. It occurred to me at this point that the real reason for my detention over the weekend was to give Heidi and Elisabeth time to collect the letters and fax them through to the police station. Elisabeth was in Drammen right now and Heidi's home was in Drammen also, so Elisabeth must have gone round to Heidi's home to retrieve the letters and fax them through.

I waited in silence whilst the interpreter read through the letters and when she had finished she told me, "There is not a single threat in any of these letters." I wondered why then the letters were given to the police at all, as having read them myself I could see that none of them were in the least bit abusive. None of the very consoling ten or so letters I had written to Heidi from Egypt, England, Switzerland and Tunisia from September 1988 to February 1989 were given to the police of course, a tactic in keeping with Heidi's usual pattern of deceit. Those six letters with the police interpreter were just factual accounts of Heidi's hitherto repulsive behaviour with repeated requests for explanations. If I were in Heidi's position, I would not want to show the letters to anyone. What was the point? It would only highlight Heidi's shameful past. Why she had them faxed to the police I am still at a loss to understand.

I then told the police interpreter in detail all that Heidi had told me about her past; the abortions, miscarriage, suicide attempts, heroin taking of Johannessen. This dear woman then quite spontaneously told me, "She [Heidi] is a sick woman." Lovely words - just the tonic I needed.

The interview concluded and I was taken in to recover my personal belongings from another senior policeman, Henrik Dugstad. Unfortunately, the envelope from the private detective and the photos he had taken of Heidi's house were left in the car and the police had retrieved them and given them to Mr. Dugstad. He asked me who took the photos and I told him that a private detective did and as they had the envelope with his company crest on it I thought I might as well tell him exactly who it was, so I did. Taking the envelope with me was a mistake and although I don't think the police reprimanded the private detective, I still felt I had wronged the man who certainly did not need the police knowing what he'd got up to.

I was now going to be released but they told me that I was not going to make the last flight out of Bergen that evening. However, they were not going to release me back into Bergen even though Heidi had departed the night before for Drammen. The police did not want me to seek out the parents or Rennaug the sister, who of course lived in Bergen. So I was told I would have to stay another night at the police station after which I would be escorted to the airport. The police moreover would not pay my return airfare to London. My original ticket was for a return flight from Oslo and was non-changeable. In any case that flight was for 8 p.m. that evening on the other side of the country. It was now 5 p.m. As I was handed back my credit card, Henrik Dugstad told me I would have to use it to pay for the fare. I protested but he said he could not help me out at all on this one. He was a very nice man, Mr. Dugstad, and proceeded to tell me about his family and his hobby of pheasant shooting in the mountains of Norway. He said he could not understand why I visited Norway to see Heidi when her child, Daniel, wasn't mine. I explained, in a tone of voice and manner that drew his full understanding, of my intense disgust at being so deceived and lied to by a woman who I had been so good to.

"All I wanted was a good wife," I told him.

"Oh, but not her," he said. "I don't think she'll ever marry anyone … a girl like that."

For the first time in two days I was allowed some fresh air - in the police yard but still handcuffed and accompanied by a police officer.

"Why the handcuffs?" I asked him.

"Regulations" he replied.

"Even though I am being released tomorrow?" I retorted.

"Yes, I'm sorry. We have to obey the rules whilst you are with us."

After another night at Bergen police station I was taken to the airport for the afternoon flight home by two very pleasant police officers in their thirties. One of them spoke of his happy walking holidays in Yorkshire in his "younger days." They waited around for me to buy my air ticket and then shook hands with me in turn and then left me. That evening, as soon as I got back to my Essex home, I telephoned Stuart. He had only been home an hour himself, having spent the night sleeping at Gatwick Airport. He had no money to catch a train home and had to wait until the next morning when his mother drove to the airport to pick him up. This inconvenience was nothing compared to what befell him after we parted company at the police station in Bergen. I listened in amazement to his story.

Within a few minutes of me being taken down to the cells, Heidi had come face to face with Stuart and bleated out, "That's the drummer, that's the drummer!" Stuart did not know what she was on about until I reminded him about my best friend Russell being the drummer with Chris Barber.

"Oh, Christ!" exclaimed Stuart. "She thought I was Russell. Well, I told them I was not a drummer but they didn't seem to believe me at first. Then some other man came in and it looked like someone old enough to be Heidi's father, and I'm telling you, they wanted you put away! That guy was remonstrating with the police for ages and you know, that young chap that got you arrested was

60

making threatening gestures to me whilst the police weren't looking, one fist punching the palm of his other hand as if to say 'I'm going to get you,'" said Stuart.

The police took no chances with Stuart. They contacted the British police to check him out - name, home address and occupation. They then took him on the overnight train to Oslo; accompanying him on the train was Heidi and a girlfriend of hers and two more police officers. Stuart continued, "I could see them behind me further up the carriage. They had their legs on the seats and were smoking all the way back to Oslo. I never spoke to them though. They were behaving like real slags as though nothing had happened."

The money I had given to Stuart was just enough to pay for his train fare to Oslo from where he still had to get to Gardemoen Airport, which was 40 kilometres away from Oslo railway station. When he arrived at the railway station, it was one o'clock in the morning - he had no money left and he tried asking one or two strangers whether he could borrow the bus fare to the airport but they weren't interested. So what did he do? He set off in the snow along the road to Gardemoen Airport hoping to hitch a lift. British army vehicles passed him but did not stop to pick him up. Hardly any other vehicles came along and Stuart, now in a desperate state, managed to walk the rest of the way to the airport, but frozen to the bone and completely exhausted. He then waited all day until 8 p.m. to catch his plane home on the return portion of his ticket. This poor fellow had gone through hell on my behalf and all as a result of a few well-placed lies from Heidi.

I had missed a day's work because of being unable to catch my scheduled flight home but had phoned work from the police station alerting them to this fact, saying that I was just taking an extra day's 'holiday.' I then worked for a big organisation and we had our own police force with whom we all ate dinner, with a silver service and waitress attendance. I arrived for dinner at the usual time on the day of my return to work and one of my colleagues, Graham, enquired of me as to why I had taken an extra day in Norway. The number two in the police force, Lance, butted in saying, "Were you arrested then?" Assuming that the Norwegian police had got in touch with him, (as they had made enquiries as to who my employers were whilst I was in custody), I replied, "Yes, how did you know?" to which Lance, the police officer said, "I didn't know you were arrested, I was only joking."

Who did I work for? Well, the only clues I'll give you are that we were named in the 1992 film 'Blue Ice' starring Michael Caine and filming took place in the vicinity of our dining quarters. Also, our old headquarters were shot in the 1966 film 'Battle of Britain' with Laurence Olivier standing on its hallowed steps. And our patch featured exclusively in the film 'The Long Good Friday' with the incomparable Bob Hoskins.

I had exposed my secret inadvertently and so decided to own up and I told my colleagues the story, which they promised to keep quiet. They all knew Stuart and Russell anyway as I had brought them in for lunch a couple of times each. The incident at lunch though was embarrassing, as I had not told my work colleague, Graham, the real reason for my extra day's 'holiday.' Lance, the policemen who caused my faux pas, was the life and soul of the party at meal times and it was certainly a feather in his cap to have succeeded in fooling me, the youngest and cockiest member at the dinner table. In due course, the last laugh was on Lance who later had a claim to fame or notoriety, depending on how you look at it. He was the father-in-law of the road manager of Big Audio Dynamite, a major rock band at the time. After he retired from the force, Lance immediately had nationwide television exposure. He had left his wife 20 years earlier for another woman who he lived with until she died of cancer. He then went back to his wife in complete distress and asked her for a new start only to stay with her for just a few months until he set up home with his Chief Superintendent's secretary whom he had got pregnant. Well, the deserted wife was having none of it and in 1991 went on television's 'The Time and Place' hosted by John Stapleton to reveal all, including telling the nation her husband's full name and how he had "got off" with someone else and so on. She even spoke of having challenged Lance on his doorstep in Norfolk after Lance's baby was born and related how Lance had suffered a heart attack afterwards. She had got her revenge all right. And now I had to see about getting some revenge of my own.

Chapter 13

It was a sickening blow not to have dealt with that wicked liar, Heidi, in Bergen. I felt totally justified in going to Bergen to remonstrate with her about her treachery in the preceding years. One person who I was sure would help me out was Heidi-Anita, the kindly neighbour whose Christian values would lend her to a sympathetic response. I wrote a letter to her asking her to furnish me with an explanation for Heidi's behaviour, which she surely must have discussed in detail with Heidi by now. But I never received a reply and for that, not surprisingly, I will never forgive her. For Heidi-Anita, Christian kindness had evaporated at the very time I needed it. It would now cost me a lot of money to discover the background to the treachery that had befallen me in Norway.

I then wrote to the private detective in Drammen who had earlier helped me out. I told him the story and sadly he wrote a long letter back to me telling me off for trying to get him "to trace a girl who clearly did not want to be found." I thought this was pure hypocrisy on his part; he had known all along that Heidi did not want to be found by me and I suspected the police had been in touch with him over the matter. But still, the letter he subsequently wrote to me just wasn't good form. The funny thing was he offered afterwards to get me Heidi-Anita's telephone number for payment but I did not proceed with the deal. Tragically this private detective, Mr. Madsen, not long afterwards died of leukaemia. I spoke to his wife before he died and she told me he was ill with cancer. Poor man. I was beginning to think that death or misfortune touched everyone who involved themselves with Heidi.

I knew the senior partner, Michael Bell, of a Norwegian law firm in London – Foyen & Bell. I got in touch with his litigation partner and wrote the whole story down from start to finish in a notebook for him. I now set out the correspondence that followed to illustrate how things went afterwards:

Letter dated 24th February 1990 to my London lawyer

Dear Mr. Whittal,

Heidi Overaa

I enclose my notes on this matter which start in 1982 when I met the girl and give a detailed account of all that has taken place since.

I am incensed over what happened to me last weekend and all I care about is achieving some form of redress. If there is any way of making a protest, then it must be done whether it be by writing to the newspapers in Norway or just, as you suggest, some strong letters to the police and the girl herself (although I would also like my feelings known to Heidi's parents and sisters).

Thank you for your efforts on my behalf so far and I look forward to hearing from you with your suggestions in due course. I enclose my business card although please write to my home address at the head of this letter.

Yours sincerely,

Letter dated 26th March 1990 from my London lawyer to me

Dear Mr. Delaware,

Miss Heidi Overaa

I enclose herewith a copy of a letter I have now drafted in preparation for sending to the Bergen police and I apologise for the delay in getting around to this matter.

I thank you for your letter of 24th February enclosing the long and detailed statement regarding this matter, which I read carefully with a good deal of concern.

In conclusion, I felt that it would probably be better not to write to Miss Overaa, as I could see no purpose in doing so. As you have, obviously, had strong feelings for this woman, she has clearly caused you a great deal of physical and emotional harm and I feel that any further contact with her can only aggravate matters.

Clearly, she has psychological problems and there is, in my view, no grounds upon which you could take an action against her in damages or otherwise.

As far as your good name is concerned, no benefit could be gained by writing to Miss Overaa, as in that respect it has not been prejudiced. As we discussed on the telephone, I do feel that your good character may possibly have suffered somewhat in the eyes of the Bergen police and, therefore, I have written the enclosed letter.

You will note that there are a number of blanks which require dates to be inserted on which I await your advice.

I look forward to hearing from you.

Yours sincerely,

Letter dated 28th March 1990 to my lawyer from me

Dear Mr. Whittal,

Heidi Overaa

Thank you for your letter of March 26th. Your draft letter I return with my comments in red. There are a few errors of fact which I have corrected.

I am very sad however to see that you have advised against a letter being written to Heidi Overaa: I feel very strongly that the point has to be made to her and also the rest of her family, otherwise they will feel as if they are in the right. A copy of your letter to the police will suffice my needs - to be sent to Heidi, her sisters and parents. It will teach them not to ignore their responsibilities. I will be left with an enormous sense of grievance unless something is done in this respect.

I have in fact written to Heidi's neighbour who quite understood the situation and I hope to hear from her. Stuart and I sat for an hour with her in her home when we visited Drammen.

Over all I feel very bitter indeed that a girl who initially - when I met her in 1982 - wanted to follow a better path, has reverted to a quite sinful and sick way of living. The problem was that she was extremely pretty (and I consider I restrained myself on her charms very well in the circumstances). I had to protest against her way of living to those who should have taken care of her - her family. Now they all hate me and Heidi is as badly off as ever. You can't win.

Yours sincerely,

Letter dated 9th April 1990 from my lawyer to me

Dear Mr. Delaware,

Heidi Overaa

Thank you for your letter dated 28th March, I note your comments in relation to my draft letter addressed to the Chief Constable of Bergen Police Station and I have made the necessary amendments. I also note your comments regarding your disappointment that I have advised not writing to Heidi, but I stand by that advice.

I can see no benefit whatsoever in pursuing a claim against Heidi or writing to her. I believe firmly that the situation can only be worsened by any further contact and that any correspondence between Heidi and yourself, albeit through the services of this office, can only lead to further acrimony and protracted misery.

I note however your suggestion that I send a copy of my letter addressed to the police to Heidi, which in the circumstances, I shall do.

I have taken a long and hard look at this matter and studied the various statements that you have provided me with very carefully. I have considered every potential legal action available to you and have to advise that none is available.

In the circumstances, I feel that this letter to the Bergen police, with a copy to Heidi, takes the case as far as I am legally able and that any further advice would be of a non-legal nature.

Yours sincerely,

Letter dated 9th April 1990 from my London lawyer to the Chief Constable of the Bergen Police

Dear Sir,

Heidi Overaa

We have been instructed by our client, Frederick Delaware in relation to the unfortunate incident which led up to his arrest and detention at Bergen Police Station between the dates of 17th February and 19th February 1990.

We have a full statement from our client regarding the background to this matter and, more particularly, the incident which took place prior to his arrest.

We are aware that our client was interviewed and gave a long statement to police officers at Bergen Police Station and, therefore, no doubt you will be fully aware of the circumstances. In summary, however, it is clear that our client has known Heidi Overaa since 1982 when they formed a platonic relationship, which has endured until now. Our client met Miss Overaa in France whilst on holiday in 1982. Clearly, both parties were very much attracted to each other and they started a normal and healthy relationship. It soon became apparent, however, to our client that Miss Overaa was suffering from a number of tragic problems, which included her early family life and her current traumatic relationships with certain undesirable youths in Norway.

In particular, we understand that Miss Overaa was exposed to a life of drugs and was extremely confused and psychologically troubled. Because of his love for Miss Overaa, our client went to considerable lengths to assist her in sorting out some of her problems. In particular, he felt that she was not obtaining the sort of care that she should have expected from her family and friends and he felt a strong moral obligation to support her himself. This our client attempted in the early years of their relationship but soon discovered that his efforts were going unrewarded. In particular, we understand that Miss Overaa on frequent occasions played on the emotions of our client and even tried to entice our client to Norway with a plea for help in dealing with a young man called Gudmund Johannessen who was pestering her. We understand that this man is violent, a drug user and a criminal convict. Unfortunately, either through insincerity, or simple psychological problems, Miss Overaa led our client into an impossible situation which ultimately led him to being unjustifiably arrested.

It would seem that our client was detained for a wholly unreasonable period of time, bearing in mind that the various Norwegian parties involved in this incident, we understand, are known to the Bergen police and, therefore, we would have thought the incident capable of being resolved in a matter of hours, rather than days. The incident subsequently led to a great deal of unnecessary expense for both our client and his colleague who accompanied him on this visit.

We understand that the allegations made against our client and his colleague were that he had travelled to Norway with the purpose of causing physical harm to certain persons in Norway. This we should like to make clear is categorically denied on behalf of both our client and his colleague. We also understand that our client and his colleague were both reprimanded and his colleague was told not to return to Norway. We are not aware that any Court Order was made deporting either our client or his colleague and perhaps you could please confirm this.

In the circumstances, we have advised our client that he is perfectly at liberty to return to Norway as is his colleague, as neither of them either intended to, or, in fact, committed any offence.

The principal purpose in writing to you now is to put on record our client's position, as he feels he was unfairly and dishonestly enticed into an extremely embarrassing situation, which has now caused him a great deal of concern.

We had initially been asked to write to Heidi Overaa by our client, seeking some form of explanation for her behaviour and putting the record straight. We have, however, advised our client that we believe it in his own interest simply to avoid any further contact with Miss Overaa, irrespective of his feelings towards her and that in the circumstances we hope this letter to you will suffice in clearing our client's name.

We would be happy to discuss this matter further, should you feel there are matters remaining unresolved.

Yours faithfully,

Letter dated 9th April 1990 from my lawyer to Heidi Overaa

Dear Miss Overaa,

We have been instructed by our above named client in relation to the incident in Norway on 17th February when our client was arrested and detained at Bergen Police Station.

We enclose herewith a copy of our letter to Bergen Police Office, which is self-explanatory.

Yours sincerely,

Letter dated 18th April 1990 from my lawyer to me

Dear Mr. Delaware,

Heidi Overaa

I confirm that I wrote to both the police and Heidi Overaa on the 9th April 1990 and enclose herewith copies of my letters.

I am anticipating a reply from the Norwegian Police, which will naturally confirm that they have received my letter.

In the event that I do not hear from them within say the next three weeks, I will write again. I have, however, no reason to believe that the letters will not find the appropriate addressees.

I look forward to keeping you updated.

Yours sincerely,

Dear Mr. Whittal,

Heidi Overaa

Thank you for your letter of 18th April with enclosures.

I telephoned the Bergen police yesterday and spoke to Henrik Dugstad who is dealing with the case. He said he has not yet received your letter but it would eventually filter through to him. He himself had not spoken to Heidi Overaa since the incident and he will find out who, if anyone, has. He is a nice fellow and I am sure he will co-operate. Whether they will make contact again with Heidi Overaa is another matter.

Between you and me, I spoke to Heidi's psychiatrist, a doctor a Lier Hospital near Drammen. He would not tell me much obviously, but what he did say gave me a little consolation.

I am relieved that an official stand has now been made and I look forward to hearing from you with further developments.

Yours sincerely,

Dear Mr. Delaware,

Heidi Overaa

Thank you for your letter dated 20th April, received here on 23rd April. I enclose herewith a copy of a letter received from the Bergen police dated 19th April and apologise for the delay in sending this to you, due to the fact that I was out of the office last week and this is the first opportunity I have had to do so.

I look forward to your comments.

Yours sincerely,

Dear Sirs,

Heidi Overaa

I am in receipt of your letter of April 9th and I have looked into the matter concerning your client.

I can inform you that Bergen Police Department have had under investigation a case of accusations reported by Ms. Overaa in December 1986. The case referred to threats and other allegations related to Section 227 of the (Norwegian) Penal Code - Threats of Bodily Harm etc.

The documents of the case consist among other things of letters from your client containing explicit threats related to Ms. Overaa's life and health.

Investigation of the case mentioned, was not finished; and not presented to the Public Prosecutor because your client in the meantime had left Norway.

In February 1990 the police was notified that your client had returned to Norway and reports were made to the police that your client had issued new threats towards Ms Overaa among other things.

Due to the then present suspicion of serious crimes, your client was apprehended by the police on Saturday February 17th. The police notified him of the serious accusations against him which he denied.

The police, however, regarded the situation as serious and found that there was an imminent possibility of further threats and also a danger of physical action.

Your client was therefore informed that the police seriously considered bringing the case before the Magistrate on Monday February 19th asking for an Order of Custody. Your client was also informed of Norwegian laws concerning entrance and stay in Norway of Foreign Subjects. The (Norwegian) Aliens Act had provisions which made it possible and reasonable for the police to consider issuing an Order of Denied Permission to stay in Norway; pursuant to the then present criminal charges against him.

In that situation, pending a strong possibility of a Court Order of Custody and/or an Order of Denied Stay in Norway, your client wished to leave Norway as soon as possible.

Based on this wish of your client, the police released him from provisional custody on Monday February 19th and your client left Norway on the same day.

On behalf of Norwegian Police Authorities, I wish to inform you that the case concerning reports of threats, are not closed. The case rests, due to the fact that your client is a resident abroad. If your client returns to Norway within the Statute of Limitations, the case might be re-opened. Any further entry into Norway might also be considered within the framework provided under the Aliens Act.

For the record, I also wish to state that the provisional custody of your client from February 17th to 19th was proper and legal; within the provisions of the (Norwegian) Criminal Procedures Act, Section 171 Sub-section 1 & 3 c.f. Section 175.

Hoping I have been able to sufficiently respond to your letter, I beg to remain,

Yours sincerely,

Svein Eric Krogvold
Commander
Head of CID

Letter dated 8th May 1990 from me to my lawyer

Dear Mr. Whittal,

Heidi Overaa

Thank you for your letter of 2nd May with enclosure.

First of all I enclose a letter from Heidi written way back in 1984 after we had resumed contact. It shows the reality of our friendship and I relied upon it as evidence of her desire to reform and follow a straighter path. When she continued to repeat her self-destructive behaviour it was little wonder I felt betrayed. The letter was written a few months after her breakdown and suicide attempt, following her miscarriage of twins when she discovered Gudmund Johannessen had been sleeping with her best friend. He - Johannessen - had got her pregnant. Please return the letter to me in due course.

The police refer to 'explicit' threats I made by letter in 1986. I can't remember what I wrote then but I probably made reference to her deserving a damned good hiding for getting pregnant again to Gudmund Johannessen. I certainly told her that she was a tramp, and had betrayed my trust in her. It made me feel quite ill that she had got pregnant again to this boy, who believe me, is trash. He used her as one of many sleeping partners, a girl who no one cared for and who needed desperately love and comfort and who eventually succumbed to his persistent attention.

I would like you to ask the police to send you copies of these 1986 letters so that I can refresh my memory. I reject the notion that I have no right to tell a girl off and especially after the time I spent on the case of Heidi Overaa.

68

The police it seems are evading the issue. They made no reference to your point that it was an impossible situation I was placed in and it was inevitable that I would return for some explanations. The point about me being asked - begged - for assistance by Heidi in September 1988 to immediately go to Norway and rescue her from Gudmund Johannessen has been ignored. This is real treachery by Heidi. She has used me when it suited her, and nothing was going to stop me from seeing her in person to let her explain herself.

In September 1988 she made another mild suicide attempt because of Gudmund Johannessen so I feel quite justified in taking matters into my own hands and returning to Norway. Her own family were powerless. And it is still continuing. Johannessen beat Heidi up at Christmas - yet no prosecution followed - after she complained to the police.

When Heidi asked me over in September 1988, I took it that our stormy friendship was repaired. Also in June 1989 she wanted to resume contact after we had a two hour phone chat from her hotel. She took one hour of the hotel's time and at their expense to talk to me. She has in the past threatened to kill me - on the phone and by letter (which was so disgusting I tore it up at the time) but also told me that Gudmund Johannessen and his brother would "break my legs" if I confronted them over Gudmund Johannessen's behaviour. When she gets another reminder of what a bastard Gudmund is she turns back to me and begs for assistance. The whole lot of them are low-life scoundrels. The fact of Heidi's suicide attempts, abortions, involvement with multiple sex partners seems to the police to be beside the point. It is ridiculous. Soon I will be made out to be on a level with the Kray twins!

As far as the February incident this year is concerned, the police have around 6 letters in their possession which led up to my visit which my interpreter certified contained not one threat. She stated she believed Heidi was sick and that was the view also of Henrik Dugstad, the policeman. If they want to check they can ask about Heidi's past of her psychiatrist - Dr. Broch at the clinic in Lier. It won't happen of course, as all hell will break lose if the Overaa family discover her doctor has been talking to me.

The police say "due to the then present suspicion of serious crimes ....." That is the doing of Heidi who is purely out for revenge after I informed the parents of Gudmund Johannessen of the sum total of events. I don't see why these people should not be told at long last of what a bastard their son has been. The police certainly couldn't prevent him from repeatedly causing her depression and as I said, two suicide attempts and actual physical violence to her.

At the police station, Heidi had the backing of some mature people and I understand from my friend - Stuart - that they were insisting I be dealt with severely. Heidi had obviously persuaded them that I had on the phone told her that I was going to beat her up - I will not stand for such nonsense. But I can see that if you want to cause maximum distress to a guy then those were the kind of remarks Heidi would make to the police. They have no idea she is lying.

The crux is that these people cannot stand being given a run for their money. The parents of Heidi wanted to prevent the embarrassment of "the facts" getting out and it is her father who I guess has been behind trying the punish me and prevent me returning to Norway. I criticised him heavily for leaving the burden of his daughter to me and he wants revenge. I am not joking; the whole Overaa family have had so much go on in their lives it would make a real good trash novel and now when someone like me has had enough, they resort to dirty tactics and that's why I am so incensed.

Their mentality amazes me and if they think like that and between themselves use and cheat me, then I'll take them all the way. They give it out but they can't take it.

Perhaps you could write to 109 Gamle Riksvei, where Heidi-Anita lives. She and her husband look after Heidi Overaa and they know the truth. This neighbour is a good woman and spent about two hours with Stuart and myself discussing Heidi. She

69

certainly did not give me any indication that Heidi was about to have me arrested. Heidi in her deceit probably didn't even tell her of what was planned.

You may think I'm taking all of this too seriously but I repeat, that too many people exist like this and they seem to be getting their own way all too often. I am making a stand. Perhaps on your reply to the police you could be very direct and ask them what they think about the filth that surrounds this girl and take account of her history. They make me feel - this letter of theirs - that I am a liar and in need of 'help' myself.

Would you agree in the light of what the police say that they might arrest me immediately I set foot in Norway - i.e. at the airport? Also regarding Stuart the police have said nothing.

The police in Norway overall could not do anything to prevent the circumstances that led up to my visit. When Heidi was raped nothing was done. When Heidi's 'grandfather' (her stepmother's father) sexually abused her nothing was done; her suicide attempt - nothing done; her continued pregnancies, sleeping around, involvement with a drug taker - all bypassed. Still the police make no reply to your letter that Johannessen is a criminal convict. Don't let them get away with it. Certainly the attitude of the psychiatrist is 'ah, poor thing - don't do it again' and they talk endlessly to no effect. They have done nothing for her over the years and it seems now they are only talking to her sister and not her father - who really is the one responsible for her. The whole thing stinks. I should be thanked by the police for trying to put a stop to this licence; I should be thanked by the Overaa family for my efforts. Instead they want me prosecuted. Tell me of one man who has not lost his temper over a woman? We all know what a pain they can be.

Yours sincerely,

<hr>

Letter dated 9th May 1990 from me to my lawyer

Dear Mr.Whittal,

Heidi Overaa

Further to my letter of 8th May, do you think it might speed things up if I telephoned the head of the CID in Norway to discuss things? It has been almost three months since the incident and the delay in getting our point across is causing me real distress. I find now after all our efforts the police have more or less ignored your letter of 9th April; they are hoping that the matter will just go away but I am not standing for it.

Due to exasperation at hearing nothing concrete from any of my contacts in Norway - specifically Heidi Overaa's neighbour - I telephoned Rennaug Overaa on Saturday and we spoke for about 5 minutes. She told me she read the "papers" at the station when the police told her that they believe I am "not right in the head." Now, over in Norway they can follow their own ways if they want but I try to follow a decent path of living, even if in times of weakness I fail, but I will not be told that I am "not right in the head" because I express my views in a very forthright manner. After all I am only trying to follow the Ten Commandments. Perhaps it would have been 'better' if Heidi had died from the suicide attempts so they could all see just what a mess they are in. All that I wrote on paper to Heidi in 1986 and in 1989, Heidi had been told orally before and she accepted what I said. After she got herself into bad company and further trouble, it affected her mind so much that she turned against me when I reminded her of her pledges to start afresh. The only way to make these people listen is to tell them, loud and clear, the facts. There comes a time when tough talk is needed. I am not asking them to become Muslim; I respect the Christian and Jewish faiths and the right of people to worship in peace as they wish. I am not forcing, nor do I ever force, Islam down anyone's throat.

So please keep the pressure up and don't let these people off the hook. I am sure Heidi Overaa's father figures somewhere in this and basically that is why I want him to be sent a copy of your letter of 9th April. He is a sly one it seems and could still do with a timely reminder of his errors of omission in letting Heidi reach her present predicament. She is now alone with an illegitimate child and she has no skill to earn a living. She is in a mess. I did leave Heidi alone for long spells and later when I did phone up I find twice she has tried to kill herself. It's not me that caused the problem. The police cannot see the wood for the trees.

Yours sincerely,

P.S. These revelations about a 1986 complaint to the police are news to me. Heidi told me that her father had advised her what to do to prevent me seeing her but I was never told actual complaints had been made. Thinking about it, perhaps the father himself complained. Heidi later - believe me - fully accepted my criticisms of her when finally she broke down on the phone to me weeping and shouting to me, "I want revenge against Gudmund" and "I am begging you now to help me against this psycho" - in September 1988. It was very sad and I felt for her. She "hated all men." Perhaps if I had had hard evidence - by letter - of all this the police would for sure know I'm telling the truth but all this took place on the phone. As I said, Heidi's psychiatrists must know all this and I have told them the whole story from my viewpoint. Unfortunately we won't be able to get their confirmation in writing due to the doctor/patient relationship of confidentiality which, of course, is to be respected.

Letter dated 12th June 1990 from me to my lawyer

Dear Mr. Whittal,

Heidi Overaa

So far I have heard nothing concrete from the Norwegian Embassy and my contact there, Vidar Kleiven. His secretary told me last week he had been in contact with Bergen but knew nothing more and that he would contact me. I can't see why there should be so long a delay but I phoned the Embassy several times and so now must leave it to them.

Unless you hear from me to the contrary by Tuesday of next week - in order to give a few more days for Vidar Kleiven to respond, would you please write back to the police in Bergen. This business of Heidi Overaa feeling threatened happened once before with a shopkeeper in Bergen a few years ago who, she alleged to me and to the police, had raped her. The police told her they would find it very difficult to prosecute him. Nevertheless she felt her life to be "in danger" because of the 'muscle' that this shopkeeper could command. I wonder what the police made of all that. Nothing happened to the shopkeeper and it seemed nothing happened to Gudmund Johannessen when he assaulted Heidi last Christmas and was reported to the police. I have never laid a finger on Heidi - all that stands against me are those letters of 1986 which was a reaction to that girls diabolical behaviour and which was the only way I had of releasing the anger inside me. My intention was always to give her a stiff lecture, in person, and no more. The letters were meant to shake her up so she would change her behaviour.

I don't know whether the police are trying to cover themselves fully, just in case my contact with Heidi causes her to try and kill herself again, or whether they are just prejudiced against me. It seems in the past they have never really got to grips with Gudmund Johannessen and he in fact is the real offender. Therefore, on your advice, a strong letter to the police might cause them to pull their finger out and come clean about the reality of this case; I am not the cause of the chaos, others are. This matter cannot go on indefinitely and also I have little or no money to spend on this case.

71

Perhaps eventually if the matter does carry on you could advise me as how best to conduct things myself.

I trust you had a restful fortnight off. I will phone you next week, if I have any more news.

Yours sincerely,

Letter dated 13th June 1990 from me to my lawyer

Dear Mr. Whittal,

I did today telephone Commander Svein Erik Krogvold at Bergen police station and spoke to him for ten minutes. He could give me no assurance that the matter would not be taken further if I re-entered Norway and said that my only safeguard was not to go back. I told him my letters of 1986 were not meant to be taken literally and that he must take into account the whole background of the matter. This he said did not concern the police - Heidi's actions and problems were between her and myself and only her withdrawal of the allegations would close the case. Regarding Gudmund Johannessen he had no information to hand on him. All in all it seems I am getting nowhere. Mr. Krogvold said no one from the Norwegian Embassy here had contacted him, which annoyed me, after promises had been made by Vidar Kleiven that he would talk to the police. I spoke to Mr. Kleiven's secretary today and left a message to the effect that I had spoken to the police etc. and she said he would phone me back.

Yours sincerely,

Letter dated 14th June 1990 from me to my lawyer

Dear Mr. Whittal,

Heidi Overaa

Today I finally got a phone call from Vidar Kleiven at the Norwegian Embassy and he managed to get something out of Commander Krogvold that I could not, when they spoke together. The police will do nothing provided I make no further contact with Ms. Overaa on any visit I make to Norway. Strange, isn't it, how it takes the Embassy to get this assurance which a day earlier Mr. Krogvold would not give me, when I spoke to him. Therefore please get this confirmed in writing by the police and of course make reference to Vidar Kleiven (who is on 071 235 7151 if you want to speak to him first). To finish things off if you see fit I wouldn't mind you composing a letter to Heidi Overaa telling her off basically saying that if she wants to live the life of a tramp and involve others in her problems, then there is bound to be a lot of bitterness created if she continues with the same behaviour after repeated attempts (on my part) to sort her life out. A letter like that from you would go a lot further than a similar one from me. But if you think the copy letter you sent her earlier is enough, I'll accept it.

Best wishes,

Dear Mr. Delaware,

Heidi Overaa

Thank you for your letters of 12th, 13th and 14th June which awaited my return from holiday.

I have written to Bergen police and enclose a copy of my letter herewith.

I note what you say in your letter of 14th June regarding writing to Miss Overaa but would very strongly advise against such a letter. In fact, I would advise strongly to the contrary that absolutely no further contact is made with Miss Overaa as this quite clearly will certainly lead to further problems for you both from a personal emotional point of view and from the point of view of your personal livelihood regarding the Norwegian police.

Having read at length the copy correspondence that you have forwarded to me and your summary of your relationship with Miss Overaa, I would not be surprised if Miss Overaa at some time in the future tried to contact you again. If, as you say, the allegations made by Miss Overaa are motivated by some misplaced spite and a deliberate attempt to cause you problems, your silence in the long term will be by far your best remedy. Writing to her or contacting her in any way can only play into her hands.

If Miss Overaa contacts you in the future, that will provide you with an excellent opportunity to forward any correspondence or inform Bergen police of any telephone contact and ask them to see Miss Overaa and tell her not to pester you. If any further emphasis of your position is required, which I doubt, then this would certainly make it.

I look forward to writing again as soon as I hear from Bergen police and thank you for keeping me informed on this matter.

Yours sincerely,

Dear Sir,

Heidi Overaa

We write further in the above matter and in particular, further to your letter of 19th April. Since then we have taken further instructions from our client and understand that the Norwegian Embassy here in London have been in touch with you.

The writer has been on holiday and, therefore, not in a position to write to you before now.

Regarding the allegations to which you refer having been made in December 1986, put into the context of the relationship between our client and Miss Overaa and, in particular, Miss Overaa's turbulent and confused life, which has included psychiatric treatment, we think the reference to the 1986 allegations are being misinterpreted and, therefore, bear little relevance to the current matter.

Firstly, we should state that our client does not recollect making any threats to Miss Overaa in 1986, although at that time he did write to her in strong terms in a genuine attempt to help her sort her life out, which was then clearly in a mess. We are very conscious that our client and Miss Overaa have had a long standing relationship and indeed we have copies of affectionate letters from Miss Overaa to our client going back as far as 1984.

We also note that despite accusations that you say were made by Miss Overaa in 1986, she nevertheless begged our client in September 1988 to travel to Norway and 'rescue her from Gudmund Johannessen.'

We are sure that you will agree that it is not uncommon for parties to such a long standing and difficult relationship, which has a history of going from very good to very bad, to exaggerate and perhaps even to become bitter when that relationship ends. We would like to reiterate that Miss Overaa has continually sought contact with our client since their first meeting in 1982 and we are, therefore, surprised that you are placing such great emphasis on some unspecified allegations made in 1986.

At the end of the day, however, it is clearly unacceptable and unreasonable that our client should be made to feel that he is unable to travel freely to and from Norway and to be threatened with possible arrest if he does so for unspecified and unsubstantiated reasons. If every couple who fell out after a long relationship was subject to such extreme measures, relationships between different nationals would very soon come to an end altogether.

Our client has no intention whatsoever of reinstating contact with Miss Overaa and he cannot, of course, be responsible for Miss Overaa's own actions and cannot prevent her trying to contact him.

We understand that Vidar Kleiven of the Norwegian Embassy has been told that the Police in Norway will do nothing in relation to our client or this matter, provided that our client makes no further contact with Miss Overaa.

Bearing in mind the comments that you made in your earlier letter which are clearly threatening, we shall be grateful if you could please confirm in writing that our client may travel freely to and from Norway without risk of immediate arrest, subject to his not contacting Miss Overaa.

We look forward to hearing from you.

Yours faithfully,

Letter dated 21st June 1990 from me to my lawyer

Dear Mr. Whittal,

Heidi Overaa

Thank you for your letter of 19th June received this morning.

I appreciate the points you made to Commander Krogvold and I wonder what he will say this time.

The point of my trip last February to Norway was to find Heidi and confront her over her treacherous behaviour. It was time for a face to face lecture. She has avoided giving explanations and proper answers for years. I was determined to correct this: now I have lost out again and this whole family are gloating over the way they have manipulated the police into persecuting me. I have still not had the opportunity to question Heidi in the presence of any responsible person. She is a slippery eel and has got away with it. Her mercenary attitude to love and life is prevalent among so many girls today. In her particular case, men are used just to satisfy her sexual needs; they have no souls or emotions. She discards men and friends as easily as she discarded the unborn children in her womb by abortions in her youth.

All we are doing now is trying to save myself from further damage because I am a solicitor, at the cost of firmly making a point to the Overaa family. I was determined not to let this imaginary fear prevent me from seeking justice. It is a pity that an arbitration procedure does not exist for cases such as this. It would be wonderful to see the Overaas humiliated for the trouble they have caused me.

Yours sincerely,

Letter dated 2nd July 1990 from my lawyer to me

Dear Mr. Delaware,

Heidi Overaa

Thank you for your letter dated 21st June, the contents of which I note. I also enclose herewith a copy letter I have now received from the Bergen police dated 26th June.

Clearly, matters have not been resolved and I will need, if you require me to pursue this matter, to address myself to higher authorities in Norway for a proper response.

Please could you let me know whether you wish me to pursue matters at this end.

In relation to your letter of 21st June, I am extremely concerned that your main concern seems to be, for want of a better word, revenge against either Heidi Overaa or her family.

I advised at the beginning of this matter that I could see no realistic civil action against Heidi Overaa which would compensate you. I, naturally, cannot and would not want to become involved in a personal course of action aimed merely at 'humiliating' Miss Overaa or her family. I still believe that, bearing in mind her personal circumstances and her previous recourse to psychiatric treatment, that such a venture is doomed to failure and will be expensive and unrewarding.

There are, of course, implications of her behaviour which could be challenged from a criminal point of view given sufficient evidence, for example perverting the course of justice. To do this I will need to ask the police in Bergen to re-open the whole matter and to investigate it properly. They are indicating that they may do this if you return to Norway in any event so I do not believe they could justifiably refuse to have the whole case properly investigated. If the Chief of CID at Bergen police does not wish to co-operate along these lines, I can again seek a higher authority to get the case properly aired.

Perhaps you could please let me have your instructions.

Yours sincerely,

Dear Sir,

Heidi Overaa

I am in receipt of your letter of June 19th 1990.

I have no further comments and refer to the information given in my previous letter of April 19th. I see no reason to go into the different aspects of the merits, which - obviously - can be considered from different angles.

The essence is that the police case rests, due to the fact that your client is abroad. The case might be re-opened if he returns to Norway. The re-opening of the case might lead to an investigation that would finally end in either a dismissal, or some kind of action (possibly a fine or theoretically a prison sentence).

I am in no position to comment any further on these matters of future possibilities.

Yours sincerely,

Sven Eric Krogvold
Commander - Chief of CID

Fax dated 3rd July 1990 from me to my lawyer

Dear Mr. Whittal,

Heidi Overaa

I telephoned Commander Krogvold this morning and he said his position stands as per his last letter to you. He told me he'd <u>not</u> spoken to Vidar Kleiven from the Norwegian Embassy so it must be that the assurances given to Mr. Kleiven were from another police officer in the station. Further, I said that I am prepared to go to Oslo with a lawyer by my side and speak to the Oslo police. Krogvold replied that this is a matter only for the Bergen police. I do not want to visit Bergen especially as the girl herself will not be there. I don't trust the police and so before any more is done, I'd like to have a rest from this and perhaps we can resume further action in the autumn, when I'll also have some money for your legal costs. I will still visit Oslo in August, but as Vidar Kleiven told me no warrant is out for my arrest, I think I'll be okay. He in fact is on holiday for several weeks. I'll phone you tomorrow just to square things off with you.

Yours sincerely,

Letter dated 13th August 1990 from me to my lawyer

Dear Mr. Whittal,

Heidi Overaa

I returned from Norway yesterday having met Heidi Overaa at her home last Saturday. We sorted out our differences and made peace.

I left for Norway on 2nd August and on 31st July received a letter from the girl in response to my letters to herself, her two sisters and her stepmother. I told them exactly how I felt and I think the message got through at last.

Anyway, I spent a wonderful evening with Heidi and her young son and we will certainly be friends again, but no more. It pleased me to hear her confession that she'd been "possessed by demons" over the period of our friendship as that was what I'd always thought. She is now a "born again" Christian following the rules as best she can. As far as we are both concerned, the matter is now closed. Again, thank you for all you've done and I wish you well.

Yours sincerely,

So, as can be seen it took almost a further six months of stress to 'resolve the situation.' But only because I took some risks and went to see the girl in person.

However, Heidi's complaint to the Bergen police in December 1986 came as a complete surprise to me. Suffice it to say that her action in going to the police came very shortly after I had exposed her past to her parents and Gudmund Johannessen's parents. Certainly in February 1990 I did not issue any "new threats." This allegation of fresh threats by Heidi was an excellent piece of deception by her based on the fact that if I had written some angry letters in 1986, then making new threats in 1990 might be quite believable. I was surprised, even so, that in sitting with Heidi's neighbour, Heidi-Anita, for an hour or so, then quietly going round to see Heidi's sister, Elisabeth, and after that sitting quietly on my own in Rennaug's apartment, still gave rise to a police suspicion that I was there to commit "serious crimes."

The business over Vidar Kleiven's roll was interesting. Ironically, I had met him at the Norwegian Seamen's Church in Rotherhithe, East London in March 1990 when he was giving a lecture on drug abuse to au pairs. After the talk, I spoke to him and mentioned my contact with the drug scene in Norway in the shape of Heidi and Gudmund Johannessen, although I didn't mention this couple by name. Vidar Kleiven gave me his business card as I said I might need to speak to him again soon. On May 17th I happened to bump into him when he was with his family celebrating Norway's National Day in London's Battersea Park and I mentioned my predicament with the Bergen Police. He took my business card and promised to find out what was going on and report back to me. I told him that all the nice letters I had written to Heidi in 1988 were not shown to the police, only the critical ones, and he acknowledged the injustice of the situation. When, after several phone calls by me, he finally got back in touch with some news, it was with quite a stern, resentful voice that he told me Heidi and her family wanted "nothing to do with me" but that I could quite definitely return to Norway without being arrested as long as I did not contact Heidi herself. The importance of getting assurances like this confirmed in writing can clearly be seen here. You would have thought one could rely with complete confidence on the word of a Norwegian diplomat but clearly this was not the case on this occasion. I am not pointing the finger at Vidar Kleivin, but whoever told him I could travel to Norway freely clearly hadn't consulted with Commander Krogvold. Krogvold's reply of June 26th 1990 to my lawyer meant I was facing an impossible situation. My London lawyer told me it could cost several thousands of pounds in legal fees to go to a higher authority in Norway to get a proper investigation done. This was money I didn't have. Thank you Bergen Police! Thank you Heidi Overaa! And people wonder why I hated her and wanted her humiliated! Her psychiatric problems may certainly have made her very difficult to prosecute but nevertheless, as could be seen, she still knew what she was doing.

I'd stayed with the families of two other Norwegian girls I had met in England for a fortnight prior to meeting Heidi. One lived in Porsgrunn, south west of Oslo, and that was Dise who I have previously mentioned, and another one in Mandal, which was a small town further down the coast close to Kristiansand. The families of these girls had treated me with the greatest kindness. On arriving in Norway in early August, I had immediately gone to Drammen to Heidi's place to see her but she wasn't in. I tried to see if Heidi-Anita her 'Christian' neighbour was in. I found only her brother-in-law at home and he spoke little English, but I gave him a present of a model fire engine to give to Heidi's son. He told me Heidi was away on holiday for a fortnight so I wished him well and returned to Oslo.

On returning to see Heidi a fortnight later, again I found she was not at home and neither were any of the neighbours. Just as I was making my way out of the compound that housed this small group of householders, Heidi-Anita, her husband and their three children came back from a shopping trip in their car. My, how angry this couple were with me for "harassing" Heidi. They gave me a stiff lecture and left me alone to contemplate my wickedness. No wonder I got no reply to my letter to Heidi-Anita - she obviously disliked me intensely for being so "nasty" (as she put it) to Heidi. She told me she thought Heidi would be back tomorrow.

On returning the next day, I knocked on Heidi's door and the window nearest to the door opened to reveal the blond head of a little boy - obviously Heidi's son. Then Heidi appeared in the window and told me to hold on for a minute. She then came to the door dressed in red shorts, greeted me and excused herself whilst she went to change into something more appropriate. I waited in the garden sitting on a chair. Out came Heidi with some tea and biscuits accompanied by Daniel. She then went to her neighbour, Heidi-Anita, to make a phone call to her stepmother to cancel the dinner appointment she had made later that day with her. Now that I was with her she would instead spend time with me but the message came back from Heidi that her stepmother had told her that if I didn't stop writing my letters to them, they would sue me. "Sue me?" I queried, and retorted, "I'll sue them if it comes to it." We started to talk calmly to one another and she told me of her conversion to Christianity. How "demons" had possessed her and made her lead a "wicked life." Indeed her new-found ability to tell right from wrong made her conclude that her late mother "was in hell" for her wrongdoing. As for Heidi's last suicide attempt in 1988 Heidi told me that Daniel's grandparents would have looked after him had she succeeded in taking her life; that she had been "obsessed" with Gudmund Johannessen but was now hoping to find a good Christian man to marry.

Surprisingly we talked little of my arrest 6 months earlier, save for her comments that they were worried I might do something drastic such as "kidnap Daniel," her son. Now this was fantasy! A former SAS soldier I certainly was not.

During our chat in the garden Daniel had come over to me and we struck up an instant friendship. I liked him straight away and held the dear boy close to me with my arms around him. Heidi told me of Daniel's great distress at seeing his mother suffer so much at the hands of Gudmund Johannessen, his father. My heart went out to him and on being invited inside the house, as it was getting a bit chilly outside, Daniel came to sit on my knee at the kitchen table and put his arms around me. Sitting with Heidi and Daniel I was enjoying the relief at the ending of the stress, at long last, and I was imagining just how enjoyable family life could be - a beautiful girl and a lovely boy. Daniel was so attached to me that he took out his dummy and gave me a big wet kiss on my cheek. A gesture I have never forgotten. This kiss immediately produced the comment from Heidi, "Be careful, you might catch AIDS." Her joke was not so funny, for in reality, after Daniel was born Heidi was so concerned that she had caught HIV from her lover's heroin taking and sexual licence that both parents had commissioned two AIDS tests each on themselves. The tenderness and love for me from Daniel filled me with happiness, so much so that after Daniel had been put to bed I told Heidi that I still had feelings for her and rather generously said, "I still love you," but these feelings were based more on my conviction that she had reformed her character and for the tender love of her son towards me. She told me she was "getting old" and I knew by this that she was anxious for a fresh start in life. She said she had not got a man in her life at present and I said I hadn't got anyone either but I told her that I hoped to find a young girl in due course, implying that I was not interested in Heidi. In fact I was looking forward to my visit the following day to see a teenage Norwegian girl living in a small town south of Oslo called Sætre. A girl called Marianne Solberg whom I had met in Brighton the previous summer.

Heidi told me that I could not spend the night in her home as her stepmother was coming the next day to visit her first thing and would be furious if she found me there. With Daniel fast asleep I spent a few minutes cuddling Heidi before she took me to the bus stop outside her home. It was dark and chilly and she gave me one of her cardigans to keep me warm. I gave her a big hug and kiss and when the bus came bade her farewell and returned happy to my hotel in Oslo. I slept very well that night and really enjoyed my breakfast next morning. Here was my day of departure for London but I was going first to see that teenage girl in Sætre. It was a lovely sunny day and I got off the bus having taken a beautifully scenic route to Sætre. The girl's mother picked me up in her car and took me to her home. Her daughter Marianne soon arrived and we had a lovely dinner together. They took me afterwards for a ride by Oslo Fjord and the beauty around me was breathtaking. A year later Marianne visited me in England on her way to seeing another boy in Taunton, Somerset, by which time her parents had got divorced.

After visiting Heidi and returning home to London, such an impression had Daniel's friendship left on me that I immediately bought him a present of a box of miniature model cars and sent it off in the post. Not long afterwards I got a call from Heidi from a phone box outside her home and she thanked me for the present. She said it had made Daniel very happy and that he was telling everyone he had a lovely friend in England. Daniel was with his mother and she asked him in Norwegian to speak to the "man from England." He could not, of course, speak English but he happily called me "funny face" a few times at his mother's prompting and we all laughed. Heidi told me how much Daniel needed a father. Heidi later sent me a couple of postcards written in Egersund on the south-west coast of Norway, where her sister, Rennaug, now lived. These postcards, however, were actually posted from Drammen. Heidi remarked in them how much Daniel liked me - "he told me so," and further how he "did not know what it was like to have a father." Heidi also told me how "nice" my name sounded.

Funny isn't it? In the space of 6 months I went from being arrested to becoming flavour of the month with my accuser. The extremely charming manner of Heidi's tone of speech to me and the joyous affection of her son really did make me think hard whether Heidi had truly changed and whether after all I could make a go of it with her and her son as a family. These were, of course, tentative thoughts, but no matter how despicably she acted in the past, she was still far more of an attraction than anything I had experienced in England. Later, in speaking to Heidi and telling her how much I liked Norway, she said to me, "Well, come and live in Norway. Come on. Come over here and stay." I asked her in any event whether I could come and visit her. She said I "certainly" could. After that I wrote an important letter to her asking her if we could discuss "the future." She was very perceptive and wrote back and spelt it out. "You are talking of marriage. Hmmmm........." then went on to tell me how it was her dream to marry a Christian man "more than anything else in the world."

Heidi had become quite obsessed with her new-found faith. Her neighbours, Heidi-Anita and Asbjørn had spent much time with her, praying with her, over her and for her. Heidi had told me Asbjørn had caused her to "speak in tongues," that one of her feet which was shorter than the other had grown by a quarter of an inch, which she told me was all due to the "power of Jesus." Therefore, she had to marry a Christian man.

Heidi phoned me to continue the theme of her Christianity, telling me that she had ordered some religious books from England and would send one of them to me in due course, which she urged me to read with an open mind. I was Muslim of course and a practising one. I believed in Jesus, but we Muslims believe the word of Christ was corrupted by those that came after Christ and that the Quran was revealed to correct this perversion and also continue the revelation of God. But converts are as keen as mustard to impress on others their new-found faith. Well, the book arrived; it was called 'I Dared To Call Him Father.' It depicted a Pakistani Muslim woman, who, ignorant of the Quran and physically and mentally abused by her cruel husband, sought solace in the Bible and some Christian friends who had been comforting her over her broken marriage.

This Pakistani woman, Bilquis Sheikh, writes on pages 42 and 43 of her book:

> ' "I am confused, Father ...." I said. "I have to get one thing straight right away." I reached over to the bedside table where I kept the Bible and the Quran side by side. I picked up both books and lifted them, one in each hand. "Which, Father?" I said. "Which one is Your book?"
>
> Then a remarkable thing happened. Nothing like it had occurred in my life quite this way. For I heard a voice inside my being, a voice that spoke to me as clearly as if I were repeating words in my inner mind. They were fresh, full of kindness, yet at the same time full of authority.
>
> "In which book do you meet me as your Father?" I found myself answering: "In the Bible" That's all it took. Now there was no question in my mind which one was His book.'

As far as I was concerned, the fact was that this Pakistani woman's husband was a wicked man who did not follow the principles of the Quran in one of its most important facets, that of being kind to women. This was no reason, however, to abandon the Quran in favour of the Bible. It is certainly the case that many Pakistani men do not act in accordance with the teachings of the Quran. Then again, many men worldwide, and especially in Norway as I have seen with my own eyes, do not treat women with any degree of respect at all.

I had been educated at a Church of England primary school and my mother had been born a Christian Protestant in Germany. My father was a Muslim and so I prided myself in knowing something about both Christianity and Islam. But I was not going to stand for Islam being rubbished by a book such as 'I Dared To Call Him Father.'

When Heidi telephoned me again I had not read the whole book but certainly quite a few pages. I told her I could not accept the logic of the book and spent a little time talking to her about Islam. At the end of this conversation, she said to me, "Why don't you give me time to understand Islam?" This was a nice gesture. She later wrote to me a very loving letter continuing the theme of her newly found beliefs. Referring to her abortions, she told me that she truly believed God would forgive her. To this sentiment, I fully agreed with her. If she truly had repented and asked God's forgiveness for her wicked acts then most certainly God would, presumably, forgive her. In a subsequent telephone conversation Heidi told me she had even refused to go and see in a theatre in Oslo a drag act performed by the well-known Norwegian troupe called 'The Garlic Girls' on grounds that it was ungodly. Her sister Elisabeth had invited her. By coincidence, I was introduced to one of the actors in 'The Garlic Girls' who in fact was gay. His cousin was the girl Dise who I stayed with in Porsgrunn and who had obtained Heidi's address for me in 1989 by phoning Elisabeth Overaa pretending to be Heidi's friend. This gay actor was a very handsome chap and he and his boyfriend were dressed in shorts that summer when Dise introduced me to them in their flat in Oslo.

However, when I had read the whole book 'I Dared To Call Him Father,' I was incensed that this piece of rubbish was intended to convert me to Christianity and I presumed that Heidi wanted my conversion so that she could then marry me. So I wrote and told Heidi just what nonsense I thought the book was and criticised her for thinking I would abandon my faith. I also took the opportunity to express my severe reservations over a few aspects of my arrest in 1990, which I had failed to obtain an explanation for from Heidi in August. She then wrote back to me explaining little and concluded that it was obvious to her that "....you hate me."

Chapter 14

I decided to go to Norway for their 17ᵗʰ May 1991 National Day to see the celebrations when everyone was dressed up in national costume and paraded through the streets. I also wanted to go and see another Norwegian girl, Tone (pronounced Toona) who I had also met in Brighton three years earlier and who lived in Arendal on the south coast of Norway, not far from Kristiansand. On 17ᵗʰ May, which was an overcast, drizzly day, I went to Drammen to first try and see Heidi but she was not at home. Another neighbour, in a different house, who I had never seen or spoken to before, told me that Heidi had left with her sister Elisabeth to celebrate the National Day in Oslo. So I left a record of my visit by suitably arranging the large stones outside her home to spell my first name. I also left a hand-written note by her door.

I then went to Arendal to see Tone and wanted it to be a complete surprise so I didn't phone beforehand. Her father was at home though, and he introduced me to his wife, son and daughter-in-law. He tried to phone his daughter, who I had come to see, who he thought was at her friend's house, but unfortunately no one was there. He told me she would probably be with her friends in the town celebrating the National Day. He kindly drove me back to the town centre and mentioned that his daughter would be going to England in September to be an au pair in Wimbledon. I left my business card with him for his daughter to give me a call. Then I wandered the streets of Arendal hoping to come across her but I didn't and eventually took the sleeper train back to Oslo.

On Saturday 18ᵗʰ May, I watched the F.A Cup Final between Tottenham Hotspur and Nottingham Forest in my hotel room, when Paul Gascoigne so stupidly came to injure himself so badly. I was a life-long Spurs fan so I was happy that they won the match but was very concerned for Gazza. Heidi, of course, had no telephone, so off again I went on the long trip from Oslo to her home outside Drammen. On the bus approaching the house, I prayed that Heidi and her son would be in, more because I was longing to see Daniel again who I liked so very much. What a faithful friend he had been. When I got there, the stones that I had arranged to form my first name had been dismantled. Again, no one was at home. I walked around the house, peered in through the windows but there was no sign of life. Not a sound. I stayed for half an hour kicking a ball around I had found in the garden. For how much longer could I wait? I decided to go to the phone box not far from Heidi's house and telephone Elisabeth, Heidi's sister, to see if she was with her. Elisabeth (surprise, surprise) was rude and un-cooperative and told me Heidi was not with her and she didn't know where she was. I wasn't at all convinced by her response so I went back to the house, waited a little while longer and soon decided I had had enough. Just to make quite sure that Heidi would know I had been round again, I wrote a message on the boarded up window that replaced a broken window pane nearest her front door and also wrote out a note which I attached on a hook by the windowsill. I remarked to Heidi how I thought her sister, Elisabeth, was "full of shit" for having been so unco-operative on the phone. I also scratched with a stone my first name on her dilapidated front door, in small letters.

When I got home to England, I wrote to Tone and also wrote to Heidi. Tone would hardly have remembered what I looked like from three years earlier so I sent her a photo of myself telling her I would give her a ring soon. When I rang she wasn't in but her parents said they would give her a message. I also had her girlfriend's number, which Tone's parents had given me telling me I could ring her to see if Tone was with her. I made the call and the girlfriend said that she didn't know for sure where Tone was but she gave me the telephone number of a place where she thought she might be at that moment. On phoning the number, a young man answered with - "Who the hell are you?" Taken aback, I explained who I was and he retorted angrily that he was Tone's boyfriend and proceeded to tell me that I was a "black, ugly, fanatic," based, no doubt, on seeing the sun-tanned photo of me on the Red Sea in Egypt that I had sent to Tone. Before I could talk further, the boyfriend, Rolf-Hakkon, put the phone down on me, so I phoned Tone's girlfriend back to discuss this incident and from her demeanour realised she had purposely set me up for a fall. So I told her that the "black, ugly, fanatic" insult would be answered for by Rolf-Hakkon. Two days later I got a call from Tone in my office at work. She asked if I could phone her back, as her parents would be "furious" with her if she spent their money phoning me long distance. So phone her back I did at my personal expense, for one hour. What did I learn? That after my phone call with her boyfriend, he had lost his temper, went out on his motor bike at speed, crashed, written the motor bike off and broken his arm in the process. This meant she couldn't go on a motor bike holiday with her boyfriend to Greece. Further, she had changed her mind about going to England as an au pair. I wondered who had changed her mind for her. Months before, Tone had made her mind up quite definitely to spend a year as an au pair and wouldn't have done so, I suspected, if she had wanted to be with her boyfriend. Now that someone else - me - had expressed an interest in her, her boyfriend must have thought hard about her worth and then persuaded her not to go away as "the black, ugly, fanatic" would then be close at hand. Tone explained that her boyfriend was jealous of my contact with her and asked me to understand the situation. To make sure I got my point home to the boyfriend, I phoned him up at his place and told him I knew he had broken his arm and crashed his bike, and he angrily said, "Who told you that?" to which I said nothing except that I would see him some time so he could apologise for what he had called me. Scratch the surface and the hatred and prejudice is there! Their relationship didn't last and by 2001 Rolf-Hakkon was still unmarried.

Heidi phoned me up to explain that when I had visited her on 18th May, she had in fact been inside her home all the time. She didn't hear my knock at the door as the television was on full volume and she and Daniel were having a bath together and talking in loud voices. But when I was there, I had noticed the bathroom window was open. I told her at what time and the exact length of time I stayed outside the house and she swore that she was definitely in at that time. I assured her that I didn't see the television on when I looked in the window and neither could I hear the television or their loud voices coming from the bathroom. All I saw was a pear core on the kitchen table. Not a sound had come from the house, which, if those 'noises' were being made, I would definitely have heard. I concluded to myself whilst speaking to Heidi that she was lying but did not push my point. She continued that her sister Elisabeth had come round to visit her in the afternoon, after I had departed, to find my note on the hook which Elisabeth had "laughed at" derisively. Heidi did not appreciate my leaving a message on her boarded-up window but she agreed that a new window pane would soon be inserted and accepted that all in all what I had written didn't matter. My own opinion was that all the time during my stay outside her house, Heidi was probably staying with her sister Elisabeth and that after I made my phone call they left it a little while and then came round to Heidi's place and found my note on the hook under the windowsill. Heidi should have known that I was going to see her on that Sunday because the previous day I had also left a hand-written message under a stone by her doorstep telling her I would turn up again next day. I believe that she stayed away on purpose.

I felt I would lose nothing now by writing to her and telling her exactly what I thought had actually happened and condemning her for her lies and treachery and that just because I could not accept the Christian literature she had sent me the previous year was no reason to take it out on me to such a degree. I got no reply to my letter.

Chapter 15

Things were left alone after that and for the next two and half years or so there was no contact between Heidi and myself but whenever my mind returned to the subject of my arrest in 1990, and my last visit to her in 1991, I felt a definite sense of injustice. But I knew I would never get a proper explanation from Heidi. The past had taught me that when it came to putting her on the spot, she either lied or evaded contact altogether. So one day early in 1994, I wrote to her stepmother in Bergen to explain fully my feelings and to let her know what Heidi had told me about her. But I did not let the stepmother know about the alleged abuse her own father had imposed on Heidi. The stepmother's son, Christian, wrote a card back to me surprisingly and just signed it "the Bizz." Christian told me off for writing such a forthright letter to his mother. His mother had been annoyed at the frankness and revelations of my letter, which were based truly on what Heidi had told me. He told me that if I wrote again, he would call the police and if they didn't help him he would get some of the security men in the Bergen disco he worked in to sort me out. He wrote further that they "knew Heidi was telling us one thing and the police another but that she is 28 years old" and it is her that I should be contacting. I wrote back to say that contacting Heidi was useless and that was why I was writing to her stepmother.

Some months later, in the middle of 1994 I believe, I decided that I just could not accept the unsatisfactory situation at the Bergen police station in February 1990. Although there had been a reconciliation of sorts in August 1990 there was still a rather large residue of dissatisfaction left in my mind from the half-truths and innuendoes perpetrated by Heidi and her family that had got me arrested in the first place. Further, I felt that the reconciliation was somewhat diminished by Heidi lying to me about being at home in May 1991.

I therefore instructed in January 1995 a top firm of lawyers in Bergen to make a full investigation of the Bergen police over my arrest there in February 1990. My frustration found a release at the same time by my writing several letters to Heidi outlining my concerns over unanswered questions of the past. I didn't get a reply. So in order to get the message through I sat down with a pack of plain postcards and wrote some home truths on all of them and posted them. This would ensure that they would be read by her. One summer's day, a few months earlier, whilst strolling by the Tower of London near my office, I took a chance and from a call box phoned the home of Elisabeth, Heidi's sister, to see what had become of Heidi. Elisabeth's son answered. He was 12 years old and alone at home. He told me Heidi had got married in March 1994 to a man called Runar Schøne and told me how the couple were doing. Heidi was "very happy" and she was waiting with her husband to move into a new home that was presently being built for them. They were staying in temporary accommodation but the nephew didn't have Heidi's telephone number to hand. As far as I was concerned, I didn't give a damn about Heidi's marriage. I thought she was quite lucky to have found someone but that it must have been a desperado who could not have known about her past - maybe someone with similar problems to herself. Anyway, I wasn't going to let external events, i.e. the fact of her marriage, deflect me from getting to the bottom of the 1990 arrest.

To go back in time, what turned out to be a disastrous mistake on my part was made in 1993, when the file I was keeping of correspondence with my London lawyers, together with Heidi's 1990 letters and postcards, was disposed of. The file's disposal was advised upon me by a friend 'in my own interests' to forget about the girl and everything associated with her. So at the same time as instructing the lawyer in Bergen to investigate the 1990 arrest, I was trying to obtain my former London lawyers' own file from 1990 with their copy correspondence to me and my original letters to them. The London office told me in 1994 that if the file was still in existence it would be stored in their provincial office in the south of England. If it was "still in existence," I thought with horror. I felt sick. On that file was the original letter Heidi had written to me in 1984 singing my praises. It was absolutely vital that this letter was found above all else. I was told the file could not easily be found even if it did exist unless I had the file reference number. I did not have the file reference number as all the original letters that were in my possession had been thrown away, so I would just have to be patient and wait and see if the provincial branch office could locate the file in their storeroom, by their own search.

A letter from the Bergen lawyer arrived in March 1995:

Dear Mr. Delaware,

Heidi Overaa

I refer to your telephone call and to your letter with enclosures.

On February 13th I received copies of the police's original documents of investigation and I have studied them closely.

From the documents of the investigation it appears that Heidi Overaa has made a formal report to the police on two occasions. The first report, in December 1986 was concerning threats, in letters and in the telephone, together with attempted rape.

Together with this report, two letters from you were presented - one dated November 17th 1986 addressed to Heidi Overaa's father and one dated October 13th 1986 addressed to Heidi Overaa herself. The report was sent in to the Bergen Police Department but the Police Department did not take any steps in the case while you were resident abroad.

The next formal report to the police was sent in on February 17th 1990 and led to you and your friend being taken into custody. On this occasion there was only a minimum of investigation, Heidi Overaa was examined and you made a statement. In addition, Heidi Overaa has sent several letters from you addressed to her and her sister Elisabeth, to the Bergen Police Department, to prove/illustrate that threats were put forward and lead to sincere fair [sic].

As you will know, I am not allowed to copy the documents of investigation and send them to you. However, I find it possible to make an exception as regards the letter from Chief Detective Krogvold dated April 19th 1990 to your London lawyers.

I draw your attention to the three last sections, stating that the case is not closed and can be re-opened in case you return to Norway.

Later the case was dismissed on December 11th 1992 as time-barred, which implies that you can travel safely to Norway without risking any criminal prosecution. However, I must add that if you - in connection with travelling to Norway - contact or try to contact Heidi Overaa - this could be interpreted as continuing (annoying behaviour), and <u>could</u>, after the circumstances, lead to re-opening of the dismissed case.

In Chief Detective Krogvold's letter, it appears that your possible entry to Norway will be considered together with the Aliens Act and under this Act's legal authority, you could be sent out - expelled from Norway/refused entry to Norway. After the dismissal of the case on December 11th 1992, this is no longer the situation. Therefore you do not risk being stopped or exposed to unpleasantness in connection with passport checks.

I understand my terms of reference are as follows:

1.   What is the situation of the criminal case today?

2.   Did the Bergen Police Department act with legal authority on February 17th 1990 and could an action for damages be raised against the Bergen Police Department/the Norwegian Department of Justice?

3.   Do Heidi Overaa's reports to the police appear as false accusations and could an action for damages be raised against Heidi Overaa based on these false and incorrect reports?

I have already answered point 1.

As regards points 2 and 3 these are closely connected. First I will consider whether the Bergen Police's way of acting was legal.

Without doubt the Bergen Police Department had the necessary legal authority to take you and your friend into custody. To be allowed to take someone into custody there must be just cause for suspicion of a criminal offence/act leading to more than 6 months imprisonment or that a corresponding criminal act will take place if a person is not arrested. Threats against someone's life or health have a penalty limit of 4 years.

On the present basis, and in accordance with the previous reports to the police, the Bergen Police Department cannot be criticised after Heidi's second report.

On the other hand, the Bergen Police Department could be criticised for not examining you until Sunday February 18th at 1 p.m. after having arrested you at approximately 7 p.m. the evening before. Surely the fact was that you were taken into custody on a weekend at a time when the Bergen Police Department were short of manning, because of the resource situation. This explanation is not a good one but undoubtedly it will be a sufficient reason if action is raised for damages.

The fact that the arrest occurred at the weekend (Saturday evening) gives the Police Department legal authority to keep a person in custody for up to 48 hours until presentation for the Magistrates Court.

From the documents of investigation, I read that you were released on Monday February 19th at 2.15 p.m. which means that you stayed in custody for another 24 hours after having given your statement to the police.

The fact that you still stayed in custody appears as a formalism as your statement revealed that the reports against you were groundless. The reasons why you were kept in custody could be several but the most obvious reason is the fact that the episode took place on a weekend and that the Superintendent in charge was not available until Monday morning (read: got the opportunity to study the documents).

In my opinion, it was an abuse of authority to keep you in custody for another 24 hours, but nevertheless, I have no doubt, arranging an action for damages on this basis, would be useless, see below.

The Police's official answer will be that the case still was considered serious, and that it was possible that you would make another effort to contact Heidi Overaa.

According to the documents of investigation, you were not deported from Norway. It appears from your own statement that you yourself chose to return to England immediately and for your own account [sic].

Thus, there was no decision of deportation in the case and if your departure was on the basis of such a decision, then the Norwegian authorities should have paid for your travelling costs.

The fact that you were escorted to Bergen Lufthaven [the airport] by representatives from the Bergen Police Department shows, however, that your return to England was close to a deportation.

My conclusion under this point is that the Bergen Police Department cannot be criticised for the arrest, but for keeping you in custody for nearly 48 hours. Nevertheless it is my obvious view that you will not win a claim for damages against the Bergen Police Department/the Norwegian Department of Justice based on abuse of authority.

As regards this point, I have no doubt.

Nor have I any doubt as regards the question whether a claim for damages can be raised against Heidi Overaa for false reports. Neither a formal report to the police from you, nor raising an action for damages against her, would reach a result. I mainly base my conclusion on the contents of the letters enclosed to the documents of investigation.

The letters show that you have strong and good feelings for Heidi Overaa. Nevertheless, when the letters are addressed to Heidi Overaa or other members of the family, the contents of the letters are strongly reproaching, sometimes amounting to condemnation. Undoubtedly some formulations could be characterised as defamation.

The letters contain only a few threats but based on the contents, Heidi Overaa will have obvious reason to interpret parts of them as threatening. On some occasions, the letters obviously contain threats, even if they represent a way of expressing oneself, more than statements of intentions.

Undoubtedly, in case of a report to a police or a claim for damages from Heidi Overaa, she will be supported in her feeling of fear. I remind you that according to Norwegian law, in connection with justifying a report to the police, her subjective understanding of the situation will be decisive.

I further remind you that Heidi Overaa did not ask the police to keep you in custody, but only for assistance to avoid you from contacting her.

I interpret Heidi Overaa's reports to the police as more as a request of assistance in keeping you from further contact with her, than as a report because of threats.

The threat aspect was toned down in Heidi Overaa's statement to the police. At the same time, she maintained that she was afraid that you, because of your moral point of view and your strong basic view, would 'punish her' for her way of living.

Based on your information, available letters and the police's documents of investigation, I have no doubt that a legal action against Heidi Overaa will be dismissed.

According to the circumstances, I find it incorrect to advise you with regard to your future behaviour against Heidi Overaa. However, it is my experience that even a friendly approach could be misunderstood as 'annoying behaviour' and therefore, reported to the police. Even if the reports are groundless, they could easily lead to unpleasantness.

I have closely studied the facts of the case and the above reflections are given after thorough consideration.

Yours sincerely,

Well the third paragraph, last line stands out, doesn't it? An allegation of attempted rape against me: as per Heidi's report to the police in December 1986. I had last stayed with Heidi in April 1985 and my account of that stay is given above so it took 20 months for Heidi to report this further allegation. But significantly the allegation was reported straight after the letter of 17th November 1986 that I sent to her father telling him of her past and warning him that as she had tried to take her life once over Gudmund

Johannessen and then in getting pregnant again to him, she was inviting disaster yet again. The attempted rape allegation mentioned in my lawyer's letter was completely false. As for the allegation of threats to her "life or health," copies of all the letters I wrote from 1986 to 1988 were sent to me in 1999 by the Bergen police and only one of them contained a threat to Heidi, and that was only a conditional threat which was more a figure of speech as will later be seen. I made no threats to Heidi on 16th February 1990 in my telephone call to her from the Alpine Hotel in Geilo but presumably she told the police I had. A pity the call wasn't recorded by Heidi with police assistance.

One good thing that did result from the Bergen lawyer's letter was his sending me the copy police letter of 19th April 1990 which contained my London lawyers' file reference: 710/1. With this reference supplied by me to the provincial office of my 1990 London lawyers, my file was located and despatched to me. Heidi's original letter of 1984 was there inside. Great!

It had taken me nine years to find out that extra allegation of attempted rape reported to the police in December 1986. It meant that on my other trips to Norway, once in 1989, twice in 1990 and again in 1991, I just might have been arrested and detained for inquiry. This allegation was unforgivable and I was also angry with the Bergen lawyer for submitting his fee note on 1st March 1995 before I had had a chance to reply to his letter of 28th February. Particularly as no details of that heinous allegation of attempted rape had been supplied to me by that lawyer. Further, whilst enclosing the Bergen Police Chief's letter of 19th April 1990, he did not enclose, or comment on, the copy of my London lawyer's letter to the Bergen Police of 19th June 1990 or the letter of 26th June 1990, being the police's reply to my London lawyers. I had only in fact been completely safe from arrest on 11th December 1992 when the Statute of Limitations had expired, 6 years after Heidi's reported allegation of attempted rape of December 1986.

Wesenberg was therefore saying that my chances of prosecuting Heidi and the police were non-existent. It was not entirely unexpected, given what I knew already of the Norwegian mentality. The trouble was, I knew the girl was a very nasty piece of work but obviously I hadn't got sufficient evidence to prove it in the eyes of Norwegian law.

I replied to my Bergen lawyer on 9th March 1995

Dear Mr. Wesenberg,

Heidi Overaa

I enclose the following copy letters, having today received my old file from my London lawyers used in 1990:

1. Letter from 1984 from Heidi Overaa: read it and see if this sounds as if just a year later I would attempt to rape her.

2. Letter dated 19th June 1990 to the police in Bergen [from Mr. Whittal.]

3. Letter dated 26th June 1990 being the police's reply to my London lawyers.

I entirely deny attempting to rape Heidi Overaa. This is a lie calculated to destroy my character and an attempt to get me into serious trouble.

I am not at all satisfied with the conclusions of your advice and I am disgusted with the police's whole attitude and approach.

You can quite clearly see from my lawyer's letter of 1990 that "unspecified allegations" were made against me. My lawyers asked for an explanation and got a reply on 26th June 1990 which was of no help at all. Do you still think the police were within their rights? I could not in fact return to Norway and the fact that I did was only possible after contacting the Norwegian Embassy.

I now discover from you that these unspecified allegations from 1986 included attempted rape. The police themselves never mentioned this attempted rape to me. I never made threats to Heidi Overaa. So please provide me with all police evidence against me: all the letters I wrote. The details of attempted rape: time, place, manner. Everything, please.

You said in your letter to me "as you will know I am not allowed to copy the documents of investigation to you…." but that you will make an exception of the April 19th police letter. I did not know that copy letters and other evidence against me can not be supplied to me. That wouldn't happen in England. People accused of crimes are entitled to see the evidence themselves, not just rely on their lawyer's opinion and own sight of the evidence.

If you can make one exception, then all the other letters and complaints in detail should be made exceptions of. Besides, I already saw that 19th April 1990 letter way back in 1990.

What you did not comment on was the two subsequent letters of 19th June and 26th June. How dare they not tell me the exact allegations being made against me by this psychiatric patient, Heidi Overaa. How dare they make me worry myself to death and have to take the trouble to contact the Norwegian Embassy.

You can see I spent hundreds of pounds on a lawyer in London. Now I spend hundreds of pounds using you and still we get nowhere. I insist the whole matter be looked into properly. Damn the police for treating me and my lawyers in the U.K like shit!

If the police believe Heidi Overaa about alleged attempted rape then to hell with them.

The police in 1990 - I see from my file - reprimanded Stuart for coming to Norway 'to threaten the lives of Norwegian citizens.' What a lie. Stuart and I never did such things. It's a case of Norwegians versus the outsider.

For God's sake: Heidi Overaa wanted to marry me in 1990 if I turned Christian.

My U.K lawyers were going to go to a higher authority than the police in 1990. If necessary, if you cannot help me properly and supply me with the evidence against me and get Heidi prosecuted for perverting the course of justice in alleging attempted rape then I will go straight to the Norwegian Embassy and contact my Member of Parliament. Everyone just wants to sweep the matter under the carpet and it will not happen.

I enclose a letter I wrote yesterday before I got my old file. Please act on it.

Yours sincerely,

I had already written to the Norwegian Embassy enclosing a full statement and they replied to me on 20th April 1995 as follows:

Dear Sir,

I refer to our recent telephone conversation and your letter dated 4th April 1995.

As I mentioned to you on the telephone, there is little I can do, but your letter, with enclosures, have been forwarded to Mr. Krogvold, Bergen Police, and I trust that you will hear from him in due course.

Yours faithfully,
Iver Stensrud
Attaché - Norwegian Embassy.

On reading the letter of 28th February 1995 from my Bergen lawyer and that filthy allegation of attempted rape Heidi had reported to the Bergen Police in 1986, I was determined now to get in some of my own real revenge. I was livid. I didn't care if the allegation was reported nine years previously because the passage of time did not reduce the enormity of the lie. I phoned the parents of Heidi and had such a go at them it must have frightened them out of their skin. I bellowed my distress at Heidi's behaviour and the decibel level would have rivalled anything coming from the London Arena just across the road from the call box. It was ballistic! After that I felt much better.

I then made a few telephone enquiries of the Folkeregistret (People's Register) at Drammen Town Hall and the local office in Solbergelva as to Heidi's new address, but without success. I then got in touch with Heidi's local post offices. Jackpot! One of the ladies who answered was an Indian woman called Camilat, who knew Heidi as she often came in to buy stamps and to post letters. This Indian woman was really helpful. She told me that she suspected that a man who Heidi had previously been associating with was selling drugs when I told her about Heidi's involvement with Gudmund Johannessen and his heroin taking. Camilat told me to phone back next week, as she knew someone who was acquainted with Heidi's husband, Runar Schøne, and who could supply her with Heidi's new address. I phoned back a few days later and true to form I got the Schønes' address and telephone number.

I then phoned Heidi and she answered. All I said was, "Attempted rape?" She must have had a fit. How did you find out my phone number, I could see her asking herself. She fumbled her words in response to my statement and I repeated the facts I had discovered. She refused to talk about it saying, "I will not say anything until you tell me what you were doing before."

"Before what," I said.

"You know," she said.

"Intercourse!" I said, "but not attempted rape and don't try and avoid the issue. How dare you tell the police such disgusting lies." She then put the phone down on me.

First thing next day, I telephoned a couple of language translation services for price quotes and for the relatively small sum of £65 plus VAT I could get 500 words translated into Norwegian. Within a week, the translated document was faxed through to me from the translators. Within another week - early May if I recall - I sent a copy of the translation by post purposely from St. Albans to all the people living two houses either side of each of Heidi's several addresses in the past ten years; in all I'd say no more than 20 letters. Now we will see what happens! Happily I went off to Denmark to visit an Egyptian friend of mine in Aarhus who ironically had married a Danish girl and they had one gorgeous blonde-haired daughter, a real diamond. Now he has three children - yes it can be done folks!

The translation that was done for me into Norwegian was a fact sheet detailing the whole of Heidi's past in beautiful clarity. Every single word was accurate and true according to the information supplied to me by Heidi. The effect on her neighbours reading this letter had a result that even I did not expect and the translation of this article is given below:

Report on Heidi Overaa

We now report as follows on the subject of enquiry, Ms. Heidi Overaa, born 20th August 1963, now living with her husband Runar Schøne at Sollikroken 7, 3058 Sobergmoen.

In 1981 Ms. Overaa went to England as an au pair from Bergen and stayed in St. Albans, Hertfordshire. She left Norway to recuperate from her second abortion. Both abortions were at the request of the prospective father, only known as Peter. Ms. Overaa had hoped to retain the affections of her boyfriend, Peter, by having the abortions. This relationship however ended and it is understood that Ms. Overaa whilst on holiday in Rhodes in the summer of 1982 had sex with two different men on the beach.

In 1983 Ms. Overaa met a gentleman called Gudmund Johannessen from Åsane, Bergen who by 1984 had got Ms. Overaa pregnant with twins. Ms. Overaa miscarried the twins when she discovered that Mr. Johannessen was sleeping with her best friend. Ms. Overaa then attempted suicide in the summer of 1984 by taking an overdose. She later took as a flatmate a 17 year old ex-prostitute, Iren.

In 1985 Ms. Overaa again got pregnant to Mr. Johannessen and on 1st April 1986 they had a son, Daniel Sebastian Overaa. At the time of their sexual relations, Mr. Johannessen was injecting heroin and also sleeping with other girls, facts Ms. Overaa was fully aware of. Indeed both had two Aids tests, each of which proved negative, after the birth of their son.

We have ascertained that Mr. Johannessen went to prison for offences committed whilst in the Norwegian Army and for which the sentence was one of six months custody, during the 1980's.

In 1988 Ms. Overaa was again rejected by Mr. Johannessen and attempted suicide by taking an overdose. Ms. Overaa then left Bergen to stay with her sister, Elisabeth, in Drammen, but was soon admitted to the B.S.S Psychiatric Clinic in Lier where she remained for two months.

Ms. Overaa's mother divorced in Heidi's early teens and unfortunately died when Heidi was 16 years old, it is understood from causes related to drink and drug abuse. Shortly before this Ms. Overaa's father had sought to put her in a home for delinquent children but this move did not materialise.

We believe Ms. Overaa has a reputation for lying and also is understood to have had numerous different sexual partners until her marriage in the spring of 1994.

Ms. Overaa on an unknown date in the early 1980s reported to the police an alleged attempted rape by a Bergen shopkeeper and in December 1986 reported another man for attempted rape which it has been ascertained was a fabrication made in order to discredit the gentleman concerned who had exposed Ms. Overaa's behaviour to her parents and Mr. Johannessen's parents. Mr. Johannessen later in 1990 beat up Ms. Overaa who reported the matter to the police.

In 1993 Mr. Johannessen married Nina Engeberg and they have one child.

On 22nd May 1995 I phoned Heidi from a nightclub in Aarhus in central Denmark to see what reaction she may have had to my communications to her neighbours as well as the same communication to her husband. I had met a Norwegian girl in the Norwegian Club in Norway House in Trafalgar Square, London, in early May and she said she would be pleased to post a letter for me when she returned soon to Norway. I sent the letter, being the above report, to her London office but could not be sure she had in fact received it before she left for Norway or, even if she had received it, whether she had posted it. It was addressed to Runar Schøne. When Heidi answered the phone I said, "I phoned just to say hello."

"No hellos thank you" and she put the phone down immediately. So I phoned again and resumed my enquiries about her lies. She wasn't going to say anything so at my request a Danish guy who was by the phone told Heidi to "Fuck off." She deserved that.

Immediately after returning to England from Denmark I received the following letter from my Bergen lawyer:

Letter dated 29th May 1995 from my Bergen lawyer to me

Dear Mr. Delaware,

Bergen Politakammer - Heidi Overaa

> For your information, please find enclosed a copy of a newspaper article in Bergens Tidende of May 24th 1995.
>
> A similar article has been printed in another Norwegian newspaper (Verdens Gang) and the main contents in both articles are that Heidi Overaa has been terrorised during the last 13 years.
>
> I assume that you will manage to have the articles translated into English.
>
> Referring to the enclosed article, I would strongly repeat my advice to you, not to contact Heidi Schøne or her family in any way.
>
> I have received your pay cheque for 250 British pounds and look forward to receiving the rest of the amount for 150 British pounds.
>
> Yours sincerely,

Shocked to my core, I telephoned a Norwegian commercial lawyer I knew who was working in London and lived near my office at Tower Bridge and made an appointment to meet him at his home so he could translate the article enclosed with my lawyer's letter.

On the front page, a full banner headline reads in translation:

Bergens Tidende 24th May 1995

13 Years of Harassment

A Bergen lady, Heidi Schøne (pictured) has been harassed and threatened with her life over a period of thirteen years by a man who she accidentally met when she was an au pair in England. Her secret addresses haven't helped against the English lawyer, whose attitude is similar to one suffering from erotic paranoia.

[On page 2 the headline is:]

Defenceless against 13 years of pursuit

OSLO:

For more than thirteen years the Bergen lady Heidi Schøne (31) has been threatened with her life and harassed because she didn't want to be the wife of a Muslim man who lives in England. Family, friends and colleagues often received written reports about Heidi's life. The Muslim lawyer has also used a private detective to trace her. People will find it hard to imagine the pressure Heidi and her immediate family have been under since the early 1980's.

A few weeks ago, a Bergen freelance photographer received a letter from Watford in England, although the letter did not have any sender's name and address. The title of the letter was 'Report on Heidi Schøne' which was defamatory and humiliating. The freelance photographer contacted Bergens Tidende who in turn contacted Heidi Schøne and her husband who lived outside Drammen and they told her about the letter.

Heidi answered the phone crying "Where shall this end? How many people will have got this letter?"

Bag with letters

Yesterday, Bergens Tidende met Heidi Schøne and her husband Runar in Oslo. Under her arm she carried a bag with letters from the Muslim man; all the letters were very rude and insulting. The last 13 years have been very traumatic. Secret addresses haven't helped. All of this started 14 years ago when Heidi Schøne was an au pair in England. On a boat trip from France to England with a girlfriend, she met a friendly Muslim man. He was very nice and he told her about his Muslim beliefs and that if he got married the girl must be Muslim as well. "I felt quite safe," she said. "In England we met him several times just as good friends. After nine months I moved back to Bergen."

Ugly and Stupid

Then he changed. The Muslim man wanted Heidi to be his wife. "He visited me several times in Bergen without being invited. He said he wished he could marry me; and said I was ugly and stupid and that he would be the only one who would love me when I was 50 years old. Arguments between us followed. Since then he has made threats on my life and has harassed me. He has also threatened to kill my family," said Heidi. In 1990 the 35 year old Muslim man was arrested in Bergen but the police didn't take the matter any further. The harassments carried on. The Muslim man didn't speak Norwegian but the aforementioned report is written in Norwegian and sent from Watford where he is living. In 1990 the police found material which indicated that the Muslim man had liaised with a Norwegian man with the purpose of following Heidi Schøne and finding her secret address, one of several secret addresses which followed for Heidi and she lost out every time.

Sent to the neighbours

Now she has given up with secret addresses. Her new neighbours have got the reports explaining to them what her old life was like as the Muslim man saw it. "How can one make sense of it? We haven't been lovers or had feelings for each other. He fantasises about it," the Bergen woman said painfully.

For six years she has lived outside Drammen. Six months ago she got married to Runar Schøne. Then the Muslim chap worked even harder on the matter. Numerous 'reports' were sent to Bergen and Drammen recently.

Her husband also got a letter sent personally to him –

"The Muslim man sent the report about Heidi to me as if I had requested it myself. The report was totally false. He did all he could to blacken Heidi's name," said Runar Schøne. He is sick and tired of the Muslim man.

Not afraid

The fear of the Muslim man has receded as the years have gone by. Heidi is not afraid anymore. The fear has changed to frustration and anger. Family, friends, colleagues and neighbours feel overwhelmed by these reports.

"Just a few years ago, I was very frightened and kept hiding under the bed," said Heidi.

"He has no limits. When he knocks on the door and finds no-one in, he writes obscene words on the door," she adds. The words Heidi refers to are unprintable. She knows that it will take a long time before the terror will stop. With her husband she has hired a lawyer called Tomm Skaug in Oslo and she has also reported the Muslim man to the police.

Heidi Schøne has been terrorised for several years by an insane man who she had earlier been friendly with but with whom there was no serious relationship. This situation is very difficult for her.

"I have seen the letters and I will follow the case. But it will be difficult so long as he is living in England and not in Norway," said the lawyer Tomm Skaug to Bergens Tidende.

EROTIC PARANOIA

A person who acts like this Muslim man against Heidi Schøne is not a new phenomenon in the view of the psychiatrist Kjell Noreik, a member of the medico legal group of psychiatrists. These people don't like to take no for an answer. The diagnosis is called erotic paranoia. One psychiatrist, Nils Rettersdøl has been writing much about Muslim behavioural patterns. Kjell Noreik doesn't place this diagnosis on the Muslim man but says that erotic paranoia is erotic delusions. He says that a person with this condition builds up a fantasy in relation to the other individual even though the former is rejected. Now this is a problem but not too serious a one. But it is very painful for the victims of this behaviour. This behaviour can carry on for years and doesn't stop even if the perpetrator is admonished. Some will also become violent.

Story: Haakon B. Schrøder   Photo: Havard Bjelland
***

On the front page of the newspaper was a picture of Heidi with a recent hair cut and she was now wearing glasses. In her left hand was a postcard I had sent to her and you could see that the picture showed the word 'LOWLIFE' on the top of the postcard. Down by her right hand were three or four other letters that I had sent to her. It was a great pity that no-one knew the contents of those letters as they were all straightforward and purely enquiring as to the abuse and hell she had put me through in years gone by.

On page two was a photo of Heidi with her husband pictured with his arms around her and holding each other's hands, sitting on a bench.

Let me briefly comment on the Bergens Tidende article.

The word 'Muslim' has been mentioned 19 times, chiefly with reference to my label, the 'Muslim man.' They didn't name me. But clearly an association is made with being Muslim and sexual and behavioural deviancy. I wonder had I been Christian would they have called me the 'Christian man' throughout? Of course not. And if I was Jewish there's no way, I'm sure, they would have called me the 'Jewish man.'

All the twenty or so letters were sent not from Watford but St. Albans. I chose St. Albans for effect, as that's where she'd been an au pair. Maybe the letters were taken by the postman to Watford Central Post Office, which nevertheless was not that close to St. Albans. In any event, I lived nowhere near Watford as they claimed but some 25 miles away. The press knew full well where I lived.

They say the report was entitled 'Report on Heidi Schøne.' It was in fact entitled 'Report on Heidi Overaa,' but obviously instructions were given to keep out of the press the Overaa family name. Runar Schøne is reported as quoting that, "The report was totally false." On the contrary, clearly the report was totally accurate as far as I was concerned. I operated on the basis of accurate facts and to report anything other than sound facts would permanently reduce my credibility to nil.

As far as her having several secret addresses was concerned, I think the press were lying. I doubt very much if she ever had a single secret address. The Norwegians will have to prove it to me. For sure, if you have no phone your name won't be in the directory, and although in every country there are varying degrees of confidentiality in giving out information on individuals in general, the only reason I found it difficult to get Heidi's address was because I wasn't Norwegian and didn't know the normal channels for finding the information.

Further, I detested the implication that I was coercing her to follow Islam and be my wife. It was stinking prejudice. Resentful of her disgusting behaviour I certainly was and wrote several times and told her so. As far as I was concerned, the attitude I have on these matters is reflected word for word in a leader article printed by The Times on Wednesday 10th November 1993:

CHOOSING ISLAM

The Muslim faith has many attractions to Western women

In the trench warfare of ideas between Islam and the West, conversions to the Muslim faith have been largely neglected or dismissed as anomalous. Yet in Britain alone there are already between 10,000 to 20,000 converts, the majority of them women. This striking pattern is also visible in America, where women converts outnumber men by four to one. Ignoring stereotypes, many Western women are turning to a religion which is widely assumed to be prejudicial to them.

As the investigation in The Times on women and Islam has shown, the intellectual clarity and moral certainty of this 1,400 year-old faith are proving attractive to many Western women disillusioned with the moral relativism of their own culture. Though some are converting to Islam after marrying Pakistani or Bangladeshi men, others are making the leap of faith as an independent act of spiritual self-improvement.

In spite of the outrageous indignities which many women suffer in Muslim countries, the principles outlined in the Koran are generally sympathetic to their interests, promising them "rights over men similar to those of men over women." The Prophet Muhammad gave to female Muslims the right to inherit and divorce and regarded his wife Aisha as one of his principal counsellors. Though the tribal and

93

rural societies in which Islam has prospered have rarely conformed to these founding ideals, many women have played a central role of their governance. Banazir Bhutto's rise to power in Pakistan and Toujan al-Faisal's election as Jordan's first female MP this week would have seemed less remarkable to those who had heard of Take Khayzuran, who dominated the Caliphate in the 8th century, or the Egyptian queen Shajarat al-Durr whose armies defeated St. Louis of France in the 13th century.

The separate spheres marked out for the two sexes by Islam certainly bear little relationship to the notions of gender which have been ushered in by the feminist revolution. But what matters is that many of the women in the West who have taken this unexpected path have done so out of choice rather than familial duty or historic obligations. They have been positively attracted by the sense of sisterhood and community they discover in Islam.

This tentative process of spiritual change suggests that increasing numbers of people are questioning the value system of their own culture. It raises important questions about the state of the Western moral tradition and how it might be fortified. Yet the effect of this (still modest) phenomenon is likely to be positive. The presence of Muslim converts in British society - many of them highly educated - can only assist the process of mutual understanding between the two cultures which the Prince of Wales celebrated last month. Only those who have crossed the divide can truly understand what lies on either side.

***

After the Bergens Tidende article was translated for me, the next day I went straight round to the Norwegian Seamen's Church in Rotherhithe, East London, where they have all the recent newspapers for the whole of Norway. One of the other newspapers that had run the story, Verdens Gang (which was the equivalent of The Sun newspaper in England) was there, with the banner headline '13 years SEX-terror' with a huge picture of Heidi on the front page. Her local newspaper, Drammens Tidende, was also there and again it had a huge picture of Heidi on the front page holding a little dog, this time with two Christian Advice Booklets on AIDS that I had sent her pictured in the foreground together with several of my letters. The photograph of Heidi in these two newspapers pictured her with long hair and a slightly receding hairline. Obviously for the Bergens Tidende newspaper they told her to have a haircut to look a little bit sexier. These two newspaper articles are translated below:

VERDENS GANG 26th MAY 1995

13 years SEX-terror

By Harald Vikøyr and Janne Møller Hansen (photos)

For thirteen years, Heidi Schøne, from Drammen has been sexually harassed and terrorised by a man she met on a holiday when she was eighteen years old.

The man started off with telephone and letter harassment. When he was rejected, he continued with terrorising her friends, showing up in person at her door, and death threats.

"I have begged, cried and threatened to make him leave me alone, but it has not helped," says the frustrated Heidi.

As an eighteen year old she gave her address to a slightly peculiar, obtrusive Englishman. In this way began thirteen years of fear and sex terror for Heidi.

When the half Arab, Muslim man was rejected by her later on, he started with obscene phone calls, death threats, threatening letters, showing up in person at her door and harassing her friends for years and years.

Psychiatrists think that the behaviour of the Englishman possesses all the symptoms of erotic paranoia: the sick person is convinced that another person is in love with him or her.

Moving to a secret address and getting a secret telephone number didn't help. Suddenly a postcard dropped into the letterbox saying

94

"Freddie's back" - taken from the horror film with the main character with the name Freddie Kruger. "He found me again! Me and my family were threatened with our lives and he came to my door many times. At one door he wrote 'Fuck you' with a knife."

"It didn't help moving to a secret address and getting a secret telephone number."

Heidi Schøne was born and raised in Bergen, and stayed for a while in England as an au pair with a family. She and her friend had a trip to Paris.

LIKED HIM

On the ferry she became aware of a person watching her from a distance. "When we came to the train, he sat down with the same group of young people that I was with. He was a Muslim, five to six years older than us and proved to have strong opinions about life, among other things. We thought that he was somehow a bit peculiar, but completely harmless."

"I liked him. We had a cup of tea together with him and later on we had some contact, but purely as friends. He would marry a Muslim girl, he said."

HELL

But sometime after Heidi had returned to Bergen, the harassment started. At the time she had a boyfriend in Bergen, but she still was followed by the Englishman.

"I let him in the beginning. He was very manipulating. He had bombarded me with telephone calls and letters telling me that I was stupid, and that nobody but him wanted me. At one point he did obscene things while I had to watch. The funny thing was that I started to believe him bit by bit."

ASHAMED

"It was all so unreal and I felt ashamed. I was more and more frightened, and isolated myself. For long periods of time I didn't go out. I lay down under the bed when the doorbell rang. I just couldn't open the door."

"Those I spoke to said that it would probably stop. He was probably just a bit too eager, a persistent sort of guy."

She involved just a few people in the case and thought for a very long time that it would stop; "The ones I spoke to said that it would probably stop. He was probably just a bit too eager. Nobody took it seriously."

PRIVATE DETECTIVE

But the Englishman had hired a private detective, and managed to trace her time after time. In strange ways he also managed to collect sensitive information about persons close to Heidi. He sent this to her, and she was able to show it to the police.

But the years went by, and when Heidi was about to marry her boyfriend, Runar Schøne, an unpleasant and obscene letter was sent to her from the Englishman indicating that he knew her sexually. "When I think about it now, about how I was manipulated, I just get so angry. I didn't understand it but after a while when I realised he had to be sick I gained my self-respect back. I have begged, cried and threatened him to leave me alone, but it has not helped," says Heidi.

THREW AWAY

Three years ago she threw away all the material she had received from the Englishman. She wanted to burn him out of her life, but in vain.

"The last half year I have received 30 to 40 consignments of letters, postcards and books. Books about AIDS or abortion. As if I have AIDS? I have also recorded him on tape."

"When I think about it today, how I was manipulated, I just get so angry."

And on this tape she has made him admit things. This and the latest consignment of letters she will hand over to her lawyer, Tomm Skaug, who will try to stop the Englishman.

EXTREME

Psychiatrists think that the threatening and lovesick Englishman who has bugged Heidi Schøne for 13 years might suffer from erotic paranoia.

"I don't know this particular case, and do believe that if this can be called erotic paranoia, this is an extreme case," says the Professor in Psychiatry Nils Rettersdøl.

MISCONCEPTION

Erotic paranoia is a disease of the mind in which a person has a misconception that another person is in love with him or her. "To wish or imagine that someone is in love with you is truly a normal phenomena, but the sick person is totally convinced that this is how it actually is, and won't be talked out of it."

In German psychiatry the suffering is called erotic self-seduction, other people call it "old maids psychosis."

MOST OFTEN WOMEN

It most often strikes woman and mostly women in their menopause. Among the known cases of this is a woman who has this relationship towards a male person who has authority and is exposed, for example the local priest. The person who is suffering from this, has no idea of it. The sick person can plan a wedding and won't be talked out of it.

EXPERT:

Erotic paranoia is hard to heal. "It just stops after a couple of years," says Professor in psychiatry, Nils Rettersdøl.

"However, persons with erotic paranoia are seldom directly mean - it can of course be unpleasant and absolutely unwanted that a woman rises up in the congregation and proclaims her imagined relationship with the priest, or another official authority.

But direct unfriendliness like in this case is not normal. The very case described here must be in some extreme form, in that case. It is hard to heal erotic paranoia; most often it just stops after some years by itself. But seldom have the sick the insight and the understanding that it is wrong and imagined," says Rettersdøl.

***

Just below a full page photograph of Heidi and her husband, sombrely looking at my letters to her with the Aids and Abortion Christian booklets on the kitchen table before them, ran the caption:

TERRORIZED:

Heidi Schøne (31) has for 13 years lived under terror of the half-Arab Englishman she met on a trip to Paris – "He sought me out regardless of where I moved to. He said that I and my family would be killed."

Then below one more photo, another sub-story:

SEVERE HARASSMENT

BERGEN (VG) "Personally, I would have reacted rather strongly to being subjected to this sort of thing," says police constable Gunnar Fossum of Nedre Eiker police office.

He received the report from the Schøne family and made the preliminary preparations for investigation. The Telecommunications Administration ('Televerket') connected up the nuisance callers search system to the Schøne family's telephone number.

"On one occasion, he did obscene things which I had to watch. The strange thing was that I gradually began to believe him." Heidi Schøne (31).

***

INTIMATE REFERENCES

Among the documents held by Fossum is a lot of written material containing apparently factual intimate personal particulars concerning Heidi Schøne. He translated these into good Norwegian before he sent them to Heidi's husband and to neighbours, family and friends.

"It was when this happened last winter that we decided to go to a lawyer and to the police," husband Runar Schøne says.

"I have seen how terribly nervous Heidi becomes, now that this is happening again. He must have got a hold of her mentally. It is unbelievable how well she manages after so many years of being terrorized," Runar says.

"I myself have had a telephone call from the Englishman. He just screamed in English what were probably swear words."

***

As far as the Verdens Gang (VG) article is concerned, the word 'Muslim' was only mentioned three times and 'Arab' twice. But sickeningly, again, the emphasis was on telling the public that I was someone who as a Muslim could not tolerate rejection at all and resorted to dirty tactics purely out of unreasonable spite.

More obviously, no mention is made of the decisive contribution of Gudmund Johannessen which produced the utter depression and despair Heidi felt after two suicide attempts, a state of mind that eventually caused her to go as an in-patient at a psychiatric unit.

The Verdens Gang newspaper went out of its way, as did Bergens Tidende, to encourage division between Islam and Christianity on grounds that had no basis in reality. As for Drammens Tidende the translation is:

DRAMMENS TIDENDE 27th MAY 1995

BADGERED AND HUNTED FOR 13 YEARS

By Ingunn Røren and Nils J. Maudal (photos)

For thirteen years an insane man has been making obscene telephone calls and has been stalking Heidi Schøne (31) from Nedre Eiker. This man has sent Heidi more than 400 obscene letters and threatened the lives of both Heidi and her family.

The man is obsessed with Heidi and has followed her movements for many years. For a long period he had a private investigator following her, and he has also several times shown up at Heidi's home and harassed her sexually.

Heidi reported him to the police many times but the police can't do much as long as he does not attack anybody physically.

TERRORISED FOR 13 YEARS

For thirteen years, Heidi Schøne from Nedre Eiker has been terrorised and chased by an insane man who has threatened to kill both her and her family.

After thirteen years of hell Heidi is now telling her story to cast light on the problem she knows that far more people than herself are struggling with; she is being chased by an insane man who is obsessed with her, and she

feels powerless. She has on several occasions reported the man to the police, but their response is limited unless he attacks someone physically.

GAVE HER ADDRESS

The nightmare started when she was eighteen years old and gave her address to a half-German, half-Arab man living in England, who she met when she was an au pair. This was to become the start of years of derision for Heidi and her family. For thirteen years the man has been making obscene phone calls to Heidi and sent her more than 400 letters - all of them with perverse contents. She has also been sent books about AIDS and abortion and audio cassettes about herself.

"The worst part though are the 'reports' about me that he has sent my neighbours, family, friends and colleagues in which he is making a number of coarse and false statements about me," says Heidi. She has moved 5 times during all these years and has had several secret addresses. Each time, the Englishman, who works as a lawyer, managed to find Heidi, by means of threatening the lives of the neighbours until they tell him where she is.

"It is an enormous strain on you when you discover that your neighbours have received these 'reports' before you have got to know them yourself," says Heidi.

GOES TO NORWAY

Heidi and her husband, Runar, have since January lived in a new house at Solbergmoen. All of her neighbours have received scandalous 'reports' which claim that Heidi lives a very wild life, and is a morally destroyed human being.

"Even though the man lives in England, he has flown to Norway eight or nine times during these years and has come to my door. The first time I let him in, because I thought he came as a friend, but the next time he came I was already becoming afraid of him, because he had wanted to know where I was if he called and I was not at home," says Heidi.

The next time when he showed up, she slammed the door in his face; he has attacked her door with a knife and scratched obscene words on the door. He has also vandalised the neighbours' doors and written 'I am going to get you' on the windows.

"I changed between being terrified by the man and being totally irritated with him. I have begged, cried and raved when he has called to make him stop bothering me, but it doesn't help. When he started making frightening telephone calls, he calls on hourly intervals the whole night through," Heidi says.

Heidi deeply regrets that she gave her name and address to the man thirteen years ago.

"I was young and stupid and had then a completely different impression of the man than what I have today. I noticed that he followed me on the ferry between England and France, but I didn't give it much thought. We got in touch, had a cup of tea and met four or five times during the ten months I lived in England. We had never had any kind of relationship," says Heidi.

What she couldn't know was the 'nice man' would become completely obsessed with her and spend the next few years following her smallest moves. For a while he had a private detective follow her. Heidi, her family, and her friends have all been threatened by this man, who has also threatened to kill her 9 year old son. In 1988 Heidi was sent funeral cards by the man who told her 'her days were numbered.'

In 1990 the man brought a friend to Bergen, where Heidi was staying, in order to get her. Heidi managed to alert the police who apprehended him and kept him in custody for two days.

"The police didn't have enough on him to charge him and had to release him. The only thing they could do was take him to the plane, and the terror continued," says Heidi, who felt powerless in the face of the methods of this man. After marrying Runar a couple of years ago, the harassment became worse than ever. Immediately after the wedding, she received a letter in which the man wrote that he would have loved to have been there at the wedding night. Only in the last month, she has had more than 40 letters and countless numbers of telephone calls, all with the same message, that she is living a morally depraved life, that the Englishman hates her and is going to get her. The words in the letter are not suitable to print but they are very mean and perverse.

When the man calls, he yells and screams into the receiver and throws curses. Heidi recorded one of these calls and has delivered most of the letters, reports and the cassettes to her lawyer, who is now considering suing the man for defamation, stalking and reduced quality of life.

The last letter arrived about a month ago.

"Early on I cried when I received these kind of letters, now I just wonder when it will end," says Heidi.

Recently she found out that the man is known to the police for a similar case in England, where he is said to have harassed a younger woman. Not long ago he received a restraining order saying that he was not allowed to come near this woman and Heidi is hoping to get something similar done for her. Heidi knows that the man's mother has tried to commit him to a mental hospital, but the man is obviously one of those most difficult psychiatric cases where the person is too sick to be imprisoned, but too well to be committed to an institution.

"The judicial system has to be able to protect normal human beings against insane people," says Heidi, who is exhausted after years of harassment.

***

Although in Drammens Tidende there is not one reference to my being Muslim, they credit me with being "half-German, half-Arab." This is an accurate label but one must remember that Germany invaded Norway in World War Two and the word 'Arab' is often synonymous with the word 'Muslim.' The reference to "half-German, half-Arab" was used in this context as a derogatory term. The contents of this article are nauseating for their wholesale perversion of the truth. I never made a single obscene phone call, let alone continuously over a thirteen year period. Come on you wankers of the press; your desperation is pathetic! As if it was not possible to record one single obscene phone call in thirteen years. Besides which, Heidi had no phone at all from 1988 to 1993. When the newspaper said Heidi recorded one of my calls, no evidence ever subsequently came out on this aspect.

As far as all my "perverse, unprintable letters and cards" are concerned, I would love the press to have printed them in full. Then all will be able to see what a total distortion their claims were.

All these attacks against me in the newspaper articles were complete fabrications by Heidi and I now had the task of trying to counter those gross defamations and terrible lies. None of the newspapers had named me. But why not? Any guesses? Well, in Norway the press do have a policy of not naming individuals who are the subject of damaging allegations or police action. To what extent this policy applies I am unsure. One thing that did occur to me was that when Heidi spoke to the press, surely she would have had no idea that I myself would have got hold of the press reports as, of course, she was not to know I was instructing a lawyer at the same time in Bergen and it was he who alerted me to the newspaper articles. Thus from Heidi's point of view she would assume that no-one would have known any better from the stories she was telling, making them, therefore, versions of fact instead of what they really were, total fiction.

Correspondence then followed with various parties:

Letter dated 9th June 1995 from my Bergen lawyer to me

Dear Mr. Delaware,

Bergen Politikammer - Heidi Overaa

I refer to my letter dated May 29th 1995.

For the time being I am very busy in Court, in Oslo, and this was will take all my time throughout August and September. As a result of this, I will therefore not be able to represent you any further in your case.

I advise you to consult another lawyer. Please find enclosed your documents.

Yours sincerely,

I then wrote to the senior partner of the London law firm that I had instructed in 1990, having spoken to him over the telephone about the newspaper articles and my letter to him of 14th June is as follows:

Letter dated 14th June 1995 to my London lawyer

Dear Mike,

Heidi Overaa

I did yesterday receive my other letters from my lawyer in Norway. I enclose colour photocopies of everything I have retained. You will see there is a postcard from 1985, letters from 1984 and 1982. One of the 1982 letters describes a discussion of Islam in her school class. In another letter, she describes her being unhappy at the way one night I had treated her - that arose from her telling me she had done something awful on top of her first abortion; so when I asked her what, she refused to tell me for ages, so I kept pressing her for an answer and she then told me: 'a second abortion' and ran down the street crying back to her house.

Iver Stensrud is a policeman at the Norwegian Embassy and he sent my long letter to him on to the Bergen police two months ago. Yesterday his secretary put the phone down on me when I asked to speak to him. He spoke twice to me before very nicely.

My lawyer in Norway says I must instruct another lawyer as he is too busy in Oslo for several months to help me. He knew he had to make proper and full enquiries of the Bergen police and now of course he won't.

So give me a call any time at work or at home. I would like to get things moving but only once we have got our own end right.

Cheers.

Yours sincerely,

P.S. Some of her letters are undated as I am afraid she was very scatterbrained.

On the 17th June 1995 I telephoned Heidi:

HS.   *Hello, Heidi.*

F.   *Yeah, hi there Heidi, Freddy here. How are you today?*

She put down the phone; I rang again. Immediately she answers:

HS.   *Hello, Heidi.*

F.   *Why don't you want to talk?*

She put the phone down again. I rang again. She answers straight away:

HS.   *Hello, Heidi.*

F.   *Why do you tell such lies to the newspaper? Huh?*

HS.   *Why do I have to talk to you? I'm not interested.*

F.   *You don't have to talk to me.*

HS.   *No, why do you call me then?*

F.   *Because I just can't believe you say these things to the newspaper.*

HS.   *I don't have to answer your questions.*

F.   *No, I know you don't.*

HS.   *You will get your answers in Court.*

F.   *I haven't heard from your lawyers.*

HS.   *I'm not interested. You will be hearing from them. They are preparing a case ... there is so much evidence you won't believe it.*

100

F.   *Yeah, but you know....*

HS.   *Bye, bye.*

I rang again:

HS.   *Yeah, hello?*

F.   *Well you know it's me, don't you?*

She put the phone down. I rang again:

HS.   *Hello, Heidi.*

F.   *So are you going to talk or are we going to go on like this all night?*

HS.   *What I'm going to tell you is that I did not go to the newspaper. They came to me. Do you know why? Because one of the photographers got your report in their mail. That was my old address in Bergen. So you really did it big there. And the journalist called me because you have written my name and everything in the report. That's why he wanted to know about the story. They think you are a nut case and you are.*

F.   *So why in 1990 do you send me a book 'I Dared To Call Him Father'?*

HS.   *Hmmm?*

F.   *Why?*

HS.   *You know why I did that.*

F.   *Why did you do that?*

HS.   *To 'witnessing' you* ["witness" being the word some Christians use in trying to convert others to Christianity].

F.   *Huh?*

HS.   *You don't have to ask me that because you know why I did.*

F.   *But did you want me to turn Christian?*

HS.   *Of course I did. I want the best for you. Of course I did. Because I know deep inside how hurt you are. I know that. That's why I said what I said in the letters. But you keep on terrorising me and harassing me. You know what your motives are. You want to destroy me. You've written it yourself.*

F.   *Yes, but look ... ...*

HS.   *No, I don't have to look.*

F.   *I'm not asking you to look but just cool down for a minute.*

HS.   *No, I don't want to cool down. You've been pestering me for all these years. I'm trying to tell you please stop it. But you won't listen to reason.*

F.   *Look ... look... Heidi look ... ...*

HS.   *That's why I have to drag you to court. There are so many other people who are so sick of you terrorising them. My family, Gudmund, his brother, my husband. They can't stand it!*

F.   *Yeah, but why does he say this and why do the newspapers write things about the Muslims in general.*

HS.   *I don't know why you're asking me - this is years ago.*

F.   *No, this was in the newspaper - why do they say in Bergens Tidende going on and on.*

HS.   *Oh, yeah yeah, because I told them. What you said in your letters. You talking about God and Allah and how bad I am to your religion. That's been your motive all the time hasn't it?*

F.   *But why does your husband ... ...*

HS.   *You're so clean and I'm so dirty.*

F.   *No, I'm not so clean... you know that I'm not that wonderful....*

HS.   *You've told everybody how bad I am. And you're so pure, so clean. So I know who you are. You've been **harassing** me. I've known you for thirteen years. Because I didn't do what you wanted me to do, then you started harassing me.*

F.   *But the newspapers said I'd been issuing death threats for ...*

HS.   *Yes, you have ...*

F.   *For 13 years ...*

HS.   *I don't say that.*

F.   *But the newspapers said so.*

HS.   *No, they don't say that. They don't say for 13 years. They say for 13 years you've been harassing me. Because you have. You've always been telling me how bad I am, and when I was really down and crying and you said "Oh, I'm so sorry for you." And then you turn your back on me and 'Boom!' in my back.*

F.   *No!*

HS.   *Because I did not do what you wanted me to do!* [she screamed]. *Yes, that's the truth and you know it!*

F.   *Don't lose your temper. At least try and talk sensibly.*

HS.   *I don't have to do what you tell me to do, don't you realise that?*

F.   *Yeah I do, I do* [I said resignedly].

HS.   *If I want to lose my temper I will. I am not ashamed anymore, you do understand?*

F.   *Yeah, I do.*

HS.   *Yeah? And if I want to raise my voice I'll bloody well do it!*

F.   *But in 1988 why did you ask me to come over and help* [but I didn't have time to add "you

102

against Gudmund Johannessen."]

HS.   *I know what you're doing now. I know you're taping this.*

F.   *I'm not.*

HS.   *Yes, you are.*

F.   *I'm not.*

HS.   *I know you are! I know what you're doing, I know. Requesting me all this because you're gonna have it in the court and everything. You know what you've done and now you have it on tape that you admit to sending these reports.*

F.   *I've admitted to the newspapers to sending letters, not reports; what reports?* [I teased.]

HS.   *But you have on my tape.*

F.   *Huh?*

HS.   *Yes, you've admitted you're sending these reports to my family, to my neighbours. I have it on tape. You have admitted twice. And you also admitted at the beginning of this conversation. OK, OK, you said?*

        [Obviously, this very conversation that I was taping, she was also apparently taping and her above comments were self-serving and false statements.]

        But you've been harassing me for years! [she screeched] *And I'm sick of it.*

F.   *Well, you shouldn't tell lies to the police about ...*

HS.   *I didn't tell lies about.... No, you've been lying. All these years.*

F.   *In 1990?*

HS.   *You've been lying and lying and lying and mixed it with the truth with my miserable life and you use it against me.*

F.   *I didn't* [lie, I was about to add.]

HS.   *You didn't?* [she exclaimed.]

F.   *No.*

HS.   *Oh, I see; we don't have any more to discuss. **Nothing** more to discuss, bye.*

        Down went the phone. I rang again. Immediately she answered:

HS.   *Hello, Heidi.*

F.   *Yeah, I mean ... ...*

HS.   *Last time you called me you said you were nearby. We traced your phone call and you were in England. You've been lying all the time.*

F.   *I was in Denmark the first time.*

HS.   *I am not!* [lying]. *We had a tape where you said it. You always ... ...*

F.   *I was in Denmark the first time.*

HS.   *No, you were **not**. You were in England last time.*

F.   *No, the very first time, but when you ... ...*

HS.   *Oh, yeah ... because I know you were in Denmark. We know all the numbers where you called from. You better not call here because we're tracing your phone calls every time you call me!*

F.   *So, what? It doesn't bother me.*

HS.   *It doesn't matter whether it's bothering you or not, I'm just telling you; I don't want to talk to you.*

F.   *If you write such nonsense to the newspapers...*

HS.   *It doesn't matter what you want because ...*

F.   *It does ...*

HS.   *It's my decision whether I want to speak to you or not and when I'm telling you I don't want it, that's what it means.*

F.   *Does it matter if you tell nonsense to the police?*

HS.   *Give me some respect; show some respect.*

F.   *Respect after what you've done?*

HS.   *Goodbye.*

F.   *Oh, to hell with you. Why don't you go to hell with your rubbish.*

HS.   *Yes, you too. Bye bye, bye bye.*

F.   *Yeah, piss off.*

She put the phone down. I rang again:

HS.   *Hello, Heidi.*

F.   *So what's the name of your lawyer then?*

Down went the phone. I phoned again:

HS.   *Hello, Heidi.*

F.   *Yeah, so anyway ... ...*

HS.   *Whatever you want, I'm not going to answer your questions.*

F.   *Why don't you name me in the newspapers?*

HS.   *I am not going to answer your questions! You have to contact my lawyer.*

F.	*What's his name?*
HS.	*You know his name.*
F.	*I don't.*
HS.	*In the newspaper.*
F.	*I can't remember.*
HS.	*And if you want to make a deal instead of going to court, you can contact my lawyer.*
F.	*A deal?*
HS.	*Bye, bye.*

I rang again:

HS.	*Hello, Heidi.*
F.	*Come on lets talk about it for God's sake.*
HS.	*No I don't want to talk about it.*
F.	*Are you tired?*
HS.	*I can't talk to you alone Frederick.*
F.	*Well I wanted to talk to you in 1990 with the police. Why did you not want to talk to me then?*
HS.	*We did talk that time didn't we?*
F.	*Not before the police.*
HS.	*You came here to my home.*

[She was in fact referring to our meeting in August 1990 with her, her son and me].

You told me you were going to stop it. Your lawyer has also said that you promised to stop this years ago. You haven't kept your promise Frederick.

F.	*When I discovered ... I only discovered last January ... ...*[and I was going to mention her allegation of attempted rape, but]
HS.	*I told you Frederick, I can't talk to you unless there are other witnesses. I can't Frederick because it doesn't serve my case. Of course it doesn't. You don't think about me. I have to think about myself. I have to stop this harassment.*
F.	*It's not harassment. Do you think it's pure harassment?*
HS.	*Of course I know beyond all this there's a lot of pain.*
F.	*The police weren't answering the questions my lawyers were putting to you - to them.*
HS.	*What is it that you want by this conversation? What is it that you want? Do you want to solve anything?*

105

F.   *Well yeah, I do.*

HS.   *Do you want to promise me you're gonna stop this?*

F.   *If we could sit round a table and get some answers.*

HS.   *Yeah, we could sit round a table with a lawyer.*

F.   *I'm willing to do that.*

HS.   *That's good.*

F.   *But where?*

HS.   *I can contact my lawyer and we can talk about it. I also got a letter from my doctor years ago and he also received horrible letters and phone calls from you Frederick. We've got so much evidence.* [This was a filthy lie again – I had spoken very politely and written one straightforward decent letter to her psychiatrist, Dr. Broch.]

F.   *Your doctor?*

HS.   *Yes, my doctor. My shrink. And he was my shrink years ago. I've got so many witnesses against you. You won't last for a minute Frederick.*

F.   *I believe I will* [last for a minute that is; indeed, a lot longer than that].

HS.   *I can contact my lawyer and you can contact me during the week. After Wednesday because I'm going to Sweden.... And then you can contact by writing or by phone and then we make some arrangement, OK?*

F.   *Yeah, well I honestly can't remember the name of your lawyer. How's Daniel?*

HS.   *Daniel can talk. Daniel can talk when we have witnesses.*

F.   *Well how's Daniel anyway?*

HS.   *But if your purpose is not to stop this and make up then it's no use. Is that your purpose, to solve this?*

F.   *My purpose is genuine.*

HS.   *That's OK then.*

F.   *Yeah, how's Daniel?*

HS.   *Hm?*

F.   *How's Daniel?*

HS.   *He's fine.*

F.   *Is he nine?*

HS.   *Sorry?*

F.   *Is he nine years old now?*

HS.   *Yes he is. You've spoken to him on the phone I've heard.*

F.   *That's right. His English is not bad.*

HS.   *You also sent the reports to my nephew. He's only 12 years old. It's so shocking. I know it's pain beyond this but it's so shocking. How you can destroy others lives because you want to get to me?*

F.   *Why do you make allegations in 1986 that are untrue to the police?* [i.e. Attempted rape.] *I only discovered it at Christmas.*

HS.   *Then we will discuss it with a lawyer. Because you don't want to listen again, only yourself....*

F.   *I am listening to you. I'm not losing my temper.*

HS.   *We have been speaking about this before and we haven't managed to solve this between us. We haven't. Time has shown that. Then we have to do it in other ways.*

F.   *You never talked to me in the police station in 1990 did you?*

HS.   *No because we were advised not to. After what you done that time of course I couldn't talk to you. I was afraid of you. I was so scared ... out of my mind.*

F.   *Oh come on, you weren't. Were you really?*

HS.   *Other people have seen me so scared of you.*

F.   *You're not scared of me......I find it incredible. You were as cool as a cucumber in the police station. You were just completely relaxed and calm. You looked fine to me.*

HS.   *I wasn't. I was a basket case.*

F.   *Were you?*

HS.   *Yes I was. But we can discuss this later. And later ... You've proved by your actions what your motives are ... I could have done you lots of things. I mean I could be spreading lies about you and do awful things to your life if I wanted to but I haven't and you have. You're trying to destroy me.* [Implying that what she told the newspapers was all true!]

F.   *Please just calmly listen.*

HS.   *I will listen when a lawyer is ... ...*

F.   *Forget war for a minute. When I was in Egypt I was there for 3 months ....*

She'd put the phone down. I rang again. She answered straight away.

HS.   *I'm sorry I don't want to upset you but I have to do what my lawyers have advised me. I am going to hang up now. You will have all the time to talk later ... You're not going to get what you want. You can tell me something later.... I'm just doing what I think is right OK.*

F.   *OK.*

HS.   *Bye Bye.*

F.   *Bye Bye.*

On the 20th June 1995 I telephoned Commander Krogvold of the Bergen Police:

F.	*Yes. Good morning, is that the Police Station?*
Answer	*Yes this is Bergen Police Station.*
F.	*Ah, good. Is Commander Krogvold in this morning please?*
Answer	*You want?*
F.	*Commander Krogvold.*
Answer	*Yes, just a moment please.*
F.	*Thank you.*
K.	*Krogvold.*
F.	*Yes, hi, good morning Commander Krogvold, it's Frederick Delaware, the lawyer from London.*
K.	*Yes.*
F.	*In connection with Heidi Overaa. I understand you know the name of her lawyer.*
K.	*No. I... I... I .....don't know. I had a letter from the lawyer but I, that's in the case and the case have gone to the files. I don't have his name now.*
F.	*Did you know what's happened in this ... in this ...er ... ...*
K.	*Nothing happening here as far as I know.*
F.	*Because ... I spoke to Heidi Overaa yesterday and she told me you are preparing some sort of case against ... ...*
K.	*No, the case here are closed from many years ago.*
F.	*Ah, OK. It's just that she's been telling me the police are waiting for me to arrest me in Drammen and I don't know the truth.*
K.	*There are no case here at Bergen Police Department ... the case here are closed from many years ago.*
F.	*Yes, OK then. Did you get some letters from my lawyer called Mr. Wesenberg?*
K.	*Yes, I've got letters from many [parties] through the years ... the letters are answered.*
F.	*I was just wanting to have some details because in 1986 Heidi made allegations that I - untrue allegations I must say - that I attempted to rape her.*
K.	*I see no reason to comment on this case any further. It's an old case, it's closed and I have no comments at all. The letters from the lawyers are answered and that's all.*
F.	*Okay then, thank you very much, bye bye.*

Followed by a conversation with Haakon Schrøder, reporter with Bergens Tidende:

F.   *Yes, hi there, is that Mr. Schrøder?*

HS.   *Yes.*

F.   *Hi, I phoned you last week, it's Mr. Delaware here.*

HS.   *Wait.* [And then immediately the phone went dead so I rang again.]

Answer   *Bergens Tidende.*

F.   *Yes, can you put me through to Haakon Schrøder again please?*

Answer   *He is not in our office at the moment.*

F.   *Oh, I thought I'd just er ... I spoke to him just one minute ago.*

Answer   *Oh, just a moment ...* [eventually] *Hello, it's not answer.*

F.   *It's not answering?*

Answer   *No.*

F.   *Well, OK I'll try again in five minutes.*

            I tried again:

Answer   *His line is opperkirk.*

F.   *Oh, is it? What does that mean, "busy"? Well OK I shall try and ring later.*

On 21ˢᵗ June 1995 I had a conversation with Tomm Skaug, Heidi's lawyer:

F.   [I've received information] *through my lawyer Wesenberg that in 1986 Heidi had gone to the police and told them that I had attempted to rape her, OK.*

TS.   *No, that's not true, I have got all the copy of the police papers... and there is nothing about rape there.*

F.   *Well there is ... in my letter; I can send you a copy of my letter from Wesenberg and in it it says that in 1986, in December, she went to the police and said that I had attempted to rape her and this I never, never, never did and I will never do this to anybody and it's made me so angry, this is the reason for all my postcards and my letters and the phone calls.*

TS.   *But what, what, what do you want her to do so that you can stop this?*

F.   *I asked the police at the end of December, the last week in December, and I wrote to Wesenberg and I said please sue Heidi - get the papers from the police and I want to sue Heidi Overaa for perverting the course of justice and I want to sue the police for wrongful arrest and they could not get ... ...*

TS.   *Why don't you do that ... but please do it in a proper ... ...*

F.   *Yeah, I tried to ...... you see I've been in contact even with the police ... the Norwegian police at the Embassy in England and I phoned Commander Krogvold yesterday in Bergen Police Station and he said the case is closed and my letters have been answered and he doesn't want to talk about it ...he says the case is closed and he said, "I don't want to discuss anything" and I told him about this attempted rape business and the thing is you see in 1985 ... ... I had sex with Heidi ... and she did not tell me that she had resumed having sex with Gudmund Johannessen who was taking heroin, injecting it ... and she didn't tell me this.*

TS.   *But this is more than ten years ago.*

F.   *It's more than ten years ago. It happened in 1985; she didn't tell me* [about Johannessen's heroin taking] *until a year and a half later and it wasn't until 1990 that I had the time and the energy and a friend to come with me to confront her about her past.*

TS.   *And to confront her with the past?*

F.   *Because I don't like being used.*

TS.   *Yes, but I think you have done that now, so now if you stop this written* [he meant 'writing'] *then it's okay.*

F.   *If only she can not tell the police these things. She's told the police before in the early 80's that she was raped by a Bergen shopkeeper.*

TS.   *But that is nothing of your business.*

F.   *No it's not ... ... it **is** my business because Heidi kept telling me about it; she told me all her past and then to go and tell the police* [and then I explained the background to Heidi's second suicide attempt].

TS.   *But why did she call the police as soon as you arrived?* [He had changed the subject to my 1990 arrest.]

F.   *When in 1990?*

TS.   *... ... and then the police arrested you as soon as you came ... ... and they asked you to go back to England ... and not to write any more letters and you did promise that.*

F.   *No, I didn't ... I didn't promise anything. My lawyers wrote that I would not send any letters but provided we got some proper information from the police ... and we didn't get anything.*

TS.   *Yes, but then if you write to me and ask what you want ... just stop these things and I will talk to Heidi about it ... I want you to ... that every connection that you want to have with Heidi ... I want that it should go through me.*

F.   *Yeah, that's OK... I phoned her up 6 times and she spoke to me. The thing is all this writing letters ... it's all nonsense because in 1990 she wanted me to marry her. She wanted me to become a Christian. She sent me postcards from Egersund where her sister is staying, saying Ah what a lovely name* [I have] *... and she sent me a book ... ...*

TS.   *Do you have a copy of these letters?*

F.   *I threw everything away after 1985* [i.e her post-1985 correspondence apart from the Christian book 'I Dared To Call Him Father'].

TS.   *I don't believe you.*

F.   *No, no, you must believe me.*

110

TS.   *No, I don't.*

F.   *Because she sent me a book called 'I Dared To Call Him Father,' about a Muslim woman who became Christian. Do you believe that, because I have the book? I kept the book.*

TS.   *I don't know anything about that but the first thing is I don't believe that she asked you to marry her.*

F.   *She did ... she said, "If you become a Christian."*

TS.   *But then you would have these letters from her, but you don't have it ... I would like to see it then before I believe it.*

F.   *I disposed of even my lawyers' letters and I had to get their file. But I have lots of love letters that I will send you... I have about six love letters. It says in the newspapers "13 years of terror" - yeah? Well I have postcards and love letters from 1984, 1985 with the postcards. I will send you those, OK.?*

TS.   *OK.*

F.   *I will send you those. But I'm telling you now I am not a liar and you can ask her ... she sent me postcards from Egersund, two of them, which she posted in Drammen and she said her son Daniel "likes you very much." I know Daniel, he sat on my knee, he likes me very much and I was in her house in August 1990 with her son and we got on very well and Heidi told me then that her grandparents would have looked after Daniel had she succeeded in committing suicide in 1988 ... ... I warned her parents about Gudmund Johannessen.*

TS.   *But she has nothing to do with him now.*

F.   *Not now, but on two occasions she could have lost her life and that made me so angry OK ... ... but I'm telling you, ask her about the postcards she wrote to me* [in 1990 which Tomm Skaug refused to believe, Heidi had written to me].

TS.   *You must send me a copy of them, OK. You have my address?*

F.   *No I don't.*

So I took his address.

F.   *I have got nothing* [letters that is] *after 1985 but she wrote to me many times and I can swear to you by God I'm not lying to you, she wrote me those postcards* [in 1990] *and she did say this to me - she wrote one letter saying "You are talking about marriage" and then she goes "Hmmm" and she goes dot dot dot dot* [on the letter] *- she says "I want to marry a Christian man more than anything else in the world; this is my dream and as you will not be turning Christian then I will not be marrying you." So I said "OK., that's what you want, fair enough," but she did want to convert me to Christianity. Do you believe that?*

TS.   *I don't know. I don't really believe it.*

F.   *You don't believe it. You will believe it because I have it on tape. I have her conversation on tape and her very words which were she wanted to "witness me" OK.? That's on tape.*

TS.   *Anyway, I don't think that matters too much now, anyway because now she has got married to a Christian.*

F.   *Yes, she's got married to a Christian, but what also made me very angry is that when I phoned him up he said to me: "Come to Jesus, come to Jesus, Allah" which is the Arabic word for God, he said "Allah doesn't exist, he can't help you. Come to Jesus." He then goes on* [and I mimicked Runar Schøne speaking in tongues] *for five minutes speaking in some strange language in tongues, yeah? And he's crazy - she's welcome to him.*

TS.   *But did you hear for five minutes?*

F.   *Yes, because he went on for five minutes and my mother heard it.* [Years later Runar Schøne actually admitted to "babbling" as will be seen later in this book].

TS.   *But why do you write all these letters to her neighbours? It's not a matter of her neighbours. You are writing letters to everybody around in Norway here, not everybody exactly but...... these letters of yours, they are in the police and they have formed a report, you know - that you are sending reports.*

F.   *You've read the reports?*

TS.   *Yes I have.*

F.   *And what do you think of them? You think they're all rubbish?*

TS.   *It doesn't matter really what you have written in them, but who you have sent them to. I mean, why do you send them to everybody who is ... it's not everybody's business this thing ... why do you send them to the neighbours?* [I thought that was obvious - to expose the bitch and punish her.]

F.   *Well I'm not going to say anything - I'm not going to say anything on that topic, but the point is she has tried to ruin me in* [February] *1990 ... she tried to ruin my career through lies ...in August she welcomes me to her home, lets her son sit on my knee, he takes his dummy out, gives me a big kiss and likes me very ... her son liked me so much that it was probably why she thought if I can make Freddy become a Christian then we get married and I felt so sorry for her son and I liked him so much that I think if Heidi, as I said to Heidi, "You can stay Christian but any children we have, have to be brought up as Muslim" and this was the one reason that she didn't take things further because she didn't accept that any of our children be brought up as Muslim.* [I went on to explain the full circumstances of my arrest in February 1990 beginning with my meeting the hypocrite Heidi-Anita Skjortnes - Heidi's Christian neighbour].

The only reason she's married is because she's married a Christian fanatic - he's mad. Anyone who says: "Allah doesn't exist, come to Jesus" and says [and I again mimicked her husband's speaking in tongues] *...... speaking in tongues. And we had a programme on this in England three weeks ago called 'Everyman' about exorcism, exorcising the devil ... ... you've got to understand the other side of it. I'm furious ... I never raped anybody or attempted to rape anybody.*

TS.   *But Heidi has not er er claimed or anyway she hasn't told me that.*

F.   *No, she hasn't told you that because that's the reason I'm so angry ... you can phone up* [my lawyer] *...phone him up... when he reported to me in January* [his] *first paragraph was "attempted rape" and when I read those words it drives me crazy. When I read "attempted rape" I think of the Muslims in Sarajevo who are being raped and it makes me feel sick, and ... she's got to withdraw that accusation from the police. If she does that then I will stop.*

TS.   *That's your main thing ... that she should withdraw?*

F.   *Yeah withdraw the allegation - she knows it's rubbish. She's not even saying rape ... attempted ... it's just nonsense and I want you to find out about the attempted ... the rape by the Bergen shopkeeper* [and I also went on to mention Heidi telling me about the allegation that Greek men had tried to rape her at knife point when she was on holiday].

I followed this conversation up with a letter to him:

Dear Mr. Skaug,

Heidi Overaa

I enclose as promised copy letters 1982 to 1985. The originals are in my possession. You can ask Heidi about the 1990 letters/book - 'I Dared To Call Him Father' and postcards written in Egersund telling me how much Daniel liked me, and how nice she thought my name sounded. You can make your own mind up about the truth. However, the fight for justice will go on if you do not believe me. Heidi and her son Daniel know the truth: it is up to Heidi to admit it to you. Remind her son of the time he spoke to me on the phone in 1990 - summer - calling me jokingly "funny face." I sent him presents on his birthday of model cars and a London bus in 1990 and 1991. He went around telling everyone he had a lovely Englishman as a friend. Heidi said in her postcard: "Daniel likes you very much: he told me so." If you cannot get Heidi to admit this, (her son will) then my fight for justice goes on, on, on and on - for ever if necessary.

The situation has been made worse by the disgusting reports in all the newspapers. I hope my reports are published. I cannot see now how Heidi can do anything to retrieve the situation. She has been a party to my assassination without naming me. Don't tell me she tried to stop the newspapers going to print for my sake! A full apology in the press plus money from the press will have to be negotiated by you if this matter is to be resolved. A complete withdrawal of the December 1986 allegation of attempted rape is a <u>must</u> plus a police acknowledgement of this. The police [in Bergen] two days ago told me that the matter is <u>closed</u>. Thus they obviously believe Heidi is a liar. Everyone knows Heidi is a liar. I will if necessary call the police interpreter from 1990 to repeat her statements to me: that Heidi is "sick." I have even contacted the drugs officer at the Norwegian Embassy in February telling him of my disgust at the AIDS/HIV scare with Heidi in 1985 and the attempted rape allegation. The police in Bergen he sent this report of mine. Still the police don't care. So there is nothing you can do. You are going to get nowhere.

You can confirm the contents of my conversation with Dr. Broch (Heidi's psychiatrist) with Dr. Broch himself, but don't ruin his career! He told me only a few months ago that he was "aware" of Heidi's marriage.

Remember, the 1986 attempted rape allegation I only was told of by my Bergen lawyer in January 1995. I have to fight this until my name is cleared. My lawyers in 1990 got nowhere with the police thanks to Heidi's lies and you will be up against them [my 1990 lawyers].

Heidi's attempt to 'witness' me - she said two nights ago, i.e. turn me Christian, and her letters of 1990 were made at the time when she was lonely and sad - she wanted me to turn Christian and then marriage was on the cards. She said "Come and live in Norway," that I could visit her at any time, on the phone. What ruined things was the book she sent me and she stayed away on May 18th 1991 on purpose and lied afterwards about being in. I have not sent you my press report - it is only for the press and if you want to help Heidi destroy me then I can not supply my life story to you. I am a lawyer like you and I know what's what. I don't think you can do anything to me. It's useless and unless I get satisfaction as indicated above the fight goes on.

Chapter 16

I then sent to the three newspapers photocopies of all of Heidi's letters to me, together with a nine page report detailing my side of the story and the absolute truth of the whole matter. I had kept a couple of Sainsbury's carrier bags full of all the letters, postcards, Christmas cards etc. that I had received in probably the last two decades and I got them out of my cupboard and rummaged through them to see if I had managed to retain any of Heidi's other letters from the 1980's. Most fortunately I had, and in all, the few that I kept are printed below:

Letter dated 24ᵗʰ August, 1982

Thank you very much for your letters and the telephone calls. Nice to hear that you are okay. I'm alright as always, (he! he!) and I hope it is the same with you. You've had your exams already haven't you? Did you pass your exams, I mean have you heard anything? Hope you passed your exams, in fact I'm quite sure you did, you used to work hard didn't you? The school starts again tomorrow, it's Sunday today and I'm sitting in my room listening to music. Nice eh? I'm looking forward to go to school again!! So do my parents! They're glad I'm back again, safe. So am I in a way though. I miss England, funny that is, because I felt quite miserable in the end. Anyway I'm sure I will 'be back' in England quicker than I thought! Have you met a girl lately? My 'old' boyfriend visited me Saturday. He is nice, good-looking, but oh I don't know... ... I suppose you have met a girl you fancy, ha? I'm right? I think so! He! He! I'm only pullin your legs! Was that right?

Did I spell it right? [She drew an arrow from the 'Did' up to the word 'pullin' on the line above]. Never mind, I can speak English but I'm not a good writer, never mind, it's not '<u>that</u>' important. I'll send a photograph of myself so if you want keep it! If not then put it in the bin! He! He!

I hope you still want to write to me!

I 'can't' write any more now, because my Mum is shouting at me up stairs!

Take care!

Love from me.
Heidi

Letter postmarked 31ˢᵗ August 1982 from Ulset Post Office, Bergen

[At the top of the letter in red biro were written the words:]

OBS! I wrote this letter three weeks ago but I'd forgotten all about it, but I thought I might as well send it!

[the body of the letter was written in blue biro:]

<u>Thank</u> <u>you</u> very much for your letter and the nice card you wrote! You're a nice person, but you're very 'funny' at the same time. I've written a letter to you but I'll send both letters to you. I'm fine but I'm not a good girl (as you expressed yourself). Well I'm a good girl in some ways but not in all ways. I don't know, but you seem to feel a bit sorry for yourself. Right? Why? You wrote you had to fight to get someone otherwise you won't get anyone. Nonsense! Look, you've got a good look, you're nice (when you want to, he! he!). I'm joking, but you've got everything, you're not ugly, far-off, you're a good person, at least that's my impression! But I wasn't very happy about you when I was in England and if you expect me to forget it you're

wrong! I won't because the way you treated me that last night wasn't too nice. Well, I've 'done' a lot wrong, but that doesn't mean that you've got the right to punish me or something. You ask me if I remember the night I begged you to stay, yes I do. I remember it all, but that doesn't mean that we shall forget all the bad things and just remember all the good things. You might think so, but <u>I do not</u>. I'm not saying you did all the wrong things, because that's not true, but you're not that good ……………. that…... Well, I won't say anymore, you know exactly what I mean. Well I wish you good luck in life. Enjoy life and I hope you'll get what you want in it, marry a nice good girl, maybe from Egypt! And that you will be happy with your work. But listen, I don't care what you think but you don't need to <u>fight</u> to get <u>something</u>. Maybe you need to fight to get <u>what</u> you want but just not for <u>something</u>. You know what you want, and I think I've got an idea about what you want in life (I mean the kind of wife and etc. etc.). Still sometimes it seems to me that you don't know <u>for sure</u> what you want. I wish you luck and if you want to, I'll keep in touch with you. Okay.

Love, Heidi

XX [i.e. two kisses]

[She then drew a picture of herself in biro showing her head and long flowing hair.]

I was at a loss to understand her reference to "all the bad things" as I hadn't done or said anything bad to her, but in the spirit of conciliation, I remember writing to her asking her to let bygones be bygones. When she mentioned, "the way you treated me that last night," this was her reference to my coaxing out of her the fact that she had had a second abortion, after which she ran home sobbing.

> Letter dated 3.10.1982 sent with postmark of 7.10.1982 from Ulset Post Office Bergen

How are you? Oh, a stupid question! I just received your letter! Thank you very much! Nice to hear from you, as well. Nice to hear that you wish me well, and that you hope the 'bad' memories can fade away with time. (As you wrote) I don't think I will forget it but I'll forgive you 'sure.' Well, I suppose it's not the right way to write it 'forgive you' but I'm not that good in English! Bad to hear about your exams, I mean you're not too optimistic, 'bad news.' Well I hope you pass them, and I wish you good luck in Egypt. Sad in a way because I might go to England just over Christmas time or before Christmas, not sure yet. But I want to take a trip to England anyway and I will! So I might not see you this year or the next. And in 1983 or 1984 you're married, four kids and you don't want to talk to a 'stupid Norwegian' girl. Alright! When are you moving into your new house? Write and tell me will you. Give my regards to your parents (if they 'won't mind.' I don't know if they like the impression about me you gave them) (of me, I mean). I guess you told them a lot, especially to your mother. Right?

[The above was written in red biro. What follows below was written in blue biro]

Hi there!

I'm back again! Now I'm 'sitting in a chair,' at school. Just now we talked or discussed religion, Islam, etc. etc. and everyone in the class said that a Muslim man has no respect for women. Right! Sure! Women have to do what their husbands and parents etc. etc. tells them. Oh, shit, make me so angry, right of course if you believe in God, that's not a bad thing. But it seems to me sometimes that the 'males' think they've got the right to punish other people when they've done something wrong, especially the women, poor 'things.' As you said, good at cleaning house 'doing the things women should do.' He! he! Some of the Muslims (males) thinks they are God 'himself.' I know this is not a nice 'way to put it,' but that's how I feel about it. So, I don't think I will turn to Islam and do what the Quran tells me to do. It's nothing wrong to believe in <u>God</u> and do what you think or God thinks is right. No, nothing. But Islam, NO NO. The woman got no rights, it doesn't surprise me that a lot of the girls and women feel unhappy, and think it must be good to be - western - American. Don't you think so!

Well, I do not want to make you upset, that's not the meaning of this letter! So, I don't think I'm in the right 'mood' to write today, but I just wanted to ask if you're all right etc. etc. And <u>again, thank you</u> for wishing me well! So take care!

Love Heidi

P.S. I'm, sorry I didn't send this letter to you soon after I wrote it. <u>Sorry!</u>

These three letters from 1982 contradict the Bergens Tidende newspaper claims that I changed into an aggressive pest soon after Heidi returned to Bergen in 1982 after her time as an au pair in England.

Undated letter contained in a black envelope with a love heart stuck to the back. Impossible to distinguish date stamp on envelope. Probably written in the spring of 1984

How are you? It was very nice talking to you again! It's always nice talking to you. You're such a nice person and you know that too. But how are you now? Have you heard anything from the Egyptian girl recently? How are your mother? Is she doing fine or what? I don't understand why your father won't leave her alone and I don't understand why he is not treating your mother better than he do. Of what you told me she is such a good and warm person. She deserves far better than this! Well, I've got nothing to tell you. There is no news. But I am doing fine and again I hope you're fine too. I haven't got the money yet but I will soon so we'll see what happens. I might come and see you, I don't know.   'Have it'!

Lots of Love, Heidi

I hope I hear from you soon.

Undated letter from summertime in 1984

Hello! Thank you very much for your letter and the phone calls! Nice to hear your voice again. I don't know why but you made me feel happy, or should I say in a good mood. I have been thinking a lot about you (after you phoned me) and that was a bit 'strange' for me. As you always do or did, you made me think of life in general, about why we are all here and what happens when we die. That dream you had was very strange, don't you think so? When did you have that dream? After you phoned me on Monday? [This was the dream referred to above when I found myself in a burning building with Heidi]. Well there's a lot of things I'd ask you but I don't know where to begin. Did your Muslim friend marry the American girl three months after he had met her? Well, I think that's crazy. That's out of order I think. I suppose it's because of the way I'm brought up. I mean, if someone got married (here in Norway) after knowing each other for only three months, they normally break up after a couple of years because they didn't know each other enough before they got married. That happens again and again and it seems to me that some people just don't learn. I mean I'm not thinking of the two persons who got married but about their kids. I think that's terrible! They give up too easily. So I don't think I will get married, at least not in the first two to three years. I hope I can come to England and see you. If I can afford it. I would like to go and visit my friend (Salamon) in St. Albans too. Shirley and Colin too. I am going to finish the school this year and then I might study law. Don't be surprised!! Well, I've always wanted to do that. Well we'll see if I'm going to study law or if I'm going to study physiotherapy. There's a lot of things I would like to do. I am a big 'dreamer' you see, but it all depends on the result next year. Well, anyway I don't think there is more for me to say in this letter so I'd better end it here. I hope I see you soon.

Lots of love, Heidi

P.S. I'll give you three photos. You asked for one but when you get three that's hopefully enough. Ha, ha.

[Heidi sent me three photographs of herself - photographs taken by her father by a fjord in Bergen, playing with their black Labrador dog. She also sent me a Muver greetings plastic card enclosed in an envelope saying on the front "Someone Special." The card itself said "Anytime, anywhere, I'll be there if you need me" and signed "lots of love from Heidi."]

This next letter was the one which for five years had stayed on my London lawyer's file in storage – the original letter! And vital to my defence.

Letter post stamped 22.8.1984 at Arstad Post Office, Bergen

Nice to talk to you again, very nice! It feels strange, but you make me feel better every time I've talked to you. I don't know what I like so much about you, but it's something that's for sure. The first time you phoned me (about two weeks ago) you asked if I've ever been thinking of you when I had my problems. Well, I told you that I never did. But that's not the truth, actually I did a lot. I don't know why but I just wanted to forget all about you but I never did. Please believe me because I'm telling you the truth now. Thank you very much for listening to me when I told you about my problems. I don't understand why you bothered. Have you ever listened to Randy Crawford? She's my favourite! Especially her first solo LP: 'Raw Silk' and 'Secret Combination.' She has got a great voice and the lyrics are just wonderful. If you haven't got any records of her, please buy one or two and listen to them. There are especially two songs I like very much. The song I like best is: 'I Hope You'll Be Very Unhappy Without Me' (Raw Silk) and the other one is: 'Trade Winds' (Secret Combination). If you don't buy them, I'll buy them to you!! If you're going to buy a record or two, please don't buy the newest records of her, they're not good at all, because that is just horrible pop-disco. She had a concert here in Bergen, in February, I think. It was and she was just super! Well that's enough about Randy Crawford. So how are you? Fine I hope. You know what! I think a lot of you!

Bloody he! ..... I don't know why I think of you. Oh, can't you marry two women! He!he! That was a joke. I can finish my studies in Norway first and then I'll come over to England and get married to ....!! You will probably be old and dead by then!! He!he! What about marrying an Egyptian and Norwegian girl!? A blonde and a dark one, that should be a good or should I say nice combination!!? Marry the Egyptian one first and when you are fed up with each other I'll come over and .... Well, what I last wrote that was meant to be a joke, because I know that you will try hard to love your wife properly. So I hope you had a laugh when you read it. There are a lot of thoughts I would like to share with you but I just don't dare to talk about that to you or anyone else. It feels good to know that you care about me as a person and not just as a "sex object!." Seriously, I mean it. It feels very nice! But still I think we're gonna lose contact when you are married. You're gonna get married first, I know that! I am not gonna get married now that's for sure. There's none I like so much that makes me think of marriage. So I better get me a good education so that I can support myself so that I don't need a fool of a man to support me if he leaves me and our children. But I hope we'll never lose contact again. And if you ever get married you would be (very) welcome to my wedding and if you have a wife, she will obviously be welcome too. Well this is only wishful thinking. I told you about the girl who has got pregnant, poor little thing. My friend, the boy is not treating her good. She phoned me yesterday and she felt so depressed. Oh, it makes me feel so sad when I hear about things like that because I know how it feels. Oh, it feels just terrible. You know what you want to do but you have to think about the other one who is involved too and if he wants you to have an abortion well, is there anything to do except for having an abortion? Because you like the boy very much and you don't want to lose him 'just because of a baby' and then you go to a hospital and ……… well you know!! Well, it's not just the baby. I'm just trying to tell you, and make you understand how it feels for a girl. And when you've had that abortion you will lose him anyway and you feel helpless. Absolutely terrible. Oh, it makes me cry when I know what she is going through now. I am too sentimental I know that, but that's something I can't change. I am sorry to tell you about this again, but there is so much I can see of myself in the girl! And all the stupid excuses the boy uses of not having the baby. Oh God, it's not fair! You go into the hospital and ………… and afterwards you feel empty, oh so empty. And in a way you start to hate him and you hate yourself after what you have been doing to your body and the baby. And you start thinking of life, why people are doing what they do in different situations and you feel, well nothing really and after a while you'll end up like me. I don't trust anybody! I don't! And I hate myself for thinking the way I do. But I can't help it. I suppose it is a way of protecting myself. I want to be realistic but people tell me I am cold and hard. Do you understand what I mean? I think that's why I think of you, just because "you make me feel me." I can talk to you without being afraid of being laughed at. Well, I haven't got any more paper left so I better end it here. Kiss and love from Heidi.

Postcard post stamped 9th April 1985 from Ulset Post Office in Bergen with the front of the postcard showing a pair of hands clasped together

Thank you very much for your letters! I just want to write this card to you to show you that I think a lot of you. I do <u>really</u> hope that you take care of yourself and that everything works out for you!!!!!!!!!!

Lots of love, Heidi xxxxxxx [i.e. seven kisses]

On 30th June 1995, after having sent him copies of Heidi's letters to me and a full report of my side of the story, I telephoned Harald Vikøyr of Verdens Gang:

F.   *So are you going to do anything about it or not?*

HV.   *I don't think so.*

F.   *You don't think so.*

HV.   *No.*

F.   *Why's that?*

HV.   *… I don't think it's relevant.*

119

F.   *Oh you don't?*

HV.   *No.*

F.   *What, to 13 years of sex-terror, you don't think it's relevant?*

HV.   *No.*

F.   *Why's that?*

HV.   *Well that's my ... ...*

F.   *That's your opinion.*

HV.   *Yes.*

F.   *Are you actually a racist? I mean do you hate Muslims for the sake of it?*

HV.   (laughing, he said:) *No.*

F.   *Putting erotic paranoia and Muslims this, Muslims that.*

HV.   *No.*

F.   *You don't?* [Hate Muslims.]

HV.   *No.*

F.   *Well anyway what about your editor, is he there?*

HV.   *No.*

F.   *He's not there today?*

HV.   *Then you have to call Oslo where the headquarters is.*

F.   *So you're not printing a follow up story, nothing?*

HV.   *It's not quite five* [o'clock] *but er I think I got your lawyer's number* [in London] *but I'm busy doing other things ...*

F.   *So why do you want to bother to ring him if you're not going to do anything?*

HV.   *Er, there might be a story later when the investigation is getting closer.*

F.   *There's no investigation, there's no court case, no nothing, no police, nothing.* [I was thinking of what Commander Krogvold of the Bergen police told me.] *I've talked to everybody and nothing's going to happen. And I tell you something, what you've done has made things worse for Heidi because if you think that I'm going to take the rubbish you've printed, then it'll be worse for her ... You can print your rubbish but if you knew her, if you bothered to investigate her past, then you'd see my statement was all true. There's not one lie in my statement.*

HV.   *Why don't you just forget her?*

F.   *Because she's made allegations to the police that could stick for the future, OK? And I only discovered those allegations nine years later* [of attempted rape.] *And if you knew what they were then you too would do something about it* [and later]... *I'm not going to have your*

120

system [i.e. the newspapers' tactics of print and be dammed] *and your legal system which costs a lot of money and all the processes - I can't be bothered with all that; that's why I wrote those letters to her OK?*

HV.   *I don't think there is anything she* [Heidi] *can do ...*

F.   *Yeah, that's right, so why are you saying there's an investigation?*

HV.   *Well there is an investigation that is started by the police where she lives.*

F.   *In Drammen?*

HV.   *Yeah ... in the article that I wrote it had a comment by the police officer* [who] *started the investigation and he has got the papers and copies of all the things.*

F.   *I got in touch with the Drugs Police Officer at the Norwegian Embassy in February. I gave him all the papers and he sent them to the police* [in Bergen.] *I said, "Do something about my case because ... ..."*

HV.   *So you think you are the one who's...* [been wronged]

F.   *Oh definitely. I asked my lawyer Wesenberg in Bergen in the last week in Christmas to re-open the matter - sue Heidi - last Christmas before I wrote all those letters.*

HV.   *May I have a talk to Mr. Wesenberg?*

F.   *He's at Court in Oslo but you can speak to him. You know his office in Bergen.*

[I then explained some more of the background to my employment of Wesenberg. I didn't tell him that the December 1986 allegation was attempted rape at this stage though.]

Letter dated 3rd July 1995 to my London lawyer

Dear Mike,

Heidi Schøne

After we spoke on Friday, I later telephoned the VG Correspondent in Bergen, Harald Vikøyr, of Olebullsplass, 8 -10, 5012 Bergen. He told me that he thought my statement and copy letters were 'not relevant,' but didn't explain why. He said it was the Drammen police who were having the investigation, but again he didn't say what the nature of the investigation was. He was however surprised to learn that I'd instructed a Bergen lawyer last Christmas to see if I could sue Heidi Overaa for perverting the course of justice and also sue the police for wrongful arrest. As you can see from the correspondence, my Bergen lawyer did not complete the enquiries I had requested of him and now he says he's too busy to act for me any more. The VG correspondent said he would contact my Bergen lawyer but I said he wouldn't get much out of him because of the lawyer/client confidentiality relationship.

Ingunn Røren of Drammens Tidende said nothing would be printed in her paper until "the Court case was over." I told her it was a fantasy that any Court case would materialise and I asked her, over what the Court case would be and where etc. She just said Heidi had told her this. So when I spoke to the Editor, he told me he would go through my statement and Heidi's letters again before considering whether to go to print. "I have your telephone number," he said and asked me to leave it at that.

Bergens Tidende and Dagbladet also have my statement/copy letters and your phone number so I think there is nothing more for us to do until you hear from them. However, I'd like you to stick to doing an absolute minimum on this matter - to save my money - and if the press want to talk to you don't waste your phone bills phoning them - maybe a quick call in due course just to see if anything is happening and arrange it so that they have to phone you back. As you can see the brick wall the Norwegians have put up is very hard and expensive to scale and it is this same hurdle I've had to put up with in using [your firm] in 1990 and my Bergen lawyer last Christmas. The information I require is just not forthcoming. That's why I took matters into my own hands - the legal route is just a waste of time so I decided on direct action myself.

I do hope the Norwegian papers are not someday soon going to print my name in any follow-up story. I personally believe the police in Drammen can't do anything, as there is nothing for them to go on, so it will be interesting as to exactly what the newspapers will do next.

For your information the newspapers' addresses are listed below:

[The names of the three newspapers who printed my story and their addresses are given in this letter together with the name of one National newspaper who did not print my story. The names were also given of Heidi's lawyer, Heidi's psychiatrist and the address of the Oslo Bar Association.]

I did once telephone [the Oslo Bar Association] when my Bergen lawyer wasn't answering my letters - he wasn't making those further essential enquiries of the police - later claiming he was too busy and the Oslo Bar Association said they could write to him and tell him to get on with it. I didn't request them to do this, but I should have. Now my Bergen lawyer who had a pipeline into the police has abandoned me.

At the moment I've had enough of it all - the work I have had to do just to get my side of the story to the press and discover what they plan to do next has drained me. Cheers for now.

Yours sincerely,

The correspondence continued:

Letter dated 17th July 1995 from my Bergen lawyer

Heidi Overaa (Schøne)

I refer to your letter of 9th July 1995 in which you asked me to make further enquiries from the Bergen police.

I regret to inform you that I'm not willing to represent you further. The main reason for my decision is that you are not willing to accept my advice.

Yours sincerely,

Helge Wesenberg

Letter dated 26th October 1995 from my Bergen lawyer

Re Heidi Overaa/Schøne

I have been informed of your phone call today requesting/demanding further grounds why I no longer will represent you. I have already stated my reasons in my letter of July 17th 1995. It is an obvious reason for an attorney to withdraw from a case when the client acts contrary to the attorney's advice and recommendation.

I remind you that my definite and unequivocal advice to you was no further approach towards Heidi Overaa or her family. Then I gave you my considered opinion as regards your question of suing Heidi Overaa and/Bergen Politikammer [Bergen police].

An attorney has the privilege of withdrawing from a case in which he has no confidence. Particularly so, when the client in addition acts contrary to the attorney's advice and in a way that the attorney strongly disapproves.

In addition to the above mentioned and despite my pressing for payments you have only paid half of my fee.

I precisely defined that the last element was not conclusive as regards my decision given to you in my letter of July 17th 1995. At that time, I believed that you would pay my fees. Today, October 26th 1995, I find that I will not receive payment and this will be an additional element supporting my decision.

Yours sincerely,

Helge Wesenberg

Letter dated 7th November 1995 from my Bergen lawyer

Re Heidi Overaa (Schøne)

Referring to your letter of October 29, 1995, I once again precisely define that I no longer represent you.

This means that I have neither further information for you, nor will I discuss with you considerations and recommendations already given in my letter of February 28, this year.

I hereby inform you that I will not answer further letters and / or phone calls.

Helge Wesenberg

Attorney

Letter dated 9th November 1995 from Heidi's lawyer, Tomm Skaug

Re Heidi Overaa

I refer to our previous telephone conversations and your letter regarding the above.

Please take notice that my client's mail is being redirected and eventual future letters from you - according to agreement - will not be reforwarded. On behalf of my client, I consider our connection as permanently terminated.

Kind regards,

Tomm Skaug

Dear Mike,

Heidi Schøne

I enclose a copy of my Bergen lawyer's last three letters to me, July 17th, October 26th and November 7th.

My comments on these letters are:

For July 17th the man said in one of his earlier letters that he could no longer represent me because he was busy in Court from the spring to the autumn: you should have this earlier letter. The story changed by July 17th when [previously] I said I'd wait until he was free again [to investigate further for me]. For 26th October refer to his second and third paragraphs - I only made further approaches to Heidi Overaa (and not her family) because my Bergen lawyer's answers in January were quite inadequate and I felt he would not bother to make further and more complete enquiries of the police. I wasn't prepared to sit in silence whilst suffering the allegation of attempted rape from December 1986. So I immediately phoned up Heidi Overaa and challenged her as to this and she gave no direct reply before putting the phone down. As you know I quickly responded to my Bergen lawyer's January letter and until now he did nothing more. My complaints as to his reports are on your file and these revolve around the Bergen police's last letter to your colleague from 1990 advising that I could in theory face prison and that I offended a certain Norwegian penal statute.

So with my Bergen lawyer prevaricating I acted on my own initiative. In a phone call to him <u>before</u> the main newspapers came out, he acknowledged to me that more needed to be done by him - but he was afraid the Bergen police would re-open the attempted rape allegation case. I assured him Heidi was a habitual liar and surely her past history by itself could lend considerable weight to my denial. I said I had nothing to fear and could he please proceed. He didn't even want to write to Heidi to put her on notice. My [last] phone call to my Bergen lawyer had to be cut short in the spring and I never spoke to him again. I just wrote - with no effect. Before those newspaper reports, the Bergen lawyer could not have known I was trying to get information from Heidi Overaa. I think it's a red herring his saying that he "withdraws" from my case when I acted contrary to his advice and recommendations. His withdrawal from my case I feel came as soon as he completed his January letter to me. I accused him of believing what he read in the newspapers, later. Again the actions of mine which he "strongly disapproved of" is another red herring. He could only have known from the newspapers of these reports reaching Heidi's neighbours. Reports which caused Heidi to tell me on the phone made her neighbours believe I was a "good person"; something she said she had to "put right by putting the truth to the newspapers": and that she "could have, but didn't, tell the papers a load of lies." Well, she told many lies and distorted much indeed. But she suspected I was recording her conversations so she was making self-serving statements.

Regarding only paying half my Bergen lawyer's fees - I repeatedly told him he'd get the rest once the additional information came forth. I politely indicated that I was not prepared to play the same old game; pay up the lot; then argue for months to come and paying more and more; on and on.

So, you have my Bergen lawyer's telephone number and if you can speak to him please get to the crux of the matter. He'll do his best to discuss his red herrings. I

124

cannot believe his contention that I cannot see copies of my own letters in the police possession. That I cannot see what the evidence is against me, especially the evidence that surfaced after I left Bergen in February 1990.

Further, it might also be a good idea to phone Tomm Skaug because all I can see is confusion on his part. I'm not entirely sure if he's spoken to 'his client' more than once. He told me that Heidi had never told him about her 1986 allegation of attempted rape. Surely, if it was true that would be the first thing she mentions to her own lawyer. And that reminds me - why can't the police in Bergen supply details of Heidi's rape allegations against the Bergen shopkeeper that was reported to the police - so Heidi tells me. Believe me, she loves making false accusations about other people's sexual associations and her own. Heidi told Drammens Tidende and VG and me that she had a great case against me and indeed the papers themselves told me this and would not print my reply until the case came to Court. I told them that there never was any such case. Heidi had been lying as I knew she was. Her lawyer keeps saying Heidi is now married and wants to be left alone. I said if things had been sorted out properly in the first place - years ago - the lingering resentment would not be there in 1995. After all it's not my fault that the matter hasn't been sorted out. I told Skaug that an allegation of attempted rape is such a serious matter for me as it is an attempt to ruin me (imagine if this came to light whilst I was still in custody in February 1990), that Heidi's conversion to New Age Christianity in 1990 was hypocrisy in the light of maintaining false allegations later to the police. Moreover the fact of her wanting to convert me to her brand of Christianity and possible marriage has been ignored by everyone.

Well, I think if you could find another Norwegian firm, in Oslo, not Bergen then I can put specific instructions to them on the basis that if they can get the specific information from the police then they will get paid. I would also be interested to see if you think my Bergen lawyer has been negligent in his advice.

Yours sincerely,

P.S. The fact that someone called 'Peter' phoned my father's home up at 2 in the morning and again at 6 in the morning a few weeks ago, saying "something terrible" had happened and could he have my phone number (which is ex-directory) and when my father's wife, (his second wife) refused, an Englishman a couple of days later phoned me up at home telling me to watch my "fucking back 'cos someone's going to break your legs" (only Heidi could have given him my phone number), means that Heidi has no legal case and so resorts to alternative tactics.

What I had resorted to in the face of being stone-walled by the Norwegian newspaper correspondents, Heidi's lawyer, and my Bergen lawyer following my correspondence and numerous and long telephone calls, was to carry on sending copies of the fact sheet detailing Heidi's past that I had had translated into Norwegian. My reasoning was that if the newspapers were not going to print my side of the story, then I would send my own 'newspaper' in the form of this fact sheet to as many people in Norway as possible. I did this by copying from tourist brochures the names and addresses of every hotel in Bergen and Oslo, together with any other business address I could find in other brochures that were stored in my cupboard at home. It was maybe this action of mine that had got back to my Bergen lawyer which had so abruptly put him off acting for me. But if anyone thought that I was going to sit here and do nothing and rot whilst total lies became established as 'true facts' then they had another thing coming; they do say that God helps those who help themselves! I knew by the desperate nocturnal phone calls from someone calling himself 'Peter from Sweden' to my father's home, whose number was listed in International Enquiries, and the physical threats of violence over the phone to me by a man presumably acting at Heidi's behest, meant that my private initiative was bearing fruit. The newspapers know they can easily beat 'the little man in the street' who hasn't got the resources to mount an effective counter-offensive. Only an unorthodox attack by me would work and in truth it worked very well.

125

Come 1996 I had begun regularly to talk to Torill Sorte, the policewoman in Heidi's local police station in Mjøndalen, who was handling Heidi's case. I recorded all of my telephone conversations with her as I did also with Heidi and everyone else I telephoned in Norway.

In March 1996 I had the following conversations.

Telephone conversation with Svein Jensen, policeman at the Mjøndalen Police Station:

SJ.   *Jensen*

F.   *Right, Mr. Jensen, it's Mr. Delaware.*

SJ.   *Hi!*

F.   *Yeah, hi there. I had these newspaper articles translated, Drammens Tidende, and Verdens Gang. I had them translated last week and in it I read that I've threatened to kill Heidi's nine year old son, that I've threatened to kill her neighbours unless they give me Heidi's address, that I've written 400 obscene letters and made obscene phone calls and that my mother wanted to put me in a mental hospital. It's rubbish all this and I obviously think this is dreadful stuff to print about me and I was wondering if you have any evidence for any of this apart from Heidi's word.*

SJ.   *No, there is nothing other than ... her word.*

F.   *I'm really upset about this threat to kill her nine year old son because nothing is further from the truth... Are the newspapers saying to you: "What are you going to do about him threatening to kill everybody?" Are they waiting for your response – the newspapers? Are they waiting for you to talk to them?*

SJ.   *Perhaps they only write it because she took contact with the newspapers. The newspapers have not tried to speak to us about it.*

F.   *The newspapers gave me your number.*

SJ.   *Our number?*

F.   *Yeah, they gave me your telephone number.*

SJ.   *They were in contact with us I think when this ... when she had contacted the newspapers, then after that we haven't heard from them.*

F.   *Yeah ... you don't believe her do you?*

SJ.   *No, I don't think I do.*

F.   *Oh good, thank God for that because ... have you got even any of her letters that I wrote to her?*

SJ.   *I'm not sure. The case is with another person who is with us [Policewoman Torill Sorte]... but there are some letters you wrote to the neighbours and things like that.*

F.   *The stuff I wrote to you in my long report ... have you been able to check any of the things to make sure you believe me?*

SJ.   *No, but there are so much in the case from how she tells us so that I don't trust her so very much ... ...*

[and later]:

F. *Am I going to be arrested if I come to Norway?*

SJ. *I don't think so, but the case isn't closed yet, but I think it will be in a short time.*

F. *Have you spoken to Heidi in the last few weeks?*

SJ. *I haven't, but I know Torill has tried to speak to her. I don't know if she has spoken to her yet.*

F. *Succeeded,* [in speaking to Heidi] *yes … thank you very much and I shall ring next week.*

SJ. *Yes, do that.*

F. *Thank you, bye bye.*

SJ. *Bye bye.*

Telephone conversation with Torill Sorte the following week:

F. *Yes, hi, good morning. Is that Torill?*

TS. *Oh yes!*

F. *Yeah, this is Frederick Delaware here.*

TS. *Yes.*

F. *I understand you've been looking into this matter with Heidi Schøne. Did you get my letter?*
[I'd sent her a full report of my side of the story plus copies of Heidi's letters to me.]

TS. *Yes I did.*

F. *Now has it been of any use to you, all my stuff?*

TS. *I have talked to Heidi's husband and he told me that they want to … um … put the case away and not do anything with it so I … he wanted to go home and talk to Heidi and I haven't heard anything about it after that.*

F. *When was that? When did you speak to them?*

TS. *Oh, three weeks ago.*

F. *The thing is you see, I'm not very happy to leave it at that because she has done dreadful things by telling the newspapers* [and I reiterated the basic facts]… *and I wanted to convince you that she was lying and I wanted you to actually talk to her in your police station and say: "Look – these are such terrible lies … how can you get this man into trouble?"*

TS. *I have tried to come into contact with Heidi but she don't want to come here and talk to me. I don't know why.*

F. *Yeah, you see that's exactly the point … she's avoiding you because she knows she's an awful liar.*

127

TS.	*I hope I come in contact with Heidi soon so we can close this case and what you want to do with it after that is up to you.*

F.	*I want you to honestly try and establish without doubt in your minds that she is telling lies ...*

TS.	*I want to come in contact with Heidi. I shall write to her again and tell her she'll have to meet me on my office ... and I shall confront her about what she has said and what you say and then we can talk again. I shall try to come and contact her next week ... if you call me in two weeks.*

F.	*Do you have the power to charge her with perverting the course of justice? In telling you this about me threatening to kill everybody she wants me to be arrested and taken to court. That is definitely perverting the course of justice.*

TS.	*Yes.*

F.	*Something has to be done to her. To make her realise she can't do these things.*

TS.	*I see, but my problem is that I never have spoken to Heidi.*

F.	*Oh, you haven't?*

TS.	*No, because she don't want to come here. Every time I ask her to come here, her husband have come to me.*

F.	*Yes, exactly ... that illustrates my case perfectly because she knows she is an awful liar.*

TS.	*But I don't want to give up before I have talked to her.*

F.	*Exactly, so ...... you take your time. But the only way you are going to talk to her is if you go and see her in her home, and you use your authority as a police officer.*

TS.	*But I will try again and come in contact with her and if she don't come here, I will go home to her and try to talk to her there.*

F.	*Ask* [Runar Schøne] *why he speaks to me in tongues and in Biblical language.*

TS.	*I shall talk to him about that.*

F.	*Finally, there is one more thing. Do you think the newspapers will print an apology to me?*

TS.	*I don't think so ... then you have to talk to the newspapers.*

F.	*Once you finish the case, would you talk to the newspapers and tell them what your conclusions are. They will want to know from you what your ...*

TS.	*I have no right to go to the newspapers because I don't have authority to talk about the case with the newspapers.*

F.	*But they came to you. They contacted you didn't they?*

TS.	*That's the right way ... but I can't go to them. But you can.*

F.	*Also when you do go down there* [to Heidi's] *speak to her neighbours. Ask them if I've threatened their lives and the rest of it. Anyway, thank you very much and I'll give you a call in maybe two weeks time.*

TS.	*Do that.*
F.	*Thank you.*
TS.	*Yes.*
F.	*OK. Bye bye.*
TS.	*Bye bye.*

Conversation with Ingunn Røren, journalist with Drammens Tidende, at her home on 25th March 1996:

A man answered.

F.	*Yes, hello good evening. Is ... I presume it's your wife, Ingunn Røren.*
Man	*Er OK.*
F.	*The journalist? Yeah?*
Man	*The journalist. One moment.* [He speaks in Norwegian to Ingunn Røren.]
IR.	*Hello.*
F.	*Yes, Hi there Ingunn, it's Frederick Delaware here, sorry to phone you at your home.*
IR.	*Ah huh.*
F.	*It's just that about three weeks ago I had your article translated into English and see that you've written that I've threatened to kill Heidi's son.*
IR.	*That you?*
F.	*...... threatened to kill Heidi's son.*
IR.	*Yes according to Heidi.*
F.	*You wrote that yeah, and you believe her do you?*
IR.	*I'm not sure but that's what she said and I'm not saying that you did, but I'm saying that's what she said you did.*
F.	*Cos, I certainly didn't and there's no way that you should print this without er ... you can't print this stuff without some evidence. You know she's been in a psychiatric unit, you know her past because you had those letters* [my fact sheet] *translated into Norwegian.*
IR.	*Yes.*
F.	*And it's just disgraceful. And my mother has never wanted to put me in a mental hospital and you could have checked that out easily. That's an obvious lie to make because her parents wanted to put her in a psychiatric unit when she was a teenager.*
IR.	*But how come you're still so interested in Heidi?*
F.	*Because I've just discovered what you've printed.*

IR.   *Yes, but I thought you read that a long time ago.*

F.   *No, no, no I didn't. I only read one article* [at the time] *which was* [Bergens Tidende.]

IR.   *Yeah, but I've only written one article.*

F.   *No, it was in all the newspapers. It was in Bergens Tidende and that's what I had translated. Only four weeks ago did I have your article translated and it's just as well isn't it? It's a good thing that I know what you've written about me and that I've threatened to kill her neighbours, her, her family ... I've written 400 obscene letters ... it's all rubbish. And you know perfectly well it's rubbish and you know also the reason I sent those books on Aids and Abortion is because she slept with someone taking heroin - she knew she could catch Aids; she knew she was putting herself at risk and she had two abortions.*

IR.   *What's that to me?*

F.   *Because I bloody well slept with her while she was ………*

IR.   *Yeah, but that's your problem.*

F.   *Yeah, but it's also her fault as well. It's my problem for sure but you should know the reason why I sent those letters, to try and teach her a lesson. You've printed something that's totally misled the public just to get a sexy....*

IR.   *Yes, but if you have a problem with that, you have to contact the editor.*

F.   *Yeah, I will contact the editor ... but she* [Heidi] *doesn't even want to contact the police. She's avoiding them because they haven't closed the case yet and they don't believe her.*

IR.   *She has contacted the police and they do believe her.*

F.   *They don't believe her.*

IR.   *They do.*

F.   *When was the last time she spoke to the police then? She has never spoken to Torill ... ... never!*

IR.   *She has spoken to Nedre Eiker* [Torill Sorte's station], *the police in the community where she's living... She has spoken to them and they have a report on you.*

F.   *You gave me her number* [Torill Sorte's].

IR.   *Yes.*

F.   *And Svein Jensen told me he doesn't believe her but they have to let Torill speak to her and Torill has been trying to get in touch with her for months and Heidi's avoiding them.*

IR.   *That's not what I've heard. If you have a problem with what I wrote you have to contact the editor.*

F.   *Yeah I will contact the editor, but ...*

IR.   *It's his responsibility.*

F.   *Yeah, but you wrote the story.*

IR.   *But it's his responsibility. He is the one who selects what to print and what not to print.*

F.   *Well OK, when the police have…. She's not bringing a case … I mean ten months* [since the newspapers came out]… *I wish she would bring a case so I can show her up in Court, because she's got no evidence. There's no 400* [obscene] *letters - she destroyed them all* [so Heidi told the newspapers] *and you'd have thought she'd have kept them wouldn't you for her case?*

IR.   *I've seen some old letters and she has not destroyed them.* [I was specifically referring to the 400 obscene letters every single one of which Heidi said she destroyed as per Verdens Gang report of 26.5.1995 but Ingunn Røren misunderstood me and referred to other letters I'd written].

F.   *And what's wrong with the letters; what have I said in the letters that's so bad?*

IR.   *There were lots of things but that's your problem; you have to take it up with Heidi.*

F.   *Yeah, I will take it up with Heidi but also I'll take it up with you when I pay you a visit and if I have to bring the police with me I will so help me God; you're not gonna get away with this. You didn't print my name either did you? Why's that?*

IR.   *What, I didn't … … …*

F.   *Why didn't you print my name in the newspapers if it's all true?*

IR.   *Why should I?*

F.   *Because every other newspaper does if they've got their facts right.*

IR.   *Yeah, but if you still have a problem on this, please call the editor.*

F.   *I will call the editor, but you are going to have to face me even if I get the police and I'll get their blessing first … I'll ask them first.*

IR.   *I don't think you'll get it.*

F.   *I think I will because they said to me that they cannot contact the newspapers themselves but I can and I will say to them - "Look, I'm gonna go round there and you're welcome to be at the front door when I do" and if they don't want to be there then I'll face you and your bloody editor and you try and deal with us, OK because you're not getting away with it …*

IR.   *Call the editor.*

F.   *Yeah, I'll call the editor but you are the one that wrote the story. It's you …*

IR.   *He's the one* [the editor] *who's responsible and his name is Odde and you have to call him at work tomorrow.*

F.   *Yeah, I'll certainly do that but don't you worry, you're not gonna get away with it…*

IR.   *Yes, yes, yes, bye bye.*

F.   *Yeah, piss off you bitch!!*

The next day I telephoned the newspaper and spoke to a Mr. Strand, another editor at Drammens Tidende:

Answer	*"Drammens Tidende,"* a woman responded.
F.	*It's your editor I'd like to speak to ... what's his name?*
Answer	*Yes, wait a minute ... Hans Arne Odde.*
	[then after a minute's wait] *I couldn't find him - he's in a meeting.*
F.	*Has he got a secretary?*
Answer	*I shall try: Just a moment please* [and I was then put through to her.]
F.	*Hello, good morning. I was wondering when your editor Hans Odde ...*
Secretary	*Yes, just a moment please.* [And I was put through to a man.]
F.	*Yes, hi, good morning. Are you Hans the editor?*
S.	*I am one of the editors, yes.* [But not the Chief Editor, Hans Odde. This chap was a Mr. Strand.]
F.	*Oh one of the editors. My name's Frederick Delaware, and you did a story on me last May about Heidi Schøne and I had that article translated only four weeks ago and it's obviously calculated to give me a lot of trouble, especially as you've written that I've attempted* [I should have said 'threatened'] *to kill that girl's son, all his neighbours and all the other stuff which is all complete rubbish and I wanted to speak to the editor who allowed this idiot - Ingunn Røren- to first of all believe that stuff and secondly your editor* [who] *allowed it to be printed because you should've known that the girl who made those accusations has been in a mental hospital. So I want to speak to your editor just to see how this was allowed to happen.*
S.	*I have never spoken to you before but I think you have been speaking to another of the editors and you have been speaking to this reporter.*
F.	*Yes, I spoke to her yesterday.*
S.	*So I know you have been in touch with many of our people.*
F.	*Yeah, that's right because what you've done is upside down and you should've known before what this girl was all about because you had reports in Norwegian that all her neighbours received. Now she's been telling lies and trying basically to get me put in prison by making up all sorts of rubbish – that I've tried to rape her. That I've tried* [I meant threatened] *to kill her, her neighbours, her son, her family. That I've written 400 obscene letters and thank God that the police, now, do not believe her ... and in fact she's avoiding them. I want to know how your story could possibly be printed, it's so.... I know you have to try and get sexy stories.........*
S.	*No ... ...*
F.	*And all the rest of it ... ...*
S.	*We don't have to.*
F.	*I cannot understand, when you knew beforehand the girl was in a psychiatric unit and all the problems that she's had and yet you go and print this stuff ... if it wasn't for the evidence I'd kept ... if I didn't keep some of her letters ... I only kept a few.... The rest I threw away.... But I kept a few and thank God I did because the police have read them. I want to try and prosecute her ... but I must first of all discover how you come to print*

this story. I'm phoning so many months later because it was only four weeks ago that I had your particular article translated and I'd never read before that I've [threatened] to kill her son and I want to know from you what day I made this threat. Whether I made it in a letter, a phone call. Whether she told her neighbours. Whether she reported this threat to the police straight away. I want to know these facts.

S.   *I have no comment on that.*

F.   *Yeah, that's right. I'm not gonna let this go because that girl, like so many people in your country, ruins lives …… those love letters that she sent me that you've got obviously disprove that I've been terrorising her for thirteen years, so I need to speak to the person who allowed your reporter to print and if I can I will have your people in Court.*

S.   *OK.*

F.   *I understand your chief editor is Hans …Odde. Is he free at the moment?*

S.   *No, he's not – he's in a meeting.*

F.   *So, when the police have finished, once they can find Heidi to talk to, I will ring you again and ask you to give them a call so that we can get to the bottom of this story, but I bet you won't print anything will you … you won't print the truth … the fact of what her past is and what she's done, will you? You'll just keep quiet.*

S.   *We'll try to print what is true – yes for sure we will.*

F.   *Well that's good to hear. That's nice to hear. OK. Well what I will do…… if you can speak to your editor and tell him… … once I've spoken to Torill Sorte and Svein Jensen in the Nedre Eiker police - once they've interviewed Heidi, I will then be in touch with you and you can ring the police so that we can have their conclusions.*

S.   *What are the names of these policemen?*

F.   *Torill [Sorte] and Svein Jensen – they are the Nedre Eiker police and the only reason I knew about them is because Ingunn Røren gave me their phone number and their phone number is (32) 878170. Torill tells me that with Heidi – "Every time I try and get in touch with her, her husband calls me to say they want to drop the case." Now if I have been threatening anyone's lives …I've been writing 400 obscene letters, making filthy phone calls … and you say my mother wanted to put me in a mental hospital, that I do obscene things in front of her [Heidi] and I make her watch, then that should be enough of a case shouldn't it to go to the Courts don't you think? Don't you think so if it's true?*

S.   *Well, I will not comment on that. All stories have at least er two … …*

F.   *Sides to it. You knew her past. You knew she was sleeping with someone taking heroin.*

S.   *I didn't.*

F.   *No, no, but the editor did because all those… I sent literally hundreds and hundreds of those Norwegian articles [my fact sheet] to everyone in Norway. Hundreds of people, everyone under 'The Sun' cos I'm sick and tired of being accused of attempting to rape someone. I'd never do this. She's been raped … she was raped by a Bergen shopkeeper in the 1980's. She was beaten up by her boyfriend in 1990 … anyway someone in your office knew about her past. They had the whole picture and they said it was false … they said I'd been making false accusations and course comments – none of it was false. I'm a lawyer and so help me God I would not tell a single lie.*

S.   *What did you say your name is?* .

F.   *Delaware. What's your name by the way?*

S.   *S-T-R-A-N-D.* [He spelt it out for me.]

F.   *Mr. Strand?*

S.   *Yeah.*

F.   *OK, it's very kind of you to be patient enough to talk to me cos I'm afraid I did lose my temper yesterday evening – well I didn't lose my temper except at the very end with Ingunn Røren.*

S.   *She felt a little threatened.*

F.   *I will call again once the police have finished with Heidi.*

S.   *Yep, OK.*

F.   *Bye bye.*

S.   *Bye bye.*

Conversation of 26th March1996 with Nils Rettersdøl:

F.   *Yes, hello, good morning, is Mr. Nils Rettersdøl at home?*

Answer   *Yes, just a moment.*

F.   *Thank you.*

NR.   *Er, Rettersdøl.*

F.   *Good morning.*

NR.   *Morning.*

F.   *Hi, I hope you speak some English – you do? Good. My name's Frederick Delaware... I'm the chap in England that you did a newspaper article on concerning Heidi Schøne.*

NR.   *Concerning?*

F.   *Heidi Schøne. ... You are the psychiatrist aren't you?*

NR.   *Yes.*

F.   *That's right, I mean, you did an article on erotic paranoia, d'you remember?*

NR.   *No, I'm not quite sure.*

F.   *Well I've got your photograph in the newspaper.*

NR.   *Yes, but I don't think I wrote an article. It must have been some sort of interview or something.*

134

F.　　　　　*Yeah, but you must have read it.*

NR.　　　　*Yeah.*

F.　　　　　*Yeah. It's just that ... um, I was rather ... ... this is ... what they've written in the newspapers is... it's all rubbish. I just wanted to tell you the truth of the matter. Now, did the newspapers show you those reports that I was sending to her neighbours, did they show you that?*

NR.　　　　*Er, no. I think I have been busy ... it was just a short interview or something.*

F.　　　　　*Yeah, well the thing is this, they have used you in a most despicable way because this girl has been in a psychiatric unit herself in Lier and before I met her she'd had two abortions, she tried to kill herself twice and the reason I went to Norway in 1990 and got arrested is because I wanted to confront her because she had been sleeping with a boy who had been injecting heroin, OK? And I had slept with her myself once ... only to discover that ... and she didn't tell me that she was sleeping with someone else and he was taking heroin ... but I went there to Norway to confront her about the heroin aspect and I was sitting in her sister's flat upstairs and the police came to arrest me. Now she has told them that I wanted to kidnap her son, and I'm reading in the newspapers ... I've just had them translated yesterday and I see she said that I've threatened to kill her son, that I've threatened to kill her, her family, that I've sent 400 obscene letters ... I've done none of this at all ... I have not sent one obscene letter ... I'm a lawyer and I would never expose myself to this shame and in fact the newspapers have said that she has destroyed all these letters [the 400 obscene ones]. Now I've kept some of her early letters and I've sent them all to the newspapers, together with a long report and they've printed nothing and I've spoken to the policeman in Mjøndalen and he understands my position and he's going to ... [and I continued with the other disturbing aspects of Heidi's life]. I thought that you were interviewed and given all the information?*

NR.　　　　*No, no. It has just been some general remarks. I think on the ...*

F.　　　　　*I thought so because initially I was extre...['extremely' I was going to say.]*

NR.　　　　*Nothing else – I didn't know anything about the case.*

F.　　　　　*She's pictured in the newspaper reading a book on Aids. Now this book ... she became a Christian [and I explained about the speaking in tongues of Runar Schøne on the phone to me].*

NR.　　　　*Are you in England now?*

F.　　　　　*Yes, I'm in England. I'm at home now, but I've got to do something about this ... I'm planning something, I don't know what ... but this is just 180 degrees off the truth. [And I proceeded to tell the whole background of Heidi and justified my writing so many postcards and letters to Heidi, questioning her actions.] Do you understand my motives?*

NR.　　　　*Yes, yes.*

F.　　　　　*When I read this about erotic paranoia, I just couldn't believe it, because I pride myself on being as decent as I can [be]... what the newspapers have said is so shameful, I just wanted you to understand this.*

NR.　　　　*Yes, yes, yes. But you can be sure that I didn't know anything about the case ... the comment from an interview ... but generally, quite generally ...*

F.　　　　　*That's right; I though so because I couldn't believe that you would basically put your reputation on the line.*

NR.   *No, no.*

F.   *They didn't even interview her psychiatrist called Dr. Broch.*

NR.   *In Lier?*

F.   *That's right; they didn't interview him ... and the newspapers... I said "Could you please print my side of the story," and they've done nothing.*

NR.   *Well that's quite ordinary for a newspaper.*

F.   *But it just seems so far from the truth that ...*

NR.   *Yes, they write it from their angle you know.*

F.   *Mmm – Sex sells. Well OK sir, I'm very grateful for you listening to me and I just can rest easy now that you know my side of the story.*

NR.   *Completely.*

F.   *Right, thank you very much.*

NR.   *Yes, all the best.*

F.   *Bye bye.*

NR.   *Goodbye.*

Conversation No. 2 with Nils Rettersdøl in April 1996:

F.   *Yes, hi, good morning. Is that Mr. Rettersdøl?*

NR.   *Yes.*

F.   *Yes, Hi. It's Frederick Delaware here.*

NR.   *Yes, yes.*

F.   *I'm sorry to trouble you at home again, but did you get my material?*

NR.   *All your papers, yes.*

F.   *Have you managed to read through it?*

NR.   *Yes, yes.*

F.   *I don't want to put words into your mouth but have you changed your ... or got an understanding of my motives?*

NR.   *Yes, well I have not had any special opinion about it before you know ... because what I said was on a very general level without knowing anything about your case actually.*

F.   *Why can you without knowing about me, why can you ... ... make these ... I know they were general statements but why ....*

NR.   *I have made no statements about you.*

F.   *What did they actually say to you then, the newspapers?*

NR.   *Just asked about these ... a general ... ...*

F.   *What scenario did they put to you? What was the picture that they gave you? About me.*

NR.   *I don't think they gave me very much picture about you actually because I told them I couldn't say anything about your case. It was more to answer on a general level.*

F.   *They must have said, you know he's um ...*

NR.   *No, I think it stands there also that you, that some doctors in Bergen had had the opinion that you had such a ... erotic paranoia or something like that.*

F.   *Yeah, well do you think that having read the stuff that I've sent you that I'm suffering from ... ... [erotic paranoia]*

NR.   *No I don't think so according to what you have written.*

F.   *Yeah. It's just that obviously I know you probably have seen a lot of patients and you have to deal with them smartly and kindly but I honestly wanted to ... ...you know, because it was such a shock to read all this about attempting to kill everybody....*

NR.   *Yes, yes, yes ... all newspapers are always ... at least some of them are ... ...*

F.   *Well it was all of them this time wasn't it? It was the three biggest newspapers ... ...*

NR.   *Verdens Gang, that is a ... sort ... like Daily Mirror.*

F.   *But Bergens Tidende ...*

NR.   *Yes, that is a rather serious one.*

F.   *They wrote a lot about how bad Muslims are and about a Muslim suffering from erotic paranoia and that bearing in mind what Heidi ... the number of affairs she's had ... it's rather hypocritical of the press to write that and you know it could have ... if 'The Sun' newspaper had got hold of that ... then God knows what I've had to ... go to the moon or something and they still can ... they still might get hold of this stuff and for your information Heidi has not spoken to the police once – she refuses to go and see them. I don't suppose you're going to ring the newspapers and tell them off are you?*

NR.   *No, I don't think ... this is rather an old history isn't it?*

F.   *Well, yeah, but it's still ... ...*

NR.   *I think the best for you would just be to drop it.*

F.   *To drop it?*

NR.   *Yeah.*

F.   *It still hurts ... it hurts very much.*

NR.   *It hurts but I think it hurts more to take all this ... and go through it all ... every thing ... it's very hurting I think.*

F.   *Do you think she is just a wicked girl or is she suffering from something?*

NR.   *Well that's difficult for me to say.*

F.   *Yeah.*

NR.   *I think you'd be best in dropping it actually because it makes always a lot of trouble if you start up again such a case.*

F.   *Forgetting about it would ...*

NR.   *That's of course impossible.*

F.   *Forgetting about it is ... particularly as she could have ruined me by those allegations ... ... is a bit much. That's why people go to court to prosecute people for perverting the course of justice. It's something that's hard to accept and I felt she had to be taught a lesson. I know she's learnt some kind of lesson because all her neighbours know about her past ... through those letters I sent. Well OK I'll leave it at that and thanks for talking to me anyway.*

NR.   *I wish you every happiness.*

F.   *Thank you very much indeed, thank you.*

NR.   *Bye bye.*

F.   *Bye bye.*

During the second week in April 1996 I spoke again to Torill Sorte:

Police Receptionist   *Lensmannkrontroller* [which means 'Police' in Norwegian].

F.   *Hi, good morning, is Torill Kjennås back yet please?* [Her full name was Torill Sorte Kjennås but she preferred to be known just as Torill Sorte.]

Police   *Yes, just a moment.*

F.   *Thank you.*

TS.   *Sorte.*

F.   *It's Freddy.*

TS.   *Hello.*

F.   *Yes, hi there. So, any news?*

TS.   *No!* [she exclaimed] *Because I tried to get her before ... Easter ... and I drove over to her and she wasn't at home. I tried to call her and I have sent her a note, so I hope to hear from her, but I haven't heard anything yet, no.*

F.   *You couldn't speak to her on the phone then?*

TS.   *I haven't get her* (ha! ha!) *I haven't ring her* [she meant spoken to her].

F.   *Huh?*

TS.   *Nobody's taking the phone.*

F.   *So you think she's in hospital or something? Is she having a baby or something?*

TS.   *No, I don't think so.*

F.   *Have they moved house?*

TS.   *No, they live at the same place. But maybe she have been out on some holiday, I don't know. So I try again and I hope to hear from her.*

F.   *Keep trying.*

TS.   *Yes I am doing that.*

F.   *I still cannot understand why she's not ... she's normally so keen to tell everyone how nasty I've been and ... ...*

TS.   *Not any longer I think.*

F.   *I think when she told these stories to the newspapers, she probably thought I would never read them ... I would never see them. It was only good luck because the lawyer I was using at the time sent me one article and then I went to the Norwegian Church and saw all the others and I nearly died of shock ... seeing them. All right, so what shall I do? Ring you in another week?*

TS.   *Um, yes. Try to call me again. I am trying but I don't have any luck yet. But I write to her the last day before Easter, so I hope.*

F.   *Yeah, so did I. I wrote to her too. I just wrote and told her that I had those articles translated and told her that ...how dare she write such rubbish. I also spoke to the newspapers and asked them why they print this stuff and they said "Because she told us."*

TS.   *OK I'll try again, ring me in a week or something.*

F.   *How do you spell your surname?*

TS.   *Torill.*

F.   *Your second name?*

TS.   *Sorte: S-O-R-T-E.*

F.   *It's Torill Sorte?*

TS.   *Yes.*

F.   *Is that Norwegian?*

TS.   *That's Norwegian. Ha! ha! ha!*

F.   *Oh is it?*

TS.   *It's 'Black' in English.*

F.   *Huh?*

TS.	*It means 'Black' in English.*
F.	*Does it?*
TS.	*Yes, ha! ha! ha!*
F.	*Well, OK. It's a pleasure to talk to you actually. You only work a few days a week do you?*
TS.	*No, I work everyday, yes, but I have a baby for a year or so.*
F.	*Oh, have you. Ah! Lovely.*
TS.	*Now, I started working again.*
F.	*Yeah, well good luck. I'll speak to you again in a week or so.*
TS.	*Yes.*
F.	*Thank you very much.*
TS.	*OK.*
F.	*Bye bye.*
TS.	*Bye bye.*

17th April 1996 conversation:

Police	*Nedre Eiker Lensmannkontroll God dag.*
F.	*Good morning. Torill Sorte please. Is she in today?*
Police	*Yes, one moment.*
TS.	*Sorte.*
F.	*Yeah, hi there Torill, it's only Frederick here again ... Er, have you any news at all?*
TS.	*Er ...*
F.	*Guess not?*
TS.	[suppressing a slight laugh] *Heidi stay here now and I talk to her now.*
F.	*Right now?*
TS.	*Yes.*
F.	*Ah, good.*
TS.	*And you can call me up later. That will be good.*
F.	*What I'd like to do actually is talk to her myself after you've talked to her.*
TS.	*She don't want to talk to you.*

F.   *She doesn't? It's just there's er ...*

TS.   *She don't want to talk to you. You can talk to me ... but not now because I have to talk to Heidi, yes?*

F.   *OK. It's just that I ... I have to sort of ask her what she's er ... these allegations about er ... her son* [threats she made alleging my] *attempting* [I meant threatening] *to kill her son. The* [allegation of attempted] *rape especially and it was important that **I** ask her, you know.*

TS.   *You see she don't like you anymore.*

F.   *Well I know that, but I don't like her, but I still have to talk to her.*

TS.   *No, she don't want to talk to you. You can call me later.*

F.   *When's best?*

TS.   *In an hour, half an hour.*

F.   *OK then thank you very much. Bye bye.*

TS.   *Bye bye.*

I spoke to Torill Sorte again later that day but the policewoman just repeated in general terms what I'd read in the newspapers, but didn't get any of the answers I for so long now required from Heidi Schøne. So I phoned again a few days later.

Call to Torill Sorte on 22nd April 1996:

TS.   *Sorte.*

F.   *Yeah, hi there Torill, it's Freddy here ... again. Sorry to trouble you... I haven't been able to get much sleep since you spoke to me on Friday, mainly because I haven't got any answers to these accusations that Heidi's been making and I just want to ask you once again where is the evidence that I threatened to kill her nine year old son?*

TS.   *They are in letters with Bergen Police.*

F.   *And what date are these letters? When were they sent?*

TS.   *Oh, I don't know. That's the old case ... I ...*

F.   *The old case? What, from 1986?*

TS.   *Maybe, I don't know.*

F.   *Her son was not nine then was he? Her son was one. And I'd have to be mad to threaten to kill a baby then wouldn't I? Huh?*

TS.   *You ask me but I don't know anything about it because I haven't read them.*

F.   *So ... I wrote to her parents in about 1986 or 1988. I can't remember anymore but her son in 1988 was two. Now how on earth am I going to threaten to kill a two year old boy, huh? How?*

TS.   *Don't ask me about that. I can't answer you about that ... if the letters say that you have threatened her son ...*

F.   *Yeah, but I haven't threatened ... ...*

TS.   *... In the letters and I will read it when I get them ... but I haven't read them yet. I don't know.*

F.   *She's saying I've threatened her son?*

TS.   *Er ... she's saying it's said in a letter, yes.*

F.   *In a letter? My God! But he's not nine though is he? The newspapers said I'd threatened to kill her nine year old son.*

TS.   *OK, I don't know anything about ...*

F.   *Well, haven't you read the newspaper?*

TS.   *No!*

F.   *Oh, you haven't?* [I couldn't believe this; the policewoman had not read yet any of the newspapers with their heinous lies. What kind of sloppy police work was this?]

TS.   *No.*

F.   *I mean what was your evidence based on. I thought ... When I spoke to Mr. Jensen* [the policeman I first spoke to] *he said to me there is so much she is saying that he didn't believe her ... now why did he not believe her?*

TS.   *I don't know why he don't believe her but what I am saying to you.. it's you who's calling her. It's you who's writing to her ...*

F.   *And why am I writing to her? Because I ...*

TS.   *Listen to me ... she want to be in peace and it's you who can't forget what's happening and that's why I'm saying that er.. er ... if you have leave her alone and she still have write to the newspapers or so then you have a good case, but now when it's you who's writing.*

F.   *Yes, but Torill, why am I writing to her? What are my letters saying? My letters are saying: "Why did you tell the police I attempted to rape you." This is a most important point to me. It's an important point to any man. A man has a right to know why false allegations of attempted rape are being made. My lawyers ... are you going to prosecute my lawyers for writing to her* [in 1990], [I added sarcastically]. *She's a lying pig that girl and you should know she's been in a psychiatric unit. Now she is driving me nuts, and ...*

TS.   *My job is not to say what's wrong with her. My job is, you see, to remember what you have told me. To remember what she has told me. And then I have to see at the case and see what I have.*

F.   *But you seem to be telling me how wrong I am to make proper legal enquiries.*

TS.   *No, I don't say how wrong you are. I say that I will give you our advice to stop to write.*

F.   *I will. But why am I writing? I want some answers. I cannot keep ...* [quiet].

TS.   *You won't get these answers.*

F.   *Well then, don't expect her to be left in peace. If we were in England, she can be arrested, taken to the police station and questioned. But you, in Norway, you're being soft with her.*

TS.   *I have talked to her.*

F.   *Yeah? But you treat her like a friend, as if "Ah, poor Heidi" you know ...*

TS.   *That's because I have no reason to hate her. My job is to investigate the case and I'm doing that. I have no reason to hate you either and I don't do that.*

F.   *Well OK. But don't everybody have a go at me for writing letters. I only write letters because she is perverting the course of justice and in England, whatever happens in Norway there is nothing you can ever do to me, there's never going to be a case, I know that. You're never gonna get me over there and if she comes to England then my lawyers can run rings around her, but I will not stop until I have exact details. The attempted rape ...*

TS.   *That, that's your choice ... but I say if I had been you I would stop to write because you are not doing anything good with doing that. We get many letters here* [My 'information campaign' was hotting up].

F.   *Well, how many letters do you get?*

TS.   *I don't know.. She's not get anything from you. The Post ... the* [Post] *Office is stopping the letters and giving* [them] *direct to me.*

F.   *So what about letters to her neighbours? How do they get to you?*

TS.   *They send them to me.*

F.   *Oh they do ... Also ... I want to know which of her neighbours I've threatened to kill, yeah?*

TS.   *I don't know anything about you have threatened someone.*

F.   *Yeah, yeah. It says in the newspapers I've threatened to kill her neighbours if I didn't get her phone number and address.*

TS.   *I haven't read the newspapers so I don't know.*

F.   *Do you want me to send them to you, the newspapers?*

TS.   *Yes, you can do that.*

F.   *Yeah, I'll do that. So it's threats to kill her nine year old son and if he's not nine,* [when the alleged threats were made] *he was two. When I went there, she never mentioned this to me once and when I went to see him in 1990 – you know he was putting his arms around me, giving me a kiss. I was sending him presents. There was nothing. I mean I ... I'd shoot myself if I ever made threats to kill him. It's nonsense and also I want to know how my mother ... how* [Heidi alleged that] *she 'knew' my mother wanted to put me in a mental hospital. I want to know how she 'knew' that.*

TS.   *I don't know.*

F.   *I want to know about the 400 obscene letters.*

TS.   *You can ask you mother about that.*

F.   *Yeah, I have asked my mother. I'll get my mother ... you just hang on a tick. Mum!*

Liane (my Mum)	*Yes.*
F.	*Come here a minute.*
TS.	*I don't need to talk to her.*
F.	*Come here. Come here* [to my Mum]. *It's about* [Heidi's allegations] *you wanting to "put me in a mental hospital" as Heidi says it … just say that you never spoke to Heidi.*
Mum	*Hello.*
TS.	*My name is Torill.* [And after the formalities were over I whispered to my mother that she had to get to the point.]
Mum	*Frederick wants me to tell you … he wishes particularly at this moment to tell you that I did not threaten to put him into a mental hospital … and … and.. which I didn't do because no mother is in a position to do that … I don't know how this phrase came about with newspaper articles being written and journalists putting their own bit into it and their own imagination. Things become distorted and it is indeed a most dreadful and unfortunate affair.*
TS.	*Heidi have very much good to say about you and your husband. Heidi have very much good to say about you. She said the newspaper contacted her, so that's why the newspaper have written about it. Heidi says she haven't said everything who's done in the newspapers.*
Mum	*Yes, that is what I thought.*
TS.	*They make up their own story you see.*
Mum	*Yes, that's what I thought. They made up their own story and Heidi has …* [and later] *The other thing he is particularly upset about is that at one stage it seems Heidi accused him of raping her – attempting to rape her. There is much media hype about this – girls accusing fellows of raping them and this I find very theatrical and he wishes that to be withdrawn.*
TS.	*I see; I understand that Frederick not can forgive her. I understand that but it's so many years since they have seen each other and it's time to stop things because you can't go on. Heidi want to be alone and in peace and she's married … But you know we, the police in Norway here, are doing what we can to try to stop this because I don't have a case to bring Frederick to court. Not in here in Norway. But I hope he understands himself that he can't go on for these … because then I have to do something. I can't let him … because Heidi is very worried …she's afraid of him … the letters and phone calls … she said she can't talk to her neighbours because they think she's nuts … because they get letters from Frederick and read them and ask Heidi what is this … so she don't know what to do and I understand that frustration, yes. So I hope you can talk to Frederick and get him to understand that we want him to stop and if he do that … maybe he don't, can't forgive her but if it's that, that's a start for him. OK! Can you tell Frederick that I have to go to the Court and if he want to call me more he can call me later.*
Mum	*All right, many thanks, bye bye.*
TS.	*Bye bye.*

This was a policewoman talking from a position of real ignorance, not having read any of the three newspaper articles. She seemed to be quite unsuitable to head any investigation. This particular taped conversation later turned out to be of vital importance in evidential value as will be seen later. My mother could not herself remember a great deal of what the newspapers had said about me as there was so much written and I had to prompt her as to what to say to Torill Sorte. Sorte was very partisan, trying to put across how oppressed Heidi felt from my 'nasty' campaign which of course was a natural response to the lies of Heidi and the newspapers. Heidi used her usual tactics of exaggerating her distress, disguising the fact that it could have come as no surprise to her that I would initiate a determined response.

Chapter 17

I wrote to Torill Sorte on 22nd April 1996 enclosing copies of the three newspapers almost a year after the newspapers went to print:

Dear Torill,

Heidi Overaa

Further to our telephone conversation this morning, I enclose photocopies of the newspaper reports from Drammens Tidende, Bergens Tidende and finally VG. Last June, I had only the Bergens Tidende article translated and it was only 6 weeks ago that I had the other two newspaper articles translated which translations are also attached. You will see that I have been accused of 13 years of sex terror, writing 400 obscene letters, making hundreds of obscene phone calls, threatening to kill Heidi's 9 year old boy, her neighbours, her family and Heidi herself and doing obscene things in front of her making her watch.

Further, I have been attacked by Norway's top psychiatrist, Nils Rettersdøl, as [possibly] suffering from erotic paranoia. I spoke to Nils Rettersdøl and sent him all the newspaper cuttings and the full report on Heidi. He told me he was told nothing whatsoever about Heidi from the newspapers and knew nothing whatsoever about me but was presented with 'a general picture' of a man suffering from whatever the newspapers told him such a person had. You will see that an explicit attack has been made upon members of the Muslim faith.

In view of Heidi's past, which you have admitted to me is all true, it is she who has been suffering from erotic paranoia, if anyone has. The evidence is there to see that men have only used her for sex and then abandoned her. She has been pregnant twice to the same boy and on each occasion he has begged her to have an abortion. Later, she twice became pregnant to Mr. Johannessen and on each occasion he did not want her children and abandoned her.

It is a most dreadful thing for you to accuse me of harassment when, through my lawyers and myself, I have only attempted to get to the truth of these accusations. I have told you before that my English lawyers firmly believe that Heidi Overaa is guilty of perverting the course of justice. It costs many hundreds of pounds to employ a lawyer and I can not carry on doing this. I have therefore written letters myself to Heidi and when I do not get replies, I send reminders. Although you say Heidi herself did not go to the press, when she did speak to the press the allegations were purely from her mouth and they printed her words. Ingunn Røren of Drammens Tidende specifically told me that she did not know whether or not to believe Heidi but the accusations she made were printed. All this coming from a girl with a proven psychiatric record and previous suicide attempts.

How on earth you expect me to keep quiet in the face of these disgusting allegations is beyond me. You have no right to tell me to keep quiet. I am physically and mentally unable to keep quiet.

I repeat, last Friday when you told me Heidi said I objected to her having a boyfriend, I would never have expected Gudmund Johannessen to resume being her boyfriend after he had got her pregnant with twins, slept with her best friend, causing her to miscarry, and then her attempting suicide. To go back to such a man, you must only be delinquent and I could not in all reasonableness be expected to foretell he would start pestering her again for sex and that she would give in. He is the one that should be accused of sex terror - besides at the same time as sleeping with each other, both Heidi and Gudmund Johannessen were sleeping with other partners. You can hardly say they had a faithful boyfriend/girlfriend relationship prior to seeking the long-term commitment of marriage. He, may I remind you, is a convicted criminal with a history of heroin and cannabis abuse.

In the face of the hysterical press reporting on me, I have every right now to make the public aware of the true state of affairs and have an opinion expressed on Heidi's psychiatric state. You say Heidi just wants "peace" with a chance to get on with her life. She should not expect "peace" when she has accused me of doing dreadful things that in England would ruin me for life. If you do not think the allegation of attempted rape is an attempt to ruin me, then I feel sorry for you. I know most people in Norway have many partners and often the children do not live with their fathers. Norway has one of the highest suicide rates in the world, one in five pregnancies end in termination (source: Statistics Office of Norway) and alcohol and drug abuse is rife. All these problems are shielded by the generous welfare state.

It is a very subtle and mischievous technique to accuse someone of harassment when all they are doing is trying to get some justice.

Finally, I will telephone you in due course to see what progress you have made with your investigations and obtaining the evidence from the Bergen police. I would also like to speak to Svein Jensen because he seemed to have the sensitivity to tell me that he did not think he believed what Heidi was saying.

Yours sincerely,

On Friday 26th April 1996 I decided to phone Henrik Dugstad, the senior Bergen police officer, who I'd quite liked from the time of my 1990 arrest:

F.   *Hello, good morning, is Henrik Dugstad in please?*

Answer   *Yes, just a minute.*

HD.   *Dugstad.*

F.   *Yes, hi there Henrik, it's Frederick Delaware. You may remember me from 1990 and a woman called Heidi Overaa.*

HD.   *Er, yes you were visit Bergen and have to go out. Leave this town.*

F.   *Yeah, that's right. The reason I'm ringing you up now is that Heidi moved to Drammen and I've been speaking to the police there and they have written to you* [I meant to the Bergen Police Station, not him specifically] *asking for ... ...*

HD.   *Nothing to me ... I think maybe they have written to the headquarters here. I am staying at another department today than I worked at this time* [1990]. *I remember my job was just to follow you to the airport or something like that from the police headquarters ... wasn't it?*

F.   *Yeah, because I did speak to you ... I was in your office for some time and I thought it was you that was dealing with this case.*

HD.   *Yes, it was quite a short case.*

F.   *The thing is you see, Henrik ... when I left you in Bergen in 1990, I went back to see this girl in Drammen in the summer and can you believe it, she wanted to marry me if I became a Christian ... and we made peace ... but she sent me some stuff on Christianity and it really was nonsense and I went back to see her a year later and she was not there. She stayed away on purpose. She's now married to a Christian guy who I think is an exorcist, you know he takes the demons away from ... she actually was exorcised from the devil by her neighbours. But anyway, a big story in the newspapers last May ... did you see the story?*

HD.   *No, no. I just read the local newspaper in Bergen. Bergens Tidende.*

F.   *Accusing me. The thing they* [the Drammen police] *have written to your police station for, is because there were some letters that I wrote to Mr. & Mrs. Johannessen as well as Mr. & Mrs. Overaa in 1986 telling them that* [Heidi] *was sleeping with someone taking heroin and apparently Heidi is saying that these letters contain threats to kill her son. Now I've never made any threats to kill her son and she has said in the newspaper that I have threatened to kill her neighbours if they didn't give me her address and that I've made hundreds of obscene ...*

HD.   *That's nonsense I believe.*

F.   *Yeah ... and that I've made hundreds of obscene phone calls and that I have written 400 obscene letters and the reason she went to the newspapers is because I ...* [and I then changed tack] *I used lawyers, a guy called Wesenberg, last year to see if he could ... ...*

HD.   *Wesenberg?*

F.   *Yeah, ... possibly get some evidence to see if she's perverting the course of justice because ...*

HD.   *What did he say?*

F.   *Oh, he said no, no chance. He doesn't want to speak to me at all anymore and the reason is this. He wrote back to me and said: "She complained to the police in 1986 that you attempted to rape her" and that again is absolute nonsense.* [She had complained that] *a shopkeeper in Bergen and* [earlier that] *Greek holidaymakers wanted to rape her. Now I have never attempted to rape her. I would never do this.* [I proceeded to relate the way the story got into the newspapers and its main allegations].

HD.   *You not staying in Norway at this time?*

F.   *No, no, no. I'm phoning in England. But I told the police in Nedre Eiker that I have not threatened to kill her 9 year old son. Then they said to me "you wrote many years ago letters to the father of Gudmund Johannessen threatening to kill her son." Now I've never done this ... ...*

HD.   *But what is your aim with the telephone call with the police in Bergen ... do you want something?*

F.   *Well my aim today is to make absolutely clear in my mind what these letters say. I want to know now that this is just another load of nonsense. I have not threatened to kill her son. Those letters ... when I left you in 1990 I got in touch with your police station and they said they had received further information, further letters saying I had made threats and if I ever return to Norway, I may be arrested and in theory go to prison.*

HD.   *I'm not quite sure what's happened. I can't believe that was the true because at this time as you visit us in 1990 you wasn't taken any – any, um, er, investigation at all. I saw you just on the plane at Fresland then we were satisfied.* [He had arranged for his deputies to take me to the airport in February 1990 to see me off.]

F.   *Yeah, that's right but when I got back home, I got some Norwegian lawyers in London to write to your police station.*

HD.   *Yeah, I know that.*

F.   .... [and again I explained the fact of Svein Erik Krogvold's letters to my lawyers of 1990] *and* [Krogvold] *simply said that there was some more evidence that had come through after I left saying that I'd threatened ...*

HD.   *But the Department of Justice as we call it in Norway, you could write to them to ask what's going on.*

F.   *Well I used Mr. Wesenberg to do this.*

HD.   *He refused?*

F.   *He said he would not send me photocopies of my letters. I understand that a lawyer cannot photocopy the file. He can only talk to you about it.*

HD.   *Yes, he has the right to see the case ... but his explanation to you, it must be true from the letters.*

F.   *... ... but Mr. Wesenberg didn't give me any details about this allegation of attempted rape.*

HD.   *Then you contact another lawyer in Bergen, maybe. Wesenberg has too much to do at the time .... He's a clever lawyer but too much to do ... you can ask another lawyer.*

F.   *..... I did not threaten to kill her son.*

HD.   *No, no, but why don't you try to forget the whole case. If I were you, I wouldn't think a minute of it.*

F.   *... ... but I did not expect to have so many lies told against me and frankly it shocks me to be arrested. I couldn't come to terms ... ...*

HD.   *... I'm sorry ... I didn't know the case.*

F.   *You see talking to Mr. Krogvold is difficult.*

HD.   *Yeah.*

F.   *He's not easy to talk to because he doesn't want to say anything.*

HD.   *But you know if I look into the case and do something outside him, I have a very difficult job, you believe* [me]. *I haven't the right to do that.*

F.   *No, I understand. I'm sorry. I thought you were in charge of the case.*

HD.   *My person ... is secondary to the case. I just follow you to the airport ... but if you* [contact] *a lawyer* [in Drammen] *he can ask to have a look into the case – that must be the best way to ... ...*

F.   *Well, thank you very much.*

HD.   *Not at all, I'm sorry, but I think if I had been you I would have forget all the case. I don't know but ... you'll do that case for the rest of your life if you do as you are now ... forget that girl it's not... ...*

F.   *I'm not interested in* [trying to win her affections I was about to add]….

HD.   *No, no. I know what you're meaning but ... ...*

F.   *I'm just interested in getting to the truth because I believe she is um ...*

HD.   *Sick?*

F.   *Yeah, well she is sick. She has been in a psychiatric unit but she has told the newspapers
         that I am mentally ill.*

HD.   *But you can tell the newspaper something else maybe.*

F.   *They don't want to print it. I've sent copies of her love letters* [to the newspapers]. *They've
         printed nothing.*

HD.   *I know ... I'm so sorry .... Have a good day.*

F.   *OK then. Bye bye.*

HD.   *Bye.*

On the 27th April 1996 I spoke to Harald Vikøyr, the Verdens Gang journalist:

HV.   *Vikøyr.*

F.   *Yes, hi there, that's Harald is it?*

HV.   *Yes, it's Harald, yes.*

F.   *Hi, there, my name's Frederick Delaware, from England. I don't know if I've spoken to you
         before. I probably did. But I've just had fully translated the article you wrote last May
         about '13 years of Sex Terror,' you remember?*

HV.   *Er, oh yes.*

F.   *Yeah, that's right.*

HV.   *Are you the one?*

F.   *Huh?*

HV.   *Are you the one?*

F.   *Yes, I just had it translated about four weeks ago. I was just wondering how on earth you
         can write such um, well, rubbish basically. I see here* [and I quoted from my translation]
         *"Psychiatrists think the behaviour of the Englishman possesses all the symptoms of erotic
         paranoia. The sick person is convinced that another person is in love with him or her."
         Well how on earth do you come to that conclusion? I was never ......*

HV.   *Isn't this nearly a year ago?* [he protested.]

F.   *It doesn't matter. I just got it translated, but the point is this, it's so far off the mark .... You
         knew she was in a psychiatric unit before you printed this story. You got my letter. I sent
         your office my letters ...*[my full side of the story and copies of Heidi's letters to me].

HV.   *Er well, I've um, I've sent them further on to the Central Newsroom because ordinarily this
         isn't my area in the country so I just got this case through another paper and she's been
         living for a while ... she was from Bergen wasn't she? What you need to know is that when
         I wrote such an article, I do not base it only on her information of course, er, er, I base it on
         er, on er, other information and information from the police so I feel pretty secure that I've
         done an ordinary news article but if you have any complaints about it, contact my editor and*

you can er, er, you can sue us.

F.   *The point is you didn't print my name, nor did the other newspapers, but you have said ...
that will make it very difficult for me to sue you, er, but ... ...*

HV.   *But of course we didn't, er, write your name.*

F.   *You said, "When the half Arab Muslim man was rejected by her later on." I mean that's
nonsense, she got pregnant to a chap who was injecting heroin.*

HV.   *Anyway, anyway, this is such a long time passed now, so I just don't remember every detail
just by having a phone in the evening by you, so I'm sorry I cannot be very helpful. I can
answer you in general terms, like how we base our articles, things like that and if you have
any complaints.*

F.   *Well I spoke to that psychiatrist Nils Retterdsøl and he told me you told him nothing about
me. You told him nothing about Heidi, just a general picture!*

HV.   *Yes, of course ... and the article, er, er, tells in the interview with Retterdsøl also in general
how this kind of phenomenon is.*

F.   *So I'm supposed to be love sick. The only reason I went up there in 1990 is because the one
time I slept with her she didn't tell me she had already resumed sexual relations with that
idiot Johannessen who was taking heroin ... now I've got every right to go up there and have
a go at her. You haven't told [the public] she's been in a psychiatric unit, nor her abortions,
her AIDS-risk behaviour or the fact she's tried to commit suicide twice.*

HV.   *If you feel she has, er, done anything wrong to you or that we have done anything wrong to
you, you need to contact the paper because I'm not interested in going into any discussion of
it. This is not a case that I follow by now. Have you been contacted by the Norwegian
police?*

F.   *I've been speaking to the Norwegian police for a long time over the past six weeks and they
spoke to Heidi for the first time in a year* [last Friday]. *She did not want to speak to the
police. For a year she kept sending her husband there to say they just want to forget all
about it. Now I've kept pestering the police to get her in because she's been lying to them.
She's been saying my mother wants to put me in a mental hospital, I do obscene things in
front of her. I make hundreds of obscene phone calls; I write hundreds of obscene letters and
it's just ridiculous. She's the one that's been in the psychiatric unit and she has a whole
psychiatric history, and it's ridiculous for you to turn the tables on me. This isn't just a
phone call of someone who's maybe slightly had a complaint against you. What you've
written is 100% rubbish. I know it's a year on but you wrote the story and I'm offended and
you yourself are going to have to face me later on. I know where you live and I don't give a
damn ... you've tried to ruin me. You've made out Muslim men... ... and all the rest of it and
death threats, obscene phone calls, showing up in person at the door ... she wanted to marry
me in 1990.*

HV.   *That if I do not write a story that says this relationship* [sic] *was a lie, completely, then you
will come to Norway to visit me in my home with a friend ... ... ha ha ha ha ha.*

F.   *What's so funny about that?*

HV.   *This is what we call a threat in Norway. So...*

F.   *Why is it a threat? I know you won't print anything* [as per my earlier written request to
rectify the matter] *because it will make you look an idiot.*

HV.   *If you tell me that you want to come to Norway to see me with a friend.*

F.   *Yeah that's right. I want a friend for company. I take a friend for company.*

HV.   *"I know where you live" ... that's a threat and I will discuss this with my editor* [to see] *if we want to contact the police about this.*

F.   *Well, contact the police. I've spoken to the police last Friday* [yesterday] *OK? ... to Henrik Dugstad in the Bergen police last Friday and I also spoke to Torill Sorte in the Nedre Eiker* [Drammen] *police and they haven't even read your story and I've sent them the newspapers and they will read your story. Now, you are not going to try and make me worried by you trying to interpret these things as threats. You wrote rubbish ...such nonsense that you are going to have to answer for it otherwise you think you can write what you want, you see. You've got my side of the story.*

HV.   *How do I have to answer for this?*

F.   *You knew beforehand* [her past, I implied]. *The only reason you printed that story was to get your own back on the "Arab Muslim man" who has taught a little Norwegian slut* [a lesson]

HV.   *You tell me that I hate Muslims?*

F.   *Huh?*

HV.   *You tell me that I hate Muslims. I try to ... ...*

F.   *Well you do ... If you put "half Arab Muslim man" and you keep going on about Muslims, especially the other newspaper – Bergens Tidende – about typical Muslim men behaviour OK – "half Arab Muslim man" ...*

HV.   *As far as I can see through this conversation, I'm more convinced that you have a problem ... and that you have some difficulties that you're going to try to solve but don't try this threatening behaviour .. 'cos ...*

F.   *Threatening behaviour? What, you don't want to face your accuser? It's as simple as that. You want to hide?*

HV.   *If you want to meet me you can meet me in the office. Of course you can.*

F.   *All right, I'll meet you in your office then.*

HV.   *Of course. Just make a date.*

F.   *All right. When I come, you're not going to hide?*

HV.   *No, of course not.* [I didn't believe him for a second.]

F.   *No, OK. Good. OK, in your office.*

HV.   *And, and what do you want?* [he asked rather worriedly.]

F.   *What do I want?*

HV.   *I'm not going to write anything more about this case.*

F.   *No, no, no. You have to be told to your face properly to convince you* [of the wickedness] *of all the rubbish you've been saying. You know ... it's nice ... because you will never forget what's going to take place in your office, I can promise you.*

HV.   *What kind of things?*

153

F.   *Well wait and see. Let's just say wait and see. Why should I give everything away after you've [written] that rubbish. That girl ... she's been to the police saying people have tried to rape her. She's told lies about her family and everything under 'The Sun' ... she's been in a psychiatric unit and you still believe her. That's just unbelievable reporting. Just to sell newspapers. I bet you didn't even think I would see the newspaper did you? Even the policeman in Nedre Eiker doesn't believe her ... so why don't you give him a ring and ask him.* [I then related my August 1990 meeting with Heidi in August with her and her son and then continued ..] *and that was 1990. That's not thirteen years of sex terror is it?*

HV.   *Well, anyway ... you know many of the details, I don't remember. I wrote one article and I checked it well with the police and I saw the documentation she had.* [He went on to tell me that he had spoken to the Bergen Police Department.]

F.   *...I understand I'm supposed to have made death threats to her son. Did you see any evidence of this?*

HV.   *I don't remember.*

F.   *I've threatened to kill her nine year old son, her neighbours ... her, her family. I've threatened to kill a lot of people according to the newspapers haven't I? Did you have any evidence for this?*

HV.   *I don't remember ... about this.*

F.   *Well, that's all in the newspapers* [and I impressed upon him my reasons for the hypocrisy of his newspaper for having Heidi being pictured with two Christian Aids booklets].

HV.   *Anyway, if you come to Norway and want to talk just give a ring and we'll make an appointment.*

F.   *All right then, thank you very much. Goodbye.*

Letter dated 29th April 1996 to the Bergen police

Dear Sirs,

Harald Vikøyr of VG Newspaper.   Article 'Thirteen Years of Sex Terror' dated May 26th 1995 - Heidi Schøne

The above article concerned myself and I enclose a copy of the newspaper report, together with my side of the story, Heidi's letters to me (1982 to 1985) and a short resume in Norwegian of her life.

Harald Vikøyr told me last Saturday that he obtained information from you, the police, on which he based his article. This article is complete rubbish and I would like to know how your information helped him come to the conclusions he arrived at.

How can you allow a girl with such a past to claim through Harald Vikøyr that she has been suffering 13 years of sex terror? Heidi Overaa wanted to marry me in 1990 IF I became a Christian. Her next door neighbours 'exorcised' her from demons, Heidi told me when I visited her in [August] 1990 after my arrest in your police station in February 1990. She has a proven psychiatric record, yet the newspapers from VG, Bergens Tidende and Drammens Tidende carried huge front page stories saying that I am insane etc. etc. What complete rubbish! I have not threatened to kill Heidi's 9 year old son (in fact he likes me very much and told

154

everyone so) nor have I threatened to kill Heidi's neighbours as Drammens Tidende (Ingunn Røren) have written. HOW CAN THIS FILTH BE PRINTED?

Please respond with your comments.

Yours faithfully,

I wrote this letter to the Bergen police after earlier phoning one of their officers who told me that the police were legally obliged to answer all enquiries that were put to them. As mentioned above, I also sent all my information to the Norwegian Embassy in London which was in turn passed on to the Bergen Police Station, namely to Commander Svein Erik Krogvold. I never heard a thing from them in writing. I phoned once again the reticent Commander Krogvold in late May:

F.   *I assume by your telling me that the case is closed that you didn't believe her that I've attempted to rape her?*

SK.   *Well I have no comment on that. But ...*

F.   *Why not?*

SK.   *I have no comment either on that or other cases.*

F.   *OK. Well that's fine. At least you've assured me that Harald Vikøyr did not telephone. I guess he must be lying.*

SK.   *No I haven't spoken to Mr. Vikøyr in that matter at all and I wouldn't comment, er ...*

F.   *You think maybe another policeman in your station has spoken to him?*

SK.   *No, I'm fairly sure that that isn't a possibility but Mr. Vikøyr have a lot of social* [contacts] *and he would get the information from the woman so ...*

F.   *Oh, yeah the woman* [i.e. Heidi] *but he said specifically that he spoke to you.* [i.e. to the Bergen police]

SK.   *No, I haven't spoken to Mr. Vikøyr in that matter at all.*

F.   *He definitely said he spoke to the Bergen police.*

SK.   *Bergen Police Department are 500 persons but er ... ...*

F.   *Ok, well I'll see, because I want to get a book out on this. I think it will sell well and I just wanted to get the facts absolutely right. I didn't want to print stuff that wasn't true. So, OK. I thank you for your time.*

SK.   *OK.*

F.   *Thank you. Bye bye.*

This was followed a few days later by another conversation with Torill Sorte. The occasion for this was after I had phoned one, Svein Updal, at the Bergen Police Station, who had retrieved my file from 1990 pursuant to my request to look at the papers to see whether they contained a letter or letters, which Heidi alleged I had sent to the parents of Gudmund Johannessen, threatening to kill her son.

155

F.   [Svein Updal] *said he didn't have the time to go through them* [i.e. my letters to Heidi on his file] *word for word. So I said get in touch with you and send the file. So he said he rang you and left a call out and you were going to ring him at 3 o'clock or something yesterday.*

TS.   *I?*

F.   *Yeah, he said he left a message for you to call him at 3 o'clock.*

TS.   *No, I haven't talked ...*

F.   *His name's I think Svein Updal*

TS.   *Yes, but I have to .... I have get some message from him. Yes! Here, I have. OK. I will try to call him.*

F.   *I'm getting a bit ... you know, it's carrying on for so long and I'd really like to know today – er, I'd like you to know today that I've not been threatening to kill her son, and I was wondering if you could ask him to get this specific letter which is written to, you say, Mr. & Mrs. Johannessen, is that right?*

TS.   *But I will talk to him and I will ask to get the case here so I can look at it. But I don't know if we can answer that question today. I ... ...*

F.   *But tell me something. You say the newspapers don't believe the story that I've written about Heidi. Now do you have the powers to obtain her psychiatric report from her doctor, Dr. Broch?*

TS.   *No, but I don't see any ... why should I do that because my case is that she has wanted an investigation because of some letters and some telephone calls you have given to her. That's my case. I don't have any authority to investigate her life you see because that's not the problem in my case.*

F.   *Yeah, but the problem in my case is that she's a liar and if you get ... You see, I can't understand why the newspapers say they don't believe me. Everything I've told them and everything I've said is true and it must be simple enough to ...*

TS.   *Yes, but you see I have your letters and I have the newspapers you sent me and as I told you some days ago that I will maybe ask the English police authorities to take you in and ask you some questions and write it in a report and then I will put it in my case.*

F.   *But what more do you want to know?*

TS.   *Yes, but that's the way we are investigating our case. That's the way to do it. My lawyer, my chief has to look at the laws in the right way and contact England if that's necessary.*

F.   *Have you read the newspapers in full now?*

TS.   *Yes, I have read them.*

F.   *Yeah, well I hope you can understand why I'm pretty furious, yeah?*

TS.   *Yes, but er somehow; I understand you are mad at everything yes. But I mean this is ... a thing ... that has happened some time ago. You have to live with things. And maybe we can't forget but we have to live with it and I think it's time to do that now.*

F.   *That's right, but can you not at least establish the truth that I have not threatened to kill her neighbours. I mean can't you simply ask Heidi which neighbours I have threatened to kill and go and get statements from the neighbours? Is that not simple enough?*

TS.   *That's simple enough, but ... you have one story, you see, and she have another one and I have talked to Heidi, her husband and I have talked to people who have get letters from you. That's some neighbours, yes?*

F.   *Yeah.*

TS.   *And it's people in Oslo, people in Drammen.*

F.   *Mmm, everywhere.*

TS.   *Yes and they don't like it and I understand that.*

F.   *Well, yes, of course they don't like it but the point is I don't like the newspapers telling the whole country. The newspapers told the whole country. I'm only telling ... as I said, this is the only thing I can do [i.e. send my side of the story directly to the Norwegian public]. I have no other means of getting my point across. Now if she says I've threatened to kill her 9 year old son then she can go to hell. And I've threatened to kill her neighbours? Absolute rubbish. And you can ask her ... all these hundreds of obscene phone calls. She didn't have a phone from the time she left Bergen in 1988 until I phoned her in 1995 at her.........*

TS.   *Why do you start to call her again then?*

F.   *Why do I? Because I found out in [March] of last year that she'd made an allegation to the police that I'd attempted to rape her and obviously I have to ask her how the hell she comes to that conclusion. And she didn't answer me. She said "What were you doing before? What were you doing before?" OK. And I had sex with her OK, and if she should allege anything it's that I raped her, but she didn't say I raped her. She said I: "attempted to." She was lying back on her bed ...I was sitting at the other side of the room. She said: "OK come on over, it's nothing, OK, it's nothing" she said to me. I didn't touch her. I didn't force her, I didn't restrain her, nothing. I'd never do that and she knows that.*

TS.   *But Heidi has never told me that you have raped her.*

F.   *No - "attempted" to rape her.*

TS.   *I know, but, er ... ...*

F.   *Yeah, but it's in the police report. Helge Wesenberg, this big lawyer in Bergen, Helge Wesenberg.*

TS.   *But, I haven't seen that report.*

F.   *Well, OK. What you can do, - Wesenberg doesn't want to speak to me anymore because he's very upset at what I've done. Now the only thing that he should be upset at is that I've sent these reports to everybody. But I asked him [in a letter], "Did you believe the newspapers that I've written hundreds of obscene letters and made hundreds of obscene phone calls, made death threats?" and he didn't answer that. He wasn't even going to speak to me. Now the day he said [i.e. wrote] "attempted rape" is the day I phoned Heidi again, yeah?*

I made a subsequent telephone call to Torill Sorte in June 1996:

TS.   *Sorte.*

F.   *Yes, hi there Torill, it's Frederick here. Good morning. Have you managed to sort things out yet?*

TS.   *Yes, I have given* [Bergen police] *a ring and they say that there is nothing in the case that we can bring something more in this case and ... I have said to my lawyer that ... I think if things are as they are now ... it wouldn't happen, - anything.*

F.   *Yeah, the reason I obviously asked you to go to Bergen is I wanted to know* [about] *these threats to kill her son and her neighbours.*

TS.   *I asked them about that and they say that it was nothing in that case who would bring something like that.*

F.   *Yeah, so there's no threats against her son are there?*

TS.   *No, they say so ... that er, there's nothing there.*

F.   *Yeah, nothing at all.*

TS.   *No.*

F.   *So, I mean, that's obviously, you know, the news I wanted to hear so I'd like you to ask Heidi ...*

TS.   *You see I have talked to Heidi.*

F.   *Again?*

TS.   *No, not again, but she said that er, these things…… say these threats and so on and, er, I have checked it and in Bergen they say it's nothing who indicates like that.*

F.   *So in other words ……*

TS.   *Then you see – if a case we work with. Always like that. One of the parties say one thing and another say other thing.*

F.   *But the point is I asked you specifically* **when** *I made these threats. She must know ... I have never made them and as I told you before in 1990 that little boy, he really liked me and you know I'll always like him 'cos he's just a poor unfortunate and wonderful little chap and it just destroyed me to think she can say these things. You must ask her when I made these threats. Are you telling me she's a liar?*

TS.   *Yes, maybe. You see if she lies about these things, it's not – what shall I call it – er, she can do that if she want to do that. I can't do something with it.*

F.   *There's nothing you can do to ...*

TS.   *No.*

F.   *You can't even tell her off?*

TS.   *People lie to me all the time.*

F.   *But why would she lie to you? Even the threats to kill her neighbours, you must ...*

TS.   *I don't know.*

F.   *You must simply ask her: "Which neighbours?" Say to her: "Please Heidi, get me one neighbour who can come to the police station and tell me that."*

TS.   *Yes, but you see, er, when I, er, investigate a case and I see that I think I don't like the way she had told me, OK, that's a lie, then I say "Maybe" I take the case and go to my lawyer and say there is nothing and we put it away and if she is not happy with that we can take the case up again, but I don't think she will do that. I have no time and I have no thinking of contacting Heidi again. If she's not happy with the things I'm doing, she have to come to me and say: "I want to take the case up again."*

F.   *Oh, I've got you. She will just be told that nothing is happening?*

TS.   *Yes, but the police mean it is not a case for the police. Maybe she is not happy with that. Maybe she want to do something more.*

F.   *Such as what?*

TS.   *Maybe she want to give a new, er, start a new case. But then she have to have new moments to come with and I don't think she have ...*

F.   *New what?*

TS.   *Er ...*

F.   *Evidence?*

TS.   *Yeah, and I don't think she have new evidence.*

F.   *Well now, that's right. Will you actually tell her that there is no evidence of threats to kill her son?*

TS.   *No, she will get a letter from us to tell what we mean about this case.*

F.   *Will you actually tell her in that letter that, "We have found no evidence that he has threatened to kill your son or your neighbours"?*

TS.   *Er, no, not specifically that, but it will tell that we have no evidence to say that this is a case for the police.*

F.   *Did the Bergen police talk to you about this allegation of attempted rape?*

TS.   *No, I talked to the investigator there and he told me that he has looked in the case and he couldn't find anything.*

F.   *Ah, was that Krogvold?*

TS.   *Huh?*

F.   *Krogvold?*

TS.   *Er, yes.*

F.   *Mr. Krogvold?*

TS.   *Yes.*

F.   *Well he told me that nothing was going to happen, but my lawyer wrote to me – Helge Wesenberg in Bergen – saying she made an allegation of attempted rape and I know it was many years ago but that doesn't really matter. It's the fact that she did it which ... that she made that allegation.*

TS.   *But I hope now when I take this case to my lawyer and say: "Put it away." I hope these things can stop and everyone can start, er, up. I understand this case have been a big problem for you.*

F.   *It certainly has.*

TS.   *I hope you can live with it in some way.*

F.   *I just wanted you yourself to be satisfied that I never made threats to kill her son.*

TS.   *Yes, but as I have told you earlier, my job is to investigate and I have to see the both sides of the case.*

F.   *Yeah, but do you believe me that I didn't do this?*

TS.   *I used to say that it's not my job to believe.*

F.   *Oh dear.*[We were going round in circles]

TS.   *I haven't found any evidence to say that you are a liar.*

F.   *Surely you can ask her: "Where's the evidence?" Just say to her "Where's the evidence Heidi?" She said it was in letters didn't she? She told you it was in letters ... but there aren't any ...*

TS.   *I can't find these letters you know but she can lie to me if she's doing that. She can tell me things who is not true and she can do that.*

F.   *Yeah, that's right. She's been doing it for many years and also it's very hurtful for her to keep taunting me about sex – she keeps going on about how I want to have sex with her and how I want her to come to England and have sex with me. That hurts me very very much. But er ...*

TS.   *My advice to you is that you have to ... forget it and er not have any contact with her. I mean if she's a liar and she thinks what she has come to the police with is just a lie, she isn't a person I want to have any contact with.*

F.   *Look ... can you sort of ring them up* [the newspapers] *and say "We haven't got any evidence for this"?*

TS.   *Er, they have called me ...*

F.   *When did they call you?*

TS.   *A week ago.*

F.   *Oh did they?*

TS.   *Yes and I have tried to contact her but she have ... there has been some holiday here.*

F.   *Which newspaper was this?*

TS.   *Er, Drammens Tidende.*

F.   *Oh good, yeah, Ingunn Røren..*

160

TS.   *Yes, but I haven't got her yet and I don't know why she have called but I will tell her what I think and this is not a case for the police.*

F.   *All right. Well, OK Torill.*

TS.   *Yes.*

F.   *Thank you very much indeed and, er, thank you for your time and everything.*

TS.   *That's my job.*

F.   *Also Svein Jensen. He was very nice as well and give him my regards.*

TS.   *I shall do that.*

F.   *Thank you very much.*

TS.   *OK.*

F.   *Bye bye.*

TS.   *Bye bye.*

Telephone conversation with Ingunn Røren next day:

IR.   *Hello.*

F.   *Yes, hi, good morning, is that Ingunn?*

IR.   *Yes.*

F.   *Yes, hi. It's Frederick Delaware here from England.*

IR.   *Mmm.*

F.   *I understand that you've tried to call the police last week.*

IR.   *Yes, I did.*

F.   *Oh, when?*

IR.   *Not last week, the week before.*

F.   *Er, Ok. Well, er, the lady, the policewoman, Torill Sorte, I spoke to her yesterday and she told me that she hadn't in fact spoken to you. You phoned last week.*

IR.   *Maybe it was last week, I don't know.*

F.   *Yeah, that's right, she says she hasn't spoken to you yet but I spoke to her yesterday and they have found no evidence at all about any death threats to her son. Heidi specifically said that I made these threats in letters which ...*

IR.   *According to the policewoman, the investigation's not over yet so ...*

F.   *Well, it is over in the sense that she will write to Heidi to say that there's no death threats to her son in letters – that's a big lie, there's ... ...*

161

IR.   *That's not what she told me.*

F.   *Huh?*

IR.   *That's not what the policewoman told me.*

F.   *Well I spoke to her yesterday.*

IR.   *Yeah, but I have spoken to her several times and that's not what she's telling me.*

F.   *What's she told you?*

IR.   *She's told me a few things I can't tell you but the investigation is still going on so she can't speak about everything. You're still under investigation.*

F.   *Well, she told me specifically yesterday that she will write to Heidi saying that there is nothing ... I mean I spoke to her yesterday and she said ...*

IR.   *Yeah, OK, when I see that letter I'll believe that.*

F.   *Yeah, well why don't you give her a ring? Give her a ring now. You know her name's Torill Sorte and she specifically said to me ... ...*

IR.   *Yeah, OK, I can do that.*

F.   *OK, but Heidi told [you] that I have made death threats to her son.*

IR.   *Yes.*

F.   *She told the police that. And the police asked her: "Where's the evidence?" And Heidi said: "In letters he wrote which the Bergen police have."*

IR.   *OK, I'll ask her.*

F.   *OK. But the Bergen police have spoken to Torill Sorte and she has said that there is absolutely nothing whatsoever in any letters indicating death threats to her son or her neighbours. And there's no obscene letters, nothing, so you know you are gonna have to print some apology eventually.*

IR.   *If it's true what you told me now I'll speak to the police and then decide what to do.*

F.   *OK, speak to the police and I will give you a call back – when can I give you a call back?*

IR.   *Today I'm leaving. I'm going to work with another ... a murder case.*

F.   *You're leaving the newspaper?*

IR.   *Not leaving for good, I'm travelling.*

F.   *Well can I call you back in say an hour?*

IR.   *No, I'm leaving the building, so I won't be here today.*

F.   *So when's best to call you?*

IR.   *Maybe on Friday.*

F.   *Friday?*

162

IR.   *Yes.*

F.   *OK. What she did say is that if Heidi comes up with some new evidence, then they may do something, but she says she doubts very much – well, Heidi would have come up with new evidence by now but the point I'm trying to make – I know you don't like me, but the point is you've been conned. You've been lied to by that girl and I'm very surprised that - you knew she was in a psychiatric unit* [as I assumed she saw my report in Norwegian specifying the BSS Clinic]………..

IR.   *No I didn't.*

F.   *Oh, you didn't know that before* [i.e. before Heidi was interviewed by the newspaper].

IR.   *I don't think she is.*

F.   *Well why don't you ring her doctor, Dr. Broch? His name is Dr. Broch at the BSS ...*

IR.   *Why do you still care about all this?*

F.   *Because I want to clear my name, that's why.*

IR.   *I haven't written your name.*

F.   *No, no. I want to clear my name in the sense ... I know you haven't written my name, but you've accused me of things that I haven't done and ... why don't you ask Heidi about the allegations she's made to them* [and I was going to add about a Bergen shopkeeper raping or attempting to rape her, but Ingunn Røren interrupted].

IR.   *I don't care about Heidi; what you say about her. I don't care.*

F.   *But, I mean don't you believe me?*

IR.   *No I don't.*

F.   *Oh you don't believe my story?*

IR.   *No I don't.*

F.   *What specifically don't you believe?*

IR.   *I've tried to tell you this before and my editor has tried to tell you this and I will give the police a call. That's all I'm going to do.*

F.   *But can you ... you must try and appreciate that I must try and understand why you don't believe me, because you can simply ring up her doctor, Broch. His name's Dr. Broch. Ring him up at the BSS Psychiatric Clinic. She stayed there in 1988.*

IR.   *What's the point about that? 1988.*

F.   *Yeah, because you don't believe she's been in a Unit. She's a sick woman.*

IR.   *Even if she's been in there, she's out again.*

F.   *Yeah, but she's still sick.*

IR.   *That's not our business.*

F.   *No, but you have ...*

IR.   *I don't have the time any more. I'll give the police a call about all this talk.*

F.   *Oh, all right then, I'll call you Friday, bye bye.*

IR.   *Bye bye.*

I made an immediate phone call to Hans Odde, Editor in Chief of Drammens Tidende:

HO.   *Yeah, Odde.*

F.   *Yes, hi there Mr. Odde, it's Frederick Delaware here. You remember I wrote to you about a week or two ago about Heidi.*

HO.   *Ya, ya, I can remember that.*

F.   *Yeah, that's right. I seem to be having a lot of difficulty in getting – being able to discuss anything with that reporter, Ingunn Røren. She doesn't seem to want to, er ...*

HO.   *No, if you have anything to discuss you should discuss it with me and not with her.*

F.   *Oh, with you. OK. It's just that, you know, **she** wrote the article.*

HO.   *That's right. But I'm responsible for everything in this newspaper ... if you have anything to discuss please discuss it with me.*

F.   *Yeah, that's fine. Yeah, I spoke to the police yesterday.*

HO.   *Did you?*

F.   *Torill Sorte and she's said there's absolutely no evidence – Heidi claimed there was evidence in letters that the Bergen police had – that I'd threatened to kill her son – and I haven't of course threatened to kill her son – it's a dreadful lie and the police have confirmed that there's no such letters. Nothing, no threats. No threats to kill her neighbours. So I was just wondering are you going to print an apology in the newspaper about this?*

HO.   *At the moment, I'm waiting for the decision from the police and when the police decide what to do with this case, I will write about that in the newspaper.*

F.   *Good. Good.*

HO.   *Yeah.*

F.   *Yeah. They have said that they will write to Heidi now and tell her there's no evidence for anything but can you not yourself telephone the policewoman now?*

HO.   *Yeah, we will and we will ask the police what they are going to do with the case and if there are no evidence, we will write about that.*

F.   *Oh, wonderful. But the point is I would like you to telephone Heidi and ask her how I made these threats to kill her son and her neighbours. I'd like you to ask which neighbours I've threatened to kill and if you could find the neighbours, please and speak to the neighbours and also if you can find any of these 400 obscene letters. I understand she threw them all away, but I haven't written any obscene letters. Whatever you have, if you've got any obscene letters then you must tell me, but I do not write obscene letters and I can't understand why you don't believe my story. Everything I have told you is 100 per cent true. I know I've been telling a lot of people in Norway about her but that's the truth, because it's very hurtful to hear that I've attempted to rape her. She has made allegations to the police I've attempted to rape her and she has also made allegations to the police many years ago that another Bergen shopkeeper has attempted to rape her and even when she was on holiday in the early 80's she said that some Greek men wanted to rape her. I know it sounds unbelievable all this to you, but I swear to you it's true. You have not asked me any questions and I'm prepared to answer whatever you want and admit to you what I have done, but I am not a pervert and I cannot understand why you have not discussed my side of the story with me, because I wrote to you a year ago. You know that and I sent you copies of her letters but you haven't got in touch with me. Why?*

HO.   *As I told you, I have your letter, your last letter and we will now phone the police and ask them what they are going to do with this case. We have asked them several times already and they have answered us that they are still working with it and when the police have decided what to do with the case we will write the decision in the newspaper. And I don't know all the details that you are talking about, but I am not very interested in all those details either.*

F.   *But what are you interested in?*

HO.   *And I do not think that it's a good idea to call Heidi now and ask her more questions about this.*

F.   *Obviously I have to know how I've threatened ... It's a dreadful thing to accuse a man of threatening to kill her son when he hasn't. I swear to you I haven't. I love that boy. He's friends with me. I've sent him presents. He's spoken to me on the telephone. He's told everybody what a nice man I am. For God's sake, I have not threatened to kill anybody. So I want you to ask her when – the circumstances, the date, the times – she didn't have a telephone for six years.*

HO.   *As I told you, we find out about the decision that the police will make in this case and I have your address as far as I remember. You wrote your address in your last letter and when we write another article about this, I think I could send you the article and you can yourself see what we are writing about this case and if you have anything to add or ask about after that you can write to me again.*

F.   *If I give you the number of the policewoman, can you phone her now yourself?*

HO.   *I'm not quite sure if I will phone her myself just at the moment, but er I could have the number.*

F.   *OK it's 32.*

HO.   *Just a moment – 32.*

F.   *27.*

HO.   *27.*

F.   *45.*

HO.   *45.*

F.   *00 and it's Torill Sorte, Torill.*

HO.   *Torill Sorte?*

F.   *Sorte, yep.*

HO.	*Is it an 'S.'*
F.	*Yes S-O-R-T-E.*
HO.	*S-O-R-T-E.*
F.	*That's right. She's been very good to me. And also there's another police officer there called Svein Jensen.*
HO.	*Jensen?*
F.	*Yeah, Svein Jensen and he told me many months ago that he did not believe what she was saying.*
HO.	*OK. OK.*
F.	*And I have to remind you that it was me who asked, who begged the police to get Heidi in. She did not speak to the police for eleven months.*
HO.	*OK.*
F.	*It took that long and only when I asked the police to investigate the matter did they call Heidi in. So I have been pressing the police to investigate because I want to clear my name.*
HO.	*I see.*
F.	*OK then.*
HO.	*Yep.*
F.	*Thank you very much.*
HO.	*Thank you very much and I will call the police now and ask them what they are going to do. As I told you when they have decided what to do, we will write an article about that in the newspaper and I will make a copy of the article and send to you.*
F.	*Yeah but ... I know you don't like me.*
HO.	*No, I've no reason not liking you.*
F.	*But what you printed about me initially, about me. I mean I've got everything translated here and it really is dreadful stuff. I know you have to sell newspapers but not at the expense of the truth. I mean you never printed she wanted to marry me if I became a Christian in 1990 and the reasons I sent her books on AIDS and abortions is not because she has AIDS. I know she hasn't got AIDS but she did sleep with the man who was taking heroin. She asked me to come and beat him up when he left her again. She had two AIDS tests; he had two AIDS tests and she knew she might catch AIDS.*
HO.	*OK.*

On 9th June 1996 I wrote belatedly to the PFU, the Press Complaints Commission of Norway. I discovered rather late in the day that I was allowed to make a complaint against the newspapers for their articles and I wrote the following letter to the Secretary of the Commission:

Dear Mr. Børringbo,

Complaint against VG, Drammens Tidende and Bergen Tidende: May 1995; Heidi Schøne

I refer to our telephone conversation some weeks ago and now that the police in Mjøndalen (Torill Sorte on telephone number (32) 274500) have completed their investigations (and I understand the newspapers are to print some more on this case) I wish to lodge a complaint on the reporting of May 1995.

I enclose copies of the 1995 [newspaper] reports together with the English translations. Also enclosed are copies of Heidi Overaa's letters to me (1982 to 1985) together with the report I sent these three newspapers in June 1995 detailing my side of the story. Also is a report on Heidi's past in Norwegian, firstly a one page commentary and then a two page commentary.

The reason the press got hold of the story was due to my sending my reports of Heidi's past in Norwegian to all her neighbours in Bergen and Drammen, past and present, in January 1995 - see report marked 'A.' The reason I did this was because I had a few days earlier received advice from my lawyers in Bergen that in the autumn of 1986 Heidi Overaa had complained to the Bergen police, that I had attempted to rape her. This was a dreadful and false allegation and I wanted to get revenge and teach her a lesson. Two or three years earlier she had complained to the police that a Bergen shopkeeper had attempted to or had in fact raped her and confirmation of this can be obtained from her best friend at the time, Ann-Kristin Horvei (tel: (55) 196405). Heidi herself told me of this Bergen shopkeeper in 1984 and she also told me that in 1981 whilst she was holidaying in Greece, Greek boys had threatened at knife point to rape her, but they gave up when she proved she was on her period.

May I tell you that this allegation against me was made 20 months after I last stayed with her, but two weeks after I complained to her father that she was a suicide risk (and indeed two years later my prediction came true: she attempted suicide even though she had a two year old son to care for). I had in fact had sexual intercourse with Heidi, so if anything she is perverse in saying "attempted rape" when intercourse took place. So I learn about this allegation 9 years after the complaint was made. The police did nothing against me. Indeed they did nothing against the Bergen shopkeeper.

However, I was so furious that I got revenge by informing all of Heidi Overaa's (now Schøne) neighbours of her past - which is one hundred percent true. Then the press picked the story up.

I have **not** threatened to kill Heidi's son, who I dearly love. Can you believe that the police in Mjøndalen could not get Heidi to come into the police station until the 17th April 1996. She only went after I begged the police to get her in to answer my complaint. Every time the police left a message for her to come in, she sent her husband round [to the police station]. She was avoiding a cross-examination. She **specifically** told Torill Sorte that I had made threats to kill her son in letters that were at the Bergen police station since 1990. The Bergen police confirmed to Torill Sorte that **no** such letters or threats existed. A big fabrication by Heidi.

I have **not** threatened to kill Heidi's neighbours if they do not give me her address. I have asked the police to ask Heidi to produce one neighbour who can testify to this - and no-one has been produced. Another bloody lie by Heidi.

My mother did not ever want to put me in a mental hospital: this was a lie, told by Heidi in revenge for my TRUE statement that she was in the BSS Psychiatric Clinic in 1988 (under the care of Dr. Broch (tele (32)804355)) and that also Heidi's

167

parents wanted to put her in a home for delinquent children when she was a teenager.

I have certainly NOT written over 400 obscene letters (surprise surprise there is no evidence for this as Heidi threw them all away 'to burn the memory from her mind' she says!). I have not made hundreds of obscene phone calls - Heidi did not have a phone from 1988 to 1994 and I would in any event not expose myself to being taped.

Further, even when the policewoman, Torill Sorte, had interviewed Heidi for the first time on 17th April 1996, Heidi did not give her any of the newspapers and it was I who had to send the newspapers to the policewoman as, can you believe it, she did not know what allegations Heidi had made in the newspapers - she had not even bothered to read the newspaper reports! Torill Sorte received the newspapers from me AFTER she interviewed Heidi and did not interview Heidi again. Heidi never made any mention of her 1986 allegation of attempted rape - she knew it was a lie and she kept quiet. The hypocrite. Torill Sorte has not gone back to Heidi asking for the evidence: time, place, manner of threats to kill her son and neighbours etc.

I have spent hundreds of pounds phoning the three newspapers to question them in order to clear my name. Ingunn Røren of Drammens Tidende had no evidence for Heidi's allegations but just told me that is what Heidi said AND they printed it. All the newspapers had my reports in Norwegian - and could have checked them out for their veracity. They knew I had grounds for revenge, but apparently none of them believed my story. No-one got in touch with me before going to press, to ask me my side of the story.

The psychiatrist, Nils Rettersdøl, told me he knew nothing about Heidi's past, knew nothing about me, but was presented with a "general picture" about my behaviour as told through the eyes of Heidi Schøne, via the journalists and that in conclusion I [may] exhibit the symptoms of "erotic paranoia." I sent him copies of Heidi's letters plus the report in English detailing my side of the story. He now knows better.

So please can I emphasise that it was I who pressed the police in Mjøndalen to investigate and get on with it. The first police officer did nothing and then left. Torill Sorte then only got on with it when I constantly phoned her up. She had little time for Heidi Schøne and I believe still there was a cover up as there was in 1990 in Bergen, when I was arrested most surreptitiously for trying to confront Heidi Overaa over her AIDS risk behaviour. Afterwards she said she would marry me if I became a Christian!

The books on AIDS and abortion [that were pictured in the photographs along with Heidi in the newspapers] were Christian booklets. Heidi says in the newspapers: "As if I have AIDS?" I know she has not got AIDS. But she told me that deep down she knew she might catch AIDS after she knew Gudmund Johannessen, the father of her son, was injecting heroin and sleeping with other woman and nevertheless she continued to sleep with him.

The further report I sent out marked 'B' was so that I could present my own 'newspaper' format with a psychiatric opinion on Heidi, and indeed Ingunn Røren of Drammens Tidende telephoned the police a few weeks ago to see what they were doing about me: the answer now is that there is no evidence to support Heidi's allegations and unless she comes up with fresh evidence the case is closed.

In 1994 I asked my lawyer to see if I could prosecute Heidi for perverting the course of justice. He said it was a non-starter but unfortunately he did not have the time or energy to investigate the matter properly. I am surprised the police in

Norway do not prosecute Heidi for trying to pervert the course of justice and for wasting police time.

Suffice it to say I would like a front page apology on all the newspapers and also damages in money for distress and mental suffering. I cannot have these allegations printed when there is no evidence - only the word of a sick woman. I'm glad I found some of Heidi's letters - others I threw away years ago.

Yours sincerely,

In that letter of 9th June 1996 to Mr. Børringbo I referred to a psychiatric report on Heidi marked 'B.' The narrative, I obtained from a Penguin paperback book from 1952 called 'Psychiatry Today' by Dr. David Stafford-Clark, the most eminent British psychiatrist at the time and his description therein I thought fitted Heidi perfectly and it is printed verbatim below under my own heading 'Heidi Schøne – abnormal mental life':

Heidi Schøne - abnormal mental life

On the mental side the outstanding feature is emotional immaturity in its broadest and most comprehensive sense. These people are impulsive, feckless, unwilling to accept the result of experience and unable to profit by them, sometimes prodigal of effort but utterly lacking in persistence, plausible but insincere, demanding but indifferent to appeals, dependable only in their constant unreliability, faithful only to infidelity, rootless, unstable, rebellious and unhappy. A survey of their lives will reveal an endless succession of jobs, few of which have been held for more than 6 months, many of which have been abandoned after a few days, very little love but often a great number of adventures, very little happiness despite a ruthless and determined pursuit of immediate gratification. Such patients are all too often their own worst enemies and nobody's real friend. If as sometimes happens, they are distinguished by some outstanding gift or talent, they may achieve apparently spectacular success only to throw it away or spoil it at least for themselves by their turbulent and exacting emotional attitude. More frequently, despite a level of intelligence which is as often above average as below, they drift from failure and disappointment to one lost opportunity after another into drug addiction, alcoholism, suicide or prostitution.

Sexual perversion, which may be acquired in the same way as neurosis, is often found among psychopaths, but by no means all sexually inverted people are psychopathic, nor are all psychopaths sexually abnormal in this sense. What in fact is characteristic of the psychopath's attitude to sexual emotion and experience is this same shallowness and immaturity combined with a frequently disastrous opportunism, which may lead not merely to the prostitution already mentioned, but also to deliberate perversions, to wanton repeated and joyless seduction and many of the more grotesque and outrageous sexual crimes.

Innumerable attempts to classify psychopathic personality have been made. Perhaps the most successful is that which divides all psychopaths into two great overlapping groups, the aggressive and the inadequate. Aggressive psychopaths include the violent, quarrelsome, unstable alcoholics, the bullies, sadists and most of the recidivists with a constant record of violent crime; the inadequate group embraces all the minor delinquents, confidence tricksters and social misfits whose plight constitutes a tremendous problem for society as well as for their families and dependants. Such people in the course of their troubled and catastrophic lives are particularly liable to encounter stresses, frequently of their own contriving, for which they can provide only neurotic solutions; it is by no means uncommon for a psychopath to seek help not for his general disorder of personality and character, but for the particular anxiety state or hysterical illness to which his way of life has at this point inevitably brought him. Running through the lives of patients with this fundamental disability seems to be a consistent impulse towards destruction. Destruction of their hopes and happiness and ultimately of their health and lives; a destruction all the more consistently sought for the apparent motives for most of the actions which lead them from one disaster to another are immediate satisfaction or short term gain.

By now, the telephone directories from Bergen and Drammen that I had ordered had reached me via British Telecom in Preston, Lancashire. The above psychiatric analysis was then randomly sent to hundreds upon hundreds of people, being individuals and also companies and other establishments in the Bergen and Drammen districts. These were sent by letter and later on, several hundred faxes went out as well. Again, I was proud of myself for continuing to furnish my own 'newspaper' reports, which, after all, were only 100% true. I had also by now typed up a full information sheet on my findings to date. Printed in full below, it went by post and fax to many hundreds of people in Norway:

PRESS RELEASE

HEIDI SCHØNE - The Real Sex Criminal

Newspaper Articles in May 1995

Owing to wholly false reports printed in May 1995, by the following, now disgraced journalists:

- Ingunn Røren of Drammens Tidende

- Haakon Schrøder of Bergens Tidende

- Harald Vikøyr of Verdens Gang

a response must be made to acquaint the Norwegian public on how they have been deceived by the editors of the above newspapers.

The facts are as follows:

1. The **SEX TERROR** referred to in the press was in fact started by Heidi Schøne's (then Overaa) first boyfriend, Petter, who twice got the teenager pregnant and on each occasion begged her to have an abortion threatening to leave her if she did not. Heidi aborted on each occasion hoping to keep her boyfriend who, however, eventually left her anyway. Psychological **SEX TERROR** by one Norwegian on another.

    THE STATISTICS OFFICE OF NORWAY state that today one in five pregnancies in Norway end in termination which probably makes **NORWAY** in percentage terms **THE LARGEST NATION OF FOETAL CHILD KILLERS IN THE WORLD. NORVEGE: NUL POINTS**

2. The **SEX TERROR** continued in the form of another so-called boyfriend of Heidi's, Gudmund Johannessen, now of Rollandslia 223, Ulset, Bergen and now married to Nina Engeberg (nice choice Nina!). Johannessen an ex-prison convict got Heidi pregnant with twins in 1984 but he slept with Heidi's best friend afterwards and when Heidi found out, she miscarried and attempted suicide. Continually pestered for sex afterwards, Heidi again became pregnant to Johannessen in 1986 whilst he was INJECTING HEROIN, purchased in China, and whilst he was also sleeping with other women: the facts of which Heidi, a delinquent, was well aware of but all she was interested in was "good sex." An illegitimate child was born and both parents had two Aids test each for

---

170

fear of having contracted HIV due to their high risk behaviour. Note the hypocritical indignation with which Drammens Tidende showed Heidi being pictured with Christian advice booklets on Aids and Abortion. Deceiving the public again! Rarely having lived together and never having married, Johannessen again rejected Heidi and their son in 1988 following which Heidi made a second suicide attempt, prepared to leave her two year old son motherless (as well as effectively fatherless), later saying her son's grandparents would have looked after him, had she succeeded in committing suicide. Psychological **SEX TERROR** by one Norwegian against another.

3. In 1986, a letter was written by the Muslim man to Heidi's father warning of her suicidal risk behaviour. The letter was ignored.

4. In the autumn of 1988, Heidi entered the BSS Psychiatric Clinic in Lier near Drammen but with no appreciable response to treatment.

5. After leaving the Clinic, Heidi was EXORCISED FROM DEMONS by her so-called Christian neighbours, Asbjorn and Heidi Anita Skjortnes, and claimed she spoke in tongues and that her foot grew by a quarter of an inch. Heidi's Christian neighbours' marriage broke up when Mrs. Skjortnes left her husband and two children for another man she met when she started work.

6. In 1989, Heidi Overaa became a 'Christian' and having failed to persuade the Muslim man living in England to convert to Christianity, she married a self-styled exorcist, Runar Schøne, well practised in the art of speaking in tongues.

7. Twice in the 1980's, Heidi Overaa complained to the Bergen Police that two different men had tried to rape her. No charges were brought. She also claimed that on holiday in Greece, Greek men had tried to rape her at knifepoint. This, the girl, who in 1982 in Rhodes had sex with two different men on the beach.

8. In 1988, after being rejected by Johannessen (but before her suicide attempt) she requested that the Muslim man living in England travel to Norway with his best friend, a karate expert, to take Gudmund Johannessen "to the woods and tie him up or something." She wanted revenge.

9. The 400 obscene letters described in the newspapers have never existed.

10. The Nedre Eiker police failed for 11 months to persuade Heidi to talk to them with regard to her May 1995 newspaper allegations. Eventually, they talked to her for the first time on 17th April 1996 after constant pressure for a full investigation was brought upon the police by the Muslim man from England.

11. The police have not been able to produce or discover any of Heidi's neighbours who allegedly have been threatened with death.

12. The police have proved Heidi to be a liar when she claimed threats were made to kill her **two year old** son (not nine year old son as reported by the newspapers).

13. Nils Rettersdøl, the Psychiatrist was tricked by the press in that he did not know that Heidi was herself, a psychiatric patient, a delinquent, habitual liar and refuge for sex starved Norwegian men: a woman whose behaviour fitted that of a passive psychopath. Mr. Rettersdøl has brought his profession and his own standing into disrepute by relying on the uncorroborated word of the press. It is Norwegians who have sexually terrorised and taken advantage of the psychopathic personality of Heidi Schøne.

14. Heidi now cuts a sad and lonely figure in Drammen having been shunned by the townsfolk for her perverted behaviour: behaviour that several hundred of them are aware of.

15. Surely the success of her marriage (which was supposed to be based on the Christian values of truth and love), must now be open to question, having so deceived her husband, family and the public in general.

THE RECORD HAS NOW BEEN PUT STRAIGHT AND THE NEWSPAPERS HAVE PROMISED TO PRINT AN APOLOGY NOW THAT THE POLICE HAVE FINISHED THEIR INVESTIGATIONS <u>WHICH DID NOT START</u> UNTIL THE MUSLIM MAN BEGGED THEM TO INVESTIGATE.

To those that accuse others falsely of sex terror let us hear the primal scream of the typical Norwegian foetus before it is killed by those using abortion as a contraceptive:

Foetus: "Don't kill me mummy ...... I'll be a healthy child when I'm born. I want to live."

Mummy: "I only wanted a fuck, not a little fucker like you, so CRUSH you to death, I will. CRUNCH, CRUNCH, CRUNCH and WHOOSH out you'll go into the dustbin. I want to live my own life first and besides your father ... is just not interested. Bye, Bye ...."

Foetus: "But mummy, mummy, I love you ....."

....

This article is dedicated to the memory of the crushed and crunched dead of Muslim Bosnia whose own primal screams were ignored whilst in parallel the anti Muslim Norwegian press attacked Muslims in a way that clearly illustrates why the attitude prevailed in Europe that enabled little or nothing to be done about the atrocities of the Serbs against the Muslims in Bosnia

In late June 1996, I spoke to Torill Sorte twice and Hans Odde, the editor of Drammens Tidende.

Conversation with Torill Sorte:

F.   *Do you think they* [the newspapers] *are going to put* [print] *something bad about me again? I think they are aren't they?*

TS.   *I don't think they have any reason to do that because there's no evidence to say that they have do that.*

F.   *Yeah, but I said to Ingunn Røren: "Why don't you believe my story. I swear to you it's all true." I admit I've sent hundreds of people those articles – my 'newspaper' – but it was all true. I haven't lied about a single word in any of those reports.*

TS.   *You see* [what you've said] *in these letters are very bad things.*

F.   *Yes, I know they are but they're all true.*

TS.   *Maybe people think "Oh! Nobody can do anything like this" and they think that the person who has written this must be crazy.*

F.   *Yeah, I can see that in a way but it is all true, but also people can find out whether it's true or not ... you've seen that letter that she wrote to me in 1984. She's mentioned her*

172

abortions hasn't she ... she's mentioned the fact [in the letter] *that there are things she can't tell anybody ...*

TS.   *But people think these things are her problem and they don't want to know anything about it ...*

F.   *But* [Heidi] *went to the newspapers herself and told such rubbish that I was glad that earlier I had sent that stuff because it's a dreadful thing to say that I've threatened to kill her son – I love that boy as if he's my son. You must have sympathy for me because she's always lied all her life about so many things. Her life is a mess and it's her doing. It's her boyfriends who've never loved her properly. They've never really loved her, so ... ...*

TS.   *No, maybe that's true, but people think that this is the problem for Heidi and if she has ruined her life so what. They don't want to know about it, you see.*

F.   *But they still read the newspapers about me.*

TS.   *That news – you see journalists write things about people that's not true. If I have a story I've worked with and it come in the newspaper sometime I don't understand that this the case I am working with. They write things that are not true. And I try to live with it, but I understand it can be difficult sometimes, yes, I understand that. But if the newspaper call me I will say what I have found out.*

F.   *Mmm, please, yeah.*

TS.   *And I won't tell anything about my ... what I mean and what I feel about this because my job is to tell what I have investigate and what it come to that.*

F.   *Do you think Svein Jensen could just tell them he didn't believe her?*

TS.   *I don't think he will do that ... that is his personal opinion of this and, er, we can't do that because we have no evidence who says one thing or another. The only thing I can say is that the evidence is not strong enough to... er, have a case.*

F.   *I would love to have confronted her and just sit down with you and her, just so that I can prove to you properly that she's lying – I mean I can't even talk to her on the phone. You won't give me her number will you?* [I asked tongue in cheek.]

TS.   *I can't do that. I am not allowed to do that.*

F.   *No, I thought so* [I laughed] *Because she always gets away with it. She's never there to be questioned by anybody.*

TS.   *I have questioned her.*

F.   *Yeah, but I know her better than you. I know the facts better than you.*

TS.   *You see, you say one thing, and she says another thing.*

F.   *Does she still maintain that I've sexually harassed her?*

TS.   *What?*

F.   *Does she still say that I sexually harassed her every time I visit her?*

TS.   *No she didn't mention that to me.* [But the newspapers printed it.]

F.   *Do you want me to send you that letter that my lawyer in Norway wrote to me about*

173

attempted rape? Do you want me to send you that letter?

TS.   *You can send it to me.*

F.   *Believe me, he did find this out from the Bergen police that she had complained in 1986 that I had attempted to rape her. He wrote that to me ... I can send you the letter if you want, because no-one seems to have picked this point up which is the reason I have sent all those letters in the first place, you see. I can't understand why the Bergen police don't mention this to you when my lawyer Wesenberg found this out last year. It was on the police file last year. So how can the Bergen police not mention this to you?*

TS.   *You tell me, I don't know.*

F.   *Mmm... I mean, I'm sure something funny's going on up there. I don't know whether her parents are putting pressure on the police or they know someone ...*

TS.   *You see the police in* [Bergen] *said to me, they could take the case* [the police file from my 1990 arrest] *and put it in the mail and I can read it, but it wouldn't give me anything you see, because it was nothing that says anything more than what I am having here, so ...*

F.   *But it's funny. I just can't understand if she makes a complaint to the police about attempted rape which from her point of view, although it's a lie, she's maintaining it, I can't understand why she doesn't mention it to you. It's a dreadful thing for a man to do to a woman and if it's true, why doesn't she mention it to you? I think the reason is because she has also made the same allegation to the police about a Bergen shopkeeper and two allegations of attempted rape don't look very good. It looks as if um, you know, people are beginning to discover that she is a liar. She is the sort of person I have always said she is and ...*

TS.   *That's why I say to you, you have to forget her.*

F.   *Oh yes, I don't want to be romantically involved with her or anything, I just want people to understand that her kind of behaviour can ruin men, it can ruin me and it's too much to take. I can't live with it.*

TS.   *I see.*

F.   *Yeah. Anyway, well, I better say goodbye and er good luck with the newspapers.*

TS.   *I shall try, yes. We'll see what's coming out of that. Yes? OK.*

F.   *Thanks a lot.*

TS.   *Goodbye.*

F.   *Bye bye.*

Conversation with Chief Editor of Drammens Tidende, Hans Odde:

HO.   *Odde.*

F.   *Yeah, hi, good morning. Did you get the letter I wrote to you last week?* [saying the police had closed the case and asking if they could print my side of the story.]

HO.   *I got your letter this morning, yes.*

F.	*Ah good. So what are you going to do?*
HO.	*I am going to do exactly what I told you I was going to do last time we talked together. Wait for the police decision.*
F.	*But they've given it.*
HO.	*No, you're not quite right there. They have not closed the case yet. Have you got a letter from the police?*
F.	*No, I have nothing from the police and I will probably never have anything.*
HO.	*OK.*
F.	*But the thing is as I have told you, I phoned the police up and they said they cannot understand why you are behaving like this because the case is closed and when she [Torill Sorte] has the time to do it she will officially close it. But the point is ... you didn't even phone her [Torill Sorte] up once in the whole year. You didn't really care about the investigation. It was me who did care about the investigation. Me who is supposed to be the, er ... the Chief Tormentor and Nasty Person and it's only when I got to call the police to complete the investigation that they did it. You didn't care, did you?*
HO.	*We care about the investigation in the way that we asked the police.*
F.	*Yeah, but you never phoned them until I phoned you.*
HO.	*OK. I don't know how often and when we phoned the police.*
F.	*Never, never – once last year and then never again.*
HO.	*But the fact is this case is not closed yet.*
F.	*Well it is closed. Ring her [Torill Sorte] up and ask her. Just say simply ...*
HO.	*We rang her up ... after we talked together last time. Some few days ago ... and we asked her "Is this case closed?" and she answered "No, not yet." And we're still waiting for it so when this case is closed we'll write about it. I promised you that and we will.*
F.	*But are you going to say something like: "This man in England has got away with it and Oh dear! What can we do about this nasty man who's still writing to everybody about this poor girl Heidi." I mean you're going to do a story in her favour. You're not going to help...*
HO.	*No, no er... I think that we will make a story according to the facts in this case and write the decision the police does.*
F.	*But are you going to write anything about what I've said about Heidi's past. Are you going to say the reason I've sent all those letters out is because I can't get this attempted rape business and the other allegation against a Bergen shopkeeper of attempted rape, and the AIDS business [cleared up] ... ...*
HO.	*I can't tell you which of these details ...*
F.	*Can you tell me even maybe one detail? Anything?*
HO.	*No, I don't think so because we are still waiting for the police and when they decide what to do about the case we'll write about the decision and before that I cannot tell you what we are going to write because I do not know yet.*

F.   *Are you even going to apologise to me?*

HO.   *I do not know because I do not know if there is a reason for apologising.*

F.   *Because I haven't threatened to kill her son. I haven't threatened to kill her neighbours. That's something I'm not going to accept and I will wait until I've seen what you've written and then I'll decide what I'll have to do, but this case is not over until I get some apologies. And front page. Believe me, because I'm not gonna have my life ruined – er ...*

HO.   *Mmm... Mmm. I can't tell you what we are going to write but as I have told you, we are going to write about this case when it is closed by the police and if there is a reason for apologising, we are going to do that. If there is a reason. If we have done ... written ... anything wrong, sure we are going to apologise that.*

F.   *Good and you must explain to your readers next time round that ... the hypocrisy of Heidi when she says: "As if I have AIDS?" You must point out ... I'm not sending books out of spite. She risked catching HIV and those are Christian booklets and you must explain the reality behind my actions.*

HO.   *Yeah, I can't tell you now ... so if you just wait for the official answer from the police when the case is closed and we're going to write the facts about this, I'll tell you that.*

F.   *OK. All right then.*

HO.   *OK.*

F.   *Thank you very much.*

HO.   *Bye Bye.*

F.   *Bye Bye.*

Next a telephone call to policewoman Torill Sorte:

F.   *Hi, good morning, is Torill Sorte in today please?*

Answer   *Just a moment please.*

TS.   *Sorte.*

F.   *Hi Torill, Freddy here again. Did you get that letter I wrote to you last week?*

TS.   *Yes.*

F.   *Yeah, so are you going to be able to write to me now and just tell me that ... this case is closed so that the newspapers can ...*

TS.   *You won't get a letter from me.*

F.   *Oh!*

TS.   *You will get it from the police in Drammen.*

F.   *Oh, in Drammen.*

TS.   *When the case is closed, you will get a message from them.*

176

F.   *When will it be closed?*

TS.   *I don't know. I can't give you some ...*

F.   *I mean, have you got a phone number for them. I can get in touch with them and ask them what's going on ...*

TS.   *The case is with me because I have to go through the case and look at all the letters you have write and the letters Heidi have write...*

F.   *So the newspapers, you know, I keep telling them you tell me the case is closed. They tell me it's not closed.*

TS.   *You see I have said to you that the case is closed, but I think that's what will happen when I send it down to Drammen.*

F.   *Oh, I've got you. But the thing is, you know, when's it going to happen because it seems it's taking too long?*

TS.   *It will take some time. I can't give you a date.*

F.   *I mean is it going to be months do you think?*

TS.   *No, I don't think so ... maybe some weeks.*

F.   *Oh, OK. So, am I going to be arrested then if I set foot ......*

TS.   *No.*

F.   *... set foot in Norway. Not at all?*

TS.   *If you come to Norway?*

F.   *Yeah.*

TS.   *Yes, I will arrest you then, yes.*

F.   *Even if I go to the airport?*

TS.   *Yes.*

F.   *But why's that?*

TS.   *Because as I have told you the proof in the case are not good enough to do something in England, as I have told you before.*

F.   *So in Norway there's proof is there?*

TS.   *No, but we don't want you in Norway because we want that Heidi shall get some peace from you.*

F.   *But what about some justice? She's a liar. I haven't done these things.*

TS.   *You say that. She don't say that.*

F.   *She says I've threatened to kill her son still?*

TS.   *Yes.*

177

F.   *Oh, does she?*

TS.   *Yes she say that but I have no proof of that.*

F.   *How does she say I've done it?*

TS.   *She said you have written some letters.*

F.   *Where are they?*

TS.   *I don't know. You see I don't have proof of that.*

F.   *Well that's right 'cos she's a sick woman and a liar. When did I write the letters and what did I ...I mean any normal person keeps these letters don't they? If you threaten to kill someone you keep the letters don't you?*

TS.   *She says she has given them to the police in Bergen.*

F.   *Yeah, and what have they done with them?*

TS.   *And they don't have the letters.*

F.   *Yeah, that's right because she's a bloody liar and I wish you'd believe me for once ... that I've written no such thing and I want to know from her when. It seems to me that I'm going to have this little bitch properly questioned and er ...*

TS.   *I don't need to hear this you see.*

F.   *You say you're going to have me arrested if I set foot in Norway. Now I'm the victim. I've only got in touch with her because I want some answers, and just because I want answers because you haven't questioned her properly, then I shouldn't be made to pay for it by being arrested in Norway.*

TS.   *You see you have sent 400 letters to people in Norway.*

F.   *But not 'obscene.' When the newspapers say "400 obscene letters," what I understand by that is that I've written 400 obscene letters to Heidi.*

TS.   *No, not to Heidi.*

F.   *So when it says "400 obscene letters"* [in the newspapers] *those are the reports ...*

TS.   *To hundreds of people everywhere in Norway.*

F.   *Yeah, that's right, but they're not obscene.*

TS.   *And the police in Norway don't like that you're doing this, but there are no proof to have a case, so ...*

F.   *So when the newspapers say "400 obscene letters" they don't mean letters I've written to Heidi? They mean letters to other people?*

TS.   *Yes, you haven't write 400 letters to Heidi.*

F.   *Oh, no, no that's what I thought the newspapers meant. What about obscene telephone calls then? I haven't made obscene telephone calls.*

TS.   *No, you say that but as I have told you before, the case have two sides. Yours and Heidi's.*

F.	*Yeah, but if she has no telephone from 1988 to 1994 how can I make obscene telephone calls? How? If she has no telephone tell me how I'm supposed to do this.*
TS.	*She have a telephone.*
F.	*She has a telephone now, but not between 1988 and 1994. OK. That's easy enough to check with the telephone companies.*
TS.	*But you see I have no proof in the case to have a case, and that's why I have to go through the letters because my lawyer in Drammen want me to do that. When I have done that we will send the case to Drammen and I think, that my* [opinion] *that the case will be closed.*
F.	*But I'll still be arrested because the police don't like me sending out the truth to ...*
TS.	*No, because Heidi says that you have um, have ... said you will come and visit her ...*
F.	*Yes... ...*
TS.	*Talk to her ... ...*
F.	*Yes, that's right because you can't do that* [i.e. they aren't competent enough to cross-examine her properly].
TS.	*But listen to me. And she don't like that.*
F.	*Oh, doesn't she? I don't like being accused of attempted rape. I don't like being accused of threatening to kill her son.*
TS.	*No, but if you are going to Norway and you try to come in contact with Heidi, then I must believe that, er, it's a reason why you're doing that. If the things Heidi says is right, then er ... er when you are coming to Norway you are in a way telling me that she is tell the truth, you see.*
F.	*Yeah, but the point is no one's given me the opportunity to talk to her about these allegations and that's not fair. That's just not fair. If I'm brave enough to come to Norway, it's not to kill her son is it? Or kill her neighbours. Have you found me one neighbour?*
TS.	*No, but I don't take that chance you see. She said you maybe want to do that. You say to me that you don't want to do that.*
F.	*She's saying that I maybe want to kill her son? Is she saying that?*
TS.	*She's saying that, yes.*
F.	*OK. I'll never forgive her for this. I tell you something, I'll never forgive her for this. If that's what she's saying. Have you spoken to her son?*
TS.	*No, he's a little boy.*
F.	*Oh, no he's 10 - he's still ...*
TS.	*Still a little boy, yes.*
F.	*OK, still a little boy but you can at least still speak to him. He's not in a court of law.*
TS.	*She has said that you have sent some letter with these – we have discussed this before.*

179

F.   *Yeah, but where are the letters for Christ's sake? – You, you ...*

TS.   *As I have told you before, I can't find the letters.*

F.   *Well ask her, go back and ask her ...*

TS.   *Yes I have ask her. She has said that the letters is at the police in Bergen but the police in Bergen don't have the letters.*

F.   *Why not?*

TS.   *That's why I'm closing the case you see.*

F.   *Yeah, so if the police in Bergen don't have the letters, you must tell Heidi they don't have the letters.*

TS.   *Yes, she know that.*

F.   *Yeah, because she's a liar. They don't exist. They never did.*

TS.   *But you are not a criminal because you are lying you see.*

F.   *Yeah, but I'm not lying, I never wrote such rubbish.*

TS.   *Yes, but Heidi says the same about her you see. You are saying one things, she is saying another and my job is to prove who is the right and I can't prove that what she's saying is right, that's why I'm closing the case.*

F.   *Yeah, and did you ask her about the attempted rapes of me and the Bergen shopkeeper? Have you got in touch with the police about the Bergen shopkeeper? My lawyer told me that on the file in the Bergen police station she made an allegation in December 1986 that I've attempted to rape her. Do you want me to send you a copy of my lawyer's letter?*

TS.   *Yes, but as you know the case in Bergen is closed.*

F.   *Yeah ... that bloody bitch. I'll never forgive her for this. If that's what she's saying, then I'll do what I want. I can send hundreds more of those things [i.e. reports in Norwegian]. There's no way she's gonna get away with still maintaining, even [though there's] no evidence; she still bloody well lies.*

TS.   *Yes, but as I have told you before, if still are sending letters, I can't close the case.*

F.   *Oh, you can't?*

TS.   *No.*

F.   *Oh, a tricky situation.*

TS.   *If you are stopping these and she is stopping these and I have no proof, yes, I will close the case.*

F.   *Well I tell you something. I am so happy that I sent those letters because she must be miserable. They must be in every single hotel, shop, hairdressers, clothes shops – everything under the sun, they all know about her and I hope the rest of her life is ... ...hell ...... I had the goodness to be kind to her and help her out and this is what I get. I get just treachery all the way. I mean you must see from her past history, all the things she's done that she's a bloody liar.*

TS.	*Yes, but I have told you I will close the case. I think that will happen. I can't promise you if you coming to Norway that you get contact with her …*
F.	*What are you going to do then? Why don't you just let me speak to her in front of you? Why don't I just come to Norway?*
TS.	*She don't want to speak to you. She don't want to see you.*
F.	*What do you mean "don't want." This isn't a social call. It's something you should investigate with me, you and her.*
TS.	*Yes, but I have done.*
F.	*Not with me sitting beside you.*
TS.	*Yes, but I am closing the case because I don't have any proof that you have done something criminal and that's why I'm close the case and you should be happy for that.*
F.	*Yeah, well I hope the newspapers can er … I tell you something, if those newspapers print any more rubbish on me, then I tell you something it's not the end of the story and I'll ruin that girl's life. I know her life must be miserable at the moment and it's probably ruined anyway, but I'll make damned sure it's ruined properly.*
TS.	*You will ruin her life but you will ruin yours.*
F.	*I won't ruin my life. I live in England. It's a miserable life anyway.*
TS.	*But you won't get it any better. The best thing for yourself is forget Heidi and I have told that many times. She's said one thing and if she wants she can do that and you say another thing. But I have no proof.*
F.	*No, no, but at least Svein Jensen told me he didn't think he believed her. He did, but you can't can you?*
TS.	*As I have told you before, my job is not to believe you.*
F.	*Well, why does he believe me then and not you? He's a policeman.*
TS.	*As I told you, maybe I believe you, but my job is to investigate.*
F.	*Well OK. If she says that there are letters with the Bergen police, I want to know where they are.*
TS.	*They have no letters in Bergen who says that you … …*
F.	*Well, why does Heidi say they have them then?*
TS.	*Maybe she's a liar.*
F.	*Yeah, good. Exactly. Even if I get another lawyer to look into this case, then as soon as he writes to you, you won't tell him anything more than you've told me will you? He won't be able to do anything will he really?*
TS.	*What do you want him to do?*
F.	*What I really want someone to do is cross-examine Heidi.*
TS.	*I have talked to Heidi.*

F.   *Yeah, but you haven't cross-examined her properly. You didn't even have the newspapers with those allegations* [that were printed in them when you saw her for the first time on April 17th - I would have gone on to say.]

TS.   *But I have the case. I asked everything. I asked her about the letters where you should have threatened her son to kill him.*

F.   *When did I send them? Can you tell me when? When did she say I wrote them?*

TS.   *Oh that was some years ago.*

F.   *"Some years ago." Yeah, when he was two. Wonderful. What a bastard I must be to write* [that].

TS.   *Yes, but she said that and I said OK, if he had write some letters and ... ... what is it ... ...her husband's father.*

F.   *Have you spoken to that stupid arsehole? Her father? Have you spoken to him?*

TS.   *What, her father?*

F.   *Yeah.*

TS.   *No.*

F.   *Never spoken to him. When I told him that Heidi was a suicide risk ... and told him about her abortions and everything, he put that letter into the police OK ... and two years later she did try and commit suicide. So that man ... he never looked after her. He didn't give a damn for his daughter and what I predicted came true. He only did that* [allowed my letter to go to the police] *because he was upset and you know it just doesn't square up. I mean, she goes to the police 20 months after I last stayed with her saying that I've attempted to rape her, OK, and the police did nothing then and they did nothing when she went to the police saying a Bergen shopkeeper had attempted to rape her. They did nothing then. It just does not add up. Can you tell me, does she go to work?*

TS.   *No.*

F.   *She just sits at home. Has this husband of hers, has he got any children of his own?*

TS.   *No, I don't think so.*

F.   *Nothing and she's not going to have any more children at 33.*

TS.   *I don't know ... she and her husband want some babies, I don't know.* [Heidi in fact was pregnant and later gave birth to a son].

F.   *Well, I'm sure they do want some, so we'll wait and see, but I hope she doesn't get a good night's sleep again because she knows she's a liar and when we all die and God judges us, you'll know for sure then that I don't threaten two year old babies. And how come that when I go and see him in 1990* he [Daniel, her son] *sits on my lap and kisses me and tells all the neighbours what a wonderful friend he's met and she* [Heidi] *lets me talk to him. What kind of a woman lets her son do that if he's* [i.e. me] *threatened to kill the son years before?*

TS.   *But we have talk* [about this] *many times and maybe I believe what you are saying. As I have told you, I've no proof to do the case that Heidi wants to. That's why I'm closing the case. You should be happy for that because, er ...*

F.   *Well that's the least I expect. Well, I think that's about as much as I'm going to get from you to say she's a liar, but you can rest assured all I've done is written [those reports] to about a thousand people ... ...but I want once and for all that evil woman to know that for the rest of her life people will know what she's all about and if the newspapers can print rubbish on me then I see no reason why I can't have my own source of truth sent out to the public in Norway ... you can call my letters a newspaper.*

TS.   *Yeah, I see. I understand what you're saying. But, I mean, these have to stop sometime.*

F.   *Yeah, it does but how can it stop when she makes these outrageous allegations?*

TS.   *But I mean when the case will be closed, you see, the newspapers will write about that.*

F.   *And what will they say about me though? They're not going to write anything nice about me. They'll just say – "this madman has again escaped justice because the police have found nothing, but we still believe Heidi and etc etc." I just cannot believe they are going [to write an apology]...*

TS.   *That you can't blame Heidi for. You see she can't say what the newspapers will write ... what they are doing, that's their business you see.*

F.   *You see it's a bit too much for them to say they were wrong. They just don't do that, the newspapers.*

TS.   *Maybe they don't will do that but that is the business for the newspapers, you see. You can't blame Heidi for that.*

F.   *Well I can certainly blame her for telling those outrageous lies.*

TS.   *That's because they're not writing nice things about you after the case is closed.*

F.   *It's because obviously they think she's a poor little girl and they ...*

TS.   *Maybe they do, yes, but as I said, if the newspaper is doing that you can't er ...*

F.   *... do anything about it ...*

TS.   *... do something about it because it's a free country and every newspaper have to write [and there my tape ended].*

The PFU wrote back on 24th June 1996 from Oslo

Sir,

We have received your letter of June 9th concerning your complaint on reports in Norwegian newspapers in May 1995.

According to the statutes of the Press Complaints Commission, Article 4.3, your complaint cannot be taken up by the Commission because it came too late. The article reads as follows:

A complaint must be filed within three months after the publication. Exemptions from this time limit can be made within a reasonable time if the complainant has had no opportunity to acquaint himself with the matter and it is a matter of principal interest.

We will, however, make reference to your complaint and this letter in the next meeting of the Commission scheduled for August 20th.

Yours sincerely,

Norsk Presseforbund
Signed Gunnar Gran, Secretary General

Letter dated 2nd July 1996 from the PFU

Case 099/96 - Drammens Tidende, Verdens Gang og Bergens Tidende

We have received your latest letter concerning the complaints against the newspapers mentioned above.

We will in front of the meeting in the Commission make reference to your remarks regarding exemptions from the time limit.

Yours sincerely,
The Press Complaints Commission
Signed by Arne Jensen, Secretary Organisation

This letter was written to me in response to my earlier letter asking for the time limit of three months to be ignored by the PFU on the grounds that I had not had all the articles translated into Norwegian (which of course cost me money) until well after the three month time limit had expired. I was extremely confident that an exception would be made to allow my complaint to be heard in full, as, basing my evidence on the truth of the matter and full investigations by me, it would then certainly be in the public interest for these newspapers to be exposed as completely fraudulent.

Letter dated 14th August 1996 from the PFU

Case 099/96 Drammens Tidende, Verdens Gang and Bergens Tidende

We have on 12.8.96 received your letter of 7.8.96 concerning the complaints against the newspapers mentioned above.

In our former letters we optimistically informed you that we had the intention to make reference to your complaints in the August meeting of the Commission. We are sorry to say that such reference can not be made until the next meeting, September 17th. That is due to great number of complaints received during the summer and due to the late arrival of your latest letter.

Yours sincerely,

For Press Complaints Commission

Signed by Kjell M Børringbo, Secretary to the Commission

In August I spoke to Torill Sorte and Svein Jensen:

TS.   *Sorte.*

F.   *Yeah, hi Torill, it's Frederick here.*

TS.   *Hi!*

F.   *Hi there! I had a chat today to the Press Complaints Commission and they told me that first of all the press in Norway are waiting for you, you know, the police to ...*

TS.   *I have talked to them today.*

F.   *Yeah, ah ... today?*

TS.   *Yes.*

F.   *Ah, and secondly they tell me that the press aren't interested in printing my side of the story. So as far as I'm concerned, then, they're worthless. Horrible people. I just can't see the justice in them* [the newspapers] *waiting for you to get in touch with them so that they can print another load of rubbish.*

TS.   *But, as I have told you before, the press do what they want. I can't tell them what they shall do and you can't tell them what they shall do. They do what they want, and they'll write what they want.*

F.   *Can you not, at least, as I asked you before, at least write to them specifically on these points. That you haven't found any evidence of threats to kill Heidi's neighbours or threats to kill her son and emphasise that ...*

TS.   *You see, I'm not in a position that ... ... I can't do that.*

F.   *But you are the police. You must, you ...*

TS.   *Yes, I am the police and I can answer questions that they ask me but I can't write to them and tell them which way a case take.*

F.   *I thought the whole investigation was based upon the fact that I've had allegations made against me that I've threatened to kill her son and the neighbours. Surely that's a serious matter for the police to investigate and for them to deny it or prove it.*

TS.   *As I have told you before, that point of the case was investigated in Bergen by now and that's not my problem. I have to take care of all the letters you are writing.*

F.   *Yes, that's right, lots of them* [I was referring to my 'reports' in Norwegian].

TS.   *Yes and look at them and that's my case. What the police in Bergen have done – they have to answer for that. I am only taking these letters I have it ... if you want a letter from the police in Bergen who said they have locked your case and don't find any evidence for going to court, you can get, maybe get that.*

F.   *I've given up with them because they won't write to me anything. I've written to them before and asked them and Commander Krogvold says he's not going to enter into any correspondence. You see, I would have liked something in writing about the attempted rape business and I've told the other newspapers the reason all these letters are going to so may people because of that allegation of attempted rape. As far as I'm concerned, there was no 'attempt' to do this and unfortunately - I know you are caught in the middle - but the press for me are evil and they have to be taught a lesson and if they can't print my side of the story then this case will never end.*

TS.   *You see the press can print what they want. If they don't want to print about you, they can do that. I can't say to them, you have to write about Freddy.*

F.   *I think that this is such a major issue to do with love and truth that I think they need a lesson. Especially Heidi. She's also complete evil and I can't let her win. And if they don't print my side of the story as far as I'm concerned the press have won, because everybody in Norway seems to ... you know if it's printed then they will think, "Oh, it's probably true" – because they don't believe that the press prints such lies.*

TS.   *We have talked about this before and my position – I mean that people in Norway have forget this case a long time ago.*

F.   *Have forgotten it?*

TS.   *Yes, I think so.*

F.   *But the thing is, I haven't.*

TS.   *No, not you, but people around* [i.e. the general public in Norway] *have done that* [i.e. forgotten it] *and when you are sending these letters saying things about Heidi, they think you are crazy. It isn't interesting for them. It isn't interesting for them what you are saying. They buy the case of Heidi and I mean that was interesting.* [An astonishing remark by Torill Sorte. The newspaper stories were "interesting" for the public, but the actual truth was not.]

F.   *Why did they find it interesting? Because it's all sexy, salacious, criminal stuff that everyone's going to find interesting. Obscene letters, obscene phone calls. Of course they'll find it interesting. But the trouble is, it's all rubbish. I'm beginning to think that people in Norway are simple in the head. You know, any fool can understand my point of view. I mean I've told people here* [about my plight] *and they can't believe it. And I want to teach Heidi a lesson, a nice good one and I'm afraid there's gonna be a lot more stress for her and I really want to 'break her back.' If you can't question her about the* [allegation of] *attempted rape whilst she's in the police station with you, right, and you say she doesn't mention this, then ... I've asked you to mention this to her.*

TS.   *Yes, but that's not my case. I'm not interested in that. Heidi is not getting* [your] *letters. She is not hearing about the case at all. She don't hear from you because all the letters you send to her they come to me.*

F.   *Yeah, that's right. But you see, the letters that come to you come from England. If I got someone to send letters from Norway or Sweden, they would get to Heidi and she would hear about the case.*

TS.   *No.*

F.   *Why not?*

TS.   *Because she has asked to have stopped all the letters she don't know who have write them.*

F.   *Oh has she?*

TS.   *Yes.*

F.   *So she trying to, um ...*

TS.   *She don't want to hear about this ...*

F.   *At all?*

TS.   *No.*

F.   *Yeah, that's right. Well she's obviously had enough.*

TS.   *Yes, she had enough.*

F.   *Yeah, but the thing is, you know if she still tells you in the police station that I've threatened to kill her son then she obviously is still lying and if she's had enough it's too bad. I can't ... ...*

TS.	But that's the case for Bergen police station who have investigated this and they said we have not go to the court with this case [i.e. there will be no prosecution of me on threats to kill a child].
F.	Can you at least tell the press this?
TS.	No, I can't.
F.	Oh, well that's ludicrous isn't it? That is really ridiculous, because that's the whole point. To prove that she's a liar. She is a liar.
TS.	I can't tell the press about any case I am [handling] you see.
F.	So why do people write to me [a private detective from Oslo - a chap called Gunnar Reklev - did] and tell me the police believe her?
TS.	You have to ask them about that.
F.	I have and they say they can't reveal their sources, but the police have told them [that they believe Heidi].
TS.	The only thing I have told the [press] is that we have not ... you live in England, she live in Norway and we have no such much evidence that we can go to the English police department and say we want to talk to Frederick about this because here in Norway it's not a big crime. It isn't.
F.	What isn't?
TS.	The case you have.
F.	Yeah, that's what I thought.
TS.	Writing letters to people around in Norway is not a big crime here in Norway.
F.	No.
TS.	That's why I'm closing the case but I have to put the case together before I send it to the lawyers in Drammen and then I think it will be closed.
F.	Why do the Press Complaints people tell me this morning that if I was living in Norway there will be a case, that I would, er ...
TS.	I think it will be yes. It will be a case that you are all the time sending letters around everywhere.
F.	But you just said to me now it wasn't a serious ... ...
TS.	Crime?
F.	I mean why is it a crime for a start? It's a civil matter. It's me telling the truth just as [and I was going to add "the newspapers tell crap"].
TS.	But you see Heidi have come to us because she want [us to] investigate you.
F.	Yeah, why?
TS.	Because she mean you have done something to her that you are not allowed to do.

F.   *Yeah, what?*

TS.   *Er, er ...*

F.   *Yes tell me, you've never told me before.*

TS.   *That's writing letters about her who you are sending around here in Norway.*

F.   *Yeah!*

TS.   *She don't like it ... I would not have like it.*

F.   *Yeah, but I don't like finding out she's lied to the police that I've attempted to rape her when I haven't.*

TS.   *But that's another case.*

F.   *No. It's the same case. That's why I wrote the letters.*

TS.   *No it isn't.*

F.   *It is. I wrote those letters because I found that out* [the allegation of attempted rape]. *So it is the same case. Why do you think I sent those letters* [reports]? *Because I send them the day after my lawyer in Norway wrote to me saying that he's found out that she's gone to the police saying that I've attempted to rape her and if you ask her about the Bergen shopkeeper that she also went to the police and said had attempted to rape her then you can build up a nice big picture that she is a born natural liar. A repetitive habitual liar who needs help.*

TS.   *These things about the letters is the only thing I'm investigating, and as I have told you that's not a big enough case to go to England and ask for help. That's why the case will be closed.*

F.   *Good, will I get a letter from you?*

TS.   *You will get a letter from me when the case is closed. We have had a murder here.*

F.   *You did?*

TS.   *Yes.*

F.   *Oh God, who, who?*

TS.   *Some people in a motor cycle group.*

F.   *Hells Angels?*

TS.   *Hells Angels and Bandidos.*

F.   *And who?*

TS.   *Bandidos.*

F.   *What are they?*

TS.   *A group who is not so big as Hells Angels.*

F.   *So it's a gang fight?*

TS.   *Yeah ... so I'm working with that and that's why your case is taking so long.*

F.   *Oh, OK, fair enough. I understand. What did the Press Complaints Commission phone you up for this morning?*

TS.   *When they called?*

F.   *Yeah.*

TS.   *Er about 10.30 I think.*

F.   *Yeah, why do they call you? Just to, er ... ...*

TS.   *They have asked me if I have sent the case to Drammen and what I will do with it and I told them what I have told you.*

F.   *Right. 'Cos they seemed quite angry with me. He [Kjell Børringbo] seemed very resentful.*

TS.   *That is [because] you are calling them and they look at it as a problem, I think.*

F.   *A problem?*

TS.   *That you are calling and ask for things and so on.*

F.   *Well, that's their function isn't it? To investigate complaints against the newspapers. 'Cos no-one else helps me.*

TS.   *But let's hear what they want to do with it.*

F.   *Well I think everyone in Norway is against me. Everyone.*

TS.   *I don't think it's personal.*

F.   *Well, huh!* [Not "personal" my arse, I thought!]

TS.   *I don't think so. But it's the way the press can write. You see ...*

F.   *I can never forgive it ...*

TS.   *I am in the newspaper sometimes and they write things about a case I have dealt with who is not correct at all.*

F.   *This is ridiculous. That's disgusting. You are a policeman and they must print exactly the truth and what you say.*

TS.   *They print what people want to read.*

F.   *In that case they're scum and they ought to go to prison. You ought to go round and arrest them. This is just terrible stuff. We're living in a fantasy world.*

TS.   *Press Freedom. They can do what they want to do.*

F.   *It's a big abuse of freedom and I hope one day to confront these journalists myself and then they'll be taught a good lesson because this is just disgusting stuff – writing about sex-terror just to sell their newspapers. I feel sorry for you as well because ... I've gone on for a year now. I'm not phoning you up pretending to be a liar. I know what I've done. I know I've sworn at Heidi and I know what I've sent and I can admit all that, but um ... ...*

TS.   *When shall you stop?*

F.   *Well, probably, - not yet - 'cos I still wake up in the middle of the night with the words that I've threatened to kill her son* [coming back to haunt me] *and I can't live with it. I can't. And I don't see why I should.*

TS.   *I don't understand why you can't live with it when ...*

F.   *Because I haven't done it and she's told ...*

TS.   *Yes, but when it's a lie then that's her problem and not yours.*

F.   *Well it's my problem because I loved that little boy and he's probably read the newspapers and everybody thinks that I'm a pervert. And ... ... the press had the chance just to say ... just for them to print: "This was Heidi's words and we have no proof of it, it only came from Heidi." But they didn't. They have not printed my side or just an apology and they are sticking by their story. They told me they believe her…… How many chances have they had to print my side of the story and just apologise? They've had a year and they've done nothing.*

TS.   *They don't want to do it.*

F.   *Well, then they have to take the penalty don't they?*

TS.   *As I told you before the press do what they want.*

F.   *Oh, well. I think... they're evil and ……*

TS.   *That's their right ... I think people will talk about the press in the future also because the press have a right to write what they want and write it when they want it and the only thing they have to think about is to do something ... what shall I say ... if they write a story that the people tell them they can write it but they can't mix a story.*

F.   *Can't what?*

TS.   *They can't mix it themselves you see.*

F.   *Mix?*

TS.   *Er Make it ... ...*

F.   *Yeah, they can't make it up themselves…… I mean even in England we have The Sun and the Mirror…… if they found out Heidi's past they would print it all. They would crucify her……*

TS.   *They don't want to look at it.*

F.   *That is right because I think it's a racist element as well – anti Muslim, anti-foreign. Everyone knows here in England that Norway's a racist nation. Very insular. It's not just me saying that. It's ordinary English people. But OK. Well, I guess that's it. I'll just wait to ... ...*

TS.   *I hope for doing something with the case when I come over this murder. But I have told the press what I have told you and nothing more.*

F.   *Well thanks for that.*

TS.   *And if they say anything else that's for them.*

F.   *They keep insisting that you* [the police] *believe them fully. Sorry, you believe Heidi fully and, er, that's upset me because I keep, er ... I'm suspicious you see.*

TS.   *As I told you before, my job is not to believe. My job is to investigate.*

F.   *Ok Torill, well thanks a million. I'll wait to receive your letter.*

TS.   *OK.*

F.   *Thank you very much.*

TS.   *Yes.*

F.   *Bye bye.*

TS.   *Bye.*

I made a subsequent phone call to policeman Svein Jensen who was at the Oslo Police Headquarters:

F.   *Yes, hi there Mr. Jensen, you remember me, Frederick Delaware.*

SJ.   *Yes, I remember you.*

F.   *Yes, hi there. I got your phone number from the Mjøndalen police station. Sorry to trouble you again, but I keep hearing from the newspapers and from other people that the police seem to believe Heidi and not me and in view of that I was just wondering how this can be?*

SJ.   *I don't know because I don't have the case. That's Torill.*

F.   *She doesn't herself tell me anything. She just says there's no evidence and all this.*

SJ.   *I see, but I don't know what's new in the case. I can't help you.*

F.   *I don't think anything's new at all. It's just that I'm not very happy the way she's* [Torill]*... she's very nice to me over the phone, but it's just that when Heidi came in after 11 months to speak to Torill, I phoned up at the very moment that Heidi was in with her and I asked to speak to Heidi because I want to challenge her over allegations that I've threatened to kill her son and her neighbours and I've written hundreds of obscene letters and made hundreds of obscene phone calls. I have not done any of this and I must have the chance to challenge her over this and, er, that's why I asked Torill to let her speak to me, and she says she doesn't want to speak to me but specifically I said please ask her about this allegation of attempted rape in 1986. That's the reason I've been sending all these letters 'cos I'm sick of it. I said that's the reason for the whole case, that she's gone and told lies to the newspapers because of these 'reports' I'm sending so please ask her about the* [allegation of] *attempted rape. And she didn't. She said nothing. She didn't mention it to her. She says: "Heidi didn't mention this to me." And to me this is just ridiculous because she's made allegations I've attempted to rape her. She's made allegations a Bergen shopkeeper attempted to rape her and unless this is investigated then what's the point of it all. I'm trying to prove this girl is a liar and a very sick woman and yet the opposite is written that I am the sick man and that I'm suffering from erotic paranoia and Muslim men are this and that ... I can't accept this and never will and I will continue my campaign against her until the newspapers print my side of the story. I can't live with this.*

SJ.   *I see, but I'm afraid, er ...*

F.   *You are her boss. You are above her* [Torill]. *You must be able to do something for God's sake.*

SJ.   *But I haven't had time to get myself into the case as has Torill.*

F.   *You see, I want a man to deal with this. I don't want a woman. I've got nothing against Torill personally, but she's just a woman with a woman and I want a man to talk to the woman. I'm a man. I want a man on my side. I can't live with these allegations. I've read them again in the newspapers in English. I can't sleep. I just cannot have this and the newspapers are refusing to print my side of the story. The Editor of Bergens Tidende told me that in the 25 years he's been in the newspapers he's never come across a case where the other person's point of view is not printed. He says: "We always print the other side" and I said: "Well you haven't printed my side and it's 15 months [since the newspaper articles]. You've got all my information" and he says he hasn't even seen my correspondence. I send my stuff to the newspapers, to the journalist and he doesn't give it to the Editor. He [the journalist] says: "Speak to my Editor" and then I speak to the Editor and then he says "I've not heard anything ... I don't know about this." What's going on up there?*

SJ.   *I don't know, I'm sorry.*

F.   *OK, well I appreciate you're busy and everybody's got their lives to live, but I've got to clear my name and you can tell Torill that I will continue to send reports to everyone I can until my name is cleared.*

SJ.   *I think if you still going on with that, er ... it will not help you.*

F.   *But nothing helps me anyway. Whatever I do doesn't help me. Nothing helps me.*

SJ.   *I'm afraid that will turn into so that it will be more painful for you.*

F.   *But no one's doing anything anyway. No one is in touch with me. No one writes to me. The newspapers, the police – no one gets in touch with me to say anything. Except the Press Complaints Commission and they will investigate my case on the 20th August.*

and again I spoke to Torill Sorte in September:

TS.   *Sorte.*

F.   *Yeah, hi Torill, it's Frederick here.*

TS.   *Oh.*

F.   *Yeah, hi there. I was wondering the other day – I haven't heard from you with this letter that was going to come. What's been happening?*

TS.   *I have talked to ... the chief lawyer in the Department.*

F.   *The prosecutor?*

TS.   *Yeah, you can call him that, and he want to take a look at the case before I do anything else.*

F.   *The case?*

TS.   *The case Heidi has sent to us when she come here with it a long time ago ... a year I think.*

F.   *What was her case?*

192

TS.   *I have talked about that many times. You know what that is.*

F.   *No, it's not just sending these bits of paper is it? [My reports.]*

TS.   *Huh?*

F.   *It's not…… the stuff that's arriving in post is it, in Norwegian?*

TS.   *No, it's her story about what she means is her problem. The letters and everything. Of course I could have sent you a letter, but I …… …*

F.   *… you have nothing much to say.*

TS.   *Yeah, so I'm sorry about that. I shall write it in my book and I shall do it I hope this week.*

Letter dated 2nd October 1996 from the PFU

Case 099/96 Drammens Tidende, Verdens Gang and Bergens Tidende

As confirmed by telephone today, the Press Complaints Commission in its meeting September 17th decided not to make exemptions from the time limit regarding your complaints.

This is the Commissions final decision and we therefore formally close the case.

Yours sincerely,

For the Press Complaints Commission

Signed Kjell M Børringbo, Secretary to the Commission.

Finally, in October, I spoke to Torill Sorte again:

TS.   *Sorte.*

F.   *Yeah, hi Torill, it's Frederick here again.*

TS.   *Oh.*

F.   *I was wondering when on earth this case or letter from you is gonna close this matter altogether.*

TS.   *I have looked at this case and I have talked to the Statenlawyer and we are doing something with it but it hasn't gone fast because, er …… …*

F.   *It's not important?*

TS.   *Yes it's important for the people who ……*

F.   *But it's not priority anyway?*

TS.   *No, it isn't.*

F.   *So what's the position then with this case?*

TS.   (Chuckling) *I hope ha! ha! ha! to send the case to my lawyer in the police in Drammen before Christmas, I hope.*

F.   *Saying what? I mean what's he gonna do?*

TS.   *The case is what Heidi have, er said in her, er.........*

F.   *Statement.*

TS.   *Yes, statement.   And my job is to prove or get evidence for one direction and the other direction.*

F.   *So let's be honest, all you've got to really do is confront her again over these allegations that she says I've written threats in letters to kill her son, yeah? Now all you've got to do is get her back and say: "Look, Mr. Delaware is terribly upset over this lie and he has to clear his name," so what if you could please, is ask her to either prove that some evidence exists or admit she's lied. I know it's very hard* [for her] *to admit she's lied but at lest you can put it to her that, "We have to assume Heidi that you have lied." And secondly you can ask her to produce these neighbours* [and then my tape ran out before I could add "that I'm supposed to have threatened to kill."]

Chapter 18

Out of the twenty or so reports that I initially sent out in Norwegian detailing Heidi's past, one had been picked up by a freelance photographer as he lived next door to Heidi's parents' old address. Her parents had moved. He passed this report on to a local Bergen journalist who told me he phoned up Heidi and read out the report whereupon she burst into tears. The rest is history.

My own 'press release' printed above was, as I have previously mentioned, sent out to hundreds upon hundreds of people whose addresses I had gleaned from the Bergen and Drammen phone directories. I had to resort to this tactic as it eventually became clear to me that no Norwegian newspaper was going to print a word of my side of the story. The last time I phoned Heidi was simply to call her "a racist pig" and as she drew breath to comment I put the phone down on her. After that she changed her phone number so my only source of information on the case was from Torill Sorte of the Mjøndalen police with whom I was in regular contact.

I wasn't at all disturbed by the phone call from some Englishman threatening to "break" my "fucking legs." He didn't specify why he wanted to do this but I knew it could only have come at Heidi's instigation. I told him to "fuck off " myself, knowing his threats to be bluff. To organise a revenge beating is a very risky business. If an Englishman is going to do it then he would be a stranger to Heidi and would not do it unless he was paid - and paid well, and there is no absolute guarantee that he wouldn't be seen or get caught in the act. So he could, being a mercenary, just take the money, do nothing and tell Heidi that the job had been done. It would be difficult for her to find out for sure whether the job had in fact been done. Also Heidi would be opening herself up to conspiracy to commit a criminal offence if the perpetrator of the violence was caught and arrested by the police. To save his own skin, or at least reduce his prison sentence, he'd probably implicate Heidi as his co-conspirator. It would take hours of stalking me, waiting outside my house possibly, following me and hoping an opportunity would arise where I would be alone and the assault could take place. As for sending someone over from Norway, the expense was something Heidi and her family would never be able to afford. There are the airline fares, hotel bills and car hire for a start. This is beside the usual risk of being caught in the act. So in all I was quite sure no one was going to break my legs, especially on behalf of a delinquent liar like Heidi.

As can be seen, the faxes and letters that I had sent all over Norway were affecting the recipients, resulting in numerous telephone calls to the Bergen and Mjøndalen police. Many of them obviously wouldn't have a clue what was going on not having read the newspapers and may have thought the person sending them was rather extreme. But, as I was at pains to point out to the Mjøndalen police, I had little alternative although I hoped that if the targets of this information knew the full facts they would sympathise with me.

Why did I liken Heidi's behaviour and that of the Norwegian press, and in this group I also include the psychiatrist Nils Rettersdøl, to that of the Serbs' behaviour and actions against the Muslims in Bosnia? The reason is that I believe the motivation for the press attack on me as for the attacks on the Muslims of Bosnia was blind prejudice and hatred of Islam. I could see in Heidi's letter of 1982 to me her prejudice against Islam and also of the boyfriend of Tone from Arendal who with no justification or provocation whatsoever called me "a black, ugly, fanatic." He knew I was Muslim. This wicked emotion lies just under the surface which, if scratched, is bared in full. No attempt was made whatsoever by the Norwegian press to corroborate Heidi's side of the story. They had relied only on her own word and numerous letters from me containing explicit and specific reference to Heidi's sexual past - all of which nevertheless was completely true. Heidi had told them it was all untrue and, maybe her denial was, at first sight, grounds for believing that she had been the victim of gross injustice. But the fact is that the 20 or so reports in Norwegian that were initially sent to several of her neighbours could easily have been verified and checked out by these journalists, who it seems on this occasion did not value their worth as investigative reporters. It was pure evil to allege to the police that I had threatened to kill her son in a letter when he was 2 years old or so. I can never forgive this. The subtle institutionalisation of Islamophobia in Norway can never be better illustrated than by the newspapers' use of psychiatrist Nils Rettersdøl's comments and whose exposure I have eagerly sought. Further evidence of press duplicity will be amply provided later in this book.

I truly believe that the Norwegian people in general fear Islam, although obviously to a lesser degree than the Serbs and Croats and in saying 'Norwegian people' I mean that expression of opinion as presented by the press who are supposed to reflect the people's traits and views. Sure, there do exist bad Muslims (i.e. hypocrites) but objectively I was not one of them on the facts. The press all too readily printed a pack of lies and it seems quite a few people believed those newspaper stories. This I equate with the eagerness of the Serb and Croat people to believe the filth that was suddenly preached by their respective leaders, Milošević and Tuđman, telling them that Muslims were their enemies and to go out to kill them if they, the Serbs and Croats, weren't to be killed first. Just as the German people proved in the 1930's and 1940's and the Serbs and Croats proved in the 1990's, so too I believe that the Norwegians have proved by their newspaper attacks on me that humanity can warp and pervert rational thinking into an insanely destructive force. The perpetrators of such fundamental lies and cruelty belong on a different planet, and they belong in hell. Bosnia is a subject I will deal with in more detail in the next chapter.

Although, unfortunately, I did not tape it as I had not yet obtained the recording device, my first telephone conversation with Mr. Runar Schøne in late summer 1995 is one I will always remember. He answered the phone himself and said to me, "Allah doesn't exist - come to Jesus, only he can save you" and immediately proceeded to speak in 'tongues' for three whole minutes. During his rantings, I gave the phone to my mother and she could not believe what she was hearing. At the time, I wasn't quite sure that he was speaking in 'tongues' but a fortnight later I saw a Biblical television programme on the BBC's 'Everyman' programme broadcast from Manchester. In it, they recited exactly the sort of language that Runar Schøne had spoken to me. His wife, Heidi, was beside him and what she thought of her husband doing this to me I cannot imagine. But as she was married to him and later gave birth to a son, I assume she was fully behind him. Runar Schøne, though, epitomised a deeply ingrained way of thinking which explains much and on which I will come back to.

Chapter 19

In one of the 'information' sheets I had been sending all over Norway, I included a short paragraph paying tribute to the Muslim dead of Bosnia and blamed their sickening plight on a certain 'attitude' deeply ingrained in Western thinking. I deliberately linked the unspeakable atrocities befalling those people to the foundation of thought portrayed by the form of words used in the Norwegian press coverage. A Norwegian artist I met at the Norwegian YWCA in West London in 1998 called Olaf Storø told me that Norwegians are brought up from a young age to consider anyone who is not Christian as "heathen" (and by "heathen" he specifically included Muslims and Jews and all other non-Christian faiths). I thought this rather ironic in that firstly the Vikings were the classic heathens before Christianity reached them and secondly, today, Norwegians are for all practical purposes Christian in name only. They are at best 'pick and choose' Christians and at worst devout atheists; Scandinavians as a whole are like this.

Olaf Storø's remarks are clearly borne out by Heidi Overaa's letter to me from 1982 ("But Islam, NO NO") and the fact that Bergens Tidende printed the word 'Muslim' nineteen times, clearly linking the word 'Muslim,' not just to my so called 'perversion' but so far as I am concerned to their perceived general defect in Muslims. Perhaps a few degrees short of the 'general depravity' that the Jews were labelled with in 1930's Germany, but much closer to the Serb and Croat propaganda onslaught against the Yugoslav Muslims. I felt the fact the Bosnians were Muslim created, to a significant extent, the apathy of the governments of Europe and America, which led to nothing effectively being done to prevent the slaughter of the Muslims in Bosnia.

Peter Maass, the heroic journalist on the Washington Post, himself a Jew, in 1996 wrote a book on his experiences in Bosnia - 'Love They Neighbour - A Story of War.' His analysis is as close as you will get to the truth of the matter of Bosnia's betrayal and the underlying causes for the carnage inflicted on the blond and blue-eyed Muslims. I give you the following extracts from his book, but before I do, I would like to pay my own tribute to Peter Maass, who I have corresponded with on Bosnia and Kosovo and spoken to, by saying that no greater friend in the world could the Muslims of Bosnia have had than him. He is quite simply a wonderful man.

"Just as David Owen did the dirty work for British Prime Minister Major and French President Mitterrand, Major and Mitterrand were doing the dirty work for Clinton. This was helpful.   Clinton could criticise the Europeans obliquely, and his aides could criticise them directly, but he never stood in their way, he implicitly encouraged them and let them take a well-deserved beating for being appeasers. The leading-edge role of Europe's leaders deserves far more attention than I can give it in this book. Why did Major follow the politics of Chamberlain rather than the politics of Churchill? Why did Mitterrand follow the politics of Pétain rather than the politics of de Gaulle? There are specific reasons. Major, an uninspiring leader, had shallow support in his own Tory party and was focused on domestic affairs, while Mitterrand, at the end of fourteen years in office, was a tired old man fighting cancer of the prostate. There are other reasons, too, many others, but they are less important than the general observation that nations, like individuals, have the ability to be brave and the ability to be cowardly, and, when the war in Bosnia broke out, the leaders of Britain and France tapped the cowardly vein in the soul of their nations, lulling their people to sleep with soothing lies. It could have been otherwise,

and perhaps next time, with a new set of leaders, it will be.

Dust in our eyes. Bill Clinton wanted us to forget about Bosnia, to write if off as an infinitely complex place in which nothing was as simple as it might seem, only the high priests of politics could figure it out, for the war was a matter of tribal rivalries and those Balkan people "have been fighting each other for centuries," blah-blah-blah. This was rubbish, and Clinton knew it. What people on this planet have not been fighting other people for centuries? Not the French and Germans, not the British and French, not the Koreans and Japanese, and not, for that matter, the citizens of the United States; if you consider the Civil War and the war against Native Americans and perhaps toss in the recent riots in Los Angeles and Liberty City, not to mention Harlem or Watts or the startling murder rate in Washington, D.C., Americans have been fighting *one another* for centuries. The point is this: if you can understand the intricacies of a draw playing football or the wild-card play-off system, as most Americans can, then you can understand Bosnia. Beginners might need fifteen or twenty minutes of instructions to grasp the basics of either subject. Unfortunately, most Americans got two-minute television stories or six-hundred-word newspaper articles that created more confusion than comprehension - on the one hand this, on the other hand that - and influential government officials, with their evasions and contradictions, made things cloudier, intentionally. In essence, Americans never had the chance to learn the rules of the game, and they were told by their government not to bother, because the game was too complex for ordinary mortals to understand.

I want to explain that in May 1993, after Clinton used the Europeans as an alibi for his own inaction, the foreign ministers of Britain, France, Russia, Spain and America met in Washington and put on another show of resolve. They put aside the troublesome question of rolling back the Serbs and decided, instead, to protect a few bits of territory held by the Bosnians. They created six "safe areas." The message to the Serbs was clear: Take everything else but not our little safe areas. Yet, illustrating that appeasement increases rather than fulfils an aggressor's appetite, the Serbs kept attacking the safe areas, restricting the amount of food delivered to them, and the world powers did little. "Mr. Clinton is going to be a great president," cheered Radovan Karadžić. The United Nations troops dispatched to the safe areas were not, it transpired, allowed to use their weapons to defend the safe areas. The troops could fire back only if their own lives were in danger, rather than the lives of the Bosnians whom, we erroneously assumed the troops were there to defend. On occasion, the world powers forgot to pretend they were serious, and in one case, hundreds of U.N. troops were sent to protect the Bihać safe area *without weapons*. Obviously, if you had the terrible misfortune to live in a United Nations "safe area," you lived in one of the most dangerous places on earth. It was not much of a surprise that U.N. soldiers surrendered their weapons when Serbs finally called the West's bluff in 1995 and mounted an earnest assault on the safe areas of Srebrenica and Žepe, capturing them.

I want to explain that Bill Clinton's rare displays of resolve were deceptions, no difference from fakes in dodgeball, shifting left before leaping right. In February 1994, a Serb shell landed in a Sarajevo marketplace, killing 68 people, a number of little consequence in a war that had killed about 200,000, but camera crews recorded the carnage in the safe area, and this led to international outrage. I want to explain that President Clinton threw dust in our eyes by saying, for example, that he had tried hard to get our allies to agree to lift the arms embargo against the Bosnians and carry out air strikes against the Serbs, but in fact he hardly tried. He sent Warren Christopher on a famous trip to Europe in May 1993, but Christopher did not argue or cajole when he stopped in Paris, London and Moscow, he merely listened and nodded his head, and then returned to Washington to say that, despite his supreme efforts, our European allies refused to budge, so the embargo would, regrettably, stay in place, and the F-16s would, regrettably, stay in their hangers. President Clinton passed on the message to the country. More than two years later, his real agenda became clear when Congress called his bluff and approved a bill to lift the embargo; Clinton vetoed it.

I can recall the precise day when, finally, I fell spiritually sick. It was April 22, 1993.

In Washington D.C., the Holocaust Memorial Museum was being inaugurated in an outdoor ceremony that featured an emotional speech by President Bill Clinton, who looked bravely into an unseasonably cold wind and hit all the right notes, as he usually does. "The nations of the West must live forever with this knowledge: Even as our fragmentary awareness of these crimes grew into indisputable facts, we did far too little. Before the war started, doors to liberty were slammed shut. And even after we attacked Germany, rail lines to the camps, within miles of militarily significant targets, were left undisturbed. Mass deaths were left to occur, enshrouded in our denial .... The evil represented in this museum is incontestable. It is absolute. As we are its witness, so we must remain its adversary. We owe that much to the dead, as we owe it to our consciences and our children. So we must stop the fabricators of history and the bullies as well. Left unchallenged, they would still prey upon the powerless, and we cannot permit that to happen again."

Elie Wiesel was on the stage with Clinton. A few months earlier, Wiesel had visited a Serb prison camp in Bosnia, and the haunted faces of the Muslim inmates reminded him of the doomed souls jailed with him at Auschwitz fifty years before. He saw many parallels, too many. And so, when he reached the speaker's podium, Wiesel, a writer of extraordinary conscience, had no choice but to turn his perpetually sad gaze away from the crowd and look into the eyes of William Jefferson Clinton, perhaps the only person in the world who could turn things around. It was not the polite thing to do, but it was the right thing to do. "Mr. President, I cannot not tell you something," Wiesel said. "I have been in the former Yugoslavia last fall. I cannot sleep since for what I have seen. As a Jew I am saying that we must do something to stop the bloodshed in that country. People fight each other and children die. Why? Something, anything must be done!"

This is when you start to feel the spiritual sickness. It can be held at tolerable levels if you convince yourself that your efforts as a journalist or aid worker or diplomat might make a difference. You soldier on. But the sickness takes over if you sense futility, if you can no longer look a Bosnian in the eye and say, in honesty, that the reason the world doesn't react is because it doesn't know what's happening or doesn't understand. When you conclude that the world does know, and does understand, and still doesn't react, your time is up. When that happens, you do unusual things. Canadian diplomat Louis Gentile, who worked in Banja Luka for the U.N. High Commissioner for Refugees, wrote an unusual letter to *The New York Times* on January 14,1994. It was a diplomat's primal scream:

> The terror continues, terror of attacks by armed men at night, rape and murder, children unable to sleep, huddling in fear behind boarded up doors and windows. The latest victims were three Muslim residents of the Banja Luka suburb of Vrbanja on December 29. In broad daylight, four armed men (two in uniform) entered the home of a couple 58 and 54 years old. The man was shot in the head and killed; his wife was shot in the hand and then beaten to death with a blunt instrument. A Muslim neighbour, who had the courage and misfortune to inquire what was happening when the murderers left carrying a television set, was shot in the heart at point-blank range ...

> To those who said to themselves after seeing *Schindler's List*, "Never again": It is happening again. The so-called leaders of the western world have known what is happening here for the last year and a half. They receive play-by-play reports. They talk of prosecuting war criminals, but do nothing to stop the crimes. May God forgive them. May God forgive us all.

Geneva is what Europe aspires to be, and Sarajevo is what Europe recoils from. They would seem to have nothing in common, these two cities, except that when you are in one of them, you cannot imagine that the other exists.

The truth, more complex than appearances, is that they are similar, underneath their contrasting garments, like a millionaire and a beggar. There is much virtue to be found in Sarajevo, even beauty, and much vileness in Geneva, even evil. All of this dawned on me when I turned down further assignments in Bosnia and was dispatched to Geneva, where, instead of soldiers tearing Bosnia apart, diplomats were doing the same thing. These diplomats were not Serbian or Croatian but American and British and French, and instead of preventing a crime, they acted as accomplices. The men with pens were every bit as fascinating and repulsive as the men with guns.

Bosnia was a circle, always leading you back to where you started, to the weaknesses of humans. It also, thank God, let you see the strengths of humans.

George Kenney quit his State Department job in the summer of 1992, and was followed a year later, in the summer of 1993, by three more diplomats, including Marshall Harris, the desk officer for Bosnia, whose letter of resignation became front-page news. "I can no longer serve in a Department of State that accepts the forceful dismemberment of a European state and that will not act against genocide and the Serbian officials who perpetrate it," Harris wrote to Secretary of State Warren Christopher on August 4, 1993. "I can no longer in good conscience allow myself to be associated with an administration that ... is driving the Bosnian government to surrender its territory and its sovereignty to the victors in a war of aggression. Accordingly, I hereby resign."

The others who resigned - Stephen Walker, the Croatia desk officer, and Jon Western, who compiled war crimes evidence in the Intelligence and Research Bureau - made similar statements about President Clinton's policy. A few months after them, another diplomat, Richard Johnson, who headed the Yugoslav desk, let his dissent be known through a private report entitled *The Pin Stripe Approach to Genocide*, in which he wrote, "My thesis here is a simple one: Senior U.S. government officials know that Serb leaders are waging genocide in Bosnia but will not say so in plain English because this would raise the pressure for U.S. action."

Izetbegović's [Bosnia's President] greatest defect was his naïveté. Whilst Serbs and Croats were obtaining weapons and organising themselves for war, Izetbegović was calling for peace and trying to keep Yugoslavia together. His effort to prevent the federation's breakup undercuts, yet again, the Serbo-Croat contention that he always wanted to set up an Islamic state in Bosnia. When the Yugoslav National Army (JNA in Serbian) ordered the disbanding, in January 1991, of all Territorial Defense units (similar to our National Guard), Izetbegović fully complied, despite the objections of some of his supporters. Izetbegović had been duped; while the JNA, whose officer corps was dominated by Serbs, disarmed Territorial Defense units in areas of Bosnia inhabited largely by Muslims, it secretly supplied more weapons to units in areas inhabited largely by Serbs. When Bosnia's secession became unavoidable, Izetbegović believed that Western countries would use their diplomatic and military muscle to prevent an attack by Serbia. Here, too, he was naïve.

I am thinking of a remarkable gathering, the International Conference for the Protection of War Victims, held in a large convention centre in Geneva. The keynote speaker was U.N. Secretary General Boutros Boutros-Ghali, whose appearance was the culmination of dozens of lofty speeches by ministers and ambassadors who arrived at the conference centre in spotless Mercedes limousines. Warren Zimmermann, the former ambassador to Yugoslavia and, at the time, still a loyal bureaucrat, represented the United States and, like every other speaker, condemned atrocities and genocide and insisted that war criminals

be brought to justice and punished severely. "Our governments meet this week here in Geneva to say enough! No more! This barbarism must stop!" And so on.

It was difficult to figure out whether such speeches should be met with applause or laughter, for just a few hundred yards away, at the Palais des Nations, Charles Redman was meeting with Radovan Karadžić, leader of Bosnian Serbs, and Slobodan Milošević, leader of Serbia, both identified by international human rights groups as the worst war criminals in Europe since Nazi Germany. Curiously, Karadžić and Milošević were treated with great respect during their frequent visits to Geneva, where, instead of arresting them, the United Nations arranged complimentary limousines for them and picked up the tab at their five-star hotels; It seemed an odd way to fight barbarism.

Back at the International Conference for the Protection of War Victims, on the other side of the Avenue de la Paix, the ministers and ambassadors wrapped up their speeches. You could almost hear the champagne glasses clinking against each other.

Was I too involved in Bosnia, am I biased, extreme in my judgements? No. There were many other people, respected and well-known, who came to similar conclusions.

Richard Nixon said: "The siege of Sarajevo can have a redeeming character only if the West learns two things as a result. The first is that enlightened peoples cannot be selective about condemning aggression and genocide … the other lesson is that because we are the last remaining superpower, no crisis is irrelevant to our interests."

George Schultz, secretary of state in the Reagan administration, said: "The Serbs have made suckers out of the United Nations. They have said, 'We're negotiating so don't use force on us because you might upset the negotiations'. Meanwhile, they're throwing the book at the Muslims, murdering them and raping them and so on… We should be prepared to conduct military strikes on gun emplacements, on supply lines, on weapons caches and ammunition depots and not just near the front lines but way back into Serbia."

In Los Angeles, a rainstorm is reason enough to keep children indoors, so on rainy days, when I was a boy, my seventh grade exercise class would be held in a small gymnasium, where, inevitably, our coach would let us play dodgeball for the fifty-minute period. Dodgeball was the most elemental of adolescent games. One boy would stand against the wall, was to duck the balls, and to do this, you would jump in the air, fling yourself to the left, to the right, up in the air again, fake a move to one side, then hit the ground, roll to your right, hop back on your feet, skip to your left, dodge to the right, hit the ground again and so on, until you got zinged, which, within a minute, was likely to happen, because only a young Nureyev could stay on his toes that long; everyone else was doomed to run out of energy and then, *boom-boom-boom,* three balls would slam into you.

The image of dodgeball is what comes to mind when I think of the way President Clinton reacted to Bosnia. The image may not be exact, perhaps inadequate, but it's the best I can come up with. Clinton was the boy against the wall. Month after month, year after year, he engaged in an array of acrobatics, ducking to his left, then his right, laying low on the ground, rising up again, jumping to one side, then the other, faking left before going right. These weren't physical movements, but political ones. Saying the fighting was a civil war, then saying it was a war of aggression; blaming the United Nations for getting in the way of NATO, then blaming NATO for getting in the way of the United Nations (even though he could dictate policy to either organisation); portraying Slobodan Milošević and Radovan Karadžić as war criminals, then sending high-level envoys to meet them, demanding that the arms embargo against Bosnia be lifted but refusing to anything about it, and then, later, opposing the lifting of the embargo!"

***

I am mindful of the Conservative Party's links with Serb interests which the Major government pandered to, particularly in the form of Douglas Hurd's business ventures. However, this was something Margaret Thatcher would never have let get in her way in punishing the Serbs, had she still been in power. Indeed, when I met a Serb woman, Sacha, in Paris at the height of the bombing of Belgrade in June 1999, she told me Milošević would never have started on his murderous campaign if Mrs. Thatcher had still been Prime Minster. At the outbreak of hostilities in 1991, Britain and her European partners were capable of handling the conflict themselves. Just after John Major became the Prime Minister, Dr. Zaki Badawi, the eminent Muslim scholar, based in London, called on Douglas Hogg, the Foreign Office Minister, to request of the British that one or two sorties – a small bombing campaign – be conducted over Belgrade on the basis of 'a stitch in time saves nine.' Hogg replied to the effect that bombing Belgrade didn't work in World War Two and that the Nazi's couldn't overcome the strongly resisting Serbs, so now the British would fare no better. But Badawi countered that: It was now the 1990's with high powered precision bombing to hand and he wasn't asking for anything more than a short sharp shock to stop Milošević in his tracks. Hogg's arguments proved vacuous when in August 1995 massive NATO bombing of Serb targets in Bosnia quickly helped bring Milošević to the negotiating table at Dayton.

On 19th September 1991, in The Hague, at a meeting of the European Foreign Ministers in joint session with the Western European Union (WEU) - a military forum - Douglas Hurd rejected a proposal that a robust peace-keeping force of 20,000 to 50,000 men be sent to Bosnia, citing the reason as the British experience in Northern Ireland. Mark Stuart in his authorised biography of Douglas Hurd, 'The Public Servant,' states:

> 'Nevertheless, the tantalising possibility remains that an intervention force, or more realistically, the earlier use of air power, might have prevented later atrocities.'

However, as the Serb and Croat aggression in dismembering Bosnia gained momentum, military intervention was something that the Europeans could only do with the help of the Americans. In practice, however, because of that 'attitude' towards the Muslims, and the fact that there was no threat to America's interest (as there was for oil in the case of the Gulf War), in spite of huge media sympathy for the Muslims in Britain, continental Europe and America, their governments didn't want to contribute troops to Bosnia; public opinion was, however, in favour of arming the Muslims and instituting air strikes against the Serbs. Still Douglas Hurd was totally against the lifting of the arms embargo against the Muslims, and in 1994 he visited Washington to beg the Americans not to lift the embargo.

Hurd was consistent to the end with his perverse attitude towards the Muslims. After the Dayton Peace Accords in 1995, Hurd went the following year to Belgrade in his capacity as Deputy Chairman of Nat West Markets when, 'he tried to persuade President Milošević to sign contracts with Nat West to privatise Serbia's electricity and oil sectors,' (quoted in Mark Stuart's 'The Public Servant'). Hurd also gave similar assistance to British Telecom's plans for Serbia's phone system. This, the man who Boris Johnson described in his Daily Telegraph article of 31st March 1999 as: "There was once a British Foreign Secretary (tall, urban, white quiff) who described him [Milošević] as the only Balkan leader who made any sense."

I believe Hurd's involvement contributed much to the insane misery of the Muslims in Bosnia and Kosovo, and so I will provide another quote from Mark Stuart's work 'The Public Servant':

> 'It is perhaps significant that before he left the Foreign Office, he [Hurd] ordered that an official account of the conflict be written, to remain confidential for thirty years. This was partly intended to act as a corrective to the over-emotive accounts which he suspected might be written in the future. But surely it also indicates a high level of lingering doubt as to whether his own policies were right?'

Indeed, the 2001 publication 'Unfinest Hour,' by Dr. Brendan Simms of Cambridge University (a brilliant work which concentrates on Britain's betrayal of the Bosnians), utterly condemns John Major, Douglas Hurd and Malcolm Rifkind in their role as appeasers. Simms called for a Government enquiry into Britain's handling of the Bosnia affair. In reviewing 'Unfinest Hour' the following commentators are worthy of mention. Nick Cohen of The Observer said, "Britain's refusal to act in the former Yugoslavia left the Serbs free to butcher thousands of Bosnians ... Simms's attention to telling detail and cool, literate anger make *Unfinest Hour* the best epitaph for the wretched years of the Major administration I've read to date." Marcus Tanner of The Independent said, "This is a book about how the British establishment grovelled before Serbia's murderous dictator Slobodan Milosevic ... Talk about a low, dishonest decade! Reading it made me want to throw my passport on the nearest rubbish heap, so total is the indictment of ... the British state."

Geoffrey Robertson writing in the Financial Times 'Books of the Year', said, "The government of John Major should be on trial for turning a blind eye to genocide. The prosecution case, in damning detail, is to be found in Unfinest Hour." Significantly before the opening to his book, Simms quoted from the Bible – Proverbs 24: 10-12:

> If you have shown yourself weak at a time of crisis, how limited is
> your strength!
> Rescue those being dragged away to death, and save those being hauled
> off to execution.
> If you say, 'But this person I do not know,' God, who fixes a standard
> for the heart, will take note; He who watches you will know; He will
> repay everyone according to what he does.

The Prime Minister of Malaysia, Dr. Muhathir, on receiving the Prime Minster, John Major, in September 1993 at an official reception, pointed his finger at him and directly accused him of being responsible for the slaughter of the Muslims in Bosnia. Major became angry and wanted to leave the reception, but the British Ambassador persuaded him to stay.

The Bosnian Muslims had consulted Dr. Zaki Badawi and were advised by him not to declare independence for Bosnia so as to save themselves from being massacred, on the grounds that no-one would care enough to come to their aid when the attacks began in earnest. Why not? We come back to the 'attitude problem' shown towards the Muslims of Bosnia – Muslims, many of whom drank alcohol, ate pork and barely followed the tenets of Islam! But nevertheless, who were Muslims in name and to some extent were practising Muslims. Muslims who the Serbs and Croats had lived with, married and intermingled with for centuries before and who all of a sudden were 'the Muslim fanatic, enemy.'

Milošević and Tuđman had been Communist Party leaders in the former Yugoslavia, but after the fall of Communism in Eastern Europe, these two undemocratic dictators, were both free to indulge their natural instincts of ultra-nationalist fascism in order to stay in power. Communism was on the way out. But tell the people you rule that they have suffered horrendous injustices at the hands of the Muslim 'fanatics' in centuries gone by and couple this with reintroducing and considerably magnifying, as the case may be, Serb grievances against Croat and Croat grievances against Serb, particularly from World War Two, and the people rise up to support the leader and keep him in power. The unarmed Muslims were caught in the middle; the Serbs and Croats attacked them from all sides, the Bosnians unable to defend themselves. They didn't even continue to insist on outside help, only the right to be given heavy weapons to defend themselves. But no - the fear of the Muslim 'fanatic' pervaded all thoughts of the Clinton administration and Major government. Thoughts which were immune to the Serb strategy of ethnic cleansing based on the 'ethic' of rape warfare devised by Milošević, Karadžić and Mladić and joyfully practised by the rank and file of the Serb army. What a way for the Serbs to take revenge for the atrocities committed on them by Hitler during the Second World War! How sick in logic! Beverly Allen, the American lecturer from Syracuse University, in her book 'Rape Warfare - the Hidden Genocide in Bosnia Herzogovina and Croatia,' (published by the University of Minnesota Press 1996) relates the words of a Zagreb psychiatrist describing the condition of the non-Serb women who survived genocidal rape:

> 'Another common trauma, she said, is the damage done to their throats! They have been strangling for weeks and months on end as a result of having repeatedly been forced to swallow vast amounts of urine and sperm.'

The 'Christian' Orthodox Serbs, prompted by Milošević's hunger for power, propagated 'the fact' that the Muslims are 'not like us.' 'Christian' Europe pondered and prevaricated. The truth was ignored on the altar of prejudice. Muslims believe in the same God of the Christians; Muslims revere Jesus. Why, the Christian King of Abyssinia gave refuge to the Prophet Muhammad and his followers when they faced persecution at the hands of the pagan Quyresh of Mecca. The Muslims protected the Jews when 'Christian' Europe was persecuting them in centuries past. But nevertheless, still the Muslims were labelled with the lie of the Serb propaganda drive, a tool later at work in Kosovo. The 'Christianity' of the Orthodox Serbs was of a type every bit as evil as the 'Christianity' of the Maronite Christians of Lebanon whose Phalange Militia butchered the Palestinian innocents of the Sabra and Chatila refugee camps in Beirut in 1982.

The complicity of the Serb Orthodox Church was very well illustrated by the Serb journalist, Gojko Berić, whose superb book 'Letters to the Celestial Serbs' published in English in 2002 I came across, ironically, at Beirut Airport in June 2003, after visiting the Sabra and Chatila camps. (The book has a Lebanese publisher, Saqi Books).

Berić's work is unique – it is written by a honourable Serb, employed by the Sarajevo newspaper Oslobodenje. He wrote: "I hated Karadžić and the Serb fascist rabble more than my Bosniak [Bosnian Muslims] and Croat neighbours would ever imagine, much more than they themselves hated them." His condemnation of the Serb and Croat peoples is absolute and his book makes essential reading.

I make no apologies at all for including extracts from 'Letters to the Celestial Serbs' in the following pages as without them the picture I want to paint on the Muslim disaster will not be complete.

On the Christian aspect of the war Berić makes the following points (written in April 1997):

> Regarding Pope John Paul II's visit to Sarajevo in 1997, 'It is natural that the Pope's visit should arouse greatest emotion among the war-depleted Bosnian Croats, while the Croats of western Herzegovina are torn between fanatical love for the Holy Father and - which is irreconcilable with true religious belief - unconcealed hatred of the Bosniaks. To the Serbs in Republica Srpska, who are living in self-imposed isolation and economic and social misery the Pope's visit means nothing. Contempt for the Vatican is one of the constants in their favourite conspiracy theory.'

*   *   *

> 'Unprecedented hatred found expression in the destruction of places of worship and the obliteration of entire graveyards, most of them Muslim. There is not a single mosque left now in Republica Srpska, and barely any in the areas under Croat control. Eye witnesses claim that those who razed the mosques with the greatest ferocity were soldiers wearing Orthodox or

Catholic symbols and invoking God.' [A similar practise to the Christian Phalange killers of the Palestinian Muslim civilians in the Beirut refugee camps of Sabra and Chatila in 1982.]

'Not only did Patriarch Pavle not once convincingly condemn Serb atrocities in Bosnia, he openly took Karadžić's part. He passed over in silence the slaughter of Bosniaks in Zvornik, Bijeljina, Visegrad and Foca, the death of eleven thousand civilians and children in Sarajevo, and the existence of Serb-run concentration camps. He did not react to the ethnic cleansing of entire regions that had belonged to the Bosniaks and Croats, and was disappointingly restrained in referring to destroyed mosques, even those of the greatest historical and cultural value. And what was the Patriarch's message to the enemies of the Serbs? "May the Lord bestow repentance upon them, and shed light on their minds and hearts," said the Patriarch. But who should repent on account of the two hundred thousand killed and butchered Bosniaks? They themselves, presumably. Nor did the Catholic Church gain any moral credit for the war in Bosnia-Herzegovina; it would be truer to say that it lost moral credit. Its condemnation of the atrocities against Croats was loud and specific but Croat malefactors were referred to in the pulpit only sporadically and allusively in the context of sermons on the general principles of Christianity.'

*   *   *

'The major victim among the three confessional communities in Bosnia was the Islamic Community. This has enabled hojjas and imams to take upon themselves the leading role in the homogenisation of the Bosniaks. Taken unawares by the aggression, with Serb knives at their throats, the Bosniaks saw their only salvation in turning en masse to religion.'

*   *   *

In March 1999 Berić continued his theme in his chapter 'The Patriarch's Travels':

'So far as I have heard, the Patriarch has never even made any reference to the twenty or thirty thousand Orthodox [Serbs] who remained in Sarajevo during the War, and who suffered and were killed alongside their Muslim neighbours. Perhaps this is because the Patriarch regards them as apostates, traitors to their faith, who should pay the penalty like any other apostate. I have reached this conclusion from the fact that the only official figure of the church in Sarajevo during the War was the ascetic monk Avakum Rosić. Do you remember this unfortunate fellow? He looked twenty years older than he was, and when journalists used to ask him for his views on the shelling of Sarajevo, he always had the same answer: "God sees all and knows all!"'

'I don't know if Patriarch Pavle will ever come to Sarajevo. Perhaps he lacks the moral fibre for such a gesture and is too old to be able to find it. He has never explicitly condemned Serb atrocities against this city and its population, although he has had countless opportunities. I noted in November 1997, the Patriarch blessed and signed a Declaration calling for the Hague Tribunal proceedings against Radovan Karadžić to be lifted. This is too many sins for one Patriarch.'

'And this is why I think that the Patriarch's duty before he joins God, is to come in contrition to Sarajevo.'

*   *   *

Berić, in effect, subscribes widespread mental illness to the Serb and Croat populations as a whole and for this aspect I quote the following extracts:

'The Bosniaks were appalled and bewildered by the brutality which the Serbs unleashed against them, the more so since both demographically and maritally the Bosniaks and Serbs were more intermixed than with the Croats. That brutality was to remain a deep and painfully mystery to them ....'

'It is easy to say now that everyone in Bosnia is vicious because they all hate each other equally. But if you set fire to someone's house, butcher his family and rape his wife, the least you can expect from the poor fellow is that he will hate you.'

'Ethnic cleansing, concentration camps with thousands of wretched inmates, mass killings of civilians and children, women raped in their thousands, robbery, plunder, arson – these were the planned objectives of this war. Wasn't this facism? I know that historians don't think so. They can wait years before formulating their judgement on something. I couldn't wait, for both moral and professional reasons. I know that every historian will say that the use of historical analogy is extremely problematic. I have already read views such as this: "If Milošević is a new Hitler, then you must show us the evidence, in the form of his racist laws and camps with gas chambers; you must point to his Himmler and his Eichmann!" 'That's their affair, which puts no obligation on me. And anyway, Hitler didn't sign any kind of decree on the "final solution" to the Jewish question, yet he killed six million Jews. A similar fate was intended for the Bosniaks [Muslims] in this war. As a human being and a direct witness of these events I have just one word for the scoundrels who committed the evil deeds in this region: fascists!'

*   *   *

'And why do the Serbs not want to live with the Bosniaks and Croats? To put it briefly: because there are many malefactors among the Serbs. It would be most accurate nowadays to compare the Bosnian Serbs with a hit-and-run driver who has caused a regular massacre in the road, and then cowardly turns tail and runs from the scene of the accident, afraid of witnesses and the punishment he deserves. That is what it's about.'

'Thanks to Milošević and Tuđman, this country will never again be what it used to be. People who for centuries lived together, though they belonged to different religions and nations will never again be brothers. At school their children are already being taught a subject called hatred. Enemies are distributed in equal measure throughout the new school textbooks, so that each of the three peoples is the enemy in the eyes of the others. There will be no shortage of hatred for the next fifty years.'

'Geography, too, has been changed to a certain extent: for thousands of displaced Bosnians and Herzegovinians, their native towns have become unattainably foreign.'

'Given that no sentence of the courts could eliminate this damage, nor alter its nature and extent, the fate of those who bear the principal guilt has become relevant only from the point of view of moral catharsis.'

*   *   *

'Six years ago, during the siege of Sarajevo, I wrote that Milošević was merely the cap on the head of the Serb mentality. If the head doesn't want a new cap, there is nothing that can be done about it. Since then Milošević has won an easy victory over the Serbs at the polls another four or five times. Although he has become officially the gravedigger of the Serbian people, they are still chanting, "Slo-bo, slo-bodo [freedom], showing a degree of faith in him that even the Nazis did not accord to Hitler. A prisoner who shouted this kind of paeon to his gaoler would be sent to a mental hospital. But how can one cure almost an entire nation of this bizarre mental illness? ......'

As long as the gadget known as television is at the service of the Greater Serbia idea, the mental hygiene of the Serbs will remain at 19th century levels. But even if Milošević should leave the scene, I don't see who will liberate the Serbs from their centuries-old mythological captivity, since they feel so comfortable in it.'

*   *   *

When Tuđman was on his death-bed in December 1999 Berić wrote:

> 'I don't believe the Croats are less nationalist than the Serbs, nor that they care much about real democracy, which implies above all respect for human rights and freedoms. Like the Serbs, they are living in a morass of xenophobia and hatred. So far as that's concerned, the Croats would have gone on voting for Tuđman as President for as long as he wanted. If they're not grieving for him as much as expected, that's because he has reduced them to the level of beggars.'

On the role played by the international community Berić is spot on:

> 'The wheels of return sank into the mud right from the start, when the international community entrusted the implementation of the provisions of the Dayton Accord to the very same people who had begun and conducted the war of extermination in Bosnia. This is as if the allies, back in 1945, had entrusted the Gestapo with arranging for the return of Jews to Germany and Central Europe. Closing their eyes to the presence of war criminals and conducting negotiations with them on the reunification of Bosnia-Herzegovina, was a really futile exercise.'

The abysmal French contribution is also condemned by Berić and this is why I personally will never accept that the French were ever truly on the side of the people (Muslims) of Iraq when they furiously protested against the U.S and British war on Iraq in 2003 on the grounds that the Iraqi people would be the biggest losers.

Writing about the French UN commander General Philippe Morillon's men in Bosnia Berić states:

> 'The Vice-President of the Bosnian Government Hakija Turajlić, was returning from Sarajevo Airport in a UN armoured personnel carrier when armed Serbs stopped his escort. Colonel Patrice Sartre agreed to open the rear door of the APC, which allowed a Serb gangster to fire an entire clip into the helpless man, who was at that very moment under official UN protection. The French soldiers behaved like cowards, completely beneath the dignity of their profession, without firing a single bullet in reply. On his return to France, Colonel Sartre received the Légion d'honneur! By not putting up any resistance against uniformed gangsters he had carried out his duties, in exactly the same way as the UN performed its duties in Bosnia.'

*　　　　*　　　　*

The same cowardice as exhibited by the Dutch battalion at Srebrenica. This fact was confirmed to me by a survivor of the massacre of the Muslims there, one by the name of Emir Suljagić. This tall dignified young man gave a talk to the Bosnian Institute in London on 7th July 2003. He told me afterwards that the Dutch, "should have and could have" prevented the atrocity but that their "cultural mentality" made them back off.

Adam LeBor in his biography entitled 'Milosevic,' states:

> 'Without air support or proper reinforcements Dutchbat certainly could not have held off General Mladić's men for long. However, the question remains if Dutchbat had resisted would General Mladić have been prepared to kill 110 UN soldiers?'

LeBor also importantly confirms:

> 'The U.S certainly knew about the Serbs preparations to take Srebrenica: U-2 spy planes were patrolling the area, and a stream of satellite intelligence was also being fed back to Washington.' .... 'Certainly if there was some kind of diplomatic understanding between the West and Belgrade over Srebrenica, it went horribly wrong over the fate of the inhabitants. ... One cause of Mladić's hunger for a blood meze [Arabic word for a long feast of many small dishes] was that [Muslim] soldiers operating out of Srebrenica had attacked his home village of Visnice, and burnt down its houses. The suicide of Mladić's daughter Ana, a medical

student in her early twenties, had certainly hardened his heart. Encouraged by their commander, the Bosnian Serb soldiers descended into a frenzy of blood lust.'

The poison of Russian hatred even warped the thinking of none other than Alexander Solzhenitzyn. Berić writes of him thus:

'A letter by Alexander Solzhenitzyn, sent from Moscow of 8 April 1999 and headed 'Law of the Jungle,' has seen the light of day in the Paris Figaro. "After flouting the United Nations and trampling on the UN Charter, before the eyes of the world and for the coming century NATO has proclaimed the old law of the jungle: might is right. Surpass in violence the opponent you condemn, a hundred times over if your technology permits. And they expect us to live in this world in the future! Before the very eyes of the world the destruction of a wonderful European country is taking place, and civilized governments are applauding. As people leave their shelters in desperation to form human chains, risking their lives to save the bridges over the Danube, is this not worthy of the heroic deeds of Antiquity? I cannot see what there is to prevent Clinton, Blair and Solana from exterminating them with fire and flood down to the very last man."

Berić continues:

'Solzhenitzyn sees things this way, but Günter Grass and certain other European writers see it quite differently. The author of Gulag expresses profound disagreement with the bombing of Serbia, while the author of Tin Drum regards it as essential.'

'I would not particularly reproach Solzhenitzyn with rebelling against violence and defending a "wonderful European country" if he had done the same seven years ago, when the regime of that "wonderful European country" – with the selfless support of Solzhenitzyn's Serb fellow writers – launched a war against multi-ethnic Bosnia-Herzegovina. At that time Solzhenitzyn said nothing, and never condemned the conversion of cosmopolitan Sarajevo into the largest concentration camp in Europe since the Second World War, though he had himself been a camp inmate and the victim of violence.'

*   *   *

Once more, I can only see hatred of Muslims at the core of the Russian policy in Chechnya. How the Russians were made to pay for their bloody-mindedness, by way of the Chechen suicide bombers. Let us not forget that Cherie Blair wife of the British Prime Minister, in the presence of Queen Rania of Jordan on her visit to London in June 2002 sympathised with the desperate acts of the Palestinian suicide bombers in Israel, because they have "no hope."

Before she was indicted to the Hague, Biljana Plavšić was for a short time the president of Republika Srpska. A woman of whom Berić writes:

"The Bosniaks will remember her for the kisses she showered upon Željko Ražnatović Arkan [the Serb warlord] after the massacre and 'liberation' of Bijeljina, where the streets were still littered with the corpses of the civilians who had just been killed." Plavšić stated to the Belgrade newspaper Duga: "I always kiss heroes."

Berić continues:

'In Karadžić's HQ Plavšić was reputed to be the major advocate of ethnic cleansing and expulsion of the non-Serb population. "She is even more evil than Krajisnik," said Carl Bildt.'

'Of course, even a devil with horns, tail and hoofs is not as black as he seems. Proclaiming herself a nationalist who was not a thief, and who was ready to take on like a man criminals and corrupt politicians, Plavšić earned several plus points in the West. She succeeded in dismissing the intractable General Mladić, and ended up being welcomed with full state honours by France's President Jacques Chirac, on the steps of the Élysée palace. Did poor Jacques really not know he was kissing the hand of a mass killer?'

Significantly for me Berić mentions George Orwell in one of his Celestial letters written in July 2000. Its importance lies in the way the nationalism spoken of can apply anywhere – even to Norway and their intense dislike for Muslims:

> 'In his essay 'Notes of Nationalism,' George Orwell remarks on a common characteristic of all nationalists: an inclination for the individual to identify himself with a single action, setting it above good and evil, and recognising no other duty except to represent its interests. A nationalist not only fails to condemn atrocities committed by his side, but is possessed of an exceptional capacity not even to hear anything about them. As an example of this ability Orwell cites the behaviour of the English during the Second World War. For quite six years the English admirers of Hitler contrived not to learn of the existence of Dachau and Buchenwald. And those who are loudest in denouncing the German concentration camps are quite often unaware ..... that there are also concentration camps in Russia. Huge events like the Ukraine famine of 1933, involving the deaths of millions of people have actually escaped the attention of the majority of English Russophiles. Many English people have heard almost nothing about the extermination of German and Polish Jews during the present war. Their own anti-Semitism has caused this vast crime to bounce off their consciousness ....'

As for Izetbegović, Berić states:

> 'The fall of communism created in him the illusion that it was possible to put an equals sign between life in Bosnia and his religious political philosophy. But he failed to see what was most important: that the freedom that had been seized was to be short-lived, and that war was already looming. Izetbegović was not for the dissolution of Yugoslavia, nor did he want war. He rejected the very possibility, even when it had become inevitable. "You can sleep peacefully, there won't be war," he assured his citizens on television, but at the same time he wasn't ready to sacrifice the sovereignty of the country for the sake of peace. When he woke up one morning it was war, right there outside his window and the windows of the rest of us.'

> 'His critics among the Bosniak intellectual and political elite now claim that war was not inevitable. But if we have agreed that Bosnia-Herzegovina was the victim of an aggression preceded by political and military plans drawn up in Belgrade, I fail to see how war could have been avoided in 1992. A full year earlier Milošević and Tuđman had reached agreement in Karadordevo on the partition of Bosnia-Herzegovina. The Bosniaks were not the ones who could have prevented the war. They could have remained in Milošević's Yugoslavia under a fascist regime, but for them that would have been the equivalent of going to hell. And even in that case, part of the country, the part over which Tuđman claimed rights, would have disappeared for good.'

> 'Izetbegović had difficulty coping with the winds of war. He behaved like the captain of a ship on stormy seas, who saw hope coming from heaven rather than the helmsman's skill. True to his ideological and religious convictions, he was reluctant to organise a civil resistance to the fascism by which the country was being attacked from without and within. He was badly affected too, by the hypocritical attitude of the West to the genocide against the Bosniak people, which reinforced him in his conviction that the Bosnian Muslims, albeit in the heart of Europe, belonged to another world.'

*   *   *

I felt tremendously sorry for Izetbegović, who passed away on 19th October 2003 aged 78. I see a bit of myself in him and I hope God blesses him in the next life. Just imagine what it must have been like for Izetbegović to have to sit at the same table with Milošević and Tuđman at the Dayton Peace Accords, knowing just how evil his adversaries were; overwhelmingly conscious of the affront to decency that the Americans had imposed on him by forcing him to negotiate in person with two devils. No wonder Izetbegović said he was depressed and always looked sullen at these talks, hardly able to look his enemies in the face. He could never have imagined that Milošević would later be a prisoner in The Hague, so hypocritical was Bill Clinton's policy at Dayton. At least Izetbegović lived to see

Milošević arraigned before The Hague War Crimes tribunal secure in the knowledge that the Serb madman would almost certainly spend the rest of his life in custody before getting hellfire in the next life. And Izetbegović outlived Tuđman (who died in December 1999), knowing that Tuđman too will probably see hellfire on Judgment Day. In the event Milošević died from a heart attack in his prison cell at The Hague on 11th March 2006.

Zaki Badawi, mentioned earlier by me in this book, told me that Izetbegović should have let Bosnia remain a part of Yugoslavia under the authority of Milošević, which he advised Izetbegović to do. Badawi thought that this would have limited the aggression against the Muslims to much lower levels than to the disastrous levels that, Badawi, it seems predicted if the Muslims declared independence. Badawi thought that Milošević could live with the Muslims as part of Yugoslavia but would never accept an independent 'Muslim' state next door. However when I spoke to author and Balkan expert Noel Malcolm at the October 2003 Bosnian Institute meeting he was much more pessimistic and told me he thought even without an independent Bosnia, Milošević would still have pursued his policy of ethnic cleansing against the Muslims. When I raised the point again with Zaki Badawi in April 2005, Badawi was adamant: the slaughter would not have happened if Izetbegović had not declared independence.

Vojislav Koštunica became President of Serbia and was seen by Berić as just a continuation of the evil that Milošević, his predecessor, represented. Said Berić:

> 'Koštunica himself, meanwhile, is controversial too. His visit to Pale has not been forgotten, nor his consistent support for the policies of the war criminal, Radovan Karadžić, Milošević's key man in the war to create Greater Serbia. Koštunica has never condemned the siege and shelling of Sarajevo, nor has he found it necessary to comment on the mass war crimes committed by the Serbs in Bosnia......'

> 'Milošević has been defeated but Serbia remains the greatest Balkan sanctuary for thousands of the war criminals who killed, raped and looted their way through Croatia and Bosnia.'

On 1st July 2004 The Daily Telegraph printed the following story with the headline, 'Ashdown sacks 60 as Karadžić stays free,' by Harry de Quetteville, Balkans Correspondent:

> LORD ASHDOWN, the international administrator in Bosnia, yesterday sacked 60 Bosnian Serb officials.

> He said they bore "a hideous responsibility" for the failure to arrest the wartime leader Radovan Karadžić or any other war crimes suspect.

> He accused them of "creating the climate of secrecy, intimidation and criminal impunity that allows indicted war criminals to evade justice." The "cancer of obstructionism and corruption" had to be removed and "nothing less than major surgery will do," he said.

> Among those sacked is Zoran Djerice, whose duties as interior minister included leading the hunt for Karadžić, and Dragan Kalinic, the parliamentary speaker, who headed the nationalist Serb Democratic Party founded by Karadžić.

> Karadžić and his military commander, Ratco Mladić, are wanted by the United Nations tribunal in The Hague for war crimes and genocide.

> Their alleged crimes include the massacre of more than 7,000 Muslim boys and men in the eastern town of Srebrenica in 1995, as well as the siege of Sarajevo, which lasted more than three years.

> Mr Kalinic insisted yesterday that he and his party were not to blame for Karadžić's escapes from dozens of Nato snatch raids since the end of the 1992-1995 war. "Many are helpless because Karadžić is most likely protected by God and angels," he said.

Bosnia-Hercegovina is now in effect divided into the Muslim-Croat Federation in the west and the Serb-run Republika Srpska in the east.

Karadžić is thought to be hiding among a network of friends in the Serb area.

***

Please let me present to you the report I prepared and sent to the Bosnian Embassy in London on 28th November 1996 after attending a speech by the former Norwegian Foreign Minister and colleague of David Owen, Thorvald Stoltenberg:

28th November 1996

Dear Mr. Karabdic,

Report on Talk by Thorvald Stoltenberg
at Norway House at 7 p.m. Wednesday 27th November 1996

Mr. Stoltenberg who I shall refer to as "TS" in the rest of this letter told the audience that he lived with his family in the former Yugoslavia in the 1960's and said that he himself would not have predicted at all that by the 1990's war would have broken out.

TS blamed the outbreak of the war on the recognition by the EU of Croatia as a separate state and TS praised Lord Carrington for his foresight in predicting that the break up of Yugoslavia in this way would lead to war. TS also blamed the war on "historical differences" between the various factions and was proud to quote the example of a delegation of American Jews that visited him and told him that he, TS, was wrong to refer to the centuries of history for the Serbs as being a relevant factor in the 1990's conflict but should look only at the facts of the matter since 1991. TS replied that there was no greater supporter of Israel than himself and that Jews themselves always carried their history with them as did the Serbs and that they, the American Jews, should recognise that the Serbs were exactly the same as the Jews. TS then said that the Jewish Delegation apologised to him and recognised that the Bosnian war was based on the grievances that the Serbs had in their past history going back centuries.

TS said that when he met Izetbegović, Karadžić, Milošević and Tuđman he promised all of them that he would do his very best to be fair and impartial, not in the sense of being impartial to the atrocities, which he condemned, but impartial in the negotiations towards an overall settlement. TS also made reference to the fact that each of the aforementioned leaders criticised him for not being impartial towards the other leaders in turn. That when negotiations were in progress over which villages were to be included in the smaller Bosnian state the 1991 census was looked at and where the Muslims were found to be in a majority of a particular village the Serbs countered by arguing that the Ustashe had during the war got rid of many Serbs who at the time formed the majority of the village and thus TS must consider making the village a Serbian village and to stay outside the new Bosnia.

Regarding the bombing of the Serbs TS said to me after he had finished his speech, "You know better than I do that this was ineffective and would be useless because of the UN hostages that were taken by the Serbs." I replied that the whole policy of the UN was flawed in that it was easily predictable that the UN soldiers would make easy targets for hostage taking and that the wrong approach was adopted from day one in that the humanitarian effort was bound to be a disaster without the collateral efforts of strong military action against the Serbs. I told him that the Serbs must have thanked God for the policy of the UN in putting in their under-equipped soldiers who were just easy targets for the Serbs.

210

I remarked also that TS mentioned nothing about the arms embargo against the Muslims in his speech. TS replied that he would mention it now to me, and told me that the war would have gone on forever if both sides were being continually supplied with arms, and besides he said that arms were getting through to the Muslims in any case. I was beginning to upset the audience by this time because their guest, TS was certainly showing his disquiet in the answers that he gave me and indeed at one stage asked (sarcastically) if I would like to give a talk myself. I replied that from the start the Muslims had practically no arms to defend themselves properly and indeed had surrendered their arms earlier to the JNA who had redistributed them to the Bosnian Serbs. I said that the Bosnian state based its existence on a multi-religious and multi-ethnic format and it certainly was not the case that the Bosnian Muslims were Islamic fanatics and cruel fundamentalists, as portrayed by some Western opinions.

TS definitely gave the wrong impression to the audience about the Muslims, also for example by emphasising the request of a Muslim General to a Bosnian Serb General for the latter to supply the Muslims with ammunition and arms to attack the Croats in exchange for money to which the Bosnian Serb General replied that the Bosnian Serbs would attack the Croats in return for payment by the Muslims, to which the Muslim General said okay.

TS said that he himself felt the prospects for continued peace were good because the Bosnians were sick of war and I replied to him, that of course they were sick of war because they hardly stood a chance in the first place and if they had been given arms to defend themselves then they would have done much better. TS said that many people did not believe that there were good prospects for peace but he said that the last elections in Bosnia were not free and fair and that the elections in 1998 had to be free and fair for the chance of a proper peace.

On the more positive side, TS said that Karadžić's version of the facts were quite out of touch with reality and that he thought Karadžić who each night slept in a different bed (to avoid assassination I suppose) should give himself up voluntarily to the Hague War Crimes Tribunal and face the music with his able American lawyers to defend him. TS said that Karadžić knew that for the rest of his life he would be hunted and TS said the same applied to Mladić but TS said that he didn't think trying to capture Mladić was worth "losing the life of one EU soldier." TS said he got very angry with people who criticised the European soldiers in the UN force for not being braver because he said they were doing a fantastic job already.

TS said that the shelling of Sarajevo was "totally unacceptable" and also mentioned the stance of Carl Bildt who asked for the indictment of Tuđman to the War Crimes Tribunal in The Hague for ordering his Croat forces to shell Serb villages. TS said that this request from Bildt annoyed the rest of the world and nearly cost Bildt his job as EU Negotiator. TS heavily criticised the USA and Clinton for speaking but doing nothing during the height of the crisis by not putting in any of their own ground troops which omission contributed most dramatically to the prolongation of the crisis. TS also mentioned Boutros-Boutros Ghali's request for 34,000 troops to be put into the "safe areas" whereas only a small proportion of this amount was offered by the contributing states.

Overall TS was talking to a largely ill-informed and an ignorant audience composed of mostly middle and upper-class Norwegian and English people who form the core of the Anglo-Norwegian Society. Their reaction to my questions to TS and the questions they themselves asked him confirmed my opinion of the audience's basic ignorance of the facts of the whole situation.

At the end of the lecture TS moved to shake my hand and said to me, "I was glad of your intervention" but I thought to myself how could he be glad when he didn't like what I had to say. I gave him a copy of Peter Maass' book on Bosnia – 'Love They Neighbour - A Story of War.' Peter Maass is a Jew - a correspondent for the

211

Washington Post and a complete and total friend of the Muslims of Bosnia. I told TS that as a Muslim I despised my Egyptian compatriot Boutros-Ghali and I said that I hoped that Boutros-Ghali would not be voted in for a second term as UN Secretary General. I also expressed the hope that when the Muslims are strong in Bosnia they will go back to war and obtain the justice deprived of them. I also told TS my opinion of David Owen making it quite clear that I didn't like him.

My best wishes to you and your staff and your continued efforts to safeguard and resurrect Bosnia and its people. May God bless all of you.

Yours sincerely,

Noel Malcolm in his book 'Bosnia - A Short History' describes the former Norwegian Foreign Minister's peace plan with Lord Owen, which would have given the Serbs 53 per cent of the Bosnian territory, the Croats 17 per cent and the Muslims 30 per cent, as follows:

> 'However, the fact that the Owen-Stoltenberg plan had conceded the basic
> principle of rewarding aggression, together with the fact that the international
> negotiators seemed willing to make more and more concessions and alterations
> to satisfy Serb demands ensured that the Serb leadership would not regard these
> proposals as a final settlement either.'

Noel Malcolm reports on Lord Owen's appointment (as replacement for Lord Carrington) as EU negotiator whereupon he then 'immediately dropped his support for threats of military action [against the Serbs] and began treating the Serbs as an equal party in the negotiations with equally valid claims.'

Owen and Stoltenberg were just two of the well-oiled cogs in the big (fait accompli) 'We can't help the Muslims' machine.

And to think Stoltenberg tried to hoodwink the Jewish delegation into believing the Serbs had a right to rely on their history when they had a policy of genocidal rape against Muslim women to further the 'justice of their cause.' Fuck the past history of the Serbs if that's what they proceed to do in the 90's.

As for the help of Europe - well the British people were far, far wiser than John Major and Douglas Hurd. The 'common man' could see the injustice of it all - but not the PM and his Foreign Secretary. The Dutch people and their government were lone voices in Europe calling for early and direct punishment of the Serbs, although to their eternal shame the Dutch soldiers, as former B.B.C journalist and later Member of Parliament Martin Bell also believes, betrayed their steadfastness by their cowardice in letting the Serb army in, to "lead away" and then execute the Muslims of Srebrenica. The various charities in the countries of Western Europe did their bit and many citizens of those countries gave money - for the Muslims to be fed, then shot. But as for the collective will necessary in Europe's governments for decisive early action, it just wasn't there because of that often denied, but in fact fully operational 'we don't really care' attitude towards the Muslims. Certain fanatical elements in the Middle East had given many people in the West the idea that all Muslims were capable at the touch of a button of extremist and brutal behaviour. But to allow this myth to justify not helping the Muslims of Bosnia betrayed Western governmental ignorance, self-delusion, self-interest and utter cowardice.

There was no oil in Bosnia and certainly the Serb Army was far superior to the Iraqi Army in the Gulf War and may have given the U.S Army more of a fight. The Americans were scared, using as an excuse their Vietnam complex. Say the Muslims of Bosnia were not Muslims at all, but Jews? Would America then have stood by? Even Israel wanted to help the Muslims of Bosnia at one stage. Ironically, in general the 'Islamic' governments of the world did little to help their 'brothers' in Bosnia, which reflected a 'couldn't care less' attitude by those governments (but not, I stress, their people) towards human rights in Bosnia.

The point is that the UN and NATO were supposed to lead the fight against genocide and oppression. The Holocaust situation that was beginning to develop for the Bosnian Muslims was one of those events that the world would 'never let happen again' so we were told. To their eternal credit, Margaret

Thatcher, the ex-Prime Minister, and Paddy Ashdown, the leader of the Liberal Democrats, had called for the hounding of the Serbs from day one. Clare Short of the opposition Labour Party went on television in 1995 to ask that the Serbs be bombed. But these were lone voices, out of power - their pleas falling on deaf ears. John Major and Douglas Hurd, in their overwhelming arrogance, thought they knew better and were not opposed at all by the Labour leadership who had no real appreciation of the situation in Bosnia 'because it was too complex to understand by outsiders.' This view was confirmed to me in 1998 by the Labour M.P Keith Darvill, a solicitor and predecessor of mine at work. I had also attended a Labour Lawyers meeting on 'Human Rights in Europe' at the House of Commons in 1995, chaired by John Wadham of Liberty. Would you believe that not a soul at the talk mentioned human rights in Bosnia, except me? When I addressed Dougie Henderson M.P, 'the fittest man in the Commons' over the Bosnia debacle and asked what the Labour Party would have done had it been in power, Henderson was lost for words. He didn't have a clue and just said we should look forward now and not look back to the past. It came as a great surprise to me, after Labour won the 1997 election, to see this same Dougie Henderson pictured in an Islamic weekly magazine voicing his support for the Muslim community of Britain in their fight for greater social justice. Maybe by then he'd read the book by Peter Maass - 'Love Thy Neighbour'- that I gave him as he walked out of our meeting to register his vote in the House. Henderson went on to become the Armed Forces Minister in the Labour Government during the Kosovo crisis in 1999.

David Mellor, Paddy Ashdown, the Saudi Ambassador and the Eastern Adriatic Department of the Foreign and Commonwealth Office on behalf of Robin Cook, replied to my letters on the subject of Bosnia, after the Dayton Peace accords. But it was all academic. The damage had been done and really, little else mattered. So very easily it could have been prevented, yet because of that 'attitude,' disaster was almost inevitable without Margaret Thatcher leading the rest of Europe in her own inimitable way. She attacked the Falklands against the advice of many and see what she brought - democracy for Argentina. Without Thatcher, the Bosnians had had it. Brave individuals (like Thatcher) can prevent catastrophe. Again, quoting from Peter Maass' book:

> Margaret Thatcher wrote 'Feeding or evacuating the victims rather than helping them resist aggression makes us accomplices as much as good Samaritans.' She also said, "I am ashamed of the European Community, for this is happening in the heart of Europe. It is within Europe's sphere of influence. It should be within Europe's sphere of conscience. There is no conscience."

The most basic function of the European Union is to prevent just the kind of calamity that befell the Bosnians, but the European governments couldn't or wouldn't agree on a damn thing and the Bosnian Serbs and Serbian Serbs would have been raising toasts to European democracy every night of the conflict. With all the sophisticated weaponry at their disposal, the Europeans cocked-up big time with their amateurish humanitarian programme. Mrs. Thatcher compared the west's inaction as "being a little like an accomplice to slaughter." Of course, it was the governments of Europe that turned cowardly and I think this situation was a defining moment in the European morality: the Muslims didn't matter enough. The European governments knew the slaughter would continue yet did nothing to intervene militarily; intervention was a non-starter, ruled out altogether. As for humanitarian aid, Mark Stuart in 'The Public Servant' says:

> 'But there are real doubts whether the humanitarian effort actually achieved anything. Rosalyn Higgins, an expert on the UN, believes that it was a mistake to establish a UN operation dedicated to the provision of humanitarian aid without a ceasefire. By choosing not to stop the violence via a military intervention force, she believes that the UN prolonged the suffering. ... Larry Hollingworth, then the co-ordinator of UN convoys, claimed that only one fifth of aid was getting through, whereas Hurd put the figure at nearly half.'

The British Army was used and abused by its government but regrettably even some of the British Generals took the piss out of the Muslims. Times may have changed since World War One but that same pig-headedness remains to varying degrees in the politicians and generals of today who give the orders. Why have an air force if it's not used? Why have an army if you're not prepared to put the soldiers lives at risk?

The appeasement of Milošević at the Dayton Peace Accords in 1995 allowed the nightmare to continue for the Muslims in Kosovo in 1999. Again, Clinton was not prepared to sacrifice the life of one U.S.

soldier to prevent the deaths of thousands of innocent civilians. This message to Milošević caused the acceleration of the purge of the Muslims which eventually came to a halt because of the bombing of Serbia. I repeat those words: 'the bombing of Serbia,' for that is what should have happened in 1992. Unfortunately, the Americans have never truly cared for the suffering of others, even with their obvious military ability to help out. For three years, from 1939 to 1941, they let Europe and the British face the Germans alone and only declared war on Japan (but not Germany) after Pearl Harbour was bombed. I believe that but for the Jewish Holocaust lobby in America, Americans in general would not back Israel. If there had been a Muslim lobby of similar stature in the U.S.A, the Bosnia and Kosovo exterminations would not have taken place. How ironic that on September 11th 2001 America itself experienced the horror of totally unbearable suffering through the attacks on New York and Washington. A taste of Bosnia came its way.

The celebrated American writer, commentator and professed atheist, the late Edward W. Said, explained much in his book 'Covering Islam' published in 1997:

> 'For most of the Middle Ages and during the early part of the Renaissance in Europe, Islam was believed to be a demonic religion of apostasy, blasphemy and obscurity. It did not seem to matter that Muslims considered Mohammed a prophet and not a god; what mattered to Christians was that Mohammed was a false prophet, a sower of discord, a sensualist, a hypocrite, an agent of the devil. Nor was this view of Mohammed strictly a doctrinal one. Real events in the real world made of Islam a considerable political force. For hundreds of years, great Islamic armies and navies threatened Europe, destroyed its outposts, colonised its domains. It was as if a younger, more virile and energetic version of Christianity had arisen in the East, equipped itself with the learning of the ancient Greeks, invigorated itself with a simple, fearless and warlike creed and set about destroying Christianity. Even when the world of Islam entered a period of decline and Europe a period of ascendancy, fear of 'Mohammedanism' persisted. Closer to Europe than any of the other non-Christian religions, the Islamic world by its very adjacency evoked memories of its encroachments on Europe, and always, of its latent power again and again to disturb the West. Other great civilisations of the East – India and China among them – could be thought of as defeated and distant and hence not a constant worry. Only Islam seemed never to have submitted completely to the West, and when, after the dramatic oil-price rises of the early 1970's, the Muslim world seemed once more on the verge of repeating its early conquests, the whole West seemed to shudder.'

And so I return to that little corner of North-Western Europe - Norway and its press. Look for it and with some investigation the picture is clear. The big lie is still alive and well, being promoted by certain evil sections of Norwegian society. Wholesale perversion of the truth was practised by the Nazi press and the Serb and Croat press, and in my case by the Norwegian press, with their subtle use of psychiatrists to denigrate me. These mass media campaigns often get their readers to believe them and sometimes the roller-coaster that is created becomes impossible to stop. Serbs and Croats, having been under the yoke of Communism for 50 years, were backward, inward-looking people, immature and uncivilised in their behaviour; easily persuaded by their tyrannical leaders.

The Norwegians are from an isolated part of Europe with a small population of just over 4½ million. On close observation, you will find them very insular in their way of thinking and xenophobic. The Serb, Croat and Norwegian peoples have demonstrably shown their anti-Muslim credentials and when I say 'peoples' I mean a sizeable number, for there are always some for whom basic common sense and tolerance prevail.

Other parts of Europe do have strong anti-Muslim, anti-immigrant and anti-black sections, giving rise to prejudice, religious and social, often on largely economic grounds. France, with its vast Arab and African population saw the rise of the right-wing nationalist, Monsieur Le Pen; Germany with its large Turkish workforce sees the rise of neo-Nazism, and Britain with its established black West Indian and Asian populations and newer east European influx (although Britain is the least intolerant society in Europe towards its immigrants), is in a constant state of tension.

However, Norway and the former Yugoslavia did not have poor immigrants in large numbers, causing economic and social strains on the system. No, their problem with these 'strangers' comes more from ideological prejudice, much of it just hype, a lot of it ignorance but nevertheless very harmful, when absorbed by its populace.

But as far as Britain is concerned, successive governments allowed immigration to proceed at far too quick a pace, unchecked. The strain on the social services and the culture clash has certainly caused friction in British society. It will not be easy to overcome these problems for they are mounting, but we must live in hope. John Major's inaction contributed significantly to Balkan immigrants seeking refuge in the UK and Western Europe. These desperate people would have stayed in their homes if the chaos had been stopped in its tracks as it could have been.

Chapter 20

Regarding Heidi Schønes' behaviour, I have relied already on Dr. David Stafford-Clark to support my assertions. I will now reproduce in full two articles from The Times:

The Times dated 3rd January 1996

Woman's lies fooled Navy commander

A woman who breached Royal Navy security was jailed for a year yesterday. Claire Marie Waller suffered from a mental condition that made her a compulsive liar, Plymouth Crown Court was told.

She adopted false identities and posed as an Army officer to trick her way into the Britannia Royal Naval College at Dartmouth, Devon. John Bush, for the prosecution, said: "She was offered accommodation as a visiting officer at, and inside, the college without having to produce any form of service identification documents, which is a worrying feature of this case."

Waller posed as Captain Claire Postgate of the 40th Field Regiment, Royal Artillery. She told Lieutenant Commander Gareth Llewelyn Hughes, whom she met in a Dartmouth hotel, that she was waiting for an Army-crewed yacht to arrive in the south Devon port.

Lieutenant Commander Hughes, a member of the college training staff, invited his "brother officer" to stay at the college. He also invited her to join cadets on a sailing weekend aboard a college boat, which she accepted.

Lieutenant Commander Hughes paid a £257 hotel bill Waller claimed she could not pay because of a "temporary financial embarrassment." But Waller, who comes from a military background, had already conned hotels and guesthouses out of payment.

Robert Linford, representing Waller, said she suffered from a form of the attention-seeking Munchausen's syndrome. He went on: "She is about the most well-spoken and, on the face of it, personable defendant I have ever represented. It's an appalling, miserable condition."

"Once the first lie is told, the next one will follow and it is going to become bigger and better."

Waller, of Bordon, Hampshire, admitted six charges of theft, deception, and perverting the course of justice. Judge William Taylor said: "I accept you are a sad, lonely young woman who lives in a fantasy world."

A police officer said security procedures at Britannia had been stepped up.

***

I believe Heidi Schøne may have a lot in common with Claire Marie Waller.

The Times, Thursday 26th February 1998

Vatican changes rites for casting out devils

A SURGE in demand for exorcisms has led the Vatican to revise the ritual and prayers used. The changes come as one of the Roman Catholic Church's leading exorcists said yesterday that he had yet to encounter a case of genuine demonic possession.

The Congregation for the Divine Sacraments and Divine Worship has nearly finished the ten-year task of rewriting the formulae for deliverance. The texts are not expected to alter the key part, where the demon is ordered to leave the person, but to shorten the accompanying prayers and invocations. The language is likely to be stronger, with instructions included for what vestments the priest should wear and how he should act, according to the *Catholic Herald*.

However, Father Louis McRaye, 83, the official exorcist for the Birmingham archdiocese, said that, in more than 80 cases in which he had been involved over the past ten years, none had demonstrated real possession. Instead, nearly all those who sought exorcisms were disturbed or psychiatrically ill.

Public demand for exorcisms has never been greater. In Italy, the number of priests carrying out exorcisms has risen from 20 six years ago to 300. Fears of demonic possession, thought to be fuelled in part by films such as *The Exorcist*, can lead Catholics and non-Catholics to turn to the Church for help.

But in Britain, symptoms that might in some countries be attributed to demonic possession are more often accounted as mental problems, and the individual referred to a doctor.

Those Catholic priests who are convinced that they are dealing with a case of genuine possession are forced to use a lengthy, Latin rite that has its origins in the Council of Trent in the 16th century and has been only partly modified in the centuries since then.

The rite was one of the few to escape updating during the reforms of the Second Vatican Council in the 1960's. It includes lines such as: "Behold the Cross of the Lord: Depart all adverse creatures" and: "I abjure you, most ancient demon … that you depart from this member of God's family." It also includes the entire eleventh chapter of Luke's Gospel.

Father McRaye said: "It is very lengthy and in some ways it is repetitive. The Lord himself in the Gospels was an exorcist, but in this case he just told the thing, the creature, the demon, to go. And it went."

"But my own experience is that I am uncertain that I have ever come across a case of real possession. Only twice have I wondered, and in one case I did read the full Latin rite over the person. But there was to my mind no sign at the end of anything supernatural."

In the Church of England, there is no official exorcism rite, the nearest thing being the "commination," or denouncing of, sinners, in the 1662 Book of Common Prayer, said in at least one Anglican church yesterday to mark Ash Wednesday.

***

The comment of Father Louis McRaye in the third paragraph provides more food for thought in relation to Heidi Schøne's claim that she was exorcised.

Heidi's behaviour was extreme but it has its origins in the problems that exist generally in mainstream European societies such as those in Britain and Holland. I reproduce a leader article from The Sunday Telegraph and then take a story from The Times to illustrate my point.

The Sunday Telegraph leader article dated 16th May 1999
Reap what you sow

According to a report in the British Medical Journal last week British teenagers smoke more cigarettes, take more drugs, drink more alcohol, have more babies, terminate more pregnancies and suffer more venereal disease than those of any other European country. The thread that connects these unpleasant facts is the abysmally low educational and cultural level of a large section of the British population. It is not entirely a coincidence that we also have the highest illiteracy rate in Europe. We are reaping what we have sown.

There is much in British popular culture that promotes, and nothing that contradicts, the idea that instant gratification is the highest good known to Man. Self-indulgence has been promoted as a sign of positive mental health, while self-restraint has come to represent a sign of mental unbalance. Our leaders have not had the courage to point out the destructive effects of our popular culture in this respect: on the contrary, the Prime Minister has been at pains to demonstrate how much he admires popular culture and even wants to participate in it.

The doctrine of non-judgmentalism - indifference masquerading as tolerance - now pervades our public service and is even accepted as unassailable by a wide section of the public. According to the doctrine, there is no virtue except a failure to condemn, and no vice except holding a belief that one way of life is better than another.

The only goal of public policy in such a climate of opinion is risk reduction. Since people will inject themselves with drugs anyway, we must make it safe for them to do so; since girls of 11 and 12 will have sex anyway, we must make sure they do so without conceiving.

In a culture of self-indulgence such as ours, however, the policy of risk reduction (always at public expense) leads to more risk taking. By implication, we teach our children that the only way to rid themselves of a temptation is to give into it.

Enough of the old values remain, however, for us occasionally to be horrified at the results of our own attitudes. After saturating our culture with crude eroticism, we are outraged to discover that more teenage girls than ever are having babies. After insisting that drug taking is merely a matter of personal choice, we are alarmed that primary school children have taken us at our word.

Even the poor and ignorant these days know where babies come from and how to avoid having them. They do not have unwanted pregnancies or babies through lack of knowledge, but because they live in a culture in which nothing matters very much and in which a baby might even seem a way out of the boredom and pointlessness of existence.

One in five British households with children is without a wage earner. The devastating consequences of this dreadful phenomenon are not hard to imagine. Children do not learn to connect their consumption of food or of anything else with any form of disciplined endeavour. They live in a world in which there is nothing to hope for and nothing to fear. The schools offer them no model of escape from their environment, but neither does the prospect of imminent hunger or destitution spur them on to personal effort.

The tax and social system, with its perverse economic incentives, is partly responsible for the degradation of British youth. And when these perverse economic incentives occur in a culture that in any case refuses to condemn any behaviour whatsoever on moral grounds, the circle is closed.

In a free society, it is not the duty of the state to produce virtuous citizens, or to enforce virtue. It can, however, refrain from the active promotion of vice. It can, for example, stop pretending that it is of no consequence whether a child has one parent or two. And its political leaders should have sufficient courage and integrity to insist that not everything that its electorate does or wants to do is right: for otherwise they are not leaders, but followers.

***

The Times, Tuesday 12th May 1999

Liberal Dutch hail purge on permissiveness

from Roger Boyes in Leiden

Dutch youths, reeling after a few beers, are being forced to think twice before urinating in the tree-lined canals that criss-cross the country's towns and cities. Police are suddenly cracking down on all minor crimes - from those who abuse the canals (so-called wilplasser) to noisy vandals - in a move that resembles New York's "zero tolerance" law and order policy.

The result is that a country long regarded by the British and other Europeans as an anything-goes society is beginning to look cleaner, safer and tamer. A trawl of brothels in Amsterdam searching for under-age prostitutes and illegal immigrants has resulted in the closure of several establishments: 15 buildings in the red-light district have been sold to the city authorities.

Throughout the country, so-called coffee shops - outlets for cannabis - are feeling the squeeze. In Leiden's most popular coffee shop, which advertises its wares with a Jamaican flag (the usual code to alert passers-by that this is not the place to seek a cappuccino), there are now strict identity controls and anyone looking remotely spotty or under-age is shown the door.

In Leeuwarden, police are imposing instant fines of £150 on youths kicking beer cans around on the streets or shouting after midnight. The town has also announced a 41-point programme called "No to Violence." One of its measures is a training course for bouncers at discotheques and pubs. They are taught how to eject troublemakers without violence. The courts have adopted accelerated procedures: youths involved in brawls will face charges within four days.

The police throughout the country have become very visible. In Leiden - an ancient university town which has always specialised in international law - students are complaining about the alleged arrogance of mounted police. But on the whole the officers' presence is welcomed by inhabitants.

The social climate has changed radically over the past few months. "For years an influential left-leaning elite of social scientists, politicians and journalists trivialised crime" the daily *De Volkeskrant* newspaper wrote. Now, it says, "people are realising that social life

deteriorates rapidly if small offences are tolerated."

The turning point seems to have come last autumn. A young man in the city centre of Leeuwarden tried to break up a fight between two young drunks and was kicked to death. The man, Meindert Tjoelker, was about to get married and the case touched Dutch hearts. The city police chief appealed to the country to demonstrate against "this growing madness." The call was printed in almost all national newspapers and 20,000 people paraded through the streets on the day the young man should have married.

Last year, 39 people were killed in The Netherlands in similar circumstances, caught up in alcohol or drug-driven street fights. Whilst this hardly puts Holland at the top of the international crime league, the Dutch clearly feel a line has been crossed. In 1985, 3,000 youths were arrested for violent crimes; now it is more like 8,000 a year.

Mieke Komen, an Amsterdam sociologist, has fuelled the debate with a best-selling book, *Dangerous Children*. She argues that relaxing external controls on youths has in no sense led to more self-control despite the thesis put forward by various Dutch liberals. On the contrary, shoplifting was largely ignored as an offence in Dutch cities for decades. Now there is a wave of serious and violent theft.

"Self-control can only be taught - and it is precisely this teaching that is missing in our society," says Dr. Komen.

***

I had spent the first three months of 1997 at the University of Amsterdam, the coldest winter in thirty years in Holland, and naturally all the canals were frozen solid and used for ice-skating. The girls at the University regarded smoking as a virtue, which practice continues in the night clubs and music bars where the volume of the music was often so high, conversation was practically impossible. The streets of Amsterdam were filthy with litter and it seemed to me as if there was a bye-law to encourage dogs to shit on the pavements. There was crap everywhere and with all the cyclists you can imagine the mess that had to be cleaned off the bicycle tyres, especially at night when avoidance became more difficult. The cafes were full of bustle and always had really polite bar staff - both men and women - who without exception spoke excellent English. Some of the girls serving were extremely welcoming and couldn't do enough for the public they served. Not quite like in Britain where the attitude of "Here's your change, now fuck off" generally seems to prevail. Now everyone knows the Red Light district for its 'usual' fare. Its 'unusual' fare amongst other things include the 'specialist' magazines, also displayed in the shop window. For example those depicting dogs, pigs and horses on heat and 'about' to have intercourse with a woman. Bad enough you may think. But give the Dutch some credit - you don't have to buy the magazine even if it is staring at all the tourists. One day, I popped into a cafe on the Leidseplein, one of the main squares in Amsterdam, and chanced to look at one of the supplement magazines that were stacked up with the Dutch newspapers reserved for customers to read. Thumbing through it out of curiosity, I came across an amazing page; it was filled with the following photographs: a pretty girl pissing into a handsome man's mouth; another young woman with her hand up a young man's arse; the face of a woman in her 70's looking at the multiple-studded genitals of a man in his 70's and a young naked woman in a crouched position staring at the three foot erection of a horse.

In the private gym where I went to take one-hour exercise classes, the men and women changed together and showered together all in full view of each other's glory. The girls dried off in front of me as if I wasn't there.

The canteens of most of the university faculty refectories had a poster with a list of the top ten sexually transmitted diseases. Chlamydia came top for the girls, an infection which if not caught early causes permanent infertility. With the age of consent at twelve in Holland, there was plenty of reason for the high profile warnings to the students, especially as the girls could be so accommodating, regarding the sex act more like a duty, than a favour.

Transvestism, transexualism, homosexuality, bisexuality, lesbianism, bestiality, sado-masochism - it all features in the red light district of Amsterdam. (The ultra-liberal Dutch also had the Gay Olympics staged in Amsterdam in August 1998). Yes indeedy! That's why allied soldiers died in World War Two in Holland, pushing back the Germans so that the Dutch could have their freedom. Freedom to fuck whoever or whatever you want; wherever you want; howsoever you want; with or without a vibrator; as a couple; male on female; male on male; two males on one female; three males on one female; female on female; bisexual men with a woman; a dog and a woman; a dog and a man; a pig and a woman; a horse and a woman; group sex; gay orgies. Chuck in some grass, heroin, coke and ecstasy (which is tested in the clubs beforehand as to its purity) together with beer and spirits and well - yeah, it's party time. But the 'real' party goers don't go to Holland any more - the real action is in Thailand, where the age of consent for all practical purposes is - well there isn't one - and need I say what's on the menu? Europe too bore witness to the paedophile uproar in Belgium in recent times. Can it be so different in Holland and Germany? Why, a week after returning to England, what did I see on British television? A documentary on a British paedophile recruiting young boys who then 'disappeared' and operating from the 'Blue Boy' - a gay nightclub in the same street as the University language Faculty.

And now back to Egypt. Hurghada on the Red Sea. I was scuba diving in May 1996 - incredible beauty; God's kingdom is truly magnificent. I was on my own and decided on a quick trip to Luxor which I had not seen for a few years. At the bus station were two girls with backpacks. Straight away I made for them and yes, they were Dutch, and yes they were pleasant, friendly and kind. They were off to Luxor having just finished their medical studies. They were both now qualified doctors. We all got on the bus - no air conditioning damn it - but the windows slid fully open. Trudy and Janneke were their names and on the journey I felt extremely happy with their company, sitting beside Trudy the whole time. The journey south west across the desert to the Nile took us through Assuit, well known for its Islamic fundamentalism, but before reaching Assuit we stopped off in a small town where I bought the girls some foul mudamis sandwiches from a street vendor. We had our bottled water to wash down the delicious food. I enjoyed the reciprocal feeling of friendship and care with the girls and by the end of our journey we had decided to book into the same hotel. Trudy particularly told me she didn't want to say goodbye. I was by now quite keen on her and I will always remember these two girls on that holiday for they came as a Godsend. So off we got from the bus, collected our luggage from the undercarriage, took a horse-drawn carriage and eventually booked in to the Luxor Sheraton. We took the cheapest rooms - away from the main hotel building. They were situated in the landscaped gardens and the girls had one room, and I took one next door to theirs.

After showering and changing, the girls met me to go to the Isis hotel where we arranged to meet Kit and Anna. Kit was an Australian boy back-packing around the world and Anna, his girlfriend, was a Danish girl who'd met him in Israel; both of them were on our bus from Hurghada. Well, the five of us enjoyed a splendid evening, even though we were all exhausted, and ate everything given to us in the pizza parlour at the Isis hotel. Kit and Anna were staying in basic accommodation in town. My new friends and I returned by taxi to the comforting luxury of the Sheraton, where we danced together at the disco, which was almost empty. I could never quite get my head around the fact of a disco existing in Egypt. It was state of the art stuff, as you'd expect - in place solely for the tourists. But I couldn't equate the ethics of basically 'Come-fuck-me-dance-disco' with the core of my own self. The king of the discos in Egypt for years had been 'The Jackies' in the basement of the Cairo Nile Hilton; they

221

imported European DJ's and all of Cairo's elite joined in with the tourists and businessmen. Egyptian girls dressed to kill, drank alcohol and the men looked cool - or at least tried to look cool. Three occasions there stick in my mind - once meeting a very pretty Saudi girl drinking whiskey, another time being asked out of the blue by a young American businessman if I liked men, and the other time recognising a guy whose mother was English and late father Egyptian and for whom I acted as solicitor in obtaining probate and administering the father's estate. But I hadn't seen Mike for some years and he'd changed a bit and we were both staring at each other. Eventually I went over to him and asked if we'd met before. He got my name pretty quickly and then I his too - Mike Chackal - and he quipped, "Yeah, I was thinking does he fancy me or do I know him?" We both laughed heartily. That's 'The Jackies' for you!

I went back to Trudy and Janneke's room where the three of us, with me in between them - all of us fully clothed - lay under the sheets as the air conditioning made the room chilly, and watched Euro-sport on TV. Both of them had their arms around me with their heads resting on my shoulders. What a rewarding end to the evening. Once again I thanked God. Trudy eventually got up to get changed in the bathroom and I was left alone in the arms of Janneke. I was surprised to hear the phone ring which Janneke answered. It was her boyfriend from Holland whose call in fact she was expecting. Detaching herself from my embrace, she spent five minutes talking to her boyfriend. Trudy afterwards came back in and in front of me took off her dress and T-shirt and hopped back into bed with us, when we watched more of the Euro-sport. There were two beds in that room and once we'd switched the TV off, Janneke went to the other bed to leave Trudy and I alone. Well, Trudy was truly exhausted and after an hour with her she'd fallen asleep. I knew I couldn't be beside her all night and still sleep so I decided to go back to my own room and obtain whatever rest I could. I extricated myself as best I could without disturbing Trudy - took their key with me, went out, locked their door and put the key back through their letterbox.

I got undressed and retired into my own large double bed and tried to relax. I was thinking of Trudy and I missed her. After a short while a knock came at the door. It was Trudy, asking me what I was doing back in my own room. More or less immediately I put my arms around her and held her tight - oh so tight. I told her how so grateful I was for having met her and that I liked her. She had put her dress back on and I drew it up with my hands until I reached the skin of her buttocks, which she obligingly let me caress all over. She said, "Go in - let me give you a massage, you are so tense." I was tense and I was lonely and sad (the garbage in those Norwegian newspaper reports was getting to me and I had been telling the Dutch girls all about it). "Lie on your front," Trudy told me. I did so on my big bed, having taken the covers off altogether. Trudy was a real professional. Oh Dutch girls! It began as a thorough all over body massage - I was only in my underpants and she used her hands expertly with just the right pressure to cause optimum contentment for me. Yes, very relaxing thank you. Without warning as if it was only natural for me to expect this, she lifted her T-shirt over her well-proportioned breasts and used them to massage my back, increasing my sense of frustrated well-being. For neither she nor I had any intention of proceeding to the ultimate act of natural pleasure, although I know it was much tougher on me than on her. I'd laid out my stall during the day and I wasn't going to let myself down. So Trudy and I just lay together in each other's arms - she refused even to take her top off altogether and entreated me to try and just relax - but this was not easy. Eventually, she left and went back to her room but I couldn't sleep at all after that - well, would you be able to?

Next morning was one of those you don't forget - ever. I felt so completely exhausted, so dog-tired and jaded that I just didn't want to face even eating a morsel for breakfast - leave alone endure the stifling heat of the Valley of the Kings and Valley of the Queens on our sightseeing trip. But I masked my condition, did have a bite to eat and a cup of tea and made pleasant conversation. The girls were tucking into a bloody great big full breakfast - third helpings if you please! The conversation went around the usual subjects: their hospital internship, their families and having children. Trudy definitely didn't want any children - ever. Then it changed to maybe one or two at most, but a long way into the future. Janneke was much softer on the subject. For the first time on our trip Trudy was also getting snappy and a bit callous. It took the edge of the previous day's euphoria altogether. Now for the first time Trudy told me she had a boyfriend back home. Well, breakfast had marked me and Trudy had shown a side to her that was malevolent - but I was glad I found out, although sorry indeed to experience it. Janneke was not like that at all; calm and understanding all the way. But it was Trudy I'd gone for and liked especially.

222

After breakfast we waited in the foyer for Kit and Anna to join us for the day's sightseeing. We took a taxi intending to take the car ferry across the Nile, but the queue to get across was so long we'd have had to wait about two hours in the heat and petrol fumes. So, instead, I paid off the taxi driver and we caught a small motor boat and crossed that calm peaceful river to the west bank of Luxor. We had gone at the worst time - mid afternoon when the sun was at its highest and when most of the other tourists had returned. The trip up and down the steps of the tombs bored me - I'd done it twice before in earlier years and with the heat and my sleepless night, I was a sorry chap. A break in the monotony came at the top of one of the stairways to a tomb when Trudy burst into tears - sobbing audibly and in great distress. I went over to her and she told me that one of her friends who'd promised her they'd share an apartment back in Amsterdam had changed her mind. Her friend had now decided to let her boyfriend move in with her and Trudy was now left to find alternative accommodation, which she said was the last thing she needed before starting her hospital internship. She had phoned the girl that morning from Luxor to hear her change of plan and what with the heat of Upper Egypt it had all got too much for her. One of the Egyptian guides did his best to comfort Trudy and me by throwing water over our faces, hair and necks. We completed the full tour of the site and returned to our hotel. I was grateful that my stint as tour guide was over for the day. We showered and met up again to go for our evening meal. Trudy had bucked up and on leaving our apartments I was honoured by my fresh-faced friend putting her arm around me as we walked off along the winding path to the main hotel building and telling me, "Oh, I'm happy with you." And I knew that she really was. We ate just the three of us this time and afterwards in the moonlight we all went for a swim in the rather cool waters of the swimming pool. How content we all were, splashing and fooling around. Again that night I spent some time in the arms of Trudy in her room and retired to sleep on my own; I did get some precious sleep that second night and my mind was calmer having had the benefit of a close talk with Trudy. She referred to her troubled childhood and remoteness from other girls at school. She had been a bit of a loner and had had no confidence at all. Indeed, Janneke herself later confided in me that Trudy had been in such a state that she needed professional help, which to some worthwhile extent had helped her. It dawned on me that my instincts on Trudy's disposition had after all been well founded and once again I found myself saying, "You do pick 'em!" But even so, Trudy was no Heidi. Trudy had a big family - three sisters and two brothers - and she related how her married sisters had told her how so good it was to wait and be patient for the right time and the right man to enjoy sex with. I liked hearing that. In fact in Southern Holland there is a strong Christian community who retain the Christian commitment to no sex before marriage and indeed in 1995 in Leiden, 2,000 students had signed a charter binding themselves to this principle. I remember at the time reading in the newspapers one liberated Dutch girl ridiculing these 2,000 "narrow-minded students" on the basis that "our parents have fought for two decades to obtain freedom from sexual repression and why should we throw it all away now?"

Life had been hard for Trudy's father. He had been a farmer but the enterprise had failed and Trudy had blamed her mother for not being more supportive of her father in the project. But 'family days' were a big feature of Trudy's life and it was touching to hear of the kinship that these get-togethers of all the relatives produced. I was later to speak to Trudy's mother and father on several occasions and even though their English was very poor, I could tell what kind-hearted people they were.

The third day of our stay in Luxor was to be our last. I was going to return to Hurghada to pick up my luggage from my hotel and the girls were going on to Aswan. We would then meet up in Cairo. Breakfast on the second morning was a much more appetising affair for me and after packing our bags we went to the pool again and were joined by Kit and Anna. It was a fairly large pool and Trudy and I had the opportunity to discreetly kiss and cuddle in the water - like honeymooners. Trudy wanted to know where the toilet was and I took her round the corner to show her. Spontaneously she stopped me when we were around that corner and said, "Just a minute - wait" and she clasped my face and kissed me for a long, long time. I'm glad no one else was around to see my own 'spontaneous reaction' - for I was truly happy and free. We sat down on a deck chair and continued exploring our feelings. They were a joyful few minutes, which I treasured for a long time afterwards and looking back now I can only give thanks to that dear girl for the glimpse of heaven she gave me. We went back to the pool side and sat on our deck chairs. We were content - but Trudy perceptively remarked, "Look, no-one's really happy around us." Too true. The holiday scene on the Nile in a five star hotel complex was almost an illusion. Loneliness seemed to bite deep into the other guests' demeanours. Single men; single women; only the odd married couple; a mother and her daughter. But then so too was my situation an illusion; I too only had myself to look forward to, but not for a little while yet.

223

Janneke went off into Luxor town centre with Kit and Anna and left Trudy and I to enjoy a sumptuous barbecue meal just up from the swimming pool. How gracious and kind she was for every single minute of that meal. From time to time we kissed like newly-weds, when no one was looking. I savoured the unaccustomed luxury of it all, for soon we had to go to the railway station and go our separate ways. I adored those moments with her. Contentedly we checked out of the hotel and we took a taxi into town and as we had time on our hands before the others arrived, we went into a café and had a Seven-up each. The owner then persuaded us to separately have our photos taken with him. It was after we said goodbye to him that Trudy and I came across one of those wretched sights that come completely out of the blue. Just across the road from us I noticed a beggar sitting in the road, with shoulder length corkscrew hair. Rather young. It was a girl with one leg missing and naked but for a flimsy T-shirt. She could have only been in her early twenties and she glided along the dirty road on her bottom, which was fully exposed to all. She came closer to us and then, with her back to us, raised one hand to the side of her face and shook it like a demon possessed. It was the action of one who was completely deranged and I will never forget my horror at the sight of this poor soul in her insanity, and Trudy's own incredulous but self-composed shock at this moment. It was as if we were witnessing something that just didn't happen except in films. This wretch was completely abandoned and ignored by the townsfolk. By this time the café owner had seen our disbelief and came out to watch for himself. He told me that she was "magnoon" ('mad' in Arabic) which was obvious already and on enquiring what happened to her leg he told me she'd lost it in a train accident at the railway station which was in front of us. What a humbling experience this was and it only increased my frustration with humanity, in that so many people, in spite of the blessing of all their faculties, are nevertheless arrogant, cruel and merciless - untouched by suffering of any degree. Suffering - that sedative to human callousness.

Trudy and I made our way with our heavy bags to the station foyer and held on to each other tight whilst we waited for our friends to arrive. Tickets were then purchased and before taking our trains - me north to Quena and then by bus to Hurghada, and the others south to Aswan, Trudy and I were left alone to say our goodbyes in the sweetest possible way. I enjoyed the companionship of those people and heartily wished them all a safe trip. I had arranged to meet them in Cairo railway station three days hence, so our parting would be brief.

I eventually arrived in Cairo from Hurghada and booked in at the Nile Hilton where, because I had Egyptian nationality, I could pay half the normal tourist rate. I went to see as many of my relatives as I could that day, including a 98 year old uncle; a truly wonderful fellow who still had all his wits about him. He died in 1998 aged 100. What he must have seen in that time - dear Zaki Bey. In the evening, I went to eat at a Kentucky Fried Chicken outlet in down town Cairo and afterwards began my walk back to the Nile Hilton. I was passing by the underground subway when I saw this dream of a girl pass me by - with a bloke who looked like someone out of the Van Halen rock group; long blond hair down to his arse, six earrings in each ear and rather scruffy too. Ordinary looking. But she was I-n-c-r-e-d-i-b-l-e. They walked on by - she in her T-shirt with BOSTON written on the front underneath which lay 40 DD breasts. He talked with an American accent and she was speaking English too. I just had to try and find out who she was. Instinctively I knew from her happy-go-lucky manner and fresh-faced looks that this was a girl I simply had to befriend; she was the one I had been waiting for. So I walked on a little and turned round to see them enter a small store. I walked back straight away into the shop and waited about three minutes for them to purchase some bottled water. I, in the meantime, was asking for some pumice stone that I genuinely wanted. Choosing my moment, I asked the guy where he was from. Tactics were important here. Never talk to the girl first or the guy will think you're taking the piss. Talk to him first and he can't complain. So he told me he was from the good old U.S of A and, as luck would have it, gave me an introduction to the girl by asking, "And where do you think she's from?" Looking at the word BOSTON printed on her T-shirt, I said, "Well the U.S.A too." "Ha, trick!" she said. "I'm Dutch." (Well you could've knocked me over with a feather - Dutch!). "Oh really," I said. "I've been to Holland a few times - where exactly are you from?" "Oh, The Hague." "You don't say," I replied. "I've stayed there in Joseph Israelslaan - a street near the railway station when I was on an Anglo-Dutch Lawyers Exchange. Where in the Hague are you living?" She responded: "Oh, you won't know it - it's a suburb of The Hague."

The three of us left the shop and I then told the guy how relaxed I'd found life in Holland and he said he was looking forward to going there to stay (with the girl) and as he was a "qualified engineer" he'd probably have no trouble finding a job, he told me. Knowing the limits of friendly conversation had been reached, I bade them farewell. They walked on ahead and crossed the road, whilst I stayed behind

224

them on the other side and I saw them enter a building which contained a cheap hotel in the upper floors. A place I was going to return to next morning.

I got up early the next day and made straight for this couple's hotel. The feeling that I'd met the love of my life was overpowering. I was sick with longing. And clearly with Trudy having a boyfriend, not wanting me and having some slight 'problems,' I was going to do my best to find out who this oh-so easy-going, uncomplicated girl from The Hague was. No real plans could be made. I just went up to the reception area and waited. I had a story ready but whether it would be convincing was another thing. What I had hoped for was to catch the girl on her own. I searched the place for them - the two dining rooms and the lounge - but there was as yet no sign of them. I waited for two hours in reception, by which time I'd had enough of watching the Euro-sport on T.V. So I went up to the reception desk and just asked for the whereabouts of the couple. The Egyptian desk clerk told me they'd left at six that morning to go to Luxor. "And have you got their names?" I asked. "Yes, here in the guest book," he said, and showed me two names - Mara K***l [her full surname shall remain confidential] and Barry Watson. Well, it had to be them. K***l was 100 per cent a Dutch name and my description of the girl was corroborated by the receptionist, although the boy's hair was not long I was told. Well, he must have tied it up in a bun, I reasoned to myself. Anyway I took out my note book and wrote their names down. I knew I probably had enough to find the girl: her town and full name. Well done son, not bad for a morning's work!

The next morning I was due to meet the overnight train arriving from Aswan with my four friends. I actually arrived at Ramses Railway Station just as the group were walking on to the station concourse and Janneke was so surprised to see me facing her, that in gratitude she gave me a full kiss on the lips. Another moment I'll always remember. We all bundled into a taxi and went straight up to my room at the Hilton. The girls spent two days with me in Cairo, and, as they were doctors, I introduced them to two of my cousins, one a surgeon and the other in his final year of medicine at Cairo University. Mohammed, the surgeon, took us on a tour of his uncle's private clinic in Mohandessin, a suburb in Cairo, catering for Egypt's elite and containing full operating theatres and other excellent facilities and staffed by one or two British nurses. Mohammed also pointed out to us a huge new hospital that the French had built but which could not open because the Egyptian government had no money to run it. Cairo University Hospital that my other cousin, Omar, took us to one evening was quite an eye-opener for the girls; standards of hygiene left a lot to be desired and, whilst I waited outside, Janneke and Trudy took a quick glimpse at one of the delivery rooms for new born babies.

We visited the pyramids. Mohammed, Janneke, Trudy and I took horses and galloped for miles around and had our photos taken to capture the moment. We visited the Citadel of Muhammad Ali - a magnificent historic mosque on the edge of Cairo with a panoramic view of old Cairo; we strolled through Khan El Khalili bazaar where Trudy was in a bad mood because I was spending too much time talking to Janneke and it took a while to sort that problem out. "Funny isn't it?" I thought to myself. When earlier back in Luxor we'd been discussing the subject of marriage, Trudy told me that even once she was married, she would still like to go out with other men who she knew, for a meal say, but "just as friends," and what did I think of that? Bollocks was what I thought of that and told her so. Bollocks was also what her boyfriend told her when she got back to Holland when Trudy told him 'everything' about her friendship with me. He lost his temper with her and was most upset. "Let my girlfriend go away on holiday and what does she do - she falls in love with the first guy she meets," he must have been thinking. I even by chance spoke to him and reassured him that "nothing" (i.e. sexual intercourse) had happened. Which was quite true. I thought, "Well that's a good lesson for this typical-thinking Dutch couple. They don't mind hurting others if it suits them, but when the boot is on the other foot and they are hurt, they just don't like it." After Trudy got back to Holland she wrote me a card and I soon gave her a call at her parents' place. We had a long, long chat and when I told her I had to go, she said, "Oh don't stop yet. I miss you." So she invited me to visit her when she would cook me a meal. Yes, we had a strong bond, but as I continued to call her, her boyfriend grew ever more anxious - he was with her several times when I called - and eventually, after she had a serious chat with him, she changed her mind altogether about me. We could meet in a café for an hour or so and then go our own separate ways, she said. No meal would be cooked. No going to sit in her flat as her flatmates would see me, and gossip. So, soon it was all over and in fact when she came to tour the south coast of England the following summer with her boyfriend, I didn't even get a phone call from her to say hello. When subsequently I spent three months at Amsterdam University, Janneke, Trudy and I met just the once. I didn't then mind, however, as Trudy, unfortunately, wasn't the girl for me. But remembering overall how she had been so caring and loving towards me in Egypt, I stood beside

225

her as she mounted her bicycle to go and told her of my gratitude and with tears in her eyes she departed, with a wave.

When I got back to England from Egypt, I wrote to the Town Hall in The Hague and gave them the sparse details of Mara K***l. They wrote back saying they had no one of that name registered in The Hague. But when studying in Amsterdam in 1997 I had discovered that there were separate districts all over The Hague - called 'gemeente' in Dutch - and each one had recorded on computer the names and addresses of its registered citizens. So after trying one or two in person, without success, I decided to go back to Amsterdam and from my room write a letter to each of the several gemeente. I then left Amsterdam for a week's work back at the office in London. When I got back, a few letters had been slipped under my door and to my enormous joy the full address and date of birth of Mara M***a K***l was there printed on one sheet of paper before my very eyes. Even her place of birth - Rheden. I posted back the small administrative charge of 10 guilders and next day set off for a street named Wateringkade in The Hague. I was really looking forward to meeting her - what a surprise she would get. And she didn't even know my name. I got to The Hague Central Station in the early evening, warmly dressed as usual for February, and took a tram to her street. I was concerned obviously as to whether or not that boyfriend, Barry, was with her but decided that there was nothing I could do but pretend to be lost or something if he answered the door and hope he wouldn't recognise me from Egypt. I surveyed the scene when I got to her flat, which was across the road from the red light district and opposite a noisy flyover. I rang her door bell. No answer. I rang again. Still no answer. So I rang the neighbour's bell. No answer. I rang again. Then a landing light came on and a middle-aged lady opened the door to me. She enquired as to my business and I asked if she knew where Mara was and she told me she was visiting her mother nearby but she didn't know where that was. Significantly, she told me that Barry, the boyfriend, was back home visiting his family in the United States and that he'd had all his long hair cut off – "to look more respectable" - and his earrings removed. The neighbour apologised for not answering the door very quickly, as it was "a bad neighbourhood." So I said I'd call on Mara tomorrow. "But make it the evening as she's got a job; she finishes at 5 o'clock," the lady told me.

Next day I got to Mara's flat a little before 5 p.m. and waited outside. About twenty minutes later I saw a girl in a heavy coat and handbag coming towards me that looked like my quarry. She had her hair in a pony tail, whereas in Cairo it was flowing loose, so I could not be sure it was Mara. I stared at her as she came towards me trying to identify that it was Mara and she smiled at my studious attentions. So I just said, "Are you Mara K***l?" and she said, "Yes - who are you?" Within literally two minutes she had invited me upstairs to her humble flat. Would you believe she was actually eager to invite me in and learn all about my quest to find her? I loved it and I liked her whole attitude over the matter. My first impressions of her on that mild Cairo night were confirmed. My instincts were correct. She apologised for the lack of warmth in her living quarters as they did not have central heating, just electric fires to plug in. And so it was; I'd found her; this cheerful, simply wonderful example of social tact. She was amazed that I'd managed to track her down and wanted to continue the evening in a restaurant, which of course I heartily agreed to. We stayed in her sitting room for some little time more, chatting about all sorts of things and she listened most attentively. Oh yes, I liked her! On the shelves that bedecked her living room wall were two bottles of coloured water and I asked what they were. Cheekily, I said, "I think I know what the yellow water is, but what's the red water?" She quipped, "Oh! that's my period." "Hmm," I thought, "very droll." Was this or was this not a very Dutch girl-like comment? Well, take 'em as you find 'em! The talk of course had to include Barry, the boyfriend, away in the U.S.A. Mara told me that his surname was not in fact Watson, as he had written in the guestbook at their Cairo hotel. He had a Jewish surname and was worried that if he used it the Egyptians would harass him. He wasn't asked to show his passport at their very basic hotel. He couldn't in fact find any job in engineering in Holland. What he could find though was a job handing out flyers to passers-by in the street. But Mara had now found him a job in the American Jean Company shop in town. Barry, she told me, liked girls' bottoms. "He loves my bottom," she exclaimed. "Are you a bum or a tit man?" she asked me. Noticing her own extremely large breasts with firm jutting nipples and tight nicely rounded bottom, I replied - truthfully - "Both, as a matter of fact" and we exchanged views in general on the human form.

Mara had chosen an Italian restaurant within walking distance and she cut out some discount vouchers from a book she had. However, I made it clear that the balance of the bill would be on me. She got herself ready and brushed her long hair and at the top of the stairs asked me if I thought she looked okay. A nice gesture, that question. She looked gorgeous. Out we went and Mara told me we'd take a short cut through the red light district and she said she was glad I was around to accompany her through it. We crossed the road and we put our arms round each other and after we crossed another side street, I kissed her on the cheek to which she said, "Oh, that was nice." Now I was so happy, you know. Our talk turned to the problems of relationships and I mentioned the high incidence of venereal diseases and I specified chlamydia as being the number one disease for young girls. "Yes," she eagerly retorted. "I had it. The boyfriend I had before Barry was Dutch and he gave it to me. I also caught an infection. Oh, I was really, really sick. It looked horrible down there - itchy, painful. I was ill in bed for weeks. But I got it treated and although it's still there, the fungus inside me, I'm alright now. I told Barry and he's okay about it. I loved my Dutch boyfriend - we'd known each other from school and he went with me to the airport to say goodbye on my way to Israel and we both cried. But then I met Barry at the Kibbutz and we were like zombies all the time. Exhausted. We made love every night until three in the morning." And whilst Barry left Israel for a trip back home to the United States, her Dutch boyfriend came to visit and was told it was all over; Barry was now her man.

Mara guided me to a right turn and we entered the red light district, which consisted of girls in windows with just their underwear on, plying their trade. Some of them were actually damned attractive and Mara, noticing the same, told me so too, and quite spontaneously and in all good faith assured me, "You can come back later and enjoy them." I was shocked at her suggestion but showed no reaction. I wanted, jokingly of course, to add, "Okay, but only if you come in and watch," but I kept quiet. It wouldn't have surprised me in the least if she'd taken me up on my 'offer' and came in to watch. The term 'going Dutch' was taking on new dimensions. No wonder she was in a mess sexually. Her parents were divorced and her mother, aged 39, had been living until very recently with a man ten years her junior. But this man, after five years of cohabitation, had now decided he wanted a younger woman with whom he could have some children. Mara's mother was alone again and miserable. Mara's father, an artist of sorts, lived elsewhere in Holland and she wasn't very fond of him, seeing him only very occasionally. She had two brothers.

We entered the Italian restaurant in a side street and it turned out to be the most romantic dinner I'd ever had. In return for her candour about her own life, I returned the endearment by telling her about my 'Norwegian experience,' which she said was the most incredible story she had ever heard. She was great company and hung on to my every word and, not unnaturally, I felt great warmth in her presence. But …. And, so feeling relaxed herself, she asked, as we were about to finish our dessert, whether we could go back to her place and have something to drink and watch the T.V. The way she said it was clearly an invitation for a 'cosy' evening. I continued talking for some time though and we were there till closing time. Mara then showed me some of the nearby landmarks of The Hague - the old parliament, the royal palace, and explained a bit of the history behind these buildings. It was getting very late however and so she walked me to the train station, having earlier invited me to return the next day for a spaghetti dinner in her flat with a girlfriend of hers. Appropriately, the next day was Valentine's day.

I returned the next evening, but I'd already made my mind up that it would be our last meeting. Whilst she was cooking the pasta, she explained how she'd phoned her boyfriend, Barry, in the United States to wish him well on Valentine's Day, but hadn't told him of our meeting for fear of his adverse reaction at her hospitality towards me. While the cat's away the mice just will play! But she had also spoken to her mother who, she said, was surprised and concerned at the ease with which I'd obtained her daughter's full personal details from a public register. Apart from this one exception, Holland was a country very keen on preserving strict privacy laws for its citizens. At Amsterdam University, the administration staff would not give any information even on a fellow student at the same university. This situation stemmed, I understand, from the occupation of Holland in the last war when the Dutch were constantly pestered by the Germans to produce their identity cards, a form of intrusion that led to Holland trying to free its citizens from all unnecessary trespass.

Mara continued by telling me that her mother thought she was "naïve" in so readily befriending me the previous evening and clearly this admonishment was having a chastening effect on Mara's intimacy with me on this second evening. That they began moralising about the situation I found a little hypocritical and shallow, bearing in mind the freedom with which both mother and daughter had conducted their own love lives up till then. Sitting on the couch together, Mara now refused to let me put my arm around her, citing as her motive her desire not to "cheat" on Barry. I thought to myself, "Hmm - so what about last night then?" And screwing Barry, a near stranger, for months on end at the Kibbutz. That wasn't naïve? And she did not want to marry Barry, she said, until she was sure he was right for her, just in case she ended up quickly divorced "like my mother, who ruined her own life by getting married too young." "But my dear girl," I mused, "screwing an arsehole you aren't married to is a situation no different from screwing an arsehole you are married to." Screwing was going to take place no matter what and both forms of relationship - married or unmarried - were probably going to end eventually because of the quality of the people involved; the 'arsehole' factor was the impediment that had to be eradicated from the union. But it was obvious to me that too many people couldn't recognise an arsehole when they saw one; still less see that the arsehole was also staring at them in the mirror. Many couples today start living together to more or less 'see how things go.' This recognises in some large part the mutual lack of trust that exists. But this recognition stops short of correcting the very shaky foundations on which they base their lives. They are often like feathers in the wind, unable to lead lives of any great spiritual meaning or purpose. Statistics have proven that more relationships in unmarried cohabiting couples break down than in married couples. With nigh on half of marriages failing as well, I think my point is proven to a large degree; human beings today are often unable to live with each other for very long.

And so it was. Mara, her girlfriend and I had our spaghetti meal and then went out to sit in a couple of disco bars. The girls were both chain smoking. The smoking, drinking, disco culture worshipped by so many seemed to represent the pinnacle of their shallow lives. Poor things. I left Mara that evening back for Amsterdam, disillusioned but glad to have found out the important things about her in only two meetings. I never contacted her again, save for a postcard from England thanking her for two wonderful evenings. She soon departed Holland to live in America where Barry had returned to find work.

I leave the subject of Holland and the Dutch by reproducing one of the leader articles from The Times of Thursday 29th September 1996 and an article in William Langley's column from The Sun on Monday 11th May 1998.

The Times, Thursday 29th September 1996

THE BLUE ORANGES

Queen Beatrix is not afraid to speak her mind

The House of Orange has produced three generations of popular, strong-minded women who have symbolised the redoubtable spirit of The Netherlands, in war and peace. Their charisma has ensured that this dynasty, implanted in a country whose libertarian spirit would otherwise make it a natural republic. Britain retains a warm memory of Queen Wilhelmina, the heroic voice in exile of her embattled nation. Her daughter, Juliana, seemed in the post-war years the epitome of the modern monarch, for whom the very phrase the "bicycling queen" was invented. And Queen Beatrix, more regal that her mother, has re-introduced a degree of distance and moral authority that is, perhaps, a necessary corrective to the despotic informality of monarchs on wheels.

Yet the House of Orange is now running into unaccustomed criticism, and discrete voices are asking whether the Queen is overstepping her severely circumscribed constitutional role.

She has spoken out against the legalisation of homosexual marriages; she has called on her Government to do more to clean up the environment; and, more controversially, she has insisted on having the Dutch Ambassador to South Africa removed before she pays a state visit because she disapproves of his living with a woman who is not his wife.

The Dutch, notoriously liberal in sexual matters, have been taken aback by this whiff of Victorianism. It looks like a case of throwing stones in the royal glasshouse. For the Dutch royal family has also had its share of scandal and bad luck - not on the scale of the

House of Windsor but enough to strain the limits of popularity. The Queen's father, a notorious philanderer, was publicly disgraced by the Lockheed affair; her husband, Prince Claus, suffered depression, and her son, Crown Prince Willem-Alexander, has been sowing wild oats by the bushel.

Queen Beatrix has clearly understood, however, that her own position must be above reproach; indeed, she is staking out the moral high ground not only to remind the Dutch of the strong national streak of Calvinist thinking but to articulate some of the older, more formal and more conservative virtues that have been overshadowed by post-war egalitarianism. The same, indeed, has been the case with Queen Silvia of Sweden, who has been outspoken in criticising her country's tolerance of child pornography. But if continental monarchies have less pomp and protocol than our own, they have shown that informality is no guarantor of universal popularity.

***

The Sun, Monday 11th May 1998

When he takes the chair for today's special Cabinet committee on welfare reform, Tony Blair might consider the disturbing case of 19-year-old single mother Ms Estelle Cruyff.

Ms Cruyff's father, Henny, fears she is about to be dumped by her unemployed boyfriend, dreadlocked former soccer boss Ruud Gullit, who already has four other children by two different women.

Henny says: "I am desperately worried. I believe he is treating my daughter badly." Gullit's ex-wife, Cristina has joined in the attack, claiming the sacked Chelsea manager had not been to see their two kids for six months.

If true, this is typical of the behaviour Blair blames for Britain's social breakdown. He points to the irrefutable evidence that children who are raised in secure two-parent homes have enormous advantages over those who aren't.

Surely the Prime Minister wouldn't attack deadbeat dads knocking up teenage girls on council estates, while ignoring the alley-cat morals of celebrities.

Gullit is currently in Holland. He would do us a favour by staying there. At the very least Blair should declare an all-ports alert to prevent this menace to public morals from slithering back into the country.

***

Chapter 21

On 8th January 1998, I wrote again to policewoman Torill Sorte pressing her to be more specific in answer to the questions I had been raising for months, if not years, on end. I want an official reply in writing from her in any event.

Dear Torill,

Heidi Schøne

I tried to speak to you today but was told you were in a meeting in the afternoon and then had to leave before 3.30 p.m.

Before Christmas, I telephoned several times Heidi's neighbours, the Weums on (32) 871882. I luckily caught one young girl in who was babysitting, and she told me a little about Heidi's baby boy. Otherwise when I phoned these people, they refused to speak English on several occasions but eventually admitted to speaking English, but a man only called me a "fucking idiot." I was only asking them to go upstairs and get Heidi Schøne down to speak to me.

I must of course get some answers to these newspaper allegations from Heidi. Phoning her neighbours is all I can do as I will not let Heidi off the hook. But the neighbours won't help.

So bearing in mind that Heidi would not have imagined that I would ever read the allegations she made in the newspapers, once again, I must ask you to re-interview her, and ask her the following:

1. The precise details and evidence of threats she claims I made to kill her son, Daniel. What you told me last time – about there being nothing on the Bergen Police file – is fine, but you told me Heidi still maintains I made threats. So I need to know the details of what form the threats took and where the evidence is. It doesn't exist, as no such threats were made by me, but I must know exactly what Heidi is saying now.

2. The names and addresses and statements from the neighbours who Heidi says I have threatened to kill if they did not give me her new "secret address." Again I never made such threats, but Heidi made the claims so she should furnish you with names and addresses and details of the threats.

3. Does she deny a single allegation I have made in the Norwegian Report detailing her past? What I wrote was all true. Does she deny any of it? This report that the journalists got hold of, prior to doing their May 1995 story, is 100% factual and would not be too difficult for you to verify.

4. My Bergen lawyer in 1995, Wesenberg, told me he did not want to further question Commander Krogvold about the attempted rape allegation of December 1986, in case Commander Krogvold re-opened the case. According to Krogvold, the 'attempted rape allegation' case was statute barred on December 11th 1992. But according to Wesenberg, the attempted rape case can be re-opened even after the limitation period has expired. Please therefore obtain details of the allegation from Krogvold and Heidi as Krogvold refused me as did my own lawyer, Wesenberg. I hope you can see

231

why I hate that stinking piece of shit, Heidi Schøne, and why I will never give up pursuing her for the truth.

5.   Will I be arrested, still, on entry to Norway, and what has become of the further enquiries you have been making into this case?

I will telephone you next week so that you can give me an update. Heidi's lawyer, Tomm Skaug will not supply me with any information whatsoever on Heidi's newspaper allegations. When I contacted the Norwegian Embassy here in London, they just refer everything to Krogvold who of course will not supply me or my lawyers (in London in 1990 and in Bergen in 1995) with details of the attempted rape, or indeed the rape of Heidi by a Bergen shopkeeper, or Gudmund Johannessen's assault on Heidi in Christmas 89-90 or his criminal conviction etc. etc. etc.

If it comes down to it, I will have to start all over again with another Norwegian lawyer - more money in legal fees - but I will ask this lawyer to enquire as to the questions I have asked you in this letter. Please do your best to get those answers now, as I feel sure, I can get Heidi prosecuted for trying to pervert the course of justice.

Yours sincerely,

Frederick Delaware

At 9.30 a.m. on 14th January 1998 I telephoned Torill Sorte:

TS.   *Sorte.*

F.   *Yes, hi Torill, it's Frederick Delaware.*

TS.   *Oh hello.*

F.   *Yes, hi there. Been a long time. Right, did you manage to read my letter that I wrote.*

TS.   *Yes I did I give it to ... ...*

F.   *Ah. Good. OK. I've got a copy of the letter in front of me, can we ...*

TS.   *I sent it to the lawyer in Drammen.*

F.   *Oh, the lawyer. Ah, OK. Is there any chance I could have his phone number?*

TS.   *Er, yes (32) 805500.*

F.   *And what's his name?*

TS.   *Lyngås.*

F.   *How do you spell that?*

TS.   *L and one you don't use* [she was referring to the "å" letter which we don't have in the English language] *Lyngås, Dag Lyngås.*

232

F.   *OK, as far as you're concerned, what can we do about you interviewing Heidi again?*

TS.   *I have talked to Heidi two times since I talked to you last.*

F.   *Oh!*

TS.   *And I have written it down and sent it to Lyngås in Drammen and he has sent the whole case to Oslo who have been in contact with England and England has answered our letter and er told us they looked at the case and we have so long put the case away and that it - it won't be a case and so ...*

F.   *So it's all over is it?*

TS.   *Yes it's all over, yes. If it comes any more thing in the case we have to look at maybe the lawyers in Oslo* [will do] *something with it but not now.*

F.   *So what were you trying to find out from the people in London and ... ... if I could be stopped somehow?*

TS.   *No, not just that but we want to see the law, how they are, er ...*

F.   *What for extradition?*

TS.   *Yes, although we need to know what English er* [law] *is, what* [it] *says about these things. What they want* [the English] *to do with the case and if they get it over to them, so that was very more, what shall I say...*

F.   *Well you had to wait a long time for the police in England to er ...*

TS.   *No, it was very quick way.*

F.   *Oh, was it?*

TS.   *But er the laws in Norway is not like the laws in England. See the difference, that's what we want to find out.*

F.   *That's what I told you from the start. This isn't a criminal ... ...*

TS.   *Yes it is.*

F.   *In England?*

TS.   *Yes, it is a criminal* [offence] *in England, but you see for the English police to look at the case ... it have ... they want some more if the case ...if Heidi have lived in England they would have done something with the case. But when Heidi lives here and you in England you have to be ... ...*

[The English newspapers would surely never have contemplated such a story as did the Norwegian press so no conflict would have arisen here in England in the first place.]

F.   *So what were the criminal things I was doing?*

TS.   *Er, to say things about Heidi in the public and ... ...*

F.   *Even though they're true?*

TS.   *Yes, but you mean it's true: she says another ...it's, er, you call it in England you say things who is not so good about her.*

F.   *What is she saying that isn't true?*

TS.   *She say?*

F.   *What things is she telling you that are not true? ... I mean it's all on that sheet of paper in Norwegian isn't it? Yeah?*

TS.   *Yeah, but she say is not agree with you.*

F.   *Yes, but on what?*

TS.   *Yes it's many things you said in your letters. But she say also for some years ago she liked you very much and she told the things about her who were true and that you now use in your letters to people in Norway [that] hurts her. But she said also that it's a mix with things who is not true.*

F.   *What are the things – I have not said a single lie in any of the things I've said.*

TS.   *She says so.*

F.   *Yes, what?*

TS.   *About doing and about ... ...*

F.   *About doing? For instance, for instance Gudmund Johannessen. Is she denying Gudmund Johannessen took heroin?*

TS.   *No, but it's the way you say it, er, what she ... ...what have that to do with her? Also she means that her life is her business.*

F.   *You still haven't told me what I'm supposed to have lied about.*

TS.   *Frederick, I don't remember exactly and I don't want to tell you things that I can't remember it correctly.*

F.   *Well could you get your file then and I'll ring back, because ...*

TS.   *I don't have it here any more. I have sent the case to Lyngås and Lyngås has sent it to Oslo, so I don't have it here any more.*

F.   *So someone eventually will be able to tell me what Heidi says I have been lying about.*

TS.   *Yes, but it's in the report I have written after talking to Heidi but you see it's a long time since I wrote this report and I don't have it here and it will be wrong if I tell you things and I don't remember it correctly.*

F.   *Well first of all she must be saying that some of the things I have written in that report are not correct. But every single piece of information in there came from her mouth to me.*

TS.   *...... she says that some things you are saying is wrong and other things you have written in the letters is mainly things that is right.*

F.   But what is she saying I've written ... when you say "wrong" do you mean that I'm making it up as lies?

TS.   Yes, she says that something that you have written is lies, yes. But as I told you I can't remember what was that so I don't want to ...

F.   Well OK, there's nothing that I've written, nothing whatsoever, once, that is a lie.

TS.   You say that. She don't say that. So you don't agree about that.

F.   That's what I'd like to find out. I'd like to talk to her because she ...

TS.   She don't want to talk to you.

F.   Well, that is not surprising because ... ...she's gonna have to   ...... the cross examination I'll give her will catch her out.

TS.   No, I don't think that. She says she has tried to talk to you. She has written letters to you. She have tried to be nice to you, but now she says she don't, er ...

F.   Well that's all rubbish, she ... the last letters she wrote to me were in 1990.

TS.   Yes, that's a long time ago.

F.   Yeah and that was purely to do with um, well I suppose re-establish a friendship and her, um, her Christianity and her wanting to marry a Christian man and hoping I would become a Christian, but it was nothing to do with trying to tell me to be reasonable and to leave her alone. But the thing is this, let's get down to some basics. Threats to kill her son. You read my letter so what's your answer to that. She alleges I've threatened to kill her son.

TS.   She said for a long time ago, I don't remember when, it came a letter, who the police in Bergen have get but I don't know what they have done with it. I have tried to get it out but I haven't made it because they don't know where it is. They have thrown all the letters she gave to the police, maybe; I don't know what they have do with it. But they can't find it and they can't give it to me. Because I have ... I wanted to get the letters to read them.

F.   So a major piece of evidence of threatening to kill a little two year old boy somehow goes missing?

TS.   Yes, and er the police in Bergen say that they get some letters from Heidi and from her husband's ... the parents and that's right.

F.   Her parents?

TS.   No, not her ... what do you call it ... her husband's er ...

F.   Her boyfriend's parents?

TS.   Her boyfriend's ...

F.   Johannessen?

TS.   No, not Johannessen. The father to the boy. The grandaddy and mother for the boy.

F.   Overaa?

TS.   *Not Overaa. No, her boy. Er ...*

F.   *Her step-brothers ... half brothers?*

TS.   *No ... the parents of her boyfriend at that time who is the father for her boy.*

F.   *You mean Schøne?*

TS.   *He's her son?*

F.   *Well Runar Schøne is her husband. In 1986 her husband ... ...*

TS.   *Yes, the father of her boy.*

F.   *Gudmund Johannessen.*

TS.   *Was that Johannessen?*

F.   *Yeah.*

TS.   *OK OK. His parents did go to the police and give up some letters.*

F.   *In 1986?*

TS.   *No, um. Maybe, I don't remember.*

F.   *Yeah I did write to them but I didn't say anything abusive in there. I just told them ... ...*

TS.   *OK, but at that time they took the letters and go to the police and write a report there. Heidi did the same, but I can't find it because they have maybe thrown the letters [away]. I don't find it. And they say they don't know where it is, so I don't know what they have done with it.*

F.   *But I have a report from the police in 1990.*

TS.   *Yes.*

F.   *They say ... ... when my lawyer wrote to them in 1990 from here they didn't mention the fact of attempted rape, you see, but when my Bergen lawyer investigated it in 1995, he somehow found the allegation of attempted rape. So in 1990 the police didn't tell my English lawyer this and that's the reason I became so angry about this attempted rape and it's those ... it's the facts of that that I've been trying to obtain without success. You see that's the reason ... it was the last straw and I just won't accept that. No I'm obviously furious that this allegation about [threatening to kill] her son has been made by Heidi because you know, I have to be insane to put that in writing. I've never wrote it at all anyway, but for someone to put that in writing is suicide. And I think there's a cover up or something going on.*

TS.   *But you can see er in the case who is in Oslo now we have based our investigation on things we can find, and I have got some letters in there from you, from Heidi to you.*

F.   *But you can see the theme of my letters is the same throughout. I don't like being told after I've had sex with her that she's ... ...*

TS.   *She deny that.*

F.   *What, she denied that I had intercourse with her?*

236

TS.   *Yes.*

F.   *Oh, that's nonsense. I had an AIDS test in 1986 because she told me that Gudmund Johannessen was taking heroin.*

TS.   *She says it happen maybe oh I don't remember, but I remember she said you have sex one time.*

F.   *Yes.*

TS.   *In Bergen maybe.*

F.   *Yes.*

TS.   *Yes.*

F.   *That's right in 19... 80...5.*

TS.   *And she has said that she didn't want to have sex with you but you want.*

F.   *Yeah, she said she didn't want, that's right, but eventually she said "OK, come on, it's nothing," but I did not attempt to rape her, I did not manhandle her. I did not touch her in anyway whatsoever. I was on the couch. She was on her bed and I was on her black couch on the other side [of the room]. But the reason she said – afterwards – that she was reluctant to have sex, she told me afterwards was because she'd resumed having sex with Gudmund Johannessen. OK, which ...... she didn't want to tell me that [before intercourse] because she would've thought that I thought she was insane after what he'd done to her, but a year or so later she told me that he'd been injecting heroin after he went to China and he bought heroin over there. Then, obviously, I was so angry it took me until 1990 to go and question her. To go and confront her about this er behaviour of hers and that's when I was arrested, but it was purely to go and visit her about her AIDs-risk behaviour. But even the first time I went to see her, we came close to having sex. It's just that I actually told her before I went to ... Bergen ...... I told her not to let me succumb to having sex and it wasn't right until we got to know each other a lot better. But um, what does she say about the attempted rape?*

TS.   *Er, she said that it was a rape from her side, yes.*

F.   *Huh?*

TS.   *She said it was a rape.*

F.   *Oh she's saying I raped her?*

TS.   *Yes.*

F.   *When?*

TS.   *I don't remember ...*

F.   *On the occasion we had ...*

TS.   *In Bergen.*

F.   *But on the occasion we had sex?*

TS.   *Yes, in Bergen. It was one time she says I mean to remember. One time in Bergen.*

F.   *Is this the same occasion I've just described to you?*

TS.   *Yes.*

F.   *Oh she says that was rape?*

TS.   *I mean so. I don't remember exactly but I need to remember that, er ... she said you have sex one or two times?*

F.   *No, just the once.*

TS.   *Once OK and that was the rape.*

F.   *Oh.*

TS.   *She says.*

F.   *So it's nothing to do with attempted rape, as the police said.*

TS.   *Maybe at that time the police mean, it was that but, er ... ...*

F.   *Well that's what they wrote. Attempted. There's a big difference.*

TS.   *Yes, I know, but I don't know that case. But I mean the police have not put the case away.*

F.   *They haven't?*

TS.   *We have yes.*

F.   *Oh, you have, but what about the police in Bergen about attempted rape?*

TS.   *Yes, that is put away.*

F.   *So why does Wesenberg tell me they can re-open it?*

TS.   *Maybe they can do that but it hasn't been done.*

F.   *Huh?*

TS.   *Maybe they can re-open the case ...*

F.   *Do they actually believe... do they believe her ... does anyone believe Heidi?*

TS.   *I believe that Heidi have a very difficult time and she have lived a life she don't not proud of, but she now try to start again and have a nice life ... All these letters from you and all the telephone to the neighbours and so on it's, er ...*

F.   *Well obviously most women when they get to her age, she's 35, they don't have many chances left in life to ... ...*

TS.   *Yeah, but I think she have a good life with her husband. I think so, yes ... she try to get on her life again ... and I think that she is making it; that she will make it. I think she will get a good life now but as she's said she has lived her life when she was young. She's not proud of it and she try to forget it but she can't when you write letters to her all the time.*

F.   *Well obviously I'm not gonna forget the allegations she's made in the newspapers. But there was also, she alleged, a Bergen shopkeeper as you know had raped her as well. Have you any information on this?*

TS.   *No.*

F.   *No, well, as I've told you in my letters her old friend Ann-Kristin Horvei - I've given you her phone number - she told me a little bit as well about this Bergen shopkeeper who was supposed to have raped Heidi because they were at a party together so that's another little piece of evidence ... Anyway, I did not rape her and er, if she wants to maintain that then her life in the future's not gonna be very happy because she's gonna have to withdraw the allegation.*

TS.   *But you see my point is that not we have put the case ... ...*

F.   *In Oslo.*

TS.   *Yes, and it's lying there and we won't do anything with it if it all stops now. I hope so. I understand that you is hurt and she is hurt.*

F.   *She's only hurt because the truth has come out about her. I'm very hurt because a pack of lies has been told about me.*

TS.   *Yes, you say that but as she said – things that is coming out er she mean it something is lies and something is truth and this is mixed together and it is much.*

F.   *So the fact that she's been in a psychiatric unit and sleeps with people taking heroin and all the abortions it means that she's really not such a bad girl*

TS.   *Yes, maybe that's right. But I see it like this. That is her life and as she says she is not proud of this life, but she want to come over it and start again.*

F.   *But she mustn't ... oh yes start again. In 1995 she didn't start a good life again; she's turned Christian and for her to print wholesale lies or have wholesale lies printed in the newspapers means to me that she's worse than ever.*

TS.   *Now the case is closed. For so long.*

F.   *So will I be arrested if I set foot in Norway?*

TS.   *Yes, if you try to contact Heidi you will.*

F.   *If I try to contact her?*

TS.   *Yes.*

F.   *But if I don't?*

TS.   *No, then I can't arrest you. I won't could do that.*

F.   *Yeah, but can anyone else? Can the Bergen police? Can the people at the airport?*

TS.   *Maybe the people in Oslo, the lawyers there mean that if you come to Norway we will try to start a case again. To end this case in a court or something. I don't know. For so long it's closed and I don't know what will happen if you come to Norway.*

F.   *So I better phone them up and ask them.*

TS.   *Hm?*

239

F.   *So the best thing for me to do is to phone them up and ask them?*

TS.   *Maybe, yes.*

F.   *So is Heidi lying or what?*

TS.   *I don't know. Maybe ha! ha!.*

F.   *Well ...I think definitely.*

TS.   *It's too possible ... ...the one is that if you have threatened them* [i.e. the neighbours]
            *they don't want to go to the police because they think they will not ... er ... make some
            more trouble for Heidi or maybe* [Heidi] *lied.*

F.   *Yes, well I can tell you something. I've never threatened her neighbours at all. The
            only way I got her address was from an Indian woman called Camillat who worked at
            the post office who knew Heidi. 'Cos someone else in the post office knew Runar
            Schøne and that's how I got her so-called secret address. And again this woman
            Camillat told me that she thought Heidi was mixing with a man who took or sold
            drugs; a drug taker. So you know .... Everything I've told you was gathered from
            other people.*

TS.   *Yes, but what I understand is that these letters phones or everything have gone on so
            long. The police have put the case away. I don't know ... I don't understand why you
            can't stop it there.*

F.   *Because it's a dreadful thing to allege that I've threatened to kill her son. That I've
            written 400 obscene letters.*

TS.   *But I'm sure that no one in Norway remember the case anymore.*

F.   *No, no, no. You see at the time the newspapers came out I couldn't do anything about
            it. I couldn't have my point of view printed and the effect obviously – the newspapers
            were printed against me and it has a much deeper affect on me than the public who
            don't care 'cos it's not them, it's me!*

TS.   *The police have taken the case serious and we have looked at it and we have
            investigated and we have put it away and I mean you have to do the same. You can't
            do this for years and years.*

F.   *To be honest I wanted to make sure that just as many people who read the
            newspapers read my ...*

TS.   *Many people have read your letters yes, because I get many of them.*

F.   *Yeah, that's why I've carried on because I had to get my point of view across and for
            that I blame the newspapers for .... Is it the case that the newspapers didn't
            believe what I'd written in Norwegian?*

TS.   *The newspapers don't believe you, you say?*

F.   *Yeah, is that why they ...*

TS.   *Maybe, I think so, yes. ... but that's nothing to do with Heidi.*

F.   *No, they printed what she told them. She told me over the phone she said... ... you
            see when I spoke to her she refused to say anything about the case. She said the case
            is er ... "I can't say anything because my lawyers have told me to say nothing." But
            what she did say was: "I could have told a lot of lies to the newspapers but I didn't"*

240

and er the reason she said that is because, she told me, ... "I know you're recording my conversation" and she said that on the recording of my conversation with her [so that] if anybody listened to it they would say "Oh look – she's telling the truth." But that girl told a hundred per cent lies. Now, I know her better than anyone because I've known her longer than anybody and that's why I don't care what anybody else says, you know ... I tried to say: "Look! You know she's alleged that I've raped her now. Now get the evidence of the Bergen shopkeeper that she says has raped her." And it was me who was always trying to help her in the 80's even when I wasn't that interested in her 'cos obviously eventually with all these suicide attempts and sex with so many men, it kind of turns me off, even though I was feeling very lonely. So you know when she says she liked me a lot in the early 80's that was true but for someone in her condition she isn't gonna like me or love me for very long because she likes going with lots of different boys you see and when I find out, you know, that she's got pregnant again and it did almost ruin her life, because she did have another suicide attempt in 1988, my letters to her parents and to Johannessen's parents were obviously warnings which they didn't take seriously. They just ignored them and said this Englishman is mad, but what came afterwards was a tragedy for her and I foresaw it. No-one else did. I did. And when I go and first simply question her about getting pregnant again, she goes crazy.

TS.   *I don't want to do something more with this case now because I have sent it to Lyngås in Drammen and he has sent it to Oslo, so if you need to know anything more……*

F.   *Phone the others ... yeah. I think you've had enough haven't you?*

TS.   *Well, but I can't help you any more because as I told you, I mean this case is so old and I mean when the police had looked at it and we have interviewed Heidi several times and I have talked to other people and……*

F.   *Oh, who else?*

TS.   *Hm?*

F.   *Who else?*

TS.   *I have talked to her husband I have talked to the police in Bergen where I get the report from and I have talked to people who send me letters ... and I can't help you anymore. I mean if I have been you, I maybe have been hurt if the things you have told me is right but I mean that this case is so old and you have to close it and start on your life and forget ... maybe you can't forget it but you can live ... I mean you have to do that. I can't help you anymore. If you want some other answers. If you want the case re-opened again, you have to talk to the lawyers. I can't help with that.*

F.   *Yeah, so ... it'll be difficult for me to get her prosecuted for perverting the course of justice would it?*

TS.   *As it looks now, yes, but maybe the lawyers in Oslo say that okay now we have so much that we want to ... prosecute again.*

F.   *Who has so much?*

TS.   *I can't deny when the case is ... I send my stuff away to them and they have to decide when they want to get the case in Court.*

F.   *So it's not definite that it's closed yet?*

TS.   *No ... but at this time it is.*

F.   *So the number of this man Dag Lyngås is 8-0-5-5-0-0- yeah. OK. Well as far as Heidi's husband is concerned, I mean he can go to hell, because he says to me, you know "Allah doesn't exist. Come to Jesus" and speaks like some lunatic 'in tongues.'*

TS.   *He's very all right. I've talked to him many times and he's very all right.*

F.   *If he says to me Allah doesn't exist and speaks to me 'in tongues' – for 5 minutes – and you're trying to tell me he's OK – he maybe ok to you but he's certainly got another side to him. But tell me something. If I don't see Heidi, right, I won't get arrested but I want to see that idiot her husband and I want to have a little chat with him. Now if I see him will I be arrested?*

TS.   *As I told you... ... ... and take contact with Heidi and her family ...*

F.   *Or her husband?*

TS.   *Yes.*

F.   *Right.*

TS.   *Her husband is included, I will, we will do something.*

F.   *Yeah, what?*

TS.   *We have to arrest you. We can't let you do that. She is terrified and her husband is a part of her life. That is one of the laws we have in Norway.*

F.   *So simply trying to get the truth out of people once they've told* [lies, I was about to add]

TS.   *You have to go the right way.*

F.   *You have to go a different way? That's what I've been trying for the last er ...*

TS.   *Yes and you have to try and talk to the lawyers in Oslo.*

F.   *... ... Three years.*

TS.   *... ... To re-open the case again.*

F.   *All right Torill, thanks for the chat. I hope I won't have to bother you again and I appreciate all the time you've put in.*

TS.   *I just hope you can ... start to have a new life. I don't think these things that is coming up now between you and Heidi is good. It's only hurting you both and I hope you can.*

F.   *I was basically ... er ... the best years of my life have gone and the shock of what she's said and done about me – I couldn't really come to terms with and that is why I was determined over the years to punish her, so, so much and continue doing it because I think there's one or two other people like her about. You know, you always read about them in the newspapers, in crime reports and I think she had to be taught a lesson that she'll never forget.*

TS.   *I think she have. She has got a lesson from you.*

F.   *Well I see in the newspapers she's lost a lot of hair. But, but ... when I last spoke to her I could tell the old lies were coming out and you know I may have ... I mean I called her a racist pig the last time I spoke to her and just put the phone down and that was the last contact I had. And I've written maybe, you know, fifty post cards just with the dates of ... . you know, she does this in 1984, she does this in 1986 and abortions this and that, but that's all, just to make the postman read it so the postman tells the whole town because I want her punished. People must know what she's all about because don't forget ... ...*

TS. *I can tell you that all the neighbours and people around her know.*

F. *Well I spoke to two of the neighbours on the phone about two years ago. And they themselves hadn't read the newspapers. But I sent them myself, full details – about nine pages – so they know the full story from my point of view, but I did say to one woman, "Can you please not believe the newspapers when they say I've threatened to kill her son because I have not" and you know that boy likes me very, very, very much indeed. Heidi wrote and told me so. And if ... is she trying to tell everybody... ... she lets her son go around telling everybody what a nice friend he has in England when two years before he's threatened to kill the boy? That's nonsense. She would say – keep away from this boy, we'll have no contact with him. You know – he's threatened to kill him and she will keep him away at every opportunity. Not let him sit on my knee and play with me and kiss me. It just doesn't make sense because allegations of threats to kill and obviously rape can put me in prison and that's why maybe in exposing her other people won't try this, but ...... I know with those kind of allegations flying around my liberty is at stake and I have to do something about it. All right Torill take care and have a restful week.*

TS. *Thank you.*

F. *All right then.*

TS. *OK.*

F. *Bye bye.*

TS. *Bye.*

F. *Bye.*

On 19th January 1998 I telephoned Dag Lyngås:

DL. *Lyngås.*

F. *Yes, hello, good morning, my name's Frederick Delaware.*

DL. *Yes.*

F. *Torill Sorte gave me your telephone number and told me that you have been dealing with this case.*

DL. *Yes.*

F. *I'm finding it quite hard to get some evidence about* [that which has] *been written in the newspapers and I was wondering if you could help me get it?*

DL. *What do want? You want the evidence?*

F. *Yes, these newspaper articles ... ...*

DL.   *What articles are you talking about? In Norwegian paper?*

F.   *Yes, that's right. In Bergens Tidende, Drammens Tidende and Verdens Gang, yeah.*

DL.   *Today or ...*

F.   *No, no, no in 1995.*

DL.   *Oh yeah ... I don't know er maybe it's in what you call the case have some copies of the articles but er ...*

F.   *Well it's just that I myself sent the articles to Torill Sorte ... and there were some very serious allegations being made in those newspaper articles by Heidi.*

DL.   *But I understand that you also now write letters to Heidi.*

F.   *Oh yes, that's right. I want to know the answers to these serious allegations ... threats to kill her son, ... rape. I want the police evidence [regarding her allegation] that a Bergen shopkeeper also raped her ....threats to kill her neighbours, sexual harassment, all this sort of rubbish that was written in the newspapers that isn't true. And my reason for asking this is because there is no evidence that exists to indicate this and I myself want to take proceedings against her for perverting the course of justice. But the reason I've written angry letters to her is because no one is giving me the answers to these questions that I've been asking for years and obviously I show my disgust and hatred for this woman by telling her in writing.   And I don't see what's wrong with that.*

DL.   *Well the police in Norway want that you have to stop this writing to Heidi Schøne.*

F.   *I'll stop writing once she tells me where the evidence is for threats she says I've made to kill her son. You see the police have had two years to look into this and I have had no answers and I obviously have to keep trying to get in touch with Heidi.*

DL.   *Yes.*

F.   *So that she explains it, because you see Torill Sorte said to me: "You must do this the proper way." Well I've tried the proper way when I went to see Heidi in [February] 1990 – she makes up stories that I've made more threats and then I'm arrested so I can't even talk to her and when we were in the police station and the police officer asked me what can we do to resolve this case and I said, "Well let me sit down with you and Heidi- just the three of us- then I'll show to you that Heidi is a liar." The policeman came back to me and said, "Heidi doesn't want to talk to you." So she gets away with it every time. I must have her confronted with these allegations.*

DL.   *If... you should .... You can't get this evidence from me, I don't know er ... but if you want this articles from the newspaper you have to ...*

F.   *No, I do have them – I have the original newspapers myself.*

DL.   *OK.*

F.   *But I've asked Torill Sorte to look into it but she hasn't come up with, you know, satisfactory answers at all and it's not good enough and I must have some one look into this for me.*

DL.   *But you have to get a lawyer who can look at this. The Norwegian authorities we maybe will send this to the British authorities for, to, of what do you call it um ...*

F.   *For extradition?*

DL.   *Yes to get a trial in England, or ... ...*

F.   *A trial for what?*

DL.   *Well, er, we mean you have threatened Heidi Schøne with your letters and things.*

F.   *Yeah when?*

DL.   *When? A lot times. You have send her several letters.*

F.   *Threatening what?*

DL.   *Threatening and what you call she can't talk I don't know the English word for it... er... you had disturb her private life, you understand that?*

F.   *Of course I understand that but the thing is you see she's tried to ruin my life by saying I've attempted to rape her or even raped ... I think it's rape now. I think she's changed her story to rape you see and that's why I have to have some answers because I believe Heidi is a very, very sick woman and I've tried to be reasonable for years about this. I've asked for the authorities in Norway to supply the evidence that she's gone to the police in the 80's saying that a Bergen shopkeeper had tried to rape her. She's told me her cousin was raped and killed. She's told me that tourists in Greece tried to rape her in 1981 and now I find myself the subject of an allegation of either attempted rape or rape. Now also she says I've threatened to kill her son in a letter and no one can find this letter. She says the Bergen police have this letter but they deny it. OK – I've never made such threats – never. She says I've threatened to kill her neighbours if they don't give me her secret addresses so I've asked which neighbours and for statements from the neighbours as to these allegations and nothing has come forward, you see ... now I must have the answers to information that I'm entitled to and the reason I'm writing letters to her is to get this information.*

DL.   *But the police in Norway not allow you to write to Heidi Schøne. We have all your letters at the police.*

F.   *Yes, I know that, I know that.*

DL.   *You have to stop this writing now or if not we have to send the case to the local authorities* [I think he meant British authorities].

F.   *Yeah, well I've taken legal advice here in England as you probably know and I'll be most happy to attend any case. I even offered to go to Norway two years ago to Torill Sorte just to sit down with Heidi and sort this out.*

DL.   *We don't want you to come to Norway. If you come to Norway we maybe going to arrest you and do the case in Norway.*

F.   *Yeah, I thought so. So, Torill Sorte told me that you'd tried to get me over to Norway. You'd taken advice from the English authorities and they have said that they can do nothing to help you. Is that right? That there'll be no extradition, no trial, nothing. Is that right?*

DL.   *Can you repeat that?*

F.   *Torill Sorte ... ...*

DL.   *Yes.*

245

F.   *She told me that the authorities in Oslo have contacted the authorities in England and asked them whether I can be sent to Norway. Yeah? Are you with me?*

DL.   *Yes. I don't know nothing about that.*

F.   *Oh.*

DL.   *Because I haven't know the case for so long time.*

F.   *OK. She says that the case is with someone in Oslo. Is that right?*

DL.   *No, the case is with me now.*

F.   *Oh, with you?*

DL.   *Yes.*

F.   *Oh. So how long have you had it?*

DL.   *Three, four months.*

F.   *And who had it in Oslo?*

DL.   *Maybe one of the District Attorneys.*

F.   *And what do he do?*

DL.   *Send it back to me.*

F.   *Oh, God. So have you been trying to see if you can extradite me? Extradite me. Make me go to Norway.*

DL.   *No, we don't want you to go to Norway.*

F.   *For trial?*

DL.   *No, we don't want you to come here at all.*

F.   *For trial? Huh?*

DL.   *No. We don't want you to come to Norway. A trial we want maybe send it to England or ... ...*

F.   *So, do you actually read the letters I write?*

DL.   *No, I haven't read all the letters you write.*

F.   *Because they're asking basically the same thing, all of them: That I don't get treated like a complete idiot and you give me the answers* [to the questions I'm putting] *to the allegations that have been made against me in the newspapers and by Heidi to the police. Now it's very naughty of all of you to start saying I'm harassing her when you know perfectly well she's been in a psychiatric unit and has a very poor sexual history, when you know all I want is information as to ... the allegations that have been made against me ... obviously eventually I'm going to get so sick of it that I'm going to start getting some revenge. Because I'm **not** going to stand this stress on me and my mother reading this rubbish in the newspapers.*

DL.   *But now you are threatening Schøne.*

F.   *I'm threatening Schøne?*

DL.   *Yes.*

F.   *Who, Runar Schøne?*

DL.   *Heidi, Heidi.*

F.   *Threatening with that? I've just said to her … …*

DL.   *You are aggressive. Have to take some step … …*

F.   *Aggressive? I'm not aggressive? She's wicked. I must have answers to her allegations and I need to talk to her face to face. She avoids talking to me because she knows she can't deal with the answers. Now I've tried quietly to ring them up to talk sensibly about it and … …*

DL.   *But she don't want to talk to you.*

F.   *No, no, no obviously they don't want to talk to me because they're wicked deceitful liars and people who are like that they don't want to talk. I want some evidence. I want to talk to them. Now if you can't get the evidence then I will try. You can't supply the evidence that I've been trying for 2½ years to get so you know I have to try myself.*

DL.   *If you want to look at the evidence you have to go to a lawyer.*

F.   *A lawyer. Yeah. That's right. I've been to a lawyer in Bergen but … he only mentioned the business of attempted rape. Now can you tell me please, because Heidi spoke again to Torill Sorte, what is the latest on this? Is it attempted rape or rape?*

DL.   *I can't answer that because I haven't look at the paper.*

F.   *OK, I'll phone you back this afternoon.*

DL.   *Oh no! I can't do it today. You have to come back in two, three weeks.*

F.   *Weeks?*

DL.   *Yes.*

F.   *Oh. Well that's another three weeks of stress for me isn't it?*

DL.   *The thing is to leave the whole thing as it is now and stop writing these letters and stop calling the police, Heidi Schøne … …*

F.   *Well obviously I can't do that because I want Heidi shown up to the world for the liar that she is. And if you think that she can just make allegations that are totally false … I mean, you amaze me. You know I'm trying to get evidence – which doesn't exist of course – that um … I'm trying to prove she's a liar as to these threats to kill the son, the neighbours, the rape and you are telling me to forget about it. It's just ludicrous. And I'm not going to because a woman like that is pure evil. She's your Norwegian blonde and I'm just the "worthless" Muslim. You know I've read the newspapers and fourteen times they mention "the Muslim man." I was better to Heidi than any man she's ever met. And if you'd read the letters that she's written to me then you can see that I have a point. I want all evidence surrounding Heidi … and I want her interviewed properly. Unless she's interviewed properly then I will continue to make public her past throughout the whole of Norway and I'll do it very big. You're gonna have a lot of people contacting you – you have to do something to get to the bottom of this.*

DL.   *Well as I said to you...*

F.   *Use a lawyer, yeah. I will use a lawyer, but will the lawyer be able to get the answers to these questions? Will the lawyer be able to interview Heidi herself?*

DL.   *No, the Police will interview Heidi, if necessary.*

F.   *"If necessary." That's right – that's the problem – "if necessary" you see and I must say that unless those answers come back to me clearly ... and once those answers come you will have to prosecute her for perverting the course of justice and I will carry this on for years if necessary because I've really had enough and I'll make it public, every inch of the way if you don't get this evidence that Heidi says exists that I've threatened to kill her son in a letter OK. And if the lawyer can't do this, then I'll carry on.*

         I spent hundreds of pounds on lawyers here in 1990 in London and they didn't get very far with the police. We got no information on this attempted rape. It was on file and I wasn't told until I found out in 1995 through my Bergen lawyer and my Bergen lawyer refused to go any further into the matter of attempted rape because he said Commander Krogvold in Bergen might re-open the case. So I said to my lawyer, Wesenberg – I have not attempted to rape the woman – go ahead and find the information and he refused.

DL.   *Is the case of rape a case in Bergen?*

F.   *Yes, it was the Bergen police station.* [And I told him the story.]

DL.   *But the case of rape, I have not the case. This is Bergen you have to ...*

F.   *Yes, I have contacted them and Commander Krogvold refuses to talk to me about it. Now my lawyer has written and told me "attempted rape." Torill Sorte is now telling me ... Heidi has told her "rape."*

DL.   *You can't discuss that case with me. You have to go to the police in Bergen.*

F.   *Yeah, but Torill Sorte has already discussed the case with Heidi ... but she said she couldn't remember* [about the case in detail anymore] *because the papers were now with you.*

DL.   *I don't know if the paper about the rape is with me.*

F.   *Well they should be because Torill Sorte told me they were. But anyway, I've got a long list of questions but you obviously won't answer them direct to me will you?*

DL.   *Oh, I just want to answer a lawyer ... and I don't want to discuss the evidence with you* [or] *your lawyer. I just can give him a copy of the paper in the case. I don't discuss the evidence.*

F.   *Oh, you don't, so I can't even see the evidence?*

DL.   *You can see what the police have but I won't discuss it with you.*

F.   *Right OK. When my lawyer eventually contacts you, will you see fit to question Heidi about threats to kill her son, her neighbours, sexual harassment, obscene words, 400 obscene letters?*

DL.   *As I said I will do it if I think it's necessary.*

F.   *Can you tell me now?*

DL.   *No, I can't, I don't have the paper.*

F.   *OK. All right. Well I've tried to write to Heidi and any person who's right – if she's right – she can simply write back to me and say ... this is a copy of the letter* [in which] *you threatened to kill my son. Here are the names of the neighbours who you threatened to kill ... and can simply write this like any normal person can, but don't start telling me I mustn't write to her because I want this information. It costs lots of money to use a lawyer and you're making me spend money – hundreds of pounds in phone calls and using lawyers just because of this lying woman. Now she's the one who's been in a psychiatric unit, not me. She's tried to kill herself twice. She's slept with someone taking heroin ... now can't you see for God's sake that this woman is a liar? I may have told her to go to hell. I may have told her to drop dead. I may have told her she's a worthless piece of shit but any man would. So would you. If any woman threatened you like this I know you'd do the same, OK.*

DL.   *I think what you are doing is not legal.*

F.   *Is it legal and nice to say in the newspapers that I'm insane, that I've written 400 obscene letters? That I do obscene things in front of her making her watch. Write obscene words on her door. Threaten to kill her son, threaten to kill her neighbours and I'm "the Muslim man, the Muslim man" – every paragraph. You think that's legal as well do you? If you think I'm going to take this then you've gotta think again because I'm not.*

DL.   *OK.*

F.   *All right. I shall have to spend a few hundred pounds more, no doubt, contacting a lawyer in Drammen and ... first of all they'll want money and then they'll read the case. Then they'll probably say they won't help me. And then I find another lawyer and on and on it goes. In the meantime, I will not stop making public Heidi's past – until the newspapers apologise on their front pages. Hm?*

DL.   *I heard what you're saying.*

F.   *OK. All right all the best and thanks for listening to me. And I shall – can I actually – the spelling of your name, your surname. It's – I know it's* [pronounced] *Lyngås but what's the er* ["spelling," I was about to say].

DL.   *What are you going to use that for?*

F.   *Well first of all I want to get it* [the spelling] *right, because I have to tell my Drammen lawyer.*

DL.   *You can get my title – it's Assistant Chief of Police.*

F.   *Don't worry, I'm not gonna make your name public.*

DL.   *I'm not afraid about that.*

F.   *No, that's OK, I won't do that. You're at which police station?*

DL.   *Drammen.* [And he gave me the address.]

F. *All right, I'll get down to getting in touch with yet another lawyer and if the answers come out then maybe we'll get somewhere, but we'll have to wait and see how things go. All right, thanks very much.*

DL. *Goodbye.*

F. *Goodbye.*

On 23rd and 24th January 1998, I instructed in writing a Drammen lawyer, Karsten Gjone, who was recommended to me by an ex-policeman now working as a private detective. My letter to Gjone of 24th January contained a list of 21 questions covering everything I wanted to know. This lawyer had full supporting documentation and all copy correspondence from the past. I also wrote to Gjone a brief letter on 4th March.

On 1st April 1998, I telephoned Torill Sorte of the Mjøndalen police:

F. *Well you'll be pleased in a way to know that I've instructed a lawyer in Norway. He's had my papers for a couple of months now but he's so busy ... it'll still be probably at least another week before he can advise me, but I understand that I've got rights to sue Heidi and also have her punished for the lies she's been telling. But my lawyer says I have to come over to Norway for that so we're gonna have to sort out this business of me making Heidi's private life public. So somehow we'll have to overcome that. But the thing is, I spoke to the Assistant Commissioner of Police in Drammen, Lyngås – and he hasn't done anything.*

TS. *That's not right. He has done the case to the chief lawyers in Oslo.*

F. *Yeah, Yeah, against me but he hasn't answered those questions that I've asked you ... a list of questions you said that you passed on with the file to him but none of those questions have been dealt with at all and he just said that "We want to get you." So we had a quick chat and I told him that I've got a lawyer and he'll be in touch in due course if I suppose he thinks there's something he can help me with. The reason I'm ringing you is that I have to clarify one or two of these [answers to] questions that I've asked about Heidi because the policeman in Drammen ... doesn't want to ask Heidi these questions at all. Can you – is it rape or attempted rape that she's alleging? Most important I know this.*

TS. *She said that she didn't want to go to bed with you and you make her to do it and she was afraid. She tried to get away but she couldn't.*

F. *Well that's not the case. No. What happened ... initially she didn't want to do it OK and I was on the other side of the room ... in the end ... from the other side of the room she says, "OK. Come on over - it's nothing." And she lies on her back and lets me do it. But there was absolutely no way I forced her, absolutely nothing. No chance whatsoever ... the words were "Come on over OK ... it's nothing. You'll see it's nothing," because I'd never done it before OK. That is not rape and it is not attempted rape. OK.*

TS. *But you see she don't tell me these because she want to get a case to you. She told me these because she will give me a picture of what a person you are.*

F. *Yeah, that's right, but I am not that person. I mean what did she actually say? Did I ... when she says I forced her - what exactly did I do? What is she saying?*

TS. *I mean she said you er ...*

F. *I held her down or I threatened her or what? Come on, she must have told you?*

TS.   *Yes she told me.*

F.   *Yeah, what did she say? Go on.*

TS.   *Er ... I can't remember exactly what she said. I mean to remember that she said that you hold her.*

F.   *I held her down?*

TS.   *Yes.*

F.   *What, by the throat or what? The arms, the hair?*

TS.   *That I don't remember. I think it was her hand, but I can't remember.*

F.   *Huh?*

TS.   *I'm sorry about that. Because you see I wrote it down in my report and I put it into Oslo months ago.*

F.   *Well it's down there in writing anyway.*

TS.   *Yes.*

F.   *Good. I can tell you something. Heidi's a very strong girl. If she doesn't want a chap to have sex with her, there's no way he can do it, because she will struggle like hell. And you know "held her down by the hands" is an absolute load of nonsense and I'm prepared to stand up in Court and swear on oath exactly what happened, you see. But is she saying it's rape or attempted rape? Which one is it?*

TS.   *She said it was rape.*

F.   *Yeah, OK. So my lawyer in telling me it was "attempted rape" – you have his letter – he's not right then?*

TS.   *I have his letter?*

F.   *Yeah, I sent you the first page of my lawyer's letter – Wesenbgerg.*

TS.   *Oh yes.*

F.   *And it's got "attempted rape," hasn't it?*

TS.   *Yes.*

F.   *So obviously...*

TS.   *But you see ... I see you mean this is a big case what this is and it's a rape. But Heidi has never come to me and said I will get you in the Court, so we can ...*

F.   *No, not you, no, but she did go in 1986 to the Bergen Police and tell them "attempted" [rape].*

TS.   *I haven't seen this sort of question.*

F.   *Well, why do you think Wesenberg wrote to me? Can't you just read Wesenberg's letter. In 1986 she went to the Bergen Police, 20 months after I last stayed with her. Twenty months after I had sex with her she went and complained. But it was two or three weeks after I told either her parents or Johannessen's parents that he was taking heroin. And about the abortions and all the rest of it ... the miscarriages. Right? She did that out of revenge. Now if she goes to the Bergen Police and tells them I've attempted to rape her, then the next time I'm in Norway, I could get into serious trouble. Obviously, because it's an arrestable offence and I'm sure if she'd had her way she'd have me held in the police custody and go to the Magistrates' Court. So that's the reason I've got revenge against her 'cos when I read those words "attempted rape," I thought, well, if you wanna tell such filthy lies, then I'll teach you a lesson. But the thing is you see, she's also gone to the police before, about that Bergen shopkeeper who again she said raped her and I am going to get details of that complaint. Because I'm building a picture about Heidi saying that she's a scheming, manipulative little liar and there's no way I am going to take this accusation of attempted rape – she's said it about Greek men on holiday – her cousin was raped and killed in Norway, so I think it will be quite easy for me to stand up in Court and convince the Judge that she's a bloody liar.*

TS. *I don't think so.*

F. *Why not?*

TS. *Because you have done some things about your letters, about the way you have – the letters you have sent to her and so on.*

F. *Yeah, what's wrong with them?*

TS. *What?*

F. *What's so wrong with them?*

TS. *The wrong thing is that you have sent many letters to people in Norway ... that write her name and put her picture on it.*

F. *Yeah good ... No, no, no, - it was the newspaper's picture. She put her picture in the newspapers. I'm only using their picture. She told the whole of Norway about my [so-called] private life without mentioning my name OK. What it was, I sent that ... [report]. First of all it was to no more than twenty of her neighbours. Twenty – where she used to live.*

TS. *Lots of letters. I don't know how many.*

F. *Yeah, yeah – [sent] after the newspapers [came out]. But before the newspapers [came out] no more than twenty [reports in Norwegian about Heidi's past]. Immediately she tells the whole of Norway through the newspapers.*

TS. *How you like that?*

F. *Huh?*

TS. *How do you like that?*

F. *How do I what?*

TS. *If someone you know write things about you who you don't want anyone to know and send it to your neighbours, to your post office, to your school, to your theatre and so on – you like that?*

F. *Well I basically wouldn't have done the things that she's um* [done in her private life].

TS. *She didn't name your name in the newspapers. You used her name and you used her husband's name and you used her ...*

F. *Yeah, but no, no. Her husband and her they put their name in the newspapers. They waived their rights to anonymity. Because if their name is in the newspapers then I have a right to tell everybody these two people that were in the newspapers, by their names, are liars and that they've done this and that and the other. It's only after the newspapers printed their story ...*

TS. *But do you mean it's right if I have picked up your name in a newspaper and I don't like what you are writing, I could have write different things about you and send it to your neighbours and call them – that would have been OK?*

F. *The newspapers do that here.* [I intended to convey the message of the existence of the right to freedom of speech and the right to reply.]

TS. *But we don't do that in Norway and it's not allowed.*

F. *Well, the thing is you see, if people want to go behaving like liars and perverts and massive cheats and they don't want anyone else to know, well I think that's fraud. That's really doing what you want and being able to cover it up. The point is, I must have some legal redress for the* [allegation of] *attempted rape. But not only that, you see, if I hadn't done what I did* [i.e. send those 20 or so initial reports about her past to her neighbours], *then I wouldn't have known what she's capable of –* [making false allegations, accusing me of] *threatening to kill her son. Now I think that's far more serious a lie than anything I've ever done. After all, all I've told is the truth. You see, I have told 100 per cent* [the truth.]

TS. *She don't say that.*

F. *No, no, but I do and ...*

TS. *You say she's a liar and she says you are a liar. She has told me that she has told you things about her that she didn't want anyone to know because it will hurt her and you told it. And she says that's the wrong she did to tell you things, because she thought she could trust you.*

F. *Well the thing is this, you see, you're talking as if she's a poor honest little girl.*

TS. *I don't.*

F. *But the thing is you see, as far as I'm concerned, all that trust is gone once she starts alleging attempted rape because to me – or rape – that is the worst thing to do and if she thinks I'm gonna keep quiet after that allegation ... and if she thinks I'm gonna keep quiet after* [an allegation of] *threatening to kill her poor little son – actually it's his birthday today, he's 12 – and if she thinks I'm gonna keep quiet after that ... what the newspapers said, everything in there was complete rubbish and lies. It wasn't as if she told even the truth about me. There wasn't one thing in there that was true, OK. So I mean, if I had a criminal conviction or if I'd done this, done that and the other and it was true, OK. But she made up things 'cos she didn't have a damn thing on me. I am still sure I can get her. Even if the lawyer tells me it's 50/50 I will still try. I want that girl punished.*

TS. *But as I told you, the case we had in Norway here where Heidi told things to me and I wrote it down and I send it to my chief in Drammen and he send it through to Oslo. That case is put away because we don't want to do anything more with it now. As I have told you, if you come to Norway and if you try to contact Heidi and if you don't stop it, we have to do something with it because it has now gone thirteen years, now fourteen and she wants peace.*

253

F.   *She wants peace?   What are you talking about?   In 1990 she was trying to manoeuvre me into marriage if I became Christian. She wants peace!*

TS.   *You told me that. She don't tell me that.*

F.   *Fair enough. So answer this then. Does she deny that in 1988 she asked me and my friend to come up to Norway to deal with Gudmund Johannessen? Does she deny this?*

TS.   *No, she don't deny that.*

F.   *She admits it?*

TS.   *Yes.*

F.   *Oh, good. That's one thing. OK. So why does she ask me to do this when in 1986 [she now alleges] I've raped her?*

TS.   *Because she want to be your friend.*

F.   *Oh, oh so in spite of my "raping" ... ...*

TS.   *And that she don't want to be your boyfriend and so on, she want to be your friend. And only that. Her side is that you don't understand what she want. And you don't stop when she says I don't want to be your boyfriend.*

F.   *Well the thing is you see, she wants one time, she doesn't want the next. She tells me she doesn't want Gudmund Johannessen to be her boyfriend. She's a sick woman. She goes from one man to the next. She's got a whole history of sexual partners.*

TS.   *That's her case. She can do what she wants. You can't stop her with that.*

F.   *If she asks me for help and er earlier on and all the rest of it ... and earlier on her psychiatrist told me I was "her favourite" at one stage. I'm not in Norway, I can't see her every day, you see and as soon as some other man she meets is with her for a few days she starts falling in love with him... The thing is ... she doesn't like Muslims and that in itself probably put her off in the end but I think the main thing is the attempted rape and the threats to kill her son. You said that she sent a letter to the Bergen police didn't you about threatening to kill her son, now ...*

TS.   *No, she was talk with the police in Bergen but ... the parents to Johannessen wouldn't talk to the police and I think it was they who get the letter there if I don't remember wrong!! They took the letter with this threat to the police.*

F.   *They took a letter?*

TS.   *I think so. I don't think it was her.*

F.   *So where is the letter?*

TS.   *As I told you before, I have written to the police in Bergen and they don't have it. They have er throw it away or so on.*

F.   *Aah! They've thrown it away!*

TS.   *They say. They say to me – I have ask to see the case and they say they can't give me the letters because they throw it away.*

F.   *Yeah. Do they remember seeing such a letter with a threat to kill the son? The police – do they remember?*

TS.   *They remember it was many letters but they don't remember what was in it.*

F.   *This one specific letter which is so important. Threats to kill a two ... [year old boy].*

TS.   *It's so long a time ago.*

F.   *Yes, but surely there must be one ... if they took that letter to ... I mean was that letter addressed to Heidi or was it addressed to Johannessen?*

TS.   *I don't remember. I thought it was to Johannessen, but I ...*

F.   *Right, so I mean that's absolutely ludicrous. I threaten ... I write a letter to Johannessen's parents threatening to kill Daniel do I? Jesus Christ! Well I tell you that's in[sane].*

TS.   *I don't remember so I can't say.*

F.   *Well someone's gonna have to remember because ...*

TS.   *I have tried. You can call the police in Bergen and I have called I don't know how many times – but I have called them many times and asked after the letters and if they can do something with it or I can talk to the investigator, but they can't help me. So I don't know.*

F.   *So it sounds as if you can't do anything – it's not worth me trying.*

TS.   *You can try.*

F.   *Well I have, haven't I? No, but if you can't succeed, I certainly won't.*

TS.   *No, I don't think so ... the last thing they said to me was the letters was thrown away and they was sorry about that.*

F.   *What, a really vital piece of evidence was thrown away? Well that's not very good of the police is it?*

TS.   *No, that's not very good.*

F.   *Not really, no. Particularly as most of those letters were really nothing anyway and I never said it, so ... ...*

TS.   *I haven't read them.*

F.   *Well OK, what about threats to kill the neighbours? Have you found out which neighbours, um – which neighbours – have you gone and asked which neighbours?*

TS.   *I have talked to Heidi and I have talk to some of the people who live around her now but they admit they have get some phones from you.*

F.   *Well obviously, yes, there's been one or two but no threats to kill them.*

TS.   *But they have said they don't want to talk to you.*

F.   *Oh, they don't want to talk to me –Oh that's the Weums [the family living beneath Heidi]. Obviously I haven't threatened to kill them, have I?*

TS.   *No.*

F.   *No, because they don't even speak to me in English.*

TS.   *Oh maybe...*

F.   *There was one other I think that I phoned just to tell them if they'd heard anything about* [the story] *and they hadn't and I said well she's told the newspapers I've threatened to kill her son and I told them, "I just want you to know that I certainly have not."*

TS.   *But what do want now? ... I don't understand ... I don't have the case anymore.*

F.   *You see, you're the one that my lawyer will get in touch with 'cos you have interviewed Heidi and you will probably have to go back and talk to her again OK. And it's these questions that I want answering because I'm basically building up a picture that she's a very unstable woman and a complete liar – and it is those answers I need to help me in my case – because I will bring it, I can tell you. If allegations have been made that I've threatened to kill the neighbours, then Heidi must supply those names and those neighbours **must** come forward, even if they're forced to by a Summons, to actually say whatever ...*

TS.   *If I get some letters of these or a report or something, I will do that yes – I will do that.*

F.   *Good, OK, because you will find not a single neighbour has been* [threatened with death].

TS.   *Then I need to get the lawyers in Oslo to re-open the case.*

F.   *Re-open the case?*

TS.   *Yes.*

F.   *Against me? Yeah, yeah, OK. I got you, yeah.* [What I think she meant was that they would need the file to look at all the documents.] *You see you won't find any neighbours that I've threatened. And also her friends. Again, Heidi must come forward with the names of the friends. She must be forced to divulge the names of the friends and then these friends again will have to swear, to swear on oath that I've threatened to kill them and again you will find nothing.*

TS.   *But why can't you put this case away now?*

F.   *Why? Well basically I think, er ...*

TS.   *I understand you're hurt.*

F.   *I think it's more than that. That kind of thing must never be allowed to happen again. That's an evil wicked thing she's done over ...*

TS.   *I don't think you can stop that.*

F.   *Over thirteen years ... especially the business about her sleeping with a guy taking heroin.*

TS.   *That's her problem.*

F.   *Well yeah – does she admit to that?*

TS.   *Huh?*

F.   *Does she admit to that?*

TS.   *She says she has done stupid things in her life and I ...*

F.   *Does she admit to the heroin?*

TS.   *I haven't talked to her about that.*

F.   *Well you should've done because it's one of the main things.*

TS.   *That's not my business if she has done er ...*

F.   *Well it will be your business because I'll ask my lawyer to make sure you do ask her that. So, I mean ...*

TS.   *Why?*

F.   *Why? Because I want ...*

TS.   *How do you and I have something to do with something she has done 13 years ago.*

F.   *Well it's because ... it's one of the reasons I wrote to her a very strong letter and got angry with her and it's the reason I went over in 1990 to have words with her because I didn't have the chance beforehand ... and why I was arrested. I wasn't arrested because I want to commit serious crimes. I was arrested because she made it up because I wrote to Johannessen's parents and spilled the beans and they found out about everything and it caused Heidi awful problems. That was the reason she made up the lies about me "threatening" the lives of "Norwegian citizens." I mean it's ridiculous. If I want to do something, I can't achieve a damn thing over the phone because she puts the phone down every time or she hasn't got a phone. So when I go over to try and sort it out in person, I get these massive allegations -and I'm not having it. I'm not used to dealing with such garbage. I mix usually with "slightly" [I was being mildly sarcastic] more decent people and it's a big shock to me to see what was going on there. And I think myself that a lot of people want to know what's going on. I mean stories like this between me and Heidi sell books. And I think that it's in the public interest that people know what's going on. Also her husband – you say he's an OK sort of guy. Have you asked him whether he said to me that "Allah doesn't exist – come to Jesus – only he can save you" and speaking to me in tongues? Has he admitted to that?*

TS.   *No.*

F.   *Have you asked him?*

TS.   *Yes.*

F.   *And what did he say?*

TS.   *He laughed.*

F.   *Oh did he? OK do you want me to get my mother to give you a call to say that she heard him?*

TS.   *No, you don't need to do that. As I told you, I don't have the case now.*

F.   *No, that's right. But the point is this: what he [Runar Schøne] did over the phone was the sort of thing that only comes from a madman OK. "Allah doesn't exist – come to*

Jesus – only he can save you." Only that sort of stuff comes from a bloody madman OK and my mother heard it.

TS. *So what!*

F. *So what? It builds up a case that these people are crazy because you don't believe it OK. Either I'm lying, OK, or he is. So, who do you think's lying?*

TS. *I don't ... I won't answer that because as I told you earlier, I have taken the case; I have talked to Heidi, her husband, I've talked to you several times and I've written down what I have heard, what I have seen and so on and that's my job. I don't have the need to answer who is lying or so I know that in a case with two people is always someone who's lying.*

F. *So if I get my mother to put in an affidavit (a) that she heard this and (b) that um ... that's another thing Heidi is saying - that my own mother wants to put me in a mental hospital – another amazing piece of rubbish. I'll get my mother to swear* [an affidavit denying that].

TS. *So do it. For me it's the same. I don't have a case now. Everything I will send to ...*

F. *Fair enough, at least I've sorted it out in my own mind. Anyway, I just want to get it straight again. When you asked him about speaking in tongues and this business about Allah doesn't exist, he denied it, basically?*

TS. *He didn't say that - he only laughed.*

F. *Oh did he? So, so did you get the impression that he was denying it?*

TS. *No he ... yes! I would say that.*

F. *Yeah, OK, good. We've sorted that one out. What about the "400 obscene letters." Did anyone else see them? She said in the newspapers there were 400 obscene letters I've sent* [all of which she said she'd destroyed].

TS. *I've seen some of them and some is in the case* [Torill Sorte misunderstood me here. As the newspapers had said all 400 were destroyed, then she couldn't have seen any of them].

F. *Yeah, but* [and I was not now referring to the "400 obscene letters" the newspapers mentioned but to other letters with Torill Sorte] *I wouldn't say they're obscene. They're not dirty sex talk. They're basically talking about her life – her sex life.*

TS. *That's not nice what you are writing I think.*

F *Yeah, but they're not obscene.*

TS. *No, no if you lie it is.*

F. *Huh?*

TS. *If the thing you have written in the letters is not the truth.*

F. *If it's not the truth it's a lie. But as I've told you, I have told the truth – 100 per cent.*

TS. *Yes, I don't know that.*

F. *No, you don't know that but I do and God knows it and so does Heidi and in a human Court of Law the burden of proof is such that you have to do your best. But I know it,*

Heidi knows it, God knows it. But also Heidi was with her husband when he was talking such nonsense over the phone and I'm sure once we get a psychiatric report on Heidi ... ...

TS.   *I don't think you will get that.*

F.   *Well I'll certainly try hard I can tell you ... he [Heidi's psychiatrist, Dr. Broch] told me long ago that it is possible to get psychiatric evidence from a Court Order and I'll certainly be trying 100 per cent for that, particularly as I've had a couple of your psychiatrists go on about erotic paranoia amongst Muslims – which again – you know – is unforgivable.*

TS.   *But you know we can talk and talk and talk.*

F.   *Yeah, I've talked enough and when my lawyer advises me he'll be in touch but it'll probably be after Easter.*

TS.   *You can tell your lawyer he can call me or come here also and I can talk to him and I can answer the questions he wants to know.*

F.   *Sure, sure, I'll tell him that. But I've told him it's Heidi that has to be cross-examined, not you.*

TS.   *No, but I can talk to him.*

F.   *Yeah, OK.*

TS.   *OK?*

F.   *Thanks very much. Bye.*

TS.   *Bye bye.*

On the same day, 1ˢᵗ April 1998, I wrote an eight-page letter to my lawyer Gjone reporting on my conversation with Torill Sorte.

On 2ⁿᵈ April 1998, I sent a fax to Torill Sorte:

Dear Torill,

Heidi & Runar Schøne

I do think that various people amongst you in Norway have been bad losers and it's a case of sour grapes. What goes around comes around they say, and I am overjoyed that so many people know my side of the story – the truth – 100% of it.

Heidi's confidences in me became worthless because she has tried in her madness to ruin me. I only went public to 20 or so of her neighbours in 1995 **after** reading Wesenberg's report to me in February. Heidi **then** told total lies to whole country. Only **after** that did I begin my nationwide campaign of correcting the deception of Heidi and the Press.

Do you not think schools, banks, hotels and a complete cross-section of the public read those stories by the shithead three journalists? So why can't the same approach be taken by me? My privacy was invaded by lies. Heidi's deception was exposed by the

---

259

truth. Yes sir! There are some bad losers in Norway! Some can't stand it that an example has been made of a sexual pervert – Heidi Schøne – and her sub-normal 'husband' Runar "Come to Jesus. He only laughed," Schøne. Perverts shouldn't have a right to privacy – they won't be allowed to get away with it.

Yours sincerely,

Frederick Delaware

On the 6th April 1998 I made a series of telephone calls to Norway as follows:

Ingunn Røren, the journalist at Drammens Tidende.

Answer   *Drammens Tidende.*

F.   *Hello, good morning, do you still have a journalist called Ingunn Røren with you please?*

Answer   *Just a moment* [followed by quite a wait and then the phone going dead. I tried again].

Answer   *Drammens Tidende.*

F.   *Yes good morning, I'm trying to see if you still have a journalist called Ingunn Røren, please.*

Answer   *Just a moment –* [the call was transferred].

IR.   *Ya, Ingunn.*

F.   *Yes, hello is that Ingunn Røren?*

IR.   *Ya.*

F.   *It is?*

IR.   *Yeah.*

F.   *Good. Well you remember me, Frederick Delaware.*

IR.   *Um, no.*

F.   *Regarding Heidi Schøne?*

IR.   *OK, yes.*

F.   *Um, I'm taking hopefully criminal proceedings against her, Heidi. I've got a lawyer now and er got enough evidence, so I was just wondering if we'll have your co-operation in coming to Court to be cross-examined on the things you've printed.*

IR.   *You want me to come to Court.*

F.   *Oh, yes, as well as your Editor, of course, but you ...*

IR.   *Yes, then you have to, to ... give us a subpoena. Your lawyer has to give us a subpoena.*

F.   *A what? Oh, yes, that's right, hopefully he will do that.*

260

IR.   'Cos we never go to Court unless the Court says we have to go.

F.   I appreciate that, but it's obviously important that you come along.

IR.   But anyway you have to talk to my Editor about that because he's the one who is deciding.

F.   I'll certainly talk to him about that but obviously, er, you gave the interview, but um …

IR.   Yeah, but he's the one who makes the decision.

F.   Yeah, that's right, but you gave the interview and you're both involved in this, er…

IR.   But he's the one who's deciding whether I'm the one who's going to go to Court or not … because it's the Editor's decision … anyway.

F.   Well … but if the Court decides you have to go…

IR.   Yeah, then I have to go.

F.   That's right, so…

IR.   Er, I should let you talk to him.

F.   Yeah, I certainly will talk to him in a minute, but the thing is this … um …, as I want to put you on the spot. That Norwegian translation that you have of Heidi's past had a reference, two references, to rape allegations. Um, did you talk to her about that?

IR.   Talk to Heidi about it?

F.   Mmm.

IR.   Yes.

F.   And what did she say?

IR.   Er, I don't remember exactly now because um, but we talked about it, yes.

F.   Mmm, well can you think hard?

IR.   I have to take a look at the interview because it's been now er two years ago or something … so I have to check the interview.

F.   Yes, it's quite important to the, er, let me say, um, conspiring to pervert the course of justice and why didn't you make any reference to that in your newspaper about those allegations?

IR.   I'm not sure. I think er it was because it was er … I don't know, I don't remember exactly because it's been a long time since we did the interview. I don't remember everything we talked about and why really.

F.   But you do have your notes from the time do you?

IR.   Yes, some notes. I'm not sure I have all the notes.

F.   Why's that?

IR.   *Because it's been so long time ago and I can't save up all the notes from every interview I do.*

F.   *No, but hers in particular?*

IR.   *No, it's not that different from other interviews so...*

F.   *But her ... her notes in particular, do you have them?* [I meant Ingunn Røren's notes on Heidi but she misunderstood me.]

IR.   *I did not ... I don't have any notes from Heidi. I have er ... she gave me some letters that you wrote to her but no notes.*

F.   *So how did the discussion of the rape allegations against two men, me included, ... um*

IR.   *We have never talk about two men.*

F.   *Well she made allegations of rape against a Bergen shopkeeper in the early 80's.*

IR.   *I've never heard about that.*

F.   *Well it was... huh! It was in the, er, Norwegian translation* [my report] *that everybody has* [that started the ball rolling in the first place.]

IR.   *Yeah, but I didn't talk about an allegation against a man in Bergen.*

F.   *Well, I wrote it in the Norwegian translation.*

IR.   *Yeah, but Heidi never told me about that.*

F.   *So what rape matters did you talk about?*

IR.   *Um?*

F.   *Which rape matters did you talk about?*

IR.   *I think I talked about er you tried to rape her once or something, I'm not sure ...*

F.   *Tried?*

IR.   *We didn't talk much about it.*

F.   *Trying?*

IR.   *Yeah, I'm not sure. I'm telling you it's a long time ago. I think it was discussed little while...*

F.   *So what was it? Trying to? Attempted? Actual?*

IR.   *I don't remember ... I have to see if I have a notes.*

F.   *Um, well let's hope those ... ...*

IR.   *Er your case is not that special. So it's not important to remember everything we said and talked about.*

F.   *No, not that special but it's special enough obviously to make three newspapers and to get er Verdens Gang to get psychiatric opinions isn't it? It's that important!*

IR.   *Yes, it was at the time, yes, but it's not that important now.*

F.   *No, obviously, er ... ...*

IR.   *I don't go around and remember everything that was said but if I find my notes I will know but er ...*

F.   *So when do you think you'll find your notes or have time to look for them?*

IR.   *Er, maybe tomorrow.*

F.   *OK, good, well I'll um, I'll certainly give you a buzz back tomorrow.*

IR.   *Er, yeah, anyway I suggest you talk to the Editor because he's the one who handles all the cases and they go to Court. So it's no use to talk to me about it, because you have to talk to him.*

F.   *Well aren't you trying to get rid of the responsibility for yourself in some way?*

IR.   *No, it's his decision. He's the one that decides everything about cases that may go to Court. It's not me. That's just the way it is. It's not er ... It's my responsibility as well but he's responsible for me again.*

F.   *Er OK, fine. Now the business of threatening to kill her son, which is again another matter I hope to have her punished criminally for. Um, what do you recall about that? It's rather, er, a vital piece of information to give to everybody and I'm sure that stuck in your mind. Now exactly how, what did Heidi tell you about alleged threats to kill her son, who was two years old?*

IR.   *She told me what it said in the interview.*

F.   *Yeah, and what did um ...what did ... how did the threats come about?*

IR.   *Um?*

F.   *How did the threats come about?*

IR.   *I guess she told me.*

F.   *Yeah, well what did she ...*

IR.   *I didn't know what had happened so yes she told me. She said what it said in the interview. You had it translated to you can read it there.*

F.   *Um. No ...*

IR.   *I'm only responsible for what it says in the newspaper.*

F.   *Yeah, that's right, that's right, but she told you ... In the newspaper it merely made reference to the fact that threats were made to kill her son and not how. Not how. So can you ... she must have told you how. And don't tell me she didn't tell you because she must have told you in detail how.*

IR.   *Anyway I'll answer these questions in Court if the case ...*

F.   *No, no, no, no.*

IR.   *I have no responsibility to answer up to you right now.*

F.   *I think you're hiding something ... I think there's a cover up.*

IR.   *What should that be?*

F.   *Huh?*

IR.   *What should I be hiding?*

F.   *Tell me **now** please......*

IR.   *No ...*

F.   *... how the threats were made.*

IR.   *You have to go to Court against Heidi.*

F.   *Yes, we will go to Court but......*

IR.   *And then I'll see if the Court tells me I have to go to the stand and testify, I'll do that. Before that you have no right to make me testify right here and right now.*

F.   *But we have a right to get evidence beforehand to present to the Court and your reluctance ...*

IR.   *Yes, my interview is the evidence you get from me. What it says in print and newspaper that's the evidence you get from me. That's it. I can't tell you what I talked to Heidi about besides what it says in the newspaper.*

F.   *So how did I make the threats? Over the phone? In letters?*

IR.   *I'm telling you, when I interview something ... someone, er, and I speak to them, I can't tell everybody else what they told me. I have stand for what's in the paper and everything else in the conversation between me and Heidi, that's between me and her.*

F.   *Yes, very good. That's a very good way of escaping, er, justice isn't it?*

IR.   *Yeah, I think so ...* [she misunderstood].

F.   *Yeah, I certainly do.*

IR.   *If the Court tells me to go, I'll go ... I won't do anything until the subpoena comes.*

F.   *OK, right. Your Editor, what's his name and could you put me through to him please.*

IR.   *I can't put you through but you can get his number.*

F.   *OK, what's his name?*

IR.   *Er, Hans H-A-N-S A-R-N-E O-D-D-E* [she spells his full name for me].

F.   *And his number?*

IR.   *That's (32) 204307.*

F.	*He's in now is he?*
IR.	*I don't know. Try.*
F.	*OK, I'll try. Thank you very much.*
IR.	*Bye.*
F.	*Bye bye.*

Followed immediately by a call to Ingunn Røren's Editor, Hans Odde:

HO.	*Odde.*
F.	*Yes. Good morning, Mr. Odde, it's Frederick Delaware from London, um, regarding your newspaper article on Heidi Schøne, er, in May 1995, you remember?*
HO.	*Mm huh.*
F.	*Good. Right. I've just spoken to Ingunn Røren and I'm hoping to take criminal proceedings in the Norwegian Courts against Heidi Schøne and I understand that we need a Court subpoena to force yourself and Ingunn Røren to testify. Is that the case?*
HO.	*Yeah.*
F.	*Good. OK, well, um hopefully after Easter when my lawyer is back from skiing, I shall get him to, er, see what he can do to achieve this. Now I've asked Ingunn Røren over the phone now and she refuses to answer, but as you were the one who printed the story what I shall be after is Ingunn Røren's notes that she took for Heidi's interview and I hope they are still intact, specifically with regard to rape allegations that you knew about before you printed the story. The rape allegations against me and a Bergen shopkeeper in the 1980's and also, just as important the threats that were made to kill her son when he was two. That and the exact discussions on how Heidi alleged I threatened to kill her son. That is the evidence I shall need from her and also why you decided to print those articles without reference to the rape allegations or to the fact that Gudmund Johannessen, her boyfriend, was in fact the one causing the sex-terror. OK. Now do you have anything to say about the rape allegations or threats to kill her son now?*
HO.	*Nothing, but er I want to tell you that er I don't want to answer any questions from you at this time.*
F.	*Why is that then?*
HO.	*If I receive letters from the Court I will probably answer the letters from the Court but I think it's right of me to be a bit formal at the moment.*
F.	*Mmm. Why's that though? Why's that … you ……*
HO.	*Because you are telling me that you have already engaged a lawyer.*
F.	*That's right.*
HO.	*And that you are going to, to, er go to Court with this case.*

F. *That's right.*

HO. *And because of that I think it's right of me to be formal now.*

F. *Yes I ...*

HO. *What I'm doing is that if I receive a letter from the Court I will probably answer the letter.*

F. *Good.*

HO. *But I do not want to answer any question for you at this moment of the case.*

F. *I accept that, quite. But the thing is you've had almost three years to answer the questions I've put to you in writing and in phone calls before and you didn't want to co-operate then either, so the fact that I'm going to Court now doesn't really in actual fact make that much difference to you. You are not going to co-operate whether or not we go to Court, and you see, I believe what you've done is criminally irresponsible and I will be getting hopefully the psychiatrists who didn't actually, er, who were tricked by the Verdens Gang newspaper basically into giving evidence. They didn't know what they were doing and getting the lot of you and um, you know, just to show that you Norwegians in general, um, are basically so dense in your newspaper articles and so hateful of foreigners, especially if they're Muslim, er, you know and also I, after ... I will discuss the matter with my lawyer but, er, I will hopefully be able to tell you that I want £50,000 compensation plus front page articles of apology and obviously if I don't get that then the campaign against you and Heidi will carry on. OK, my lawyer will be in touch. That's all I have to say.*

HO. *OK.*

F. *Thank you very much.*

HO. *OK.*

F. *Bye bye.*

On 6th April 1998, I wrote another update to my lawyer Gjone.

I made a follow up call to Ann-Kristin Horvei on the 20th April 1998:

A-K. *Hello.*

F. *Yeah, hi Ann-Kristin, it's Freddy.*

A-K. *Oh, hello.*

F. *I rang you a couple of weeks ago and also a week ago. Have you been on holiday?*

A-K. *No.*

F. *Oh, well I just missed you then. Do you know Heidi's had another baby?*

A-K. *Oh, did she? When?*

F. *I think a year ago – a boy... I think it's called David.*

A-K.   *All these things you know!*

F.   *Yeah, well I've tried to talk to her neighbours and they ...*

A-K.   *Does she still live in Drammen?*

F.   *Yeah, she lives in Solbergmoen... she lives in one big house and there are two families and I asked the neighbours to go and get Heidi and they won't even speak to me in English. They pretend not to speak English and just called me a "fucking idiot" and put the phone down, but they don't like me at all because I suppose Heidi's telling them that I'm ...you know, everything under 'The Sun'. But when you were still friends with Heidi at that time, what did she have to say about ... did she say that I've raped her, to you?*

A-K.   *No.*

F.   *Never?*

A-K.   *No.*

F.   *I wonder why. I mean she's your friend and she would have told you wouldn't she?*

A-K.   *Yes, but I don't know, er - no, I don't know.*

F.   *Did she tell you about the Bergen shopkeeper?*

A-K.   *Yes, I think she told me, yeah, yeah, but I have told you, yes, but not about you ... so when you told me er ... when you called me last time for an hour ... that you told me that you have sex with Heidi ... that is new for me ... I never heard about that.*

F.   *Oh yeah ... when you see ...*

A-K.   *I don't think you have told me that before.*

F.   *Didn't I?*

A-K.   *No.*

And later, regarding the 1998 rape allegation I discussed the matter with Ann-Kristin:

F.   *And she told the police that I've held her down. Now no one can hold Heidi down, having sex. If Heidi doesn't want to have sex with someone ... she's a strong girl and there's no bloody way unless you're holding a knife or a gun to her head. I know Heidi's strong and she's a ...liar. There's no way that happened. And that is why the story: I got so angry that I thought I've had enough of these bloody lies and I told lots of her neighbours – the neighbours where she'd lived before and unfortunately one of the neighbours was a photographer and he gave the information to a journalist and the journalist couldn't believe Heidi's past ... and she and Gudmund Johannessen had two AIDS tests each after Daniel was born.*

A-K.   *After?*

F.   *Oh yeah, after ... **after** Daniel was born.*

A-K.   *Not after she was pregnant?*

F.   *No, no if I remember ... ...*

A-K.   *Here in Norway all people will be check ... they take of everyone.*

F.   *Yeah, I know that but what Heidi told me was that ... and I remember her words - that she was "worried for Daniel."*

A-K.   *But not the father. They don't check the father.*

F.   *But in this case she told me that both herself and Gudmund Johannessen had two, two AIDS tests each and her words were that she was "not worried" for herself she was "more worried for Daniel" in case, you see. So I'm not making this up about Johannessen's heroin taking, because she told me he'd bought the heroin when he was on a trip to China.*

A-K.   *Yes.*

F.   *And that ... I knew he smoked cannabis because he smoked it in front of me, and um knowing Johannessen as I do, it didn't surprise me he was injecting heroin, and the rest of it ... that I wrote to Heidi's father because he's the father, he's responsible for her life ... and I also knew he didn't like me and I wanted to say ... look man if you don't like me then um ...you know...*

A-K.   *Can I ask you for something?*

F.   *Yeah.*

A-K.   *Heidi's mother. She was dead. When and why did she die? Do you know that?*

F.   *Well, I asked **you** didn't I? I asked you why and the information ... All I knew ... Heidi told me that ... when I went to see Heidi in 1990 for the second time 'cos I went twice ... the first time in February I got arrested ... the second time everything was sorted out and I sat with her and we hugged and cuddled and she told me that her mother was "in hell" ... Heidi had supposedly found God and she told me that her mother was in hell because she was always taking pills, drinking and trying to kill herself. And I didn't actually go on to ask her how she died in detail, but I asked you once and you told me you thought she ... or was it Heidi ... that her mother fell and hit her head and had a brain ... a blood clot on the brain or something like this ...*

A-K.   *Yes* [agreeing].

F.   *But I talked to you about this before and you weren't quite sure but that's all I know - is that they got divorced ... parents were divorced and the mother was in a dreadful state ... pills, drinking ... and I'm afraid also ... she's got two sisters, Heidi, and there's one of them ... the one that now lives in Egersund. Heidi told me that she* [the sister] *would've killed herself if she hadn't had her children. And she's on doctor's prescription ... pills, tablets for depression. Because her husband and her had divorced. So it's something they turn to ... drink and pills and that's why Heidi tried twice to kill herself with pills. But why do you ask about her mother?*

A-K.   *I only have think about it and wondering.*

        [and later:]

A-K.   *But they didn't write about you in England?* [in the English newspapers]

F.   *They didn't write about me in England 'cos no one knew it was me. But I think, you never know. It could've got out into the newspapers in England. It's something that they like to write about and I suppose I'm lucky. But Heidi has to be taught a lesson ... I like that boy Daniel very very, very much and he liked me very much and he was telling everybody ...his neighbours ...*

A-K.   *I see Daniel last summer.*

F.   *You did?*

A-K.   *Yes ... me and my children we are playing out and there was ... yep play station or something and I know. You know Gudmund ...he is living here in Åsane and Nina, Gudmund's wife, her sister is living er ... yes ... in a place here where we are. I saw there was a boy and Gudmund was there and he have a football T-shirt and Daniel is [written] on back and I saw him ... he looks like Gudmund ... yes it was him.*

F.   *Did you say hello to Daniel?*

A-K.   *No, no, no.*

F.   *He doesn't know you?*

A-K.   *Oh, no, no, no.*

F.   *I have seen him.*

A-K.   *So I think Daniel is visiting his father for holidays.*

F.   *But you haven't seen Heidi?*

A-K.   *No, no, no... I've not have seen Heidi. Last time I saw her it was 17th May, Norwegian National Day, and I think it must be ... oh my God ... hundreds of years ago.*

F.   *Yeah, I remember you telling me she was dressed in green.*

A-K.   *Yes, not in nice clothes for a National Day.*

F.   *No, that's right – she's obviously unhappy at the time.*

A-K.   *Very many years ago.*

F.   *But ... I haven't seen Daniel since ... August 1990 and I am **not** going to have written in the newspapers that I have threatened to kill him. And I've asked where's the evidence and Heidi told the police that I wrote in a letter ... saying that I will kill Daniel ... and how old was he? Two! Two years old. And what's happened to this letter? Heidi said she gave it to Gudmund Johannessen's parents ... who gave it to the police ... so the policewoman in Drammen phoned the Bergen police to ask where the letter is ... No one kept a photocopy and so I have to ...*

A-K.   *There are not a letter.*

F.   *Well, I know I didn't write a letter so it looks ... I've asked for my lawyer to get in touch with Gudmund Johannessen's parents to ask them about this allegation. It's a dangerous thing to do because they could lie – because they don't like me, Johannessen's parents, because I think they went to the police. They are all very unhappy you see because they didn't know that Heidi had had abortions. They didn't know that Gudmund Johannessen had got Heidi pregnant with twins and that she miscarried. They didn't know any of this and ...*

A-K.   *If it's true.*

269

F.   *Well ... ...*

A-K.   *I don't know.*

F.   *Did Heidi tell you that she was having twins? Pregnant with twins? This was before I knew you. She said she tried to take her life in maybe July at er um ... July 1984. In July 1984 she got pregnant with twins to Gudmund Johannessen. He slept with her best friend ... Heidi found out and miscarried and tried to commit suicide by taking pills, but her sister found her and took her to the hospital and she had her stomach pumped. It was maybe for two weeks she said she wasn't washing, she wasn't eating. Now she was below your parents' place ... Heidi was living below your parents' home – you remember, in 1983?*

A-K.   *Eating or and ... ...*

F.   *Not eating nor washing – she'd just tried to kill herself ... ...*

A-K.   *For two weeks?*

F.   *Yeah and she wasn't eating, washing ... well maybe she was eating a little bit but her ... she'd given up. Do you remember any of this?*

A-K.   *No.*

F.   *Nothing?*

A-K.   *No, I remember that she told me the thing about the twins.*

F.   *Ah, so that's true.*

A-K.   *I don't know!*

F.   *But she told you ...*

A-K.   *I have listened but er ... but should I believe her? I don't know, maybe.*

F.   *'Cos she told me also about the twins and I definitely believed her because of the way she told me. You know 'cos one evening she introduced me to Gudmund Johannessen. She just said quietly, "That's the boy I told you about" ... and she just said "It was twins." And you know I thought: "What the hell are you doing with him now? Why are you introducing ... why is he near you?" Do you think it's true? Do you think she's lying?*

A-K.   *I don't know.*

F.   *Obviously she must have lied to you about other things or else you wouldn't suspect she's lying. What things? Has she lied to you before?*

A-K.   *About what?*

F.   *Anything – anything that's quite serious.*

A-K.   *No ... I can't remember something.*

F.   *So why do you think she may be lying about the twins? Why?*

A-K.   *I don't know the story was ... yeah ...*

F.   *What? Did it sound too farfetched?*

A-K.   *What?*

F.   *Did it sound um ... you know that ...*

A-K.   *It was so er ...*

F.   *Unbelievable?*

A-K.   *Yes ... and I remember myself ... when I was in her ... yes, 16... and you was in love and a boy, yes ... it was finished and ... you find, yes ...*

F.   *Someone else?* [I added quickly]

A-K.   *Fantasy. No! No, the fantasy, er OK. you find a liar.*

F.   *Huh?*

A-K.   *I remember when I was young yes ... and when I was young I remember myself ... I don't tell ... anything correct. You understand what I mean? When I was young I lie for myself and lie for my friends ... you know ... when I was very young ... yes so when I have a story I maybe think maybe it's a lie because myself in that time when I was young I can tell somebody a story it was not true. Maybe something was little true but you know and er but I don't know if that story of Heidi is that true. But she had never told me she would kill herself – never. And you told me much of time she want to do it.*

F.   *Twice she tried.*

A-K.   *Twice, yes.*

F.   *Twice she tried.*

A-K.   *She have never told me.*

F.   *Well she told me things ...*

A-K.   *I remember when I was in her ... when I was very young, I do the same. I'm not trying to kill but I told people* [trouble with] *my boyfriend ... oh oh ... I don't want to live anymore ... it was not true.*

F.   *She actually told me she took the pills ... the thing is you see, in her circumstances it was serious because if she got pregnant with twins ... and your boyfriend sleeps with your best friend and you miscarry, then a lot of girls are going to be seriously affected, mentally ... they're going to feel terrible. That's why I believe she ... and I still believe it ... but I never spoke to her parents about this ... but her ... stepmother told me not to believe everything.*

A-K.   *Told you, you shouldn't believe her?*

F.   *She told me in general don't believe everything Heidi tells you.*

A-K.   *Yes.*

F.   *But the thing is her stepmother was worried about the things Heidi was telling me probably about her. 'Cos Heidi told me her stepmother was sleeping with lots of men in America where she was a model, OK and I once ... actually asked the mother about this. I wrote to the mother saying Heidi's been saying all this about you and then her*

271

son, Christian, he wrote back a letter threatening me with er ...[at which point A-K broke off to help her child put a coat on to go out, then we resumed some chit chat] [and later]:

F.   *Yours is the only relationship that's lasted. Everyone else I know ... let's say many other people I know in Norway they're all divorced and separated.   They're beginning on second marriages and ...*

A-K.   *All the people I know, my friends ... they are married with the same man and much of children and happy ... Do you remember the boy? ... Bjorn-Morten ... he was a very nice boy.*

F.   *The one who was a model?*

A-K.   *Yes, he was very pretty.*

F.   *I remember him ...*

A-K.   *I remember I think Heidi was with him ... she start to meeting Gudmund again ... and then he find out Heidi was with Gudmund ... but ... after that he meet a friend of me ... one of my best friends now and they married and she, the wife, had one kid with another man for many years ago and they tried to get kids and they don't get kids and then they go to hospital and get some help. So after some time they get four kids.*

F.   *Oh, Jesus Christ! All at once, and they all lived?*

A-K.   *Yes – four kids and I think they are six years old.*

F.   *How old is the wife?*

A-K.   *She is 35.*

F.   *The same age as the man. Well if you see him give him my regards. I'm sure he remembers me.*

A-K.   *Yes, I think so*

F.   *He remembers me and a lot of people must ... ...*

A-K.   *I think I have say something to him about you when you have called me up.*

F.   *'Cos what happened was that when I went to see Heidi the first time, she wanted me to go home after one day ... in the Christmas I met you ... because I didn't want to stay up all night talking to her friends. And I think one of them was him ... this boy ... whatever his name is, and a few days later Heidi told me that she likes him and they spent half an hour or an hour in the car ... in his car ... trying to sort something [a future together] out ... but then she told me it wasn't going to happen and I couldn't understand why 'cos she wasn't with Gudmund at the time, you know, when I saw her the first time she didn't like him anymore, Gudmund, you see, and so she was free ... so ... but that boy if he thinks that Heidi was still with Gudmund then he's not right, he's wrong. Heidi had finished with Gudmund. Why did he think that Gudmund was still with Heidi?*

A-K.   *I don't know, but I think Heidi must have been pregnant so maybe she ...*

F.   *No, not ... ...*

A-K.   *Yes, she must have been pregnant when she was with, er ...*

F.   *Not in 19 ... not when* [I was going to say '84 the Christmas visit of mine].

A-K.   *She must have been having sex with Gudmund when she was with this boy, because after that he is wondering: "Oh my God, could I be the father to the boy because later if you are counting up the months..."*

F.   *Did he sleep with Heidi?*

A-K.   *Yes, they was together a few months I think.*

F.   *When?*

A-K.   *In that time.*

F.   *In 1984?* [I actually meant 1985].

A-K.   *I don't remember the year, but in that time...*

F.   *But after I ...*

A-K.   *After the wondering Oh my God could he be the father, because he not could get babies.*

F.   *Hey?*

A-K.   *He have problems. They don't find out why. He don't could have babies, normal.*

F.   *He's infertile? His sperm ...*

A-K.   *It was nothing wrong with he, it was nothing wrong with her, but she have get baby before ... some people are not er ... so they was married many many years before they go to get some help in hospital ... he was boyfriend with Heidi.*

F.   *So what happened was ... you see I'm a bit confused because I saw you at that Christmas and Heidi had told me she liked that boy and wanted to have a relationship with him ... they were going to try ... the last week in December of 1984 when I visit you in Bergen for the first time... but ...*

A-K.   *She was boyfriend with him when we was in England.* [Which was summer 1985.]

F.   *Oh was she?*

A-K.   *Yes, I think she was.*

F.   *So she must have been sleeping with Gudmund and him at the same time?*

A-K.   *Yes*

F.   *Yeah ... well I didn't know that ... because Gudmund ... he's the father is he? Definitely?*

A-K.   *Yes, yes.*

F.   *That's for sure?*

A-K.   *Yes, you can see it when you see Daniel.*

F.   *I see, so, yes that's news to me. Ah! God! ... that's quite shocking that I didn't know that at all.*

A-K.   *It's not shocking.*

F.   *Well for me it is ... because ... so after I left at Christmas Heidi must have gone back to see this ... what's his name?*

A-K.   *Bjorn-Morten.*

F.   *Gone back to see him and then they started having sex ... so why did she have sex with Gudmund at the same time? Why did she do this ...?*

A-K.   *That is love Frederick ... that is love.*

F.   *So she loved two boys at the same time?*

A-K.   *Maybe she like Bjorn-Morten, she like him very much, but when the right man is ... ...*

F.   *Available ...*

A-K.   *Maybe she can't say no ... you can't understand it. Nobody can understand it ... that's life.*

F.   *... I know Heidi's slept with a lot of men. Would it be possible, you know, if it was necessary for you to come to Court just to tell me these things?*

A-K.   *Huh?*

F.   *Could you come to Court in Norway ... in Drammen if my lawyer wants you to help me ... to give your opinion ... 'cos I need someone basically to help me, just to say that I'm not er ...*

A-K.   *What shall I tell them?*

F.   *Just tell them these things about Heidi ...that you've told me today ... 'cos a lot of people believed the newspapers. A lot of people have thought: "I'm sure that what has been printed is true" ... If it was necessary just to come along and say ... I would ask you questions in Court myself and you would have to basically say the truth. How you felt ... it wouldn't be difficult. Could you do this, if necessary? ... I'm certainly going to try and take Heidi to Court in Norway, because I find what she's done is so unforgivable ... to call me ... you know, 13 years of sex terror ... when it wasn't me. It was Gudmund Johannessen that caused the trouble as well as Heidi and about being a Muslim as well ... the Muslim man.*

A-K.   *You are still a Muslim?*

F.   *Yeah, of course I am. I've always been a Muslim, I always will be ... but ...*

A-K.   *Do you practice?*

F.   *Yeah, yeah, I pray, fast, don't drink, yeah.*

A-K.   *Oh, maybe I'm a Muslim too, I do not drink.*

F.   *Well, that's nice to hear. But it's too important and I don't think people should get away with these lies ... it's very upsetting ... you see Heidi when she became a Christian, after Gudmund beat her up ... I thought maybe she's changed but her kind of Christianity is perverse. It's pretty sick. She says she was exorcised from the Devil and spoke in tongues and her husband ...*

A-K.   *Who's speaking in tongues, her husband?*

F.   *Yeah, he spoke to me in tongues over the phone.*

274

A-K.   Yes, but is that correct or was he having some fun with you?

F.   No, I think it was absolutely the case because two weeks later they had a programme on television in England [Everyman broadcast from Manchester] and I heard exactly the same things ... the same accent ... the same way of speaking, and he says to me: "Allah doesn't exist ... come to Jesus ... only he can save you." He hates Muslims ... Heidi believes that I'm going to go to hell. A lot of Christians think that if you aren't Christian you'll go to hell ... because you don't believe Jesus is the son of God. She sent me a book in 1990 about a woman ... a Pakistani woman who became a Christian and Heidi wanted me to become a Christian and I know that ... she said I could come and live in Norway and, I, actually - to be honest with you ... both of us were thinking of trying for marriage. She ordered the book from England ... to Norway and then she sent it to me here. I read ... and it was such a load of rubbish ... [and later]:

A-K.   You think there will be a case?

F.   I don't know, I hope so, I'm trying for it.

A-K.   Here in Norway?

F.   Yeah, I have to go to Norway. But you see I have told hundreds of people in Norway now about Heidi ... I publicised my side of the case in a big big way. I can't understand how even Gudmund Johannessen's wife, Nina, I mean she won't speak to me, she puts the phone down and gets very angry ... I don't know how she can marry Gudmund Johannessen, I really can't believe ...

A-K.   He's not the same one, in that time you know him.

F.   Oh, no, but the point is, a lot of people change but I'm not interested in what they've become, I'm interested in the trouble they cause at the time when they're young. Because it's when you're young and you're full of sexual power that you go sleeping with lots of woman, like Gudmund did ... and that's the reason for all the problems from that behaviour at the time. It's no good learning your lessons afterwards ... you mustn't do them in the first place ... because if Heidi tries to kill herself twice and all the rest of it, it doesn't matter what Gudmund Johannessen becomes afterwards. He's been to prison. Did Heidi tell you he's been to prison?

A-K.   No, maybe he do something wrong when he was in the military.

F.   Yeah, that's right he did.

A-K.   Not in prison. We don't call it "in prison" when you are in military. But there are a sort of prison in military. But it's not ... ...

F.   Yeah, it's a military detention or something. Yeah, but you see what these people have done... what Heidi's done and everyone else and the newspapers and the lies ... it's all the same thing. It's all: "We hate Freddy ... We hate the Muslim ... he's a love-sick fanatic" and that's precisely the reason I'm not married ... because being Muslim is being shit and not wanted. No-one wants anything to do with the Muslim man. No-one wants to marry him because ... I know and I was told that people in Norway are taught at school and it's part of the culture that Muslims ... should be left alone ... Muslims are wrong ... and Heidi told me this years ago ... that her parents would be furious if she married a Muslim and she wrote and told me in a letter that they were discussing Islam in school and how the Muslim men treat the women like shit and how, Heidi told me that ...

A-K.   Yes, that's the thing we hear.

F.   Yeah, that's right, you see and maybe some of that does happen. It certainly does happen in the Middle East a lot. A lot of men aren't kind to their women, but the thing with me is that it's not me ... I'm not one of them and also a lot of Norwegian men are not kind to their

275

women. People like Gudmund. And it's very unfair to ... 'cos after all Heidi wrote to me ... she loved me at one stage, she wanted to marry me on two different occasions ... so it's not as if I am out of bounds.

A-K.   *Do you think there are many people like Gudmund?*

F.   *Yes, I think there are quite a few because ... and I think there are many women... the same ...let's face it, there are a lot of men who've slept with a lot of women ... a lot of sexual partners ...there's a lot of divorce ... a lot of suicide in Norway, depression ... ...*

A-K.   *I don't know any of them.*

F.   *Well, I heard that maybe ten people a year commit suicide in Drammen ... for every five pregnancies in Norway there is one termination ... so things aren't so wonderful in Norway ... I've tried with other girls in Norway and they don't like Muslims ... that is absolutely clear to me.*

A-K.   *Yes* [agreeing.]

F.   *And they treat me like shit. I have to fight to prove to people that I'm not shit ... that I'm a human being and I'm worthy of being looked upon on as a human being, suitable to marry someone from Europe, as I live in Europe and I cannot have the newspapers saying that Muslims are shit, and that I personally threaten to kill ... a young boy ...I cannot have this, so I must wipe the past out and establish the facts and the truth. I know it's going to be difficult for me now ... so at least I have to get some satisfaction from correcting the rubbish that's been spoken about me. Especially as Daniel liked me very much. I'm sure he'd been horrified ... so upset ... to see what his mother has been saying about me. I think Heidi is evil ... really wicked ... to try and ruin me.*

[and later] Heidi wrote to me and I have the letter in my cupboard where Heidi admits to having had abortions and it was you ...you know about Heidi's abortions? You knew about them didn't you?

A-K.   *Only this twins story so I don't know ...*

[So I explained the background ... and referred to the two abortions]

A-K.   *And you believe it?*

F.   *I do believe it, although ... ...*

A-K.   *All this abortion you believe?*

F.   *There's two abortions and a miscarriage of twins.*

A-K.   *Oh, that's much.*

F.   *... ...I personally believe it's true. I'm convinced it's true but the thing is ... I know some people lie... ...*

A-K.   *Yes.*

F.   *But Heidi told me one of her sisters did lie about having an abortion.*

A-K.   *Yes.*

F.   *I don't know which sister lied. She said she* [the sister] *had an abortion but she didn't.*

A-K.   *No.*

F.   *And I can't remember what the reason was, the circumstances.*

A-K.   *One upset her.*

F.   *Do you know about this?*

A-K.   *No ... but when you're telling me ... I say the same thing, when I was very young I can say about abortion – it was lie.*

F.   *It's easy to find out.*

A-K.   *There must be some papers in the hospital.*

F.   *I tell you another reason I do believe, because she told me she went to hospital the second time and the nurses treated her ... the nurses were very angry with Heidi for coming in again.*

A-K.   *It was the same nurse?*

F.   *It was the same hospital ... and they would know about the previous abortion ... so she said, "The nurses were very angry with me" ... oh coming in again pregnant wanting a second abortion. She said her stepmother called her "a whore" ... so that's why I believe it ... I assumed that because Heidi wrote and told me, she is telling the truth ... do you not believe her?*

A-K.   *No ... I tell you that because I only know myself and there was something maybe me and Heidi could have ... so ... yes ... we have the same things ...*

F.   *Did you tell people that you would have abortions yourself when you didn't?*

A-K.   *Yes, I do when I was 14 or 15 maybe.*

F.   *Oh you did. But you didn't have abortions?*

A-K.   *No, no, no, no. I was not pregnant – nothing.*

F.   *But why did you tell them this?*

A-K.   *Only ... I think I was together with a boy ... I must be 16 ... 17 because I have a boyfriend one year ... after one year I should still be going to school in another town and I come into the school and all the things were OK and he asked me: "Oh no, drop the school and come and live here in Bergen. So we can, er ... being ... seeing each other every day" and I was in love OK and I dropped this school ... I don't go this second year ... I have take one year ... and come back to him and after one week the school starts he dropped me ... it was finished and I was so angry because one year of my school ... I can't go back to this school because I have left ... so I must only find me a little work or something ... I was so angry because he only was ... finished.*

F.   *You wanted to get revenge or something?*

A-K.   *What?*

F.   *You wanted to get revenge?*

A-K.   *Yes, yes. I call people so he know, my friends how I do that, so everyone should believe it ... I should go to take this abortion, I go to take the bus up to the hospital and sit there for many hours only for fun and I take the bus away so if somebody has seen me or something ... I was*

277

very desperate that time and do much other things later ... now I grew up and OK. I can laugh and think now but ... that is the only thing, maybe she is lying, maybe because I know myself could do it.

On 22ⁿᵈ April 1998, I spoke to Torill Sorte of the Mjøndalen police again:

F.   *Now you've told me that in 1985 after Christmas, that she's telling you that she had a boyfriend, yeah?*

TS.   *That she has a boyfriend? Oh, yes when you come and visit her?*

F.   *Yeah.*

TS.   *Yes, she has a boyfriend.   She was together with the father of her son wasn't she?*

F.   *Yeah – was this after my first visit or before my second visit or in between, do you know roughly?*

TS.   *I seem to remember that she said she had a boyfriend when you went to visit her the second time [April 1985].*

F.   *The second time, yeah. Was this the only boyfriend she had?*

TS.   *At that moment? Yeah, I think so.*

F.   *Yeah. So she didn't tell you that she was also have sexual relations with another man?*

TS.   *No.*

F.   *No. Well, she was having sexual relations with a chap I knew, called Bjorn-Morten and he also thought he was the father of Daniel, you see. So it's not really honest of Heidi to say that she had a boyfriend, because she was sleeping with two men at the same time.*

TS.   *Maybe she have two boyfriends.*

F.   *Yeah that's right and she also – I visited her – [1984] and then she had another boy visit her from England who used to be her boyfriend in England, so it's ...*

TS.   *You say that but she don't say that.*

F.   *Yes, well I know both these men and Heidi knows she visited him [i.e. the boyfriend she used to have here in St. Albans] after I visited her for the second time. I mean he saw her parents. Her parents saw him. I mean there's no dispute about that. She knows who he is - an Italian boy. She may not have told you this but there were actually four of us who were seeing her in this time after Christmas and up to Easter 1985. So she was sleeping with two of them and I visited her and then another chap so, you know, she liked lots of men so it's not really fair to say that she had a boyfriend because she said the only thing that she had in common with Gudmund Johannessen was "good sex" and you know with her personality and background it's not really love. I don't think you can call it love because ... you don't have two boyfriends on the go at the same time. Because this other chap, Bjorn-Morten, was a good-looking chap and I knew she liked him because when I visited her at Christmas she told me she liked him and she wanted to be friends with him and they met and I met him – you know – he's a nice chap. He's now got – he had quadruplets. His wife*

278

gave birth to four at once – anyway Heidi obviously didn't tell you about Bjorn-Morten did she? Huh?

TS.   *No, I can't remember.*

F.   *No that's right. Well that's something obviously that's a little bit sneaky of Heidi because – I'm trying to prove that she is a bit of a slut.*

TS.   *But you don't have anything to do with that.*

F.   *No, I don't but my point is that she's hiding things from you and you know everybody says that [I] can't be telling the truth about these things – it's too much.*

TS.   *Yes, but you know if a case come to the Court in Norway, it's the way that things Heidi have done in her early life – the Court don't have anything to do with. The only thing they have to care about is the things happening between you and her. So other things are her things and the Court and people in Norway don't have anything to do with that.*

F.   *Yeah, but my point is that she's a liar and she hides things.*

TS.   *But you can't prove it by trying to tell that she's a hooker and ...*

F.   *Well she's not paid but she likes sleeping with a lot of men.*

TS.   *Maybe that's right, that she have three or four boyfriends at the same time, but I don't have anything to do with that.*

F.   *But the point is you see I am trying to tell people her past and I have not lied about it and ... my case is that she told the whole country about me.*

TS.   *Yes, that's her right.*

F.   *Doesn't matter! She still told lies about me and one or two people did know it was me, the people I knew in Norway.*

TS.   *They know about the case before it goes in the newspaper didn't they?*

F.   *Well they didn't know obviously there were allegations I'd threatened to kill her son and neighbours and that I've written 400 obscene letters ... and they were quite shocked and I'm sure one or two of them maybe believed it and it's a hard job for me to disprove it. I've been told by one or two Norwegians that are very sympathetic to me that the story wouldn't have been printed if I was not a Muslim.*

TS.   *No, that's not true.*

F.   *Oh I think it certainly is.*

TS.   *I don't think so ...*

F.   *One or two Norwegians tell me that people are brought up in Norway from a young age to think that Muslims are basically 'heathen' – that they are really awful rubbish because they are not Christian. Even one of the first letters Heidi sent me in the early 80's was to say basically what a load of rubbish Muslims were. She told me how angry she thought her parents would be if they thought she was marrying a Muslim man and also for her husband to tell me: "Allah doesn't exist, come to Jesus" – all these things, it's so obvious that Muslims are not liked in Norway.*

279

TS.   *They are. Some people don't like Muslims but some people don't like Catholics or ...*

F.   *Yeah, but the thing is these people are telling me voluntarily that the story wouldn't have been published if "you weren't Muslim ... ..."*

TS.   *I don't think you shall think about that because I don't think it's right. I think that the newspapers have written about this because they have found the things* [that have been] *said to them interesting not because you are a Muslim.*

F.   *Yeah but they also said to me that this little sheet in Norwegian that I've sent to everybody, they said they didn't believe it – it was crap.*

TS.   *No, they don't believe it. People call me and say what this – what crap this is.*

F.   *That's right exactly. Has she admitted for instance that she's had two abortions?*

TS.   *No, but I haven't anything to do with that.*

F.   *No, but you see ... ...*

TS.   *I can't ask her about that – those things I don't want to know.*

F.   *The newspapers have said it was this one sheet that they have said is crap. Now what exactly is crap about it? What's wrong about it? What is a lie about it?*

TS.   *What's wrong is that you are writing things about that. Maybe some of the things is true, maybe something is lie, I don't know. The point is that you have writing letters with her picture and her name and you send it to people around Norway.* [Heidi's photo was transposed from the newspaper on to my fact sheet and then distributed all over Norway.]

F.   *No, no, no – that was after the newspapers printed the story.*

TS.   *No, no – it was then the case came into the police, not before.*

F.   *So what am I supposed to do when she say's I've threatened to kill her son?*

TS.   *You should have gone to the police and give the police a case and send it to Norway.*

F.   *I did, I did many times.*

TS.   *What happened with that?*

F.   *Absolutely nothing. I sent everything to the Norwegian Embassy here in London at the time... ... and Iver Stensrud – one of the attachés ... and I have a letter from him on my file and he said all he could do is send everything on to Krogvold in Bergen. I have sent everything to Bergen.*

TS.   *I have never seen that.*

F.   *No, no in Bergen, I sent ...*

TS.   *But I have never seen them – never. I haven't heard about the Embassy taking a contact with me and all that.*

F.   *Not with you, but with ...* [Krogvold in Bergen].

TS.   *Was that before I got the case?*

F.	*I spoke to the Embassy here in London and they sent the papers to Bergen, not to you.*

TS.	*I see, but have you talk to the Embassy after that?*

F.	*Yes I did and eventually they said there was nothing [they] could do here – they've given everything to Krogvold – so I phoned up Krogvold and he said he's not going to do anything. So obviously when I see such injustice, then I began my campaign. But I told the newspapers – I sent my whole case to them and I expected an apology – I expected some understanding and I expected my side of the story to be printed. And I told them, OK, if you don't - you've got her letters [to me.] You've got [the story of] her past. I'm willing to discuss it. They discussed nothing. They were slimy little rats. So I said fair enough, if that's the way you wanna play. If you wanna play dirty with me then you see what happens. And I only sent the stuff afterwards, OK. So I've done my best to bring a Court case and don't forget I was using Helge Wesenberg in Norway at the time as the only reason I found out about these newspaper stories is because he sent me the [one] article which I had to pay for to get translated – I had to wait a long time before I got all three newspaper articles translated. And I had to pay for them.*

TS.	*Me and you can talk all the day I think.*

F.	*The point is what is Heidi saying I've lied about?*

TS.	*Yes but as I told you what's lies and what's not lies and what you have said and what she has said is er ...*

F.	*It's not the point?* [I suggested.]

TS.	*Yes, it is the point, but it is there and you and I have talked about these things many times but as I told you if you want to do something, I hope your lawyer will contact me and I'll talk to him and we can see the case together and see what we can do.*

F.	*The thing is, you see, I feel you are going to try to put him off, aren't you?*

TS.	*No, I will talk to him and I will listen to him and I hope he will listen to me when I tell him what I have done and where the case is and what's been done in the case and what the State lawyer is saying about it and I hope he can understand something of it. If he find things is wrong, that I have done something wrong, or the State police have done something wrong, I hope that I will do something with it.*

F.	*Don't try and tell me that the newspapers are blameless. They're the ones who are at fault. Because if someone is accused of threatening to kill three sets of people – you know, a little boy - I'm not going to stand this. Also the rape. Something funny's going on. If Wesenberg tells me in 1995 "attempted rape" and it turns out to be rape, then I'm not having it. And I need to know which police station Heidi complained about the rape [or attempted rape allegation concerning] the Bergen shopkeeper. I need to know which police station to get in touch with then because I need to support my evidence.*

TS.	*But as I told you, I will give everything to your lawyer and he will look at the case and I'm sure he will give me his thoughts about it ...*

F.	*You've said you've done your very best to find out about this so-called letter that I've written threatening to kill that little boy. Now why can't you get the Bergen police to get in touch with the parents of Johannessen?* [Who Heidi says were sent 'the letter.']

TS.	*The Bergen police said that they get the letters.*

F.	*"The letters" – many letters?*

281

TS.   *I don't remember how many, but it was more than one.   And they said they don't know where they are now.   So I don't know what shall I do with this – they're gone.*

F.   *The thing is this, when I was arrested in 1990, they had several letters in the police station.*

TS.   *But they don't have any anymore.*

F.   *Well they were copies so Heidi must have the originals.*

TS.   *She don't have the originals.   She have looked to her things and she can't find any. She throw it away when she have talked to the police because she think that: "Oh, I don't need them any more."*

F.   *When I was with the police in 1990, no letters came up threatening to kill her son ... the police in 1990 had several of those letters but they did not ever tell me and they never mentioned once, anything about threatening to kill her son.   Now this is a serious allegation and I'm sure that they knew about it at the time [i.e. one way or the other.]   Now Krogvold, who is in charge of the case, he must remember if a letter came in saying I've threatened to kill that son – now I never wrote any letter and I'm gonna go all the way on this ... I won't have the public thinking that a 'Muslim man' threatens to kill little boys.*

If Heidi says Gudmund Johannessen's parents had this letter, then the proper thing to do is to get back in touch with them. OK? Isn't that right?

TS.   *Yes, but I don't still have the letters.   The letters is gone.*

F.   *No, no, no.   They will remember – if Gudmund Johannessen's parents had the letter, then they will remember if they saw the words threatening to kill that little boy, won't they?*

TS.   *Yes, I thought you were talking to the police in Bergen about that, because...*

F.   *I've written, I've kept a copy of the letter.   I've sent them everything.   I've spoken to a very nice chap – another policeman, a chap called Henrik Dugstad ......*

TS.   *If you come to Norway now, you will be arrested.   But if we can come to an arrangement with your lawyer, then maybe you can come to Norway.*

F.   *I think within two weeks he'll have spoken to you ... but to be honest I'm still campaigning against Heidi ...*

TS.   *Yes I know that.*

F.   *You still getting calls today are you?*

TS.   *Yes.*

F.   *Yeah, that's right – good.   You see I want to make Norway in general [aware] – I want to raise the profile ... you will have to make Norwegians aware ... that a lot of Norwegian men do not treat their women well and that is obvious by this case between me and Heidi......   Also I'm very much against abortion.   I like to publicise this.   And the fact that many – so much cheating goes on that I think maybe half of Norway is on second marriages.   The kids don't know who their fathers are or they take a long time to discover who their fathers are and I'm making a social statement as well, you see.*

TS.	*Yes, but talk to your lawyer and we'll see what we can do.*

F.	*Well OK. I'm prepared to come to an arrangement so long as I have my day in Court ... but I'm also worried that I'm not going to get a fair trial.*

TS.	*Be sure we are doing that.*

F.	*Because I know how the [Bergen] police treated me when I got back here to England [in February 1990].*

TS.	*You have to believe the Court system – that it's fair.*

F.	*The police certainly weren't ...*

TS.	*No, maybe they don't.*

F.	*I'm afraid ... and I've been told that Norwegians stick together against the foreigner.*

TS.	*I don't think so.*

F.	*No? Or families stick together anyway.*

TS.	*Well blood is thicker than water isn't it?*

F.	*Yeah, that's absolutely true. Quite right there. Well anyway, you must remember one or two things. What am I supposed to have lied about?*

TS.	*I don't want to talk about that now. You can talk to your lawyer.*

F.	*You see if you don't want to tell me, will you tell* ['my lawyer' I was about to add]...

TS.	*I have told you many times – what she* [Heidi] *has said. What she don't have said, what she has lied about.*

F.	*Is she saying that her boyfriend didn't take heroin? Is she saying that she had no abortions?*

TS.	*As I told you before, things Heidi have done in her life is not my thing. My thing about the case is between you and her ... and all the other things I don't have anything to do with it.*

F.	*I read in the newspapers that Runar Schøne, her husband, said that these reports* [my fact sheets] *were "completely false," you see. So basically Heidi's private life is part of this case because what I'm saying is that it's not "completely false," it's completely true, so these things have to be of concern to you. They are central to the case. When we have a Court case, the lawyers in the Court always try and talk about the past – the sexual past, the lies and everything about the defendant.*

TS.	*OK, but I will talk to your lawyer. I will explain to him what we are talking about and I feel that that's the right way to do things, so if you can get him to call me. OK?*

F.	*OK Torill, thanks a lot, Bye bye.*

TS.	*Bye.*

On 27th April 1998, I wrote to Karsten Gjone enclosing a copy of that day's Sun newspaper:

Dear Mr. Gjone,

Heidi Schøne

I enclose a copy of an article in today's Sun newspaper, Britain's biggest selling tabloid daily. It worries me that even now my own story could get into the British newspapers. It could have and it still can. That is why the journalists and editors of V.G., Bergens and Drammens Tidende must be part of my prosecution case.

Torill Sorte has told me that the police might do "a deal" whereby I can sue Heidi if I stop publicising my case. It seems I am beginning to get through to the authorities that I will not be abused, without a right of reply. But if the police wanted to extradite me [previously], then I will need guarantees from them that I will not be arrested in Norway. I don't want any tricks.

I believe there is a cover up with the Bergen police and the newspapers. I also think that Helge Wesenberg is part of the cover up and has a lot to answer for. Certainly the PFU are playing games. I waited until the police investigation was over before complaining to the PFU only to discover I was "out of time" and further they would not afterwards exercise their discretion in my favour to make an exception to my complaint.

Cheers for now

Yours sincerely,

Frederick Delaware

P.S. I spoke last week to Christian Overaa, Heidi's half brother. He was OK, and he told me that his father had a serious heart condition, so I promised to leave his father, Severrin and his mother alone and would not make enquires of them over Heidi. Christian told me that the first his mother knew of the press story was when she saw the papers on the news stand. I feel Heidi's parents and brothers understand that Heidi is prone to making up stories and Christian accepts that I have to 'go all the way' to clear my name.

I reproduce The Sun article in full below. Although the subject of the story, an Englishman called David Coombs, gladly co-operated with The Sun, this alternative sex-scandal is instructive in certain aspects. The Norwegian newspaper Verdens Gang earlier did a big story on him as well and identified him by name and by photo; although again it is obvious he freely consented to the whole project.

The Sun [banner headline] of Monday 27th April 1998

I'VE BEDDED 227 GIRLS

Brit conman seduces lonely Norway lasses

Exclusive

From Kathryn Lister in Bergen

A CASANOVA conman told yesterday how he has bedded 227 girls – and tricked them out of a fortune.

Boastful David Coombs, 34, had sex with a host of lonely beauties in Norway before fleeing them of £100,000 worth of cash and jewellery.

Now police in the Scandinavian country have put out a nationwide alert to women about the penniless painter and decorator from

Southampton. They have plastered his photo across Norway's top newspaper under the headline: 'Impossible to get rid of.' One duped victim also put up wanted posters.

Coombs has been kicked out of Norway four times as cops had 63 complaints from tricked lovers. But he sneaks back. He is also wanted in Finland.

Coombs woos targets by pretending to be a dashing pilot, then cons them into funding his high life.

The Sun tracked him down to Rick's Café in Bergen, Norway.

The conman said:

"Norwegian women are easy and with charm and good sex they open their handbags. I know I'm a bad boy but I love women and they love me."

Coombs, who holds on to conquest's business cards so he can keep a tally, breaks no laws with his cheating.

But one victim, Kari Masterson, 29, warned: "If you meet him, run home, lock the door and phone the police."

NORWAY TO TREAT A LADY

Girls here are stupid so it's easy to bonk em... then con them...

Rat David Coombs

By Kathryn Lister in Bergen, Norway

Cocky conman David Coombs claims Norwegian girls are easy to dupe because they are bimbos.

He told The Sun: "They are fairly stupid – and the police here aren't too bright either."

"That's why I've managed to get away with it for so long."

Cheat Coombs, 34, also believes the girls are "easy prey" for sex because Norwegian fellas are hopeless lovers.

And he boasted: "I've never had a single complaint about my performance between the sheets. I'm very well endowed, keep myself in good shape and never suffer from brewer's droop."

Coombs – who has loved and left 227 Norwegian women, including a string of blonde beauties – added: "I know I'm a bit of a cad but I adore sex and women and have an in-built desire to flirt with them."

"The most I've slept with in one night is three, one after the other. And I've also had a threesome with two sisters."

His oldest victim was a 51 year-old hairdresser and his youngest a student aged 18 whom he swindled out of her grant.

Coombs, a former painter and decorator from Southampton, is not ashamed to talk about his "favourite" cons.

And he is well aware Norwegian authorities cannot throw him in jail because he never actually breaks the Scandinavian country's deception laws. He said: "Over here it's not illegal to borrow money and possessions if you give a person a guarantee that you will pay them back."

"I give them the guarantee – but I never pay them back."

CHEAT HAS EVEN CONNED PARENTS

Police in his main hunting ground of Bergen have managed to expel him from Norway four times. But Coombs, who has even swindled his mum and dad back in Britain, always manages to slip back.

He bragged: "When I was booted out for the third time in 1993, two officers accompanied me to London on the plane to make sure I got there."

"I jumped off, bought a ticket on a return flight and was back in Bergen before they were."

He added: "Since my last expulsion in 1995 they have relaxed the immigration laws, which has made it easier for me to keep coming back."

285

The conman first went to Norway nine years ago. He met a Norwegian girl in Britain and flew to Scandinavia to marry her, but dumped her eight days before the wedding.

He set up with another blonde but walked out on her when she was six months pregnant with their son. He has only seen the lad, now eight, twice. And he does not pay any maintenance. These days, the oily-haired creep seeks most of his targets in Bergen's cafés and bars.

Revealing his technique for snaring another sucker, he said:

"Usually I start by going into a bar and looking around for an attractive woman to make eye contact with. If I'm in a hotel I buy them a drink but I always put it on their room bill when they're not looking.

I prefer smartly-dressed slim blondes aged between 20 and 38. I can't stand ugly, overweight women in tight-fitting clothes."

After an initial bit of flirting with my eyes, I walk over and bowl them over with one of my famous chat up lines.

The ones that work the best are either 'You have a beautiful smile and should use it more often' or 'Hi. I'm not chatting you up but I'd love to sit and talk to you.'

"I usually score the first night and if it doesn't happen after two dates then I move on to the next woman. I'm not waiting around for weeks just to s**** a woman."

He added: "If I met the right girl I'd like to settle down and start a family but for the moment I'm having too much fun. I'd like to see my son but I'm denied access to him because his mother hates my guts."

Without batting an eyelid, Coombs moved on to describe how he fleeces his victims.

He said: "My favourite con is getting a woman to agree to a date but then convincing her I've left my suit somewhere."

"It never ceases to amaze me how many hand over their money or credit cards so I can buy some new clothes."

'COPS ARE FED UP TO BACK TEETH'

"I always shop at Armani or Hugo Boss. I've had a whole new wardrobe out of them."

"The police are fed up to the back teeth with me but I'm too sharp for them. I always stay one step ahead of everyone."

He said he totted up his tally of conquests while "languishing in a police cell one night."

And he added: "I have a fantastic memory and keep the business cards of most with marks out of ten for their performance written on the back."

Coombs heartbroken victims queued up to condemn him last night. His most recent, Borghild Oksland, 34, wept as she said:

"He was very charming and told me he worked as a helicopter pilot and had gone to a public school in England.

He said his parents were extremely wealthy and he had several well-known showbiz friends.

I met him at a friend's party and he swept me off my feet.

He went to get some money out of a cash machine but told me he had punched in the wrong numbers and his card had been swallowed. He was very convincing and clung to me like a leech.

The next day he persuaded me to lend him my Escort car. He called several times to say he was returning it, but never showed up."

Beautiful Borghild added: "I realised my terrible mistake and stuck 'Wanted' posters with his photo on lampposts around town." Coombs was arrested in the sporty white Escort, worth £13,000 last Thursday.

But he was released hours later after telling the police he had merely borrowed it. And Borghild got the car back.

Conned computer consultant, Kari Masterson, 29, said: "I lent him money which he promised to pay back. But his promises are empty, like his affections."

"I want to warn other women to keep well away from him."

Bergen's police chief Jan Johnsen branded Coombs a "menace to women." He said: "He has broken the hearts of women all over Norway and has more chat-up lines than there are cases against him."

"Usually he tells them he is a helicopter pilot and he flits like a fly from one to another."

"He always promises the women he will pay them or return whatever he has borrowed, but it never happens."

"I currently have 63 complaints about him on file but the true figure must be at least double that. Most women are too embarrassed or ashamed to come forward or leave police their name."

The police chief added: "We just want to kick him out of the country and keep him out."

Back in Britain, Coombs's parents learned not to trust him after he took them for several rides. He owes them around £1,000 in loans and unpaid bills.

Coombs once sold his dad Barry's car to another man while he was out. Barry, 63, a retired boat skipper of Hythe, Hants, said: "I had to go and get it back from the bloke."

He added: "David is a smooth talker who could sell anything to anybody. But I would never leave him alone in my house – I don't trust him enough. When he lived with me he tapped into my bank account to get money."

Coombs's mum Barbara, who split up with Barry 16 years ago, said: "David would spend a night in a hotel when he was in England and in the morning just walk out without paying."

"Then, because he'd left my address with them, they'd ask me to pay the bill. Other times he would run up a taxi fare to around £80 and then get out without paying. The drivers always turned up at our door."

"He once took back a pair of shoes I'd bought him as a present and exchanged them for a more expensive pair – using my money of course."

Coombs's older brother Michael, 37 – a dad of three who has been happily married for 16 years – refuses to speak to him.

Barbara, 62, who also lives in Hythe, said Coombs calls her up to eight times a day and always has a dramatic story to tell.

But she added: "He believes all his lies – he lives the part. I'm afraid he has been nasty and not a very good son. Wherever he goes he causes havoc. I do get a bit cross with him."

***

On 4th May, I wrote to Karsten Gjone and Helge Wesenberg:

Dear Mr. Gjone,

Heidi Schøne

Further to our useful telephone conversation this afternoon, I enclose a copy of a letter written to Helge Wesenberg today. Please talk to him on these points. I have been so angry with him for his conduct. I feel it is high time I wrote again to him.

I look forward to hearing from you with your letter.

Yours sincerely,

Frederick Delaware

287

Dear Mr. Wesenberg,

Heidi Schøne

I refer to our correspondence in 1995. I have instructed Karsten Gjone to bring proceedings in Drammen against Heidi Schøne (formerly Overaa).

However, I will also be insisting that you yourself be subpoenaed to attending at the trial for your role in the matter.

I refer to your letter of February 28th 1995 and the third paragraph where you mention "attempted rape" being alleged by Heidi Schøne, with no details. Earlier this year Heidi Schøne had told Torill Sorte – policewoman in Nedre Eiker, Mjøndalen, that I raped her. Not "attempted rape" as reported by you, but actual rape, by holding her down. Your explanation please!

Torill Sorte has made extensive investigations of the Bergen police to discover that they have lost or disposed of the letters of mine written to Heidi in the 1980's. Letters which you tell me were on file in 1995. Heidi has alleged I have made threats by letter to kill her son, Daniel, when he was 2 years old. That I made threats to kill her neighbours and friends. All written in the newspapers in 1995. Why did you not report on the fact that you saw no evidence at the police station for written threats to kill a two year old child?

And you wonder why I campaign against Heidi?

Did you believe the newspapers? Why did you lie to me in your letter of June 9th 1995 – saying you were too busy to help me when the real reason was stated in your letter of July 17th 1995 – that you didn't like the fact that I questioned your judgement.

I wrote a full and very sad letter to you post dated 9th January 1995. It would be obvious to anyone that the newspaper allegations were all lies – especially as you had letters Heidi wrote to me, and knew that she had been a psychiatric patient. I believe you have been negligent in your investigation and attitude and I will, through either Karsten Gjone or a British lawyer be pressing you for a FULL explanation. I note that you gave neither Michael Bell, my lawyer in 1995, nor Karsten Gjone, any explanation as to your conduct.

I have personally launched a 3 year long investigation of the Bergen police, Mjøndalen police, PFU, Editors and journalists of the three newspapers, Nils Rettersdøl the psychiatrist, and others into this case and I believe I have enough evidence to bring Heidi Schøne to court. But you yourself, as I have said, will have to be subpoenaed to Court because what you have done was unforgivable. You were supposed to be acting for me, not Heidi!

At the end of the day your decision to drop me has cost me very dearly indeed because I lost faith in Norwegian lawyers. I have since embarked on a nationwide information campaign against Heidi as you probably know, and thankfully many, many hundreds if not thousands of people know the truth of the matter.

Yours sincerely,

Frederick Delaware

Copy to: Karsten Gjone, Drammen

Once in a blue moon you come across someone who understands everything you are trying to say and who, moreover, sympathises with you. One such chap was Arne, a Norwegian who was living and working in London in January 1998. He was kind enough to make himself available to translate the article from Bergens Tidende into English so that for the first time I could actually write down the translation word for word. We sat down at a table in his residence at the Norwegian YWCA in Holland Park, and I wrote down his translation. After we'd finished, it turned out that poor Arne had been shit upon by his own 'dear' wife. Arne had been married for a little while and he and his wife had a daughter. But one day, after five years away in Japan, the best man at Arne's wedding turns up, with no place to go. Feeling sorry for him, Arne allows his old friend to stay with him and his wife until he can find suitable alternative accommodation. The arrangement came unstuck when Arne's best man started screwing Arne's wife. Well, the marriage collapsed and Arne had to put up with the additional false claim from his wife that he'd brought girls into the sitting room to have sex with him whilst she was upstairs asleep.

Arne had got divorced and from his experience he told me how he could sympathise with me, a fellow victim of false accusations. We said goodbye and I left Arne thinking I'd never see him again as he was going back to Norway in February.

A few months later, I think in May, I returned to the Norwegian YWCA and asked for Arne's phone number in Norway as I wanted just to say thanks once again for his efforts that night translating the article, but more particularly to ask him another favour. So I got in touch with Arne and he was all in favour of helping me out. So what he did was this; he phoned up Heidi's neighbour in the apartment below, telling them he'd received this report in his mail entitled 'Heidi Overaa' with their (the neighbours') phone number on it, which report said: "Ring this number for further information." Well, the ruse had worked and at Arne's request the neighbour dutifully went to get Heidi's husband, Runar Schøne. Arne explained that loads of people down his street had got the report and asked Runar Schøne what it all meant. Runar gave his wife's version of events and added that if she knew that these reports were still being sent to everyone, Heidi would go crazy. It was good news to hear all this from Arne but even better news was to come. Without my asking for it, Arne had, via a friend of his, obtained Heidi's telephone number, which was unlisted. I will not divulge how the number was obtained or who got it for Arne, but it was one of the sweetest acts of friendship anyone could do for me. Obtaining that number was a very risky thing to do, but in doing it unsolicited it just goes to show someone in Norway believed in me, and really wanted to help me.

So on the 3rd July 1998, I telephoned Heidi Schøne:

HS.   *Hello Ann.* [It certainly sounded like 'Ann' to me but it was Heidi's voice.]

F.   *Yes hello Heidi, it's Frederick here.*

HS.   *Huh.*

F.   *Hi ... still there?* [She'd put the phone down.]

            I rang again ...

HS.   *Hello.*

F.   *Yeah, hi.*

HS.   *I'm not interested in talking to you Frederick.*

F.   *Well, we've got a Court case coming up.* [i.e. my intended prosecution of her.]

HS.   *I'm not,* [going to court] *so don't call back here.* [In other words she was no longer asking the police to prosecute me.]

            She put the phone down. I rang again. The phone was picked up and put down immediately. I rang again and the phone rang for quite some time, then....

289

HS.   *Hello*

F.   *Yes, hi there.*

HS.   *Get lost, Frederick.*

Down goes the phone. I rang again …

Answer   *Hello.*

F.   *Yeah, got something to hide then have you?*

Answer   *Huh?*

F.   *Got something to hide have you?*

Answer   *No.*

F.   *So why don't you talk?*

Answer   *No.*

F.   *You're not Heidi are you?* [I suspected Heidi had got her neighbour down to answer the phone which was quickly put down on me.]

I rang again … It wasn't answered so I gave up finally.

On 3rd July 1998 I also phoned the Deputy Chief of Police in Drammen, Dag Lyngås:

DL.   *Lyngås.*

F.   *Yes, hi there Mr. Lyngås. It's Frederick Delaware here from London, regarding Heidi Schøne. My lawyer has been in touch with you, I understand.*

DL.   *Yes.*

F.   *Well he tells me that you're gonna put me on a plane straight back home* [the moment I land in Norway.]

DL.   *Yes, that is correct.*

F.   *So how am I supposed to attend Court to sue Heidi?*

DL.   *That's your problem.*

F.   *Well, I know it's my problem but what do you propose to do to help me get some justice? So that I can finally question Heidi. Are you attempting to pervert the course of justice?*

DL.   [Ignoring my last question, he replied] – *Yes, but I think you are … have … you should stop writing about Heidi* [i.e. the reports] *… these several …*

F.   *I told you that the newspapers* [must] *first give me compensation and apologise, then I stop. I've told you this long ago.*

DL.   *Yes.*

290

F.   *So they are the ones who must come to some deal.*

DL.   *Yes but I have intended to try to prosecute you in England now, so I going to send the case [to] the authorities, the police in England if you don't stop.*

F.   *Well I won't stop so you can certainly carry on and try but I thought you'd tried before and failed.* [Failed to get the police in England interested which Torill Sorte had months earlier told me, the outcome of which was that the law in England was "different" from that in Norway and the case was "put away."]

DL.   *We have tried before but you don't stop the ... [reports].*

F.   *Yeah, but how are you going to succeed now if you've failed before? Because the principle is still the same. I have the freedom to write my side of the case and tell the people of Norway. Your newspapers have……*

DL.   *Has the freedom to tell the people of Norway as I said before.*

F.   *……I have the same freedom of speech.*

DL.   *That's not correct, so … …*

F.   *Why not?*

DL.   *I think we have to go… …*

F.   *Why's that not correct?*

DL.   *… …to the police in Britain.*

F.   *Well, they're not gonna help you. I can assure you of that. But I've spoken to Heidi this morning. I have her number – 871898 - and she still refuses to talk to me because she's got too much to hide. You see, so I've got her number. You can give her a call on that number. Have you got her number?* [I was egging him on, happy to tell him I'd obtained her unlisted number.]

DL.   *No, I haven't got ...*

F.   *Have you a pen?*

DL.   *No I don't want her number.*

F.   *Oh, you don't want her number, OK. Well I'm just trying to ring her up to ask her about these lies, you see and you yourself are unable to tell me anything about threats to kill her son.* [i.e. a confirmatory letter.] *About the rape. So I am entitled to get answers to these questions and you will not succeed in doing anything about me in England because we have laws here that give us freedom of speech.*

DL.   *Yes.*

F.   *So you're wasting your time, but I hope you try 'cos you'll waste your time and your money and ...*

DL.   *Not my money.*

F.   *Well not your money but the State's money. But the thing is I will carry on no matter what. I've been carrying on for three years already because of what those newspapers have said and what Heidi did before. Now I believe there's a cover up with your police, not just in*

Drammen but mainly in Bergen.

DL.   *Have you spoke to your lawyer?*

F.   *Yes I did. I spoke to him this morning. He's just got back from holiday, so I'll speak to him again on Monday. But I've told him I don't care what it costs. I want that girl in Court. I want to expose her in Court.*

DL.   *OK.*

F.   *If you can ring the newspapers up and you tell them that it's most unfair that they don't print my side of the story. And I've obviously got a case. Er, and you must blame the newspapers and not me. If I had had any doubts, if I was wrong, I'd have stopped long ago. But I know I'm right. I just have to know why a girl goes to the police and says I've raped her. I cannot have things being said to the whole of Norway that I've threatened to kill her son.*

DL.   *You know you have to ask the police in Bergen with the* [rape]. *I can't answer that.*

F.   *Torill Sorte* [who served under Lyngås] *has certainly tried to get some answers from the Bergen police. She has tried. So she tries. Why can't you try? But the thing is this, my lawyer* [Wesenberg from 1995] *who told me this information* [attempted rape] *is also a bit funny. He's covering up something 'cos I've asked him repeatedly to give me the details* [of the attempted rape] *and he refuses. And it costs a lot of money to employ another lawyer. I have employed another lawyer and I've told him four months ago – he's had my stuff for* [four] *months but because he's so busy he hasn't had time* [to investigate] *so in the meantime I do my own stuff. You must put the blame on the newspapers and Heidi, not me. I'm only doing something that any embittered man would do who's suffered terrible injustice.*

DL.   *Well, well. That's your point of view.*

F.   *So what are you going to do to let me sue Heidi 'cos I have to come to Norway to the Court.*

DL.   *If you come to Norway, we are going to put you in jail, you know.*

F.   *So you're not going to put me on the plane, you're going to put me in jail first?*

DL.   *Yes.*

F.   *So why did you say you're going to put me on a plane back home?*

DL.   *I haven't said that.*

F.   *Well my lawyer told me that you would put me on the plane straight away back to England. Is he lying?*

DL.   *Maybe we can do that too.*

F.   *Huh?*

DL.   *Maybe we will do that too, yes.*

F.   *You see, I'm only coming to Norway for one purpose. The Court case. You see...... I'm not interested in going to talk to her on her doorstep.*

DL.   *Your lawyer will help you with the ... ...*

F.   *How can he help me if you are going to arrest me? He won't be able to help me will he?*

DL.   *Well I think that's so.*

F.   *He will be able to help me?*

DL.   *Yes ... Your lawyer Gjone – Karsten Gjone.*

F.   *Yeah ... so how will he be able to help me if you are going to arrest me?   What's the deal? You said* [in a previous conversation I had with him] *that there's gonna be some deal. What am I supposed to do to enable me to prosecute Heidi? And the newspapers of course.*

DL.   *Are you going to prosecute the newspapers?*

F.   *Oh yes definitely.*

DL.   *Oh.*

F.   *Yeah, I'm suing the newspapers and Heidi at the same time. Heidi I'm suing personally for lying and perverting the course of justice and I can prove it in Court. I've got lots of evidence and I'm also suing the newspapers on the same grounds. I've told them already. I've spoken to the newspapers and they're pathetic. They're like little children and I know I'll win. I just have to get to Court.*

DL.   *Well, well. I think I'm gonna send this case as I said to the Norwegian prosecutors and that they gonna send it to England.*

F.   *Who they gonna send it to – the Embassy?*

DL.   *No, the police in England I think.*

F.   *I've been talking to the Norwegian Embassy quite a few times in the past trying to get their help.*

DL.   *They can't help you.*

F.   *No, that's right. They can't help me. You're quite right. And I've written long ago to the Bergen police and obviously to Torill Sorte in 1996 with no ...* [response]

DL.   *You know, no one in Norway will help you with this case.*

F.   *Except my lawyer.*

DL.   *Maybe he will do it, yes.*

F.   *Mmm. Yes 'cos ... ...*

DL.   *Ok I can't talk any longer with you now. You have to do ... what you have to do and I er ...*

F.   *You're certainly not prepared to find out for me these people* [neighbours] *I've threatened to kill or investigate any of the truth. You're not prepared to investigate the truth?*

DL.   *I will not help you with this.*

F.   *Mmm. Yeah OK then.*

DL.   *OK. Bye.*

F.   *Cheers, bye bye.*

Chapter 22

On the 14th July 1998 I was sitting at home in the morning wondering why I still hadn't received my first letter yet from Gjone. So I decided to call him. He said he still hadn't managed to send me a letter but he had in front of him at that very moment a copy of that morning's local newspaper, Drammens Tidende, in which he said I was featured on the front page and again inside. So I asked what it said and instead of telling me even the gist of it, he said he would put a copy of the article in the post to me. I asked him why he hadn't yet written to me and he said he'd now have to wait until I read the article. Great! It meant getting the whole damn thing translated first.

Furious, I phoned Ingunn Røren the Drammens Tidende journalist who wrote the story (14.7.1998):

IR.   *Ya, Ingunn.*

F.   *Yes, hi Ingunn, it's Frederick Delaware here.*

IR.   *Yes, hello.*

F.   *Hi, I see you did a story today.*

IR.   *Yes, I did.*

F.   *Yeah, good, so I'll be getting the newspaper from my lawyer and if you've said anything that's rubbish I shall look forward to seeing you in Court.*

IR.   *That's OK.*

F.   *What have you said then?*

IR.   *Hm?*

F.   *What have you said?*

IR.   *In the story?*

F.   *Mmm.*

IR.   *You have to read it.*

F.   *Look, for fucks sake, I'm phoning you up to ask you what you've said. Are you some kind of idiot? What did you say?*

IR.   *I just printed a story.*

F.   *What the fuck was it? Are you dumb or something? Are you scared? What did you say?*

IR.   *I'm not scared.*

F.   *Yes you are, well say something.*

IR.   *If your lawyers are sending you the newspapers, you can read it yourself.*

F.   *`Yeah, but I have to translate the whole damn thing first, all right. It's a pity I found her* [i.e. Heidi's] *phone number isn't it. I suppose that's why er* [you did a repeat story]*... because none of you will answer the questions but I will see you in Court. And it will continue. You see if you think writing an article is gonna do anything it won't. The hundreds of letters* [reports in Norwegian] *and they're still going through – another 200 arrived this morning ...*

IR.   *200 letters?*

F.   *Yeah, 200, to everyone in Norway – all over with her photo, her past ...* [i.e. my report].

IR.   *Why would you wanna do that?*

F.   *Well why do you want to do your article?*

IR.   *Because you're sending all the letters.*

F.   *And all because you're doing your articles. You said I threatened to kill her son, three years ago. You lying shit! I did not threaten to kill her son and her neighbours. Which neighbours? I haven't attempted to rape her. She's saying I've raped her now. I haven't raped her. So I send the fucking letters.*

IR.   *She said that you **tried** to rape her.*

F.   *No, she didn't. She told the police* [this year in Mjøndalen] *I've raped her, OK, raped her.*

IR.   *She told me you <u>tried</u> to rape her.*

F.   *She told the police ... ...* [this year it was rape, I was about to add.]

IR.   *It was an **attempt** to rape her.*

F.   *She told the police I have raped her ... she's a fucking liar. And if you can't understand - the girl's been in a psychiatric unit, then I feel sorry for you. You need to go in psychiatric unit yourself. You know, you think I'm gonna take all that crap and do nothing about it.*

IR.   *You can do anything you like, yeah.*

F.   *Oh, can I? Well I'll certainly sue you in Court. I'd like to see how you're gonna get out of it. Why not give my lawyer a ring?*

IR.   *Who's your lawyer?*

F.   *His name's Karsten Gjone. You can have his number.*

IR.   *Can you spell it for me – the name?*

F.   *Gjone, G - J - O - N - E. Karsten, and I'll give you his phone number 'cos he's in Drammen. He's had my papers since January.*

IR.   *Yes.*

F.   *(32) and then his number is 837818.*

IR.   837818.

F.   *Yeah, that's right. He's had the papers for months and unfortunately as he's so busy in Court all the time he hasn't had time to do much. 'Cos I sent him the whole file from years and years – everything, with instructions to take you to Court. You personally, your editor and Drammens Tidende and Verdens Gang.*

IR.   *Then I'll see you in Court.*

F.   *Yeah, I will see you in Court. Anyway, your editor, where is he?*

IR.   *My editor – why do you want him?*

F.   *I want to speak to him obviously.*

IR.   *Yeah but he's on vacation.*

F.   *He's what?*

IR.   *He's on vacation.*

F.   *He's on vacation. So who allowed the story to go through?*

IR.   *Hm?*

F.   *Who allowed the story to be printed? You say the responsibility is always with your editor.*

IR.   *Yes.*

F.   *Yeah and who allowed it to go through?*

IR.   *It's another editor.*

F.   *What's his name?*

IR.   *His name is Bjorn.*

F.   *Bjorn?*

IR.   *Dramdal.*

F.   *How do you spell that?*

IR.   *D-R-A-M-D-A-L.*

F.   *Bjorn Dramdal. OK. You photographed Heidi again?*

IR.   *Hm?*

F.   *You photographed Heidi again?*

IR.   *No, it's an old picture.*

F.   *Oh, it's an old picture is it – so you've obviously gone round and interviewed her again have you?*

IR.   *Hm?*

F.   *You've obviously gone round and interviewed her again.*

IR.   *No, I've just been spoken to her husband.*

F.   *Oh her husband.*

IR.   *Yes.*

F.   *And not her. Oh, because the police are keeping quite a lot from her. They're not telling her the whole country [are being sent reports by me on her] – there must be a good few thousand of those letters now over the whole country and the process will continue.*

IR.	*That's up to you.*
F.	*Well it is up to me obviously, but you see you if you write a load of rubbish then obviously I have to 'print' my own 'newspaper.'*
IR.	*You think people want those letters?*
F.	*Well, I think actually quite a few of them, I understand, are quite interested in the other side of the story.*
IR.	*Because most of the people who get those letters they call us and ask us what it is. They want us to have them ...*
F.	*They ask you what it is but you thrust your rubbish in their faces with your newspapers and you present a story of lies.*
IR.	*You have told me you are going to sue me last year or something, so now you have to sue me.*
F.	*Well that's right, but when you phone my lawyer you will know he's had my papers since January and I ...*
IR.	*I'll give him a call.*
F.	*I can't force him to issue proceedings. I keep telling him to get on with it but he's a busy man but you give him a call and you will see because if you think I'm not going to do it then think again, 'cos I certainly will because I know I'll win. So anyway, can you put me through to Bjorn Dramdal please?*
IR.	*I'm sorry I can't do that from this phone. You have to phone to the paper.*
F.	*All right I'll do that then. Bye.*
IR.	*Bye.*

I rang the main switchboard for the paper:

F.	*Yes morning, Bjorn Dramdal please.*
Answer	*Just a moment.*
F.	*Thank you.*

A man answered.

F.	*Yes, morning, Bjorn Dramdal please.*
BD.	*Er, who would you like to talk to?*
F.	*I would say he's one of your editors, Dramdal.*
BD.	*Yes, that's me.*
F.	*Oh, that's you. Yes, hi there. Name's Frederick Delaware. You did a story on me today, with Heidi Schøne.*
BD.	*Ah ha!*

F.   *I was wondering what the reason for that was.*

BD.   *Excuse me?*

F.   *What was the reason for you doing the story?*

BD.   *With?*

F.   *Heidi Schøne.*

BD.   *Because she has this problem you know. Yes, who are you?*

F.   *I'm Frederick Delaware. I'm the chap that you are writing about.*

BD.   *OK.*

F.   *Yeah.*

BD.   *So you are the chap that is sending round the faxes.*

F.   *Oh, faxes, hundreds of letters, yeah ... all over the country. I think another 200 arrived today.*

BD.   *You think so?*

F.   *Well I hope so unless the post office stop them.*

BD.   *OK.*

F.   *Yeah, because I've spoken to your journalist this morning and I've given her the name of my lawyer in Drammen...... he's had my papers for five months with instructions to sue your newspapers. I've got a lot of evidence over three years now and I told him to issue proceedings. So the sooner he does this the better so that the truth can come out. But what have you been saying today?*

BD.   *I think I have to put you over to the Editor in Chief, that's Mr. Aaraas, just a moment please.*

F.   *Well you, oh, OK.* [Passing the buck again!]

A.   *Ya, Aaraas.*

F.   *Yes hello there, good morning, the name's Frederick Delaware. I understand from my lawyer that you've done a story on me today.*

A.   *I have, yes.*

F.   *Heidi Schøne. My lawyer's had my papers for five months now. I asked him five months ago to sue the three newspapers in Norway, but unfortunately he hasn't time, because there's so much to read and he's so busy. But I spoke to him this morning and he told me there's another story and he's going to read through it.* [Gjone hadn't himself had the time he told me to read through it but would put it in the post.] *But the thing is, what have you said today?*

A.   *What we have said today? Well er there's no name in it* [i.e. they hadn't named me.]

F.   *Why's that then?*

A.   *But ...*

F.   *Why's there no name?*

A.   *What?*

F.   *Why have you not mentioned my name?*

A.   *Well why should we but we thought that we communicate through your lawyer. That's the best.*

F.   *Well, yes, you will communicate with my lawyer but I'm asking you a simple question. I haven't got the newspaper in front of me so I can't read it. I'm just asking you simply why did you not name me, because ... ...*

A.   *I, I, I, do not answer any questions at the telephone. We communicate through your lawyers, OK.*

F.   *You see, the thing is we had a very big story here in the English newspaper ''The Sun'' a few weeks ago about an Englishman sleeping with lots of women in Norway. The newspaper in Norway named him and the newspaper in England named him, so why don't you name me? Have you got something to be afraid about?*

A.   *I don't answer any questions. Ask your lawyer to contact us.*

F.   *I have. Can you ring him yourself please if I give you the number?*

A.   *No, no, no. I've no reason to ring him. If he has anything to tell us I think he will write. That's the way we do it, OK.*

F.   *OK. You are aware that another 200 letters arrived all over Norway today? And 1,000 in the last month.*

A.   *OK.*

F.   *I just wanted to tell you that because if you want to write things er like three years ago that I've threatened to kill her son, which is complete rubbish ... and she told the police three months ago that I have raped her; she first of all tells them [in 1986] that it's attempted rape ...*

A.   *Well, I, I ...*

F.   *No, let me finish ...*

A.   *I have no reason to talk to you, so please ...*

F.   *Anyway, what's your – you're the Assistant Editor are you or the Chief Editor?*

A.   *I am, I am ...*

F.   *Well, Assistant or Chief?*

A.   *I'm the Deputy Chief Editor.*

F.   *So Hans Odde is on holiday is he?*

A.   *Yes.*

F.	*Deputy Chief Editor, and what's your name please?*
A.	*Aaraas.*
F.	*How do you spell that?*
A.	*A-A-R-A-A-S.*
F.	*A-A-R-A-A-S?*
A.	*Yes.*
F.	*Well I understand her husband gave the interview but you can tell Heidi that if there's anything in that newspaper, as I think there will be, that is lies and nonsense and it's the same old stuff, then you know the campaign will continue in ways that you won't believe, OK and the basic thing that will go out ... is the one page Norwegian translation of her past. OK?*
A.	*Well ring your lawyer and he have to write to us then OK.*
F.	*OK, right, bye.*

After these heated conversations, I phoned Arne to relate the news of another newspaper exposé and he went out, bought the newspaper and late in the evening called me back and translated the document in its essential aspects for me.

Two days later, I received from my lawyer the offending Drammens Tidende article. On the front page was the single column title, "Pursued by a madman for 16 years." On page five the main article was entitled "Sexually harassed for 16 years." Gjone hadn't even bothered to send a covering letter much less the oft-promised report on my enquiries and his advice. The article is translated here:

Drammens Tidende 14ᵗʰ July 1998

SEXUALLY HARASSED FOR 16 YEARS

For 16 years Heidi Schøne from Solbergelva has been pestered and followed by a mentally ill Englishman. In only the last year the man has sent more than 300 letters to Heidi and made numerous phone calls

The Muslim man has been obsessed by Heidi Schøne (34) since she was 18 years old. His long time pestering of Heidi and her family has been a huge strain. DT-BB first covered this case three years ago. Still, the family is being badgered by the same man.

Want to be left alone

"All we want is to be left alone. This man is very ill and his countless letters and phone calls put an enormous strain on us all," says Heidi's husband Runar Schøne. For years the Schønes have been living with a string of secret phone numbers and addresses, but each time the man manages to find them and the terror continues until they manage to hide themselves away again.

'Reports'

In the course of the 16 years this man has sent out many 'reports' to Heidi's family, friends, neighbours, colleagues and a number of strangers. These reports are grossly defamatory and the information listed has no basis in reality. Once again, many people from Drammen have received 'reports' about Heidi in their mail box. The reports are modelled like answers for questionnaires from Drammens Tidende, VG and Bergens Tidende, but none of the newspapers mentioned have ever asked for such a report.

Extreme evil

"I do not know who Heidi Schøne is and I didn't understand anything when I opened the

301

envelope containing pictures of Heidi Schøne and her husband together with revelations of filth, I have never seen the likes of. It must be awful for the Schøne family to be exposed to something like that. The entire letter reeks of extreme evil," says Per Leiblein from Konnerud who received a letter on Monday.

The harassment has been reported to the police. Nedre Eiker Constabulary has been investigating this case for three years.

No extradition

The problem is that the circumstances this man is being charged for are not enough to have him extradited from England. He has on the other hand been clearly told that he will be arrested if he comes to Norway, says local policewoman Torill Sorte Kjennås at Nedre Eiker Constabulary.

Screening Mail

To protect Heidi and her family, all their mail is screened at the Constabulary. So far this year Sorte Kjennås and her colleagues have dealt with more than 300 letters from the man. The family has got a secret phone number, and Telenor have been notified by the police that the number is confidential and is not to be given out to anyone, no matter what the circumstances. The family's address is secret and is barred from disclosure by the National Registration Office (Folkeregistret).

Threats

"In spite of all this the man has nevertheless managed to trace us down a couple of times, and when he does, the phone terror starts again. The man spends all his time tracking Heidi and passes himself off as different persons in order to get hold of our number," says Runar Schøne. The man has previously threatened neighbours of the family with lethal force to know where they have moved.

Drank tea together

Heidi Schøne met the Muslim man when at the age of 18 she was in England as an au pair. She regarded the man as a friend and drank tea with him on a couple of occasions. They have never had any relationship, but for 16 years the Englishman has been obsessed by the idea of marrying Heidi. For a long period he hired a private investigator to follow Heidi's every move. The harassment increased nine years ago when Heidi got married.

Psychiatrists believe the Englishman suffers from an extreme case of erotic paranoia.

[Under Heidi's photo]:

For years Heidi Schøne and her family have lived with a number of secret phone numbers and secret addresses. But a mentally ill Englishman has time and time again traced their address and is sending harassing letters.

***

I then telephoned Deputy Chief Editor Aaraas of Drammens Tidende:

A.   *Aaraas.*

F.   *Yeah, Hi Mr. Aaraas, it's Mr. Delaware here.*

A.   *Yeah, OK.*

F.   *I got your newspaper this morning.* [i.e. the 14th July edition which my lawyer had posted to me.]

A.   *Yeah.*

F.   *Had it translated and I see you've written that, er, the first thing you've written is "the Muslim man" obviously trying to "get" the Muslims again and secondly you've put I've written 300 letters to Heidi in the last year.*

A.   *OK, I haven't seen the ... today. Just a moment. Well we have nothing in the ... Thursday.*

F.   *No, no, in Tuesday's newspaper.*

302

A.   *Oh Tuesday, I see, ah.*

F.   *I see you've put* [in the sub-title]: *"Heidi was sent 300 letters in the last year."*

A.   *OK.*

F.   *To Heidi yeah? To her address, yeah?*

A.   *OK.*

F.   *That's what it means right.* [Referring to the actual Norwegian words used.]

A.   *Well, I haven't ... just a moment.*

He went to get Tuesday's newspaper.

A.   *Ya.*

F.   *Yeah, page 5, yeah?*

A.   *Yes.*

F.   *You see – "sent Heidi over 300 letters in the last year."*

A.   *Yeah.*

F.   *OK, now what's that mean – 300 letters to her?*

A.   *Yes.*

F.   *To her address?*

A.   *Yes.*

F.   *And have you got them?*

A.   *I think so.*

F.   *I **don't** think so. Because I know how many I've written and you'll have to prove it, which you can't. I've written to her five times.* [My estimate.] *Five times, and the only letters I've been writing to her is telling her that I've got a lawyer. I'll be seeing her in Court, OK. And also another letter telling her that I'd discovered* [a matter relating to] *her first child Daniel, OK. There were two men who thought they were the father of Daniel and one of them was Gudmund Johannessen and the other was Bjorn-Morten. They both thought they were the father* [of Daniel]. *Now I've written maybe five, six letters to her and you will not find 300 letters in the last year – that's 100% certain. As far as telephoning her is concerned, I've phoned her once in the last two and a half years. Once. And you will have no proof to the contrary, all right? So that's a couple of lies I'll be happy to expose in Court because I will go to Court, no matter what. I've got the money and I'll be taking you to Court as well as the other two newspapers. Now you've mentioned a psychiatrist - repeating this trash of "erotic paranoia."*

A.   *Er if you go to Court, I have no reason to talk to you. As I said some days ago, we communicate through the lawyers.*

F.   *No, no, not really, because it's* [the Court case] *a long time off. I'm simply asking you ... you know ... I mean you obviously have got a lot to hide. I have nothing to hide, that's why I'm telephoning you, right. But you seem to have a lot to hide. You wrote the newspapers, man. Now unless you're from a mental hospital, you can explain to me - my simple questions, OK. Now, you've mentioned a psychiatrist at the last paragraph again repeating this trash* [about erotic paranoia] *um, I mean... ...*

A.   *Er, er, as I said ...*

F.   *Don't avoid me.*

A.   *We look forward to er get a letter from your lawyer, but I don't want to communicate...*

F.   *Why's that? Have you got something to hide?*

A.   *I don't answer any questions.*

F.   *Why not?*

A.   *Bye.*

F.   *Yeah, fuck you then.*

I then sent a fax to Karsten Gjone on 16ᵗʰ July 1998:

Dear Mr Gjone,

Heidi Schøne

I received the newspaper article this morning from you, thank you. As I told you yesterday, a Norwegian friend of mine translated the Drammens Tidende article for me over the phone. It is all 100% rubbish and lies. I have written maybe 5 letters or so to Heidi Schøne in the last year, simply pointing out that I will be suing her and informing her of important discoveries I have made about her past. I am fully aware in any case that none of my letters get through to her – so why bother to send 300? Ask to see the "300 letters" sent in the last year; they don't exist.

I phoned Heidi once – about two weeks ago – in the last two and half years. Just to let her know, because you yourself in the near 6 months you have had my papers have not had the time to put her on notice, by letter, of my intention to bring her to justice – that I am still "on her case."

My latest thinking is to sue Heidi personally and subpoena everyone else to her trial. This would presumably save costs were it the case that by the system of Norwegian law I would be liable to pay the newspapers' legal costs were I to sue them instead. I await your advice.

However, there is much you can do without it costing much. The preliminary enquiries of the newspapers, police, Heidi and Mr. Wesenberg especially are questions that must be answered first.

You say Ingunn Røren phoned you and I'm glad she has satisfied herself that I am serious about taking legal action. However, the main thrust of my actions over the last three years has been:

1.   To collect evidence and I have achieved this to my complete satisfaction, and

2.   To publicise my side of the case and to draw to the attention of the Norwegian public the complete deceit and hypocrisy of the newspapers and the girl. This has produced great results – my campaign has worked and I am happy about this.

I will call you on Monday with – yet again – a request that you get in touch with Wesenberg and get some answers to my other questions.

I had expected last Monday your letter that had been promised and I trust you can send me something now.

Yours sincerely,
Frederick Delaware

This time the Press Complaints Commission in Norway (the PFU) would have to deal with my complaint and I wrote to them on 19th July 1998:

Dear Mr. Børringbo,

New complaint relating to article by I. Røren
Drammens Tidende of 14th July 1998

I enclose a photocopy of the offending article hereon. This matter follows on from Case 099/96 and your correspondence to me of 24th June, 2nd July, 14th August and 2nd October 1996.

Fortunately, I am within the three-month time limit for lodging a complaint. The whole of this article, as for those in 1995, is false. There is no evidence to support their claims; in particular, I have not sent 300 letters to Heidi Schøne in the last year. I have sent maybe five or so to tell her of forthcoming Court proceedings against her and also to inform her of further evidence against her and there's nothing wrong in that – besides she isn't even receiving them – the post office intercept them and they go to the police.

Ingunn Røren has repeated the allegations of her 1995 story. I therefore repeat my contentions contained in my letter to you dated 9th June 1996.

I have appointed, in January 1998, a lawyer – Karsten Gjone of Drammen on (32) 837818, to prosecute Heidi Schøne and once that case is over to prosecute the newspapers. I will therefore liaise with him over your conduct in handling my complaint this time round. No reasons were given in your letter to me of 2nd October 1996 for not exercising your organisation's discretion in my favour, so as to make an exemption for me from the time limit. Most surprising when one considers the enormity of the deception and lies by the three newspapers. Indeed, for an obvious fraud by the newspapers, I wonder at the point of the very existence of the PFU.

This time round it'll be interesting to see what happens.

Yours sincerely,

Frederick Delaware

P.S. I enclose, for your information, three fact sheets on this case.

On the 24th July, a ten-page letter that had been dictated in January had only now been typed up by Janet my former secretary who was typing up this book. I updated the letter and sent it off to Gjone. At least he'd have a clearly worded and complete history of the case to date (which only repeated all my earlier correspondence to him). Gjone's English was not good at all – in fact on one or two occasions, once we'd finished having our conversation, instead of saying "goodbye," he said "hello." So at least with a letter from the word-processor, he could not complain that he couldn't read my writing.

On 29th July 1998, Kjell Børringbo of the PFU wrote to me in response to my complaint of 19th July and sent me a copy of a letter in Norwegian that he'd written to my lawyer Gjone. The PFU's letter said:

Mr. Frederick Delaware,

Enclosed you will find a copy of the letter we today have sent your lawyer in Drammen. He will be back from vacation August 10 and we will wait to receive his answer.

Kjell Børringbo

A copy of the letter to Gjone had also been sent to the Editor of Drammens Tidende, Hans Arne Odde.

On 14th August 1998, I wrote once more to Gjone:

Dear Mr. Gjone,

Heidi Schøne

Once again, despite trying several times to speak to you today at your office and on your mobile phone, I have been unable to contact you to properly discuss this case. It is six months now since I first wrote to you and having phoned you, probably fifty times, I have yet to receive a single letter from you. Clearly, I have a right to wonder whether you will have the time to act on this case at all. But I will give you some more time – but there has to be some immediate progress. Just as in the case of the lawyer Wesenberg, I have the money to pay your fees but I will only pay on results. Wesenberg for me is an arsehole – I feel he got pleasure in telling me of the 1995 newspaper reports then telling me to instruct another lawyer. Anyone can see that Heidi is a terrible liar – but not Wesenberg, the papers or it seem the police. There is something 'mental' about the attitude of these people to my case and their attitude as you can see, is being punished by me through my protest of informing the Norwegian public of the truth.

What I would like you to do immediately is:

1.   To personally deliver a letter to Heidi Schøne herself stating that you are acting for me over her false allegations to the press and the police, and that I will be suing her for attempting to pervert the course of justice. I don't care if she is penniless: I must get her into Court and expose her. Now I hope you can see why I wrote to her so many times in the past - everything is being done to prevent me getting any answers or any legal redress. She, Heidi, is a nutter and is running scared. She must be punished.

        If you send a letter to her in the ordinary post, it will not reach her. The police stop all letters going to her from people she does not know.

2.   Commander Krogvold in his 1990 letters to Føyen and Bell and Wesenberg in his 28.2.1995 letter to me, mentioned nothing about alleged threats to kill Heidi's son. Heidi alleges these threats were made in a letter I wrote to Gudmund Johannessen's parents. So what have Krogvold, Wesenberg and Mr. & Mrs. Willy Aksel Johannessen got to say about this letter that cannot be found; not even a copy?

3.   Similarly, why was I not told about the allegation of attempted rape in 1990 when Krogvold wrote to Føyen & Bell? Why is it now actual rape? Where are the details now of the allegation Heidi made to the Bergen police of alleged attempted/rape by a Bergen shopkeeper?

4.   What did your reading of the papers in the Drammen police station reveal? Is there anything you read that I don't know about?

306

5.   Have you satisfied yourself that Drammens Tidende are lying when they say I have written around 300 letters to Heidi in the last year? And what exactly will you tell the PFU?

As you have learnt, there are Norwegians who can quite easily see that Heidi is a lying scumbag and these Norwegians have helped me in spite of certain risks to themselves. I see no reason therefore why you yourself cannot simply just get on with it now and get all the information I require and proceed to find a way of letting me into Norway to prosecute Heidi Schøne.

I will call you next week.

Yours sincerely,
Frederick Delaware

Things with Gjone had by now become a complete joke. I had told him of my friend Arne ringing up and talking to Runar Schøne, but I was careful not to disclose Arne's surname. Gjone had surprisingly wanted to talk to Arne but didn't specify why to me, so I told Arne to ring him from a call box and on no account reveal his surname. It materialised that Arne was asked very little, save, strangely, as to whether it was he that had recommended Gjone to me, which I thought was ridiculous as in fact the private investigator had written to Gjone telling him that he'd recommended Gjone to me. Gjone it seems was very forgetful.

Right up to this point, Gjone had kept on telling me that I could sue Heidi for perverting the course of justice and also sue the newspapers. When in February he'd phoned Wesenberg to enquire of his input into the case, Gjone, in spite of my express request, told me that he did not ask Wesenberg why the latter had refused to answer my further letters in 1995, including Wesenberg's refusal to get the whole story of Heidi's allegation of "attempted rape."

I realised that Gjone was not going to tackle Wesenberg at all. When I wrote to Wesenberg on 4th May 1998, Gjone said I should wait for Wesenberg's reply. I told Gjone that there was no way Wesenberg would ever reply and it was up to him, Gjone, to confront Wesenberg over the phone!

On 21st August, Mrs Berit Peruzzi at the Consular Section of the Norwegian Embassy in London faxed to my office the name of the lawyer in Bergen who handles complaints against other lawyers. On 23rd August I sent him a full complaint against Wesenberg which although out of time (there was apparently a six month time limit which had passed in the Autumn of 1995) there was a discretion to make an exception and besides which I wanted to put on record, the criticisms I had of Wesenberg's conduct. Further, in not answering my letter of 4th May 1998, I felt Wesenberg had something to hide.

On 24th August 1998, I phoned Gjone again. I had been asking him for some time to get a letter to Heidi by taking it round in person. After all, she only lived fifteen minutes away by car. Still he had not gone round. So I asked him again to do this on the 24th August – just to communicate to her my intentions. Gjone then replied: "But don't you want to see her in Court?" He then said that any letter he sends to Heidi will be intercepted by the police. Exasperated, I repeated again that that was the reason he had to give the letter to her himself. He said he'd spoken to Torill Sorte and had asked for Heidi's phone number so that he could talk to her. Torill Sorte had refused to give it to him. "Why?" I asked. Gjone replied that he didn't know. He didn't ask Torill Sorte why. He then said that I would have to lodge a guarantee in Court for Heidi's legal costs if I didn't win my case, a requirement of foreigners suing a Norwegian citizen. He said he'd ring up the Court to find out how much.

So I wrote to Gjone on 24th August 1998:

Dear Mr. Gjone,

Heidi Schøne

I write further to our conversation this morning. Torill Sorte will not give you the phone number of Heidi, which obviously you need in order to talk to Heidi, because then you can pass the number on to me. But I don't want to talk to Heidi really. I want her in Court to face cross-examination as to her lies.

I don't care if you think it will be difficult for me in Court against Heidi. I just want the chance to expose her as a liar. Please just get a letter off to her and deliver it yourself to her in person. Is that too difficult? You told me long ago that it was legally permissible to prosecute Heidi Schøne for her lies. I am sick and tired of the delay in such a simple matter. We can worry about my getting into Norway later. For the moment, just get a letter to Heidi.

Yours sincerely,

Frederick Delaware

On 27th August 1998, I phoned Gjone once again and he told me to my surprise that he had finished reading the police papers and that I could neither sue Heidi Schøne, nor the newspapers because they hadn't named me. I faxed a letter to Gjone repeating my misgivings, again asking him to put his advice in writing. As far as I was concerned, he was wrong on both counts. Heidi was a dreadful liar and I could sue the newspapers as in Norwegian law, even though a plaintiff is not named, it is sufficient grounds to bring a claim if at least one person knows the article is referring to the plaintiff. I had at least three people – Ann-Kristin Horvei, the lawyer Wesenberg and the policeman Henrik Dugstad who between them had recognised me from the newspaper articles in Verdens Gang and Bergens Tidende in 1995.

I began to look for another lawyer. I got back in touch with the private detective who had recommended Gjone to me to ask him to question Gjone as to why he'd not written once to me and to enquire in more detail as to why he thought I couldn't sue Heidi or the newspapers. The private detective came back to me passing on the worn out comments of Gjone as to the newspapers not naming me and little else of substantial explanation. However, the detective told me that he didn't think Gjone was interested in helping me, which is what I thought all along.

On 16th September 1998, I wrote to Kjell Børringbo of the PFU, after our telephone conversation that morning:

Dear Mr. Børringbo,

Heidi Schøne and Drammens Tidende

I write for the record with regard to our telephone conversation this morning:

1.   Since your letter to me of 29.7.1998, you have heard nothing from either my lawyer or the newspapers.

2.   That in any event you refused my request to deal with me directly over the complaint relating to the 14th July 1998 article, saying that you will be doing "nothing … nothing … nothing" to help me as you were "sick" of me and that "this is trash" and you told me last time (i.e. in 1996) you "would be doing nothing." But this is a fresh complaint and I am within the time limit.

It is clear to me that there is something deeply wrong with your character. For such disgusting and untruthful press allegations not to be investigated is a disgrace. Your total inability to explain your reasoning now and in the past for your inaction, indicates to me that your organisation has no integrity. At least I have had the satisfaction in ensuring Heidi Schøne has been severely punished for her filthy allegations. But it's not enough: I must have her in Court to expose her properly. You protect 'your own' at the expense of justice and the truth.

Yours sincerely,

Frederick Delaware

Kjell Børringbo was extremely rude to me. His tone of voice was aggressive and he was completely unco-operative so I just put the phone down on him. In November I got my old friend, the private detective, to give Børringbo a call to ask him why he wasn't investigating my complaint. Børringbo, I was told, had not investigated the allegations made in the press because "they did not name me." In all the letters I had received from the PFU in 1996, and one in 1998, there was never any mention of the papers not naming me as being the reason that prevented the PFU investigating my complaint. I was under the impression the function of any Press Complaints Commission was to investigate the veracity of a press story, irrespective of whether a complainant was named. Surely, wholesale lies and deception by the Norwegian press had to be exposed by their regulating body?

On 22nd September 1998, I faxed Karsten Gjone a short letter:

Dear Mr. Gjone,

Heidi Schøne

Your failure to supply me with any of the details I have asked for in my many letters has forced me to try and find another lawyer. Please forward my file on to him when I give you his address in due course.

However, your complete inability to deal with my questions over almost eight months is totally unacceptable and I'm afraid I will be asking for the Den Norske Advokatforening [the Norwegian Lawyers Complaints Bureau] to investigate fully your involvement in this case.

Yours sincerely,

Frederick Delaware

I was now hunting around by phone for another Norwegian lawyer. I'd sent a full set of papers to Advokat Steiner Sørvik in Oslo. His English was excellent but he wrote back saying he didn't have the time to give me the proper service that my case needs. He was good enough though to talk to me and told me that it was indeed possible for me to sue both Heidi and the newspapers. He also informed me that the psychiatrist, Nils Rettersdøl (who spoke to Verdens Gang on the subject of erotic paranoia) was well known for being interviewed by the newspapers for his psychiatric opinions.

The next lawyer I contacted was, it turned out, Norway's top libel lawyer, Tor Erling Staff. I myself was a Commercial Property lawyer and at my office I looked up Halsburys Laws of England, Volume 28, under the section for Defamatory Statements. In paragraph 39 it states that it is not essential that the plaintiff should be named in the statement: 'Where the words do not expressly refer to the plaintiff they may be held to refer to him if ordinary sensible readers with knowledge of special facts could and did understand them to refer to him.' In other words, presuming the laws in Norway were similar if someone in Norway recognised it was me the newspapers were talking about, I had a prima facie claim for defamation. There were, as I have already mentioned, at least three such people I knew this applied to – Ann-Kristin Horvei (Heidi's former friend), who had told me she'd read the newspaper Verdens Gang adding: "Who else could it be, but you," Helge Wesenberg and Henrik Dugstad.

So I put this point to Tor Staff when I phoned him and he confirmed that the position was indeed similar in Norway. Further, he told me that Heidi Schøne could personally be taken to Court and asked to prove her allegations made via the press. Staff however told me I was out of time to sue the newspapers for libel for the May 1995 articles; there was a three year time limit which had expired at the end of May '98. This meant Karsten Gjone was facing a potential negligence claim and immediately I put his insurance company, Vesta, on notice.

After my conversation with Tor Staff, he asked me to write to him with copies of the newspapers, a résumé of my association with Heidi Schøne and a cheque for £1,000. He replied on 25th September returning all my papers and my cheque saying his son was too busy as he was himself: "I think after having considered it, your case requires too much time and immediate attention."

309

I phoned him up afterwards to ask him if there was anyone else he would recommend to me and he said he never made recommendations, because if things went wrong "all hell breaks loose." He said he would only be blamed for making the "wrong" recommendation. Wise thinking. Staff also said he was put off by my complaints against Wesenberg and Gjone, and I feel this was a major factor in Staff not wanting to act for me. I was told by others in Norway that Staff was a fearless advocate for the little man oppressed by the newspapers. There was no greater challenge for him than my case.

I continued to try and find a competent lawyer to act for me. Next I was recommended Scøth & Co of Oslo, only to find out that their clients included the newspapers Verdens Gang and Bergens Tidende. One of the secretaries there recommended a "first class" libel lawyer called Per Danielsen in Oslo. His involvement is worthy of a chapter in itself.

On 30th September, I lodged a full complaint against Karsten Gjone to the Lawyers Disciplinary Committee in Norway. Gjone had missed the time limit and not written to me in eight months. What else could I do? His secretary pleaded with me not to complain after I patiently explained my predicament to her. She understood but her principal obviously didn't.

Chapter 23

I wrote to Advokat Per Danielsen a brief letter. I then spoke to him over the phone and I told him Tor Erling Staff didn't have the time to act for me and that Gjone didn't do anything in eight months, to which Danielsen replied: "Well perhaps you didn't pay him enough." I replied that I'd given Gjone £100 with my first letter, but he'd turned down my suggestion for another sum on account (presumably on the understanding he'd be paid when he'd finished his investigations). To prove I was not mean, I told Danielsen that Tor Staff had asked me for £1,000 on account. So now in turn Danielsen asked for the same, which I sent him, together with copies of all the newspaper articles and other relevant documents and correspondence, i.e. I sent him all he needed, with my covering letter of 6th October 1998:

Dear Mr. Danielsen,

Heidi Schøne

Further to our telephone conversation this morning, I left a message with Gjone's secretary asking for the file to be sent to you, but I suspect I'll have some problems with him sending it on to you. Tor Erling Staff did today already put in the post to me the papers I sent him. So to save time, I have today photocopied the whole of my file and enclose:

1.   Copies of four newspaper articles from 1995 and 1998.

2.   A summary of events entitled "Heidi Schøne" and "Press Release" which please read through first to get an overview of the case.

3.   Copies of letters I managed to find (thank God!) from 1982-1985 from Heidi Overaa (now Schøne) to me.

4.   All the correspondence in this case from 1990 – 1998.

No matter what, I want this girl and the newspapers in Court. The girl must be shown to be a liar.

The newspapers did not name me but at least two Norwegians knew it was about me and that in law is sufficient to sue the newspapers.

Enclosed is your cheque. I'll be in touch.

Yours sincerely,
Frederick Delaware

I had already explained that morning on the phone to Per Danielsen that I was out of time to sue for the three May 1995 articles but wanted to sue over the 14th July 1998 Drammens Tidende article.

I had phoned Karsten Gjone's secretary with the request that she send my file on to Per Danielsen.

After he'd had all my papers for a week, I phoned Danielsen to see how things were going and he specifically told me to phone him a fortnight hence – 30th October, so I could discuss his review of my papers. On the 30th I phoned but he was too busy to speak to me. He was not too busy on the same day, however, to dictate a letter as follows:

Dear Mr. Delaware,

Heidi Schøne

We have just received a letter from your former lawyer, Mr. Karsten Gjone. Enclosed was a big pile of documents.

In order to get to the bottom of this, I am afraid we will have to ask you for more money up front, before we can get back to you.

We would therefore appreciate if you could pay an additional NOK 10,000 – as soon as possible.

We look forward to hearing from you again.

Sincerely yours,

Per Danielsen
Attorney at law

I wrote back to him on 2nd November by fax:

Dear Mr. Danielsen,

Heidi Schøne

Thank you for your letter of 30th October. I also wrote to you on 30th October so you should receive that letter soon.

Please ignore the file you received from Karsten Gjone. You already have a duplicate set of papers sent with my letter of 6th October. Keep Gjone's file safe. He did not write to me once in eight months and refused my request to send him more money.

In order for you to get to the bottom of this quickly, all that is necessary for you to do is, from my file, read the 9 page typed report: 'Heidi Schøne,' my 10 page fax letter to Gjone dated 24th July 1998 and the typed up: 'Press Release.' Also read Heidi's letters to me, as well as, of course, the newspapers. You will then have an excellent idea of my case. The other letters are incidental.

I have already supplied you with a cheque for £1,000 – which you have cashed. It seems to me that you have not managed to make a start on my papers. I must insist that you now telephone Arild Pedersen, Private Detective and former policeman on (69) 273300. He knows my case and will put you in the picture straight away. This will save you a lot of time and will keep my costs down.

However, I must make it clear to you that, as I have pointed out to you in my letter of 30th October, you must send Heidi Schøne a 'By Hand' (not posted) letter informing her that you have instructions to take civil proceedings against her for lying and trying to pervert the course of justice. Arild Pedersen can take the letter round if a member of your staff cannot. This must be done very soon and is a prerequisite to my instructions. I will telephone your office to enquire as to your availability to discuss this fax.

Yours sincerely,

Frederick Delaware

He wrote back on 5th November saying:

Dear Mr. Delaware,

HEIDI SCHØNE

Referring to your letters dated October 30 and November 2, please let me establish some ground rules:

I am not willing to threaten a person I do not know with a lawsuit without have considered whether you have grounds for doing this or not.

Likewise I cannot start lawsuits against newspapers before having studied your case more carefully.

In order to complete our preliminary work, we must, therefore insist on you paying an additional NOK 10,000, -, before we can get back to you with our advice.

We look forward to hearing from you again.

Sincerely yours,

Per Danielsen
Attorney-at-law

Considering I sent him the relevant papers on 6th October, he had had the best part of four weeks to establish easily that Heidi was lying and in my opinion could have written a letter putting her on notice of a possible claim. As far as suing the newspapers was concerned, I had not asked him to issue a Writ forthwith. Deep down I felt Danielsen was not going to help me either and I was not in the mood to give him the benefit of the doubt. I had lost all patience. So I wrote to him by fax on 9th November as follows:

Dear Mr. Danielsen,

Heidi Schøne

Thanks for your letter of 5th November. I feel a degree of hostility in your letters and I think it will be best if you return all my papers and money (save for your administrative expenses).

I sent you all the necessary papers a month ago and it was you who specifically set a date about two weeks ago for a telephone chat, an appointment you could not keep. I had assumed that with £1,000 already in the bank and four weeks or so with the papers, this would be enough time to see that I have a prima facie case against Heidi Schøne. A letter to her simply stating that your client was "considering" taking a case against her is surely appropriate now.

For you to come back to me on 30th October with the letter that you need another NOK 10,000 as you have received more papers from Gjone told me that you did not read properly my letter of 6th October. You already had all the necessary papers: Gjone's file was a duplicate.

Tor Erling Staff had required £1,000 only, but returned the papers because he didn't have the time to take on the case. All he had asked for was £1,000 and by even British legal fee charging rates, this is enough to be getting on with.

After Wesenberg's pathetic performance and Gjone's when he refused me sending him more money, I will not start paying out huge sums of money until I have the knowledge that the lawyer can overcome the police cover up.

Everyone is going out of their way to protect Heidi Schøne and so if I ask you to speak to Arild Pedersen, then there is a good reason. If you can't form an initial opinion on £1,000 then I get suspicious.

So I will find another lawyer and will not now send all these papers to him. I will write a two-page letter asking for the proof to back up the allegations that have been printed in the newspapers against me. The new lawyer can then ask the police for the proof and issue a writ against Heidi to force her to answer for her lies.

You see in spite of my own great efforts to obtain evidence and proof from the police, it has not been forthcoming. And this makes me feel that the evidence against me doesn't exist: well I know it doesn't exist as I didn't do the things that have been printed. But getting the police to confirm this is very difficult. Heidi Schøne is suffering terribly because of the great success I have had in telling the Norwegian people my side of the story. The police want to protect her from a civil court case and will make it their job to influence any lawyer to lay off her. So until I see some real action £1,000 is all I'm prepared to pay.

Please then return the papers.

Yours sincerely,
Frederick Delaware.

I later phoned Danielsen and confirmed my request. He said he'd send back my papers and wanted to end the conversation and say goodbye. But I said: "Hold on. Have you spoken to Karsten Gjone?" "Yes, I have," he replied, and on my further enquiry promised that he did not allow himself to be unduly influenced by what Gjone had said. "No," I thought suspiciously, "of course not. Only ask me for another 10,000 kroner for the preliminary work and refuse to talk to me on the phone for our scheduled telephone conversation!"

I feel I just might have made a mistake in telling Gjone of the new lawyer, Danielsen. In case my hunch was right, the next lawyers I instructed, Elden & Elden of Oslo, I sent absolutely no copy correspondence from the 1990's but only the newspaper articles, copies of Heidi's letters and the story in English I'd sent the newspapers in 1995, together with a covering letter with specific questions to obtain answers from Heidi Schøne.

While all this had been going on, my dear friend, Arne, recovering from a near fatal road accident in which he had broken both legs and an arm, had translated into Norwegian some extra wording for my 'Report' as follows:

Heidi has claimed that she was exorcised from possession of demons in 1988 by her Christian neighbours in Solbergelva, Asbjorn and Heidi-Anita Skjortnes. Heidi-Anita Skjortnes later left her husband Asbjorn for another man whom she met when she started work in a Drammen department store. She now goes by the name of Heidi-Anita Dahlen-Nilsen. After her so-called exorcism, Heidi Overaa met and married Runar Schøne, a Christian man who claims to speak in tongues and who rejects utterly all people of faiths other than his own peculiar brand of evangelical Christianity. The Schønes had a baby boy in 1996, Heidi's first legitimate child in six conceptions.

It has also emerged that Heidi Overaa in 1985 was having full sexual relations with one Bjorn-Morten, who in fact thought he was the father of Daniel Overaa but Daniel subsequently turned out to be the son of Gudmund Johannessen.

> Bjorn-Morten unwittingly exposed himself to the risk of H.I.V infection as a result of Ms. Overaa's resumption of sexual relations with Mr. Johannessen, the intravenous drug user.
>
> Heidi Schøne is presently awaiting prosecution in the Norwegian Courts accused of attempting to pervert the course of justice in connection with allegations that were printed in the above-mentioned newspapers in 1995 and 1998. It is believed Mrs. Schøne is suffering from the psychiatric illness known as Munchausen's Syndrome, a terrible affliction which involves the patient in serial lying, which has not been cured in spite of Mrs. Schøne's supposed conversion to Christianity.

I thought this was well-merited punishment for the hypocrites Heidi-Anita Dahlen-Nilsen and her ex-husband, Asbjorn Skjortnes, and of course extra exposure for Heidi Schøne.

I had spoken at length to Heidi-Anita Dahlen-Nilsen on 17th October 1997, obtaining her number from a private detective. She told me she didn't want to get involved in my case and that's why she never replied to my pleas for help in 1990. She'd had no idea Heidi made the newspapers, hadn't seen her since 1990 and moreover didn't want me to send her the newspapers. She confirmed that Heidi Overaa had never mentioned to her allegations of "attempted rape" against me.

I had kept my promise to the newspapers to continue to fax the updated 'Report' to hundreds of fax machines in Oslo, Bergen, Drammen and many other towns in Norway. The campaign I knew was still bearing great fruit when Torill Sorte in September refused to talk to me. I wanted to question her over her comments printed in the 14th July 1998 newspaper article.

I had sent a complaint to Gjone's insurance company, Vesta, over his failure to observe the time limits to sue the newspapers. Vesta were waiting on the outcome of my complaint against him to the Disciplinary Tribunal. On 1st December 1998, Danielsen wrote to me :

Dear Mr. Delaware,

HEIDI SCHØNE ETC.

In accordance with your telefax dated November 9, 1998, we have now closed your file.

Because you only have sent me duplicates, I see no reason for returning the papers we have received.

In any case we would like to keep a full set of copies, for file reasons. If you still want something returned, please let us know. We will then have to charge you copying expenses.

I am sorry you stopped our assignment in the middle of the process. I am also sorry you don't appreciate us not taking too many initiatives before we feel we have our feet on the ground.

Our asking for an additional up front payment has nothing to do with being more expensive than other lawyers in Oslo. It simply has to do with the fact that having to study approximately one kilo of documents requires more man hours than your £1,000 would cover for.

Before you stopped our work, I'm sorry to say that we reached the preliminary conclusion that you do not have a case against any newspaper. We could however be wrong, but then we would have to go through more careful studies, and we did not get to that.

Enclosed please find our invoice. Please advise what we should do with the rest of your money.

Sincerely Yours,

Per Danielsen
Attorney at Law

On 7th December 1998 I phoned him up, recording the conversation:

PD.   *Danielsen.*

F.   *Yeah, hi Mr. Danielsen. It's Frederick Delaware here. Morning to you. I got your letter.*

PD.   *Yes.*

F.   *Thanks, but it's Mr. Gjone's file that I'd like to have back. You can keep what I sent you* [on 6th October 1998] *but it's his file that I really must have back 'cos I want to see what he's done on it. There's obviously no reason at all for you to keep that.*

PD.   *I'll think about it, OK.* [Said in a tone of voice that did not make me feel optimistic at getting Gjone's file back. And as it's my absolute right to have my files back, what was there to think about!]

F.   *Well it's something that I won't stand for you keeping at all. Not for a minute longer, because as you know full well there's a complaint against Mr. Gjone and in law I understand there's no reason whatsoever to justify you keeping it, you see.*

PD.   *I'll just copy it then.*

F.   *Well, there's no reason for you to copy it.* [Because he had his own full set of papers sent with my letter of 6th October 1998. And he still implied he'll charge me for the copying. Further, when I no longer wanted him to act for me, why would I want such a man to keep sensitive and personal records on me for ever, so right then I thought I should have the lot back and said:] *Why do you want to keep anything then?* [What were his "file reasons"?]

PD.   *I don't have time to argue with you on the phone* [Read: I don't have time to even discuss this with you or let you test my knowledge of what I've said I've done].

F.   *I'm paying for the call.*

PD.   *You want to pay for my time as well?* [What, on top of his 8,500 kroner bill?]

F.   *I don't think I have to pay for your time in law* [to discuss your professional conduct or lack of it.] *You see I'm a lawyer, I know what goes on. I see your invoice hasn't got one word of what you've done for me.*

PD.   *OK.*

F.   *You're supposed to put a list of how you justify the 8,500 kroner.*

PD.   *We've done that.*

F.   *No, you haven't really explained what you've done for ... ...*

PD.   *We have.*

F.   *Well in the covering letter you've just said you've read through it* [the papers] *but that's not*

316

sufficient. I know what I'm saying because I've been a lawyer for ten years.

PD.   *Ah huh.*

F.   *The thing is you didn't explain to me why you have to read through "a kilo" of documents when I told you to ignore Gjone's file. You never took my call on that or explained that. That obviously leads me to think something funny's going on … … You understand!*

Then astonishingly a full 8 second silence in which Per Danielsen ignored me, followed by:

F.   *Are you still there?*

PD.   *No, not really.*

F.   *Well what's the matter, why aren't you talking? Is there a problem?*

PD.   *I'm busy* [i.e. you Frederick Delaware don't matter a damn].

F.   *Huh?*

PD.   *I'm busy. If you want questions answered, just write us a letter or a fax.* ["No thank you," I thought. "Just like my other letters and faxes were 'answered.' "]

F.   *I don't want to write. I've been writing enough. I was told by the Complaints Bureau you must send Gjone's file back to me and I will be putting in a complaint about you immediately if I don't get that file back. There's no way you can justify what you've done. It's ludicrous. I will be putting in a complaint.*

PD.   *Pardon?*

F.   *I will be putting in a complaint about you.*

PD.   *You can do whatever you like.*

F.   *Yeah, I will. Goodbye.*

PD.   *Bye-bye.*

And followed this by a letter faxed the same day, 7ᵗʰ December 1998:

> Dear Mr. Danielsen,
>
> **Heidi Schøne**
>
> I refer to your letter of December 1ˢᵗ 1998 and our subsequent telephone conversation this morning.
>
> I am writing formally to request that you immediately make available for collection Gjone's file. This will be picked up by Arild B. Pedersen, who is associated with his brother's law firm in Moss (Tlf: (69) 27330).
>
> I have spoken to Rune Jensen this morning, the lawyer handling my complaint against Gjone. He has confirmed that I am entitled to have my papers back. You have two sets of papers – Gjone's and your own. Keep the papers I sent you with my letter of 6ᵗʰ October, but I must have back Gjone's file. This will show me what he's done and is something you will

not be allowed to deprive me of. Your second and third paragraphs of your letter of 1st December make no sense at all.

Regarding stopping your assignment "in the middle of the process," I rather had the impression from your secretary, and from your refusal to talk to me on 30th October (a date after all, which you yourself asked me to call you on), that you hadn't had time to make much, if any, of a start on the papers. I gather you were still busy in Court. So you must have got a lot of reading in after that.

Regarding your refusal to take "too many initiatives" (your fourth paragraph), there was only one initiative I wanted you to take and that was communicated to you in my letter of 30th October, i.e. to ensure a letter was delivered to Heidi Schøne "informing her that I have instructed lawyers to consider taking civil action against her for lying/attempting to pervert the course of justice." The scale of her deception must have been obvious to you if you charge me NKR 8,500 for work done up to the time I terminated my instructions on 9th November (yet on 5th November you indicated in your letter you had not had the time to consider basically whether Heidi was liable to face proceedings).

I find it strange that in eight months Gjone cannot get off one single letter to Heidi Schøne and neither yourself, after taking £650 sterling [his 8,500 Kroner bill] of my money, a simple letter to Heidi was refused. Remember she lied – not me. A fact supported by policeman Svein Jensen as long ago as 1995. Heidi Schøne and the newspapers brought on themselves the firm response I initiated.

In your penultimate paragraph you say your preliminary conclusion was that I don't "seem to have a case against any newspaper. We could be wrong." But what are your reasons for this preliminary conclusion?

I already told you – twice – the first time being in my first letter to you of 6th October that two Norwegians who knew me, read the newspapers of 1995 and knew it was me the articles referred to. I already know that the time limit for suing the newspapers for the May '95 articles is passed. Hence my complaint against Gjone. That leaves the July 1998 article only, so in all I don't need much of your time to consider the case against the newspapers. I knew I had a prima facie case against the newspapers up until May 1998. But I wanted the journalists of the newspapers and their editors to be subpoenaed to the trial of Heidi Schøne. You spoke to Gjone. I asked you to speak to Arild Pedersen, who knew my case well enough – why didn't you?

A few minutes on the phone to discuss these matters was denied me by you – why? And why not a word of advice on Heidi's lies? Your silence on her false accusations is a serious omission. Indeed, it follows on from Gjone's ten months silence on the specifics of Heidi's deception.

I must say it is not just Heidi Schøne and the newspapers I am up against is it? Please provide me with a detailed summary of the work you have done to justify your charge of NKR 8,500.

Yours sincerely,

Frederick Delaware

Cc. Arild B. Pedersen and
Rune Jensen (tlf (33) 46 22 22) Disciplinary Bureau

The next day I put in a complaint against Per Danielsen to the Norwegian lawyers Disciplinary Tribunal enclosing a copy of the taped conversation. My correspondence with Danielsen continued.

Letter dated 8th December 1998 to me:

> Dear Mr. Delaware,
>
> **HEIDI SCHØNE**
>
> Referring to your letter dated December 7, we have now copied the documents you want, in accordance with your instructions. The pile can be picked up in our office as you wish.
>
> Your letter is full of incorrect allegations, but I see no point in pursuing this because we have already closed the file.
>
> The work done is in accordance with hours spent. Because you ordered us to stop in the middle of the process and refused to pay additional funds as requested, I see no point in going into more details than simply stating that you certainly would have had problems winning cases against the newspapers and Heidi Schøne. That would at least require more work and money than you were willing to invest.
>
> I hope this answers your questions.
>
> Best regards,
>
> Per Danielsen
> Attorney at law

My reply dated 12th December 1998:

> Dear Mr. Danielsen,
>
> **Heidi Schøne**
>
> I am in receipt of your letter of 8th December. Your letter does not answer any of my questions. Moreover how am I to place much reliance on what you tell me in view of the manner of your last telephone conversation with me? Your conduct fell way, way below that expected of a professional man.
>
> The allegations I have made in my previous correspondence, if you have nothing to hide, must be answered by you. Are you trying to tell me that an explanation will not be forthcoming just because you have "closed the file." A file that it seems you are extremely anxious to hold on to? Why, when I have told you I no longer wish you to act for me?
>
> A complaint by me against you has been received by Rune Jensen and he is passing it on to the correct Complaints Bureau for your area.
>
> For your information, in the Spring of 1996 the policeman Svein Jensen of Mjøndalen told me he did not believe Schøne's story when she was at the police and nor did Mr. Jensen trust her. Further the journalist Ingunn Røren had told me in the Spring of 1996 that she did not know whether or not to believe Heidi's story about her allegation of my threatening to kill her son and specifically told me that she is not saying I did make the threat, but that is what Heidi said I did.

This evidence, which I have on tape, is sufficient to give me a good chance in the courts. If you had allowed me to speak to you – something I always insisted on – you would have allowed yourself the chance to hear me tell you this. It is in the papers you have been given by me anyway. I told you that we must have a telephone conversation to get to the bottom of the matter quickly. But no! You would not speak to your client, over a matter that after all had made huge headlines in Norway. A matter that took Karsten Gjone eight months to do God knows what! After all the time I have had to wait, still you would not to speak to me, a fellow lawyer, in spite of having cashed my cheque for £1,000.

It is the detail that is important in this case – you are just being evasive and this leads me to believe you are hiding much. You are frightened to let me test your knowledge of what you say you have done. I want conclusive proof from you.

You had the newspapers and you had a two page statement 'Press Release' telling of my discoveries after 1995. I had to do a huge amount of research and investigation myself, but I'd condensed it into two pages. You had a résumé on one page of Heidi's past in Norwegian. That would not take long to read through. Yet you give me no comments on it? What do you think of Heidi's past – of her being in a psychiatric unit? Of her sleeping with a man she knows to be taking heroin? Why don't you tell me?

I want all my money back. Your past correspondence, your last phone call, your complete refusal to answer my questions, discuss the case over the phone etc. etc. justifies me telling you that your 'service' has been a complete disservice. I got more advice over the phone from two other Oslo lawyers – at no charge whatsoever – than I did from you. These other lawyers were unfortunately too busy to take on my case, but they gave me great hope.

I also want **all** the documents, papers etc. back that I gave you on 6th October, PLUS Gjone's whole file. I don't want you to keep anything, in fact. If the Complaints Bureau decides you are entitled to keep copies of what I sent you on 6th October then so be it, but no more.

Yours sincerely,

Frederick Delaware

cc Norwegian Complaints Bureau

On 15th January 1999 Per Danielsen wrote to the Lawyers Disciplinary Tribunal:

Dear Sirs,

SAK NR. 129/98: DELAWARE – ADVOKAT PER DANIELSEN

Referring to the Disciplinary Committee's letter dated January 12, 1999, I have the following comments:

He informed me that he was not satisfied with work done by his former lawyer, Mr. Gjone in Drammen.

As I understood he wanted a "second opinion" and assistance with regard to initiating libel suits against several newspapers and a special lawsuit against a woman named Heidi Schøne.

320

Our office asked for £1,000 to be payed in advance, which Mr. Delaware actually paid.

Having received a large pile of documents from Mr. Gjone, I started working with the different cases.

After having done substantial work, I found that more man hours than Mr. Delaware's up front fee would cover for, would be needed. We therefore asked for an additional sum of money, but Mr. Delaware never paid this.

Instead Mr Delaware started acting irrationally.

He instructed me to warn Ms. Heidi Schøne that I was considering starting a law-suit against her.

I refused to do so, without being sure that he had grounds for pursual.

Mr. Delaware did not like this, and started to send a number of telefaxes and in addition called me a number of times.

In accordance with Mr. Delaware's instructions, I stopped working in the middle of the process.

I have billed him for a total of NOK 8,500 corresponding with the number of man hours spent.

Mr. Delaware then wanted his documents, which have been made available for him. He has stated in a telefax that the documents would be picked up, but we have not heard from anybody.

I refer to my relevant letters to Mr. Delaware, already enclosed with the complaint, to substantiate what I write.

As to the particulars of his complaint, please let me state the following:

Delaware's letter dated December 7, 1998

It is not clear to me what Mr. Delaware is complaining about, but it seems to have something to do with the returning of his file.

We have acted in accordance with Mr. Delaware's instructions and wishes. Please read my letter dated December 8, 1998.

We have not charged anything, although we certainly are entitled to charge for copying.

Mr. Delaware has forbidden us to mail him his file in the post, and that's okay with us. His associate has however not picked up the file yet.

Delaware's letter dated December 8, 1998

Mr. Delaware in this letter asks if a lawyer can charge NOK 8.500 - with, in effect, nothing but his word that he has done anything.

It is difficult to interpret what Mr. Delaware means by this. If he really is asking whether we have charged him too much or not, it is clear that we have charged him for man hours spent, as explained in letters to him. In the mentioned letters we also have explained what work has been done.

321

Mr. Delaware further refers to the fact that he has instructed me to ignore Mr. Gjone's file – in writing. Then he asks if I am entitled to ignore the request, then charge him for reading the file.

Here Mr. Delaware clearly misunderstands.

First I must remind Mr. Delaware that he wanted me to go through Mr. Gjone's file in the first place. This was of course necessary in order to evaluate whether he had cases or not.

Then, suddenly, when we asked for more money, he later instructed me not to do the work I had already done. Of course Mr. Delaware is entitled to instruct his lawyer, but then the lawyer in return is entitled to refuse carrying out the instructions by cancelling the assignment. It did not come to this. However, I certainly do not want to work for Mr. Delaware. Among other things because he gives confusing instructions.

Mr. Delaware's letter also contains allegations against the undersigned personally. I do not find it necessary to comment on this.

Mr. Delaware's letter dated December 13, 1998

Here Mr. Delaware says he wants a refund of "all my money." I cannot agree, because Mr. Delaware is obliged to pay for the hours spent, before he stopped the assignment for unnecessary reasons.

Mr. Delaware also states that "he denied me any talks." This eventually came to be true. I do not want to spend more time on this busybody who seems to be creating problems not only for myself, but also for several of my colleagues.

General Comments

Mr. Delaware's letters and complaints are not clear. I therefore urge him to explain if I have understood his complaints correctly or if I have missed any.

Closing arguments

Mr. Delaware has asked me to consider law suits against several newspapers and a girl he knew many years ago, named Heidi Schøne.

I have told him he does not seem have grounds for the law suit against the woman Schøne. This however does not imply that we are not entitled to be paid for the advice given. The same goes for the cases against the newspapers, a work we were not allowed to finish.

To say it bluntly, Mr. Delaware seems to want to harass a girl in Norway. As a professional lawyer I am not willing to do this, even though Mr. Delaware complains (on the surface about other things, really he is just frustrated, in my opinion).

Best regards,

Per Danielsen

Attorney at law

I replied directly to Danielsen on 22nd January 1999:

Dear Mr. Danielsen,

Complaint against you ref: SAKN129/88

I received a copy of your letter of 15th January 1999 addressed to the Disciplinaerutvelget for Oslo etc. I will reply to them in full shortly but in the meantime enclose for your information the result of my complaint against Karsten Gjone, who you spoke to. My complaint against him has been upheld and I certainly hope my complaint against you will also be upheld.

I see what you really think of me: that all I want to do is "harass" Heidi Schøne and that I am a "busybody" creating problems for you and your colleagues, i.e. Gjone and Wesenberg. Well, Gjone has been found unprofessional. I submit that you have also been very unprofessional and will try and convince the adjudicators of this.

Rune Jensen, the [Disciplinary Committee] lawyer of Sandefjord, was very helpful to me on the phone. He told me more about the newspapers self-regulation rules than you ever did. His attitude was right. Your attitude is all wrong. I smelt a rat early on and I feel justified in all I've done, said and will say about you. I got more advice in 'free' phone calls from Tor Erling staff and Steiner Sørvik than I did from you for NKR8,500. You ripped me off.

Your letter of 15th January is evasive and empty of substance. You have added great insult to my substantial injuries inflicted by the lies of the newspapers and from things other people in their ignorance and prejudice may, I suspect, have told you.

Yours sincerely,

Frederick Delaware

On 23rd January 1999 I wrote again to the Lawyers Disciplinary Tribunal. I knew that it was essential that the Tribunal have sight of the whole picture in detail. As the saying goes, 'the Devil lies in the detail.'

Dear Madam,

Case No. 129/98 Frederick Delaware vs Per Danielsen

Thank you for your letter of 19th January 1999 with enclosure from Per Danielsen.

I have no particular wish to overburden the Tribunal with too many papers on this matter but I'm afraid this will be somewhat inevitable if you are to fully appreciate my position. Background information is necessary. I therefore enclose one set of the following (all of which Per Danielsen has already):

1.	A copy of each of the four newspaper articles; three from 1995 being V.G., Bergens Tidende and Drammens Tidende, and one – Drammens Tidende from 1998.

2.	To be read in the light of Heidi Schøne's actual life translated into Norwegian, a copy of which I enclose: it is 100% true and verifiable.

---

3.   Two letters from Heidi Schøne: one post-dated 22.8.84, the other a card post-dated 9.4.1985, which thank God I happened to have kept. These obviously refute the newspaper allegation "13 years of sex-terror" from 1995. I suspect Heidi thought I would never have retained letters from so long ago. But I did!

4.   My full report from 1995 sent to all the newspapers entitled 'Heidi Schøne' x 2.

5.   My own findings from 1996 after painstaking investigation by myself headed 'Press Release' x 2.

6.   A full set of correspondence with Per Danielsen x 2.

I immediately want to refute Per Danielsen's attempt to denigrate my character by saying I have been "creating problems" for himself and "several of his colleagues" (who could only be Karsten Gjone of Drammen and Helge Wesenberg of Bergen, lawyers over whom I have also complained). I always felt total justification for my complaints and so far with Karsten Gjone I have been vindicated. Gjone has been found guilty of failing to uphold the standards required from a lawyer and I enclose a copy of that report dated 13th January 1999 x 2, sent by Rune Jensen to me last week.

I had asked Gjone to enquire of certain vital omissions of Wesenberg's work for me in 1995 over Heidi Schøne. Gjone spoke to Wesenberg but repeatedly failed to ask Wesenberg the questions I wanted asking. After I dropped Gjone and complained about him Per Danielsen spoke to Gjone, but Danielsen refused to tell me what was said between them. Gjone would naturally have little good to say about me to Danielsen as he, Gjone, was under investigation. Wesenberg also would have nothing good to say about me, either, to Gjone. But I have been proved right over Gjone as you can see.

Rune Jensen, I am most pleased with. He told me last week what Wesenberg, Gjone, Danielsen, the PFU or anyone else has failed to tell me since May 1995. That the newspapers 'rules' require them to consult a 'victim' BEFORE they go to print, to obtain the 'victim's' opinion. The newspapers – all 3 of them – failed to consult me and easily they could have found me. Further, that once a story HAS been printed the newspapers are obliged to print my response. Again all three papers failed in their duty. Rune Jensen sympathised with me for my telling him that I had been forced to generate my own form of 'newspaper,' in my massive campaign by fax and letter to random members of the Norwegian public. I was not going to let the newspapers totally deceive their public and make them believe that Muslims are so, so bad. Would Bergens Tidende have mentioned the "Jewish man" 16 times? I don't think so and nor does Rune Jensen. But it's OK for Bergens Tidende to say "Muslim man" 16 times.

The trouble was that my campaign against the newspapers was so widespread and so successful that the police were getting hundreds of enquiries from members of the public and as a result had to cocoon Heidi from the publicity by stopping all correspondence from any source anywhere. As a result, I can't even get a lawyer's letter to Heidi. Moreover, Drammens Tidende said last July that "in the last year" I have written over 300 letters to Heidi. A big lie. I wrote 5 or so letters telling her I would do all I could to get her into Court for her lies. Besides which I knew none of the letters got to her anyway (they ended up at the police station). I just wanted the police to know that I was still on her case as Gjone refused to write to her once (or me – his own client!). No proof exists about "300 letters **to** Heidi in the last year." They don't exist.

The Drammen police decided to try and extradite me to Norway two years ago. They consulted British police who told them that British laws are different and I was a free man. The police objected to me telling the public my side of the story on the grounds I was violating Heidi's private life. BUT she had named herself in the newspapers and allowed herself to be photographed. Only after that did I begin an en masse information campaign, using her public name and her public photo. **After** the newspapers had failed to observe their rules. Hence the sympathy of Advokat Rune Jensen.

Heidi Schøne – the girl from the Lier B.S.S. Psychiatric Unit. The girl who alleged I attempted to rape her in 1986 (as well as alleging a Bergen shopkeeper raped her, as well as Greek youths attempted to, on her holiday) but who changed her story in 1998 to actual rape by me. All the allegations against me are false. Yes, Heidi – the best form of defence is attack! Even if it means telling filthy ruinous lies. Say the story was picked up by the English papers? The Sun did in fact do a story on an English 'Casanova' in Bergen a couple of years ago (not me).

I asked Advocat Helge Wesenberg last year to explain the [attempted rape/rape] discrepancy – no reply. I asked Danielsen to investigate – no comment. It was the attempted rape allegation that so infuriated me which began the troubles again in 1995, together with my misgivings over treatment meted out to me in 1990 in Norway. I only knew of the attempted rape allegation (from 1986) in 1995. Now it is rape.

So am I not entitled to have this investigated by Danielsen? Does he believe I really – IN WRITING – threatened to kill a two year old boy – Heidi's son Daniel – who I dearly loved when I met him. And he made known his fondness for me.

Does Danielsen believe I threatened to kill Heidi's neighbours? Even when there is no evidence whatsoever?

Does Danielsen believe that the 400 obscene letters I am alleged to have written and have all been destroyed by Heidi, were really written at all, by me, a practising solicitor whose career is most certainly finished if it were proven true?

Does Danielsen believe I made hundreds of obscene phone calls – when I could lay myself open to being taped – yet none were made and no single record of any such conversation exists? When Heidi had no phone from 1988 to 1993? Need I go on?

1.   Per Danielsen in his wisdom having "done substantial work" (see the 7th paragraph on the first page of his letter to you on 15.1.99) makes NO COMMENT on any of Heidi's lies. What, pray, does the "substantial work" consist of? Tell me please.

2.   I know the newspapers didn't name me – clever weren't they! But I knew the position in English law – a copy of which I enclose, and which Tor Erling Staff told me over the phone was the position also in Norwegian law. Staff charged me nothing for this phone advice and returned my £1,000 cheque as he was too busy to take on my case. So why no comment on this simple point by Per Danielsen – the so-called expert. If he had bothered to talk to me properly he'd have been told that Ann-Kristin Horvei of Bergen had told me long ago that from Verdens Gang she recognised me as being the one to whom the articles referred. She had no idea of the allegations that were made in the press and asked me if they were true. Until I told her they were all false, her doubts made her feel they might be true and I had to explain for ages the whole damn story. The point

325

is I have a prima facie case against the newspapers on this particular point, so why no explanation from the "expert" Danielsen. The reasons please! Ann-Kristin Horvei has not spoken to Heidi Schøne for 10 years!

3.   You will see from the correspondence a call was arranged for 30th October 1998. This was essential to me. I did not want Per Danielsen to read through pages of unnecessary correspondence. Why in particular should I be penalised financially for the proven incompetence of Gjone? I had to tell Danielsen this and guide him through the copious correspondence. Yet despite his being, I was told, "too busy" (maybe in fact he had no desire to speak to me because I was "a busybody" who "harasses" Heidi Schøne – and how was that conclusion reached?) Danielsen still had time to write to me the same day asking for more money as he now had a "big pile of documents" from Gjone. A quick look at the "big pile" would reveal it is correspondence and documentation that Danielsen already has. So why the need for more money? To read duplicates?

Before addressing my point on duplication, which in fact was never addressed, I'm asked to provide more money. So I smelt a rat. I felt £1,000 was down the drain already. Another 10,000 NKR would also go straight down the drain. There is a strong smell of unprofessionalism here. Many people are unjustly accused of murder and other atrocities and it is a client's right to have a lawyer defend impartially the accused. Danielsen was no such defender, even of me in my circumstances.

Per Danielsen's last paragraph of his letter to you of 15.1.99 betrays his true feelings. I was right to smell a rat. My instincts, as with Gjone, were soundly based. I have been a lawyer since 1987 in both private practice and as an in-house lawyer for a major public British organisation. I know bad practice and evasion when I see it.

Again, on December 1st 1998, Per Danielsen refused to address my comments on duplication. I had to speak to him. NO REASON was given for his "preliminary conclusion" as to why I cannot sue the newspaper (as Tor Staff indicated I may be able to do). What great advice - to give no reasons - for "substantial work" and no comments on obvious FILTH from Heidi Schøne. Not a word of sympathy. Not a word of legal reasoning. Not a single quotation from a legal statute. Nothing! It seems to me there was never any intention to provide helpful advice.

Specfically P.D. cannot charge me photocopy expenses. Rune Jensen told me this explicitly, but why photocopy at all? There were already duplicates! Why no breakdown of what I was charged for? Hourly rate. Degree of difficulty. Number of hours spent. Analysis of my case, legally and morally. Why? Why nothing at all?

So I don't have a case against Heidi or the newspapers at all, eh? Well, read the copy letter sent to Gjone's insurers, Hans-Arnt Skjølberg of Vesta. Rune Jensen has, I believe, listened to the tape. The letter is dated 11th December 1998.

Per Danielsen's comments on his second page of his latest letter (15.1.99) about my letter of December 7th are deliberately deceptive. He knows full well what my complaint is all about. In his letter of December 1st to me, he is refusing to send me back either of my two files. It is irrelevant if the papers are duplicates. My letter of December 7th was written immediately after the telephone conversation we had, which I taped, which tape you already have and which, after his secretary confirmed on December 7th that Per Danielsen had still not returned Gjone's file (despite repeated requests), goes as follows:

[The telephone conversation of December 7th referred to above was handwritten here. The Tribunal had already received a copy of the tape recording but told me that they would only listen to it if I wrote out the words first]

So it was very clear to Per Danielsen what I was complaining about. So the same day, having had quite enough, I wrote to P.D. copying in Rune Jensen. I wrote separately on 7th December to Rune Jensen initiating my complaint over Per Danielsen's general conduct, having already consulted Rune Jensen.

Yet from Per Danielsen's comments in his letter of 15.1.99 he conveys the impression that he's acted reasonably.

Next day – 8.12.98, a no doubt chastened Per Danielsen wrote to me having overnight photocopied all the documents "I want." He has duplicates already. Why photocopy Gjone's file when he has two sets to begin with?

Again he refuses to answer my questions on the false grounds that he has already "closed the file." I am being played with and wound up.

Per Danielsen gave me the distinct impression that (by his letter of 30.10.98) he would do no work on Gjone's file (nonsensical as he already had all he needed) or the other file until he had got another 10,000 NKR. What on earth does he mean by saying I tell him not to do work he has "already done" by ignoring Gjone's file?

If there is confusion for Danielsen (which I reject) then why no phone call to clear things up? Per Danielsen would not speak to me on the case ONCE until December 7th and you see how that went. There is no truth in Per Danielsen's statement in response to my being "denied any talks" when he says this "eventually came to be true." Nonsense. There is no "eventually" about it. The correspondence and my comments herein indicate that any meaningful talks were denied me throughout, i.e. nothing was ever granted.

All I can say is that Rune Jensen was a gentleman and gave me great advice – more than Danielsen ever did. Tor Staff was great. So was Steinar Sørvik. What a shame the last two were too busy.

In this last page to you – 2nd paragraph – Per Danielsen says he does "not find it necessary to comment on the personal allegations" I have made against him. A complaint by its very nature is personal. My allegations go to the heart of his competence to give proper client care.

Per Danielsen's silences, omissions and failure to give reasoning, his rudeness and evasion are clear for all to see. He only adds insult to the gross injuries and real distress inflicted on me by the newspapers. I don't need this again after a year of "nothing doing" from Gjone.

Yours faithfully,

Frederick Delaware

P.S. Apologies again for the length of this letter. But I trust you will understand.

P.P.S. One thing I forgot to emphasise is that Mr. Danielsen's "substantial work" if indeed this was performed, must BE SEEN TO BE DONE by a client. I refer to my letter of 7th December faxed to Mr. Danielsen. I have not been convinced in the slightest that "substantial work" has been done.

> So as I terminated instructions on 9th November, I see that days 6th, 7th and 8th were left to do "substantial work." It's all so hard to believe him on what I've been told, bearing in mind all that's gone on. It just does not ring true at all.

Danielsen to his regret would now know he'd been taped as the above letter would be sent to him by the Norwegian Disciplinary Tribunal.

On 18th February 1999 Per Danielsen replied to the Disciplinary Tribunal:

> Dear Sirs,
>
> **SAK NR. 129/98: DELAWARE – ADVOKAT PER DANIELSEN**
>
> Referring to Mr. Delaware's last letter dated January 23, 1999, please allow me to present the following comments:
>
> If Mr. Delaware had not stopped the assignment in the middle of the process without any rational reason, all of his questions would have been answered at length.
>
> Based on the work we had done, it proved necessary to consider whether the allegations against Mr. Delaware were true or not. We would have had to go through this in detail, after having confronted Mr. Delaware with a great number of questions. (Please see the complex allegations in e.g. Verdens Gang's article).
>
> It however never came to this, because of his irrational behaviour.
>
> Mr. Delaware's irrational thinking is clearly demonstrated in his comments following the transcript from the taped conversation with me.
>
> I also refer to his statements: "So I smelt a rat" and "There is a strong smell of unprofessionalism here."
>
> On the time I worked with the assignment, I was loyal to Mr. Delaware. I felt obliged to present possible problems to him. My statement about "busybodyness" is of a retrospective nature. Looking back on his reactions, I certainly feel annoyed because he, which he now proves, has behaved extremely irrationally. Mr. Delaware said he was a professional lawyer and I treated him as such.
>
> I refuse to believe that Mr. Tor Erling Staff has advised Mr. Delaware to say he would have been able to sue the newspapers. Without having studied the harassment allegations from Heidi Schøne, it would similarly not have been possible to evaluate whether he had a case against her or not.
>
> I am sorry I on one occasion was too busy to talk to Mr. Delaware and see now that this particular incident has led to Mr. Delaware believing smelling a "rat." If he would have been more patient, I would have given him valuable advice.
>
> I found it fair to ask for money up front, because Mr. Delaware was living abroad.
>
> I have never said Mr. Delaware "can not" sue the newspapers. Here again Mr. Delaware misunderstands.
>
> Mr. Delaware, in addition, however, may have had problems with the time limit, depending on when the contents of the newspaper articles came to his

328

knowledge, because the three year time limit does not start to run before he has actually read the articles.

To repeat myself: We have not charged Mr. Delaware for photocopying expenses. The amount of NOK 8,500, - represents 7,5 hours with an hourly rate of NOK 1.200, given a small discount.

In my last letter I urged Mr. Delaware to comment on whether I had understood all of his complaining points or not. Mr. Delaware does not comment on this. I again urge him to explain whether I have understood everything completely or not.

Best regards,

Per Danielsen
Attorney at law

I replied on 3rd March 1999:

Dear Madam,

Per Danielsen

Thank you for your letter of 1.3.99 enclosing a copy of Per Danielsen's letter to you dated 18th Feb 1999.

Mr. Danielsen now urges me again to explain whether he has understood everything completely. It is beyond me to explain any more than I did in my large submission of 23rd January 1999. I note that few of my points have been answered by Per Danielsen.

Tor Erling Staff advised me on the phone on the basis of my representations to him that the newspaper allegations were false. I refer to my copy letter (submitted to you on 23.1.99) dated 11th December 1998 to Hans-Arnt Skjølberg of Vesta, wherein policeman Svein Jensen did not believe Heidi Schøne and the Drammens Tidende journalist admits she went to print without knowing whether what Heidi said was true or not.

Tor Staff asked me if I had any friends or others in Norway who recognised me from the newspaper articles – as I was not named. I told him: "Yes, at least two people." And he told me of the legal position in Norway which is similar to that in England on libelling unnamed people. There was a prima facie case for me. But then Tor Staff asked me when the articles were written. 1995 - May, I told him, so he replied that I had missed the time limits. I spoke to Staff in September 1998.

On the question of suing Heidi Schøne personally for lying/attempting to pervert the course of justice, Tor Staff told me Heidi Schøne must herself prove her allegations that she made via the newspapers.

For your information I was in possession of all the Norwegian articles – three of them – within about ten days of their publication in May 24, 25 and 27, 1995. Anyway, it's all too late now to sue the newspapers for 1995 articles and I must rely on my negligence claim against Karsten Gjone's insurers.

I maintain that Mr. Danielsen's conduct was irrational, not mine. I've set out my case already. I certainly wasn't treated like a fellow lawyer. Mr. Danielsen says on one occasion he didn't have time to talk to me – 30th October 1998 – but he had time to write to me that day asking for more

329

money. He had my phone number at work and could have phoned me up. He hadn't used the money up I'd already sent him, before asking for more. I want a report on the basics for the £1,000 I'd sent him which included a phone call conversation – after all Tor Staff and Steinar Sørvik spoke to me giving advice – for free.

To make hostile statements such as I'm "a busybody causing problems for his colleagues" and I'm just out to "harass Heidi Schøne" because "really he is just frustrated" are the kind of comments which give support to my gut reaction of smelling a rat after being asked for another NKR 10,000 for looking at a duplicate file.

My present lawyers have been paid NKR 5,000 and then they reported to me; then NKR 6,000 and they reported to me. They let me speak to them on the phone for as long as I want. They have obtained the Bergen police papers and have asked for the Drammen police papers. They have told me at last, after my 3½ years of trying, that Heidi Schøne has not made a full statement to the police in Bergen on her false allegation of attempted rape. She merely said I'd "attempted to rape" her. There is no other information from 1986 on this. In 1998 she says now that I've raped her. It took her 12 years to change her mind. She also alleged a Bergen shopkeeper had raped her in the 1980's. But in 1995 she told Ingunn Røren at Drammens Tidende that I'd **attempted** to rape her. Ingunn Røren told me this but they chose not to print that allegation. I have all this on tape in case you are wondering.

My new Oslo lawyers have corresponded with the PFU and told them to get on with investigating my complaint over the 1998 D-T article. These lawyers have told me Heidi Schøne is not obliged to help enquiries unless a writ is issued. I have given instructions that I want a writ issued. I have had much, much better value for money.

It is clear Mr. Danielsen made a mistake in earlier correspondence claiming he would charge me photocopying expenses. Why not just admit it? Only now do I see his hourly rate and basic advice on the three year time limit for suing the newspapers.

I got more advice in two free calls to Sørvik and Staff than I did from Danielsen at NKR 8,500. The phone was an essential medium for me.

You are welcome to phone Tor Staff to confirm that what I have reported is true. He is on (22) 20 31 60. Steinar Sørvik told me the psychiatrist, Nils Rettersdøl, talking about erotic paranoia, is a well-known contributor to the newspapers. He is paid for it – and Rettersdøl told me he only based his comments on what the newspapers told him. He knew nothing much about me, in fact and nothing about Heidi's past, e.g. being in the BSS Psychiatric Unit, after two suicide attempts. So clearly being a Muslim is akin to being like filth for the Norwegian press. I won't have it. I will be bringing to Court two white Norwegian citizens who will bravely give evidence that in their opinion Norwegians are brought up to despise anyone who isn't Christian. Thanks to the Holocaust, Jews are no longer denigrated in the press in Europe. Maybe now after Serb atrocities, Muslims will in due course not be denigrated, merely for being Muslim. Still it didn't stop the fucked-up (words I chose carefully and mean) – fucked-up Norwegian press printing total crap when the big story was the mental case Heidi Schøne. A true story about her past which the press could have looked into.

I have had enough of Norway and its press and lawyers and police (save for good men like Jensen).

It is time for me to get some long overdue justice and Heidi Schøne will be pursued to Court. The campaign against her will continue unless the newspapers – all three of them – print FRONT PAGE apologies in bold print. The newspapers don't want that so there is a dilemma for them.

On top of anti-Muslim detestable insults and flagrant filthy lies I have to spend hundreds of hours fruitlessly trying just to get simple things done AND I have to pay for it. Well, Heidi Schøne can expect no favours from me. She is worn out and paying the price for lies calculated to ruin me: the man who in 1990 she would have married had her attempt to convert me to Christianity succeeded. She has admitted to me – it is on tape, that she wanted to "witness me," i.e. convert me in 1990 and I have the book she sent me in her attempts at conversion.

Yours sincerely,

Frederick Delaware

On 1st March 1999 the Secretariat to the Disciplinary Tribunal put the papers in to the Disciplinary Committee consisting of three lawyers.

On 25th June 1999, Per Danielsen sent me back Karsten Gjone's papers.

On the 13th November 2000 the Committee made their decision and their seven page report was forwarded to me on the 21st November. The report concluded:

1. That Per Danielsen, Attorney at Law, was not in breach of the rules of proper professional conduct in refusing to write to NN [they did not name Heidi Schøne but gave her the anonymity of the reference "NN"] to inform her that he had been retained by Frederick Delaware to consider legal action or to bring legal action against her.

2. That Per Danielsen, Attorney at Law, was in breach of the rules on proper professional conduct on 1st December 1998 in refusing to release the case documents received by him to the Complainant.

3. That Per Danielsen's fee was reasonable in relation to the assignment and the work to be performed.

Well, point 1 was no great surprise to me. Point 2 obviously was in my favour, but point 3, I was not happy with. So I appealed as follows:

Sekretaer
Den Norske Advokatforenings sekretariat
Kristian Augusts gate 9, 0164 OSLO
Norway. Telefax: 22 11 53 25
FAO: Gro Grasbekk

23rd November 2000

Dear Ms. Grasbekk,

Case Number: 129/98 – Per Danielsen

Thank you for your letter of the 21st November enclosing the decision of the DNA dated the 13th November 2000.

I write (in duplicate) to inform you that I wish to appeal against the findings of points 1 and 3 in the Chairman's conclusion.

I will write again shortly when I have had more time to reconsider the ample documentation in my possession. Suffice to say that I do not believe at all that Per Danielsen did seven and a half hours work for me as this work should have been

331

reflected in a proper report as opposed to the completely unsubstantiated assertion that he had done a lot of work for me costing 8,500.00 kroner. I myself am an experienced solicitor in England and would never get away with what Per Danielsen has done in justifying this fee to a client without explaining precisely what he has done and the conclusions reached after seven and a half hours of work. Per Danielsen's true attitude is shown by the fact that later he thought I was suffering from "frustration." What exactly does he mean by this – "sexual"(?) frustration as the newspapers indicated whilst at the same time making repeated references to me as "the Muslim man" (16 times in Bergens Tidende in 1995). It is quite apparent now by the Drammen Byrett's [Drammen City Court] decision of September this year in allowing me to proceed to a full trial that I do have a case. It is quite apparent also to my new lawyer that enormous lies have been told about me and none of this was mentioned in Mr. Danielsen's so called report to me. In England lawyers must give a full breakdown of exactly what work they have done and what conclusions they have come to on the amount of work they have so far done. Although I cannot prove for certain that Mr. Danielsen is lying, until I see proper evidence for the amount of work he has done I suspect he is not telling me the truth. In England we require a solicitor to furnish a client with a remuneration certificate if the client is not satisfied with the legal charges incurred whereby the solicitor must detail fully how he can justify time spent on work. Danielsen must be seen to justify his work and fees to me, not just say so.

Moreover, the Committee have failed to comment on the disgusting manners shown by Mr. Danielsen in the taped conversation. To say that he had the manners of a pig is no overstatement. For these manners alone a full refund is justified, and I expect the judge on this appeal to be given the tape to listen to.

The fact is, that for £1,000.00 Mr. Danielsen did not even comment on the basic law of the case, i.e. what a plaintiff has to prove in such a case which information incidentally was supplied free of charge to me by the Drammen Byrett in the summer of 1999 whereafter I proceeded to issue the writ in person. This proved successful whereafter an amended writ was issued by my present attorney who has told me that he cannot understand at all the newspapers comments in the light of NN's letters to me. Letters which Mr. Danielsen had copies of which blatantly proved NN and the newspapers were liars. If my present lawyer can tell me this then why in seven and a half hours of work can Mr. Danielsen not do the same? No! Danielsen's conduct was totally unacceptable.

I note that the Committee have found Per Danielsen to be in breach of the rules of proper professional conduct in relation to point number 2 of their conclusion which obviously I am pleased with.

With regard to point 1 in view of what Mr. Danielsen later on said about my "frustration" I think that he would never have written to NN in any event. I repeat, it would have been quite clear from even a cursory glance at NN's letters to me compared to the comments in the newspapers that NN was a terrible liar and an initial letter could easily have gone out especially after seven and a half hours work. I therefore wish to appeal on point 1 as well, of the Committee's conclusion.

The fact of the matter is that I have Mr. Danielsen's shockingly impolite conversation on tape and his conduct speaks for itself and certainly brings the Norwegian legal profession into disrepute especially as he was dealing with a fellow professional.

Would you please acknowledge receipt of this letter.

Yours sincerely,

Frederick Delaware

Followed by another letter:

Sekretaer
Den Norske Advokatforenings secretariat
Kristian Augusts gate 9, 0164 OSLO
Norway
Telefax: 0047 22 11 53 25
FAO: Gro Grasbekk

27th November 2000

Dear Ms. Grasbekk,

Case Number: 129/98 – Per Danielsen

Further to my letter of the 23rd November I have now been able to review my papers properly and now write again in duplicate.

I would like the judge considering this appeal to report on the following matters with the object of returning not only my £1,000.00 up front payment but also ordering further compensation as he sees fit for the time, stress and inconvenience incurred by me in making this complaint.

1. Per Danielsen's letter to me of December 1st 1998

    In this letter Per Danielsen says he reached a "preliminary conclusion" that I "do not seem to have a case against the newspaper." For Per Danielsen's alleged seven and a half hours work at 8,500.00 kroner I deserved to know the reasons for Per Danielsen's preliminary conclusion. Where is the substantive legal advice? I should have been given a precise statement on the legal principles governing my case e.g. standard of proof, burden of proof, time limits etc. without having to request such basic information. I should have been told exactly what Per Danielsen's proposed "more careful studies" involved and were designed to reveal, as to me, seven and a half hours of work is easily sufficient to discover what the basic bones of the case are all about. In effect I am being fobbed off with hollow excuses that give the appearance of a lawyer who hasn't done his job or at least part of a job for which he charged 8,500.00 kroner. When Per Danielsen says that I stopped the assignment, I only stopped it because he forced me to stop it owing to his previous misunderstanding which he could not bring himself to correct.

2. Exactly which papers did Per Danielsen read through in his seven and a half hours of work and how can he fail to see the enormous difference between NN's letters to me and my other evidence on the one hand and the newspaper allegations on the other hand? Why no comment on the fact that in all the newspaper articles I am being referred to as "the Muslim man"?

3. My letters of the 7th and 12th December 1998 to Per Danielsen are clear enough and remain to this day substantially unanswered. Clearly the committee looking into this complaint have ignored the comments made in these letters and I trust the appeal judge will now consider these comments.

4. Per Danielsen's letter to me of December 8th 1998 refers to the fact that I "would have problems in wining cases against the newspapers and NN." Per Danielsen is therefore asserting that he knows of these problems and he should therefore communicate the nature of these problems to me. He never did this and should have done at the time.

5. Per Danielsen's letter of the 15th January 1999 to the Den Norske Advokatforening referred to his belief that I had been "harassing" NN and that I was a "busybody" and that I was "really just frustrated." However no reasons were given for his claim. This is further evidence that he cannot give impartial advice, leave alone proper advice. Such comments together with the contents of my taped telephone conversation with Per Danielsen on December 7th 1998 indicate to me that he had little grasp of the basics of the case which remotely resembled seven and a half

333

hours of work. There wasn't <u>that</u> much to read anyway and an experienced lawyer like Per Danielsen should know how to be selective in his perusal of the papers in front of him. I had in any case, in correspondence, indicated exactly which papers he should read through to help him form an opinion for the £1,000.00 I had paid him.

6. In his letter to me of the 30th October 1998 the clear message from Per Danielsen is that he needs another NKR 10,000 to read the extra documents that he has just received from my previous lawyer. Documents that were in fact just duplicates of what he already had. That was why I refused payment of another 10,000 kroner as it was demanded on a mistaken assumption.

7. Connected to this is Per Danielsen's refusal to discuss the case on the telephone with me (see my letter to him of 12th December 1998). My intention was to guide him directly to the issues that mattered and to save his time and to get telephone advice on the legal position on the basic principles. He had, after all, requested me to phone him on the 30th October, an appointment that I kept but which when I tried to speak to him I was told he was not available. Instead I get a letter the same day asking me for more money.

8. It is quite obvious from the evidence, which anyone can see, that I am, if nothing else, a victim of hatred for Muslims. To be referred to in Bergens Tidende in 1995 at least 16 times as "the Muslim man" and also to have similar references in Drammens Tidende and Verdens Gang to being "a Muslim" speaks for itself. No Norwegian newspaper would put "the Jew" or "the Christian" to such an extent. Moreover the association of my religion with a speculative and degrading assessment of my character will never be forgiven or forgotten by me. I wonder what the wider Muslim public would think of this institutionalised attack on Muslims. I suspect that the Norwegian newspapers still want revenge on the Muslim world for what happened to William Nygaard, the Norwegian publisher of Salman Rushdie's book 'The Satanic Verses.' Nygaard, a man who only last month went on British terrestrial television to proclaim how happy he was to publish this book, in effect saying that it was his moral and public duty to publish the book. The former British Foreign Secretary, Lord Howe, in the same programme described the book as being utterly perverse and offensive to Muslims. The appeal judge on this case only needs to read the translated transcript of my conversations with the Drammens Tidende journalist Ingunn Røren, to see the lengths this journalist went to, to pervert the image of Islam. Certainly Ingunn Røren's taped evidence deserves to go public – she can sue me if she wants to.

9. Per Danielsen I suspect is lying and even if he isn't he gives the clear appearance of having ripped me off. I repeat, that it is no exaggeration to describe him as having the manners of a pig in his taped conversation with me of 7th December 1998. I want the appeal judge on this case to give a specific ruling on this conversation as to whether it is unworthy of a lawyer to react like this. It certainly brings the Norwegian legal profession into disrepute. Danielsen was trapped by his own arrogance on that occasion and must bitterly regret being caught out.

10. Only a fool would be unable to see the full extent of NN's lies and the newspapers' real agenda. Per Danielsen represents himself as a libel expert yet his attitude and unsubstantiated legal comment are worse than useless.

I want all my money back, not just the outstanding fee. I also deserve on top of this, further compensation as indicated above.

As things presently stand NN along with Drammens Tidende, Ingunn Røren and Hans Odde will face trial next year, as declared by Judge Anders Stilloff of the Drammen Byrett in September. So I have got in part what I set out to achieve. However it should have been easy to get to this stage long ago. I have paid a high price and I will make sure that those in Norway who have so tried to ruin me and denigrate the founding values of Islam will never be allowed to forget it.

334

Yours sincerely,

Frederick Delaware

Danielsen didn't reply at all to these comments and on 18th May 2001 the Appeal Committee reached its decision:

Report of 18th May 2001:

By letter of 23 November 2000 Complainant, Frederick Delaware, filed in appeal with the Disciplinary Board against points 1 and 3 in the Disciplinary Committee's conclusion. He also sent the Board a letter dated 27th November 2000 in which he claims, inter alia, compensation for the time and unpleasantness the complaint proceedings have caused him.

Per Danielsen has not entered a reply to the appeal. It is therefore accepted that he adheres to his earlier statements in the matter.

The appeal to the Disciplinary Board has not brought forth any fresh information and therefore the position with regard to the complaint is the same as in the first instance.

With regard to the facts of the case, reference is made to the presentation given by the Committee.

The Disciplinary Board has reached the same result as the Disciplinary Committee and in essentials agrees with the reasoning given by that Committee. The Disciplinary Board considers it obvious that a lawyer must be allowed an opportunity to examine a matter and decide whether there is due cause for legal action before notifying the other party that such action will be instituted. If in such a case the client is unwilling to accept the lawyer's advice, the lawyer is entitled to refuse the assignment. This similarly applies in a case where the client does not pay a retainer or furnish security for the fee and costs when so requested. With regard to the complaint regarding the fee charged, the Disciplinary Board agrees with the Committee. The total fee of NOK 8,500 – based on 7.5 hours of work, is in reasonable proportion to the scope of the work, the nature of the assignment and the circumstances otherwise, and it is considered that the work performed by Per Danielsen was necessary for proper performance of the assignment.

This decision is unanimous.

Conclusion:

The decision of the Disciplinary Committee is upheld.

Knut Glad

Chairman

As can be seen, the Disciplinary Board, in considering my appeal, mentioned nothing whatsoever about the points I had raised in my letters of 23rd and 27th November 2000. When the Board referred to Per Danielsen's failure to reply to those letters, I see it as his ducking the questions I had posed. The Board also stated that I had not brought forth any "fresh information." I was merely asking for answers to my original complaints to be addressed by the Board in writing. This 'fresh evidence' obstacle was the same ploy imposed by the Press

Complaints Commission to cover up the shortcomings of the defendants. Again, this abysmal response would not happen in England.

Finally, the Danielsen saga was brought to an end when on 5th June 2001 I asked the Norwegian Bar Association to ask Danielsen to reimburse me the balance of monies due to me after deducting his fee. On 21st June I received a cheque for £338.65 from Danielsen's correspondent bank, the Royal Bank of Scotland.

Chapter 24

With regard to the lawyer Helge Wesenberg from Bergen, I was very annoyed still that no answers had been forthcoming from him, which I had employed Karsten Gjone to obtain. Clearly Gjone wasn't going to bother, so on 23rd August 1998, I put in a complaint against Helge Wesenberg to the Lawyers Disciplinary Tribunal in Bergen. They had told me on the telephone that there was a six-month time limit, so as Wesenberg had last written to me in 1995, I was well outside the time limit. As usual there was a discretion for the Tribunal to hear my complaint out of time. My heads of complaint were:

1. The refusal of Wesenberg to send me any details of the serious allegation of attempted rape, on the grounds that the Bergen police may re-open the case. I'd made it clear to Wesenberg in 1995 that I didn't attempt to rape her and asked him to look into it. He refused as has been seen.

2. Wesenberg's excuse to me that he was too busy to represent me (his letter of 9th June 1995) only for him to tell me his real reasons on 17th July 1995 and 26th October 1995.

3. Wesenberg's complete silence on Heidi Schøne's past (as told by me), including the fact she'd been in a psychiatric unit and his absence of comment on her letters to me which clearly contradicted the newspaper assertions of continuous harassment and sex terror.

4. Wesenberg's failure to comment on the fact that the Bergen police in 1990 did not mention a thing to my London lawyer about the attempted rape allegation made to the police station in 1986 by Heidi.

5. I also wanted Wesenberg's comments on the supposed letter I'd written threatening to kill Heidi's two year old son, which letter was supposed to have been given to the Bergen police, whose files he'd examined.

6. Importantly, I wanted to know why Wesenberg failed to comment on my London lawyer's letter to Krogvold at Bergen police regarding police comments that I faced (in theory) a prison sentence regarding the police's unspecified allegations.

On 19th October 1998, Attorney Tor Hauer, Chairman of the Disciplinary Tribunal, made his decision which was that I was outside the six month time limit, in order to succeed in my complaint being considered.

Further the Tribunal stated: "Section 5(2) of the procedural rules lays down that the Disciplinary Committee, even though a deadline has been exceeded, may consider the complaint under consideration is deemed to be reasonable for special reasons. The Disciplinary Committee does not find that there are special reasons in favour of considering the case on its merits. Emphasis has also been placed on the fact that the deadline has been exceeded considerably. The complaint is accordingly rejected."

However, I had three weeks in which to appeal the decision and on 23rd October 1998 I sent in my appeal arguing that my case should be looked into as it did have special merits particularly as Heidi Schøne's allegation had been changed from "attempted rape" to "actual rape." My appeal was now to be considered by District Judge Knut Glad, President of the Disciplinary Tribunal, who, I was told on 16th November, would give "a decision on whether the case should be considered on its merits."

On the 29th April 1999, the Disciplinary Tribunal wrote to me with a full translation of Judge Knut Glad's decision, which is reproduced here:

THE DISCIPLINARY COMMITTEE

has   on 28ᵗʰ April 1999

dealt with Appeal No: D105.98 Professional Ethics

Complainant: Frederick Delaware

Respondent: Helge Wesenberg, Attorney at Law

Participated in the proceedings: District Court Justice Knut Glad

The Disciplinary Committee announced the following:

RESOLUTION:

On 23ʳᵈ August Frederick Delaware complained to the Norwegian Bar Association about the conduct of Attorney Helge Wesenberg in a case he had undertaken for him.

The Complainant is resident in England.

Briefly told, he engaged the attorney to conduct investigations directed against a woman acquaintance of Complainant who lived in Norway. According to the Complainant, the said woman had directed against him serious and untruthful accusations of assault.

The Disciplinary Subcommitee for Aust-Agder, Vest–Agder, Stavanger and Haugesund districts of the Norwegian Bar Association pronounced on 19th October 1998, through the President of the Subcommittee alone, a resolution with the following **conclusion:**

   "The complaint is dismissed"

The grounds for the dismissal of the complaint was that it had been presented more than six months after the Complainant became – or ought to have become aware of the circumstances of the complaint. The complaint period was exceeded and the Subcommittee did not see any special reason for nevertheless dealing with the complaint.

The Complainant, on 23 October 1998, appealed from the Subcommittee's decision to the Disciplinary Committee. He referred to the problems that had been caused to him by the necessity of having to engage a new attorney, after Respondent refused to continue handling his case. He claimed that Respondent had cooperated in a cover-up and thus shamefully prevented Complainant from getting full information of importance to his contestation of the said woman's accusations against him of assault.

The case appears before the Committee essentially as before the Subcommittee.

By letter of 16 November 1998 from the secretariat of the Disciplinary Subcommittee, the parties were informed that the case had been forwarded to the president of the Disciplinary Committee for consideration of the dismissal on the ground that the period allowed for complaint had been exceeded.

The Disciplinary Committee has come to the same result as the Disciplinary Subcommittee, but on somewhat different grounds.

338

The Attorneys Regulations provide in § 5-4 that when three years have elapsed from the date on which a complainant became – or ought to have become – aware of the circumstances on which the complaint is based, a complaint can no longer be presented. This is an unconditional rule which prevents the Disciplinary Committee from dealing with a complaint, even if the facts of the case might have made it reasonable to consider it.

Respondent declined to continue handling the case for Complainant by letter dated 9th June 1995. The reason he gave was lack of time. After renewed application from Complainant, Respondent declared by letter of 17th July 1995 that he was no longer willing to represent Complainant because the latter failed to accept the advice he was given by the attorney.

The period for filing complaint must be regarded as having begun at the latest when Complainant received this letter. His complaint against the attorney was filed only by letter of 28 August 1998, i.e. after the absolute period for complaint had expired.

The complaint is accordingly dismissed.

The decision has been adopted by the President of the Disciplinary Committee alone pursuant to § 5-5 (1), see § 5-4, of the Attorneys Regulations.

Conclusion
The decision by the Disciplinary Subcommittee is upheld.

Knut Glad
President

You will see then, that in fact I was only 6 weeks out of time according to the Judge, which on the face of it was very bad luck. The Judge made my receipt of the letter of 17th July 1995 from Wesenberg the point from which the three year time limit ran. I sent a fax on 4th May 1999 to Bodil Ekrem, Administration secretary of the Disciplinary Tribunal:

Dear Madam,

Thank you for your letter of 29.04.99 with enclosures.

The attached copy letter from Helge Wesenberg is dated 7.11.95. This was the last letter I received from him before I made my complaint. Negotiations by me were continuing up to this time to try and resolve the matter with Wesenberg.

Surely, by the Attorney's Regulations in § 5-4 the three year period in which to make a complaint runs from 7th November 1995 – in which case my complaint should be heard?

Is it not right that I should make every effort to resolve a dispute with the attorney himself, first, before making a complaint? Only once it was absolutely clear that Wesenberg would not co-operate should the time limit run. Am I right?

Yours faithfully,

Frederick Delaware

The next morning I was told there was nothing I could do when I phoned the Tribunal offices. So I wrote to the Judicial Secretary, on 5th May 1999:

Dear Mr. Wishman,

Helge Wesenberg

I refer to Bodil Ekrem's letter to me of 29.04.99 and my reply of 4.05.99. In England a time limit would run from the date of the last letter from the lawyer in a series of correspondence. I believe it is quite incorrect for the letter of 17th July 1995 to be taken as the three year time limit commencement date. Did the Judge actually see copies of my letters of 26.10.95 and 7.11.95? If so, how could he possibly conclude that it was the letter of 17th July 1995 from which the time limit ran? I mean no disrespect to the Judge but there must be a mistake on this. Bodil Ekrem told me on the phone today there is nothing more I could do, but how can this be? If the Judge has unwittingly made a mistake then that is something I wish to remedy.

Please help me on this point and confirm that you understand my argument.

Yours sincerely,

Frederick Delaware

I received Mr. Wishman's rather bland reply in his letter of 11th May 1999:

COMPLAINT CONCERNING PROFESSIONAAL ETHICS:
FREDERICK DELAWARE ADVOKAT HELGE WESENBERG

Dear Sir,

We refer to your letter of 05.05.99.

In resolution of 28.04.99 The Disciplinary Committee upheld the decision made by the Disiplinary Subcommittee that says that your complaint is dismissed. The decisions made by the Disciplinary Committee are not subject to appeal. I refer to the courts of law act § 227. This means that you have to bring the decision in for a Court of Law.

I am sorry to inform you that we no longer can help you.

Yours sincerely,

Carl-Chr. Wishman
Jurist

If you refer in Chapter 16 to Wesenberg's letter of 26th October 1995, you can see that he offers further advice on why he will not represent me. Advice which he was telling me for the first time. I was still not satisfied with his unsubstantiated explanations and enquired further of him on 29th October 1995 so he wrote again on 7th November 1995. It surely was arguable that either of these later two letters from Wesenberg should be taken as the starting point from which the three year time limit should run.

Regarding my complaint against the lawyer, Karsten Gjone, he wrote twice in Norwegian to the Disciplinary Tribunal with his version of events, the translations for which are:

Letter dated 30th October 1998 from Karsten Gjone:

Grievance Committee for Oppland, Buskerud
Vestfold and Telemark districts of
The Norwegian Bar Association
Per chairman Rune Jensen, barrister at law
Postboks 278, 3201 Sandefjord

Case of complaint No. 36/1998: Frederick Delaware – Karsten Gjone, barrister at law

I refer to your letter of 15th inst.

The undersigned received at the end of January this year a communication from lawyer Ronald Pedersen, Moss, enquiring whether I could help an English lawyer residing in London.

The help would consist in establishing contact between the person concerned and a woman residing in the district of Drammen, and also appraising the action against Bergens Tidende, VG and Drammens Tidende with a claim for damages.

It is correct that at the end of January I received a file containing copies of newspaper articles and a very large amount of correspondence, including a number of communications from Frederick Delaware addressed to individuals/authorities.

Immediately after receipt of the documents, the client began making telephone calls to the undersigned. He was informed that I had to spend some time examining the material sent to me. At the same time, a number of letters began to arrive for me, as documented in his complaint of 30 September this year. His innumerable communications delayed the proceedings, of course.

During the proceedings, I was asked by the client to contact the previous counsel, lawyer Helge Wesenberg, Bergen, police constable Torill Sorte at Nedre Eiker police office and also police inspector Lyngås at Drammen police station. I have had conversations with all three of them. The information that I obtained was used as the basis in my counselling for Frederick Delaware. The complainant states in his complaint that he did not receive a single reply from the undersigned.

In conclusion, I would like to mention that the client's innumerable verbal and written communications have caused considerable extra work which has not been recorded, and now finally I would just mention that, at the start of the assignment, the client paid £100 and has not subsequently been invoiced for my work.

With kind regards,
Karsten Gjone

Then by a letter dated 17th November 1998 Karsten Gjone wrote again:

Grievance Committee for Oppland, Buskerud
Vestfold and Telemark districts of
The Norwegian Bar Association
Per chairman Rune Jensen, barrister at law
Postboks 278, 3201 Sandefjord
Case of complaint No. 36/1998: Frederick Delaware – lawyer Karsten Gjone

I refer to your letter of 6 November this year with the complainant's letter of the same date enclosed, presumably sent by fax.

I adhere to that which is stated in my reply of 30 October this year. I still maintain that I did not act in breach of the Rules for good lawyer's practice. The proceedings were delayed mainly owing to continual communications from the complainant to myself, and I would refer in this connection to the annex to the complaint, the letter of 24 July 1998, a 10-page letter which it also became necessary to examine.

The complainant wanted actions against newspapers mentioned earlier to be appraised, which I advised against unequivocally, and he also wanted the action against Heidi Schøne to be appraised – which I likewise found I could not recommend.

If the Grievance Committee wishes to have a further statement from my side before the decision is taken, I assume the parties will be contacted.

With kind regards,

Karsten Gjone

On 13th January 1999, the Disciplinary Tribunal found in my favour and the translation of their decision is produced below:

[hand-stamp]

[heraldic shield]

The Norwegian Bar Association, Grievance Committee for Oppland, Buskerud, Bestfold and Telemark districts.

On 13 January 1999

Tried the case of complaint No.   36/1998 – Good lawyer's practice

Complainant: Frederick Delaware

Summonsed party: Lawyer Karsten Gjone

The following participated   Marit Eggen
In the proceedings   Gunnar A. Jahren
                                             Lars Skjelbred

Certified a true copy of the original
[hand stamp]

LAWYER

RUNE JENSEN

SANDEFJORD

[signed]
Berg Nilsen

The following

DECISION

was pronounced

By letter dated 30.9.1998, Frederick Delaware summonsed lawyer Karsten Gjone before the Bar Association's Grievance Committee for breach of good lawyer's practice. The complaint was submitted to lawyer Gjone, who gave his opinion on the matter.

Facts of the case

Frederick Delaware communicated with lawyer Gjone by letter dated 23.1.1998, requesting assistance in his case, after having previously received assistance from another lawyer, without the desired result being achieved. The latter lawyer was also summonsed before the Grievance Committee by the same complainant, but in another district.

The case concerned a Norwegian woman, NN, who had reported Delaware in 1986 for (attempted?) rape, and who subsequently had given the press information which resulted in 3 Norwegian newspapers (VG, Bergens Tidende and Drammens Tidende) printing in 1995 stories about him, dealing with, among other matters, various forms of harassment of NN over several years. Delaware did not wish to have assertions of this kind applied to himself, and what he requested assistance for in the letter to lawyer Gjone was "to get NN to answer the allegations she has been making in the newspaper articles, e.g. threats to kill her son Daniel – who was 2 years old at the time! And threats to kill the neighbours, herself, her friends, etc., etc." In addition, he wanted to sue the 3 newspapers and demand a public apology, as well as damages for himself and on behalf of the Muslim religion, as being offended via the complainant.

A large amount of written material exists, from the complainant to lawyer Gjone. Lawyer Gjone for his part, did not send any written replies to his client, but gave his advice over the telephone. The advice is reported to have been that the complainant did not have any case to pursue further within the Norwegian legal system.

Substance of the complainant's pleading:

During the 8 months that had elapsed since Delaware's first letter to lawyer Gjone of 24.1.98 and until the complaint was lodged on 30 September of the same year, the complainant had not received a single written reply from the lawyer, nor were the actual tasks carried out which the complainant had asked his lawyer to perform, such as to contact a few named persons – within the police service, for example. So eight months had elapsed without anything whatsoever happening in the case – and this proves also to have resulted in it becoming too late to sue the newspapers for damages. The main point in the whole case has therefore disappeared.

The complainant states that he had a similar experience with another Norwegian lawyer, whom he also summonsed before the Grievance Committee, and on the basis of the experience he is now having with Norwegian lawyers, police, etc., he is convinced that there is a conspiracy against him here, since he writes:

"I am sick and tired of inept Norwegian lawyers and I resent having to tramp around law firms asking for someone to do a proper job. To have had nothing in 8 months is a disgrace. I know there is a cover-up, so please don't forget to find out exactly what is going on."

In addition, he writes, a further letter dated 06.11.98

"I believe that Gjone has done next to nothing. He refused my request to send him more money. Many of my telephone calls were met with the response that he was busy or in court or that he hadn't had the time to make contact with the relevant people. Delay, delay, delay and inaction. His English is poor and he is incapable of understanding the details. Gjone repeatedly told me he was "just about to write" to me – but he never did. He did FOR THE FIRST TIME tell me in late August that I could not sue the newspapers or NN. The reason with the newspapers he said was because they didn't name me – but clearly, as I have explained, he was wrong. The first thing Tor Erling Staff told me when I rang him up was to ask me if anyone I knew in Norway recognized that the articles referred to me. Yes, I told him. But then he told me there is a three-year time limit to sue – which I now had missed – May 95 to May 98, for the three articles in late May 95.

Gjone gave no reasons whatsoever as to why I could not sue NN herself. This is not the work of a competent lawyer. There was no indication at all that he had obtained the necessary information I had asked for to enable him to give that opinion."

Substance of the summonsed party's pleading:

He was asked by a colleague in January 1998 to help an English lawyer to make contact with a Norwegian woman and appraise the case against three Norwegian newspapers with claims for damages. In this connection, he received from Delaware a file containing a number of documents: copies of newspaper articles and "a very large amount of correspondence, including a number of communications from Delaware to individuals/organisations."

The summonsed party also writes in his reply to the complaint of 30.10 this year:

"Immediately after receipt of the documents, the client began to make telephone calls to the undersigned. He was informed that I had to spend some time on examining the material sent to me. At the same time, a number of letters began to flow in for me – as is documented, incidentally, in his complaint of 30 September this year. His innumerable communications delayed the proceedings, of course."

The summonsed party otherwise states that he contacted the people whom Delaware had asked him to contact, and the information he received in these conversations was used as the basis in the advice to the client. The summonsed party goes on to write:

"The complainant alleges in his complaint that he did not receive a single reply from the undersigned. This is not correct. I have made it known repeatedly that I cannot recommend suing the abovementioned newspapers, first and foremost because none of the articles refers to him personally. I have not reported this in writing, but I have stated it clearly several times.

I have constantly appraised the factual and legal questions, so that the complainant has no 'case,' either against the abovementioned newspapers or against NN.

The assignment was concluded by the complainant telephoning my office to say that he would "seek other assistance.""

The summonsed party maintains that the client was kept fully informed of the handling of the case in innumerable telephone calls, that the advice given was clear, but that the client did not wish to follow the recommendations.

The summonsed party denies that he acted in breach of good lawyer's practice, and is of the opinion that the case was "handled with reasonable speed," since the proceedings were delayed somewhat owing to the client's innumerable calls.

The Grievance Committee shall note:

The complaint was lodged within the time limit and dealt with in the usual way.

The complaint against the lawyer is considered to contain assertions of several blameworthy situations:

1. Dilatoriness during execution of the assignment

2. Absence of replies to questions

3. Failure to execute actual assignments

4. Exceeding the time limit for suing the newspapers

In general, it may be noted that communication between lawyer and complainant in this case has been rather special, in that the complainant has sent very many written requests to the lawyer during the period of the client relationship, with, in some instances, clear expression of what he wants the lawyer to do. Copies of these letters – or in any case some of them – have been sent to the Committee together with the complaint. The lawyer, on his side, has not, according to the Committee's understanding, sent anything in writing back to his client, so that all communication from his side has been verbal, over the telephone. It is therefore impossible to document the lawyer's statements in connection with the complaint.

1. Dilatoriness

Under the rules for good lawyer's practice, point 3.1.2., the lawyer shall take care of the client's interest "quickly, conscientiously and carefully."

The assignment given by the complainant to the summonsed party was a quite complicated task which could not be expected to be done very quickly. It seems that the complainant agreed with this at the beginning. There was a regular flow of documents from the complainant's side to the summonsed party as the case proceeded, and communication existed between the lawyer and client, even though it certainly seems as if the client has been considerably more active than the lawyer.

The Committee cannot see that the summonsed party acted in breach of the ethical rules on this point.

2. Absence of replies to questions

The complainant maintains that he has not received replies to his questions. However, the main question in this case is the one embraced by the assignment itself and the summonsed party asserts in his reply that he has given clear answers to the complainant over the telephone to the effect that the case is not a "case." This has not been documented; nevertheless, there is no reason to doubt the lawyer's statement. On the basis of the letters which the complainant has continued to send to his lawyer, it seems, however, that this viewpoint, and the advice which then followed naturally regarding not going further with the case, did not reach the client, since he was still requiring actual tasks to be carried out in the same way as he had done earlier, right up to the ending of the relationship in August. The lawyer should have reacted to this.

Since the advice not to go further was completely decisive for the relationship between lawyer and client, the summonsed party should have ensured that his advice reached its destination, by giving it in writing. If the advice not to go further with the case meant that the lawyer considered the assignment finished – and this would be the logical consequence – then this, too, should have been clarified in writing, so that there was no doubt as to whether or not a client relationship existed at all.

On this point, the Committee's view is that the summonsed party infringed the ethical rules.

3. Failure to carry out actual assignments

The lawyer states that, following a request from the client, he contacted three named persons with knowledge of the case, namely the previous lawyer, the rural policeman and a police inspector. Other requirements, such as delivering a letter in person to NN, or starting to take evidence from a number of people, were not fulfilled.

This cannot be considered to have any separate significance in the case and the summonsed party did not breach the ethical rules on this point.

4. Exceeding the time limit for suing the newspapers

The normal time allowed for claiming damages or redress is 3 years, according to § 9 of the statute of limitations. It is difficult to know from the documents in the case whether the 3-year term expired in May 1998 – 3 years after the articles concerned were printed in the Norwegian newspapers. However, it has not been stated by the summonsed party to the Committee that this important question was considered, even though it was an essential part of the complaint. It is possible, therefore, that the time limit for litigation was exceeded without the complainant being aware of it.

The expiration of time limits which have a binding effect is serious for a party and, regardless of the summonsed party's conception of the reality of the case, this question should have been taken up directly and clearly so that it was clear that the client understood the problem and could relate to it. He did not get an opportunity to do this.

The decision is unanimous.

FINDING:

Lawyer Karsten Gjone acted in breach of good lawyer's practice.

[signature]   [signature]   [signature]

In response to my earlier complaint, Gjone had pathetically replied to the DNA that the reason he did not write to me in all that time was because I kept ringing him up and his time was taken up in speaking to me, thus preventing him from writing to me. This was a total lie. As I've explained earlier, most of the time he wasn't available when I phoned and when he was available he had little to say of any practical value. He didn't even offer the DNA a proper explanation as to why I couldn't sue my opponent Heidi Schøne.

So what is the punishment for a Norwegian lawyer completely wasting a client's time? In Gjone's case the punishment was absolutely nothing – unless you take the DNA's decision letter itself as sufficient humiliation. There was no fine for Gjone, no compensation for me. And although in Gjone's case his inaction was not sufficiently bad to warrant appearing in person before the Norwegian Bar Association's Disciplinary Committee, I discovered that in Norway they never publicly name lawyers who have been disciplined as the English Law Society Gazette regularly does. No, in Norway they print an annual report on the offending lawyers but just refer to them by reference to a number. No naming and shaming. I wrote to the DNA's lawyer, Rune Jensen, and told him that I hoped one day the Norwegian Law Society would name and shame its errant lawyers and sent him a copy of the Law Society's Gazette, which had a section on the disciplined solicitors. However, I'll give Rune Jensen his due. He was the one who brought it to my attention for the first time that the newspapers in Norway were obliged by their self-regulating rules to contact me before going to print and get my side of the story, and once they print a story they are obliged to print the victim's point of view afterwards. Well, for the four newspaper stories on me, no-one contacted me at all. Shame on Wesenberg and Gjone and the PFU for not telling me this. Shame also on Wesenberg for not advising me of my right to complain to the PFU and of their three month time limit regarding the May 1995 stories. They just couldn't give a damn, could they?

I had already been in touch with Gjone's insurance company, Vesta Forsikring AS, who on 15th January 1999 replied saying:

OUR CLAIM NO/OUR REF. : HAS 98-908329

CLAIM FOR DAMAGES AGAINST SOLICITOR KARSTEN GJONE

Dear Mr. Delaware,

We are in receipt of your letter of 11th December 1998 with enclosed tapes.

We have listened to the tape but do not find it appropriate to comment on your situation with Mr. Danielsen.

Concerning your claim against Mr. Gjone, you do not in any circumstances have a case against him unless you can prove that there was a case against the newspapers.

We have read the newspaper articles you have provided us with. As far as we can see there is nothing in these that connects or identify your person to the content of the articles.

Consequently, we find it quite unlikely that you would have won a possible trial against the newspapers and your claim against Mr. Gjone is therefore rejected.

Sincerely yours,
For Vesta Forsikring AS,

Hans-Arnt Skjølberg

I wrote back on 21st January 1999:

Dear Mr. Skjølberg,

Karsten Gjone

Thank you for your letter of 15th January. Your rejection of my claim of course ignores the quick advice given to me by Tor Erling Staff that it is not necessary for me to be named so long as a reader(s) identifies me from the articles. Ann-Kristin Horvei of Bergen who I have known since 1984 identified me from Verdens Gang, saying, "Who else could it be?" She has not spoken to Heidi for 10 years and had no idea previously of any of the allegations made by the newspapers. Ann-Kristin asked me if the allegations were true. I said they were false. Shall I get her to provide a statement?

I look forward to your response on this before I get John Christian Elden, my Oslo lawyer, to deal with you.

As requested, I enclose a copy of the Norwegian Disciplinary Tribunal's Report dated 13th January reprimanding Karsten Gjone. Kindly acknowledge receipt.

Yours sincerely,

Frederick Delaware

I spoke later to the insurance Company's lawyer Hans-Arnt Skjølberg who acknowledged Gjone had been at fault, but told me it was up to me to provide the legal evidence to prove my claim that the newspapers would be liable to compensate me.

Chapter 25

Merely at random, from a list I had of Oslo lawyers, I chose a chap called John Elden, simply because I thought that he was an Englishman who had settled in Norway and was practising law. I was quite wrong! He was very Norwegian indeed and he asked me to write in to him. I did so on 10th November 1998. My tactics this time were not to send in any previous correspondence at all or even mention that I had used Norwegian lawyers before. I sent John Elden copies of the four newspaper articles; copies of three of Heidi's letters; the one page résumé in Norwegian of Heidi's past (my famous - 'Report'), my 'Press Release' and the nine page story that I'd sent to the newspapers three years earlier. I hadn't got a reply by 13th December 1998, so I sent another reminder together with the tape recordings of policeman Svein Jensen and the journalist Ingunn Røren from Spring of 1996.

I then received a letter dated 11th December 1998 being simply an invoice, nothing else, requesting I transfer 5,000 Norwegian kroner into their account (about £405). I sent it off by bank transfer on 15th January 1999 and on 21st January wrote again to Elden and Elden, enclosing the result of my successful complaint against Advokat Karsten Gjone. I made it quite clear in that letter that I thought I was entitled to bring a case against Heidi for the lies she told in the press but told Elden & Elden that I wasn't quite so sure about my ability to successfully sue the newspapers as I wasn't named, save for the fact that one or two people recognised me from the articles. I asked Elden & Elden to look up the case law on this "recognition" point and to correspond with Karsten Gjone's insurance company, Vesta. I also asked them to pursue the Press Complaints Bureau (the PFU) whose Mr. Børringbo had, I told them, refused to look into my complaint against Drammens Tidende as "they had not named" me.

On 28th January 1999, Elden & Elden wrote to me:

> Dear Mr. Delaware,
>
> **HEIDI SCHØNE**
>
> In reference to your letter dated 10 November.
>
> We have contacted both Bergen and Drammen police districts (including Nedre Eiker police station) and requested that the case files be forwarded. When I have received the files, I will examine them thoroughly.
>
> In libel-cases the police seldom seems to be of much help to the defendant, [Elden & Elden should have said "plaintiff "] and we must therefore be prepared to take the necessary measures ourselves.
>
> Until I have received the police files, I will not be able to comment any further on the possible false statements given to the police by Heidi Schøne. On this basis, I recommend that any further action be delayed until the files have been examined. Neither Ms. Schøne nor any other involved parties have any obligations towards me as to enlighten the case.
>
> I am also obliged to point out that our legal fee in cases as this one, at this time is NOK 1000, - per hour. I urge you to consider the costs versus the possible gain in conjunction with the case closely, as I must also point out that most of your up-front payment has been used. To conduct further work on the case, I therefore will require further payment made to my account no. [****.**.*****] in the Union Bank of Norway.
>
> Finally, may I also refer to Norwegian libel-law; possible criminal punishment and damages payable by the defendant may be waived by the court in the case of self-infliction through conduct that may be criticised in the first place, or through reversed libel or physical retortion. On this basis, we may be met by accusations that the possible libel from Ms. Schøne was "nullified" by reversed libel.
>
> It is, however, much too early to make any predictions as to the result of a legal process before the Norwegian courts. Even true statements can be considered libel

in Norwegian law, should the statements have been made without reasonable cause or based on the way in which the statements were made.

In case you should doubt Ms. Schøne's mental state, I must also point out that Norwegian law does not accept the conviction of people considered legally insane, and this state may also free the accused of paying any damages. The court may, however, declare the statements made nullified.

Kind regards,

ATTORNEYS AT-LAW ELDEN DA

For John Christian Elden advokat

John Christian Elden was the son of John Elden Senior who I initially spoke to.

I replied on 2nd February 1999:

Dear Mr. Elden,

Heidi Schøne

Many thanks for your letter of 28th January. I am grateful for your comments. I will arrange for another payment of NKR 5,000 to be made to your account.

I am painfully aware of the costs implications in this case. Maybe however we won't have to go to court if Heidi Schøne can be properly exposed and dealt with beforehand. My confidence comes from the direct evidence I have from policeman Svein Jensen that he doesn't really believe Heidi and they only have her word on what she's alleging.

First of all I'm looking forward to you writing to her once you've read the police papers. If you are concerned about the costs implications as I am, then the much avoided letter to Heidi Schøne is really an obvious and minimal requirement. Is she so out of reach, so untouchable? I have corroborating taped evidence from her best friend at the time about the event of the Bergen shopkeeper raping or attempting to rape Heidi.

I know the Bergen police papers well enough. But why in 1990 did they not tell me about the allegation of attempted rape from 1986 or the allegation of threats in writing to kill her son?

The failure of the newspapers to follow their own rules and give voice to my side of the story will surely be in my favour. How can the "libels" possibly cancel each other out when what I wrote is all true but what she wrote must to any normal person be seen for what it is – trash and lies.

As for Heidi Schøne's mental state: yes she was in the BSS Psychiatric Clinic in Lier; she has, she says, been "exorcised" and her husband did speak to me "in tongues." She is clearly very disturbed indeed but still clever enough, with criminal intent, to know exactly how to play things with the newspapers and police in order to give me maximum damage. But Svein Jensen didn't fall for her lies. The only pity is that Torill Sorte took over the case from him. A case, may I remind you, that didn't start to be investigated until April 17th 1996 at my own behest.

I am a lawyer. You are a lawyer. Put yourself in my position. How would you like it? I might well have been in much more trouble than I was and I will not forgive her motives in trying to ruin me. It's not my fault I didn't discover her allegation of attempted rape until nine years later – after all, my London lawyers should have

350

been told in 1990 and the statute of limitations ran out at the end of 1992. Besides, twelve years on she is saying that it's actual rape – for the first time, when it was me who constantly pressed Torill Sorte to investigate the circumstances of the allegation of attempted rape (as well as the Bergen shopkeeper event).

I don't mind a battle of words in court. I'm confident I can win.

And what of the PFU? Have they contacted you? Don't let them off the hook. I want their participation now. It is high time.

Yours sincerely,

Frederick Delaware

On 3rd February 1999, Elden & Elden wrote to me:

Dear Mr. Delaware,

HEIDI SCHØNE

In reference to your letter dated 21 January 1999.

I have today received the PFU files. PFU have in it's meeting on 17 September 1998 decided not to make exemptions from the time limit regarding your complaint. This decision is unfortunately final, or in other words inappealable.

I must also point out that your up-front payment now has been consumed. To conduct further work on the case, I therefore will require further payment made to my account no. [****.**.*****] in the Union Bank of Norway with NOK 6,000 this time.

Kind regards,

ATTORNEYS AT LAW ELDEN DA

For John Christian Elden advokat

This matter had in fact been passed over to another lawyer in the firm, Eric Lindset. He hadn't read the PFU papers properly. The date of "17th September 1998" was an Elden & Elden error. On 17th September 1996 the PFU rejected my 1996 complaint (refer to the letter from the PFU printed in Chapter 17 in this book dated 2nd October 1996). So on 6th February 1999 I wrote back to Eric Lindset:

Dear Mr. Lindset,

Heidi Schøne

Further to our telephone conversation yesterday, I enclose as you requested a copy of my letter to the PFU dated 19th July 1998 and their reply dated 29th July 1998. You will see that my complaint is <u>in time</u> in relation to the article of 14th July 1998 in Drammens Tidende. Please deal with the PFU and tell them to stop being a pain in the arse and investigate my complaint.

I also enclose a list of questions I gave to Karsten Gjone to be asked of Heidi Schøne. I want the answers, no matter what, and therefore once you have read the police papers please issue a writ against Heidi Schøne (and her husband if necessary). I must have your assurance, once you have read the police papers that a letter and then a writ will be issued.

You will find in the Bergen police papers an allegation of attempted rape from December 1986. This allegation is now actual rape (since 1998) as you will see on Drammen police papers. Don't blame me for telling everyone about Heidi's life if (a) false allegations of attempted rape and now rape are made against me as well as an allegation of rape by Heidi against a Bergen shopkeeper in the 1980's and (b) the newspapers disregarded their own rules in allowing my story to be printed to deny me the right to refute allegations that I threatened to kill her son, neighbours, friends etc.

This is a big case in Norway and I will not have things hushed up and kept quiet to save the newspapers, police and Heidi Schøne further embarrassment. She had her public say in the newspapers. Let me now get the answers to my questions. If she is legally insane, then the Court can declare this. Until they do on we go.

Yours sincerely,

Frederick Delaware

I also wrote on 8th February 1999:

Dear Mr. Elden,

Heidi Schøne

I am in receipt of your [firm's] letter of 3rd February this morning. Your colleague Eric Lindset will be in receipt soon of a letter of mine dated 6th February.

I telephoned the PFU this morning and Kjell Børringbo answered the phone. He told me that nothing has been decided yet on my complaint dated 19th July 1998 over the 14th July 1998 Drammens Tidende article. Børringbo wrote to Karsten Gjone on 29th July 1998 [and sent] a copy of that letter to me [on the same day]. I am clearly within the time limits and the PFU expect you to progress the matter. I expect nothing less than a full enquiry of Drammens Tidende.

May I please hear from you immediately that you have cleared up the confusion and that the PFU will look into my complaint of 19th July 1998. For ease of reference I enclose all the 1998 correspondence with the PFU.

Yours sincerely,

Frederick Delaware

P.S. Regarding my up-front payment, this of course has been spent reading the papers but what you have you to conclude so far? What of Anne-Kristin Horvei and Vesta? I see what you have written in your letter to me of 28th January but as Heidi Schøne's statements are outrageous lies, and my statements are true, then the burden of proof being on her to prove her newspaper allegations, the only way forward is for a writ to be issued asking her to prove her allegations. There are two aspects here: Heidi Schøne in court for her lies; the newspapers disobeying their self-regulatory rules; - your comments please, and Vesta dealing with the libel matter after Gjone's involvement. No matter what Norwegian laws are, I am in no doubt that I am entitled to get answers to my questions regarding Heidi's lies and she must prove what she said. Svein Jensen doesn't believe her - your comments please. As for Gjone, apart from his name being published in the legal journals for his failure to get answers to my questions, what else can be done to punish him?

Yours sincerely,

Frederick Delaware

And I wrote again on 14th February 1999:

Dear Mr. Lindset,

Heidi Schøne

I write further to our conversation last Friday. I expect the NKR 6,000 will arrive in your account in the next two or three days.

Now that you have the Bergen police papers and will soon have the Drammen police papers, please get answers to these questions:

1.   For the Bergen papers, please give me a list with dates of all the papers they have. Any letters of mine, please copy and send me. Please obtain an exact translation of Heidi Overaa's statement alleging attempted rape. I have correspondence between Foyen & Bell and Krogvold from 1990 but my lawyers were not happy with Krogvold at all and this time I want to sort things out once and for all.

2.   Please ask Krogvold why he didn't inform Foyen & Bell in 1990 of the allegation of attempted rape.

3.   Please ask Krogvold to supply evidence of Heidi Overaa's complaint of rape by a Bergen shopkeeper in the 1980's. Heidi told me herself and also told Ann-Kristin Horvei who told me too.

4.   Heidi told Torill Sorte that a letter was given by Gudmund Johannessen's parents in 1988 to the Bergen police wherein I was alleged to have threatened to kill Heidi's two year old son. The Bergen police do not recall ever having received such a letter, which is obviously not on the police file. How come such vital "evidence" is lost? Answer: because it never existed in the first place. And the fact that the Bergen police didn't report this to my lawyer in 1990 confirms this.

5.   On the Drammen police papers, please obtain the statement from Heidi saying that in fact she alleged I raped her. I want to compare statements of "attempted rape" to "rape." Why change her story?

6.   Please ask Policeman Svein Jensen why he didn't believe Heidi. He must have based his opinion on something, i.e. her statements. What papers did he look at and what was it exactly that made Svein Jensen think Heidi is lying? Remember it was quite a few months from Svein Jensen seeing Heidi and/or her statements to the time that Torill Sorte interviewed Heidi. I feel that the police had already made their minds up that Heidi was a liar. It was me who kept insisting for Heidi to be interviewed again. She kept avoiding the police until April 1996. Did Svein Jensen ever interview Heidi? After Svein Jensen there was another policeman handling the case: he did nothing, Torill Sorte told me, and then left. Next it was Torill Sorte's turn.

7.   Please obtain confirmation and details from the Drammen/Mjøndalen police of Heidi Overaa's complaint in Christmas 1990 to the police of the assault on her by Gudmund Johannessen. I want to know Johannessen's reasons for beating Heidi to the ground. It was this assault that I believe made Heidi want to get revenge on me and which she proceeded to do in February 1990 when I was arrested. I believe Johannessen was angry with Heidi for her telling me about Johannessen's heroin abuse.

N.B. Heidi has admitted to Torill Sorte that she asked me and my best friend over to Norway in 1998 to deal with Gudmund Johannessen prior to Heidi's second suicide attempt.

353

8. Please enquire of the newspapers why they failed to observe their own rules with regard to consulting me and printing my side of the story. Also did they pay Heidi money for her 'story'?

Please in future send me copies of all correspondence you have with others on my behalf.

Yours sincerely,

Frederick Delaware

On 18th February 1999 I received the following fax from Elden & Elden:

Dear Mr. Delaware,

HEIDI SCHØNE

In reference to your letters and copies, telephone calls and telefaxes.

I have been in touch with Mr. Børringbo at PFU, and he has also informed me that your last complaint is received within the correct time limit. In a letter dated 12 of February, the PFU has also informed me that they were uncertain as to whether you will try the case before the Courts. If so, the PFU rules implies that it may not rule on the complaint until the court action is finished.

I do not recommend legal action against Mr. Gjone. I have noted that you have issued both the PFU as well as «Drammens Tidende» (the newspaper) with copies of the Bar Association's decision against Mr. Gjone.

As you know from our telephone conversations, I have received the documents from Bergen police district. The case is too old for you to press charges, but I must let you know that the case files contain several letters from you. Some of these do contain what in Norwegian law is considered as threats, including threats of violence. Other letters contain what is here considered to be harassment, regardless of whether the contents is true or not. Norwegian law prohibits me from making you copies or translations of the police files without the police's written consent. The police does not normally consent in cases such as this one. You are however free to read the documents yourself in my office or at a police station.

I'm still waiting for the documents from Drammen police district. Until I have received these, I still cannot comment any further the case. I recommend that any further action be delayed until the files have been examined.

Furthermore, I must strongly emphasize that I must recommend against you contacting the other parties directly while we are handling the cases.

For your information, I enclose copies of all correspondence in the case this far.

Once more, I am also obliged to ask you to consider the costs versus the possible gain in conjunction with the case closely, as all the time we use on the case is being billed at 15 minute-increments. At present, we have used a total of 10,5 hours. Provided that you have recently made a payment of NOK 6,000, I must ask for another NOK 10,000 in advance based on the fact that this case seem to become work-intensive. Further work on the case requires such payment as mentioned.

Kind regards,

ATTORNEYS AT LAW ELDEN DA

354

As for "some of " my past letters containing "threats of violence," later in the year I got copies of all of those "several letters" – eight in all and only one from 1986 contained a threat of violence to Heidi and even that was a conditional one, hardly meriting great consideration now so many years later. More of the actual wording used in this "threatening" letter later.

Concerning the PFU rules, I was puzzled to be told on the telephone by Eric Lindset that the PFU required me first to promise not to sue the newspaper, Drammens Tidende, over their 14th July 1998 article, if the PFU were to proceed to investigate my complaint.

I replied on 18th February 1999 by two letters:

Dear Mr. Elden,

Heidi Schøne

I refer to your letter dated (mistakenly) 28th January faxed to me today by Eric Lindset. I await the hard copy plus 5 enclosures.

The NKR 6,000 should be in your account today or tomorrow. It has already been sent by my bank.

I note all you say. I have spoken to Eric Lindset this morning. I confirm that I will not be suing Drammens Tidende for the July 1998 article. They did not name me and I will not be able, I think, to find someone who recognised me from the article. [I was forgetting of course that my previous lawyer Karsten Gjone had recognised me.] However, the 1995 articles and Vesta/Gjone missing the time limits and Ann-Kristin Horvei recognising me must be carefully looked into.

Please therefore ask the PFU to look into my complaint.

Please also send me the lawyers journal with Gjone's name and negligence report. [I was yet to discover disciplined lawyers were never named.]

With regard to Bergen police dept. papers, I see that it seems a girl can do whatever she wants and in fact cannot be told off. I guess the fact that she later tried to take her life, again, over Gudmund Johannessen is, perversely, irrelevant. That I am far away in England, and was subjected to the behaviour of a disturbed woman seems to be of no concern to the police (who later told me that Heidi was sick). Also in 1988 I sent her many nice letters but they weren't given to the Bergen police.

Eric Lindset also told me [on the phone] that Heidi Schøne did not in 1986 make any sort of full statement concerning the allegation of attempted rape. She just mentioned the allegation. A pity because I would like to have compared statements from 1986 to 1998 when she told Torill Sorte that I raped her "by holding her down." Still, Heidi told the journalist at Drammens Tidende that I had "attempted" to rape her. Drammens Tidende did not print this. I told Drammens Tidende Heidi is now saying rape.

I appreciate your concern at my writing to the third parties. I did this to save my costs with you and to make these parties realise they must get on with helping you. But I won't write to them again.

As far as the Drammen police papers are concerned, there is nothing in them for you to worry about. The police only investigated the case because I asked them to and because of my information campaign against Heidi and the newspapers.

As Eric told me today, my claim against Heidi Schøne is for false accusations she made in 1995. As she will not voluntarily help me, then a writ to force her to prove the accusations is surely the only way forward.

I myself know more or less everything from the Drammen police papers. I was spending hundreds and hundreds of pounds phoning the Drammen police/Bergen police/newspapers/lawyers etc. I don't want you to spend much time looking at the Drammen papers. Save that I want to know exactly what papers Svein Jensen based his opinion on, that he did not believe Heidi. Did he see her? As for my information campaign, the newspapers are to blame. They did not follow their own rules to let my point of view be made public.

So if I had my way, I would say try not to penalise me in costs for information I mostly know of the Drammen police papers. Particularly as you feel you cannot even write to Heidi Schøne, the untouchable, for unproven false allegations in the press. I do realise that as you have not seen the Drammen papers, you cannot commit yourselves to acting against her, but you will soon see there will be nothing stopping you issuing a writ.

I will send more money but only once you have given me your word that a writ and letter will be given in person to Heidi Schøne over false allegations, on the basis that there will be nothing new for me in the Drammen police papers. You can wait until you receive the papers for a brief look and perhaps a telephone call to the investigating officer to cut down reading time.

Yours sincerely,

Frederick Delaware

Dear Mr. Elden,

Heidi Schøne

I refer to the Bergen police papers and the letters of mine they have. I remember well my time in the Bergen police station in 1990 in February. The police certified that <u>none</u> of my letters contained threats. These letters I read with my police interpreter, who told me she though Heidi was "sick." When I got back to England the police told me they'd been handed another letter by Heidi in which I'm supposed to have issued threats. One letter only. Yet the fact she's been sleeping with someone injecting with heroin – no comment by the police. Don't expect me to keep quiet or write nothing. I'm not in Norway. I have to write. And if I repeat my questions to her don't blame me – if she doesn't answer then I keep writing. When I went to Norway I was arrested on false accusations. Even the shit of a journalist with Verdens Gang told me the police had supplied him with "facts" for his story – the Bergen police. I asked the Bergen police in writing for an explanation, which I was told they were obliged to reply to. They never replied. So I had to pressure Heidi Schøne to overcome the cover-up. Are you telling me that the only way to get answers is to pay you to basically then tell me how so awfully much it will cost me, with the charge that I am wasting my money? Well, in other words, justice and answers are inaccessible in Norway. It won't work on me. I hold the Bergen police in complete contempt as I also do the newspapers and Karsten Gjone. They think just because I'm over here, and I'm not Norwegian, then they can say and write utter rubbish. Besides, it's racist and anti-Muslim crap that was printed. I've never hit Heidi or touched her, ever. But the pig she slept with – Johannessen – did abuse her and assault her. But he's 'OK.' No mention of him in the newspapers.

So why should I not resume my campaign against the newspapers? It is the duty of the newspapers to print my story. They disobeyed their own rules. They are in great difficulty because they know that if they don't print my [side of the] story, then my campaign will resume in due course.

The Bergen police – Krogvold, did not tell me of the allegation of attempted rape in 1990 – ask him why. Confront the man. He even said in theory I could face a

356

prison sentence, when the diplomat Vidar Kleiven said I was free to travel to Norway. So after that, do you think I'm just going to keep quiet?

I have every right to get Heidi Schøne to prove her allegations and she'll have to do just that. She won't be able to prove them and I will win. That is reward enough against an arrogant 'do-whatever-I-want' bitch along with the perverted press of Norway. The press was exactly like the Nazi press and more recently Serb press. And they cannot get away with it.

Frederick Delaware

On 19th February 1999 I wrote to Elden & Elden enclosing some of the 1990 correspondence between my London lawyers and the Bergen police, which indicated the brick wall we'd come up against at that time. I remarked how odd it was that the PFU were now looking into my case, now that I had another Norwegian lawyer, whereas they refused, wrongly, to deal with me directly once Advokat Karsten Gjone had given up.

Slowly I was building up a fuller picture for Elden & Elden.

On 23rd February, 1999 I wrote to Elden & Elden:

> Dear Mr. Elden,
>
> **Heidi Schøne**
>
> I have once again spoken to Ann-Kristin Horvei, who recognised me from the Verdens Gang article of May 1995. She knew me well – since December 1984 – but knew none of the 'facts' quoted by Verdens Gang and my reputation was damaged in her eyes. She had been a close friend of Heidi Overaa (now Schøne) until 1987 since when they have not spoken. She also told me that another chap who we both know, recognised me from the newspapers – he is Bjorn-Morten (I don't know his surname).
>
> Ann-Kristin Horvei told me she is willing to give a statement to you. Please write to her at:
>
> Laeirvåg, 5153 Fonnas. (Tlf (56) 16 86 24).
>
> You will then be able to proceed with Vesta and my claim against Karsten Gjone, for missing the three year time limit in suing the newspaper V.G.
>
> I was assured by Tor Staff that such a statement (from Ann-Kristin) may well form the basis for a successful claim against the newspapers.
>
> Yours sincerely,
>
> Frederick Delaware

The correspondence continued:

> Dear Mr. Delaware,
>
> **HEIDI SCHØNE**   24.2.1999
>
> In reference to your most recent letters and copies, telephone calls and telefaxes.
>
> I understand by your letter dated 19th February that you will handle the PFU-case without further assistance from me from now on.

I'm still waiting for the documents from Drammen police district. Until I have received these, I still cannot comment any further on the case. A new letter has been issued to Drammen police district. Once again, I recommend that any further action be delayed until the files have been examined.

Your case against Bergen police district/Krogvold is precluded because of the legal time limits, and I therefore recommend no further action on this aspect of the case.

I find from time to time your handwriting complex to read, particularly in telefaxes.

At present, we have used a total of 13.75 hours. We have recently received a payment of NOK 6,000, and I must ask for another NOK 10,000 in advance based on the fact that this case seems to become very work intensive. Further work on the case requires such payment as mentioned.

Kind regards,
ATTORNEYS AT-LAW ELDEN DA

For John Christian Elden lawyer

Dear Mr. Elden,   28.2.1999

Heidi Schøne

By the time this letter reaches you, I trust some more money will have entered your account. I also hope the Drammen police papers will soon be with you.

Please send me a copy of your letter to the PFU telling them to investigate my complaint. Now that you are handling my case with the PFU, please continue with them. The point I had been trying to make was that when I told the PFU last year to deal with me [directly], as Gjone had done nothing, they refused. That is just not on, as in fact it doesn't really need a lawyer to progress the matter. But as the PFU don't respect me at all and only get down to business by pressure from a Norwegian lawyer, then please yourself, help me out. [I had in fact never told Eric Lindset I would handle the PFU case on my own "from now on." He misread my wishes completely. The opposite was the case. The PFU's hostility towards me meant a Norwegian lawyer's involvement was indispensable]

I am not satisfied with continued silence from the Bergen police. I enclose their letter to my lawyers dated April 19th 1990. Their words in the fifth paragraph: "present suspicion of serious crimes" may be thrown back in my face at any trial I attend in Norway. I have to know the substance of these allegations for once. The passage of time should not deflect you from the injustice I have suffered in the 1980's and 1990. It is a fact that when I was in the police station in 1990 the police interpreter certified that none of my letters contained threats. I resent the implication that strong letters to a sick woman – a crafty, manipulative, scheming, sick woman – are wrong in principle and are interpreted to be threatening. When none of my letters in 1990 were declared threatening, what wording did I use in the letter or letters that later turned up?

I will have to look at your file in your office myself, so please hold on to it. Given that the Drammen police have told me and the press that I will be arrested on entry to Norway, I will have to risk an overland trip from Sweden, rather than the possibility of arrest at Oslo airport.

Sooner or later, I expect you to write to Krogvold at Bergen and ask him the questions I want asking. Particularly as to why I wasn't told of the attempted rape allegation and also what comment they have to make on Heidi's statement that a letter I wrote containing threats to kill her son was handed in to the Bergen police by

358

Gudmund Johannessen's parents. Torill Sorte told me that the Bergen police do not ever recall having received such a letter.

Also a girl who's slept with a man whom she knows to be taking heroin was not commented on by the Bergen police. That's the reason I went over there in February 1990: to confront Heidi over her sick behaviour. After all, she didn't write with an explanation. So much for my trying to combat drug abuse. The spirit of my actions was completely ignored by the Bergen police.

Yours sincerely,

Frederick Delaware

Dear Mr. Elden,   2.3.1999

Heidi Schøne

Thank you for your letter of 24th February which I have received this morning.

You will have received my letter of 28th February and a further 6,000 kroner, which I trust is enough to be getting on with for now. You will see my comments on the PFU; please yourselves, push them into action and ask if they can reply to you in English; they are quite capable of this. The PFU investigation may take a long time. Is there a chance of a quick answer from the newspapers as to why they didn't follow their rules over my right to reply?

As far as I can see, they will never print my story. Any apology will be a small paragraph which few readers will notice – and although this may be a symbolic victory for me, it won't be enough and the newspapers know what I will do if I don't get a full front page apology with my story printed. So the newspapers are in a dilemma.

Can you not also ask the newspaper – D.T. for evidence of the 300 letters "written to Heidi in the last year" by me. They are lying, so at least this will help you to have more confidence in what I am saying. They will have faxes; letters in the form of my 'reports' – many of those, yes, but only about five or so letters **to** Heidi and if you read them they are self-explanatory.

The one letter in which I have allegedly written threats to Heidi in 1986 was quite natural and understandable – [probably] a reaction to the girl sleeping with Johannessen, a man injecting heroin. This was a dreadful risk which indeed may have had disastrous consequences for me, and indeed Bjorn-Morten of Bergen who also slept with Heidi several times in 1985 without knowing of Johannessen's drug abuse. Bjorn-Morten is well known to Ann-Kristin Horvei and she will confirm Bjorn-Morten's relationship with Heidi. It is a fact that Heidi and Johannessen had two AIDS tests each **after** Daniel Overaa was born.

So the letter in which I issued threats – which were not in any case carried out and were meant to be an expression of my disgust and anger more than anything – is being used by Heidi as a platform for a long list of lies, i.e. threats to kill her son, her neighbours, herself; hundreds of obscene phone calls, hundreds of obscene letters, sexual harassment. There is no proof for any of this so surely prosecuting Heidi for these lies will be successful. I will stand firm and take my chances in court. But I don't want to wait until a court hearing to get a response to a writ. Surely when a writ is given to Heidi she is obliged to provide answers, i.e. proof of her allegations, straight away? And if she can't do this: she will definitely fail I promise you, then going to court will be a formality just to pronounce her guilty.

Regarding the Bergen police, I do not want to sue them. I just want answers to my questions. There aren't many questions. A one page letter to Krogvold will do. After all, Torill Sorte asked the Bergen police questions last year as to this fictitious letter threatening to kill Heidi's son that Heidi insisted was given to the Bergen police in 1988. What an evil allegation! Pure evil.

I am sorry you could not read my faxes, so here are the originals: two for 18th February and one for 23rd February.

Yours sincerely,

Frederick Delaware

On 13th March 1999, Eric Lindset wrote to the Press Complaints Bureau (PFU). He referred to me as "N.N" to give me official anonymity. The translation is as follows:

PFU (Press Professional Committee)
Postboks 46 Sentrum
0101 OSLO

N.N. VERSUS "DRAMMENS TIDENDE · BUKSERUD BLAD"

I refer to your letter of 8th inst. and also earlier correspondence.

N.N. wishes Law Firm Elden DA to represent him in relation to yourself in the present case, and we have taken on the assignment.

It is not opportune at present for N.N. to bring to court his case against *Drammens Tidende·Buskerud Blad*. N.N. therefore requests that his complaint of 19th July 1998 should now be subjected to your consideration of the facts.

N.N. has filed a suit [complaint] against *Drammens Tidende ·Buskerud Blad* on the basis of the newspaper's notice concerning him on Tuesday 14th July 1998, on pages 1 and 5. A copy of the article was enclosed with the complaint.

N.N. asserts that the abovementioned article constitutes a breach of *good press practice*. N.N.'s allegations can be seen from both the complaint itself and his fax and other letters, as well as telephone calls to yourself and the summonsed party. I will mention below his main points, however.

N.N. got to know several people among the readership of *Drammens Tidende·Buskerud Blad* during his stay in Norway and contact with the woman interviewed in the article. The latter recognized/identified N.N. as the person spoken about.

N.N. finds it offensive to be given the description *mentally disturbed*, and points out that the statement is completely without foundation.

In addition, N.N. emphasizes that the other allegations about him in the article are also false and, at the same time, liable to offend both his self-esteem and his reputation. Even if it is beyond PFU's competence to give an opinion on what is true or not, N.N. thinks that the very serious allegations made, demand adequate treatment of the newspaper. The press must show concern to present correct, factual information, particularly when it is a matter of material that can discredit the good name and reputation of people. In this case, it looks as if the newspaper did not take into consideration that N.N. may be innocent of the allegations. This kind of thing is usually not established until after the final verdict. In any case, the criticism could be made that *Drammens Tidende·Buskerud Blad* uses a verificatory form in the notice and does not make clear to the readers whether it is a matter

---

only of private allegations or a police statement or charge. According to N.N., this reflects a lack of quality of reporting. A minimum would have been to allow N.N. to put his version of the case. According to N.N., this omission must certainly provide a basis for criticism on the grounds of press ethics. In other words, the gathering of information was one-sided, since N.N. did not have any opportunity to make objections or remonstrations. N.N. alleges that *Drammens Tidende-Buskerud Blad* did not take into consideration the possibility that the interviewed woman used the newspaper as a means of smearing him without reason worthy of any attention. In penal action the press should presumably be careful about repeating statements from the alleged offended person and hence a potential witness.

Furthermore, N.N. deems it inadmissible, irrelevant and offensive for him and other Muslims that his religious persuasion should be given prominence in the notice.

In conclusion, I would like to ask whether it is possible to obtain PFU's decision in English translation.

With kind regards,
LAW FIRM ELDEN DA

Eric Lindset
Lawyer

Eric Lindset wisely left it open for me to sue Drammens Tidende after the PFU had dealt with the matter. In his eighth paragraph Eric Lindset refers to the fact that the PFU has no power to look into the truth or falsehood of a newspaper allegation. Lindset should have told me this directly and at the first opportunity. For a long time I was unaware of this crucial point as his letter of 13th March 1999 was not translated into English until many months later. The Press Complaints Commission (PCC) in England do look into the accuracy of press statements depending on the context in which they are used and the degree of insult / damage / loss of reputation caused. The PCC can order the newspaper to make an apology.

All Elden & Elden were doing now was sending me copies of the correspondence they had been entering into with the Bergen and Drammen police and the PFU, in Norwegian. They were not providing a translation of even the shortest letters (often just two or three sentences) to save costs, so I had to ring them up for an update from time to time. It was tedious work having to go over the same ground – often repeatedly – with the new lawyers. Some of the 'advice' given to me by Eric Lindset over the phone was of a very uncertain general nature. That's why I wanted advice put in writing. As far as the Drammen police were concerned, Elden & Elden wrote to them in January, February and March asking for the police papers to be sent to them, but with no success. So on 19th April, they threatened the police with a Court application to force them to produce the papers. On 27th April, the police wrote to my lawyers saying that after 14th May my lawyers could visit the police station to look at the police files, once the police had got everything together.

Drammens Tidende then made it clear that they did not want to deal with the Press Complaints Bureau (PFU) if I still intended taking the newspaper to Court. On 17th May, I had been told by Elden & Elden that, once more, the newspaper wanted to wait until after I had sued them before they dealt with the PFU. With no immediate prospect of a writ being issued, I reminded Elden & Elden of my instructions of 18th February: that I would not sue Drammens Tidende – and this was confirmed by Elden & Elden to the PFU on the 24th of May in unambiguous terms. At all times, it was my intention in fact to prosecute Heidi Schøne and Drammens Tidende in getting them to prove what they said was true as advised to me orally by Tor Staff. I wrote on 21st May 1999 to Eric Lindset at Elden & Elden with a full list of the statements made in the four newspaper articles to date that I wanted Heidi Schøne and Runar Schøne to prove in court were true. Unfortunately, I was labouring under a misapprehension. I thought, wrongly, that Norwegian law allowed two separate causes of action: one where the defendant had to prove what was printed was true, even if no one recognised the unnamed plaintiff from the offending article; and the other the usual complete libel action, which involved a recognition of the unnamed plaintiff by a reader or readers, plus the requirement of the defendant proving what was written was true. I thought that the former cause of action would just give a lower form of compensation than the latter. Hence my letter to Elden and Elden dated 18th February 1999 promising not to sue Drammens Tidende (which I meant but didn't specify was) for a full libel action. Hence the value of proper written legal advice, which I had never received from anyone up to now. There was, of course, in reality only one legal cause of action which was the full libel action - finding someone who recognised me and asking the defendant to prove the truth of what was written. I was later to discover also that the newspaper could be sued for libel under the criminal law for negligence as well as the civil law.

On 7th June, my lawyer wrote to me saying that they still hadn't managed to get to the Drammen police station to see the papers. As far as I was concerned, this hurdle was all that was preventing a writ being issued. On 24th May, 30th May and 7th June Elden & Elden sent copies of the latest correspondence on the case, each letter in Norwegian consisting of just two sentences. They couldn't be bothered to tell me in English what was written.

On 10th June, Elden & Elden wrote back to me enclosing a copy of a three page letter from Drammens Tidende to the Press Complaints Bureau dated 7th June 1999.

On 20th June 1999, my lawyers, Elden & Elden, sent me copies of 8 of my letters from 1986 to 1989 that the Bergen police had on file since March 1990. On 6 of those copy letters, I could see the sender's fax reference: 'From Drammen Politkammer 03 8 31212 [being the fax number of the Drammen police] 90.02.18 [being the 18th February 1990 – the date I was in the cells in Bergen police station] pages 1 to 15.' There were six letters that the Bergen police interpreter had read through and certified as not containing a single reference to any threats. Four of the letters, dated 4th August 1989, 7th October 1989, 11th October 1989 and 17th December 1989 were addressed to Heidi's sister, Elisabeth. Only two were addressed to Heidi, dated 2nd August 1989 and 16th December 1989. They were letters containing very personal and private details on Heidi's family and her related problems and I remember telling the police in Bergen in February 1990 (after Heidi's sister Elisabeth gave the letters to the Drammen police to fax them to the Bergen police) something like: "Elisabeth could see for herself that these letters contained no threats at all and that they were so private in nature that surely she wouldn't want you [the police] of all people to see the family's dirty washing."

However, together with the six letters sent to Elden & Elden were two more from 1986, one undated (probably because the date was missed out when the original was photocopied) and these two were the extra letters that obviously the Bergen police in 1990 must have been referring to as containing "explicit threats to the life and health of Ms. Overaa," when writing to my London lawyer on 19th April 1990.

The one apparently undated letter that was interpreted as threatening had been written in October 1986 some weeks after I returned home to England following that August evening – eventually spent alone with Heidi – after my tasteless meal of "sheep." Heidi, to remind you, had told me, when we were alone, that she was at home earlier in the day when I knocked on the door, but she couldn't be bothered to answer the door, having seen me through the spyhole. The offending paragraph in my letter had been underlined by the police; it read on the third page:

> "Well, I've given up with you, just as everyone else has, and I do not want to hear from you unless you change completely. One day I'll be back though and obviously I'll kick the shit out of you if you ever keep the door closed on me again."

This surely was the letter that the police in Bergen in 1990 used as the foundation for taking on board Heidi's claims of heinous verbal threats, allegedly made by me "to commit serious crimes," uttered allegedly on my February 1990 visit, with Stuart, to Norway. The police couldn't be sure one way or the other whether Heidi was telling the truth or lying about my alleged "verbal threats." I knew, of course, she was lying. But the police weren't taking any chances. That letter was in fact the one Wesenberg (the lawyer from Bergen) said was dated 13th October 1986.

The other letter was one I wrote to Heidi's father, dated 17th November 1986:

Dear Mr. Overaa,

Rather than suffer in silence any longer, I feel that I have to know the answers to one or two questions that have always bothered me concerning your daughter, Heidi. I write to you now only after being totally convinced that Heidi is a dead loss as far as integrity and good manners is concerned. I do not feel guilty about writing to you, as appealing to Heidi's reason has proved quite fruitless, and therefore as her father and the person responsible for her well-being, I appeal for your understanding.

Quite frankly I really hate Heidi and when you know why I'm sure you will sympathise privately, even if you don't tell me openly.

I remember the hours I spent on the phone with Heidi discussing her problems – mainly derived from her association with boys, of the wrong sort altogether. The hundreds of pounds I used up in phone bills. And all for nothing it seems, for the big criminal, Gudmund, has ended up where he began. How sickening it was to hear that that madman nearly caused Heidi's death by getting her pregnant, then sleeping with her best friend <u>and</u> others, causing Heidi to miscarry her twins, which in turn made Heidi take all those pills and lie down to die, only to be rescued by her sister just in time. Gudmund, the drug taker, the drunk, the womaniser. But it took two, and it only reflects on Heidi that she could associate with such a despicable character. It's funny – the crying and desperation Heidi felt when she was down. With no one to help her. The parents of her [first] lover can only let them go to their own bedroom and make love: then console her when she has her abortions. She had had two when I met her in St. Albans in 1982 – and she was only 18! Any normal person would have thought that she'd have learnt some sort of lesson. But no, again a disastrous event in 1984. How useless was my concern and worry.

You may be asking yourself why I didn't marry her, or at least ask before it was too late. Well, unfortunately the "right time" was when she was 18 and, I guess stupidly or otherwise, I didn't ask her. Firstly because I was in the middle of studying for my solicitors exams when I met her and secondly I was put off by her past. But at least then it wasn't too late to save her. Anyway, just because I didn't ask her at 18, didn't mean, in theory, that it couldn't have waited till later. But by 1984 it was too late, even though she was 'free' when I came for the first time to Bergen at Christmas 84/85. Her manners and behaviour reflected the agony and frustration she had suffered at the hands of Gudmund and her many other lovers. In truth she was quite a handful: what I saw and heard was sickening. She was not the same girl I had met in 1982. Anyway, I doubt if there had been any others who've spent so much time and money on her; only it's impossible to win this battle: the devil had won here. You can imagine my fury when Heidi again got pregnant last year to this idiot: still she has no confidence in him and they are not married; judging by what she told me last August the future is bleak, but this time I have no sympathy for her. She has brought it all upon herself: it is a really sickening feeling to see this futility. Now she is 23, with an illegitimate child and no proper father. That bodes ill for the future, when Daniel discovers the facts of his birth. One hears of the problems of children because of their stupid parents and here is a prime example it seems.

Is it the case that absolutely nothing could have been done to prevent this? Could you do nothing? Didn't it bother you that Heidi was doing what she did? Am I at fault for associating with this crazy girl? I know she was a "difficult child" on her own admission and I know that at one point you considered putting her in a home for difficult children. I feel cheated. I blame, in truth the pagan way of life amongst the youth of Norway, and the total lack of parental concern. These are the people who 'enjoy' their youth at the expense of the future, an orgy of sex and drunkenness, of venereal disease, illegitimacy and Godlessness. The people whose behaviour is responsible in some part for the spread of AIDS. People can have bad luck through

363

no fault of their own. But these people create misery and are the authors of evil. The perpetrators of mental illness.

What annoyed me more than anything was not having the door answered by Heidi, when she was in, when I rang on one occasion last August. I had waited all day for her. It was only through great self-control that I didn't kill her the next day. However, I did come for a visit of friendship, and the next day when I did see her, we got on OK but it was still infuriating to hear her uncaring attitude towards everything.

I hope you will not criticise me and tell me to mind my own business. I cared very much for Heidi – when no one else did, and I think that you are lucky that she is alive today. But the wickedness that has surrounded her and infected her to the core, has beaten me. I can't take any more of this disgusting way of life and I just want you to know how much I have suffered as a result. The wicked may have won for the time being, but it is to God we all have to return, and when the day comes to face Him, the truth will stand out, and the truth will be the winner. Not like on this earth, where evil is the (temporary) winner.

I know this letter might distress you and I'm sorry if it has but without it perhaps you would have remained ignorant of a few home truths. Heidi to me is a cheat and my temper is lost; my patience exhausted. It grieves me to say and write this, for I wanted to be her friend for ever, but the pain I've endured overrules this desire. She cannot be my friend as long as she lives in the sewer of ignorance she is in. That kind of friendship destroys me and is not worth having.

Yours sincerely,

Frederick Delaware

This 17th of November 1986 letter reflected all that I maintained in my Norwegian language 'Report' and in my submissions to the newspapers and police in 1995 and afterwards to be the truth of the situation. The newspapers and others in 1995 had been suggesting that I was making up Heidi's past, as they just couldn't believe it. My predictions and warnings to Heidi's father turned out to be pretty accurate; witness her second suicide attempt over Gudmund Johannessen and subsequent stay at a psychiatric unit in 1988.

Mr. Overaa showed and gave this letter to his daughter Heidi obviously asking her to explain herself. My sentence: "It was only through great self-control that I didn't kill her the next day," didn't help but it was only a figure of speech meant to convey my frustration. The fact is I've never hit her in my life, as the newspapers in 1995 acknowledged. I have no history of violence, but Gudmund Johannessen did assault Heidi in 1990. The 'threats' in those two letters from 1986 related to one incident which anyone would find utterly cruel if it happened to them. And who on this earth has, in any case, never uttered such 'threats' meaning them merely as a serious expression of frustration rather than a literal expression of intention? My first lawyer Helge Wesenberg recognised this fact.

It was poetic justice that these two 1986 letters containing 'threats' had, after 1999, apparently been "lost" by the Bergen police department together with the other six non-threatening letters and would not be presented in evidence against me in any future proceedings. I suspected the police had misfiled them. Surely they had not disposed of them assuming they would no longer serve any purpose?

Chapter 26

For the whole of June 1999 I was in fact abroad in Paris, so none of the correspondence sent to me that month was looked at until July.

However, on 18th June from Paris I telephoned Eric Lindset in Oslo for a progress report and he told me he'd received a response from Drammens Tidende (dated 7th June 1995) addressed to the Press Complaints Bureau (PFU). I asked him what it said and he told me it was a long letter but "it didn't say anything new." He did say, however, that he would delay replying to it until I'd had a chance to read it on my return to England at the beginning of July. I told him on the phone that as he'd told me there was "nothing new," then he might as well respond as he saw fit and refer again to his original submissions to the PFU.

The next day, 19th of June, I'd changed my mind and wrote to Eric Lindset telling him to wait until I got home so I could consider the Drammens Tidende letter. On 21st June, from Paris I wrote to my lawyer again:

Dear Mr. Lindset,

Heidi Schøne

I write further to my letter of 19th June. As I told you in that letter, I'll wait until I get home now to consider the Drammens Tidende letter and get back to you.

However, I only want you to reply to the D-T letter once you have gone to the Drammen police station. You can then yourself confirm that there is no evidence for the several serious allegations Heidi made to the press. This will be of much weight to the PFU.

I hope D-T will comment, or have commented, on the taped conversations I had with Ingunn Røren and Svein Jensen. I hope D-T have commented on their refusal to consult me before they went to print and their refusal to print my side of the story. I expect, still, my side of the story to be printed with the admissions Svein Jensen and Ingunn Røren made to me.

Also I would like you to telephone Svein Jensen or call on him to ask him on what he based his comments on not really believing Heidi. Did he interview her himself? Did he read the newspapers?

Further, do D-T accept that what Heidi did - make false allegations of attempted rape in 1986 and of actual rape in 1998, along with her other behaviour over the years - resulted in my campaign against her?

Do D-T believe the résumé of Heidi's past life written in Norwegian? Do D-T accept that what was written by all three newspapers in 1995 most of which was anti-Muslim and utter rubbish, meant that I would continue a big campaign against her?

I do not want there to be a cover-up by the PFU and Drammens Tidende, neither of whom like me at all.

I very much hope that by the time I get back to England at the end of this month, you would have had the time to have visited the Drammen police station. Then the question of the writ and Vesta/Gjone can be addressed.

Yours sincerely,

Frederick Delaware

When I got home from Paris on 30th June, I found that Eric Lindset had written to me on the 24th June:

Dear Mr. Delaware,

HEIDI SCHØNE

In reference to your letters of 18 and 24.06.99.

For your information, I enclose a copy of my letter to PFU of today.

Kind regards,
ATTORNEYS AT-LAW ELDEN DA
For John Christian Elden Lawyer

Well I hadn't written to him on either the 18th or the 24th June but on the 19th and 21st June, which were my two letters from Paris. He must have made a simple mistake. His letter of 24th June to the PFU read:

PFU (press professional committee)
Postboks 46 Sentrum
0101 OSLO

N.N. VERSUS "DRAMMENS TIDENDE·BUSKERUD BLAD"

I refer to your letter of the 9th inst. and also earlier correspondence.

On behalf of N.N. I wish to make clear that the newspaper's reply does not give rise to further additions from here and that which was stated earlier is adhered to.

With kind regards,

LAW FIRM ELDEN DA

Eric Lindset

The PFU replied on 25th June:

Adv. Eric Lindset
Adv. –firma Elden og Elden
Prinsens gt. 21,

CASE 119.98 – NN VERSUS DRAMMENS TIDENDE/BUSKERUD BLAD

We have received your communication to the effect that there is nothing to be added in the abovementioned complaint case.

This completes the round of replies and the complaint will be dealt with at PFU's meeting on 24.08.99. The Committee's opinion will then be sent to the parties.

With kind regards,
For the PRESS PROFESSIONAL COMMITTEE

Kjell M. Børringbo
Organization Secretary

Copy: Drammens Tidende/Buskerud Blad, per ansv. Red. Hans Arne Odde   PB.
7033.3007 DRAMMEN

On 30th June, Eric Lindset wrote to me:

Dear Mr. Delaware,

HEIDI SCHØNE

In reference to your letters of 18 and 30.06.99.

For Your information, I enclose copy of new letter from PFU dated 25.06.1999.

I have now examined your letters, telefaxes and postcards to Heidi Schøne and others in the Drammen police archive. It is my opinion that the phrases used in them, is a hindrance for you to gain a judicial victory against Schøne at Norwegian tribunals.

Kind regards,
ATTORNEYS AT-LAW ELDEN DA
Eric Lindset
For Christian Elden lawyer

On the 3rd July 1999, I drove up to the Norwegian Church in Rotherhithe, East London, and asked an assistant there to translate verbally the letter from Drammens Tidende dated 7th June 1999 (which much later was professionally translated in writing), which went:

PFU
Postboks 46, Sentrum 0101
OSLO

With reference to the report from PFU of 31.5, and to lawyer Elden's letter to PFU on 24.5, I take it as the basis that PFU is dealing with the practical aspects of the complaint against the newspaper.

In connection with the proceedings, I ask PFU to consider the case as a whole – from the first article in 1995 and to the provisional final news report on 14th July 1998.

1. Background

DT-BB mentioned the case for the first time on 27 May 1995 enclosure 1) following an article in VG which showed that Heidi Schøne had moved to N. Eiker. Our journalist Ingunn Røren contacted Schøne, who agreed to be interviewed. Her reason for appearing in the newspaper was to give people an explanation for all of the 'reports' on her that had been sent to very many people – to neighbours, colleagues and occasionally firms. She produced examples of such letters which had caused her a great deal of trouble. Both Heidi Schøne and her husband Runar Schøne gave an impression of being nice and believable. The newspaper's staff also saw a pile of letters that she had received from the Englishman, as well as several extreme books and newspapers dealing with AIDS and abortions. The Schøne family had reported harassment to the Nedre Eiker police office.

The journalist cannot remember whether she tried to contact the Englishman, but shortly after the first article was printed he rang her at the newspaper. He was calm during the first few minutes of the call and expressed himself well. Gradually he became more and more excited and shouted out a number of allegations against Heidi Schøne. Most of them were to the effect that she was a "sex criminal." The man said that he had a number of letters which could prove what he said about Heidi and offered to send them to the newspaper together with replies to Heidi's statements.

The journalist received a pile of papers from him a few days later. The papers were copies of cards which Heidi Schøne had sent to him and also a letter on two A4 sheets

---

that were clearly replies to her statements. The letter (Enclosure 2) had obviously been written by a confused person and contained serious allegations against Heidi Schøne, assertions that Norway is the country in the world which kills most foster children ["foster" is the Norwegian word for "foetal" and was mistranslated by the Norwegian interpreter. What was meant here was that Norway performs the world's highest percentage of abortions], a "conversation" between a foster child and a mother, exorcising of demons and a footnote which says that the letter is dedicated to the memory of all crushed Bosnian Muslims. Following discussions in the editorial office, we agreed that neither the letter nor any other of the man's statements could be used, because he had to be protected against himself and because it was impossible to reproduce any of the statements in print. The letter confirmed the impression Heidi Schøne had given of the Englishman as a mentally disturbed person.

Later on, the journalist received a number of telephone calls from the Englishman, who was in a rage because the newspaper had not printed his letter. He mentioned several statements that he wanted to have in print, but these were very serious personal attacks upon Heidi Schøne, the journalist and editor-in-chief. The Englishman also telephoned the editor-in-chief, who refused to print the man's two-page letter. The man also contacted the journalist privately and abused her live-in boyfriend because they were living in sin. The many conversations with the man strengthened the journalist's impression that it was right to protect him against himself. On one occasion, he said that he would sue DT-BB, Bergens Tidende and VG in order to get money for a court case against Heidi Schøne. He rang back later and said that it was only DT-BB that he would sue, because the people involved in the other newspapers were men. The journalist had offended against the Quran as a woman by speaking in public. The man's frequent telephone calls diminished after a while, but when the newspaper discussed the Schøne case again in July 1998, he rang repeatedly.

The background to resumed discussion for the case was that several firms, private individuals, schools, institutions and Drammen Municipality had already had reports sent to them by post or fax concerning Heidi Schøne. Several of the recipients contacted DT-BB, because the reports were formulated as if they were replies to enquiries from the newspaper concerning Heidi Schøne.

The man rang several times but was too excited and off-balance for anything reasonable to be got out of him. He denied having sent letters to Schøne, but stated at the same time that he would send 200 new letters within a week. Shortly afterwards, we received a number of new communications from people who had received letters concerning Schøne. We discussed the matter again in the editorial office and concluded that nothing the man had said could be published.

2.   The complaint to PFU

On the factual points in this case:

a) The complaint: "NN has been recognized/identified by DT-BB readers"

NN's name is never printed in DT-BB, nor other particulars that can assist identification. He is mentioned as "the Englishman." When he nevertheless claims that he has been recognized, this is due only to the fact that he himself hunted for Heidi Schøne, gradually, as she had to move, and the readers of DT-BB whom he had contacted had understood that he must be the Englishman whom the newspaper spoke about. Constantly, from the newspaper's side, it has been emphasized that he should not be identified or be made identifiable in the articles – in order to protect him, among other reasons.

b) "mentally disturbed"

The description "mentally disturbed" has been used. In addition, that he is suffering from "erotic paranoia." The documentation in the case confirms that proof of the assertion exists and that relevant information can be provided for the readers to have full understanding of the case. Without this information, the readers would be left with fundamental questions regarding both the man's behaviour, Heidi Schøne's sufferings for 16 years and the lack of opportunity for the investigators to intervene and stop the harassment by the man.

c) "false allegations"

According to the complaint, NN maintains that "the other allegations about him in the article are also false …"

DT-BB has not printed false allegations and we are prepared to document all assertions if PFU finds this expedient for trial of the case. It is not actually stated in the complaint, either, which allegations have been made and are said to be false.

d) "smears him for no reason worthy of attention"

The newspaper is accused of smearing NN for no worthy reason. This assertion fails on its own unreasonableness. Seldom, if ever, has anyone experienced more pointless, schematic harassment as that which NN has been responsible for in relation to Heidi Schøne. The newspaper has discussed the harassment because NN spread hundreds or thousands of false, malevolent 'reports' about her and gave the impression that the reports were commissioned by the newspaper. The discussion has provided local people with the explanation for the horrible reports and the sender has been protected by the use of non-identifiable descriptions of him.

e) "his religious persuasion is given prominence …"

The complainant considers it inadmissible, irrelevant and offensive for him and other Muslims that his religious persuasion is given prominence.

It is relevant for the case and the readers' understanding of it to reveal that NN is a Muslim. This has also been an important point for him in the information and the conversations he has had with the newspaper staff and in the reports which he had made and distributed.

3. Finding

The complainant complains that he was not contacted before the newspaper printed the article on 14 July 1998 and that his written and verbal statements have not been put into print.

The newspaper had several good reasons for not contacting him or printing his statements, for example:

a) On several occasions, the newspaper staff tried to interview NN, but his statements were such that they could not be printed.

b) The newspaper considered printing all or parts of the written information that NN sent, especially the letter he sent after the first article appeared in print in 1995. The contents showed that nothing could be printed.

c) NN was not identified and no information was provided that can help the readers to identify him.

d) Internally within the newspaper the question was discussed several times as to how we could pass on the man's views, but the outcome each time was that the man had to be protected against himself. In future, the newspaper can be

369

criticized for not having made clear to the readers that this was the reason why his statement was not printed.

When NN brought DT-BB before PFU via a lawyer, we in the newspaper hoped that the lawyer would be able to help the man's views be submitted in a form such that it could be printed. The complainant rejected the offer of space.

With kind regards,

Hans Arne Odde
Editor in Chief

Enclosure 1: Article in DT-BB 27 May 1995.
Enclosure 2: NN's 'reply' to the article.

I went straight back home from the Church and wrote two letters – one to the PFU and one to Eric Lindset.

Dear Mr. Lindset   3rd July 1999

Heidi Schøne

Thank you for your letters of 30th May, 7th, 10th, 12th, 20th, 24th and 30th June 1999.

I, today, have had roughly translated the Drammens Tidende letter of 7th June 1999 to the PFU. I enclose a copy of my reply to the PFU dated 3rd July. Suffice it to say it is total crap from the newspaper and in particular, as the tape recordings will prove, I did not tell off Ingunn Røren's partner for "living in sin," neither did I tell Ingunn Røren that I would only sue D-T and not the other two newspapers, because she is a woman who spoke publicly (which she says I told her is against Quranic principles). What a liar she is. And how she hates Islam.

I have read the copy letters I wrote to Heidi Schøne in the 1980's. The "threat" is contained in a letter which is undated – "and obviously I'll kick the shit out of you if you ever keep the door closed on me again." I have used the words "**if** you ever," etc. I will maintain it's a figure of speech. Note that I have never hit her.

You say in your letter of 30th June that my letters and postcards are a "hindrance" regarding victory in court. Well it's up to me to decide if I want to take the risk of going to court. I want to go to court against Heidi Schøne.

However, I will wait for your FULL REPORT on the evidence you have found in the Drammen police station. You have seen the facts that I want Heidi Schøne to prove, with my letter to you of 21st May 1999. I expect that you have found no evidence to enable Heidi Schøne to prove her lies. Particularly, that I have not written 300 letters or even a fraction of that amount to Heidi Schøne in 1998. If Svein Jensen doesn't believe her and Ingunn Røren is "not sure" whether to believe her, this should be enough to give me the right to say to you: I want you to issue a writ. After all it is for Heidi Schøne to prove what she told the newspapers was true.

After reading the trash from D-T of 7th June I am more determined than ever to get Heidi Schøne into court. But let me have a written report from you on the evidence or lack of it that exists at the police station which supports Heidi Schøne's statements to the press.

Yours sincerely,

Frederick Delaware

PS. Ask the PFU to accept and consider the tape recordings PLUS transcript of my conversations with Røren, Odde, and Nils Rettersdøl. I don't want another cover up.

Dear Mr. Børringbo,   3rd July 1999

Heidi Schøne, Drammens Tidende SAK119/98

I have spent the whole month of June abroad and have only today had roughly translated Drammens Tidende's letter to you of 7th June 1999. I am writing to you direct to save time.

First of all, many thanks to Drammens Tidende for not providing me with a translation to English. Secondly, and of utmost importance, is the complete rubbish they – D-T and Ingunn Røren speak.

I have recorded on tape the entire conversations I have had with Ingunn Røren (and the editor Hans Odde, as well as the journalists and editors of B-T and VG).

1.   It is a wicked lie to say I would only sue D-T because Ingunn Røren is a woman who has done something against the teachings of the Quran because women should not speak publicly. I NEVER SAID THIS. I have a record of the conversation on tape which will be sent to you shortly. Ingunn Røren is a wretched liar.

2.   I NEVER SPOKE ANGRILY to Ingunn Røren's partner telling him he is living in sin with her. This is a total lie. Again, she is making this up. She is sick-minded and hateful.

3.   The public have a right to know Heidi Overaa/Schøne's past which is comprised in the reports I have sent. They are true accounts of her past.

4.   Heidi Schøne has accused me (and another Bergen man) of attempted rape in 1986. In 1998 she changed her story to say I in fact raped her. A LIE. This and H-S's other behaviour started the trouble.

5.   Heidi Schøne has told total crap to the newspaper. Svein Jensen, the policeman is ON TAPE ADMITTING TO ME HE DOES NOT BELIEVE Heidi Schøne. Ingunn Røren is on tape admitting she does not know if Heidi is telling the truth.

6.   The Psychiatrist, Nils Rettersdøl, was told nothing of Heidi Schøne's past life: and very little of mine. He is on tape too. He was tricked by VG. It is total crap to say D-T wanted to protect me against myself. They didn't want to print my name because it would have made it easy to sue them. They didn't print my response because it would make the newspaper look like liars and deceivers.

7.   I have told the PFU in 1996 of the false accusations made by the three newspapers in 1995 which were repeated in 1998 by D-T. I told D-T long ago exactly what was false in their story.

8.   D-T have never tried to interview me and you will clearly see this from the tape recordings. Ingunn Røren knows very well she never tried to contact me once.

371

9.   I have not sent 300 letters **to** Heidi Schøne in 1998. Why the silence from D-T? Where is their response to my denial?

10.   What of Gudmund Johannessen?

11.   It is beyond doubt that Ingunn Røren and her editor Hans Odde who allowed the story to be printed have very little integrity and should not be allowed to get away with their deceit. The tape recordings prove this.

Yours sincerely,

Frederick Delaware
Copy of this letter to: Eric Lindset of Elden & Elden.

On 4th July I sent to Mr. Børringbo at the PFU the tape recording of Ingunn Røren and her partner (who answered the phone to me) dated 25th March 1996 (printed above) and the two recordings (printed above) with the psychiatrist Nils Rottersdøl, policeman Svein Jensen and the various other conversations (printed above) with other journalists.

Again on 4th July, I wrote to Eric Lindset asking him to proceed to issue a Writ against Heidi Schøne, using the list of newspaper (and other) allegations supplied to him on 21st May by me. Once again, I had to ask him to provide me with a full report on his findings in the Drammen police station. His one sentence report was obviously not enough. Again, on 12th July I wrote a full résumé to him of my requirements.

However, I still had another phone call to make to Ingunn Røren, the journalist and liar with Drammens Tidende over her allegations made in her editor's letter to the PFU dated 7th June. On 13th July 1999 I telephoned her at her office in Bergen - she had left Drammens Tidende to work for Bergens Tidende. As you will see, God was smiling on me that day for Ingunn Røren walked right into my trap:

Answer   *Bergens Tidende.*

F.   *Hello, Good morning, can I speak to Ingunn Røren please?*

IR.   *Yeah, Ingunn.*

F.   *Yes, hello Ingunn Røren, it's Frederick Delaware here in London.*

IR.   *Yes.*

F.   *Hi there, I just wanted to have a chat to you to ask you why you find it necessary to lie to the PFU about me saying that you and your partner are living in sin and that I won't be suing your newspaper* [whereas I meant and continued] *I will be suing your newspaper because women mustn't speak publicly and it's against the Quran. I mean, why do you have to lie. You know I didn't say that. In your heart you know I didn't say that, and I think it proves to you the lengths you want to go to, er, I don't know, to falsify things. You know I didn't say that. You've no proof. You've no nothing. I didn't say it. So why did you ...*

IR.   *I've told the PFU what you've told me ... ... and I told you also that I won't speak to you about this matter anymore.*

F.   *Yes, but why do you lie?*

IR.   *So you have to take this case to the PFU and they're taking their actions.*

F.   *I want to speak to your partner because I never told him this. When did I tell him this?* [i.e.

that he was living in sin with Ingunn Røren.]

IR.   *When you phoned my apartment.*

F.   *I phoned your house once.*

IR.   *Yes you did.*

F.   *And are you telling me in that one phone call I told your partner ... ...*

IR.   *Yes you did.*

F.   *Well, you're lying because I didn't say that and your partner ... um ... I spoke to your partner for two or three seconds and I said to him: "Can I speak to Ingunn Røren please... I presume that's your wife." That's all I said to him and he went to get you.*

IR.   *As I told you, I won't discuss this matter with you. You have to speak to the Chief Editor.*

F.   *It's nothing to do with him. It's personal between you and me.*

IR.   *No, it's not personal.*

F.   *It is. It is personal because it's your word and your editor doesn't know whether you tell him the truth or not. He can't prove it. But your partner, where is he? Is he still in Drammen? Is he with you here? Is he with you in Bergen?*

IR.   *He's none of your business.*

F.   *He's left you hasn't he?*

IR.   *He's none of your business.*

F.   *I think he's left you and not surprisingly. But the thing is ... I have to find him. I will find him because I never said anything of the sort.*

IR.   *Then you have to find him. It's none of your business.*

F.   *Well, then, can you at least give me his name?*

IR.   *No. He's none of your business.*

F.   *He is, because you ... ...*

IR.   *It's part of the PFU case ... ... I'll await what the PFU has to say about this. I've told you before, I'm not gonna talk to you anymore about it.*

F.   *You're scared. You're scared. You've got something to hide.*

IR.   *I'm not scared.*

F.   *That's why you don't want to talk to me.*

IR.   *You're the one that should be scared.*

F.   *I'm not scared in the slightest. Why should I be scared? You know I'm not scared. I couldn't give a damn about any of you stupid idiots 'cos you're a liar. You make up stories and you know it. In your heart ... ...*

IR.	*I don't care what you think about me. I really don't care. I couldn't care less actually.*
F.	*I think you could or else you wouldn't lie. And you're all very upset because of the huge amount of publicity. All the phone calls to your office and the police and the newspapers about the truth about Heidi Schøne. I know you're all terribly upset.*
IR.	*Why should we be terribly upset?*
F.	*Because of the lies ...[her frustration causes her to say and print]*
IR.	*Why should you hold the truth about anything. Who told you that you have the truth ...*
F.	*I know what I've done is all true. All I've said ... ...*
IR.	*Why's Heidi Schøne your matter at all?*
F.	*Well she's a ... ...*
IR.	*She doesn't matter to you at all.*
F.	*Well she's a liar and so are you. You're enormous liars.*
IR.	*She doesn't care about you. She doesn't want to speak to you.*
F.	*She's a sick woman. Been in a psychiatric ...*
IR.	*Why should you care? She lives in another country.*
F.	*Because she's a liar.*
IR.	*Who do you care. She doesn't speak to anyone that you know. I don't think she's a liar.*
F.	*The point is ... well you're just as sick as her if that's what you think. But the thing is you have started telling lies. So you categorically tell me that I told your partner he's living in sin.*
IR.	*Yes, you did*
F.	*OK, well ... ...*
IR.	*I told you and I'll tell you once more I'm not gonna speak to you about this matter anymore because you're just making out all these accusations without any proof.*
F.	*What accusations?*
IR.	*I told you ...*
F.	*Which accusations?*
IR.	*I've told you. I don't wanna speak to you.*
F.	*See, 'cos you're a liar.*
IR.	*Speak to the Chief Editor.*
F.	*No, no, no. He's just as bad as you. He wants to close up and say nothing.*
IR.	*Maybe you should think about it. Why doesn't anyone want to talk to you?*

374

F.   *Because you're a bunch of arseholes all of you. You're liars.*

IR.   *So why should you care?*

F.   *Well **you do** care. I don't know. You're probably twisted. You hate Muslims for a start. And where on earth does it say in the Quran that women shouldn't speak publicly? That's all rubbish.*

IR.   *I don't know.*

F.   *You made that up.*

IR.   *I don't know.*

F.   *The Quran says women can, must and [they] do speak publicly. And should speak publicly.*

IR.   *Yeah, but I told you if you have anything else to say you should call the Chief Editor because he's the one who's handling this.*

F.   *No, no, it's personal.*

IR.   *I don't want to talk to you, I told you.*

F.   *This is personal and I don't think it's anything to do with your Chief Editor. You're just covering up and lying.*

IR.   *You still have to talk to him 'cos I'm not gonna talk to you.*

F.   *Well, I have to find your partner or your ex-partner. I think he's dumped you because you're on the other side [of the country]. He's probably working in Drammen and you're here, you know. But ... ...*

IR.   *I'm not going to tell you anything.*

F.   *If I do find him, I'm sure he'll say that I didn't say that.*

IR.   *Then talk to him if you can find him 'cos I'm not gonna tell you anything about him.*

F.   *The thing is Ingunn, I taped that whole conversation [of 25.3.96, which proved I did not tell off Ingunn Røren's partner for living in sin] at the time, OK. I've got it.*

IR.   *Yeah you probably did.*

F.   *OK.*

IR.   *It's illegal but you have ... ...*

F.   *Well it doesn't matter ... But the thing is it proves ... ...*

IR.   *It's illegal so you can't use it in Court in Norway ... 'cos it's illegal to tape records.*

F.   *Well it's direct evidence that proves you're a liar. 'Cos you've lied to me again just now. And this business about erotic paranoia – I spoke to the psychiatrist, Nils Rettersdøl, and he told me that whoever phoned him up from the newspapers told him nothing about Heidi Schøne – nothing – and told him very little about me. You twisted it. You gave a hypothetical situation and that's another dreadful thing you've done yourself. The point is you're so full of shit, I'm surprised ... ...*

375

IR.   *It wasn't me who call him* [being Nils Rettersdøl.] [Her article still said I was suffering from an "extreme case of erotic paranoia."]

F.   *I'm surprised you can live with yourself for being such an awful liar. Why don't you just give up and re-educate yourself in proper manners?*

IR.   *Why don't you just give up? The Heidi Schøne ... ...*

F.   *Because, you're the one ... ...*

IR.   *She doesn't want to talk to you.*

F.   *Well, I'm not interested in the stupid idiot for Christ's sake.*

IR.   *Leave her alone.*

F.   *Well, you started lying. She started making completely false allegations. OK.*

IR.   *I told you I'm not going to listen to you anymore. So you have to call the Chief Editor.*

F.   *I will call the Chief Editor but I think you know exactly what kind of a real liar you are and ...*

IR.   *I'm not gonna listen to this.*

F.   *Well, you don't have to ... bye bye. Bye.*

On the 14th July, I sent a copy of the two damning taped conversations with the liar Ingunn Røren of 25th March 1996 and 13th July 1999 to my lawyer, the PFU and finally Ingunn Røren's new editor, Hans Nyberg at Bergens Tidende, telling him, "I expect you to sack her. After all, who wants to employ an obvious liar."

Once again, I had direct evidence of the fundamental hatred that the Norwegian media had for Islam. Ingunn Røren had been living with the man I presumed to be her husband. They were not in fact married and in common parlance were 'living in sin.' But this was not a comment I levelled at either one of them. Most young couples in Scandinavia do not marry until they are into their late 20's, if that. It is a popular form of relationship and has no stigma attached to it at all any more, which is also true for having children born out of wedlock. Ingunn Røren tried to put me into the unpopular minority, Muslim 'fanatic' corner by attributing to me that I had angrily told her partner he was "living in sin." Further, her comments regarding my alleged views on women speaking in public being forbidden by the Quran was a calculated attempt to bury both me and the religion of Islam. You have seen The Times newspaper leader article from 1996 printed above evidencing how the founding values of Islam give women equal rights to men. My own personal support for women's rights can be found in the letter I wrote to Paddy Ashdown, leader of the Liberal Democrat Party, shortly after the May 1997 General Election. I had met and became well acquainted with Aina Khan, a Muslim woman, who stood as the unsuccessful Liberal Democrat candidate in Ilford South, an East London constituency. She was also a practising solicitor. I quote extracts from my letter of 21st May 1997 to the Rt. Hon. Paddy Ashdown M.P.:

Dear Mr. Ashdown,

Aina is a very well balanced Muslim with views that I would class as entirely compatible with the idea of Islam. I was greatly impressed by Aina's speech at her adoption meeting in Ilford. The way she spoke and the things she spoke about convinced me that she would make an excellent Member of Parliament for all her constituents, not just Muslims and other ethnic minorities. I believe that she would as a Muslim have more success as an M.P. than a man in her position. There are many shades of opinion amongst the Muslim voices in Britain and some of these opinions unfortunately can be very harmful. But Aina's opinions I feel would be acceptable and understood by supporters of traditional Christian values in this country. I myself went to a Church of England school and I feel I know what I am talking about. Aina is a very confident public speaker and I have little doubt that if she did ever become an M.P., she will not let anyone down. Please, if you can, give her every chance to try again for Parliament.

I would also like to thank you most profusely for your fantastic support for the Muslims of Bosnia. May God bless you for that ......

Yours sincerely,

On the 11th June 1997, Paddy Ashdown replied, saying in his third paragraph: "I share your view that Aina Khan was a first class Parliamentary candidate. I have copied your letter to Nick Harvey M.P. in his capacity as Chairman on the Joint States Candidates Committee for his information."

Auberon Waugh spoke the truth in an article in The Sunday Telegraph of 10th October 1999 when trying to explain, as he put it, "the West's terror of Islam."

'It is said that certain Muslim states have persecuted and continue to persecute Christians. No doubt this is true, but it is not a major truth. The main truth is that practically nobody in the West gives a fig for Christianity, and this is the explanation for everything. After the collapse of socialism, the crumbling of Christianity leaves the West with nothing to believe in, apart from some vapid ideal of "progress."

As Christians prepare for the new millennium with hymn books that feature soccer chants and topical references, we are acutely aware that Islam is the only creed left that believes in itself. That is what terrifies us all.'

***

On the 20th July 1999 at 11.10 a.m. I telephoned Eric Lindset, my lawyer and spoke to him for nearly an hour. He told me he was extremely unhappy with the comments he had seen at the Drammen police station included in my information campaign against Heidi, but sternly refused to specify exactly which of my comments troubled him. I knew what I'd written so why couldn't he explain himself so I knew where he was coming from? I have already described all the contents of my campaign earlier in this book. Indeed, all these contents were already on show for policeman Svein Jensen when he spoke to me in March 1996, save for maybe the article entitled 'Heidi Schøne - Abnormal Mental Life.' Eric Lindset told me now that he didn't want to issue proceedings against Heidi, having "less sympathy" for my case. However, he said he would have to consult his boss, John Christian Elden, to see what his opinion was as to whether they could carry on and draw up a writ for me. He would then get back to me. I asked Eric Lindset if there was a cheaper libel forum in Norway than for a formal court procedure and without specifying the name of it, he told me there was such a system consisting of a panel of professional laymen in more informal proceedings than the Court.

Put off by Eric Lindset's pessimism, just after 1 p.m. I phoned the Oslo Courthouse that Eric Lindset said covered the jurisdiction to issue my Writ, but they told me to call again tomorrow. After four short calls to the Oslo Courthouse on 21st July, I was told that the correct jurisdiction to issue a writ was the Courthouse covering the district wherein the main defendant resided, i.e. Drammen. So just before 1 p.m. I phoned the Drammen City Court (called the Drammen Byrett) and was, to my amazement, put straight through to a Judge. He spoke excellent English and for five minutes explained the procedure for issuing a writ after I explained my predicament. Five minutes of free advice, none of the specifics of which in my 7 months of using them Elden and Elden advised me on. The Judge told me it would cost 2,650 Norwegian kroner (£215.00) to issue a writ against Heidi and the newspapers, which seemed cheap enough to me; and that I could act for myself and, significantly, so long as my writ "looked like a writ" they would accept it. The writ, however, would naturally have to be submitted in the Norwegian language.

Using the checklist I'd sent to Elden & Elden on 21st May 1999, I hand-wrote a 15 page writ in my own words and sent it off to be translated into Norwegian via an English translation agency. It needed in fact to be sent over to Norway where the legal expertise for the translation could readily be found. I paid my £442.39 translation fee in advance, which included typing up the English version for me.

I then received a letter dated 20th July 1999 from Elden & Elden:

Dear Mr. Delaware,

HEIDI SCHØNE

In reference to your letters of 3, 12 and 14 July 1999 plus today's telephone conversation.

I hereby confirm in writing that you now has ended the engagement of our firm. For your use I enclose an address list for the Norwegian Courts of Conciliation (FORLIKSRÅD). The standard court fee is NOK 530 and had to be paid in advance/together with the application for conciliation proceedings/writ (FORLIKSKLAGE).

I have as formerly mentioned examined your letters, telefaxes and postcards to Heidi Schøne and others in the Drammen police archive. At your request I can verify that there was lesser than 400 of them. Besides, neither of them contained threats of killing Heidi Schøne or others. It is my opinion that the phrases used in them, nevertheless is a hindrance for you to gain a judicial victory against her at Norwegian tribunals.

Kind regards,
ATTORNEYS AT-LAW ELDEN DA
Eric Lindset
For
John Christian Elden Lawyer

I replied on 28th July 1999:

Dear Mr. Lindset,

Heidi Schøne

Thank you for your letter of 20th July.

However, your sentence: "I hereby confirm in writing that you now has ended the engagement of our firm," is obviously completely incorrect. From previous correspondence and our conversations I never at any time myself ended my engagement with your firm. Besides which the PFU are still in correspondence with you **and** you have still failed to write a full written report on your findings at the Drammen police station. I waited around 6 months for that 'report.'

You state in your 3rd paragraph that "there was lesser than 400 of them." What is this? The newspapers mentioned "300 letters in the last year." Where does "400" come from? You must have counted how many letters "in the last year" I sent to her. I estimated 5-10 at most. What is the figure, in fact? Please put it in writing. I need written evidence please!!

You also know that I have been after **details** of Heidi Schøne's statement of her allegation of rape. I know there are details, as Torill Sorte told me, there was a record. I await your report.

378

You know the police will not write to me directly. So I use you to obtain things I cannot get. But it must be a proper lawyer's report. Also a short letter to the Drammen police asking for copies of my letters and postcards, doesn't take much to do. Even asking them at the station to do this?

The fact is, the newspapers and Mr. & Mrs. Schøne have to prove what was said in the newspapers was true. And they can't. If they wanted to appear so good and so wronged by the Muslim man, then they shouldn't have lied. Their lies will hang them. I suspect they never imagined I would see the newspapers.

I am using the Drammen Byrett and the writ is being translated now. The Judge I spoke to was very helpful and told me that I can force the journalists to come to Court as well.

I note for the record you have failed to deal with the law regarding being recognised by the likes of Ann-Kristin Horvei in the Vesta claim.

As far as I'm concerned, it doesn't matter if the 1986 allegation of attempted rape was only discovered by me in 1995. The police could have told me in 1990 in Bergen when my lawyers wrote to them. It's not my fault. There are quite a few things I haven't been able to do because it is "too late." Besides, as I told you, the bitch is alleging, now, rape and still I note nothing has been confirmed about her allegation of rape against the Bergen shopkeeper.

I now realise how extremely easy it is for me to handle the Court case myself. I should have done it months ago. I have drafted a full writ and I thank God that at long, long last the Schønes and the journalists will be put "on the spot."

Yours sincerely,

Frederick Delaware

P.S.   As I recall, you were going to ask John Christian Elden for his opinion as to whether your firm were going to carry on and issue a writ for me. You were of the opinion my case would be "hindered" by my correspondence to Heidi Schøne. So in fact I had not ended my engagement of your firm at all and for you write this because you "felt" I wanted to proceed with a writ personally is surely wrong in fact. As it turns out in phoning the Drammen Court and speaking to the Judge after I spoke last to you, I discovered it would take me no time at all to [draft the writ] myself. But I didn't know this until after we last spoke. Enormous effort has been put in by many people to ensure Heidi Schøne is not brought to Court. I will now ensure she is brought to Court, if she has the courage to appear. We'll see what happens.

On 10th August 1999, I sent ten copies of my Writ to the Drammen Byrett, by International Datapost at a cost of £48.95. I had already got permission from the private detective, Arild Pedersen, to use his brother's law firm as my address for service of documentation in Norway. Arild Pedersen said his brother's firm did not do libel work. But as he knew me from previous advice I had sought from him over the last three years and it was he that had recommended Karsten Gjone to me, he obligingly persuaded his brother to allow me to use their office address as the address for service, without which I could not issue a writ.

The cause of action I had included in my Writ stated as follows:

'By the laws of Norway the Defendants are required and are asked to provide material and other proof of the truth to the unsubstantiated and other allegations printed in the newspapers including those allegations listed below.'

I was the plaintiff and there were eight defendants: Heidi, her husband Runar, Ingunn Røren (plus her newspaper Drammens Tidende), Haakon Schrøder (plus his newspaper Bergens Tidende) and Harald Vikøyr (and his newspaper Verdens Gang).

I attached copies of the four newspaper articles. I asked for more witnesses to be subpoenaed, including the editors of the three newspapers, the psychiatrist Nils Rettersdøl, and policeman Svein Jensen.

In English law, the defendant must satisfy the Court that the statement (which the defendant claims is justified) is true in substance and in fact. In a civil action, the standard of proof is proof on the balance of probabilities, although the more serious the allegation, the higher the degree of probability required.

In my Writ I asked for each and every one of the listed newspaper allegations to be proven and included the relevant quotes from my taped conversations with Ingunn Røren of 25.3.96 and policeman Svein Jensen of March 1996. I had included the allegations made in the 1995 articles and 1998 article. At this stage, I was still under the (wrong) impression that I could sue for the 1995 articles on the grounds that the defendants had to prove what they said was true. The question of a time limit had not even entered my head for this specific cause of action.

I also included my translation of Heidi's past into Norwegian in the Writ, explaining why I used it in my 'nationwide information campaign.' I also put in my nine page Summer 1995 response to the newspapers, plus copies of the three most vital letters from Heidi to me, one undated from 1984, the others dated 22.8.84 and 9.4.85. Importantly, I included a photocopy of the front cover of the book 'I Dared To Call Him Father,' plus the relevant paragraphs on pages 42 and 43 (quoted earlier in this book).

I requested general damages for pain and suffering and also for the three newspapers to print apologies. I had asked too for terms of imprisonment and fines for the three journalists and their editors.

On the 13th August 1999, Elden & Elden wrote to me again:

Dear Mr. Delaware,

HEIDI SCHØNE

In reference to your telephone call and letter of respectively 22 and 28 July 1999.

I don't agree that the my sentence («I hereby confirm in writing that you now has ended the engagement of our firm») repeated by you, «is obviously completely incorrect». It's caused by your sayings during our telephone conversation of 20 July 1999. Furthermore, I was at the same time informed that you will personally write and send in a application for conciliation proceedings yourself, and now also have directly taken charge of the case and correspondence with PFU. In the telephone call to me of 22 July 1999 you even affirmed this discontinuance. Besides, you are not abreast of the up-front fees/payments we called for. This terminates a task by itself. Finally I find it infeasible to continue relations with clients which would not follow my advises.

It's unknown to me that I was obliged to give a full (proper) written (lawyer's) report on the findings at the Drammen police station. I recommend just that (considering doing) further action (application for conciliation proceedings) was delayed until these files has been examined by me.

The number of 400 is your own and comes from letters dated 21 May 1999 and 10 November 1998.

My advice in our telephone conversation 4 March 1999 was to not proceed with a claim against Vesta. You assured me at the same time of that this was both understood and accepted.

Kind regards

I replied on 16th August 1999:

Dear Mr. Lindset,

Heidi Schøne

Thank you for your letter of 13th August which I received this morning.

Regarding the "400" letters, you have misread the position. In my letter to you of 21st May I sent an extra list of press statements. You yourself make reference to Drammens Tidende's May '95 [allegation that] 400 OBSCENE LETTERS WERE WRITTEN. This is not what I am referring to. I am referring to [the allegation] in Drammens Tidende's July 1998 article: "300 letters sent to her in the last year," i.e. the year 1997-98. The newspapers have already said that **none** of the alleged 400 obscene letters exist as Heidi has destroyed them all. Why would I use "400" when none of them exist and according to the liar, Heidi, have all been destroyed? Clearly you have failed to understand the position.

Regarding ending the engagement of your firm, I can only refer to my "P.S." comment in my letter to you of 28th July 1999.

I have sent a writ in Norwegian to the Drammen Byrett – the judge has accepted it and it will now be issued to the defendants: Heidi Schøne, Runar Schøne, and the three journalists. I have subpoenaed 15 witnesses and asked for prison sentences to be considered for seven people: Mrs Schøne and the three journalists and also the three editors. One of the Judges at the Court gave me excellent advice. At 2,650 NKR to issue the writ, this is good value for money and the Byrett is most appropriate for a case of this magnitude. Conciliation proceedings would be a very poor substitute indeed.

In England, lawyers do not terminate a client's retainer without **first** telling the client the position and reason. Not being up-front with fees and payments you called for was not how we operated: I paid you what I could, regularly, and you accepted this way of dealing. But if you want to use this as a reason now, you must first write and tell me. In myself writing to the PFU I was saving you the job as clearly it was necessary to write quickly to them. You were on holiday and I doubt you could have coped with the detailed explanation that had to be given to them.

As far as "not following your advices" which is another reason for not continuing "relations" as you put it, what advice was that exactly?

It must have been obvious to you that I would want to know the details of the Drammen police papers, e.g. details of the 1998 rape allegation, details of how many letters were written in the last year, i.e. 1997-98. I asked in writing on several occasions for these questions to be answered.

Regarding Vesta, your "advice" was not put in writing. Indeed, you put very little in writing. I don't remember your advice being given [that I agreed not to pursue Vesta Insurance Company over the lawyer Karsten Gjone's failure to issue a writ against the 3 newspapers for missing the time limits] on 4th March and certainly this is something that **must** be confirmed in writing with reasons. After all, lawyers deal with the written word. At no time would I have "understood and accepted" this as you allege. I relied on advice given to me by Tor Staff on this point and intend to pursue it with Vesta.

You saw the complaint I put in against Gjone had succeeded because of his failure to put anything in writing. You should have known from this that I expect a clear understanding of events and correct advice put in writing. In particular a full report on what was discovered at the Drammen police station. Svein Jensen had all the evidence before him at the police station in 1996 and he didn't believe Heidi Schøne or "trust her so much." The press statements will have to be proven in court as true in fact. I know this can't be done by the Schøne's or the press and they will have to spend the next six months worrying about the trial and being found to be liars. Clearly, the tape of Ingunn Røren exposes her as a liar.

Yours sincerely,

Frederick Delaware

P.S. I'll have to insist on a full police report and receipt from the police in Drammen of copies of all my letters and postcards. I refer to previous correspondence.

On 31st August the private detective's law firm wrote to me enclosing a copy of a letter the Judge had written them. It had transpired in fact that questions regarding the Court's jurisdiction had arisen, as well as time limits and the Judge wanted sections from the relevant Norwegian statutes to be quoted in my Writ. Stig Lunde, one of the partners in the law firm was willing to help me, even though he was not a libel lawyer.

When I phoned Stig Lunde, whose firm already had a copy of my Writ, he told me briefly that he had to check out the right Court jurisdiction as three of the defendants, Heidi, her husband Runar and Drammens Tidende, were based in Drammen, whilst the other two newspapers were based in Oslo and Bergen. Regarding the question of time limits, I was surprised to hear this was a problem. I knew there was a three year time limit to sue for libel, but I had assumed I wasn't proceeding under that cause of action. I thought I was suing on the related but alternative ground (unique to Norway) of requiring the defendants to prove what they said was true. Stig Lunde said he hadn't looked at my Writ yet, but would try and find the time to do so and get back to me.

On 1st September 1999, Elden & Elden wrote to me again:

Dear Mr. Delaware,

HEIDI SCHØNE

I will hereby confirm that your letter of 16 August 1999 is received by us.

What is written in our letter of 13 August 1999, we uphold.

Anyway, we have recently received a letter for you from PFU dated 25 August 1999, which is enclosed in original.

Kind regards,
ATTORNEY AT-LAW ELDEN DA
Eric Lindset
For
John Christian Elden
Lawyer

Just one sentence in direct answer to my many questions! I was furious. The letter from the PFU to Elden & Elden dated 25th August 1999 incorporated the PFU's 8 page report dated 24th August 1999 ruling on my complaint against Drammens Tidende. It was all in Norwegian.

On 2nd and 3rd September 1999, I wrote to Stig Lunde giving him some background information.

On 4th September, I made the 2½ hour round trip to the Norwegian Church to get an oral translation of the PFU report.

My complaint to the PFU had been rejected. None of my direct evidence had been mentioned in their report at all. I went straight back home and faxed the following letter (dated 4th September 1999) to Elden & Elden, as well as sending a copy to the PFU:

Dear Mr. Elden,

I am in receipt of your [firm's] letter of 1st September. I see that the hostile PFU have not given you an English translation which you requested of them. Nevertheless I got the main points translated briefly for me today. D-T have not been found to be in breach of good press reporting. A cover-up. The PFU report was dishonest and ignored all my evidence – the tape recordings of Svein Jensen, Ingunn Røren and Nils Rettersdøl. The police in Drammen, as you told me, had only five or so letters from me to Heidi "in the last year" not 300 as D-T reported.

What use are the PFU if they don't investigate the truth?

You should have reported yourself to them more adequately. They ignored all the evidence I painstakingly collected and supplied to them.

If the police are recorded on tape saying they don't believe Heidi this should be referred to in the PFU report as should Ingunn Røren's taped conversations and Nils Rettersdøl's. The fact of Ingunn Røren being a proven liar should also have been in the PFU report. Total exoneration for dishonest Norwegians!

The PFU are a dishonest organisation and I contest and appeal against their decision. They will be subpoenaed to the Court case due next year to explain their deceit.

Yours sincerely,

Frederick Delaware

Copy to PFU OSLO – Sak 110/98 on 0047224050 55

I then faxed immediately afterwards a second letter just for Eric Lindset of Elden & Elden:

Dear Mr. Lindset,

You have let me down over the PFU case. You should have made sure my own written evidence and tapes – vital, vital evidence – would be taken into consideration by the PFU. No mention is made of my tapes and findings at all. The PFU are quite hopeless anyway, but you should have made sure my evidence would be considered.

Also you refuse to answer basic questions requested many times in correspondence. Get John C. Elden to read my letters. He must see that you cannot be understanding what I have asked of you.

I will have to report you to the Norwegian Bar Association for a poor standard of work. It will take you hours to deal with the paperwork and I expect to win. You had many chances to comply and had Gjone's example to learn by.

> When I want a report – a full report – on your findings at the police station in Drammen, it has to be in writing. You told me little I didn't know already. I shall be asking for all my money back.
>
> Frederick Delaware

I was sick with frustration. I wanted answers to my questions now and phoned the Norwegian Bar Association to enlist their help.

I got a reply from Elden & Elden dated 6th September 1999:

> Dear Mr. Delaware,
>
> **HEIDI SCHØNE**
>
> I will hereby confirm your telefaxes of 6 September 1999 is received by us.
>
> Furthermore your contact (Wenche Siewers) in the Norwegian Bar Association called me today.
>
> What is written in our earlier letters, we uphold.
>
> I have as formerly mention examined your letters, telefaxes and postcards to Heidi Schøne and others in the Drammen police archive. At your request I can again verify that there was lesser than 400 (/300) of them. Besides, neither of them contained threats of killing Heidi Schøne or others. In the end I have to point out that your request of a full (proper) written report on the findings at the Drammen police station arrived here after my visit there.
>
> Kind regards,
> ATTORNEYS AT –LAW ELDEN DA
> Eric Lindset
> For
> John Christian Elden
> Lawyer

Now the man was being idiotic. I replied immediately on 9th September 1999:

> Dear Mr. Lindset,
>
> **Heidi Schøne**
>
> Thank you for your letter of 6th September. It is obvious to me that still you have not managed to understand the facts.
>
> 1.   Drammens Tidende have said in their article of 14th July 1998 that I have "written 300 letters <u>to</u> Heidi Schøne in the last year." These 300 letters are purely that – letters **to** her. Even you told me on the phone that [at the Drammen police station] there were only a handful, i.e. 5-10 in the last year. So how can you report in writing "lesser than 400/300"? I know I wrote only 5-10 letters in 1997-98 **to** Heidi. This fact should have been confirmed by you to the PFU. But I need this confirmed, myself, in writing from you.
>
> 2.   Drammens Tidende said in their article of 27th May 1995 that I had written "400 obscene letters to her all of which she destroyed to burn the episode out of her mind," i.e. none of them are in existence. I didn't write any obscene letters to her – she lied. You'd have thought she'd have kept some at least, as evidence.

I have pointed out to you in the clearest of terms in previous correspondence that you have misunderstood the position. You are confusing points 1 and 2 above and each time you reply to me you make it worse for yourself. That is why I asked you to refer the matter to John Christian Elden for a second opinion.

I made it clear to you on 6th February 1999 in my letter by enclosing a list of questions put to Karsten Gjone, that I wanted "details of the date, time of day, manner of the attempted/actual rape" Heidi alleges against me. Plus the details of the same allegation she made against a Bergen shopkeeper.

In my letter to you of 14th February point 5) I have specifically asked you to obtain details of the rape allegation in the Drammen police papers. In point 6) I asked you to ask Svein Jensen exactly why he didn't believe Heidi's story. In point 7) I wanted details of Gudmund Johannessen's assault (reported to the Drammen police) on Heidi. None of these details are supplied by you.

I also made my concerns clear to John Elden on 18th February 1999 in a letter.

So it is entirely wrong of you to say in your letter that my request for a full report arrived at your office after you went to the Drammen police station. The basics – the **details** of the rape allegation (made 12 years later by Heidi), Svein Jensen's opinion and the crap about 300 letters in the last year were core elements in the report I wanted, known to you in advance.

I spend all that money on you and get nothing, in effect, of what I asked for, put in writing.

I'm afraid there's no way your conduct can be accepted. And believe me you'd never get away with it in England, where the Office for the Supervision of Solicitors have effective powers to punish solicitors, whereas in Norway the DNA are almost a waste of time complaining to. They have no powers worth speaking about.

Furthermore, how can you stay silent on the total crap printed by the PFU in their report of 24th August? Where's the English translation you requested of them? Why is there no reference made to the fact of my cast-iron proof that Ingunn Røren's had lied to the PFU? Where is the reference to Svein Jensen's and Ingunn Røren's taped conversations? Did you follow up my letters and tapes to the PFU with a request that they consider and include my evidence? No, you didn't did you? Now the PFU are going to reprint their crap in two journals and put it on the internet. All my evidence was ignored. No wonder I have to campaign myself !

There is more, as you have seen in my previous correspondence with you. Even a simple letter to the Drammen police asking for them to photocopy the letters and postcards you cannot manage. It's all been a total waste of time because of your poor service. You really don't care at all.

I will not tolerate it anymore and this letter together with the copy correspondence listed below will be sent to the Norwegian Bar Association to form the basis of my complaint. You must deal with the outstanding points.

Does it not occur to you that a single sentence is just not enough to form the full extent of your report on your findings at the police station in Drammen – after all the questions I have previously put to you?

Yours sincerely,

Frederick Delaware

Copy to Wenche Siewers of the Norwegian Bar.

This letter formed the basis of my complaint to the Norwegian Bar Association whom I wrote to on the 9th September as well.

On 16th September 1999 I was requested and sent a cheque for £1,500 to my new lawyer Stig Lunde – how many had I used now? – on account of costs.

On 1st September 1999 Elden & Elden wrote to me:

Dear Mr. Delaware,

HEIDI SCHØNE

I will hereby confirm that your letter of 9 September 1999 is received by us.

Anyway, we have recently received a letter for you from Drammen police district dated 9 September 1999, which is enclosed in original.

Kind regards,
ATTORNEYS AT-LAW ELDEN DA
Eric Lindset
For John Christian Elden Lawyer

The Drammen police had refused to send me any copies of my own postcards and letters addressed to Heidi. The letter from the Drammen police consisted of three sentences in Norwegian which Elden & Elden didn't even bother to translate. As luck would have it, I met a Norwegian girl from Oslo working as a sales assistant in a jeans shop at the Lakeside Shopping Centre in Essex and she gave me the 'good news' of the Drammen Police's refusal to send me copies of my postcards and letters.

On 23rd September 1999, I sent a 3 page fax to my new lawyer giving him the further background information he had requested. On 21st September 1999 the Norwegian Lawyers Association wrote to me:

Dear Mr. Delaware,

REGARDING COMPLAINT RAISED AGAINST ERIC LINDSET AND HIS PRINCIPAL JOHN C. ELDEN

With reference to your letter the 9th September 1999, I do have to ask for the complaint to be addressed to the Ethics Committee (Disiplinærutvalget). This is necessary for the complaint to be taken into consideration.

The complaint should contain: short facts, the relevant incidents and the dates of the incidents complained upon. Try to be specific and short. This is to ensure a quick and correct evaluation of the lawyer's work which both parties will benefit from.

Bundles received from you will be useful as evidence/documentation and is not wasted. The bundles will be stored safely until we hear from you again.

If you have any further questions please do not hesitate to contact the writer.

Phone +47 22 03 51 06

Yours sincerely,

Jørn A. Nyborg
Legal Secretary

I sent a holding letter of 23rd September 1999 to them. I decided I would need a couple of days at home to formulate a concise, easily understood, complaint against Elden & Elden, including photocopies of all the relevant correspondence.

On 24th September 1999, I wrote to the Chief of the PFU, Per Edgar Kokkvold:

Dear Mr. Kokkvold,

Heidi Schøne and Drammens Tidende

I refer to our recent telephone conversations and look forward to hearing from you with the English translation of the PFU Report 24th August 1999.

Earlier this week, I received [back] from the PFU the three tapes, recording various conversations I made in past years. These tapes were for the PFU to keep for your records, that proved the deceit of the newspapers. They are copies of the original tapes which I keep here.

In returning these tapes to me, there is no covering letter and obviously no mention is made of whether you listened to the tapes. Did you or Mr. Børringbo listen to them?

What I can't see in the PFU Report [by just looking at the Norwegian version] is any reference to my evidence provided to you:

1.   The taped conversation by Policeman Svein Jensen saying he did not believe Heidi Schøne's story.

2.   The taped conversations with Ingunn Røren relating that she did not know whether Heidi was telling the truth in relation to alleged threats by me, reported in 1995, to kill Heidi's son when he was two. This was reported as a fact in the newspaper.

   Also the fact that clearly Ingunn Røren has lied regarding her statement that I told her partner he was "living in sin," has not been referred to in your report. I said nothing of the sort to her partner and did not tell Ingunn Røren either that "I would only sue her because she is a woman – who shouldn't speak publicly." She is talking total crap and I caught her out as you would have found out by listening to the short tape. Her lies render all her evidence suspect. She is worthless. She used these lies to justify printing the fact that I was a Muslim and to portray to readers that Muslims are bad people – linking me to erotic paranoia and sex-terror. She's a fucking piece of shit – good words for this evil woman.

3.   The tape recording of Psychiatrist Nils Rettersdøl clearly indicating he was used and tricked by the newspapers is not referred to in your report.

4.   Long ago, I sent you copies of Heidi's love letters from 1984 and 1985 which clearly contradict the newspaper story "16 years of sex-terror." No mention of my evidence is in your report.

5.   Elden & Elden told me there was no evidence that I wrote "300 letters to Heidi in the last year." I wrote her 5 or so letters telling her I'd see her in Court. Did you ask the newspaper for evidence of 300 letters in the last year **to** Heidi?

Clearly my evidence should be reported in your final report. The fact that Heidi Schøne has been in a psychiatric unit should also be explained to readers of your report – as it [the PFU report] is going on the internet and three other publications.

387

So this is what I am going to do. I will create a Home Page on the Internet with my 'report' in Norwegian (you have it) plus the report 'Heidi Schøne – Abnormal Mental Life' plus using the scanner to transmit the newspaper photos of Heidi Schøne and her husband.

Yours sincerely,

Frederick Delaware

On 29th September 1999, Kokkvold sent me just a one page translation of a portion of the 8 page PFU report of 24th August 1999. It went like this:

STATEMENT FROM THE [NORWEGIAN] PRESS COMPLAINTS COMMISSION:

The complaint concerns a report published in *Drammens Tidende – Buskeruds Blad*, in which the newspaper related the story of a woman who asserts that she has been stalked by a mentally disturbed Englishman for some 16 years. The man submitted a complaint through a Norwegian lawyer that the newspaper had given a partisan account of the woman's version without giving him the opportunity refute what he refers to as "unsubstantiated, fallacious allegations." The complainant regards it as defamatory that the paper unquestioningly characterises him as mentally disturbed, and claims moreover that he has been identified as a result of the report. Furthermore, the complainant considers it irrelevant and offensive that his religious beliefs as a Muslim are pointed out.

Drammens Tidende – Buskeruds Blad considers that it has solid evidence that the woman's version is correct and regards it as manifest that the complainant is mentally disturbed. As far as the paper is concerned, there was no reason to obtain the complainant's side of the case in view of the telephone calls and letters received by the editors after an earlier report on the woman's situation. The paper deemed that it would be protecting the complainant from himself by refraining from putting his statements in to print. The editors now acknowledge that it should have informed the readers of this consideration. The newspaper denies having carried any information about the complainant that would serve to identify him, but regards it as relevant to inform its readers that the complainant is a Muslim.

As a general point, the Press Complaints Commission wishes to refer to the Code of Ethics of the Norwegian Press, paragraph 4.14, which states that: "Persons who are the object of serious allegations should as far as possible have the benefit of corresponding attention to the facts as they exist."

Notwithstanding, in the present case, the Commission does accept the editors' decision not to obtain the complainant's comments. However, the Commission duly notes that the newspaper subsequently considered that it would have been correct to inform the readers of the reason why the complainant was not given the opportunity to provide his version at the same time.

It is the opinion of the Commission that the disputed report should be regarded as a plea for help from the woman in question. The Commission finds it evident that the woman has for many years had a great deal to endure. The newspaper's new report on the case, giving an account of the complainant's behaviour, was aimed at the woman's neighbours and others and as such was intended to ease the woman's situation.

The Commission wishes on this point to refer to The Code of Ethics of the Norwegian Press, paragraph 1.5, which states that: *"It is the duty of the press to protect individuals and groups against infringements or acts of negligence perpetrated by public authorities and institutions, private enterprises or others."*

> The Commission is likewise satisfied that the complainant was given full anonymity by the newspaper.
>
> *Drammens Tidende – Buskeruds Blad* is found not to be in breach of best ethical practices established for the Norwegian Press.
>
> *Oslo 24 August 1999*
>
> *Sven Egil Omdal,*
> *Odd Isungset, Catharine Jacobsen, Thor Woje*
> *Helen Bjørnøy, Grete Faremo, Jan Vincents Johannessen*

I replied to Kokkvold on 1st October 1999:

Dear Mr. Kokkvold,

Drammens Tidende Case No. 119/98

Thank you for sending me your letter post-stamped 29th September enclosing the translation into English of the Press Complains Commission's Report of 24th August 1999.

I refer to my fax and post letter to you of 24th September 1999 and add the following.

The "solid evidence" mentioned by D-T in the second paragraph is their own self-serving unsubstantiated assertion, which "evidence" the PFU have, I presume, not seen. In contrast, the PFU have seen my evidence; again: namely that the policeman Svein Jensen did not believe Heidi; Ingunn Røren has admitted she didn't know whether to believe Heidi and Ingunn Røren has been found - on taped evidence - to be a fabricator of evidence regarding her contention that it is important to tell readers that I am a Muslim. We all know D-T wanted to promote the association of the word "Muslim" with their belief that Islam is a religion for weirdos and is not a religion for "us."

Heidi Schøne is a woman with a proven psychiatric background and her troubles are either self-inflicted or caused by the likes of Gudmund Johannessen. I only reacted to her lies and the newspapers lies.

The Commission Report is a complete cover up. They have ignored completely fully substantiated evidence from me: in tapes; in Heidi's letters to me and, therefore, the Report can hardly be taken seriously.

My objections must be considered by the PFU. Although the matter is going to court, a trial will be several months away provided of course there is no vast financial impediment put in my way.

The fact that the police did not believe Heidi should be mentioned in the PFU report and should have been reported by all the newspapers. The fact of her love letters to me clearly contradict the rubbish printed. Only the blind cannot see and the deaf of heart cannot hear. It is not as if I am trying to trick you or defend an indefensible position.

Perversely, the 14th July 1998 article in D-T has saved my skin: without it, I would have been outside the time limits to sue Heidi Schøne and D-T. The VG and Bergens Tidende journalists will be subpoenaed as witnesses only.

I await your response and perhaps if it isn't satisfactory, I will try and subpoena some of the Commission to Court so a proper cross-examination of the decision

389

making process can be investigated by the Judge. I feel that the Internet will be my quickest remedy in any event, as previously explained. Kindly acknowledge receipt of this letter.

Yours sincerely,

Frederick Delaware

PS. I enclose copies of three letters from Heidi Overaa to me for the Commission to read; clear evidence that the bitch lied.

On the 2nd October, I spoke to Stig Lunde, my newest lawyer. The judge had given him two weeks to sort out what needed amending in my own Writ. I was told now that I was out of time to sue the three newspapers for their 1995 articles, even on the sole basis of getting them to prove what they printed was true. We had to proceed only against Heidi Schøne, Ingunn Røren and her newspaper Drammens Tidende on the basis of the 14th July 1998 article. We were within the 3 year time limit. However, in the amended writ we were going to leave in the 1995 articles so as to explain and support my later campaign against the newspapers and Heidi, which directly resulted in the July 1998 article. I was too late to ask for any of the defendants to be imprisoned, even for the 1998 article. The position was that if the police themselves do not prosecute Heidi or the journalist(s) involved for attempting to pervert the course of justice which I was advised they would certainly not bother to do, then I myself had three months in which to bring my own private prosecution, and the time limit of three months started on 14th July 1998. So I was out of time as at 13th October 1998!

On 15th October 1999, my lawyer, Stig Lunde faxed the judge a letter requesting a further extension of time in which to amend my Writ. Lunde kindly faxed me a copy of that letter (in Norwegian) as a gesture of good faith. The judge gave us as long as we reasonably needed to do what was necessary.

On 27th October 1999, I faxed Mr. Kokkvold at the PFU the following letter:

I refer to my letters to you of 24th September and 1st October. Would you please acknowledge receipt of these letters and yourself provide me with a proper response to the questions asked.

I feel it is appropriate to instruct English lawyers to phone you and get those answers if you can't deal with me. I will give you a week to respond.

Frederick Delaware

He replied next day, 28th October 1999:

Dear Sir,

I refer to your letters of September 24 and October 1, and your fax of October 27.

Your letters were submitted to the PFU on October 26 1999. The Commission did not find your letters to contain any relevant new information, and saw no reason to reopen the case. The case is now closed as far as the PFU is concerned.

Yours sincerely,

Per Edgar Kokkvold, Secretary General.

I replied in turn:

> I am in receipt of your letter of 28th October 1999.
>
> It really is unworthy of the PFU to deliberately ignore the questions posed in my letters of 24th September and 1st October 1999. Why the continued cover-up, as in 1996?
>
> The PFU letter of 25th August 1999 to my lawyer Eric Lindset of Elden & Elden consisted of 8 pages. Your translation to me was only 1 page.
>
> How can you live with yourself over the deceit occasioned by the PFU conclusions in the 24.8.99 report? You had the chance to put the record straight and you failed miserably – how cowardly. Certainly your organisation and the press you are meant to control and admonish are Serb-like: lying to the public and suppressing the truth. In due course my 'usual' campaign will re-start. It would be appropriate for a personal hearing to be granted me now, but I expect you'll turn me down.
>
> Frederick Delaware

The PFU – an organization funded by the Press Association and whose Secretary General, Per Edgar Kokkvold, used to be a newspaper editor!

The full translation of the PFU Report of 24th August was obtained by my paying my UK based translators in May 2001 and which repeated the sequence of events as earlier reported to me, but in greater detail.

On 11th November 1999, I sent a full 14 page complaint about Eric Lindset of Elden & Elden to the Norwegian Bar Association, enclosing all the relevant correspondence, newspaper articles and full résumé of the case so far. I sent the Bar Association a copy of my own Writ and its case number proving that it was legally possible to get the Writ up and running. It went off by International Datapost to the Norwegian Bar Association in duplicate at a cost of £44.25. It guaranteed delivery in two days.

When I spoke to my lawyer, Stig Lunde, he told me what I had never heard from any of the lawyers I'd contacted; that he couldn't recognise what the newspapers were talking about having read Heidi's letters to me (three of which he had, as contained in my Writ). Lunde was so astonished he went on to suggest that he could ask a handwriting expert to certify for the Court that Heidi's letters had been written in fact by her and had not been forged by me. But I told him, even she would never attempt to deny she wrote them. "I have the originals with me," I reassured him.

Still, my lawyer was a very busy man and things were going slowly. So, on 22nd November, as he had not been previously made aware, I sent by recorded delivery to Hans Odde, Chief Editor of Drammens Tidende, a tape of the recording of Ingunn Røren's conversation as incontrovertible evidence that she was a liar, in response to Odde's filthy letter of 7th June 1999 to the PFU.

On 13th December 1999, Stig Lunde, at midnight, tried to send me a 10 page fax in Norwegian on the matters he wanted to discuss with me over the phone. For some reason, the fax couldn't get through. I mention this only to show the total commitment of the man to my cause in trying to send me a fax when he got back to his office after a full days meetings in another town. It was a token of his utter good faith to try and fax me 10 pages of his internal memorandum in a language I couldn't understand. Next morning, at 9.52 a.m. the fax came through and I spent 3½ hours on the phone to him in the afternoon going through his letter as he explained each point in turn to me.

We were trying hard to give Heidi Schøne, Ingunn Røren and Drammens Tidende a Christmas present of service of the Amended Writ. But we had too much to do and the Christmas 'present' would have to wait until the New Year. However, Stig Lunde had by now listened to the tape recording of policeman Svein Jensen from March 1996 and those two Ingunn Røren conversations and told me he quite understood my "frustrations" with that journalist.

I had already anticipated that an Amended Writ might not be served on Heidi in time for the Christmas and New Year festivities, so I sent a copy of my original Writ to Heidi's sister, Elisabeth, in Drammen on which I had written the words: 'A taste of things to come.' I was not prepared to carry on waiting after 4½ years for yet more time to pass without communicating my serious intentions to Heidi. I sent the document to her sister of course, as Heidi's mail, I suspected, would still be intercepted by the police. I doubted whether Elisabeth would be able to keep the contents of the Writ to herself for long. Hopefully it would spoil their Christmas.

Given that nothing would now be done until January 2000, I sent Stig Lunde extra background information consisting of the PFU report of 24th August 1999 and other papers to enable him to have the clearest possible understanding of the last 5 years activities. I asked him to put in a full complaint to the PFU over their refusal to answer properly my letters, and also to deal with Karsten Gjone's insurance company, Vesta, as clearly it needed a Norwegian lawyer to handle the reticent insurance giant.

Chapter 27

On the 13th January 2000, Stig Lunde sent an Amended Writ (a 'Korrigert Stevning') to the Drammen City Court whereby four parties were named as Defendants – Heidi Schøne, Ingunn Røren, Drammens Tidende and Hans Odde, the Editor. The Summons was 11 pages long with 13 Exhibits and we'd asked for all the Defendants to prove the truth of the 14th July 1998 newspaper allegations and for damages of NOK 50,000 (around £3,700) from Heidi Schøne, NOK 30,000 (around £2,300) from Ingunn Røren and NOK 300,000 from the newspaper (around £23,000). My lawyer thought it best to go for damages on the low side in order to impress on the judge that we wanted mainly to win out of principle and not to appear greedy for money. I didn't agree with that reasoning and I thought what the Defendants had done was so obviously wrong that, say NOK 150,000 (about £11,500) from the chief instigator Heidi Schøne and NOK 200,000 (about £15,400) from Ingunn Røren (a journalist, who, after all had deliberately tried to pervert the course of justice in her evidence) was justified. As for the newspaper itself, NOK 500,000 (£46,000) for repeating their crap was more appropriate. Claiming these higher amounts, of course, didn't mean I'd be awarded them necessarily but it was a good starting point to impress the seriousness of the matter without being over the top.

Amongst the Court exhibits were the three 1995 newspapers articles and my 'campaign article' in Norwegian and the 9 page memo I'd sent the newspapers in summer 1995. We wanted to link the 1995 articles with the 1998 article and ensure the whole story was explained in Court. We'd be up-front about my fax and letter campaign in between the 1995 and 1998 articles. The pick of Heidi's letters to me were included in the exhibits. The Amended Writ was really a fresh beginning altogether and my original Writ would never be seen by the Defendants. Nevertheless, my original Writ made everything that followed possible and it sickened me to think that if I'd done the same thing for the three 1995 articles within the time limits, instead of relying on Karsten Gjone, I would've got the big fish – Verdens Gang and Bergens Tidende – into Court.

On the 30th January 2000, I sent a full type-written letter to the PFU detailing every aspect of their cover up and I enclosed the transcripts of phone conversations. This was a letter that just had to be done as most of my other letters to the PFU had been handwritten and would be tedious to read for evidential purposes. I later had Stig Lunde put that letter into the Drammen Court for the Judge to see the full story of the PFU involvement. It was equally important that the Drammen Court see the transcript of my conversations with Svein Jensen, Torill Sorte, Ingunn Røren and Professor Nils Rettersdøl and in January I sent these off to Stig Lunde.

In early February, my previous lawyers, who I had complained against, Elden & Elden, put in a full reply to my complaint which at my request the Norwegian Bar Association had translated into English at their own expense. This letter is dated 31st January 2000:

> The Disciplinary Committee of the Oslo Chapter
> Of the Norwegian Bar Association
> C/o the Secretariat of the Norwegian Bar Association
> Kristian Augusts gate 9
> 0164 OSLO
>
> **FREDERICK DELAWARE – ERIC LINDSET, ATTORNEY AT LAW REPRESENTED BY JOHN CHRISTIAN ELDEN, ATTORNEY AT LAW**
>
> We refer to your undated communication containing a complaint by Mr. Frederick Delaware dated 11 November 1999.
>
> Mr. Delaware approached our office on 10 November 1998 requesting assistance. The case concerned a woman who had allegedly reported him to Bergen Police District for (*attempted*) rape in 1986. In 1995, this same woman also reported Mr. Delaware to Nedre Eiker Rural Constabulary Office for violating her right to privacy over the last 13-14 years. Moreover the woman agreed to be interviewed about Mr. Delaware by several Norwegian newspapers in 1995 and 1998. The newspapers wrote articles on this subject.

Mr. Delaware was not mentioned by name, but was described as inter alia an English, half Arab, Muslim. Mr. Delaware initially wished to bring a legal action against the woman so that she would account for/prove her accusations.

Mr. Delaware had also reported the newspaper articles to the Press Complaints Commission and also requested that we represent him in the future proceedings before that body.

Mr. Delaware was also of the view that he had a claim for damages against a former legal counsel *(the insurance company of said legal counsel)* in this matter. This was based on an alleged failure to comply with time limits for bringing legal action against the aforestated newspapers on the grounds of the newspaper articles in 1995.

I have been responsible for this case on behalf of this firm (John Christian Elden, Attorney at Law). However, most of our contact with Mr. Delaware has been through our Eric Lindset, Attorney at Law. Our dealings with this client have involved a not inconsiderable number of telephone conversations, telefaxes and letters.

Mr. Delaware has lodged nine complaints against my handling of this case(s) which he contends has been contrary to proper professional conduct. I have the following comments on these complaints:

1. ORIGINATING WRIT

Our firm gave advice on the matter of the issuing of an originating writ. This advice was offered both by telephone and in letters. With regard to the latter, I refer to the following letters from our firm to Mr. Delaware [copies of the 5 letters were enclosed as exhibits].

Admittedly six months passed from the time our involvement with this case commenced until our advice not to proceed with this action *(against the aforementioned woman)* was first given in a letter (Exhibit 4) dated 30 June 1999. Our precondition for giving final advice was that the evidence in the case *(seizures made by Drammen and Bergen police districts)* had been reviewed, cf. letters (Exhibit 1, 2 and 3) dated 28 January 1999, 16 February 1999 and 24 February 1999. The main cause of the delay was that it took time to elicit a response from the police. Please find enclosed for your information the following inquiries and reminders to both Drammen and Bergen police districts:

- Request (Exhibit 6) dated 24 January 1999 to Bergen Police District to inspect documents.

- Request (Exhibit 7) dated 24 January 1999 to Drammen Police District to inspect documents.

- Reminder (Exhibit 8) dated 24 February 1999 to Drammen Police District concerning the request to inspect the documents.

- Reminder (Exhibit 9) dated 13 March 1999 to Drammen Police District concerning the request to inspect the documents.

- Reminder (Exhibit 10) dated 19 April 1999 to Drammen Police District concerning the request to inspect the documents.

Bergen Police District promptly responded to the request in their communication (Exhibit 11) dated 9 February 1999. Drammen Police District, on the other hand, did not respond to our approach until their letter (Exhibit 12) dated 27 April 1999. The original case documents were attached to the letter. The Police District also noted that any examination of seizures would have to take place at the police station.

In a telephone conversation on 6 May 1999 Mr. Delaware and Eric Lindset agreed that the latter would travel to Drammen to review the material. The two also discussed whether Eric Lindset should travel to Drammen immediately expressly for this purpose or whether he should seek to combine this with some other business visit to Drammen. In the event of the latter alternative Mr. Delaware would not be charged for travel or per diem expenses or for fees for work performed outside the office. Mr. Delaware preferred this latter approach to an immediate visit, and Eric Lindset reviewed the documents on 30 June 1999. In my letters (Exhibits 4 and 5) of 30 June and 20 July 1999 and in a number of telephone conversations with Eric Lindset, Mr. Delaware was advised not to bring a legal action against the above stated woman.

2. COMMENTS TO THE EVIDENCE

Mr. Delaware has been notified of our/my assessments of his various tape recordings and the letters written to him by the woman in question. This took place in the many telephone conversations between Mr. Delaware and Eric Lindset.

3. THE PRESS COMPLAINTS COMMISSION

It should be noted that during its review of this matter the PCC had the audio cassette in question to hand. Moreover the PCC had been informed of Mr. Delaware's wishes/requests as regards various comments and responses.

4. TRANSCRIPTS, TRANSLATIONS AND/OR COPIES OF THE DOCUMENTS IN THE CRIMINAL CASE

In a letter (Exhibit 13) dated 13 March 1999 to Bergen Police District we requested permission to provide Mr. Delaware with copies of the Police District's documents in the criminal case against him. In a letter (Exhibit 14) dated 13 April to ourselves Bergen Police District requested (further) grounds for the request. We responded in a letter (Exhibit 15) from this office dated 19 April 1999. In a letter (Exhibit 16) dated 24 April 1999 Bergen Police District rejected the request p.t. with the exception of seized letters written by Mr. Delaware himself, which was the essential point. Following a letter (Exhibit 17) from this office dated 30 May 1999, these letters were received in a communication (Exhibit 18) dated 14 June 1999. The material was forwarded in its entirety to Mr. Delaware in a communication (Exhibit 19) dated 20 June 1999.

As regards the items seized by Drammen Police District I/we have by no means undertaken to transcribe and/or translate the material in question.

This could in fact entail a breach of §16-3 of the Prosecution Instructions. Moreover, given the scope of the seizure this would be a time-consuming and costly task. However, Drammen Police District was explicitly asked for copies for Mr. Delaware in a letter (Exhibit 20) dated 22 July 1999. This request was refused by Drammen Police District in a letter (Exhibit 21) dated 9 September 1999.

5. CLAIM AGAINST FORMER LEGAL COUNSEL/SAID COUNSEL'S INSURANCE COMPANY

In my letter (Exhibit 2) dated 16 February and in a telephone conversation (cf Exhibit 22, letter dated 13th August 1999, final paragraph) with Eric Lindset on 4 March, Mr. Delaware was advised not to proceed with or expend resources on a claim against his former legal counsel/said counsel's insurance company. The reasons given by this office related solely to my assessment of the tenability of the claim. In the aforesaid telephone conversation Mr. Delaware expressed that he both understood and accepted our advice.

6. TRANSLATIONS

The question of translation of the correspondence was discussed by Mr. Delaware and Eric Lindset on the telephone. On the grounds that he could secure translations at a lower cost than us, Mr. Delaware asked for the written material to be forwarded in an untranslated form. Nevertheless Eric Lindset regularly informed him of the contents of the various written documents by telephone. This is clear inter alia from my letter (Exhibit 23) of 9 May 1999 to Mr. Delaware.

7. TERMINATION OF THE ASSIGNMENT

In a telephone conversation on 20 July Mr. Delaware informed Eric Lindset that he no longer wished to retain our services. Written confirmation (Exhibit 5) to this effect was sent to Mr. Delaware on that same day. In a subsequent telephone conversation on 22 July 1999 between Mr. Delaware and Eric Lindset the former reiterated his termination of our assignment. Mr. Delaware has subsequently totally or partially changed his mind on this point. In any event, we decided to terminate the client-attorney relationship with Mr. Delaware and he was informed of this in a letter dated 13 August 1999. Our reason was that Mr. Delaware made direct contact with the opposing party despite our instructions to the contrary (cf. Telephone conversations and Exhibit 2, third paragraph from the end). Furthermore he was not prepared to follow our advice not to take legal action against the aforementioned woman and his former legal counsel/said counsel's insurance company. Finally Mr. Delaware had fallen behind in (*advance*) payments.

8. THE NUMBER OF LETTERS SENT BY MR. DELAWARE TO THE WOMAN IN QUESTION

It is not the case that we have not confirmed to Mr. Delaware that the letters and postcards seized by Drammen Police District numbered less than 300/400 items. Admittedly, Eric Lindset has not performed a precise count, but there were many. Mr. Delaware was therefore informed by telephone that the difference was unlikely to have any effect on the outcome of the case since some imprecision is generally accepted under Norwegian libel law. Furthermore we could not be entirely certain that the seizure covered anything that was in fact received at the address of the woman in question.

9. LETTER FROM THIS OFFICE TO THE WOMAN IN QUESTION

Initially our unambiguous advice to Mr. Delaware was to wait further measures until we had received the police documents against him (cf. Exhibit 1, fifth paragraph from the end, Exhibit 2, fourth paragraph from the end and Exhibit 3, fourth paragraph from the end). Having done this our advice, as noted earlier, was that he should not proceed with legal action against the woman in question.

Accordingly I refute that I directly or through the person who assisted me in respect of Mr. Delaware (Eric Lindset, Attorney at Law) acted in contravention of proper professional conduct.

Yours faithfully,
ADVOKATFIRMAET ELDEN DA

My response was dated 11th February 2000:

Gro Grasbekk
Den Norske Advokatfug
Oslo, Norway

Dear Madam,

Case No: 4/2000 – Eric Lindset and Elden & Elden

Thank you for your letters of the 4th and 9th of February 2000 with enclosures. I much appreciate the translation into English of Elden & Elden's letter of 31st January.

I reply as follows:

1. ORIGINATING WRIT

My new lawyers in Norway (whose name shall remain confidential) issued the (enclosed) Amended Writ dated 13th January 2000 which was served by the Drammen Byrett on 19th January 2000 (see copy of their letter enclosed) on Drammens Tidende, its editor Hans Odde, its journalist Ingunn Røren and Heidi Schøne: 4 defendants.

My original writ which you have, had to be amended, as my new lawyers told me I was also out of time to sue the 3 newspapers over their 1995 articles for the cause of action in asking the newspapers to prove the truth of their allegations (copy original Writ enclosed for Elden).

My new lawyer has agreed to deal with Vesta Insurance Company over Karsten Gjone's negligence in missing the time limits to sue for libel asking the newspapers to prove what they said was true: the burden of proof is on V.G; B-T and D-T and Heidi Schøne.

I also enclose a copy of my lawyer's internal notes to indicate the correct level of advice that should have been considered by Elden & Elden and communicated to me.

I must insist that my original Writ of 20th August 1999, the Amended Writ of 13th January 2000 and my lawyers internal notes of 14th December 1999 are not disclosed or talked about to anyone whatsoever, by Elden & Elden, except in connection with this complaint being handled by the DNA.

Elden & Elden's "firm advice" as they put it can be seen as wholly inadequate.

2. COMMENTS ON THE EVIDENCE

I was <u>not</u> informed at all on the telephone of Elden & Elden's assessments of my tape recordings or Heidi Schøne's letters to me. You will see that my subsequent correspondence bears this out. Besides, lawyers should always follow up oral advice by written advice. We lawyers deal in the written word for obvious reasons. Elden & Elden knew the risks inherent in not putting advice in writing, from Karsten Gjone's example.

3. THE PRESS COMPLAINTS COMMISSION (PFU)

Elden & Elden gave up with the PFU at the vital time which can be seen from the correspondence with you.

I therefore have continued to take the matter up personally with the PFU (see my enclosed copy letter of the 30th January 2000 to them) with instructions to my lawyer to deal with the PFU's cover up.

My questions raised in my letter of 11.11.99 to Elden & Elden have not been answered by Elden & Elden.

The PFU's report of 25.8.99 was a cover up and referred to none of my vital evidence as my letter of 30.1.2000 will reveal.

4. TRANSCRIPTS, COPY DOCUMENTS AT BERGEN & DRAMMEN POLICE STATIONS

I was pleased to receive copies of my old letters held at the Bergen police station, which was one good result obtained for me by Elden & Elden.

However the complaint put in my letter of 11.11.99 has not been answered properly. If I put a question I mean it to be answered. I only wanted it confirmed in writing that Eric Lindset saw the police papers in Bergen indicating an (untrue) allegation of attempted rape in 1986; an (untrue) allegation of actual rape (no longer attempted) made by Heidi Schøne in 1998 to the Nedre Eiker police. I also wanted a report on Heidi Schøne's allegation of rape to the Bergen police by a Bergen shopkeeper in the early 1980's (for which I have taped corroborating evidence of Heidi Schøne _telling_ her best friend at the time that the incident allegedly took place).

Regarding my request for a full report from Eric Lindset on his visit to the Drammen police station he implied in his correspondence to me that he could have done a full report had he known he should have done one for me. He knew long before his visit what I wanted, but is he now telling me it is against the rules to give a full report? Why not tell me that in the first place? His one line report was a complete waste of time.

5. CLAIM AGAINST KARSTEN GJONE

The fact is that Elden & Elden didn't give me the advice that my present lawyer did. There is a valid claim _now_ for Gjone's failure to issue a writ (in the form of the Amended Writ against Drammen Tidende) against VG, Bergens Tidende and Drammens Tidende for the 1995 articles.

I did _not_ express my acceptance or understanding of Elden & Elden's advice; what real advice was that? As far as libel was concerned I think apart from Ann-Kristin Horvei, six or so others recognised me. [Although I only had concrete evidence of three witnesses having recognised me over the 1995 articles.]

6. TRANSLATIONS

Exhibit 23 obviously I know about. But there were so many short 1-3 line/sentence letters in Norwegian that I was not going to and did not phone up Elden & Elden every time for a translation. Besides, Eric Lindset told me that they charged clients for phone calls in increments of 15 minutes or part thereof. Why not save me some of their time and my time and my money by doing the simple thing in the first place: a quick translation; even the gist of the meaning would do.

I repeat that I was not asking for the longer letters to be translated.

7. TERMINATION OF ASSIGNMENT

I repeat that I did **not** inform Mr. Lindset that I no longer wanted him to act for me in a phone conversation of 20th July. He knows the truth of the matter as I wrote later, in my post-script (P.S.) to my letter to him of 28th July 1999.

Exhibit 5 is a self-serving misrepresentation: a complete untruth. It was only **after** I spoke to the judge at Drammen Court on 21st July 1999 (at 12.47 p.m. English time for 22 minutes and 25 seconds at a cost of £5.512 pence – as per my phone bill which is available on request) that I knew I could issue a writ myself. I had hitherto been of the firm impression that only the lawyers could issue a writ.

By the time of my next conversation with Eric Lindset on 22nd July at 11.36 a.m. for 8 minutes and 48 seconds, I **then** knew I could dispense with Eric Lindset's 'help' in drawing up a writ. I did **not** "re-iterate" my termination of Elden & Elden's assignment. For the first time that day - 22nd July - I told Eric Lindset I would issue the writ myself and Eric said he would pass on to me further correspondence he received. But I state again: Eric Lindset said on 20th July that he would get back to me after his professional requirement to consult his boss John C. Elden over my request that his firm draw up a writ for me. Eric didn't want to draw up a writ (indeed his advice earlier indicated he was incapable of doing this) so I asked him to tell John Christian Elden that I insisted a writ be drawn up. So I waited for word from Eric as to what John C. Elden had decided. On the same day by letter I'm told that I have terminated my instructions. Very unprofessional.

Elden & Elden say in their letter of 13th August 1999 that their reason for terminating the client/attorney relationship was that I made "direct contact with the opposing party despite our instructions to the contrary" and they refer to Exhibit 2. Exhibit 2 is dated 16th February 1999 and I heeded that advice. However, my writing to this 3rd party – the PFU – was clearly explained in my letter of 11.11.99 to the DNA: It was an emergency because Eric Lindset was on holiday for two weeks and he would never have had the time to go into the matter as I myself could, as I had a much better understanding of the issues involved. Crucially I could not risk the PFU deciding that my vital, later evidence was inadmissible for being tendered out of time. Besides, I copied Eric Lindset in, on **all** my correspondence with the PFU. I had made sure the PFU knew exactly what they had to do and instead of Eric Lindset appreciating how much time and effort I'd saved him, I get condemnation for writing to a third party.

The point is also that no mention was made in Elden & Elden's letter to me of 13th August 1999 of their objection to my contacting this 3rd party. This reason is only mentioned now – in their letter of 31.1.00.

Falling behind in advance payments is a false reason advanced by Elden & Elden. I have already dealt with this in my letter of 11.11.99 and of course no response is given in E & E's letter of 31.1.00. What is this: Elden & Elden's right to silence being exercised??

8. "OVER 300 LETTERS" SENT TO HEIDI SCHØNE IN 1997-1998 AS REPORTED IN DRAMMENS TIDENDE ON 14.7.98

Again what kind of response is this from Elden & Elden? Their reply is of no value at all. I did not write 300 letters "in the last year" (almost one a day) to Heidi Schøne. I wrote 5 or so telling her I am taking her to court.

Heidi Schøne could not bear to be confronted with answering my questions on her disgusting behaviour. So she side-stepped the matter by asking the post

399

office to send all her mail from any source to the police for them to vet first. Also she would not want letters from other people asking her about my "information campaign," regarding her filthy lies to the press.

Would it not be easy then for Eric Lindset – he had been given 6 months notice of my requirements – to simply ask the police to see the 300 or so letters I allegedly wrote in 97-98 to Heidi Schøne?

I'm a bit confused also, as Eric told me on the phone that indeed I only wrote "5 or so letters in the last year." So I told him to confirm it in writing – see what ensued!

The fact is the police do not hold 300 or so letters for the period 97-98 – on that you can rest assured and for the newspaper D-T to print that in 1998, is a lie which I wanted to expose – BUT I NEEDED ERIC LINDSET TO CONFIRM IT IN WRITING FOR EVIDENTIAL PURPOSES.

9. LETTER FROM ELDEN & ELDEN PUTTING HEIDI SCHØNE ON NOTICE

First class advice – I don't think: that Elden & Elden's advice was that basically I don't have a case against Heidi Schøne. So, I've attempted to rape her, (allegedly): I've raped her (allegedly), I've threatened to kill her, her family, her two year old son (in writing). I've written 400 obscene letters (allegedly); I fantasise about Heidi Schøne who never had any feelings for me. My mother wanted to put me in a mental hospital (she, Heidi says). And more. And this from a girl who has been in a psychiatric unit; who's slept with a man knowing he was injecting heroin; who had two abortions before I ever met her and who twice tried to take her life.

Oh yes – good advice from Elden & Elden: have they bothered to look at my evidence? Anyway, sarcasm aside, the writ is issued and served, and on a very sound foundation.

Yours faithfully,

Frederick Delaware

To this Elden & Elden had no further comments and on the 22nd August 2000 the Disciplinary Committee found as follows:

> 1. Neither John C. Elden, Attorney at Law, nor Eric Lindset, Attorney at Law, acted in contravention of proper professional conduct.
>
> 2. There are no grounds for reduction of payment of the defendant's fee.

The Disciplinary Committee continued:

> "By way of introduction the Committee notes that the task of the Disciplinary Committee is to assess the ethical aspects of the attorney-at-law's handling of the case, and not the quality of the legal advice that was offered.
>
> The Disciplinary Committee notes that all the complaints presented by the complainant are generally based on the defendant's allegedly inadequate handling of the legal matters of the complainant. Accordingly, the Committee concludes that none of the matters are censurable on ethical grounds.

As regards the complainants allegation that the assignment/client relationship was unilaterally and unjustifiably terminated (point 7), this point is in a somewhat different position since termination of the client relationship is permissible only within the framework that follows from the section 3.1.6 of the ethical regulations. There seems to be some disagreement as to whether the assignment/client relationship was in fact terminated by the complainant or by the defendants …….. Notwithstanding this disagreement the assignment appears to have been terminated largely on the basis of disagreement about the way in which the case was being handled, and the Disciplinary Committee will not censure [Elden and Elden] in connection with the termination of the client relationship.

According to section 3.1.2 of the ethical regulations, the defendants are required to advise their client and to properly promote their clients' interests. If correct the complainant's complaints could provide grounds for censure of [Elden and Elden]. Nevertheless, the Disciplinary Committee find that on the subject of the complainants 1. [issue of Writ] and 9. [letter to Heidi Schøne], [Elden and Elden] insisted from the time at which they took on the assignment that they must be provided with an overview of the facts of the case before the measures specified therein would be taken.

"Having gained an overview of the facts in the case [Elden & Elden] explicitly advised the complainant against pursuing such measures" [being the issue of a Writ against the newspapers and Heidi Schøne and a letter to Heidi Schøne putting her on notice] "Accordingly the Disciplinary Committee cannot see that there are any grounds for censuring [Elden and Elden] on these points.

As regards point 3 [the Press Complaints Commission] evidence has been presented to show that [Elden & Elden] did contact the Press Complaints Commission and promoted the interests of the complainant in this respect. Moreover it is clear from the letter from [Elden & Elden] dated 24th February 1999 that the complainant notified [Elden and Elden] that he would personally handle the relationship with the Press Complaints Commission. Accordingly the Disciplinary Committee finds that there are no grounds for censuring Elden & Elden on this point.

As regards [taking action against Karsten Gjone's Insurance company, they, Elden and Elden] advised against the implementation of the measures specified therein, their advice being that it was too late to pursue this course of action. Accordingly the Disciplinary Committee finds that there are no grounds for censuring [Elden and Elden] on this point.

As regards the other points in the complaints all of which concern Elden and Elden's attitude towards evidence in the cases in question and the reporting of this to the complainant, the Disciplinary Committee finds it particularly difficult to establish the facts in this matter …. Although [Elden and Elden] did not provide a full report on all the facts they reported their understanding of the main case against the woman in question based on the facts that they considered significant in the case. Here too the Disciplinary Committee concludes that there are no grounds for censuring Elden & Elden."

So I appealed on the finding by letter dated 4th September 2000 and to summarise, my points were:

1. I enclosed a copy of Stig Lunde's amended writ of 13th January 2000 as evidence that it was possible to issue a writ on clearly explained grounds.

2. Why did Elden & Elden offer no comment at all on the taped telephone conversations or Heidi's letters to me, which I said constituted the whole basis of my case.

401

3. That the Committee were wrong in concluding that I had notified Elden & Elden that I would personally handle the case with the Press Complaints Commission. I enclosed a copy of my letter of 28th February 1999 in which I specifically corrected Elden & Elden's mistaken impression and told them to continue on my behalf, which they did. But it was important for them to ensure that the PFU considered the evidence I'd given them. Elden & Elden did not do this and it led to a PFU cover up, particularly over the journalist Ingunn Røren's lies to the PFU.

4. That it was not too late to claim against Advokat Karsten Gjone's insurance company for his negligence in missing the time limits to issue a writ against the newspapers for the 1995 articles. So I enclosed a copy of Vesta Insurance Company's letter to me of 24th November 1999 in which they acknowledged receipt of my claim and which my present lawyer was dealing with.

5. I repeated my protest that I clearly deserved a full written report on the evidence at the Drammen police station which I'd been after for months.

On the 11th September 2000, I wrote to the Disciplinary Tribunal enclosing a copy of Judge Anders Stilloff's decision after the 25th August 2000 hearing (described later in this chapter) in which I was allowed to proceed to full trial, having won all the points argued before the judge. Clearly, the judge thought Heidi Schøne, the journalist and editor of Drammens Tidende had a prima facie case to answer.

Elden & Elden replied as follows on 6th September 2000:

The Disciplinary Committee of the Norwegian Bar Association
Kr August gt. 9
0164 Oslo.

APPEAL BY FREDERICK DELAWARE

I refer to your letter of the 5th of this month, and hereby confirm receipt.

We refer to documents already submitted by this side. Should the Committee require further comments we are at its disposal.

As regards the quality of the advice not to take out a writ against Heidi Schøne, I note that the Public Prosecutors in Oslo/Drammen Police Districts have imposed a fine on the Complainant pursuant to § 390a of the Criminal Code for privately taking out a writ against Schøne in an action before Drammen City Court.

Yours faithfully,
ADVOKATFIRMAET ELDEN DA
John Christian Elden (initialled)
Attorney at law

I replied on the 16th September 2000:

Beate Sundstrøm
Disiplinaernemnden
Den Norske Adv. OSLO

Thank you for your letter of 14th September 2000 with enclosures.

The Public Prosecutor in Drammen has asked for a fine to be imposed on me for my giving as evidence in my writ – the enclosed fact sheet of Heidi Schøne's (formerly Heidi Overaa) past life, x 2.

How am I supposed to predict; indeed how is my lawyer supposed to predict, that including this highly relevant piece of evidence in a civil action is going to lead to a fine under § 390a of the Criminal Code?

My lawyer has written to the Public Prosecutor justifying my action and his action, as a response to disgraceful newspaper allegations against me in 1995 and 1998. The Public Prosecutor has also been informed that Judge Stilloff accepted all my lawyer's arguments and has allowed my case to proceed to trial (you have the Judge's decision).

Further, at no time did Elden & Elden ever advise me about this specific point so they are now just being wise after the event.

I have informed the Public Prosecutor that this action against me is without foundation and malicious and an interference in the due process of law in my civil case. I have told him that I will <u>not</u> pay the fine. My lawyer and I await further developments on this matter with the Public Prosecutor.

The point is, there are fundamental issues here at stake that must be tested in the Courts. I needed and I have at last found a lawyer who believes in furthering my legitimate interests. Once again, it is clear that in allowing me to proceed to trial, Judge Stilloff accepts also that I have a right to sue Heidi Schøne, Ingunn Røren (journalist), Hans Odde (Editor) and Drammens Tidende. Let us not forget that Ingunn Røren has been proven (as per the evidence) to have attempted to pervert the course of justice in her evidence to the PFU – something that escaped Elden & Elden's notice, despite my pointing it out to them. Further action by my lawyer will be taken against the PFU – an absolutely useless organisation when it came to serving my interests. Their involvement must be exposed for all to see for what they really are.

Yours faithfully, Frederick Delaware

On the 17th September 2000 Elden & Elden replied:

The Disciplinary Committee of the Norwegian Bar Association
Kr. Augusts gt 9
0164 Oslo

THE APPEAL BY FREDERICK DELAWARE

I refer to your letter of 14 of this month with attachments.

The submitted documents do not provide grounds for changing our advice to the complainant not to issue an originating writ against Heidi Schøne.

We submit that the advice offered by an attorney at law should not be confined to whether it is possible in practice to issue an originating writ and for the writ to be heard by the Court – and to succeed in a legal action. It is the duty of an attorney at law to prevent unnecessary legal actions and, if possible, to prevent the unnecessary escalation of existing conflicts. The complainant, who states that he is "an experienced British solicitor," should be aware of this, as it also applies to British attorneys at law. The fact that the complainant secured a different opinion from Mr. Lunde does not mean that the initial advice was contrary to proper professional practice.

Yours faithfully,
ADVOKATFIRMAET ELDEN DA
John Christian Elden (signed)
Attorney at Law

This letter spoke volumes for me. Clearly, Elden & Elden had every intention of doing their best to ensure a writ would not be issued. A perverse attitude.

The Disciplinary Board gave their decision on 20th December 2000 which is produced below:

THE DISCIPLINARY BOARD

Reviewed Complaint No.   D89/00 Proper professional conduct/calculation fee

On   20 December 2000

Complainant: Frederick Delaware

Defendants   Eric Lindset and John Chr. Elden
Attorneys at Law:

The following persons
reviewed the case: District Court Judge Knut Glad

                                               Ole A. Bachke, Attorney at Law
                                               Trine Buttingsrud Mathiesen, Attorney at Law
                                               Monica Vinje, Senior Consultant
                                               Jan Fredrik Haraldsen, Assistant Director

In a letter dated 11 November, Frederick Delaware lodged a complaint against attorneys at law Eric Lindset and John Chr. Elden to the Disciplinary Committee of the Norwegian Bar Association. The attorneys assisted the complainant in three cases, all of which were based on the filing of an allegedly wrongful complaint to Bergen Police District for attempted rape in 1986. The complaint concerns the calculation of the attorneys' fees and breaches of proper professional conduct.

The Disciplinary Committee of the Oslo chapter of the Norwegian Bar Association reviewed the complaint and gave its decision as follows on 22 August 2000:

1.   *Neither John C. Elden, Attorney at Law, nor Erik Lindset, Attorney at Law, acted in contravention of proper professional conduct.*

2.   *There are no grounds for reduction/repayment of the fee.*

In a letter dated 30 August 2000, Frederick Delaware appealed the decision of the Committee in due time to the Disciplinary Board. A letter dated 4 September 2000 expands upon the appeal. The complainant submits that the Committee failed to properly assess the matters raised by the complainant, and that where such matters were considered, the wrong decision was reached. It is not entirely clear whether the appeal also relates to the decision on the fee, but it is assumed that this is the case.

John Chr. Elden submitted a reply on 17 September 2000. He refers to earlier submissions.

As regards the facts in the case, nothing new of significance has been raised in this round of the appeal, and reference is made to the outline provided by the Committee.

The Disciplinary Board has reached the same conclusion as the Committee, and concurs with the grounds given in the Committee's decision.

According to Section 3.1.2 of the Rules on Proper Professional Conduct, an attorney at law is required to advise his/her client and to promote the interests of his/her client in a satisfactory manner. Nevertheless, the attorney at law must be given free reign in determining how he/she wishes to handle the client's case and in the professional advice he/she wishes to give. For an attorney at law's performance of an assignment to be viewed as a breach of the Rules on Proper Professional Conduct, he/she must have committed clear errors or have been negligent. In the view of the Disciplinary Committee, this is not the case in this instance.

Under Section 3.1.6 of the ethical rules, an attorney at law may withdraw from an assignment if the client does not follow the advice given by the attorney. The documents in this case suggest that the situation in this instance was such that the attorney against whom the complaint has been lodged was justified in unilaterally terminating the client/attorney relationship.

This decision is unanimous.

Conclusion:

The decision of the Disciplinary Committee is upheld.

Knut Glad
Chair

Another whitewash.

In March, my lawyer informed me that Drammens Tidende, its editor Hans Odde and the journalist Ingunn Røren had asked the Court to dismiss my case because I had used the PFU. They were, it seems, arguing that I couldn't take them to Court if I'd used their Press Complaints Commission. My lawyer was also very apprehensive for my chances of getting anywhere as all the Defendants had asked the Court to give a ruling that I should put up a guarantee for their costs should I lose the case. They had asked the Court for a NOK 300,000 bond from me, i.e. about £23,000, money which of course I did not have. My lawyer had asked me to look into how I could raise this money. Things looked as if they were on the verge of total collapse and I began to think again of starting another 'information campaign.' I asked Stig Lunde to research thoroughly the position as to costs guarantees and he said he would do so. Lunde was a commercial/company lawyer so he was chartering new territory in handling my case.

It was therefore an anxious call I made to him a week later. His further research had mercifully discovered that the Court would only require a costs guarantee against me if the merits of my case were poor and also if I had no other assets to pay costs if in due course I happened to lose the case. So I had to give Lunde copies of the title deeds to my house, which had no mortgage, and tell of my income as a solicitor.

I knew my case was very strong and that we were in with a good chance of getting the case on for a full trial. On 29th March 2000, Lunde put in a large bundle of evidence including the transcripts in typewritten English of my aforementioned tape-recorded telephone conversations. He'd done a lot of work. Unfortunately, his Amended Writ of 13th January 2000 and his submissions of 29th March 2000 to the Court were not immediately intelligible to me as it was all in Norwegian and it would cost me a fortune to get them professionally translated. I therefore just trusted that he'd done a proper job. In time, I would have to find a Norwegian in London who would roughly translate what was written. However, for the moment I could see from what Lunde had sent me that Wahl, Nøkleby & Co acting for Drammens Tidende had been crafty enough to send the Court a copy of the PFU decision of 24th August 1999 but did not send to the Court Drammens Tidende's letter of 7th June 1999 to the PFU which detailed the lies and deceit Drammens Tidende justified as explaining their reference to me in the 14th July 1998 article as being "Muslim." So I asked Lunde to send the 7th June 1999 letter of Drammens Tidende to the Court together with my letter to Paddy Ashdown M.P. of 21st May 1999 and his reply of 11th June 1999, evidence which clearly contradicted the lies of Ingunn Røren. I posted my response on 2nd April to Stig Lunde. On 4th April I got my mother to write to Stig Lunde detailing firstly the fact of her listening to my conversation with Runar Schøne in 1995 when he spoke in tongues to me, and secondly the fact that Heidi Schøne's 1995 newspaper allegation that my mother had wanted to put me in a mental hospital was a "total invention" by Heidi Schøne.

405

On 11th May, Stig Lunde informed me that we had been given a preliminary hearing date of 25th August 2000 at the Drammen City Court which pleased me in that we had the whole summer in which to prepare for it. Unfortunately, the Judge had requested that all my transcripted phone conversations be translated into Norwegian. I had myself spoken to the Judge the previous December and knew that his command of the English language was not so good, so I sympathised with his need to clearly understand the evidence. A pity they couldn't let a judge fluent in English hear the case.

On Sunday 11th June 2000, I went round to the Norwegian Church in Rotherhithe, East London, with all the Norwegian documentation that my lawyer asked me to get translated to ensure that I fully understood what he'd done for me. I got there during the morning service and it soon became obvious that no one had the time to orally translate the stuff. One of the staff, though, was going to ask if anyone knew of a good translator, so I sat chatting away whilst some of the youngsters in the church had their photos taken with Christian, one of the members of the boy-band A1. My old friend, the Pastor, later came up to me with the address of a translator in Surrey. It seemed after all that I would have to pay a good bit to have the papers translated. I left the church and made my way back to north of the River Thames by taking the narrow Rotherhithe tunnel in my car.

As I came out of the tunnel, on my left-hand side, I noticed a very good-looking blonde with long waist-length hair. Well, not to miss an opportunity, I kept my eye on her as she crossed the traffic lights and I managed to do a 'U' turn in the car and quickly parked on the side of the road along which she had begun to walk. She turned left into a side street and I had to walk fast to catch up with her. "Excuse me," I said to her, "you wouldn't know where the sales office is, would you, for the flats in this development?" She replied: "Not really, but it might be in that building over there," she said pointing to a block across Limehouse Dock. "I'm not so familiar with the area, although I do live here," she added. "Where are you from?" I enquired. "Norway," she said.

Three and a half hours later we parted company at the 'Riverside' pub after she had orally translated my papers, for which I paid her £80. Her name was Celia Høyden and she was living with her English boyfriend nearby, having just returned from Middlesborough working on behalf of Cambridge University on a police forensic course. My lawyer had done an excellent job in his submissions to the Court and I was now at last familiar with his arguments.

For 6 weeks during the summer, my lawyer had been away on sick leave preventing him sending off my taped telephone conversations for translation. It was crucial that the judge had these translations before him by the day of the preliminary hearing on Friday 25th August 2000. I was getting worried but fortunately Stig Lunde recovered just in time and got the tapes translated. The judge got the package on the Monday before the hearing. The Defendants were of course sent the translations and I was glad that at long last they could see that the journalist, Ingunn Røren had tried to pervert the course of justice in her representations to the PFU.

On Tuesday 22nd August, I spoke to my lawyer for four hours on the phone and it was only at this time that I discovered exactly what I had to prove in my case – that someone recognised me from the 14th July 1998 newspaper article. There were about 20 or so people in Norway who might have recognised me but only one who I knew did know it was me and that was Karsten Gjone, the lawyer who did nothing for me, but who was reading the story on the 14th July 1998, the very day I happened to phone him. So that was the only name I could confidently give to the Judge – Karsten Gjone, a sacked lawyer who I complained against and who was found in breach of the rules of professional conduct.

I had up to now believed that the basis of my case rested on the sole ground that the newspaper had to prove what they said was true. But as I have already stated, I had been under a misapprehension. I also had to name someone who knew it was me and furthermore it was similar to orthodox English libel I was suing for, save that the judiciary decided the verdict and not a jury.

On the morning of my departure, the 23rd August, I received a copy of Lunde's letter to the Court submitting the translated transcripts and my correspondence with Paddy Ashdown, which I quickly skimmed through. Another first class job by Lunde, albeit a bit late in its delivery to the Court. The translations of the transcript telephone conversations ran to 26 pages and cost me £1,400.

I had long ago decided it was too risky for me to fly straight into Oslo from London. I did not trust the Norwegian police to let me leave the airport in Oslo. There was an unquantifiable risk that they would sabotage my appearance at the Drammen Court by arresting me on some trumped-up charges and hold me in custody until the hearing was over. I couldn't be confident that my name was not on the police computer at Oslo airport. So I had booked a flight to Gothenberg in Sweden from where it was a four hour train journey north to Oslo. At Gothenberg airport, I picked up my luggage along with the Coleraine football team from Northern Ireland, who were in town to play the second leg of a UEFA Cup match. My heart went out to those lads – bravely managing to keep their minds on football with "the troubles" blighting their lives. I spoke to one of their party who told me their match was a "backs to the wall" job against a good Swedish side. He was right, as Coleraine went out of the tournament the next day.

I got out from the train at Moss (45 minutes south of Oslo) to meet my lawyer for the first time, in his office. He had waited for me after close of business and we went through our papers discussing what we'd do next day in Court. He had been working very hard for me in the last few days and would continue to do so in his hotel room in Drammen the night before my big day.

I arrived at the District Courthouse in Drammen early, well before our 9 a.m. start. No one else was around except for a Court attendant sitting at the Reception Desk. I told him who I was and he told me on which floor my hearing was scheduled for. I checked out the courtroom and returned to sit in the ground floor reception area. A little while later in walked a shaven-headed, thick-set man in a blue outfit who made enquiries at the Reception Desk. He then walked up to me and mentioned my name, telling me he was a police officer with instructions to serve a criminal Summons on me, which I refused to accept so he left it there on the bench beside me and walked out, not best pleased with my reaction. Eventually, I picked up the Summons and read it. They had had an English version done for me.

As the judge walked in to the Courtroom, everyone was present except Ingunn Røren, the journalist, who somehow had managed to get her editor (also a Defendant) Hans Odde, to represent her. I thought this was a bit audacious. She had saved herself a long trip from Bergen on the West coast where she now worked for the Bergens Tidende newspaper. At least Heidi Schøne was present, together with her overweight husband, dressed as if he was about to go to work on a building site. He smiled at me but I couldn't make up my mind what was behind the smile.

Judge Anders Stilloff was a dignified, quiet man. The first thing he did after the preliminary introductions were over was to ask the Defendants whether they wished to settle the action. I half-smiled at this immediate slap in the face for my opponents. I had sitting beside me an interpreter, a Scottish gentleman by the name of William Mulholland, who'd been living in Norway since the 1960's. The lawyer representing the newspaper, Ingunn Røren and Hans Odde said they would not be making any offer to me and in any case first needed the Board of Drammens Tidende to approve any offer. As for Heidi Schøne and her lawyer, they were taken completely by surprise and had obviously not prepared themselves for such a question, so the Judge made them leave the room to consider the matter. They returned defiant; they would not offer me anything either.

The Defendants had in the weeks leading up to the hearing indicated that they would object to the admission to the trial of my taped conversations with Ingunn Røren. It was vital these be admitted and so it came as a great surprise to me and my lawyer when at the hearing the lawyer for the newspaper did not object to them going in.

However, the newspaper proceeded to ask for my case to be dismissed because I had used the Norwegian Press Complaints Commission (the PFU) and couldn't therefore afterwards take the matter to Court, as I had agreed not to sue the newspaper through my previous lawyers Elden & Elden. My lawyer countered this by arguing that at the time I made this statement it was true, but subsequently I had changed my mind and decided to sue. Up to this point and for several months afterwards, I was under the impression that in Norway a complainant could not sue a newspaper in Court once he had used the PFU. My lawyer had mentioned to me the previous autumn, before he issued his Amended Writ, that a problem of this nature might arise because I had agreed not to sue Drammens Tidende. This much was true: I had agreed not to sue the newspaper for libel as I knew it would be hard to find a totally independent witness who recognised me from the article, but I was under the impression at that time that another entirely separate ground existed in Norwegian law to bring the newspaper to Court; that they had to prove what was printed was true. I made my opinion known to the PFU on 30.1.2000 in the last paragraph of my letter, but I had been wrong. I first had to find someone who recognised me and in which case the newspaper then had to prove what they said was true; the common understanding of a straightforward libel case. Karsten Gjone, my sacked lawyer, had recognised me.

The reality of the law only became clear to me in October 2000. I had by then rung up the English Press Complaints Commission (PCC) to confirm what I had thought to be the position here. I was given the comfort I needed. The PCC will not look into a complaint if *at the same time* the complainant wants to take the newspaper to Court. The PCC, however, will look into a complaint first and when they have adjudicated on the matter, the complainant is then free to proceed to take Court proceedings if he wants to. The position I then discovered was in fact "supposed to be" exactly the same in Norway: but this had not been explained to me by my then lawyers, Elden & Elden, and I wondered if in the many letters the PFU wrote to Elden & Elden the PFU made mention of the alternatives available. If it had been put to me that I could put in a complaint and then after the PFU decision I could still sue the newspaper, then obviously that is the path I would have taken. Only a complete fool would cut off his opportunity to go to Court if he didn't have to. What counted was Elden & Elden's own statement in Norwegian to the PFU in 1999 that I "didn't have a case against the newspaper" to enable me to go to Court and so I would "not be suing the newspaper." I had agreed to let the PFU look into the matter because I thought they would investigate all the circumstances of my complaint including whether or not the allegations were true.

Heidi's own lawyer, in spite of all the evidence in my possession, went on to claim that my case against her should be dismissed as well as I was using the Writ as an instrument of harassment, and that, in effect, there was no case against her. What a perverse misuse of his right to defend his client.

We broke for lunch and the moment the judge had entered his chambers I went over to Heidi Schøne and shouted, "How dare you make allegations that I've threatened to kill your two year old son," to which she stared blankly at me, whilst walking towards her husband who said, "We have proof," as they walked out of the room. My lawyer confirmed to me that he heard this retort from Mr. Schøne. I had for 5 whole years been unable to confront Heidi in person over this and knowing, of course, that my case could be dismissed, I took the opportunity to vent my frustration.

In the afternoon session, my lawyer continued to present as much of the background to my case as possible in the limited time given to him by the judge, who was anxious to wind things up. I was put on the stand and had to give evidence as to my financial standing. I made sure I brought one or two more of my opinions to the attention of the judge. Before the end of proceedings, Heidi Schøne asked to be let go and the judge agreed she could go home. The Judge allowed the three sets of lawyers a closing speech and then dismissed us all. He would make his decision in due course.

Afterwards, the Editor Hans Odde, spoke to my lawyer telling him that he would write in his newspaper about my being served with a criminal Summons. After discussing this Summons with my lawyer over a lemonade in the town centre, I walked over to the newly built police station to deal personally with the police Summons. It was just after 4 p.m. and the Assistant Chief of Police and Chief Prosecutor had just gone home. In attendance was a police officer with slightly long blonde hair and I explained the situation to him. To my surprise, he told me he didn't like Ingunn Røren, the journalist, and that my previous lawyer, Karsten Gjone was "no good" either. Being a criminal lawyer, Gjone was well-known in the local court house. So this policeman told me to go over to the table and chair in the corner and write my reply to the Summons.

I had been summonsed to attend the Magistrates Court in Drammen on 9th October 2000 to answer the following allegations under Section 390(a) of the Penal Code:

1. That I had violated "the privacy of another person through frightening or annoying behaviour or any other inconsiderate behaviour," the grounds for which were set out as follows:

   For years and until August 1998, he phoned from England on numerous occasions and wrote more than 200 letters/postcards to Heidi Schøne (formerly Overaa) and/or to various private persons, public and private firms/institutions, in which he stated/wrote that Heidi Schøne had had an abortion, that a person with whom she later had a child had injected himself with heroin at the time they were having sexual relations, and that he also named the child's father and the child. He also stated/wrote that Schøne and the child's father had been tested for AIDS after the child was born, that the child's father had been remanded in police custody and that Schøne tried to commit suicide by taking an overdose and that she was later admitted to a psychiatric clinic in Lier. He also wrote/stated that Schøne's mother died from alcohol and drug abuse and that Schøne's father, a short time prior to this, had tried to send Schøne to a children's home, etc. and that through his attorney, Stig Lunde, in a Writ of 13th January 2000 (private criminal case), he mainly reiterated the above accusations.

The offended party has requested prosecution, which is also called for in the public interest.

For the violations(s), you are hereby ordered to:

Pay a fine of NOK 10,000 – ten thousand kroner – or, if the fine is not paid, serve 25 – twenty five – days in jail.

2. Further, a Restraining Order had been issued against me under S. 268 of the Criminal Procedure Act and I could at the police station see the case documents. Heidi Schøne and also the policewoman, Torill Sorte, would be witnesses against me. I had a time limit of just 3 days to put in my response. If I attended the Magistrates' Court on 9th October, I faced the possibility "that the prosecuting authority is free as regards which penalty claim shall be submitted, and that in addition to a penalty, a claim to pay public legal fees will be submitted."

Alternatively, I could accept the Restraining Order and whereupon "the prosecuting authority will withdraw the request for adjudication and the indictment."

The prosecution had asked for the Restraining Order to last for one year but failed to mention the starting date. Violation of the Order was punishable by up to 6 months in jail pursuant to s. 342(2) of the Penal Code.

At the police station, I wrote on my copy of the Summons:

1. I do **not** agree to pay the fine (under S. 390(a) of the Penal Code).

2. I have not seen Heidi Schøne since August 1990. I have not visited Norway since 1991 before today's hearing. I do not want to see Heidi Schøne except in Court. I reject the basis of the Restraining Order. This is a malicious prosecution.

I also reiterated a few of the basic points of my own case which justified my 'information campaign' and enclosed a full copy of my own original Writ in Norwegian of August 1999 which would give the police a good understanding of matters that were not mentioned in my Amended Writ.

Further, the police were wrong to mention that I had offended their Penal Code by allowing my lawyer to mention Heidi's past in the Amended Writ of 13th January 2000. I was protected by the so called rule of legal privilege which allowed mention of relevant facts to be presented in Court.

Heidi Schøne, the police and their co-conspirators, Drammens Tidende, had all got together to try and teach me a lesson, but they only showed themselves up to be desperados, clutching at straws.

I handed in my reply to the police who gave me a photocopy for my own records. I then left to go back to my hotel in Oslo, exhausted. I spent the next day, Saturday, enjoying the sights of Oslo including a wonderful three hour boat trip around Oslo Fjord. In the evening, I was walking down the street to my hotel when two girls approached me to ask whether there was a cashpoint nearby, to which I replied that I didn't know. They spoke good English, asked my name and where I came from and proceeded to tell me their names – Heidi and Aina. Well, I just couldn't believe it. Another Heidi. And Aina, the same name as the parliamentary candidate I'd supported in 1997, evidenced by my letter to Paddy Ashdown M.P. which was read out in Court the previous day. It took me a while to dismiss the notion that I was being set up. The girls were desperate to go to the toilet so I invited them to come to my hotel room, which they gratefully accepted, going in together in the toilet to piss. Aina was in fact a huge breasted single mother of 25, who was, nevertheless, still living under the same roof as the father of her 3 year old boy. Both girls were from Trondheim and were in Oslo on a short holiday with other friends. Heidi wrote her phone number down for me. When I proceeded to ask her about her boyfriend, she told me she was a lesbian who had an older lover. She'd gone off men after finishing a long-term relationship with her last boyfriend. They invited me out to meet their friends in one of the local bars and I experienced the noisy delights of Oslo night life before returning to my hotel at 2 in the morning.

Next day, I left Oslo railway station back for Gothenberg airport, grateful that at least the first hurdle was over. I congratulated myself on having taken the decision not to fly directly into Oslo; my fears of police action had been justified. Even though I had stopped my 'information campaign' exactly two years earlier, the police were still determined to teach me a lesson for exposing the past of that wretched liar, Heidi Schøne. Not least because the public had taken up a lot of police time with enquires as to the purpose of my 'scandalous' reports. The risk of being taken into custody at Oslo airport was unquantifiable, so it was better to be absolutely safe, by not flying into or out of Norway.

On the 28th August, my lawyer sent the full set of PFU rules to the Court and the Defendants, so the Judge could fully consider the case. It was clear that even the people at the PFU did not know how to apply their own rules properly.

In the first week of September, my lawyer was urging me to pay the police fine indicated in the Criminal Summons, but I said I will not until at least I had received a reply in English to my defence to the Criminal Summons. Lunde admitted to me that he was not a criminal lawyer and that it may be necessary for me to take separate advice from a Norwegian criminal attorney. However, he was convinced that if I turned up at the 9th October hearing, I would lose and face the possibility of a larger fine and in theory a prison sentence. He said that by making public Heidi's past, I was facing an offence of strict liability, i.e. no matter what my defence or justification what I had done by my 'information campaign' was to have broken the law. Nevertheless, on 6th September he faxed the Assistant Commissioner of Police a two page letter defending my actions.

On the 7th September, the Drammen judge, Anders Stilloff, made his decision on the preliminary hearing of 25th August. I had won a total victory. I was considered within my rights to issue proceedings against the newspaper at the Drammen Court, after having used the PFU, so my case was not dismissed. I did not have to put up security for costs for any of the Defendants, which crucially conveyed the fact that the judge thought I had a strong case. Immediately I received a copy of the Judgement, (see Appendix 1 at the end of this book), I sent copies to the Norwegian Bar Association, which was dealing with my complaints against Elden & Elden and Per Danielsen. These lawyers would now see for themselves just what a Norwegian lawyer with the right attitude could achieve. After 5 long years, I'd got myself a trial. Furthermore, on hearing of my victory, the police postponed my 9th October Magistrates' Court hearing pending attempts to do a 'deal.'

On the 15th September, Lunde informed me that the newspaper had put in notice of an appeal to the Oslo Appeal Court. They were claiming that I had entered into a binding agreement with Drammens Tidende that in using the PFU I had agreed never to sue Drammens Tidende. This "binding agreement" took the form of Elden & Elden's 1999 letter – which I had received but for months didn't know what it meant as Elden & Elden never translated anything for me – telling the PFU that I would not sue Drammens Tidende, as I "didn't have a case against the newspaper." I did of course ask Elden & Elden to tell the PFU that I would not sue Drammens Tidende, to enable the PFU to proceed with their 'enquiry.'

On the 22nd September 2000, Drammens Tidende did another story on me which had also been placed on the newspaper's internet website. Lunde told me briefly that it was a harmless article but due to his heavy workload he only managed to fax me a copy of the internet article on 13th December. As it was in Norwegian of course, I was unable to recognise it myself when I had previously logged on to the Drammens Tidende website. It's translation read:

Came to demand money – was fined

The Englishman came to Drammen in order to demand nearly 400,000 kroner in compensation from a Nedre-Eiker woman and Drammens Tidende, but was met with a fine of 10,000 kroner. He got the fine for having violated the 38 year old woman's private life over a number of years. Together with the fine, he was banned from contacting the woman in any way whatsoever.

Police Inspector Dag Einar Lyngås sent to the county court for approval the application for a ban on visits. The Englishman did not accept the fine and was immediately summonsed for the main hearing in the county court on 9th October.

In fact, he came to Norway and Drammen in order to demand money from Drammens Tidende and the woman. Three years ago, the woman appeared in Drammens Tidende with the story of how, at the age of 16, she had been pursued by the man she met while she was an au pair in England. The man sued successively both the newspaper, editor Hans Arne Odde, the journalist who wrote up the case and the Nedre-Eiker woman. He is demanding 50,000 kroner compensation from her, while the claim against newspaper and journalist totals 330,000 kroner.

When it became clear that he had come to Norway in connection with the lawsuit, the police took advantage of the opportunity. According to the understanding of Drammens Tidende, the police could not have demanded extradition of the man to Norway.

The 38 year old woman reported the Englishman several years ago. For a number of years, it is reported, he telephoned her and sent innumerable letters. Other people, public institutions and private firms also received letters and faxes, which were traced back to the man. The contents of the letters and faxes were information greatly to the discredit of the woman.

In reply to questions from Drammens Tidende, the man's lawyer, Stig Lunde, says that he does not have any comments to make on the fine and the ban on visiting.

Now the newspaper had reduced Heidi's age to 16 as the starting point for the saga.

I happened to phone the Appeal Court on 31st November 2000 to see what was happening with the Drammens Tidende appeal to be told by a female court officer that "the case was dismissed" by the judge on the 24th November. I asked whose case was dismissed and came off the phone with the distinct impression that the newspaper's appeal had been dismissed. The court officer did not speak good English but so convinced was I that Drammens Tidende had lost their appeal that I said to her, "God bless the judge."

I phoned Stig Lunde next day to tell him I knew of the great news, but I was, alas, mistaken. Drammens Tidende had won their appeal in fact. It was my case against the newspaper, it's journalist and editor that had been dismissed. Only my claim against Heidi Schøne stood. Stig Lunde never did send me a copy of this judgment dated 24th November 2000 and after several of my own attempts to obtain it in 2004, the Supreme Court of Norway finally faxed it to me on the 18th June 2004. The English translation from my agency was received in late July 2004 (see Appendix 2). We now had to consider an appeal to the Supreme Court and we had until 29th December 2000 to put in a submission.

One piece of good news I received in early December 2000 from my lawyer was that the Drammen police had abandoned their request for a restraining order against me in favour of Heidi Schøne. They had also removed from the Summons the accusation that I had broken the criminal law by reiterating Heidi Schøne's past in Stig Lunde's Amended Writ to the Drammen Court, and had reduced my fine to NOK 5,000 (about £370). They had produced a new statement for me to sign in English which was the same as the earlier one save that the words in the last sentence " … and that, through his attorney Stig Lunde in a writ of 13th January 2000 (private criminal case), he mainly reiterates the above accusations," were crossed out and initialled by the police. So they had now recognised the fact that I was allowed to state Heidi's past in my amended Writ. Still, I had no intention of signing anything.

411

On 29th December 2000, my lawyer sent off my appeal (against the Court of Appeal decision) to the Supreme Court of Norway, asking it for leave for the Supreme Court itself to look into the whole case against Drammens Tidende, which included a further statement of claim that the Drammens Tidende newspaper had broken the criminal law by publishing untrue statements about me. We were in fact bringing a private criminal prosecution against the newspaper, as the police, surprise, surprise, had chosen – or more accurately probably not even bothered to consider – not to prosecute the newspaper themselves.

The only problem was that very late on my lawyer had discovered his original information of a time limit of 28 days in which to appeal had been wrong. The time limit was in fact only 14 days. We had therefore missed the time limit to go to the Supreme Court! However, Lunde reassured me that the Court rules allowed a discretion for a reprieve if the justice of the case demanded it be investigated by the Supreme Court, and further, the Court rules allowed a discretion in instances of this nature for late appeals to the Supreme Court, if it was not the fault of the plaintiff himself, but the fault of the lawyer (whose mistakes are usually seen as the mistakes of his client). As I could hardly have know of the correct time limits, then we were "safe" on the issue of missing the time limits, said Lunde. Lunde faxed through to me his six page submission to the Court having explained to me as best he could what he'd written (see Appendix 3). I rushed round the local shops to photocopy my thin fax paper, signed the photocopy of Lunde's fax and then faxed the six sheets of A4 back to Lunde, who then posted it on to the Court.

Once again, after some intensive research by Lunde, including consulting an academic at Bergen University – who thought the Court of Appeal was harsh to allow Drammens Tidende's earlier appeal – I was back on track.

It was with great anguish that in the second week of March I spoke to Stig Lunde who told me my appeal to the Supreme Court had been dismissed out of hand (by their decision of 16th of February 2001) because he had missed the time limits. The Supreme Court did not exercise the discretion that lay within their power, to look at my appeal. This, in spite of the fact that new case law was going to be created by me by deciding exactly what the PFU rules were in relation to a complainant's rights against the newspapers. Lunde had earlier told me how anxious the PFU themselves were to know where they stood as they were unclear as to their own rules! The Court had taken the easy way out, Lunde said. We were left to proceed with the criminal trial against Heidi Schøne on her own. Lunde told me he could still issue civil proceedings against the newspaper and the other defendants, in effect starting the same case under the civil procedure rules, which would be an easier burden than the criminal rules of evidence. The Supreme Court judgment of the 16th February 2001 was eventually also sent to me by the office of the Supreme Court in May 2004 as Stig Lunde never managed to provide me with a copy. On the 17th June 2004 my translation agency sent me the English version (see Appendix 4).

In April 2001, Lunde phoned to tell me that the Drammen police were anxious for me to sign their Charge Sheet and send it back to him along with payment for the fine of 5,000 Norwegian kroner (£370). I told him I would not sign anything or pay a penny of the fine. Lunde advised me that I was doing the wrong thing as it was a small fine, that at any subsequent prosecution I faced the reasons for my 'campaign' would be of no concern to the Magistrates Court and by signing, it would get the matter out of the way and the police off my back. I disagreed entirely, so Lunde said he'd look into appointing me a criminal lawyer to defend me when the time came for the police to prosecute me again in the Magistrates Court. The prospect of another Court case with yet another lawyer loomed. Poor Lunde. In his efforts to "save" me money and his time in looking for a good criminal lawyer, he had earlier suggested I go back and use Karsten Gjone, who he said was a "good criminal lawyer." Flabbergasted at his suggestion – Gjone had been useless when I really needed him, had been found guilty of negligence by the Norwegian Bar Association, and I was still claiming against his insurance company – I said this proposal was out of the question. Lunde nevertheless said he completely understood my position and would find me someone else to defend me in the Magistrates Court.

The next piece of news was that the trial date had been set for 15th January 2002 in my private criminal prosecution of Heidi Schøne, with four days given over to the case.

The day before the three year time limit was up for the 14th July 1998 Drammens Tidende article, Lunde issued separate civil writs against Drammens Tidende, Ingunn Røren, and Heidi Schøne, i.e. on

412

13th July 2001. These three civil actions began at the lowest level of the Norwegian judicial system – the forliksrådet, in effect conciliation tribunals presided over by laymen with obviously only the basics in legal training. Lunde was worried that if he didn't start at the forliksrådet and instead issued the writs in the local City Courts, the defendants would ask for the cases to be dismissed for our failure to follow correct procedure. When he phoned up Drammens Tidende's lawyer to try and agree the proper venue to issue the proceedings, the lawyer, Nøkleby, offered no co-operation and left it to Lunde to make the decision. So to be on the safe side, Lunde issued the three writs in, respectively, Ingunn Røren's local forliksråd in Bergen, in Heidi Schone's local forliksråd in Nedre Eiker and in Drammens Tidende's local forliksråd in Drammen, all, as I said, on 13th July 2001.

The main reason for this civil suit was to again try and get the Drammens Tidende newspaper into court. Unfortunately, the Drammen forliksråd dismissed my writ, relying on the Court of Appeal decision in my earlier criminal prosecution: that I'd promised not to sue Drammens Tidende and would let the Press Complaints Commission decide the matter. Lunde had appointed agents to put our case at the forliksrådet and I expected the point over my being misled as to my rights to sue the newspaper vis à vis the PFU procedure, to win the argument and allow me through to full trial. But the only information Lunde could supply me with was a simple statement over the phone that my case was dismissed. He did however appeal.

As for Heidi Schøne, I had some unexpected success in the forliksråd. In Norway you could send your spouse along in your place to represent you at the proceedings. Along went Runar Schøne, but judgement was awarded in my favour. The couple had recently got divorced and this 'spouse rule' obviously no longer applied. Heidi Schøne should have turned up herself. I marvelled at the way Lunde, by chance, casually told me of their divorce and his total disinterest in this fact and ignorance as to the reason for it. Whilst on the subject of divorce, Gudmund Johannessen's parents had also got divorced as had Gudmund Johannessen himself from his wife, Nina Engeberg.

Well, it must have been a fairly amicable divorce if Runar Schøne was still supporting Heidi and I puzzled at the workings of the Norwegian mind regarding this event. Still, Heidi had the right to appeal and this she did, asking at the same time for my case to be dismissed. We had to reply to this pleading and on the last day possible, 18th December 2001, Lunde put in his response to the Drammen City Court.

Regarding the journalist Ingunn Røren, by 2nd January 2002 Lunde had still not heard a word from the Bergen forliksråd as to what had become of my writ - a wait of 5½ months. But I expected the worst. As she was part and parcel of my case against the newspaper, which case was dismissed, then surely my case against the journalist would also be dismissed in due course.

Chapter 28

On the 11th October 2001 at 9 a.m. I was surprised to get a telephone call from my local police station. The policewoman who spoke to me was our local community liaison officer and she wanted me to collect something at the police station. "What is it you want me to collect?" I enquired. "Oh, it's too complicated to explain over the phone, but it won't take long," she replied.

"Could it have anything to do with Norway?" I asked myself, as that was all it could possibly be.

"Yes," was the answer when I was led into a side room at the police station. The Norwegian police had used Interpol to serve on me a Summons to attend a Magistrates Court hearing on Tuesday 30th October at 9 a.m. in Hokksund (near Drammen). The only information on the Summons was that I was "charged with the violation of Section 390(a) of the Penal Code" and was "to appear and give testimony during the main hearing."

Of course, it all related to my large information campaign conducted from 1995-1998, acquainting the Norwegian public with my side of the story giving the life history of my accuser.

I immediately phoned Mr. Lunde and then wrote to him telling him that I would not attend any hearing until I got outstanding replies with regard to my two letters of 25th August 2000 to the Drammen police, in response to that earlier Summons served on me in the Drammen City Courthouse on the morning of my own private criminal libel prosecution. In particular, I wanted to see what the exact extent of the 'evidence' against me was.

So on 17th October, I faxed a letter to Torill Sorte, the policewoman in Norway, telling her that Mr. Lunde had appointed a criminal lawyer for me, to whom the police evidence must be sent, together with replies to my letters to the police of 25th August 2000. I also mentioned to her that there would not be enough time for my new criminal lawyer, Harald Wibye, to look through so many years worth of my own papers, plus the police 'evidence' and to take proper instructions from me, in time for the trial on 30th October. I thought it oppressive for me to face a trial in the midst of my own criminal and civil prosecutions. There was enough paperwork for me to attend to as it was.

The real agenda for the police in Norway was, of course, to trip me up by forcing an abrupt criminal trial, and give me a fine in time for the conviction to be presented to the court in my own criminal and civil libel prosecutions, thus undermining my case. For I had been assured by Mr. Lunde that I would be found guilty, as it was a strict liability offence I had committed, i.e. telling my side of the story about Heidi's life to the Norwegian public whereby I had named her. It was no defence, I was told, that she had waived her anonymity by allowing her name to be published and photos printed in her national and local press. Perverse isn't it? Their press hadn't named me, allowing them to print total crap. They had named her, but I couldn't name her in my retaliatory campaign. I could respond but only by leaving her name out, when of course no-one would take any interest as they wouldn't know who I was talking about.

I was also concerned that Heidi Schøne wouldn't turn up to the Magistrates Court. She was the chief police prosecution witness, along with policewoman Torill Sorte. Heidi Schøne was now back under the supervision of her psychiatrist from 1988, Petter Broch. Not unnaturally, she was under some stress. This psychiatrist actually wrote to Heidi's lawyer giving reasons as to why his patient should not face me in any legal proceedings. The letter was given to the Court. I paid for the letter to be translated into English but before I received the translation I phoned up the doctor to ask him if his letter was "for" or "against" me. He said it was neither for nor against me and that I would have to wait until it was translated. He did say that he had no recollection of ever having told me in 1990 that Heidi had told him I was her "favourite," or that "she made a lot of other men very angry." Dr. Broch was now very reticent and icy in his talk with me. His letter dated the 6th September 2001 said:

Re: our patient Heidi Cecilie Schøne, DOB 20.08.63

My communication concerns the imminent legal proceedings in connection with the British citizen Frederick who is bringing an action against the abovementioned person for defamation.

415

I have known Heidi Schøne since 1989. She has consulted me mainly for difficulties she has had in her adult life after an unusually stressful adolescence. She is currently a patient of the psychiatric ward of Buskerud Central Hospital for similar problems, but also to a considerable extent for the stress and anxiety caused to her by the imminent legal action and the long sequence of events leading up to the action.

Heidi Schøne was roughly 18 years old when an au pair in England. While there, she became acquainted with a man of Egyptian origin, Frederick, with whom she spent some time together; as I understand, this was not in the form of a sexual relationship. The contact with this Egyptian was very difficult. He was insistent and tried to behave as if she was his property. I am under the impression that he had also had similar relationships with women previously.

His taking over of Schøne (at the time Heidi Overaa) gradually became such that she virtually had to run away. She has since been pursued by this man throughout the rest of her life. He has sought her out no matter where she was when she attempted to hide herself away, and he has published long malicious articles about her in Norwegian newspapers. He has sent similarly malicious audio tapes to family and friends etc. I assume that the sequence of events and the details surrounding this are known. I myself also received audio tapes from him in so far as he traced me as the person treating her. The content of these articles and the audio tapes is as far as I can understand of such a nature that they could destroy all the relationships Heidi Schøne might have with other important people in her life. I myself did not retain the material I received because at the time I did not yet fully appreciate the depth and seriousness of the matter. This activity is of such an intense and comprehensive nature that the driving force and the motivation behind the pursuit must be assumed to have a morbid nature. In international literature, such activity is described as "stalking" and has gradually become a clinically recognized concept. I have myself this year also attended an international conference at which experience of this phenomenon was gathered.

The conclusion is that the activity is of a very serious nature for the victim and that the underlying motivation and driving force of the pursuer have various psychological causes, but are of an obviously morbid nature. The driving force behind the actions is virtually uniquely to obtain one form of contact or another with the victim again. Every such contact with the victim or those closest to the victim functions as a type of reward which generates new motivation and perseverance. It is, therefore, central to managing the problem that the pursuer **does not** achieve the desired contact. Contact is sought if necessary in attempts at prosecution, the contact with the victim being more important than the outcome of the action.

It is against this background that I am writing this in order to contribute to finding a solution to an imminent legal action in such a way that the plaintiff does not have contact with Heidi Schøne through the action. It is in keeping with the guidelines which also [were given] at the American Psychiatric Association's conference earlier this year with reference to some internationally known legal cases in recent years. It is thus of great importance, partly for Heidi Schøne's mental state, but first and foremost in order to make a contribution to bringing this situation to a conclusion, that the plaintiff does not achieve any contact with Heidi Schøne through the legal action by Heidi herself being represented by her lawyer without her being present or in any way whatsoever accessible to the plaintiff.

Regards,

Petter Broch
Consultant

So neither "for" nor "against" me, eh? This misuse of psychiatry to denigrate the foreigner/the Egyptian was appalling. It was also an insult to Lunde, who had issued the criminal and civil writs against Heidi Schøne and the newspaper – as if Lunde didn't have a mind of his own and was just meekly complying with my requests.

Dr. Broch's letter served to remind me of the use psychiatry was put to in Nazi Germany and Soviet Russia. Surely the man could have asked to see a copy of Lunde's criminal and civil writs to see why I was suing. He had no grasp of the reality of the situation and his facts were wrong. He was relying on hearsay. What he was basically saying on behalf of his own psychiatric patient was that I myself was an evil lunatic. I had never sent audio tapes to family and friends of Heidi. Obviously I had not published long malicious articles in Norwegian newspapers. This particular assertion in Dr. Broch's letter showed a complete lack of care on his part. I had 'published' my own articles on her in response to long malicious articles about me in the Norwegian newspapers.

With about a week to go to the Magistrates Court hearing, I made contact with my new criminal lawyer, Harald Wibye. I was entitled to state financial assistance (legal aid) in Norway as this time I was being prosecuted, but Wibye would still be out of pocket so I sent him a cheque for £450. He'd known about my case for many weeks as Stig Lunde had warned him to expect a Summons after I refused to settle out of court with the police. Wibye had been sent some papers by Lunde on the case but it was only in the week leading up to the case that he read through them. We discussed the case over the phone as best we could and to make sure he had all the relevant papers, I sent copies by International datapost on 25th October.

The Drammen police 'evidence' arrived at Mr. Wibye's office whilst I was speaking to him on the 29th October – the day before the hearing. My own datapost package had not reached Wibye on the 29th October, so I hurriedly did an 8 page fax to him of the essential papers he did not have. The datapost package only arrived *after* Wibye had departed for the hearing on 30th October.

Harald Wibye was a first class criminal lawyer who, as a favour to Stig Lunde, was defending me at the Magistrates Court. He had spent two years at a boarding school in Wales and his English was excellent. He told me that the police evidence against me was so overwhelming that it wasn't worth me attending the trial. To repeat, my offence was one of strict liability, i.e. there was no defence available as I had named the woman and described her lurid life history. I, of course, naturally protested that the bulk of my 'reports' on Heidi had been sent in response to the 1995 newspaper articles so as to acquaint the Norwegian public with the background of the woman who had told such nonsense to the press. Wibye insisted that this was not a defence; the press stories and Heidi's lies was one case, and the police prosecution of me was another. The two were not related. Wibye was frustrated at my inability to understand this "straightforward" point.

Harald Wibye told me that after strenuous pre-trial negotiations with the police prosecutor, the latter had agreed only to ask the Court to fine me 10,000 Norwegian kroner. This replaced the police's initial desire to ask for a 3 month prison sentence, which they had asked for because they were annoyed I didn't pay up on their 5,000 kroner request from August 2000. However, the judge could still send me to prison if it was in the interests of justice.

After the hearing was over, I spoke to Wibye on his mobile phone and he related the day's events. He'd spent a full 6 hours in Court and the judge – a woman – was going to deliver her verdict within the next few days. When he arrived at Court, Heidi Schøne was nowhere to be seen, so Wibye insisted to the Court that Heidi Schøne be forced to attend the hearing for cross-examination. The judge agreed to adjourn the case for Heidi Schøne to be brought to Court. When she arrived, she sat next to the policewoman, Torill Sorte, and waited with Wibye in the foyer of the Court building. Then a stranger came up to Heidi and said: "You're Heidi Schøne aren't you? I received a letter about you with your photograph!" and he walked off. This was one of my reports on her past life with a newspaper photo transposed on the back of the report that had been sent to so many hundreds of people in her town. This incident was another sign of the success of my campaign. I was well pleased.

During the hearing itself, Wibye behaved as a true defender should. He gave Heidi Schøne a hell of a time. She admitted in Court to having been sexually abused by her stepmother's father. She refused to talk about the alleged rape of her person by the Bergen shopkeeper but admitted she'd made the allegation to the police. Looking at my evidence of her past, Wibye remarked: "You've been abused by quite a lot of people haven't you?" implying that she was a serial complainer.

Importantly, another version seems to have been given by Heidi Schøne as to my threats to kill her two year old son, but Wibye couldn't with clarity recall the exact form of words used in this long drawn-out day. What seems to have been said by Heidi is that I phoned her up one day and told her that her son was "a bastard" (i.e. illegitimate), that "bastards don't deserve to live" and therefore "I shall kill your son" which words Heidi said her son overheard and asked his mother: "Why does Frederick want to kill me?" Wibye was stopped by the judge in pursuing this line of enquiry, which was a great pity. No dates were given by Heidi Schøne as to this new version of events. Even this allegation in itself perplexed me, as when I spoke to Daniel in 1995 his English was not very good at all. Obviously, in 1988 when he was two, he couldn't speak or understand a word of English and when he was 4½, when I met him, his understanding of English was still nil. Nothing, however, was said by Heidi about the alleged letter I'd written putting my threat to kill the boy in writing, which letter she had previously said was given to the Bergen police.

Wibye nevertheless told the Court that I should not be convicted because my letters and campaign had been provoked by my 1990 arrest, false allegations of attempted rape/rape plus the 1995 and 1998 newspaper stories and he read out in Court Stig Lunde's writs.

On being questioned about her allegation of rape against me, Heidi agreed that if she did not tell a chap she doesn't want to have sex with him, how is he supposed to know different? Her 1998 allegation of rape "by holding her down" was at odds with her 1986 statement of attempted rape in 1985.

On the subject of the police charge of my telephoning Heidi, well, earlier in this book I have detailed the sort of experiences I had on that front when trying to talk to her. Wibye told me that the police had tapped Heidi's phone for only a week in May 1995 but even then, as they had not managed to get the full numbers of the callers, the judge dismissed the 'evidence' as inadmissible. Strangely, no tape recording of the conversations were even made. It was all so amateurish. My calls to Heidi in May 1995 included the one I made from a Danish nightclub.

By the end of the cross-examination, Heidi Schøne was in tears. At long long last, probably for the first time in her life, she had been put on the spot. At least by my absence from the hearing, she had no excuse for not turning up at Court. There might have been difficulty in getting her along if I had turned up, but I'd have thought no right-minded judge would have allowed her – the chief prosecution witness – to stay away on grounds of my alleged mental condition of only wanting contact with her, which her psychiatrist said was an end in itself, regardless of the outcome of the trial.

On 2nd November, the verdict came through and as expected I was found guilty of the strict liability offence and given a fine of 10,000 Norwegian kroner. A fine I had no intention of paying if I could help it. The offence under Section 390(a) of the Penal Code was that "he did with frightening or annoying behaviour or other inconsiderate behaviour or conduct violate another person's right to be left in peace." Further, the Verdict continued inter alia:

'The basis for the indictment or for being an accessory thereto is the following:

Over a number of years and until August 1998 he telephoned on several occasions and wrote from England over 200 letters and cards to Heidi Schøne (formerly Overaa) and/or to various private individuals and to public and private firms and institutions, in which he said/wrote inter alia that Heidi Schøne had had abortions, and that a person with whom she had later had a child had injected heroin at the time they had sexual relations, and in which he also named the child and the father of the child. He also said/wrote that Schøne and the child's father, were tested for Aids after the child was born, that the child's father was detained in custody, that Schøne had tried to commit suicide by taking an overdose, and that she was subsequently admitted to a psychiatric clinic in Lier. Furthermore, he said/wrote that Schøne's mother had died of alcohol and drug abuse, and that Schone's father had shortly before tried to have Schøne sent to a children's home etc. He has also repeated in essence the above accusations in notice of proceedings dated 13th January 2000 (private prosecution) issued in the person of his advocate, Stig Lunde.

The complainant has brought proceedings which are also necessitated in the public interest. The main hearing in the case was held on 30th October 2001 in Courtroom No. 3 in Tinghuset [the Courthouse] in Hokksund. The defendant did not appear at the main hearing. At the request of the public prosecuting authority, the Court decided to let the case proceed, cf. *Straffesprosessloven* section 281.

Police Inspector Knut Halvard Austad of Drammen Police District appeared for the Prosecution, and Advocat Harald Bjelke Wibye appeared for the Defence. The Court heard testimony from 3 witnesses and such documentation was produced as shown in the Court Records. Tape recordings were made of the testimony of the defendant and the witnesses, cf. *Straffesprosessloven*, section 23.'

I will repeat in its entirety the Court's deliberations concerning the question of guilt:

II The Court's deliberations concerning the question of guilt:

The defendant and the complainant, that is to say Heidi Schøne (formerly Overaa), first met each other approximately 20 years ago. Schøne was then 18 years old and working as an au pair in England. They met when she was on a train trip with some girlfriends, when the defendant came into contact with her, got talking to her girlfriends and later had a cup of tea with them in a café. The complainant gave him her address and telephone number.

The Court has heard that the defendant and Schøne had a certain amount of contact after that, including by letter. It is clear that at first the tone between them was friendly and that the desire for contact was mutual. Schøne has stated how she came to trust the defendant. He is described as charming and well-spoken. She talked openly with him and told him about a number of personal things, including her difficult childhood and adolescence. She had problems in relation to her immediate family and the defendant became her confidante. However, there was no romantic relationship between the defendant and Schøne. Schøne has told the Court that this was not a possibility since, because of his Muslim faith, the defendant wished to marry a Muslim girl who was a virgin.

After Schøne returned to Norway following her stay in England, the two continued to correspond. The defendant was living in England. The complainant told him in her letters about her life in Norway, amongst other things. Correspondence from the period 1985-1986 shows that there was a warm tone to the letters/cards that the complainant sent the defendant. Schøne has also told the Court that the defendant visited Norway two or three times in the 1980's, and that on at least one occasion he stayed in her home during his visit.

Gradually, a change took place in the tone of the letters Schøne received from the defendant. The tone in the letters gradually became more unpleasant. Many of these letters were destroyed by the complainant. The complainant has stated that she also received many telephone calls at her home, which became increasingly unpleasant. He arrived unannounced at her home, which she found troublesome and annoying.

Schøne has told the Court that she had difficulties in saying no and rejecting the defendant. The defendant was good at persuading people and gaining their sympathy. The Court has gained the impression that the defendant had a certain power over the complainant because of his knowledge of details from her childhood. The complainant has also stated that, following incidents of sexual abuse by a close family member in her childhood, she had had difficulty in setting limits. In addition, the defendant could at times be kind and pleasant, which made it more difficult to reject him.

Schøne has stated that she tried in various ways to stop the defendant, but was unsuccessful. She obtained a secret address and an unlisted telephone number. The defendant managed to find her again, however, using a private detective. This fact is mentioned by the defendant himself in the notice of proceedings of 13th January 2001 which he brought as a private prosecution in Drammen Byrett (Drammen District Court).

The letters presented to the Court show a very unpleasant tone towards the complainant. The defendant is clearly indignant over what he believes are her poor morals. Themes repeated over again in the letters are her sex life, abortions, suicide attempts and her partner's drug abuse. The defendant's reaction to abortion was expressed, for example, in March 1995, when he sent her a copy of a crime article from an English magazine in which he drew parallels between the complainant and the woman described in the article. The woman had killed two of her children. The spring of 1995 appears to represent a peak with regard to the unpleasant communications by letter.In a card postmarked 7 April 1995, he writes, "Heidi, in Norway it may be normal for a slut like you to sleep with tens of men (even taking heroin!) – 'for company' as you told someone but I have been scared by your sick behaviour. Your stepmother called you "a whore" after your second abortion. She was so right and she also told me you were *[incomprehensible text].* The fact that you were in demand for sex doesn't mean you fuck like an unpaid whore. Your unborn children you put in the dustbin – the reality is even garbage like your lovers want someone better than you. Christian pervert!"

Schøne has stated that the defendant sent out a 'report' about her which he distributed to her neighbours, friends and relations, amongst others. This occurred in March/April 1995. The report is written in Norwegian and gives the impression of being a reply to a communication from someone who had requested the report. The report begins: "We are now in a position to make a report concerning your queries." The report consists of about one typewritten page and relates the defendant's version of the complainant's life story. He writes inter alia about several abortions she is alleged to have had, her sex life, her boyfriend's unfaithfulness, her suicide attempts, and her mother's death because of alcoholism and drug abuse. In a longer version of the report (undated), which has also been presented to the Court, it is evident that the defendant is highly provoked by what he regards as the Norwegian family mentality.

The witness Runar Schøne, who at that time was married to the complainant, has stated that a journalist learned of the 'report' and wanted to write about the case. This led to newspaper headlines in Norway in Verdens Gang on 25 May 1995, in *Drammens Tidende* on 27 May 1995, and in Bergens Tidende. On the front page of Verdens Gang, the headline read "13 years' sex terror." The complainant talked in the newspaper articles about what she had experienced, without naming the defendant.

The newspaper articles appear to have triggered a fresh wave of unpleasant communications from the defendant. Again he sent out copies of the mentioned 'report' to various private individuals, public offices, etc. The Court finds it proven that the report was sent to a large number of addresses, 50-60 of which have been documented by the Court.

The frequency and intensity of the defendant's communications by telephone and letter varied. The complainant has stated that they would come "by fits and starts." At certain periods there could be many communications per day, and then again it could be quiet for a couple of months. Over a period of two years, there were no communications from the defendant.

Since 1998, Schøne has received no communications from the defendant. However, on 13 January 2001, the defendant issued notice of proceedings in a private prosecution against the complainant, amongst others. In the notice of proceedings, the defendant repeats in essence the previously mentioned description of Schøne's past and personal circumstances.

The Court finds it difficult to date exactly when the defendant's unpleasant communications to Schøne began. This is also to do with the fact that Schøne has destroyed many of the letters. However, the Court finds it proven that the period in question stretched over many years and until August 1998. The Court refers to the letters presented in court and to the complainant's own testimony, which is also supported by the testimony of her ex-husband, Runar Schøne.

The Court is in no doubt that both the nature and, at times, the intensity of the defendant's communications were annoying and inconsiderate. The Court also finds it proven that the defendant's conduct violated the complainant's right to be left in peace within the meaning of *Straffeloven,* section 390(a). Here, the Court refers to the fact that

Schøne felt so harassed that she did not dare collect her mail, that she had to move to a secret address and obtain an unlisted telephone number, and that during certain periods she was afraid to go out. She has also told the Court that it has been very difficult for her that so many people in her immediate environment have received the 'report' from the defendant and thus become aware of circumstances that are of a highly personal nature. The fact that parts of the 'report' are true has made it even more painful and difficult to protect herself against the accusations, she told the Court.

Statutory period of limitation:

Counsel for the Defence has argued that the defendant be acquitted, since in his view the statutory period of limitation for the offence has expired. The Court refers to the period of limitation for offences under *Straffeloven*, section 390(a) as two years, cf *Straffeloven*, section 67. It has been established that the prosecuting authority brought a preliminary charge within this two-year limit. Counsel for the Defence maintains that the charge was incorrect, as the correct penal provision should have been *Straffeloven* section 390, which also concerns "public information." The Court holds that the matter is not barred by lapse of time. In this context it is sufficient for the Court to refer to its view that the prosecuting authority's application of the law in the charge is correct. Admittedly, parts of the correspondence for which the defendant has been responsible can also be regarded as being in the nature of public information, but in the Court's view the totality of the offence is best encompassed by the description of the offence in *Straffeloven* section 390(a).

Provocation/retaliation

Counsel for the Defence has argued that the defendant should be acquitted since his behaviour has been in response to provocation on the part of Schøne. He refers to an accusation of rape brought against the defendant by Schøne in 1990, and to the newspaper articles referring to the defendant's conduct. The Court holds that these circumstances cannot be grounds for acquittal. Firstly, *Straffeloven* 390(a) includes no reference to *Straffeloven*, section 250, as is the case in section 390. Counsel for the Defence appears to believe that the exculpatory principle where there is provocation should nevertheless apply by analogy. The Court has not found grounds to go any further into that matter, as it has not been demonstrated to the Court that Schøne, by any of the actions referred to by Counsel for the Defence, has been responsible for provocation of such a nature as would give grounds for acquittal. The charge of rape was made because she believed that an assault had occurred and not in order to provoke the defendant. With regard to the writings in the newspapers, these came about on the initiative of journalists, and the defendant's name was not mentioned in the articles.

Straffeloven's scope of application:

Since the issue has been raised by the Prosecution, the Court also notes that the offence falls within the scope and application of Straffeloven, cf. section 12, second paragraph of the Act.

On the basis of the facts described above, the Court finds it proven beyond all reasonable doubt that the defendant has behaved as described in the charge, and that he acted wilfully. Both the actus reus and means rea elements of a crime are deemed present. The defendant will be sentenced as charged.

The points I wish to make are:

- There certainly was much romance in our friendship; the evidence is there. Just as she had slept with half of Norway, Heidi enjoyed physical contact with me. The usual red herring, my Muslim faith, was another piece of misinformation given by Heidi Schøne.

421

- Regarding Heidi obtaining a secret address and unlisted phone number, I used a private detective in 1989 and at that time her address was not a secret and she had no phone at all; she could not afford one.

- The postcard marked 7th April 1995 was just another attack on her after I'd discovered the false allegation of attempted rape. The judge's reference to "Christian pervert" could seem to the ordinary reader without special knowledge of the facts as an attack on Christianity in general. But it wasn't in fact. It was a reference to Heidi Schøne's and her husband's abuse of proper Christian values; her exorcism, her husband's slander of Islam and his speaking in tongues and the fact that a good Christian doesn't tell so many lies to the press.

- Significantly, Heidi Schøne had admitted that at least "parts" of the 'report' on her past were true, whereas previously the newspaper Drammens Tidende had stated my report on her life had "no basis in reality" and Runar Schøne said the reports were "totally false." Harald Wibye told me that he asked Heidi Schøne which parts of the report were false. She had refused to say, so Wibye said: "Well then, we shall assume it's all true."

- Regarding the accusation of rape, you can see here that Wibye, with all that he had on his plate, misinformed the judge about the facts. 1990 was the wrong date for the allegation. It was 1998 that the new allegation of actual rape surfaced and no mention is made of the earlier allegation to police in 1986 of attempted rape. But, note the cunning of the police in bringing the prosecution. Section 390 of the Penal Code (as opposed to Section 390(a) which was what I was charged with) allows a defence of provocation and justified public comment. If I'd been charged under that Section, I could have legitimately raised the issue of Heidi's false allegations to the police and the newspapers, and I would most certainly have turned up at the Hokksund Magistrate's Court.

  Even so, Wibye tried desperately to get the police charge in under Section 390 in order to get in my defence of provocation and justified public comment and had to explain to a clueless judge, Marianne Djupesland, the difference between the two sections. His point was that the police should have charged me under Section 390 but didn't and therefore their case should be dismissed. That panicked the prosecution and the judge who adjourned the case to look up the law in her chambers, but Wibye's argument was eventually rejected by the judge.

- The words, "the accusation of rape was made because she believed that an assault had occurred and not in order to provoke the defendant" is another example of what can happen when the police do not allow the defence sufficient time to prepare. No discussion was made of the obvious contradiction between making an attempted rape allegation in 1986 and an actual rape allegation in 1998 out of the same incident in 1985. Further, as the allegations were false as far as I'm concerned, then what else but a wicked provocation could they be?

Finally, let us look at paragraph III of the Court's deliberations concerning sentencing:

> The defendant is hereby convicted of an offence that bears a maximum sentence of fines or imprisonment of up to six months. In the Court's opinion, the offence for which the defendant is sentenced would normally be in the upper bracket of the sentencing framework. However, on grounds of procedural economy the prosecuting authority has elected to request sentencing in the form of a fine of NOK 10,000. The reason is that the defendant lives in England and that extradition would be inappropriate. For those reasons, argued by the prosecuting authority, the Court is therefore minded to elect such a lenient criminal sanction as a fine of NOK 10,000, alternatively 25 days imprisonment.

The Norwegian police had, in response to Harald Wibye's request, promised to send him a translation of the verdict in English in order to help me decide whether I should appeal. The translation he would send to me whereafter the time for my right to appeal (14 days) would run. Wibye earlier told me that the verdict contained the word "rape" and the Norwegian police could use Interpol to give the verdict to my local police to serve on me. So I told him there's no way I wanted the Norwegian police to libel me to my local police and Wibye said he'd make sure the police sent the translation to him for onward transmission to me with a letter of receipt that I was, in good faith, to sign and return to Wibye. The police would of course have to pay for the translation.

On 1ˢᵗ December 2001, I received the English translation of the verdict - delivered by a local police officer to my door via Interpol! He came into my sitting room, told me the police had read the whole verdict and wished me good luck in my private criminal prosecution and civil prosecutions.

Of course, I wanted to appeal and right up to the European Court of Human Rights as I thought it was utterly wrong that this state of affairs should come to pass. After great persuasion by Harald Wibye, I decided not to appeal as Wibye assured me I would definitely get a prison sentence – a victory Heidi Schøne certainly did not deserve, he said.

On the 14ᵗʰ November, Harald Wibye telephoned me to give me some "important" news. A journalist from the newspaper Drammens Tidende had phoned him up having now perused a copy of the Court's verdict. Wibye had given a comment to this journalist, Lars Arntzen, who had promised to call me to get my side of the story. Wibye's first question to me was: "Has the journalist called you?" I said, "No" and added that I severely doubted whether such a call would come. Wibye was less sceptical and told me that I now had a "golden opportunity" to put my side of the case. No call came.

On 17ᵗʰ November, I was on the Internet looking specifically for an article on the case and I found it. Next day I went up to the Norwegian Church, and someone there kindly let me have the newspaper of Friday 16ᵗʰ November 2001 whereupon I had made banner headlines on the front page. I got the story professionally translated and it ran as follows:

Drammens Tidende   Friday 16ᵗʰ November 2001

Fine for serious sex terror

By Lars Arntzen

Pestered woman for 16 years – must pay 10,000 kroner

A 43 year old man who sex-terrorized a woman from Nedre Eiker with countless phone calls and letters and postcards over 16 years escapes imprisonment. The Court considers a 10,000 kroner fine is an appropriate punishment. The fact that the man is resident in England is the reason why he is escaping imprisonment. The Court makes no secret of the fact that this punishment is extremely lenient. The charges on which the man has been convicted carry a maximum penalty of up to six months imprisonment.

10,000 fine for 16 years of sex terror

Escaped imprisonment because he lives in England.

A 43 year old convicted of terrorising a woman from Nedre Eiker with countless phone calls and around 200 letters and postcards over 16 years escapes imprisonment. The Court considers a 10,000 kroner fine is an appropriate punishment.

The 43 year old Englishman was fined 10,000 kroner last autumn but refused to pay this.

That concluded the action in the County Court, in which he lost in all respects. The fact that the man is resident in England is the real reason why he is escaping imprisonment. The prosecutor, police inspector Dag Einar Lyngås, opted to ask for a fine instead of imprisonment because

423

extradition from England would be too expensive.

Lenient punishment

However, the Court is making no secret of the fact that this punishment is extremely lenient. The charges on which the man has been convicted carry a maximum penalty of up to six months imprisonment, and the Court is of the view that the punishment would normally have been approaching this maximum penalty.

Lawyer Vegard Aaløkken represented the woman in the case, and he has advised his client not to speak to the media. But he confirmed that the woman is pleased that the man has been convicted in the County Court.

"She is first and foremost pleased to have been believed by the Court," Aaløkken told Drammens Tidende. Asked about her reaction to the man not having been sentenced to imprisonment, he replied:

"A stronger reaction would normally have been natural, but she is in full agreement with the Court's remarks. The most important thing for her is that the man has been convicted."

Report on life

The telephone calls, the letters and the postcards to the woman are said to have been marked by in part extremely serious malice. Some of the letters and the postcards, in which the woman is referred to in condescending terms, are also said to have been sent to other private individuals and public and private businesses. The subject matter of the letters was on the whole concerned with her sex life, abortions, suicide attempts and partner's drug abuse.

According to the woman, the man also distributed a 'report'

about her to neighbours, friends and relatives. The note began "We can now submit a report about your life" and was his version of her life story.

In Court, the woman explained that it was extremely difficult for her that so many people in her immediate circle had received "the report" from the 43 year old. The fact that some of the content was true only made the whole thing even more difficult for her.

The Englishman and the woman from Nedre Eiker first met over 20 years ago when she was an au pair in Britain. Initially, the contact is said to have been marked by friendliness, and the man was described as charming and eloquent. The woman chose to confide her personal problems in him gradually, and this was how he gained an insight into her life. Over the years, the woman made a number of attempts to prevent the defendant from making contact. Among other things, she obtained a secret address and telephone number, but to no avail. The 43 year old managed to trace her again through a private detective.

"The threats were provoked"

The 43 year old continues to deny culpability for the telephone calls and the letters to the Nedre Eiker woman. His lawyer is of the opinion that everything was provoked by the woman herself.

In Court, lawyer Harald Bjelke Wibye therefore asked for his client to be acquitted. In his view, the response to the provocations is not a good enough reason to convict the Englishman.

In 1990, the woman reported the man for rape. Later, she also appeared in the newspapers and gave an account of his behaviour. The Court nevertheless refused to accept that these are provocations which could exempt the 43 year old from punishment.

In its sentence, the Court states that the rape report was made because in her opinion an assault had taken place and not in order to provoke the defendant. As far as the items in the papers are concerned, these were arranged on the initiative of journalists, and the name of the defendant was not mentioned in the articles.

Lawyer Bjelke Wibye is not satisfied with the sentence, but will for the time being not say anything about a possible appeal. The sentence is in the process of being translated so that the Englishman can read it as well. They will then assess what happens next in this case, but in all likelihood there will be an appeal.

"My client feels he has been wrongfully convicted. He believes the woman's statements are wrong and grossly defamatory. Among other things, the rape report is down to her own unreasonableness," the lawyer said.

In any case, this is not the last time Bjelke Wibye's client and the Nedre Eiker woman have met one another in Court. They are to meet again as early as in January. Then, it is a private criminal case the man has brought against her that is to be dealt with.

***

Harald Wibye had received a fax of the Internet newspaper article and told me that on subsequently speaking to the journalist, the latter told him that after all he'd had "no time" to call me to get my opinion. Oh what a surprise!

So not to be outdone, I got out my Drammen phone directory and wrote down 1,000 fax numbers covering almost the entire Drammen district. I then wrote out in English my response to the newspaper article and sent it off to be translated into Norwegian. When the translation arrived I took it round to my usual commercial agency together with the list of Drammen fax numbers which were all fed into the computer. In two overnight sessions on 23rd December 2001 and 2nd January 2002, my response was faxed to the Norwegian public. The English version is as follows:

The 'Englishman's' Response to Drammens Tidende headline 'Fine for Serious Sex Terror' 6th November 2001 by Lars Arntzen

In accordance with his right to reply the Englishman referred to in the above articles states as follows:

1. The Englishman did not attend the Court hearing on 30th October 2001 as he had no time to prepare for the case, particularly as his lawyer only received the police 'evidence' the day before the hearing, a lot of which was in fact not proven and inadmissible to the Court.

2. No journalists attended the hearing. The above Drammens Tidende article is a complete misrepresentation of the Court proceedings.

3. The fact is that the Drammen police were prepared to settle the matter if the Englishman paid a 5,000 kroner fine, which he refused on grounds of principle.

4. The evidence which convicted the Englishman consisted merely of 'reports' to the Norwegian public giving his side of the story to criminally libellous newspaper stories from 1995 which included provocative and wholly false allegations from the Norwegian woman – presently and in the past a psychiatric patient. There has

---

never been any so called "16 years of Sex Terror," unless one counts the sex terror inflicted by Norwegian men on this woman.

5.   The 'reports' were sent for a three year period, 1995 to 1998 and that in essence was the reason for the police prosecution.

6.   Why did the Englishman respond in this manner? Only a handful of 'reports' on the woman's life history were initially sent due to extreme provocation by the Norwegian woman (a false allegation to the police of **attempted** rape), followed by more 'reports' after extreme provocation by Verdens Gang, Bergens Tidende and Drammens Tidende in 1995 and 1998, which newspapers showed many photographs of the woman and named her. The Norwegian woman had voluntarily waived her right to anonymity. However, the three newspapers did not think the Englishman would find out about the articles as he was of course living in England. But he did immediately find out as he had earlier, in December 1994, asked a Norwegian lawyer to investigate the woman for her attempts to pervert the course of justice.

7.   The police charge of 30th October 2001 was for a strict liability offence, i.e. sending out details of the woman's life history, for which there is no defence available as the Norwegian woman was named in 'the reports.'

8.   However, the Norwegian newspapers in targeting a defenceless foreigner did not name him, meaning that in the unlikely event that he did find out about the articles, he would have to face the almost impossible task of finding a Norwegian who recognised him from the articles in order to enable him to sue for criminal and civil libel and at enormous personal, financial and emotional cost.

9.   By the time she was 18, the Norwegian woman had had two abortions to the same Norwegian man. She then claimed she got pregnant later to another lover carrying twins, but miscarried after discovering his infidelity. She then attempted suicide. Later she resumed sleeping with the unfaithful man and at the same time with yet another Norwegian man, trying to get pregnant to both, or either. The unfaithful man was injecting heroin having been in military prison previously. She succeeded in getting pregnant to the I.V. heroin user and a son was born. The father again rejected the girl and a further suicide attempt followed by the girl who said all she had in common with the father was "good sex." They had rarely lived together. The woman then entered a psychiatric clinic and in 1994 married a man who claimed to "speak in tongues." Her marriage failed and she was divorced in 2001.

10. Throughout the period 1982-1990 the Norwegian woman was asking the Englishman for help in solving her problems with men, but repeatedly kept on with disastrous liaisons, much to the exasperation of the Englishman, who naturally was forced to tell her some "home truths."

11. Drammens Tidende intimated that the Englishman betrayed the woman's confidences about her promiscuous private life and personal problems. The Englishman decided that by the woman's treachery towards him, she has waived her right to these confidences being kept.

12. In 1995, the Englishman discovered that in December 1986 the woman had complained to the Bergen police that the Englishman had **attempted** to rape her in April 1985. There was a delay of 20 months in making this (false) allegation, which complaint was made a mere two weeks after the Englishman had warned her family of her unsafe sexual practices and suicidal tendencies. The complaint was in revenge for the Englishman's revelations of her past to her own family who had been ignorant of the sex terror inflicted on her by Norwegian citizens.

426

13.	At the Drammen Court hearing on 30ᵗʰ October 2001, the Norwegian woman admitted also that she made an allegation against a Bergen shopkeeper in the 1980's of rape. The police did not bring charges. In the 1980's, the Norwegian woman also claimed Greek men had tried to rape her at knifepoint. In 1995, she alleged to Drammens Tidende that the Englishman had **attempted** to rape her. In 1998, she changed her story. At the request of the Englishman of the Drammen police to investigate the allegation of **attempted** rape, the woman now claimed it was actual rape. The police have never brought charges. Notwithstanding this, these false allegations against the Englishman, designed to ruin him and at the very least get him arrested and questioned, were sufficient provocation for the Englishman to release the woman's past history to the public to highlight the problems he had been facing from a sick woman. Initially, only her neighbours were told.

14.	The Drammen public must also be made aware that the woman told Drammens Tidende in 1995 that the Englishman had in 1988 allegedly threatened to murder her two year old son. Without any corroborative evidence Ingunn Røren printed this allegation as 'a fact.' Later enquiries revealed that the woman told police that the alleged murder threat was made by the Englishman in a letter which was "given to the Bergen police." The Bergen police told the Drammen police they had no such letter. Of course, the allegation is false and designed to cause much trouble to the Englishman, if not to ruin him. Such a malicious allegation is surely provocation enough for the Englishman to be able to acquaint the Norwegian public with the truth of the girl's past so they knew the background of a woman making such allegations against him, via her national and local press. The Englishman had no other means to reply.

15.	Besides which the Norwegian woman has admitted to the Drammen police that even after making allegations of attempted rape and threats to murder a two year old against the Englishman, she still proceeded in 1988 to request the Englishman's help in restraining the abusive father of her child. No woman in her right mind asks an alleged rapist and alleged potential child killer over to help her. The fact is that the father of her child assaulted her in 1990 and he was reported to the police.

16.	In 1990, August, the Norwegian woman resumed a cosy friendship with the Englishman even sending him postcards and letters and Christian literature.

17.	The Englishman believes the woman is a lunatic who far from being the 'innocent victim' as portrayed by her xenophobic press, is a calculating, scheming opportunistic liar with little regard for normal standards of civilised behaviour.

18.	The former Drammens Tidende journalist Ingunn Røren in on record as having given perjured evidence to the Norwegian Press Complaints Commission; facts presently with the Drammen City Court.

19.	In England, newspapers print the name of their victims if they've got their facts right. The extensive cover up by the Norwegian establishment is a permanent stain on its reputation.

You will see I didn't name the girl this time, but concentrated on correcting the usual newspaper crap. At least the newspaper printed a little of Wibye's opinion. Again, the lie of "16 years" of serious sex terror was repeated. Drammens Tidende had copied particular phrases directly from the police wording on the charge sheet. But the evidence of countless phone calls was not proven, still less the contents of the phone calls. The number of letters and postcards produced by the police was not mentioned in the verdict either. And in England, no great reliance would be placed on the testimony of the likes of Heidi and Runar Schøne.

Where Drammens Tidende refer to the fact that "Lawyer Vegard Aaløkken represented the woman in the case," Aaløkken wasn't even present in Court and his press statement, "She is first and foremost

427

pleased to have been believed by the Court," has to be taken with a large pinch of salt. Now the newspaper was calling me just "the Englishman" with no more references to being mad or suffering from erotic paranoia. To have called me the "Muslim man" again would have been inconsiderate as their article came out on the first day of Ramadan!

Harald Wibye on 5th November had faxed me six out of the 30 or so letters of mine that the police had sent him. Three were from 1995 reminding her of her treachery to me in 1990 over my winter arrest and the facts of her none too rosy private life, and another three were from 1998 simply telling her I was still quite intent on taking her to Court for the 1995 and 1998 articles. In fact, there was no evidence in letter form pre-1995.

Overall, however, the result of my not agreeing to pay the small initial 5,000 kroner fine was pleasing in that once again the newspapers had shown themselves up for the frauds they were. The Magistrates Court had shown its immaturity and one-sidedness and the police had demonstrated their prejudice and underhand methods in dealing with me.

When earlier I went to the Norwegian Church in East London to pick up the newspaper of 17th November 2001, I had two bits of good fortune. Firstly, Drammens Tidende had in the same week printed on their front page a full picture of their editor, Hans Odde, in colour. This was a Godsend and was immediately put to good use by scanning his photograph onto my website which then turned into the face of a pig with a cigarette in its mouth. Certain appropriate comments were added to the illustration. Secondly, I met a mature gentleman called Patrick Byrne who had suffered at the hands of the Norwegian system when his Norwegian wife had divorced him. He well understood my predicament and later wrote to me a nice letter in which he said about my case:

> "I do not know how long these sagas have been running but there seems to be a tendency for Norwegian women to firstly invite and welcome Brits with open arms and then when things go sour they hit them with the SYSTEM and resort to personality murder backed up with an hysterical support group of immediate acquaintances and the Nationalistic establishment of xenophobes."

My new acquaintance sent me two old newspaper articles. One, I reproduce in full from The Times newspaper of 27th December 1990 written by Tony Samstag:

The Times 27th December 1990

Norwegians' charity to foreigners ends at home

Aslam Ashan, aged 48, is a graphic artist who came to Norway 20 years ago from his native Pakistan, settling in a suburb of the capital. Recently he had what must have seemed a good idea; a Christmas party for those residents of Oslo, particularly the elderly, who would otherwise be alone. Mr. Ashan and his friends, mainly Muslims, reasoned that their willingness to work during the Christian holiday was, as he put it, "an exploitable resource."

According to what statistics you read, up to half the population of Oslo may be living alone, ironic in a society crippled by religious fundamentalism where the sanctity of family life is cited as justification for a depressing shortage of social amenities.

The local council was happy to put up about £3,000 for the party. But weeks passed and not one Norwegian had accepted the invitation. So Mr. Ashan went on a national religious radio programme to repeat his offer. This time the lonely responded in force, from all over the country; not, however, with even one grateful acceptance, but with scores of abusive telephone calls. A consensus emerged that the bloody foreigners, not content with taking their jobs, social benefits, women and so on, were now trying to steal Christmas from the Norwegians as well. This seasonal tale from the folk who claim to have invented Father Christmas illustrates the Dag Hammarskjöld Syndrome; the tendency of small, provincial countries to wax idealistic over exotic, impoverished peoples, while abhorring the stranger in their midst.

Norway is justly proud that it gives 1.11 per cent of its gross national product to development aid, one of the highest percentages in the world. At the same time, few foreigners actually living in Norway, perhaps 4 per cent of the population, will be surprised by the natives' response to Mr. Ashan's generous impulse.

There is an elegant variation on the Hammarskjöld Syndrome – the Brundtland Effect; a preoccupation with wide-ranging threats to the environment while allowing one's own immediate habitat to be plundered and despoiled. This phenomenon is named after Gro Harlem Brundtland, the prime minister. She is well known as chairman of the United Nations World Commission on Environment and Development. Her exhortations about sustainable development and the like have earned her many international awards. At home, however, she and her ministers have consistently demonstrated a talent for evading sensitive conservation issues.

This year's crop of scandals includes the continuing illegal slaughter of Scandinavia's last wolves by Norwegian farmers and the proposed siting of an Olympic skating hall at a protected wetland.

***

The other article was a long and critical Sunday Times piece dated 7th May 1995 entitled 'Gloom with a View; Norway' by Roland White. Of particular interest to the British will be the following paragraph:

'A colleague spent two years living on the outskirts of Oslo as a child and recalls this period with a shudder. "People pushed notes through our door saying: 'Go home, British pigs.' And they drew pigs in the snow outside. As if this was not enough, it was so boring. We went to bed at about 7 p.m. because there wasn't anything else to do."'

When I later spoke to Roland White – on the 21st April 2005 to be precise – he told me his Sunday Times article caused outrage in the Norwegian press and he received a lot of hate mail; subsequently he later confirmed to me it was *"polite hate mail."*

Chapter 29

My own prosecution on a four day trial was to start on Tuesday 15ᵗʰ January 2002, so I left England on Sunday 13ᵗʰ bound once again for Gothenberg by plane. The next day I caught the train from Gothenberg to Oslo Central Station. In the main concourse of Oslo Station, I bumped into a Norwegian girl, Torill, now aged 30, whom I had met years earlier in England whilst she was working at the Romford YWCA in Essex. Her parents came from Drammen and I filled her in on the reason for my trip. She gave some very useful advice on the press's methods as she had herself taken a course in media studies. Remarkably, she had been interviewed by Drammens Tidende on the subject of her studies whilst in England. She told me she hardly recognised the article so different was it from the interview she gave to the journalist.

I went on to Drammen by train and booked into the Rica Park Hotel and within a minute, by pure chance, my lawyer Stig Lunde phoned me and I agreed to go round to his hotel nearby for a pre-trial discussion. The trial of Heidi Schøne was to be transferred from the criminal mode to the civil mode as the criminal element had only related to Drammens Tidende's involvement and now that they were no longer part of the proceedings, Heidi Schøne's involvement was only on a civil basis. This meant that only one judge would consider the case and not three judges, which was the case for criminal libel trials.

In correspondence with the Court, Heidi's lawyer had tried very hard for her not to have to sit in the same court as me, saying it would cause her psychological damage as per Dr. Petter Broch's opinion. I knew this to be bullshit – Heidi was exploiting the situation. They were trying to make out that I was a sort of Charles Manson figure and eye contact with me would hypnotise her into deeper distress. But the judge agreed with us – her presence would be required. But in accordance with Norwegian law, there was no sanction if she didn't turn up. It would just look bad for her case if she chose to be absent, I was told.

We had been allocated the same courtroom as in August 2000, the same judge – Anders Stilloff, and the same interpreter, the dour Scotsman, William Mullholland. Heidi's appearance on the first day lasted all of 5 minutes. She was told she could go home as she would not be required to give evidence that day.

Stig Lunde opened the proceedings on my behalf stating that my honour and reputation had been sullied by Drammens Tidende; that my rights to freedom of expression had been restricted by the newspaper refusing to print my response; that Heidi's statements defamed me and I was the victim of her and the newspaper's negligence or deliberate action; that my patterns of reaction were natural, i.e. anger and the desire for revenge; that my reaction to the 1995 articles doesn't justify another article in 1998; that I was accused of attempted rape in 1986, which accusation was upgraded to rape in 1998; that we must be able to look at the 1995 articles as they shed light on the 1998 article; that my limited sending of 'reports' to Heidi's neighbours in no way justified the vast newspaper coverage against me. Stig Lunde stated that we were only demanding 50,000 Norwegian kroner from Heidi Schøne as she was of limited means but we were also claiming my legal costs from her otherwise I'd be out of pocket. Lunde spoke of the ethical norms for the press as per the revised edition of their Code of Ethics (2001 edition). This stated that journalists are responsible for the journalistic content of their material; that freedom of the press is there to help against unfair treatment of individuals; that journalists are meant to be critical of their sources and check that the information they receive is correct; that the victim of their coverage must have a chance to answer; that when I was told by the PFU that I had forfeited (by trickery) my right to sue, this explains my reaction. As for the burden of proof for Heidi, it was she who had to prove what she was claiming. Lunde then went through our evidence in full.

Vegard Aaløkken addressed the court in the afternoon and began by telling the judge that I was a complete madman who had terrorised Heidi for either a 16 year period or, alternatively, a 14 year period. The only documentary evidence he had concerned my letters and postcards starting in 1995 lasting until 1998. For the pre-1995 period it was all anecdotal and hearsay; not a single letter pre-1995 was produced in evidence.

Two of the articles I had sent Heidi in 1995, and which were mentioned in October 2001 by the judge in the police prosecution of myself, were then presented to the Court by Vegard Aaløkken. These articles concerned an American woman who had killed her two young children by drowning them, but whose life otherwise contained many of the features present in Heidi's. One article was from the Hello! magazine and the other from The Times newspaper of Saturday 8th July 1995. In sending these articles to Heidi, I had underlined the similarities in her life to that of Susan Smith of South Carolina, U.S.A. Relevant quotes from the Hello! magazine were:

- Family court documents were released showing that at the age of 16, Susan was sexually abused by her stepfather ...

- Susan herself attempted suicide at least twice. The first known time was when she was 13. She overdosed on over-the-counter drugs. Shortly after her graduation from high school in 1989, Susan again attempted to take her life in a similar fashion.

- "She's someone who lost out," says Laura Walker, the owner of an antique shop in Union. "She has been betrayed by most of the men in her life – a father who committed suicide, a stepfather who abused her and a husband who cheated on her."

- The reverberations from her crime and betrayal have affected all those around her.

The Times article of Saturday 8th July 1995 is reprinted in full below:

The Times 8th July 1995

Jury to hear Gothic ordeal of child killing mother

FROM: BEN MACINTYRE IN NEW YORK

What was Susan Smith thinking last October when she strapped her two young sons into the back of her car by a lake in South Carolina, eased off the handbrake, and watched it roll into the deep water; that question is a matter of life and death for the former secretary, whose trial begins on Monday.

In the nine days after the disappearance of her sons, Michael, three, and Alex, 14 months, Ms. Smith, 23, became a familiar figure on U.S television screens as she tearfully begged a fictitious black carjacker, who she claimed had kidnapped her children, to return them unharmed.

When Ms. Smith finally confessed that she had drowned her sons near her home in Union, South Carolina, she seemed, to many, to epitomise the purest evil.

Yet a far more complex picture has emerged of a troubled young woman caught up in a Gothic tale of grim, small-town life involving suicide, promiscuity and sexual abuse. Many residents of Union have come to see Ms. Smith as a

tragic, even insane, figure, who requires psychiatric treatment rather than the electric chair.

Although she is described as "seriously depressed and suicidal," doctors have found Ms. Smith mentally competent to stand trial. The case, however, will hinge on what was going through her mind on October 25 when she rolled her car into the depths of John D. Long Lake.

She had appeared to be a normal, middle-class girl who excelled at school, where she was voted the "friendliest student," and showed every sign of adoring her two sons. But her lawyers are expected to argue that beneath the veneer she was so traumatised by sexual and emotional abuse that she could not distinguish right from wrong.

Her father, despondent over his collapsing marriage, committed suicide when she was six. She first attempted suicide at 13. Three years later she told a school counsellor of a pattern of sexual abuse by her stepfather. In 1991, when two months pregnant, she married David Smith, a supermarket worker, and though a second child followed the marriage soon collapsed in acrimony.

In 1993, Ms. Smith began a relationship with Tom Findlay, a wealthy young man. But just two weeks before the drownings, he broke off the affair and in a letter accused his former girlfriend of being "boy-crazy." It has also been reported that, on the day of the killings, Ms. Smith told Mr. Findlay she had also slept with his father.

Her lawyers are expected to argue that the sordid combination of promiscuity and emotional and sexual trauma drove Ms. Smith again to thoughts of death, and in an irrational state of mind she killed her children in a botched suicide. But her chilling lies in the aftermath may undermine any case for sympathy. The trial is expected to last at least ten weeks.

[Susan Smith was found guilty of the murder of her children and executed in 2003.]

***

Heidi's defence lawyer's main theme continued to be that I was "mentally ill," and a sexual deviant for writing to Heidi telling her she was "a bitch" and "a whore" and berating her for her past sexual behaviour. I was meant to be "sex-focused" and "sexually obsessed" by my references to Heidi's own sexual conduct. I was also "a rapist" although the defence lawyer did not get round to explaining exactly why or the reason for the revised allegation of actual rape in 1998 from the allegation of attempted rape in 1986. He justified my being called "a Muslim" in the 1998 newspaper article on the grounds of my strong support for the Bosnian Muslims, omitting to state the obvious to the judge, that the real reason I was referred to as "a Muslim" by Drammens Tidende had nothing to do with my sympathies for the Bosnians. In none of the six articles done on me was Bosnia ever mentioned to the readers. The 'Muslim pervert' label was the newspapers' real agenda.

After he'd finished, I went up to Vegard Aaløkken, Heidi's lawyer and pointedly told him that if he really thought I was mentally ill then it was he who must be sick in the head. I was really shocked at this awful attempt by him to mislead the Court. At one point during the defence submissions I was reprimanded by the Judge for interrupting defence counsel even though it was just to correct Aaløkken's pronunciation of the word "prick" (he pronounced it "pryke"). The Judge told me he would tell me to leave the courtroom if I interrupted again; not a good omen.

Next it was my turn to be questioned by my own lawyer and I gave evidence as to Heidi's own obsession with sex, which included some of her own sexual fantasies related by her to me down the years. I also stressed some of the main points of my own case to the Court. I confirmed that I had never been in a mental hospital or had any form of psychiatric treatment. Nor had I ever had a restraining order (a criminal conviction incidentally) made against me in England, as alleged by Heidi in the press.

Then began my cross-examination by the defence lawyer which continued into the following day for part of the morning. He emphasised to the Court that my information campaign against Heidi was a symptom of my "continued mental illness," and read out again some of my letters to Heidi calling her "a whore" and "a bitch."

What really incensed me though was hearing for the first time on Heidi's behalf that I had allegedly told Heidi when visiting her in the 1980's that if she didn't let me kiss her and touch her breasts, I would tell her neighbours about the sexual abuse she'd suffered at the hands of her stepmother's father.

Next up were the defence witnesses. Dr. Petter Broch, Heidi's psychiatrist was the first to give evidence and his rather frank appraisal of Heidi's life included the following:

- Heidi's stepmother had abused her mentally, and made Heidi "very compliant."

- Heidi's stepmother's father had sexually abused her.

- Heidi had a tendency towards sexualised behaviour.

- When she was in a proper relationship Heidi had problems functioning sexually.

- Heidi didn't get far with her psychiatric treatment with Dr. Broch because of her "identification" with him "as a man," as men were her main problem.

- Heidi's stepmother had reported her to the Child Protection Unit "on false grounds."

- Heidi had faced subtle forms of punishment from her two older sisters.

- That my 'reports' and letters on Heidi's life contained "a core of truth."

- That the letter (and tape recording of the letter) I'd sent Dr. Broch [in 1990] he threw away, although he did not, he said, listen to the whole tape.

- That my 1995 letters to Heidi's neighbours and my information campaign against her was "stalking" on my part.

- That when asked by the defence lawyer whether I was suffering from "erotic paranoia," he said he didn't know what it was and would have to research the phenomenon.

- That he'd read the Verdens Gang article on me from May 1995 and "probably" also the Bergens Tidende article.

- Regarding my alleged threats on Heidi's life, Dr. Broch confirmed this was just Heidi's word.

- When asked by Stig Lunde about the meaning of a sense of honour and sense of self-respect, which had propelled me to act, Broch said that it was not easy to define these concepts in Norwegian culture. And when asked by Lunde about the normal range of reactions when one's sense of honour is attacked, Broch answered that it depends on the sort of person who is attacked; that rage, the desire to protect oneself and revenge were a reasonable reaction as was the converse reaction – that of "withdrawal." That these varying reactions were more developed in different cultures.

- That Heidi's problems are still there as she has still got contact with her stepmother.

Heidi was next on the stand. She began by stating that due to her mental condition she was on a 100% disability pension which had recently been granted by her social services department. And that I was responsible for this state of affairs! Then, at the prompting of her lawyer she launched into a one-hour attack on me in which she best described me as a sexual pervert and deviant, repeating her accusation of blackmail threats if I couldn't kiss her or touch her breasts; that I constantly phoned her up asking what underwear she had on etc. etc. She gave an incredible performance and if I hadn't known better I would have believed her.

When I first visited Heidi at Christmas 1984, to try and console her in her distress I had given her a copy of the Quran. What kind of a hypocrite could I be to commit so many alleged sexual and other misdemeanours with her in the course of the next 18 months?

She admitted that Gudmund Johannessen smoked cannabis and took amphetamines but was adamant that he had never injected heroin. I marvelled at this claim as it was obvious from my many letters to her discussing the subject of HIV and her own AIDS tests and Johannessen's heroin abuse, plus the fact of my own AIDS test in December 1986, that my information came straight from Heidi. Either that or I was a complete liar and fantasist and therefore quite mad.

She admitted Johannessen abused her and hit her (which included the time I guess when he beat her up in 1990 and she reported him to the police).

Further, she claimed that she never told me she was moving to Drammen in 1988. (What a lie!) And I had at one time told her in a postcard that, "If you don't get pregnant your breasts will fall off." Needless to say, no such postcard was presented in evidence. Nor were the "funeral cards" saying her "days were numbered" as the press had in 1995 reported in Drammens Tidende.

Stig Lunde's cross-examination of Heidi was very perfunctory and he began by acknowledging that she was under stress and should ask him to pause if necessary. Lunde had warned me that his cross-examination of Heidi would be quite soft so as not to give the impression that we were out to totally destroy an already clearly disturbed woman. So, on the crucial point of the truthfulness of my 'reports' on her life, Stig Lunde asked what parts were untrue and she replied that she would not answer the question as she regarded it as "harassment." Then Lunde objected and continued that the purpose of her being in court was to answer the questions. She then said that "parts" of my report were true, but not which parts. Lunde did not press her further.

Things got even better for me when Heidi admitted that the three 1995 newspaper articles had at the time all been read out to her over the phone by the journalists and she did not correct any of it! The judge then interrupted and pointed out to her that she had therefore adopted the contents as all true herself as if it came from her own mouth including her husband's comments in Drammens Tidende that my 'reports' were "totally false" and that as she was not interviewed for the July 1998 article (her then husband was) she had by implication continued to adopt all that the July 1998 article said.

As for "death threats" to Heidi's son, she did not mention, when asked, the 1998 allegation to the police about it being "in a letter" sent by me to Gudmund Johannessen's parents who gave it to the Bergen police. This time she said I told her in a phone call that her son was "a bastard" and that "bastards don't deserve to live" and secondly that on one occasion on my August 1990 visit I had "stared hard" at her son in such a way that she took that as a menacing gesture intended by me to mean that I "could kill him." I only ever met her son once, in 1990, August, when on that lovely day for me she now described how it utterly disgusted her when she saw me cuddling Daniel and showing my affections towards him. I felt sick. Heidi proceeded to tell of her nausea when I left her son a present of a toy bus with her neighbour and later sent him a set of model cars from England. The implication she tried to convey was that I was a danger to her child. I swore to myself that I would never forgive her.

Surprisingly, Heidi admitted she had told me in Easter 1985 at the Bergen Aquarium that the fish were having "group sex" but justified it on the grounds that I did not understand the irony of her humour at seeing a school of fish. I understood perfectly well her observation but I only brought it to the attention of the court as an example of the sexualisation of her own behaviour.

Heidi also admitted to sending me in October 1990 the Christian booklet 'I Dared To Call Him Father' and when asked by the judge whether a letter had accompanied the book, she answered, "Probably, yes."

Further, Heidi admitted that I'd made no "concrete" threats to her former neighbours to get her new address and phone number, adding, "I can't remember if he's issued death threats against my neighbours."

Amazingly, Heidi stated that on my visit in 1986, I wanted to apply for a residence permit for Norway and that when on one occasion Heidi had telephoned my mother, Mum had told her that she would do all she could to "stop me" harassing her, and if she couldn't, Mum would try to put me into a mental hospital.

Heidi did admit to having "an abortion" and admitted to receiving from me in 1988 Brian Wilson's music cassette tape ('Love and Mercy'). As for my attempted rape/actual rape of her, she never got round to explaining the discrepancy, but just said that one night I'd woken her up with "heavy breathing" whilst playing with myself and proceeded to have sex with her. Nothing was mentioned about "holding her down," as Policewoman Torill Sorte had alluded to in one of my 1998 conversations with her (printed above).

When Heidi had finished the judge asked her if there was anything else she'd like to say. "No, I just want peace," she said. And that was that. She was excused from further attendance and went home. Hers was not the performance of a terrified woman. Nay, she deserved an Oscar. I had wondered if perhaps she had even conned her social services into giving her a 100% disability pension.

The next witness was the Drammens Tidende editor, Hans Odde. After he'd got the preliminaries out of the way he mentioned how his own sister, who was a kindergarten teacher, had been called in by her principal to explain the meaning of a faxed report he had received with my usual heading, 'Heidi Overaa: Bergens Tidende, Drammens Tidende and Verdens Gang.' The kindergarten principal thought that Drammens Tidende were up to some innovative stunt and he wanted some answers from the editor's sister! Apart from that it was all quite mundane from Odde. He'd got the story from Verdens Gang and as Heidi was a local girl his journalist had invited her for an interview. When asked why, before the story was printed, efforts were not made to contact me to get my side of the story, Odde replied that they didn't know how to get in touch with me. Lunde then said that they could have asked Heidi to give them that information; (she always had my phone number and everyone had my address).

Ingunn Røren was on next and she clearly was embarrassed knowing she'd already been caught out lying from the taped conservations. The judge knew this so Lunde didn't spend much time on her, especially as the judge said aloud that, "The newspapers are not in the dock." Still, as I told Lunde, an English barrister would, for effect have began his cross-examination by saying, "Ingunn Røren, you're a liar aren't you?" Nevertheless, Ingunn Røren tried to get out of it by saying I'd phoned her many, many times and I was unintelligible and totally unreasonable. She repeated her claim that the newspapers did not print my side of the story "so as to protect him from himself."

Runar Schøne was next up. He said he was a taxi driver by occupation and had met Heidi in late 1993. They'd got married on 25th March 1994 but were now divorced. His evidence was ironically to be of great assistance to me.

He said he "couldn't remember" if he'd spoken to me in tongues, but did admit to "babbling." Then he said he hadn't in fact technically spoken "in tongues." He was presumably worried that if he denied "babbling" I'd produce a tape recording of it, thus proving he'd perjured himself. What I knew of course was that I hadn't recorded him "babbling" (in summer 1995) and had only after that bought a recording device. But he wasn't taking any chances!

He proceeded to compare me with Osama Bin Laden and Lunde later told me that he was watching the judge and Lunde himself raised his eyebrows to the judge on hearing this Bin Laden comment, whereupon the judge raised his eyebrows back and smiled in amazement at Runar Schøne's crass remark. (The spectre of the Muslim fanatic is never far away!).

Runar Schøne went on to state how he'd liked to have come to London to "kill" me. Then came Runar Schøne's accusation that his neighbours "were afraid for their lives" because of my information campaign, although he would not confirm whether I'd threatened any of his neighbours with taking their lives (as he'd twice been quoted as saying in Drammens Tidende). This, in spite of his insistence that an "old lady" neighbour of his had been "threatened" by me. Schøne neither produced her name, address or a witness statement from the "old lady" to the police. He finished off by saying that this saga was more incredible than any film ever made and that Heidi deserved "a million pounds in compensation" for all she had endured.

Once each witness had been called in from outside to give their evidence and been examined by either side, they left the courtroom, so none of them got to know what was said about the rest of the case. Policewoman Torill Sorte was the last witness. For a start she didn't even acknowledge me. She began by saying she took over "the case" in April 1996 but that in 1995 the police had traced some of my phone calls to Heidi's home which came "from abroad" but had not recorded the contents. (A pretty useless operation then wasn't it?). The telephone numbers traced were incomplete even! I thought to myself, so what if they were traced! I had spoken to Heidi from England and then Denmark in May 1995 and I'd brought along to Court later taped conversations with Heidi and myself from June 1995 to be used if necessary.

Next came the big surprise. Torill Sorte stated that my "despairing" mother had spoken to her telling her that she had put me into a mental hospital. I blurted out to Torill Sorte, "You liar." The judge said

436

nothing. I swung round to Lunde, "You've got to save my neck on this one," I told him, and Lunde with the 22nd April 1996 transcript of the telephone conversation between my mum and Torill Sorte in his hand, said to Torill Sorte, "That's not what this conversation states from a 1996 recording." Gotcha! Sorte then protested: "I didn't know he was recording my conversations." Sorte was flustered and came up with this excuse – It was a long time ago and a report had been put in by Heidi years ago which stated that she (Heidi) had spoken to my mother and there were some "rumours" of me being put in a mental hospital, and it was this report by Heidi to the police, said Torill Sorte, that was "the more accurate account" of my supposed encounter with a mental hospital. The judge had not heard the tape before or seen the transcript as it had not been put in evidence, as I had so many taped conversations. I couldn't afford to pay for all of them to be translated into Norwegian which the judge had insisted on before he accepted them in evidence. However, it was good that this particular conversation with Sorte and my mum had not been put in as evidence, otherwise we may not have caught Torill Sorte out.

The judge said he would listen to the tape in the morning and if necessary Torill Sorte would be called to give evidence to explain herself. Torill Sorte then left and I knew she would be furious with me for my trap. Two other conversations from 1998 with Torill Sorte (reproduced in Chapter 21) had been sent to the Court but only arrived three days or so before the trial, so Torill Sorte obviously did not know about them.

After the day's proceedings had finished, I gave Lunde the relevant tape and in the foyer of the Courthouse on the ground floor he listened to the tape for the first time and, eventually satisfied, told me he would talk to Torill Sorte in the early evening to discuss her evidence and the taped conversation prior to deciding if she should be brought into court again at 9 a.m. the following day, Friday.

At 10 p.m. I phoned Lunde to ask what his decision was on Torill Sorte. He told me he would not be calling her the next morning. He said he'd spoken to her and she told him that if she was asked to come back to court, she would swear on oath that this recorded conversation from 1996 was not the only one she had had with my mother; that she would say, unbeknown to me, my mother had later phoned her to tell her I *had* in fact been treated in a mental hospital! I was not happy with Lunde's refusal to bring Sorte in. It was obvious from the content of the 1996 conversation that it was the first conversation my mother had with Sorte, who in speaking to my mother at my insistence had not even read the three 1995 newspaper articles. So what in effect my mother had allegedly done was to betray me by finding the telephone number for an obscure police station and gone out of her way to tell the policewoman she had, after all, put me in a mental hospital. Some mother!

Clearly for me, Sorte had perjured herself and was prepared to do so again and Lunde said it would look bad for me if a policewoman insisted in court that my mother had phoned her to retract the 22nd April 1996 conversation, to insist I had "in fact" been "put" in a mental hospital. Lunde's command of spoken English was not perfect. His written English was pedestrian and it angered me to think that this language impediment was a major stumbling block to a proper assessment by Stig Lunde of the taped telephone evidence.

So on Friday morning, the tape was played to the judge and translated into Norwegian by William Mullholland, my interpreter. The judge now knew that my mother had specifically told Torill Sorte she had not threatened to "put" me in a mental hospital as told by Heidi to the newspapers in 1995. Still, on my return to England, I was going to get my mum in on this in an effort to get Sorte charged with perjury.

This determination to medicalise my behaviour and go all out to ruin me was later to take another twist in the closing statements of the two lawyers.

Stig Lunde began his summing up by ridiculing Heidi's interpretation of my allegedly "staring hard" at her son as a death threat, and that Heidi Schøne's mental aches and pains had roots going back long before she met me, so it was not correct for her to say that I was responsible for the fact she is now receiving a disability pension. Mr. Lunde then referred to a 1997 police report that I had never before known about, which stated, "On one occasion he was committed for treatment by his mother." This information, said Lunde, was submitted by Torill Sorte in a 1997 report after an alleged conversation between my mother and Torill Sorte. However, no such information was ever given by my mother to

Torill Sorte, said Lunde, who emphasised that no such conversation took place. Further, that it was incorrect that 300 letters had been sent to Heidi in the year 1997 to 1998. Any 'letters' included the reports sent to the public about Heidi's past. [I had in fact sent 10 postcards and one letter 'to' Heidi.] He continued that Heidi had acknowledged receiving from me a (Brian Wilson) music cassette whilst she was in a mental hospital in 1988; our letters to one another were part of "an exchange of views." Lunde stressed that crucially none of the above facts and background were mentioned in any of the newspaper articles that Heidi herself approved; that the word "Muslim" was linked to sexual harassment and which only increased my aggression because I felt tainted by the connection and aggrieved that Islam itself was being degraded; that my so-called "obsession" with Heidi Schøne ended in 1990 when she sent me the book 'I Dared To Call Him Father,' but that there had in any case never been any such obsession, and that in 1995 there definitely was no obsession with thoughts of marriage to Heidi; indeed there was no interest in that respect whatsoever. That as for a 16 year period of harassment even if there were differences between us, up to 1990 there was both negative and positive contact; that Heidi did not give a contrary impression. Moreover, that there had also been periods where there was no contact at all, periods of calm and positive contact; that it is only from 1995 that I acted in a way that could have been regarded as harassment; that talk of harassment of her family "year in, year out" was incorrect; that the newspaper allegation that my 'reports' to the public had "no roots in reality" was incorrect and, more seriously, this newspaper statement reinforces the opinion that the 'reports' were the work of a madman; that Heidi had refused to go into details of the contents of my 'reports' but that much of the veracity of the 'report' had been confirmed in Dr. Broch's testimony. Further, that references to "a secret telephone number and address" in the context of the article reinforced the false impressions given by the rest of the article. [No documentary evidence was given as to Heidi's address being "secret."] That the phrase Heidi and I "drank tea together a couple of times" [in England when we met] as per the Drammens Tidende article of July 1998, trivialised the actual contact and again reinforced the impression that I was a madman; that there was "never any romantic attachment" was incorrect as the evidence showed the contrary was the case; that the harassment "increased in extent" when Heidi got married was false as the increase in contact had to do with my need to know the reason for my arrest in 1990 and it was a coincidence that this took place after Heidi married; that the Drammens Tidende article could have been done in a more balanced way without defaming me; that all the articles printed were read out to Heidi and she didn't correct any of them. Lunde finished off by quoting examples in Norway where the press hadn't first checked the facts of articles they printed.

I thought Lunde's summing up was excellent. The defence lawyer then began his summing up. He first emphasised the fact that I'd obtained a criminal conviction the previous November and a 10,000 kroner fine and that, in spite of this conviction, I'd proceeded to fax the whole of Drammen and his office my point by point response to the Drammens Tidende article of 17th November 2001. [In fact only 200 or so of the faxes got through]. The judge then spoke up to ask me why after my conviction I did another campaign. I told him that I did it in accordance with my right to reply and that it was indeed no coincidence that I'd sent my statement to Vegard Aaløkken's office, the reason being that he had misled the public by stating in the newspapers that "Heidi was glad the Court believed her," when he himself was not present at my criminal trial the previous October and was only relying on the word of Heidi. And that as my offence was one of strict liability there was no alternative to my being convicted. Aaløkken followed on by saying that both Heidi and Torill Sorte stated in 1997 statements that they both spoke to my mother, who told Sorte in particular she had put me into a mental hospital. And further that I had insisted to know what kind of underwear Heidi was wearing.

On a surprising departure, Aaløkken then climbed down on several points. He agreed that there was no basis for the newspaper saying that "300 letters" were sent to Heidi Schøne from 1997 to 1998. He also agreed that it was not proven that for 16 years I had been "obsessed" with Heidi and had "wanted to marry her" throughout this period as alleged by the press. He also agreed that it was not true that the extent of my "harassment" increased on her marriage to Runar Schøne; that the reference to (my alleged condition of extreme) erotic paranoia in the July 1998 Drammens Tidende article was not Heidi's responsibility; that Nils Rettersdøl had (in the Verdens Gang article in May 1995) stated he was speaking "generally" and not about my specific case; that as Heidi had not herself made the statements in the 1998 article that were false, she herself must be found "not guilty" of the charges; that although there was no documentary evidence to corroborate the defence claim that there was 16 years of sex-terror, "proof " in Norwegian law doesn't have to be documentary. (I could have jumped out of the window on hearing this. He was no doubt relying on the testimony of his witnesses as being 'safe' evidence).

438

There was then a break for five minutes after which Stig Lunde was to be allowed a reply. I told Lunde that it was grossly unfair for the defence to put in evidence two 1997 police witness statements, sent on 13th January 2002 to the Court. One was a 1997 report by Torill Sorte of the Drammen police which stated that in 1992 my mother spoke to Heidi Schøne and my mother allegedly told Heidi that if I didn't "stop" my harassment my mother would do all she could to see I went to a mental hospital. The other was a 1997 report by Torill Sorte stating that Sorte herself had spoken to my mother who told her I had been "put" in a mental hospital. So I told Lunde to ask the judge to ignore these 'Reports' as I had had no opportunity to consider and rebut them. Lunde agreed it was essential to put this to the judge.

So in his reply Stig Lunde made three points:

- that the two 1997 (Norwegian language) mental hospital 'Reports' of Police Sergeant Torill Sorte should be withdrawn from evidence as they were sprung on me by being submitted in evidence 3 days before the trial started.

- that in relation to identification of myself by readers of the 1995 articles who knew both Heidi and/or myself wherein I was identified as the "Muslim, English lawyer," her friends and acquaintances would realise that there was only one such person that Heidi knew, further increasing my chances of being recognised, which applied also for the words "half-German, half-Arab" and

- that Heidi should pay damages to me because she was responsible for using the media in such a deceitful way.

Defence counsel then got up to agree that the 1997 mental hospital 'Reports' should not be considered in evidence as they came in to Court too late. So the Judge agreed that he would not take them into account. The trial had now ended.

I felt totally vindicated. Lunde shook hands with his counterpart and my interpreter shook hands with both lawyers. I knew it was coming and so it turned out: Vegard Aaløkken came up to me to shake my hand and I did so, saying, "All the best." Did I really say that?

Lunde and I left the Courthouse to relax in a local café. For the first time in many, many years, I felt a huge sense of relief. I felt that my hard work had paid off. I joked with Lunde that as Heidi was now single, he should take his chance and move in for her.

I saw Lunde off in his taxi and hugged him with genuine gratitude for all that he'd done for me. He had got up at 4.30 a.m. that day and did four hours work on his summing up prior to our 9 a.m. start. He was a lawyer with a cool head and a mind that could take in huge amounts of information without overloading and exploding. Essential ingredients for a courtroom lawyer.

That same night I took the train from Drammen Railway Station to Sandefjord and then the coach to Torp airport to take the 10 p.m. plane back to Stansted in Essex. I was pretty confident I wouldn't be prevented from leaving Norway without first being asked to pay my 10,000 kroner fine, imposed by the Magistrates Court the previous autumn.

After getting home, on the following Tuesday, my incensed mother wrote to Judge Stilloff asking him to throw the book at policewoman Torill Sorte for lying on oath about her "conversation" on the mental hospital incarceration.

Chapter 30

The judgement was given on 11th February 2002 and is reproduced here in its entirety. I had it professionally translated into English.

COURT RECORDS

FOR

DRAMMEN DISTRICT COURT

In the year 2002, on 11th February, the court was set in Drammen courthouse.

Judge:	District Court Judge Anders Stilloff.
Clerk of the court:	The judge.
Case No.:	1318/99 A.
Plaintiff:	Frederick Delaware.
Counsel:	Lawyer Stig Lunde, postboks 1064 Jeløy, 1510 Moss.
Respondent:	Heidi Schøne, Sollikroken 7, 3058 Solbergmoen.
Counsel:	Lawyer Ellen Holager Andenæs through advokat Vegard Aaløkken, C.J. Hambros plass, 0164 Oslo.
The case concerns:	Claim for compensation (reparation).
Present:	No-one except the judge.

Judgment was pronounced as follows:

JUDGEMENT

Frederick Delaware filed a writ on 10.08.99, amended on 13.01.2000, in which he claimed kr. 50,000 – in compensation (reparation) from Heidi Schøne (maiden name Overaa) under the Law concerning compensation (skadeerstatningsloven) § 3-6, 1st part, for defamation. The background to the claim lies in a newspaper article in Drammens Tidende/Buskerud Blad, editor Hans Arne Odde and journalist Ingunn Røren, demanding annulment and compensation (reparation). This part of the case was rejected through the binding decision of the Borgarting circuit court on 24.11.2000, because the right to request prosecution for criminal offences was considered to have been withdrawn by Delaware's lawyer at that time, in conjunction with grievance procedure within the Norwegian Press Council (PFU).

According to the decision of the circuit court, only Delaware's civil claim against Schøne remains – which means that the rules of the Law concerning civil litigation (tvistemålsloven) now apply. Cf. Bjerke/Keiserud (2nd edition 2001) page 29 and HRD I Rt. 1994 page 348 (349).

The main proceedings were held on 15, 16, 17 and 18.01.2001. Delaware and Schøne attended, with their counsels, and gave evidence. Five witnesses were heard and documentation was carried out as shown in the Court records.

The facts of the case can be summed up as follows:

Delaware and Schøne met each other whilst she was staying for a few months in England in 1982 as an au pair. He is English and lives and works in England. When she went home to Bergen, they corresponded with each other, and he also visited her at her home.

The following is an excerpt from a letter dated 13.08.83 which Schøne wrote to Delaware:

Dear Frederick,

Nice to talk to you again. It feels strange, but you make me feel better every time I've talked to you. I don't know what I like so much about you, but it's something that's for sure.

The following is from a letter Schøne wrote in 1984:

Dear Frederick,

How are you Frederick? It was very nice talking to you again! It's always nice talking to you. You're such a nice person, and you know that too.

On a postcard date-stamped 09.04.85, Schøne writes:

Frederick,

Thank you very much for your letter(s)! I just want to write this card to you to show that I think a lot of you. I do really hope that you take care of yourself, and that everything works out for you!!!!!!!!!!

Lots of love Heidi xxxxxxx

Delaware and Schøne agreed that it was a good intimate relationship between them initially. This means that Schøne confided in him, including the fact that she had been sexually abused during adolescence by her stepmother's father, that she had subsequently been with a number of boys and had sexual experience, and also that she had aborted after unwanted pregnancy.

At Easter in 1984, Delaware was invited by Schøne to Bergen. At Christmas in the same year, he invited himself. At Easter in 1985 he came on a visit uninvited and for the first (and last) time they had sexual contact going beyond kissing and caressing. Schøne reported him later to the police for attempted rape on this occasion. In May/June 1985 Schøne was in London with a girlfriend and encountered Delaware by chance (without agreeing to meet), but no contact took place.

On 01.04.86, Schøne gave birth to a son, Daniel. The father is Gudmund Johannessen, contact with whom she broke off in the autumn of 1988 before moving from Bergen to the Drammen area. Delaware had visited her unannounced in Bergen before this, in the summer of 1986.

After she had moved to the Drammen area, Delaware engaged a private inquiry agent in 1989 to trace her. He succeeded in doing this and telephoned her at the hotel where she worked. She refused to meet him, however.

In February 1990 Schøne was on a visit to her sister in Bergen. Delaware got to know about this and travelled from the Drammen area – where he had gone to meet her – to Bergen. Schøne refused to meet him and notified the police, who arrested him. The upshot was that, after two days in custody, he voluntarily left Norway. The last time Delaware and Schøne met was in August 1990.

In April 1995 Runar Schøne (who had married Schøne in 1994) reported Delaware to the police on behalf of himself and his wife.

Delaware wrote quite a lot to Schøne, and in court she produced a number of letters and cards dating from early in 1995. Earlier correspondence was not kept. He also telephoned her.

On a postcard dated 27.02.95, Delaware writes, among other things:

> *Congratulations on your marriage!! A long time to wait Heidi – 31 is a bit late; hope you enjoyed your wedding night (I should be so lucky!!) Well, Runar (translate for him Heidi) – Heidi always liked a big prick – I guess you are no different; obviously you've reached your turn in the queue – what number were you – 50?*

On a postcard date-stamped 07.03.95, Delaware writes, among other things:

> *The birth of a child a joy? No, a horror – abort – abort. "Yes Petter, of course love." Pregnant with twins a blessing? Not really, a real drag says Gudmund so I'll screw her best mate; oh she lost 'em and tries to kill herself, c'est la vie.*

On a postcard stamped 07.04.95, Delaware writes:

> *In Norway it may be normal for a slut like you to sleep with tens of men (even taking heroin) – "for company" as you told someone but I have been scared of your sick behaviour. Your stepmother called you "a whore" after your second abortion. She was so right and she also told me you were a liar. The fact that you are in demand for sex doesn't mean you fuck like an unpaid whore. Your unborn children you put in the dustbin: The reality is even garbage like your lovers want someone better than you, Christian pervert!*

On another postcard stamped 08.04.95, Delaware writes, among other things:

> *Talking like a whore again last night? Trying to annoy me with your filthy talk when you know I'm still single? How can I be proud to marry you – after the disgusting things you've done to me. Stick to the fanatic moron you've got. He's on your level. I just can't understand why he hasn't gone for a younger woman – he must be desperate. Just when I tried to make you decent and I truly once cared for you. You think I still do after what you've done? The reason I hate you so much is because you destroy lives. No one managed to stop you in your quest to sleep with as many men as possible ... ...*

On a third postcard stamped 08.04.95, Delaware writes, among other things:

> *You were so busy screwing on the beach in Rhodes/screwing your lifetakers – your 'loving' boyfriends – there was never an opportunity to get to know you. You hated God & his values.*

As early as around 1990 Delaware sent a tape recording and letters to senior medical officer psychiatrist Petter Broch at Buskerud General Hospital (now Buskerud Hospital), psychiatric department, where Schøne was being treated. Tape recording and letters are assumed to have similar contents to a 'report' which Delaware sent in the spring of 1995 to Schøne's family, friends and neighbours in both Bergen and the Drammen area. How many he sent is rather uncertain; but it may have been as many as about 35. The report is as follows:

[See 'Report on Heidi Overaa' sent to her neighbours mentioned in Chapter 15 in this book]

This report came to the knowledge of Bergens Tidende, without Schøne's co-operation, and she was contacted by a journalist and interviewed in the newspaper of 24.05.95. A few days later, Verdens Gang and Drammens Tidende/Buskerud Blad also carried interviews after contacting Schøne.

Delaware's name is not mentioned in any of the newspapers. He is described as English of Arabic/German origin, lawyer, Muslim, mentally disturbed. Professor of psychiatry Nils Rettersdøl was interviewed and states that the man may be suffering from "erotic paranoia."

The newspapers produced a reaction from Delaware. He then issued a new 'report' in considerable numbers, probably up to 3,000 of them. The report was distributed entirely at random, partly on the basis of fax directories, to both private individuals, firms and public/private institutions of various kinds. The new report, which may appear to have been submitted in response to an inquiry from three named newspapers (this proved to be untrue), runs as follows:

[Here the Judge reproduced my 'Report on Heidi Overaa' mentioned in Chapter 15 but slightly updated to which I had now added a new heading 'Heidi Overaa – Bergens Tidende and Drammens Tidende and Verdens Gang.']

Delaware also distributed a number of reports in English, with rather similar content. Some addressees also received a general article in English (of unknown origin), on mental conditions, entitled 'HEIDI SCHØNE –ABNORMAL MENTAL LIFE.'

On 17.11.97 Delaware wrote to Schøne the following, amongst other things:

You know, I really wish you were dead and buried, you filthy pervert. It's hard to imagine anyone more evil and sick than you. I bet you helped kill your own mother. Even after her death you paid her memory the compliment of two abortions. You are a disgusting piece of dirt.

Fuck off and die and go to hell. I don't know how you sleep at night. You hate Muslims, you hate life and only associate with criminals and odd crazy people. You represent the sickness that is in Norwegian society and for as long as I live I'll make sure you pay for the wickedness you've inflicted on me. Maybe a living death is better for you – as you get older, things will get tougher. I hope Daniel turns against you just as you turned against your mother and me.

I will do all I can to ensure the truth is spread far and wide about you – killer!

Drammens Tidende/Buskerud Blad discussed the case again in an article of 14.07.98, on the basis of an interview with Schøne which the newspaper initiated. The following is taken from the newspaper's front page:

[The Judge reproduced the whole of the Drammens Tidende Article of 14th July 1998]

The newspaper article resulted in Delaware lodging a complaint against the newspaper with the Norwegian Press Council (PFU). From the presentation of the case there, it emerges that the newspaper held the view that Delaware's statement (reactions to the article) could not be printed because he had to be protected from himself, but that the paper subsequently acknowledged that this should have been made clear to the readers of the newspaper. PFU declared on 24.08.99 that the newspaper had not breached good press practice.

Delaware was sentenced on 02.11.2001 by Eiker, Modum and Sigdal County Court (herredsrett) to a fine of kr. 10,000 -. Alternatively 25 days imprisonment, for infringing

§ 390(a) of the Penal Code. In an exhibit which had been drawn up on 24.08.2000, replacing the indictment, the general findings used by the Court as a basis are reproduced as follows:

[The criminal charge against me was repeated here.]

The Judgment was reported in Drammens Tidende and Buskerud Blad on 16.11.2001 under the title "Fine for extreme sexual harassment" ("sex terror") and Delaware then distributed a new 'report' in reply, from which the following is quoted:

In 1995, the Englishman discovered that in December 1986 the woman had complained to the Bergen police that the Englishman had <u>attempted</u> to rape her in April 1985. There was a delay in 20 months in making this (false) allegation, which complaint was made a mere two weeks after the Englishman had warned her family of her unsafe sexual practices and suicidal tendencies. The complaint was in revenge for the Englishman's revelations of her past to her own family who had been ignorant of the sex terror inflicted on her by Norwegian citizens.

The Drammen public must also be made aware that the woman told Drammens Tidende in 1995 that the Englishman had in 1988 allegedly threatened to murder her two year old son. Without any corroborative evidence Ingunn Røren printed this allegation as 'a fact.' Later enquiries revealed that the woman told police that the alleged murder threat was made by the Englishman in a letter which was "given to the Bergen police." The Bergen police told the Drammen police they had no such letter. Of course, the allegation is false and designed to cause much trouble to the Englishman, if not to ruin him.

Such a malicious allegation is surely provocation enough for the Englishman to be able to acquaint the Norwegian public with the truth of the girl's past so they knew the background of a woman making such allegations against him, via her national and local press. The Englishman had no other means to reply.

The Englishman believes the woman is a lunatic who far from being the 'innocent victim' as portrayed by her xenophobic press, is a calculating, scheming opportunistic liar with little regard for normal standards of civilised behaviour.

The plaintiff Frederick Delaware's pleading was essentially as follows:

The case concerns Schøne's reactions to Delaware's actions and his claim to personal protection of his sense of honour (Penal Code § 247). Her statements in the newspaper articles of 14.07.98 which must be considered against the background of the newspaper articles in 1995, are offensive, and go far beyond that which can be substantiated and justified in his earlier conduct towards her. If, contrary to expectation, substantiation of the accusations is provided, they will be punishable, nevertheless, cf. Penal Code § 249 No. 2.

Schøne could have made direct contact with the recipients – in reply to Delaware's 'report' in 1995 – in order to protect her interests.

Alternatively, she could have ensured that the newspapers had given a balanced presentation of the case; she approved the articles for printing. She could also have reported Delaware to the police and requested inclusion of a civil claim in the criminal case. She did not show due care at all. This applies also regarding the newspaper article in 1998, which is the direct cause of this case – although this must also be considered against the background of the newspaper articles in 1995. The fact that Delaware distributed the great majority of the reports, etc., **after** the articles in 1995, is central to the case. This was necessary because he did not speak to the newspapers.

The required conditions for compensation (reparation) for the unlawful accusations therefore exist, cf. Law concerning compensation § 3-6.

That which particularly incensed Delaware is the accusations that he raped, or attempted to rape, Schøne, and that he threatened to kill her son Daniel.

From that which emerges in Drammens Tidende/Buskerud Blad's article of 14.07.98, the following statement, in particular, is said by Delaware to offend his sense of honour and reputation, and is essentially untrue (direct quotation [translated] in quotation marks):

- Delaware did not "persecute," "pester," "harass sexually," "harass," "terrorize," "threaten to kill."

On the contrary, for a long time a very good and intimate relationship existed between them, with mutual kissing and caressing, right up until around the time when the newspaper articles appeared in 1995, even though the relationship suffered at times under her very volatile mental condition. But she still sought him out – for example, after Gudmund Johannessen had deceived her in 1988, when she telephoned for help and support. When it was wrongly claimed in the newspaper article that they only "drank tea together" and that they never had any "love relationship," this strengthens the impression given by the accusations which she makes against him.

Schøne was very open about her sex life, and this resulted in her sexual morals becoming a subject of discussion and in Delaware finding a reason for constructive criticism in an attempt to help her. He was concerned about her conduct in life and mental health. If Schøne did not realise this, but took his involvement with her to be persecution and intimidation ('terror'), she should have let him know this. He never made any death threats, although his description of Schøne's son Daniel (a bastard not deserving to live) was certainly unnecessarily harsh.

"Madman," "mentally disturbed," "very ill," "mentally ill," "erotic paranoia."

Delaware has never been hospitalised or treated for mental illness, as was claimed – unlike Schøne.

Delaware's behaviour must be assessed on the basis of the desperate situation he had got into, and of his obvious need to justify himself and disprove Schøne's accusations. It was very important for him to be able to convey the correct version. Nor does he wish to conceal the fact that the reports according to the newspaper article in 1998 also had a motive of vengeance; he wanted to avenge the wrong he had suffered because of her. Emotional, irrational reactions were natural and understandable.

Delaware did not send "300 letters this year alone" to Schøne (prior to the newspaper article in July 1998). On the other hand, it did not emerge that the considerably fewer letters he wrote to her were often agreeable. On one occasion when she was admitted to the psychiatric department, Lier, he sent a music cassette to cheer her up and she wrote letters to him, which he answered.

The background to the letters that Delaware wrote to Schøne after the visit to Bergen in February 1990 was a desire to clarify why he had been arrested and to determine what the purpose was of the reports against him. In addition, there were elements of an exchange of opinions between them concerning ethical questions and views of life.

Although it is true that Delaware is the "Muslim man" he considered it offensive that his religious faith should be stressed in the article and related to accusations of sexual harassment.

Delaware was never "obsessed with the thought of marrying Heidi." Up to 1990, he certainly wanted to get to know her, with a view to possible marriage, even though he also had contact with other women. But this was not obsession, and he gradually came to realise that the desire had nothing to recommend it. His distribution of 'reports' and letters was not prompted by jealousy. It is not correct to say that "the harassment increased when Heidi got married nine years ago."

- "16 years of sexual harassment" would imply that Delaware had behaved towards Schøne in this way since they first met in 1982. This is not true. Right up to 1990, Schøne wanted to contact him. 1995, after the newspaper articles appeared, was the earliest time that Schøne can – wrongly - have considered Delaware's actions to be harassment.

- Delaware's "years of harassment of Heidi and her family." He certainly wrote some letters, but this was based upon his concern for her and a need to let her know this.

- The newspaper article in 1998 indicates that Delaware's reports "are not rooted in reality." This is definitely wrong; the reports are founded upon what Schøne had told him. When it is stressed that the reports are untrue and, moreover, that Schøne had to get a secret address and telephone number, this strengthens the erroneous impression of it being the work of a madman.

Frederick Delaware has submitted the following:

Claim:

1.   Heidi Schøne should be ordered to make within 14 days to Frederick Delaware a reparation payment in the sum of NOK 50,000, plus 12% interest as from the due date and until payment is made.

2.   Heidi Schøne should be ordered to pay to Frederick Delaware, within 14 days the costs of the case, plus interest at 12% p.a. as from the due date and until payment is made.

Respondent Heidi Schøne's case was essentially as follows:

Schøne can substantiate by evidence the central argument in the case, namely that for a number of years she was persecuted by a mentally disturbed/mad/mentally ill man, in the popular understanding of those terms. In addition, she can essentially provide evidence without loss of quality – which is enough. Cf. Andenæs/Bratholm: Spesiell strafferett (3rd edition) pages 207 – 208. Alternatively, provided that such proof is adduced, § 249 No. 3 of the Penal Code will apply. Alternatively again: in any circumstance, it is not reasonable that Delaware should be granted redress under § 3-6 of the law concerning compensation.

Considerable importance must be attached to Schøne's view of the relationship with Delaware. He was in love with her and wanted to marry her. At the very beginning they had good contact with each other, it is true, and Schøne really had nothing against maintaining this contact. But Delaware's conduct soon assumed more and more the nature of persecution, harassment, pestering and terrorizing. He wrote, telephoned and sought her out, despite her clearly stating that she did not want this type of contact. As early as in 1985 in London, he suddenly turned up outside a restaurant that she was visiting with friends who had to protect her and ensure that he was refused admission. In February 1990 she had to call the police, because he was pestering her in Bergen. He sent a tape recording to the psychiatrist Petter Broch (who was treating Schøne), who found it "repellent," and he sent the report on her, with contents of a private, sensitive nature, to about 35 addresses in Bergen and the Drammen area. According to the newspaper articles in 1995, he distributed thousands of reports. The fact that Delaware was capable at times of behaving nicely towards her is of no significance in this connection; she has full proof of her descriptions of his behaviour towards her and also her family.

Both Delaware's letters to her and the reports about her are pathologically obsessed with sex, and the discussion of her is blatant sexual harassment. She still thinks that he raped her – or at least attempted to – in Bergen at Easter 1985. On other occasions she was subjected to unwanted kissing and touching. He could ring up and ask her what kind of underwear she had on. It was not her who stated that he suffers from erotic paranoia.

Finding out that Delaware was a Muslim was a journalistic point, because his letters have a clear religious undertone.

Schøne did not state that Delaware uttered death threats against her neighbours. This statement is attributed by the newspaper to Runar Schøne.

Schøne's main plea is that substantiation by evidence was provided, so the required condition of criminal defamation does not exist, cf. § 249 No. 1 of the Penal Code. Schøne had a valid reason for her statements to the newspaper, so § 249 No. 2 of the Penal Code does not apply.

In so far as sufficient substantiating evidence cannot be considered to have been provided, § 249 No. 3 of the Penal Code will apply. Schøne justifiably looked after her own interests; she had to protect herself against the massive violation to which Delaware subjected her. It is very important that Delaware should maintain complete anonymity and that there should be little risk of him being identified. She could not be required to confirm publicly the correctness of the information that he disseminated about her concerning sexual matters, abortions, etc.

If statements which can be attributed to Schøne should nevertheless be considered criminal, then following a probability assessment consideration cannot be given to granting Delaware redress under § 3-6 of the Law concerning compensation. The case is turned completely on its head and Schøne becomes the victim. Delaware wanted to smear her and destroy her life.

Heidi Schøne has submitted the following:

Claim

1.   Heidi Schøne should be acquitted.

2.   Heidi Schøne and/or the State should be awarded the costs of the case plus annual interest of 12% as from the due date and until payment takes place.

Remarks of the Court

The case concerns only claims for compensation (reparation) pursuant to § 3-6, 1st part, final point, of the Law concerning compensation. This provision which gives the court an opportunity to award this compensation for such non-financial damage or loss as is deemed reasonable pre-supposes, however, that the required conditions for punishment for defamation of character are fulfilled, cf. §§ 246 ff of the Penal Code does not preclude liability for compensation if the defamation is due to negligence.

The alleged defamations relate to the newspaper article in Drammens Tidende/Buskerud Blad of 14.07.98. It was the newspaper that contacted Schøne in order to hear her opinion of Delaware's written communications. Even though Schøne received the article for perusal prior to printing, she cannot be held liable for the information, opinions and forms of wording in the article for which others are the source and which the newspaper wished to convey. In particular, it is mentioned that the expression "erotic paranoia" originates from an interview with professor of psychiatry Nils Rettersdøl. It was Runar Schøne who provided the information that neighbours had received death threats from Delaware. Prior to the newspaper article in 1998, by agreement with the post office, the police took delivery of all mail from Delaware to Schøne and also had reports sent to them from various other addresses. Taken together, this constituted a considerable volume of mail – about 300 items, according to the police. The article does not mention attempted rape against Schøne or death threats against her son Daniel.

The Court's starting-point is that Delaware obviously had a very intense interest for a long time in Schøne, far beyond that which follows from normal acquaintance. Despite the fact that Schøne – after 1985 in any case – opposed the form of attention he came

448

gradually to show her (something he must have been aware of), he continued to send her letters, telephone her, spy on her and seek her out. There can be no doubt that she rightly regarded this as persecution and harassment. The whole situation culminated in Delaware's reports being sent out to neighbours, friends and family of Schøne even before the articles appeared in 1995. These reports and many thousands of similar reports which Delaware distributed around the country after the newspaper articles, constitute a serious breach of trust against Schøne. They fully reveal the pathological interest he showed in her and his motive of revenge after being rejected. The court thus does not give credence to the notion that the vengeance motive which Delaware acknowledged was confined to that which he regarded as accusations of rape and death threats against Schøne's son Daniel.

There can be no doubt that Delaware's very special interest in Schøne was of an erotic nature. Letters and postcards and, not least, the reports he sent to her, largely relate to her sexual morals and relationships with other men. Sexual harassment is an appropriate designation for these written communications. Schøne cannot be reproached for dissociating herself publicly from very personal, sensitive items of information concerning, for example, abortions, sexual circumstances and attempted suicide, even though the information may have been more or less correct.

Schøne cannot be censured – after having been called a "Christian pervert" (postcard dated 07.04.95), a "filthy pervert" who "hate(s) Muslims" (letter of 17.11.97) and having received other accusations with religious undertones – for mentioning that Delaware is a Muslim. This does not indicate any lack of respect for people of other faiths. Delaware called himself "the Muslim man" and pointed out his religious faith and his consideration for those of his own faith (in Bosnia). Cf. his undated "PRESS RELEASE" (doc. 48 annex IV 1).

Following a general appraisal, the court has concluded that the information, opinions and forms of wording for which Schøne must bear responsibility, are in essence true and not improper, either. Also, that she had a valid reason to allow herself to be interviewed by Drammens Tidende/Buskerud Blad in 1998 (and the three abovementioned newspapers in 1995); it is very understandable that she should want to rectify the impression of herself which Delaware's letters and cards gave to the addressees. On the other hand, she did not reveal Delaware's name, which is not mentioned in the newspaper article. His circle of acquaintances in Norway is very small and the Norwegian newspapers are not read in England; there is no mention of the English media having shown any interest in the case.

For Delaware to be able to be granted compensation (reparation) under the Norwegian Law concerning compensation, § 3-6, part 1, the requisite objective conditions under §§ 246 and 247 of the Penal Code must exist, in addition to the subjective requirements for punishment having to be fulfilled, or lack of care shown.

The court concluded above that the required conditions for punishment do not exist, and in the opinion of the court Schøne did not show negligence, either. The court wishes to add that it would not in any circumstance be reasonable to require Schøne to make reparation payment, in view of the obvious necessity for her to limit the damaging effects of Delaware's writing about her; it is difficult to see that Schøne's conduct in any way justifies his reactions.

Schøne is accordingly acquitted.

Costs of the case

The court has not been in any doubt about the result, and Delaware will be ordered to pay costs, cf. Law concerning litigation. (tvistemälsloven) § 172, part 1; part 2 does not apply.

Lawyer Aaløkken has submitted a costs statement, claiming costs amounting to kr. 100,386.-. The statement covers work from submission of pleas, including a court session for preparation of the case. Of this sum, kr. 14,356.- is value-added tax. Schøne has been allowed conduct of the case without charge by the regional commissioner, but without waiver of the supplementary share of costs. The basis of calculation for the additional share includes total legal-aid costs less value-added tax and amounts to kr. 85,000.-. This means that the basic own share amounting to kr. 300.-, plus 25% of the excess will fall upon her, a total amount of kr. 21,6754.-, while the remainder amounting to kr. 78,711.- falls upon the State. Delaware will therefore be ordered to pay costs of the case to Schøne and the State, in the abovementioned amounts, plus the statutory interest at 12% p.a. on delayed payment, from the due date and until payment takes place.

JUDGEMENT OF THE COURT

1. Heidi Schøne is acquitted.

2. Frederick Delaware is ordered to pay costs of the case within 14 days after the pronouncement of judgement, as follows:

    a. To Heidi Schøne kr 21,675.- plus statutory interest on delayed payment of 12% p.a. as from the due date and until payment is made.

    b. To the State, kr 78,711.- plus statutory interest on delayed payment of 12% p.a. from the due date and until payment is made.

The parties shall have the judgement announced through their respective counsels.

Court adjourned.

[signed] Anders Stilloff   (hand-stamp)

CERTIFIED TRUE COPY OF THE ORIGINAL

[signed]

Drammen District Court

The judgement as a whole was perverse. Everything Heidi Schøne said about me herself was according to the judge "in essence true." I was presumably, then, a rapist and potential child killer aside from being a sexual pervert. Judge Stilloff's criticism of the newspapers was very well camouflaged. Significantly at least the judge had accepted that my report on Heidi's past was "more or less correct." He did not accept that she was capable of telling lies. Judge Stilloff had set out my postcard to Heidi dated 8th April 1985 beginning with the words, "Talking like a whore again last night?" To put this in context I had phoned Heidi on the 7th April 1985 to try and get some sense out of her over her attempted rape allegation, but she only responded by saying, "You want to have sex with me don't you? You want me to come to England to warm your bed." To which I sarcastically replied, "Are you still attractive then?" To which she responded, "Yes I am."

On deadline day (as usual) Lunde himself put in a six page Appeal to the Borgarting Lagmannsrett (Court of Appeal), after I had paid the £2,600 appeal fee to him. The main extracts from the Appeal went as follows:

The appeal concerns: Assessment of evidence and application of the law in the case with regard to redress in accordance with The Injuries Compensation Act § 3-6 for Defamation of Character.

3. More details regarding the appeal and the grounds for the appeal

The District Court's judgement is appealed in its entirety. The appeal relates both to the District Court's assessment of the evidence as well as application of the law.

The appellant will cite the same statements and evidence before the Court of Appeal as placed before the District Court.

With regard to the assessment of the evidence this involves a claim that it is wrong for the District Court to have regarded the relevant accusations as being true. It is further wrong for the District Court to have taken the position that the appellant has displayed an intense and long-term interest in the opposing party to the appeal, and then far in excess of what follows from a normal acquaintanceship. It is also wrong to accept that the opposing party to the appeal had objected to the attention from 1985, and that she could justifiably have perceived the behaviour of the appellant after this as constituting persecution and pestering. The actual situation is, on the contrary, that she has herself contributed towards contact for several years after 1985, for example by sending a book to the appellant (1990) and by having personal conversations with him on the telephone. From the statement given by the opposing party to the appeal to the District Court, it transpired that she had had contact with the appellant on several occasions after 1985, and that long conversations were conducted without any indications emerging that she did not wish to have this contact.

The book that the opposing party to the appeal received from the appellant in 1990 led to him losing interest in her. This was because, among other things, he felt, against the background of the contents of the book, that she was attempting to convert him to Christianity. The contact between the parties reduced in scope after this.

During the parties' acquaintanceship the appellant discovered circumstances that caused him to be bewildered and worried. He was of the opinion that the opposing party to the appeal had exposed him to an HIV risk, that, against the background of conversations with her, he was worried about her way of life and that he was, at times, worried about her mental health, and also that he was arrested by the police upon visiting Norway in 1990. Despite many efforts the appellant never received any explanation regarding the background to the arrest, nor did he get any response from the opposing party to the appeal in this respect. In his attempts to obtain an answer he attempted, on several occasions, to contact the opposing party to the appeal, and he clearly expressed at that time his indignation about an arrest that he perceived as being unwarranted. It is stated that this contact had not been of any offensive or troublesome nature and that, in any case, it must be viewed in the light of the appellant's justified wish to obtain an answer regarding the background to the arrest.

As the appellant, in spite of several attempts, was unable to find out the background to the arrest in 1990, he engaged a lawyer in November 1994 to ascertain the reason. The lawyer discovered that the opposing party to the appeal had reported the appellant for alleged rape in 1986, against the background of a rape that was alleged to have taken place in 1985. This knowledge made the appellant livid with rage, and he wishes to state that no rape had ever taken place. The case was also then stated to have been shelved by the police. The appellant became aware of the rape allegation upon the lawyer advising him accordingly by telephone after having himself received information regarding the matter on 28 February 1995. In indignation about the unwarranted reporting to the police, the appellant sent crass letters and cards to the opposing party to the appeal.

In the opinion of the appellant, both the reporting of him to the police in 1986 as well as the arrest in 1990 were based upon a wish for revenge on the part of the opposing party to the appeal. First of all, as a reaction to the fact that, prior to the reporting to the police in 1986, he had written a letter to her father motivated by concern for her lifestyle and mental health. Secondly, because, prior to the arrest in 1990, he had been in contact with the grandparents of the son of the opposing party to the appeal.

As a result of what he regarded as unwarranted reporting to the police and problems that the opposing party to the appeal had caused him, motivated by pure revenge, the appellant sent some accounts to the neighbours, and erstwhile neighbours, of the opposing party to the appeal. This was to a very limited extent, however, involving around 20-35 reports.

After this the appellant became the subject of several newspaper reports in 1995. Prior to the newspaper reports the appellant had expressed his indignation directly to the opposing party to the appeal, had been in contact with her immediate family, added to which he had contacted a psychiatrist

451

who had treated her, and had also approached 20-35 persons in a very limited circle of the general public.

The newspaper reports in 1995 were one-sided, contained many major mistakes, created a totally wrong picture of the parties' relations, and otherwise went far beyond what was necessary against the background of the appellant's behaviour. It was by means of the statements to the press in 1995 with the subsequent articles, that the situation became known to the general public.

The appellant was not confronted with the situation prior to the articles being printed, nor did he manage to bring about a clearer presentation or a correction afterwards. This, combined with the extreme anger he felt as a result of the violations, caused him to start to send information himself to arbitrary recipients in the catchment areas of the newspapers that had published material about the case in 1995. These mailings were far smaller in number than the reports in the relevant newspapers.

It is alleged that the appellant's reactions are natural in relation to the violation to which he had been subjected by the reports in 1995, which is reinforced when viewed in the context of the revenge-based actions to which he had been subjected by the opposing party to the appeal in 1986 and 1990.

It will be further alleged that the behaviour of the opposing party to the appeal must be viewed in the light of her history of mental problems. Also included here is that she is said to have made incorrect accusations of rape in respect of person/persons other than the appellant.

The District Court was wrong when it took the view that the appellant's interest in the opposing party to the appeal had been of an erotic nature. After 1990 the appellant's interest had first and foremost consisted of gaining answers to specific situations with which he felt discomfort. That out of indignation and anger he made statements of an erotic nature does not mean that he has had a "special interest in Schøne … of an erotic nature," as the District Court has taken as a basis. Nor is it correct when the District Court takes the view that the opposing party to the appeal may justifiably have regarded the appellant's behaviour as "persecution and pestering."

The depiction of the appellant has been made in such a way that he can be recognised. And Norwegian newspapers are also read in England, for example in a Norwegian-English society where the appellant was a member. In addition, he had many acquaintances in Norway. Irrespectively, the statements involve a violation of his self-respect.

The reports made about the appellant in the newspaper article in 1998 are untrue and constitute a violation under both § 246 and § 247 of the Penal Code. It is wrong when the District Court takes the view that the opposing party to the appeal shall be free of responsibility for this. She had received the article for approval and is obliged to ensure that what is published in terms of both factual information and, by no means least, in terms of an overall impression, is correct and covers the factual circumstances. This includes the need for both her own statements as well as the context in which they occur to provide a correct picture, and for them not to extend further than what may be justified in the underlying circumstances. Even if the report had been true, it goes much further than what may be accepted against the background of the underlying circumstances, and is thus nevertheless punishable under § 249 no. 2 of the Penal Code.

Nor has it been necessary for the opposing party to the appeal to employ the newspaper in order to protect her own interests. In this context, the extent to which the appellant's notifications to the general public was a consequence of the unjustified reporting in 1995 is pivotal. Before the opposing party to the appeal herself made the relationship known via national press coverage in 1995, the appellant had, as stated above, made only very limited approaches to the general public. Notwithstanding this, the requisite care has not been displayed, both in terms of the presentation having to be limited to what is regarded as necessary and ensuring that a sufficiently clear and whole picture is presented. This has not been fulfilled. Consequently, exemption from liability under § 249 no. 3 of the Penal Code does not obtain.

To the extent that the opposing party to the appeal believed that she had been subjected to violation from the appellant, then it should have been dealt with in a totally different manner than by exposure through the press.

Natural alternatives could have taken the form of formal notification, issuing a claim related to defamation, or necessary information could have been presented to the extremely limited group to which the appellant had made approaches. Grounds for exposure through the press, including nationwide press, did not exist. That the appellant's public notifications to the world around became more extensive after the newspaper articles in 1995, does not alter this, cf. that his behaviour was caused by the wrong to which he had been subjected in 1995 and that had made the matter known to newspaper readers throughout the entire country.

The District Court was consequently wrong when it took the view that the opposing party to the appeal had grounds for allowing herself to be interviewed in 1998, that the conditions for punishment are not present and that she acted in a careful manner.

The District Court was further wrong when it takes the view that, notwithstanding, it is not reasonable for the opposing party to the appeal to be ordered to pay restitution. The opposing party to the appeal has inflicted considerable damage and disadvantages upon the appellant by her actions in 1986 and 1990. She has herself been a central cause to that which led to incorrect and defamatory comment regarding the appellant in newspapers in 1995 and, thereby, also to his subsequent actions.

Also with regard to the question of legal costs the judgement of the District Court is wrong. The case gives rise to matters associated with an extremely central legal benefit that are difficult with regard to both evidence and law. Moreover, the opposing party to the appeal has, through her behaviour, contributed towards such reference to the appellant in newspaper articles in 1998 that he has reasonable grounds for having the matter tried by law. Consequently there cannot, notwithstanding, be any basis for ordering the appellant to cover the costs of the opposing party to the appeal.

Insofar as mentioned, it is relevant for the appellant to submit further statements and evidence, and inasmuch as in the law's instances a judgement by default is called for, there is respectfully submitted the following provisional:

Claim

1. Heidi Schøne be ordered to pay to Frederick Delaware, within 14 days, restitution in the sum of NOK 50 000 with the addition of 12% interest p.a. from the due-by date until payment is effected.

2. Heidi Schøne be ordered to pay to Frederick Delaware, within 14 days, the legal costs relating to both the District Court and the Court of Appeal, with the addition of 12% interest p.a. from the due-by date until payment is effected.

Moss, 13 March 2002
Stig Lunde, Lawyer

Lunde had himself got an important fact wrong. It was attempted rape that Heidi Schøne alleged in 1986 not actual rape. Further, I had never made any statements to her of an erotic nature. I merely reminded her of her own sexual conduct.

I myself had to add my own opinion on Judge Stilloff's judgement, which I did once I'd paid nearly £500 to have the judgement translated into English.

My response was as follows and it cost me £2,300 to have it translated into Norwegian which I then sent to the Court of Appeal:

SUPPLEMENTAL APPEAL   **Date: 12th June 2002**

TO

BORGARTING LAGMANNSRETT

Drammen Tingrett Case Number 1318/99A and Borgarting Lagmannsrett Case Number 02-01546 A/03

I, Frederick Delaware, the Appellant in this matter write further to my lawyer Stig Lunde's appeal dated 13th March 2002, now that I have had translated into English Judge Anders Stilloff's judgment dated 11th February 2002 from Drammen Tingrett.

I intend to take this case as a litigant-in-person - as is my right under Norwegian law - and hereby subpoena the same witnesses as appeared in the Drammen City Court but will cross-examine them myself: Heidi Schøne, Dr. Petter Broch, Torill Sorte, Ingunn Røren, and Hans Odde.

The judgement is wrong for the reasons that follow:

1. My letter dated 13.8.83 was wrongly dated by Heidi Overaa on the front page. The post stamp on the envelope was 22.8.84 and Heidi Overaa will readily agree that this was the actual date the letter was posted. Heidi Overaa often wrote me letters but posted them several days later. I presume she wrote it on 13.8.84 but posted it on 22.8.84. It is important to get the facts right.

In 1983 there was no contact of any sort between Heidi Overaa and myself.

It is misleading not to reproduce the whole of the contents of the letter post-stamped 22.8.84 in the verdict as this letter gives a full picture of Heidi Overaa's feelings, especially expressing her desire to marry me and her disappointment at my rejection of her in favour of another girl. The contents of this letter will indicate that no dramatic and sudden change in my behaviour would be likely to have taken place because of Heidi Overaa's so called later rejection of me. Her description of my behaviour in this letter is the exact opposite of her description of my behaviour in the newspapers and in Court in January 2002. A remarkable swing! In this letter, Heidi Overaa also expressed her hope that we "never lose contact again." Bergens Tidende of 24th May 1995 have Heidi saying that "we never had feelings for each other." That I "fantasised" about her. Heidi Overaa clearly lied to that newspaper and other newspapers, obviously confident that I would never read the 1995 newspapers or have kept her letters. A precedent has therefore been established that Heidi Overaa is a liar of the highest order.

2. Heidi Overaa will agree, contrary to Judge Stilloff's ruling of "fact" that:

My first visit to Norway was actually in December 1984 through to January 1985 – a stay of 10 days;

I did not visit Norway in Easter 1984;

My visit at Christmas 84/85 was agreed in advance with Heidi Overaa and she was at Bergen Airport to meet me with her friend, Knut, who gave us a lift in his van back to Heidi's flat in Åsane, and Knut stayed with us for two hours.

I did visit Bergen in Easter 1985 having phoned Heidi beforehand and she agreed I could come. Just before my visit I received Heidi's postcard dated 9.4.85 which is quoted in Judge Stilloff's verdict. The contents of this card hardly indicate that my imminent visit was unwanted, as Judge Stilloff infers. Moreover Heidi left a pot of blackcurrant tea on her coffee table for me and told me to let myself in, taking the key from above the window-ledge, as she would not be in when I arrived because she planned to be out skiing. This trust of Heidi in me is hardly the action of a woman to an unwanted visit by a rejected man. Heidi came back after one and a half hours with her skiing partner, another man I had never met before, and he took us on a scenic trip around Bergen in his car and spoke of his brother being in a local Bergen jazz band. Heidi was living alone in her flat.

454

3. At Christmas 1984/85, Heidi told me, as we were about to meet her parents at their Bergen home – Asligrenda 4 – that her stepmother's father "is always asking me for sex." I was given no information as to whether intercourse actually took place and nothing more was said about the topic on this Christmas trip of mine.

In Easter 1985, when Heidi mentioned her stepmother's father in a sexual context, she gave me the impression that she masturbated him, and nothing more.

I made no mention of the above information [on Heidi's stepmother's father] to anyone until my nine-page report to the newspapers in summer 1995 detailing my version of Heidi Overaa's association with myself.

Heidi has now gone on record publicly in Eiker, Modum and Sigdal Court in October 2001 saying that she was sexually abused by her stepmother's father who died, I believe, in 1988 or 1989. Heidi told me of his death when I spent the day with her and her son, Daniel, in August 1990, the day she also told me she had been "exorcised from demons" and her "foot grew by a quarter of an inch," as a result, as one foot was shorter than the other.

Of course we only have Heidi's word that she was sexually abused by her stepmother's father. Heidi's psychiatrist, Dr. Petter Broch, now establishes this abuse as fact, but on what grounds, other than Heidi's word?

The above description is the correct chronology of my knowledge of Heidi's sexual allegations against her stepmother's father, which Judge Stilloff did not make clear in his verdict.

4. In April 1982 when Heidi and I were cuddled up together on the easy chair in her hosts' home, Heidi volunteered to me that she had had an abortion and later said the same day there was something else she had done "wrong," but was reluctant to tell me. Having put me in suspense, I pressed her for an answer and she very sadly told me she'd had a second abortion to the same boyfriend, who in fact had earlier visited her in England.

5. I note that in Court Heidi has admitted Gudmund Johannessen took cannabis and amphetamines, but she denied he ever injected heroin. It was Heidi herself who told me that Johannessen had gone on holiday to China for two weeks, purchased heroin and injected it with her knowledge, whilst having unprotected sex with her. This information was imparted to me by Heidi in the autumn of 1986 and I went to have an AIDS test myself, having had intercourse with Heidi in Easter 1985. I have the certificate to prove it. I also wrote some letters to Heidi, which are with the Court, reprimanding Heidi for knowingly sleeping with a junkie, especially as she had constantly sought my advice as to how to improve the quality of her life. Only a delinquent would behave like this. The fact is Heidi also told me she and Johannessen had two AIDS test each after their son was born. Heidi was worried for her son, Daniel, she told me. Heidi's willingness to sleep with Bjorn-Morten at the same time as Johannessen put Bjorn-Morten at risk too – clearly Heidi's behaviour is criminally irresponsible. Heidi also told me Johannessen had earlier in his life contracted a venereal disease.

So with all the above information already with Judge Stilloff, I believe Heidi Overaa lied on oath when she said Johannessen "never injected heroin."

6. Judge Stilloff infers that 1985 was a watershed for me because Heidi Overaa "rejected me." What did this "rejection" consist of ? In Easter 1985 Gudmund Johannessen visited Heidi and myself in her flat in Åsane and rolled a cannabis joint and smoked it in front of us. Johannessen had just had his hair permed. When Johannessen had left I scolded Heidi for associating with a man who smoked cannabis and this upset her. Unbeknown to me, Johannessen was also injecting heroin, purchased in China, sleeping with Heidi and other girls and Heidi was also sleeping with Bjorn-Morten. Then Heidi got pregnant and wrote and told me. I was amazed at Heidi's crass stupidity after all that Johannessen had done to her and told her that her actions would spell disaster. This turned out to be an accurate prediction. Heidi got very upset at my commentary and for a little while did not want to speak to me, and refused to see me on her August 1985 trip to England.

I could hardly, therefore, be accused correctly by Judge Stilloff as being "rejected" in the conventional sense by a normal woman. It is not as if I have missed out on a 'great catch' – Heidi Overaa. She cannot succeed with any man – she is alone again. And what a strange sort of rejection. I hardly had time to draw breath before being told she was pregnant to a man, Gudmund Johannessen, who had earlier so abused her mind, body and soul. Johannesson, yet another abuser.

Yet I repeat my genuine claim. In 1988 in August Heidi phoned me at my central London office begging for help against Gudmund Johannessen who had told his friends to tell Heidi AND her son to "fuck off." It was Heidi who suggested I and my best friend, one of Britain's top rock drummers, who she already knew to be a karate expert, punish Gudmund Johannessen by travelling to Norway and "take him to the woods and tie him up or something." Heidi's own specific intention was to take physical revenge on Gudmund Johannessen.

This request from Heidi was hardly that of a woman who I had attempted to rape (now changed to rape) and whose son in 1987/88 I had threatened to kill. For it is, I believe, a 1997 'report' that was put into Court by Heidi Overaa in which I am alleged to have threatened Daniel Overaa's life, although I have still yet to see this report so I may have to comment further.

Of course, I did not have a clue as to the 1986 attempted rape (now changed to rape) allegation or 1987 allegation of threats to kill Daniel until 1995 and onwards, so for Heidi to ask me up in 1988 to help her, knowing of her allegations, tells me she is an even sicker woman than I thought. She herself is a manipulative schemer, with evil intent. Does any woman who has really been raped by being "held down" (as per Torill Sorte's taped evidence) and have her son threatened with murder, then later invite the same accused man to help her out? I don't think so.

Heidi told Torill Sorte, the policewoman, that I had written a letter threatening to kill Daniel. I did not write this letter and obviously it has not been produced in Court, and it never will be. It never existed in the first place.

In the Eiker, Modum and Sigdal Court, on October 31st 2001, which hearing I did not attend, my lawyer Harald Wibye told me Heidi admitted to being allegedly raped by a Bergen shopkeeper, but she did not want to talk about it in Court. Yet another abuser of Heidi.

Harald Wibye also related to me how Heidi told the Eiker Court that I telephoned her (and remember she had no phone from 1988-1993 as far as I know) on an unspecified date and told her that her son was a bastard and that bastards don't deserve to live and therefore I would kill Daniel, whereupon Daniel asked his mother: "Why does Frederick want to kill me?" This entire telephone conversation never took place. It is an invention by Heidi and for Judge Stilloff to state as a fact that I told Heidi her son "is a bastard and bastards don't deserve to live" is outrageous. I said no such thing. However, Heidi's allegation has parallels with the journalist Ingunn Røren's accusation that I told her boyfriend off for "living in sin" with her. This has conclusively now been proved to be a lie by Ingunn Røren. Yet both accusations by these women have as their foundation determined attempts to make me out as a religious fanatic – a Muslim one; nothing sweeter of course for the Norwegian establishment to tack on to.

On the occasion I met Daniel Overaa – the sweetest most kind and loving child in the world who for years I dearly missed – in August 1990, aged four and a half, Heidi alleged in Court that I gave him a "hard look" which she interpreted as a "death threat." I never gave the dear fellow anything other than love, cuddles and fun – and presents. Hardly consistent for someone who "doesn't deserve to live." Besides, illegitimacy is not the fault of the child is it? Why afterwards did Heidi phone me from the public call box in Gamle Riksvei, outside her Solbergelva home, in September 1990 letting Daniel speak to me, jokingly telling him to call me "Funny face," which he did? Why did Heidi write me two postcards from Egersund where her sister Rennaug lived, telling me how much Daniel liked me and how nice the name "Frederick" sounds? Heidi took Daniel with her to Egersund. How on earth can I know this without Heidi telling me? Why did Heidi go to the trouble of ordering a religious book – 'I Dared To Call Him Father'– from England and then send it on to me? This book was produced in Court and Heidi admitted sending it to me in October 1990. I have a taped conversation with Heidi from 1995 in which she admits wanting to "witness me," i.e. convert me to Christianity. All this effort by Heidi for a rejected man? The fact is she wanted a future with me.

7. Heidi also told me in August 1990 that she feared I might have kidnapped her son Daniel in February 1990.

8. To correct Judge Stilloff's impression, I state that in April 1985 during my stay with Heidi Overaa, Heidi told me she was planning to visit England with Ann-Kristin Horvei to look at second-hand clothes shops and they wanted to open their own shop in Bergen. Subsequently, Ann-Kristin Horvei did open a shop but by then – 1986 – Heidi had dropped out of the venture. I visited Ann-Kristin in her shop at this time, when, I believe, Heidi and Ann-Kristin Horvei were no longer on speaking terms. Indeed they have not spoken since.

In August 1985, Heidi wrote and told me she was pregnant and that she was very shortly coming to England to visit the clothes shops. I assumed she was pregnant to Gudmund Johannessen because Heidi didn't herself specify. The truth as I now know from a 1998 conversation with Ann-Kristin Horvei (with the Court) is that Heidi herself did not know who she was pregnant to as she had been sleeping with two men at once. After she conceived, I wrote to Heidi to reprimand her for her pregnancy to the abuser Gudmund Johannessen and predicted it would only cause her grief in the future.

So, in August 1985, on a hunch, I phoned another English friend of Heidi's, now a lawyer, Carmine, who lived in St. Albans in Hertfordshire with his parents. He told me Heidi and Ann-Kristin were staying with him as their hotel in central London proved of very poor quality.

I was determined to know from Heidi how on earth she could possibly have gone back to such an abuser as Johannessen, so I walked up to Heidi (in Luton town centre in Bedfordshire) as she was getting out of the car, parked some way from any disco or restaurant. I said to her simply, "Heidi are you really pregnant?" Her two male companions had no idea about Heidi's circumstances and years later I met one of them, Carmine, when he told me what a fool Heidi was, getting pregnant to an "arsehole" like Gudmund Johannessen. Carmine himself had visited Heidi in Bergen just before my visit in Easter 1985 and met Gudmund Johannessen, so knew about him.

There was never any wild confrontation outside her hotel in central London as Heidi stated in Drammen City Court. I never knew where her hotel was as she never told me the address. Importantly, the very next day after Heidi got back to Bergen from England, she telephoned me to explain herself. Heidi also told me after her return to Norway that Carmine had sex with Ann-Kristen Horvei in front of her, as there were two beds in Carmine's parents' spare room which the two girls were given to sleep in. Heidi told me she was disgusted with Carmine's behaviour because he had a girlfriend called Debbie. However, in 1990 Heidi told me that her allegation against Carmine was not in fact true and that she had lied. Ann-Kristen Horvei insisted also that she had never had sex with Carmine.

9. My visit to Heidi in August 1986 was not unannounced as Stilloff records. I wrote beforehand to Heidi to say I would visit her before going to see another girl in Hønefoss. Heidi phoned my mother after I had departed to ask her what time I was arriving. Heidi greeted me warmly, let me stay alone in her flat overnight and gave me her only key, as her son was already at his grandparents and she was to stay the night with all of them. Heidi introduced me to Gudmund Johannessen's mother but told me not to tell her anything about Gudmund Johannessen's past treatment of Heidi, as Johannessen's mother was ignorant of her son's vices.

On the last evening of this visit, Heidi, myself and Johannessen had a meal together, watched the TV – the film 'Grease' with John Travolta – and then Johannessen left to go back to sleep the night at his parents. I expressed my surprise at this and wondered whether Johannessen would object to me staying with Heidi alone. She told me it was none of Gudmund's business what she did. "He does what he wants, I do what I want," said Heidi. So we stayed together and at the end of the evening cuddled and chatted warmly outside her front door before I left for my Bergen hotel. The next day I went to Hønefoss. I totally deny blackmailing Heidi as she alleged in Drammen City Court on this or any other occasion, threatening to tell her neighbours of the alleged sexual abuse she suffered at the hands of her stepmother's father, if she did not let me kiss her and touch her breasts. In any event, I could not be 100% sure her grandfather's abuse was true. Besides, in practice it is a ludicrous undertaking; was I supposed to knock on all her fellow flat owners' doors and tell them of the abuse? This is a foul lie from Heidi Schøne, made public for the first time in January 2002, 16 years after my 1986 visit.

By the time of the January Court case Heidi Overaa had plenty of motive for telling outrageous lies, in revenge for my exposing the truth of her past. She had been coached on what to say and prepared her tissue of lies with some precision.

10. In early summer 1989, close to midnight, Heidi phoned me out of the blue for one hour in a very tender call from her hotel, where she worked nights. I did not know where Heidi lived. To share the cost, I then phoned her back for one hour at the Muller Hotel – now Central Hotel – in Drammen. I told her of my bewilderment at her recent past behaviour and said I'd written and told her off in a letter which she would soon get, but told her not to read it and tear it up as it would upset her. But she couldn't later resist reading it and I didn't hear from her again. When I visited the hotel in August 1989, she had left their employment, I was told.

After that, I decided that it would be best to find out where Heidi lived to sort things out once and for all with a face to face talk. So I employed a private detective simply to find her address, which he did. That is what the detective earned a living at and finding someone's address for earnest motives is hardly a crime. Heidi was, after all, a confused, abused woman who from hour to hour changed her moods wildly and to this day no man has managed to tame her. Moreover, I will use a private detective in Norway again if I so choose, to obtain evidence against Heidi Overaa to help prove she has lied on oath.

Thus I want to make it clear that the sequence of events reported by Stilloff is wrong. As I employed a private detective first, I would not then phone and go to Heidi's hotel, having already got her home address.

Besides, trying to sort out personal differences by face to face involvement is an age-old practice. Gudmund Johannessen did it at Christmas 1990 and beat Heidi to the ground and she reported him to the police. Was he fined or sent to prison? No, as far as I know. Besides, when Heidi left the hotel, I spoke to one of her ex-colleagues on the phone, who told me Heidi was always taking away the boyfriends of other girls. This staff member had the right impression of Heidi alright, and was most willing to talk.

11. I knew Heidi Overaa was in Bergen in February 1990, because I spoke to her from her neighbour's home, Heidi-Anita Skjortnes, in Solbergelva, Drammen, who had invited me and another friend – not the rock drummer – into her home for two hours to discuss Heidi Overaa. It was Heidi-Anita Skjortnes who volunteered the information that Gudmund Johannessen had two months earlier assaulted Heidi who had reported him to the police. I'd be most interested to know why Johannessen did this. I have my suspicions. But I think Heidi blamed me for her being beaten up so got revenge by telling wholesale lies to the Bergen police in 1990 when my English friend and I later travelled to Bergen to see her.

12. My postcard of 27.2.1995, mentioned on page 4 of Stilloff's judgement, indicates that Runar Schøne does not speak passable English (which he admitted in Court), further indicating the fact that I had spoken to him before that postcard was written. I got the impression in my conversation with him that he was a fool and called him such – a prick. My impression was confirmed by his later behaviour of saying to me "Come to Jesus, only he can save you. Allah doesn't exist." And by his speaking 'in tongues' to me and my mother (and in relation to which he admitted in Court to "babbling").

I had earlier written some very reasonable letters to Heidi questioning why I had been arrested in 1990; letters written in, I believe November and December 1994 to which I got no reply. So in January 1995 I wrote to a lawyer in Bergen to investigate my arrest to be told on 28th February of an allegation of attempted rape made in December 1986. This was news to me; the Bergen police never told my London lawyers in 1990 of this allegation. Only after 28th February 1995 did I inform Heidi's direct neighbours – 20 or so – of her past, in revenge for her totally false allegation of attempted rape (changed in 1998 to actual rape "by holding her down"). I require policewoman Torill Sorte to produce Heidi Overaa's statement made to her in her office in 1998 that I had raped Heidi in 1985 "by holding her down." I also require Heidi's lawyer to produce her statement of attempted rape arising out of the same incident made to the Bergen police in 1986. Further, I require Heidi's lawyer to produce her statement of an allegation of rape she made in the early 1980's to the Bergen police against a Bergen shopkeeper.

I had tried to question Heidi on the phone in February 1995 about those past events in February 1990 in Bergen and spoke by chance to Runar Schøne. As can now been seen, my bewilderment at my arrest has been justified by subsequent events, which reflect on what Heidi Schøne in fact is: a registered mental patient on a 100% disability pension. She is moreover incapable of telling the truth, an opinion shared by independent evidence which is with the Court, but not mentioned by Judge Stilloff in his verdict – amazingly.

On the 4th April 1995, I wrote to the Norwegian Embassy in London to try and enlist their help in getting the very unco-operative Mr. Krogvold of Bergen police to send me details of the alleged attempted rape. The Embassy wrote back on 20th April 1995 – copy enclosed (Exhibit 1). Krogvold never replied to me.

13. So my subsequent letters to Heidi, and an initial 20 reports to her neighbours, after learning of an untrue allegation of sexual assault, in turn criticised her own perverse sexual conduct, but in no way can my criticism be seen as taking an "erotic interest" in her as Judge Stilloff claims. My subsequent and various reports on her life – all factual – were in direct response to filthy newspaper lies in May 1995. I was sickened that I was the third person in her life to be accused of a serious sexual assault. I had a legitimate right to respond to a woman who had voluntarily waived her right to anonymity by her stories and photos in the newspapers.

14. Let me state what Dr. Petter Broch, Heidi's psychiatrist, said on oath in Drammen City Court last January:

- Heidi has a tendency to display sexualised behaviour.

- Heidi's two older sisters used subtle forms of punishment on her.

- Heidi's stepmother reported Heidi to the Child Protection Unit "on false grounds."

- Heidi's stepmother's father sexually abused Heidi.

- Heidi's stepmother mentally abused Heidi, making her "compliant."

- Frederick Delaware's reports on her life (several different reports) contained "a core of truth."

- Heidi cannot sexually function in a proper relationship.

- Heidi could not respond to his (Dr. Broch's) psychiatric treatment because she associated him with the source of her problems: men.

- Heidi is still having problems because she is still in contact with her stepmother.

Judge Stilloff, surprisingly, did not think any of this relevant to mention in his judgement. Importantly, Heidi reveals three more 'abusers' in her life: her stepmother and both her sisters. The list grows and grows. Again, we only have Heidi's word for it.

Let me remind the Court that Heidi Overaa was a registered psychiatric patient (an in-patient) at the BSS Psychiatric Clinic in Lier in the autumn of 1988 and has been taking 'therapy' on and off ever since, precipitated in no small part by her association with Gudmund Johannessen.

I too, of course, have been described in January 2002 by Heidi, on oath, as an abuser:

- a blackmail threat in 1986, if she did not let me kiss her or touch her breasts, as described above;

- that I regularly phoned her up asking what sort of underwear she was wearing (she had no phone from 1988 to 1993);

- that I wrote to her telling her that if she did not get pregnant her breasts would fall off.

Again, all lies, but in keeping with her aforementioned sexualised behaviour attributed to her by her own psychiatrist.

How disgraceful that in all the 20 years I have known Heidi Overaa, I have never heard many of her allegations against me until last January's Court hearing, especially those numbered (i) – (iii) above. What happens in England is that we have a procedure of discovery of documents and interrogatories - questions on evidence - before the case comes to trial. This is a major failing in Norwegian legal procedure as is the entire law of libel allowing one judge such power, and the discretion to accept the 'word' of a witness, a mental patient, as true, used in this case to make such a flawed decision based on unsubstantiated and confused reasoning. Perhaps the fact that Heidi is Norwegian and I am not may have something to do with it.

15. I produce a copy of my London lawyer's letter of June 19th 1990 to the Bergen police indicating that all of Krogvold's claims were "unspecified and unsubstantiated" relating to my 1990 arrest (Exhibit 2). After that, I would never trust the police in Bergen again. I was to do my own thing, my own way.

How readily the Drammen and Bergen police co-operated with Vegard Aaløkken, Heidi's lawyer, last January in her defence, the Drammen police even giving him the police files with my surname name incorrectly spelt on the spines of the lever arch files. Hardly an independent police force, but we will come to the perjury of the policewoman Torill Sorte, unreported by Judge Stilloff, later.

16. Let us not forget that the Court found Runar Schøne to be a proven liar when he insisted in the 1998 Drammens Tidende article (and the 1995 articles) that I had threatened with death Heidi's neighbours if they did not give me her address.

17. In August 2000, in Drammen City Court, Runar Schøne shouted to me that: "We have proof" that I threatened to kill Heidi's son. No such proof has been produced. Heidi has alleged I threatened to kill her son in a letter via a statement produced to the Drammen Court in January made in a 1997 report from the Mjøndalen police station. Does the Court believe her or not? Am I also a potential child killer as well as a rapist, spy (the word used by Judge Stilloff), sexual deviant, liar and sex terrorist, as alleged in the six newspaper articles on me, alluded to in Court judgements and witness statements? If Judge Stilloff believes Heidi's 'word' that I told her "Bastards don't deserve to live," is Judge Stilloff also saying that I did as a matter of fact (relying solely on Heidi's word again) threaten to kill Heidi's son in a letter as well as on the phone? Judge Stilloff says he "believes" Heidi but does not particularise in all respects, which of course is perverse, bearing in mind the large amount of evidence totally ignored by Stilloff.

Runar Schøne on oath uttered threats of violence towards me and compared me to Osama Bin Laden, in January of this year.

18. Let us not forget that journalist Ingunn Røren is a proven liar in evidence long since with the Court that she did not dispute whilst on oath to Judge Stilloff. Her justification for calling me a Muslim in the first paragraph of her 14.7.98 article has been conclusively exposed as a pack of lies.

19. Let us not forget that policewoman Torill Sorte is a proven liar – having perjured herself on oath before Stilloff. On the day before my case last January, the Defence put in a police report stating that Torill Sorte had spoken to my mother and that my mother told her I had been "put" in a mental hospital. My lawyer, Stig Lunde, then said he had the transcript of a telephone conversation which stated the exact opposite: that my mother told Torill Sorte the newspaper report from 1995 (stating "Heidi knows Frederick's mother wanted to put him in a mental hospital") was totally false and that she, my mother, had never wanted to put me in a mental hospital.

On hearing this, Torill Sorte stated that she had no idea I was taping this conversation from April 22nd 1996. This policewoman had trapped herself by her own lies. Indeed she stated earlier that I telephoned her many times myself with unreasonable annoying calls. Well, I have taped those calls and given some of them to the Court, in the days leading up to the trial – all translated into Norwegian. The calls are polite, interesting and most informative, quite the opposite of the description given by Torill Sorte. But the lie was made by her, on oath and it cannot be undone. My mother has put in a written complaint to the Judge, who it seems has totally ignored it.

My mother only ever spoke to Torill Sorte once and is incensed at the lies of this policewoman. The moral is clear, for Ingunn Røren, Torill Sorte, Runar Schøne, and Heidi Overaa: if you want to tell lies make damn sure you don't get caught out!!

Torill Sorte will be cross-examined in the Court of Appeal by me personally and as I have never been in a mental hospital I hope this policewoman's blatant attempt to try and pervert the course of justice, in turn causes her to face criminal charges for perjury. If the Court believe Torill Sorte to be telling the truth, then let it rule that I have as a matter of fact been "put in a mental hospital by my mother" (when the reality is I have not). But as Judge Stilloff turns falsehood into fact by saying it is true that I told Heidi that, "Bastards don't deserve to live" (when I didn't), as her son, Daniel, was born out of wedlock, why not continue the practice of Norwegian judicial perversion in relying on the word of someone which is completely uncorroborated, as being true, by asking the Court of Appeal to believe the 'word' of policewoman Torill Sorte that my mother told her she had put me in a mental hospital. If the Court of Appeal does not believe Torill Sorte, then it must pronounce her as being a liar and she must face the consequences.

The fact that Vegard Aaløkken withdrew Torill Sorte's statement regarding my mother's alleged conversation with her was only because a tape recording was played in Court flatly contradicting this policewoman's allegations. I therefore believe that Vegard Aaløkken was trying to save himself from possible criminal charges of conspiracy to pervert the course of justice - conspiracy with the liar Torill Sorte and the liar and registered mental patient, Heidi Overaa. It was a filthy trick to play on me to put Torill Sorte's statement into Court two or three days before the trial calculated to give me no time whatsoever to consider it and disprove it. Fortunately, from the material I had with me, I proved Torill Sorte to be a liar. She admitted in Court she had no idea that I had recorded her telephone conversations with me and her one telephone conversation with my mother, which caught her out completely. What happened to all the time in the previous sixteen months for the defence to put in its statements?

20. Let us not forget the evidence that is with the Court from other parties. The Drammen policeman Svein Jensen (Norwegian version enclosed) (Exhibit 3), the policeman of Bergen, Henrik Dugstad (Norwegian version enclosed) (Exhibit 4) and Heidi's former best friend Ann-Kristin Horvei (Norwegian version enclosed) (Exhibit 5), who all cast severe doubts on Heidi Overaa's ability to tell the truth.

Also, how do we know Heidi's stepmother did not have good reason to report her to the Child Protection Unit?

21. Regarding the witness, Dr. Petter Broch, I confirm again that after my arrest in Bergen in 1990 I telephoned him in exasperation at the assortment of lies Heidi gave the police, to see if he could shed some light on the matter. Broch did not betray any detail about his patient Heidi Overaa but did tell me two important things:

that Heidi told him I was her "favourite"; and

that Heidi told him she made a lot of other men very angry.

I followed up my conversation with Broch by sending him a letter and a tape-recorded repetition of the exact contents of that letter (for easy listening). He stated in Court that he'd thrown away the letter and tape, which he found "repugnant." An allegation which I dispute entirely. Broch should have kept the material. Broch is not an independent witness and his letter to the Court of 9th September 2001 betrays his lack of knowledge of the true facts.

The 'facts' quoted in Dr. Broch's letter are clearly wrong:

In his third paragraph, he says that in 1982 in England, "The contact with this Egyptian was very difficult. He was insistent and tried to behave as if she was his property."

The letters from Heidi Schøne from 1982 to 1985 to me will clearly indicate that the above statement from Broch is completely untrue. He is just trying to fit me into his prejudiced and false stereotypical view of the Egyptian/Muslim male. I was born in England and have a German mother.

461

On this basis, the reliability of Broch's evidence must be open to question. I presume Broch has not seen any of the letters Heidi Overaa wrote to me.

I marvel at how so much of my alleged "disgusting," "repugnant," "obscene" evidence has all been thrown away including 400 obscene letters I was supposed to have written to Heidi Overaa and a letter threatening to kill her son. Such vital damning evidence 'no longer' exists. All we have is the 'word' of those who allege the evidence existed.

Again, on my hearing of the allegation of attempted rape in 1995, I phoned Dr. Broch to see if he had notes which he could refer to in Court as I wanted to subpoena him to give evidence as to Heidi's condition. He told me that he could not remember that far back – to 1988/9 - but that even if she did tell him of this allegation, he would not know "whether it was true." Dr. Broch has admitted in Court that we have had some conversations during which I was "always polite." At no time did Dr. Broch ever tell me or write to me that my letter and tape was "repugnant." Such strong language and such serious allegations will need more than the 'word' of any witness, regardless of background.

22. My evidence before the Court clearly reveals that there is no basis for the quote that I "may be" suffering from erotic paranoia. Clearly I did not imagine Heidi Schøne was very fond of me and Professor Nils Rettersdøl was told nothing by the Verdens Gang journalist about "the foreigner," "the Muslim man."

23. I enclose a copy of the original letter retrieved from my London lawyer of 13th August 1990 – a contemporaneous record – evidencing the fact of my meeting a few days earlier with Heidi Schøne that summer (Exhibit 6). Heidi communicated often with me afterwards, as already mentioned, even telling me her son Daniel needed an operation on his nose, and that he doesn't know what it's like to have a father.

24. Let me relate the fact that on oath before Judge Stilloff, Heidi Overaa said that I had applied for a residence permit for Norway. Another lie. What on earth would I do with myself in Norway without being able to earn a living? Heidi's desperation is pathetic. She is quite simply a liar of the highest order. And mentally ill.

25. Neither Heidi Schøne nor the newspapers saw my letter dated 17.11.97 as it went, as I well knew (see copy letter 9.11.95 from Heidi's former lawyer, Tomm Skaug, to me) (Exhibit 7) straight to the police as Heidi's mail was diverted. Diverted to stop her receiving enquires from other Norwegians as to my reports sent to third parties; my own 'newspaper' if you like, giving people an idea of my accuser's own sexual background to present a more balanced view to hysterical newspaper reports from 1995. In the period mid-1997 to date, I have written no more than a handful of letters to Heidi in single figures, telling her basically that I wished the ground would swallow her up so I could forget the filth she conspired to have printed on me, and also telling her I would take her to Court. But this was information for the police to read, in the hope they would pass it on to Heidi, and understand my frustration.

I called Heidi "a killer" in a postcard with reference to her two abortions, in reaction to her telling the newspapers I had threatened to kill her son. Even the author of this report – Ingunn Røren – told me (in my taped conversation) that she is not saying I actually made such a threat, only that Heidi said that is what I allegedly did. The Association of Lawyers for the Defence of the Unborn (ALDU) of Great Britain themselves describe abortion as "killing," so I am not alone in using this description for abortion.

Heidi Overaa's 'abortion mentality,' that of destroying anything that gets in her way, has never gone away. Her objective in those 1995 newspapers articles was to destroy my character.

26. The PFU has been proven to be an ineffective, virtually useless organisation, when looking at my evidence with the Court. Their report of 24.8.99 is a work of capitulation that does not withstand hard scrutiny.

27. Heidi Schøne admitted to the Court to adopting the untruths and lies printed in the 1995 and 1998 newspaper articles, on oath. So how can her evidence as to my conduct as a whole – for which there is no documentary evidence pre-1995 – be reasonably believable, let alone "true"?

28. Judge Stilloff should have made it quite clear in his **conclusion** that both my lawyer and Vegard Aaløkken agreed that I did not write "300 letters to Heidi Schøne in 1997 to 1998" as quoted by Drammens Tidende on 14.7.98. This was one of the reasons I went to Court; to clearly establish that this allegation was an outrageous lie as it would then totally discredit all of Drammens Tidende's various reports on me.

29. The Judge is no psychiatrist and is way out of line in saying that my reports on Heidi's life "fully reveal a pathological interest in her." They fully reveal the truth of her past and my intense anger at her outrageous lies. How many thousands of copies of Verdens Gang, Bergens Tidende and Drammens Tidende were sold on the 'sex sells label' in May 1995? Tens of thousands. My reports on Heidi's past do not reveal an "erotic interest" in her. They describe her sexual conduct and other events which the public must be made aware of.

30. The desire for the newspapers to give me anonymity "so as to protect me from myself " is humbug. They didn't name me for fear of being successfully sued in Court. Besides, it is clear that the newspapers have lied on a grand scale.

I believe Heidi may well have been paid for her many newspaper stories and ask her lawyer to admit or deny this.

31. Heidi Schøne herself DID NOT even give an interview to Ingunn Røren for the 14.7.98 article, contrary to Stilloff's claim – her then husband did – as evidenced by the very word of Ingunn Røren in my concrete [taped] evidence before the Court. It was the journalist who called me the "Muslim man" in the first sentence of her article and as we now know she based her reason for doing this on her own lies to the PFU – exposed by me in my own documented evidence. Heidi Schøne never herself called me a Muslim in that 1998 article. [Judge Stilloff wrongly claimed that Heidi herself called me a "Muslim" in that article whereas of course it was the journalist who personally labelled me a "Muslim."].

32. I called Heidi Overaa "a Christian pervert" only because she perverted the true values of Christianity by her wholesale lies **after** she claimed to be a born-again Christian. My own mother was born a Christian Protestant. I went to a Church of England primary school. I have written articles in the English press praising prominent Christians. This must be made very clear by me. Again, neither the press nor Heidi saw this "Christian pervert" letter at the time – it went straight to the police.

33. I had only referred to myself as "the Muslim man" because Bergens Tidende in 1995 called me the "Muslim man" sixteen times. They and Verdens Gang began the "Muslim man" line, something that would cause riots if it were printed in such a context in England. I had to maintain my anonymity but at the same time allow the Norwegian public to know who it was that wrote my 'PRESS RELEASE' responding to the 1995 articles, which the Court has.

The Muslim cause in Bosnia was a very tragic and noble one which I have in this country very publicly associated myself with. To relate my association with this cause to justify calling me the "Muslim man" in the Norwegian press coverage without reference to the Bosnia tragedy, but with specific connection to mental illness, erotic paranoia, sexual harassment and perversion is a crime. The Judge's reasoning in condoning the use of the words "Muslim man" in Drammens Tidende is utterly perverse and must be exposed as such.

34. The Judge doubts my only motives for revenge on Heidi Overaa were "just" allegations of attempted rape and threats to kill her son (as if these were just insignificant allegations). He is right. The other motives so very obviously include the numerous other lies she told in the newspapers printed in 1995, together with her ex-husband and the journalists – lies which Heidi Overaa has admitted to adopting in their entirety.

35. Judge Stilloff on 25th August 2000 allowed me to proceed to trial knowing fully of my 2,500 plus reports in four very different formats – English and Norwegian – and said nothing condemnatory then about the rights or wrongs of my reports or my actions. He had plenty of time before this to consider my evidence and even asked the lawyers for Drammens Tidende and Heidi Schøne to settle the case. He accepted and the Defence accepted my transcribed phone calls of various conversations with Norwegians yet Stilloff mentioned nothing at all on them in his judgement.

463

36. Advokat Karsten Gjone recognised me from the Drammens Tidende article of 14.7.98 and has, I believe, written to the Court to confirm this. He recognised me on the morning the article was printed, relying on his own special knowledge of the facts already within his grasp. My reputation was damaged. Moreover Karsten Gjone was found negligent by the Norwegian Bar Association in his treatment of my case having missed the time limits to sue Verdens Gang, Bergens Tidende and Drammens Tidende for their 1995 articles. Stig Lunde also unfortunately missed the time limit to go to the Supreme Court on the appeal of the 1998 Drammens Tidende article, the Judge mysteriously refusing to exercise his discretion to consider our appeal due to the fact it was Stig Lunde's fault and not mine. Karsten Gjone's recognition of me in the 1998 Drammens Tidende article is sufficient basis for a libel claim and must be ruled on specifically by the Court.

37. Daniel Overaa is now 16 years old and I will subpoena him to the Court to let me reassure him that his mother's allegations regarding "threats" etc. are totally false. There are also one or two questions I would like to put to him.

38. I ask for Heidi Schøne to be found guilty and for my costs to be paid by her. Judge Stilloff should not have penalised me in costs in any event as in August 2000 he clearly ruled that I had a good case against Schøne and Drammens Tidende in spite of my telling him about my information campaign and already having a copy of one report on Heidi's life: amongst the reports that I told him 2,500 of which had been circulated in Norway. Besides, I am not liable to pay Value Added Tax on her costs, as I am not a Norwegian citizen and am domiciled abroad.

Further, Heidi's legal costs must be taxed by a law costs draftsman to ensure that her costs are justified.

The law gives me a month to appeal, yet Judge Stilloff orders me to pay costs within 14 days of the date of his judgement. Another contradiction in this seriously flawed verdict.

39. The serious falsehoods and the racist/anti Muslim comments made in the newspapers in 1995 and 1998 against me and Judge Stilloff's incompetent judgement would never be accepted by the English judiciary as fair in the least. Also, it is unsafe in the circumstances to rely on the word of Heidi Overaa – a state registered mental patient and proven liar with a history of mental and sexual instability.

40. I appeal directly to the Court to forward to me the following evidence which I have not seen:

- Heidi Overaa's 1997 report to the Mjøndalen police that I threatened to kill her son in a letter.

- Advokat Tomm Skaug's report to the Drammen police of 1995.

- Torill Sorte's 1997 statement submitted to the Drammen Court on or around 13th January 2002 that my mother told her she had put me in a mental hospital.

41. I ask Vegard Aaløkken to produce to me the name and address of Heidi's doctor in Bergen at the time of her pregnancy to her son Daniel in 1986 as I will have to subpoena him regarding the two AIDS tests she told me she had <u>after</u> her son was born because she was worried about catching HIV as a result of Gudmund Johannessen's intravenous heroin abuse. Similarly, I would like the names of all private Aids test clinics in Bergen that Heidi and Gudmund in the alternative may have attended. Heidi has denied in Court that Gudmund ever injected heroin, so I ask Heidi to allow her doctor to waive his obligation of confidentiality to her (as she did for her psychiatrist, Dr. Petter Broch) in order to prove that she did not have two AIDS tests **after** giving birth to Daniel. I know all women are compulsorily AIDS tested before giving birth in Norway. If Heidi does not waive the doctor/patient confidentiality relationship in this regard I ask the Court to assume that she has been lying on oath when she says Gudmund Johannessen did not inject heroin. There would be no reason whatsoever for them to have two Aids tests each after Daniel was born if Johannessen had not been injecting heroin.

I estimate that in the region of 600,000 newspapers from Verdens Gang, Bergens Tidende and Drammens Tidende were sold on my story. The publicity I have generated against Heidi Overaa to put my side of the case in the face of evil rubbish, is insignificant compared to what I faced for the last eight years. I do not want to hear again complaints by Vegard Aaløkken, the Norwegian police, or

464

Even after my Easter 1986 visit when I allegedly blackmailed her she continued for two more years until she left for Drammen, to speak to me on the phone, relating for example how she had got a job in a photographic processing laboratory. That the boss of this laboratory often delivered flowers to her home in gratitude for her good work. In 1987 he invited her and her son Daniel to Disneyland in Florida with his own family. Heidi told me they only went for a week but at the end of it she had "had enough." They stopped off in transit at Copenhagen Airport on the way home to Oslo. I also learnt from Heidi that Gudmund Johannessen's parents had given her an old Volvo to drive and that they had a snack shop (which they later sold).

Stig Lunde had recently given me the 'good news' that a Norwegian Revenue ruling from July 2001 had decreed that Value Added Tax had to be paid on all legal services, even to foreigners living outside the jurisdiction. The Norwegian Bar Association had told Lunde it was not payable but the Norwegian Revenue disagreed and one Saturday morning Lunde pleaded with me to immediately send him £3,000 for the VAT or else he'd be in trouble with the revenue. So I sent him the money on his promise that he'd write a letter to the revenue trying to get me a refund for the tax. In England, non-E.U. citizens do not pay VAT on legal services. In Norway VAT was 24%.

Of course, my claim against the Vesta Insurance Company for lawyer Karsten Gjone's negligence was now in jeopardy, so it was very important I got this Appeal in. I'd written to Judge Stilloff to ask him for more time to get his judgement translated and also pressed him to take action on policewoman Torill Sorte's perjury. Whilst he wrote to me on other matters, he did not reply on my two specific aforementioned requests but told me that he'd spoken to Stig Lunde who had agreed to help me put in a proper appeal. I was totally dependent on Lunde making the appeal in time using his own judgement and it was nerve-racking seeing him get the Appeal in on the last possible day - 13th March 2002 - being exactly one month after he'd received the judgement from the Court. Knowing the Norwegians as I do, had it been one day late, I'm sure the Appeal Court would have rejected it altogether. When I got Lunde's Appeal translated nine days later, I then formulated my Supplemental Appeal.

Lunde told me it could be months before the Appeal would be heard. But this time I wanted to handle the Appeal trial myself, to ensure that Heidi Schøne and the witnesses got the proper cross-examination their evidence deserved. Lunde himself had demonstrated that cross-examination was not his forte.

The trouble that a good looking woman can inflict on the innocent was amply illustrated by the 2001 story of the former Dutch supermodel, Karen Mulder. She convinced the French prosecuting authorities to investigate allegations that she was raped by royalty. The Independent newspaper of Friday 30th November 2001 reported thus:

The Independent 30th November 2001

Former Supermodel claims she was raped by royalty

A FRENCH magistrate is investigating allegations by the retired Dutch supermodel Karen Mulder that she was raped by a member of a European Royal Family, other famous people and leading figures in the French modelling industry.
Ms Mulder, 33, first made the allegations during the recording of a French television programme before a studio audience last month. Her claims were regarded as so devastating and so potentially libellous, that the interview was cut from the show.
However, Ms Mulder had made almost exactly the same accusations in a statement to French police several days earlier. The public prosecutor's office in Paris confirmed

yesterday that it was taking her allegations seriously enough to start a criminal investigation for "rape by persons unknown."

Her allegations will be investigated by an examining magistrate Jean-Pierre Gaury. Sources in the public prosecutor's office said he would be looking at physical and other evidence which appeared to corroborate at least part of Ms Mulder's story.

Ms Mulder, born in the Netherlands in 1968, was for many years among the 10 best-paid models in the world. She retired a year ago and is currently being treated in a private psychiatric clinic in Paris.

The former supermodel was invited to record an interview on 31 October for a show on France 2 television, called Tout le Monde en Parle (Everyone is talking about it). The intention was to revisit allegations made by a BBC documentary two years ago that young models were often sexually exploited by leading figures in the modelling industry. To the astonishment of the show's presenters and the studio, Ms Mulder dissolved into tears and said she had been persistently raped from her childhood up until last April.

She alleged that she had been "hypnotised" and raped by modelling agency executives and a series of well-known men, including a member of a continental royal family.

The interview was cut from the show and the studio audience was sworn to secrecy. Nevertheless, accounts of what happened have been circulating on the internet and by e-mail for the past four weeks.

An e-mail account by a person claiming to have witnessed the television show says Ms Mulder claimed to have been raped by an "incalculable number of famous people in France and abroad."

Yesterday the newspaper Le Parisien reported that Ms Mulder had previously approached French police and made a formal statement containing very similar allegations to those made on the show. The public prosecutor's office confirmed yesterday that it had ordered an investigation against "X" (or persons unknown) for rape.

"Considering the celebrity of the complainant, but also taking account of evidence which she has provided which could form the basis of proofs, we have decided to appoint an examining magistrate to investigate the case," a judicial source told Le Parisien.

The source said the information to be examined included "physical evidence." The newspaper said the judge would now be seeking a medical report on Ms Mulder, who was said to be in a state of "acute distress."

Friends of the model told Le Parisien that her psychiatric problems might be connected to her difficulties in adjusting to her retirement a year ago.

But Ms Mulder's friends also pointed out that the former supermodel had been known as a level-headed person, who had always been prepared to lend her celebrity to help charitable causes.

Her modelling career was launched at the age of 17 when she won a competition organised by the French modelling agency Elite. She later worked for Yves Saint-Laurent, Chanel, Valentino and Versace. She stopped appearing on the catwalk in 1997 and retired from modelling last year, saying she wanted a new career as a film actor or singer.

***

Many people would have thought, 'No smoke without fire.' On 24th December 2002 the Hello! magazine reported the supermodel's retraction of her allegations and her apparent suicide bid:

Karen Mulder
Supermodel in 'Suicide Bid' Drama

Supermodel Karen Mulder, who a year ago suffered a highly publicized breakdown and spent several months in a psychiatric clinic, was last week at the centre of confusing 'suicide bid' story.

First, press reports across the world claimed that the 34-year old Dutch-born beauty had taken a near-fatal overdose of sleeping pills in her luxury Paris apartment and been rushed to the American Hospital in a coma. After having her stomach pumped, doctors pronounced that she would survive.

According to the reports, Karen had been saved by the quick thinking of a former boyfriend, French playboy and property developer Jean-Yves Le Fur. He had known that Karen had been feeling depressed and, when she did not answer the phone, he smashed through the front door to find her unconscious. Had emergency services arrived just one hour later, it was claimed, it would probably have been too late.

Shortly after the overdose story made headline news, however, Karen's father Ben Mulder told the Dutch press that it was "nonsense." Instead, he said his daughter was suffering from hallucinations and over fatigue and had checked herself back into the French psychiatric clinic from which she had been discharged earlier this year. "Karen went to her psychiatrist last Saturday and he convinced her that she should have herself committed again" he told the Dutch Daily *De Telegraaf.* "And that's what she has done. I'm sure now that she'll have a peaceful and quiet Christmas. She's been admitted into one of the best clinics in France and I hope that Karen will now take the time to fully recover."

Then, last Thursday, a third version of events emerged, Karen's former boyfriend Jean-Yves Le Fur, the man who had supposedly discovered the supermodel lying unconscious in her apartment, apparently denied that she had taken an overdose or that she had been rushed into hospital. While he refused to make a statement on the matter, sources close to him supplied some further information. They said Le Fur had gone to Karen's apartment on the day in question to pick her up and take her to a lunch appointment. Two Paparazzi were waiting outside the building and a row ensued. Le Fur apparently hit one of them and the photographer then took "revenge" by putting out the story about Karen's attempted suicide.

Since retiring from modelling, Karen has been enjoying some success as a pop singer and Le Fur's sources indicated that rather than being in hospital in Paris, she was elsewhere in France writing songs for her first album. Meanwhile, they said, Karen herself would not talk about what had happened and wanted the whole matter to die down.

By the end of the last week, mystery still surrounded exactly what had gone on. However, the furore brought fresh expressions of concern from Karen's friends about how she is adapting to life away from the modelling limelight.

A decade ago, she was one of the world's best-paid supermodels, appearing at glamorous parties on the arm of Prince Albert of Monaco or racing driver Eddie Irvine. However, she hit rock bottom last year when she recorded an interview with a French TV chat show in which she made untruthful claims – which she later withdrew – that she had been raped by former members of her model agency and been forced to sleep with various men, including Prince Albert, to advance her career.

Her claims were so wild that the producers felt they could not transmit the interview and destroyed the tape. Fearful about her paranoid state, they contacted her family and she was taken to the psychiatric clinic.

Karen's father Ben blamed the incident on drugs and the end of her career. "I'm convinced her sad breakdown is a result of her using cocaine" he said in an interview last year. "But she's also exhausted. For ten years she'd been flying all over the world and worked very hard. Physically and mentally she is burned out. And then her career was suddenly over."

Karen, meanwhile, later denied drugs had triggered her breakdown, but admitted she'd suffered from depression. "It was so bad that I couldn't get up" she said.

467

However, after several months of treatment at the psychiatric clinic, she checked herself out and declared that she was "moving back towards the light." She revealed she had written to Prince Albert to apologise for her untrue allegations and she lined up a role in a small French film. Karen then found immediate success as a pop singer when she released a version of Gloria Gaynor's hit I am What I Am, which made the top ten in France.

However, friends last week expressed concern that there might not be anyone close by to pull her up again should Karen plunge back into depression. As one French magazine recently pointed out: "Karen Mulder has no love, no man and no children."

***

Chapter 31

On 13th March 2002, when Stig Lunde put in my Appeal, I had to pay 16,750 Norwegian kroner (£1,434) in Court fees. On 5th April I sent Heidi Schøne's lawyer and the Court of Appeal my own Supplemental Appeal, in English, promising to have it translated into Norwegian in due course. I had to let the Court of Appeal know quickly, for my own peace of mind, just how monstrous an injustice had been meted out on me by Judge Stilloff. They could all read English.

Soon Lunde rang me up to tell me I had done the wrong thing by submitting the document in English, adding that I should have waited until the Appeal Court judge contacted him with directions as to a time limit for final submission of documents. Then I could send my version in Norwegian. As things stood, Lunde thought the Appeal Court judge would reject my Supplemental Appeal as it was not in the Norwegian language. Lunde continued by telling me that the points I raised on my own Appeal should in any case only be raised at the Appeal itself (at least a year away). I told Lunde that the Appeal hearing was so far off that I wanted my opponents to know the strength of my arguments now. Also that I could not guarantee the Appeal hearing would in fact ever take place, so distrustful was I of the Norwegian justice system, so it was better that I defend my position now.

My fears proved very real when on 23rd May 2002 Lunde faxed me a letter he had received from the Appeal Court dated 21st May 2002 which stated that the Court of Appeal wanted another 5,360 kroner (£460) from me in court fees to reach them by 5th June 2002 or else my Appeal would be dismissed! Say I'd been on holiday at the time? I was not happy! The reason for the extra fee was because the Appeal Court "discovered" that my Appeal would take more than a day to deal with – so the fee was higher, as the original fee was based on a one day trial.

On 24th May 2002 I asked my bank to urgently transfer the extra money straight to the Court's bank account at Gjensidige Bank in Oslo. It was received into the Court's account on 27th May 2002.

And what became of my three separate parallel civil proceedings against Drammens Tidende, Ingunn Røren and Heidi Schøne, commenced in the lowest form of court in Norway – the forliksrådet? Regarding my case against Drammens Tidende in the Drammen forliksråd, to recap, my argument was that the PFU did not inform me that I had the right to take legal proceedings against the newspaper after they had investigated my complaint. I was led to believe I could either use the PFU or the Courts, not both. Lunde eventually told me that my case against Drammens Tidende had been dismissed simply on the grounds that I had used the PFU and could not, therefore, go to court. Lunde had no information as to whether my argument on this point had been made at the hearing by the legal agents he appointed to represent me. I wasn't even told who the agents were by Lunde.

I 'won' my civil case against Heidi Overaa because her ex-husband mistakenly turned up for her and she stayed at home when she should have been present. If they had still been married then he could have represented her. She quickly appealed. Subsequently, my original criminal prosecution against her became a civil action only, as the criminal element had been removed by Drammens Tidende dropping out of the action. So now there were two civil actions which merged into one and that trial took place in January 2002 at the Drammen City Court, which I had lost.

As for my civil action against the journalist, Ingunn Røren, what happened here was beyond belief. Lunde had issued proceedings on 19th July 2001 in the Bergen forliksråd – the local court to Ingunn Røren – as she was now a journalist at Bergens Tidende. In the winter months I had asked Lunde a couple of times whether he'd heard anything on this case and he said, "No, nothing." So before Christmas I asked him to call the Bergen forliksråd to see what was happening. Unfortunately he did not get around to ringing them. So after Christmas I rang the court myself and no record of the case could be found on their computer system. I told the court clerk to ring Lunde when he had located the court records to give him an update as to when a hearing date was to be given.

Then one day in April 2002, after close of business, (in Norway office hours are 8 a.m. to 4 p.m.) Lunde gave me a call to say that the Bergen forliksråd had recently written to him saying that my case had been dismissed. Dismissed because "we" had not attended the hearing, for which the court said it had notified him in writing. Lunde told me that he in fact never received any notice from the court of the hearing date. It was now 4.35 p.m. Norwegian time and he said, "Today is the last day possible for an appeal." So long as he put the appeal in that evening's last post we would not miss the time limits. The appeal would consist of "trying to convince the Appeal Court" that we had not received the notice of hearing date, so that the Bergen forliksråd would be ordered to set another date for the case to be heard. However, Lunde added that there was a heavy burden of proof on him to prove he had not received the notice and it was unlikely he would win the appeal but he would try. And could I send him some money for the appeal? I just about managed to hold myself together! I said that in the circumstances it would be appropriate not to appeal. Lunde tried to change my mind saying that after all the money I'd spent "a little bit more now" wouldn't make much difference, especially as he blamed Ingunn Røren for so much of the mischief. But I was adamant. There was no point appealing if it was almost certain we were going to lose. I said goodbye and once again marvelled at the wonders of Norway's legal system and Lunde's part in it.

Chapter 32

Over the next few months there followed three written demands from the Statens Innkrevingssentral (SI) (the State Agency for the Recovery of Fines, Damages and Costs) for my settlement of the 10,000 kroner fine awarded against me by the Eiker Modem and Sigdal Magistrates Court in October 2001. With interest and costs it was, as at 1st June 2002, 11,005.00 kroner. I ignored the demands. Indeed, I was now intent on getting the verdict for the fine overturned due to the abuse of the legal process by the Norwegian Prosecutor, Dag Lyngås and the lies of Torill Sorte. On the 12th June 2002, I wrote a letter of complaint to the Norwegian Police Directorate in Oslo regarding Sorte's perjury. They wrote back to me on the 2nd July 2002, to say I should instead direct my complaint to the Complaints Investigation Commission (SEFO). Instead of passing my letter on to SEFO, they asked me to write to SEFO myself in Hønefoss, which I did on 6th July 2002.

I had at the end of June telephoned the Court of Appeal in Oslo to see if I could speak to a judge, a Mr Dag Stousland. He was responsible for the pre-trial administration of my appeal and I needed some information about the pre-trial processes and in particular wanted to ask him for a date by which the Norwegian translation of my Supplemental Appeal should be submitted. His secretary asked me to ring back at 2 p.m. Norwegian time as the judge told her he would have to look at the case file first. I phoned back at 2 p.m. precisely to be answered by, presumably, another judge who spoke perfect English. He was most accommodating and tried to put me through to Judge Dag Stousland. Unfortunately, Mr. Stousland was out of his room so I was asked to leave my office telephone number. I expressed my surprise that a Norwegian judge would bother to make an overseas call to me, but was assured such a favour was perfectly feasible. No call materialised. In eight years I had never received a single call from any Norwegian institution, despite several 'promises.' Instead, Judge Dag Stousland wrote to me on 2nd July – in Norwegian. On 5th July, Stig Lunde phoned me and left a message on my voicemail to very urgently call him back. When I did, the news was that he'd also received a copy of Judge Stousland's letter of 2nd July which gave me a time limit of 22nd July to submit my translated Supplemental Appeal. The English version was already lodged with my translation agency, so I immediately faxed them a letter at 8.51 p.m. on the Friday evening asking them to urgently translate the document. On Monday 8th July when business resumed, the Agency began the process of instructing the translator. The document was 15 pages long and so it would be a race against time. On 16th July, the translators e-mailed the Norwegian version to my office and I immediately sent it on to the Oslo Court of Appeal by Swiftair courier at a cost of £45.80. The document was signed for by the Court at 12.32 p.m. on Thursday 18th July – which left me just two spare working days to the deadline.

Lunde himself also made further submissions to the Court, similarly sending a copy of my Supplemental Appeal in Norwegian and adding three new witnesses to give evidence at my trial: my mother, plus an English journalist to speak on the lack of ethics used by the Norwegian press and an English psychiatrist specialising in adolescent behaviour, including Munchausen's Syndrome. In the event I did not have the funds or the time to enlist these two experts and dragging my mother over to Norway would have been too much of an imposition on her. I even had to have translated into Norwegian the short letter from the Norwegian Embassy to me of 20th April 1995 as well as my lawyer Reg Whittal's letter to the Bergen police of 19th June 1990 and the copy of my letter to Reg Whittal of 13th August 1990. I sent Lunde another £750 for his own legal fees. Finally, on 19th July 2002, Stig Lunde sent me the two Drammen Court Exhibits dated 22nd January 1997 and 23rd April 1997 being Mjøndalen Police Reports compiled and signed by Torill Sorte. On 29th August 2002, these were translated and I reproduce them in full below.

Nedre Eiker Police Station, Mjøndalen district – 22nd January 1997 – Report by Police Sergeant Torill Sorte

Case No. 3346/95

In April 1996, the author of the report took over the case involving Heidi Schøne (Overaa). At this time, Heidi and her husband Runar Schøne were called to the office. They did not have anything more to add to the statement.

It was clear that Heidi had been affected by this case. She was unable to tell anyone where she lived. She had changed her telephone number many times. Somehow, Frederick Delaware managed to find out where she lived. He also found out her telephone number. Heidi did not like to go out and socialise with her neighbours anymore. This was because Delaware had sent slanderous letters to all her neighbours, regardless of where she lived.

Heidi was also regularly called by people who had received letters from Delaware. It seemed as though Heidi had given up hope of getting rid of Delaware.

Since the author took over the case, Delaware has called 2-3 times a month from England. He has also sent many letters, see Appendix III.

Delaware feels as though he was exposed by Heidi, and is therefore using the letters to restore his reputation. The only thing that will get him to stop writing letters is meeting Heidi in a legal case. He believes that this will give him an opportunity to tell the world what a "whore" she is.

Delaware has also threatened to come to Norway. The author has said that everything would then be done to have him apprehended and sent back to England. Delaware believes that it is important that he comes to Norway in order to talk to Heidi face to face.

The author has also been in touch with Delaware's mother. She is an elderly woman who has given up trying to help her son. She says that he is sick and needs help. This is something they have always struggled with, and on one occasion he was admitted for treatment. His mother could not cope with all the trouble again, and therefore just lets him carry on.

Other girls have also been harassed by Delaware, and it was in connection with this that he was admitted for treatment.

Delaware has himself said that he uses a "detective" to find out where Heidi is at any one time, and what she is doing about him as a problem.

The author has read the letters that have been sent to various people. Many of these letters are identical, and Delaware claims that he has made about 200 copies of each letter he has sent out. The letters contain things that are insulting to Heidi, but no threats have been found.

There are reportedly threats in letters in connection with a statement from Bergen. These letters could not be found at Bergen police station.

See also the enclosed letters.

(Signature)

Nedre Eiker Police Station, Mjøndalen district – 23rd April 1997 – Report by Police Sergeant Torill Sorte

Case No. 9883/96

	Wednesday 16.04.97 10.30 a.m., taken at residence at Sollikroken 7.
Complainant	SCHØNE, Heidi Cecilie, national ID no. 200863-38298, Førde, lives at Sollikroken 7, 3058 Solbergmoen, tel. 32 87 17 25

Informed about the case, informed about statements and the responsibility to testify, willing to testify, she explains.

The complainant stands by the explanation that was given when she made the statement. She remembers that it was her husband, Runar Schøne, who signed the explanation, but she considers it her own.

The complainant has not heard from Delaware recently, but she has heard via neighbours that he is still calling in order to smear the complainant's reputation.

When asked how long this letter sending had been going on, the complainant answered that it had been ongoing for about 10 years. In the beginning, she used to answer the letters. She discovered that if she communicated with him, it would satisfy him and he would not contact her for a while. Gradually she grew tired of his letters, and since then things have just got worse and worse.

The reason why he is harassing the complainant is that he feels rejected. The complainant travelled as an au pair to England in 1981 and lived there for one year. While she was there, she lived in a suburb of London, called St. Albans.

The complainant knows that the parents of the complainant's alleged father, Solveig and Willy Johannessen (Solveig lives at Naustvegen 32, 5088 Mjølkeråen and Willy lives at Ullsberglia 125, 5091 Flakktveit) have reported Delaware. She believes that the statement was made to Åsane sheriff's office.

According to Willy, a letter was submitted with the statement, which contained death threats against the complainant and her son Daniel. The complainant believes that this threatening letter was written 7-8 years ago. The complainant will see if she can find copies of these threatening letters.

The parents of the complainant have also made a statement against Delaware on a number of occasions. The last time was about two years ago. Daniel's father reported Delaware a year ago. These statements were also given at Åsane sheriff's office.

When asked whether other people have been harassed by Delaware, the complainant replied that she was aware of two others. One was a fiancé of Delaware from Egypt. The complainant does not know whether this was reported. Delaware also harassed a schoolgirl, who was 16 at the time. This happened about 5 years ago. At this time, Delaware's mother called the complainant and she had discovered how Delaware harassed the complainant. She promised to commit Delaware if he did not stop.

The father of the 16 year old girl was a policeman. Delaware was apprehended outside the girl's school. He was reported at this time. Delaware has told the complainant about this.

The complainant wishes Delaware to stop his terrorising, and if it takes a legal case to do this, she wants this to take place as soon as possible.

The complainant requests that Frederick Delaware be charged and punished, because he has systematically, by telephone and letter slandered and threatened her and her family for 14 years. The complainant has no compensation claim relating to the case.

She has been informed of her right to submit a claim for insult and injury, and she will come back to this.

Read out, read through and approved

Sign. on draft copy

(Signature)

On 20th and 24th August and 3rd September 2002, I wrote to Judge John Morten Svendgård of the Oslo City Court who was handling the complaint against Torill Sorte. I had spoken to him for a good 10 minutes on Monday 19th August discussing the procedure.

I sent the judge the transcripts of my telephone conversations with the policemen Svein Jensen and Henrik Dugstad as well as nine conversations with Torill Sorte ending with those of 1st April and 22nd April 1998, plus two copies of the actual tape recording of my mother speaking to Torill Sorte on 22nd April 1996.

My letter to Judge Svendgård of 3rd September 2002 said:

For the attention of
Judge John Morten Svendgård
of Oslo Tingrett

Dear Mr. Svendgård,

Policewoman Torill Sorte

I have this morning received the translations in English of two Reports from Torill Sorte dated 22nd January 1997 and 23rd April 1997. I enclose copies of the Reports in Norwegian and in English.

I comment as follows:

<u>22nd January 1997 Report</u>

(a) The 5th paragraph: "He believes that this will give him an opportunity to tell the world what a "whore" she is.

It must be clear from the transcripts of my telephone conversations with Torill Sorte that there was much more to this case than Heidi Schøne's promiscuity. The emphasis by Sorte on the word "whore" is malicious and deceitful. Ironic, when all the newspapers accuse me of "16 years of sex-terror," from a girl, Heidi Schøne, whose own mental illness is attributed to her promiscuity, from her psychiatrist, Dr. Petter Broch.

(b) The 6th paragraph: "Delaware has threatened to come to Norway … … in order to talk face to face with Heidi."

You will see from the transcript of my 'Further conversation with Torill Sorte in June 1996' as per the last paragraph that I wanted to sit down with Heidi Schøne <u>and</u> Torill Sorte. Sorte implies that I am threatening trouble, when all I want is to expose Heidi Schøne in the same room with Torill Sorte present.

(a)   The 7th paragraph: "The author has been in touch with Delaware's mother … …" etc.

You have the tape with the conversation between my mother and Sorte. Sorte is lying big time.

My mother is <u>not</u> elderly.

My mother has never told Torill Sorte that I am sick and need help as you will see from my mother's letters.

I have never been admitted for treatment anywhere, ever. (Unlike Heidi Schøne, ironically).

<u>23rd April 1997 Report</u>

(a) 6th paragraph: ".... the statement, which contained death threats against the complainant and her son Daniel. The complainant believes that this threatening letter was written 7 - 8 years ago ..."

Daniel Overaa in 1989 or 1990 would have been 3 – 4 years old respectively. Where is the original "letter"? If it is at Åsane police station let them produce it. Heidi Schøne has had several years to do this. Such a vital piece of evidence too!! No copies? No original? No – because the letter was never written; it never existed.

(b) 8th paragraph: ".... At this time, Delaware's mother called the complainant [1992] ..... she promised to commit Delaware if he did not stop."

Another lie. You have seen my mother's evidence. In 1992, Heidi Overaa, I believe, didn't even have a phone.

I am sick and tired of Schøne's lawyer calling me "mentally ill," "a rapist" and other untrue descriptions in court and now to the Court of Appeal. Heidi Schøne is a mentally ill woman and a liar. She must be prosecuted for trying to pervert the course of justice. In 1986 she insisted I had "attempted" to rape her. In 1995 Ingunn Røren, journalist, insisted to me (it was taped) that again Heidi alleged "attempted" rape and "not rape." In 1998 Heidi changed her allegation to "actual rape" by "holding her down."

Heidi Schøne has complained about other men raping or threatening to rape her. She certainly knows the difference between attempted rape and actual rape. I have to this day, despite years of effort, never seen the "attempted rape" police report, or the "actual rape" police report. This is monstrous.

For your information let me enclose one or two of Heidi's letters to me from 1984 to 1985. If you read them you will see the reality of Heidi Overaa's feelings for me. She did not think I would have kept letters from such a long time ago, but fortunately they were not thrown away. From these letters it is clear that Schøne's statement in the last but one paragraph of the 23rd April 1997 Police Report "... ... threatened her and her family for 14 years ..." is not true. The 14 years would go back to 1983. Besides which she asked me to help her in 1988 to deal with her drug abuser/criminal convict boyfriend Gudmund Johannessen, a fact admitted in Drammen City Court. This request is hardly consistent with her later fabricated evidence.

Yours sincerely,

Frederick Delaware

Up to now, Stig Lunde himself took no part at all in helping me complain against Torill Sorte, nor for that matter did Harald Wibye. Lunde, indeed, tried to discourage me by saying I was making "very serious allegations" against Sorte. Lunde refused even to discuss the matter with my mother! Why on earth not?

What Torill Sorte was alleging was that between my mother's conversation with her (which I had recorded on tape) on 22nd April 1996 and Torill Sorte's report of 22nd January 1997 my mother had spoken to her again to say that I had been "admitted for treatment." And to think Torill Sorte continued to talk to me in 1998 without telling me that my "elderly" mother (she was 62 in 1997) had spoken to her again to tell her I had after all been committed to a mental hospital! Moreover, when lawyer Eric Lindset of law firm Elden & Elden visited the Drammen police station to look at the papers in June 1999 he never told me about these two 1997 reports.

On 22nd August 2002, I received a copy of a submission in Norwegian from Heidi's lawyer to the Court of Appeal. Vegard Aaløkken had, some months before, phoned Stig Lunde alleging that I myself was directly responsible for sending a "false notification" to the credit reference agency Dun & Bradstreet in Oslo dated 5th April 2002, for a 50,000 kroner court judgement against Heidi Schøne. I told Lunde that I was not "behind it" and asked Lunde to make further enquiries as to the nature of the Dun & Bradstreet Report. Lunde told me he'd wait to see whether Vegard Aaløkken wrote complaining to the Court of Appeal. I told Lunde I would speak to Dun & Bradstreet to find out what was going on but he implored me not to, in case Aaløkken "used it against" me on accusations of fraudulent conduct. Aaløkken did complain to the Court. On 19th July Lunde faxed me a copy of Dun & Bradstreet's letter to Vegard Aaløkken which stated that the 50,000 kroner award arose from the judgement in my favour against Heidi Schøne obtained in the Nedre Eiker forliksråd in the autumn of 2001, when her ex-husband turned up for her as she didn't want to represent herself. I was given immediate judgement as an ex-husband could not represent his former spouse.

I told Lunde that it was obvious the Nedre Eiker forliksråd themselves had told Dun & Bradstreet of my judgement (which Heidi Schøne appealed against) but Lunde disagreed, saying the forliksråd had no power to do this.

When Vegard Aaløkken's submission of 22nd August 2002 to the Court of Appeal was sent to me, I promptly phoned Dun & Bradstreet in Norway – the gentleman dealing with the case was called Tore Lia. He got the details up on his computer and told me that the Nedre Eiker forliksråd informed them of the judgement but that reference to it was deleted a few days later because Heidi Schøne had appealed. I then faxed him Aaløkken's letter to the Court of Appeal of 22nd August 2002 so he could tell me in English what it said. As I'd hoped, it was indeed an apology acknowledging that he, Aaløkken, had not appreciated that the Nedre Eiker forliksråd had notified Dun & Bradstreet of the judgement. Lunde had not seen this submission of 22nd August 2002 from Aaløkken so when I spoke to him on 5th September 2002 he expressed his surprise insisting that the forliksråd itself was not allowed to inform Dun & Bradstreet of the judgement.

Lunde would now write to the Court of Appeal trying to persuade them that I should be allowed to act for myself and not use a Norwegian lawyer, which latter method the Court had indicated was their preference.

Chapter 33

I had for two years now been operating a website on which I had scanned in all Heidi Schøne's photographs from the Norwegian newspapers and given my own side of the story without, of course, giving my own name.

I had also scanned in numerous articles on sexual health from the English newspapers over the last 10 years or so. It was a huge site and I had spent a lot of money on it. The most compelling aspect was my anti-abortion campaign which included real photographs of aborted foetuses from 8 weeks up to 24 weeks old. I was advertising this website extensively in Norway via fax and email. This new fax and email campaign and website promotion infuriated the Norwegians and the leading Norwegian newspaper, Aftenposten, made enquiries by email of my website. It coincided with my Internet Service Provider (ISP) taking the website off the internet after receiving a complaint but the ISP refused to tell me who complained. I quickly transferred the website to another ISP and normal service resumed. So on 10ᵗʰ April 2002 I phoned Aftenposten's inquisitive journalist, a Mrs. Reidun Samuelsen, who said she was in the process of collecting material to do a story on this matter. She was most upset when, at the end of our chat, I informed her that I had taped the whole conversation. She slammed the phone down on me. For weeks afterwards I could not find any Aftenposten article on me on their website so I assumed Reidun Samuelsen had, eventually, not bothered to do a story on me. But on the 23ʳᵈ April 2002 her newspaper did three large articles on abortion and teenage sexual attitudes and behaviour. I took it as a back-handed compliment. These articles were put on my website.

Earlier in this book I reproduced The Sun newspaper article of the 27ᵗʰ April 1998 regarding the Englishman David Coombs who claimed to have bedded 227 Norwegian girls. True or not, The Sun happily otherwise promoted the widespread belief that Scandinavian girls were easy going in their sexual morals. Heidi Schøne was certainly one of them. But just how much the Norwegians hate being criticized by outsiders for their promiscuous girls was amply illustrated by the newspaper Aftenposten's English language website article dated the 6ᵗʰ February 2002 reproduced below:

Minister rebukes sex-obsessed imams

Minister of Local Government and Regional Development Erna Solberg is shaken by the condescending attitude by Islamic religious leaders in Norway and what she feels is their labelling of Norwegian women as 'whores.'

Minister Solberg is most worried about the potential damage the imams may cause by spreading their attitudes in immigrant communities, the newspaper Bergens Tidende reports.

Solberg believes that Muslim leaders impart an image of Norwegian women as more than generally promiscuous and unfaithful.

"I have personally met with imams and it strikes me that several of them live and work here without learning to know Norwegian society. They come here and barely learn how to speak Norwegian. This has to be a serious problem for Muslim communities," said Solberg.

Solberg believes that the attitudes held by imams give immigrant boys a mistaken view of Norwegian girls.

"It damages Norwegian immigrant youth, because by their behavior they strengthen prejudices against Norwegian society," Solberg said.

At a Conservative Party conference in Bergen on Tuesday Solberg announced that problems concerning integration have a central spot on the agenda. Solberg said the government would see that a far more effective and demanding Norwegian language education program would be put in place. So far such education has been offered, now it will become mandatory.

***

Again, such language would, I believe, never be used by a British newspaper and further illustrates Norwegian prejudice against Muslims. Did the imams actually use the word "whores"? How on earth can the imams be properly described as "sex-obsessed," when all they were probably doing was making a social comment much like, say, the Daily Mail newspaper in Britain does every day?

How ironic that on Tuesday 26th November 2002 the same newspaper, Aftenposten, printed a headline story on its English language website as follows:

Norwegians top list over 'one-night stands'

Young, sex-happy Norwegians are the quickest to hop in bed with casual conquests, according to a new survey. Perhaps they're only bragging, but 72 percent of those questioned said they've had "one-night stands."

Next in line were the South Africans, with 70 percent claiming one-night stands. The survey was conducted by condom maker Durex over its web site, with 50,000 men and women in 22 countries taking part.

The Norwegians also scored highest among those reporting sex on the first date. A full 32 percent of the 2,500 questioned claimed that first dates often ended with more than a kiss.

The French, however, lived up to their reputation as the world's most amorous. The average French man and woman, according to the survey, has sex 167 times a year.

That compares to 152 times a year for the Danes and 144 times a year for the Norwegians. The average among all 22 countries taking part in the survey was 139 times a year.

Only half of all Norwegians said they used condoms during their "one-night stands," even though half of all Norwegians believe HIV and AIDS are major problems.

"This means that both we and the health authorities still have a lot of work to do, in encouraging people to have safe sex," said Arianne Gravdal of SSL Healthcare, which owns Durex. The survey, she said, shows that Norwegians are willing to take a big risk to have sex.

Kjell-Olav Svendsen, a doctor and lecturer at the University of Oslo, said he finds the survey results disturbing.

"It's worrisome that so many fail to use a condom during casual sex," he said.

***

Other newspapers in Norway, Verdens Gang amongst them also covered the 'One-Night Stands' story. This unlikely source of support, I felt, vindicated the position I had taken over sexual issues arising from my own 'Norwegian experience.'

On Tuesday 17th September 2002, Judge John Morten Svendgård of the Oslo City Court telephoned my mother and they spoke at length on the matter of Police Sergeant Torill Sorte's perjury. This was the first time ever that anyone other than my lawyer, Stig Lunde, had phoned England. It was obviously essential that my mother confirm matters herself to the Judge. Immediately thereafter the Judge called

478

me on my mobile phone whilst I was driving home, updating me and asking that I give my permission for him to speak to Stig Lunde who had witnessed Sorte's perjury in Court the previous January. I gave my permission.

Later on, speaking to Lunde, he was of the opinion that Judge Svendgård would not investigate whether Sorte had perjured herself but would only look into the matter of a "breach of confidentiality" by Sorte. I didn't understand. "What has breach of confidentiality got to do with it?" I asked Lunde. "The reason I have asked the Judge to investigate is solely on the grounds of Sorte's perjury." Lunde retorted by saying that Sorte should not have disclosed to the Court my alleged mental illness. I angrily told Lunde that I had not been put in a mental hospital and that Sorte had definitely lied on oath! It was enough to drive me crazy, all this clap-trap!

On the 22nd October 2002 the Borgarting Lagmannsrett (Court of Appeal) wrote to me in Norwegian notifying me that the appeal trial had been set for a year hence: Monday 13th October 2003 at 9.30 a.m. I later phoned Heidi's lawyer Vegard Aaløkken and he told me that he would only respond to Stig Lunde's appeal and my own supplemental appeal if the Court of Appeal forced him to. The Court had in fact given him a deadline by which to reply but there was no sanction if he didn't comply.

On the 4th November 2002 Vesta Insurance Company's Claims Department wrote to me regarding my claim for compensation for lawyer Karsten Gjone's negligence:

Dear Mr Delaware,

Claim for Damages against Solicitor Karsten Gjone

We refer to previous correspondence and numerous telephone conversations concerning the above.

We have considered the matter in view of all information sent us, your fax of 21st August 2002 included. Our conclusion is the same as the one we expressed in our letter to you of January 15th 1999.

Consequently, we are maintaining our rejection of your claim against Gjone and Vesta.

We beg to inform you that we consider the claim against Gjone to be time barred as no necessary steps have been taken to suspend the expiry of the Limitation period of 3 years.

Concerning your claim against Vesta we hereby inform you that Vesta will plead that the case is barred by lapse of time unless court action is taken or the matter brought in before the Insurance Complaints Office (Forsikringsklagekontoret) within 6 months from the date of this letter.

Sincerely yours,
Vesta Forsikring AS

Hans-Arnt Skjølberg

I faxed my reply to Skjølberg telling him that the Court of Appeal trial had been set for the following October and so it was premature for his company to reject my claim, but that in any event full reasons had to be given for this rejection. On 18th November 2002 I telephoned him and he told me that he was not legally obliged to give me reasons for rejecting my claim. He did say that my cards/letters to Heidi Schøne mentioned in Judge Stilloff's verdict "were not very nice" and that "the Drammen Court believed Heidi." In England insurance companies do give full reasons out of moral obligation and also because it would look bad for their case if they stayed silent. Vesta in Norway, however, were going to leave me completely in the dark only giving me the option of suing them in Court or appealing to the

Insurance Complaints Office. So by recorded delivery letter dated 3rd December 2002 I appealed to the Insurance Complaints Office emphasising that Vesta should not be allowed to operate a secret decision making process. Regarding my claim on Vesta that the law firm Elden and Elden had been negligent for not ensuring that they gave me accurate information as to my rights vis-à-vis the Norwegian Press Complaints Bureau (the PFU), Skjølberg merely told me on the phone that Elden and Elden did not think that they were at fault. Again no attempt was made to address my complaint with any legal analysis in writing.

Previously, I had been in touch with Henrik Lund of the Anti-Racist Centre in Oslo having sent him the main documents and all the newspaper cuttings on my case. He agreed with me that it was very wrong of the newspapers to call me the "Muslim" in the context that they did, but that he was unable to assess the tangle of allegation and counter-allegation in the paper work I had sent him.

The festive season was soon to be upon us. I was preparing a large celebration of my own. I would enjoy it. The Norwegians wouldn't. Not for the first time I employed a commercial operator who typed afresh onto his computer hundreds more fax numbers from the Bergen and Drammen telephone directories. A one page fax was prepared. As before, it contained Heidi's 'past' in Norwegian, her psychiatrist Dr. Broch's courtroom analysis of her in English and the address of my website. Overnight and every night for the two week period leading up to Christmas the faxes were sent by the computer. Happy Christmas Norway!

Chapter 34

In early January 2003 another 'sexual harassment' story hit the Norwegian press. This time it concerned Berit Riise the mother and agent of the Liverpool footballer John Arne Riise. She had accused the coach of her son's former Norwegian club, Aalesund, of sexual harassment during "a conversation" the two had in a meeting during the summer of 2001. The coach, Ivar Morten Normark, was quoted thus on Aftenposten's English webdesk:

> "This has been completely taken out of context," he said. He claims he was only joking when he tried to tell Berit Riise what Norway's soccer community thought of her. "I told her how my acquaintances view her and that it wasn't always positive," Normark said. He claimed there are always two questions soccer players and officials get when they say they're from Aalesund: "Do you know Berit Riise and how many times have you had sex with her?"

Berit Riise had made her sexual harassment charges during a televised debate on the Norwegian TV2 show. I saw on the Norwegian language website for Aftenposten and Verdens Gang extensive quotations on the legal aspects of the allegations from the lawyers Per Danielsen and Tor Erling Staff. Stig Lunde told me that eventually the soccer coach and Berit Riise shook hands and made up.

On 30th January I wrote to Heidi's psychiatrist, Dr. Broch, telling him that Monday 13th October 2003 had been fixed as the commencement date for the Court of Appeal trial and that I personally would cross-examine him. I sent him copies of Heidi's 1982-1985 letters to contradict his opinion detailed in his letter dated 9th September 2001 to the City court that said, "The contact with this Egyptian [in England when Heidi was an au-pair] was very difficult. He was very insistent and tried to behave as if she was his property." I told the doctor that Heidi had lied to him about our previous friendship and that it was "extremely unprofessional" of him to "happily go along with her deceit" and that his "creditability as a reliable witness was open to question." When I phoned him up later to discuss the matter he acknowledged receipt of my letter but told me his opinion about me had not changed.

The insurance complaints office in Norway – the Forsikringsklagekontoret – dealing with the Karsten Gjone negligence claim, wrote back to me on the 28th January 2003:

> Dear Mr. Delaware,
>
> I refer to your case against Vesta at our bureau. We have now received the relevant documents from Vesta.
>
> The reason for your claim seems to be that your lawyer Mr. Gjone let your case against three Norwegian newspapers be time-barred.
>
> Vesta, as Mr. Gjone's insurance company has rejected your claim. In your letter to our bureau you ask about the further reasons for this.
>
> In order to get compensation from Vesta you must prove that you have suffered economic loss because of Mr. Gjone's behaviour.
>
> In the letter from Vesta to you of January 15th 1999 [they quoted]:
> "...... consequently we find it quite unlikely that you would have won a possible trial against the newspapers and your claim against Mr. Gjone is therefore rejected."
>
> In other words Vesta rejected your claim because you, in their opinion, did not have a very strong case against the newspapers. According to Norwegian law, insurance companies are not obliged to explain in detail why they reject a claim.
>
> In order to consider your claim against the newspaper, an actual consideration of the evidence must be made. The court system is better suited for considerations like this than our bureau. According to the mandate of our bureau I am allowed to reject cases where an actual consideration of the evidence has to be made.

I hereby reject your case and advise you to go to the court system if you want to follow your case any further.

Yours sincerely,
Jørgen Urbye

On 2nd February 2003 the Independent on Sunday newspaper wrote a long piece in their magazine supplement entitled 'Sleeping with the Enemy.' It dealt with the appalling post-war abuse suffered by children born to Norwegian women and occupying Nazi soldiers. Now grown up, many of the victims gave interviews to the Independent's journalist, Julia Stuart. The article is reproduced in full below:

SLEEPING WITH THE ENEMY

Spat at, abused, shunned by neighbours. Their crime? Being the offspring of Norwegian women and occupying Nazi soldiers. Sixty years on, Julia Stuart meets the war children who are fighting back.

As a child growing up in Norway, Tove Laila Strand learnt to take the pain of being whacked with a wooden clothes hanger. It was the names her mother and stepfather called her during the assaults that hurt her more. "Hit me all you want, but please don't call me a German child," she would beg. For children born of a Norwegian mother and a soldier from the occupying German forces, this was a particularly vindictive insult. Today, sitting in a cafe in Oslo, the 61-year-old grandmother's eyes fill with tears as she recounts eight years of abuse, which included being repeatedly raped by her stepfather. "It wasn't that strange," she says. "I was, after all, the child of the enemy."

Some weeks ago, Laila Strand was spat at while shopping in Oslo. That too made her cry. No doubt she had been recognized from her recent television appearances as one of an estimated 10,000 to 12,000 "war children" born in Norway. Such was the level of abuse meted out to them after the war that, last December, Norway's parliament finally agreed to formally apologise and award them compensation. If Laila Strand and other claimants consider the amount to be insufficient, they will take their case to the European Court of Human Rights.

Norway declared itself neutral at the start of the Second World War, but was invaded by Germany in April 1940. The following June, the country's government, king and crown prince fled to London to continue their fight against Hitler, and the remaining troops capitulated. A Nazi government was formed under the auspices of the leader of the Norwegian National Socialist Party, Vidkun Quisling, whose name became a byword for traitor.

That December, Wilhelm Rediess, the chief of the SS and German police in Norway, wrote to SS leader Heinrich Himmler about the increasing number of relationships between Norwegian women and occupying troops. "Individual cases are already arising... of Norwegian women, made pregnant by Germans, seeking the aid of the German Reich, above all on the ground that they are despised and boycotted by the Norwegian population because their pregnancy was caused by a German," he wrote. It was a matter of particular interest to Himmler. In 1935, concerned about the falling birth rates among Aryans in Germany, he set up the Lebensborn (Spring of Life) association to care for unmarried, racially valuable pregnant mothers. The mothers, who otherwise may have had an abortion, checked into specially set up secretive maternity homes, where they received free, high-quality nursing and medical care. Some Lebensborn mothers had their children adopted, and the Lebensborn placed them with staunchly Nazi families.

As the vast majority of women in Norway were Nordic – the purest Aryans in

482

Nazi terms – the fraternizing mothers could not have been more racially valuable. In his letter, Rediess noted that only a small proportion of the German fathers wanted to marry the pregnant women and bring them back to the German Reich. There was another potential problem. If they failed to do anything for Norwegian mothers, they could increase the number of opponents to Germany's occupation. To add to the "stock of racially valuable blood in our racial community," Rediess suggested establishing German-controlled maternity homes.

In March 1941 – six years after the scheme had been set up in Germany – the Lebensborn arrived in Norway, the first of such ventures outside Germany. Hotels and villas were requisitioned and around 10 centres were established. As well as paying all the costs for the birth, the association gave the mothers substantial child support, and money for clothes and a pram or cot.

Most mothers took their children home, some took them to Germany to live with the father's family. Around 200 children were adopted by families in Germany and 100-odd were taken in by Norwegian couples.

It was the most successful Lebensborn outside Germany (there would eventually be two such homes in Austria and one each in Belgium, Holland, France, Luxembourg and Denmark). By the end of the War, 8,000 children had been registered. Many more were born outside the scheme by women who refused to reveal, or could not prove, the identity of the father, making the estimated number of war children in Norway as high as 12,000. It is believed that around 10 per cent of all Norwegian women between 15 and 30 had a German boyfriend during the war.

There have been claims that the homes operated as "stud farms." However, Kare Olsen, an historian at Norway's National Archives and author of *Children of War, The Norwegian War Children and Their Mothers,* dismisses this idea. "Having read through hundreds of files in the Lebensborn archive, I am convinced that nearly all the women had their children as a result of a 'normal' relationship," he says. "The soldiers were encouraged to be polite and behave well towards the Norwegians, who were considered to belong to the same race as them. It was largely a peaceful occupation. Many of the soldiers came from cultivated parts of Germany to the farming areas of Norway and were seen as exciting strangers."

One woman who found herself captivated was Agnes Moller Jensen, now 79, who met her German lover, Toni Mensch, in a coffee shop in Larvik, where she still lives. She was 20 and he was 24. "I just liked him, as you would anyone," she says. Many of her friends also had a German boyfriend. "People didn't like it so we hid by taking trips to the woods. People didn't dare say anything at the time. That started in 1945 [although the war ended in that year, many of the occupying soldiers were unable to leave Norway until 1947]." The couple had a child, Bjorn Toni, but didn't marry as Moller Jensen would have lost her Norwegian citizenship. The pair kept in touch until Mensch's death last year. The Norwegian government in exile in London, who had heard of these liaisons, warned of the consequences through BBC broadcasts. One stated that: "Women who do not reject contact with Germans, will have to pay a dreadful price for the rest of their lives." Another declared the women imbeciles.

When the war ended, many Norwegians needed no further encouragement and took it upon themselves to cut off the hair of many of the "German whores." Though the women hadn't broken any law, several thousand were arrested and many interned. A large number lost their jobs, some just for having been seen talking to a German. "The reaction against these women was far stronger than those who collaborated economically," says Olsen.

While this was echoed across Europe, what appears to be unique to Norway was the rabid hatred also shown to the resulting children. Immediately after the war, letters and articles started appearing in the Norwegian press condemning them.

In July 1945, one writer in *Morgenbladet* feared the boys would "bear the germ of some of those typical masculine German characteristics of which the world has now seen more than enough." Many insisted that the children would grow up to become a "fifth column," and there were loud calls for them and their mothers to be sent to Germany. In August 1945, the Norwegian government brought in a new law stating that any women who had married a German soldier would lose her citizenship and be sent to Germany. Several thousand were duly sent packing.

Perhaps the cruellest claim was that many of the children were mentally retarded. Else Vogt Thingstad, a doctor who took part in a meeting on European war children in Zurich after the war, wrote an article in *Arbeiderbladet* in December 1945 claiming that many of the "German women" were retarded. "...and that we therefore expected their children to a large extent to have hereditary weaknesses." One doctor said these children had as much chance of growing into normal citizens as cellar rats had of becoming house pets.

Twenty-seven children in Godthaab, the Lebensborn home just outside Oslo, were considered to be mentally retarded. Seventeen of them – including Paul Hansen (see below) – were sent to Emma Hjorth, the state asylum nearby. The rest to other institutions. Many spent their lives there, a situation believed to have been repeated in other parts of Norway. In 1990, one of the doctors at Emma Hjorth said: "If the children had got the possibility of a new start and a normal life in 1945, they probably would have grown up normally."

At one stage, Norway's Children of War Committee, set up by the Ministry of Social Affairs after the War to decide what should be done with these children, offered all 8,000 to representatives from Australia, who had approached Norway looking for new immigrants. The idea was abandoned.

In the end, around 3,000 children grew up with their single mothers, and between 2,500 and 3,000 were raised by their mothers and stepfathers. Around the same number were adopted. About 100 lived with their fathers in Germany, and several hundred grew up in orphanages or other institutions in Norway. Many mothers tried to conceal their children's heritage, by giving them their own surname or that of their stepfather.

But for some, there was no escape. "If the mother was a 'German whore' then the child was the same, and you were free to do whatever you wanted with them. Nobody cared," says Tor Brandacher, spokesman for the War Child Organisation Lebensborn. "Everybody hated them, everybody beat them, everybody sexually abused them, everyone urinated on them. Every perversion known to man was performed on them," he claims. "One boy was raped by nine men, who then urinated on him to clean him up. Another woman told me that when she was four, and in a foster home, she would be hung up inside a barn and when the farmer needed oral sex he just opened the door and helped himself."

In a children's home in Trysil, youngsters were force-fed until they vomited, and were made to eat the vomit, says Brandacher. A war child himself he started researching the subject in 1987 when adoption laws changed to allow people to know the identities of their biological parents. Elsewhere, he says, people came to the homes at night, paid staff half a ham and a bottle of alcohol, and were let in the back door to abuse the children. One group of men branded a girl's forehead with a swastika. It has also been claimed that 10 of the war children were subjected to official experiments with LSD. Four or five are said to have died as a result. At least six are believed to have committed suicide – the most recent a former academic at Oslo University, died last November.

Agnes Moller Jensen's son, Bjorn Toni, drank himself to death at the age of 37. "They called him terrible things in school and all the time he was growing up," she says. "It built up inside and he tried to forget it by drinking. I can't describe the pain of losing him. But I don't regret what I did. There was nothing wrong with my son. There was something wrong with the people." Nearly 60 years after the war, Moller Jensen – known locally as the Mother Teresa of Larvik for her work with homeless people – is still discriminated against. Like all women who had a relationship with the enemy, if her Norwegian husband dies, the state will not pay her his war pension.

For some, the torment is still to come. After the War, 30 children found living in a home in Germany were secretly sent by the Norwegian authorities to Sweden. Their names were changed and they were adopted by couples who were told that their parents were resistance fighters or that they were Jewish orphans. "One woman, a war child, suffered great psychological trauma when she found out the truth," says Lars Borgersrud, who is working on a research project funded by the Norwegian government. "The majority probably don't know even today. I know their true identity; but it's not my task as a historian to inform them as it will create a huge change in their lives." Some mothers fled with their children to Sweden after the War to escape harassment. One such woman was the mother of Frida Lyngstad, of Abba whose father was a German soldier.

Brandacher believes the "whore children" were treated so badly because of the nation's guilt over the occupation. "Around 250,000 men volunteered to work for Nazi Germany. Norway was the biggest collaborative state that has ever existed in Europe," he says. "There was high employment and a building boom like none other in Norwegian history. The resistance in Norway was a joke. After the war people needed somebody to hate to get rid of all the shame they felt."

After appeals for redress failed, in 1999 seven war children started legal proceedings against the state claiming that it had violated the European Convention on Human Rights, seeking between £50,000 to £200,000 each. They have since been joined by a further 115. "The stigmatisation, the shame, the oppression was so absolute it took us 50 years to come forward," says one, Gerd Fleischen.

Prime minister, Kjell Magne Bondevik, apologised to the war children in his New Year's speech in 2000. Last December, Norway's Supreme Court determined that the case fell under the statute of limitations. On the same day, the country's parliament unanimously voted, however, to pay compensation and to formally apologise. The details are still to be decided by the government.

Finn Kristian Marthinsen, a member of the Justice Committee that recommended to parliament that the war children be compensated, said: "Norwegian society has to say that we are sorry. It was wrong because these children did nothing criminal. It is a black spot on the history of Norway."

Randi Hagen Spydevold, lawyer for 122 claimants, says she will wait to see the government's proposals before deciding whether to take their case to Strasbourg. "This is an embarrassment for Norway. It seems that parliament has been shamed into action," she says.

Gerd Fleischer, whose Norwegian step-father, a former member of the resistance, was particularly violent to her, believes the state felt compelled to act because of embarrassing international press coverage. "There has not been much public pressure inside Norway about this. The press has written about it, but very silently. It started coming out in the foreign media and then the Norwegian embassies starting reporting back."

"Norwegian society is not an inclusive one. The same discrimination exists today. It has only changed focus. Before it was the Sami, the German children and the gypsies. Now it's the dark ones. But officially racism doesn't exist in Norway. We don't do those bad things here," says Fleischer.

While most in Norway support parliament's decision, in some cases, the hatred lingers. When Laila Strand appeared on television, a neighbour, whom she considered a very good friend, ignored her. When asked what was wrong, the woman sneered: "I don't say hello to whore children and my tax money will certainly not go to paying your compensation." Kristian Marthinsen has been accused of being a traitor. "There are still people who call me or write saying that I'm not a supporter of Norway because I'm giving the children of the enemy a kind of reward," says the MP.

For a number of war children, finding their German relatives has finally given them a sense of identity and a unique source of comfort. Solvi Kuhrig Henningsen, 59, still lives in Sandefjord where she grew up and keeps her past quiet as she still feels hostility. She was mistreated by her stepfather, her mother turned to drink and her neighbour refused to allow her to play with her daughter.

In 1995, encouraged by her husband and children, she traced eight relatives in Germany. "At last Otto's daughter has found us," was her delighted aunt's reply. Kuhrig Henningsen, whose face still carries the pain of her childhood, says: "I became a new person when I met them because not only did they look like me, they loved me."

***

This article spoke volumes about the sexual mores and mentality of the Norwegian people; past and present; both those at the time who collaborated with the Germans and those who turned on the collaborators after the War. An aggravated form of character assassination was practiced on these Norwegian women and their children through the hysterical medicalisation of their personas. There were definite parallels there with the attacks made on me by the Norwegian press. I have a German mother and they knew this from Heidi who may also have told them that my grandfather was a German soldier. Coupled with being a Muslim, I was certainly an ideological enemy.

On the 10th April 2003 I received from my translation agency the English translation of the decision of the Special Investigation Authority in Oslo (SEFO) regarding my complaint against policewoman Torill Sorte. Judge John Morten Svendgård had given his written opinion on 10th January 2003. The government lawyer, Bjørn Feyling, administering the investigation on behalf of SEFO said an English translation was being prepared for me. He said the police would send it to me. My good friends the police! Weeks passed. So eventually, tired of waiting I spoke to Judge Svendgård's secretary and she faxed me a copy of the Norwegian version in late March. I then paid my usual agency to translate the document for me. It went as follows:

THE SPECIAL INVESTIGATION AUTHORITY IN OSLO (SEFO) DEPARTMENT II

SEFO CASE NO: 103/02

Report of civil servant in Søndre Buskerud police district for making false statement and breach of confidentiality.

SUBJECT OF COMPLAINT: Torill Sorte

COMPLAINANT: Frederick Delaware

SØNDRE BUSKERUD POLICE DISTRICT CASE NO. 9866/02

This document is sent with enclosures to **Oslo Public Prosecutor's Offices, Post box 8021 Dep. 0030 Oslo,** as it is proposed the case be dropped because of the state of the evidence as far as the report for making a false statement is concerned, and no criminal offence is considered proven as far as the question of breach of confidentiality/gross negligence in performance of duty is concerned.

The complainant primarily reported the subject of the complaint for making a false statement in connection with the with the subject of the complaint giving evidence in the libel case between the complainant and Heidi Schøne before Drammen court (15-18.01.02, cf. doc.02) but SEFO has on its own initiative

---

486

found reason also to review the circumstances with regard to a possible breach of statutory confidentiality/gross negligence in performance of duty.

As far as the question of making a **false statement** is concerned, the subject of the complaint acknowledged in interview (doc.04.03) that she made a statement in the libel case on circumstances which the complainant's mother explained to her over the telephone in connection with the hearing of earlier criminal proceedings against the complainant (cf. doc.06). The subject of the complaint asserts, however, that the complainant's mother made statements to her as accounted for in her own report of 22.01.97 (cf. doc.02.02), and this was also confirmed during the complainant's statement in court. SEFO has been in contact with the complainant's mother (cf. own report in doc. 04.02), and the complainant's mother denied to the undersigned that she said anything like the subject of the complaint stated in her own report and in court. The case appears to one party's word against the other's as far as this is concerned, and further investigation with a possible interview of the complainant's mother cannot be expected to clarify this situation sufficiently for it to be possible to institute a prosecution for making a false statement.

As far as the question of **breach of confidentiality** is concerned, reference is made to correspondence from Søndre Buskerud Police District, police official Lyngås, (doc. 02.08), which confirms information provided by the subject of the complaint about the question of confidentiality before testimony having been taken up and clarified with a senior lawyer before she gave evidence in the libel case. Against this background, the evidence weighs heavily against the subject of the complaint having intentionally or inadvertently breached confidentiality (cf. penal code s.121) or for the matter having behaved carelessly to an extent which may be said to constitute gross negligence in performance of duty (penal code s. 325).

There are some unlisted documents which were submitted by the complainant and are associated with earlier cases and the recording of telephone conversations, which are enclosed. In SEFO's opinion, these documents are to be assessed and returned to the complainant when the case is settled.

The case was considered by lawyer Solveig Høgtun, police chief inspector Tom Søreide and the undersigned.

The recommendation is unanimous.

Oslo, 10.1.03
[signature]
John Morten Svendgård

Copies: The Public Prosecutor
         SEFO II, FAO district recorder Marit Nervik

On 12th April 2003 I sent Judge Svendgård the following fax:

Subject: SEFO Case No. 103/02 Torill Sorte

I have today received from my own English translators the translation of your letter dated 10-1-03.

You have covered up for your lying police sergeant Torill Sorte and not replied to my correspondence.

Firstly, why do you not just ask me for a letter from my own family doctor to confirm that I have never been a patient in a mental hospital? I give you my professional undertaking as a solicitor that I have never been in a mental hospital.

Secondly why have you not investigated, as I requested, when Torill Sorte spoke for an alleged second time to my mother: the date, time, phone records, attendance note?

You are covering up police corruption. Is it so important for you to put Norway first - right or wrong? I will appeal, but I have still to receive Bjorn Feyling's official letter.

On the same day I delivered a letter to my family doctor outlining the story and enclosing some of the relevant papers for his information. I wanted a 'To whom it may concern' letter from him stating that according to my medical records I had never been hospitalised in a psychiatric unit. (A few days earlier I had been round to speak to my doctor about this Norway saga and he told me that I had to put my request in writing, specifically giving him permission to release information from my medical records to the Norwegian authorities).

On 22nd April 2003 I went to collect my doctor's letter which was dated the same day. It said:

To whom it may concern

Re: Frederick Delaware [my date of birth and address were inserted]

I confirm that I am the general medical practitioner of the above named gentleman.

On careful perusal of Mr. Delaware's medical records, I can state categorically that I can find no evidence that Mr. Delaware has been committed as an inpatient to any psychiatric hospital.

I trust this is satisfactory for your requirements.

Please do not hesitate to contact me should you need any further information.

[Signed by my doctor]

On 25th April 2003 I appealed Judge Svendgård's decision by writing a recorded delivery letter to the Riksadvokaten in Olso as follows:

25th April 2003

Dear Sirs,

SEFO Case number 103/02
Sondre Buskerud Police District Case number 9866/02
Police Sergeant Torill Sorte of Nedre Eiker

I write to appeal against the decision of Judge John Morten Svendgård. A copy of his letter of the 10th January 2003 is enclosed together with the English translation. I myself arranged and paid for the translation which SEFO faxed to me recently. I am no longer prepared to wait for the promised Recorded Delivery letter from the Drammen police enclosing Statadvokat Bjorn Feyling's decision letter.

I enclose again all the correspondence relating to this case plus the tape recording of the relevant part of a conversation between my mother and Torill Sorte dated 22nd April 1996. You will see that Judge Svendgård has not addressed my enquires at all by his letter of the 10/01/03. My correspondence to Judge Svendgård is dated 20th August 2002, 24th August 2002, 3rd September 2002, 24th September 2002 and 16th January 2003.

I myself am a solicitor in England. Heidi Schøne of Nedre Eiker, who I am suing for libel is a registered mental patient at the BSS Psychiatric Clinic in Leir.

You will see that on the 22nd April 1996 my mother told Torill Sorte at my request that the newspaper Drammens Tidende of the 27th May 1995 was lying when it said - "Heidi knows the man's mother tried to commit him to a mental hospital." My mother told Torill Sorte (on tape) that this was a fabrication by Heidi Schøne and the newspaper.

As per Torill Sorte's false statement in her report of the 22nd January 1997 and her oral testimony in Court in January 2002, Sorte claimed there was a conversation with my mother wherein my mother told her I had been committed to a mental hospital. So, according to Torill Sorte my mother made a complete U-turn!! After clearly telling Sorte she never wanted to put me in a mental hospital my mother could hardly later say that I had in fact been **committed** to a mental hospital.

Sorte admitted in Court that she did not know I had been recording my conversations with her. She had to think quickly after giving her false evidence in court and by the time my lawyer Stig Lunde phoned her in the evening she made up a story that there had been a second conversation with my mother. But exactly when this alleged second conversation took place Sorte has never revealed. I demand to know the date and time from Sorte's records of when she had this so-called second conversation. Where are the police phone records and phone bill?

My mother has clearly stated in writing and told Judge Svendgård that no second conversation took place at all.

Importantly I enclose a letter from my family doctor dated 22nd April 2003 which unequivocally states that I have never been committed to a mental hospital. This proves that Sorte has attempted to pervert the course of justice by her false statement. I enclose copies of the transcripts of my telephone conversations with Sorte which clearly contradict her Court statement that my calls to her were annoying and harassing.

Furthermore my mother is not and was not 'elderly' as described by Torill Sorte in her statement of 22nd January 1997. Sorte is a malicious liar.

I demand a discussion with your department in order that Torill Sorte be prosecuted for perverting the course of justice. I will write to the Minister of Justice if she is not prosecuted.

Yours sincerely,
Frederick Delaware

On 29th April 2003 I received the following letter dated 27th February 2003 from Bjørn Feyling at the Public Prosecutor's Office:

Oslo Public Prosecutor's Office

Frederick Delaware

Your reF.	Our ReF.	Date:
	03-0157-06/bfe	27 February 2003

NOTIFICATION OF PROSECUTOR'S DECISION
COMPLAINANT: FREDERICK DELAWARE
COMPLAINEE: POLICE OFFICER AT SØNDRE BUSKERUD POLICE PRECINCT REGARDING CHARGES OF FALSE TESTIMONY AND NORWEGIAN POLICE INTERNAL AFFAIRS' (SEFO'S) ASSESSMENT

OF POSSIBLE BREACH OF DUTY OF CONFIDENTIALITY AND DERELICTION OF DUTY

The Norwegian police internal affairs division (SEFO) in Oslo has investigated your charges brought against a policewoman at Søndre Buskerud police precinct of Drammen.

SEFO recommends that the charge of false testimony be dismissed due to lack of evidence. SEFO has on its own initiative considered the possibility of violation of duty of confidentiality and dereliction of duty, and recommends that those charges be dismissed due to lack of evidence of legal wrongdoing.

The Oslo Public Prosecutor's Office agrees with SEFO's assessment and dismisses the case on the ground set forth by SEFO.

Regarding the various grounds for dismissal, reference is made to the circular of 28 December 1988 part II, No. 3/1988:

"In cases where the regular investigation shows strong evidence against legal wrongdoing, the decision should be 'dismissal due to lack of evidence of legal wrongdoing.' This formulation covers, e.g., cases that would have been dismissed at an earlier stage, without investigation, as obviously groundless. Otherwise, the formulation 'dismissal due to lack of evidence' should be applied. Dismissal based on 'lack of evidence of legal wrongdoing' shall be applied only when the described events are not embraced in penal provision."

For the sake of order, it should be added that the ground for dismissal, "lack of evidence," entails no gradation of the strength of suspicion.

Please be advised that in order to press charges, the prosecuting authority must be convinced both that the person charged has committed the offence(s) in question and that it can be proven in a court of law without reasonable doubt. There is thus a heavy burden of proof in criminal cases. The Oslo Public Prosecutor's Office has concluded that it does not have sufficient grounds for prosecution. Our dismissal may be appealed to the Director General of Public Prosecutions. Any appeal should be filed as soon as possible and no later than 3 - three - weeks after you receive this notification of our decision. For practical reasons, please send any appeal to our address, and we will forward it to the Director General.

Sincerely yours,
Bjørn Feyling

On the 3rd May 2003 I complained by fax to the Norwegian Bar Association on the conduct of Heidi Schøne's lawyer Vegard Aaløkken:

Dear Sirs,

Complaint against Advokat Vegard Aaløkken of Ellen Holager Andenæs of CJ Hambros plass 5, 0164 Oslo

I am engaged in libel proceedings against Heidi Schøne for whom Vegard Aaløkken acts. We are due to appear in the Court of Appeal in October in Drammen.

Since January 2002 I have been trying to obtain certain evidence which Aaløkken is obliged to give me.

1. Part of the evidence I want is referred to in two court witness statements from police sergeant Torill Sorte dated 21/01/97 and 23/04/97 which Aaløkken himself submitted to the court. Within these statements mention is made of "a statement" signed by Runar Schøne which Heidi Schøne "considers her own." It is this statement from Runar Schøne that I want. Vegard Aaløkken and the

Drammen Police are working hand in hand on this case. Police Sergeant Torill Sorte is however under investigation by the Riksadvokaten in relation to perjury and an attempt to pervert the course of justice so neither she nor her police department will co-operate in giving me the evidence. SEFO have ignored my requests for this evidence. Aaløkken has passed the buck by asking me to contact the police for this evidence, knowing full well that nothing will be done by the police to help me. Aaløkken is avoiding his own responsibility, because he does not want to disclose as he put it "evidence prejudicial to my client's case." Aaløkken has easy access to all the police evidence and must be forced to co-operate and supply me with the evidence which is directly within his power to procure, if he hasn't got it already on file.

2. Further I also want from Aaløkken, Heidi Schøne's statement taken by Torill Sorte that I allegedly raped Heidi Schøne "by holding her down." I have been waiting 5 years for this statement. As Aaløkken himself called me "a rapist" in court and Drammens Tidende in 2001 printed the same allegation, so I am entitled as of right to see Heidi Schøne's statement to this effect.

For the record Heidi Schøne in 1986 told the Bergen Police I had **attempted** to rape her in 1985. She confirmed her allegation of **attempted** rape in 1995 to journalist Ingunn Røren of Drammens Tidende. In 1998 after I insisted the (false) allegation of attempted rape be investigated by Torill Sorte, Heidi Schøne then changed her story to allege I had actually raped her by holding her down. Heidi Schøne admitted in Court she has made a similar allegation against a Bergen shopkeeper "but didn't want to talk about it."

3. I require Aaløkken to have the professional courtesy to answer my supplemental appeal in order to clarify the arguments to be discussed in court, by eliminating now, points of issue that can be agreed in order to save time at the trial.

4. Finally Aaløkken should not call me "a rapist" and "mentally ill" in court when there is no evidence at all for this. What independent psychiatric evidence was offered to the court to support Aaløkken's opinion that I am mentally ill? None. As for being an alleged rapist Aaløkken should in the least supply me with Schøne's statement to the police. How ironic it all is when Heidi Schøne herself is in fact a psychiatric patient on a 100% disability pension who brings her psychiatrist in to Court to allege that almost all her family have abused her.

Yours faithfully,
Frederick Delaware

The Bar Association wrote back on 6th May saying their decision process would take about 6 months, which would make a decision unlikely until after my Court of Appeal case. Would I still like to file a complaint? On 8th May I faxed them in the affirmative. On 9th May the Bar Association wrote to Aaløkken enclosing a copy of my complaint. Aaløkken wrote back to the Bar Association on the 26th May, in Norwegian. After their initial refusal, the Bar Association decided it would be proper for them to translate Aaløkken's letter into English, so I could know what was said, in case I wanted to appeal against the Disciplinary Committee's eventual decision. On 10th September 2003 the translation was sent to me:

ADVOKATENE VED TINGHUSET
ADVOKAT ELLEN HOLAGER ANDENÆS

The Disciplinary Committee of the
Norwegian Bar Association
Oslo Chapter

Oslo, 26 May 2003

Case no. 93/2003, Ref. no. 7363V1 -
Reply to complaint submitted by Frederick Delaware

491

Opening remarks

Reference is made to the Disciplinary Committee's letter dated 9 May 2003, received at this office on 12 May 2003 enclosing the complaint made against me by Frederick Delaware.

The Committee requests that my reply be written in English. I am unable to accede to this request. This reply requires a degree of linguistic accuracy that I would be unable to achieve in the English language.

About the case

Concerning the individual points in the complaint, I hold that the complaint cannot be dealt with by the Committee as these questions have already been dealt with by the court, alternatively that the case must be dismissed as my assignment has been to take care of the interests of my own client, cf. Section 2, 3rd and 4th subsections of the Procedural Rules for the Disciplinary Committees.

Initially, it will be appropriate to submit a brief outline of the factual and legal aspects of the case.

Frederick Delaware met Heidi Schøne while Schøne was an au-pair in England in 1982. They had a friendly relationship to start with and exchanged letters and visits.

This changed in the mid-eighties. Heidi Schøne has been exposed to unwanted and extremely troublesome attention on the part of Frederick Delaware. She has been subjected to the worst type of harassment.

Delaware has telephoned her and sent innumerable letters of an offensive nature to Heidi Schøne. There has been less of this slanderous behaviour in recent years, probably due to the fact that the plaintiff has been unable to make contact with Schøne.

Delaware has also persecuted Schøne by repeatedly telephoning and writing letters to numerous persons (family, friends, acquaintances, neighbours, companies, institutions, etc.) in which he has made different insulting allegations concerning the defendant. This behaviour continues. Among other things, Heidi Schøne has been held to ridicule on an address on the internet and it is assumed that Delaware is behind this. I enclose the material aimed in particular against Heidi Schøne on the address www.norway-shockers.com. The attached 'article' will be found in both Norwegian and English versions under 'Pretty Face.'

Exhibit 1: Print-out from the Internet.

By judgement passed by Eiker, Modum and Sigdal District Court on 2 November 2001, Frederick Delaware was found guilty of acting in a harassing manner towards Heidi Schøne.

Exhibit 2: Judgement passed by Eiker, Modum and Sigdal District Court on 2 November 2001.

From the above, it can be seen that this harassment comprised among other things contacting Heidi Schøne's circle in different ways and spreading private information about her. As a countermove, Heidi Schøne found that it was necessary for her to go to the press with her story. The theme in the articles that appeared in Drammens Tidende/Buskerud Blad and VG in 1995 and 1998 was that Heidi Schøne had been exposed to sex harassment by an insane man, namely Delaware.

On 10 August 1999 Delaware filed a writ claiming NOK 50,000 in damages from Heidi Schøne on the grounds of defamation. The claim for damages was

492

based on a newspaper article in Drammens Tidende/Buskerud Blad on 14 July 1998.

On 11 February 2002 Drammen District Court passed judgement in favour of Heidi Schøne and awarded legal costs.

Exhibit 3: Judgement passed by Drammen District Court on 11 February 2002.

This judgement has been appealed and the appeal is to be brought before Borgarting Court of Appeal in the week commencing 13 October 2003.

The individual points in the complaint

Concerning the documents requested in items 1 and 2, I must advise you that Delaware has also requested the Court of Appeal to order me to submit these documents. Reference is made to the attached letter dated 15 February 2003 from Delaware to the Court of Appeal and the reply from the Court dated 24 February 2003 in which it is stated that the Court "has no basis for ordering the Respondent to submit the document you require." I therefore hold that this issue has already been dealt with by the Court and cannot therefore be processed by the Disciplinary Committee.

Exhibit 4: Letter dated 15 February 2003 from Frederick Delaware.

Exhibit 5: Letter dated 24 February 2003 from Borgarting Court of Appeal.

It may appear that a refusal to send this document is due to a lack of willingness. However, I must state that during a telephone conversation with Delaware on 11 February 2003 he told me that he intended to use the documents "to discredit Heidi Schøne." As this is the opposing party's intention, I am of the opinion that by refusing to send the document to Delaware, I am doing no more than looking after my client's interests in a normal manner. This item in the complaint could therefore no doubt be dismissed for this reason.

I would add that the documents were obtained from the police prior to the main hearing in Drammen District Court. Delaware would no doubt be given access to the documents in the case by applying to the police in the same manner. We are dealing with a finalised criminal case in which the condition concerning legal interest is fulfilled and Delaware is therefore entitled to access, cf. Section 4-2, 3rd subsection of the instructions to the prosecuting authority.

In item 3 it is stated that I must reply to the questions raised in "my supplemental appeal." I attach the supplemental appeal for your information. This question has also been dealt with by the Court of Appeal and must therefore be dismissed by the Disciplinary Committee. In item 1 in the letter dated 7 January 2003 to the Court of Appeal, Delaware demanded that I should reply to these questions. In the letter from the Court of Appeal dated 9 January 2003 it is stated that Delaware "cannot expect replies to the questions raised."

Exhibit 6: Supplemental appeal dated 12 July 2002.
Exhibit 7: Letter dated 7 January 2003 from Frederick Delaware.
Exhibit 8: Letter dated 9 January 2003 from Borgarting Court of Appeal.

In item 4 it is stated that I must discontinue using the words "rapist" and "mentally ill" about Delaware. In Exhibit 3 there is a summary of my arguments before Drammen District Court. These were based on Heidi Schøne's statement and other evidence in the case.

In order to present clear and convincing proof that Heidi Schøne had been exposed to harassment of a sexual nature, it was appropriate to refer to the episode in which Heidi Schøne was subjected to a sexual attack by Delaware. In this connection I referred to the statement made to the police concerning a rape,

493

or at least an attempted rape in Bergen at Easter 1985. Reference is made to Exhibit 3, page 15.

With regard to Delaware's mental condition, I held that Heidi Schøne had been victimised for years by a mentally ill/insane/psychologically disturbed man. On my part it was not held that Delaware had received any professional diagnosis and it was stated that the words were used in the more popular sense. Reference is made to Exhibit 3, page 14.

In Exhibit 3 it is shown that the Court fully supported Heidi Schøne's arguments. My description of Delaware was made in conjunction with my normal duty to take care of my client's interests in the case. This item in the complaint must therefore also be dismissed.

I find no reason to comment on certain points in Delaware's letter as in my opinion they are either self-contradictory or without relevance to the case. It is possible that I have overlooked questions that should have been answered due to my inadequate command of the English language. Should this be the case, I request that the Disciplinary Committee bring this to my attention.

Yours faithfully,
Vegard Aaløkken

I responded in full on 17th September 2003 by fax:

Jostein Moen
Den Norske Advokatforening

Dear Mr. Moen,

CASE NO. 93/2003-VEGARD AALØKKEN

Thank you for your letter of 10th September 2003 enclosing the English translation of Mr. Aaløkken's letter dated 26th May 2003.

I respond as follows:

a) In relation to points 1 and 2 of my letter of the 3rd May 2003 my lawyer Stig Lunde has recently informed me that Mr. Aaløkken, a few days ago, told him that he believes the 2 documents I need were sent to Stig Lunde before the January 2002 trial. Mr. Aaløkken has asked Stig Lunde to search his ample records for these two documents. Why can't Mr. Aaløkken just send these two documents again to Stig Lunde? The principle has been established that Aaløkken admits having the documents and admits that he believes he has already sent them long ago to Stig Lunde. These documents, to remind you, are a witness statement from Heidi Schøne to Torill Sorte in 1998 alleging violent rape against me and a statement made by Runar Schøne which Heidi Schøne "adopted as her own." These documents are already referred to in a 1997 witness statement of Torill Sorte who is working on the same side as Mr. Aaløkken and his client Heidi Schøne. Full and frank disclosure of documents, that Aaløkken now tells us are in his possession, should be made and it is irrelevant if the documents prejudice his client's case. It is his professional duty not to withhold sight of documents from me that he has access to, has informed me exist and has in his possession. Mr. Aaløkken, in now saying that he believes he has sent those documents to my lawyer, should render irrelevant what he has said to you in his letter of 26th May 2003 on withholding the material.

494

b) Besides which, I repeat that I have been trying for five years to get Heidi Schøne's statement from the police and in the last year from SEFO (also Runar Schøne's statement) but I have been ignored. The police will **not** co-operate with me or my lawyer at all. They are fighting hard to save their reputations as one of their officers, Torill Sorte has been investigated for perjury and attempting to pervert the course of justice. Also the police in Norway used Interpol to prosecute me for my campaign against the newspaper stories. I am **not** going to read in the newspapers that I am a potential child killer (solely on the word of Heidi Schøne) and do nothing about it. By my spreading her past about, I wanted to inform Norwegian people just what kind of a person Heidi Schøne is. I was convicted in absentia under section 390(a) of the criminal code for the strict liability offence of telling the public about Heidi Schøne's background. Does anyone seriously think that after all that, the police will readily give me the documents I need? In theory they should, but in practice I will never get them. I ask Aaløkken simply to send me these two documents.

c) Mr. Aaløkken knows very well that his client got pregnant again in 1985 to Gudmund Johannessen who previously got her pregnant with twins, slept with her best friend making her lose the twins causing her to make an attempt on her own life. When getting Heidi Schøne pregnant again Johannessen was a drug taker, a convicted criminal and in 1988 left Heidi Schøne and their son, causing Heidi Schøne to try to take her life again in September 1988. In Christmas 1990 Mr. Johannessen beat up Heidi Schøne on her doorstep and she reported him to the Drammen police. I suspect Heidi Schøne concealed future addresses, if at all, so as to prevent Mr. Johannessen from contacting her. I reprimanded Heidi Schøne in the summer of 1985 for getting pregnant again to such an abuser as Gudmund Johannessen and I also warned Heidi Schøne's father that Heidi's life was a complete mess. My fears proved real but were ignored at the time.

Mr. Aaløkken knows too that (i) Heidi Schøne asked me and a friend to help her out against Mr. Johannessen in August 1988 just prior to her second suicide attempt and (ii) Heidi Schøne sent me Christian literature in October 1990 after her so-called exorcism and attempt to become a born again Christian. Hardly the behaviour of a woman to a man who years later accused me of 13 years of sex terror beginning in 1982. All of Heidi Schøne's evidence prior to 1995 is only on her word. This the word of a registered mental patient on a 100% disability pension, under the care of Dr. P. Broch at the BSS Clinic in Leir. She was first an in-patient at the clinic in 1988. So Aaløkken is not telling the full picture.

d) You have seen the contents of my appeal and if Aaløkken thought his client had a good case then why doesn't he reply to my numerous points in my appeal? Answer: because his client has a very poor case and he should advise her to plead guilty. What seems to count in her favour is that she is Norwegian and I am not and I am Muslim (which by Bergens Tidende in May 1995 calling me the "Muslim man" 19 times, obviously counts against me). It is self evident that Judge Stilloff has made many mistakes in his judgment and we have an appeal case in October. I reply to every point made by my opponents as soon as time permits. Mr. Aaløkken says nothing in response to my appeal because his client's position is indefensible.

e) As for Mr. Aaløkken saying my behaviour has been slanderous – what nonsense is this? In Judge Stilloff's own verdict he specifically states that Dr. P. Broch says that my comments on Heidi Schøne's past life contain "a core of truth" and Stilloff himself has said in his judgment that my comments on Heidi Schøne's past are "more or less correct." So I have not been slanderous at all. I have been very careful to accurately describe Heidi Schøne's past and the court has vindicated me.

f)   Further, contrary to Mr. Aaløkken's claim I have on the whole **always** been able to make contact with Heidi Schøne. She has been living at the same address for the past 10 years. The only time I couldn't is when she was hiding from her abuser Gudmund Johannessen.

g)   I told the newspapers as far back as 1996 that if I don't get an apology I will institute a commercial campaign to put my side of the story to contradict their racist motivated nonsense. My campaign was so successful that the police, unable to cope with public enquiries instituted a malicious prosecution against me under section 390(a) of the penal code and I was convicted in absentia. The website www.norway-shockers.com only took off on 18th October 2000, five years after the newspapers first printed stories on me. I have a right of reply under the European Convention of Human Rights and that is what the website achieves. Besides, I think the public in Norway should know that Heidi Schøne kills her own unborn children (two abortions) when she falsely accuses me in the press (Drammens Tidende, May 1995) of threatening to kill her son. The burden of proving this [threat to kill her son] is on Heidi Schøne and she has failed to do this.

h)   As for Exhibit 2 submitted by Mr. Aaløkken he was not present himself at the trial. What happened was that for one hour my criminal defence lawyer was trying to change the charges from section 390(a) to section 390 which latter section gave me a defence of justified comment. But unfortunately the judge that day could not understand the legal arguments presented to her so wrongly proceeded under section 390(a). I was not present but was convicted in absentia having been given a mere 3 weeks notice of the hearing date. Hardly time enough to prepare when I was in the middle of preparing my own civil and criminal prosecutions of Heidi Schøne. The police used dirty tactics as of course did the newspapers. Mr. Aaløkken presents a false picture himself which again is unprofessional and worthy of censure.

i)   The reason the newspapers in 1995 called me "insane" and "mentally ill" etc is because they thought that only a madman could attribute to Heidi Schøne the past I described her as having. They now know different: Judge Stilloff has said that my description of her past is "more or less correct." I know obviously the hatred that exists for Muslims in Norway is a major factor for the press to link the words "mentally ill" and "erotic paranoia" with the words "the Muslim man." I note also similar labels have been used by Norwegians against the children of German soldiers and Norwegian women during the occupation. For the whole story in the Independent newspaper article from earlier this year, click on Norway Uncovered Part 2 on the www.norway-shockers.com website.

j)   The judgement of Drammen District Court found Heidi Schøne "not guilty." What Mr. Aaløkken has ommitted to say is that Judge Stilloff alluded to the fact that the newspaper journalists lied and that Runar Schøne lied but as they were not on trial they could not be dealt with. Also as Mr. Aaløkken will readily admit, Heidi Schøne said in court that she was given all six newspaper articles before they were printed and adopted the contents fully failing to correct anything. She herself thus adopted the lies in the newspapers and this aspect is one of the cornerstones of my appeal.

k) Mr. Aaløkken refers to Heidi Schøne's statement to the police "concerning a rape or at least an attempted rape." What misleading nonsense is this? Aaløkken knows perfectly well that in December 1986 Heidi Schøne went to the Bergen police (20 months after I stayed with her but 2 weeks after I warned her father she was a complete mess) to make an allegation against me of attempted rape. She maintained the allegation of attempted rape in 1995 to journalist Ingunn Roren (insisting "**attempted**"). All of a sudden in 1998 Heidi Schøne's 'revises' her allegation to one of violent rape to policewoman Torill Sorte. This is the statement I had been asking for ever since. It must be stated that in court Heidi Schøne admitted to being allegedly raped by a Bergen shopkeeper in the early 1980's. She also claimed to me that she has been threatened with rape at knife point by Greek men when on holiday and that her cousin was raped and killed. Also, in court, her psychiatrist stated that she was sexually abused by her stepmother's father and mentally abused by members of her own family. Her list of abusers is very long.

l) Mr. Aaløkken specifically said in court that my information campaign consisting of fact sheets etc. to put my side of the story was "a continuing symptom" of my "mental illness." He repeated in his summing up that I am "mentally ill and a rapist." The mental illness allegation was **not** used in the "popular sense" as Aaløkken states. Aaløkken made a determined effort, as did many of his fellow countrymen, to convince people that I am clinically mentally ill. As for being a rapist Mr. Aaløkken himself has it seems backtracked by alleging that "at least" I am an attempted rapist.

m) Mr. Aaløkken comments at the end of his letter that certain points of mine are either "self contradictory or without relevance." But he does not say why or which points. This is very condescending. I am a lawyer just like he is and I know bullshit when I read it.

Yours sincerely,
FREDERICK DELAWARE

On 23rd May 2003 Aftenposten's English language webdesk produced the following:

Why Norway?

The news that Norwegian interests in Muslim nations were now targets of al-Qaida terrorism stunned Norwegian authorities. Security at embassies was immediately stepped up as baffled experts and politicians tried to fathom why Norway had made the list.

Confusion was rampant after Osama bin Laden's closest adviser Ayman al-Zawahri added Norway to the more predictable list of the USA, Great Britain and Australia - active partners in the alliance against Iraq - as targets for a new wave of terrorist attacks.

The threat was being taken very seriously, but one of the first reactions was that Norway must have been confused with another country. Several theories were quick to emerge.

Mullah Krekar?
The editor for Britain's leading pro-Arab newspaper Al-Quds al-Arabi, Abdel Bari-Atwan, believes Norway's treatment of mullah Krekar, alleged leader of the guerilla group Ansar al-Islam operating in northern Iraq, is reason enough to come on al-Qaida's list.

Krekar's group has been linked to al-Qaida by various sources. Krekar faces prosecution and expulsion from Norway for links to terrorism, and this would be considered a serious offense in Krekar's extremist Muslim circles.

Afghanistan?
Bari-Atwan, speaking to newspaper Stavanger Aftenbladet, also mentioned Norway's active role assisting allied forces in Afghanistan as possible factor in the al-Qaida threat.

Norwegian special forces are still helping hunt al-Qaida and Taliban forces in Afghanistan, and newspaper VG cited an "intelligence source" as saying Norwegian forces and fighter jets in Afghanistan "had clearly hit the terrorist network, directly and hard."

The Norwegian Defense Intelligence Service (FO/E) has also played an active role in aiding US colleagues, VG reported. The newspaper also speculated that the death of al-Zawahri's wife and three daughters in a bomb attack on Kandahar might have some links to Norwegian efforts in Afghanistan.

Norway to be an example to others?
"I have twisted my brain trying to find an answer, and after rejecting most theories I am left with this: Al-Qaida knows a local group is ready to attack a Norwegian target," Stein Toenesson of the International Peace Research Institute Oslo (PRIO) told Aftenposten.

"I fear a Norwegian target has been chosen, and this will increase the fear of terrorism in the USA and other countries on the list. But the idea of all this could be just to create fear," said a baffled Toenesson.

Vigilance, not panic
Norwegian Prime Minister Kjell Magne Bondevik called for Norwegians abroad to be extra observant.

"We take the threats seriously and have informed Norwegian embassies, businesses and citizens in relevant nations," Bondevik said.

Norway has not followed the lead of the USA and Britain in closing embassies in nations considered to be at special risk.

"In contrast to those nations Norway has not received concrete threats against named targets," said Foreign Ministry (UD) spokesman Karsten Klepsvik.

***

On the 27th May 2003 Aftenposten did a follow-up article on their English language webdesk:

Al-Qaida stops Norwegian garage

Employees at an Oslo building firm were so shocked and outraged by the Al-Qaida threats against Norway that they have refused to carry out assignments for Muslims. One customer, born and raised in Norway, has had his plans to build a garage derailed, newspaper VG reports.

"You are probably a Muslim and after the recent Muslim terror threats none of my employees want to work for Muslims," read the letter sent by company head Olav Oeye.

The letter arrived the day after the terror threats, and while the 27-year-old Muslim was waiting for Oeye's firm to deliver a price after surveying the plot for the garage.

"I had an offer from Grimstad Garages. In the offer they gave the names of three contractors who I could call to build the foundation. Olav Oeye Inc. said they could come Saturday at 11 am," the man told VG.

"I could hardly believe what I was reading. I am just as Norwegian as others, even if I have brown skin and have another religion. I have never had my feelings hurt so badly before," the ex-customer said. He will now charge Olav Oeye Inc. with religious discrimination and promises legal action.

"The garage will get built anyway but now it has become an important matter of principle for me to pursue this. My Norwegian friends are the most shocked," the Norwegian-Pakistani said.

Olav Oeye remains unrepentant, and is not swayed by the argument that the 27-year-old is born and raised in Norway.

"After reading the papers and listening to the radio it wasn't amusing thinking about working for Muslims. We have it a few times before and there are always problems with the bill. No, why should I (regret) it? I am retired and have five or six employed who do what I want," Oeye said.

Lawyer Abid Q. Raja said he had never heard such a clear case of religious harassment and, according to VG, nearly began to laugh when he heard the contents of the letter.

"This must be the most unprofessional firm in Norway. But it also indicates that there are very many who have similar opinions in Norway but are not brave enough to say so," Raja said, and said the letter clearly violates the law.

The National Association of the Building Industry also expressed shock and said they would consider reactions if Oeye Inc. was a member, but did not believe they had the jurisdiction to exclude the company.

"This is so odd that our ethical rules don't cover it. It is irrelevant if a prospective client is a Muslim or not, regardless of threats to Norway. This is completely unreasonable. It is just not on," said Association director Odd Trender to VG.

***

For a good while now I was finding the whole project extremely wearing: fighting so many opponents in Norway was completely draining me. On 6th April 2003 by recorded delivery letter I wrote to the British Embassy in Oslo telling them the story so far. I pleaded that, "I have reached the stage where I need help from yourselves as I cannot cope with the enormity of the task confronting me." I also wanted to make them aware of the torment that the Norwegians were putting me through. I sent them a copy of Tony Samstag's 27th December 1990 Times newspaper article 'Norwegians' charity to foreigners ends at home' and Julia Stuart's article of 2nd February 2003 in the Independent on Sunday magazine 'Sleeping with the Enemy.' I made a follow up call to the Embassy a few weeks later hoping to discuss the matter. I spoke to a Norwegian lady working for the British Embassy called Patricia Svendsen who said she would be dealing with the matter but hadn't had time to read my letter yet. She would now read it and asked me to call back the next day. I found it ironic that in trying to enlist British help against the Norwegians I had to deal with a Norwegian citizen employed by the British Embassy (because of her Norwegian language skills and familiarity with the Norwegian system).

When we spoke the following day, I went into some detail with Miss Svendsen on the matter. She heard me out but said the Embassy couldn't get involved in my civil case. As a lawyer I understood this but my problem, I told her, was that the Norwegians were not playing fair at all and I could not handle that oppression on my own. Miss Svendsen then indicated that my ultimate remedy lay with the European Court of Human Rights – "if they accepted the case," she added. Quite so, I thought to myself, but at what cost to me in terms of money, stress and the time would it take to get a case to Strasbourg? Why should one individual have to go to those lengths when having to fight the perversion of a whole country, situated moreover, in Western Europe? But I knew long ago that that was the direction I had to go in. However 95% of Applications to the European Court of Human Rights were currently rejected. Hardly a practical remedy therefore.

I finished our conversation by saying that due to my continuing "information campaign" (I didn't tell her about my website) I feared being arrested on my return to Norway in October. In that case, Miss Svendsen said, the Embassy would want to know that the grounds for the arrest were proper and ensure legal representation was to hand. But that in Norway they had "freedom of speech" and no criminal offence was committed unless one targeted a particular racial group. I countered this by reminding her that I had a conviction and fine which I had not paid under the Norwegian Penal Code for publicizing Heidi Schøne's past in response to the newspaper articles and would have got 6 to 12 months imprisonment if I'd been present in Norway. But just like me Patricia Svendsen could not understand what the Norwegians were playing at.

I was still unhappy at the impasse with the Norwegians regarding my (unpaid) fine. I suspected that the police would try and teach me a lesson for my efforts in trying to get Torill Sorte charged. So on the 17th June 2003 I wrote again to the Embassy in Oslo asking them to "intervene on my behalf and obtain an explanation as to why I was charged under a strict liability penal section: Section 390 (a) [instead of] Section 390.....I fear arrest and detention in Norway, especially as I have cast-iron evidence of a police officer's perjury - the State Prosecutor is presently investigating my complaint."

When a few weeks later I telephoned Patricia Svendsen she explained that she didn't reply to me because my letter added nothing to what we had previously spoken about. Only if and when I was arrested would assistance be given, she said.

All the while I had been writing to the Court of Appeal asking for them to send me the witness statement of Heidi Schøne given to Torill Sorte alleging that I had raped her "by holding her down." I was getting nowhere. Judge Stousland wrote back in Norwegian to say neither Heidi Schøne nor her lawyer were legally obliged to give the document to me. When I asked the judge to write to me in English if he could, he replied – in Norwegian – that the court rules allowed him to write to me in Norwegian and that if I wanted him to write to me in English I would have to pay the court a sum on account, for his letters to be translated. That as a favour he would continue to let me write to him in English. I still had the able assistance of Patrick Byrne for the longer Norwegian documents I needed translating. I had for some time been posting them off to him and within a week he would send me back a translation of the more important sentences.

As a litigant in person now, I myself was responsible for complying with the directions of the Court of Appeal. The court supplied help to a litigant in person but for a fee. I paid directly into one court official's private bank account – Monica Gran – the amount of £1,355 to enable her to collate and photocopy six sets of all the documentation needed for the trial; one set for each of the three judges, one for me, one for Heidi's lawyer and one for the court office. I spoke as often as necessary to Monica Gran who was cheerful and very pleasant. She received the money on the 29th August and then began her tedious administrative task. I had sent some supplemental evidence to the Court of Appeal on the 19th August including my family doctor's letter confirming I had never been a patient in a mental hospital.

The insurance company Vesta had written to me on the 19th August 2003 regarding my claim against Elden and Elden for failing to tell me the correct procedure when using the Press Complaints Commission (PFU) in Norway in conjunction with suing Drammens Tidende. The insurance company acknowledged that I "more or less had to choose between suing Drammens Tidende and letting the PFU look into the matter" and continued, "You decided for the PFU and according to Lindset you were fully aware that this meant you had to waive the possibility to sue Drammens Tidende after a decision from the PFU. Accordingly, he, Lindset does not accept liability on this matter."

On the 6th September 2003 I replied to the insurance company's lawyer as follows:

Dear Mr. Skjølberg,

Claim Number: HAS 98-908329   Elden and Elden

Thank you for your letter of 19th August 2003. I note the second sentence of your second paragraph which is an accurate record of the choice I faced as presented to me by Elden and Elden at the time. However the correct choice that the PFU should have presented me with according to their own rules is that I should have been told that I could still sue Drammens Tidende after the PFU had concluded their investigation. Elden and Elden's job is to present me with the proper legal choices and unfortunately they failed to do so.

Elden and Elden were at fault for not ascertaining the correct position and they were therefore negligent. I need you specifically to confirm that Elden and Elden did not present me with the correct choice by Norwegian law. You know full well this was exactly the nature of my complaint for many many months. You must get to the bottom of this.

I'm in the Court of Appeal in October and it may well be that Heidi Schøne is convicted. In which case my claim against Karsten Gjone will succeed and you will have to award me financial compensation. Until I reach the end of the judicial line, being the European Court of Human Rights you cannot disbar my claim against Gjone.

Yours sincerely,
Frederick Delaware

Vesta replied on the 17th September 2003:

OUR CLAIM NO/REF. HAS 98-908329

CLAIMS FOR DAMAGES AGAINST LAW FIRM ELDEN & ELDEN

Dear Mr. Delaware,

Thank you for your letter of September 6th 2003.

According to Mr. Linset you were made aware of the fact that choosing to let PFU look into the matter meant that you had to waive to sue DT. You still choose to present the case to PFU. This decision was yours only. Therefore Mr. Lindset does not accept liability. In addition we refer to our letter of August 19th 2003.

Sincerely yours,
Vesta Forsikring AS

Hans-Arnt Skjolberg

When I phoned him to discuss the matter, Skjølberg became angry saying even if Eric Lindset was negligent I still had to prove to Vesta that I would have won the case against Drammens Tidende which he thought was highly unlikely; that moreover he'd seen my website. When I told him I had a right to reply to all the newspaper stories, especially the "racist" anti-Muslim attack, he told me, "After you lose a case you say it's because of racism. You say that just because you lost! What does it matter if the newspapers called you "the Muslim man"?" It was no use debating the issues with him. He gave me the name of a woman in his company to whom I could complain when I told him I wanted to take the matter further over his belief that calling me "Muslim" in the newspapers was quite alright. But I let the matter be. What I had forgotten to mention in my correspondence with Vesta was the fact that Elden & Elden should also have told me from the outset that the PFU did not have the power to investigate the truth or falsehood of a statement made by a newspaper. Elden & Elden knew this all along but I myself did not know this for quite some time.

On the 27th August 2003 the Public Prosecutor's office sent me their decision on my appeal to them regarding Torill Sorte's perjury:

COURT ENDORSEMENT PAPER
The Public Prosecutor's Office
P.O Box 8002 Dep   **Oslo 06-03/0157**
0030 Oslo

ReF. RE 02-1185 AG/mw
   15.07.03

APPEAL SUBMITTED BY DELAWARE REGARDING THE DECISION NOT TO PROSECUTE THE SEFR (COMPLAINT INVESTIGIATION COMMISION) CASE

Enclosure: the District Attorney's Office in Oslo

We point to the Appeal of April 26th 2002 submitted by Frederick Delaware regarding the decision of February 27th 2003 to drop the case against Chief Inspector Torill Sorte. The report dealt with a perjured statement, but Sefo also considered the reported incident in accordance with the regulations regarding breach of professional secrecy and gross neglect of duty. The case of perjured statement was not prosecuted due to insufficient evidence and the part that dealt with breach of professional secrecy and gross neglect of duty was not prosecuted because there was no evidence of any criminal offence being committed.

The report regards a testimony given by Sorte to Drammen District Court in January 2002 where she explained that the plaintiff's mother, during a telephone conversation, told her that the plaintiff had been hospitalized at a mental clinic. The plaintiff's mother has informed Sefo's chief executive that she has never said this. This disputed information is dealt with in the reported person's own report of January 22nd 1997, and the telephone conversation might possibly have taken place before this date. There are conflicting statements and based upon the existing information there is evidently no evidential foundation to charge for perjured statement, nor is there any foundation of assuming that further investigations will reveal information of vital importance to the prosecution.

Consequently, the appeal is dismissed.

The Public Prosecutor's decision could not be appealed, cf. the Criminal Procedure Act Section 59, letter a.

The right to institute a private prosecution is described in the Criminal Procedure Act, Chapter 28.

Please notify the parties. Please notify the plaintiff and enclose a translated copy of this endorsement paper in English. A transcript of the Criminal Procedure Act, Chapter 28 in English should be enclosed with the notification.

THE PUBLIC PROSECUTOR'S OFFICE, P.O BOX 8002 DEP, 0030 OSLO

On behalf of Anne Grøstad, Public Prosecutor, signature of Ingunn Fossgard.
Copy to: Sefo Oslo, Varargan II (Case no. 103/02)

Together with this decision letter I received a large parcel. Inside I found three police files containing an assortment of material. There was a whole bundle of my 1996 to 1998 'reports' on Heidi Schøne's life history together with the envelopes they were posted in, that had been handed in to the police by the addressees. I also had returned to me all the original letters and other papers I had sent to police officers Torill Sorte and Svein Jensen, asking for their help. One was to Svein Jensen dated 4th November 1995. Ten were to Torill Sorte – six from 1996 and four from 1998. I didn't get a single reply. As well as this I had returned to me the Norwegian language translations (in triplicate) of the transcripts of my recorded telephone conversations with Torill Sorte. Even my five postcards and one letter written 'to' Heidi in 1997 and five postcards written 'to' her in 1995 (after I'd learnt of her attempted rape allegation) and one postcard dated 27th February 1995, were enclosed.

On the 1st September 2003 I sent the following fax to Anne Grøstad of the Public Prosecutor's office:

Dear Madam,

Police Sergeant Torill Sorte

I refer to your letter of the 15th May 2003, the decision letter of the 15th July 2003 of your office (copy English translation enclosed) and our recent telephone conversation.

As I informed you over the telephone, I believe your office's decision not to prosecute Torill Sorte amounts to a cover up. I sent you a letter from my family doctor declaring categorically that I have never been treated in a mental hospital. No reference is made in your decision letter of 15th July 2003 to my doctor's letter. It follows that it would be impossible for my mother to say to Torill Sorte that I have been in a mental hospital. Futhermore no reference is made in your decision letter as to whether or not Torill Sorte was asked exactly when this phone call took place between her and my mother.

You have also been given a tape of a conversation between Sorte and my mother wherein my mother, at my request, explains to Torill Sorte in 1996 that she has never threatened to put me in a mental hospital (to contradict newspaper allegations). No mention is made in your 15th July 2003 report of this taped conversation.

You yourself in effect are covering up police corruption. As a lawyer yourself, for you to allow this cover up to happen is a complete disgrace. I will therefore have to subpoena you to attend the Drammen City Court trial on 13th – 17th October 2003, Court of Appeal, in my case against Heidi Schøne. I will inform you of the exact time you are required to appear.

The fact is, as you must know, your department was instrumental in using Interpol to prosecute me last year under section 390(a) of the Criminal Code just because I publicized my side of the story to numerous front page newspaper stories against me. It was a malicious prosecution. Moreover I was not even afforded a defence of justified comment under section 390. There is thus the added ingredient of a conflict of interest in your department's involvement.

Yours faithfully,
Frederick Delaware

On the 6th September I faxed Anne Grøstad again with details of the time and date she would be subpoenaed to attend court: 2.30 p.m. on the 16th October 2003. And then I faxed the judge with a full letter explaining my reasons for subpoenaing Anne Grøstad. My last sentence read, "I'm convinced there is a cover up to protect the Drammen police, in particular Torill Sorte and the only forum to investigate this is at the Court of Appeal in October, when Anne Grøstad will be questioned about her department's involvement in all matters relating to myself and Torill Sorte."

Anne Grøstad wrote back to the court on the 10th September 2003 saying that she was going on holiday to Tenerife from the 14th to the 28th October and that the Attorney General himself Tor-Aksel Busch would go in her place provided the court ruled that he had to go. The Court of Appeal wrote to me and said the judges at the trial would decide if Tor-Aksel Busch would have to turn up.

About four weeks before the trial the Court of Appeal wrote to me (in Norwegian as usual) to tell me that I had to find and pay for an interpreter myself. I couldn't understand why, as on the two previous hearings the court had appointed and paid for William Mulholland. Stig Lunde though, said he had spoken to Judge Stousland (who was preparing the case) who was adamant that the court rules declared that I myself had to requisition an interpreter. Lunde thought the lower court had been wrong to pay for my interpreter and that I should be grateful for their mistake. A year earlier Stig Lunde had told me I would have to get and pay for two interpreters to simultaneously translate at the trial; that it would cost me almost as much as paying him to do the case for me. Stig Lunde had wanted £10,000. At the time I was confident, however, that Lunde's advice was questionable as following on from the previous arrangement, when the court paid for the interpreter, surely the Court of Appeal would be required to pay this time. But no, my hopes that this argument would prevail were dashed when Lunde now told me his advice last year was based on a fax he had, at the time, received from the judge. I contacted the interpreter for the last two hearings, William Mulholland who said he would do all five days for a fee of £1,271. I faxed my confirmatory letter of agreement to him on the 17th of September telling him of my website address so he could refresh his memory about the case. The same evening he sent me an email to say, "My wife has just come home and reminded me that we are due to visit her family in northern Norway in the week beginning 13th of October, so regretfully I cannot assist you in court in Drammen at that time. Please accept my sincere apologies." Bad luck!

So I telephoned my Norwegian based translation agency in Stavanger who said they would make some enquires. The following day they told me they could certainly get me one translator - a woman - who insisted she would not be able to cope all on her own and would require the assistance of another translator: half a day each for the five-day trial and the total cost including value added tax (at 24%) would be around £8,000. Not surprisingly I didn't accept.

I can't remember who, but someone told me to look on the Internet to find a translator on www.statsaut-translator.no and this led me to Kevin Quirk, an Englishman living in Tønsberg, Norway who was a state registered translator. He had studied Norwegian at university in London and had married a Norwegian girl. He agreed to do the whole week in court on his own - simultaneous translation if necessary - for £1,400. I was mighty relieved at this offer as without a translator, Stig Lunde told me, my appeal would be dismissed. I sent Kevin Quirk some court papers for his perusal, and telegraphically transferred £1,400 into his bank account. I also sent Stig Lunde £455. On top of this I had sent £1,355 by a bank transfer to the Court of Appeal official, Monica Gran, to enable her to prepare the court documentation. The documentation, consisting of 622 pages bound up in three volumes including Norwegian language exhibits, arrived on 7th October giving me only six days to check through it all. I hated all this last-minute pressure. But it seemed inevitable given the nature of the Norwegian system.

On the 8th October, I had a long conversation with Stig Lunde. The night before, he sent me a long fax of an exhibit that Vegard Aaløkken had submitted to the court: it was a printout of that part of my large website that related to Heidi Schøne. Stig Lunde told me also, that journalist Ingunn Røren had now told him she could not fly from Bergen to attend the trial in Drammen as she was seven months pregnant. (Earlier she had said she would come but not on the date I had arranged for her). I told Stig Lunde that she would therefore have to travel by train. But even at this suggestion Stig Lunde was pessimistic: she would probably request a doctor's certificate that she was not fit even to travel by train whereupon her evidence to the court would have to be given over the phone.

I had in fact subpoenaed nine witnesses to the trial: Heidi Schøne, Henrik Lund of the Norwegian Anti-Racist Centre, Ingunn Røren, policewoman Torill Sorte, my former lawyer Karsten Gjøne, Dr. Petter Broch (Heidi's psychiatrist), Hans Odde editor of Drammens Tidende and Anne Grøstad of the Public Prosecutor's office. Stig Lunde had sent the subpoenas off to the Court of Appeal for them to stamp and send out to the witnesses. But Judge Stousland then sent them all back to Stig Lunde saying he had just discovered that the court rules had changed and it was for Stig Lunde to send out the subpoenas to the witnesses which he immediately attended to. Stig Lunde told me the subpoenas would probably reach the witnesses by Thursday the 9th October; the trial began the following Monday. Lunde assured me that as the witnesses had for a couple of weeks now been informed by him of the exact date and time they were to turn up, actual service of the subpoenas at such an advanced stage would not present a problem. The week before Stig Lunde managed to serve the subpoenas he had been away from work, ill with the flu. This delayed things and made me nervous. I guess if it came down to it he would have forced himself to go into the office even if he had not fully recovered, as of course it was essential that the subpoenas be served as I was pretty sure certain witnesses, for example Ingunn Røren, Dr. Petter Broch, Karsten Gjøne and Anne Grøstad would not otherwise turn up. Anne Grøstad of course was now going on holiday to Tenerife during the trial and her boss – the Attorney General, Mr. Busch would go in her place, if the court ordered him to attend. When I phoned Mr. Busch he told me he would not go to court, that he didn't want to speak to me and promptly put the phone down on me.

In my 8th October conversation with Stig Lunde he was most insistent that I send him, straight away, a good sum of money to cover the extra work that he had been forced to do over the preceding days. "If you want a happy lawyer, please send me the money." I was exhausted and literally had to spend every spare moment working on the court papers and preparing my case. I didn't want to go to the bank yet again to fill in a form to transmit the monies. Surely this could wait until after my return, I protested. But no, Stig Lunde would have none of it. He wanted more money now. So I said, "Maybe you know I'm gonna be put in prison or something for the website. Is that what you're trying to tell me?" He replied, "My dear friend, I think you are far off now. If this is the way it's going to be then I won't have nothing to do with it…" To which I said, "Well, no. I have always paid you and you know that." But Stig Lunde continued, "I think you have to be a little bit more polite if you want to have me on your side here… You are going to have to be polite, if not you are going to have a problem with me working for you… When I ask you for my money I don't want a long speech about it… You are saying that maybe I know something about you going to prison or something… Now I will use the words you have used a lot of times - this is "absolute rubbish" and I don't like it." I retorted: "Well, I don't trust the police and that is always a worry at the back of my mind." But it was no use. "Now we have been talking for 12 minutes," he said and again confirmed that he knew nothing about any police action. When I finally asked him whether he could tell me if Heidi Schøne had a new address for the subpoena he had just served on her he said she did have a new address but that he had been made to promise not to reveal it to me. Whom had he given the promise to? That, Stig Lunde would not tell me either.

On Saturday morning, 11th October, I went round to my bank and filled in the bank transfer form for another £800 to be sent over to Stig Lunde.

Sunday 12th October was the date of my departure from Heathrow airport. I took the KLM Air UK flight to Amsterdam and then took the connecting flight to Oslo. From there I went by train straight to Drammen, where I checked in at the Comfort Hotel.

Chapter 35

I arrived at the courthouse at 9 o'clock on Monday morning carrying my heavy rucksack full of legal papers. I had also brought with me two sets of tapes, recording 42 conversations I had had with various Norwegians over the years to play any of them if necessary. Kevin Quirk, my translator soon came and then one of the judges - who I thought was a court usher - collected old jugs of water and replaced them with fresh jugs of water. Three judges were hearing the case - Mr. Agnar Nilsen Jnr., who had replaced the water jugs, Mr. Thore Rønning and Mrs. Anita Lund. Judge Nilsen Jnr. spoke fluent English with an American accent. He was the senior judge on the bench for this trial. The other two judges did not, it turned out, speak good English.

When I asked Kevin Quirk whether he had read any of the newspaper stories on me, he said he had found a report on the Internet from the Drammens Tidende website.

Just before proceedings began Heidi Schøne came into court even though she was only scheduled to give evidence and be cross-examined by me the next day. She spoke for five minutes to the judges in Norwegian and then left. Judge Nilsen Jnr. then ruled that it was essential that Ingunn Røren come to court, but debate then followed as to who was to pay her fare. I thought I'd already given enough money to Stig Lunde for all the witnesses' fares to be paid. Judge Nilsen Jnr. said that as Vegard Aaløkken had also requested the attendance of Ingunn Røren then her fare should be split 50-50 between myself and Heidi Schøne. To which Vegard Aaløkken replied that Heidi Schøne had no money to contribute and therefore Ingunn Røren should not have to come at all. To which I quickly interrupted to say that I would pay all of Ingunn Røren's fare. Judge Nilsen Jnr. agreed and told Vegard Aaløkken to phone Ingunn Røren during lunch to tell her she had to attend court.

Discussion then took place as to whether Tor-Aksel Busch, the Attorney General, should be required to attend court. Judge Nilsen Jnr. wondered whether his participation had any relevance to my case against Heidi Schøne. I told him that a police officer - Torill Sorte - had lied on oath; that Tor-Aksel Busch in his decision letter of 15th July 2003 had not referred to any of my evidence when ruling that he would not prosecute Torill Sorte. That this meant there was no way of knowing if my evidence had been considered and that therefore Tor-Aksel Busch had to be called to explain his decision, as, I told the court, I suspected a cover up. Judge Nilsen Jnr. *seemed* to understand my argument and said the court would give its answer tomorrow.

Judge Nilsen Jnr. then told me that this trial was a totally new trial and the decision of the previous judge, Mr. Stilloff, was not relevant now. The judge casually remarked that he had looked at my website.

I would have liked in my opening speech to have properly run through all the points made in my supplemental appeal document, but I knew this would not be possible due to the lack of time. I had to explain the basic structure of the whole story first to the court and try to incorporate only the key points made in my appeal. It wouldn't be easy.

I began by saying that Heidi Schøne should be found guilty under both sections 246 and 247 of the Norwegian Penal Code for being responsible for "telling or adopting or being the primary source for the untruths," written in the Drammens Tidende article of the 14th of July 1998, since Heidi had admitted receiving the article for prior approval and had corrected nothing and I quoted the main examples of her deceit. I then carefully examined Heidi Schøne's own background with the object of convincing the court that her mental condition and high volume of outrageous and uncorroborated accusations made her a witness whose word could not safely be relied upon to be true; that she could not prove 16 years of continuous harassment and so should be found guilty. I repeated what Dr. Petter Broch, her psychiatrist, told the court last time about his patient's condition, including his assessment that my 'reports' on her past life "contained a core of truth." I emphasized that all the evidence against me pre-1995 was only on Heidi Schøne's word and I referred to the tape-recorded conversations of policemen Svein Jensen and Henrik Dugstad who did not believe Heidi. Overall, I hoped that I had put in everything of relevance. I had also to draw the court's attention the relevant documents in the three bundles of court documentation which made for a lot of tedious to-ing and fro-ing and many interruptions for Kevin Quirk to translate when necessary.

Next I proceeded to deal with Vegard Aaløkken. That he had not answered Stig Lunde's appeal document or my lengthy supplemental appeal document and so the court should draw adverse inferences from Aaløkken's silence. And that I didn't know if Vegard Aaløkken had even presented the appeal documentation to his client Heidi Schøne. I examined Vegard Aaløkken's motives by referring to his "absolute bad faith" and attempts to deceive the court, using the following facts. That at the very first hearing in August 2000 he said that my writ and Stig Lunde's supplemental writ were a form of "harassment" of Heidi Schøne. I said that as a man who had faced so many serious allegations I had the right to defend my reputation by issuing a writ. Further, that Vegard Aaløkken was "quick to jump to another perverse conclusion" when he informed the court that I had fabricated the Dun and Bradstreet report which declared I had (rightly) won 50,000 kroner against Heidi Schøne in the lower courts system, the forliksrådet. That he didn't even ring up Dun and Bradstreet to ask what the report was all about, putting the onus on me to prove that I did not fabricate the facts within the report. That only when I had telephoned Tore Lia at Dun and Bradstreet in Norway did Vegard Aaløkken apologize to the court and withdraw his allegation. I continued attacking Vegard Aaløkken by saying that at the previous hearing he had called me "mentally ill" as well as saying that my sustained "information campaign" against Heidi Schøne was a "continuing symptom" of my "mental illness." I made it clear to the court that Vegard Aaløkken had tried to persuade Judge Stilloff that I was clinically mentally ill, not as he later suggested to the Norwegian Bar Association that I was a "madman" in the "popular sense of the word." I asked the court exactly what "madman" in the "popular sense of the word" was supposed to mean, when all the newspapers had called me "mentally ill" and "sick" and "suffering from an extreme case of erotic paranoia," press descriptions designed to give the impression that I was possibly a registered mental patient or at least should have been. I continued that Vegard Aaløkken in his own "madness" had last time called me "a rapist" knowing that for 12 years his client insisted, falsely, that I had only attempted to rape her.

I went on to refer to policewoman Torill Sorte's attempt to persuade the court at the first trial that my mother told her I had been "put" in a mental hospital, and I read out my family doctor's letter to refute this. And that for Bergens Tidende to identify me 16 times as the "Muslim" man clearly indicated that religious prejudice was the real motive behind the press onslaught from 1995 onwards.

I told the court I did not want Vegard Aaløkken now to be allowed to mislead the court, by repeating the nonsense of continuous sex terror from 1985 onwards without first answering the points raised in my appeal, as otherwise I asked, what was the point putting in an appeal if all its arguments were completely ignored. I requested that Aaløkken answer each point (knowing full well the court would not oblige him to) or that I would alternatively get answers from Heidi Schøne in my cross-examination of her.

I emphasized the "positive" contact I'd had with Heidi: in 1988 when she requested my help against Gudmund Johannessen; in 1989 when she phoned me from her hotel and spoke to me for two hours and my August 1990 visit for which she did not report me to the police and her admission to sending me Christian literature in the autumn of 1990.

When I'd finished, Judge Nilsen Jnr. told me that it was not the practice in Norway to attack the character of opposing counsel: "You are not in England now." A remark which surprised me as Aløkken had attacked me, albeit in my capacity as the plaintiff, for which surely I was entitled to respond. In any event I was going to say my piece.

Vegard Aaløkken then made his opening speech. He repeated most of what he had said in the last court case: that Heidi was not responsible for many of the comments in the newspapers, for example that I had written Heidi 300 letters from 1997 to 1998 or that I had threatened with death her neighbours if they did not give me her new address or that I was suffering from an extreme case of erotic paranoia. Aaløkken ignored the fact that Heidi Schøne had approved the 1995 articles and 1998 article beforehand but did not correct them. He announced that I was uninvited in April 1985 (ignoring the fact that before leaving to go skiing Heidi had left her door key for me under a stone on the window-ledge with a pot of hot blackcurrent tea waiting inside); that in 1990 I had "distributed tapes to people" - (I had sent one tape to Dr. Broch which merely recorded word for word the letter I sent him, my reasoning being that it might be easier for him to listen to a tape than plough through my long letter); Vegard Aaløkken conceded that my information on Heidi Schøne's past was "in large part true."

Vegard Aaløkken then went through several of the letters and postcards I had written to Heidi in 1995 and onwards when I had communicated my disgust at her lies and her hypocrisy in calling herself a Christian; in one letter dated 6th March 1995 I simply said "Gotcha! At last" and "Freddie's back" which Vegard Aaløkken wanted to convey as another example of harassment, when in fact I wrote this immediately after receiving the letter dated 28th February 1995 from Helge Wesenberg, my Bergen lawyer, informing me of her allegation of "attempted rape." I knew this to be false and at the time I thought I had cornered Heidi and would be able to lodge a complaint about this allegation. The court, with much amusement, tried to recall which films Freddie Kruger had appeared in. I had to tell the court 'Nightmare on Elm Street,' but that my nickname, obviously, was (as a matter of fact) Freddie in England. [The truth was that I knew at the time I wrote these words how they were related to Freddie Kruger]. Vegard Aaløkken then produced a Hello! magazine article I had sent to Heidi - sent to her after the May 1995 newspaper articles. This featured Susan Smith, the American woman who was executed in 2003 for murdering, by drowning, her two small children. In this article I had circled the similarities between Smith's life and Heidi's: there were many comparisons to be made. (See The Times newspaper article on the Smith case printed in Chapter 29 of this book).

Again, Vegard Aaløkken referred to my postcard calling Heidi a "Christian pervert." He ignored my full explanation in my appeal document that these words meant she in fact "perverted the true values of Christianity."

Vegard Aaløkken continued: that my communications with Heidi indicated I had a "special sexual interest" in her, ignoring the fact that her own life was dominated entirely by sexual adventure and disaster, which I in turn had criticized in my letters to her. He referred to a police witness statement by Heidi dated 17th February 1990 - a Norwegian language document - in which it was alleged by Heidi that I had made threats to her sister Elisabeth in the snow outside her house in February 1990 (when I was accompanied by Stuart McQueen) and then vandalized a car. Completely untrue on both counts and which accusations were not in any case put to me on my arrest in Bergen on 17th February 1990. They were fabrications by Heidi. This witness statement was included for the first time, as far as I could see, in the three volumes of court documentation sent to me on 7th October 2003 by Monica Gran, the Court official. And as it was in Norwegian I had no idea what it meant – until now.

Vegard Aaløkken referred to policewoman Torill Sorte's 22nd January 1997 report (printed above) when he repeated her comments that my mother was an "elderly" woman (I repeat she was 62 in 1997) who said that I was "sick and need help" and that I'd been "admitted to hospital for treatment." Vegard Aaløkken then told the court I had made death threats against Heidi's son, Daniel, referring to Heidi's police witness statement (see Chapter 32) of the 23rd April 1997. And that I used to "grope" her and had "forcibly kissed" her and told her that if she didn't let me continue I had threatened to tell her neighbours that she'd been sexually abused by her stepmother's father. That I forced her to have sexual intercourse with me. That I had a Restraining Order imposed on the 24th August 2000 on me by the Norwegian police - which Vegard Aaløkken omitted to mention had been withdrawn by the police when I pointed out to them at the time that I hadn't seen Heidi in over 10 years. That I had received a fine of 10,000 kroner in 2001 under section 390(a) of the Norwegian Penal Code - Aaløkken forgetting to mention that I was convicted in absentia. And finally that my harassment continued in the form of my website www.norway-shockers.com. (The fact was that Drammens Tidende still covered me on their own website).

Before the start of Tuesday's proceedings (14th October) Vegard Aaløkken gave the court and myself a letter from Dr. Broch, Heidi's psychiatrist, dated 13th October 2003 which stated that Heidi Schøne's mental state was such that she was unfit to face any cross-examination by me. Kevin Quirk told me that the letter said that Heidi had had a "pathological relationship" with her parents and amazingly a "pathological relationship" with me. Vegard Aaløkken then argued that her psychiatrist's recommendation should be heeded by the court. The same tactics were employed now as for the court case in 2002. I argued that it was absolutely essential for me to cross-examine Heidi Schøne and that the opportunity to do this was a fundamental aspect of my case. The court said they would delay their decision on this matter until after Heidi Schøne gave her evidence. But the judges had reached a decision on whether or not they would ask Tor-Aksel Busch, the Attorney-General, to present himself for cross-examination: he would not be asked. No reasons were given by Judge Nilsen Jnr., who pronounced the ruling.

Heidi Schøne entered the courtroom looking ill and exhausted from stress. She had long hair now but I guess it had to be another wig. She began by stating that she promised to tell the truth. She added that she'd been on a state disability pension for the past 18 months, had a prolapse of the vertebrae in her neck, had problems remembering things and had a terrible headache as well. That she'd had an alcoholism problem in the family (a reference to her late mother) and she'd been sexually abused by her stepmother's father. She then implored the court that something must be done to "stop" me. That if only she had the money she would sue me in England. And that she wished I was dead.

More 'facts' about our relationship now emerged: that I used to have "way out" discussions with her; that I had been forcing her to convert to Islam; that I called her a "whore" on my 1985 visit to her; that I "shouted and wailed" over the telephone; that I talked of "stoning women to death" (a practice that I believe has no part whatsoever in Islam, but I knew Heidi was now raising to blacken my character); that I called English and Scandinavian women "pigs." That I tried to have intercourse with her on my first visit to Norway in Christmas 1984, had "penetrated" her but "couldn't manage to ejaculate." That I'd criticized her "fat thighs." That I said to her she was "just a bitch." And that my temper was capable of making her life terrible. That I'd written many cards and letters to her calling her a "bitch" and "a pig" and "a swine" but that she had thrown them all away. That indeed there was a long period when she didn't have a phone "probably" from 1988 to 1993 she said; that there was "a woman" I had "scared to death" and another woman who had become "hysterical" because of me. Heidi did not mention who these women were. That from 1985 to 1990 she had two bags full of my letters which she threw away; that I sent cassette tapes to her neighbours (none were produced in evidence); that when I visited her Drammen hotel in 1989 one of her colleagues - no name was given - had told her that I was in her eyes "completely mad." That on one occasion I telephoned her all night repeating that I would "kill" her; that my "comments" to Heidi that her son was "a bastard" and I would "kill him" terrified her. That I had also written to her saying that because her son Daniel was "a bastard, he didn't deserve to live."

She admitted she wanted my help in 1988 against Gudmund Johannessen but stated that I had called her. (What a lie. She had called me at my office within minutes of her being told to "fuck off " by Gudmund Johannessen. I was the only real friend she had and she knew it!). She admitted she wanted Gudmund Johannessen beaten up. Further that there were many people around her who were scared of me - she gave no names; years ago, she said, I told her I loved watching horror films.

Judge Nilsen Jnr. asked Heidi to leave the courtroom and then quickly decided he would not allow me to cross-examine her. He would do so himself. Did I have any questions? Yes, about three hours worth I thought to myself. Off the top of my head I rattled off several questions, which the judge wrote down. The honorable Judge Agnar A. Nilsen Jnr., judge and cross-examiner - cum - prosecutor at the same time!

Heidi came back in and in response to the judge's questions said the following: that a distant cousin of hers was indeed raped and killed; she had certainly been raped by a Bergen shopkeeper; that when asked about what her condition was to justify a 100% disability pension she replied "extreme post-traumatic stress syndrome." When asked whether she had been exorcised from possession of demons in 1990 she hit the roof in a histrionic outburst intended to convey to the court that only a lunatic - me - could allege such a thing. I have to say again she was an extremely good actress. When asked for clarification on her court statement in 2002 that I had "applied for a residence permit" she stated that I had "shouted over the phone" to her or "maybe written" to her that I was "going to get a residence permit." That in 1995 she had the three newspaper articles read out to her over the phone, from Verdens Gang, Bergens Tidende and Drammens Tidende; that in 1998 Ingunn Røren contacted her prior to the 14th of July 1998 article but that she "couldn't remember" if it was read out to her. (At the 2002 trial she said it was read out to her). That I had pestered and harassed her for so many years that the Post Office "offered to filter" her post; when asked whether she could remember any neighbours I had threatened with death she replied, "No," as she "withdrew" herself more and more, but that "Runar Schøne can remember the names of neighbours threatened." Had she kept any of the alleged cassette tapes I'd sent her? No, she'd thrown them away she said. Further, that Aftenposten did a story on me last year. That I had used "morphine" obtained from my father (a general medical practitioner, now retired); that I wrote "horrible things" on a boarded-up window of her home in August 1990; that she was burdened by looking after her almost blind and handicapped (second) son; that in the middle of London (in 1985) near her hotel there was a confrontation with me and she had to get "security" to take me away. That on one of my visits to her in Norway I had sinisterly just "appeared" at her window.

510

Judge Nilsen Jnr. did not allow me to cross-examine Heidi on any of her new and varied evidence, saying I would have the opportunity to "comment" in my closing speech. Oh what a travesty! I also noticed that Heidi had referred to me in a Norwegian police witness statement as a Shia Muslim, when in fact I was a Sunni. The Shia branch of Islam, of course, was associated with Iran and in Norway Iran did not have a good image at all since the Salman Rushdie affair, when the Norwegian publisher of his book 'The Satanic Verses' was shot and wounded in Norway.

Next to give evidence was Henrik Lund of the Anti-racist Centre of Oslo. I had a quick chat with him outside the courtroom informing him also of Heidi's courtroom antics. Once in the witness box Henrik Lund confirmed, in relation to Bergens Tidende's article of May 1995 calling me in the "Muslim" man 16 times that no newspaper in Norway would write similarly when the subject was Jewish or Christian, so that to do it when the subject was Muslim can be seen to be an attack on the Muslim religion. I myself told the judge that this was bound to provoke a strong reaction from me.

At the close of business I left the courthouse somewhat deflated as I knew that Heidi Schøne had escaped cross-examination yet again. I walked over the bridge across the river back to the town centre and looked around the shops for a little while. I then stood outside the entrance to Steen and Strøm, the department store, when I was confronted by a familiar face. It was Margot Iqbal, a Norwegian lady who had once been married to a Pakistani and whom I had met many times in the Norwegian Church in East London. What a surprise to see her now. Neither of us could believe it. We went to a café close to Drammen Cathedral and talked for an hour or so. I told her that she was welcome to visit the courthouse to attend my case.

The next day was Wednesday 15th October 2003. One of my previous lawyers, Karsten Gjone, happened to be in the courtroom opposite us that week for one of his own cases and before his day's business began he made himself available to give evidence. In a quick appearance he confirmed he recognized me from the 14th July 1998 Drammens Tidende article and that I had previously instructed him to sue Drammens Tidende, Bergens Tidende and Verdens Gang. I did not attack him for his failure to issue writs against the three newspapers for their 1995 articles as I suspected the judge would object. Besides, I had the Bar Association's decision confirming Karsten Gjone's negligence to hand into the court.

Hans Odde, the editor of Drammens Tidende was next to give evidence. He mentioned that he knew he was the subject of a strong attack by me on my website. He confirmed that he had no evidence that I had sent 300 letters to Heidi Schøne from 1997 to 1998. When questioned on his newspaper's statement that my reports on Heidi's life had "no basis in reality," he stated that, "At the time it was difficult to evaluate the evidence," and he did not check out whether my reports were true. (Yet he had three years to do so, from 1995 to 1998). That the information for his 14th July 1998 article came from Verdens Gang. He finally then admitted that his newspaper should not have said my reports had "no basis in reality." Regarding Drammens Tidende's emphatic claim to "16 years of sexual harassment," I reminded Odde in cross-examination that in 1995 I had sent him copies of Heidi's letters to me from 1982 to 1985 and a full resumé of my side of the story. When I asked whether Heidi had corrected any of his newspaper's draft articles he said, "No, she didn't." Further that he did not know what "erotic paranoia" meant when he allowed those words to be printed in 1998! When I questioned him on the source and accuracy of various statements (including the one that I had "threatened to kill" Heidi's son) in his newspaper he said that his newspaper should have researched the matter "much better" than they did. I was surprised to hear Odde then say that his newspaper had to a certain extent "fallen out" with Heidi Schøne when she accused Drammens Tidende of not doing enough for her.

Next up was policewoman Torill Sorte, born, she said, on 30th April 1968. I immediately referred to my family doctor's letter indicating that I had never been put in a mental hospital. How come, I asked her, could my mother have told her this, particularly when we also had a recorded conversation with my mother saying the opposite? Torill Sorte responded by saying that she had spoken to my mother "several times" and that my mother had told her I had been put in a mental hospital. I told her she was a liar and pressed her to reveal who phoned who and when. Her reply was that she "couldn't remember." I told her I had the transcripts of 18 of our conversations from the time we started speaking in 1996 to when we stopped in 1998 (a set of which I had given to Vegard Aaløkken). I went through the salient points of each conversation with Torill Sorte. Once again I put it to Torill Sorte that she was a liar and asked her to explain herself with more clarity but Judge Nilsen Jnr. interrupted to say that the court would draw its own conclusions from her statement.

When I had finished and Torill Sorte had left the courtroom, Judge Nilsen Jnr. reprimanded me for my "outburst" for calling Torill Sorte "a liar" and that if it happened again to another witness I would not be allowed to continue any further cross-examination.

Then came Runar Gottlieb Schøne who came hobbling in on crutches and proceeded to tell the court he had had an operation on his leg some hours earlier. Once again he admitted to "babbling" over the phone to me in his "Come to Jesus, Allah doesn't exist" phone call. He confirmed that at our last court appearance in January 2001 he compared me to Osama bin Laden and wanted to kill me. Again, he could not provide any evidence as to which of his neighbours he said in the newspapers I had "threatened to kill." He did mention that from the time he met Heidi in 1993 she was always telling him about me and that he'd seen many letters from me. His appearance on the stand didn't last long: he was not in a good mood and I knew that Judge Nilsen Jnr. would not let me perform the sort of cross-examination I had in mind for him. So I let it go.

Ingunn Røren appeared next. She had in fact taken a plane that morning from Bergen airport to Oslo. So much for her earlier claim that she was not in a fit state to fly due to her pregnancy. She had just been trying it on, as I suspected. I asked her what material she based her 14th July 1998 article on. She said: "Heidi's word and the other newspapers." When I challenged her to justify her words: "Psychiatrists think the Englishman is suffering from an extreme case of erotic paranoia," she replied that she didn't at the time know what the words "erotic paranoia" meant but just lifted the words from the newspaper Verdens Gang. She did now know what these words meant. Importantly she also confirmed that she had contacted Heidi in 1998 prior to writing her 14th July 1998 article.

I had prepared in England extensive notes for my cross-examination of Ingunn Røren but Judge Nilsen Jnr. made it clear that I was going to be given little time to complete my task as he wanted all the witnesses to be cross-examined by close of business on that Wednesday. So now I could test Ingunn Røren on only a few of the important points. With regard to her accusation that I had abused her boyfriend in 1996 for "living in sin" with her, my intention was to play the tape of my one brief conversation with him, in court to refute this and ask for this boyfriend's name and why he hadn't put a witness statement in, to support her claim. But none of this I could do as Judge Nilsen Jnr. would not permit it. After I referred Ingunn Røren to the Norwegian translation of this conversation with her boyfriend, she froze and in the face of incontrovertible evidence still maintained her original claim! I was about to go in for the kill but Judge Nilsen Jnr. prevented me going any further saying the court would draw its own conclusions from Ingunn Røren's statement and the other evidence. Yes, I was indeed not in England now.

Dr. Petter Broch came on at 12.35 p.m. In cross-examination he told me Heidi was suffering from an "enduring personality disorder." When I asked whether she was suffering from schizophrenia he said, "Definitely not." Dr. Broch went on to confirm as correct his seven-point statement on Heidi Schøne made on oath in 2001 regarding her various 'abusers.' He stated that he thought my "pursuit" of her had a "pathological" basis and was a form of "stalking" according to American Psychiatric Association journals on the topic. I asked him to try to appreciate that as I had been accused of threatening to kill Heidi's son, family and neighbours and had been described as suffering from an extreme form of erotic paranoia in the newspapers, then I had the right to take legal action and a right to reply with my version of events. And that this could hardly amount to "stalking." I could see that Dr. Broch was fumbling for an answer and when I tried to continue Judge Nilsen Jnr. stopped me; the judge had had enough. (Stig Lunde had told me when I was still in England that Dr. Broch was not at all happy to have to come to court yet again as he was a very busy man. I reminded Stig Lunde that Vegard Aaløkken had himself requested the presence of Dr. Broch and further, that it was essential Dr. Broch be called to confirm to the court exactly what he gave in evidence last time, as Judge Stilloff did not make mention of it in his judgement).

After lunch Vegard Aaløkken made his closing speech. Again he called me "mentally ill." Again he said Drammens Tidende were justified in calling me a "Muslim" as that was how I had "represented" myself. That Drammens Tidende's accusation of "300 letters to Heidi" from 1997 to 1998 (for which there was no evidence at all), was not Heidi Schøne's accusation but that of the newspaper as it also was for the "extreme erotic paranoia" comment. However, this time Vegard Aaløkken did not call me a "rapist." He confirmed that Norwegian law does not require absolute precision and that because of my 1982 to 1985 letters the "sex terror/stalking" period had to be reduced accordingly (presumably by four years although Vegard Aaløkken didn't specify). He said the evidence amply indicated that I was responsible for "stalking" for the "remaining period" and that Heidi should be found not guilty. Vegard Aaløkken ignored in particular, once again, Heidi's 1988 request for help from me and our friendly contact during the second half of 1990. I marvelled at how in effect I had to have hard evidence and plenty of it, to counter allegations of harassment and that my word often counted for little. Yet Vegard Aaløkken argued all Heidi had to have was her word to support her claims as sufficient evidence of the truth. I have no doubt at all that if I had not kept those 1982 to 1985 letters then my word on the subject of those letters would have counted for nothing. No one would have believed these letters were ever written to me. As it was, the fact that I had not kept Heidi's few post-1985 letters and cards to me was taken as clear evidence that the "harassment" started shortly after 1985.

On Wednesday evening back at my hotel I put in five hours on my closing speech. I was very happy with the finished product. I turned up in court next morning in bullish mood determined to emphasize that in no shape or form was there 16 years of continuous sex terror/harassment or stalking. I told the court that the years 1982, 1983, 1984 and up to summer 1985 when I was told Heidi was pregnant to Gudmund Johannessen again, were entirely "good" years. I said that no complaints were made during the course of 1985 against me and only after I spilled the beans to her father in November 1986 did the first complaint come, two weeks later in December 1986, when she backdated her allegation of attempted rape to Easter 1985: a long time to wait to make such a complaint; and only then, I emphasized, out of revenge for telling her father of her sordid past. And that no details have ever come to light of the exact nature of the "attempted rape." That significantly no harassment allegations were made to the police or anyone else in 1987, 1988 or 1989. Only when I tried to visit Heidi in February 1990 to confront her over her incomprehensible past did she then complain to the police and backdate her vague and unsubstantiated allegations. That she didn't contact the police at all regarding my alleged 400 obscene letters that were later "thrown away." That we have no confirmation from any member of her family or friends that they have seen with their own eyes the 400 obscene letters or even a proportion of them. That Heidi took revenge on me because I had written to Gudmund Johannessen's father telling him of his son's abuse of Heidi which his father was completely ignorant of.

I mentioned the year 1987 when Heidi told me she had visited Disneyland in the U.S.A with her son and her employer's family. That she was working in a photographic processing laboratory in Bergen; living alone as a single mother. That she had been given a second-hand Volvo to drive by Gudmund Johannessen's father who had also recently sold the family snack shop. That Heidi told me Daniel needed an operation on his nose. That 1987 was a friendly, good year. As was 1988 when Heidi had admitted trying to enlist my help against Gudmund Johannessen. And which girl, I yet again emphasized, would request such help from a man who had attempted to rape her and (in the alternative) "somehow" raped her and also threatened to kill her son? For 1990 I made the usual points in some detail. For 1991, 1992, 1993 and 1994 I said there were no complaints made by Heidi to the police in those years. Then came 1995 when, once again, she backdated her allegations solely relying on her own word: the word of a woman who was in 1988 subject to psychiatric treatment and was now suffering from a permanent mental disorder. I told the court that Heidi had made up her claim that I had obtained and used morphine from my father. That photographic evidence should have been obtained at the time, as proof of my writing "horrible things" on Heidi's door and boarded-up window. That the documentary evidence in possession of Heidi Schøne from February 1995 clearly discloses my annoyance at her silence on questions I had asked her regarding my February 1990 arrest. And when I learnt of the attempted rape allegation I sent my initial 20 reports to her neighbours past and present, as a lesson for making this false allegation. And on seeing the 1995 newspaper articles I initiated a large information campaign in response. I referred again to the independent taped evidence from policemen Henrik Dugstad and Svein Jensen and from Ann-Kristin Horvei doubting Heidi Schøne's ability to tell the truth and to psychiatrist Nils Rettersdol's comments on the nonsense of my "erotic paranoia."

As for Dr. Broch I tried to cut him down to size by examining his letter of 6th September 2001 in which he said in his fourth paragraph that the contact in England [in 1982] with "this Egyptian was very difficult" and that I treated Heidi like my "property." I declared that if this was true

Heidi would hardly write to me such considerate and loving letters from 1982 to1985. I repeated again Broch's confirmation of those very revealing seven points he made on Heidi's life on his first court appearance in 2002.

I asked the court for a declaration to be made in its judgement that Ingunn Røren had lied on oath with regard to her telling the PFU that I had "abused" her boyfriend for "living in sin" and for a declaration that Drammens Tidende had lied when it said I had written "300 letters to Heidi Schøne in the last year" (1997 to 1998) and a declaration that policewoman Torill Sorte had lied on oath with regard to my mother telling her I had been put in a mental hospital. I also pointed out that if Ingunn Røren had insisted in 1998 that Heidi Schøne had told her in 1995 that I had "attempted" to rape her then that was proof enough that Heidi had fabricated her later allegation of actual rape.

That Heidi Schøne had been contacted by Ingunn Røren in 1998 and in having the 1998 article to approve or at least read out to her over the phone, in not correcting it Heidi had the intention to adopt it as true, in effect of making it her version also of the truth. Therefore it cannot be right to direct the fault for false allegations solely at the door of Drammens Tidende.

I repeated the fact that in a libel claim I needed someone to recognize me from the article: that Karsten Gjone was this person and that my reputation had further suffered in his eyes.

I also rubbished the PFU decision of the 24th August 1999 which declared that Drammens Tidende were not in breach of good journalistic practice over their 14th July 1998 article and referred to my letter of the 30th January 2000 to Per Edgar Kokkvold of the PFU. As For the Eiker Modum and Sigdal Magistrates Court fine of the 2nd November 2001, I again went briefly into the reasons as to why that was a totally unacceptable decision.

I then went on to clarify, refute and explain certain comments made by Vegard Aaløkken on the 1995 and post-1995 evidence and made certain the judges were fully aware that after November 1995 I myself knew that none of my letters to Heidi Schøne reached her as they were filtered by the Post Office, yet I continued to write "to" her to let the police know my frustrations.

I finished by saying that if the court was to rule in my favour by finding Heidi Schøne guilty, on this occasion only, I would not enforce my claim for damages or legal costs, to save her from living in poverty for the rest of her life. And that if the court decided only Drammens Tidende is guilty the court should insert a declaration that, even though the newspaper is not on trial, they have failed to prove many allegations, which the court should itemise. And I asked the court to remember that this case began as my prosecution of both Drammens Tidende and Heidi Schøne and told them that due to Stig Lunde missing time limits to go to the Supreme Court, Drammens Tidende had dropped out of the action. And because of that I should not in any event have Heidi's legal costs awarded against me nor have to pay Value Added Tax on them as I was not a Norwegian citizen and I was resident abroad.

When I had finished, Vegard Aaløkken was entitled to reply to my closing speech. But before Vegard Aaløkken was allowed to start Judge Nilsen Jnr. said this: "I want an immediate message to be sent to Heidi Schøne that I have been ashamed to take part in this trial." Quite taken aback I asked why. Judge Nilsen Jnr. said, "Look at the state she was in." I replied that her problems had been self-inflicted, as she knew long ago I would take things all the way after what was said about me in the newspapers. Ignoring me, Judge Nilsen Jnr. angrily retorted, "You know, I can fine you for bringing this appeal to court." So I calmly said that if necessary I would take the case to the European Court of Human Rights.

After this highly charged exchange Vegard Aaløkken made his final comments and by one o'clock the court rose, one and a half days earlier than scheduled. Vegard Aaløkken quickly went outside the courtroom to speak to someone and I packed my rucksack with the court papers. I thanked Kevin Quirk. He asked me what I was going to do now and I said I was catching the plane home that evening. I was relieved it was all over but I knew I'd lost my appeal; Judge Nilsen Jnr. had made that quite obvious.

As I walked towards the door of the courtroom my heart sank. I saw two policemen immediately outside in the foyer waiting for me. The Drammen police had obviously liased with Judge Nilsen Jnr. who must have told them exactly what time the trial would finish. I knew now I would not be going home that evening and possibly for many evenings to come. The policemen apprehended me, then gave Kevin Quirk some paperwork to translate for me. It was a summons for my arrest for promoting my website in Norway and for a small fax campaign over the last 18 months, detailing Heidi Schøne's past. Once again, I was charged under section 390(a) of the Norwegian Penal Code. The summons was dated the 8th October 2003, the very day I challenged Stig Lunde on the telephone as to whether he had any information as to a possible arrest. The police of course knew I was coming and had prepared themselves in good time. This more recent campaign of mine was in fact very limited as few people in Norway had actually hit on my website and the number of faxes sent was around 40 to 50. The problem as I saw it, was the nature of the things I put on the website: that Torill Sorte had lied on oath. And that the Public Prosecutor Anne Grøstad had covered up for Torill Sorte. I had also attacked the editors of the three newspapers and their journalists and had scanned in every single anti-Norway article from the British press I could find. I coupled this with articles from Aftenposten's own English news website whose headlines described Norwegians, among other things, as "the least religious in Europe," and "world leaders in casual sex"! The chapter in this book on Bosnia was also on view. Concentrated all on one website it was guaranteed to upset the Norwegian establishment. So the police officers then arrested me and took me downstairs to their van parked in the car park.

We travelled to a place I knew well - the newly built Drammen police station and my escorts drove into the underground car park. One of the police officers was the spitting image of the Brazilian World Cup footballer Ronaldo, and when I told him this he laughed, "Yes, I know - many others tell me this too." Well, 'Ronaldo' relieved me of my jacket and trouser belt, the contents of my pockets, my wallet and my wrist watch. All my Norwegian money was counted and placed in a separate plastic bag and put in the police safe. My rucksack and other belongings were put in a locker by 'Ronaldo.' He told me I could make a phone call. I immediately rang the British Embassy in Oslo to explain my predicament and was put through to the Vice-Consul. I told him of my contact with Patricia Svendsen earlier in the year and that she said I should contact the Embassy if and when I was arrested. I told the Vice-Consul that I had now been arrested and the reasons for it and could he send someone round to help me? I told him the address of my website and explained that its existence was basically the reason for my arrest. He said he'd send Patricia Svendsen round as soon as possible, who he said had worked for the British Embassy for 10 years. But the Vice-Consul added, "You do know there is only so much we can do in these situations." I replied, "Yes, I know that." I made a second phone call - to Stig Lunde. "Hello Stig, I'm in Drammen police station because I've just been arrested," I complained. "You're joking," he replied. "No I'm not ..." And I explained the chain of events after I had finished prosecuting my civil case. Whilst I was talking to him he tried to contact Harald Wibye on his other phone, but Wibye was busy with a client and would call back. We continued to talk in the hope that his ongoing efforts to contact Wibye would succeed but Wibye remained busy. Eventually we said goodbye in the knowledge that I would most probably be kept in the cells overnight, until, hopefully, Harald Wibye could visit me the next day.

I was then led to the cells and locked in, minus my shoes which I had to leave outside the door. Maybe half an hour later, the officer in charge of the case (when I'd earlier asked him his name he said, "That's not important") unlocked my door to say that he would like to ask me some questions so that they could sort this matter out whereupon I could leave the police station. That I would also have to pay my outstanding fine. Alternatively, he said, I could wait until the people from the embassy arrived. I said I'd wait for the people from the embassy. About one and a half hours later the same officer came to my door to announce that the people from the embassy had arrived. Patricia Svendsen, I was surprised to see, was of Asian origin - brown skin. Her colleague was Neil Hulbert, an 'Entry Clearance Officer.' Their news was not good. Patricia Svendsen informed me that the police wanted to keep me in custody and charge me in the magistrates court the next day and ask for a custodial sentence of eight months. Patricia Svendsen was not happy at this and told me I would not be going to prison if she had anything to do with it. So much for the officer in charge earlier offering to "clear the matter up" and let me go! Patricia Svendsen took down some particulars of my story and she recalled the warning letters I had written to her earlier in the year. I guess she must now have realized how disappointed I felt at her failure to help me then, before it got to this stage. I showed Patricia Svendsen the May 1995 Bergens Tidende article and their "erotic paranoia" commentary and read out a paragraph from one of Heidi Schøne's letters. However, it was clear to her that nothing was going to be resolved that day as she wanted me to get proper legal advice before I talked to the police and such assistance would not be forthcoming until tomorrow. I gave her Stig Lunde's phone number as well as my mother's phone number so she could tell my mother what had happened. "She won't have a heart attack will she?" queried Miss Svendsen. "I hope

515

not," I replied. Miss Svendsen then asked me for a photocopy of my passport particulars which photocopy I had stored in my wallet. I left the interview room but the police desk was deserted - we were all alone down there. So I went to my locker, retrieved my wallet and took out the one-page photocopy showing my passport details and photo. I put my wallet in my front trouser pocket and returned to the interview room. Soon the embassy officials bade me farewell and told me they would continue their efforts to try to free me.

The officer in charge of the case then gave me a signed copy of a Restraining Order made against me dated 8th October 2003, under section 222(a) of the Norwegian Criminal Procedure Act whereby I was barred from visiting Heidi at her residence or contacting her in any other way. I had no idea where she now lived as she had, of course, apparently moved. And again, I had not visited her in 12 years or attempted to do so. So I looked upon this restraining order as akin to the engineering of crime by the police in their bloody-mindedness. Further, the Order stated that I was "barred from distributing information about the aggrieved party to third parties either by letter, telephone, telefax, e-mail or the Internet." The Restraining Order was to last until 8th October 2004. Violation of the Restraining Order "was punishable by fines and imprisonment of up to six months or both and repeated violations punishable by up to two years imprisonment."

I was put back in the cells. It must have been evening time when two policemen opened my door holding some food. Vegetable soup with stewed beef, two rolls and a yoghurt. I wasn't going to eat though. I knew that by eating I would soon have to go to the toilet and there was no toilet paper. And no soap to wash one's hands with. For water, one pressed a button in the wall above the toilet and a thin stream of water shot out. And I wanted to stay clean. Every half an hour a policeman checked on me - to see if I was still alive. This carried on all night save for the small hours, when the checks were less frequent. I got no sleep - just lay there on my bunk under a blanket to keep me warm, dozing in the full light of my cell. I exercised a little by walking around this confined space and eventually ate the yoghurt. The next time a policeman opened my door he told me it was 8.30 in the morning. It was one of my arresting officers from the day before who, surprised to see me said, "Are you still here?" No breakfast came - not even a cup of tea. Later, the door opened again and one well built blond-haired policeman appeared. He said he just wanted to know what I looked like - obviously curious as to who this longtime adversary was. Time dragged on. At 11.30 a.m. the door opened again and I was told I would shortly be taken to the magistrates court. About half an hour later two policemen arrived to take me to the Eiker Modum and Sigdal Magistrates Court. "Your lawyer will be at the court," I was told. They let me wash my hands and face with soap and warm water in the adjoining toilet facilities. I was then taken around the corner to my locker where I put my belt on as well as my watch and leather jacket and took my rucksack out.

Outside, frost lay on the ground as we drove for half an hour to the courthouse. I was relieved to be out of that claustrophobic cell. Twice in the night when I had coughing fits and needed assistance - even just a cup of tea - I rang the bell in my cell but no one came. If I had been dying in between their half hour checks the police would have been none the wiser. I prayed very hard that I would not have to go to prison. Knowing the Norwegians as I did I knew it would be a close call.

We arrived at the courthouse early and had to wait for the judge and lawyers to arrive. The court session was being specially and hastily convened for me. Eventually my lawyer arrived. Not Harald Wibye but a local Drammen lawyer, Svein Olav Duesund, who had been given the papers two hours earlier. No official interpreter was available so they brought along another policeman who spoke reasonable English, to translate for me. Mr. Duesund took me to an interview room and told me negotiations were presently taking place on my case but that if I were to plead guilty to the charges I may - he wasn't certain - escape with a fine and a suspended prison sentence. Would I be prepared to accept this? "Yes," I said. I knew it would be a pointless exercise trying to reason with my accusers. The police lawyer turned up - Ingunn Hodne - and my lawyer conferred with her. When the courtroom was unlocked I went in with my lawyer who discussed my options in more detail with me. I was not going to debate with him why I could not be charged under section 390 of the Criminal Code which gave me the defence of justified comment. After the trouble Harald Wibye had had two years earlier in trying to bring that section in to cover me I was in no mood to try to argue the point myself now. I was exhausted and would do whatever it took to get out of the country. Mr. Duesund then went out. I sat in the witness box with only the translator policeman sitting behind me in the room. When my lawyer came back in it was to tell me that the police lawyer had agreed that if I paid my outstanding fine of 10,000 kroner plus interest together with another 10,000 kroner fine for the present offence for which I was to plead guilty, they would let me leave Norway that evening in return for a prison sentence of eight months suspended for two years. At the same time I was to close my website and do no more faxing. I told my lawyer it was all agreed. Mr. Duesund said, "All this is subject to the judge himself agreeing that you shouldn't go to prison."

The judge then came in and after I promised to tell the truth, he made sure I understood the charges. He asked me if I pleaded guilty or if I wanted to contest the charges. I pleaded guilty. He was at the same time typing away on his computer. More pronouncements were then made as to what was expected of me. The judge mercifully agreed that I did not have to go to prison. Then the hearing was adjourned and we all left the courtroom to sit in the waiting area. After 15 minutes we all went back in again and the judge handed my lawyer and the police lawyer a copy of his verdict. This was read through to me by my translator. I was given seven days to close my website as they did not want Heidi Schøne's name, photos or life history being made available "to the world." So much for the right to reply. That the newspapers had written such rubbish on me elicited no comment at all from the police lawyer or the judge. The Norwegians were determined to silence me. Judge Eric Stillum signed three copies of the verdict and gave one to my lawyer who passed it on to me. Good, I was finally safe.

We all went into the waiting area outside the courtroom whilst discussions took place as to how I was to pay my 22,205 kroner fine. It had to be cash and the question was to which bank was I to be taken to get the money. After a little while the police lawyer, Ingunn Hodne, gave me her mobile phone to take a call from Harald Wibye. Harald told me that behind the scenes he had been working overtime to get me out of an eight-month prison sentence. To do this he had to put his own neck on the line by assuring the judge and the police lawyer that I would definitely obey his command to cease publicising Heidi Schøne all over Norway by fax and would shut down my website. Harald Wibye told me that at first the police lawyer was sceptical that he, Harald, had such influence over me. He however managed to persuade them after many phone calls that I would obey his orders. And that he didn't want to get in touch with me beforehand in case he gave me false hope. Harald Wibye now asked me to abide by his request and I agreed knowing full well that the court's verdict would never be enforced, at the request of the Norwegians, by the British courts. But I knew Harald Wibye had done terribly well to get me off the hook so I was not going to argue with him.

Eventually I went back with my two police escorts to the police van and we drove to the nearest bank, the Sparebanken in Hokksund. There, one of the policemen came in with me and explained to the bank clerk that I had to pay a 22,205 kroner fine and that I would pay with my Visa card. I showed the bank clerk, a lady, my passport as evidence of my identity. After spending a very long time on the phone waiting for Visa Norway to get clearance from Visa England the bank clerk told me that as I did not have a second form of identity I was only allowed to withdraw 10,000 kroner. We attended to the formalities. I put the money in my wallet. We would now have to go back and report to the police station and get permission to go out to another bank's cash point to get the remainder of the money. The trouble was I could not remember my Visa card pin number as I had not withdrawn cash on my credit card for a very long time. I had my Natwest card with me but my withdrawals on it were limited to £500 a day. I needed the equivalent of another £1,000.

We drove back to the underground car park at the police station. I was led back to the cells minus my belt, wrist watch, jacket and rucksack. Off came my shoes. A new police shift was due on now so I had to wait until fresh officers were ready to take me back out again into the town centre to get the rest of the money. This time it was the Gjensidige bank a police car took me to. My Visa card pin number came back to mind thank God, and I tried for 10,000 kroner. Rejected. So with a strong prayer I tried for a smaller amount – 5,000 kroner. Accepted! Out came the cash. Next I put in my Natwest card. Success. Another 5,000 kroner came out. Together with the 3,000 kroner still in the police safe I had just enough to pay the 22,205 kroner fine and get the train to the airport. We drove back to the police station. After half an hour, attending this time at the main police reception when I obtained a receipt for payment of my fines, I left on foot and walked joyfully back to the town centre.

The first thing I did was to telephone my mother from a public phone. She wasn't in but I left a message: that I was out of custody and on my way home. The second thing I did was to inquire if there were any Ryan Air flights back to London but the answer was no - the last flight was fully booked. The third thing I did was to go back to the Gjensidige bank to see if I could squeeze any more money out of the cash machine. Luckily, I got another 500 kroner (£44) which I would need to last me the night. The fourth thing I did was to go to the nearest shop, a Chinese supermarket, and buy a Snickers bar of chocolate. I hadn't eaten for almost 24 hours. I then walked the short distance to the railway station and from there on down to my hotel.

On being arrested the previous day I had asked Stig Lunde to phone the hotel to tell them I would be a day late in paying my bill, trusting he would think of a good reason to explain my absence. I had packed my suitcase on that Thursday morning and taken it down for storage near the reception, intending to return after the court case finished, settle up and leave for the airport. Now at 5.50 p.m I walked up to the reception desk, apologized for being 'late', and ask the lady on duty to fetch the bill. With her permission I helped myself to two glasses of fruit juice from the restaurant – I had had nothing to drink since a mouthful of water in the police cells that morning. I paid the bill and then phoned British Airways to see if I could catch a flight from Oslo's Gardemoen airport. But the BA office was closed. So I tried SAS. I was in luck: they had a seat - in business class - at cost of 5,649 kroner (£498) leaving at 8.10 p.m. I had to be there for the self-service check-in half an hour before departure. But would I make it in time to the airport? I asked the hotel receptionist how long it would take to get there by train - about an hour was her reply. So I paid for the flight with my Visa card. I had already ordered a taxi for the short trip back to the railway station. In my happiness I told the receptionist that I had made the newspapers many times in Norway and had responded by opening my own website. I wrote down the site's address for her, adding, "For the rest of your life you will never forget me." She said she would look at my website in the evening (presumably when her shift had finished). I would of course have left the country by then. I bade this lady a fond farewell. When the taxi dropped me at the railway station I found at the ticket office that a train was leaving directly to the airport in five minutes. I paid the 151 kroner fare and walked with my luggage to platform one. I asked a girl on the platform how long it would take to get to the airport - about an hour and a quarter she said. No good! I would only reach the airport as the plane was leaving. I went back to the ticket office - was there a quicker train? No there wasn't. I returned to platform one and took the train when it came in. Maybe there was a later British Airways flight I could take or even another airline. I crossed my fingers. Hoping also that the hotel receptionist would not complain to the police that evening that she had seen my website, only for the police to eagerly turn up in the departure lounge to re-arrest me for informing a third party about my website. Well, I was fantasizing this time surely?

The train arrived at the airport at exactly 8.10 p.m. I made my way quickly to the SAS check-in desks and to my surprise an attendant was still seated at one of them. And? The flight had been delayed due to fog! Prayers answered. Luggage checked in. With a feeling of triumph I walked the long distance quickly to gate 56. This was a superb airport – clean, modern and beautifully designed. The passengers were not yet boarding. I bought a bottle of apple juice and drank it in two goes. There was one public phone box only for the whole section of this end of the airport. I phoned my mother. With great joy I told her I was just about to board the SAS flight back to London Heathrow. She had got my message earlier to her great relief. But unfortunately when Patricia Svendsen from the Embassy telephoned her with the bad news, my mother told me she had momentarily fainted and banged her lip on the Ottoman in the bedroom. Ten minutes or so later the phone rang again when it was Stig Lunde with the second edition of the bad news.

We had to wait for another 40 minutes on the plane for the pilots to come from another flight and which was late in arriving. I certainly enjoyed the evening meal given to me by an extremely gracious SAS stewardess. The plane landed just after 11 p.m. at Heathrow. I took the courtesy bus to the long stay car park, paid the £81 parking fee and drove home.

The next day I phoned Patricia Svendsen at the British Embassy in Oslo and told her I had received an 8 month prison sentence suspended for two years and that my mother had fainted on receiving her phone call. Miss Svendsen had no particular comment to make and I didn't hear from her again. I made a courtesy call to Stig Lunde who was surprised that I was home so soon. And then I went out to an Internet café and typed in "Heidi Schøne" on the search facility on two Norwegian newspaper websites. Sneaky bastards! Verdens Gang had a front-page article dated 7th July 1998. Drammens Tidende had two more front-page stories on their site from 1998. Aftenposten's article on me mentioned by Heidi in court, I found by typing in the word "Muslim" on the newspaper's search facility. It was dated 20th April 2002 by Reidun J. Samuelsen. Four stories that I never knew about. Their translations are as follows:

Impossible to shake off sex-crazed Englishman

By Alexander Nordby

For 16 years a sex-crazed Englishman has terrorised Heidi Schøne with his letters, telephone calls and threats.

The Englishman is completely obsessed with the Norwegian woman, and since 1982 he has bombarded Heidi Schøne with terrorising phone calls, death threats, intimidating letters, and by turning up on her doorstep and harassing her friends.

The man has also sent to random individuals in Norway hundreds of letters containing serious sexual allegations and intimate claims about the Norwegian woman.

"I have begged, cried and threatened him to get him to leave me alone," said Heidi Schøne when VG spoke with her three years ago.

Ms Schøne and her family still have a secret address and an unlisted telephone number. Her post is sorted by the local police force, who so far this year have received more than 300 letters from the 40-year-old Englishman.

Forces himself on people

When Heidi Schøne was 18, she travelled to England to work as an au pair. While on a train, she met a man who was half Arabic. The man behaved strangely and was pushy, but she liked him and spoke to him in a friendly manner. Her life of hell began when she returned to Norway.

While she was staying in Bergen, the Englishman suddenly appeared on her doorstep. To begin with she let him in, but he gradually became extremely bothersome. He called her incessantly, sent her countless letters, and on one occasion he forced her to watch while he did obscene things.

After he had been rejected, he carved the words "fuck you" on a door with a knife. She moved to a secret address, but a postcard nevertheless appeared containing the words "Freddy's back" – taken from a horror film where the main character is called Freddy.

The case was previously investigated by the police force in Bergen. Three years ago, Ms Schøne reported the matter to the police in Drammen.

"It will be up to the public prosecutor to decide whether a request will be sent to the English authorities," says Dag Einar Lyngås, assistant chief of police.

[A photograph of Heidi Schøne was printed here.]

Caption: HARASSED: The Englishman has sent 300 letters to Heidi Schøne so far this year. Photo: VG

Erotic paranoia

Psychiatrists believe the threatening and lovesick Englishman may suffer from a case of extreme erotic paranoia.

This condition is a delusional disorder in which the individual is convinced that another person is in love with him or her.

Erotic paranoia most frequently affects women, particularly menopausal women. The disorder generally passes by itself after a few years.

People who suffer from erotic paranoia seldom act in an ill-willed manner, as is the case with the Englishman.

(VG 07.07.98   06:43)

***

This Verdens Gang story of 7th July 1998 was published four days after I had last spoken to Heidi (3rd July 1998) and the reason the newspaper took the matter up again was, presumably, as a reaction to the fact that I had obtained Heidi's unlisted 'secret' telephone number.

Drammens Tidende   **5th October 1998**

Hopes the Public Prosecutor can stop her nightmare

For 16 years Heidi Schøne has lived a continuous nightmare. She now hopes that the public prosecutor will be able to stop the man who has persecuted her since she was 18 years old.

By Ingunn Røren

Heidi Schøne, 35, from Solbergelva has been persecuted and harassed by an Englishman for 16 years.

"During the course of these years he has sent out hundreds of letters, both about me and to me. In addition, he has telephoned me at all hours of the day for some periods," says Heidi Schøne. Since 1995 the case has been under investigation by the district sheriff's office in Nedre Eiker after Heidi reported the Englishman to the police for victimisation and harassment. The case has been fully investigated, and has now been sent to the public prosecutor's office.

"The problem is that the legislation is far too weak in cases where one is subjected to the type of harassment that I've had to live with for the last 16 years. I'm terribly tired of this, and hope now that the police and the public prosecutor will be able to stop this persecution," says Heidi Schøne.

Under Norwegian law, harassment is generally considered to be a misdemeanour and not a criminal offence. Norway has no extradition treaty with England for individuals who are charged with misdemeanours and not criminal offences.

"This case is special, however, since the harassment has continued for very many years and to such a great extent," says Toril Sorte Kjennås, police officer at the district sheriff's office in Nedre Eiker.

The decision now rests with the public prosecutor.

Heidi Schøne first met the Englishman when she was 18 and an au pair in England. She drank tea with the Englishman a couple of times, and gave him her address in Norway when she left England to return home.

"I didn't know then that the man had become completely obsessed with me, and that he would bother me for the next 16 years. Since 1982 he has sent me an average of one letter every single day, and called on countless occasions. I have begged, pleaded and cried, but he just won't leave us alone," says Heidi. In addition to the letters he has sent Heidi, the man has sent highly offensive 'reports' about Heidi to her neighbours, colleagues, friends and family.

The Schøne family have moved several times and have had several unlisted telephone numbers, but the man has managed to trace the family each time.

"This puts an enormous strain on me and on the rest of my family," says Heidi, who is married and has two children.

On countless occasions she has had to explain to complete strangers why they have received reports about her.

"Our neighbours here in Solbergelva have been great and have supported us, but it naturally puts a strain on us when everyone around us is pestered with letters and telephone calls from the man," says Runar Schøne, Heidi's husband.

Recently the district sheriff's office in Nedre Eiker has begun to intercept letters that the man sends to Heidi.

520

"We have taken charge of more than 400 letters," says police officer Toril Sorte Kjennås.

"It's been a relief not to have these letters in my letter box. Of course, I know he's still sending me letters, but it's good that the police sort through our mail," says Heidi.

In recent months the man has once again sent several letters about Heidi to a number of individuals, public institutions and companies in the Drammen area. The letters have a grossly defamatory content, and contain a number of untruths about Heidi and her family. The most recent letters have been formulated so that they look like they are answers to an enquiry from Drammens Tidende, but DT-BB has never sent out such an enquiry about Heidi Schøne.

"I am tired, angry and desperate about the situation. The letters he sends to everyone have made me isolate myself more and more. I sincerely hope that the public prosecutor can find a solution so that the man can be sentenced. More than anything else I want the court to ban him from approaching me or contacting me. Perhaps then we'll finally be able to get some peace, and will not have to have a secret address and unlisted telephone number, and be frightened every time the telephone rings," says Heidi.

*****

Drammens Tidende	**9th December 1998**
Harassed and persecuted – case put on hold	

A decision has been taken: The police are to step down their efforts to apprehend an Englishman who over a period of 16 years is alleged to have harassed and persecuted Heidi Schøne (35) from Solbergelva.

By Morten Wold

"Of course we're disappointed," says Runar Schøne, Ms Schøne's husband, to DT-BB. Dag Einar Lyngås, police superintendent at Drammen Police Force, can only apologise that the police find they are unable to continue to employ the resources necessary to apprehend the Englishman. Since 1982 he has harassed, persecuted and spread untruths about Heidi Schøne in the form of letters and telephone calls to her relations, friends, employers, and to newspapers in Norway.

A disappointed family

"The case will be put on hold and will be under periodical observation," says Mr. Lyngås to DT-BB.

He stresses that the case has not been closed, but that the police will follow developments to see whether the harassment continues. Runar Schøne says the police decision is disappointing and that this means the family will have to continue living in a virtual "exile."

"We have a secret address and an unlisted telephone number, which we have had to change several times. We haven't done anything wrong, but are being punished with a poorer quality of life as a result of this man's activities, while he goes free and can do whatever he wants," says Mr. Schøne.

Heidi Schøne's nightmare began in 1982, when she met the Englishman while working as an au pair in England. He allegedly became obsessed with her and has since then sent her letters almost every day and managed to trace her address and telephone number – even though she has moved and obtained an unlisted telephone number several times.

Post sorted

Things became so bad that the district police force in Nedre Eiker now sort her post in order to stop any letters that may be from the man. More than 400 letters have been stopped and stored by the district police force – to shield Heidi Schøne and her family.

521

The case has been under investigation since 1995 and was sent to the public prosecutor some time ago. Heidi Schøne hoped then that this would lead to the man's conviction.

The public prosecuting authority has encountered problems in dealing with this matter, however, and will have difficulty in remanding the man in custody since he has been charged pursuant to section 390A of the Norwegian General Civil Penal Code, which carries a maximum sentence of six months' imprisonment. In order to be held on remand, a minimum sentence of more than six months is required plus the danger of repetition of the offence.

"There is most certainly a danger of repetition here, but at present the conditions have not been met," says Dag Einar Lyngås to DT-BB.

This means that the police will now remain relatively passive, but will arrest the man if it is brought to their attention that he is coming to Norway.

***

For the 5th October 1998 Drammens Tidende article Heidi had been interviewed and yet again her emphasis was on continuous harassment for 16 years from 1982. Both Heidi and the newspaper knew they were lying on this point and on a number of other allegations. Similarly in their article of 9th December 1998 Drammens Tidende had deliberately and persistently lied.

I retrieved the tape recording of my conversation with Reidun J. Samuelsen of 10th April 2002, transcribed it and reproduce it here for comparison with her article.

To recap, I had telephoned the newspaper as once they had seen my website they e-mailed my ISP to ask me to make contact:

Answer: *Aftenposten*
F.　　　*Yes, good afternoon. Have you got a journalist called Reidun Samuelsen?*
Answer: *Yes……I'll try for you.*
RS.　　*Samuelsen.*
F.　　　*Oh hi there, you're Miss Samuelsen?*
RS.　　*Mrs. Samuelsen, yes.*
F.　　　*Oh Mrs. Oh. Ok. Hi there um …I understand you're doing a story on Heidi Schøne or want to.*
RS.　　*Yes that's right.*
F.　　　*Well I'm the chap that's taking her to court.*
RS.　　*OK.*
F.　　　*And I'm just wondering what your angle's going to be this time.*
RS.　　*I haven't written about this before…..Actually I haven't decided yet…..I'm in a phase where I'm collecting material…*
F.　　　*There have already been some big stories on this in 1995…*
RS.　　*Yes, I know…*

[And then I related briefly a little bit about Heidi's psychiatric past.]

RS.　　*For me the story here is not her past it's why are you writing [on the internet] about this?*
F.　　　*Because the newspapers wrote about me.*
RS.　　*Is that how it all started?*
F.　　　*Yes….she's made some pretty awful allegations against me…*
RS.　　*In public or…*
F.　　　*Well to the police…and in public…..in the newspapers. She says I've threatened to kill her son…a terrible lie…kill her neighbours…She doesn't get on with her stepmother…you know the story on her stepmother because you've seen the website haven't you?*
RS.　　*I have seen the website, yes.*
F.　　　*Have you been in touch with her?*
RS.　　*I've talked to her briefly but I'm gonna talk to her again, yes.*
F.　　　*The thing is you see, she's supposed to be mentally ill…I mean she had her psychiatrist in court [and she talks about] how I rung her up asking what underwear she's wearing, [that] I've written to her saying that if she doesn't get pregnant then her breasts will*

522

fall off…[that] *I've written 400 obscene letters to her that she's thrown away…*[that] *I wrote a letter to her threatening to kill her son…*

RS. *I…I'm not familiar with all of that stuff. What I've been seeing is the website. For us this is more of a - how can I say - an example of the use of the internet.*

F. *Well it's the abortion images isn't it…the pictures of the abortions that er…there's been a lot of complaints I understand…I mean have you seen the pictures?*

RS. *Yeah.*

F. *The thing is…one of the main things about why I've been so upset is because your newspapers called me "the Muslim man." Bergens Tidende called me "the Muslim man" 18 times.*

RS. *I can't answer for what other newspapers have been writing about….the thing that I would like to ask you is why are you putting all these stories about Heidi into the public* [domain]?

F. *I'm putting it into the public because nobody….you see when the newspapers started this story off they are supposed to ring me for my side of the story OK…I know that from the PFU - and no one did - no one rang me.*

RS. *Now you are calling me so that's a good thing.*

F. *Huh?*

RS. *And now you are calling me so then I don't have to call you afterwards. That's a good thing.*

F. *I'm supposed to have my side of the story printed.*

RS. *Yes so please tell me why you are doing it.*

F. *Well, so that people know my side of the story. People don't know she's mentally ill you see…and I've taken her to court…and we're still in a legal process so….*

RS. *But you actually lost the last court case didn't you?*

F. *Well, I've appealed. The only reason I've lost is because I think it's more of a political decision.*

RS. *I see…*[and later] *For me I'm not very interested in - what can I say - printing the details here because it will be your word up against hers and… the important thing for me is that you chose to put it out in public by the internet and I guess you must see that this will affect her life…*

F. *My life has been affected too because of the rubbish that has been printed….I do not write letters threatening to kill two year children…I did not write 400 obscene letters to her…but the point is this - it's never going to go away is it? This story will never go away because it's basically something your newspapers should've apologized for once they knew that my story was true on Heidi…*

RS. *From my point of view that's not the most important thing here because I can know many bad things about a friend, a neighbour but the moment I put it out in public that's another* [thing]…

F. *But she put out in public – in the newspaper – that I've threatened to kill her son. Is that not…?*

RS. *Did they put your name in print or something?*

F. *No they didn't put my name…the main thing is that I'm Muslim…they don't care about my name. They care that I'm Muslim. You've seen the* [newspaper] *articles on the website …You people in general do not like Muslims. I know that because I've spoken to enough Norwegians, OK. And the main thrust of the* [May 1995 Bergens Tidende] *article…they don't care what my name is…they know and want to attack me as a Muslim.*

RS. *I didn't know that you were a Muslim….*[Obviously she hadn't in fact looked at my website for very long because the three 1995 newspaper articles were up there in Norwegian together with the English translations]…*Nobody told me that and it doesn't matter for me…*

[And later]:

F. *You've got so many dishonest people up there* [in Norway] *and I've exposed them because I tape all my phone calls - I'm taping this phone call with you now just in case you…*

RS. *That's something you should have told me before we started.*

F. *Well, I don't do that, otherwise…I tape all my phone calls with the police, journalists…*

RS. *OK, I think I've got your side of the picture now and I don't think I need to talk to you anymore. OK.*

523

F.	*OK but I'm warning you if you print anything bad then there'll be pretty tough consequences for you.*
RS.	*So are you threatening me?*
F.	*With a law suit, yeah. With a law suit. See, you've already changed your attitude so I can tell how sorry you feel for Heidi and your people over there but as I said, we'll get a photograph of you and put it up there* [on the internet as I had already done for several of my other Norwegian adversaries] *and...*
RS.	*This is actually a threat.*
F.	*Well it's not...putting a photograph of you* [I was not allowed to finish]....
RS.	*It's a threat OK. I'm not talking to you anymore.*
F.	*Well I'll talk to your boss then.*
RS.	*Bye-bye.* [And she put the phone down on me.]

Aftenposten   **15th April 2002**

Started after an au pair job 20 years ago

British Muslim terrorizes Norwegian woman on the Internet

For 17 years an Englishman has terrorised a woman from the Drammen area. Now he has begun to use the Internet.

"He has taken many years of my life," she says.

By Reidun J. Samuelsen

Intimate details

The women first became acquainted with the Brit when she was an au pair in England around 20 years ago.

Although they have never had a boyfriend-girlfriend relationship, he nevertheless urged her to convert to Islam in order to marry him during a visit he made to Norway three years later. She refused, and that was when it all started. Since then he has threatened her directly and spread erroneous information about her over the telephone and by means of letters.

"He has made this his goal in life. He regards me as a despicable and worthless person. Yet at the same time he is obsessed with me," she says.

The Englishman has sent out e-mails in which recipients are urged to read the web pages he has created. In addition, he has faxed the same message to people who live near the 38-year-old woman. His intention has been to get as many people as possible to visit the web pages where the woman is described in strong terms.

She is accused of being mentally unstable and of having lived a wild life. The Englishman lists her previous relationships, regularly citing intimate details. Everything is richly illustrated with photographs of the 38-year-old. He also makes a point of the fact that the woman is alleged to have had an abortion.

The title of the e-mail that has been issued is "Censured" Pictures of Aborted Foetuses.

"It's been terrible, and my self-confidence has taken a beating. At times I have feared for my life," says the woman.

The long period of harassment has taken its toll on the woman.

New report to the police

According to the Englishman, the woman has made incorrect allegations against him, both to the police and to the media. He says he has posted the information about her on the internet so that people can hear his side of the story.

In January of this year he was convicted of defamatory behaviour towards the woman, for which he was fined NOK 10,000. It was in the wake of this case that he began in earnest to use the internet to spread his campaign of harassment, which resulted in the 38-year-old reporting him to the police once again. Police officer Torill Sorte of Nedre Eiker Police Force, who was a witness in the case in January, has also reported the Englishman.

"We hope to bring a new case against him," says Ms Sorte.

She has been profiled on the web pages with her full name and address, and has been accused of making false statements in court.

"Actions of this nature require a reaction," says Torill Sorte. She is interested in receiving copies of e-mails and faxes that the man has spread.

Internet harassment can be stopped in the following way A new EU directive makes it possible to shut down web pages containing defamatory statements.

By Reidun J. Samuelsen

The host is liable. "A new directive, the so-called E-business Directive, orders web hosting providers to take greater responsibility for the web pages they host," says Professor Jon Bing at the Norwegian Research Centre for Computers and Law at the University of Oslo.

If the web hosting provider is aware that the content may be illegal, he is automatically responsible for what may be found there. The new provisions are to be enacted in all European countries by February. When Aftenposten contacted Skymarket, the web hosting provider that hosts the web site containing information about the woman from Drammen, the site was closed in a matter of hours.

"The problem is of course that anyone wishing to use the internet to spread harassment can shift to another web hosting provider who is not familiar with the content on his pages. He may also find web hosting providers in countries who do not comply with the E-business Directive," says Jon Bing.

The professor is of the opinion that people themselves can make an effort to stop web pages by tracing the web hosting provider and inform him that a web site may be illegal. This is a far simpler process than going through the courts.

"It is difficult to shut down web sites overseas by means of a court ruling," says Professor Bing.

Erik Moestue, a police lawyer at the computer crime centre in Økokrim, the Norwegian National Authority for Investigation and Prosecution of Economic and Environmental Crime, says that the Norwegian authorities have no opportunity to grant orders in other countries.

Odd Einar Dørum, the Norwegian minister of justice, feels that this area requires attention. The government has commissioned the Computer Crimes Committee, which was appointed in January, to investigate whether the Norwegian Criminal Law's geographical scope is appropriately delimited as regards illegal material on the internet. The committee shall also consider whether the police have sufficient opportunity to demand that such material be removed from web sites.

***

It was surely no co-incidence that Aftenposten, as I have already mentioned, published three features on abortion and teenage sexual attitudes and behaviour in their 23rd April 2002 issue. My website also had numerous articles from the English newspapers on abortion and sexually transmitted diseases scanned onto it.

The deadline for me to close my website was Friday the 24th October 2003. I had no intention whatsoever of closing it down. Two thirds of the contents on the website had nothing whatsoever to do with Heidi Schøne. And what the Norwegians were asking me to do was wrong. But to please Harald Wibye I removed all references to Heidi Schøne and Heidi Overaa and called her Heidi Munchausen and replaced Runar Schøne with Runar Schyte. Exactly! I had in 2001 scanned on to my site the newspapers' own photographs of the couple and put my own comments underneath the photos. I now put black bands across the eyes of Heidi and Runar Schøne so that they couldn't easily be recognized. The original ten newspaper articles were left fully intact on another part of the website! The (Norwegian) lawyers could sort that one out!

By the following Tuesday, the 28th October my website had disappeared from the Internet. I telephoned my website designer. He told me my Internet Service Provider (ISP) had sent him a letter from Økokrim, the National Authority for Investigation and Prosecution of Economic and Environmental Crime in Norway who were, it said, "investigating a criminal case regarding threats and harassment posted on a website..... The website in question contains text and images which is clearly offensive. Several people mentioned on this have filed complaints to the Norwegian police regarding the content. Økokrim requests the website should be closed and that the Webmaster should lose access to the domain. If a court order is necessary Økokrim will start the process of contacting the UK government on this matter. However, Økokrim is hoping [for] your cooperation....."

The website did not contain any threats. The reference to "offensive images" must have been connected to the photographs of aborted fetuses – my site doubled up as an anti-abortion website.

Well, I phoned my ISP and while I explained the history of the case to him, he put the website back on the Internet. Interestingly the Law Society Gazette of the 19th December 2002 wrote a piece entitled 'Call to review Net defamation law.' It said among other things:

> 'The Law Commission has called for a full review of the law of defamation over fears that it puts Internet service providers (ISP's) under pressure to remove potentially damaging material without considering whether there is actually a problem.... Law Commissioner Professor Hugh Beale QC said some ISP's receive more than 100 defamation complaints a year - including solicitors letters from companies objecting to websites set up by disgruntled customers - and that because of the law, ISP's often remove the sites without considering whether the information is in the public interest, or true. "There is a possible conflict between the pressure to remove material, even if true, and the emphasis placed on freedom of expression by the European Convention on Human Rights," he said'.

The next day I phoned Økokrim's special investigator Thomas Dahl and told him that I had his letter of 28th of October 2003 in front of me. He acknowledged that there were in fact no "threats" on my site. I told him I had just returned from Norway prosecuting my own civil libel action and that I had in fact now removed all references to Heidi Schøne from my own text in accordance with a 'police request.' I did not tell him that strictly speaking the 'police request' was that I had to remove the whole website. I did add though that I thought the 'police request' was illegal under the European Convention on Human Rights, and that I hoped to take my civil case to Strasbourg. He said, "You got to do what you got to do." I also mentioned my distress at the four Drammens Tidende articles and the one Verdens Gang article from 1998 still remaining on these newspapers' own respective websites. I gave him the police lawyer Ingunn Hodne's telephone number so he could liaise with her.

Two very interesting articles then appeared on Aftenposten's English website as follows:

Aftenposten   **5th November 2003**

Bishop critical of minister's advice to Islam

Oslo's bishop, Gunnar Staalsett has warned Minister of Local Government and Regional Development Erna Solberg of the dangers of criticizing Islam after she told Norway's Muslims that they should modernize their religion. Staalsett fears that the statement will create a warped view of Islam.

"There is naturally a need for reform in all religious communities, but an initiative from the government sounds a special note," Staalsett told Norwegian Broadcasting (NRK).

Staalsett is concerned that the minister's remarks can cause provide a mistaken image of Islam as a whole.

"One should be very careful about portraying a religion from its worst sides," Staalsett said.

Aftenposten English Web Desk. Jonathan Tisdall

***

Aftenposten   **8th November 2003**

Facing Mecca frightens pious villagers

Residents of Bykle, population 864, are reportedly deeply troubled that their new church, currently under construction, faces Islam's holy city of Mecca. Fear of the anti-Christ runs through the town, newspaper Faedrelandsvennen reports.

The old church in Bykle lay east-west with its entrance from the west. The new church points southeast. Hallvard Gjerden, 64, of the Norwegian Lutheran Mission (NLM) was one of the first to make a connection.

"The church is facing directly towards Mecca - to the millimeter. I've checked," Gjerden told the newspaper.

"People fear that the Muslims will seize the church and use it as a mosque. You don't dare write this, but the mosques are the church's greatest enemy. The Muslims want to conquer the earth and kill Christians," Gjerden said.

The head of the building commission for Bykle church, Tor Mosdoel, was only amused by Gjerden's theories.

"This is just something people have made up," said Mosdoel, who has no fear of Muslims whatsoever. "The church had to have a northern entrance because the building site gave us no choice," he said.

Aftenposten English Web Desk. Jonathan Tisdall

***

527

Once again Jonathan Tisdall, an American who manned Aftenposten's English Web desk, was writing stories that helped confirm my long-held impressions on Norwegian attitudes to Islam. Ironically, Hans Erik Matre, the former editor at Bergens Tidende in 1995 responsible for overseeing the disgraceful "Muslim man" article on me, had just been appointed chief editor at Aftenposten.

I made inquiries of the Supreme Court in Norway as to the procedure for appealing to them from the Court of Appeal. The court official Margaret Meder told me only 20% of appeals are accepted by the Supreme Court and if they do not accept an appeal, then the appellant was free to go directly to the European Court of Human Rights in Strasbourg. The appeal fee depended on the number of days in court. They ranged from 17,700 kroner (£1,547) for a one day hearing to 24,400 kroner (£2,132) for a four day hearing to 35,500 kroner (£3,103) for an eight day hearing. Crucially only the partys' lawyers were required to attend. And I had "one to three months" to appeal from the date I received the Court of Appeal judgment.

On 19th November 2003 I telephoned Ingunn Hodne, the police lawyer. She was not satisfied with my amendments to my website. She said I had promised in court to take the website off. I said, "Yes, but only under duress. If I didn't agree you would have sent me to prison." I added that only a small proportion of the website dealt with Heidi Schøne and that in any case I believed the Norwegian conviction would be illegal under the European Convention on Human Rights. But the police lawyer replied that it was a conviction under Norwegian law which I should respect. I rebutted that by saying I should have been charged under section 390 of the Penal Code which gave me a defence of justified comment: a section which Harald Wibye, I reminded her, two years ago had tried to persuade the Magistrates Court judge to change the charge to. The police lawyer told me that the judge had rejected Harald Wibye's argument but I insisted that, according to what Harald Wibye told me, the judge did not appreciate or fully understand his hour-long argument. The police lawyer continued with, "What if you send faxes to people all around you about your neighbour. Isn't that against the law in your country?" I told her that I only responded with so many faxes after the newspapers printed their stories on me. "But we regard that as harassment in our country," she said. I countered that with, "So why do your newspapers print headlines on Prince Charles involving "homosexual rape." Isn't that harassment of him? Isn't calling me the "Muslim man," "half-German half-Arab," suffering from "erotic paranoia" harassment of me?" The police lawyer couldn't or wouldn't understand my arguments. She said they would now try and get me imprisoned for eight months either in England or if they could extradite me, in Norway. I told her that her efforts would get nowhere: that the freedom of speech we have in England allows a person's past life to be made public if it basically served the public interest.

On 22nd December I telephoned the Court of Appeal in Oslo to enquire about the judgement. I was told by Ingerid Sandberg, the court clerk, that it had been sent to Stig Lunde "two weeks ago" and that it was assumed he'd received it. I said that I had not heard from Stig Lunde and asked why I had not been sent a copy by the Court. Because I was abroad, came the reply! Amazing, when for months the court had regularly been writing to me. Ingerid Sandberg told me to ring back tomorrow when she would have spoken to the judge for guidance. I immediately phoned Stig Lunde who said he had got the judgement and had in fact tried to phone me. We discussed my right to appeal and Lunde said he would get advice from one of the Court of Appeal judges as to the date from which the time limit for my appeal was to run. He quickly faxed through to me a copy of the judgement which was dated 14th November 2003. I in turn faxed it through to my home based translation agency who would translate the document over Christmas for me. Later that day Lunde told me that he had phoned the Court of Appeal, when Judge Agnar Nilsen Jnr. told him the time limit for my appeal - one month - would run from the date I received the judgement from Lunde in the post. Lunde told me he would now put the judgement in the post.

On 29th December 2003 I had entered the Norwegian word, "Engelskmann" (Englishman) onto Drammens Tidende's website search engine. Two new articles on me came up dated 26th October 2003 and 18th November 2003. Their translations are below:

By Herborg Bergaplass

An Englishman who had persecuted a woman from Nedre Eiker for more than 20 years sued her for libel. While in court, he was arrested and charged with severe persecution on the internet.

The 45-year-old man, who made the acquaintance of the woman from Nedre Eiker when she was a young au pair in England, has harassed and persecuted her for 18 years. In the autumn of 2001, he was sentenced to pay a fine of NOK 10,000, which he did not pay. Instead the Englishman sued the woman for libel, because she had told her story to the media. Last week the civil case was heard in the Court of Appeal, but before the Englishman had time to leave the courthouse in Drammen he was arrested. The background for his arrest was new, severe instances of persecution, including allegations posted on the internet.

Withdrew cash to pay fines.

The 45-year-old was remanded in custody, where he made a full confession, which opened for sentencing in the court of examination and summary jurisdiction. The man appeared as a repentant sinner, and stated that he understood that he had subjected the woman to a lot of pain.

Erik Stillum, the municipal court judge, felt that a suitable punishment would be eight months' conditional imprisonment, under the following terms: All information about the woman from Nedre Eiker that has been posted on the internet is to be deleted, the web page where the persecution appears shall be removed and the content shall not be republished in any form. Furthermore, the 45-year-old is not permitted to have any form of contact with the woman, nor shall he in any way communicate information about her to third parties (e.g. newspapers). In addition, the man was sentenced to pay a fine of NOK 10,000.

The Englishman accepted the verdict on the spot, and willingly went to a cashpoint machine together with the police and withdrew funds to pay both the new and the old fine, i.e. NOK 20,000 in total, after which he left the country of his own accord. "A reasonable verdict, and a good solution to the whole case," said Svein Duesland, who was appointed defending counsel for the man in the court of examination and summary jurisdiction.

Alteration of terms under consideration.

On Friday, the staff of Drammens Tidende accessed the web site, which in no way has been deleted. The harassing content is still there. The Englishman has merely changed to a fictitious name the real name of the woman from Nedre Eiker, and covered up her eyes on the pictures posted on the internet. Ingunn Hodne, the police lawyer in Søndre Buskerud Police Force, has also noted that the web site is still operative.

"We will consider applying for an alteration of the terms of the judgment. He is already in breach of the terms," says Ms Hodne.

The police lawyer had hoped that the man would give up now, since the regret he showed in court represented a change of tone. If a petition is lodged to have the judgment altered, Ms Hodne will claim that he be sentenced to unconditional imprisonment. The man will then be summoned to a main hearing via the British police, and will be ordered to appear in court. If he fails to do so, a judgment by default may be delivered. According to Ms Hodne, it will be decided whether a request will be issued for his extradition from the UK to attend the main proceedings in Norway, or whether the case will be transferred to England for sentencing there.

"If he is in breach of the terms of the judgment, the case can be brought before the court for alteration. However, I cannot ascertain whether the terms have been breached," says advocate Svein Duesland.

***

Drammens Tidende	18th November 2003
Libel appeal dismissed	

By Herborg Bergaplass

The court of appeal has dismissed an appeal by a 45-year-old Englishman who for years has harassed a woman from Nedre Eiker, and who had sued her for libel.

The Englishman has twice been convicted of harassing the woman. The 45-year-old has sent her hundreds of letters, telephoned her countless times, and sent 'reports' containing various allegations about her to several newspapers and other entities in Norway. The woman from Nedre Eiker met the man when she was an au pair in England over 20 years ago. When their relationship ended, the harassment began. And when the woman told her story to Drammens Tidende and other Norwegian newspapers, the man responded by suing her for libel and demanding NOK 50,000 in compensation for non-pecuniary damages. He lost the case in the municipal court, and was ordered to pay costs. The 45-year-old appealed to Borgarting Court of Appeal, and in October the parties met in the courthouse in Drammen.

"My client is pleased that the verdict delivered by the municipal court has been upheld, and that the man has been ordered to pay court costs," says the woman's lawyer, advocate Vegard Aaløkken.

Arrested in court

No later than 14 days after service of the verdict, the Englishman is required to pay court costs totalling NOK 105,000. He was arrested by the police immediately after the proceedings in the court of appeal were concluded and he was charged with new cases of severe persecution, this time on the internet. The 45-year-old was brought before the court for a remand hearing, and appeared to be a repentant sinner. He pleaded guilty to harassing the woman, and was sentenced there and then. The judge felt that eight months' conditional imprisonment was appropriate, on condition that all information posted on the internet about the woman be deleted.

Terms breached

All he did was to give the woman a fictitious name on the web site, which is not enough for the police.

Ingunn Hodne, police lawyer at Søndre Buskerud Police Force, will apparently file for an alteration of terms. Ms Hodne says to Drammens Tidende that she has not had time to consider the case yet, but will do so shortly.

***

On the 10th January 2004 my agency sent me the translation of the Court of Appeal's judgement:

BORGARTING COURT OF APPEAL

makes known its

JUDGEMENT

of 14 November 2003

in appeal case no. 02-01546 A/03: Delaware – Schøne

Appellant: **Frederick Delaware**

Respondent: **Heidi Schøne**
Counsel: **Vegard Aaløkken**

Members   **1   Appeal Court Judge Agnar A. Nilsen Jr.**
of the   **2   Appeal Court Judge Thore Rønning**
Court: **3   Judge called from Probate and Bankruptcy Judge Anita H. Lund**

May be reported publicly.

The case concerns a claim for damages for alleged libellous statements in a newspaper article.

On 10 August 1999, Frederick Delaware filed a writ of summons at Drammen city court (now district court), corrected on 13 January 2000, in which he claimed NOK 50,000 in damages from Heidi Schøne (formerly Overaa) for libellous statements contained in a newspaper article of 14 July 1998 in Drammens Tidende/Buskerud Blad. The writ also included a claim for a judicial declaration that the defamatory statements were null and void and damages against the newspaper, editor Hans Arne Odde and journalist Ingunn Røren. However, this part of the case was dismissed because the right to request prosecution for criminal conduct was deemed waived in connection with complaint handling within the Professional Committee of the Press, cf. Borgarting Court of Appeal's ruling of 24 November 2000.

The alleged libellous statements are listed as follows in the writ:

i)   "Pursued by mad man for 16 years."
ii)   "For 16 years a mentally ill Englishman has pestered and pursued Heidi Schøne...."
iii)   "Sexually harassed for 16 years."
iv)   "For 16 years Heidi Schøne from Solbergelva has been harassed and pursued by a mentally ill Englishman."
v)   "So far this year Sorte Kjennås and her colleagues have dealt with over 300 letters the man has sent to Heidi."
vi)   "The man has previously threatened the life of neighbours of the family in order to find out where they moved."
vii)   "..for 16 years the Englishman has been possessed with the idea of marrying Heidi."
viii)   "The scale of the harassment increased when Heidi got married nine years ago."
ix)   "Psychiatrists think that the Englishman is suffering from an extreme case of erotic paranoia."
x)   "But a mentally ill Englishman has time after time tracked down the address and sends harassing letters."

531

Drammen district court passed judgement on 11 February 2002 with the following conclusion of the judgement:

1. Heidi Schøne is held not liable.

2. Frederick Delaware is ordered to pay the following costs within 14 days of announcement of the judgement:

a. To Heidi Schøne NOK 21,675, plus statutory overdue payment interest of 12% p.a. from due date until payment takes place.

b. To the State NOK 78,711, plus statutory overdue payment interest of 12% p.a. from due date until payment takes place.

For further details of the case, refer to the judgement of the district court and the remarks of the Court of Appeal below.

Frederick Delaware appealed against the judgement to Borgarting Court of Appeal in due time. Heidi Schøne opposed the appeal.

The appeal hearing was held in Drammen courthouse from 13 to 16 October 2003. The appellant, Frederick Delaware, appeared without counsel and made a statement. He had an interpreter with him however. The respondent made a statement on 14 October 2003 and was moreover represented by her counsel. Seven witnesses were heard, and documentation as shown in the court record was prepared. Refer to the court record also with regard to procedural decisions.

The appellant, Frederick Delaware, asserted in substance the following before the Court of Appeal:

Heidi Schøne's statements to Drammens Tidende/Buskerud Blad in the article of 14 July 1998 must be seen against the background of similar and other statements reported in newspaper articles in Drammens Tidende/Buskerud Blad, VG and Bergens Tidende in 1995. Schøne's statements are untrue, offensive and go far beyond what can be substantiated and justified in his previous behaviour towards her. Schøne must also be accountable for the statements of others, because the articles were referred to her before they were printed, but she did not correct the content.

Delaware began sending out 'reports' about Heidi Schøne after he found out that she had reported him for attempted rape in 1986. Moreover, most of the reports were sent out after the newspaper articles in 1995 because he could not make himself heard as far as the newspapers were concerned. What particularly upset Delaware were the allegations in the articles from 1995 that he had raped or attempted to rape Schøne and that he had threatened to kill her son Daniel.

The appellant did not "pursue," "pester," "sexually harass" or "threaten" Schøne. Nor did he cause "terror" or "threaten" Schøne's family or neighbours. On the contrary, the parties had an extremely good and intimate relationship for a long time, especially up to 1990. The relationship was nevertheless characterized by Schøne's extremely changeable state of mind. He was worried about her way of life and mental health. Delaware has never been put in a psychiatric hospital or been treated for mental illness. Police inspector Sorte was being untruthful when she stated that she was told in a conversation with the appellant's mother that the mother had tried to have him put in a psychiatric institution.

It is also untrue that Delaware sent "300 letters" to the respondent in the year before the newspaper article in 1998. He wrote only a few letters, and these were positive. The background to the letters was a wish to clear up why he had been arrested in 1990 and what the complaints regarding him were about. Moreover, they were a link in an exchange of views between them on ethical questions and outlook on life.

Delaware finds it offensive that the newspaper refers to him as the "Muslim man."

He has never been "possessed with the idea of marrying Heidi." His sending out of reports and letters was not explained by jealousy, and it is not correct that "the scale of the harassment increased when Heidi got married nine years ago." If Schøne had been "sexually harassed for 16 years," this would mean that Delaware had behaved in this way towards Schøne from when they met in 1982. This is not correct. In any case Schøne wanted contact with him right up to 1990.

It is positively incorrect that Delaware's so-called reports "(are) not founded on facts." His reports are based on what Schøne herself told him.

The conditions for compensation (damages) for the unlawful allegations therefore exist, cf. Damages Act § 3-6. The allegations are punishable in accordance with Penal Code § 246 and § 247. The allegations were under no circumstances made for respectable reasons and are altogether improper, cf. Penal Code § 249 no. 2. The conditions for exemption from punishment in accordance with Penal Code § 249 no. 3 do not exist.

Irrespective of the outcome, Delaware should not be ordered to pay costs before any court because he had good reason to take legal action. As he is resident abroad, costs imposed should not include value added tax.

There is no basis for imposition of a procedural penalty in accordance with the Courts of Justice Act § 202.

The appellant has requested that:

1.   Heidi Schøne be ordered to pay to Frederick Delaware within 14 days damages of NOK 50,000, plus 12% interest p.a. from due date until payment takes place.

2.   Heidi Schøne be ordered to pay to Frederick Delaware within 14 days the costs of the case before the district court and Court of Appeal plus 12% interest p.a. from due date and until payment takes place.

The respondent, Heidi Schøne, asserted in substance the following before the Court of Appeal:

It is only the statements in the 1998 article which are under consideration. Furthermore, Schøne is accountable only for the statements she herself made. She has not stated anything about Delaware suffering from erotic paranoia. The information that Delaware sent her approximately 300 letters comes from the police who as time went by had Delaware's letters sent directly from the Post Office. The statements about threats to neighbours originate from her husband, Runar Schøne.

Heidi Schøne has produced convincing proof of the central issue in the case, namely that she has for a number of years – though not as long as 16 years – been pursued by a mentally afflicted/mad/psychologically ill man, in the popular sense of the words. Delaware pursued her by writing, ringing and seeking her out despite her having made it clear that she does not want such contact. He also phoned neighbours and family and sent 'reports' to a number of other people/institutions. There were also threats against neighbours and family. The son's grandparents reported Delaware for threats.

Both Delaware's letters to her and the reports about her are morbidly preoccupied with sex, and the discussion of her is obviously sexual harassment. Referring to the fact that Delaware is a Muslim was a journalistic point because his writings have a clear religious undertone. Today Schøne is harassed on websites Delaware has on the Internet. She had respectable grounds for making the statements in question, cf. Penal Code § 249 no. 2.

533

To the extent that Schøne is deemed not to have produced sufficient evidence, Penal Code § 249 no. 3 will apply. Schøne has justifiably looked after her interests; she had to defend herself against the massive assault Delaware subjected her to. Delaware was not identified by name in the article.

If statements attributable to Schøne should nevertheless be deemed punishable, it will, after an assessment of reasonableness, be out of the question to award Delaware damages in accordance with Damages Act § 3-6. The case has been turned completely upside down; it is Schøne who is the victim. Delaware wanted to blacken her name and destroy her life.

The respondent has requested that:

1. Drammen district court's judgement be upheld.
2. Heidi Schøne and/or the State be awarded the costs of the case before the Court of Appeal, plus 12% interest from due date and until payment takes place.

The Court of Appeal has arrived at the same conclusion as the district court and can concur entirely with the grounds of the district court. In other respects, the Court of Appeal would add and sum up as follows:

It is only the statements in the newspaper article in Drammens Tidende/Buskerud Blad of 14 July 1998 that became the subject of dispute in the case by virtue of the writ of 10 August 1999. Delaware is not understood to be intending to widen the case by asserting that accountability can be based directly on statements in the articles from 1995. Accountability on such a basis would in every circumstance be statute-barred.

The information, expressions of opinion and formulations for which Heidi Schøne is held accountable are considered to be substantially true and indeed not improper. Of the evidence that emerged during the appeal hearing, the Court of Appeal would refer particularly to those of Delaware's letters and reports which are included in the district court's judgement, the party statement of Heidi Schøne, and the testimonies in particular of Runar Schøne and consultant Peter Broch. There is furthermore reason to call attention to the fact that, by a judgement of Eiker, Modum and Sigdal rural district court of 2 November 2001, Delaware was convicted of violation of Penal Code § 390a – invasion of privacy – by virtue of having pestered Schøne "over a number of years and up to 1998."

The number of harassing letters Delaware sent to Schøne before the 1998 article is of no significance for the reason alone that it was the police who took care of the post and spoke to the newspaper about the number. Nor is it of decisive importance whether the harassment had been for as long as 16 years in 1998, as long as the "core" of this allegation is true, cf. Bratholm and Matningsdal: Penal Code with commentary, part two, page 645. Schøne was persecuted, in some cases very seriously, in any case right back to around 1984/85, see inter alia Schøne's complaint to the Bergen police authorities of 1 December 1986. If there is such overwhelming written documentary evidence from early 1995 and up to today for serious harassment, including harassment which may be described as sexual harassment, Schøne must be believed when she says she previously threw away lots of similar offensive letters and postcards. The fact the Schøne at times chose to deal with the situation by acting pleasantly and politely towards Delaware does not alter the view that what is involved here is continuous harassment. It is not crucial either to what extent the 'reports' Delaware sent out contain true information about Schøne which had been confided to Delaware.

Schøne had respectable reasons for being interviewed by Drammens Tidende/Buskerud Blad in 1998. In 1998, the newspaper was following up a corresponding article from 1995 which had come about because the case had become well-known via the reports Delaware had sent out. The objective conditions for punishment in accordance with Penal Code §§ 246 and 247, cf. § 249 no. 2, do not therefore exist.

Even if the conditions for punishment in accordance with the said provisions had been satisfied, the question of whether to award Delaware damages in accordance with Damages Act § 3-6, subsection one, point two, would depend on an assessment of reasonableness. To award Delaware damages would have appeared to be a further offence against Heidi Schøne. On the whole, the case appears to be an abuse of the court apparatus. A procedural penalty in accordance with Courts of Justice Act § 202, subsection one, was considered but not imposed because there may be doubt about whether the subjective conditions for punishment exist.

The district court's judgement is accordingly to be upheld, the Court of Appeal also agreeing with the district court's decision on costs.

The appeal has been in vain. In accordance with the basic principle of the Civil Procedure Act § 180, subsection one, Frederick Delaware must pay the costs of the respondent before the Court of Appeal as no special circumstances exist which may justify exemption from liability for compensation. Mr. Aaløkken has submitted a statement of costs for a total of NOK 112,541.78, of which NOK 110,003.50 is his fee, the rest being travel expenses etc. in connection with the appeal hearing having taken place in Drammen. Value added tax is calculated to be NOK 21,782. It appears from the duties that the fee demand also includes work in connection with Delaware having made a complaint against Mr. Aaløkken before the ethical committee of the Lawyers' Association. Such expenses fall outside what can be claimed as covered in the appeal case. Supplementary work performed is also reduced from 4 to 2 hours. Overall, the fee demand is reduced by NOK 11,235 (12 hours @ NOK 755 plus VAT). Costs are to be awarded including VAT even if Delaware is resident in England.

Also to be paid are the travel expenses of NOK 3,578 of witness Ingunn Røren, which were advanced by the State. Delaware is accordingly ordered to pay costs of NOK 104,885. Heidi Schøne is granted free conduct of the case. NOK 300 of the costs – in accordance with the personal share she has to pay – are awarded to her, but the rest is awarded to the State.

The judgement is unanimous.

Conclusion of judgement:

1. The district court's judgement is upheld.

2. In the matter of costs of the case before the Court of Appeal, Frederick Delaware shall pay within 14 – fourteen – days of the of announcement of the judgement:
    -        to Heidi Schøne NOK 300 – three hundred - plus interest in accordance with the law on interest on overdue payments § 3, subsection one, point one, from due date until payment takes place, currently 12% per annum.
    -        to the State NOK 104,585 – one hundred and four thousand five hundred and eighty five - plus interest in accordance with the law on interest on overdue payments § 3, subsection one, point one, from due date until payment takes place, currently 12% per annum.

Agnar A. Nilsen Jnr.   Thore Rønning   Anita Lund

Certified for
Senior Judge of the Court of Appeal:
[signed J.H. Sandberg]

By the second week in January 2004 I had still not received Stig Lunde's letter with the judgement. So I phoned him to ask exactly when he posted it but he couldn't remember, whereupon he said he would put another copy in the post.

On 10th January 2004 I visited my website designer and we deleted all references to Heidi Munchausen and Runar Schyte on my website and replaced their "fictitious surnames" with their real one – Schøne. But I left in place on their respective photographs the bands across their eyes to retain a bit of mystery.

On 12th January 2004 Lunde's letter with an original stamped copy of the Court of Appeal judgement arrived. Another letter arrived next day from Lunde with a declaration for me to sign authorizing Lunde to write to the Court to tell them that the judgement had been served on me in the proper way. I signed it and faxed it back to Lunde on 14th January.

My very supportive acquaintance, Patrick Byrne, had earlier (11th January) paid me a visit in order to translate some of the court documentation that I had seen only for the first time the previous October, when the court official, Monica Gran, sent me the three volumes of evidence amounting to 622 pages in all.

The police witness statement dated 1st December 1986 of Heidi Overaa (as she then was) was the document that I understood contained the allegation of those magic words "attempted rape," which Helge Wesenberg my lawyer from Bergen had reported to me on 28th February 1995. Ever since then I had, of course, been trying to obtain sight of that document. In my bundle of court documentation, this 1st December 1986 statement consisted of only one page, numbered 143. And even then Heidi's actual statement only began half way down the page with no evidence of her signature in sight. It was a very brief statement in Norwegian. The only words I recognized were "Shia Muslim," which puzzled me as I was in fact a Sunni Muslim. What did the page say? Patrick told me that it said I had told Heidi I was a Shia Muslim when I met her [in 1982]. Heidi was a clever girl! Shia Muslims formed almost the entire population of Ayatollah Khomeini's Islamic Republic of Iran and were not 'flavour of the month.' So for Heidi to associate me with the Ayatollah's followers at the Ulset police station in Bergen, did me no favours. Patrick told me there was nothing on that one page statement mentioning "attempted rape." Was there another page or pages that had been withheld we wondered?

Heidi's witness statement of 17th February 1990 to the Bergen police stated among other things that from 1982 to 1984 I wrote her "nice letters," but "after 1984," I wrote a letter "threatening to kill her" saying also that she would "burn in hell." That when I visited her sister, Elisabeth (with Stuart McQueen in February 1990), I had "for one hour jumped up and down shouting abuse" and had "damaged a motor car." That I had used a passport under another name. That my mother had phoned them three years earlier to tell them to treat me kindly because I was "unbalanced," had "attacked a door" and was "on medication." That in June 1989 Heidi had voluntarily admitted herself to the Lier Psychiatric Clinic because of all the trouble I had caused her and that all this had been explained to Dr. Broch and was on the hospital records. That I had threatened her and her child's life and harassed her over the years.

In a witness statement of 18th February 1990 to the Bergen police Heidi stated I told her that if she married someone else I would "kill her."

In her 3rd October 1997 witness statement to the Mjøndalen police Heidi mentioned that she threw away cassettes I had recorded and had sent to her neighbours and close acquaintances wherein I had called her "a whore" and a "terrible person." That all the cassettes were dumped in 1998 after she got notification from the police that she could not do anything with them. [I in fact had sent no cassettes to any such people.] Heidi continued that she had been living with Iren in Bergen but could not remember her surname. That she could not remember the surname of Kristina, the au pair from Sweden, who had been her friend in England in 1982. Neither could she remember the surname of "her lover" in England at the time, a chap called David, as it was "so long ago." That "a month" after meeting me on the train I began contacting her mainly by telephone and she "seemed to remember" that I visited her "a couple of times." That the family Heidi was living with were "racists" and they didn't want me to visit them but in any case I went there "once" on which occasion "Kristina was not there but the wife and children were at home. After that whenever we met it was at Kristina's." [The actual facts were that I went to Kristina's home once in Harpenden and only then after spending time alone with Heidi at her residence before we were picked up in Kristina's car in St. Albans. A Danish au pair was also with us on the journey. Heidi's host family were not racists at all and I went to their home many times and even slept on the couch overnight twice, with Mrs. Warwick's permission.]

Stig Lunde had until Monday 16th February 2004 to lodge an appeal to the Supreme Court. The appeal had to be put in the post by this date but had to be sent to the offices of the Court of Appeal in the first instance. Lunde concentrated his efforts in the preceding week and stayed up until 3.30 a.m. on Wednesday 11th February working on the final draft. The working day of that Wednesday was spent by Lunde refining the appeal text. I kept in touch all day by phone until the finished product in Norwegian was e-mailed to me at 6.45 p.m. Lunde had, during the day over the phone, translated as best he could the text and I was satisfied with his work. I printed off five copies of the document, signed them all and faxed one back to Lunde. He in turn countersigned it and faxed it on to the court. However, Lunde told me that my fax was not very legible so it was put in the post to the court together with a clear copy of the appeal so that the judges could readily read the contents. Lunde paid the court fee by internet transfer: 17,760 kroner (£1,410) based on the need for only a one day hearing. The next day, Thursday, I went to the post office and by International Datapost sent my five signed copies of the appeal to Lunde. He would receive them on Monday 16th February, countersign them and in turn send them onto the court. The previous week I had paid Lunde £2,000 for his legal fees having already sent him £1,500 to cover the court fee.

The appeal is translated as follows:

Borgarting Court of Appeal
11 February 2004
Postboks 8017 Dep.
0030 OSLO

REGARDING

NOTICE OF APPEAL

TO

THE SUPREME COURT

WITH APPLICATION FOR EXEMPTION FOR THE
VALUE OF THE SUBJECT OF THE APPEAL

Borgarting Court of Appeal case no.: 02-01546 A/03

Appellant:	Frederick Delaware
Respondent:	Heidi Schøne, Sollikroken 7, 3058 Solbergmoen.
Counsel:	Vegard Aaløkken, CJ Hambrospl. 5, 0164 Oslo.
The appeal concerns:	Appeal against Borgarting Court of Appeal's judgement of 14 November 2003, in appeal case no. 02-01546 A/03, in case relating to damages for libellous statements reproduced in a newspaper article on 14 July 1998.

* * * * *

---

1. Introduction

Borgarting Court of Appeal passed judgement in appeal case no. 02-01546 A/03 on 14 November 2003 with this conclusion of judgement:

1. The District Court's judgement is upheld.
2. In the matter of costs of the case before the Court of Appeal, Frederick Delaware shall pay within 14 – fourteen – days of pronouncement of the judgement:

-        to Heidi Schøne NOK 300 – three hundred - plus interest in accordance with the law on interest on overdue payments § 3, paragraph 1, point 1, from due date until payment takes place, currently 12% per annum;
-        to the State NOK 104,585 – one hundred and four-thousand five hundred and eighty five - plus interest in accordance with the law on interest on overdue payments § 3, paragraph 1, point 1, from due date until payment takes place, currently 12% per annum.

The judgement related to an appeal against a judgement from Drammen District Court which had passed judgement on 11 February 2002 with the following conclusion of judgement:

1.   Heidi Schøne is held not liable.
2.   Frederick Delaware is ordered to pay the following costs within 14 days of pronouncement of the judgement:

a.   To Heidi Schøne NOK 21,675, plus statutory overdue payment interest of 12% p.a. from due date until payment takes place.

b.   To the State NOK 78,711, plus statutory overdue payment interest of 12% p.a. from due date until payment takes place.

In light of the fact that the appellant is resident in England, the Court of Appeal wished the judgement to be pronounced via the lawyer who had assisted the appellant at certain stages of the appeal case. In accordance with a special power of attorney, lawyer Lunde accepted pronouncement of the judgement of the Court of Appeal on 16 January 2004 on behalf of the appellant. This notice of appeal is filed in due time after this.

Lawyer Vegard Aaløkken has been counsel for the respondent before the District Court and the Court of Appeal, and is given as counsel before the Supreme Court as well, cf. Civil Procedure Act § 44, paragraph 1, point 2.

2. Further information about the appeal and grounds for appeal

The appeal concerns the Court of Appeal's judgement in its entirety, and it is asserted that the decision is wrong in respect of both application of law and assessment of evidence. The appellant furthermore asserts there have been procedural errors.

The appellant asserts the same arguments and evidence as before the Court of Appeal and the District Court.

The case concerns a report about the appellant in Drammens Tidende/Buskerud Blad on 14 July 1998. Before the report, the newspaper had had contact with the respondent. The claim against the respondent is based on the information she gave in conversation with the newspaper and the fact that she did not ensure that corrections were made when the newspaper article was gone through with her before publication.

The Court of Appeal's basis is that the respondent had a respectable reason for being interviewed and that the remarks were not improper. This is against the background of aspects of the behaviour of the appellant. For an accurate and overall picture, however, it is necessary to see the behaviour of the appellant in the context of the newspaper reports which had already appeared in 1995 (VG, Bergens Tidende and Drammens Tidende/ Buskerud Blad) and the parties' contact before these reports. The Court of Appeal does not go into this in its assessment.

The appellant disputes that the respondent had a respectable reason for being interviewed and that the remarks were not improper. The appellant also disputes that the statements are true. This applies seen in isolation, and in any case with regard to the overall impression conveyed by the article.

In the remarks about the appellant to the newspaper in 1998, the respondent went beyond the acceptable. The characterization given of the appellant is crude and unbalanced. For a report to have been acceptable, it should have been more balanced and placed in an overall context with regard to the relationship between the parties. Since the respondent was aware that her remarks and characterizations would be conveyed via the newspaper to the public, there was a special requirement incumbent upon her to ensure that the remarks were not unnecessarily insulting to the appellant. In addition to this, the accusations were untrue.

The appeal against the Court of Appeal's procedure is moreover connected with the fact that the appellant did not succeed in cross-examining the respondent. He also argues that the court did not deal with this in a way which led to sufficient clarification of the case. The appellant is aware that, in accordance with Civil Procedure Act § 219, it is up to the court to ensure that examination takes place in an appropriate way. However, it is asserted that the examinations were carried out in such a way that the necessary and sufficient light was not shed on central aspects of the case.

3. Further information about the parties' contact and the statements

The parties have known one another since 1982 when they met while the respondent was an au pair in England. The parties stayed in contact after the respondent moved to Norway in July 1982. Among other things, the appellant visited her for 10 days at Christmas 1984 and a week at Easter 1985. The appellant has stated that the parties had sexual intercourse once during this latter visit, and also that he was then also informed that she had had unprotected sex with another person. The respondent explained to the appellant in 1986 that this person had been in China early in 1985 and bought heroin, and that he used this himself and was a user when she had unprotected sex with him in 1985. The appellant found it incomprehensible that the respondent had had unprotected sex with a person he regarded as being in the risk group for HIV at the same time as she also had sexual intercourse with the appellant. This information made the appellant concerned, for his own health and also with regard to the respondent's way of life. As a consequence of his concern for his own health, he took an HIV test in December 1986, which was negative.

Against the background of continued concern, he has stated that he made contact with the respondent's father in 1986, and that he then informed him of his concerns about the respondent's way of life and mental health. The parties had contact after this as well. The appellant has in this connection stated that, in 1988 for example, he was contacted by the respondent in connection with insecurity she then felt in the relationship with her cohabitant.

He has also stated that in 1988 he sent her comforting letters and music cassettes when she was admitted to hospital for 4 to 8 weeks in 1988. The appellant asserts that up to this point in time there was nothing to indicate that the respondent did not wish to have contact with him.

The appellant emphasizes that there was no connection between the contact between himself and the respondent and the fact that she was admitted to hospital. The appellant states that he has been advised that the cause was among other things problems she had in the relationship with her then cohabitant.

When the appellant was visiting Norway in February 1990, he attempted to make contact with the respondent. He was then arrested by the police in Bergen. This was incomprehensible to him, but he subsequently became aware that the respondent had reported him in 1986 for attempted rape and that this report was made 2 weeks after the appellant had sent the letter to the respondent's father regarding his concern. He states that he interpreted this as pure and simple revenge because she had not liked the fact that he had expressed the concern he felt, which was expressed with the intention of being of assistance to her.

The appellant has also stated that it was only in the letter from lawyer Helge Wesenberg of 28 February 1995 that he became aware that he had been reported for attempted rape. It was only at this point that the background to the arrest in Bergen in 1990 became clear to him.

Until he became aware in 1995 of the reason for the arrest in 1990, this had been incomprehensible to him and had caused great anxiety. He attempted to make contact with the respondent to clarify this, without success. As a consequence of the uncertainty and the despair about not having the situation clarified, he sent letters and cards to the respondent and her then husband. Among other things in frustration at not having cleared up why he had been treated as he had been, and in indignation at having been exposed to what he regarded to be the risk of HIV, he made such accusations in letters and postcards against the respondent as have been documented in the case.

After the appellant became aware in 1995 that the respondent had reported him in 1986 for attempted rape, something which she much later corrected to actual rape, he felt rage and despair, in addition to the anxiety and concern he had already endured previously. This resulted in him in March 1995 sending out an account about the respondent. This was done on a very limited scale – roughly 20. These were sent to the respondent's then and previous neighbours. Before the appellant committed this desperate act, he had since the arrest in 1990 attempted through both English and Norwegian lawyers to clarify the background to the arrest. This was without having had any success in obtaining clarification of this in the contact with the police. The appellant emphasizes that neither attempted rape nor rape of the respondent ever took place on his part, and that the sexual intercourse at Easter 1985 was voluntary.

The newspaper report in 1995 was occasioned directly by the accounts mentioned above. Even though there might well be some people who had questions about what the background to the accounts they had received was, the report in the newspaper went far beyond what was necessary in order to shed light on this. Furthermore, the presentation was one-sided and stigmatized the appellant, without the actual background to his accounts being sent out emerging – namely that this was a desperate act which resulted from the despair, frustration and indignation he felt.

When the appellant became aware of the newspaper report, he became desperate and furious and wanted to defend himself. He was not given an opportunity to correct or disprove the report in the newspaper. He therefore instead sent out his accounts to addressees in the distribution areas of the newspapers concerned. The number of these sent out was considerably smaller than the newspapers' circulation.

Even though these accounts would have appeared strange to those who received them, the appellant asserts that it was nevertheless entirely wrong to refer to this as the work of a madman, as was done in the newspaper report in 1998, in particular without in any way putting it in the context of the parties' previous contact and what had provoked such a reaction from the appellant. The appellant asserts that it was the responsibility of the respondent to pass on the whole situation and the development between the parties which had led up to the accounts being sent out. It is also asserted that to the extent that there was occasion to give the public information about the personal circumstances of the appellant, this must in any case be limited to what was necessary as an explanation and sufficient to defend the respondent. The newspaper article in 1998 goes far beyond this, and appears as a one-sided and stigmatizing denunciation of the appellant.

The presentation of the appellant in 1998 completely omitted to mention that the respondent had also received positive and pleasant letters and cards from the appellant, and that she had received comforting cassette tapes when she was in hospital. There is no mention either of the fact that she herself took the initiative in making contact with the appellant, at least up until November 1990. The appellant also argues that the volume of letters indicated in the newspaper article is incorrect, but more important is the fact that the presentation gives the incorrect impression that these were exclusively massive communications from him with offensive content. This is without it emerging that for long periods there were only positive communications from him, and that on many occasions there was also contact from her, and also without it emerging that the respondent was religiously and sexually fixated in her contact with the appellant.

The appellant also reacted to the fact that he was a Muslim being brought up. He regarded the context in which this was presented as an insult to his religion and as such a provocation as well. He also reacted strongly to it being said that he had threatened to kill the respondent's son. This was difficult for him to take, at the same time as it also felt provocative to him, because in the first place it concerned a child and in the second place a child he cared about and had only positive feelings for.

The appellant asserts that no circumstances existed which constituted a basis for characterizing him in any of the ways as were the case in the newspaper article in 1998.

4. Further information about the basis for damages and assessment of the affronts

Authority for damages is given in E § 3-6. Compared with Penal Code chap. 23, this gives 3 basic conditions for damages:

1. The description of the offence in Penal Code §§ 246 and 247 must be complied with, looked at objectively.
2. The statements must be unlawful, as it is clearly established in case law that a reservation of unlawfulness exists.
3. Negligence must be shown, or it must be shown that the conditions for punishment are present.

The requirements with reference to addressee in Penal Code §§ 246 and 247 respectively are met.

The statements are untrue, individually and in any case in the overall impression presented by the newspaper article in 1998.

Notwithstanding truth, the statements are in any case improper, and there was no respectable reason for making such accusations as were made. In this connection, reference is briefly made to:

-   The respondent could originally in 1995 have looked after her interests by providing clarifying information to the few neighbours who had then received accounts.
-   To the extent it had nevertheless been necessary to use newspaper reports, a more balanced presentation should have been given. When the respondent chooses to make remarks to the media, she has a duty to ensure that she passes on balanced, comprehensive and correct information.
-   The respondent had alternatives for action with regard to looking after her interests, according to which it was not necessary to make the kind of report about the appellant she made via the media. She could have reported the appellant if she thought there were criminal circumstances. Either in connection with such an action, or independently, use could also have been made of the institution of libel.

541

When the respondent as it has emerged nevertheless consciously chose to use the newspapers against the appellant, she had a duty to stay within what is necessary out of consideration for the protection of his person. Instead a massive and unlawful denunciation is undertaken, which goes far beyond what is necessary in order to provide factual information to those who may have received the accounts and the public besides. A desire to put a stop to the appellant's conduct does not justify the use of unlawful and offensive accusations.

The respondent should have ensured that the journalist was given balanced information. Not having done this, she is responsible for the accusations made. Furthermore, she had the article read out for approval, which also entails a requirement to point out circumstances which appear incorrect or which give a wrong impression. This was not done. The respondent has not shown "due care," cf. Penal Code § 249 no. 3.

In this context, it is mentioned that the judgement included in Rt 1999 page 1541 is understood as being based on a legal principle that a person who makes an accusation has a duty to ensure a balanced presentation and that all circumstances which are important to the overall picture are made clear. The respondent has not fulfilled this requirement in her report about the appellant.

Even though the judgement included in Rt 2003 p. 1190 relates directly to the responsibility of the press for reports, reference is made to the assessment criteria indicated in paragraph 73 of the judgement, with further reference to Rt 2002 p. 764. The criteria applied to the case in question must lead to the accusations having weak protection. The statements in the case in question clearly lie outside the area of free expression. Especially given that they were made against another private person as part of internal disputes, this must lead to the accusations being without protection and amounting to libel as they appeared.

5. Further information about the procedure of the Court of Appeal

As emerges from the Court of Appeal's judgement, a number of the appellant's arguments were not dealt with or commented on at all in the grounds. The appellant is of the opinion and argues that this amounts to a procedural error.

He also argues that the Court of Appeal's decision not to allow the appellant himself an opportunity to cross-examine the respondent amounts to a procedural error. The appellant is of the opinion that a thorough and in-depth examination would be necessary in order to clarify the case satisfactorily, in order to bring out both the whole situation in the case and also circumstances he considers were of importance for shedding light on the reliability of the respondent. He points out that several hours of cross-examination would have been necessary for adequate examination, while the court spent only around 15 minutes on the respondent.

It is the opinion of the appellant, and he argues accordingly, that in reality no cross-examination of the respondent took place; furthermore, that the result of this is that it has not been possible to check the accusations she made to the newspaper in 1998 by confronting her, the upshot being that the Court of Appeal has found the accusations true. This also made it impossible to demonstrate shortcomings in coherency in various parts of the respondent's explanation, and to relate her explanation to the actual events. Apart from the fact that this led to inadequate and one-sided clarification of the factual aspects of the case, it also meant that circumstances of significance for assessment of the respondent's reliability did not emerge before the court either.

The appellant is of the opinion that it would have been impossible for the court to carry out an appropriate and adequate cross-examination and at the same time ensure the necessary neutrality, cf. in this context ECHR art. 6.

As, according to the above, the court did not handle the cross-examination in an appropriate way, and the appellant was not given an opportunity to ensure that the case was clarified sufficiently by cross-examination either, the appellant asserts that this also amounts to a breach of the requirement for fair procedure according to ECHR art. 6.

6. The assessment of damages

The appellant argues that his behaviour after the newspaper report in 1998 cannot be considered in the assessment of whether the affront offered in 1998 is unlawful or not. On the other hand, he agrees that subsequent behaviour may generally be a relevant criterion for the assessment of damages. Regarding his behaviour, however, he argues that importance must be attached to the fact that his remarks after the newspaper article in 1998 lie within his right of expression which follows from ECHR art. 10. Furthermore, in an overall assessment, importance must be attached to the fact not only that the case has been stressful for the respondent, but that both the treatment from the respondent and the reports about the appellant in newspapers in both 1995 and 1998 have been a considerable strain for him.

Moreover, the appellant argues that the claim is submitted on the basis of an overall assessment, and is in spite of everything very modest. There is no reason to reduce it further.

7. Conclusion

In other respects, the same arguments and evidence are cited before the Supreme Court as before the previous instances, including what emerges from the 'supplementary appeal' to the Court of Appeal of 12 June 2002 also.

At the same time as this appeal is sent in, the court fee is transferred to the Court of Appeal's account on behalf of the appellant. It is assumed that one day for the main hearing will be sufficient. In accordance with the telephone conversation with the Court of Appeal today, 24 * R, NOK 17,760 is being transferred to the Court of Appeal's account.

It is relevant for the appellant to bring forward supplementary arguments and evidence. Reserving further arguments and evidence, the appellant consequently submits the following respectful

Claim:

1.   Heidi Schøne be ordered to pay to Frederick Delaware within 14 days damages of NOK 50,000 plus the overdue payment interest applicable at any time from due date until payment takes place.
2.   Heidi Schøne be ordered to pay to Frederick Delaware within 14 days the costs of the case before the City Court and the Court of Appeal as well as the Supreme Court plus the overdue payment interest applicable at any time from due date until payment takes place.

CONCERNING APPLICATION FOR EXEMPTION FOR THE VALUE OF THE SUBJECT OF THE APPEAL

With reference to Civil Procedure Act § 359, application is hereby made for exemption from the requirement relating to the value of the subject of the appeal according to Civil Procedure Act § 357.

In the opinion of the appellant, the case raises questions of significance beyond the case in question.

Furthermore, it is pointed out that the case concerns an important social benefit where the value of the subject of the appeal is of minor significance. In this connection, reference is made to what is argued under section 6 "The assessment of damages" above, where it emerges that the claim is set low on the basis of an overall assessment and on the basis of a consideration that a high amount in itself is not the central factor in remedying the affront to which the appellant has been subjected. The protection of the personality has been violated in such a way that the decision will have "great significance" for the appellant, cf. Civil Procedure Act § 359, point 1 "if." If necessary, the application can be substantiated further.

It is presumed that the application for exemption for the value of the subject of the appeal will be dealt with before the notice of appeal. In order to limit the volume of work necessary, it is consequently requested that the respondent's counsel be asked, to begin with, to limit the work to that which concerns the application.

* Notice of appeal with application in 5 copies *

London, England
11 February 2004

Frederick Delaware
Countersignature

If the case is allowed to be brought before the Supreme Court, the appellant will engage a lawyer who will be counsel for him. For the time being, however, he has wished to limit expenditure. As the appellant does not himself speak Norwegian, and in order to relieve the Court of Appeal from receiving the appeal orally from the appellant and thus writing it down, the notice of appeal has been written by me in accordance with instructions received. In this connection, I have exercised control over ensuring that the appeal has been made as clear as possible and that it is free of errors. Any responsibility and costs associated with the content of arguments and the appeal lie fully with the appellant himself. I am not answerable for fees or incidental costs.

With reference to Civil Procedure Act § 364, the notice of appeal with associated application for exemption for the value of the subject of the appeal is hereby countersigned.

Moss, 11 February 2004

Stig Lunde
Lawyer

On 11th March 2004 Heidi Schøne's lawyer submitted his response. As soon as Lunde sent it to me I passed it on to my agency for translation and it went as follows:

[Letter from office of ELLEN HOLAGER ANDENÆS, Oslo, dated 11 March 2004.]

RESPONSE TO APPEAL

TO

SUPREME COURT

Borgarting Court of Appeal case no. 02-01546 A/03

Appellant:	Frederick Delaware
Respondent:	Heidi Schøne
Counsel:	Vegard Aaløkken

The appeal concerns:	Appeal against Borgarting Court of Appeal's judgement of 14.11.03, in case no. 02-01546 A/03, in case relating to claim for damages for libellous statements reproduced in a newspaper article on 14.7.98.

1. Introduction

Reference is made to the letter dated 18.2.04 from Borgarting Court of Appeal, in which Frederick Delaware's appeal against the abovementioned judgement is notified. The time limit for response is three weeks from 19.2.04, which is the date when the appeal was notified.

Heidi Schøne wishes to argue that the Appeals Committee of the Supreme Court should not give consent to proceed with the case because the appeal concerns a financial value of less than NOK 100,000.

In the event that consent is given, Heidi Schøne argues that the appeal must be rejected. The judgement of the Court of Appeal is correct, and it is not full of procedural errors.

I agree with the appellant that it is appropriate that in my response I will, to begin with, limit the work to making comments on the application for exemption for the value of the subject of the appeal. Please advise if this is not sufficient.

2. Application for exemption for the value of the subject of the appeal

The case does not raise questions of significance beyond the case in question. There is therefore no basis for deviating from the basic principle that consent shall not be given when a financial value of less then NOK 100,000 is concerned, cf. Civil Procedure Act §§ 359 and 357.

There is no doubt that Heidi Schøne has for years been subjected to annoying and unwanted attention from Frederick Delaware.

This is described in Drammen District Court's judgement of 13.1.00, the appealed judgement and Eiker, Modum and Sigdal District Court's sentence of 21.2.02, included in the abstract of appeal page 515.

After the appeal hearing in the Court of Appeal was completed on 16.10.03, Delaware was arrested by South Buskerud police district, charged with violation of Criminal Procedure Act § 390(a), for annoying behaviour towards Heidi Schøne in the period 25.2.02 to 31.8.03. The next day he was brought before Eiker, Modum and Sigdal District Court with a request for remand in custody.

In the court session, Delaware admitted guilt, and the same day a guilty judgement was delivered, in which Delaware was sentenced to eight months in prison. The sentence was suspended on condition that he inter alia delete all information relating to Heidi Schøne posted on the Internet and remove the web page www.norway-shockers.com.

Enclosure 1: Eiker, Modum and Sigdal District Court's judgement of 17.10.04.

Delaware accepted the judgement. He was released the same day. I have been informed that the judgement is legally enforceable.

After the conviction, Delaware continued the annoying behaviour towards Heidi Schøne. This included, a short time afterwards, breaking the conditions for the sentence being suspended. This was done by Delaware continuing with the undesirable spreading of information about Heidi Schøne at the Internet address mentioned. Heidi Schøne was now referred to as Ms. Munchausen. The pictures were censored by lines over the eyes. The accompanying enclosure was taken from www.norway-shockers.com on 24.10.03.

Enclosure 2:   Printout from www.norway-shockers.com dated 24.10.03.

As a matter of form, I would point out that the website has now been removed. I do not know whether Heidi Schøne is subjected to corresponding annoying behaviour elsewhere. By his behaviour, Delaware has demonstrated clear contempt of court.

In his behaviour, he also shows that he wishes to continue the persecution of Heidi Schøne. It is difficult to see the appeal to the Supreme Court as being the consequence of anything else, and there can therefore be no basis for consenting to the application for exemption for the value of the subject of the appeal. In this connection, reference may be made to the accompanying statement dated 13.10.03 from consultant Peter Broch in which, on page 2, it is evident that he thinks the persecution must have a "pathological motivation" (known as "stalking" in international literature).

Enclosure 3:   Statement dated 13.10.03 from consultant Peter Broch.

Accordingly, I submit the following respectful

r e q u e s t:

1. Consent is not given for exemption for the value of the subject of the appeal.

Subsidiarily

2. The appeal is rejected.

In every circumstance

3. Frederick Delaware is ordered to pay to Heidi Schøne within 14 days the costs of the case before the District Court, the Court of Appeal and the Supreme Court, plus the overdue payment interest applicable at any time from due date until payment takes place.

Five copies of the response to the appeal are sent to Borgarting Court of Appeal. Two copies are sent directly to Frederick Delaware.

Yours sincerely

[signature]

Vegard Aaløkken
Lawyer

Enclosures

Copy w/enclosures: Frederick Delaware

I told Stig Lunde it was important we replied to this and we discussed the form of the pleading. On 6th April 2004 Lunde emailed me the further pleading in Norwegian for me to sign and fax directly back to the Supreme Court. This I did, as well as, by recorded delivery letter send five originals to the Supreme Court and two originals to Heidi Schøne's lawyer. The English translation is as follows:

WRITTEN PLEADING

TO

SUPREME COURT

Case no.:   HR-2004-00551-U

Appellant: Frederick Delaware.

Respondent: Heidi Schøne, Sollikroken 7, 3058 Solbergmoen.

Counsel: Vegard Aaløkken, C.J. Hambrospl. 5, 0164 Oslo.

* * *

Reference is made to the respondent's response of 11 March 2004.

* * *

The case concerns protection of the personality, contains a number of questions in relation to the ECHR, and relates to fundamental rights. In addition to the fact that it is of great importance for the appellant that the case is brought before the Supreme Court, more detailed clarification of the protection of the personality and the relationship with the ECHR is also of significance beyond the case in question.

Civil Procedure Act § 357 in any case gives occasion for consenting to an appeal without regard to the value of the subject of the appeal, even if the case should not raise questions of significance beyond the case in question. Firstly, reference is made to the fact that the provision provides a "can rule." Consequently, it does not exclude consent also being given outside the alternatives for which the provision gives instructions. Secondly, reference is made to the fact that it has great significance for the appellant that the case is subjected to examination and correct hearing.

In this connection, reference is made to the fact that the comments to which he was subjected were reproduced in the media. Furthermore that they were coarse and offensive and that they continued over time – after the articles this dispute concerns as well. The comments of which he was the object were not justified and went far beyond what can be considered acceptable on the basis of the situation as it existed when the comments were made. The assessment should also attach importance to the fact that it is fundamental rights that have been violated.

* * *

During the hearing of the case, the respondent has repeatedly referred to the appellant having behaved annoyingly towards her and shown her unwanted attention.

The central issue is whether the behaviour the appellant had demonstrated at the time the comments were made and were reproduced in the media was of such a nature that it justified the respondent's remarks to the press. The behaviour after this time is not to be used as a basis for assessing whether the appellant's honour was illegally offended.

* * *

In the response, a new document, Eiker, Modum and Sigdal District Court's judgement of 17.10.04 is submitted.

It follows from the judgement that it is based on a charge for offences in the period 25 February 2002 – 31 August 2003 and 1 September – 16 October 2003 respectively.

This is consequently a long time after the remarks the dispute in question concerns. The behaviour must moreover be seen in the light of the frustration the appellant felt as a consequence of the treatment he himself was subjected to.

* * *

The statement from consultant Peter Broch was submitted during the main hearing before the Court of Appeal, and the appellant first became acquainted with it when it was handed over in court on 14.10.03.

The appellant was given a brief and immediate introduction to the contents by his interpreter. This is not sufficient for him to be able to look after his interests properly. Furthermore, he was not given an opportunity to cross-examine Dr. Broch either.

Dr. Broch's information about abnormal behaviour and "stalkers" was not substantiated or documented in any way. Nor did it emerge which behaviour and traits of the appellant he thinks would justify such a label. The appellant wishes to deny that he behaved as Dr. Broch has indicated.

In his statement, Dr. Broch states that the appellant systematically persecuted the respondent "with harassment spread across most of the major newspapers in Norway." The actual situation is that the appellant, who was the object of newspaper articles, was himself not in any way involved in reports about the respondent in newspapers.

As emerges from the statement, Dr. Broch was the respondent's therapist and psychiatrist. As the comment quoted above shows, he lacks knowledge of the parties' relationship and the comments this dispute concerns. It is emphasized that he never treated the appellant and consequently has no basis for assessing him from such a connection. Dr. Broch's knowledge of the appellant was acquired through being the respondent's therapist and psychiatrist. Moreover, it cannot be ruled out that Dr.Broch's assessments and opinion of the appellant may have been influenced by his closeness and connection with the respondent which developed as her therapist.

Given the above, no importance can be attached to Dr. Broch's assumptions with regard to the appellant's behaviour.

It emerges clearly from the statement that the respondent has carried considerable suffering with her from childhood, and also that the relationship with the appellant may have been influenced by this. The appellant does not in any way wish to trivialize the considerable problems the respondent has had in her life, but it is important, and in accordance with what the appellant has stated, that the respondent's conduct and accusations towards the appellant must be seen in the light of her previous history.

* * *

The appeal to the Supreme Court is exclusively a consequence of the fact that the appellant considers that incorrect assessment of evidence and application of law have been used as a basis, and the stated procedural errors before the Court of Appeal.

It is important that the case be submitted to examination by the Supreme Court, and within this that the comments about the appellant be assessed in relation to the behaviour he had demonstrated at the time of the comments and the newspaper report.

* Written pleading in 7 originals, 5 of which are sent to the Supreme Court and 2 directly to lawyer Aaløkken. *

London, 6ᵗʰ April 2004
[signature]
Frederick Delaware

Also sent by fax to:
Supreme Court of Norway – fax: 22 33 23 55
Lawyer Aaløkken – fax: 22 41 31 04

Within days of my posting these documents to the Supreme Court they returned them all to me together with a copy of the Supreme Court judgment – in Norwegian – dated 17ᵗʰ March 2004! Lunde did not, as I asked him to, check with the Supreme Court whether they had given their judgment before submitting the pleading of 6ᵗʰ April 2004. The Supreme Court later translated into English their verdict and sent it to me on 22ⁿᵈ April 2004:

THE APPEALS SELECTION COMMITTEE OF THE SUPREME COURT

On 17 March 2004, the appeals selection committee of the Supreme Court, Comprising judges Gjølstad, Tjomsland and Bruzelius, in the matter of

HR-2004-00551-U, (Case No. 2004/454), Civil Case Appeal:

Frederick Delaware
Versus

Heidi Schøne   (Vergard Aaløkken, Attorney at Law)

rendered the following

JUDGEMENT:

Frederick Delaware has applied for leave to bring an appeal before the Supreme Court without regard to the value of the subject – matter of the appeal, the appeal being against the judgment rendered by the Borgarting Court of Appeal on 14ᵗʰ November 2003 in the action against Heidi Schøne, cf. section 357, cf section 359, of the Civil Procedure Code.

The Appeals Selection Committee of the Supreme Court finds that there are no grounds for granting such leave.

The respondent has entered a claim for costs in the case, with the addition of interest. This claim is granted. Costs are at NOK 3,000.

CONCLUSION:

Leave to appeal to the Supreme Court without regard to the value of the subject-matter of the appeal is denied.

Frederick Delaware is to pay Heidi Schøne the cost of proceedings before the Appeals Selection Committee of the Supreme Court in the amount of NOK 3,000 – three thousand kroner – upon service of this judgment, with the addition of ordinary interest on late payment, pursuant to section 3, first paragraph, first point of the Act concerning interest on late payment, calculated from the expiry of the time for performance and until payment is affected.

Steinar Tjomsland   Liv Gjøstad   Karin M. Bruzelius

True transcript certified: Birgitte Janecke Lund

549

Regarding my complaint against Vegard Aaløkken the Bar Association wrote to me on the 12th March 2004 enclosing a copy of their English translation of its decision of the 4th March 2004:

Disiplinærutvalget for Oslo krets av Den Norske Advokatforening

Has on   04-03-2004

Resolved complaint nr.   93/2003

PlaintifF.   Frederick Delaware

Defendant: Advokat Ellen Holager Andenæs
                                              v/ advokat Vegard Aaløkken

Responsible for the matter has been: Terje Aakvaag, Halldis Winje and Terje Løyning

By his letter dated the 3rd May 2003 Frederick Delaware has filed a complaint against advokat Ellen Holager Andenæs by advokat Vegard Aaløkken, holding that the Defendant has conducted his affairs in violation of applicable regulations regarding professional ethics. By his letter dated May 8th 2003, the Plaintiff has reiterated his complaint. The Defendant has responded to the complaint in his letter dated May 26th 2003.

The merits of the matter would appear to be as follows:

The Plaintiff filed a suit against a client of the Defendant to the Drammen City Court. The Drammen Court resolved the the matter on February 11th 2002 in favour of the client of the Defendant's.

The Plaintiff has appealed against the award of the Drammen Court and the appeal hearing is scheduled for week 42 in 2003.

The complaint relates predominantly to certain documents which the Plaintiff believes is in the possession of the Defendant and which the Plaintiff believes are relevant to the dispute before the appeal court. The purpose of the complaint appears to be that the disciplinary body should instruct the Defendant to surrender the said documents. The complaint further relates to certain statements which the Plaintiff believes have been made by the Defendant's client.

The Plaintiff holds that the Defendant has the relevant documents available and that they should be produced in evidence in the dispute before the appeal court. The Defendant should have a responsibility to ensure that all relevant factual circumstances are available to the appeal court in order that the court be given a correct and balanced bases for its decision.

The Defendant holds that the complaint should be dismissed as the matter relates to issues that have been or will be decided upon by the appeal court. In any event the Defendant holds that the substance of the complaint relates exclusively to matters in which he has acted in the best interests of his client.

The Disciplinary Body holds:

The matters brought forward in the complaint are exclusively of a nature that will be - or have been – addressed and decided by the appeal court in due course.

550

It consequently follows that the complaint falls out side the competence of the Disciplinary Body, cf. Article 2, section 3 of the regulations regarding the organisation of the Disciplinary Body. Additionally, it follows quite clearly from the presentation in the complaint from the Plaintiff, that the complaint relates only to matters in which the Defendant has acted within his brief from his client. Consequently, the matter must be dismissed.

Conclusion:

Following this discussion, the Disciplinary Body has arrived at the following

DECISION:

The complaint is dismissed.

Terje Aakvaag
Subcommittee 5

I appealed on 15th March 2004 to the Disciplinary Council. The Court of Appeal case had taken place now and I had appealed to the Supreme Court. I asked the Disciplinary Council now to ask Vegard Aaløkken to supply Heidi Schøne's police witness statement alleging "attempted rape" and police witness statement alleging "rape by holding her down," adding that the Court of Appeal had not dealt with these matters. That the Court of Appeal only dealt with the evidence that was before them.

I had resumed corresponding with Svein Erik Krogvold of the Bergen police in a determined effort to obtain the "attempted rape" witness statement made by Heidi. On the 15th March 2004 I asked Krogvold to send me what I had assumed was the missing page or pages from Heidi's 1st December 1986 witness statement. The correspondence went as follows:

> **Letter dated 17th March 2004 from Assistant Chief Constable Svein Erik Krogvold:**
>
> I am in receipt of your telefax of March 14.
>
> The document you refer to has not more than one page.
>
> The police have previously responded to communication from three different law firms, claiming to represent you. In 1990 from the law firm of Foyen & Bell in London, in 1995 from the law firm of Roll, Komnæs & Wesenberg in Bergen and in 1999 from the law firm Elden & Elden in Oslo.
>
> I can see no reason to responding any further to communication from you or your representatives, in this case which has been closed for over 12 years now.
>
> Yours sincerely
> Svein Erik Krogvold
> *Assist. Chief Constable*

> **My fax of 20th March 2004 in reply to Mr. Krogvold:**
>
> I am in receipt of your letter of 17th March. I know "the case" has been closed for 12 years. And that's 12 years of silence has to **exactly** what Heidi Schøne's allegation of "attempted rape" involves. Plus 6 more years of silence **before** the case was closed, i.e. 1986 to 1992.
>
> Enclosed is exhibit 177 [Heidi Overaa's 1.12.86 police witness statement] in the civil case documentation from the Borgarting Lagmannsrett. The letter of February 28th 1995 from Helge Wesenberg, you will see states in the 3rd paragraph, last line, "attempted rape." This information was gathered from your police records as per Heidi Overaa's witness statement. A statement that must be

contained in the missing page(s) to the 1.12.86 statement. Where is Heidi Overaa's signature?

Please send me Heidi Overaa's statement containing her allegation of attempted rape. This civil case has gone to the Supreme Court. Heidi Schøne, as she later became, has made an allegation in 1998 and onwards that I raped her (no longer "attempted") "by holding her down." So I want the 1986 statement to compare the wording. I want the details for the purposes of [getting evidence to prove] her lying on oath - perjury - and for presentation to the Supreme Court/European Court of Human Rights.

You willingly helped Schøne's lawyer, Vegard Aaløkken, by sending him all the evidence in this case, including Heidi's signed statements on other occasions. But this one statement on "attempted rape" – read by Wesenberg – is missing.

Please send me the "attempted rape" statement from December 1986.

I also want to know **who** gave in a report to the Bergen police saying I threatened to kill Heidi's son "in a letter." **Who** brought the letter in? Where is the "death threat" letter?

This matter has made 12 front page stories in your country's newspapers, so don't imagine the matter will disappear. If I do not get your co-operation I will have to refer the matter to the Minister of Justice.

Letter dated 24th March 2004 from Mr. Krogvold:

I refer to your telefax of March 20.

The document you refer to has only one page. I have now repeated it twice and intend not to do it anymore! Heidi Overaa's signature is at the bottom of the page (below the text: "opplest og vedtatt"). I do not know where you got your copy, but it is not my problem if the signature is missing due to the fact that the document evidently has been placed a bit low in the photocopy machine.

I have no comments to what Mr. Wesenberg might have stated in a letter to you, of **his interpretation** of what might be the content of the case documents he has had access to.

Yours sincerely
Svein Erik Krogvold
Assist. Chief Constable

I replied by fax dated 28th March 2004 to Mr. Krogvold:

I refer to your letter of 24th March. You know perfectly well what I want: the document that Helge Wesenberg read from your office that allowed him to write to me "attempted rape." I have sufficient grounds to suspect these words were on "missing page(s)" to the 1.12.86 statement. You tell me there is only one page with Heidi's signature right at the bottom. Not good enough!

Heidi Overaa's statement of 18-2-90 (two pages) has her signature at the bottom of the first page but there is a second page as well, with her signature at the bottom. Bearing in mind my lawyer Reg Whitttal at Foyen & Bell in London, wrote to you on June 19th 1990 – in the 8th paragraph – of your "unspecified and unsubstantiated reasons" for your threat to arrest me, I have every reason to question your good faith.

So please send me the document which Mr. Wesenberg based, in your words, "his interpretation" of my actions of "attempted rape" **and** tell me who brought

552

the alleged "death threat" letter to Daniel Overaa into the Bergen police. Not only has all evidence of this "death threat" letter been withheld from me, so has evidence of the police record of the receipt of the letter. Who gave the letter in and which officer received it at the police station? Has it all gone missing?

I see what your Drammen police did to me – in particular police sergeant Torill Sorte of Nedre Eiker – as criminal in nature. And you have all been trying hard as hell to finish me off. Your Attorney General, Tor-Aksel Busch, is covering up police corruption. You know the whole story as it is on the internet.

So, Odd Einar Dørum [Norwegian Minister of Justice] will be contacted, in good time, to look into the Bergen and Drammen police actions and Tor-Aksel Busch. Everything is related.

On 14th July 2004 the Disciplinary Council of the Bar Association sent me the English translation of their decision on my appeal to them dated 29th June 2004:

The Disciplinary Council rendered the following

DECISION:

On 3 May 2003 the Complainant filed a complaint with the Norwegian Bar Association alleging that the attorney-at-law who is the subject of the complaint had acted unprofessionally when appearing as counsel for the Complainant's female opponent in a legal action brought by the Complainant for damages for defamation. According to the judgment of the city court in the case in question, the Complainant had pursued and harassed the woman for several years, in amongst other ways by sending out a 'report' on her to neighbours, friends and family. The harassment largely focused on the woman's sexual morals and relationships with other men. The 'report' came to the attention of a newspaper in the area in which the woman lives, and as a countermove against the harassment she agreed to be interviewed by the newspaper. The Complainant's claim for damages for defamation is rooted in these interviews.

The complaint to the Disciplinary Committee of the Norwegian Bar Association concerns the attorney-at-law's failure to cooperate with the Complainant in acquiring police documents, allegedly containing false accusations made by the woman against the Complainant, the attorney's failure to counter the Complainant's submissions to the court and the fact that the attorney-at-law apparently described the Complainant as "a rapist" and "mentally ill" during the court proceedings.

The subject of the complaint refuted the complaint in a letter dated 26 May 2003. He submits that the complaint should be dismissed both because the circumstances raised by the Complainant have already been reviewed by the court, and because he acted only with a view to safeguarding the interests of his client in the case.

The Disciplinary Committee of the Norwegian Bar Association rendered its decision on 4 March 2004, concluding as follows:

The complaint is dismissed.

The dismissal was based on the submissions entered by the subject of the complaint.

In a letter dated 20 March 2004, the Complainant appealed the decision of the Disciplinary Committee to the Disciplinary Council within the due time. The subject of the complaint has not commented on the appeal of the Complainant. Accordingly, it is assumed that the subject of the complaint stands by his submissions to the Disciplinary Committee.

This case is primarily in the same position before the Disciplinary Council as when it was heard by the Disciplinary Committee, and reference is accordingly made to the Committee's outline of the facts in the case.

In a letter dated 29 March 2004 from the secretariat of the Disciplinary Council, the parties were notified that the case had been submitted to the chairman of the Disciplinary Council for an assessment of whether the merits of the case should be reviewed, cf. Section 5-5, first paragraph, of the Rules for Advocates.

According to this provision, the chairman of the Disciplinary Council has the authority to dismiss a complaint if it has not been filed within the due time, if it is patently unfounded, if the complainant has no legal interest in the complaint, or if the circumstances to which the complaint pertains have been brought before the courts.

The Disciplinary Council has reached the same conclusion as the Disciplinary Committee. In justifying its decision, the Disciplinary Council has concluded that it is sufficient to refer to the right and duty of an attorney-at-law to safeguard the interests of his or her clients within the applicable ethical guidelines.

The subject of the complaint represented the Complainant's opponent in a very unusual case, which was based on the prolonged and serious harassment of the attorney-at-law's client. No proof has been submitted to support the contention that the subject of the complaint's handling of the case on behalf of his client was blameworthy, and contravened the requirements as to professional and ethical conduct expected of an attorney-at-law in the performance of an assignment.

The Disciplinary Council notes that a party may often disagree with - and be dissatisfied with - the way in which the opposing party's attorney-at-law performs his or her duties. The adversarial system can of itself easily result in antagonisms of this nature. It may be difficult to appreciate that the attorney-at-law has an obligation to safeguard his client's interests in a conscientious and careful way within the framework of what constitutes professional and correct conduct. The complaint is dismissed as patently unfounded. This decision was adopted by the chairman of the Disciplinary Council pursuant to Section 5-5, first paragraph, of the Rules for Advocates.

Conclusion: The decision of the Disciplinary Committee is upheld.

Knut Glad
Chairman

True translation certified: Robert Hans Lovering Government Authorised Translator

So, the Disciplinary Council decided that my complaint against Vegard Aaløkken was "patently unfounded."

I had made complaints against five lawyers now. My complaint against Karsten Gjone had been upheld. For the other four lawyers – Helge Wesenberg, Per Danielsen, Eric Lindset of the firm of Elden & Elden and Vegard Aaløkken – the same judge, Knut Glad sitting on the Disciplinary Council of the Bar Association, heard my appeals. Each time he dismissed my complaint. A seperate judge should surely have sat on each appeal to avoid the appearance of bias.

On 24th May 2004 I had sent a five page fax to Odd Einar Dørum (see Appendix 5) the Norwegian Minister of Justice in Oslo asking him to explain his Aftenposten newspaper comments of 15th April 2002. I referred the minister to my website to help him on the detail of the case. I mentioned the deceitful involvement of Aftenposten's journalist Reidun J. Samuelsen (who had spoken to the minister regarding my "internet harassment"). Mr. Dørum was, I presumed, also responsible for the conduct of the police and I asked him to investigate the cover up over the enquiry into policewoman Torill Sorte's perjury. On 10th August 2004 a deputy director and senior advisor at the Royal Ministry of Justice and the Police replied saying, "The Ministry of Justice have acknowledged your opinion on the matter and we have noticed [sic] your allegations." I expected a full response in due course as had been promised by the minister's spokesman, Gunnar Johannessen, to whom I had sent my fax on 24th May 2004.

In July 2004 I received from my translation agency two further legal documents, so now I could begin work on my application to the European Court of Human Rights. The language would now be English. The 6 month time limit to lodge an application to the European Court ran from the date of the last judgment that exhausted Norway's judicial apparatus, or the date when I (as a litigant in person) received notice of the judgment, whichever was the later. The date of the judgment was 17th March 2004, which the Supreme Court sent to me on 22nd April 2004. To be on the safe side I submitted my letter of application to the European Court on the 10th September 2004. This would stop the 6 month time limit running but I was required as soon as possible thereafter to submit the full application and all supporting documentation. On the 16th September 2004 the ECHR acknowledged my letter of 10th September 2004 and told me to send the balance of papers "without undue delay." I was extremely busy at work and so to buy myself enough time I asked the ECHR for an extension until "early December 2004" to submit the Application form and supporting papers. My request was granted. It took a monumental effort – hours and hours and hours of preparation and photocopying – to gather what was needed. Almost 1,300 pages of original documentation were selected and photocopied twice. On 25th November 2004 at a cost of £56 I sent my parcel of documentation by International Datapost to the European Court in Strasbourg. My application letter of 10th September 2004 (with the additional comments in my letter of 24th November 2004 shown in square brackets) went as follows:

BY FAX AND POST

The Registrar,
European Court of Human Rights,
Council of Europe,
F-67075 Strasbourg Cedex,
FRANCE.

Date: 10th September 2004

Dear Sirs,

Mr. Frederick Delaware v. Norway

I, Frederick Delaware, am a practicing solicitor of the Supreme Court of England and Wales. I represent myself in this case and am writing to introduce an application with the Court under Article 34 of the European Convention on Human Rights. I was born in London on [** *** ****] to a German mother and Egyptian father and am a citizen of the United Kingdom.

In libel proceedings brought in Norway my Norwegian lawyer, Stig Lunde, filed on my behalf an Amended writ on 13th January 2000 by way of a private criminal prosecution of the Norwegian newspaper Drammens Tidende, its editor Hans Odde, its journalist Ingunn Røren and a fourth defendant called Heidi Schøne (maiden name: Heidi Overaa). The claim was for judicial declaration that the newspaper's defamatory statements about me printed in an article dated 14th July 1998, were null and void and compensation for non-pecuniary damage. The article was entitled, 'Sexually harassed for 16 years.' It repeated much of what was printed in a very similar article in Drammens Tidende dated 27th May 1995 entitled, 'Badgered and Hunted for Thirteen years.' Drammens Tidende's 27th May 1995 article lifted much of what was said in Verdens Gang's article of 26th May 1995 entitled, '13 years of Sex-terror' and Bergens Tidende's article of 24th May 1995 entitled, '13 years of Harrassment.'

A former lawyer, Mr. Karsten Gjone, missed the three year time limit to issue writs against the three newspapers over the May 1995 articles and was found guilty of professional misconduct for his negligence by the Norwegian Bar Association after I lodged a complaint.

To my knowledge there have been twelve prominent, usually front page, national and provincial newspaper stories on this subject in Norway from 1995 to 2003. The main source of information to the newspapers was the defendant Heidi Schøne, a Norwegian au pair who I befriended in England in 1982. She was for a short period in 1988, after a second suicide attempt, a psychiatric patient in a hospital in Norway but is now on a full disability pension for mental disorder which her psychiatrist, in evidence, attributed in large part to sexual and mental abuse suffered at the hands of Norwegian citizens including her own family, over the years. By the age of 18 she had had two abortions to the same Norwegian man.

Heidi Schøne has added me to the list of abusers and the end result, helped by a pernicious nine year press campaign in Norway, is that I find myself branded by the Norwegian courts as, inter alia, a rapist, a stalker, a sex fiend and a potential child killer, solely on the uncorroborated and untested word of Heidi Schøne, now aged 41, whose testimony was ruled "in essence" to be true.

Moreover, because I publicized my own side of the story via an information campaign, including a website, I was given a sentence of 8 months imprisonment suspended for 2 years under Section 390(a) of the Norwegian Criminal Code on 17th October 2003, the day after I finished prosecuting my Court of Appeal libel case. The prison sentence is no longer suspended because I refused to close down my website on my return to England. I cannot now travel to any Scandinavian country due to the mutual enforcement law, without fear of arrest and deportation to Norway and to prison.

Significantly, up to the time of the May 1995 newspaper stories, the Norwegian police had never received complaints from Heidi Schøne in the nature of endless years of sex-terror/harassment. Specific allegations printed in the newspapers in 1995 had not been reported to the police at all, eg., that I sent her 400 obscene letters (all of which she said she threw away!), that I threatened to kill her son (in 1988 - in writing!). Her 1998 allegation to the police of aggravated rape was withheld from the police for thirteen years after the time of the alleged incident. And it was only after I issued my writ against Drammens Tidende and Heidi Schøne in January 2000 that the police, on very flimsy grounds, acted against me and then only by, eventually, asking me to pay a small fine of 5,000 kroner which I refused to do. Even a senior officer at the Bergen police and a senior officer at the Drammen police told me in 1996 that they did not believe Heidi Schøne's claims and direct evidence of their opinions was submitted in evidence to the court, and accepted as admissible.

A preliminary hearing took place in Norway on 25th August 2000 before Judge Anders Stilloff who ruled that I was allowed to sue Drammens Tidende, its editor, journalist and Heidi Schøne over the newspaper's article of 14th July 1998.

Drammens Tidende then appealed and on 24th November 2000 the Borgarting Court of Appeal dismissed my action against the newspaper Drammens Tidende and editor and journalist on the grounds that I had in 1999 waived my right to sue the newspaper because I had agreed to this to allow the Norwegian Press Complaints Commission (the PFU) to look into my complaint to them.This, in spite of the fact that the PFU were not allowed, on their own admission, to adjudicate on whether the statements made in the newspaper were true or false: a position that I had not been made aware of. My lawyer, Stig Lunde, then appealed to the Supreme Court on the grounds that the Court of Appeal had misinterpreted the law. By their decision of 16th February 2001 the Supreme Court dismissed my appeal because my lawyer had missed the two week time limit to appeal, by 14 days.

This left only Heidi Schøne as the defendant in my action which under Norwegian law automatically turned into a civil action.

When we knew that Drammens Tidende had dropped out of my criminal libel prosecution, my lawyer Stig Lunde, began a civil action against the exact same set of defendants. This was in the hope that the civil courts would adopt a different approach to the question of my use of the PFU. But to no avail as the civil court of first instance, the forliksradet – whose adjudicators are not lawyers but laymen arbitrators – simply adopted the Court of Appeal ruling from my criminal prosecution and dismissed my action against Drammens Tidende its editor and journalist, but not Heidi Schøne.

The two actions merged into one civil action against Heidi Schøne culminating in a four day trial on 15th January 2002 before one judge, Anders Stilloff – the same judge who sat on the preliminary hearing on 25th August 2000 at Drammen City Court. There are no jury trials for libel cases in Norway: the judiciary decide the case. On 11th February 2002 Heidi Schøne was acquitted and awarded costs. On 13th March 2002 my lawyer, Stig Lunde, submitted an appeal against the judgement in its entirety on the grounds that the decision was wrong in respect of both application of the law and assessment of the evidence. A supplemental appeal pleading was submitted on 12th June 2002. The appeal was heard on 13th to 16th October 2003 before three judges. I was acting as a litigant in person with an interpreter at my side. On 14th November 2003 my appeal was dismissed.

On 11th February 2004 my lawyer, Stig Lunde appealed to the Supreme Court against the Borgarting Court of Appeal judgement in its entirety, asserting that the decision was wrong in respect of both application of the law and assessment of the evidence.

On 17th March 2004 the Supreme Court refused to give me leave to appeal to them, giving no reasons. Under Norwegian law the Supreme Court are not obliged to give reasons where a claim for damages is under 100,000 Norwegian kroner. My claim for non-pecuniary damages against Heidi Schøne was only 50,000 kroner. The costs of the whole action were awarded against me.

I submit that in the circumstances of this case there has been a violation of Articles 6, 10, 13 and 14 of the European Convention on Human Rights, detailed below.

I ask for compensation plus costs under Article 41 which will include all my legal costs, translation fees and other reasonable expenses incurred in this case.

This letter has been introduced within six months of the exhaustion of domestic remedies in Norway in accordance with Article 35(1) of the European Convention. A completed application form, together with a file of relevant copy documents and reports on the court proceedings will be submitted shortly.

Violations of Article 6 – Right to a fair trial

1. Judge Thore Rønning sat on both Court of Appeal cases for the judgements of 24th November 2000 (which I did not attend) and 14th November 2003, in breach of the rules of natural justice which gave rise to a potential conflict of interest including an appearance of bias. I did not know Judge Rønning sat on the earlier appeal as the Court of Appeal only sent me the 24th November 2000 judgement this year.

2. For the 13th to 16th October 2003 Court of Appeal case, in front of three judges, which I took as a litigant in person, it became apparent that neither Judge Thore Rønning nor Judge Anita Lund had a sufficient working knowledge of English. This was a relevant factor in this case as the presiding judge, Agnar Nilsen Jnr., who spoke fluent English, allowed me to present my case in English which for the most part was not translated into Norwegian by my interpreter. This considerably reduced the effectiveness of having three judges sit on and then decide the case, especially given the hostility of Judge Nilsen Jnr. towards me. I could not be confident that he had communicated my representations to his colleagues on the bench. No reference or assessment whatsoever is made in their judgement of 14th November 2003 to any of the arguments detailed in my appeal papers, leaving me with the impression that none of my arguments were even considered. The substantial points at issue were not dealt with at all by the Court of Appeal which constitutes an error in law. [I refer the Court to the case of *Van de Hurk v Netherlands* (1994) 18 EHRR 481 whereby it was held that Article 6 (1) obliges domestic courts to give reasons for their decisions but not necessarily a detailed answer to every argument. I submit that the Court of Appeal and the Supreme Court failed this test.]

3. At the start of the October 2003 Court of Appeal case Judge Nilsen Jnr. told me of his unhappiness with my website **(called www.norway-shockers.com)** which he had looked at: an ill omen. The website contained several articles exposing xenophobic attitudes and ill treatment by Norwegians of the outsider, including newspaper articles from The Times and The Independent of London.

Judge Nilsen Jnr., without giving reasons, ruled against my request to call the Attorney-General of Norway who I had subpoenaed to give evidence in his role in the cover-up over the inquiry into the earlier perjury of police sergeant Torill Sorte.

This policewoman swore on oath at the January 2002 trial and by a 1997 witness statement (only given to me in 2002!) that my mother told her that she, my mother, had put me in mental hospital! My mother, furious, wrote to Judge Stilloff in Spring 2002 to say that Sorte was a liar. Torill Sorte, now committed to maintaining the lie, later repeated her claim on oath at the October 2003 trial. My family doctor's letter given to the Court stated categorically that I have never received treatment in a psychiatric hospital.

At the end of the October 2003 trial, Judge Nilsen Jnr. then explained in stark terms how he was "ashamed" to have taken part in the trial because, he told me, Heidi Schøne was so stressed out and that he would now consider fining me for bringing the appeal (which presumably would also include a fine for my lawyer, Stig Lunde, who drafted the appeal papers). I was then immediately arrested at the door of the courtroom (something Judge Nilsen Jnr. must surely have co-operated on) and charged by two policemen under Section 390(a) of the Criminal Code for promoting my website which only went on-line in October 2000. I received a prison sentence of 8 months suspended for two years (now no longer suspended). These machinations only reinforced my firm belief that the Court of Appeal was not interested in giving me a fair trial. They had already prejudged the matter.

4. The Drammen City Court civil judgement of 11th February 2002 referred to and used against me a criminal conviction given on the 16th November 2001 under Section 390(a) of the Criminal Code, whereby I was fined 10,000 kroner for a three year campaign (1995-1998) publicizing my side of the story which included reference to the defendant Heidi Schøne's life history. I was tried and convicted in absentia and the Magistrates Court declared that it would have considered a prison sentence but for the practical difficulty of extraditing me from England. This criminal conviction violated my right to freedom of expression under Article10 and also violated Article 6(3)(b) in that only three weeks notice of the Magistrates Court hearing was given to me via Interpol and the criminal defence lawyer who took my case only received full police statements and 'evidence' the day before the trial. I was in the midst of preparing for my own imminent civil libel prosecution case and did not have the time to prepare for my defence on the criminal charges. Besides which, the Police Prosecutor had ignored my earlier written submissions to him requesting substantiation of his various charges, when he wanted to do "a deal" and fine me 5,000 kroner in return for me pleading guilty under Section 390(a) of the Criminal Code. I had argued that it was my right to respond to horrendous newspaper allegations, only to be told much later by my defence lawyer Harald Wibye, that Section 390(a) was a strict liability offence. I wanted to appeal but Mr. Wibye told me it would be hopeless and in attending any appeal trial personally I would "definitely" receive a 6-12 month prison sentence. Section 390 of the Criminal Code provides for a defence of justified comment and Harald Wibye had argued in the Magistrates Court that this was the section that I should have been charged under. Even the magistrate herself had to retire to refer to her legal texts, but for unexplained reasons still decided to proceed with the original charge under Section 390(a).

[I have enclosed with my Application an account of the events leading up to and following that conviction including the trial itself as related to me by my defence lawyer Harald Wibye. I would however also like to add that in this criminal trial there was no equality of arms with regard to the disclosure of evidence for the "attempted rape" / "actual rape" allegations arising out of the same incident. In the case of *Rowe and Davis v. United Kingdom* No. 28901/95 of 16-2-00; (2000) 30 EHRR1, the Court declared that failure of the prosecution to disclose documents to the defence may impair the fairness of the proceedings. In her verdict 16th November 2001the judge indicated that she seemed to believe Heidi Schøne's allegation of actual rape (which allegation was then repeated in the newspaper Drammens Tidende). Before the 30th October 2001 criminal trial my defence lawyer, Harald Wibye should have been given an opportunity to see both Heidi Schøne's 1986 police witness statement alleging attempted rape and her changed 1998 police witness statement alleging actual rape, but the police prosecutor disclosed neither. Harald Wibye was therefore unable to see the detail of the statements and cross-examine Heidi Schøne on the conflicting statements in order to examine her credibility as a reliable witness.]

The banner headlines in Drammens Tidende's newspaper of 16th November 2001 read, 'Fine for Serious sex-terror' and '10,000 fine for 16 years of sex-terror.'

The Public Prosecutor in Norway was desperate to obtain the conviction in time for it to count against me in my own civil libel prosecution at the Drammen City Court and this purpose was achieved with consequent breach of Article 6 for the civil libel case.

5. I was denied the right of proper cross-examination of defence witnesses at both first instance and Court of Appeal libel trials either through my lawyer or as a litigant in person, which thereby destroyed one of the primary purposes in bringing and progressing the action: the need to test the evidence. Moreover, at the Court of Appeal trial in October 2003 Judge Nilsen Jnr. refused to allow me to cross-examine Heidi Schøne at all and instead took on the responsibility himself and then for only 15-20 minutes.

This created a conflict of interest for the judge in his primary role as an impartial administrator of justice. He could not be both judge and prosecutor at the same time. I had waited eight long years to cross-examine Heidi Schøne and importantly it had been agreed several weeks earlier between myself and Heidi Schøne's lawyer that four hours would be set aside for this. No indications were given that Heidi Schøne was too ill or unwell to face cross-examination – not until the day of her appearance, when her lawyer submitted a letter from her psychiatrist, written the previous day, saying she was unfit to face cross-examination by me.

She was, however, fit enough to introduce entirely new allegations that were so ridiculous (for example that I used morphine obtained from my father, a general medical practitioner and that I blackmailed her), that when I pleaded with Judge Nilsen Jnr. for the opportunity to cross-examine Heidi Schøne on these matters he refused saying that I could comment in my closing speech at the end of the trial. My lawyer Stig Lunde told me weeks before that Heidi Schøne's psychiatrist, Dr. Petter Broch, was not at all happy at being subpoenaed by me to attend cross-examination as he was too busy. His presence was essential and it was of enormous disappointment to me when Judge Nilsen Jnr. prevented me from putting vital questions to Dr. Broch, in particular why he associated my right to present my side of the story to the public as "stalking" and "pathological" in nature. I could not even ask whether he thought his patient was capable of telling lies in view of the fact that he had himself, at the previous trial, sworn on oath that she sexualized her behaviour and had implicated all the members of her own family in mental abuse or in the case of her stepmother's father, sexual abuse. Indeed, Dr. Broch, at the previous trial confirmed that Heidi Schøne's stepmother had once reported her to the Child Protection Unit. [Heidi Schøne's psychiatrist, Dr. Petter Broch wrote a letter to the Court dated 13th October 2003 (copy enclosed with my Application) saying that Heidi Schøne should be excused from being cross-examined by me due to her "mental state." This letter was handed to me by Heidi Schøne's lawyer in its original Norwegian language format at the start of the second day of the Court of Appeal trial (14th October 2003) and translated to me in its essential points by my interpreter, Kevin Quirk. The court accepted that Heidi Schøne should not face cross-examination and this destroyed the main highlight of my appeal: the absolute need to cross-examine Heidi Schøne. The submission of this letter so late – after the trial had in fact started – was unfair on me. Heidi Schøne should have been prevented from relying on it: it was a deliberate attempt to sabotage a fair trial. Heidi Schøne's lawyer had agreed weeks before with me on a full witness schedule for the trial allowing 4 hours for his client to face cross-examination by me. There was bound to be a degree of anxiety for Heidi Schøne (as there was for me) but she had had months to prepare herself for the trial. I suspect that she had feigned her complaint in order to get out of being cross-examined as she had tried via a similar letter from her psychiatrist at the first trial. Her mental state did not stop her from introducing for the first time further ludicrous allegations (see my account of the Court of Appeal trial submitted with my Application)].

Similarly, with the other defence witnesses, being: Hans Odde the editor of Drammens Tidende, Ingunn Røren the writer of the article and police sergeant Torill Sorte I was stopped by Judge Nilsen Jnr. from asking questions of these three in relation, specifically, to their own previous perjuries and in relation to Heidi Schøne's various perjuries and evidence. I was reprimanded by Judge Nilsen Jnr. for putting to Ingunn Røren and Torill Sorte that they were blatant liars and my respective requests that they explain themselves was interrupted and stopped by the judge - at the very point when each witness was on the verge of being caught out. I was denied my moment of vindication.

6. The burden of proof was on Heidi Schøne to prove 16 years of sexual harassment from 1982 to 1998. This naturally implied 16 years of **sustained** action. For the years 1982 to 1985 Heidi Schøne was forced to concede there was no harassment due to my presentation to the court of her love letters to me for that period. One of these letters described my character as particularly honourable and as someone who did not treat her as a sex object. Yet remarkably, in 1995, I had for many years, according to Heidi Schøne, been the exact opposite in absolutely every aspect of my behaviour. Without her letters, which fortunately I had stored away at the time, I am sure Heidi Schøne would have continued to insist that the alleged harassment began in 1982 as this is precisely the claim she made in the May 1995 newspaper articles – that the harassment began the moment she left England in June 1982. At the time of the 1995 newspaper articles Heidi Schøne would not have suspected that I would have known of their publication or that I would have kept her early letters.

But what she did not count on was that, by coincidence, I was using at the time a Norwegian lawyer to make enquiries of the Norwegian police as to certain matters relating to Heidi Schøne. It was the lawyer who sent me one newspaper article and alerted me about the other two. Heidi Schøne admitted in court that she had been notified of the contents of the May 1995 articles (and 14th July 1998 Drammens Tidende article) prior to their publication and had approved of the contents and corrected nothing. She had therefore adopted the wording as the truth. In saying this in court in January 2002 she thereby repeated and confirmed all of the contents of the 1995 newspaper articles and so I was doubly entitled to cross-examine Heidi Schøne on the 1995 articles.

For the period mid-1985 to mid-1995 there was no documentary evidence presented by Heidi Schøne as to harassment. Her evidence consisted solely of her uncorroborated word. Even then she admitted in court that in Summer 1988 she requested the urgent help of myself and my best friend, Russell, to travel to Norway to help restrain her abusive boyfriend, the father of her child. This, in spite of her making a false allegation to the police in December 1986, that I had attempted to rape her twenty months earlier in April 1985 (in revenge for my writing to her father two weeks earlier, in November 1986, warning him about his daughter's catastrophic lifestyle). This 1986 allegation was only made known to me in March 1995 by the Bergen lawyer I was using to make enquiries of the

Bergen police, in my attempt to prosecute Heidi Schøne for attempting to pervert the course of justice.

In 1998 she changed the allegation to one of actual rape "by holding her down"! What girl would request the help of a man she had two years earlier reported to the police for attempted rape (later changed to actual rape)? Heidi Schøne admitted in court that she made a complaint to the Bergen police in the early 1980's about a Bergen shopkeeper who had allegedly raped her. No charges were brought. She also admitted receiving from me a music tape I had sent her in 1988 to console her after a second suicide attempt, on again being rejected by the father of her child. She admitted in court that in October 1990 she sent me a book (ordered from England) in an attempt to convert me to Christianity after she had supposedly become a born-again Christian. This was a very friendly period for us. I had not kept the letters she sent me in1990. I had kept the book and put it in evidence.

For the period 1995 to 1998 the evidence used against me to prove harassment, consisted of my letters and campaign leaflets which formed the basis of my public protest (as is my right under Article 10) in response firstly, to my suspicion that Heidi Schøne had been making false allegations to the police, secondly when my suspicions were confirmed by my 1995 lawyers report to me and thirdly to outrageous 1995 newspaper allegations. Neither the police nor the newspapers nor the Press Complaints Commission (the PFU) took the slightest interest in responding to my written complaints. I even protested to the Norwegian Embassy in London in 1995 but all they could do was forward my papers on to the Bergen Police, who in spite of their apparent legal obligation to reply stayed silent.

The Court at first instance accepted that for long periods there was no contact between myself and Heidi Schøne. Indeed, from 1982 to 1991 she confided in me every intimate detail of her life which I gave in written evidence to the Court at first instance who certified my account as "more or less correct."

The Court of Appeal somehow failed to appreciate my argument that Heidi Schøne could not have it both ways: confiding her innermost secrets over the best part of a decade was incompatible with her later (and constantly adapted) evidence of a decade and a half of sex-terror. The appeal judgement never explained this inconsistency (and many others) and the Supreme Court refused me leave to appeal. The Court of Appeal could not even tell me, when asked, how high the standard of proof had to be for one such as Heidi Schøne. I argued that for a woman with a delinquent past, a history of mental illness and obvious motives for revenge after having her own past exposed, then the standard of proof for her evidence ought to be a high one, especially as her own word formed the most part of her defence.

Heidi Schøne's description of her alleged torment at my hands had similarities to the description she gave me of the suffering she encountered, over the years, at the hands of Gudmund Johannessen, the father of her first son. He was an intravenous heroin user according to Heidi Schøne (they had two Aids tests each after the birth of their son), a felon (6 months in military prison in Norway) and was directly responsible for her two suicide attempts (in 1984 and 1988).

In Christmas 1990 he assaulted her and she reported him to the police. Heidi Schøne blamed me for this as I had earlier informed Gudmund Johannessen's parents of the enormous abuse he had inflicted on her, which so upset the parents and had consequently caused her "enormous problems." Not least because Gudmund Johannessen felt betrayed by Heidi Schøne by her telling me of his despicable conduct, so he in turn took his frustrations out on her by beating her to the ground. Out of revenge, when I went to visit Heidi Schøne in February 1990, she told the police I had made threats against her and I was arrested, held for two nights in the cells, then released without charge. When things had blown over and I visited Heidi Schøne in August 1990 she apologised for the torment she had put me through and told me she had been "possessed by demons" which

561

had now been "exorcised" by her Christian neighbours. Later in the day, paradoxically, she said that she was worried when I visited her in February that I might have kidnapped her son!

I was always intrigued as to exactly what Heidi Schøne had told the police in February 1990 to get me arrested. My curiosity came to the fore in early 1994 when I wrote to Heidi Schøne to enquire. I got no reply. Her silence I took as an admission of past duplicity, so I wrote a batch of postcards to her to express my feelings. Once I had, in March 1995, discovered her false December 1986 allegation of attempted rape, I felt such a sense of betrayal that I retaliated by informing her neighbours of her colourful past. In 1995 she was still adamant that it was attempted rape. I had from 1995 to 1998 been pressing her local police in Drammen to ask her about her 1986 attempted rape allegation, made to the Bergen police. Finally in the middle of 1998 she told the local Drammen police it was actual rape "by holding her down." This disturbed me even more. Her newspaper allegation that I had threatened to kill her son incensed me. It is my public 'information campaign' that the Norwegians regard as harassment. I regard it as a right under Article 10 provoked by Heidi Schøne and the newspapers.

7. My public protest stopped from mid-1998 to October 2000 when it resumed with the launch of a website. The newspapers have their own websites and three of them still have their articles on me posted. My 2001 criminal conviction plus my website were used in evidence against me at the October 2003 Court of Appeal trial, even though my 'campaign' evidence for this arose **after** the Drammens Tidende article of 14th July 1998 over which I was suing. This is a clear breach of Article 6.

8. Direct evidence was presented by me – including from Heidi Schøne's former best friend and two honorable policemen – indicating that Heidi Schøne was a liar. This evidence was completely ignored at every stage of the trial process and was not referred to in the court judgements.

9. In refusing me leave to appeal to them and without giving reasons the Supreme Court, by their judgement of 17th March 2004, continued the breach of Article 6 initiated by the earlier judgements.

10. The dispute resolution procedure regarding my complaint to the Press Complaints Commission (the PFU) over the Drammens Tidende article of 14th July 1998 violated Article 6 because of the total absence of any form of public hearing or meaningful consultation: it was a secret decision making process (see the case of *Wickramsinghe v. United Kingdom* [1998] EHRLR 338). In the circumstances I had a legitimate expectation to be consulted. The PFU refused to deal with any of my itemized complaints against the newspaper. In 1996 the PFU refused to exercise their discretion to look into my complaints against the three May 1995 newspaper articles giving no reasons. I was not told that the PFU could not look into the truth or falsehood of the statements made by Drammens Tidende in their 1998 article. On 24th August 1999 the PFU ruled that Drammens Tidende had not breached good press practice. I had been misled by the PFU and Drammens Tidende, for why else would I agree to use the PFU if not to have a proper investigation into the truth or falsehood of the newspaper's statements? The PFU are a body funded by the print industry in Norway and their chairman, Per Edgar Kokkvold, was a former newspaper editor. The PFU ruling of 24th August 1999 was used in evidence against me in my action against Heidi Schøne. Subsequently, at the Court of Appeal trial in October 2003 cross-examination of the editor and journalist made it clear that their newspaper had lied and misled the public but by then Drammens Tidende were not on trial.

11. The dispute resolution procedure regarding the judicial inquiry into police sergeant Torill Sorte's perjury and attempt to pervert the course of justice was also in breach of Article 6 because of the total absence of any form of meaningful consultation, public hearing or even involvement of the suspect herself. The decision making process was completely secret. The Police

Complaints Authority decided not to prosecute Torill Sorte and their decision was upheld by the Director of Public Prosecutions but at no stage was any of my evidence referred to in the official decisions, giving the impression that it was not even considered: a cover-up for a police officer who should have lost her job. No substantive reasons were given for not prosecuting Torill Sorte in the face of overwhelming evidence against her.

12. The defence lawyer for Heidi Schøne, Mr. Vegaard Aaløkken, withheld crucial evidence from me: his client's witness statement from 1998 that I raped her in 1985, apparently by holding her down. I wanted this direct evidence to see the detail of the alleged assault but its non-disclosure was justified by Mr. Aaløkken on the grounds that it "was not in his client's interest" to give it to me. Further, despite asking the Bergen police for nine years now I have not been sent Heidi Schøne's witness statement from December 1986 alleging attempted rape out of the same incident. I wanted to cross-examine Heidi Schøne on these conflicting statements to cast doubt on her credibility. In 2001 Drammens Tidende printed an article saying that I had allegedly raped Heidi Schøne. Without being able to test her evidence at any of the trials the court judgement at first instance ruled Heidi Schøne's testimony "in essence" to be true and this was upheld by the Court of Appeal. [The equality of arms argument will equally apply to my own libel prosecution trial. I had complained to the Norwegian Bar Association over Vegard Aaløkken's (Heidi Schøne's lawyer) failure to produce Heidi Schøne's 1986 and 1998 conflicting witness statements. My complaint was rejected on the grounds that Vegard Aaløkken was under a duty to protect his client's interests. A copy of the Bar Association's decision in 2004 has been submitted with my Application.]

Vesta insurance company, acting for the lawyer Karsten Gjone who missed the time limits to sue the newspapers over their 1995 articles, refused to compensate me on the grounds that the Drammen City Court believed Heidi Schøne was telling the truth in the 1995 articles.

Violations of Article 10 – Freedom of Expression

1. Heidi Schøne had herself given interviews in May 1995, no doubt for money, to three newspapers: Verdens Gang which is Norway's biggest tabloid, and Bergens Tidende and Drammens Tidende - provincial newspapers with large circulations. This because I had told a few of her neighbours of her colourful past in retaliation for her surreptitious attempt to ruin me through her false allegation of attempted rape. Large photographs were printed of Heidi Schøne and her husband (including on the front pages) and both of them were named and their home district given. The headlines were: '13 years of harassment' in Bergens Tidende of 24th May 1995, '13 years of Sex-terror' in Verdens Gang of 26th May 1995 and 'Badgered and hunted for 13 years' in Drammens Tidende of 27th May 1995.

I was referred to among other things as "insane," "mentally ill," "suffering from erotic paranoia," as one who had "threatened to kill her son" and also "threatened to kill her friends, family and neighbours." Bergens Tidende called me "Muslim" sixteen times associating me with these medicalised and sexualized descriptions. Verdens Gang also associated my religion in the same context.

Heidi Schøne had thus waived her right to anonymity and forfeited her right to privacy for her own private life. She had opened herself up to public scrutiny in return.

I put my own side of the story over to the Norwegian public by way of a moderate publicity campaign when the three newspapers refused to print my response. Under their self-regulatory rules, the Norwegian press are obliged to contact the subject (or victim) of a proposed story and seek his views and moreover once a story has been printed they are obliged to contact the subject and print his response. Out of the six occasions when these three newspapers were obliged to make contact not one attempt was made, even though I was easy to find. So by way of a moderate fax and letter campaign including a life history of Heidi Schøne, I exercised my rights under Article 10 (see the case of *Handyside v United Kingdom* (1976) 1 EHRR 737 at para. 49). For this campaign from 1995 to 1998 I received a criminal conviction for invading Heidi Schøne's privacy which was used in evidence against me in my civil prosecution, again in breach of Article 10.

2. My continued exercise of my right to freedom of expression and public protest under Article10, in particular via my website set up in October 2000, was breached by my second criminal conviction on 17th October 2003: a fine and a prison sentence of eight months, suspended for two years, provided I removed my website within 7 days. I did not remove the website. The Norwegian government want it closed down not least because they cannot tolerate the criticism leveled at their institutions on the website. Their criminal and economic crime unit, Økokrim, have threatened to contact the United Kingdom government to begin the process of closing it down. I pleaded guilty to the charge under Section 390(a) of the Criminal Code for promoting the website, under duress: I was given the choice of either pleading guilty to the charge and relying on the mercy of the court to give me a suspended sentence of imprisonment and a fine, or instead plead not guilty and face certain conviction and 8 months imprisonment as my offence was one of strict liability. This, after I had spent the previous 24 hours in police custody. Again no reasons were given by the police prosecutor as to why I was not charged under Section 390 of the Criminal Code which gave me a defence of justified public comment. Any appeal would have been a waste of time and the ECHR recognizes that hopeless cases do not have to be pursued. I cannot travel anywhere in Scandinavia due to the mutual enforcement law covering these countries, as the Norwegian authorities want to put me in prison.

[(i) The Norwegian authorities incorrectly applied the Criminal Code in that they should have charged me, if at all, under Section 390 of the Criminal Code (as opposed to Section 390 (a) of the Criminal Code) which gave me a defence of justified public comment.

(ii) The measures taken against me were not "necessary in a democratic society for the protection of health or morals." How does my website and fax / letter campaign to the public offend against morality? On the contrary, my communications condemned and highlighted immorality.

(iii) What "pressing social need" did the public authorities in Norway have in mind in wanting to prohibit me putting my side of the story across via faxes, letters and a website (see the case of *The Sunday Times v. United Kingdom* (1979) 2 EHRR 245)? The Norwegian Authorities gave themselves far too wide a margin of appreciation in prosecuting me: they wanted unlimited power of appreciation which they were not entitled to.

(iv) If my information by fax / letter / website offended shocked and disturbed the Norwegian state or a sector of its population I submit that it does not matter, as such information is permitted by the ECHR in the interests of "pluralism, tolerance and broad mindedness" – see paragraph 49 of *Handyside v. United Kingdom*. My information in any case is as nothing compared to the vitriol written in the Norwegian newspapers (12 articles from 1995 to 2003) about me for which there was no substantive evidence. Besides which, the Drammen District Court, with Judge Anders Stilloff presiding held that my information on Heidi Schøne was "more or less correct."]

I also ask the European Court for compensation and costs under Article 41 for violation of Convention rights in relation to my prison sentence given in breach of Articles 6 and 10.

I have every right to continue my website, especially as Norway's top newspaper, Aftenposten did on the 15th April 2002 print a front page story with the headline, 'British Muslim terrorizes Norwegian woman on the Internet,' with comment from the Norwegian Minister of Justice, Odd Einar Dørum and police sergeant Torill Sorte. I have written to the Minister who has so far sent me a letter of acknowledgement. The Norwegian Courts must surely have been under some political pressure to ensure I failed, which caused the civil and criminal courts to violate Articles 6 and 10 in my respective trials in October 2003. Furthermore, Verdens Gang newspaper did another front page story on 7th July 1998 entitled, 'Impossible to shake off sex-crazed Englishman,' referring to me as "half Arabic" and that I "may suffer from a case of extreme erotic paranoia," repeating much of what they had printed in 1995. Twelve separate newspaper stories have been printed on me to my knowledge, from 1995 to 2003 including articles on how difficult it was for the Norwegian authorities to bring me to justice while I remained in England. This institutional and media campaign made it impossible for me to get justice in Norway.

Violations of Article 13 – Right to an effective remedy

1. The Supreme Court decision of 17th March 2004 refused me leave to appeal, giving no reasons. Under Norwegian law where an action involves a claim for an amount under 100,000 kroner, the Supreme Court are not required to give any reasons for refusing leave to appeal. In my original writ I had claimed 50,000 kroner against Heidi Schøne – a token sum because she was of very limited means – but more importantly I had asked for a declaration that her libelous statements be declared null and void. I had claimed 300,000 kroner against Drammens Tidende but they dropped out of the action when the Supreme Court refused me leave to appeal to them out of time, after my lawyer had narrowly missed the time limit. Even if my claim against Heidi Schøne had been for over 100,000 kroner the Supreme Court still do not have to give full reasoning for refusing leave to appeal. The main purpose of my writ and for my appeal to the Supreme Court was to clear my name. The Supreme Court has clearly demonstrated that there is no effective practical remedy in Norway to enable me to do this in the face of outrageous and ruinous allegations. Besides facing prison in Norway, I have to pay all Heidi Schøne's and the Norwegian state's legal costs as Heidi Schøne was legally aided.

2. Further, the remedy required by Article 13 applies not only to court proceedings but also to other enquiries: in my case the investigation by the Norwegian Press Complaints Commission (PFU) after my complaint to them over the Drammens Tidende article of 14th July 1998 and the Police Complaints Authority enquiry into the perjury and attempt to pervert the course of justice by police sergeant Torill Sorte. Both of these enquiries lacked all credibility. There was no effective access for me to the investigatory procedure. The standard of investigation was abysmal. The decision given by the PFU in 1999 and the decision given in 2003 by the Director of Public Prosecutions (to whom I had appealed from the Police Complaints Authority) indicated respectively, that all my evidence was ignored in the investigatory process and not even referred to in their decision letters. They both gave substantially inadequate reasons for their decisions. The Director of Public Prosecutions had a conflict of interest, in that they were the body ultimately responsible for twice charging me under Section 390(a) of the Criminal Code (November 2001 and October 2003), for exercising my right to reply.

For years before this the Director of Public Prosecutions was trying to extradite me but were told by the British authorities that there were no grounds to do this. Again, the PFU and the Police Complaints Authority demonstrated that in practice they provided no effective remedy for my complaints to them.

Violation of Article 14 – Prohibition of Discrimination

The Drammen City Court verdict of 11th February 2002 found nothing wrong in the Drammens Tidende article of 14th July 1998 calling me "the Muslim man" in the first line of their report, followed by character assassination. The judgement declared that I had "represented" myself as a Muslim because of my documented support for the Muslims of Bosnia. The Bosnia tragedy, however, was never mentioned by the Drammens Tidende article as the reason for calling me Muslim. The article only associated the words "Muslim man" with my alleged sexual harassment, mental illness and erotic paranoia. The Drammens Tidende article of 14th July 1998 must be read in conjunction with the mindset of the Norwegian press as a whole. The 24th May 1995 Bergens Tidende article made mention of me as "Muslim" sixteen times associating me with mental illness, sexual harassment and erotic paranoia. The Verdens Gang article dated 26th May 1995 associated the words "Muslim man" with erotic paranoia and sex terror. They did a repeat article in July 1998 and associated the words "half Arabic" man with "sex crazed" and "erotic paranoia." The Aftenposten newspaper of 15th April 2002 had the front page headline: 'British Muslim terrorizes Norwegian woman on the Internet.' The journalist who wrote the article told me in my earlier tape recorded conversation of 10th April 2002 that she did not even know I was a Muslim and that my religion was irrelevant! Runar Schøne, the ex-husband of Heidi Schøne, giving evidence in court in January 2002 compared me with Osama bin Laden and my lawyer, Stig Lunde, who was present will confirm this.

The expert witness Mr. Henrik Lund of the Anti-racist Centre in Oslo gave evidence at the Court of Appeal trial in October 2003. He said that no newspaper in Norway would write similarly if the subject was Christian or Jewish so that to do so when the subject was Muslim can be seen as an attack on the Muslim religion. The Court of Appeal in its judgement of 14th November 2003, made no comment at all on Henrik Lund's evidence. For the Drammen City Court and then the Court of Appeal not to acknowledge such blatant religious vilification is clearly a breach of Article 14 and can be said to have contributed in turn to a breach of Article 6.

[Heidi Schøne referred to me as a Muslim fanatic and extremist as follows:

(i) In her police witness statement of 1st December 1986 that I was a "Shia Muslim" when in fact I am a Sunni. Shia Islam, which Heidi Schøne wanted to associate me with, has particularly dark overtones in Norway arising out of that country's intense antipathy to the Iran of Ayotallah Khomeni. For many years therefore the Norwegian police presumably believed I was a Shia Muslim follower of Ayotallah Khomeni. Heidi Schøne knew perfectly well all along that I was not a Shia Muslim.

(ii) At the Court of Appeal trial in October 2003, for the first time Heidi Schøne alleged (falsely) that I believed in stoning women to death. I believe passionately that stoning women to death has no part whatsoever in true Islam.

(iii) In the first trial in January 2002 Heidi Schøne had (falsely) alleged that I had been coercing her into becoming a Muslim. Heidi Schøne's true feelings for Islam were shown in her 1982 letter to me (enclosed with my Application) when after having a lesson at school on Islam she wrote, "Islam – NO NO" at a time when we had very friendly relations.

The Norwegian courts gave the impression of accepting as reasonable the use by the newspapers of the word "Muslim" in the context in which it was used – not just in the Drammens Tidende article of 14th July 1998 which I was suing on, but also in the earlier 1995 newspaper articles which were inextricably linked to the 14th July 1998 article in Drammens Tidende. The three 1995 articles were put in evidence at the outset of the proceedings.

The Norwegian courts gave the impression of accepting as true Heidi Schøne's 'evidence' on my Islamic credentials for they made no comment in their judgments to suggest otherwise despite my requests for them to do so. The courts were therefore not impartial from either a subjective or objective point of view. I concluded that I was being tried by a religiously/racially prejudiced court

566

in violation of Article 6 (1) – see by analogy the case of *Sander v. United Kingdom* (2001) 31 EHRR 14, where in my case the Norwegian judges should have reacted in an appropriate manner to dispel the perverted way the press and Heidi Schøne described my Muslim credentials. In *Sander v. United Kingdom* the ECHR stressed that the eradication of racism has become a common priority goal for all contracting states. France has taken the lead in this respect by repeatedly fining Bridgette Bardot for "incitement to racial hatred" for her written descriptions of Muslims (see the article enclosed with my Application from 'The Independent' newspaper of 11th June 2004).

I believe the only reason I ever made the Norwegian newspapers was because I am a Muslim. The huge number of times that I have been referred to as a "Muslim" in the Norwegian newspapers from 1995 to 2003 is ample evidence to justify my claim. Article 14 has certainly been violated].

Please would you acknowledge receipt.

Yours faithfully,
FREDERICK DELAWARE

On the 14th January 2005 I telephoned the European Court who said they had written to me that very day. I was told that my Application papers were all in order and that my case would now join the queuing system. It would take up to a year for the Court to get round to considering my Application. On 23rd February 2005 I sent to the Court by recorded delivery post a full set of the tape recordings of my conversations with all the Norwegians I had spoken to over the years: ultimate proof and best evidence to back up the transcribed recordings sent earlier to the Court. The Court wrote back on the 9th March acknowledging receipt confirming the tapes had been included in the file with my Application.

The 7th June 2005 marked Norway's centennial celebrations. On 6th June 1905 Norway's Union with Sweden had been dissolved.

I could at last rest easy for a few months now.

On Friday 22nd April 2005 Aftenposten, on their English language website, published an article entitled, 'Norwegian preacher kindles religious strife.' Its first two paragraphs went as follows:

'Celebrity Pentecostal preacher Runar Søgaard is under protection by Swedish police after receiving death threats. A high-profile sermon where Søgaard called the prophet Mohammad "a confused pedophile" has triggered fears of religious war.

Søgaard, 37, enjoys celebrity status in Sweden after his marriage to recording star and Eurovision song contest winner Carola, even though they are now divorced'.

I end this chapter with an extract from Cyril Glassé's 'The Concise Encyclopaedia of Islam,' Revised Edition 2001, published by Stacey International of London. The following words are included in Cyril Glassé's entry for **Iblis**, 'a personal name of the devil':

'Among the traditional signs of "dark spirits" are the following: first, that they say the opposite of the truth; second, that they deny their own faults and attribute them to others, preferably to someone who is completely innocent; third, that they continually change their position in an argument, the purpose of argument being only to subvert, to turn aside from truth and goodness; fourth, that they exaggerate the evil of what is good, and the good of what is evil, that is, they define good as evil because of a shadow of imperfection, and evil as good because of a reflection of perfection; they glorify a secondary quality in order to deny an essential one, or to disguise a fundamental flaw; in short, they completely falsify true proportions and invert normal relations.'

Chapter 36

On Monday 6th June 2005 a Norwegian woman by the name of Merete Underwood, married to an Englishman, was jailed for 12 months at Middlesex Guildhall Crown Court, West London, for perverting the course of justice, in lying about an alledged rape on her person by a man who she had a one night stand with. The story made all the tabloids and the pick of the bunch are featured below. Merete Underwood had a good deal in common with Heidi Schøne.

Daily Express	**Tuesday 7th June 2005**
WIFE WHO CRIED 'RAPE' IS JAILED	

She lied to cover up a one-night stand, putting the man she accused through hell.

By **Sarah White** and **John Twomey**

A Mother of two was jailed for 12 months yesterday for crying rape to cover up a sordid one-night stand with a stranger.

Merete Underwood, 32, claimed she had been kidnapped, sexually abused and raped by a least two men, prompting a police investigation costing at least £20,000.00.

She told detectives about her "terrifying ordeal," drew up an E-fit and finally identified one of her "attackers."

The man was arrested, held in a cell for 24 hours and endured 15 months of hell before the Norwegian-born blonde confessed she made up the whole story.

Underwood showed no remorse yesterday as she was jailed after she admitted perverting the course of justice at London's Middlesex Guildhall Crown Court. Last night her husband Toby choked back tears as he condemned his errant wife and told how he has been left to bring up the two-year-old son she had by another man.

Mr Underwood said: "This is just one part of what has been a horrible situation. She has put so many people through so much and now I'm left bringing up her son on my own.

"I've already had to spend £30,000 in court costs fighting for custody while she has got legal aid despite moving away and abandoning her son.

"She hasn't even visited him since last November. I'm just another one of her men." The court heard how the man she seduced then accused of rape had been "terribly □ounselorF.d" by the false allegations and he felt his reputation had been devastated.

Far from being abducted, Underwood had simply deserted her husband and her little boy in a west London pub because she was bored.

In a nearby wine bar, she met the 34-year-old interior designer, seduced him and later had sex in a hotel.

Underwood, who also has an eight-year-old son by another man, was so ashamed of herself that she cried rape in a bid to keep her night of shame a dark secret.

But police saw through her story and even found CCTV footage of her laughing and joking with the man she claimed had attacked her only hours before.

Jude Andrew McCooey told Underwood: "You have shown no remorse in any meaningful way. If you had any contrition or sorrow you would have done all you could to clear this man's name.

"You were only concerned for yourself. There is the impact this had on the innocent man, not to mention he waste of public money running to thousands of pounds.

"This was a pack of lies and you did not have the decency and honesty to admit it and put this man out of his misery."

The saga of sex, binge-drinking and false allegations of rape began in February last year when Underwood turned up unexpectedly at her husband's office with her two-year-old son.

Her husband, who is a procurement manager for an engineering firm, said: "She came up as a surprise. She'd been sending me messages saying how much she loved me and brought her son up to meet me.

"We arranged to meet my boss and had a couple of drinks. I thought it was nice of my wife to want to do that.

"My boss left and I said I wanted to go home because it was February and the temperature was minus six and her son was young and I thought he needed to go home. I tried for nearly two hours to get her to leave the first pub we were in, then we started having an argument and she agreed to go home."

Underwood later went into another pub to use the lavatory. After 10 minutes of waiting outside, Mr Underwood decided to take the little boy home.

When she did not return the next day he contacted the police. Mr Underwood, who lives in Kingston, Surrey, later received a text message which read: "Merete is OK but cries and wants to go home. But we are not finished with her."

He said: "I thought that was it. She has come up against exactly that sort of thing I'd warned her about, she's going to end up in some body-bag somewhere." Underwood later told police she had been raped and indecently assaulted by two men in a flat in London's Bayswater.

Officers took detailed statements and drove her around the area looking for any of the "suspects." She later identified the man she had spent the night with and he was arrested. After 24 hours in a cell at Paddington Green police station, he was released pending further inquiries.

Mr Underwood met his wife in Norway in February 2001. Five months later they married and enjoyed a honeymoon in Bali.

"In hindsight, this was a big mistake," he said. "She was a fantastic party girl and great for having a good time."

"When she goes out drinking she goes off with people and is completely unreasonable. She's a different person. I tried to get her help with her binge drinking by making her seek medical help and a counselor."

Mr Underwood said he would have done anything for his now estranged wife. "All she had to do was flutter her eyes and I would have supported her," he said. "I loved her and would have done anything for her."

***

570

THE WIFE WHO CRIED RAPE OVER HER ONE-NIGHT STAND

'You didn't have the decency to put this man out of his misery'

By **Stephen Wright** and **Fiona Macrae**

A cheating wife was jailed for 12 months yesterday after crying rape to cover up a one-night stand with a stranger.

Merete Underwood, 32, left her husband and two-year-old son in a pub to seduce another man in a nearby wine bar.

The Norwegian blonde spent the night in a hotel with him before telling her husband she had been kidnapped and raped.

Underwood then wasted thousands of pounds of taxpayers' money and hundreds of police hours by giving a statement about her 'ordeal' and helping draw up an e-fit image of one of her 'attackers.'

The 34-year-old interior designer she spent the night with then faced 15 months with the finger of suspicion pointing at him and has been left traumatised.

Even when she was charged with perverting the course of justice, Underwood continued to lie. It was only as the jury was about to be sworn in to try her that she confessed.

Underwood – who is being divorced by her husband Toby – wept as the judge said her belated plea and previous good character could not save her from jail.

'Rape is an extremely serious offence and quite rightly any allegation of rape is dealt with very seriously by police.' Recorder Andrew McCooey told her.

'I have heard from the prosecution the impact this had on this innocent man, not to mention the many thousands of pounds that has been wasted, all brought about by your pack of lies.'

Underwood, of Kingston, South-West London, had taken her son to meet her husband for a drink after he finished work on the evening of February 25 last year.

A few drinks in one pub were followed by several more in another, in Paddington, West London.

'Then   at about 9.30 p.m. she went to the bathroom.' Joanne Hacking, prosecuting, told Middlesex Guildhall Crown Court, West London. 'A few minutes later her husband, curious as to why she had not returned, asked bar staff to check the toilets. There was no sign of her there and no sign of her outside.'

Although worried, Mr Underwood took the view that his priority was their son's welfare and took him home.

'He eventually went to bed, woke up at 5 a.m. and realised his wife was still not home,' said Miss Hacking. 'He was astounded by this and very worried.' Later that day he reported his wife's disappearance to the police.

Not long afterwards he received a text message from her mobile saying: 'Merete is OK but she cries and wants to get home to you but we are not finished with her here. Good f***.'

Mr Underwood was 'obviously desperately concerned' but very soon after that received a phone call from his boss to say his wife had been found outside their office and had been taken to a police station.

She claimed she had left the pub for some fresh air when a stranger approached, grabbed her by the hair, forced her into a car and drove her to a hotel where two men took turns to rape her. She said she was held captive for 12 hours.

Miss Hacking said the defendant gave a full description of one of the so-called rapists and later 'identified' the interior designer.

The court heard significant police resources were wasted by her deceit. Besides the officers involved in the investigation, forensic laboratory facilities were tied up and CCTV footage had to be examined.

Miss Hacking said the 'unfortunate victim' did everything he could to convince police he was innocent.

He explained he had been with a group of friends in the wine bar when Underwood walked up to him, began chatting, kissed him on the mouth and held his had. Later they left the wine bar and went to his hotel where they shared a can of beer and had sex. They had sex again the following morning.

Then they left his room and went to a post office where surveillance cameras captured Underwood 'laughing and smiling and entirely at ease' with her lover.

'The impact of the allegations on this man were to leave him terribly traumatised,' said Miss Hacking.

'He had never had any problems with the police before and as a result of all this he became very nervous and insecure. He has been left always wondering whether people know of the allegations made against him.

'He still feels ashamed and is very worried that his reputation has been tarnished.'

Told that Underwood was now 'full of remorse,' the judge retorted: 'Words come cheap. The fact is she kept the finger of suspicion and accusation pointing for 15 months at an innocent man. As far as I can see her sorrow is directed at her plight, not the victim.'

Perverting the course of justice carries a maximum sentence of life imprisonment. But the culprits in most serious cases are jailed for between one and two years.

Underwood will serve a maximum of six months behind bars but could be out a few weeks earlier if considered eligible for electronic tagging.

***

Daily Mirror	Wednesday 8th June 2005

CRY RAPE WIFE DID IT BEFORE

One-night stand liar exposed……… by her mother

By **Greig Box**

The wife jailed after she cried rape had falsely accused a man before, her mother said yesterday.

Jane Nordhaug said she was shocked by the 12 month sentence handed out on Monday to Merette Underwood.

Underwood 32, who is Norwegian, invented the rape story to cover up a one-night stand and fool husband Toby.

Mum Jane said: "There has been a lot of trouble with many boys in the past. It is not the first time she has cried rape. It happened here about 10 years ago."

Mrs Nordhaug speaking from Fauske in Norway, said police found no firm evidence.

She added: "They dropped the investigation. All the problems with her different boyfriends have led to psychological problems for my daughter."

"I talked to her last Saturday and she did not mention it was this serious. But I knew there was some kind of trouble."

She now wants Underwood transferred to a Norwegian prison.

Mrs Nordhaug said: "It is so expensive to fly to England, so I don't know if I can afford to see her."

"I am not mad or angry with her. I just feel sorry for her."

Underwood was sentenced in London for lying to police over a sex session with an interior designer she met in a bar.

She had left husband Toby and her two-year old son in another pub.

Meanwhile, builder Kevin Blakey, 36, who has been living with Underwood in Sussex, plans to wait for her release – then take her to Norway "away from all this."

***

Daily Mirror   **9th June 2005**

JAILED... BUT IS HE CRY RAPE WIFE'S 3rd VICTIM?

DOUBTS OVER HER CLAIMS

By **Stephen Moyes**

A man was jailed for two years after being accused of raping Merete Underwood, the women sentenced for lying about another sex attack.

She received a 12 month prison term this week after lying to police over a sex session with an interior designer she met in a bar in London.

She had invented the rape story to cover-up a one-night stand to fool her husband Toby.

Now doubt has been raised over the conviction of a man who Merete, 32, claimed raped her in Norway in 1992. On that occasion the Norwegian, then 18, said she was grabbed off a pavement in Fauske and bundled into a car and attacked.

After her claims a 24-year-old man came forward to tell police he had met her after getting out of his car to relieve himself. He said they chatted and she willingly had sex with him, although they were strangers. But he was not believed and jailed for two years. His appeal was rejected and was ordered to pay £7,000 compensation.

It has also emerged in 1997, Kai-Magne Hansen, a 39-year-old foreman, was accused of raping Merete in the street after a disco in Fauske.

He recalled: "She was very drunk and came over and tried to sit on my lap. I asked her to get off. That was the only time I spoke to her."

But after she picked him out at an identity parade he was charged with rape and held in a cell for two weeks before being released without charge.

She later tried and failed to claim £20,000 in compensation from him.

Last night it was reported she plans to appeal against her jail term for perverting the course of justice.

***

Daily Mirror	**10th June 2005**

MY CRY-RAPE EX IS SO EVIL

'She was out every night drinking and picking up men. She said she'd been raped before and she'd had a brain tumour'

Exclusive from **ROBERT STANSFIELD** in Stavanger, Norway

The first husband of rape liar Merete Underwood told yesterday how her boozing and cheating tore his life apart too.

Frank Ogried said she went out nightly to meet men in bars, sometimes dumping their baby son in a pushchair outside.

He blasted: "Merete is pure evil and has ruined my life. She might be locked away for her evil crimes, but every night I sit alone as our son sleeps. Hers is a prison sentence, mine is for life."

Underwood, 32 now serving 12 months for perverting justice, even lied that she had a brain tumour to cover up her flings.

Her chequered past also includes a bid to drown herself in a bath and rape claims in 1992 and 1997, the first of which saw a man jailed for two years.

Frank, 36 of Stavanger, southern Norway, was so concerned about her mental state that he even had her put in a mental hospital for six months.

They met in a local bar in 1995 and within a year she was pregnant with Michael, now eight.

Although he begged her to have an abortion as he felt she was not ready for motherhood, she insisted she was, and cleaned up her act.

But three months after their son was born she was back on booze. Shipping manager Frank said: "She was desperate to have a child and well-behaved when she was pregnant. But after the birth being able to drink again sent her into a spiral of destruction."

"She was out every night, drinking and picking up men while I was left to look after Michael."

"She wouldn't come home at night and made up crazy excuses, such as all the taxis refused to take her because she had cancer, which she didn't."

574

Even when Michael was with her she did not stop. Frank said: "Friends would tell me they saw her in bars drinking while our son was left in a pushchair outside."

"I worked hard but any money I made she wasted on men and alcohol." After walking out on him in 1999, she began fighting for custody of Michael. But she gave up to spend more time with a new lover. Her ex revealed: "She had visiting rights but didn't turn up half the time as she was too hung over. When she did take Michael out, she just left him in bars."

This week Middlesex Guildhall Crown Court heard Underwood, of Kingston, Surrey, falsely accused a stranger of rape after a one-night stand. She picked him up in a bar after leaving second husband Toby Underwood, 34, and son James, two, in another.

Frank blames her behaviour on her troubled history. As well as the two rape claims in the 90's and the suicide bid, she hardly knew her father. "She told me she'd been raped in 1992 and someone was jailed," he said. "I believe it happened as it made her funny in the head. She tried to kill herself."

"She became desperate for attention. In 1997 she lied about being raped again and said she had a brain tumour."

"None of it was true, so me and my mum put her in a mental hospital but it didn't help."

"She only met her dad once. I think she's searching for a man to take his place. And boy, has she been through a lot of them."

Frank added: "Michael visited her last year has had little contact since. He asks, 'When's Mummy coming home?' Now I have to tell him what she's done."

"He misses her terribly. The truth will hit him badly when he realises she's deserted him once and for all."

***

The Sun   10th June 2005

Fifth fella accuses cry rape woman

From Martin Phillips in Stavanger, Norway

A fifth man yesterday told how he was falsely accused by "cry rape" wife Merete Underwood.

The 34 year old oilman, who asked not to be identified, bedded the blonde hours after she picked him up in a bar in Stavanger, Norway in 1999.

She left his house before he woke next day - and soon afterwards cops knocked at his door.

He said: "They questioned me then let me go. They said they knew all about her. They knew she'd made claims before."

Underwood 32 of Kingston, Surrey, is serving a year in jail for perverting the course of justice. She left her husband and young son in a pub to pick up a stranger.

She claimed she had been kidnapped, sparking a huge police probe – but this week admitted in court she had lied.

Underwood has cried rape at lease **six** times, The Sun has discovered. But she pleaded from jail yesterday: "I don't belong here. I want to go home."

***

Chapter 37

On Thursday 4th August 2005 Aftenposten's English language website carried the following article:

Experts baffled over aborted condolence mission

A strange thing happened on the crown prince's way to Saudi Arabia Wednesday. He and the Norwegian oil and energy minister turned the plane around, after being told they'd land too late to offer Norway's official condolences.

Crown Prince Haakon and Oil and Energy Minister Thorild Widvey made up Norway's official delegation to Saudi Arabia, to offer condolences on the death of Saudi Arabia's King Fahd on Monday.

The king was buried quickly, within a day of his death in accordance with local tradition. But on Wednesday, national leaders from around the world were expected to stream into Saudi Arabia to attend an official ceremony and offer condolences personally to King Fahd's successor, the former Crown Prince Abdullah.

Norway's official participation was aborted, however, when the country's Foreign Ministry "got the message that we couldn't offer condolences after 3:30 in the afternoon," said ministry spokeswoman Anne Lene Dale Sandsten.

The plane carrying Crown Prince Haakon and Widvey would have landed too late, Sandsten said, so they decided there was no point in continuing the trip.

Sandsten wouldn't speculate as to why the Saudis suddenly put restrictions on the condolence mission, but said several other countries were given the same message as Norway.

Middle East experts are baffled by the incident. "This sounds very strange," Kari Vogt, professor and Islamic expert at the University of Oslo, told newspaper *Aftenposten*. She can't think of any religious reason, or diplomatic etiquette, for the message.

The crown prince and the oil minister weren't travelling unannounced, she noted, adding that it's not normal to set a time limit on condolence visits to Arab countries.

Aftenposten English Web Desk
Nina Berglund

***

It wouldn't surprise me if the Saudi action had something to do with the Norwegian preacher Runar Søgaard calling the Prophet Mohammad "a confused paedophile" earlier in the year (see Aftenposten's article above).

On the 25th August 2005, I wrote again to the Minister of Justice in Norway, Odd Einar Dørum:

Dear Mr. Dørum,

Aftenposten headline of 15th April 2002 by Reidun J. Samuelsen: 'British Muslim terrorises Norwegian woman on the Internet'

I am an English lawyer, born in London to a German mother and Egyptian, Mulsim, father. The above Aftenposten article is about me, and you yourself are quoted in the piece after you spoke to Mrs Samuelsen.

I sent a fax to Gunnar Johannessen on 24th May 2004, which until now, despite promises from Håkon Skulstad, has not been answered. Mr. Skulstad refuses to tell me "over the phone" after 15 months, whether you are aware of my enquiry. I have been the subject of 12 front page headlines in Norwegian newspapers from 1995-2003. I have been engaged in extensive litigation in the Norwegian courts which has now ended.

The outcome is that I have been given an 8-month prison sentence under Section 390A of the Norwegian Penal Code for refusing to take down my website. Simply for exercising my right of reply to hateful rubbish in your press who only ever refer to me as 'the Muslim man' or 'half German, half Arab man.' Your police were previously trying to extradite me, but the British government would not co-operate.

The name of my website is **www.norway-shockers.com** and the full nature of my complaint to you is to be found there as well as in my fax of 24th May 2004 which is with your Deputy Director General, Håkon Skulstad. There has been a cover up by your department to protect the primary cover up of Tor-Aksel Busch and Anne Grøstad over the SEFO investigation into the perjury and attempt to pervert the course of justice of Drammen police officer **Torill Sorte**. A police officer who was quoted in the same Aftenposten article as yourself.

It is hardly right that such a large scale deceit be allowed to go unpunished and yet that is exactly what your department has allowed to happen. Just silence. And now with a General Election coming up it is possible that, depending on the outcome, no reply will be forthcoming from you personally.

Yours sincerely,
Frederick Delaware

I received the following reply on the 19th September 2005 from The Royal Ministry of Justice and the Police after Mr Dørum's party lost the Norwegian General Election and Dørum lost his job:

Concerning Aftenposten's headline of 15th April 2002, by Reidun J. Samuelsen: 'British Muslim terrorizes Norwegian on the Internet'

In reference to your letter of 25th August 2005, concerning the above mentioned article in Aftenposten.

The Ministry of Justice has acknowledged your opinion on the matter. No further enquiries will be answered in the matter.

Yours sincerely,

Magnar Aukrust
Deputy Director General

Line Nersnæs, Senior Adviser

I responded on the 12th October 2005:

For the attention of Magnar Aukrust and Line Nersnæs The Royal Ministry of Justice and the Police, Norway.

Dear Sirs,

Aftenposten article of 15th April 2002 and Policewoman Torill Sorte of Drammen.

I refer to your letter of 19th September 2005.

My letter of 25th August 2005 was addressed to the Minister of Justice, Mr. Dørum and if you yourselves are replying on his behalf, then the correct thing to do, surely, is to tell me that Mr. Dørum knows of my complaint.

My complaint is not just about the Aftenposten article. It is also about that wretched liar, Torill Sorte and your department's cover up for her and Anne Grøstad and Tor-Aksel Busch over the SEFO investigation. Large scale deceit.

So in this case I will require an answer from the organ grinder and not his monkey.

I will send a copy of this letter to the Prime Minister's office.

Yours faithfully,
Frederick Delaware

The Office of the Prime Minister wrote back on the 26th October 2005:

Private situation

Reference is made to your letter of 13 October 2005.

In Norway the Office of the Prime Minister does not deal with complaints concerning the handling of specific cases by the sectorial ministries or by the courts of law. We therefore regret to inform you that we may not be able to help you with your case.

Yours sincerely,

Malin Soltvedt Nossum
Senior Adviser

I then called Malin Soltvedt Nossum to clarify what the word "may" in the last sentence of her letter actually meant, as I suspected her intention was to mean "will." I was right. The Prime Minister's office would not investigate. Malin Nossum told me that in any case the Office of the Prime Minister was small and they didn't have the staff to investigate the matter. And that my only remedy lay with the Ombudsman.

On 20th September 2005 Aftenposten's English language website carried the following article:

Psychiatric problems plague one of [sic] four Norwegians

Norway seems to be offering living proof that money can't buy happiness. The country often is referred to as among the world's wealthiest, and the best place to live, but a new study indicates that 25 per cent of the adult population falls mentally ill every year.

The study, conducted by the Psychiatric Institute at the University of Oslo, is based on data collected by health authorities in eastern Norway.

The amount of people seeking psychiatric treatment amounts to 25 per cent of all adult Norwegians. Another 450,000 Norwegians are believed to suffer psychiatric problems, but don't bother visiting the doctor.

[Under a picture of the Prime Minister was the following caption:]

Norwegian Prime Minister Kjell Magne Bondevik has been among those seeking psychiatric help, after being diagnosed with a "depressive reaction" during his first term in the late 1990's. He and other government officials have been calling for more openness and funding for mental health programs.

Anxiety and depression are the most common ailments, reported Norwegian Broadcasting (NRK) on Tuesday morning.

"The health authorities and the population itself is having great difficulty comprehending the enormous amount of psychiatric problems, and the enormous need for treatment that exists," Professor Per Høglend, who led the study, told NRK.

The study results come just days after newspaper *Dagens Næringsliv* ran a front-page story hailing Norway as "the richest country of all time" based on its foreign trade surplus and balance of payments. Norway's oil wealth continues to fuel its economy, but it's clear that not everyone is enjoying the results.

On the same day, newspaper *Dagsavisen* ran a front-page story noting how local crisis telephone lines were ringing off the hook with people seeking help. "We can't manage to answer more than 50 per cent of the calls," said Mette Kammen of Mental Helse.

Paradox

It's clearly a paradox, and the question is why so many Norwegians are so unhappy. There's always the old clichés about Norway's long, dark winters, but one expert suggests the threshold for identifying someone with a problem as "depressed" has been lowered, and that people are more willing to seek professional counselling.

She also cited a reluctance by many Norwegians to openly discuss relatively common problems such as grief, divorce or the loss of a job with friends or family. A high percentage of Norwegians live alone, and loneliness is a problem in itself.

"There are lots of lonely people around the country, without a social network," said Kammen, "Many just need someone to talk to."

Aftenposten English Web Desk
Nina Berglund/NTB

***

In early December 2005, I noticed on the Aftenposten and Dagbladet Norwegian language websites that readers could send in their comments on the topics of the day. Blogs, so called. I thought I'd have a go myself. On Friday 9th December, for my first blogging attempt I wrote in the space left for 'Title' the name of my website which was **www.norway-shockers.com** and in the space for 'Comments' I asked what was happening to "Policewoman Torill Sorte of Drammen, liar and perjurer." I signed off in a fictitious English name. Immediately my comments were accepted – unedited! The fact that my comments were in English would stand out and attract attention as the other blogs, of course, were in Norwegian. I followed this up with several more goes, as there were many topics of the day listed for commentary on both newspapers' sites. I also promoted the alternative name I had for my website **www.norwayuncovered.com**. Soon, I noticed from my tracking facility for my website that the hits from Norway were going up considerably. So I continued doing the same thing at intervals throughout the day. The total count for Friday 9th December was 139 hits. For Saturday 10th December it was 57 hits and for Sunday 11th December just 10 hits. On Monday 12th December I resumed my blogging but by midday Aftenposten had blocked my comments from my computer. Dagbladet continued to accept them. For Monday 12th December the hit count was 228, for Tuesday 13th December it was 300, for Wednesday 14th December it was 128, for Thursday 15th December it was 90, for Friday 16th December it was 106, for Saturday 17th December it was 116, for Sunday 18th December it was 39 and for Monday 19th December it was 316. On 20th December 2005, I looked at my website tracking monitor at 10.15 a.m. and there were already over 300 hits. How come so many? I went to Aftenposten's website to see if they had done a story on me. They had not. I then went to the Dagbladet website. Bingo! The premier article on their site detailed my blogging efforts to promote my own website. Dagbladet's article was only in Norwegian (they did not have an English language website) so I couldn't understand what was said about me, but I recognised the Norwegian words for "half-Arab Muslim" on the second line of the article. As usual I had not been named. I also recognised a sentence saying that I had been in a "psychiatric unit in Great Britain."

By the end of that day the hits on my site numbered 1,758. And lots of emails were sent to me the pick of which were, verbatim:

- U Arab pigsvine pervert.

- I would like to give a big laugh to you. Most stupid cracy fuck, have u gotten ur head examined lately. I would like to point out to you that beeing stupid knows no color. I was once a muslim. But when I realised that [the prophet] Muhammed couldn't be anything else than a confused peadophile. I knew that a true God would never speak to such a looney. So you think that killing a featus that has not gained consciouness is more wrong than reaping children. It is more and more clearly that you are insane. The only humane thing to do is to place a gun to your head and pull the trigger. But I suspect it wouldn't do to much damage, hence the damage is clearly well done. I heard that your mother got you into hospital, bad muslim taking orders from a woman. May I recommend a rope around your neck since you are never coming to paradise. Better to end your misory right?

- I have to laugh….What a pathetic little muslim bastard you are. You're obviously insane….just like most of your kind.

  I can understand your fascination and envy of Norway and our women. However, you can never in your entire lifetime have such a great life as we have. The world isn't made that way.

  I strongly advice you to immediately shut down your website at least all references to Norwegian persons. We don't like it when you and your people publish such crap.

- Hey you. I am from Bergen in Norway and I have read all your stories and the Norwegian side. I don't really know what to belive but yours seems more likely. I dunno. In Norway you are made out to be a sexed up maniac who was a freak from the first meeting. Well I dunno but today it is all over the net in Norway about you and how they had to block you from lots of Norwegian internet sights coz u were disturbed. Well I dunno but I hope it all gets sorted out and I think… I'm not sure but I think I support you.

- Sick devil, go fuck Allah the Camel.

- You are gonna get what you deserve if you don't take down your website you sick fuck! People will find you sooner or later, mark my words you loser! You got one week…. You sick fuckin muslim fucker! Leave the Norwegian girl alone and take down the website, otherwise we'll come and pay you a visit!

  Stalkers

- You are the sickest fucker I ever let my eyes on!!!! Come to Norway, and I will show you what a real man will do to you!!!! You are a little man with no balls and a big dangerous mouth!!!! Too dangerous for your health!!!! Maybe you like a visit??? Stay of Heidi's back! You should be lobotomized!!!! Sick Sick Fuck!

- May allah put you back behind bars where you belong!!! Fucking creep!!

- Wow, I just browsed your website and I must say you strike me as the most filthy, pigeating muslim maniac I have ever encountered.

  When you eat pigs, do you lick the pigs asshole clean before digging in?

  I have one advice for you, take out your willy, that is your mangled penis, and showe it into a pigs ass, maybe you'll get some weird looking kids, I seriously doubt that anything other than a pig would take your seamen.

  Best regards and good luck on dying pigfucker!

  By the way, you really do a great job in showing of Muslims as crazy, even better than Osama!

  Oink Oink Fucker;)

  Burn in hell!

- We have put an 10,000 Euro reward on your head…. we going to get you man, we going to clear the world from an idiot like you…:)

  Burn in hell..

  ps. Going to FUCK your mother…she like WHITE man…

- You are a very disturbed guy. You only write lies about Norway and the girl you have terrorized for many years. And last but not least you only have lies on you'r site. And you don't mention that you have been in a mental institution. So you see you are the disturbed one not everybody else.

- You stink, please die

I called Stig Lunde, my lawyer, in the evening and alerted him to the article, which he had, until then, no knowledge of.

I sent a fax that night (20th December 2005) to the new Norwegian Minister of Justice Knut Storberget:

Dear Sir,

www.norwayuncovered.com

I am now getting death threats by email (enclosed) and the worst kind of religious abuse possible (again enclosed) after today's Dagbladet article (enclosed).

I have asked your predecessor and Deputy Director General to investigate Policewoman Torill Sorte of Drammen for perjury in SEFO'S cover up. But just silence!

Isn't it about time you came clean and stop putting the 'mental patient' label (a total lie) on me?

Yours faithfully,
Frederick Delaware

The next day, 21st December 2005, the Dagbladet internet article was still there in plain view on their website. Good! I had also made the front page of the Dagbladet newspaper itself on 21st December with the banner headline, 'Pursued by SEX-MAD man for 23 years,' in a three page article (although I did not discover the existence of this article until March 2006). The hit count for that day was 572. And more emails were sent to me including the following, (verbatim):

- After visiting your website, I can now understand why your mother had you "put away" for a while.

  Clearly the best option

- are you by chance a catholic priest? and did your daddy touch your penis and/or dropped you on the head when you were born? or maybe your parents suffered for BSS (baby shaking syndrome) eitherway you are one fucked up dude.

  did someone touch your bum bum in the mental ward? oh hell, all Norway knows you are crazy as fuck man. but I think you are funny, very sad but funny. I give you, lets say… 10 years and I bet that you have killed yourself or at least gotten another hobby than harassing women you cant get, haha such a wanker.

  what triggered your funny behaviour? are you sick or just a horny helpless looser? tried prozac combined with viagra? oh wait, im sure someone tried that combo in the mental ward when they made love love to your bum bum. do you call your penis king kong?

  happy Christmas motherfucker. oh wait, i bet you are inbreed! your dad is your son is you mum is your sister is your uncle is your bum bum.

  ps. I EAT FOETUSES FOR BREAKFEAST

  AND ITS MR.AMERICUM.

- You most be the sickes fuck ever! Muslims are root to all evil and you are the living proof of it.

***

On 5th January 2006 I sent the Dagbladet internet article and copies of the above mentioned emails to the European Court of Human Rights, asking them to add the papers to my file.

On 19th January 2006 I received the translation in English of the Dagbladet internet article from my UK based agency:

Dagbladet.no Home news	20th December 2005
Sexually pursued by mad Briton	

For 23 years, Heidi Schøne (41) has been sexually harassed by the man she met when she was 18. Now he is using the Net as a weapon of terror.

MORTEN ØVERBYE
Tuesday 20.12.2005, 10:08
updated 10:30

(Dagbladet.no) Yesterday Aftenposten.no closed its Internet pages to the half-Arab, Muslim Briton, after he had swamped their blogs with contributions. Several other Norwegian online newspapers have also been overrun by contributions from the man.
"He has succeeded in taking too many years of my life. That is what is so tragic. He has pursued me for 23 years. He had pursued another Norwegian girl as well, right in the middle of all this," Schøne told Dagbladet.no.

583

For her the nightmare began when as an 18 year old au pair she met a half-Arab Briton on a boat trip between France and England. She was travelling with a girlfriend when she noticed a five-six years older man looking at her.

"I felt a little uncomfortable, so I moved away. But when we were queueing to embark, he was there again and tapped me on the shoulder. We went a long way in to sit down. But of course he followed and sat down there as well."

The strange man was persistent but all the same pleasant company for the two girlfriends during the trip.

After the trip, they stayed in contact.

"We were never going out. But I did let him visit occasionally as time went by. I felt sorry for him so he was allowed to celebrate New Year's Eve with us," says Schøne.

During the time in the UK, he became increasingly persistent.

"I was only 18 at the time. I did not know what I had done to him. The only thing I had done was that I did not want to marry the guy. I did not want to become a Muslim."

Terrorized

She did not want to have any further contact with him when she later moved back to Norway. He then turned up there.

"He was extremely manipulative. If I didn't let him in, he created hell and pounded on the neighbours' doors. He bombarded me with telephone calls and letters the whole time. In these he told me how stupid and nasty I was," says Schøne.

The terrorizing continued right up to 1992. The man was then committed to a psychiatric hospital in the UK. A Norwegian police official who investigated the case explained later that it was his mother who had him committed.

When he came out again two years later, it carried on – worse than ever.

He began to send other people letters about Schøne. All translated into fluent Norwegian. Hundreds of letters were sent to everybody from Den Nationale Scene in Bergen to the local bailiff's office, neighbours, friends and acquaintances, all the letters containing intimate statements about the woman.

Took legal action, was fined

When she went to the newspapers with the story, he came to Norway to bring a legal action against her.

Instead he himself was punished.

In November 2001, he was fined NOK 10,000. The District Court observed that the punishment was very mild. But the court chose to fine him because he was resident in England. He never paid.

In October 2003, he lost the civil action in the Court of Appeal, where he himself was arrested and fined again. He then appeared as a repentant sinner. After a full confession in the magistrate's court, the Briton was given a suspended eight month sentence and again fined NOK 10,000.

In addition, he promised to remove the Internet pages where he was conducting the persecution.

The Briton accepted the judgement on the spot, accompanied the police to a cash dispenser where he withdrew NOK 20,000 and then boarded the plane to England. Then he carried on as before.

Appealing to The Hague

When he lost the civil action in the Court of Appeal as well, he appealed to the Supreme Court – which dismissed the case in March 2004. On his Internet pages, the Briton says that he wants to appeal the case all the way to the court of human rights in The Hague.

At the same time he is continuing the persecution on the Internet.

"The worst thing – not just for me but for everybody who is living through it – is how little society reacts to it. It is crazy how he can simply continue," says Schøne.

"In other countries, there are much stricter laws. If it had been in England, he would have been punished properly. Here he is allowed to get off with a fine time after time," she says.

PS! A policewoman who conducted the investigation into the Briton is now being persecuted by name on his Internet pages.

CLOSED: Several Norwegian Internet sites, including Aftenposten and Dagbladet, have in recent days closed their servers to the Briton's IP address. This is a facsimile of contributions he posted on VG Nett.

***

The actual Dagbladet newspaper article of 21st December 2005 is translated as follows:

Dagbladet	**21st December 2005**
Pursued by SEX-MAD man for 23 years	

"He has kept his promise to ruin my life." HEIDI SCHØNE (41)

SEXUALLY harassed for 23 years

23 years ago, Heidi Schøne (41) met a half-Arab Briton on a boat trip between France and England. Since then her life has been a nightmare.

Words: **Morten Øverbye**
morten@dagbladet.no

Anders Holth Johansen
ahj@dagbladet.no

In recent days, the Briton has swamped online newspapers' blogs with malicious contributions to such an extent that the major Norwegian online newspapers have been forced to block the man's access. But threats and accusations are nothing new for Heidi Schøne. She has lived with them for the last 23 years.

"It has been a nightmare, but now I am not so scared any more. Now I am more angry at society which did not take the signs seriously early enough," says Schøne.

The threats and the harassment have been a strain for her whole family. Today she is divorced and has two children.

"I had a small child he thought should die. In other countries, he would have been punished severely for that kind of threat," says Schøne.

Several letters a day

The sexual harassment has continued regularly for the last 23 years.

"New letters with "Fuck You!" written on them in red were constantly coming through the letter box. The number of letters varied with his mood. I could receive three or four letter a day," says Schøne.

In the end, the post office agreed to sort out the letters from the man. But the mad Briton could not be stopped. He got others to send letters for him and to phone. Friends and colleagues also received letters and faxes containing intimate statements.

"At times he sought me out frequently. Suddenly he could be there outside my window," says Heidi Schøne.

The nightmare began when as an 18 year old au pair she met the half-Arab Briton on a boat trip between France and England. She was travelling with a girlfriend when she noticed the five-six years older man looking at her.

The strange man was persistent but all the same pleasant company for the two girlfriends during the trip. After the trip, they stayed in contact.

"We were never going out. But I did let him visit occasionally as time went by. I felt sorry for him so he was allowed to celebrate New Year's Eve with us," says Schøne.

During the time in the UK, he became increasingly persistent.

"I was only 18 at the time. I did not know what I had done to him. The only thing I had done was that I did not want to marry the guy. I did not want to become a Muslim."

Committed

She did not want to have any further contact with him when she later moved back to Norway. Then he turned up.

"He was extremely manipulative. If I didn't let him in, he created hell and pounded on the neighbours' doors. He bombarded me with telephone calls and letters the whole time. In these he told me how stupid and nasty I was," says Schøne.

The terrorizing continued right up to 1992. His mother then arranged for him to be committed to a psychiatric hospital in the United Kingdom. When he came out again two years later, it carried on – worse than ever.

He began to send other people letters about Heidi Schøne. All translated into fluent Norwegian. Hundreds of letters were sent to everybody from Den Nationale Scene in Bergen to the local bailiff's office, neighbours, friends and acquaintances, all the letters containing intimate statements about the woman.

"He wants people to dislike me, and he can be very good at persuading people," says Schøne.

Took legal action

In 1999, the Briton took action against Heidi Schøne for libel because she had been interviewed about the situation. That ended with the man himself having to pay NOK 10,000 for invasion of privacy.

In its judgement of 14 November 2003, Borgarting Court of Appeal stated that "Overall, the case appears to be a misuse of the legal system." The Court thought that there was overwhelming documentary evidence of sexual harassment and ordered the Briton to pay NOK 104,585 in costs.

Insulting web page

The man has a web page which is intended to reveal "Norway's exotic, erotic and extremely psychotic mentality." The web page contains a series of gross lies about Heidi Schøne's intimate life.

The man has been ordered to delete all information about Heidi Schøne from his web pages. He has not done so.

"I am not afraid of him any more. But I don't understand why we in Norway do not take this more seriously. This is about human life after all," says Schøne.

Captions:

INTERNET HARASSMENT: On this web site, the Briton carries on harassment of Heidi Schøne (inset). In spite of the fact that he was ordered to remove the web pages in 2003, they are still on the Internet.

NIGHTMARE: Since Heidi Schøne (41) met the Briton 23 years ago, he has been obsessed with her and has sent hundreds of letters with intimate statements about the woman, both to her and to those around her.

"He wants people to dislike me, and he can be very good at persuading people." Heidi Schøne (41), persecuted.

Investigator was also harassed

Police inspector Torill Sorte of Nedre Romerike police district was the investigator in the case against the Briton. Then she herself was harassed.

"It finally ended with me having to ask to be taken off the case, because I myself wanted to report the man," says Sorte.

"There were faxes and e-mails which said I was mad and that I am a liar. It was quiet for a while but he has started again in recent weeks," says Sorte.

The man has today been ordered to stay away from the police inspector.

***

On the Drammens Tidende website blogging section, I had been adding my comments on policewoman Torill Sorte's perjury regarding her "mental hospital" allegations. By chance on the 17th February 2006 I came across a website called 'Roy's PRESSETJENESTE' (Roy's PRESS SERVICE) which had posted an article on my quest to expose Torill Sorte as the liar and cheat that she clearly was.

Roy's PRESS SERVICE had taken the article from another small newspaper in the Drammen area called Eiker Bladet which published the article on the 11th January 2006. For the first time ever, I had been named. The translation is:

By Roy Hansen, 11.01.06

Briton Frederick Delaware is continuing his harassment of Norwegian women. After having harassed Heidi Schøne from Solbergelva for years, he is now attacking police inspector Torill Sorte at Nedre Eiker police station.

The Briton has continued his smear-campaign against police inspector Torill Sorte at Nedre Eiker police station through a series of 'contributions' made recently to Drammens Tidende's Internet pages. This takes the form of among other things him posting links to an Internet page he was ordered to remove from the Internet as recently as 17 October 2003. DT's Internet head Lars Lager Espevalen is now promising that they will monitor their pages more closely in order to delete undesirable contributions as soon as possible.

"The man has plagued Heidi Schøne and her family since 1982, and it has proved very difficult to stop him," says Torill Sorte. In 2003, she led the investigation in the case which ended in a two year suspended sentence and a fine for severe harassment in Eiker, Modum and Sigdal district court. Since then, the Muslim man has also made the police investigator the object of his hatred.

Sent faxes
A number of public bodies, newspapers and media organizations as well as private businesses have received faxes from the man about her involvement in the case, and what he writes about her is not very flattering. "I deal with it and know that I did not do anything wrong in the matter. Not even an internal inquiry revealed anything wrong," says Sorte.

She nevertheless takes the harassment through DT's Internet pages seriously because they are easily accessible and owing to the fact that the man was ordered to remove the pages from the Internet. Harassment is moreover a growing problem in society, and Nedre Eiker is no exception.

Difficult cases
"Harassment cases are difficult cases because it takes a lot for us to be able to bring a prosecution. As a rule, the harassment occurs when relationships break down and, even though we can impose fines, this rarely helps," she says. Nedre Eiker police station handles 25-30 such cases a year on average, but few are as serious as the case against the Briton.

"There are several forms of harassment, and if, for example, it is a spurned husband who is sending text messages to his ex, it rarely stops even though fines are imposed. On the other hand, if it is a question of defamation and annoying behaviour which involves a number of people, it is a little easier to get a sanction imposed," says Torill Sorte.

Raising the issue
She now wants to raise the issue of harassment against herself with the administration of Southern Buskerud Police District. Last summer, the Briton sent a fax to the police directorate, and this was forwarded to her through official channels for comment. Even though she says that it is not bothering her personally, Torill Sorte does not want this matter to be allowed to develop. We also understand that an initiative has been put before the justice department aimed at having the legislation in this area changed.

"The man is obviously mentally unstable and must be putting an incredible amount of time and energy, not to mention money, into harassing Heidi Schøne and the undersigned, in addition to some other women we know about. Unfortunately, the laws are such that we cannot apply for him to be extradited for further criminal prosecution," says Sorte.

(Published in Eiker Bladet 11.01.06)

Police inspector Torill Sorte at Nedre Eiker police station has recently been subjected to harassment through DT's Internet pages.

***

The "other women" I was now allegedly "harassing" was, as usual, just another total lie.

The saga over the Danish cartoons of the prophet Mohammad had also just erupted and Dagbladet.no carried the cartoons on their website on the 10th January 2006. The Times newspaper of London carried the following story on 31st January 2006:

The Times   **31st January 2006**
Denmark faces international boycott over Muslim cartoons

BY ANTHONY BROWNE

DENMARK faced the full fury of the Muslim world yesterday as a long-simmering row over newspaper cartoons depicting the Prophet Muhammad finally erupted.

There were street demonstrations and flag-burnings in the Middle East. Libya joined Saudi Arabia in withdrawing its ambassador from Copenhagen. Islamic governments and organisations, including the Muslim Council of Britain, issued denunciations and a boycott of Danish goods took hold across the Muslim world.

The Danish Government warned its citizens about travelling to Algeria, Egypt, Jordan, Lebanon, Pakistan, Saudi Arabia and Syria, and withdrew aid workers from the Gaza Strip.

Last night EU foreign ministers issued a statement in support of Denmark, and the European Commission threatened to report any government backing the boycott to the World Trade Organisation.

The fury echoed the outcry that followed the publication in 1988 of the Salman Rushdie novel *The Satanic Verses*. The trigger for the latest clash of cultures was the publication by the Danish newspaper *Jyllends-Posten* on September 30 of 12 cartoons of Muhammad. A biographer of the prophet had complained that no one would dare to illustrate his book, and the newspaper challenged cartoonists to draw pictures of the prophet in a self-declared battle for freedom of speech.

One submission showed Muhammad wearing a bomb-shaped turban; in another he tells dead suicide bombers that he has run out of virgins with which to reward them. Any portrayal of Muhammad is blasphemous in Islam, lest it encourages idolatry.

In October ambassadors from ten Muslim countries complained to Anders Fogh Rasmussen, the Danish Prime Minister, who refused to interfere with the press's freedom.

But the issue began to boil this month after the cartoons appeared in *Magazinet*, a Christian newspaper in Norway, and on the website of the Norwegian newspaper *Dagbladet*.

Imams denounced Denmark from their pulpits, the Arab press inflamed pent-up Muslim anger at the West and last Friday the Saudi Government recalled its ambassador, but still Mr Rasmussen refused to apologise. He condemned attempts to "demonise people because of religious beliefs," but argued: "The Government can in no way influence the media."

By yesterday governments across the Arab world were responding to public outrage. Libya closed its embassy in Denmark and the Egyptian parliament demanded that its Government follow suit. The Kuwaiti and Jordanian governments called for explanations from their Danish ambassadors. President Lahoud of Lebanon condemned the cartoons, saying his country "cannot accept any insult to any religion." The Justice Minister of the United Arab Emirates said: "This is cultural terrorism, not freedom of expression." In Gaza, gunmen briefly occupied the EU office in Gaza and warned Danes and Norwegians to stay away. Palestinians in the West Bank burnt Danish flags. The Islamic groups Hamas and Hezbollah and the Egyptian Muslim Brotherhood demanded an apology.

Supermarkets in Algeria, Bahrain, Jordan, Kuwait, Morocco, Qatar, Tunisia, the United Arab Emirates and Yemen all removed Danish produce from their shelves. Arla Foods, a Danish company with annual sales of about $430 million in the Middle East, said that the boycott was almost total and suspended production in Saudi Arabia.

The Muslim Council of Britain, whose leaders are to meet the Danish ambassador tomorrow, deplored the newspapers' refusal to apologise for printing "sacrilegious cartoons vilifying the Prophet Muhammad."

Bill Clinton, the former US President, added his voice, telling a conference in Qatar that he feared anti-Semitism would be replaced with anti-Islamic prejudice. He condemned "these totally outrageous cartoons against Islam."

Per Stig Moeller, Denmark's Foreign Minister, insisted in Brussels last night: "We condemn blasphemy. We want respect for religions. But we cannot intervene. We have sent explanations but, as we have said before, freedom of expression is a matter for the courts, not for the Government."

A spokesman for Peter Mandelson, the EU Trade Commissioner, said that if the Saudi Government had encouraged the boycott of Danish goods, Mr. Mandelson would take the matter to the WTO.

Carsten Juste, editor-in-chief of *Jyllends-Posten*, which has hired extra security after staff received death threats, said that the drawings "were not in violation of Danish law but have offended many Muslims, which we would like to apologise for." He added that the drawings were "sober and were not meant to be offensive" to Muslims.

***

The President of the New York branch of the World Jewish Congress wrote a letter to The Times on 1st February 2006 as follows:

A free society must respect all its religions
From the New York President of the World Jewish Congress

Sir, Although freedom of religion and freedom of speech are both fundamental rights, they sometimes come into conflict which each other, as is the case with the caricatures recently published in the Danish newspaper *Jyllands-Posten* depicting the Prophet Muhammad (report, Jan 31). This has provoked an uproar among Muslims, not just in Denmark, but across the Islamic world, as it is widely understood that Islam forbids the depicting of Muhammad.

The issue at stake here is not "self-censorship," which Flemming Rose, the newspaper's culture editor, claims has befallen Europe since the murder of the Dutch film-maker Theo van Gogh. It is whether respect for other religious beliefs, traditions and practices really applies to everybody, including Muslims.

We prefer the word "respect" to "tolerance" because to be "tolerated" is not a positive notion, and in addition "respect" is not a one-way concept; it is mutual. If the cartoons in question were deliberately made and published to provoke Muslims and to stir up public opinion in Denmark, as Mr Rose seems to suggest, something has gone wrong. What the cartoons managed to do was to offend all Muslims instead of focusing on those fanatics that actually merit criticism.

Sometimes, provocations are necessary to wake people up. Over the past 30 years, the World Jewish Congress has been no stranger to that. But religious customs, practices, beliefs, should be respected by followers of other religions and non-believers alike, because this is a prerequisite for being respected oneself.

Mutual respect and understanding between members of different religions is the key to ending hatred and to creating a better world. We consider desecration of any holy book an insult to ourselves. Desecration of the Koran, the Torah or the Bible, or any religious site, should be offensive to all of us.

To consciously provoke and offend the fairly small Muslim minority in Denmark was wrong. Yes, immigrants must integrate in their host societies, be they Muslims, Jews or Christians, while retaining their own identities, beliefs, customs and faiths. Parallel societies can easily become a breeding ground for fanatics, zealots and, ultimately, terrorists. Immigration sometimes fails because immigrants do not make enough effort. But sometimes it is made harder because of an intolerant and harsh host country.

It is the job of governments and lawmakers to make sure that immigrants are not treated as newly conquered, but with respect. Those who make an effort to integrate should be welcomed with open arms, and allowed to make more than just financial contributions to their new countries' tax coffers.

Over the past 2,000 years and until the creation of the state of Israel, Jews have always been a small minority in every country they have settled in. Our ancestors have suffered from pogroms, anti-Semitism and, finally, the Holocaust.

Lies about Jews, the Jewish faith and traditions have never disappeared. In fact, they are staging a comeback, especially in Western democracies which we thought had become immune to anti-Semitism after the horrors of the Holocaust.

Nonetheless, Jewish intellectuals and politicians have always been at the forefront of the fight for human rights, democracy and free speech. But there are limits to the latter that should be respected, and publishing materials considered offensive by a small religious minority is going too far. It is as wrong as the discrimination against Christian or Jewish populations that takes place in some Islamic countries. Democracies are tested on how they treat their minorities.

Over the decades since the publication of the Second Vatican Council declaration *Nostra Aetate*, the Catholic Church and the Jewish community have been engaged in dialogue with each other. Christians, Jews and Muslims are all children of Abraham, and we should learn what we have in common.

EDGAR M. BRONFMAN

New York

The world was able to see on a grand scale the real feelings of the Danes and their Norwegian cousins towards Islam, something I had already myself been trying to highlight for the past ten years.

591

On 10th February 2006 the following email was sent to me by a Norwegian gentleman whose name shall remain confidential:

> Dear Sir(s?),
>
> I have incidentally come across this page on the net and found many interesting notes about my home country.
>
> I just want to say that I find most of your experiences credible and to the point. In my opinion Norway is lacking in true professionalism in many aspects of public life, leaving quite a number of people, also "native norwegians," victims of circumstance and ill-doers.
>
> As I gather from the internet page, your bad experiences and interest in the "dark side" of Norway started with Heidi Schøne. I can only offer my sympathy, and also add that there has been a number of such women exposed as liars and criminals the last decade.
>
> Unfortunately, political correctness is a disease under which the Norwegian society suffers heavily. "Women are poor and defenseless" and "All men are rapists" are only two of the politically correct (incorrect!) statements in Norway. Coupled with a lack of professionalism in the newspapers and the judicial system these politically correct statements have paved the way for a large number of miscarriages of justice.
>
> The most common case is that of a divorce involving children. A very common practice, I am ashamed to say, has been for the wife to claim some sort of sexual abuse towards her or a child (when in reality no such thing has occurred). The reason for such a claim is to obtain full parental control of the children after divorce. This will make sure that the wife can control the husband's contact with the children (making it NO contact usually), and at the same time make sure that the husband will have to pay VERY substantial amounts of money to the wife regularly until all children are considered adults by law, that is 18 years of age. The very unfortunate fact about the Norwegian judicial system is that until recently the wife (and her lawyer) usually backed this claim only by "expert" statements from psychologists. Except for one or two outrageous cases that was appealed all the way to supreme court, the Norwegian courts never contradicted these expert psychologist claims. This situation was revealed to the public in a series of articles in the Norwegian newspaper Adresseavisen in 2000 or 2001 (cannot remember exactly), when a number of lawyers wanted an end to the shameful practice. The lawyers also said that lawyers dealing with divorces knew a number of psychologists willing to give any kind of "expert statement" in court for money. Thus, they could arrange a divorce to whatever outcome just by false accusations, through a very severe lack of professionalism on the behalf of both lawyers, psychologists and courts.
>
> The use of psychologists in Norwegian courts have now been changed, also due to their abysmal part in the "Bjugn case," where a vast number of children were falsely claimed to have been abused by a number of men. The Norwegian society of psychologists have also publicly excused the misconduct of some of their members involved in these cases.
>
> This is just to say that I think part of your impression of a Norwegian general disliking of Moslems and Islam is that you have experienced the kind of injustice many "native Norwegians" also have experienced. I don't think it makes your experiences better, but one should always try to call a spade a spade.
>
> I think there has been a change in attitude of the courts in Norway the last years and a number of people have had their cases reopened and gotten their names cleared. These cases were given major headlines in the newspapers when they were first run, but when they are now reopened, the newspapers does not care about them. This goes only to show that the papers are not very serious in this country, but I think it also shows that even here a lie is a lie and will only take

you so far. I also feel that even though the feminist movements still are a major factor for establishing what is "politically correct" in Norway, they also have begun to feel some embarrassment by some of the acts of their "sisters."

My thoughts on abortion mirrors yours I think, and even if you might not think so from the public debate in Norway, there is a number of people that is really frustrated by the abortion laws. For instance it has been very difficult for the hospitals to find (enough) doctors and nurses willing to work at the abortion clinics. This is a fact that the media and official Norway has been wanting to stay out of public knowledge. In fact, abortion is such a sensitive subject it is not seen as a proper subject to discuss at all. The government does not want a public debate on abortion, and I think this is so because they know that a majority or at least a large minority of the Norwegian people is against it, and the way it is practised. It is a disgrace, but people who officially protest about the abortion laws are frozen out of the society.

I hope you will continue this webpage as I find it to be an important addition to the shallow Norwegian debate on our society. However, I think the way some part of it is written now, many Norwegians will feel offended before they manage to get to the truth in it.

If you are interested in reading about the "Bjugn case" I can recommend this link:

http://home.online.no/~eraagaar/

Knut Erik Aagaard has written many interesting articles presented here, but the ones titled "Overgrepslæren 1-10" are about the "Bjugn case." They were all published in the Oslo newspaper Arbeiderbladet, which today is called Dagsavisen.

Best regards,

On the 17th February 2006, I telephone the Ministry of Justice in Norway to be told that the Minister, Knut Storberget, had personally asked one of his senior advisers, Line Nersnæs, to investigate my complaint against policewoman Torill Sorte following receipt of my letter of the 20th December 2005 to the Minister.

On the 19th February 2006 I sent a fax to the Minister:

Subject: Policewoman Torill Sorte of Drammen

Dear Sir,

I telephoned your office last Friday morning to be told by one of your staff that you have asked Line Nersnæs to look into the issues raised in my letter to you of 20th December 2005.

Last month I found on the internet, by pure chance, an article on Roy's Pressejeneste from Eiker Bladet dated 11th January 2006 (enclosed). You will see that I "the Muslim man" have been named and accused by Torill Sorte of the usual falsehoods. She has clearly lied again. And why in particular is she qualified to say that I am "obviously mentally unstable"? Just because I use my website to exercise my right of reply to state that she has perjured herself in her evidence in earlier litigation, does not entitle her to perpetuate her outrageous nonsense.

What was her perjured evidence? It was that she stated in a witness statement and again in open court that my mother told her that she, my mother, had me committed to a mental hospital. Who phoned who to discuss this and when? Torill Sorte said in court she could not remember. What, no contemporaneous notes? The fact is that the courts and SEFO have my family doctor's letter stating categorically that I have never been a patient in a mental hospital. I see now that

593

Dagbladet say I was in a mental hospital for "two years" and that Torill Sorte again explains to the newspaper that my mother had me "committed" to a mental hospital. And readers in your country believe this! My mother has given evidence to Judge J. Morten Svendgård when he phoned her up, to say that Sorte is a complete liar. Why on earth Sorte was not prosecuted for perjury, in the face of incontrovertible and overwhelming evidence, after SEFO's 2003 inquiry, indicates a cover up.

So, I expect nothing less than for Torill Sorte to be sacked along with Anne Grøstad and Tor-Aksel Busch who signed the 2003 letter stating, with no substantive reasons given, that Torill Sorte would not be prosecuted. Now Sorte is saying she did not do "anything wrong." So it is absolute fact is it that I have been a mental hospital patient when I haven't? Or perhaps in the alternative my mother is a lunatic as well? I guess that fact that Heidi Schøne is a mental patient herself on a 100% disability pension is irrelevant.

Amazingly I read in the Eiker Bladet article that the police have petitioned your department to change the law in this area! Presumably to make it possible for your prosecuting authorities to extradite me for speaking out?

For your information my website did not go online until October 2000 - 5 years after your country's newspapers began their campaign of demonisation. Including saying that I threatened to kill Heidi Schøne's son. So I am entitled to a right of reply, especially as the PFU are totally useless in enforcing the newspapers own self-regulatory rules.

It is your authorities that used Interpol to deliver a Section 390(a) Norwegian Penal code writ to me in England a few years ago, offended that I was putting my side of the story out to Norwegians. These same authorities arrested me at the door of the courtroom, the minute I had finished my civil Court of Appeal case in Drammen in 2003. I was set up and ambushed. I was given an 8 month prison sentence, suspended for 2 years, if I did not take down my website, under the strict liability section 390(a). What happened to section 390? So much for freedom of speech. Presumably I will go straight to prison if I ever set foot in Norway again.

Anyway, it all boils down to one thing. I have committed the offence of being a Muslim. For 11 years now your country's newspapers have made that quite clear. The Dagbladet.no article is a clear incitement to religious and racial hatred. Those emails that you have bear this out.

Yours faithfully,

Frederick Delaware

Knut Storberget, the Minister of Justice, had on 23rd February 2006 "personally" given my complaint the Ministerial Reference Number of 13113, as so advised to me on the 22nd March 2006 by Mr. Hemming Velde of the Documentation Section in the Ministry of Justice. One would think it would be fairly straightforward thereafter for a proper investigation to take place. But not in Norway. On Monday 20th March the secretary to Line Nersnæs told me that no ministerial instruction had been received by Line Nersnæs. My calls to speak with Line Nersnæs were not even accepted. Hemming Velde at the Documentation Section had told me it was my right to have another adviser look into my complaint against Torill Sorte. So I sent a fax to Wenche Hovland, the Minister's personal secretary on 22nd March 2006 asking for a replacement investigator and for there to be no secret decision making process. No reply came from the Minister. Instead, after some persistence, I was allowed to speak to Line Nersnæs, who promised to call me back, after I told her that the Minister himself had authorised an investigation and given it a Ministerial Reference Number of 13113.

Eventually, in May, I received two calls in the space of a week to my office in England from Line Nersnæs when she at last acknowledged officially that the Minister had authorised an investigation. She said she would now consult her colleague Håkon Skulstad to see if an investigation would actually be instituted, and call me back in a week or so. I asked Line Nersnæs if she was a lawyer by training. No, she said, she was a sociologist. Line Nersnæs and Håkon Skulstad were not the right people to conduct the investigation after their refusal two years earlier to deal with my complaint to the then Minister of Justice, Odd Einar Dørum, about Torill Sorte.

Advertising my website (www.norway-shockers.com) by blogging on the websites of Drammens Tidende, Aftenposten and Dagbladet, continued with great success. However, by April 2006 these three newspapers had blocked my access to their blogging facility from my lap top computer. Previously, none of them during the daytime had sufficient staff to continuously monitor my blogged comments, which often included the phrase: "Police cheat Torill Sorte. See www.norway-shockers.com." This meant that my comments lasted up to two hours before the newspapers took them off. Time enough for a good few hits, before I repeated the blogging and so on. Once these newspapers had blocked my laptop computer IP address, all I did was go to another computer in my local library, although the best time to blogg was when I'd finished work, as of course, that was the time the Norwegian newspapers' staff had also departed for home. The result was that my rasping comments were left on their sites for the whole evening with the ensuing fruitful number of hits. Weekends were also very rewarding. One Saturday in May got me over 450 hits as no staff were on hand at the newspapers to delete my messages. The Norwegians' frustration was publicised by the Norwegian Broadcasting Corporation (NRK) doing the following interview from their local Buskerud office with Chief Inspector Torill Sorte on the website NRK.no on 13th June 2006. The NRK.no site showed a large photo of Torill Sorte and a reproduction of my blogg phrase 'Police cheat Torill Sorte on…' the words 'www.norway-shockers.com' having been blacked out by the Norwegian Broadcasting Corporation.

NRK Buskerud	13th June 2006
Englishman harasses policewoman	

[Photo of Torill Sorte]

[Picture caption]   Chief Inspector Torill Sorte at Nedre Eiker district police office.
Photo: Maria Kommandantvold/NRK

An Englishman harasses a policewoman via the discussion fora in several Norwegian Internet newspapers.

By Morten W. Røkeberg and Maria Kommandantvold.
Published 13.06.2006 17:23

Chief Inspector Torill Sorte at Nedre Eiker district police office is now lodging an official complaint against an Englishman who has harassed her for several years.

Over the last half a year the man has written defamatory articles in the discussion fora in several Norwegian Internet newspapers, with references to his own homepages.

Sorte hopes that by lodging an official complaint against him, she can have him punished.

"Will not accept being harassed"

"This has, in fact, been going on for several years, while the harassment via Norwegian Internet newspapers has taken place since before the New Year. I do not believe that one should accept being harassed by other people without doing something about it."

"Do you believe it will help by lodging an official complaint against him?"

"I don't think so, but he will have a legal case brought against him at any rate, and
hopefully he will receive a suitable punishment," says Sorte.

Found guilty of persecution

The man has previously been found guilty in this country of having persecuted another woman in the district. This woman got to know him in England in the 1980's. She took out a case against him and he was found guilty. Torill Sorte was the head of the investigation team in that case and she subsequently became a victim of his persecution. Initially through him telephoning to friends and acquaintances and sending letters but, since December last year, also persecution on the Internet.

"He accuses me of having written falsely in the case for which he was sentenced. He maintains that I am dishonest and corrupt," says Sorte.

Yesterday statements from this man were displayed on the Drammens Tidende discussion forum for a couple of hours, with reference to his Internet page on which he harasses several people in Norway. Sorte says that it is difficult to stop him because he constantly finds new ways round things.

Blocked Internet page

"We have blocked the Internet page but he constantly finds new ways of putting it out, so it is difficult to maintain control over such a page."

What can the police do?

"We can initiate an official complaint and take action in relation to it. The problem is that he does not live in this country and that makes things more complicated."

What do you known about him?

"I know a great deal about him. I know that he does not live here in this country and I know him through the investigation into the other matter."

What does this do to you?

"I have had many approaches from people who feel that this is awful, something that I really appreciate. Even though I am in the police, it has an affect on me

596

that there are constantly unjustified assertions about me on the Internet," says Torill Sorte.

***

The claim by NRK.no that I telephoned Torill Sorte's "friends and acquaintances" and sent them letters was completely untrue.

On 14th June 2006 Drammens Tidende did an article on their website as follows:

Drammens Tidende	14th June 2006
Harassment of policewoman	

[Front page / News / Harassment of policewoman]

An Englishman uses Internet newspapers in order to harass a policewoman from Nedre Eiker.

Erik Modal

Chief Inspector Torill Sorte at the Nedre Eiker district police office is now lodging an official complaint against an Englishman who has pestered her for a number of years. One of the Internet newspapers the Englishman often employs is dt.no.

Over the last half a year the man has written defamatory articles in the discussion fora of several Norwegian Internet newspapers, with references to his own homepages, states NRK Buskerud. [Local office of state broadcasting company.]

Sorte hopes that by lodging an official complaint against him, she can have him punished.

Has been going on for several years

This case dates back over several years. The harassment through Norwegian Internet newspapers has taken place over the last half year.

The man has been previously found guilty in this country for having harassed another woman in the district. This woman got to know him in England in the 1980's.

She took action against him, and sentence was passed against him. Torill Sorte headed up the investigation into that case, and it was then that she became a victim of his harassments.

"He accuses me of having written falsely in the case for which he was sentenced. He maintains that I am dishonest and corrupt," says Torill Sorte to NRK.

Difficult to stop

He uses the discussion fora in order to disseminate advertising for the network. One of the newspapers that is frequently used is Drammens Tidende's Internet edition dt.no.

Sorte says that it is difficult to stop him because he keeps on finding new ways round things.

"We have blocked the Internet page, but he keeps on finding new ways of putting it out, so it is difficult to maintain control over such a page," she says to the channel.

The problem with putting a stop to the harassment is that the man does not live in Norway. It makes the task of stopping the man that much more difficult.

Dt.no does something

The Editor, Lars Lager Espevalen at dt.no says that the Englishman has abused the debating function on dt.no and other Internet newspapers for a long time.

"We have initiated measures that have made the man's activities more difficult. This has been of importance for us because named individuals have been defamed. We are constantly working on quality assurance in respect of this part of dt.no. During the course of this summer we have already initiated new measures designed to prevent the misuse of the debating function."

Published: 14.06 09:42. Last amended: 14.06 10:27

***

On the same day, 14th June 2006, I sent a two page fax to the Minister of Justice, Knut Storberget alerting him to these two internet articles and asking him personally to acknowledge receipt of my faxed letter and confirm that something was being done to help me. I also gave a precise recap on my suffering at the hands of his justice system in years gone by.

An interesting article appeared in Aftenposten's English website appearing on 5th May 2006:

Aftenposten	5th May 2006
Drunk Norwegian tourist nearly lynched in Egypt	

Two Norwegians, part of a group of intoxicated Scandinavian tourists on holiday in Egypt, were nearly lynched at the resort town of Hurghada this week, after their antics deeply offended the local population.

The two Norwegians and three Swedes ended up being arrested by local police, who protected them from an angry mob.

The troubled started after the five Scandinavian tourists got drunk, dressed themselves up like Muslim pilgrims and started dancing around the statue of a mermaid located in a town square, and pretending she symbolized Allah.

The Scandinavians apparently were trying to parody Muslim pilgrimages to Mecca. When they started stripping off their clothes, the local Egyptians had had enough and went on the attack.

A local policeman told Swedish newspaper *Aftonbladet* that his colleagues had to step in to protect the tourists from angry local residents. "If they hadn't been arrested, they probably would have been lynched," an Islamic expert told *Aftonbladet.*

The tourists were initially held on charges of indecent conduct, since some of the men exposed themselves. The charges were later raised to blasphemy, which can be punished severely.

Norway's foreign ministry was pulled into the case, but an official at the Norwegian Embassy in Cairo said he hoped to be able to get the Norwegians released and sent home.

He said the embassy had been in contact with Egyptian authorities. An official at the Norwegians' tour company, Apollo, could confirm on Friday that the men, all aged 35-40, had been released and were free to leave Egypt.

Hurghada is a popular tourist destination for Scandinavians, and the local population generally tolerates the partying and scanty clothing so foreign to their own culture.

Aftenposten English Web Desk. Nina Berglund

***

On 9th June 2006 Aftenposten's English website made mention of Trine Skei Grande of the Liberal Party in Norway who had initiated a co-operation programme with the Muslim world in order to clear up "prejudice, misunderstanding or even sheer ignorance," in the aftermath of the Danish and Norwegian cartoon saga on the Prophet Mohammad.

On 26th June 2006 an article appeared on Drammens Tidende's website declaring that the free debate forum on their newspaper will be stopped because of its abuse through racist and harassment bloggs being posted. A picture of Editor Hans Arne Odde was shown beside the article looking concerned and thoughtful. In early July they had a change of heart and decided that free blogging would be allowed, but only from 8 a.m. to 6 p.m.. I had to laugh. Once their staff had gone home no monitoring or editing could be done! Aftenposten had by now also stopped their free blogging facility on the news items of the day. Contributors now had to register and were given a password.

On 26th June 2006, I received a letter from the European Court of Human Rights dated 16th June 2006:

ECHR-LE11.OR(CD1)
SCP/kh

Application no. 33144/04
Delaware v. Norway.

Dear Sir,

I write to inform you that on 2 June 2006 the European Court of Human Rights, sitting as a Committee of three judges (N. Vajić, President, E. Steiner and S.E. Jebens) pursuant to Article 27 of the Convention, decided under Article 28 of the Convention to declare the above application inadmissible because it did not comply with the requirements set out in Articles 34 and 25 of the Convention.

In the light of all the material in its possession, and in so far as the matters complained of were within its competence, the Court found that they did not disclose any appearance of a violation of the rights and freedoms set out in the Convention or its Protocols.

This decision is final and not subject to any appeal to either the Court, including its Grand Chamber, or any other body. You will therefore appreciate that the Registry will be unable to provide any further details about the Committee's deliberations or to conduct further correspondence relating to its decision in this case. You will receive no further documents from the Court concerning this case and, in accordance with the Court's instructions, the file will be destroyed one year after the date of the decision.

The present communication is made pursuant to Rule 53 § 2 of the Rules of Court.

Yours faithfully,
For the Committee

Santiago Quesada
Deputy Section Registrar

Note that no substantive reasons were given for the ECHR rejection of my Application. But the ECHR are under no obligation to give reasons. One of the books I used to help me make my Application to the European Court was Philip Leach's 'Taking a Case to the European Court of Human Rights.' In chapter 2 of the 2001 edition, paragraph 2.5 **Procedure leading to Admissibility** states as follows:

2.5.1   The Judge Rapporteur

Once registered, an application is assigned to one of the Court judges, known as a 'Judge Rapporteur,' whose function is to examine the case and consider its admissibility. The identity of the Judge Rapporteur is never disclosed to the applicant.

The Judge Rapporteur may ask either of the parties to provide further information, documents or other relevant material, within a specified time. The Judge Rapporteur will decide whether the admissibility of an applicant should be considered by a committee of three judges or a chamber of seven judges.

2.5.2   Admissibility decided by a committee

Convention cases which appear on their face not to satisfy the admissibility requirements are referred by the Judge Rapporteur to a committee of three judges which may declare a case inadmissible provided that the committee is unanimous (Article 28; Rule 54). In reaching its decision, the committee is required to take into consideration a report prepared by the Judge Rapporteur which includes brief statements of the facts and of the reasons underlying the proposal to declare the application admissible, or to strike a case out of the Court's list of cases (as to striking out, see below at 3.3). The Judge Rapporteur may take part in the deliberations of the committee.

The decisions of the committees usually take up no more than a page and provide no reasons relating to the particular case other than a formulaic response referring to the admissibility criteria under Article 35. The committees fulfil the role within the Convention system of disposing of the weakest cases. For example, in 1996, the committees (then of the Commission, rather than the Court) dealt with 2,108 of the 2,776 cases declared inadmissible….. The decision of a committee is final. There is no right of appeal against an admissibility decision, whether of a committee or a chamber.

Applicants may be very dissatisfied if their case is declared inadmissible by a committee, particularly because of the lack of specific reasons. The applicant will not be able to obtain further reasons for the committee's decision, but, where cases are likely to be declared manifestly ill-founded, it is the general practice for the Registry lawyer to write to applicants (or their advisers) *prior to* a referral to a committee to set out the reasons why it is likely that the case will be declared inadmissible.

If a committee cannot reach a unanimous decision as to the inadmissibility of an application then it passes to a chamber for consideration.

***

N. Vajić, President, was obviously a Yugoslav name (Croat I guessed) and I immediately went to look at the ECHR website for the President's country of origin. The judge was indeed Croatian, a Mrs. Nina Vajić. Croatia of course, along with Serbia, being responsible in the 1990's for the slaughter of those thousands of Bosnian Muslims. I also wondered who the other judges were. E. Steiner was a Mrs. Elizabeth Steiner of Austria, born on the 21st March 1956. Who was S.E. Jebens? He was in fact Mr. Sverre Erik Jebens, a Norwegian! Appointed to the European Court of Human Rights in November 2004. His c.v. included a stint as Chief Superintendent at Trondheim police from 1980-1983. He was appointed a judge in Norway in 1988.

I had to protest, so I phoned up the ECHR in Strasbourg and they put me through to a lady called Hannah who told me that so long as the Norwegian judge did not sit on my domestic Norwegian court cases, he could consider my Application to the ECHR. And further that only a 2:1

decision was needed to reject my Application. The Convention and Rules of the Court clearly stated that it had to be unanimous, i.e 3:0 to reject an Application, otherwise the case goes to a Chamber of seven judges. I said that there was no way a Norwegian judge should look at an Application against his own country, so Hannah told me to write in and complain. The next day, 27th June 2006, I faxed a two page letter to Santiago Quesada, Deputy Section Registrar as follows:

European Court of Human Rights
Council of Europe
F-67075 Strasbourg Cedex

FAO: Santiago Quesada
Deputy Section Registrar

& by fax on: 00 33 3 88 41 27 30
TWO PAGE FAX AND POST.

Dear Sir,

Re: Application No. 33144/04
Delaware v. Norway

I am in receipt of your letter of the 16th June.

I have spoken to one of your officers today, and she told I could write in with a complaint. A very serious complaint.

The complaint relates firstly to the fact that one of the judges considering this matter was Norwegian, a Mr. Sverre Erik Jebens and in spite of the fact I was told that he did not sit on my case in the domestic courts in Norway, this does not dispel the suspicion of bias, for me, as Norwegians, well known to me as they are, hate their country being criticised in the manner that I have done on my website in particular. I see Mr. Jebens only became a judge at the European Court in November 2004. This meant that whilst in Norway he would have had every chance to become acquainted with the numerous newspaper articles on this case, being twelve in all from 1995 - 2003 on the front pages of local and national newspapers. He would also have known the judges involved in the extensive litigation in Norway that twice went to the Supreme Court in that country. Norwegians moreover, are very nationalistic and stick together more than any other nation in Europe. The fact that their own newspapers write articles expressly associating my religion and myself with sexual perversion and yet the European Court does not feel that there has been any discrimination in this case indicates quite clearly to me that proper consideration for my Application has not been given and that Mr. S. E. Jebens should definitely not be a judge looking at this case. I will not stand for this at all and you almost let this fact of him being Norwegian slip past me.

Furthermore, Nina Vajić is a Croatian judge and after the performance of the Croatians in their hatred and massacre of the Muslims in Bosnia in the early 1990's I certainly do not want a Croatian judge looking into my case, as I am Muslim. Moreover, I have campaigned very strongly for the Muslims of Bosnia and a chapter on Bosnia from my book is on my website www.norway-shockers.com for which website I was given an eight month prison sentence suspended for two years in Norway if I did not remove the site – a site that was put up in response to newspaper articles printed on me in Norway, and to which my application to the Court relates. The site is still online.

This particular case has caused a huge rumpus in Norway, and for the Court - even though it has many cases and is very busy - not to give reasons for its finding that my Application "did not disclose any appearance of a violation of the rights and freedoms set out in the Convention or its Protocols" breaches the very spirit of the Convention in that reasons for refusal must be given. The whole purpose for going to the ECHR in the first place is because the Norwegian courts never gave any reasons for their decisions, and I could not even test the evidence at any stage in the Norwegian justice system.

Therefore, I am going to have to make a further complaint to the highest Judge in the European Court if my application remains denied.

Yours sincerely,

Frederick Delaware

I followed that letter up with another one on 28ᵗʰ June 2006 to Søren C. Prebensen, the Danish gentleman administering my case, as follows:

European Court of Human Rights
Council of Europe
F-67075 Strasbourg Cedex
France

FAO: Søren C. Prebensen

ECHR-LE11.0R (CD1)
SCP/kh

& by fax on: 00 33 3 88 41 27 30
TWO PAGE FAX AND POST.

Dear Mr. Prebensen,

Re: Application No. 33144/04
Frederick Delaware v. Norway

I refer to Santiago Quesada's letter to me dated 16ᵗʰ June 2006, wherein my Application was dismissed with no substantive reasons given.

I spoke to one of your female colleagues yesterday, who after discussing my matter told me I had the right to send a written complaint to your good self, as you are administering the case. I did also send a complaint to Santiago Quesada by fax and post yesterday.

My complaint relates to the fact that I have discovered, by chance, that one of the judges on the Committee considering my Application was a Norwegian – Mr. Sverre Erik Jebens. There is no way whatsoever, that a Norwegian judge should be involved on this case given the huge vitriolic publicity over twelve years that I have received in the national press in Norway from 1995 to 2006, which may have influenced Mr. Jebens. It is quite clear from the documentation in your possession that the Norwegian judiciary, police and press hate me so completely with both the press and police having used abusive psychiatry in their campaign against me. Last December I received the sickest Muslim-hating emails imaginable from Norwegians after Dagbladet newspaper's front page story on me of 21ˢᵗ December 2005 - copies of which emails were sent to you by recorded delivery. Mr. S.E. Jebens was a judge in Norway for the whole period for which my Application specifically relates being 1995 to 2003 and he would have mixed with the many judges who were involved in my domestic litigation and would quite possibly have been friends with them. He could hardly have failed to read the newspapers on my case. So in spite of the fact that he personally did not sit on my domestic Norwegian Court hearings, there is still a suspicion of bias, because Norwegians usually tend to support their country's system and especially a judge who has been brought up in that system. Indeed, Mr. Jebens should have automatically refused to sit on the Committee. That he didn't is an abuse of power. My main complaint against the Norwegian Government is that they are fundamentally dishonest in their dealings with the outsider and no Norwegian ECHR judge seeing this accusation is going to take kindly to my Application. The impression given is that the Norwegian Government has their own man – Mr. Jebens - in place by way of covert arrangement with the ECHR.

You will have seen from my website called www.norway-shockers.com and for which the Norwegians gave me an eight month prison sentence, that the slaughter of Muslims in Bosnia features very heavily, so it is also out of the question that a Croatian judge - Nina Vajić from a country of Muslim haters and killers of Muslims in Bosnia, sit on this case. I am a Muslim, a fact that is central to this case as you must surely realise. No appearance of bias must be given. How odd that it just happened to be the turn of a Norwegian and a Croatian judge on the Committee to look at my particular case?

There has therefore been a major blunder by the ECHR. Further, your female colleague told me yesterday that the ECHR has so many cases and is so busy that it does not necessarily have the time to give reasons for refusing an Application. Having a Norwegian judge in the shape of Mr. Jebens sit on this case - who may be friendly with those judges in the Norwegian courts who decided my case and which judges are furious with me for my website - gives rise to a conflict of interest for Mr. Jebens. I trust you can see this. It is Mr. Jebens who was one of the judges that have found that my Application "did not disclose any appearance of a violation of the rights and freedoms set out in the Convention or its Protocols." How is this, when at no stage in any of the domestic Norwegian court hearings could I test the evidence against me, and I was given an eight month prison sentence for my website in response to the vilest press allegations on which I was suing. So much for my freedom of speech. **Are you telling me that the Norwegian courts are correct to leave the impression in their judgement that I am maybe capable of killing a child in my capacity as a Muslim, without my being able to test the evidence of that accusation which was solely on the uncorroborated word of a Norwegian mental patient?**

As I now distrust your secret adjudication process, I expect new judges to be appointed and full reasons given for any future refusal of my Application. Can I respectfully suggest that the Turkish and Bosnian (Muslim) judges be chosen?

I will also send a copy of this letter to Santiago Quesada.

Yours sincerely,

Frederick Delaware

I had still heard nothing from the Minister of Justice, Knut Storberget in Norway regarding my complaint to him. So, on 12th July 2006 I paid a visit to my local police station – the same one which in October 2001 had asked me to drop in so as to surreptitiously serve me with the Interpol facilitated criminal summons from Norway. I now handed in a written complaint regarding the religious hate crime inspired by Dagbladet's internet article of the 20th December 2005 and newspaper article of the 21st December 2005. I had included copies of those wicked emails send to me immediately after the articles were published. Two weeks later the Hate Crimes Unit of the Essex Police in Harlow telephoned me at work to arrange for me to attend at my local police station to make a full statement, with a view to taking the matter further with Interpol. This I did on Saturday 29th July 2006. I had asked for the Dagbladet internet editor and Dagbladet principal newspaper editor to be arrested when they next entered Britain.

On the 5th September 2006 the Aftenposten English website wrote an article entitled 'Hate crimes set off alarms' wherein Justice Minister Knut Storberget was described as proposing [quoting Dagbladet]: 'a so-called "hate paragraph" in Norway's criminal code that would allow judges to hand out tougher punishment to people convicted of crimes that are grounded in others religious beliefs, skin color, nationality or ethic origins…….. "It's extremely important that we fight this kind of crime," said Storberget to Aftenposten.

603

The European Court of Human Rights wrote back to me on 8th September 2006:

FIRST SECTION

8 September 2006

Re: Application No. 33144/04
Frederick Delaware v. Norway

Dear Sir,

The President of the Court has asked me to acknowledge receipt of your letters of 28th June 2006, from which it appears that you are calling in question the impartiality of two of the judges.

I can assure you that your doubts are unfounded. The Court is an independent and impartial judicial institution. Its judges sit in their individual capacity only (see Article 21 § 2 of the Convention), not as a representative of any State or group of persons. Safeguards to ensure their independence and impartiality are contained both in the Convention and the Rules of Court (see Article 21 of the Convention and Rule 28 of the Rules of Court).

Lastly, you will appreciate that the Court and its Registry are facing a very heavy workload. As a result, I am not in a position to continue the correspondence with you on this matter.

Yours faithfully,
Santiago Quesada
Deputy Section Registrar

I set out Rule 28 of the European Court of Human Rights Rules of Court and Article 21 of the European Convention on Human Rights as follows:

Rule 28
(INABILITY TO SIT, WITHDRAWAL OR EXEMPTION)

1. Any judge who is prevented from taking part in sittings for which he has been convoked shall, as soon as possible, give notice to the President of the Chamber.

2. A judge may not take part in the consideration of any case in which he or she has a personal interest or has previously acted either as the Agent, advocate or adviser of a party or of a person having an interest in the case, or as a member of a tribunal or commisssion of enquiry, or in any other capacity.

3. If a judge withdraws for one of the said reasons, or for some special reason, he or she shall inform the President of the Chamber, who shall exempt the judge from sitting.

4. If the President of the Chamber considers that a reason exists for a judge to withdraw, he or she shall consult with the judge concerned; in the event of disagreement, the Chamber shall decide.

***

Article 21 of the European Convention on Human Rights – Criteria for office

1. The judges shall be of high moral character and must either possess the qualifications required for appointment to high judicial office or be jurisconsults of recognised competence.

2. The judges shall sit on the Court in their individual capacity.

3. During their term of office the judges shall not engage in any activity which is incompatible with their independence, impartiality or with the demands of a full-time office; all questions arising from the application of this paragraph shall be decided by the Court.

***

In spite of Santiago Quesada's rebuff I replied to the Court on 18th September 2006 after telephoning them to express my dismay:

European Court of Human Rights
Council of Europe
F-67075 Strasbourg Cedex, France

ECHR-LE11.OR (CD1)
SCP/kh
& by fax on: 00 33 3 88 41 27 30
TWO PAGE FAX AND POST.

Dear Sirs,

Re: Application No. 33144/04
Frederick Delaware v. Norway

I refer to Santiago Quesada's letter of 8th September 2006.

I will not be fobbed off with Mr. Quesada's nonsense. He insults my intelligence as a lawyer. My doubts are definitely not unfounded.

The Court do not seem to be aware of just how much the judiciary in Norway are enraged at my critical website called www.norway-shockers.com which plays a central part in my Application to the Court. The Norwegians will put me in prison if I ever go back there, and coupled with the fact that their newspapers have basically committed hate crimes, then I have every reason to question the Court's assessment of the case: that my application fails ECHR criteria for acceptance. Mr. Quesada has admitted that the Court is facing a very heavy workload, so I suspect the Court has not even had the time to consider my case properly.

In spite of Article 21 of the Convention and Rule 28 of the Rules of Court, there is a strong suspicion of bias in the unique circumstances of my case which rules Mr. Jebens out from sitting on this case.

It is a shame the Court won't give reasons for refusing my Application. The Norwegians did the same all along.

The theory of judicial impartiality is one thing. In practice I have seen the way the Norwegian judiciary and executive - from a small xenophobic country - stick together against the outsider. Under Rule 28.3 Mr. Jebens had a "special reason" to withdraw from the case. He should have known from the details of my Application that it was highly inappropriate for a Norwegian judge to sit on the case. Under Rule 28.4 the President of the Chamber should have deemed this reason enough to consult Mr. Jebens who should have withdrawn from the case. But the President can only go on the information he receives from his case advisors. Again, as the Court is so short of time to devote to a proper consideration of Applications the President should now reconsider and reconvene another committee.

It is an abuse of power and a direct breach of the rules of natural justice that a Norwegian judge should sit on a case involving an Application against his own country, particularly where the judge concerned - Mr. Sverre Erik Jebens - would have known the judges involved in his home country as he was only appointed to the ECHR in November 2004.

Mr. Sverre Erik Jebens must be subjectively **and** objectively impartial. Mr. Jebens is neither. He would have seen on my Application that I am severely critical of his former colleagues and the very legal system he grew up with and used as a lawyer. It was an attack against everything Norwegian, due to the hate crimes that their newspapers permitted and establishment covered up for. These hate crimes were anti Muslim and this leads me on to the complaint I made about the Croatian judge who also sat on the case. She should not have been sitting in view of the nature of her country's involvement in the killing of Muslims in Bosnia.

Please consider the above and revert to me.

Yours faithfully,
Frederick Delaware

I replied also and for the record directly to Santiago Quesada by fax and post on 3rd October 2006:

Dear Mr. Quesada

Re: Application No. 33144/04. Delaware v. Norway

Thank you for your letter of the 8th September.

It is not right that you brush me aside with your rather derisive comment that because you are facing a "very heavy workload" you do not want to continue corresponding with me on this matter. I have had a very heavy workload on this case for the last twelve years, with no respite whatsoever. **You treat me like a nuisance, when the fact is you are not familiar with my case and you refuse to recognise the obvious injustice that has been inflicted on me by the Court.**

You are completely wrong when you say my doubts about the impartiality of two of the judges are unfounded. I refer in particular to Sverre Erik Jebens of Norway. The whole of the judiciary in Norway have known for several years about my website, www.norway-shockers.com which has been online since the year 2000. This would have included Mr. Jebens. I believe it is the first time in Norwegian legal history that a prison sentence has been handed out, in this case to me, for a website critical of Norwegian legal practice and the practice of its newspapers and police. This website of mine is prima facie allowed under Article 10 of the European Convention of Human Rights, but not allowed, obviously, in Norway. The prison sentence was given to me in October 2003, the very next day after I finished my Court of Appeal libel case on the subject of my Application to the European Court of Human Rights. So much for Norway's requirement of giving me a fair trial. Mr. Jebens was working as a judge in Norway during the entire period of my litigation in Norway. Moreover, during Mr. Jebens time in Norway there were several front page national newspaper articles as well as local newspaper articles on me written in the most xenophobic and hateful terms. Sverre Erik Jebens would hardly have failed to read some of these newspapers. He would undoubtedly have been discussing the matter with his fellow members of the Norwegian judiciary, as they all knew he was Strasbourg bound. My website contains a lot of information that is highly embarrassing to the Norwegian judiciary, press and government and includes several British newspaper articles which are condemnatory of Norwegian practices.

It is therefore only fair to say that, human nature being what it is, Sverre Erik Jebens would most certainly have been offended by my website and affected by the numerous newspaper articles in his country's press on me. A total lack of co-operation from the Norwegian judiciary during my litigation in Norway indicates a high degree of animosity towards me. I doubt Sverre Erik Jebens would have acted any differently from his colleagues had he himself taken part in the litigation on my cases in Norway. He would no doubt have been very supportive of the procedural aspects of the Norwegian legal system.

It is therefore, I repeat, totally wrong of you to claim that Sverre Erik Jebens is completely independent and impartial in my particular case. I can just imagine the pressure he was under not to accept my Application, given the condemnation he would have got on his eventual return to work in his native Norway, if he had accepted my Application. I am probably Norway's most wanted man.

I am fully aware of Article 21 of the Convention and Rule 28 of the Rules of Court. Under Rule 28.3 Mr. Jebens did have a "special reason" to withdraw from the case. The vast amount of publicity over the best part of a decade that my case generated in Norway and Mr. Jebens undoubted knowledge of my website certainly ruled him out from sitting on this case. Under Rule 28.4 the President of the Chamber should have deemed this reason enough to consult Mr. Jebens who should have withdrawn from the case. It was for Mr. Jebens to volunteer to stand down from my case. Information that he had in his mind on this case could not have been known to the Court in general. There is a strong suspicion of bias therefore. Sverre Erik Jebens must be **subjectively and objectively impartial.** He was neither. A website that is severely critical of his former colleagues and the very legal system he grew up with and used as a lawyer could not enable Mr. Jebens to be impartial.

Please therefore reconsider the matter and revert to me.

Yours sincerely,

Frederick Delaware

I had tried four or five times without success to speak to Mr. Terje Pedersen, State Secretary to Minister Knut Storberget. On 27th September 2006 Mr. Pedersen actually telephoned me at my office to inform me that he knew nothing at all about my December 2005 complaint under the ministerial reference number 13113. And that Minister Knut Storberget would not have "personally" given the case this number, but only a member of his staff. Mr. Pedersen quoted from the letter that his Deputy Director General, Magnar Aukrust and Senior Advisor, Line Nersnæs wrote to me on 19th September 2005, finishing with: "The Ministry of Justice has acknowledged your opinion on the matter. No further enquires will be answered in the matter." This, in response to my complaint to the previous Minister of Justice over the Aftenposten article on me of 15th April 2002. I queried how he could know nothing of my complaint when his ministry had long been in receipt of several letters from me relating to the more recent matter of the Dagbladet articles of December 2005. I told him Line Nersnæs had called me twice many weeks ago to acknowledge that ministerial reference number 13113 had been given to my complaint and that she would look into it and call me back – but that she had since stayed silent. Terje Pedersen said he would now speak to Line Nersnæs and get back to me. On 17th October 2006 I called him for an update, to be given a message by his assistant that he, Terje Pedersen, was "waiting to hear" from me! I faxed him back the same day to ask him "what exactly" he was waiting to hear from me on and reminded him that his documentation centre had told me on 16th October 2006 that they had in their possession all my correspondence on this matter, being seven letters dating from 20th December 2005 to 20th July 2006, "Yet still no reply from your department," I wrote. I asked him to action my complaint.

On 20th October 2006 and continuing on into November my website tracking monitor revealed that 'Norwegian central governmental offices' were looking at my website. Indeed on Monday 6th November 2006 at 1.10 p.m., 1 hour 29 minutes and 39 seconds was spent by them looking at my website. My blogging efforts on the public commentary sections on the Dagblaget and Aftenposten websites had resumed from my laptop computer as I had obtained a free ISP connection whereby every time Aftenposten blocked my ISP address I just disconnected, redailed and got a new ISP address and so on and so forth. Aftenposten had resumed their free blogging facility. My tracking monitor showed I was getting hundreds of hits a week from Norway. But by the third week of November 2006 Aftenposten managed to block completely any comments I made inspite of my free ISP connection. So I just continued with Dagbladet.

I was getting next to no emails from Norway now but one that I did get dated 8th November 2006 said:

- By reading your homepage, I know the true story about muslims.

  What the heck! You are not humans, you are pigs all of you! Because your website is so atrocious I don't have words to describe what I feel.

  But you make me really believe all muslims are the son of the devil!!

I had also reported the whole Norway saga to my Member of Parliament in late October 2006.

After my July 2006 complaint to the British police about those vicious emails in December 2005, Interpol were now investigating the matter.

On the 30th November 2006 I faxed for the attention of Judge Sverre Erik Jebens at the ECHR, a copy of my letter of the 3rd October 2006 to Santiago Quesada, asking Mr Jebens for his comments.

I telephoned the ECHR at 1.30 p.m. on the 4th December 2006 and was put through to the usual lady, Hannah, who confirmed they had received my "recent faxes" but all she could tell me was that if I did not hear from them soon I could write in again. And that it was against policy for me to speak to Santiago Quesada as my Application had been rejected.

On the 9th January 2007 Professor Robin White, Head of the Department of Law at the University of Leicester, responded to an email enquiry of mine by stating that there is no European Court of Human Rights requirement for a national judge to sit on a Committee, but that in his opinion, "it follows that there is nothing inappropriate about a 'national judge' sitting on a Committee considering admissability….Such evidence as there is suggests that national judges at the Strasbourg Court do not make decisions on a purely partisan basis. To do so would be a breach of their duty of impartialty under Article 21."

It was about time I challenged Torill Sorte over her shameful comments in the press in the winter of 2005/6. I had held off doing this as I had been hoping that the Minister of Justice in Norway would investigate her, but that hope was evidently a false one.

I had looked up on the internet the telephone number for the Oslo Police Headquarters and eventually on Monday 12th February 2007 I phoned them.

A policewoman answered:

F.   *Hi there, good afternoon. I am ringing from England. I am a lawyer and I just wanted to find out which police station Torill Sorte, a lady called Torill Sorte …..*

Policewoman: *Yeah…..*

F.   *… is working at …*

Policewoman: *She is working here at the office in the Union.*

F.   *In the Union?*

Policewoman: *Yeah… she is a police officer but she has another job – temporary.*

F.   *So… she's still a policewoman is she?*

Policewoman: *Yeah she is.*

F.   *She hasn't been sacked?*

Policewoman:	*No, ... I don't know what the exact word for it .... She has .... What do you call it in English? Temporary as another ... she's chosen at work here in Union.*
F.	*What, the police Union?*
Policewoman:	*Yeah. Do you want to talk to her?*
F.	*I do, yes.*
Policewoman:	*Yeah, one moment.*

And she puts me through. But there was no answer.

Policewoman:	*Er.. she is not at the office right now. Do you want to have her cell line number?*
F.	*Yeah, that's fine thank you.*
Policewoman:	*Yeah. It's 00 47 for Norway. And it's 45 29 77 72.*
F.	*So, I mean, do you think she will be in later today?*
Policewoman:	*Yeah, probably she will.*
F.	*OK, so I can phone you maybe a little later?*
Policewoman:	*Yeah.*
F.	*And, OK that's good.*
Policewoman:	*Yep.*
F.	*Thank you very much.*
Policewoman:	*You're welcome.*
F.	*Bye bye.*
Policewoman:	*Bye.*

About an hour later I called again, was put through, but no answer came from Torill Sorte's phone.

I tried again three days later on Thursday 15th February 2007.

A policewoman answered:

F.	*Hi good afternoon, um, I am ringing from England trying to speak to Torill Sorte, please.*
Policewoman:	*Er, yeah, she's not here.*
F.	*Where is she today then, do you know?*
Policewoman:	*No, I don't know.*
F.	*When will she be back?*
Policewoman:	*I really do not know, I am sorry. I've ..... I don't really want to give you any information about her.*
F.	*OK. Well, I guess you know who is speaking. It's Mr Delaware the lawyer from England and I have got a little bit to speak to her about these newspaper*

comments she made last year. So it is about time I spoke to her. So I think I better speak to her commanding officer please.

Policewoman: *Er..... there is no commanding officer here.*

F. *Well, who is in charge, who's in charge ....*

Policewoman: *I am sorry, just hold on a minute....*

She put me on hold and then returned to speak to me:

Policewoman: *Hello?*

F. *Yes hi there.*

Policewoman: *Yes I will put you through to my boss. One moment.*

F. *OK.*

A policeman answered:

F. *Yes, hi, good afternoon. My name is Mr Delaware, a lawyer here in England. Obviously well known to you in relation to the police officer Torill Sorte and the other matters that you have been doing to me over the years. Now I understand she is working at your police station.*

Policeman: *Yeah .... er, what did you call the girl, you said?*

F. *Torill Sorte.*

Policeman: *She is not working with us.*

F. *Well I was told that she was a couple* ["of days ago," I was about to add.]

Policeman: *She moved.*

F. *Yeah? And where to?*

Policeman: *Er, it's a small police station on the west coast that's called Lensmanskontroller Igulen.*

F. *Oh, have you got the phone number?*

Policeman: *No. Could you find it on the internet?*

F. *So.... How do you spell the town that she's in?*

Policeman: *Excuse me, I have a higher police officer coming in so I have to speak to him, alright.*

And he put the phone down.

So I phoned the Police Headquarters again. The same policewoman as before answered:

F. *Hi, good afternoon. Well it's Mr Delaware here again. You put me through a minute ago but your chap put the phone down on me.*

Policewoman: *OK.*

F. *So, I have to speak to someone who has got the good manners to have a conversation, because I have got something else to have a little chat about. About why you are not co-operating with Interpol over the newspaper article that Torill Sorte 'wrote' last year.*

610

Policewoman:	*I really don't have anything to say about that and I won't put you through to her so, er, stop, just stop calling her.*
F.	*Well, I er ....*
Policewoman:	*I don't have anything else to say.*
F.	*Well I want to speak to .....*
Policewoman:	*Goodbye Mr .....*
F.	*..... I want to speak to her superior officer.*

But she had already put the phone down on me.

I then phoned Torill Sorte's old police station in Nedre Eiker near Drammen and they confirmed that she had left for Oslo Police headquarters two years earlier.

On 1st March 2007 I finally succeeded in speaking with Mr. Terje Pedersen at the Ministry of Justice. After listening to me reminding him about the nature of my 14 month old complaint, he yet again referred to his ministry's earlier letter of 19th September 2005 wherein he said his ministry had acknowledged my opinion and that no further enquiries would be answered. I retorted by yet again telling him that my December 2005 complaint was a "subsequent complaint.....a fresh complaint on completely new grounds" that he was supposed to deal with. He responded by saying that this was a matter that would not be handled by the Ministry of Justice in Norway. That the complaint should be handled by the police. I said that the matter had been given a ministerial reference number and that his ministry should have replied to me and not just ignore me. He said I had to go to the prosecuting authority, the Riksadvokat, who was of course the Attorney General Tor-Aksel Busch, who I had tried to subpoena to court in October 2003, without success. And Terje Pedersen continued that the ministry could not help me and it was no use me making phone calls to the ministry. "At least you could have told me that a year ago," I protested. To which he replied, "But...I tell you now." I voiced my doubts that Tor-Aksel Busch would want to deal with me but Terje Pedersen said I had no alternative as there was no higher authority than Mr. Busch whose duties lay outside the jurisdiction of the Minister of Justice. That Tor-Aksel Busch was responsible only to parliament.

How difficult could it have been for the Ministry of Justice long ago just to have forwarded my papers to Tor-Aksel Busch? Once again it was up to me to progress the matter and on the 2nd March 2007 I sent a 28 page fax to Mr. Busch, being all the necessary papers including those horrendous emails, and then again by recorded delivery post.

I was still trying to get some sense out of the European Court of Human Rights over the appointment of Judge Sverre Erik Jebens to the Committee of three judges. On 1st March 2007 I telephoned the Court to be put through, as usual, to Hannah. I told her I wanted to speak to Søren C. Prebensen who was the legal secretary (a lawyer) appointed to handle my postal application. He had not replied personally to my letter of complaint to him of 28th June 2006 (printed above) leaving it to Santiago Quesada to give his evasive response. Hannah told me that Søren C. Prebensen was on vacation that week, so I could call back on his return next week but to leave it till Tuesday or Wednesday as there was, "always a lot to do" on a Monday, and "We'll see what we can do." I phoned back in fact on 14th March and specifically asked for Søren C. Prebensen. Instead I was put through to a Ms. Nascović who, when I enquired, told me she was from the "former Yugoslavia." She told me I would not be allowed to speak to Søren C. Prebensen and that I had already been told that the Court would not be corresponding with me any further. Ms. Nascović also said that it was standard procedure for a judge from the home country to look at the national court judgements and other paperwork to check that it was all correct and in order. I said I could understand that, but I enquired whether it was also the case that this same judge sat on the Committee of three judges voting on an application? She did not know and could not point me to a particular Court Rule governing this procedural aspect. I had hoped to put to Søren C. Prebensen my concerns, including that maybe my application was not considered fully enough owing to the vast number of applications the Court had to deal with; 83,000 or so applications were pending in 2007. The rejection rate was presently 95%. Indeed

Søren C. Prebensen himself made an error when he wrote to me on 24th November 2004 in reply to his receipt of my Application Form. He said in his second and third paragraphs:

> 'I note that despite the indications in our previous letter **you have not submitted all the information** required by Rule 47 subsection 1 and 2 of the Rules of the Court. In particular you have not provided a succinct statement on your compliance with the admissibility requirement of exhaustion of domestic remedies and the six-month rule laid down by Article 35 Section 1 of the Convention.
>
> That being so, **the case can not be examined by the Court.** You are therefore requested to supplement the application by submitting the missing information. I should again emphasise that you must **reply to this letter as soon as possible; if you do not do so within one year of it being sent to you, the file on your case will be destroyed.**'

I had written back to say that I had in fact submitted all the required information, and referred Søren C. Prebensen to the exact paragraph in my earlier letter stating this. There was no missing information. Søren C. Prebensen just hadn't read my letter properly, and he now stood corrected. So there, the Court do make mistakes! I suspected that the reading of my detailed Application by the unnamed Judge Rapporteur (a Court judge who looks at the case and prepares a report for the three judges on the Committee) had been passed over with insufficient care. I had always thought it would be a formality that the Court would accept my Application.

I phoned again the next day - 15th March 2007 - in a final attempt to speak to Søren C. Prebensen. I was again put through to Ms. Nascović who this time told me, "In Norwegian cases we have a Norwegian judge in a Committee of three; in Swedish cases we have a Swedish judge; in Polish cases a Polish judge and so on ....." "So it is standard procedure?" I asked. "Yes, definitely," replied Ms. Nascović. So she was more clued up this time round. Why had Santiago Quesada not told me this when he wrote to me in response to my complaints? Previously, Hannah had told me "it just happened" to be the turn of Judge Sverre Erik Jebens to look at my Application. Hence my confusion. Ms. Nascović confirmed they never put phone calls through to the lawyers after applications had been rejected, so I would not be able to speak to Søren C. Prebensen. I had now done all I could with the Court and would not now phone them again.

I noticed at the beginning of March that Aftenposten.no had provided a new format for readers to add their blogg comments to their news articles. Once again, I found myself being able to advertise my website address without my comments being blocked. Very quickly the hits on my website shot up and the rate only slowed down when my comments were removed by Aftenposten's staff. By the middle of March Aftenposten were monitoring their website blogging facility all day long so the hits were fewer. By the end of that month I was blocked again completely.

On Sunday 18th March 2007, I phoned Torill Sorte on her mobile phone, and it went like this:

Sorte:	*Torill.*
F.	*Yes, hi Torill it's Frederick Delaware here.*
Sorte:	*I don't want ...... hello?*
F.	*Yes... it's about time I had a word with you about, your, er, newspaper comments isn't it?*
Sorte:	*I don't think I have something to talk to you about.*
F.	*Well, I certainly have something to talk to you about. Just because ....*
Sorte:	*Yes, then you have to write to me. I don't talk to you at the phone.*
F.	*Write to you?*
Sorte:	*You have to write a letter to me.*
F.	*You're not going to reply. You ... you ...*
Sorte:	*Yes.... Send it to Nedre Eiker Lensmannkontrol and I will get it there...I do not want to talk to you.*

F.	*Well that's not surprising is it, because writing* [about me that I am allegedly] *"obviously mentally disturbed" in the newspapers because you've lied, er, about all this mental hospital rubbish....*
Sorte:	*Sorry but I don't want to talk to you. If you want to talk to me you have to read* [she meant "write"] *because I don't not want to talk to you.*
F.	*Well you didn't even talk to me in court. You lied in court again, you know...*
Sorte:	*Bye bye.*

And she put the phone down. So I called her straight back. The phone rang three times.

Sorte:	*Hello.*
F.	*Yeah, so why don't you want to talk over the phone?*
Sorte:	*Well I ....*
F.	*Got something to hide have you?*
Sorte:	*If you call me one more time, I will go to the police OK?*
F.	*Oh big deal. And what the hell are they going to do?*
Sorte:	*Bye bye....*
F.	*..... Nothing.*

Again she had put the phone down. So I called straight back, only to get Torill Sorte's voicemail message (in Norwegian of course). I did not leave a message. I tried calling her again on the evening of the 20th March 2007 but once more her voicemail facility came on.

On the 21st March 2007, I telephoned Anne Grøstad, the Chief Public Prosecutor at the Attorney General's Office. She had been given conduct of my Dagbladet and Torill Sorte complaints, but told me she had not yet had the time to consider the papers, although she had read through them including those emails. I told her, truthfully, that the British police had that day told me that Interpol in England had two days earlier contacted Interpol in Norway over the hate crime matter but that Interpol in Norway still had no response to give. I told her that this time she had a second chance to properly prosecute Torill Sorte. She acknowledged that I was "unhappy" at her decision in 2003 not to prosecute Torill Sorte to which I said nothing, suppressing my desire to remind her of my opinion on that score. I could not upset her too much, now that I needed her co-operation again. She said she would do her best to investigate the matter as soon as possible and would have to send the papers also to the Police Investigation department regarding my complaint against Torill Sorte. So I left it at that and said goodbye. On 27th March 2007 I received a letter of notification from the Spesialenheten for Politisaker (Norwegian Bureau for the Investigation of Police Affairs) confirming receipt of the papers from Anne Grøstad regarding my complaint against Torill Sorte. They would be in touch again in due course they said.

I had also incurred the wrath of my professional body in England, being the Law Society, on a completely different matter. For two years I had run a website called legaljackass.co.uk which featured my various negative experiences with the numerous law firms I had worked for as a locum solicitor. I also mentioned on the site that low to mid-level property fraud is not prosecuted by the authorities due to lack of resources. I spoke in general of my experiences but made specific mention of one law firm in particular, who I had taken to court. The senior partner of that law firm had taken severe exception to what I had written about him and his firm on the internet and complained to the principal I was working for at the time, being an ex-policeman turned solicitor. He told me that the angry solicitor, Tom Harrison, had told him about my website and also tried to persuade him that I should be sacked as I was "a risk." My boss had looked at my website and saw nothing wrong with it, and supported me fully. I then complained to the Law Society that it was quite wrong for Tom Harrison to try and get me sacked just because I wrote about the failings in his law firm. The Law Society then decided that ringing up my present employer was not unprofessional conduct on the part of Tom Harrison who, they said, was "not seeking to take unfair advantage" of me. I replied to the Law Society saying what else could it be but Tom Harrison trying to "take unfair advantage of me by trying to persuade my employer" (according to my employer) to have me sacked! Instead the Law Society charged me with bringing the legal profession in England and Wales into disrepute for promoting my website. I had, by the way, very heavily criticised the Law Society on my website. I defended myself in copious correspondence with the Law Society who then put the matter to an independent Adjudicator to rule on whether my website breached the rules of professional conduct for solicitors. On the 21st December 2006 the Adjudicator decided in my favour: I had not brought the legal profession into disrepute and, moreover, I was told that my highlighting bullying in the workplace was worthy of publication on my website. A delightful slap in the face for the Law Society. And a decision that probably saved my career from being irreparably damaged, as the Law Society had called for me to receive a "severe reprimand" as well as have restrictions placed on my practicising certificate. I then got in touch with the Law Society Gazette (circulation: 113,000 copies each week) who on the 22nd March 2007 published the following article, written by Rupert White:

Web win for bloggers

Writing derogatory and potentially libellous comments about law firms does not necessarily count as bringing the profession into disrepute, according to a recent Solicitors Regulation Authority (SRA) adjudication seen by the *Gazette*.

The SRA has ruled that a website set up by a London locum solicitor detailing strident complaints against a law firm he worked for 'does not amount to a breach' of rules governing conduct. The ruling could mean less worry for lawyers who want to use the web to speak out about conduct and practice.

For legal reasons the *Gazette* cannot mention any of the firms involved or the website's name, but the website details a London locum property lawyer's allegations against a law firm which he alleges inaccurately labelled his work as sub-standard as a reason to remove him after he complained about bad practice.

The adjudicator warned the website owner about potentially libelling parties online, but ruled that 'his decision to draw attention to the difficulties often faced by locums' by publishing his highly disparaging views online did not amount to professional misconduct.

The adjudicator said: 'Bullying in the workplace, unfair practices and exploitation of employees are issues which are worthy of serious debate; what [the website owner] published was a contribution to that debate.'

The website owner told the *Gazette*: 'It took the common sense of this particular adjudicator to establish the right for a lawyer to publicly express criticism over his subjection to bullying in his role as a locum property solicitor.'

But he may still be sued for libel, as the adjudication does nothing to prove or disprove his comments said Helen Morris at media firm David Price Solicitors & Advocates.

'An adjudication by a professional body will probably be based on very specific criteria to that organisation,' said Ms Morris. 'Accordingly there is no guarantee that, if you're off the hook with the regulator, you can sufficiently establish the often complex and technical grounds required to defend yourself against a libel action.'

Rupert White.

***

Initially the Gazette said they were going to print the address of my website. Rupert White later told me they were advised they may face libel writs themselves on account of pointing the way to my commentary.

Chapter 39

On 12th May 2007 I spoke with Morten Øverbye of Dagbladet. This was a conversation that was long overdue.

I called him on his mobile phone, having been given his number by the Dagbladet newspaper office in Oslo:

M.O.   *Hello.*
F.   *Yes, hi there, is that Morten Øverbye?*
M.O.   *Hello?*
F.   *Yes, hi there, is that Morten Øverbye?*
M.O.   *Yeah.*
F.   *It is. Yes. Hi there. I thought it was about time I gave you a ring. My name's Frederick Delaware. You're the chap that did a couple of filthy articles on me, er, in December 2005.*
M.O.   *Oh you're the crazy Briton?*
F.   *Well, you're the inbred Norwegian, yeah?*
M.O.   (laughing derisively).

So I retorted:

F.   *You're the one whose mother probably put* [you] *in a mental hospital.*
M.O.   *You're the person who has been, er, following Heidi Schøne for the last 15 years....*
F.   *I haven't been following her at all...*
M.O.   *.....setting up entire websites about her.*
F.   *Well no it's.....*
M.O.   *It looks like you are obsessed with her.*
F.   *You're the one who is sick in the head if anyone.... An inbred Norwegian. But let me ask you this. Are you going to have the courage to talk to me or are you er...*
M.O.   *Yes of course.*
F.   *You are. OK. So where's this information you got, er, about me being in a mental hospital for two years? It's absolute rubbish. I've never been in a mental hospital for two minutes, but who gave you that information?*
M.O.   *Maybe you are not even aware that you have been in a mental hospital, I'm not sure. It is in the Norwegian court documents.*
F.   *Well, no it isn't because the Norwegian court documents have a letter from my family doctor saying that I have never been in a mental hospital. Now you are a fucking liar. You are a real piece of shit, OK and you've lied without checking it....You're a journalist with no principles and you don't check your facts.*
M.O.   *Your language in this, er, conversation, sir and your entire website.....*
F.   *Don't give me........Don't give me....*
M.O.   *....and your entire website....your entire website dedicated to Heidi Schøne and Norwegians and Norway is enough for me to set a diagnosis of you sir.*
F.   *You've had your fucking chance you arsehole.... You've printed stuff....You didn't write* [to me], *you didn't ring me, you didn't give me a chance. You're supposed to follow your newspaper rules* [self regulatory rules] *of phoning up a person you do a story on...*
M.O.   *I tried contacting you. You're not in the phonebook.*
F.   *You're a lying bastard. You could have emailed me.* [My website had the email address.] *You could have emailed me but the thing is....*
M.O.   *You even set up the website so I couldn't even contact you through the website...*
F.   *Yes you can. It's the email address that's been on* [the website for seven years]*....*
M.O.   *It's not your telephone number that's in the 'Who is' contact information for the website.*
F.   *No, no but you can email me. Everyone has got my phone number. But the point is this. You write that "a small child" I thought "should die" and that this is "a threat that in any other country - in normal countries" I would be "prosecuted for," you son of a bitch. You've put that I've threatened to kill that boy* [Heidi's first son] *in other words. You've put* [inferred] *in your 21st December article that I've threatened to kill that boy, that's the meaning, that's the inference from you printing that Heidi Schøne....*

M.O.	*Could you repeat the sentence... I can't remember me writing that you were....*
F.	*You have put in that.... It is quoted in there that I thought a small child should die, OK. Heidi's.....*
M.O.	*What's the exact wording of my article?*
F.	*Well the exact wording* [and I was going on memory as I did not have the article to hand] *is that "a small child he thought should die" and that Heidi Schøne has put "in a normal country he would be prosecuted severely." That's the wording that is in your article. Now you've informed* [the Norwegian public] *that I'm a fucking potential child killer and for this I'll never forgive you. And you are a sick son of a bitch. And you've lied......*
M.O.	*You started this conversation asking if I wanted to speak to you. I would really, I would love to meet you.*
F.	*You started that bullshit in the newspaper.*
M.O.	*I would love to meet you with a photographer. Is that possible?*
F.	*Well, I've got your..... your photograph* [his photograph was on the internet and I had transferred it to my website adding suitable commentary]....
M.O.	*Yeah please do..... in your context......on your website.....you are welcome to write anything you want about me and put any photograph.*
F.	*Well it's up there* [on my website] *your photograph.*
M.O.	*Ha, ha, no one takes your website seriously sir.*
F.	*Oh don't they? A lot of people do.*
M.O.	*They are lunatics, OK.*
F.	*Your two articles....*
M.O.	*I'd really like to meet you with a photographer....*
F.	*Where, in England?*
M.O.	*In England, Norway, wherever. You could tell your entire story.*
F.	*I'm not coming to Norway, but....*
M.O.	*Why not?*
F.	*You can certainly come to England.*
M.O.	*We could pay* [for] *your plane tickets.*
F.	*Oh really? Yeah, you know damn well I'm going to be put in prison, OK. You come to England and it would be good to meet you.*
M.O.	*I won't be put in prison in England so that might be the fairer way around it.*
F.	*I think you might well be* [put in prison]*....Because you've incited religious hatred. You've put "half-Arab Muslim," and you don't even know where the European Court of Human Rights is. You put "The Hague."* [In his 20th December 2005 internet article.]
M.O.	*You're not a Muslim?*
F.	*I am a Muslim, yeah, but you don't..... you associate "half-Arab Muslim" with 'sexual madman' and 'potential child killer.'*
M.O.	*I associate them with you sir.*
F.	*......and "mental hospital," so you....*
M.O.	*I put them in the context with you sir.*
F.	*No, no, no.*
M.O.	*If you feel that's embarrassing for other Muslims I understand your view. I share your view on that.*
F.	*You're just a sick son of a bitch. I don't know how you got a job....you are inbred. You are a typical Norwegian arsehole who writes things with pure hatred and bigotry. But thanks to you I'd got 30,000 hits in the last year on that website. And a lot of people......*
M.O.	*If you let me report from this conversation I will give you even more hits.*
F.	*You.......you give as many hits as you want. It's a pleasure to get hits. But the thing is you are a bigot and a cheat and er....*
M.O.	*Coming from you... I take that as a compliment.*
F.	*No journalist in England would ever print the rubbish you've done because you're a second rate nobody, but....*
M.O.	*Coming from you that's a compliment, sir.*
F.	*Oh is it? Yeah. That's because you are so full of shit you can't, you can't speak a proper conversation. You never check your facts. So "two years in a mental hospital." Who told you that?*
M.O.	*It's in the Norwegian Court documents, I already told you.*

F.	*It's not. You're a liar.*
M.O.	*No, no. I already told you that.*
F.	*You say it's definitely in the Norwegian* [court documents] *that I've been two years in a mental hospital, is it?*
M.O.	*It's in the Norwegian Court documents.*
F.	*It isn't.*
M.O.	*How come you cannot travel to Norway, sir?*
F.	*Huh?*
M.O.	*How come you cannot travel to Norway, sir?*
F.	*Well, because of the website. I think it was eight months prison suspended for two years wasn't it?*
M.O.	*Yeah.*
F.	*That's right, that's why I'm not going back to Norway. But the thing is this, you are a liar. Because nowhere in the newspaper, alright, sorry – in the court documents – does it say "two years in a mental hospital." They* [the courts] *know that's not the case and you're a liar.*
M.O.	*How many years was it then?*
F.	*Well, it wasn't two minutes, but the thing is it's Heidi Schøne who's* [been in a mental hospital].…
M.O.	*It wasn't two years and it wasn't two minutes. How long was it?*
F.	*Nothing at all, as you damn well know, so stop fucking around with words, alright. You're inbred. That's right. You're a typical inbred bigot.*
M.O.	*And you accuse me of fucking around with words. Ha, ha, ha, ha, ha.*
F.	*What I'll do man, is I will ring you again on Monday alright?*
M.O.	*Yes, please do.*
F.	*You get the court document, alright and you can tell me where it says "two years"* [in a mental hospital]…… *You lot are so upset. You get people back without even telling them you put an article up there.*
M.O.	*I tried contacting you, I already told you.*
F.	*No you didn't* …… *bullshit.*
M.O.	*There's no contact information on your website.*
F.	*There is, there's an email address. Not only that, Heidi Schøne's got my number. But the thing is you were so upset OK…. by that stuff on there* [my website] *- even from the British newspapers alright, that you got me back as a Muslim and all you represent* [to the public] *is Muslims in general as being….*
M.O.	*I really don't think you represent Muslims, sir. You might think so. I really don't think so. I think you represent yourself. You can't be representing an entire religion. That's er… ludicrous.*
F.	*No, you've represented, you've put it across to the people* [his readers] *– "half-Arab Muslim," "madman."*
M.O.	*I never put that across to anyone….. I wrote you were a Muslim.*
F.	*Yeah, that's right.*
M.O.	*I never wrote that you represented them.*
F.	*No, no. You put it across….*
M.O.	*You know the difference? You understand the difference?*
F.	*I'm a Muslim, I don't have to be told about my religion. You represented "the Muslim," as all your newspaper have done….*
M.O.	*That's what you do, sir. You meet one Norwegian and you say every Norwegian is like that. I have never done that, sir.*
F.	*Your newspapers in 1995 started that off. They* [Bergens Tidende] *put nineteen times the "Muslim man," suffering from "erotic paranoia" and you should know that….*
M.O.	*You did that even back then?*
F.	*Well, it's on the website* [all the newspaper articles]. *You should look at the website.*
M.O.	*I know, I know.*
F.	*All the newspapers are up there. But the thing is, Heidi Schøne is the lunatic. She's the one….. that's been in a mental hospital.*
M.O.	*Everybody else, everybody else but you.*
F.	*She's been in a mental hospital.*
M.O.	*You're the normal one, everybody else is lunatic.*
F.	*No, not everybody else…. There's some good….*
M.O.	*OK, just most, most….*

F.　　There's some good Norwegians that have sent me emails and those emails are up there [on the website] *but the point is this OK. You have put total lies....inferring that I am a potential child killer and for that I will pursue you for the rest of your life, and I hope you get arrested.*

M.O.　*You will?*

F.　　*Oh yes. I hope you get arrested when you come here because you have committed a hate crime ["incited" one I should've said]. I'm surprised the police – Interpol – haven't....*

M.O.　*It's a 'hate crime' to put the word 'Muslim' in a newspaper article? Well, well, well.*

F.　　*Have you seen the emails I got after your articles?*

M.O.　*Well, I didn't write those emails.*

F.　　*No, no, no, no. You've seen them and they are the sickest emails imaginable and they're up there* [on my website]. *But you know, you are a real son of a bitch. I don't care* [about] *any more bullshit you give, your words. You're trying to play smart and cocky and laughing. You are the meanest son of a bitch going. Yes that's right – you're laughing....*

M.O.　*You're just a completely normal person without any obsessions, er, dedicating your life to writing about Heidi Schøne on the internet.*

F.　　*No, your newspapers have dedicated all* [their] *time to writing total rubbish – "erotic paranoia" - and the fact that Heidi Schøne's a lovely girl, normal girl. Of course you don't tell them* [your readers] *she's been in a mental hospital. You don't tell them about that son of a bitch Gudmund Johannessen. You don't tell* [them] *she's accused different men of raping her... You don't mention any of that. She's a sick mental case and you've listened to her because she's Norwegian. It's her.....*

M.O.　*How many internet providers have kicked your site out of their service?*

F.　　*Well, it's been up there for four years with the same one.*

M.O.　*Yeah and before that? How many?*

F.　　*Well, I think, one.*

M.O.　*One?*

F.　　*Yeah, that's right yeah. But the thing is we've got freedom of speech here. We're allowed to do it.*

M.O.　*You got kicked out by the server? Why?*

F.　　*Well, I think because of the images of abortion* [aborted foetuses] *but that's nothing to do with Norway. It was the aborted foetuses, OK* [that offended the server] *because as you well know I'm against abortion.*

M.O.　*So am I.*

F.　　*Yeah, OK, so that was the reason. But the thing is you know... you're not a professional journalist because you've lied. I've never been in a mental hospital for two years.*

M.O.　*You have been writing about me on the internet but you obviously haven't been researching me on the internet. Just look it up.*

F.　　*Well, I know from what you've written in your articles that it's total bullshit that you've written. OK.*

M.O.　*If you had looked it up on the internet you would know that CNN President Chris Kramer has, er, written highly of me.*

F.　　*Well, I don't care what he has written about you.*

M.O.　*Well you are claiming that I am not a professional journalist, ha, ha, ha.*

F.　　*Anyone who writes lies about "two years in a mental hospital," that my mother 'arranged' for me to be put in a mental hospital....*

M.O.　*She didn't?*

F.　　*Well, I've never been in one so the question doesn't arise.*

M.O.　*You've never been in a mental hospital?*

F.　　*No.*

M.O.　*Never?*

F.　　*Never.*

M.O.　*Never.*

F.　　*Never. I can swear on my mother's life. Never been in one ever, OK. And you know that. I think that you know that OK. That is such a terrible thing* [to write]. *And to infer that I am a potential child killer... your separate newspapers – you're all the same. You all share the information. Because it's on there, that I've threatened to kill her child OK. And you've just adopted it, put it in different language but the inference is there.... My lawyer Stig Lunde has got my number. You could easily have done it* [phoned me]. *You're just giving the usual bullshit, but I...*

618

M.O.	*He's still your lawyer?*
F.	*Stig Lunde is still my lawyer, yeah.*
M.O.	*OK. I would like to follow up on this story about Heidi Schøne, er, so...*
F.	*The more the better... I hope you are arrested eventually because I'm trying very hard for that.*
M.O.	*Are you?*
F.	*The British police, OK, I've informed them. Those emails are the filthiest fucking shit words you can imagine..... Do I "lick a pig's arsehole".....*
M.O.	*Yeah.*
F.	*You've seen them?..... "before" I "dig in".... and that's all coming directly as a result [of your articles]. So I'm going to pursue you for as long as it takes because......*
M.O.	*You're going to pursue me because someone else writes [hateful emails] because of my article. That's a long shot, a very long shot.*
F.	*No, no, no. You've incited religious hatred.*
M.O.	*No, no, no.*
F.	*You have, you have.*
M.O.	*No, no, no.*
F.	*Listen, lets put it this way, it's a crime here. It may not be in your country OK. Because you haven't got many Muslims....*
M.O.	*Of course, of course to incite religious hatred is a crime in most countries. You should know that as a solicitor. You say that a newspaper article..... just because they are mentioning somebody is er... that somebody is a Muslim is inciting religious hatred. That's a long shot, a very, very, very long shot.*
F.	*It's not a long shot because the British police have accepted it.*
M.O.	*No they haven't.*
F.	*Well, why don't you ring up Interpol.......I'll call you during the week.*
M.O.	*And you are calling me a liar!*
F.	*You are a dreadful liar.*
M.O.	*You are calling me a liar. You are telling me that Interpol has documents about me. That's stupid, that's just stupid.*
F.	*You probably haven't been informed. I'm not lying. Why don't you ring up – who is it – Anne Grøstad, the Director of Public Prosecutions. Why don't you ring up Anne Grøstad?*
M.O.	*Why should I ring her up?*
F.	*Well, because she's the one that's looking into it.*
M.O.	*If I believed you in the slightest I might be interested in calling anybody but I really don't believe you ... I believe you are full of nonsense.*
F.	*No 'cos you're a coward.*
M.O.	*No.*
F.	*If you ring her up...*
M.O.	*I really don't.....*
F.	*I don't have to keep pleading with you.*
M.O.	*I called your bluff. I called your bluff.*
F.	*Well call her then. Go on call Anne Grøstad, OK on Monday morning or Tor-Aksel Busch [the Attorney-General]. Tor-Aksel Busch's office.*
M.O.	*(laughing) ......Sure, ha, ha, ha like Tor-Aksel Busch would really be interested in me. You must be crazy.*
F.	*You ring her [Anne Grøstad] up. What I'll do.... I call you up during the week, either at your office or on your mobile and then you can establish [my proclamations] with Anne Grøstad and you can take your words back alright? No look, incitement to religious hatred....*
M.O.	*The funny thing is that I've got this entire conversation on tape. You wouldn't mind me publishing it would you?*
F.	*I wouldn't mind you publishing it at all. You're welcome to publish it. But the point is....*
M.O.	*Thank you, I will.*
F.	*......The point is you are a liar and a cheat. Putting, as I said, OK, 'maybe' that I'm a potential child killer and that my mother's put me in a mental hospital.... I mean..... has your mother put you in a .....*
M.O.	*Do you have any other comments to what I wrote about you and Heidi Schøne?*
F.	*I think they are on the website. But the point is has **your** mother put you in a mental hospital?*
M.O.	*The problem is I can't link to your website.*

F.   Has your mother put you in a mental hospital?

M.O.   If my mother? No, I'm not crazy.

F.   Well, I think you are.

M.O.   *You* think I am. Well thank you.

F.   Well, that's right …… when you can't research facts and say "his mother put him in a mental hospital for two years" and it's entirely rubbish OK. And there's no court documents [to prove this]. You're a liar OK. There's no court documents saying I've been in a mental hospital for two years. You ring up Anne Grøstad if you're the great journalist…. You wouldn't get a job on a comic here, because you're second rate and a bigot.

M.O.   I have worked…. I have worked for CNN in Europe…. They have their main headquarters in London.

F.   I know that, because I've seen that on the internet…

M.O.   (laughing) …. You're funny.

F.   You've got a portion of you that's a real bigot.

M.O.   You're funny, you're very funny.

F.   Well, I'll tell you what. I'll give you a ring during the week. Are we settled on that, yeah?

M.O.   Yeah.

F.   I'll give you a ring during the week.

M.O.   And we'll try and meet. We'll try to meet in London if you're not being able to come to Norway …. And I will bring a photographer and you will tell your story.

F.   Well, I'm not having any photographs taken of me. You can bet your life on that…. You come on your own like a real man…. You are going to have to retract and do something to apologise as I've not been in a mental hospital for two years. I'm not a potential child killer OK.

M.O.   I have never wrote that you were a potential child killer.

F.   ….You fucking well inferred it….. I'm going to ring you in the week and you find that court document that says, as you've quoted, that I've been in a mental hospital for two years. OK….You've got the bigot about you, right, like the Serbs. You're just like those Serbs and Croat killers.

M.O.   Oh… I was in Bosnia during the war. Where were you?

F.   Well… I wasn't in Bosnia.

M.O.   Yeah, of course, so you shouldn't be talking about things you don't know anything about. You should have respect for the people in Bosnia.

F.   I know enough about Bosnia, but I certainly don't….

M.O.   You should have some respect for the people down there.

F.   What do you mean "respect"? I'm Muslim, I have written about Bosnia.

M.O.   I was in Sarajevo during the war.

F.   …..I don't need you to tell me about Bosnia.

M.O.   It was you that brought it up…..You were the one who brought up Serbs and Croats without mentioning Bosnia, you know that.

F.   Look at my website. There's enough about Bosnia on there. There's pages of the stuff on Bosnia, so you don't have to talk to me about Bosnia. But all I'm emphasising is you are a liar. You are the one who put "half-Arab Muslim" associating those people with that filth about sex…..

M.O.   That person is you.

F.   ….You are going to have your work cut out because you have lied on a massive scale. You've even said that I've lied about Heidi Schøne – "gross lies" in the newspaper. There's nothing I've lied about. Not one. Even the court said everything I said about her was "more or less correct." Those were the words.

M.O.   Were they the same courts that you were running from? The same courts that you say you can't fly back to Norway because you are… you say they will put you in jail? Is it those courts you are referring to?

F.   It was the first court, the lower court. [i.e. the Drammen Byrett who said, "more or less correct."]

M.O.   OK, so it's not that court [i.e. the Magistrates Court who gave me an 8 month suspended prison sentence] you are referring to OK.

F.   It's all on the website. You don't have to talk double-dutch with me, OK. You have been caught out because you have put one of the biggest fabrications going – "two years in a mental hospital." So you double check your facts.

M.O.   I'll put this conversation on the web and let my readers decide.

620

F.   *You let your readers....? No you find out the facts.... You have said: "It's in the court documents" – "two years in a mental hospital." So you get those court documents and you come back to me.... You've done something so, so bad that you are going to have to apologise for it in a proper way OK. You find the court documents – "two years in a mental hospital." Ask Heidi Schøne about lies made up [by me], threats to kill her son and all the rest of it and look at the website properly and we'll have another chat. Yeah?*

M.O. *And you'll call me next week?*

F.   *Yeah I will.*

M.O. *Yeah great.*

F.   *Are you gonna take the call?*

M.O. *Huh?*

F.   *You're gonna take the call are you?*

M.O. *Of course I'm going to take the call.*

F.   *So, as I said, you ring up Anne Grøstad and you get those facts and then we'll have another chat, yeah?*

M.O. (chuckling) *Have a nice weekend sir.*

F.   *Bye.*

M.O. *Goodbye.*

Fifteen minutes later the phone rang:

F.   *Hello.*

M.O. *Hello sir, this is, er, Morten Øverbye calling from Dagbladet in Oslo.*

F.   *So, you got my number on your mobile?*

M.O. *Yeah, I got it.*

F.   *Yeah, so what do you want?*

M.O. *But now there can't be any problem to reach you anymore.*

F.   *No, that's right.*

M.O. *That's fortunate. Um, I just, er, read the article I wrote. And it says, "A Norwegian police serviceman who investigated the case later explained that it was his mother who got him," er, "committed."*

F.   *Yeah, well, that's a lie because I've never been in a hospital.*

M.O. *Well, but that's my sentence.*

F.   *Your sentence is that he's been.... "his mother put him in a hospital for two years."*

M.O. *No, er, my sentence is: "The harassment," er, "sustained all the way until 1992."*

F.   *Look, in the article you did on the 21ˢᵗ December [2005] on the front page it's got that.... "When he came out two years later...."*

M.O. *"Then the man was committed to a psychiatric hospital in Britain. A Norwegian police serviceman who investigated the case said that it was his mother who got him committed."*

F.   *Well that's obviously a lie because I've never been in one and the court.... There are court documents to say exactly that. But the sentence you put in the Dagbladet newspaper itself [of 21ˢᵗ December 2005], not the internet article [of 20ᵗʰ December 2005]. You've put......*

M.O. *OK, just let me look at the internet article now. I'll just check the....*

F.   *It's all on my website OK and every single newspaper article is up there. On the 21ˢᵗ December [2005] the front page with Heidi Schøne's photograph OK. And, er, in there, you've put, "When he came out two years later"!*

M.O. *OK.....Yeah. I'm not on the internet now. I'm outdoors – outdoors.*

F.   *Well it's all up there anyway. I had [all the newspaper articles] translated by a..... top company into English.*

M.O. *Yeah. But what I wrote in the internet edition was that there was a Norwegian policeman who, who [has] checked it.*

F.   *That's right. That's why I, um, she was, er, I put in a complaint and a judge, er, I think it was John Morten Svendgård phoned my mother and my mother told him it's absolute rubbish. Because I got my mother to, er, I involved my mother in this to try and get Sorte, er, sacked. But the thing is there's a letter from my family doctor which I got purposely from my own doctor to give the facts and it's with the courts, that I've never had any psychiatric treatment anywhere.*

M.O. *You have no psychiatric history?*

F.   *None whatsoever, no.....As much as you want me to have [a psychiatric history].*

M.O.	*Except for.... No, I was about to say, except for your website.*
F.	*Well that's another bullshit opinion. I'm not going to.....I'm not going to lower myself to answering that rubbish. The fact is you've put, "Two years in a mental hospital" and I want to know where that information came from.*
M.O.	*It says so in the article "a policeman said so."*
F.	*Are you looking at the 21ˢᵗ December article?*
M.O.	*I just searched, er, Torill, for Heidi's name on our website.*
F.	*It was only thanks to a Norwegian chap that I got your article of the 21ˢᵗ [December]. You've put "two years" on the 21ˢᵗ.*
M.O.	*Yeah, I just told you I said that I wrote that.*
F.	*Yeah, "two years".....*
M.O.	*"Said a police officer."*
F.	*No. You haven't put that Torill Sorte said that. You have put separately, "When he came out two years later," OK, "he continued." "His mother had him committed" and "When he came out two years later" - that is in the 21ˢᵗ December 2005 newspaper article.*
M.O.	*Which article is published the 20ᵗʰ....*
F.	*No, the 21ˢᵗ. You did two articles....dagbladet.no on the 20ᵗʰ and that was when we had about 1500 hits on the website..... because you made it quite easy for people to find the website. So, you did a repeat article because on that one of the 20ᵗʰ you put, "Going to the European Court of Human Rights in The Hague." OK.*
M.O.	*"Chased by sex-crazy man for 23 years."*
F.	*Well I know what's on there.*
M.O.	*"Sexually harassed for 23 years."*
F.	*Yeah that's right. That's what you put on there. Yeah? OK.*
M.O.	*"23 years since you met Heidi Schøne."*
F.	*Well I met her here in 1981. [1982 in fact.]*
M.O.	*And you are still writing about her on your internet.*
F.	*Well **you** are. You're writing in your newspapers.... Let's just go back to why you're ringing.....You've got on the web – you're trying to establish whether or not you have put on your article, "Two years in a mental hospital." Now can you just find that....are you looking at my website? You're not are you? What you want to do is, you want to look at my website properly then you.....*
M.O.	*"The harassment lasted until 1992 when his mother had him committed to a psychiatric hospital in Britain. When he came out two years later ..."*
F.	*That's right.*
M.O.	*"... he continued worse than ever."*
F.	*That's right. That's what you put, yeah.*
M.O.	*Yeah. What's happened for those two years? Why didn't you write anything about her or do anything about her in those two years? Why did you continue two years later then? [He was in fact referring to a two year period before my first court case in 2001 when I did not campaign against Heidi Schøne as my lawyers at the time told me to stop my "information campaign" against her as it would prejudice my case. So reluctantly I stopped.]*
F.	*I don't know why you put that because, er.... First of all ...First of all... Do you admit you have lied about "two years" in a mental hospital?*
M.O.	*No, I wrote up the website on the 20ᵗʰ December that a police officer said so and in the wording ...*
F.	*And you believe her do you?*
M.O.	*It came from a police officer explaining, er, it went, I think, but it's er....*
F.	*No, did you speak to Torill Sorte to ascertain your facts?*
M.O.	*But I spoke to her, yeah of course. You have been harassing her as well haven't you?*
F.	*No. I've not been harassing her. I've just been questioning her. OK. She's been harassing me, by saying that I've been in a mental hospital. Or my mother wanted to put me [in one], or I have been [in one]. Now where do you get the "two years" from?*
M.O.	*I just told you that the sourcing on the website is, er, a Norwegian police officer.*
F.	*So Torill Sorte is the source for the two years, yeah?*
M.O.	*Yes and um, on the bottom of my first story it says, "P.S! Also a police woman who led the investigation of the Brit is now being harassed by name on his website."*
F.	*Well it's not "harassing" - it's a right to reply. Do you not understand? I mean, you're a journalist. Obviously my point is that you are a second-rate nothing. You wouldn't get a job in a British newspaper in a million years. Because....*
M.O.	*CNN in London and you know that.*

F.   It doesn't matter man. Your "two years" [in a mental hospital]…. That's not [CNN] a
        British newspaper is it? "Two years"…..
M.O.   No, I think it…. The Sun [newspaper] is not usually looked about as CNN. It's usually
        not as highly regarded as CNN.
F.   There are lots of newspapers in Britain… [for example]…The Times….any serious
        newspaper journalist would check with me and with the court documents if that's what
        you've done. You know perfectly well I've never been in a mental hospital, OK. So for
        you to print "two years" is a falsehood. OK?
M.O.   According to the police.
F.   According to Torill Sorte yeah?
M.O.   Who worked for the police and led the investigation.
F.   Well…. It is good that you can confirm that because er…er…that she's the source for
        that. And you believe her do you?
M.O.   …..(just silence)
F.   No, you're not sure now are you ?
M.O.   When we put it in the newspaper we obviously believe it. You complained about some
        articles to the PFU [the Norwegian Press Complaints Commission] didn't you?
F.   They're not worth shit. They're nothing. What's his name – Per Edgar Kokkvold, the
        Anglophile. The one who loves Britain and all the rest of it. He's pathetic. And their
        getting out of it and their time limits!
M.O.   ….How come you are so angry at me now. It been more than a year since I wrote this
        article.
F.   Well, because, as I said, I was trying hard as hell to get the Norwegian police to, um, to
        do something about you, but because obviously they regard me as an enemy, then
        they're protecting you 'cos you are a Norwegian, OK. But at last, as I said…. I hope
        that…. Interpol can do something about you and your editors.
M.O.   When you called me just prior to this conversation, you said that they were already
        doing something.
F.   Well that's right, they've [the Norwegian Bureau for the Investigation of Police Affairs]
        written to me to say that they are looking into it but whether they've made a decision to
        do anything yet…because they're under a little bit of pressure from Interpol in Britain
        OK, who regard it as a hate crime.
M.O.   And what's the hate crime?
F.   Well, incitement to religious hatred by printing falsehoods and connecting my religion
        with, er….
M.O.   With you….. with you….
F.   Well, obviously I am Muslim but you see those emails are the result of what you've
        written, OK.
M.O.   What emails?
F.   Well, if you look on my website. Have you not seen my website? Do you not look at it?
        If you look at the, er, are you on it now?
M.O.   I am on it, er, in just a few seconds.
F.   OK.
M.O.   It's norwayuncovered.com

He saw the email address and added:

M.O.   You ask people to contact you, don't you?
F.   Well I don't ask for those kind of comments, obviously, do I?
M.O.   No, but if you ask people to contact you, you really don't know what kind of
        words….you only want nice comments.
F.   Well, no. I don't want the filth, er, that those…..
M.O.   You didn't want people to say their opinions about you.
F.   Before you, um, you know, jump in without knowing what you're talking about, look on
        these 'sickest emails' as you want to know what the investigation about the hate crime
        is.

And I guided him to the link the 'sickest emails imaginable' on my website. He found them and
said:

M.O.   Yeah, I really understand that's not nice emails.
F.   That right, and there's so many of them that I've gotta say that there is a general
        hatred of Muslims among a significant sector of your population. Particularly every

623

time your newspapers write about me it's "Muslim man," "sick," "erotic paranoia," "mental hospital," 'potential child killer'..... that I've "raped" her.....

M.O.   *My question is... you met her 23 years ago, 24 year ago. How come... and you tell me that you are very upset and I understand you, very much... and you tell me that you are upset about these emails that come to you. But the link between Heidi and you now is your website. There is no other link. If you didn't have this website people wouldn't be sending you emails.*

F.   *And if Bergens Tidende hadn't [done] their article in 1995 none of this would have happened and if Heidi's Schøne doesn't go to the police saying I've threatened to kill her son and raped her... I sent all my side of the story to Verdens Gang and Bergens Tidende 1995 – very quickly – they printed nothing and it went on. They were printing articles without me knowing.*

M.O.   *But if ....if your problem now is that Norwegian newspapers are writing about you and that people are sending you emails all this happens because of the website. Why don't you just take down the website?*

F.   *Well, because I think the world ought to know what sort of things go on in Norway.....*

M.O.   *But as long as you keep that website up you can't stop people from emailing you.*

F.   *Only after your article - your two articles - then the bulk of those emails came as a direct result. Because they came on the day and the next day. But I haven't had anything [since]. I've had one or two bad ones, you know, but most of them, well almost all of them, were as a result of your articles. That is completely unforgivable because you've told people that I, in my capacity as a Muslim, am filth.*

M.O.   *No, no, no.*

F.   *That's the information...*

M.O.   *I never told anybody you have done this in your capacity as a Muslim. I have many Muslim friends. None of my friends would ever dedicate their lives to a website regarding one person, one woman.*

F.   *It's not dedicated to one female. It is dedicated to all the other....*

M.O.   *Oh there is lots about Heidi in it.*

F.   *Yeah, because she's the catalyst. She's the one that started it all.*

M.O.   *Now there's Heidi, it's er, policewoman Torill Sorte, it's Karsten Gjone, it's Per Danielsen, Elden, Helge Wesenberg, Vegard Aaløkken, Tony Samstag, the Norwegian police, Agnar Nilsen.*

F.   *Yeah, that's right, so not just Heidi Schøne. Not just Heidi Schøne.*

M.O.   *She's the catalyst?*

F.   *Yeah, it's an exposé of Norwegian life in general. And I do have people in Norway – as you will see from those emails – who agree with me, OK?*

M.O.   *So while I state very clearly that you are not a representative for Muslims....you feel that Heidi's representative of Norwegians, don't you?*

F.   *You didn't say that in your newspaper article. You gave the inference.....*

M.O.   *No, because....that's obvious, that everybody.... every normal person knows that one people, one person does not represent an entire religion. Everybody knows that.*

F.   *Yeah, but you make out as if it does. No one knows that kind of inference better then me because **all** your newspapers - you look at the first newspaper article from, um, Bergens Tidende, OK. They put "Muslim man" nineteen times, OK. And associated me with "erotic paranoia"...... But you see the link: every time a newspaper [does a story it's] "Muslim man," "sick," "mentally ill" and you've perpetuated it by giving it some kind of form and cast-iron certainty in the mind of Norwegian readers. Because you've seen on these emails, those 'sickest of emails' that they said, "Oh, you haven't told people on your website that your own mother put you in a mental hospital. Why don't you mention that? You are the sick one." That's what they tell me because they believe you.*

M.O.   *So my newspaper article is worse than the others you think?*

F.   *Well, I think after all that's been on there, the amateur way and vindictive spite and the lack of research that you [put into it] on there is so so bad. It's a terrible thing you've done. Because it's not true.*

M.O.   *You are convicted in Norwegian court for harassment aren't you?*

F.   *No, well yes, but the thing is they said to me either you plead guilty or we will put you in prison straight away.*

M.O.   *And you as a solicitor believe that?*

F.   *Oh I very much did. Your police wanted me bad. Because I'd put stuff up [on my website] from British newspapers long ago from The Times in 1990 and other stuff. Even the judge [Agnar A. Nilsen Jnr.] before the court [of Appeal] case, he said to me,*

624

"I've seen your website. Not very good stuff in there." And he knew I was going to be arrested the minute that [civil libel] case finished......... He knew and he never told me that the minute that case is finished I was going to be arrested, because the police were waiting at the door of the court. It was a trap and no one was interested in [a fair trail at] the Court of Appeal. And in fact when I was cross-examining Torill Sorte about this, er, mental hospital thing, the judge stopped me because I was getting very close. Sorte was floundering. She didn't know what to say. She was stumped, OK. She is a wretched liar. No one has the right to be a policewoman.... to lie like that.

M.O.   So you believe most, most Norwegians are liars?

F.   No I don't. I've said to you ... I mean how can I? You've got four and a half million people. I've put some decent emails up there from people OK. And I had many friends from Norway. I visited a lot of people in Norway, not just Heidi Schøne.

M.O.   So it's just the media, the police and the lawyers, the courts and the people you met?

F.   You've lied to me, talking like a Serb. As if oh, everyone's against the Serbs...you know....why does everyone hate us? The Serb police, the Serb media. You are all one and the same. You're a small country. You feel isolated, OK. And when someone attacks then everyone clubs together. Everyone joins up. That's why all your newspapers do the same story without bothering to research their facts.

M.O.   So you think, er, all Norwegians and all ... are like Serbs?

F.   Well, I think your press have a lot in common with the Serbs. In your morbid hatred of, er, "the Muslims".... I've said that [before] explicitly and I think that the proof is there because every time you write about me - your press – it's "Muslim man," "sick." The association.

M.O.   What we write is that you are sick, that you are very obsessed with Heidi Schøne.

F.   That's right.

M.O.   And the proof we are providing for this obsession is your website. [The Norwegian newspapers wrote that I was "sick" in 1995 and onwards, long before my website went online in 2000.]

F.   Well, no, I think it's just a right to reply and you're upset because of it. It's a big one [i.e. big website] and successful, upsetting a lot of people in Norway from top to bottom and I think there are many grievance websites in the world, especially in England, on many things, on lawyers, on everything and you are just picking on me, er, because the object of the website is Norway.

M.O.   All because it's a good story. And poor Heidi Schøne being harassed by this crazy Briton for 23 years now.

F.   Well it isn't 23 years is it, because, er, that's just made up. What, every month [for] 23 years? I've replied on a website to her bullshit. And your bullshit. That's not harassment. That's a right to reply and putting my opinion forthrightly.

M.O.   You've put up this website in 1995?

F.   No, in 2000.

M.O.   In 2000, five years after 1995.

F.   That's on the website. You've got to have a good read of that. Because all the questions you are asking me, the answers are already on there.....

M.O.   If I flew to England and knocked on the door of the Interpol there, they wouldn't, er, they wouldn't sacrifice one minute of their work for your case.

F.   Well they have because we have got a hate crimes unit here. And it's the hate crimes unit who are dealing with it and they have sent it to Interpol in Norway....

[And later]:

M.O.   We could go to the Interpol together and if Interpol arrested me it would be a good story for my newspaper, you know.

F.   You want to be a martyr?

M.O.   No, I don't think there is any chance of that.

F.   But you want to be? You want the publicity.

M.O.   I don't think there is any chance of Interpol, ever, ever stopping two seconds talking to me if I knock on their door.

F.   But why don't you try? Give it a go.

M.O.   Could we go there together with a photographer? It should be a nice story.

F.   What? What, to Interpol in Norway? You must be kidding.....

M.O.   Or England.

F.   I told you I am not going to Interpol, in Norway.

M.O.   No, because there you would be arrested you said.

F.	Well, that's right, yeah.
M.O.	Because you flew away from a sentence in Norway.
F.	Well, no other country on earth would be so perverse and bigoted as to get their own back....Isn't it some kind of criminal offence to insult Norway by printing the truth about their ... certain institutions? That's what it's all about.
M.O.	I don't think so.
F.	Oh, just because the "Muslim man" hit back and put something up [on a website.]
M.O.	I don't think this is about you being a Muslim, sir.
F.	Well to me the association.....so why every time print [the word] "Muslim"? Why every time print that? And also there's one article that says I'm....Torill Sorte printing in Eiker Bladet that I am "clearly mentally unstable." [The actual translation from my agency was "obviously mentally unstable."]
M.O.	Torill Sorte the policewomen says that you are mentally unstable?
F.	Yeah... "clearly mentally unstable" is the quote.
M.O.	She was the person who investigated the case against you. She was the lead investigator.
F.	Oh yeah, top woman! Yeah, fantastic investigative policewoman!
M.O.	Where did she have that thought from? [That I was "clearly mentally unstable."]
F.	'Cos she's nuts. Anyone who say's that I've been two years in a mental hospital when I haven't is clearly a spiteful vindictive bitch and I've told her [as much]. In fact I phoned her up a few weeks ago. She didn't have the guts to speak to me. If it's not true that I've been in a mental hospital, then clearly she's a wicked liar. Agreed?
M.O.	(Silence).
F.	You can't even agree on that?
M.O.	Of course I can. If she says you have been in a mental hospital and you have not been in a mental hospital, then she's lying.....
F.	Yeah, exactly.
M.O.	.....That's a no brainer.
F.	Exactly, but there's no way you're going to print that on the front page.... that clearly Torill Sorte has.... lied. No way you're going to put that, but I can tell you, that my family doctor's letter is in those court documents.
M.O.	You have papers saying you are not crazy? That's what you are saying.
F.	My family doctor's letter states categorically that I have had never had any psychiatric treatment and that letter is with the court, OK.
M.O.	So you have papers stating you are not crazy?
F.	Well, yeah, exactly. I mean "crazy" that's er... and there are plenty of papers saying Heidi Schøne's crazy, but you don't print that 'cos you protect her. Poor Heidi.
M.O.	Most people don't have papers saying they are not crazy.
F.	Well, the exact allegation was that my mother put me in a mental hospital so the doctor's letter says that I've never been in a mental hospital. OK. So for you to print that I've been in one for two years is clearly an outrageous lie .....

[And later]:

F.	You don't care to establish what's right or what's wrong. OK? Correct?
M.O.	I'm trying to.
F.	Oh you're trying to **now** yeah. Just because [my website] is against Norway you mustn't be so bigoted to call it an obsession, yeah.
M.O.	You are making an entire website to a lady you met, er, 23 years ago.
F.	No, you just said there's a lot more people on it – there's lawyers, there's police.
M.O.	But you said Heidi was catalyst for all the other people.
F.	Something's got to be the catalyst but it's the whole cross–section of [Norwegian society such as] your psychiatrists writing in the newspaper that I am "definitely" or "maybe" suffering from erotic paranoia .... There's nothing more provocative than writing one article after the other, especially behind my back. I think there were one or two, well, maybe four or five [articles] I didn't know had been printed for two or three years. Very luckily I found them by a search by typing in "Muslim man" [on a search engine] on the internet then up came Verdens Gang and Aftenposten....
M.O.	You are a one person mission to take down Norway. Good luck to you.
F.	Well, how am I going to do that? You know perfectly well that, er, you...you...
M.O.	I know that.
F.	You do everything. You people do anything to cover up and lie and cheat, you know.
M.O.	Norwegians do that?

F.   *Huh?*

M.O.   *Norwegians do that or.....*

F.   *You do it, your press colleagues, the police. Torill Sorte. She never knew I was recording her telephone conversations. Every single one of them. And that's why she was caught out in court.*

Morton Øverbye then asked for my mother's phone number and my doctor's phone number so as to try and verify my account, but I told him everything he needed was in the court documents.

F.   *Have you got access to the court records or not?*

M.O.   *Er, it depends on how all the case are.*

F.   *So why don't you ring up that arsehole of a judge, what's his name at the Court of Appeal? Er, Agnar Nilsen Jnr. You ring him up and say, Dear Mr Nilsen Jnr, is there a letter from my doctor and he'll say, "I'll go and have a look at the records," or alternatively he will say, "I'm not allowed to show you anything." You research from there.*

M.O.   *And it would be OK for you if we put those court documents online?*

F.   *Of course it wouldn't 'cos you're not allowed to. The court wouldn't allow you to do that. You can look at them but you're not allowed to do that [- put them on the internet].*

M.O.   *I don't ask the court's permission, I ask your permission.*

F.   *No, no, no. No permission 'cos, as I said, I don't trust you. You've just said again that my website's an obsession. It's not. It's just a record of what you've [i.e the Norwegians have] done. A record of what you've done.*

M.O.   *To me it looks like an obsession.*

F.   *To me your newspaper are obsessed as well. Because no one else would do that. You wouldn't have done anything if I wasn't Muslim, and half German. German mother.*

M.O.   *Of course, if any person were sexually or in any other way were harassing a Norwegian woman for 23 years it would be a story....if it was a German, if it was a Frenchman, an Italian, a Swede, whoever.*

F.   *There you go again – "23 years." I haven't even gone to see the woman ...since....1990 was the last time I met her OK. And all this business about threatening to kill her neighbours. What bullshit!*

M.O.   *Have I written that you have threatened to kill the neighbours?*

F.   *Your colleagues in the press have. But what you've done at the end of it all is, in a way, so much worse 'cos you've had all the benefit of the information that's already there [on the website.] [He was reading the Aftenposten headlines back to me as we spoke.] Total bullshit. Have a good long read and look at those recorded conversations and we'll have another chat...*

M.O.   *Next week.*

F.   *Yeah, that's right*

M.O.   *OK.... Have a nice weekend.*

F.   *Yes, cheers.*

M.O.   *OK, bye.*

I rang Morton Øverbye back on the afternoon of Sunday 20th May but he had not followed up anything due, he said, to his busy schedule so said I would call him again at the beginning of June.

On Saturday 26th May 2007 I set off from Heathrow airport for Reykjavik, Iceland. Uriah Heep were playing with Deep Purple on Sunday in the capital's premier sports hall, the Laugardalshöll. With my best friend, Russell Gilbrook, now the drummer in Uriah Heep, this was a concert I was not going to miss. It was Russell's third appearance with Heep after he joined them the previous February. I arrived at Reykjavik just before midnight after a three hour flight and as it was summer it was still light, so after depositing my luggage in my hotel room, I went into the town centre to see for myself Reykjavik's nightlife. It was unremarkable: a lot of drinking and a lot of drunk men and women in the streets. Many celebrating the end of the school year.

Next morning I joined Uriah Heep at breakfast in their hotel, the Nordica. We reconvened at 1 p.m. for the short walk to the Laugardalshöll where lunch had been laid on for the band. We all returned in time for the 5 p.m. soundcheck. The soundcheck was a moment for me to savour, as I watched Russell go through his paces on his expansive drum kit. His joining the group was a triumph for both of us. Add to that, however, a large element of good fortune. Back in early

February I happened to look at the official Uriah Heep website, which I rarely did, and saw that the band were looking for a new drummer as Lee Kerslake had retired at Christmas. I immediately called Russell and told him the news, adding that he just had to apply. We both wondered if it wasn't too late. Trevor Bolder, the bass player in Heep was a big fan of Russell's as he'd seen him play in Trevor's home town of Hull at a drum clinic Russell had given. But that was three or so years previously and sometime after that they had lost touch. Russell had moved house and changed all his telephone numbers including his mobile number. I told Russell I'd see what I could do to get hold of Trevor using one of my own contacts, but I hadn't managed to by the time Russell called me again three days later. What to do? Then Russell had an idea. On his other mobile phone he rang up the Hull music shop where he'd done his drum clinic and luckily they had Trevor's number. Russell called me back ten minutes later to say he had now spoken to Trevor. Heep had in fact got in mind another drummer to fill the vacancy, but were still giving auditions. Moreover, Mick Box could not remember with any great clarity Russell's playing in 1999 when Deadline, the band Russell was in at the time, supported Uriah Heep on a short tour of the U.K. But Trevor wanted Russell in the band.

So, Bernie Shaw - the singer, and Mick Box went along one Saturday evening to see Russell drum for his covers band in east London. They were very impressed. They invited Russell along the following week to an audition near London Bridge along with eleven other drummers. I gave Russell a selection of my Uriah Heep CD's and a couple of videos containing the songs he was told to learn. Russell was the last drummer to audition and he later told me he knew he'd got the job after just "four bars" by the looks on the faces of the others members of the band. Mick Box went on to say:

> "Russell came to the auditon and blew us all away. He is one of the heaviest drummers I have ever heard. We spent two days auditoning a shortlist of twelve drummers from 120 applicants and once Russell started playing we just knew he was the man for the job. There were smiles all around and he made the drum stool his. We were never looking for a clone of Lee Kerslake as that would have been an impossible task as there is only one Lee. Had we taken that stance we would have in effect stood still. We were looking for someone who can come into the band and energise it and have a wealth of ideas, especially for the new songs and give us a new lease of life. Russell did just that and his appointment comes at the start of an exciting new phase in the band's career. We hope the fans will feel the same way once they have heard him play and sing."

The Reykjavik concert was a 5,500 sell out. Uriah Heep came on first for one hour and Deep Purple, on the final leg of their world tour, then followed for two hours. It had been 13 years to the day since I had seen Uriah Heep and Deep Purple perform together in Den Bosch, Holland. Mick Box charged me with taking all the photos of the concert on his digital camera and these were all put on the Uriah Heep website. Uriah Heep left back for London the next day, Monday morning, but I stayed on for three more days to do some sightseeing. This included a fabulous bathe in the famous Blue Lagoon, which is a pool of seawater naturally heated by the geothermal activity below the surface. The extra days in Iceland enabled me to pick up the newspaper reviews on the concert. I got the three articles translated into English and on 14th June they all went up on the Uriah Heep website. The band were especially pleased with two of the articles which both gave them five star ratings and Deep Purple only two star ratings. The articles are reproduced below:

DV Newspaper	Tuesday 29th May 2007
URIAH HEEP STOLE THE SHOW	

Deep Purple & Uriah Heep
Laugardalshöll, Sunday 27th May
Uriah Heep *****
Deep Purple **

There is no denying that the concert featuring Deep Purple and Uriah Heep last Sunday was a show in two parts. The latter band was much crisper and had the edge on Deep Purple in almost every department.

When I walked into the hall, Uriah Heep had just started playing their first song. The place was buzzing, and whether it was the drunken old rocker beside me, or the housewife from Gardabær in front, everyone was in the mood. Bernie Shaw's energy was immediately obvious and pleasantly surprising because I thought he would have lost some of his vocal power. The band's instrumental work was almost perfect, and it was especially enjoyable watching drummer Russell Gilbrook, who recently joined the band after Lee Kerslake was forced to retire for health reasons. Gilbrook's fantastic energy was an almost menacing force on the drums - we were waiting for his seat to break. But his amazing ability was clear to see, and it comes as no surprise that Gilbrook is a highly-respected drummer and a tutor at the Brighton Institute of Modern Music, despite looking more like a debt collector. Mick Box produced some incredible guitar work, and he seemed to be able to conjure up brilliant solos at will.

Unfortunately, Deep Purple couldn't match any of that. Ian Gillan didn't seem to be up to the job as he once was. He struggled unconvincingly for long periods. Of course, the band's big hits like Smoke on the Water were superb, but that wasn't enough. Half of their numbers included instrumental solos lasting several minutes from guitarist Steve Morse and keyboard player Don Airey, which was tedious, even though they are outstanding musicians.

Ásegeir Jónsson

***

MORGUNBLAÐIÐ Newspaper	Tuesday 29th May 2007
	Voices from the past

MUSIC

Uriah Heep and Deep Purple in Laugardalshöll.
Whit Sunday.

Uriah Heep *****
Deep Purple **

WHEN two remarkable and respected bands like Uriah Heep and Deep Purple join forces and play in Laugardalshöll, we can expect fireworks, and that is just what we got in Sunday evening's concert. I didn't arrive in time to hear all of Uriah Heep's performance, much to my regret, but I did hear July Morning and Easy Livin.' The band exuded power and energy that was unbelievable given that its members are well into their prime. Actually, only one of the original members is still active, guitarist Mick Box, but given Sunday's performance, guitar playing must be like good wine – it improves with the years. Trevor Bolder has played bass with Uriah Heep since 1976, and he showed his vast experience with some rock solid playing. Bernie Shaw provided the vocals, but he showed his age with his choice of trousers, although he clearly hasn't lost his hair or his voice. Bass guitarist Bolder managed Easy Livin' with consummate ease, a rendering that gave us goose pimples.

Unfortunately, the goose pimples faded when Uriah Heep were replaced by Deep Purple, with original members, singer Ian Gillan, bass player Roger Glover and drummer Ian Paice, who reminded me of our beloved radio announcer Gudni

Már. The band played a two-hour set of around 20 songs, giving us a mixture of their biggest hits and some new material. The only song from their best collection, "In Rock" from 1970, was "Into the Fire." It was too early on the programme, and Gillan had not warmed up sufficiently to give us his best presentation. That was disappointing, because this is a song that really stands out when done well. Gillan's voice improved slightly as the evening wore on. He was fine when he restricted himself to the lower notes. His best patch was when he sung "Strange Kind of Woman," "Perfect Strangers," "Space Truckin" and "Black Night."

"Black Night" was the final encore and I felt it was the best of all Deep Purple's songs, enough to bring back those goose pimples. The audience, both young and old, went home humming the song's bass line, and it was obvious that everyone was very happy. This concert was probably a little better than when Deep Purple came over three years ago. The playing was solid, although Ian Paice was rather subdued on the drums compared with how he used to be. It was a fine evening, but I regret missing some of Uriah Heep's early songs, and I hope the band comes back soon to play a concert on their own. I will be on the front row.

Ragnheidur Eiríksdóttir

***

The abiding memory I left with from Reykjavik though was the sheer beauty of some of their women. It blew my mind, especially as they were so sweet on top of it. And it was certainly a topic of conversation among the Heep boys. Iceland was a desolate volcanic island with endless miles of black lava landscape. The population was only 302,000 (including 10,000 Poles) and there wasn't a single railway - too expensive to build. None of us could ever see ourselves living there - except for the sake of the beautiful women.

On Monday 25th June 2007, the Essex Police at Harlow telephoned me at work to say that they had now received documentation from Interpol in Norway via Interpol in London. Interpol in Norway had apoligised for taking nearly a year to deal with the matter of those hateful emails to me. But the outcome was that Interpol in Norway were not going to do anything as "the matter had already been dealt with." The Essex policeman (the Hate Crimes Liason officer) who related this conclusion to me said he was duty bound not to tell me anymore in spite of having a sheaf of paperwork from Interpol Norway in front of him. I reminded him that those emails only came after the two December 2005 Dagbladet articles and so, quite obviously, my complaint last year was a first complaint and absolutely nothing had been investigated previously. The police officer did not even have information as to whether Morten Øverbye or his editors had been questioned by Interpol. The Norwegians had not given an apology for the contents of those emails. The policeman acknowledged that clarification was required from Interpol in Norway, so he promised to phone Interpol in London straight away and to pass on my reservations. He soon called me back to give me some comfort and took the correct spelling of Morten Øverbye's name so that Interpol in Norway could, hopefully, question him and reconsider their position.

On 28th June 2007 I called the Norwegian Bureau for the Investigation of Police Affairs (Spesialenheten For Politisaker) to try and speak to someone dealing with my complaint against Torill Sorte. This was about the fifth time I tried this and so far no one had returned my calls. But now I was told that a decision had been made – which they were not allowed to tell me over the phone – but I would soon be informed in writing what it was. Yet again that essential requirement of consultation in the decision making process was denied me.

On 11th July 2007 I received the Bureau's decision by way of a letter dated 28th June 2007 which contained a three page report in Norwegian and its English translation dated 19th June 2007. It went as follows:

Decision on whether to prosecute

CASE NO 070188

FREDERICK DELAWARE (DATE OF BIRTH .. ..) HAS REPORTED DAGBLADET AND EIKER BLADET FOR PROMOTING RELIGIOUS HATRED AND POLICE INSPECTOR TORILL SORTE FOR HAVING GIVEN FALSE INFORMATION TO THE PRESS

In the complaint submitted by Frederick Delaware to the Public Prosecution Authority on 2 March 2007, he reports Police Inspector Torill Sorte for giving false information to the media, and the media for its coverage of him. The Public Prosecution Authority passed on the complaint to the Norwegian Bureau for the Investigation of Police Affairs on 22 March 2007. The Public Prosecution Authority has concluded that pursuant to the third subsection of Section 34-9 of the Norwegian prosecution guidelines, the Norwegian Bureau for the Investigation of Police Affairs should also consider the complaint against Dagbladet and Eiker Bladet.

The Complaint

Frederick Delaware accuses Dagbladet and Eiker Bladet of promoting religious hatred. He refers to an article published on Dagbladet.no on 20 December 2005 and two articles in Dagbladet on 21 December 2005 and Eiker Bladet on 11 January 2006. The articles are enclosed with the complaint.

Police Inspector Torill Sorte is accused of giving false information to the press. The articles state that Delaware was involuntarily committed to a psychiatric institution in 1992. In the article in Eiker Bladet, Police Inspector Sorte is quoted as saying that she considers Delaware to be mentally unstable.

16 e-mails sent to the e-mail address norway_2003@hotmail.com were enclosed with the complaint. This is the e-mail address for messages sent to Delaware's website www.norway-shockers.com and the e-mails are reactions to the contents of the website. All of the e-mails express disgust at the contents of the website, and Delaware is referred to in extremely negative terms.

The complaint also contains a declaration by a doctor that Delaware has never been involuntarily committed to a psychiatric institution.

The investigation of the Norwegian Bureau for the Investigation of Police Affairs

The Bureau has looked at Eiker Modum and Sigdal District Court's verdict 03-00945 of 17 October 2003. In that case Frederick Delaware was found guilty of breaching Section 390a of the Norwegian Penal Code by harassing Heidi Schøne, and was given an eight month suspended sentence, on the condition that he deleted all of the information that he has published about Heid Schøne on the internet and that he removed the website www.norway-shockers.com from the internet. He was also ordered to pay a fine of NOK 10,000. The verdict makes it clear that Delaware has also previously been found guilty of harassing Schøne.

Frederick Delaware has previously reported Police Inspector Torill Sorte to the Bureau for perjury at Drammen District Court in 2002. The case was dropped due to insufficient evidence. Delaware appealed, but the Public Prosecution Authority upheld the decision. The Public Prosecution Authority has sent us its verdict in the case.

Delaware has not closed down his website in accordance with the terms of his suspended sentence. The Norwegian Bureau for the Investigation of Police Affairs has looked at some of the content of www.norway-shockers.com.

The assessment of the Norwegian Bureau for the Investigation of Police Affairs

<u>The complaint against the newspaper</u>

The articles on Dagbladet.no and in the paper version of Dagbladet are mainly about Heidi Schøne's description of being sexually harassed and stalked by Delaware for 23 years. The articles in Eiker Bladet is about Delaware's harassment of Police Inspector Torill Sorte, and also mentions that Delaware has been bothering Heidi Schøne and her family since 1982.

There is no doubt that the articles contain defamatory remarks, including the claim that Delaware is a sex manic. This and other assertions, in so far as they are unlawful, may be covered by Sections 246 and 247 of the Norwegian Penal Code, both with regards to the person who has made the clam and the person who publishes it (abetment). The Bureau has not found it necessary to consider the individual claims of the article with respect to their lawfulness and the question of freedom of speech, as the facts of the case suggest that it would be possible to provide sufficient justification for the assertions for them not to be punishable; cf. Section 249 no. 1 of the Norwegian Penal code. We have refer to the information that came out at Drammen District Court in 2002, to Eiker, Modum and Sigdal's verdict of 17 October 2003, and to the information on Delaware's website www.norway-shockers.com. It is therefore the view of the Bureau that there is no relevant information to suggest that the newspapers have been guilty of any punishable offences in publishing the abovementioned articles.

With respect to the ethical aspects of the articles, this is matter of the Norwegian Press Complaints Commission. We assume that Delaware is familiar with this organization as it is mentioned on www.norway-shockers.com.

The Bureau has noted that the articles which have been reported to the police, can also be read by anyone on Delaware's website www.norway-shockers.com.

<u>The complaint against Police Inspector Torill Sorte</u>

The information that Delaware's mother helped to have him committed to a psychiatric institution was previously made public at Drammen District Court. In conjunction with that case, the Public Prosecution Authority did not find any reason to prosecute Police Inspector Sorte for perjury. The statements of Police Inspector Sorte were also investigated by the Special Police Investigation Commission (SEFO), who found it proven that no offence has taken place pursuant to Section 121 and sub-section 1 of Section 325 of the Norwegian Penal Code. We therefore cannot find any reason to reopen the case in relation to breach of confidentiality. The only question that remains is thus whether the contents of the articles in Dagbladet and Eiker Bladet are ground to suspect Police Inspector Sorte of gross negligence in the performance of her duties.

For there to be gross negligence in the performance of her duties, a specific investigation must uncover *"established, culpable behaviour which results in severe reprimand for lack of due care."* This has been specified by the Supreme Court through several verdicts, including Rt. 1986 page 670 and Rt. 1995 page 1195.

It is not clear from the articles in Dagbladet and on Dagbladet.no that, in connection with the writing of the articles, Police Inspector Torill Sorte made any comments about the involuntary committal of Frederick Delaware, or about who may have played a part in having him committed. In the article of 20 December 2005, Police Inspector Sorte is only mentioned in a postscript to the article. The whole of the article appears to be based on the comments of Heidi Schøne, who we also assume to be familiar with Police Inspector Sorte's testimony to Drammen District Court. In the article of 21 December 2005, Police

Inspector Sorte is quoted, but only in relation to Delaware's harassment of her. It is therefore not considered likely that she repeated the contents of her testimony to Drammen District Court to Dagbladet. Regardless, it is unlikely that this in itself would constitute gross negligence.

With respect to the comment to Eiker Bladet that Delaware is clearly mentally unstable, we consider it neither punishable as negligence nor defamatory. We here refer to the contents of Delaware's website and the other facts of the case.

The Bureau has decided that on the basis of the above, there do not appear to be any grounds to investigate further whether Police Inspector Sorte has been guilty of any punishable offence in terms of her statements in the three articles referred to.

Decision

The case against Police Inspector Torill Sorte, Dagbladet and Eiker Bladet will be dropped, as there are no reasonable grounds for investigating whether any punishable offences have been committed; cf. the first subsection of Section 224 of the Criminal Procedure Act.

Frederick Delaware, Police Inspector Torill Sorte and the editors of Dagbladet, Dagbladet.no and Eiker Bladet will be informed of the decision.

A copy will be sent to the Chief Police of Sondre Buskerud for his information.

This case has been decided under authority to prosecute delegated by the Chief of the Norwegian Bureau for the Investigation of Police Affairs, cf. subsection 2 of Section 34-3 of the prosecution guidelines; cf. subsection 1.

The Norwegian Bureau for the Investigation of Police Affairs, Hamar, 19 June 2007

Johan Martin Welhaven
Deputy Director

I sent in my appeal by fax immediately:

Spesialenheten For Politisaker

Ref. 070188/200700177
For the attention of Johan Martin Welhaven

12th July 2007

2 PAGE FAX AND POST

Dear Mr. Welhaven,

Dagbladet, Eiker Bladet and Torill Sorte

I received yesterday your letter dated 28th June 2007 and please accept this letter to you as my appeal against your decision on all counts.

I note that your department have purposely not returned my calls, in keeping with the usual cover up that precedes all your police investigations into my complaints.
I note also from your decision that you have not spoken to Morten Øverbye, the journalist with Dagbladet who wrote those stories on me on 20th and 21st December 2005. If you had then he would have confirmed to you that Police Officer Torill Sorte was the source of the (false) information which led him to print that I had been in a mental hospital for 2 years. As this is clearly not the case, then Torill Sorte is an abject liar and has purposely given false information

633

to the newspapers to help blacken my character. Morten Øverbye himself, as you will see from the transcribed telephone conversation I had with him on 12th May 2007, all of which can be read on my website, has told me that, presuming the fact that I have never been in a mental hospital to be correct, then Torill Sorte is a liar. The whole conversation is on tape ready to be sent to you. But speak with him first.

In particular you yourself are in dereliction of duty for not speaking to Morten Øverbye or Torill Sorte or indeed myself to obtain clarification and certainty as to the facts.

Your personal opinion that Eiker Bladet, quoting Torill Sorte, are correct to call me "clearly mentally unstable" is an indication of your complete bad faith and bigotry in this investigation. You say that my website and other facts in the case support the allegation that I am "clearly mentally unstable." You do not mention which facts and what in particular in my website supports your belief. Reasons must be given. The fact is that if someone like me writes certain home truths about the Norwegian system that upsets Norwegians, then automatically the offender is "mentally ill." This approach is an age old inbred Norwegian trick. And it is probably the reason why the British authorities have not co-operated with your police in any way over your ardent desire to have my website shut down. In England we call it freedom of speech. Your Police authority's dirty tricks to get me prosecuted and fined mean nothing to anyone over here. What you people have done to me is unforgivable and your people's perverted actions must continue to be exposed on the internet.

Dagbladet, in their articles on me have specifically mentioned my religion and coupled this with slanderous allegations which resulted in those many emails denigrating me as a Muslim and the religion of Islam. Dagbladet have therefore clearly incited religious hatred and it is just another reflection on your inbred mentality that you cannot accept this. The British Police accept that those emails are in the nature of a hate crime and it is deceitful of Interpol Norway (composed of partisan Norwegians) to lie to Interpol London on this matter. That is why I have asked Interpol London to request Interpol Norway to reassess the matter with clarification and explanation.

Please also understand that as Torill Sorte is quite clearly a liar and perjurer then it is my absolute right to have the freedom of speech to say this on a website. It is not harassment of her. Just as I have the same right to express my side of the story on the mental patient Heidi Schøne. You will see in any case I have support for my views from others whose contributions are quoted on my website. You people establish a whole series of falsehoods and build on them to create a sick fantasy. The world deserves a website such as mine to see the scale of bigotry and hatred that exists in your country.

I look forward to hearing from you on this appeal.

Yours sincerely,
Frederick Delaware

Suing in the British courts for libel over the Eiker Bladet article was a non-starter. I would have to have shown "substantial publication" of the article in the United Kingdom, meaning sufficient readers (who understood Norwegian) accessing the article here. The number would have been negligible and consequently with little damage to my reputation in Britian. In any case how was I to discover how many people had in fact read the article here?

On the afternoon of Friday 13th July I spoke to Johan Martin Welhaven and he acknowleged receipt of my fax and said that it would be translated into Norwegian and then considered. He told me he didn't think it was necessary to speak to either myself, Torill Sorte or Morten Øverbye as the documentation that I had submitted was enough to go on. I told him why it was essential to speak to the parties involved and that he had better do so on this my appeal. I tried to discuss other aspects of his decision, including the concept of incitement to religious hatred but he said he couldn't do that because he didn't have the papers in front of him. I also rebuked him for agreeing with Torill Sorte's quote in Eiker Bladet that I was, "clearly mentally unstable." He was now going off on holiday but he said he would speak to me again in due course.

On Wednesday 18th July 2007 I faxed Johan Martin Welhaven another letter with a short extract from my telephone conversation with Morten Øverbye on 12th May 2007 detailing his admission that it was Torill Sorte who was the source of his information causing him to print that I had been in a mental hospital in Great Britain for two years. The next day I sent this letter to Mr Welhaven by recorded delivery post including a disc with the recording of the extracted conversation with Morten Øverbye burnt onto it. This same extracted conversation was also put onto my website. Everyone could now hear the truth for themselves.

On the afternoon of Monday 23rd July 2007 the Hate Crimes Liason officer at the Harlow, Essex police telephoned me to say that he had heard again from Interpol in London that the Norwegian police had told them that they did not believe Dagbladet or Torill Sorte had committed any offence and therefore they would not be taking the matter any further. There was still no apology either from the Norwegians with regard to those hateful emails. The Norwegian police had written to the English police before receiving my evidence of Torill Sorte being the source for the "two years" in a mental hospital. Again, the Hate Crimes Liason officer told me he could not divulge any of the details communicated to him by Interpol in London. He did say however that the Norwegians were unhappy that I had not taken my website down.

I received a brief confirmatory letter dated 23rd July 2007 from Harlow police. I replied to it making one final effort in which I asked whether the Crown Prosecution Service could issue summonses against the editors of Dagbladet coupled with arrest warrants were they ever to set foot in England. I was asking for reciprocation following the Norwegians' use of Interpol in 2003 to serve me with a magistrate's court summons. The Hate Crimes Liason officer telephoned me a few days later to say that Interpol in London had already made a firm decision to close their file on this matter and in spite of his best efforts there was absolutely nothing more he could do to help me. He emphasized once more that the specifics of what Interpol had told him were not to be disclosed to me.

I called Johan Martin Welhaven on Thursday 16th August 2007 but his assistant said he could not speak to me as he was very busy preparing for a court case starting the following Monday and he would be in court all week. She confirmed to me that they had received my recorded delivery letter with disc. Nevertheless the very next day Mr. Welhaven sent me a letter in Norwegian. It was a copy of a letter he had addressed to the Public Prosecutor dated 17th August 2007. No English translation came with it, but I noticed it contained reference to "cd-plate." He had sent my cd disc to the Public Prosecutor along with his recommendation regarding action on my case.

I had not chased up Morten Øverbye again because I was waiting for some closure on the Norwegian police investigation into Torill Sorte. I had on my website placed a large photograph of Morten Øverbye together with his home address and the transcription of my conversation with him on 12th May 2007. On the 19th August he sent me the following email:

> I ask you to kindly remove my address from your website. As I am sure you understand, by publishing my address you don't only target me but also other people living on the same address.

> The photographer who has taken the photo would also like me to notify you that he will bill you for the breach of his copyright unless you remove the photo.

> As for your text regarding my person, you are entitled to your opinion however wrong it is - but remove the address asap.

> Morten

I replied the next day as follows:

> Morten,

Your address and photo are freely available on the net, so it is not privileged information I am disclosing to the public on you. Moreover you are a journalist and you have allowed your photo to be used on another story in connection with your professional work. You like to promote yourself - as is often the custom in your profession. In principle you agree to your photo being shown. You have also got to expect to be made the subject of my right to reply to your outrageous stories in December 2005. And to expect a very robust reply. You have to be able to take the rough with the smooth.

Your name and photo as well as your address are shown on the norwayuncovered.com website, so nobody will get you mixed up with anyone else at that address. So what is the worry for the others?

As for any breach of copyright of your photo you will have to begin an expensive commercial court action in London to assert your claim.

As a gesture of goodwill I will remove your address if you do the following:

1. Print in Dagbladet a prominent apology for your December 2005 stories with wording to be agreed between ourselves, to include, crucially, a statement that Torill Sorte has lied to you with regard to her ludicrous claim that I was in a mental hospital for 2 years.

2. Write to Johan Martin Welhaven of the Spesialenheten for Politisaker on fax number 62 556102 under his reference 070188/200700177 and confirm to him that you spoke to Torill Sorte and that she is the source for your false information causing you to print that I have been in a mental hospital for 2 years. And email me a copy of the letter. He is dealing with my complaint and has a copy of my family doctor's letter from 2003 which states categorically that I have never been in a mental hospital. This proof will enable you to write in your newspaper that Torill Sorte is a liar. Johan Welhaven is on phone number 62 556100. He is in court all this week. I will also need Welhaven to begin proceedings to sack Torill Sorte. He should not be allowed to cover up. After all such a lie must be a sackable offence, I'm sure you will agree.

Frederick

He replied immediately:

I am sure you are a man of principle, able to take the responsibility for your own words and actions. Thus, if you don't remove my address from your web page, I will make sure your name and address is forever connected with your website.

I find it only fair that your name and address is connected to your website, so that nobody will get your website mixed up with anyone else.

I will have the photographer send you an invoice for the photo.

You have 24 hours to remove the address.

Morten

I did not remove his address or photo and did not reply to him.

On the 28th August 2007 I phoned Johan Welhaven's office to be told by a female assistant that he didn't want to speak to me anymore as he had sent all the papers to the Public Prosecutor for them to decide what, if anything, to do. The assistant told me that the Public Prosecutor was the one who would be looking at my appeal, "not Johan Welhaven." I nevertheless insisted on being put through to him as it was vital that I hear from his own mouth his views on the disc I had sent him exposing Torill Sorte. Still, the assistant tried to put me off but after I persisted she said she would go and look for Mr. Welhaven. I was then put through to him. I asked him about the disc and described what was said on it. The converstaion then went as follows:

"So can you at least see that Torill Sorte has been lying?" I put to him.

He told me that the case was sent over to the "National Prosecutor" and it was "difficult to give a comment on this case now." I retorted: "Why, have you not listened to the words or read the words?" [On the disc and transcript.] He continued, saying that all documents were sent by him to the Public Prosecutor. That he had no documents with him (presumably then he had not kept a set of photocopies) and he found it, "not right to comment on this case while we are waiting for the conclusion from the Prosecutor."

He told me that he had not listened to the disc but that he had read, "all the other documents." And that the Public Prosecutor may refer the case back to him to re-investigate.

I then asked him what the copy letter he had sent me in Norwegian, addressed to the Public Prosecutor, had said. He replied that he was "quite sure" that he had concluded in his report that he "did not find it necessary to change" his conclusion that Torill Sorte had not committed any punishable offence. And that it was, "now up to the National Prosecutor to make a decision." I rebuked him for not being able to discuss with me this vital disc evidence. I told him he should have spoken to the journalist Morten Øverbye. He replied, "I'm not taking orders from you." And that they had had an investigation. That he would not discuss the case now because he was waiting for "a conclusion from the Prosecutor." I then went on to discuss his written comment that he believed Torill Sorte's Eiker Bladet newspaper assessment of me as being "clearly mentally unstable," was neither negligent nor defamatory etc. He said, "Everytime you are calling us this is your main criticism......... What do you want from me?" I replied that I wanted to know exactly what it was on my website that made him think that I was "clearly mentally unstable." He retorted with: "I will not tell you anything about what I think." I interrupted him: "You've written what you think. You've written [previously] that you think I'm clearly mentally unstable." He continued, "I must repeat. We have had an investigation. It's closed from our side. You [appealed] it and it's sent to the Prosecutor. The Prosecutor will make his [decision]..... I find it not right to discuss the case with you now." I asked him, "Will you discuss the case with me ever? Is there any time you will discuss the case?" He replied, "Only if the Prosecutor concludes that we must investigate more or we have done something wrong." He advised me to contact the Public Prosecutor directly. I told him that his own investigation was a cover up. That a proper investigation meant speaking to Torill Sorte and Morten Øverbye. Surely he was duty bound to ask Torill Sorte, the maker of the statement, why she thought I was clearly/obviously mentally unstable? Johan Welhaven concluded, "I heard your point of view. I understand it. But we can't continue this kind of discussion now." I finished by asking him, "Is anyone putting pressure on you - above you - to cover up or something?" He replied, "No." I had now done all I could so I thanked him and finished the call.

The next day I telephoned Anne Grøstad at the Public Prosecutor's office. She confirmed she had received all the papers from Johan Welhaven including the disc. She had not yet had time to look into the case. And had I requested the case be handled by someone else other than her? I said I had not made any such request. I was happy for her to deal with it. (It was a chance for her to make amends for her previous cover up over her 2003 enquiry into Torill Sorte).

I made sure that Anne Grøstad knew exactly what was on that disc and I went through the implications of that evidence in some detail. Anne Grøstad however would not discuss my concerns at all. She said it was not her department's policy to discuss the case with a complainant. And she had to consider the case first anyway. She did say that if they do find evidence of a police officer committing "a crime" then they do prosecute. I asked her if telling lies to the newspapers constituted "a crime." She could not say as everything depended, she said, on their investigations into this particular case. I couldn't understand her logic. When I asked if Torill Sorte had to have permission from her superiors to go to the press to talk about me, Anne Grøstad said she could not "speculate." I asked of Anne Grøstad that in due course she discuss the evidence with me. She said that they do not go through the evidence "with the parties." I made it clear that I did not expect Torill Sorte to be let off this time. I asked Anne Grøstad if she had ever prosecuted a police officer for telling lies. She said she did not want to discuss "any cases." I told her I wasn't asking her to give any names away, but said, "In principle, do you prosecute [police officers for telling lies]? She replied, "If we find evidence of a crime committed by a police officer we do prosecute, yes." I added, "Does that include lying to the press?" Anne Grøstad replied, "I don't want to go into any more discussion." She assured me that she would handle the case in a way that they "believe is correct." But they do not themselves examine or interview any of the parties, but "can instruct the Spesialenheten"

(Norwegian Bureau for the Investigation of Police Affairs) to do so, if they see fit. I left it at that. Anne Grøstad said I would be informed about the outcome of my appeal to her office.

In the meantime I paid for the translation to be done of Johan Welhaven's letter of 17th August 2007 to the Public Prosecutor:

Doc. 01,07

SPECIAL UNIT FOR POLICE CASES
Postboks 93
2301 Hamar
Norway

ENDORSEMENT FORM

Report no.: 070188

APPEAL AGAINST CASE DISMISSAL – FREDERICK DELAWARE REPORTS POLICE SERGEANT TORILL SORTE OF SØNDRE BUSKERUD POLICE DISTRICT FOR HAVING GIVEN FALSE INFORMATION TO THE PRESS

Sent with enclosures to the **Norwegian Director General of Public Prosecutions, postbox 8002 Dep, 0030 Oslo, Norway**, with reference to the appeal of 12 July 2007 from Frederick Delaware (cf. doc. 08) concerning the Special Unit's decision of 19 June 2007; cf. doc. 08.

The appeal is being sent to the Director General of Public Prosecutions in accordance with Section 59a, first paragraph of the Criminal Procedure Act; cf. Section 34-8 of the guidelines on criteria for prosecution. The appeal is deemed to have been duly submitted.

The appeal has not been sent until now, as it has taken a little while to have it translated into Norwegian; cf. doc. 17.

In addition to the appeal, Delaware has provided additional information and views in a letter dated 18 July 2007. Enclosed with the letter is a CD with a discussion between Morten Øverbye of the Norwegian daily newspaper Dagbladet concerning Torill Sorte.

The Special Unit's dismissal of the case was justified through the claim that there are no reasonable grounds on which to investigate whether a penal offence has been committed; cf. Section 224, first paragraph of the Criminal Procedure Act.

The Special Unit sees no reason to reconsider the prosecution decision on the basis of what is stated in the appeal.

Special Unit for Police Cases, Hamar, 17 August 2007

(Signature)
J. Martin Welhaven
Assistant Manager

During the night of 28th September 2007 I received two emails from the same person who wrote to me anonymously:

The story...
From: l*****s m*******r
Sent: 28 September 2007 03:04:57
To: norway_2003@hotmail.com

Dear Frederick,

I have read quite a lot of your story regarding HS. There is no doubt in my mind, based on your taped conversations
(http://www.norwayuncovered.com/Torill%20Sorte%20Convos.htm) that you have experienced grave injustice. Mainly from norwegian newspapers and PFU, but also from HS and the embarrassing fact that norwegian officials and law enforcement officers hardly speak english.

That said, I am supprised that you are so harsh regarding Toril. From what I read, she is the only person that understands you? Did she do something wrong regarding your case after what is referred to in the page mentioned above? (and PLEASE do not send me everything you have. I understand it is quite a lot...) why have you not pressed civil charges against the newspapers or PFU? It seems obvious that they either have made up large parts of your story based on bad oral translation OR relied on lies from their source? In either way they (or HS) are doing to you exactly what they claim you do to HS: "Invade the sovereignty of your privacy" / "bring shame on your good name" (or whatever it translates to in english). Not mainly because they wrote false articles (in witch they did not name you), but because PFU have done a dreadful job in gathering facts (if they tried at all) to decide your complaints.

It should be perfectly simple to find out wether you have been admitted to some treatment or not, and if you have actually threatened to kill anyone. Their failure to do so would only strenghten the suspicion that things have gone wrong since the alleged letter in witch you are supposed to have threatened HS's son got "lost" in Bergen.

The most disturbing thing is that PFU not only rules in favour of the newspapers, but that they reclaim that you are a mentally disturbed individual that is not given the right to have your side of the story heard to "protect yourself for your own good". To me, the newspapers claim you have sent HS 400 letters. Based on this again, you are "sexually ill" in some way. Based on this ... aso.

If there is no mental illness of relevance to the matter, this is infinitely more worrying than the wrong doings of HS in the past or the fact that you are not able to forgive HS for her wrongdoings (not that i blame you. I know how disturbing it is when someone never askes for forgiveness but recieves it from God / Jesus etc instead).

Your webpages
I have no idea why you do not focus on the simple matter of HS. Every other article on your pages are (as you probably know) highly offensive to most people, -giving them perfect excuse to regard you as insane (much more convenient than to believe you). Personally I think it is wrong of you not to separate your views rooted in your religion that collide with "common norwegian sence", and your views (truths) regarding your experience with the norwegian legal system, newspapers and PFU.

If you do not see that comparing people with pigs and claiming that most people are maniac idiots killing unborn children and fucking around on drugs ruins your case as a serious bringer of truth, you might very well be completely insane. (You would still be right about your claims regarding HS, PFU and newspapers, but noone will ever listen to you...). If you REALLY most of all are interrested in being believed regarding HS, you could simply try to look beyond the fact that we are not all Muslims.

You have the tapes from page mentioned above still? They must be a completely devastating blow if accepted in a court of law (but they probably will not. I assume they are made without concent...). They might also serve you justice if you redesigned your pages, removed the "general hatred" to everyone (and norwegians in particular), and simply put up the transcripts of your conversations with Toril and the other law enforcement officers / lawyers aso

639

alongside digitallized mp3 files. Torils statements alone, not to mention the obvious confusion rising every time you speak to a new office, pretty much clears your name in telling you what can be proven, what is lies and what is error thanks to poor language skills and BUREAUCRACY (the one thing that all norwegians understand and relate directly to problems and injustice). And if you maintain you "hatredpages" I dont blame you for one secound. You have the right to say what you wish in my book. Even if I disagree.

Finally, I would like to offer my deepest sympathy and support regarding the HS-case. I wish this wrongdoing undone and I am embarrased that my countrymen does not serve you justice and are generally complete morons (provided you are not manipulating transcripts from your conversations of course).

Hope you find peace somehow. You deserve it!

Sincerely
P

Oh my god...
From: l*****s m*******r
Sent: 28 September 2007 08:02:39
To: norway_2003@hotmail.com

Dear Frederick,

I found what I missed earlier (i googled keywords regarding an article in dagbladet.no since the norwegian search-engine "kvasir" did not give many results). First I only found fragments of your story, but realize now that the whole thing is on your "hatepages".

No wonder you hate us...

I dont know what to say. You probably had no Idea who Tor Erling Staff is, what position Faremo used to have, aso. You should have had someone by your side all the way to ensure you got correct advice enabling you to maneuver our corrupt labyrinth of bureaucracy.

I hereby declare my unconditional support of you regarding the HS case. (still doesnt mean we are all killer maniacs on drugs;). I can only in my wildest dreams imagine what you have had to fight over the past years, and I guess I as a norwegian is "supposed" to be amazed that you have taken all this so far. Usually we just bend over and take it up the ass when the mighty troll turns his ugly head our way.

I am lost for words as to your taped conversations (witch I now know to exist for a fact). Still corruption is clearest to me in the PFU / Elden case (Faremo), but the policewomen lying under oath and the writer that claims you accused her of living in sin is really just ... mindboggling... -where does this end? Does it end? I for one have never been brave enough to tape conversations with officials displaying the same kind of behaviour as your villains, but you actually give me hope. Instead of fleeing this god forsaken country I might start my own wars from now...
Thank you!

Still hope you find peace, truth and justice. Change the layout of your page, and we will all follow eventually :)

Sincerely

P
(same... -and I know you respect people enough to erase my email from header when / if referencing this)

MSN Music ...Finn din favorittmusikk blant nesten 1 million låter

On 13th October 2007 I received the following email from a Norwegian man now living in the United States. To protect his identity I have deleted certain of his comments (as shown by blank spaces within the square brackets):

Hi There!
From: **P******* (r*******@gmail.com)
Sent: 13 October 2007 20:24:57
To: norway_2003@hotmail.com

Wow. I mean...WOW!

I've just read much of your norwayuncovered.com page and I am absolutely blown away. I'm not yet sure if it is in a good or bad way, but the message that you bear in this site is Very revealing. I'm an "utvandrer" and was born and raised in Norway till I moved overseas at the age of 14. Today I am an american citizen living in the US. I would like to share my experience with you because much of what you write about in this webpage hits so close to home it is damn frightening.

Upon returning home to Norway at the age of 16, after spending 2 years in a fascist asian country, I was delighted to be back home in the land of the free. Although [.......... ....] had begun, I began to realize that the home I was yearning for was a place I no longer knew. It was not the home I had left. Not because it had changed, but because I realized that my perception of home*norway* was not at all what I had identified with overseas when talking to brits, americans, chinese etc. After a year at home it was time to travel overseas, once again.

This time I was gone for a year before my [...... ....] I moved back to Norway at the age of 18 on my own, convinced that this is where I "belonged." I spoke norwegian, I grew up skiing in the mountains, played football, drank excessively on the weekends, and this was after all where all my childhood memories, friends, schools, kindergarten, family etc etc. was.

Unfortunately, this time around I was not able to adapt into mainstream norwegian society. I felt different and like I did not fit in. My friends treated me different, what I remembered was no longer reality. [....... ....
....]

It has been my experience that people in Norway that are interested in studying or becoming a psychiatrist, wants to work at a mental ward, or institutionalize themselves for pleasure, are all part of a perverted intrinsic obsession of the sick and evil. A select few in this system are there to genuinely help and work to guide the mind, body and spirit on a positive journey, but they are easily overshadowed by the morbidly sick and demented chariots of mental health professionals in Norway. And for the Christian personnel there, I would say that they are extreemely Selfish in seeking out to do Gods work on the weak, not by aiding them towards god, but using them to justify their own path towards god by labeling the mentally ill as being posessed by lucifer and therefore must be cast into FURTHER hell. Fuck those pieces of shits! If there is a hell, that is where they will go themselves. How are sick people supposed to help sick people get well? This makes absolutely no sense at all.

I would have to say, though, that the line between reality and paranoia in this case might be a bit skewed. However, there is no doubt that ALL of norwegian society is sick, sick, and more sick. Alcoholism, sexual perversion, drug addiction, Christianity, quasi satanism, take from the rich and give to the poor (Take from the rich and make the sick even SICKER), social angst, and a painful self-consciousness that turn secrets into truth, denial and deep-rooted fear shedding light in the dark closets, filled with skeletons and death as Edward Munch tried to show the world with his expressionistic art.

Nisser are not cute little dwarfs with beards, the are evil little soul stealers, as the Novel of Peter Pan is really not as innocent as portrayed by Disney. This is Norway in a nutshell, a fairytale with a King, Queen, Prince and Princess, with fairytale weddings. There is blood on their hands, and people have always bled for the Norwegian LIE. It is time to stop this and begin to fight for the truth! Fuck socialism, make people stand up against the authorities by showing themselves worthy of existence, or let them die. I hate to say this, but it is better to be dead than to live in shame, guilt, oppression, all because those in power wish to continue their legacy of lies. It is not fair that people fall pray to this illusion, and we should not let them suffer more by allowing them to self-destruct.This will never make up for it, nor will taking on the worlds problems through human aid and asylum. This is just an attempt at covering it up even more. It is time to wake up and smell the fresh air, because there is plenty of it for everyone, and it is time to let the truth prevail for all Norwegians. I'm speaking from personal experience, not from political idealism. I have suffered it and I have found a solution which I am living today. Fortunately, away from Norway. I have a plan which I could write 10 volumes on. Please help me.

p***

On Friday 9th November 2007 the Aftenposten.no English language website published the following article:

Memoir insults Muslims

The autobiography of outspoken Progress Party politician Carl I. Hagen "Ærlig talt" - Speaking Honestly - has offended Norwegian Muslims.

A passage where the controversial Hagen calls the prophet Mohammad a warlord, man of violence and abuser of women has, unsurprisingly, caused offense.

"That the Islamic council is disappointed and angry and furious is as expected. I had more or less counted on this to happen when I wrote that," Hagen told newspaper *Vårt Land*.

Norway's Islamic Council asked Norwegian Muslims to refrain from reacting to Hagen's book.

Hagen's remarks come in connection with the massive trouble linked to the publication of caricatures of the prophet Mohammad.

Hagen writes that the government's handling of the matter led to freedom of speech "taking a back seat to respect for the warlord, man of violence and woman abuser Mohammad, who murdered and accepted rape as a method of conquest."

"If one puts religious feelings high, one cannot remain indifferent to such talk," said Islamic Council Norway leader Senaid Kobilica to Vårt Land.

The council is now working on a statement taking exception to Hagen's remarks and asking Norwegian Muslims not to react in an unsuitable way.

Hagen's memoirs has also received attention for the denigrating comments rained over most of Norway's leading politicians.

**

On 21st December 2007 I received a letter from the Spesialenheten for Politisaker (the Norwegian Bureau for the Investigation of Police Affairs) dated 21st November 2007 enclosing the decision on my appeal:

MEMORANDUM OF RESPONSE
5 November 2007

APPEAL FROM FREDERICK DELAWARE REGARDING DECISION NOT TO PROCEED WITH COMPLAINT AGAINST POLICE SERGEANT TORILL SORTE AS WELL AS DAGBLADET AND EIKER BLADET

Sent with enclosure Norwegian Bureau for the Investigation of Police Affairs.

We refer to the appeal of 12 July 2007 from Frederick Delaware of the decision of 19 June 2007 by the Norwegian Bureau for the Investigation of Police Affairs not to proceed with the case, as well as his letter of 18 July 2007. The case concerns the complaint of 2 March 2007 made by the complainant against Dagbladet and Eiker Bladet as well as Police Sergeant Torill Sorte after press reports in December 2005 and January 2006.

The Director of Public Prosecutions has reviewed the documents in the case. No grounds have been found for reversing the decision not to proceed with the case made by the Norwegian Bureau for the Investigation of Police Affairs. In addition to the legal decisions that the Bureau for the Investigation of Police Affairs has specified, reference may also be made to the Borgarting Court of Appeal's judgment of 14 November 2003 (Case no. LB-2002-546 A/03, appeal of a judgment of Drammen District Court (tingrett) of 11 February 2002). Reference is also made to the assessment of the Norwegian Bureau for the Investigation of Police Affairs, with which the Director of Public Prosecutions can in essence concur.

In accordance with this, the appeal is not allowed.

It is requested that notification be given, including information that the decision of the Director of Public Prosecutions cannot be appealed, cf. Section 59a first subsection last sentence of the Criminal Procedure Act (straffeprosesslove). Access to institute a private prosecution is governed by Chapter 28 of the Criminal Procedure Act.

OFFICE OF THE DIRECTOR OF PUBLIC PROSECUTIONS, P.O.BOX 8002 DEP, 0030 OSLO

By authority

[Signed]
Knut H. Kallerud
Chief Public Prosecutor

[Signed]
Anne Grøstad
Public Prosecutor

Yep, just as I thought: Norwegiannaires' disease has no known cure.

THE END

Judgment dated 31st August 2000 at Drammen City Court:

COURT RECORD
FOR
DRAMMEN CITY COURT

On 25 August 2000, proceedings were opened in Drammen courthouse.

Judge:	City Court Judge Anders Stilloff
Clerk:	The judge.
Case no.:	1318/99 A.
Plaintiff:	Frederick Delaware.
Counsel:	Lawyer Stig Lunde.
Defendant:	1.Heidi Schøne.
Counsel:	Lawyer Ellen Holager Andenæs fao lawyer Vegard Aaløkken.
	2. Ingunn Røren.
	3. Drammens Tidende and Buskeruds Blad AS
	(fao chairman of board), postbox 7033, 3007 Drammen.
	4. Responsible editor Hans Arne Odde of Drammens
	Tidende/Buskeruds Blad, Øvre Lianvei, 3400 Lier.
Counsel:	Wahl, Nøkleby & Co. fao lawyer Erik
(defendants)	Nøkleby, Nedre Storgate 13, 3015 Drammen.
2, 3 and 4)	

The case	Claim for judicial declaration that
concerns:	defamatory statements are null and void and redress in case for defamation.
Present:	Nobody besides the judge.

The court made the following

D E C I S I O N:

On 13.1.2000, Frederick Delaware filed a writ through lawyer Stig Lunde with Heidi Schøne, journalist Ingunn Røren, Drammens Tidende and Buskeruds Blad AS (fao chairman of board) and responsible editor Hans Arne Odde as defendants and with a claim for judicial declaration that defamatory statements were null and void (Drammens Tidende/Buskeruds Blad and Hans Arne Odde) and compensation (redress) for non-pecuniary damage (all defendants).

Through their counsel, all the defendants submitted replies with requests which will be referred to below. Here, it will be mentioned briefly that Heidi Schøne is demanding that Frederick Delaware furnish security for costs, while Ingunn Røren, Drammens Tidende and Buskeruds Blad and Hans Arne Odde are demanding that the action be dismissed because Frederick Delaware waived the right to hearing before the courts in connection with a complaint having been submitted to the Professional Committee of the Press (PFU), and in the alternative that Frederick Delaware furnish security for costs.

Preparatory proceedings, cf. Criminal Procedure Act § 412, paragraph 3, were held on 25.8.2000. The parties (with the exception of Ingunn Røren and the chairman of the board of Drammens Tidende and Buskeruds Blad AS) appeared, along with their counsel. Frederick Delaware and Hans Arne Odde made statements, and documentary evidence was produced as the record shows. It was made clear that there was no basis for conciliation solutions at that time.

The court will now consider the questions of dismissal and furnishing security.

The case circumstances with regard to the complaint-handling at the PFU can be summarized as follows:

On 19.7.98, Frederick Delaware lodged a complaint about a report in Drammens Tidende and Buskeruds Blad on 14.7.98 (which is also the basis of the present case). PFU regulations § 4, paragraph two, state:

> If the committee is asked to deal with a matter which has been reported or brought to court or which clearly will be brought to court, handling of the complaint is to be deferred until a legally binding ruling exists. In all cases, the committee may deal with the case if the press organ against which the complaint has been made agrees to this.

In a letter dated 27.4.99 to the PFU, Drammens Tidende and Buskeruds Blad, through Hans Arne Odde, referred to the provision quoted and requested *"that the committee postpone dealing with the complaint until a legally binding ruling exists, or alternatively that the complainant withdraws the threats of legal prosecution and makes it completely clear that legal proceedings are not a relevant issue."*

The PFU wrote to lawyer Eric Lindset, who represented Frederick Delaware then, on 7.5.99 and requested *"unambiguous clarification as to whether or not legal action is a relevant issue."*

In a letter dated 24.5.99 to the PFU, lawyer Eric Lindset stated on behalf of Frederick Delaware his *"wish to clarify unambiguously that taking legal action"* against Drammens Tidende and Buskeruds Blad *"is not a relevant issue for him"* and requested that the complaint to the PFU be subjected to a consideration of substance.

The PFU took the case up for consideration and concluded on 24.8.99 that Drammens Tidende and Buskeruds Blad had not breached good press practice.

Frederick Delaware has essentially argued:

The letter dated 24.5.99 from lawyer Eric Lindset does not imply that Frederick Delaware unreservedly and definitively renounced the possibility of hearing before the courts. The content of the letter is limited to confirming that bringing action was not a relevant issue for Frederick Delaware at that time. He wanted first to see the result of the handling of the complaint to the PFU and then have a free hand. That this is right is confirmed by the statement on page 3 in PFU case no. 119/98 (doc. 8 exhibit 5) that *"the PFU cannot under any circumstances go into who is telling the truth or not telling the truth in the specific case."* The keyword in § 4 of the PFU's regulations is *"clearly"*; it was not clear that Frederick Delaware would bring the case before the courts. Moreover, any renunciation of consideration by the courts can apply only in relation to the newspaper, and not the journalist and the responsible editor.

The basic principle of the law is that security for costs cannot be demanded, and the rule on exceptions in Criminal Procedure Act § 413 should be used with caution. Frederick Delaware has explained his financial situation. He will without doubt be capable of paying costs he may be ordered to pay. Compulsory recovery in England, if necessary, is not problematical; he is the owner of unencumbered properties and earns well. There is moreover no obvious possibility, in the sense that there is more than a preponderance of probability, that he must pay costs. Reference is made to decisions included in Rt. 1996 page 113, 1990 page 1183, 1990 page 914 and 1990 page 587.

In the case itself, Frederick Delaware has submitted the following

requests:

In the action against defendant no. 1, Heidi Schøne

1. Heidi Schøne be ordered to pay to Frederick Delaware within 14 days damages of NOK 50,000, plus 12% interest p.a. from due date until payment takes place.

2. Heidi Schøne be ordered to pay to Frederick Delaware within 14 days the costs of the case, plus 12% interest p.a. from due date and until payment takes place.

In the action against defendant no. 2, Ingunn Røren

1.   *Ingunn Røren be ordered to pay to Frederick Delaware within 14 days damages of NOK 30,000, plus 12% interest p.a. from due date until payment takes place.*

2.   *Ingunn Røren be ordered to pay to Frederick Delaware within 14 days the costs of the case, plus 12% interest p.a. from due date and until payment takes place.*

In the action against defendant no. 3, Drammens Tidende and Buskeruds Blad AS

1.   The following allegations included in Drammens Tidende and Buskeruds Blad on 14 July 1998 be declared null and void:

i)   "Pursued by mad man for 16 years."
ii)   "For 16 years a mentally ill Englishman has pestered and pursued Heidi Schøne...."
iii)   "Sexually harassed for 16 years."
iv)   "For 16 years Heidi Schøne from Solbergelva has been harassed and pursued by a mentally ill Englishman."
v)   "So far this year Sorte Kjennås and her colleagues have dealt with over 300 letters the man has sent to Heidi."
vi)   "The man has previously threatened the life of neighbours of the family in order to find out where they moved."
vii)   "...for 16 years the Englishman has been possessed with the idea of marrying Heidi."
viii)   "The scale of the harassment increased when Heidi got married nine years ago."
ix)   "Psychiatrists think that the Englishman is suffering from an extreme case of erotic paranoia."
x)   "But a mentally ill Englishman has time after time tracked down the address and sends harassing letters."

2.   Drammens Tidende and Buskeruds Blad AS (fao chairman of board) be ordered to pay to Frederick Delaware damages of NOK 300,000, plus 12% interest p.a. from due date until payment takes place.

3.   Drammens Tidende and Buskeruds Blad AS (fao chairman of board) be ordered to pay to Frederick Delaware within 14 days the costs of the case plus 12% interest p.a. from due date and until payment takes place.

In the action against defendant no. 4, responsible editor Hans Arne Odde

1.   The following allegations included in Drammens Tidende and Buskeruds Blad on 14 July 1998 be declared null and void:

a.   "Pursued by madman for 16 years."
b.   "For 16 years a mentally ill Englishman has pestered [and] pursued Heidi Schøne...."
c   "Sexually harassed for 16 years."
d.   "For 16 years Heidi Schøne from Solbergelva has been harassed and pursued by a mentally ill Englishman."
e.   "So far this year Sorte Kjennås and her colleagues have dealt with over 300 letters the man has sent to Heidi."
f.   "The man has previously threatened the life of neighbours of the family in order to find out where they moved."
g.   "...for 16 years the Englishman has been possessed with the idea of marrying Heidi."
h.   "The scale of the harassment increased when Heidi got married nine years ago."
i.   "Psychiatrists think that the Englishman is suffering from an extreme case of erotic paranoia."
j.   "But a mentally ill Englishman has time after time tracked down the address and sends harassing letters."

2.   Hans Arne Odde be ordered to pay to Frederick Delaware within 14 days the costs of the case plus 12% interest p.a. from due date and until payment takes place.

With regard to dismissal and furnishing security, Frederick Delaware has submitted the following

requests:

Heidi Schøne.

1.   Frederick Delaware not be ordered to furnish security for costs.

2.   Frederick Delaware be awarded costs of NOK 2,500.

Ingunn Røren, Drammens Tidende and Buskeruds Blad AS and Hans Arne Odde.

1.   The case be proceeded with.

2.   Frederick Delaware not be ordered to furnish security for costs.

3.   Ingunn Røren, Drammens Tidende and Buskeruds Blad AS (fao chairman of board) and Hans Arne Odde be ordered – jointly – to pay NOK 4,500 to Frederick Delaware for the costs of the case.

Heidi Schøne has essentially argued:

It is not disputed that Frederick Delaware has financial capacity. But he lives in his native country England, which could considerably complicate the recovery of costs. Cf. the consideration underlying the corresponding provision in Civil Procedure Act § 182. It is moreover an obvious possibility that Frederick Delaware will be ordered to pay costs to Heidi Schøne. He has tormented her for years, and it was not unlawful for her to seek help from Drammens Tidende and Buskeruds Blad in order to defend herself against him. It is by no means reasonable that she should pay him damages.

Heidi Schøne has submitted the following

requests:

1.   The plaintiff be ordered as a condition of proceeding with the case to furnish security of NOK 150,000 for costs which he may be ordered to pay to Heidi Schøne.

If the case is proceeded with:

2.   Heidi Schøne be acquitted and awarded costs plus 12% annual interest from due date until payment takes place.

Ingunn Røren, Drammens Tidende and Buskeruds Blad AS and Hans Arne Odde have essentially asserted:

Frederick Delaware has by agreement waived the right to proceed with the case in the courts; lawyer Eric Lindset's letter of 24.5.99 contains a clear and voluntary declaration of intent which of course includes the journalist and the responsible editor, not just the newspaper. Through his lawyer, Frederick Delaware was fully aware that he had the choice between the PFU and the courts, and he made his conscious choice on that basis. There is no room for pleading invalidity or unreasonableness.

The situation is similar to when the right to application for prosecution is waived, cf. Mæland: Ærekrenkelser [defamation] (1986) page 272.

It is very likely that Frederick Delaware will be ordered to pay costs. He is taking up an old case, cf. the newspaper articles in Verdens Gang and Bergens Tidende as long ago as in 1995. There is no identification, and Frederick Delaware himself provoked the article in Drammens Tidende and Buskeruds Blad in 1998 by spreading his malicious reports about Heidi Schøne in large numbers. The article is entirely marginal seen against the background of the articles in 1995 and is not unlawful.

Even if Civil Procedure Act § 182 cannot be applied, there must be occasion to consider the fact that Frederick Delaware lives in England, so that recovery will be protracted and onerous, cf. the decision in Rt. 1998 page 517.

Ingunn Røren, Drammens Tidende and Buskeruds Blad and Hans Arne Odde have submitted the following

requests:

Principally:

1.   The action be dismissed.

2.   Ingunn Røren, Drammens Tidende and Buskeruds Blad AS and Hans Arne Odde be awarded costs plus 12% annual interest from due date until payment takes place.

In the alternative:

The plaintiff be ordered as a condition of proceeding with the case to furnish security of NOK 150,000 for costs which he may be ordered to pay to Ingunn Røren, Drammens Tidende and Buskeruds Blad AS and Hans Arne Odde.

If the case is proceeded with:

Ingunn Røren, Drammens Tidende and Buskeruds Blad AS and Hans Arne Odde be acquitted and awarded costs plus 12% annual interest from due date until payment takes place.

Observations of the court

The situation with the Professional Committee of the Press (PFU)

As the court sees it, the sense of lawyer Erik Lindset's clarification in the letter of 24.5.99 to the PFU has to be judged against the background of what the PFU was asking for an answer to, in its letter of 7.5.99 to the lawyer.

The PFU asked for "<u>unambiguous</u> clarification as to whether or not legal action is a relevant issue," and reference is made to § 4 of the PFU regulations, according to which complaint-handling is to be deferred "until a legally binding ruling exists" "if the committee is asked to deal with a matter which has been reported or brought to court or which clearly will be brought to court ...."

In the opinion of the court, it is unclear what the PFU's wording implies. It is therefore doubtful whether the PFU has reserved for itself a final and irrevocable renunciation of the matter raised being heard before the courts after the committee has finalized the case as well. This doubt must be to the disadvantage of the PFU and to the advantage of Frederick Delaware in so far as, on the basis of lawyer Erik Lindset's clarification, it could not rightly be argued that a lawsuit was "*clear.*"

The court will therefore not dismiss the action on this basis, in relation to the journalist, the newspaper or the responsible editor. The case is therefore to be proceeded with.

Furnishing security

Criminal Procedure Act § 413 is in practice interpreted in such a way that
►   the general rule is that security for costs cannot be demanded and that the provision on exceptions must be used with caution,
►   there must be more than a preponderance of probability that the plaintiff will be ordered to pay the opposite party's costs, and
►   the plaintiff must be considered incapable of honouring the request to pay the costs he may be ordered to pay.
Cf. in particular the decision in Rt. 1998 page 509.

According to the available information, the starting point of the court is that it is likely that Frederick Delaware could meet costs he may be ordered to pay, if necessary by compulsory recovery if he does not pay voluntarily. He has therefore – in a statement to the court subsequent to assurance given, cf. Criminal Procedure Act § 411 – declared a gross income of 4,300 GBP per month, comprising salary and rental income from 2 properties (without mortgages or other encumbrances) where the value of one is stated to be 160,000 GBP and the other (co-owned with brother) 260,000 GBP. This information is not disputed by the defendants.

In the opinion of the court, the fact that Frederick Delaware is resident in England is of no major significance in so far as this will hardly complicate to a decisive extent recovery of costs he may be ordered to pay. Reference is made to the "civil agreement" of 12.6.61 with the United Kingdom which it is assumed will also apply in the event of recovery of such costs from Frederick Delaware in the present case; it is chapter 13 of the Civil Procedure Act on costs which is to be applied, cf. Criminal Procedure Act § 440, paragraph 1.

One of the cumulative conditions for applying Criminal Procedure Act § 413 in respect of Frederick Delaware is therefore not present, which means that he will not be ordered to furnish security for costs.

C O N C L U S I O N:

The action is proceeded with in relation to all defendants without the plaintiff being ordered to furnish security for costs.

* * * * * * * * * * *

The Court also gave the following

RULING:

Costs

The question of costs in connection with the court's hearing of demands for dismissal and furnishing security is deferred until the decision which closes the case, cf. Criminal Procedure Act § 440 compared with Civil Procedure Act § 179, paragraph 1.

CONCLUSION:

The question of costs is deferred until the decision which closes the case.
The parties were not present when the decision was made and the ruling given. The decision, which can be appealed, is advised/pronounced through counsel.

Court adjourned

[signature]

Anders Stilloff   Certified true copy   Drammen City Court

Court of Appeal judgement dated 24th November 2000:

BORGARTING COURT OF APPEAL

makes known:

On 24 November 2000, the Court of Appeal heard the appeal of Ingunn Røren, Drammens Tidende/Buskerud Blad and Hans Arne Odde against Drammen City Court's ruling of 31 August 2000.

Appeal case no. 00-02997M04.

Judges: Senior Judge Fosheim, Judges Skjæggestad and Rønning

The following

r u l i n g

was given:

by writ dated 10 August 1999 and subsequently by corrected writ dated 13 January 2000, Frederick Delaware, resident in England, brought action before Drammen City Court against Heidi Schøne, Drammens Tidende/Buskerud Blad, responsible editor Hans Arne Odde and journalist Ingunn Røren, with a claim for judicial declaration that defamatory statements were null and void and compensation for non-pecuniary damage.

Before the writ, Frederick Delaware lodged a complaint on 19 July 1998 about a report in Drammens Tidende/Buskerud Blad on 14 July 1998 which contained allegedly offensive comments about his character based on information from Heidi Schøne communicated by Ingunn Røren who was a journalist for the newspaper. The basis for the complaint was similar to the present action before Drammen City Court.

In a letter dated 27 April 1999 to the Professional Committee of the Press (PFU), the editor of Drammens Tidende/Buskerud Blad, Hans Arne Odde requested that the committee postpone dealing with the complaint:

'The reason is that lawyer Lindset writes in his complaint (13.3.99): "It is currently not a relevant issue for my client to pursue his case against Drammens Tidende/Buskerud Blad," compared with the complainant's own wording in a letter to the PFU of 19.7.98 where he writes: "I have appointed, in January 1998, a lawyer – Karsten Gjone of Drammen on (32) 837818 to prosecute Heidi Schøne and once that case is over to prosecute the newspapers."

In accordance with the PFU's regulations § 4, I would therefore request that the committee postpone dealing with the complaint until a legally binding ruling exists, or alternatively that the complainant withdraws the threats of legal prosecution and makes it completely clear that legal proceedings are not a relevant issue.'

On this basis, the PFU wrote to lawyer Eric Lindset on 7 May 1999 enclosing a copy of editor Odde's letter:

"As is evident, the editor is requesting that the complaint-handling be suspended until a legally binding ruling exists, or alternatively that the complainant withdraws the threats of legal prosecution and makes it completely clear that legal proceedings are not a relevant issue."

On this basis, and in the light of PFU regulations § 4 (to which we also referred in our letter of 18.03.99), the secretariat must ask for <u>unambiguous</u> clarification as to whether or not legal action is a relevant issue. If we do not receive a clear answer to the effect that legal action against the newspaper is <u>not</u> a relevant issue, we will have to ask the committee to decide whether the complaint is to be dealt with or suspended."

PFU regulations § 4, paragraph two, to which reference is made in the letter, state:

"If the committee is asked to deal with a matter which has been reported or brought to court or which clearly will be brought to court, handling of the complaint is to be deferred until a legally binding ruling exists. In all cases, the committee may deal with the case if the press organ against which the complaint has been made agrees to this."

Lawyer Eric Lindset answered the letter on 24 May 1999 as follows:

"Reference is made to your letter of 7th inst. and previous correspondence. On behalf of my client, I wish to clarify unambiguously that taking legal action against Drammens Tidende/Buskerud Blad is not a relevant issue for him. My client again requests that his complaint of 19 July 1998 now be subjected to your consideration of substance."

As mentioned, Frederick Delaware nevertheless brought private criminal cases against Heidi Schøne, Ingunn Røren and Drammens Tidende/Buskerud Blad.

During the preparation of the case before the City Court, the defendants represented by lawyer Ellen Holager Andenæs c/o lawyer Vegard Aaløkken and lawyer Erik Nøkleby argued that the plaintiff should furnish security for costs according to Criminal Procedure Act § 413 before the case could be proceeded with before the City Court. All the defendants with the exception of Heidi Schøne also demanded that the action be dismissed because the plaintiff had waived the right to legal action.

Drammen City Court made the following decision on 31 August:

The action is proceeded with in relation to all defendants without the plaintiff being ordered to furnish security for costs.

Drammens Tidende/Buskerud Blad, responsible editor Hans Arne Odde and journalist Ingunn Røren appealed the decision to Borgarting Court of Appeal by appeal in due time dated 11 September 2000 through lawyer Erik Nøkleby. The appeal related exclusively to the question of whether the right to bring action before the courts had been waived, so that the action should be dismissed.

Frederick Delaware submitted his reply dated 2 October 2000 through lawyer Stig Lunde. In a letter dated 20 October, the Court of Appeal set a time limit of 27 October 2000 for the parties for comments before a decision was made on the case. The parties each submitted a pleading within the time limit.

In brief, the appellants have argued:

Frederick Delaware has by a clear and voluntary statement waived his right to bring action against the appellants. In a letter of 27 April to the PFU, chief editor Hans Arne Odde refers to Delaware's earlier threat of action for damages, and asks the committee to postpone dealing with the case – until a legally binding decision exists or Delaware has made it clear that legal proceedings are not a relevant issue.

The editor's request for postponement is communicated by the PFU to Delaware's lawyer in a letter of 7 May 1999 in which it is evident that Delaware has a choice between confirming that taking action against the newspaper is not a relevant issue, or waiting for the committee to consider the editor's request for postponement until a legally binding decision exists.

Delaware's lawyer replies in a letter of 24 May 1999 to the PFU: "On behalf of my client, I wish to clarify unambiguously that taking legal action against Drammens Tidende/Buskerud Blad is not a relevant issue for him." There is nothing unclear in the wording to the PFU's organization secretary.

How the committee itself would judge the case according to the regulations, if Delaware had not waived institution of legal proceedings, is not relevant. The fact is that Delaware did not want to take the risk of the PFU postponing the case. In order to ensure that it was dealt with, he waived his right to take legal action without question or reservation.

Lawyer Lindset's statement on behalf of Delaware in the letter of 24 May 1999 is a binding promise in relation to the appellants as well. The subject of his complaint to the PFU is, as far as the PFU's regulations are concerned, the same matter as the present action against the journalist and responsible editor.

The following request has been made:

1.   The action be dismissed.

2.   Ingunn Røren, Drammens Tidende/Buskerud Blad and Hans Arne Odde be awarded costs before the City Court and the Court of Appeal plus 12% annual interest from due date until payment takes place.

In brief, the respondent has argued:

It is argued that it was not agreed to waive the right to bring the case to court after consideration by the PFU. The letter dated 24 May 1999 from lawyer Eric Lindset does not imply that Frederick Delaware unreservedly and definitively renounced the possibility of hearing before the courts. The letter merely confirms that bringing action was not a relevant issue for Delaware at that time. The legal system allows the offended party an opportunity to bring action before the courts as a consequence of defamation, and if the intention had been to stipulate renunciation of the right to judicial hearing, this would have to have emerged much more clearly than is the case.

The statement in the letter must be understood against the background that reference was expressly made to the regulations § 4 in connection with the question in the PFU's letter. The point of these regulations is that cases which will in any case be heard by the courts should not be dealt with by the PFU as well. The regulations cannot be cited in support of the right to hearing before the courts having to be waived in order for the case to be dealt with. Neither the actual situation nor the PFU's regulations should dictate that it was desirable or necessary to renounce the right to consideration by the courts in order to bring the case before the PFU. The keyword in the regulations is "clearly." It was not clear that Frederick Delaware would bring the case before the courts.

At the time the statement was made on behalf of the respondent, bringing the case before the court was not judged to be a relevant issue, and the PFU's regulations accordingly did not constitute an obstacle to the case being considered. He wanted first to see the result of the handling of the complaint to the PFU and then have a free hand. Moreover, any renunciation of consideration by the courts can apply only in relation to the newspaper, and not the journalist and the responsible editor. If the intention had been to ask questions about whether bringing action against the journalist or the editor was a relevant issue, it must be expected that a clear and precise question about this would have been asked. The complaint lodged dealt exclusively with the newspaper's handling of the case, and there was consequently no obvious reason to understand the statement as also including subjects other than that which emerges from the wording.

In the alternative, it is argued that such an agreement in any case appears invalid on the basis of both the circumstances surrounding entering into it and the content. Given the situation a person who feels offended by a newspaper is normally in and the discomfort a judicial hearing often involves, it will also appear as undue pressure if the right to consideration before the courts has to be given up in order to have the case examined by the PFU at all. Reference is made to the Contract Act §§ 33 and 36.

The following request has been made:

1.   Drammen City Court's decision be confirmed.
2.   Ingunn Røren, Drammens Tidende and Buskerud Blad (attn. chairman of board) and Hans Arne Odde be ordered to pay to Frederick Delaware within 14 days the costs of the case before the City Court and the Court of Appeal plus 12% interest from due date until payment takes place.

The Court of Appeal has come to the conclusion that the appeal must succeed and observes:

The action concerns a claim for compensation and judicial declaration that defamatory statements were null and void, and it is therefore to be considered according to the rules of the Criminal Procedure Act as far as possible and unless otherwise provided, cf. Criminal Procedure Act § 402, paragraph one, no. 2, cf. § 409. The action cannot therefore be proceeded with if the right to apply for prosecution for the criminal offence has been waived beforehand, cf. Criminal Code § 82, paragraph two and Andenæs – Alminnelig strafferett [General Criminal Law], 4th edition, page 483.

The Court of Appeal finds that there is no doubt that, in lawyer Eric Lindset's letter dated 24 May 1999, the plaintiff waived the right to proceed with private criminal cases when this is read in connection with chief editor Hans Arne Odde's letter dated 27 April 1999 and the PFU's letter dated 7 May 1999.

Lawyer Eric Lindset's letter showed that Frederick Delaware wanted a consideration of substance of the complaint at the PFU and that instituting legal proceedings was not a relevant issue. The letter makes no reservation with regard to the possibility of instituting legal proceedings after the consideration of substance at the PFU. The purpose of chief editor Odde's objection to the PFU considering the case before consideration by the courts was precisely to prevent such a development – something which Frederick Delaware had to understand.

There is no basis for the possibility of Delaware having misunderstood the PFU's enquiry as the committee only wishing to clarify whether, according to the regulations, there was authority to subject the complaint to a consideration of substance. The PFU also wished to clarify the possibilities of legal action in accordance with chief editor Odde's request. The plaintiff was assisted by a lawyer, and he also has legal training himself. The plaintiff must have understood the connection in this and that the right to take legal action was definitively waived when he wished in the letter "to clarify unambiguously that taking legal action was not a relevant issue for him."

The Court of Appeal considers the right of prosecution to be waived in respect of journalist Ingunn Røren and chief editor Hans Arne Odde as well. The fact that the letter refers only to Drammens Tidende/Buskerud Blad cannot have decisive significance. The complaint to the PFU concerned the same issue as the cause of action against Odde and Røren, and it was therefore natural for them also to understand the letter as a waiver of the right of prosecution.

The Court of Appeal wishes to add that the purpose of the newspaper's request to the PFU to have the complaint-handling postponed unless legal action was stated not to be a relevant issue would not have been achieved either if it nevertheless had to go through with legal proceedings with its own editor and journalist as defendant. The newspaper would then clearly be involved in the legal proceedings. Waiving the right of prosecution in respect of the newspaper therefore implicitly had to involve a waiver as far as the editor and journalist were concerned in order to have any meaning – a connection it is difficult to argue the plaintiff was unaware of.

The Court of Appeal does not find either that the undertaking not to institute legal proceedings is invalid according to Contract Act § 33 or § 36. As is evident from the discussion above, Frederick Delaware must himself have been clear about the content of the undertaking and the significance it would have for the right to institute legal proceedings after consideration by the PFU. The fact that subsequently, when the PFU's decision has gone against him, he nevertheless finds reason to institute proceedings cannot indicate that the undertaking is invalid. Frederick Delaware has not been subjected to any undue pressure here.

The appeal has accordingly succeeded, whereupon the legal action against the defendants is to be dismissed.

The question of costs is to be decided in accordance with the rules of the Civil Procedure Act, cf. Criminal Procedure Act 440, paragraph one. In accordance with the result in the Court of Appeal, the respondent shall compensate the appellant for the costs of the case before the City Court and the Court of Appeal in accordance with Civil Procedure Act § 180, paragraph two, cf. § 175, paragraph one. The respondent can be reproached with taking out the writ before Drammen City Court despite the prior waiver of the right to legal action. The legal basis for dismissal was beyond doubt.

Lawyer Erik Nøkleby submitted a statement of costs before the City Court dated 25 August 2000 for NOK 42,872 including disbursements of NOK 272. Lawyer Nøkleby has not submitted a statement of costs for the hearing of the appeal by the Court of Appeal.

Lawyer Stig Lunde protested against the claim for costs in a pleading to the City Court dated 30 August 2000. He argues inter alia that a time of 36.5 hours is considerably longer than can be deemed necessary in order to take care of the defendants' interests in a reasonable way. Lawyer Nøkleby was aware of the objections to the statement of costs but has not commented on this situation before the City Court or the Court of Appeal.

The Court of Appeal finds that lawyer Erik Nøkleby's claim for costs before the City Court is higher than was necessary in order for the case to be conducted satisfactorily, cf. Civil Procedure Act § 176, paragraph one.

The Court of Appeal's starting point was that it was necessary to invest quite a few working hours in going through the writ with annexes and carrying out the necessary investigations and consultations. However, lawyer Nøkleby had been requested to limit this work until it was clear whether the case would be examined on its merits, cf. demand for dismissal in reply, alternative request for provision of security. The problems for the City Court before the court made its decision which is the subject of this appeal were essentially connected with the question of dismissal, provision of security and exclusion of evidence. The Court of Appeal cannot see that these problems had such a degree of difficulty that it was necessary to spend very many working hours on them. However, the Court of Appeal must also take account of the fact that certain aspects in the preparation of the case may nevertheless have been particularly time-consuming. This requires that lawyer Nøkleby be granted a relatively large margin of doubt in his favour.

After an overall assessment of these circumstances, the Court of Appeal finds that the fee should be reduced discretionarily. The statement of costs shows that 8.5 hours were spent on preparation for the court session in the City Court, while 5.5 hours were spent on the court session itself. The remaining time spent relates to preparation of the case. As mentioned, the total time is 36.5 hours. The Court of Appeal finds that the time necessary can be reduced by ten hours, roughly two hours for preparation for the court session and the rest for the remaining case preparation. Based on an hourly rate of NOK 1,200 this results in a fee reduced by NOK 12,000 before the City Court. The total approved claim for costs before the City Court is then NOK 30,872.

As mentioned, a statement of costs was not submitted for the hearing by the Court of Appeal. The Court of Appeal sets the fee discretionarily at NOK 5,000.

Accordingly, Ingunn Røren, Hans Arne Odde and Drammens Tidende/Buskerud Blad are awarded costs before the City Court and the Court of Appeal of in total NOK 35,872 plus interest in accordance with the law on interest on overdue payments § 3, paragraph 1.

The ruling is unanimous.

Conclusion:

1.   The action is dismissed.

2.   Ingunn Røren, Hans Arne Odde and Drammens Tidende/Buskerud Blad are awarded total costs of NOK 35, 872 – thirty five thousand eight hundred and seventy two – before the City Court and the Court of Appeal plus interest in accordance with the law on interest on overdue payments § 3, paragraph 1, point 1, until payment takes place. The period for compliance is 2 – two – weeks from the pronouncement of the ruling of the Court of Appeal until payment takes place.

Berit Fosheim   Wenche Skjæggestad   Thore Rønning

Certified
for Senior Judge President:

Appeal to the Supreme Court dated 29th December 2000:

APPEAL

to

THE APPEALS COMMITTEE OF THE SUPREME COURT

with

REQUEST FOR REDRESS

Lower court case no.:	**Appeal case no. 00-02997 M04**
Appellant:	Frederick Delaware.
Counsel:	Stig Lunde.
Respondent 1:	Ingunn Røren.
Respondent 2:	Drammens Tidende and Buskerud Blad AS (attn. chairman of board), postbox 7033, 3007 Drammen.
Respondent 3:	Responsible editor Hans Arne Odde.
Counsel for respondents:	Svensson Nøkleby ANS attn. Erik Nøkleby.
The appeal concerns:	Continued appeal – appeal against ruling of Borgarting Court of Appeal in appeal case no. 00-02997 M04.

****

1. Introduction

On 31 August 2000, Drammen City Court gave a ruling with the following conclusion:

> "The action is proceeded with in relation to all defendants without the plaintiff being ordered to furnish security for costs."

The ruling was appealed by three of the four defendants with regard to the question of dismissal.

On 24 November 2000, Borgarting Court of Appeal gave a ruling with the following conclusion:

> "1. The action is dismissed.
>
> 2. Ingunn Røren, Hans Arne Odde and Drammens Tidende/Buskerud Blad are awarded total costs of NOK 35, 872 – thirty five thousand eight hundred and seventy two – before the City Court and the Court of Appeal plus interest in accordance with the law on interest on overdue payments § 3, paragraph 1, point 1, until payment takes place. The period for compliance is 2 – two – weeks from the pronouncement of the ruling of the Court of Appeal until payment takes place."

The basis of the decision of the Court of Appeal is that the appellant waived the right to apply for public prosecution, cf. Criminal Code § 82, paragraphs 1 and 3. This involves a question of whether "the case ... falls under the courts," cf. Criminal Procedure Act § 388 no. 1. According to this provision, the Appeals Committee of the Supreme Court has full competence.

The decision of the Court of Appeal is in any case based on incorrect interpretation of Criminal Code § 82, paragraph 3 cf. paragraph 1. This can be examined by the Appeals Committee of the Supreme Court in accordance with Criminal Procedure Act § 388 no. 3. According to this provision, the competence is limited to examining the general legal interpretation.

The continued appeal applies to the Court of Appeal's decision in its entirety.

2. Redress

The appeal was received here on 29.11.00, with a request, as counsel, to accept pronouncement. This was done the same day.

Against the background of harmonization of time limits for judicial remedies, the task of clarifying the applicable appeal time limit was delegated internally in the office, after which it was reported to be one month.

The appellant lives in England and is English-speaking. He does not speak Norwegian. The ruling of the Court of Appeal was gone through with the appellant in a telephone conference, and it was then communicated to him that the appeal time limit was one month.

According to Criminal Procedure Act § 409, the appeal time limit in § 379 of two weeks applies for private criminal cases. According to paragraph 1, point 2, of the provision, § 318 applies correspondingly for appeals, so that the appeal does not have to be dismissed, even if the time limit is missed, if the court finds that "the failure to meet the time limit should not be blamed on the [appellant]." It is mentioned that there is no such identification as in accordance with Courts of Justice Act § 153.

The appellant has been made aware that it was concluded in the office that the appeal time limit was 1 month. Moreover, he has no knowledge of Norwegian rules, and it will not be easy for him to check the information he is given either. Irrespective of whether I as counsel can be reproached, redress for failure to meet the appeal time limit is requested on this basis.

3. Brief overview of the case

The main issue concerns a claim for judicial declaration that defamatory statements were null and void and compensation against the background of comments made about the appellant in Drammens Tidende/Buskerud Blad on 14 July 1998.

The appellant was first referred to in the newspaper as early as 1995. Although the comments included serious allegations and offensive characterizations, the appellant was unable to make the newspaper correct the impression it had given. Against this background, the appellant himself prepared a report concerning the underlying circumstances and distributed this to people in the sales area of the newspaper.

Irrespective of the action of the appellant, the newspaper was not entitled to portray him as it did on the front page and inside the newspaper in 1998. The newspaper's comments and characterizations are untrue and appear as insults in accordance with Criminal Code §§ 246 and 247 and in any case lie far outside what could be justified by the public's need for information.

The appellant complained to the Professional Committee of the Press (PFU) about the comments made by the newspaper in 1998. Against the background of a letter from editor Hans Arne Odde and with reference to the PFU's regulations § 4, the PFU asked the appellant in a letter of 7 May 1999 for

"unambiguous clarification as to whether or not legal action is a relevant issue."

On behalf of the appellant, lawyer Eric Lindset sent a reply on 24 May 1999, in which inter alia the following emerged:

"On behalf of my client, I wish to clarify unambiguously that taking legal action against 'Drammens Tidende/Buskerud Blad' is not a relevant issue for him."

The basis used by the Court of Appeal was that this statement implies a waiver of the right to proceed with a private criminal case.

660

4. The question of dismissal

Reference is made to statements before the previous instances and to Drammen City Court's ruling with which the appellant agrees. In brieF.

* The enquiry in the letter from the PFU of 7 May 1999 must of course be understood against the background of the PFU's regulations § 4, where, in the second paragraph, inter alia the following emerges:

  "If the committee is asked to deal with a matter which has been reported or brought to court or which clearly will be brought to court, handling of the complaint is to be deferred until a legally binding ruling exists."

* If the PFU had meant the appellant to make a wider statement than was necessary on the basis of the PFU's regulations § 4, it must be demanded that this emerge clearly. This was not the case; on the contrary, the PFU referred precisely to the PFU's regulations § 4 in its letter.

* There was no reason either for the appellant to waive the right to bring the case to court at a later stage.

* The statement in the letter of 24 May 1999 was confirmation that hearing before the courts was not a relevant issue at that time, after which the case could in accordance with the PFU regulations be taken up for consideration. Apart from the fact that this follows from the wording, the background to the statement being made cannot lead to a broader understanding of it either.

* Had the PFU intended the appellant to do something as very extraordinary as waive the right to hearing before the courts in order to have the case examined at the PFU, it must be demanded that this be presented in a clear and precise way. This was not the case.

* No significance can in any case be attached - as has been by the Court of Appeal - to the fact that the appellant himself has legal training from England. Given that different legal systems are concerned, this implies much too demanding role expectations.

* Any waiver of the right to hearing before the courts would in any case appear as invalid and unreasonable, cf. Contract Act §§ 33 and 36.

The statement can in any case not be made to apply to parties other than the newspaper, as has been done by the Court of Appeal. Neither the wording nor the enquiry gives grounds for this. The appellant had no cause to think that either the enquiry or the statement would also apply to the editor and the journalist. If the object of the newspaper's enquiry was as taken as a basis by the Court of Appeal that this would of course mean that the statement would also apply to the editor and the journalist, this should have been conveyed to the appellant in a clear and precise way. This was not the case.

5. Criminal Procedure Act § 388 no. 1

By legislative amendment of 24 August 1990 no. 54, the wording was changed so that the area of application of the provision was broadened.

The provision affords an opportunity for full examination of decisions which relate to the right to have a case examined before the court and must be applied irrespective of the grounds for the right to hearing before the courts possibly not applying. The provision must consequently also be applied where the question of whether the right to examination by the courts is waived by agreement is concerned.

Accordingly, the Appeals Committee of the Supreme Court can examine all aspects of the Court of Appeal's ruling and come to a decision as to whether the appellant has waived the right to bring the case to court. This applies for the case against both the newspaper and the editor and the journalist.

6. Criminal Procedure Act § 388 no. 3

The Court of Appeal's decision is in any case based on incorrect interpretation of Criminal Code § 82, paragraph 3 cf. paragraph 1.

According to the provision, an application for prosecution can be "withdrawn" before prosecution is initiated. It is taken as a basis that the provision also applies to waiver, so that the right to apply for public prosecution can be waived on a contractual basis.

The law is framed against the background of legislators having found it desirable that waiver could for example be included as part of a compromise.

Neither the wording of the law nor the background of the provision gives grounds for statements regarding possible institution of legal proceedings being interpreted as a matter of course as the waiver covered by Criminal Code § 82. It must be demanded that the waiver appear as clear and precise. The degree of clarity and precision may be expected to vary on the basis of the actual situations. In a case where the alleged waiver does not arise as part of an otherwise mutual agreement, however, stringent demands for clarity and precision must be made. This requirement has not been complied with in the case in question, after which the Court of Appeal took as its basis too broad an understanding of the demand that must be made according to the law in order for the right to apply for public prosecution to be considered waived.

7. Costs of the case

The appellant wishes to request that he be awarded costs before all 3 courts.

The lack of precision and clarity in the approaches made to the appellant before the latter's statement and the fact that the statement does not appear as a clear and unconditional waiver of the right to apply for public prosecution mean that the appellant had good reasons for having the question of proceeding with the case examined before the courts.

8. Conclusion

The appeal has been sent to the appellant for approval by fax. The approved original will be forwarded as soon as it is received by post.

On behalf of the appellant, the following requests are made:

1. Redress be given for failure to meet the appeal time limit.

2. Drammen City Court's ruling of 31 August 2000 be confirmed and the action also be proceeded with in respect of Ingunn Røren, Drammens Tidende and Buskerud Blad AS (attn. chairman of board), and Hans Arne Odde.

3. Ingunn Røren, Drammens Tidende and Buskerud Blad AS (attn. chairman of board), and Hans Arne Odde be ordered – jointly and severally – to pay to Frederick Delaware within 14 days the costs of the case plus 12% interest p.a. from due date until payment takes place.

Appeal in 4 copies, and 4 copies sent directly to respondents' counsel

Moss, 29.12.00

Stig Lunde, Lawyer

I hereby declare that I want to appeal against the ruling from Borgarting lagmannsrett and demand reparation. I support the above-mentioned.

Place and date 29th December 2000

Signature

Frederick Delaware

Judgement of the Supreme Court dated 16th February 2001:

APPEALS COMMITTEE OF THE SUPREME COURT

On 16 February 2001, in

case no. 2001/47, private criminal case, appeal:

Frederick Delaware (lawyer Stig Lunde)

versus

Ingunn Røren
Drammens Tidende and Buskerud Blad AS
Hans Arne Odde (lawyer Erik Nøkleby)

the Appeals Committee of the Supreme Court consisting of judges Lund, Aarbakke and Oftedal Broch gave the following

R U L I N G:

By writ dated 10 August 1999, subsequently by corrected writ dated 13 January 2000, Frederick Delaware brought action before Drammen City Court against Heidi Schøne, Drammens Tidende and Buskerud Blad, responsible editor Hans Arne Odde and journalist Ingunn Røren, with a claim for judicial declaration that defamatory statements were null and void and compensation for non-pecuniary damage.

Heidi Schøne demanded in response that Delaware, who is resident in England, should furnish security for costs, while the other defendants demanded that the action be dismissed because Delaware had waived the right to hearing before the courts in connection with a complaint having been submitted to the Professional Committee of the Press.

Drammen City Court made the following decision on 31 August 2000:

> "The action is proceeded with in relation to all defendants without the plaintiff being ordered to furnish security for costs."

The City Court also gave a ruling with the following conclusion:

> "The question of costs is deferred until the decision which closes the case."

Ingunn Røren, Hans Arne Odde and Drammens Tidende and Buskerud Blad appealed the decision to Borgarting Court of Appeal. On 24 November 2000, the Court of Appeal gave a ruling with the following conclusion:

> "1.   The action is dismissed.
>
> 2.   Ingunn Røren, Hans Arne Odde and Drammens Tidende/Buskerud Blad are awarded total costs of NOK 35,872 – thirty five thousand eight hundred and seventy two – before the City Court and the Court of Appeal plus interest in accordance with the law on interest on overdue payments § 3, paragraph 1, point 1, until payment takes place. The period for compliance is 2 – two – weeks from the pronouncement of the ruling of the Court of Appeal until payment takes place."

Frederick Delaware appealed the ruling of the Court of Appeal to the Appeals Committee of the Supreme Court.

In the appeal, it is in outline argued that:

The appeal was not submitted in due time. The appellant, who lives in England and is English-speaking, was advised by his counsel that the appeal time limit was one month. The appellant does not speak Norwegian and does not have knowledge of Norwegian rules. In accordance with Criminal Procedure Act § 318, which applies correspondingly for appeals in private criminal cases, cf. § 409, cf. § 379, the appeal is not to be dismissed if the court finds that the failure to meet the time limit should not be blamed on the appellant. In accordance with this provision, no such identification between party and counsel is made as is in accordance with Courts of Justice Act § 153. Redress is requested irrespective of whether the counsel is to be reproached for something.

It is further argued that the Appeals Committee of the Supreme Court has the competence to examine all aspects of the ruling of the Court of Appeal, cf. Criminal Procedure Act § 388, paragraph 1, no. 1. This provision must also be applied where there is a question of whether the right to consideration by the courts is waived by agreement. The appellant refers to the statements before the previous instances and to the decision of Drammen City Court. In any case, the legal interpretation can be examined in accordance with Criminal Procedure Act § 388, paragraph 1, no. 3, and it is asserted that the decision of the Court of Appeal is based on incorrect interpretation of Criminal Code § 82, paragraph 3, cf. paragraph 1.

Frederick Delaware has requested:

1. Redress be given for failure to meet the appeal time limit.

2. Drammen City Court's ruling of 31 August 2000 be confirmed and the action also be proceeded with in respect of Ingunn Røren, Drammens Tidende and Buskerud Blad AS (attn. chairman of board) and Hans Arne Odde.

3. Ingunn Røren, Drammens Tidende and Buskerud Blad AS (attn. chairman of board) and Hans Arne Odde be ordered – jointly and severally – to pay to Frederick Delaware within 14 days the costs of the case before the City Court, the Court of Appeal and the Appeals Committee of the Supreme Court plus 12% interest p.a. from due date until payment takes place.

Ingunn Røren, Hans Arne Odde and Drammens Tidende and Buskerud Blad AS countered in response to the appeal.

In outline, it is stated:

Primarily it is argued that the appeal must be dismissed as having been submitted too late. In the present case, the appellant is the plaintiff in a private criminal case and cannot invoke the principle for public criminal cases that the negligence of a defence counsel shall not go beyond the convicted, cf. Rt. 1962 page 527.

Subsidiarily it is argued that the appeal must be rejected. Criminal Procedure Act § 388, paragraph 1, no. 1 does not apply. The action is not dismissed because it "does not belong under the courts" but because an elementary procedural condition – application for a prosecution – is lacking. The Court of Appeal's interpretation of Criminal Code § 82 is correct. The court's assessment of fact cannot be examined, nor can the subsumption.

The Court of Appeal has reduced the respondents' claim for costs from NOK 42,872 to NOK 30,872. It is maintained that this is incorrect and that the decision must be changed.

The respondents have requested:

"Primarily: The appeal be dismissed.

Subsidiarily: The appeal be rejected.

In both cases: Ingunn Røren, Hans Arne Odde and Drammens Tidende and Buskeruds Blad AS be awarded total costs of NOK 47,872 before the City Court and the Court of Appeal, plus 12% annual interest from due date until payment takes place.

Ingunn Røren, Hans Arne Odde and Drammens Tidende and Buskeruds Blad AS be awarded costs before the Appeals Committee of the Supreme Court of NOK 7,200 plus 12% annual interest from due date until payment takes place."

The Appeals Committee of the Supreme Court finds that the appeal was submitted too late and must be dismissed.

The appeal was pronounced to the appellant's counsel on 29 November 2000, while the appeal was not submitted until 29 December 2000. It was therefore submitted too late, cf. Criminal Procedure Act § 409, cf. § 379.

In accordance with Criminal Procedure Act § 318, paragraph 1, cf. § 379, paragraph 1, cf. § 409, an appeal in a private criminal case which is submitted too late is to be dismissed, unless the failure to meet the time limit should not be blamed on the appellant.

In the appeal statement, it says with regard to the reason for the failure to meet the time limit:

"The appeal was received here on 29.11.00, with a request, as counsel, to accept pronouncement. This was done the same day.

Against the background of harmonization of time limits for judicial remedies, the task of clarifying the applicable appeal time limit was delegated internally in the office, after which it was reported to be one month.

The appellant lives in England and is English-speaking. He does not speak Norwegian. The ruling of the Court of Appeal was gone through with the appellant in a telephone conference, and it was then communicated to him that the appeal time limit was one month."

From this, the Committee finds that it is clear that the failure to meet the time limit must be blamed on the appellant's counsel. In private criminal cases, *the plaintiff* is in this connection identified with his counsel, cf. Rt. 1962 page 527, cf. for illustration also Rt. 1971 page 423 and Appeals Committee ruling no. 2439S/1994.

The appellant has requested redress for failure to meet the appeal time limit as he himself cannot under any circumstance be reproached for the failure to meet the time limit. It is a little unclear whether the request is also made in the event that the appellant has to be identified with his counsel. As a matter of form, it is pointed out that the Criminal Procedure Act does not contain any rules on redress corresponding to the provision for disputes in the Courts of Justice Act § 153.

The appeal must be dismissed. The respondent has requested in its response that the Court of Appeal's decision on costs be changed. The Committee finds that the decision cannot be examined in connection with the appeal being dismissed for having been submitted too late. No independent appeal against the decision on costs has been submitted. The respondent has furthermore contended that it should be awarded costs before the Appeals Committee of the Supreme Court of NOK 7,200 plus interest. The Committee finds the claim much too high. Costs are set at NOK 2,500.

The ruling is unanimous.

CONCLUSION:

1.   The appeal is dismissed.

2.   In costs before the Appeals Committee of the Supreme Court, Frederick Delaware shall
        pay to Ingunn Røren, Hans Arne Odde and Drammens Tidende and Buskerud Blad AS
        jointly NOK 2,500 – two thousand five hundred – within 2 – two – weeks of
        pronouncement of this ruling plus ordinary overdue payment interest in accordance
        with the law on interest on overdue payments § 3, paragraph 1, point 1, currently 12 –
        twelve – per cent annual interest, from the expiry of the time limit for compliance until
        payment takes place.

Magnus Aarbakke   Ketil Lund   Lars Oftedal Broch
      sign.   sign.   sign.

True copy:

[signature & stamp]

5 page fax to Odd Einar Dørum, Minister of Justice dated 23rd May 2004

From: Mr. Frederick Delaware, England

Date: 23rd May 2004

SUBJECTS: 1. Aftenposten articles of 15th April 2002 by Reidun J. Samuelsen – 'British Muslim terrorizes Norwegian woman on the Internet' and 'Internet harassment can be stopped in the following way' and 2. Policewoman Torill Sorte of the Nedre Eiker Constabulary, Drammen.

Your name has been used in the second of the above mentioned newspaper articles and Policewoman Torill Sorte has been quoted in the first article. The story is directed against me, a practicing solicitor, born in London to an Egyptian father and a German mother.

Only last October, when I returned from prosecuting my Court of Appeal civil case against Heidi Schøne in Drammen, did I discover the two articles, by typing in the word "Muslim" on the Aftenposten website search engine.

I spoke recently with Gunnar Johannessen at your department and he confirmed that you did indeed speak to Aftenposten on this matter. The impression given by Reidun Samuelsen's articles is that you had seen my website (www.norway-shockers.com) and backed her story.

For your information, my website only started in October 2000, six years after three Norwegian newspapers - Verdens Gang, Bergens Tidende and Drammens Tidende printed headline stories on me in late May 1995. These headlines included: '13 years of Sex terror' by Verdens Gang, associating me with the psychiatric illness "erotic paronoia" and referring to me as the "half Arab, Muslim man." Bergens Tidende called me the "Muslim" sixteen times. Drammens Tidende described me as a potential child killer, calling me "insane" and "a half-German, half-Arab man." In 1998 VG and Drammens Tidende repeated their stories. To date there have been 12 front page stories on me (1995 to 2003), several of which I did not know of for some years. Quite a few of these bigoted articles are still on the websites of these newspapers.

So I trust you will understand my desire and my right to defend my reputation via a website, a right enshrined in Article 10 of the ECHR. I take great exception to being sexually and religiously humiliated by your country's press whose source of information – Heidi Schøne – has herself been a psychiatric patient on and off since 1988. She is now on a permanent disability pension for a severe personality disorder. The medicalisation and sexualisation of my behaviour reminds me of the attack made by elements in Norway on the children of German soldiers and Norwegian women after the War. My own grand-father was a German soldier killed in Stalingrad whilst serving with Von Paulus' Sixth Army. A fact not lost on your press. The blatant Islamaphobia trumpeted in your press would constitute, in England, the offence of incitement to religious hatred and possibly also incitement to cause a breach of the peace.

There has been a cover-up of unprecedented dimensions by your police and Attorney General on issues arising out of this saga. Before I detail these aberrations you will have to familiarize yourself with the relevant facts by looking at my website. After clicking on 'Enter' click on the link 'A general hatred of Muslims?' which deals with the Norwegian role on the subject. Scroll down and you will see the links for the 12 stories on me in Norwegian and English. When you come to the Aftenposten articles of April 2002 you will see the link to the transcription of the taped telephone conversation I had with Reidun Samuelsen on 10th April 2002. You can have a copy of the tape if you want. You will see that you have been duped by a real hypocrite of a journalist. Secondly go to the link on the home page called 'Pretty face' and then click on the link 'Norwegian version of the Norwegian perversion.' You will then get an excellent overview of the court proceedings and the substance of my complaints against Torill Sorte, Anne Grøstad the Public Prosecutor and in turn Tor-Aksel Busch, your Attorney General.

For the record and although I repeat some of what is on the website consider this: Torill Sorte, quoted with you in Aftenposten, continued the pattern of medicalisation of my character by alleging in her witness statement of 22nd January 1997 that my mother told her that I am "sick" and need "help" and "on one occasion he was admitted for treatment," a witness statement that I only received for the first time on 19th July 2002 and the English translation of which I paid for and received on 29th August 2002. In two separate court appearances in January 2002 and October 2003 Torill Sorte swore on oath that my mother had told her that she (my mother) had actually "put" me in a mental hospital. All fabrications by Sorte. She had no idea, of course, up to the January 2002 libel trial that I had recorded our telephone conversations (which started in 1996 and stopped in 1998 with myself making all the calls) which can be seen on the website by clicking on the link 'transcripts.' In the call of 22nd April 1996 I brought my mother to the phone in order that she could tell Torill Sorte that Heidi Schøne's May 1995 newspaper allegation that she "knows the man's mother wanted to put him in a mental hospital" was a fabrication. My mother duly obliged. When we eventually got to court in January 2002 Sorte stated that my mother told her that I had been put in a mental hospital. I immediately shouted out, "Liar!" to Sorte and my lawyer, for the first time, revealed to her that he had a taped conversation with my mother saying the exact opposite to her! The proceedings for that day then immediately finished. The tape was to be played next morning. In the evening my lawyer phoned Sorte who told him that my mother had spoken to her on a second occasion and had made a complete U-turn: telling Sorte that I had in fact been put in a mental hospital by her (my mother)! Sorte was not called for cross-examination, contrary to my wishes, but the tape was played before the court the next morning.

In my appeal to the Public Prosecutor, Anne Grøstad, over Torill Sorte's perjury, I produced a letter from my family doctor who stated that I had never been a patient in a mental hospital. I have in fact never had any form of psychiatric treatment. I also insisted to Anne Grøstad that she ask Torill Sorte, who phoned who for this alleged second conversation and exactly when. If Sorte had phoned my mother then there would be a record of the phone call on the police station's bill. There should also be a written note by Sorte of the time and date of the conversation. I can guarantee that Sorte never once phoned me or my mother. It was always me who phoned her as I was pressing Sorte constantly to interview Heidi Schøne over her vile press allegations. This, after her colleague, the honourable Svein Jensen told me in 1996 that he did not believe Heidi Schøne or trust her so much. And the now retired police officer from Bergen, Henrik Dugstad also told me in 1996 that he thought Heidi Schøne's newspaper allegations were "nonsense." I did record these conversations and they were translated into Norwegian and accepted as court exhibits in my libel prosecution. Add to this the fact that when investigating judge John Morten Svendgård telephoned my mother she told him she had only ever spoken to Torill Sorte once (the recorded conversation of 22/04/96) and said that Sorte had fabricated her allegation about her telling her I had been put in a mental hospital. Yet Sorte herself was never questioned. No prosecution would follow. In my appeal to the Public Prosecutor, again Torill Sorte was not interviewed; again none of my evidence was mentioned in Anne Grøstad's decision letter and again no [substantial] reasons were given as to why Torill Sorte would not be prosecuted. A cover up. When I subpoenaed Anne Grøstad to the Court of Appeal trial for cross-examination, she successfully excused herself by saying she was going on holiday to Tenerife during the week of the trial. Instead she stated that Tor-Aksel Busch would go in her place if forced to go by the court. When I called him to discuss the matter he told me he would not attend court, did not want to speak to me and put the phone down on me. Judge Agnar Nilsen junior refused to compel Busch to attend. At the October 2003 trial Judge Nilsen prevented me from properly cross-examining Torill Sorte and reprimanded me when I called her a liar after she again repeated that my mother told her I had been incarcerated in a mental hospital. Judge Nilsen made no decision in his judgement about Sorte's repeated perjury even in the face of overwhelming evidence. An obvious breach of the rules of natural justice. In fact the moment the civil trial finished I was arrested at the door of the court and the next day given an 8 month prison sentence, suspended for two years, under Section 390(a) of the Criminal Code for promoting my website. The police lawyer prosecuting me, Ingunn Hodne, was a colleague of Torill Sorte. Why was I not charged under Section 390 giving me the defence of justified comment? The same Drammen constabulary were instrumental in utilizing Interpol to serve me with a criminal summons through my local police on 11th October 2001 for contravening S.390(a) of the Criminal Code after I had refused to pay a 5,000 kroner fine for publicizing my side of the story by means of a moderate but effective information campaign in Norway. I was convicted in absentia, unable to attend the magistrates court because I was too busy working on my civil libel prosecution. My 10,000 kroner fine was used in evidence against me in my civil prosecution which I lost in January 2002. There are many conflicts of interest in your police force's application of their duties.

This whole matter started when Heidi Schøne complained in December 1986, twenty months after I last saw her, that I had allegedly attempted to rape her in April 1985. Her complaint to the Bergen police was made a mere 2 weeks after I complained to her father that she had been abused for several years by a so called boyfriend of hers who had been injecting heroin and that something had to be done to stop the debauchery. She had on two occasions in the 1980's tried to take her life over this 'boyfriend' when she lived in Bergen. At Christmas 1990 this same man, Gudmund Johannessen, assaulted Heidi Schøne and she reported him to the Drammen police where she now lived. However, I was not told about this false allegation of attempted rape until January 1995 by a local Bergen lawyer who I employed to make enquiries over other matters at the Bergen police. Heidi Schøne insisted in 1995 to journalist Ingunn Roren that it was "attempted" rape. In 1998 when a lot of pressure was being put on Heidi Schøne to give a clear explanation to the police over her newspaper pronouncements she changed her allegation to one of actual, violent rape. Ingenious! Torill Sorte, who was handling the case, has refused since January 1998 to supply me or my lawyer with Heidi Schøne's witness statement [regarding actual rape] that she told me had been documented before her. Further, the details of the allegation of attempted rape have never been revealed to me. My Bergen lawyer in 1995 refused to tell me. So did subsequent lawyers. Krogvold, of the Bergen police, all along, in my personal dealings with him has refused all information, save that a few weeks ago he wrote to tell me that the allegation was my lawyer's "interpretation" of what he read from the police papers in 1995. I replied to Krogvold that it was only fair that I see the statement that allowed my Bergen lawyer to give his "interpretation" of attempted rape. Krogvold has not responded. It is very bad practice to only let a lawyer see police papers to the exclusion of the client.

Yet Commander Krogvold in Bergen and Torill Sorte at the Drammen police co-operated fully, in every way possible, with Heidi Schøne's Oslo lawyer. Deliberately withholding evidence from me told me that Heidi Schøne was being protected. Heidi Schøne has admitted in court that she was raped by a Bergen shopkeeper in the early 1980's although no charges were brought. She has also admitted in court that her stepmother's father allegedly sexually abused her and that her two older sisters mentally abused her.

Furthermore I have only been met with continuous silence from Krogvold over the whereabouts of a letter that Heidi Schøne says was handed into the police in

671

the late 1990's by Gudmund Johannessen's father wherein I was alleged to have threatened to kill her 2 year son Daniel. Another false allegation, but particularly hurtful as I had enormous affection for the little fellow as he had for me. Krogvold could not even tell me whether there was a written police report noting when this letter was handed in to his police station and by whom. The letter was not produced in court. Of course I never wrote any such letter. However Heidi Schøne repeated her allegation in court. The court believed her on this as they did for everything else she said about me, solely on her word, even though I was unable to conduct any cross-examination of her. In the eyes of Norwegian law I am a potential child killer and a rapist and there is nothing it seems I can do about it, unless you intervene. Heidi Schøne's lawyer and psychiatrist admitted in court that all my reports on her past were correct.

Now I cannot even travel to any Scandinavian country without fear of arrest under the mutual enforcement law and deportation to Norway to serve an 8 month prison sentence for continuing to maintain my website.

The civil process has finished in Norway now, after the Supreme Court refused me leave to appeal on 17th March 2004, in my civil case against against Heidi Schøne, giving no reasons. This is the second time the Supreme Court have refused to exercise their discretion in my favour. The first time, in 2001, new case law was going to be created in my criminal prosecution of Drammens Tidende, regarding that most corrupt of bodies, the PFU. But no - the Supreme Court copped out.

Has all this been going on with your knowledge?

Could you initiate an enquiry into this police and judicial corruption?

It is also not correct either to allow a judge the right to fully cross-examine a witness to the exclusion of the opposing party's lawyer, as happened in my case. How can a judge exercise impartiality by being prosecuting counsel and presiding judge at the same time?

I look forward to hearing from you. Please in the first instance acknowledge receipt of this letter.

Yours faithfully,
Frederick Delaware

Acknowledgements

I wish to thank the following publishers for giving me their permission to use extracts from the publications listed below:

Love Thy Neighbour – A Story of War by Peter Maass. Published by Pan Macmillian, London. Copyright © Peter Maass 1996.

Bosnia – A Short History by Noel Malcolm. Published by Pan Macmillian, London. Copyright © Noel Malcolm 1994, 1996.

Rape Warfare – The Hidden Genocide in Bosnia-Herzegovina and Croatia. Published by the University of Minnesota Press. Copyright © 1996 by the Regents of the University of Minnesota.

Covering Islam by Edward Said. Published by Vintage 1997. Reprinted by permission of The Random House Group Ltd. Copyright © Edward W. Said 1997.

Douglas Hurd – The Public Servant by Mark Stuart. Published by Mainstream Publishing Company (Edinburgh) Ltd. Copyright © Mark Stuart 1998.

Letters to the Celestial Serbs by Gojko Berić. Published by Saqi Books, London. Copyright © 2002 Gojko Berić. Translation and notes: Copyright © 2002 Saba Risaluddin.

The Concise Encyclopaedia of Islam, 2001 Revised Edition, by Cyril Glassé. Published by Stacey International, London. Copyright © Stacey International and Cyril Glassé 2001.

Taking a Case to the European Court of Human Rights, 2001 Edition, by Philip Leach. Published by Blackstone Press Limited. Copyright © Philip Leach 2001. By permission of Oxford University Press.

Milosevic – A Biography by Adam LeBor. Published by Bloomsbury Publishing plc. Copyright © Adam LeBor 2002.

21ˢᵗ Century Norwegian proverb:

'Cursed be the Internet for it hath exposed our nakedness unto Man'